"If all those who manage and love wilderness followed the principles and techniques described in *Wilderness Management*, America's wilderness areas would receive the quality management they deserve."

—Congressman Bruce F. Vento
Chairman, House Subcommittee on
National Parks and Public Lands

"Wildlife conservationists need to be involved in wilderness management because of the close link between wildlife and wilderness. *Wilderness Management* is our blueprint for that involvement."

—Jay Hair
President, National Wildlife Federation

"Throughout history, wilderness has been a source of inspiration to all of humankind. *Wilderness Management* will guide our efforts in the future to protect wilderness for people of all countries."

—Ian C. Player
Vice-Chairman, Wilderness Leadership School

WILDERNESS MANAGEMENT

WILDERNESS MANAGEMENT

Second Edition, Revised

John C. Hendee
Dean and Professor
College of Forestry, Wildlife, and Range Sciences
University of Idaho
Moscow, Idaho

George H. Stankey
Senior Research Professor
Department of Forest Resources
Oregon State University
Corvallis, Oregon

Robert C. Lucas
Wilderness Management Research Project Leader, retired
Intermountain Research Station
Missoula, Montana

Issued under the auspices of the International Wilderness
Leadership Foundation in cooperation with the USDA
Forest Service

North American Press
An Imprint of Fulcrum Publishing
Golden, Colorado

North American Press
An Imprint of
Fulcrum Publishing
350 Indiana Street
Golden, Colorado 80401

Library of Congress Cataloging-in-Publication Data
Hendee, John C.
      Wilderness management / John C. Hendee, George H. Stankey, Robert
   C. Lucas. -- 2nd., rev.
         p.   cm.
      "Issued under the auspices of the International Wilderness
   Leadership Foundation in cooperation with the USDA Forest Service."
      Includes bibliographical references and index.
      ISBN 1-55591-900-6
      1. Wilderness areas—United States—Management. 2. Wilderness
   areas—Management.   3. Nature conservation—United States.
   4. Nature conservation. I. Stankey, George H.   II. Lucas, Robert
   C. III. Title.
   QH76.H46 1990   90-47810
   333.78'2—dc20   CIP

Cover: Canoeing, here on the Snake River in Wyoming, is a growing and appropriate use of a designated wilderness area. Photo by Robert P. Huestis © 1990.
Cover design: Jay Staten, Fulcrum Publishing
Interior design: Karen Groves, Fulcrum Publishing
Printed in the United States of America
10 9 8 7 6 5 4 3 2 1

CONTENTS

Publisher's Preface

Wilderness is a key part of a well-balanced natural resource program. We need wild places where biological evolution can proceed naturally to produce the genetic diversity upon which our society is built. These remote and relatively unspoiled areas provide important research opportunities for monitoring changes in the earth's climate and natural systems. They also provide a benchmark for clean water and important habitat for wildlife. Increasingly, wilderness areas are recognized as popular tourist destinations which generate economic benefits, in addition to being places for recreational retreats where we can be strengthened in body, mind, and spirit.

Thus, wilderness areas are valuable. But if we do not manage them correctly, we will lose them as surely as if they were never designated.

This book presents state of the art information about wilderness management by leading authorities in the field. The co-authors and their associates trace the history and philosophy of the wilderness system and look beyond U.S. boundaries at the growing international recognition of the wilderness concept and the need to manage for its values.

The U.S. Forest Service, through the Government Printing Office, published the first edition of *Wilderness Management* in 1978, has supported this revised second edition, and continues to provide outstanding leadership in the field of wilderness management.

This book is meant for everyone who is concerned about wilderness—managers, scientists, users, teachers, students, natural resource developers, consultants, planners, and policy makers. We all have a stake in the future of wilderness.

Vance G. Martin, President
International Wilderness Leadership Foundation

In recognition of the biological, economic, cultural, and spiritual values of wilderness, the International Wilderness Leadership Foundation (IWLF) was established in 1974. Our worldwide goals are to increase the understanding and protection of wildlands; to enhance the role of meeting human needs; and to inspire an ecological conscience among current and future leaders. For more information on the IWLF. contact our office at 211 West Magnolia, Fort Collins, Colorado, USA, 80521.

FOREWORD

The 1964 Wilderness Act stands the test of time, virtually unamended in 25 years. There are now 91.5 million acres in the National Wilderness Preservation System, managed by the Bureau of Land Management, Fish and Wildlife Service, Forest Service, and National Park Service. We face the challenge of taking care of these vast resources "to leave them unimpaired for future use and enjoyment as wilderness." Even as political decisions remain about the designation of additional land as wilderness, the managing agencies' responsibilities for the existing wilderness grow.

The toughest challenge will be to keep wilderness "affected primarily by the forces of nature, with the imprint of man's work substantially unnoticeable." Threats will come from outside the wilderness and from inside, from visitors, and from wilderness users. In a world that becomes more urbanized and developed each day, wilderness strains under such pressures as air and water pollution, development or encroachment along its edges, motor vehicle trespass, and influences on water that originates outside its boundaries.

Wilderness management must maintain the naturalness of wilderness and protect it from human influence. Management of range, minerals, wildlife and fish, and other resources must be compatible with the wilderness concept, to preserve natural conditions and minimize the impact of non-conforming activities. Fire, insects, disease, and other natural forces must be allowed to play their ecological role within wilderness as long as they do not threaten resources and properties outside the wilderness boundary. As development and global environmental changes alter land more dramatically in the future, it is wilderness that can provide reservoirs of gene pools and stand as a yardstick against those imprints of man's work and impact on the land.

Wilderness is a "special place," somewhere to experience solitude and unconfined recreation and natural surroundings. Each visitor has a special responsibility to act in a way that does not influence the wilderness experience of other visitors and does not degrade the resource. Professionals and the public alike need to understand and abide by the "leave no trace" ethic, each a "visitor who does not remain."

The wilderness management heritage that began in the Forest Service with the first administrative designation of the Gila Wilderness in 1924 has been richly enhanced by years of experience in all four agencies in the 25 years since the Wilderness Act was passed. The three principal authors were Forest Service researchers when the first edition was written and when this edition was begun. Since then, Dr. Lucas has retired and Drs. Hendee and Stankey have moved on to academic positions. We are grateful to them, and to a long list of other contributors and reviewers.

More than a decade of progress, challenges, and conflicts have taken place since the first edition of this textbook was published. Wilderness acreage has increased more than six-fold, and it has become increasingly clear that wilderness management is more than setting land aside and leaving it alone. It is the breadth of the wilderness management challenge and opportunity that this book addresses. We are pleased to jointly endorse this second edition in the expectation that it will help wilderness managers and users, resource policy makers, and concerned citizens better care for this enduring resource of wilderness.

F. Dale Robertson
Chief, Forest Service

Cy Jamison
Director, Bureau of Land Mangement

James M. Ridenour
Director, National Park Service

John F. Turner
Director, Fish and Wildlife Service

AUTHORSHIP AND SPONSORSHIP

For more than two decades, the authors, working closely with wilderness managers, have studied the problems of wilderness management. They have also participated in countless research projects, workshops, and consultancies with different universities, agencies, and management units. All three have taught university courses in wilderness management—John Hendee at the University of Washington, 1969-1976, and George Stankey and Bob Lucas at the University of Montana. During the writing of the first edition (1974-77), all three coauthors were U.S. Forest Service recreation research scientists. Now, more than a decade later, John Hendee has been assistant director of the U.S. Forest Service's Southeastern Forest Experiment Station in Asheville, North Carolina, has spent a year on Capitol Hill as a congressional fellow and a year working in the agency's legislative affairs office, and is currently dean of the College of Forestry, Wildlife and Range Sciences, University of Idaho, Moscow. George Stankey has completed a two-year teaching-research position at Kuring-gai College, New South Wales, Australia, and is now senior research professor in the Department of Forest Resources, Oregon State University, Corvallis. Bob Lucas has retired as leader of the Wilderness Management Research Work Unit of the U.S. Forest Service in Missoula, Montana. His position has been filled by David N. Cole, who authored chapter 16.

The initial writing and revision of this book was sponsored by the U.S. Department of Agriculture, Forest Service. The International Wilderness Leadership Foundation was involved in the editing and publication of this second edition, and Fulcrum Publishing was involved with production and support. The book is directed toward wilderness managers in U.S. federal land management agencies—the U.S. Forest Service, the National Park Service, the Fish and Wildlife Service, and the Bureau of Land Management—and toward teachers, students, resource managers, conservationists, and wilderness users. Our technical reviewers, case examples, and background material represent the expertise of all these agencies and, while we recognize specific policy differences among them, we have sought a level of presentation that transcends agency differences. This is not a book constrained by any agency policy—our goal is to inspire creative management of the National Wilderness Preservation System independent of current organizational perspectives, policies, or practices.

Although each agency is directed by internal policies and federal guidelines, all operate under the Wilderness Act and all have high aspirations for preserving classified wilderness under their management. Wilderness managers in all four agencies are far more interested in getting the job done than defending or criticizing "company policy"—a sign of the increasing professionalism and maturity of wilderness management.

This book was conceived in 1971 at a U.S. Forest Service-sponsored symposium, "Management Implications of Wilderness Research," where managers, researchers, and environmentalists discussed mutual concerns for wilderness management and the need for new and relevant information. Preparing the original edition spanned several years (1974-77); likewise, this revised edition has required several years (1981-90).

Where topics were beyond our expertise, we solicited chapters from colleagues who are experts in these areas—Roderick Nash on Historical Roots of

Wilderness Management, Chapter 2; Jerry Franklin on Wilderness Ecosystems, Chapter 10; Bruce Kilgore and Miron "Bud" Heinselman on Fire in Wilderness Ecosystems, Chapter 12; Jim Blankenship on Wilderness Air Resource Management, Chapter 13; and David Cole on Ecological Impacts of Wilderness Recreation and Their Management, Chapter 16. We are also grateful for the collaboration and coauthorship of Vance Martin and Roderick Nash on International Concepts of Wilderness Preservation and Management, Chapter 3; Joseph W. Roggenbuck and Dennis M. Roth on The Wilderness Classification Process, Chapter 5; Russell von Koch on Wilderness Management Planning, Chapter 8; Stephen McCool and Gerald Stokes on Managing for Appropriate Conditions, Chapter 9; and Clay Schoenfeld on Wildlife in Wilderness, Chapter 11. Except for these contributions, all parts of the book bear the imprint of all three coauthors.

John Hendee provided overall coordination for writing, editing, and technical reviews and made administrative arrangements. He led the development of the photo plan, preface, and introductory material; as well as, Chapter 1, Wilderness Management: Philosophical Direction; Chapter 7, Principles of Wilderness Management; Chapter 8, Wilderness Management Planning; Chapter 11, Wildlife in Wilderness; and Chapter 18, Future Issues and Challenges in Wilderness Management.

George Stankey had principal responsibility for Chapter 3, International Concepts of Wilderness Preservation and Management; Chapter 4, The Wilderness Act; Chapter 6, The National Wilderness Preservation System and Complementary Conservation Areas; and Chapter 9, Managing for Appropriate Wilderness Conditions. He coauthored Chapter 5, The Wilderness Classification Process, and Chapter 18. He also coordinated chapter study questions.

Bob Lucas headed work on Chapter 14, Wilderness Use and Users; Chapter 15, Wilderness Recreation Management; and Chapter 17, The Wilderness Experience and Managing the Factors that Influence It. He also coauthored Chapter 18.

Among the coauthors, leadership for preparation of individual chapters is noted at the beginning of each chapter with acknowledgments at the end. Wherever the word "we" appears (outside of direct quotations), it refers to an opinion held by the three coauthors.

Readers may notice that many of the specific examples—but not as many as in the first edition— are based on U.S. Forest Service experience in managing wilderness. These selections do not reflect the preference or even the personal experiences of the authors. Rather, they express the degree of wilderness management experience and responsibilities of the wilderness management agencies. So far, U.S. Forest Service involvement with wilderness has been considerably more widespread than that of other agencies. But growing use of national park backcountry and wilderness has steadily increased the involvement of the National Park Service. Along with the Fish and Wildlife Service, the National Park Service has acquired enormous tracts of wilderness in Alaska, and both agencies are making steady progress toward meeting their management responsibilities. The Bureau of Land Management has also gained experience in completing studies of the suitability for wilderness of public domain lands and establishing and implementing a wilderness management policy for the growing number of those areas that Congress has classified as wilderness.

Thus, as we review the progress in wilderness designation and wilderness management that has transpired since the first edition of this book, we find that all federal land management agencies have made great strides. We are confident this progress will continue.

We are particularly grateful to our many colleagues in universities, the U.S. Forest Service, National Park Service, Fish and Wildlife Service, Bureau of Land Management, and the conservation community who provided encouragement and constructive review in both the first and revised editions of this book. We have not included a detailed list because of the risk of omitting colleagues who contributed directly or indirectly to our efforts which span 20 years. We do acknowledge a few colleagues who made recent contributions to specific chapters.

To the reviewers we offer our sincere gratitude— their review and input was invaluable but they share no responsibility for our interpretations or statements. We want to give special thanks to U.S. Forest Service editor, Martin Onishuk; to editor, Amy E. Lockwood for working on the final text and for coordinating the glossary and index; to the proofreader, Lisa S. Williamson; to Jack Armstrong for his assistance; to Vance G. Martin for his executive management of the production, editing, and publication process; to Bob Baron, president of Fulcrum Publishing for accepting the challenge of publishing the text; and to the U.S. Forest Service for employment during the majority of our time we worked on the book.

John C. Hendee   September 1990
George H. Stankey
Robert C. Lucas

PREFACE

Wilderness is the topic of a substantial and growing amount of literature. Hundreds of books, articles, reports, and brochures describe wilderness values (the rationale for preservation, public appeals, political movements), wilderness places (histories, geographies, noteworthy areas, biographies of people intimately linked with specific areas), and wilderness activities (how, where, and what-to-do guides). Faced with such a bewildering selection of wilderness readings, a reader could easily conclude that everything worth knowing about wilderness has already been written. But when readers turn to wilderness management—how to preserve naturalness and opportunities for solitude in areas set aside for this purpose—they soon discover that readings are in shorter supply. This subject—wilderness management—is widely scattered among short articles, research reports, graduate theses, and government manuals. This textbook corrects that.

The first edition of this book was inspired by our concern about the lack of any systematic, comprehensive synthesis of information about wilderness management, and our goal was to provide such a volume. Today the importance of wilderness management is even greater than before. The National Wilderness Preservation System has grown to almost 91 million acres. Although most of the wilderness allocation decisions have been made, the system will still grow, perhaps by another 20 percent. And, once decisions have been made to set aside land as wilderness, the long-term preservation of those values that originally led to its wilderness classification will depend on management.

The material in this book is organized into six sections, each intended to present a comprehensive summary and synthesis of pertinent information. The book's 18 chapters bring together both published material and new information and viewpoints pertaining to wilderness management. Topics include management philosophy and concepts, research data, and management experience in all four of the federal wilderness managing agencies. Specifically, our objectives are as follows:

1. To introduce readers to pressing wilderness management issues, the implications of alternative methods of dealing with them, pertinent literature, and current research.
2. To describe differences and interrelationships between wilderness allocation and wilderness management; and between management of wilderness and management of contiguous non-wilderness lands.
3. To describe the evolution of the National Wilderness Preservation System: its philosophical and historical origins; its current size, number of areas, and distribution; and its probable future.
4. To propose principles and concepts from which management policy and actions to preserve wilderness might be derived and to describe currently available management policies, procedures, and techniques.
5. To provide a common reference for managers, students, scientists, educators, and citizens, who must work together in managing the National Wilderness Preservation System.

We recognize that readers harbor diverse views about wilderness management, and we do not expect universal agreement with our treatment of this emotion-laden topic. We have tried to avoid the polarity of opinion common to discussion of wilderness and have attempted to maintain a broad, con-

ceptual perspective. Rather than offer stock solutions, we have tried to identify alternatives and their implications. Where we do advocate a specific management action, we clearly state our position and our reasons. Although individual agencies and the public continue to hold various notions about wilderness and its management, we are gratified by some convergence of views in the past decade. We hope this book will stimulate even more discussion and consensus to meet the challenge of wilderness management that faces both governmental agencies and the public in the decades ahead.

JOHN C. HENDEE

John C. Hendee is dean of the College of Forestry, Wildlife, and Range Sciences at the University of Idaho and professor of Forest Resources and Resource Recreation and Tourism. Prior to becoming dean at Idaho in 1985, he served 25 years with the U.S. Forest Service in diverse assignments including production forestry, fire and recreation research in the West, legislative affairs in Washington, DC, and research administration in the Southeast. For ten years, 1967-1976, he led a U.S. Forest Service research program in Seattle focusing on human behavior aspects of resource management, serving also as an adjunct faculty member at the University of Washington where he initiated and taught for several years a course in wilderness management.

GEORGE H. STANKEY

George H. Stankey was a Research Social Scientist with the U.S. Forest Service Wilderness Management Research unit in Missoula, Montana for 20 years. At present, he is senior research professor in the Department of Forest Resources, Oregon State University, Corvallis.

ROBERT C. LUCAS

Bob Lucas was a U.S. Forest Service research scientist, studying wilderness recreational use patterns and visitor characteristics and attitudes as they related to wilderness management. For 28 years he served as a wilderness research project leader in St. Paul, Minnesota and in Missoula, Montana. In 1984 he received the Department of Agriculture's Superior Service Award for his contributions to wilderness management. He retired from the Intermountain Research Station in 1989 and lives in Missoula, where

John C. Hendee
George H. Stankey
Robert C. Lucas
September 1990

Organization of the Book

Wilderness Management contains 18 chapters divided into six topic areas, as follows:

Area 1—the setting—contains an introductory chapter on the differences between allocation and management, the need for wilderness, the philosophical and pragmatic bases for wilderness management, and a common-sense policy to meet today's needs. The second chapter, contributed by Roderick Nash, professor of history and environmental studies, University of California, Santa Barbara, explores the history of the wilderness management idea and the beginning of its acceptance in the United States. Chapter 3, by George Stankey, Vance Martin, and Roderick Nash, reviews international concepts of wilderness preservation, underscoring the unique cultural features of the concept as it has emerged in the United States and describes the growing international interest in wilderness.

Area 2—legal basis for wilderness—contains three chapters explaining the enabling legislation and subsequent status of the nation's Wilderness System. Chapter 4 explains the wilderness acts; chapter 5, by Joe Roggenbuck, professor of forestry, Virginia Polytechnic Institute and State University, George Stankey, and Dennis Roth, U.S. Forest Service historian, describes the wilderness allocation and classification process under the acts; chapter 6 explores the current and projected status of the National Wilderness Preservation System and related areas.

Area 3—management concepts and direction—contains three chapters identifying some broad direction and concepts for managing wilderness. Chapter 7 proposes 13 general principles to guide wilderness management; chapter 8, by John Hendee and Russell

von Koch, recreation planner with the Bureau of Land Management, discusses the importance of planning to implement management, reviews planning policies of the various agencies, and suggests a planning framework illustrated by excerpts from several actual plans; and chapter 9, by George Stankey, Steve McCool, professor of forest recreation, University of Montana, and Gerald L. Stokes, Chesapeake Bay Foundation, Virginia, reviews the basic concept of carrying capacity as applied to wilderness. Both McCool and Stokes have served as staff officers for Recreation, Wilderness, and Lands, on the Flathead National Forest, and have provided leadership in writing management plans for the Bob Marshall Wilderness Complex.

Area 4—important elements for management—contains four chapters exploring aspects of wilderness that must be managed; that is, ecosystems, wildlife, fire, and air quality. Chapter 10, by Jerry Franklin, chief plant ecologist for the U.S. Forest Service's Pacific Northwest Research Station and professor of Forest Resources at the University of Washington, Seattle, discusses wilderness ecosystems, including a review of some basic concepts that control ecosystems everywhere. Chapter 11, by John Hendee and Clay Schoenfeld, emeritus professor at the University of Wisconsin, Madison, reviews wildlife values and problems and proposes some management guidelines for wildlife in wilderness. Chapter 12, by Bruce Kilgore, National Park Service, formerly with the U.S. Forest Service's Fire Sciences Laboratory in Missoula, Montana, and Miron Heinselman, formerly with the U.S. Forest Service's Lake States Experiment Station and adjunct

professor (retired), Department of Ecology and Behavioral Biology, University of Minnesota, St. Paul, discusses the natural role of fire in wilderness and the need for management to maintain or restore this role. In chapter 13, Jim Blankenship, retired air quality specialist with the U.S. Forest Service, discusses management of the wilderness air resource.

Area 5—wilderness use and its management—moves to the problem of visitor use and how to manage it. Chapter 14 discusses the various uses of wilderness and current and projected levels of use. Chapter 15 explores direct and indirect approaches to managing visitor behavior. Chapter 16, by David N. Cole, research biologist and project leader of the U.S. Forest Service's Wilderness Management Research Work Unit, Intermountain Research Station, Missoula, Montana, discusses the ecological impacts of recreational use and how to manage them. Chapter 17 discusses managing the quality of visitor experiences.

Area 6—problems and opportunities—offers a concluding chapter, 18, which identifies some current issues and challenges. Included is an appeal for a wilderness management system that incorporates the thinking of educators, the public, and federal agencies. The chapter also calls for more research, increased professionalism and funding, and use of wilderness for human development, education, and science.

Terminology—Throughout the book, unfamiliar terms, or words used in a special way, are explained where they occur in the text or by means of footnotes. Several recurring terms, however, will be defined here and then used without additional explanation.

Before 1964, the term *wilderness* was used to describe humanity's changing perception of unknown areas or lands modified primarily by natural forces. But since 1964, while retaining this historic and familiar meaning, the word has acquired a new, more precise definition. The word *wilderness* now refers to areas allocated by Congress to the National Wilderness Preservation System. For readability and clarity, we have elected to capitalize wilderness only when it is used as a proper noun, for example, the Bob Marshall Wilderness, the National Wilderness Preservation System, or the Wilderness Act. All other references to wilderness as a general term or in the legal sense use a lowercase *w*.

The term *act* used alone might occasionally raise questions. As it is used in this book, if it applies to a period before January 1975, the term also refers only to the Wilderness Act of 1964. After that date, the term refers to the general intent or provisions of the Wilderness Act for areas in the eastern United States that were clarified by Congress in the so-called Eastern Wilderness Act of 1975, which really extended the Wilderness Act. The term *wilderness classification acts* refers to legislation designating specific areas as wilderness. The term *wilderness acts* refers collectively to all the above, usually in some generic reference to congressional direction for the National Wilderness Preservation System.

A Note to This Edition

Statistics concerning the National Wilderness Preservation System used in this book are from information published by The Wilderness Society in March 1989 and have been used to provide a consistent baseline information source (Appendices B and C). To assist those in federal land use agencies, we have included Appendix F which contains statistics recently agreed upon by the four federal land use management agencies. Authoritative sources differ on several statistical characteristics of the National Wilderness Preservation System, including the number of units, their acreage, and the agency that manages them. Several factors affect these figures and account for the discrepancies:

units may be in more than one state; land acquisitions may have been changed; boundaries may have been adjusted; measurements may have been refined; and official mapping may have been completed after publication of the statistics. This disagreement, especially concerning unit acreage, is insignificant in assessing total area of the National Wilderness Preservation System since nearly two dozen Alaskan wilderness areas only report acreage to the nearest 100,000 acres.[1] In addition, because the majority of the world uses the metric system, we made conversions to metric in Chapter 3, International Concepts of Wilderness Preservation and Management.

---

1. Reed, Patrick. 1988. The national wilderness preservation system: The first 23 years and beyond. Wilderness benchmark 1988: Proceedings of the national wilderness colloquium in Tampa, FL. January 13-14, 1988, p.20.

WILDERNESS MANAGEMENT

Once an area joins the National Wilderness Preservation System, preservation of its wilderness quality depends largely on its management. View southeast from Silver Pass in the John Muir Wilderness, Sierra National Forest, CA. Photo courtesy of the USFS.

1

WILDERNESS MANAGEMENT:
PHILOSOPHICAL DIRECTION

Lead authors for this chapter were John C. Hendee, George H. Stankey, and Robert C. Lucas.

INTRODUCTION

In the United States, the past three decades have been marked by significant progress in wilderness preservation. This progress has been the result of the combined efforts of conservation organizations, concerned citizens, federal agencies, and the U.S. Congress. The Wilderness Act of 1964 (P.L. 88-577) and subsequent allocations of land to wilderness are intended to maintain a portion of the nation unspoiled for future generations.

But our final achievements in wilderness preservation are yet unknown because allocating areas to a National Wilderness Preservation System (NWPS) is only part of the task. As George Marshall, former president of the Sierra Club and brother of wilderness advocate Robert Marshall, notes, "At the same time

that wilderness boundaries are being established and protected by Acts of Congress, attention must be given to the quality of wilderness within these boundaries, or we may be preserving empty shells" (Marshall 1969, p. 14). This is the challenge of wilderness management—to formulate and implement programs that will achieve the objectives underlying the NWPS.

Wilderness management is a relatively new and evolving field that has been subordinate to interest in wilderness allocation. Such management is becoming increasingly important because of growing direct pressures from various users and indirect human impacts on all lands. The need for assigning a high priority to management has been stated as follows (Hendee 1974, p. 28):

In the controversy surrounding wilderness allocation, equally important questions about wilderness management are being slighted.... Simply allocating an area as wilderness does not assure its preservation. Enlightened wilderness management also is needed.

Most of the areas to be set aside as wilderness will be staked out within the next few decades. From then on, the fate of those areas will rest *solely* upon their management. This is a sobering responsibility for resource professionals, and future generations will be our critics.

Resource professionals are challenged to develop effective approaches to wilderness management now—while there is still time to develop management policies and strategies by design—rather than wait until problems are racing out of control and our efforts can, at best, be reactions to pressing needs.

WILDERNESS AND OTHER LAND USES

This book focuses on the management of *classified wilderness*—areas formally protected by the 1964 Wilderness Act, and its extension to eastern lands by the "so-called" Eastern Wilderness Act of 1975 (P.L. 93-622), to public lands by the Federal Land Policy and Management Act of 1976 (FLPMA, P.L. 94-579), and to Alaska by the Alaska National Interest Lands Conservation Act of 1980 (ANILCA, P.L. 96-487). The NWPS consists of 90.8 million acres of wilderness, administered by four federal agencies: U.S. Forest Service (USFS), National Park Service (NPS), Bureau of Land Management (BLM), and Fish and Wildlife Service (FWS). Our ambition is to further the protection and use of these legally designated wilderness areas through their proper management. We have skirted the issues of *how much* wilderness should be set aside, *where* it should be located, *how large* wildernesses should be, and so forth. We believe that such issues are primarily political and will be decided largely through the political process. Resource managers can best facilitate that process by helping define and assess the potential land use alternatives for areas proposed as wilderness. Although managers' recommendations are certainly useful, they are not always as important as their analyses.

Providing a full spectrum of natural environments is a desirable response to the broad range of tastes and interests in our society. We are fortunate in the United States to have a variety of environments that range from the "paved to the primeval" (Nash 1982), and that provide a Recreation Opportunity Spectrum (ROS) that includes urban recreation areas, rural countryside, highly developed campgrounds, inten-

sively managed multiple-use forests, national parks, recreation and scenic areas, roadless wildlands, and wilderness (Clark and Stankey 1979). Through the Wilderness Act, society has chosen to preserve, unimpaired for future generations, a selection of our least modified environments.

Although wilderness is the least modified extreme on the spectrum of land uses, it is sensitive to a wide variety of uses, including uses in adjacent nonwilderness. Thus, wilderness managers must not only consider the compatibility of uses within a given wilderness, but must also be responsive to the interrelationships among uses and management on adjacent lands.

Moreover, because federal agencies that manage wilderness—the NPS, FWS, BLM, and USFS—also manage lands devoted to many other purposes and activities, wilderness management must be carefully coordinated within the spectrum of agency and interagency land management plans.

WHAT IS WILDERNESS?

What is wilderness? This crucial question affects all allocation and management decisions. At one extreme, wilderness can be defined in a narrow legal perspective as an area possessing qualities outlined in Section 2(c) of the Wilderness Act of 1964. At the other extreme, it is whatever people think it is, potentially the entire universe, the *terra incognita* of people's minds. We can call these two extreme definitions *legal wilderness* and *sociological wilderness*. Deriving a universally accepted definition of sociological wilderness seems unlikely because perceptions of wilderness vary widely. For example, for some urbanites with scant experience in the natural environment, wilderness might be perceived in any relatively undeveloped wildland, uncut forest, or woodlot. And, as illustrated in chapter 3, people from different cultures may have widely different perceptions of wilderness.

On the other hand, legal wilderness as defined by the Wilderness Act (Sec. 2c) is much more precise. "A wilderness, in contrast with those areas where man and his own works dominate the landscape, is hereby recognized as an area where the earth and its community of life are untrammeled by man, where man himself is a visitor who does not remain." This legal definition places wilderness on the "untrammeled" or "primeval" portion of the environmental modification spectrum. Furthermore, it is sanctioned by the traditions of land use in America and rests on ideas espoused decades ago. For example, Aldo

Leopold envisioned wilderness as "a continuous stretch of country preserved in its natural state, open to lawful hunting and fishing, devoid of roads, artificial trails, cottages, or other works of man" (Leopold 1921, p. 719). Robert Marshall offered a similar definition (Marshall 1930, p. 141):

> I ... shall use the word *wilderness* to denote a region which contains no permanent inhabitants, possesses no possibility of conveyance by any mechanical means and is sufficiently spacious that a person in crossing it must have the experience of sleeping out. The dominant attributes of such an area are: First, that it requires any one who exists in it to depend exclusively on his own effort for survival; and second, that it preserves as nearly as possible the primitive environment. This means that all roads, power transportation and settlements are barred. But trails and temporary shelters, which were common long before the advent of the white race, are entirely permissible.

Because this book is about managing legal wilderness, our definition of wilderness mirrors that outlined in the Wilderness Act (see preface). This definition prescribes conditions for areas included in the NWPS and indicates the purposes that management programs for these areas are designed to achieve. The Wilderness Act has lent both quantitative and qualitative substance to the traditionally elusive question, what is wilderness?

But while recognizing that wilderness has taken on added precision in its legal definition, we should not forget the evolution of the concept. Wilderness is still largely a phenomenon of twentieth century North America. Recently, however, its recognition has spread internationally. Chapter 3 describes in greater detail the status of such lands in Europe, Asia, Australia, Latin America, Antarctica, Africa, and elsewhere, and the cultural uniqueness of the United States wilderness concept. Even in the United States, the perception of wilderness has evolved from that of a forbidding landscape to that of a valued cultural resource.

The intent of this chapter, or for that matter this book, is not to trace in detail the origins of the word *wilderness* and its cultural evolution, or to annotate the extensive literature about the many values and philosophies of wilderness. Many other books and articles do this; a complete listing is beyond the scope of this book.[1] Readers should understand the origin of the term *wilderness* and the diversity of human values associated with it. This is necessary if they are to understand the Wilderness Act and be able to relate it to ways in which these values can be depreciated or enhanced through wilderness management. The remainder of this introduction briefly reviews the origins of the wilderness concept and basic values that underlie its legal definition and management.

HISTORICAL ORIGINS OF THE WILDERNESS CONCEPT

A strong religious flavor influenced the early origins of the word *wilderness.* The word appeared in the fourteenth century English translation of the Bible from Latin and was used as a synonym for uninhabited and arid lands of the Near East (Nash 1982). Lands described as wilderness were typically virtually uninhabited, desolate and arid, and vast (ORRRC 1962). In such lands, man could not long survive.

The inhospitability of these lands was due to low precipitation, and because climatology was poorly understood, such lands were perceived as evidence of God's displeasure. Wilderness was a cursed land, and when the Lord set out to punish, through act or parable, the wilderness was often the setting—witness the fate of Adam and Eve after being driven from the Garden of Eden. Conversely, the greatest blessing to be bestowed on mankind was to transform the wilderness—to make it "blossom like a rose."

The experience of the Israelites reinforced and added another dimension to the Judeo-Christian notion of wilderness. Wilderness was not only the setting for their 40-year wanderings, the Lord's punishment for their misdeeds, but it was also a place where they could prove themselves worthy of the Lord and, subsequently, the Promised Land. The wilderness, thus, was a place where one might purge and cleanse the soul in order to be fit in the sight of God. Jesus' 40 days in the wilderness, fasting and resisting the temptations of Satan, were preparation for speaking to God (Nash 1982).

Wilderness, then, in early Judeo-Christian thought, was the place of punishment and penitence. But even if wilderness had been seen as beneficent of a place to enjoy oneself—early Christians would

---

1. Important readings include: Hans Huth, *Nature and the American,* Berkeley, University of California Press, 1957; Clarence Glacken, *Traces on the Rhodian Shore,* University of California Press, 1967; Roderick Nash, *Wilderness and the American Mind* (3d ed.), Yale University Press, 1982; and "Wilderness and Recreation—A Report on Resources, Values, and Problems," Outdoor Recreation Resources Review Commission, Study Report 3, 1962, especially chap. 1. A good summary is "The Wilderness Idea as a Moving Force in American Cultural and Political History" (Evans 1981).

hardly have allowed themselves the luxury of a pleasure trip into the mountains. The mission of the early Christian was to forgo worldly pleasures and seek salvation.

In its origins, Christianity was a highly human-centered religion (White 1967). God created Adam in his own image, and humans stood distinctly apart from nature. But Christian tenets gradually evolved until it became inappropriate or at least unnecessary to insist on the dichotomy of humankind versus nature. The first proponents of this view were regarded as heretics. St. Francis of Assisi, who insisted that animals, too, had souls, was excommunicated. Rather than interpreting natural phenomena (storms, appearance of islands, earthquakes) as evidence of God's wrath, people came to see nature as a revelation of His handiwork. Eventually, with the rise of the physical and natural sciences, people began to associate wilderness with inspiration, not terror, and to explain wilderness and other natural phenomena on the basis of science rather than theology.

This new appreciation of nature was reflected in many ways. For instance, the symmetrical, formal gardens commonly found in the latter 1700s (e.g., the Garden of Versailles) gradually gave way to more informal, pastoral, and natural settings. In art and literature, the wild, turbulent panoramas of the Alps became favorite scenes. A favorite literary hero was the person who knew how to live in harmony with nature (McCloskey 1966). This gradual evolution of thinking about relationships of humans to their environment represented an important precondition to the recognition of wilderness as a source of human values and to the eventual development of programs for its preservation.

WILDERNESS AND THE EARLY AMERICAN SCENE

When the first European explorers reached what is now the conterminous 48 United States, they found a continent of almost unbroken wilderness. In less than 500 years, this 1.9-billion-acre wilderness estate has been reduced by 98 percent. But concurrent with its diminishing size has been the increase in appreciation for wilderness values. McCloskey (1966) and Roderick Nash in chapter 2 discuss that scarcity of wilderness is a necessary precondition for recognizing its value. And, as chapter 3 points out, both the American experience and that of other nations confirm this hypothesis.

Clearly, the wilderness was a barrier and a threat to sixteenth- and seventeenth-century settlers. It hindered movement, it harbored hostile Indians, and it frequently possessed little that could help settlers prosper. But as settlement rolled back the curtain of wilderness, a movement was begun to retain some unmodified lands for perpetuity. Nash (1982) has argued that interest in maintaining these wildlands was motivated in part by the desire to lend a distinctive quality to American culture. While literary and artistic accomplishments were almost nonexistent in the young nation, it did possess one thing for which there was no European counterpart: wilderness. Thus, even while strong motivations existed to conquer the wilderness, there were also stirrings of opinions that valued its retention.

One early observer who foresaw the need for long-term protection of the natural environment was George Catlin, a nineteenth-century lawyer, painter, and student of American Indians. Following a series of trips through the northern Great Plains, Catlin concluded that rapid slaughter of the buffalo, the deterioration of Indian cultures as they collided with white culture, and the general disappearance of the primitive landscape were losses American culture could ill afford. Thus, in the early 1800s, he called for establishment of *"a nation's park,* containing man and bear, in all the wild and freshness of the nature's beauty!" (Nash 1982, p. 101).

Catlin's remarks received little attention, but the seed was planted. In 1858, writing in *Atlantic Monthly,* Henry David Thoreau asked "why should not we ... have our national preserves ... in which the bear and panther, and some even of the hunter race, may still exist" (Nash 1982, p. 102). Thoreau was a primary spokesman for a viewpoint that credited wilderness with the values most important in the molding of humankind—a perspective summarized in the oft-cited statement "in wildness is the preservation of the world" (Nash 1976). He provided a philosophical framework for literary and artistic expressions of feelings about wilderness as a uniquely American asset—the one attribute of the new nation that made it superior to the tired, settled lands of the Old World (Evans 1981). Gradually, this idea became a great force among the leaders of American thought and culture.

More than 100 years passed between the warnings of Catlin and Thoreau and passage of the Wilderness Act. During that time, numerous advocates argued for the preservation of some of the remaining wilderness landscape, and some important governmental acts indicated increasing recognition of the importance of reserving lands for public purposes. Yellowstone National Park was established in 1872,

the first in a long series of significant reservations. Earlier, in 1864, the federal government had granted Yosemite Valley to the State of California "to hold … inalienable for all time" (Ise 1961). While it is almost certain that neither area was intended to remain wilderness (see chap. 2), this action set a precedent for the federal government to allocate lands for nonexploitive purposes. Moreover, these parks represented official recognition of values and philosophies expressed by people like Thoreau.

HISTORICAL WILDERNESS THEMES AND VALUES

The Wilderness Act of 1964 was the product of more than eight years of debate in Congress (see chap. 4). To fully understand the meaning of that legislation, however, one must reach back many generations. The Wilderness Act and the movement leading to it reflect a synthesis of diverse philosophical values which evolved over many years. As McCloskey (1966, p. 295) notes:

> The evolution has blended many political, religious, and cultural meanings into deeply felt personal convictions…. Those who administer that law must look to these convictions to understand why the law exists.

The diversity of motives and values among individuals and groups supporting the wilderness movement has been instrumental in its success. We need to understand the appeal of the wilderness idea that inspires such broad endorsement by a majority of Americans and intense commitment by a fervent minority. All these values, however we might describe or measure them, are the products sought from the NWPS. The success of our wilderness management efforts depends on how clearly we understand these wilderness values and how effectively we protect and produce them.

The contributions of many wilderness proponents suggest distinct themes around which the wilderness cause has been argued. Although wilderness means something different to everyone, three central themes have consistently emerged: *experiential,* the direct value of the wilderness experience; the value of wilder-ness as a *scientific* resource and environmental baseline; and the *symbolic* and *spiritual* values of wilderness to the nation and the world.

EXPERIENTIAL

The wilderness experience is seen as valuable in its own right, and as a factor in forming our national character—part of what makes Americans unique. Historically, American writers have extolled the closeness to nature, education, freedom, solitude, and simplicity, as well as spiritual, aesthetic, and mystical dimensions of the wilderness experience.

John Muir, who founded the Sierra Club in 1892, was an articulate and influential early proponent of experiential values of wilderness. Muir was a Scottish immigrant, raised on a Wisconsin farm. Although a talented inventor, Muir was more intrigued by the ideas he found in science and literature. He was heavily influenced by the writings and philosophies of Thoreau and Ralph Waldo Emerson (Davis 1966-67). Nevertheless, he found them both wanting in some respects. Muir thought Emerson had failed to express an appropriate amount of excitement after hiking in the mountains at Yosemite (Davis 1966-67), and he was amused that Thoreau, who had proclaimed, "In wildness is the preservation of the world," could refer to orchards as forests (Nash 1982).

To Muir, the essence of wilderness was the freedom, solitude, and beauty of the mountains. These qualities, he felt, could satisfy all human needs. The wilderness experience to Muir was spiritual—the forests were temples and the trees sang psalms. In the Sierra wilderness, "everything … seems equally divine—one smooth, pure wild glow of heaven's love." The wilderness also offered personal insight; during a raging windstorm in the California Sierras, Muir climbed a tree and lashed himself to it in order to experience nature more closely. The experience, he later recounted, led him to realize that "trees are travelers…. They make many journeys…. (So are) our own little journeys … only little more than tree wavings—many not so much" (Muir 1938).

The experiential theme was also reflected in many of the writings of Robert Marshall. Marshall was an extraordinary individual. In a brief but fruitful lif (he died at 38), he accomplished much for wilderness. In 1935, along with Aldo Leopold, he helped found The Wilderness Society, and in 1939 he formulated the U Regulations; both actions strengthened protection of roadless areas prior to passage of the Wilderness Act in 1964. As an extremely enthusiastic hiker, Marshall routinely logged 35 to 40 miles a day, and set a goal of walking 30 miles a day in every state (Edwards 1985). To Marshall, wild scenery was similar to great works of art. In a major paper outlining the future of wilderness, he wrote, "Wil-

derness furnishes perhaps the best opportunity for ... pure aesthetic rapture" (Marshall 1930, p. 145).

Marshall believed the restorative powers of wilderness could help prevent moral deterioration. Without the outlet of wilderness to counteract the tension and unhappiness brought by civilization, he reasoned, people might turn to the "thrills" of crime and war. Wilderness, in Marshall's mind, offered a "moral equivalent to war" (Marshall 1930).

Like Marshall, Aldo Leopold was a USFS employee who helped form that agency's wilderness concept. As a young forester in New Mexico during the years following World War I, he became apprehensive about the expansion of USFS road systems into the backcountry he loved. His prompting led to administrative protection of the Gila River country as a wilderness—the first in the nation. Over the years, his wilderness ideas developed and matured, and his *A Sand County Almanac and Sketches Here and There*, published after his death in 1948, is a classic in American conservation literature.

In the early 1920s, Leopold argued especially hard for wilderness designation because he wanted to preserve a particular kind of recreational experience, the pack trip. Unless steps were taken to preserve large tracts of land, he stated (Leopold 1925, p. 403), the day would come

> when a packtrain must wind its way up a graveled highway and turn its bell-mare in the pasture of a summer hotel. When that day comes the packtrain will be dead, the diamond hitch will be merely rope, and Kit Carson and Jim Bridger will be names in a history lesson.

Leopold pressed for preservation of areas that provided recreational experiences he thought developed both individual and national character (Leopold 1921). Another young forester of the period, Arthur Carhart, agreed with Leopold's philosophy and pressed for protection of an area surrounding Trappers Lake in Colorado. To Carhart, recreation was not merely an incidental use of forests; it ranked among the highest of all possible uses because of the moral benefits associated with it (Carhart 1920, p. 268):

> Recreation in the open is of the finest grade. The moral benefits are all positive. The individual with any soul cannot live long in the presence of towering mountains or sweeping plains without getting a little of the high moral standard of Nature infused into his being.

Carhart's immediate superior in Colorado was Carl J. Stahl, a firm supporter of the Trappers Lake proposal. Stahl also saw forests as a source for strengthening moral values. In a *Journal of Forestry* article, Stahl (1921, p. 529) wrote:

> An appreciation of nature, a stimulation of vigor of the mind and body, and the contentment of soul contributed by association with the forests, go far toward making a useful and contented citizenry. If the American population can be made to feel contented and its effort directed to useful channels, enlistment in the Red organizations of this critical period of unrest can be averted. I can conceive of no more useful purpose the forests can be made to serve.

Thus, more than 60 years ago, contact between humans and nature was seen as a counterforce to the threat of communism.

Today, many experiential education programs—Outward Bound, National Outdoor Leadership School (NOLS), Wilderness Vision Quest, various religious groups, and a host of others—use wilderness experiences for personal growth, leadership development, therapeutic, and environmental educational purposes. These programs aim at growth in desirable personal qualities such as self-esteem and confidence, independence, improved group skills, and performance through leadership and team building, as well as environmental education and outdoor skills. Many programs are aimed at disadvantaged groups and individuals. They help people in crisis or transition find inspiration and new goals. They help those dealing with the trauma of domestic instability and chaos or abuse; those adjusting to emotional losses such as death and broken relationships; those fighting substance abuse and delinquency.

All these programs derive from a belief that, in the natural environment (ideally in wilderness), away from social pressures, excessive stimuli, and diversions, we can confront our true selves, identify our values and priorities, and recover a sense of wholeness. Such programs reflect a modern day search for essential human values (Hendee 1985). They reflect one of the central beliefs of the founding fathers of our wilderness system: that the character-building values of wilderness are vital to our society (Scott 1984).

An estimated 8,850 adventure/education programs exist in North America (Hendee 1988). Many of these programs take place in designated wilderness because the kinds of physical challenge or solitude they frequently seek are particularly appropriate to these unmodified environments. For example, every year more than 17,000 people participate in courses conducted at five American Outward Bound

courses (Thompson and Bacon 1988). In a real sense, such programs fulfill Aldo Leopold's dream. He believed that wilderness areas should be places where primitive travel and subsistence skills could be perpetuated (Leopold 1949). Today, such programs challenge management in its dual role of providing opportunity for human growth and enrichment while protecting the wilderness resources.

SCIENTIFIC

Another recurring theme is importance of wilderness to science. Because of its generally undisturbed setting, wilderness is an important source of information about the world around us—how it evolved, how the impacts of civilization have altered natural systems, and what the unmodified environment holds for us.

In today's interdependent world economy, where industrial impacts extend to every corner of the globe, areas where natural processes remain intact are increasingly scarce. Wilderness areas are valuable assets: as natural baselines that reveal the extent of impacts elsewhere; as sites where scientists can study natural processes; as gene pools maintaining the diversity of nature and providing a gene reservoir we are only now learning to use; and as sanctuaries for certain flora and fauna that cannot survive outside of wilderness.

The intricate interrelationships among all organisms have been important to the scientific theme. Muir, for example, saw in wilderness a place where people could feel "part of wild nature, kin to everything" (Nash 1982, p. 129). And it was Muir who expressed the fundamental principle of ecology: Whenever you pluck up something, you find everything in the universe attached to it.

Leopold saw scientific value in wilderness as a laboratory for the study of land health. Paleontology offers abundant evidence that wilderness maintained itself for immensely long periods: component species were rarely lost, neither did they get out of hand; weather and water built soil as fast as or faster than it was carried away (Leopold 1941). In 1935, Leopold, Marshall, and others founded The Wilderness Society to promote the protection of lands retaining such naturalness. Although Leopold had long recognized historical and recreational values of wilderness, in 1935 his justifications for such areas predominantly turned to ecological and ethical reasons (Flader 1974).

Because wilderness areas have remained undisturbed over long periods of time, they are reservoirs of genetic constructs that have evolved over eons of time (Cowan 1968). Such gene pools hold answers to

questions yet unasked; once lost, they are impossible to replicate. Similarly, it is important to retain species whose chemical and biological makeup might be useful in the future—as the source of important drugs, for example. The genetic diversity in a system of large, undisturbed tracts is an important source of stability in animal and plant populations, our best hope for retaining that genetic pool (Ghiselin 1973-74).

Sometimes the relationship of humans to the world around them can be understood only by analyzing biological systems that have escaped human impact. Wilderness offers an important opportunity to examine ecosystems as they have evolved outside human influence. Understanding such evolution can help prevent errors, at best careless and at worst catastrophic, as we shape and modify the earth to our purposes. As Leopold once noted, the first principle of intelligent tinkering is to save all the parts. A large and geographically representative collection of wilderness tracts could be of immeasurable scientific importance.

Many important physical-biological systems are represented poorly or not at all in the current system of wilderness reservations. An NPS study found that in many cases natural phenomena had been eradicated by human activities (USDI NPS 1972). The USFS second Roadless Area Review and Evaluation (RARE II) specified representation of the nation's ecosystems, landforms, and wilderness wildlife as important criteria for identifying candidate areas for wilderness classification. An analysis revealed that of the nation's 261 ecotypes, 157 are included in the NWPS (Davis 1988).

Does it really matter if a natural system disappears? In a plea for an end to wilderness destruction, E. O. Wilson (1984, p. 15) gave this example:

> Natural products have been called the sleeping giants of the pharmaceutical industry. One in every ten plant species contains compounds with some anticancer activity. Among the leading successes from the screening conducted thus far is the rosy periwinkle, a native of the West Indies. It is the very paradigm of a previously minor species, with pretty five-petaled blossoms but otherwise rather ordinary in appearance, a roadside casual, the kind of inconspicuous flowering plant that might otherwise have been unknowingly consigned to extinction by the growth of sugarcane plantations and parking lots. But it also happens to produce two alkaloids, vincristine and vinblastine, that achieve 80 percent remission from Hodgkins' disease, a cancer of the lymphatic system, as well as 99 percent remission from acute lymphocytic leukemia. Annual sales of the two drugs reached $100 million in 1980.

Dr. Jay Hair, president of the National Wildlife Federation, states (1987, p. 8):

> Worldwide, everytime a prescription drug is bought, there is a fifty percent chance that the purchase owes its origin to materials from wild organisms. In the United States, the annual commercial value of these medicines is approximately 14 billion dollars. Around the world, the commercial value tops 40 billion dollars a year.

From a scientific perspective, wilderness is also valuable because it provides large tracts of unmodified habitat that some threatened species, for example, the grizzly bear and the timber wolf, need to survive. Such wilderness offers the opportunity to study these species to assure their maintenance. Wildlife issues are discussed further in chapter 11, but it is important to note here that wilderness tracts have served as a laboratory for greatly increasing our knowledge of the biota around us (Cain 1960). Studies of wildlife such as wolves (Allen 1974; Mech 1970), grizzly bears (Cole 1974; Craighead and others 1974), and cougars (Hornocker 1970) carried out in wilderness settings have substantially enlarged our understanding of these animals. Similarly, the presence of extensive tracts of undeveloped land has made possible important baseline research on vegetative communities (Ohman and Ream 1971), fire history (Heinselman 1973), and other natural biological systems that simply could not have occurred without such tracts.

Wilderness also provides an important laboratory for scientists concerned with human behavior. How individuals relate to one another, how they react to stress and challenge, and how natural environments affect behavior are important topics for wilderness research (Scott 1974). Ultimately, studies of wilderness users can provide important insights on the experiential values espoused by Muir, Marshall, and others. One of the practical goals of such studies is gaining insight into the importance of the humanistic values and devising means to increase them through management.

SYMBOLIC AND SPIRITUAL

Finally, there are symbolic and spiritual values of wilderness. In a world characterized by rapid change and complexity, both exciting and frightening, wilderness symbolizes comforting stability and simplicity. The existence of wilderness reflects self-imposed limits on the technological imperative that we must subdue all the earth just because we can (Hendee 1985, 1986).

The Outdoor Recreation Resources Review Commission (ORRRC) in 1962 called on Wallace Stegner, head of the Creative Writing Center at Stanford University, to comment on the significance of wilderness as "an intangible which has altered the American consciousness" (ORRRC 1962, p. 34). Stegner's reply argued forcefully for the maintenance of wilderness for the sake of survival:

> Something will have gone out of us as a people if we ever let the remaining wilderness be destroyed; if we permit the last virgin forests to be turned into comic books and plastic cigarette cases; if we drive the few remaining members of the wild species into zoos or to extinction; if we pollute the last clear air and dirty the last clean streams and push our paved roads through the last of the silence, so that never again will Americans be free in their own country from the noise, the exhausts, the stinks of human automotive waste.

Wilderness is needed, he concluded, because it is "a means of reassuring ourselves of our sanity as creatures, a part of the geography of hope" (ORRRC 1962, p. 34).

The extensive writings of Sigurd Olson reveal many of the important human values derived from wilderness. In a series of books published over the last two decades, Olson articulately recorded wilderness experiences. He finds wilderness a source of inspiration, insight, and personal peace: "The singing wilderness has to do with the calling of the loons.... It is concerned with the simple joys, the timelessness and perspective found in a way of life that is close to the past" (Olson 1957). While exploring the Knife River in the Quetico-Superior country, Olson found himself nearly overwhelmed by the environment around him: "I was aware of a fusion with the country, an overwhelming sense of completion in which all my hopes and experiences seemed crystallized into one shining vision" (Olson 1963).

RELATING WILDERNESS THEMES AND VALUES TO MANAGEMENT

The above review categorized some of the basic wilderness values identified by early and contemporary authors under three broad themes—experiential, scientific, and spiritual. A more detailed inquiry would identify and sort out many more values. For instance, McCloskey (1966) identified 11 wilderness values that have emerged since the arrival of European settlers in North America.

Actually, most observers have embraced all three themes. For example, Muir's strong experiential philosophy was backed by an intense scientific curiosity. Similarly, Marshall (who held a Ph.D. in plant

pathology) recognized both the spiritual and scientific contributions of wilderness. Leopold's ethical and scientific perspective was complemented by a well-developed appreciation for the recreational values of wilderness. Studies of wilderness users show that contemporary wilderness users also identify many values in wilderness.

McCloskey's statement cited at the beginning of this section is the key to this discussion—that to understand the Wilderness Act, we must understand its historical and philosophical origin. The philosophies and perspectives discussed above increase our understanding of what wilderness is, why we have it, and what it should provide society. These issues are important in applying the Wilderness Act—in the designation of wilderness and its subsequent management. Once wilderness allocation decisions have been made, the extent to which the values espoused by early philosophers like Muir, Marshall, and Leopold are realized will depend on wilderness management. It is essential that managers, educators, and citizens be guided in their efforts by a personal philosophy of wilderness that recognizes the basic values set forth by these early philosophers. We turn now to a discussion of wilderness management and its relationship to allocation of lands to wilderness.

WILDERNESS MANAGEMENT AND WILDERNESS ALLOCATION

A fundamental difference exists between wilderness allocation and wilderness management. *Wilderness allocation includes all processes and activities of government agencies and interested publics to identify areas for potential protection as wilderness and for their classification by Congress under the Wilderness Act. Wilderness management includes government and citizen activity to identify—within the constraints of the Wilderness Act— goals and objectives for classified wildernesses and the planning, implementation, and administration of policies and management actions to achieve them.* Wilderness management applies concepts, criteria, guidelines, standards, and procedures derived from the physical, biological, social, and management sciences to preserve naturalness and outstanding opportunities for solitude in designated wilderness areas.

In general, the wilderness allocation process has typically operated as follows (more detailed information appears in chap. 5): The managing agency of a national forest, national park, wildlife refuge, or BLM-administered land unit reviews its roadless areas, and with public involvement, identifies lands

to be studied intensively for potential wilderness designation. Often intense public interest in classifying a particular area precipitates the process. Then the agency studies these selected study areas, again with public involvement, to determine their suitability, the demand and need for their legal classification as wilderness, and the values and developments (timber, ski resorts, etc.) that would have to be given up. Based on this study, a wilderness proposal may be submitted by the president to Congress for study and review, and possible legislation, to classify the area as wilderness (fig. 1.1).

Fig. 1.1. Wilderness allocation refers to agency and public actions taken to identify potential wilderness areas and to secure their protection through congressional classification. Debate often becomes intense over what lands should or should not be so classified, marked by protests such as this one concerning wilderness protection for the French Pete drainage in the Willamette National Forest, OR. Photo courtesy of the USFS.

The wilderness study and review process of Congress include formal public hearings and extensive deliberation in congressional committees as alternative bills are proposed, debated, revised, and perhaps finally enacted to legally designate a specific area as wilderness. During this process, interested groups may submit alternative wilderness proposals. For example, a wilderness study on the Mount

Baker-Snoqualmie and Wenatchee National Forests in Washington State led to a USFS wilderness proposal to Congress for a 292,000-acre Alpine Lakes Wilderness—with the addition of 82,000 acres if money were allocated to purchase private land. But the Alpine Lakes Preservation Society proposed a larger, 575,000-acre wilderness surrounded by a 437,000-acre national recreation area. The Alpine Lakes Coalition Society representing industry and recreation vehicle interests, proposed a 216,000-acre wilderness in two separate parcels. Congress studied all these proposals and, after public hearings and congressional debate, finally passed compromise legislation establishing a 303,508-acre Alpine Lakes Wilderness. An additional 86,000 acres of intermingled private and public land was defined as "intended wilderness," and Congress authorized (but did not appropriate) $57 million for acquisition of the 43,543 acres of private land needed to include the full intended wilderness in the Alpine Lakes Wilderness. A protective management unit of 527,000 acres surrounds the wilderness and is managed by the USFS for multiple-use purposes.

The Alpine Lakes example illustrates the political nature of wilderness allocation issues and the complexity of considering competing demands for use of the area. Congress seeks resource management proposals and advice from federal agencies during the allocation process, but agency views are sometimes given no more consideration than the formal proposals of vested interest groups. In the 1980s, when wilderness classification proposals typically embraced all new areas in a state, the number of areas and acres proposed for classification by different interest groups might vary from one another initially by severalfold. The determination of the public interest in wilderness allocation issues is arrived at through political processes—public debate over alternative proposals, and ultimately a decision by Congress based on compromise (fig. 1.2).

Wilderness management basically involves the application of guidelines and principles to achieve established goals and objectives. Management seeks to achieve the overall purposes established through the allocation process. It generally is not as political as wilderness allocation, although the process of establishing management objectives, policies, and actions must address the desires of competing users. In some classification acts, Congress gives special direction for handling a specific management issue for a particu-

Fig. 1.2. Citizen participation in the wilderness allocation process is essential to gain data on resources and use, to determine public sentiment, and, ultimately, to make sound decisions. Public meetings, such as this one conducted by the NPS during its wilderness study of Mount Rainier National Park, WA, have become a common part of the planning process. Photo courtesy of the NPS.

lar area.[1] Also, the management challenge facing an agency is a direct function of the attributes of the classified areas. The agency must manage as wilderness what it inherits through the allocation process. If that process yields heavily impacted areas, with high levels of established or incompatible uses, providing "naturalness and solitude" will be more difficult.

THE EFFECTS OF ALLOCATION DECISIONS ON MANAGEMENT

Wilderness allocation affects wilderness management several ways: (1) interim management prior to classification; (2) precedents, purity, and nondegradation; (3) classification of areas that include unusual management problems; and (4) limitations on uses and management.

INTERIM MANAGEMENT

Areas under study or consideration for wilderness classification must be managed during the review period in a way that does not preclude their being classified by Congress as units of the NWPS. In other words, the decision to *study* an area for possible wilderness designation is also a decision to temporarily *manage* that area as a wilderness. The management of roadless lands to maintain their wilderness character

1. Chap. 5 summarizes important provisions included in the wilderness classification acts passed through 1987, and a summary of management provisions in *103 Wilderness Laws* is found in Browning and others 1988.

until Congress decides is based on Wilderness Act directives that only Congress has the right to permit or deny any area's designation as wilderness. If interim management allows the wilderness character of a proposed area to deteriorate before congressional review, it has effectively reduced the options for wilderness designation by Congress.

While wilderness study and the classification process go on, nonconforming uses or inappropriate or excessive levels of use can become well established and protected by their own advocates. Irreversible damage can result from unmanaged use. Concentrations of visitors can disastrously compact and erode wilderness soils. Threatened wildlife dependent on wilderness can be further jeopardized. Correction is always far more difficult and controversial than prevention, so an important management task is preventing damage to areas for which wilderness designation is likely, or possible, but pending.

Thus, roadless areas identified as candidates for possible addition to the NWPS are generally managed and used essentially as wilderness, pending classification decisions. This principle has evolved so strongly that a major point of conflict in wilderness classification legislation concerns the release of roadless areas from any further consideration for wilderness classification: that is, whether roadless areas considered by Congress but not designated should be released from further consideration, freeing them for uses that would preclude their inclusion as wilderness.

PRECEDENTS, PURITY, AND NONDEGRADATION

Concern exists that wilderness allocation of areas with substandard qualities of naturalness and solitude, requiring special management attention, could establish precedents affecting the classification and management of other areas. This is the so-called purity issue. The fear is that if areas that are not really pristine are classified as wilderness, the standards used in admitting such areas will set a precedent for classifying other substandard wilderness, and for violation of the more pristine areas already admitted (Allin 1982; Costley 1972). Likewise, if an area classified as wilderness required special management for some existing feature or established use, purists argue that this would establish a precedent for similar management in other wilderness areas. Purity has been a major wilderness allocation issue as Congress has increasingly considered and classified wilderness areas with impacts

and features that some argued should disqualify them for consideration (such as abandoned roads and railroads, cabins, and homesteads). Now, as wilderness allocation nears completion, the implications of precedent focus on past management. If one wilderness contains undesirable conditions, such as intensively developed campsites, or allows aerial fish stocking or limited use of motorboats and airplanes, should those standards apply to all wilderness areas?

The issue of purity in wilderness allocation and management will remain, but fears of setting a precedent have been largely quieted by adopting the principle of nondegradation, widely used in managing urban air, water, and noise (Mihaley 1972), to wilderness (see chap. 7).

Under nondegradation, management's obligation is to prevent further environmental degradation of individual areas that meet wilderness standards, while managing to upgrade areas below minimum standards. Thus, no one area sets a standard for another, since each in effect is managed to maintain its own conditions of naturalness and solitude, as long as it is above some minimum standard. For example, the presence of high-use levels requiring tight management controls in the San Gorgonio Wilderness in California does not constitute a precedent that would permit similar conditions to evolve in the relatively pristine Selway-Bitterroot Wilderness in Idaho and Montana. Likewise, practices essential for managing the typically smaller wilderness areas in the East do not establish standards for western areas that are typically larger.

CLASSIFYING AREAS WITH UNUSUAL MANAGEMENT PROBLEMS

Wilderness allocation decisions can affect management if an area presents problems for which technical solutions are limited, unavailable, or unfeasible. For example, the location of boundaries in vulnerable or unwieldy places can make wilderness management difficult, as can the inclusion of inholdings or popular locations already impacted by recreational use.

The Wilderness Act explicitly recognized that allocation criteria can affect management; in Section 2(c)2, the act prescribes the minimum size of a wilderness area: "at least five thousand acres of land or … of sufficient size as to make practicable its preservation and use in an unimpaired condition." Below some minimum size, the act is saying, management to preserve an area's wilderness qualities becomes extremely difficult. Maintaining naturalness and solitude in smaller areas is now a challenge in many

wilderness areas in the East, where less than 5,000 acres[1] have been considered "of sufficient size" to be classified as wilderness. In addition, boundaries with pronounced bulges or indentations, boundaries that do not follow easily recognized terrain features, boundaries that adjoin areas of commodity production or urban development, can all accentuate management problems. Agencies have generally attempted to keep wilderness boundaries along ridges or other easily recognized topographical features, arguing that such boundaries make management easier. For example, debate between the USFS and environmentalists over the appropriate location of one section of boundary in the San Rafael Primitive Area tied up the wilderness proposal for more than a year, even though the disputed area involved only 2,000 acres of the nearly 150,000-acre total. Managers favored a ridgetop boundary that facilitated fire protection of the wilderness but reduced its size; environmentalists favored a midslope boundary that enlarged the area.

Some areas cannot easily be managed as wilderness for other reasons. Marion Lake in the Mount Jefferson Wilderness in Oregon illustrates the difficulties that can occur when an accessible and popular area is included in a wilderness. This lake, an easy l-mile hike from the road, had a long history of heavy use before its inclusion in the wilderness system. Nonetheless, environmentalists strongly supported its inclusion, even though a permanent USFS cabin already shared space at the lake with scores of private boats stored along the shoreline. The USFS contended it would be extremely difficult to scale back this established use to a level consistent with that required by the Wilderness Act. Congress disagreed, and the area was included in the Mount Jefferson Wilderness. Despite a substantial reduction in boating (accomplished in part by the sale of some abandoned boats at auction and the burning of others), Marion Lake continued to attract heavy use—heavier than managers consider appropriate in wilderness. To deal with the undesirable impacts and resulting intensive management required at the lake, Oregon Senator Mark Hatfield sponsored legislation to remove it from the Mount Jefferson Wilderness.

---

1. Concerning wilderness areas of less than 5,000 acres: of the 81 total areas in the NWPS of less than 5,000 acres, some areas stand independently while others are adjacent to larger designated wilderness areas which are managed by the same or different agencies. These adjacent areas share management with the larger areas and do not require the same management considerations as the areas which stand alone. Islands, such as Pelican Island (FL) and the other smaller isolated areas, require unique management.

His proposal, however, failed to attract the support necessary for enactment. A decade later, with the wilderness system much larger, many similar situations arise where easy access to popular locations poses a challenge to wilderness management.

The potential for mining in many USFS-managed and BLM-managed wilderness areas is another complication with which wilderness managers must deal. The Wilderness Act allowed staking of mineral claims and the operation of mineral leasing laws through December 31, 1983, in areas that had been open to such claims and leasing before the act's passage. Some wilderness classification acts withdrew areas from mineral operation. In 1982 and 1983, Congress added a rider to the budget bill that blocked the secretaries of agriculture and the interior from any mineral leasing in wilderness. That rider remained in effect in later years, serving as imminent protection for Wilderness Study Areas (WSAs) and areas recommended for wilderness should they be classified. Mining claims can be staked on BLM study areas until they are classified as wilderness. Valid claims with valuable deposits discovered before the cutoff can be activated in the future. While BLM and USFS regulations attempt to ensure that mining activities conform to the mandates of the act, balancing the legal rights of miners with the preservation of wilderness values presents managers with yet another complicated challenge (The Wilderness Society 1984).

LIMITATIONS ON USE AND MANAGEMENT

The allocation of an area to wilderness limits the range of uses, and of management alternatives and techniques. Areas managed as wilderness will offer only part of the spectrum of recreation opportunities the area might otherwise provide—for example, motorized recreational activities such as trail bike use are not allowed. Certain management activities are likewise generally restricted by wilderness classification—use of motorized equipment and mechanical transport, for instance.

The issue of what management actions, facilities, and equipment are allowed in wilderness was an important point of debate in the Endangered American Wilderness Act of 1978 (P.L. 95-237), which sought to classify more than 20 new areas as wilderness and was a forerunner of the RARE II. Opponents claimed that such designation would mean wildfires could not be suppressed, trails would be abandoned, and hunting and fishing would be drastically reduced. To clarify the issue of what is permissible in wilderness, Congressman James Weaver of Oregon, a leading proponent of the bill, engaged the new Assistant Secretary of Agri-

culture, Rupert Cutler, in a colloquy of 12 questions and answers about USFS wilderness management policy at an Interior Committee hearing. That colloquy (published later in the *Journal of Forestry*) was an important clarification of management latitude. It exploded several misconceptions about the extreme purity of USFS wilderness management policy, which was much less restrictive than opponents of wilderness claimed (Weaver and Cutler 1977). Subsequently the Endangered American Wilderness Act passed and the RARE II was initiated.

The restrictions on recreational and management activity in wilderness make it all the more important for land managers to provide a broad spectrum of opportunities in areas that are roadless but not official wilderness: use of motorized vehicles, concentrated recreation use requiring intense management and development, and so on. It is important to have a broad range of opportunities at the roadless end of the land use spectrum, with relatively clear standards for recreational and other uses and management. This will help meet the public's desire for diverse kinds of off-road recreation and ease the demands on wilderness to accommodate all kinds of roadless recreation activities. Provision for roadless but nonwilderness land use designations will also provide an alternative to classification of areas that cannot be successfully managed as wilderness.

THE NEED FOR WILDERNESS MANAGEMENT

Managing wilderness is a new idea. Only in the past 20 to 30 years has wilderness management become an issue—as chapter 2 explains in detail. The early leaders of the wilderness movement, men like John Muir, Aldo Leopold, and Robert Marshall, whose roles were discussed earlier in this chapter, were primarily concerned with saving wilderness from development. They assumed that designating lands as wilderness and prohibiting road construction, logging, and similar uses would assure the preservation of wilderness—at least for the time being. (See chap. 2 for a discussion of the origins of wilderness management.)

"Draw a line around it and leave it alone" pretty well describes the prevailing opinion not so long ago. Even today, it is shared by some. But a great many concerned people have concluded it just will not work with the kinds of pressures now descending on wilderness. Already some of the public fervor directed at getting areas classified as wilderness is being directed at how they are to be managed.

THE MANAGEMENT PARADOX

The term *wilderness management* is a paradox (Nash 1982). *Wilderness* is supposed to be an area where the influence of modern man is absent (or at least minimized), but *management* suggests man controlling nature. In most kinds of resource management, humans do alter and control natural processes. A dam turns a river into a lake. Forest management changes the number, size, distribution, and even species of trees.

Many people react negatively when wilderness management is mentioned, because they envision bulldozers and environmental manipulation. But wilderness management does not necessarily require this kind of activity. *Wilderness management is essentially the management of human use and influences to preserve naturalness and solitude. It includes everything done to administer an area—the formulation of goals and objectives, and all policies, standards, and field actions to achieve them.* Specifically, management includes the planning and implementation of visitor educa-

Fig. 1.3. Wilderness management includes the planning and implementation of policies and actions to achieve objectives of the Wilderness Act. To a substantial degree, it involves the management of human use and influence to preserve naturalness and outstanding opportunities for solitude in a wilderness. Wilderness rangers are one important tool in the management of human use. Photo courtesy of the USFS.

tion and, when necessary, rules, regulations, and visitor management to control overuse; facilities such as trails and signs; decisions on access roads to the wilderness boundary; regulations for recreation stock and in some places livestock grazing; wilderness patrol to monitor conditions and use; and public education, including information provided for visitors at information points, in maps, brochures, and guidebooks, and by wilderness rangers in the field (fig. 1.3). We will deal in much greater detail with the components of wilderness management in subsequent chapters.

Wilderness management does not need to be—and should not be—heavyhanded on people or on resources. In recent years, the emphasis is on educating and informing wilderness users (Frome 1985). Wilderness managers are guardians, not gardeners or guards. Later we will discuss a key idea—that managers should not mold nature to suit people. Rather, they should manage human use and influence so as to not alter natural processes. The guiding rule is: *Wilderness managers should do only what is necessary to meet wilderness objectives and use only the minimum tools, regulation, and enforcement required to achieve those objectives.*

MORE USE—LESS AREA

Why is management necessary now if the founders of the wilderness movement apparently were not concerned about it? The main reason is the overwhelming increase in the number of users. Today, at least 25 times as many people visit wilderness compared to the 1930s, in the time of Marshall and Leopold. The real danger may be that people will love wilderness to death. Soils and vegetation take a pounding far beyond anything experienced a generation or more ago (Frome 1974). And some features of the wilderness experience—the quiet and solitude—that were once assured are now difficult to find in many places and impossible to experience in others.

The enormous growth of wilderness use stems from many factors: new developments in lightweight camping equipment and dried foods; changes in society such as higher education levels (the most distinguishing characteristic of wilderness visitors in every study), rising incomes, greater mobility, and growing interest in the environment and outdoor recreation; and increased interest in health and physical activity. Heightened interest and increased use of wilderness are also logical outgrowths of the intense controversies and publicity over the classification of particular areas. These battles tend to be lengthy, sustained by dedicated local environmentalists, and accompanied by continued publicity (Allin

1982; Evans 1981; Frome 1974). They have occurred throughout the nation. Public recitation of the virtues of and threats to particular areas contributes to the continued growth of wilderness visitation appreciation. Inevitably, this interest has been accompanied by a growing realization of the necessity for wilderness management.

Paralleling increased use has been a decline in acreage of undeveloped land that might qualify as wilderness. In fact, some growth in wilderness use has been caused by displacement of users from areas that ceased to be wild, roadless, and undeveloped. The amount of land that has wilderness potential is fixed; more cannot be created within any reasonable time span. Classification as wilderness assures only that development will not occur; it does not create additional acreage or raise its capacity for use. In other words, the wilderness was there, and it was being used as such before it was classified. The chief benefit of classification is better management and protection of existing wilderness (Simmons 1966; Zivnuska 1973). When managing wilderness and other dwindling resources, our attention must be focused on the intensive margin—better management of the existing supply—and not the extensive margin—increasing the amount (Lucas 1973).

PAST DISRUPTION OF NATURE

Quite apart from recreational requirements, wilderness management is needed to restore the equilibrium that has been disrupted by human interference with natural processes. For example, fire prevention and control has limited fire as a natural ecological force in some ecosystems for more than 50 years. This constitutes control of nature just as surely as does a dam across a brawling, wild river. Before modern fire prevention and control, fires occurred much more frequently and thereby prevented unnatural accumulations of fuel that could produce fires more intense than those that might otherwise occur. Fire management to restore natural conditions is needed in many areas, and wilderness management agencies are implementing fire policies to allow fire a more natural role (see chap. 12). Recent fire management trials show that fire occurrence close to historical levels can be maintained by modern management practices (Saveland and Hildner 1985). The implementation of updated fire management policies in central Idaho wilderness is also resulting in a more than tenfold decrease in costs compared to USFS policy before 1978 when control was the only appropriate suppression response (Saveland n.d.).

The nature and occurrence of fire is difficult to

predict and thus complicates using fire to restore and maintain natural conditions. But research in the Selway-Bitterroot and Gospel-Hump Wildernesses in Idaho indicates that fire danger and fire occurrence can be predicted with at least 80 percent accuracy by mid-July, thus helping fire management decisions for the rest of the season (Saveland 1985).

More fire research is needed to improve fire management in wilderness, but the past decade has yielded significant progress. Commitment to manage fire to restore natural conditions in wilderness ecosystems is growing. A technical conference in 1983 on "fire in wilderness ecosystems" attracted participation of 650 scientists and agency managers (Lotan and others 1985). But public understanding must be strengthened for fire management programs to draw necessary support.

GIVING MEANING TO WILDERNESS CLASSIFICATION

Wilderness classification loses much of its meaning if subsequent management policies do not define what classification will actually accomplish. Without management, wilderness classification verges on being an empty symbol—a mere name designation.

Some people who recognize the need for management want it to wait until all the wilderness classification decisions have been made: "We'll worry about management when wilderness designation is all done." We think this is an indefensible stand. Even though most wilderness classification decisions have been made, many areas are still under consideration. Use has increased about twentyfold in the past 40 years, and large increases will certainly continue to occur. The impacts of such use in that long a period would be substantial.

ALTERNATIVES TO MANAGEMENT?

Is managing wilderness the only alternative? Two policies could obviate that necessity. First, all use could be prohibited. Some problems, like fire management, would still require action, but essentially no use would perhaps justify no management. But the Wilderness Act and wilderness philosophy make clear that wilderness is for the use and enjoyment of people. Public use is legally mandated. Second, we could just classify areas and forget about management. Any kind of use not clearly illegal under the Wilderness Act would thus be allowed in unlimited amount, and environmental damage or changes in the ecosystem would simply be accepted. Under this option, wilderness would vanish from most places (Frome 1974). This result would violate the wilderness acts, which require the protection

and perpetuation—the preservation—of wilderness.

NOT WHETHER, BUT HOW

The middle ground between these two extremes requires management. We see no other course of action and agree with Zivnuska (1973) that managed wilderness is the only possible kind. The real question is not whether to manage but rather how to manage. That is the topic of this book. Although such interest is comparatively recent, experience and research have developed enough knowledge to greatly strengthen wilderness management. But the knowledge is scattered; we have synthesized and summarized it for ease of application.

WILDERNESS PHILOSOPHY AND WILDERNESS MANAGEMENT

Each federal agency having responsibilities under the Wilderness Act has developed policies and guidelines for its application. Such direction is important so that management does not significantly deviate from place to place. Nevertheless, policy cannot and should not be so detailed as to cover all contingencies. Managers need to retain some flexibility to respond to unique conditions occurring in individual areas. The gap that exists between specific policy and unanticipated contingencies—the need for broad guidelines on the one hand and flexibility on the other—is filled by the manager's philosophical perspective.

HUMAN VALUES OF WILDERNESS

Before considering philosophical perspectives, attention must be called to a principle discussed in more detail in chapter 7—*that wilderness is preserved and managed for the benefits and values it provides people.* Many laws—among them the Rare and Endangered Species Act, the Wild and Scenic Rivers Act, and the Wilderness Act—have been enacted to protect and preserve the natural environment for its own sake, but under the assumption that the retention of natural features provides important human benefits. Even the statement that a feature is unique and worthy of protection is a human judgment, based on the belief that such things are valuable for our pleasure, survival, and well-being (Murdy 1975).

Sometimes these benefits can be assessed as economic values (Krutilla 1967). For example, the Hell's Canyon portion of the Snake River in Idaho was found to be of greater economic value to society in its

natural state than in its development for hydroelectric power (Krutilla and Cicchetti 1972).

The idea that wilderness is for use and enjoyment by people has clear statutory support. The Wilderness Act specifically notes that wildernesses will be administered "for the use and enjoyment of the American people." But what kinds of use? The act clearly rules out some uses; for instance, motorized equipment, with some minor exceptions, is not permitted. Still, the act permits considerable diversity in styles of use and in the accompanying developments. Simply arguing that wilderness is for public use only states the obvious. It does little to resolve the issues of what kinds of use and how much. Obviously, one's philosophical perspective about wilderness and its values is important in considering the issue.

ANTHROPOCENTRIC AND BIOCENTRIC PERSPECTIVES

Let us consider two alternative philosophical notions about wilderness and the basis for its value. On the one hand, the *anthropocentric* position takes the "use and enjoyment" phrase of the Wilderness Act quite literally. Under this philosophy, wilderness is viewed primarily from a sociological or human-oriented perspective; the naturalness of the wilderness is less important than maximizing direct human use. Programs to alter the physical and biological environment to produce desired settings are encouraged: big trees, open vistas, lots of fish and wildlife. Developed facilities to increase recreational use of wilderness are appropriate. In fact, increasing direct human use would increase human values and benefits. The concept of wilderness carrying capacity would not exist, because people's ever-changing adaptation to their environment (and vice versa) would continually change standards of crowding and naturalness. The character of wilderness would change to reflect human desires and contemporary standards of naturalness. Wilderness would still be one extreme on the environmental spectrum, but a shifting extreme, not grounded in absolute standards (Burch 1974). "Let's open up our wilderness areas" (Julber 1972) might serve as a slogan for believers in pure anthropocentrism.

In contrast to the anthropocentric perspective, the biocentric perspective emphasizes the maintenance of natural systems, if necessary at the expense of recreational and other human uses (Hendee and Stankey 1973). The goal of the *biocentric* philosophy is to permit natural ecological processes to operate as freely as possible, because wilderness values for society ultimately depend on the retention of naturalness. To the extent that naturalness is distorted, the experiential, spiritual, and scientific values of wilderness are lessened.

Labeling these alternative philosophical perspectives *biocentric* versus *anthropocentric* might create a false distinction between "wilderness for people's sake" and "wilderness for wilderness' sake." As discussed earlier, wilderness is for people. *The important distinction between these philosophies is the extent to which the human benefits of wilderness are seen as dependent on the natural integrity of the wilderness setting.*

These alternative perspectives have been argued persuasively by their respective proponents. Before turning to a more detailed look at each, two points should be emphasized. First, these philosophies represent extreme, polarized concepts about wilderness management, and it is unlikely either could be slavishly followed. But they do highlight alternative orientations toward wilderness management. Second, it is difficult, if not impossible, to say that either idea is wrong or right. It seems more important to examine the long-range implications of each and judge the appropriateness of each in light of society's objectives as reflected in the Wilderness Act. With that in mind, let us look at each perspective more closely.

The Anthropocentric Philosophy

Advocates of this idea would have us facilitate direct human use of wilderness. Wilderness managers would emphasize recreation and comfort. They might develop high-standard trail systems; expand stocking of fish to most wilderness lakes; increase and upgrade campsite facilities, shelters, toilets, and similar features; and generally increase recreational carrying capacity, aesthetic satisfaction, and user convenience. The perception of wilderness held by the largest number of users would be the most important guideline for managers.

This orientation, emphasizing society's demands on wilderness, not its natural condition, would have important implications for both users and the environment. Initially the emphasis on the aesthetic and recreational qualities of wilderness settings could lead to substantial alteration of the environment, particularly the vegetation. Given current knowledge and technology, we could engineer the wilderness scene to produce specific environmental conditions (Spurr 1966). For example, some have argued that a wilderness should represent a "picture" of an early point in our history—perhaps the land as it was at the time the continent was first settled by Europeans. To create such a setting would require sharp interference with natural processes to steer

ecological succession in the desired direction. Fire, chemicals, or machines might be used. Some desirable results—from an anthropocentric point of view—might be achieved: increased scenic views from well-cropped viewpoints; additional forage for stock from intensively managed (perhaps irrigated and fertilized) range; alpine meadows enlarged and maintained by uprooting invading conifers; more observations of wildlife stimulated by strategic salting. Traditional forestry, silviculture, and habitat management would be in order. Wilderness managers could be gardeners rather than guardians.

The anthropocentric approach would mean the loss of an essential wilderness quality—naturalness. Furthermore, such an approach (at least after a certain point) would be illegal in classified wilderness. The Wilderness Act says quite clearly that wilderness should be a setting where the forces of nature operate free from human influence. That influence on ecosystems is already pervasive worldwide, ranging from the introduction of atmospheric pollutants to direct recreational impacts. But minimal influence with natural evolution seems to be the clear intent of the Wilderness Act (Sec. 2a): "In order to insure that an expanding settlement and growing mechanization does not occupy and modify all areas within the United States ... [and] ... to secure for the American people of present and future generations the benefits of an enduring resource of wilderness." Meeting this goal would not be possible under the anthropocentrism described above.

An anthropocentric approach would also be particularly detrimental to the scientific values of wilderness. The notion of wilderness as a genetic pool, an environmental baseline, and a refuge for the survival of species especially sensitive to human influence would be lost in a wilderness manipulated and altered to fit changing human tastes. Because the loss of naturalness would in many cases be irreversible, there would be incalculable costs in terms of forgone scientific opportunities.

Styles of recreation tuned to this anthropocentric management philosophy would be convenience oriented. With the production of recreational experiences as a primary goal, actions to increase access, reduce difficulty and danger, and facilitate use would be encouraged. Conversely, programs that hinder or restrict use would be rejected. The argument has been forcefully made by some authors (e.g., Behan 1972; DeFelice 1975; Foote 1973) that wilderness is for use and that programs that limit use (e.g., wilderness permit systems, rationing, rough trails, minimum party size) are bureaucratic hindrances that should be eliminated. Under an anthropocentric philoso-phy, then, if problems of environmental impact or excessive congestion did arise, the managerial response would involve such measures as hardening sites, revegetating, installing more facilities, upgrading trails, and otherwise "gearing up" the wilderness to handle increased levels of use.

Management under this philosophy would be consistent with the view that current wilderness regulations discriminate against many people (e.g., the elderly, the ill) and, in effect, close off public lands (wilderness) to the majority of the public (Julber 1972; Netboy 1974). As a model, these authors point to the European Alps, where large numbers of people are accommodated with relatively minor impact on the environment through use of extensive road systems, cog railways, and mountain chalets. The authors argue that these methods retain democratic values, protect the environment, and serve the greatest number of people.

The Biocentric Philosophy

The biocentric perspective places primary emphasis on preservation of the natural order. Its principal goal is to encourage management programs that most nearly approximate natural energy flows within wilderness ecosystems as they existed in the absence of human influence (Houston 1971). This requires controlling the introduction of unnatural levels of energy into the ecosystems from sources such as excess recreational use, and eliminating restrictions on normal energy flows caused by such policies as fire prevention and suppression. Recreational use in wilderness would be consistent with this perspective only to the point that it does not unduly alter this energy balance. Like the anthropocentric philosophy, a biocentric approach also focuses on human benefits. The important distinction between them is that, biocentrically, these benefits are viewed as being dependent on the naturalness of wilderness ecosystems.

The biocentric approach to wilderness management also has specific implications for both the environment and users. Over an extended period of time, we would expect to see the evolution of environmental conditions that reflect historical patterns of ecological succession. The natural processes that have shaped and altered the landscape (e.g., erosion and fire) would continue to operate much as they always have. One consequence would be a wilderness that might often be aesthetically unattractive. Insect infestation, erosion, fire, forest disease, and similar processes would be allowed to run their course without human interference; as a result, wilderness landscapes would sometimes reflect these natural

perturbations. This approach would also mean that particularly desirable recreational features such as high mountain meadows, important stock forage areas, or areas of wildlife production would gradually shift with advancing ecological succession or following natural disturbances.

The management challenges offered would present little opportunity for traditional forestry skills. Silviculture and habitat management, for instance, would not be needed. Rather, much more emphasis would be placed on activities such as monitoring conditions and controlling visitor behavior to preserve dynamic natural processes. Nature would roll the dice to determine ecological outcomes.

Under biocentric management philosophy, recreational use of a wilderness would be secondary to maintenance of the natural order. Management actions to increase and facilitate use, such as high-standard trails and campsite facilities, would not be appropriate. Where use caused significant impacts, management would modify visitor behavior or curtail or disperse use rather than instituting methods to absorb greater impact. Moreover, management programs would promote opportunities emphasizing the primitive environment, challenge, and solitude—activities with narrower appeal than those available on nonwilderness lands or emphasized under an anthropocentric philosophy. A biocentric philosophy requires recreational users to take wilderness on its own terms.

IN SUPPORT OF BIOCENTRIC MANAGEMENT

Which is the most appropriate management philosophy—biocentric or anthropocentric? As noted earlier, the question of which approach is right and which is wrong has no absolute answer. But the answer must be related to the long-term implications for the legal mandates set forth in the Wilderness Act.

Facilitating maximum use within wilderness would gradually diminish its naturalness and solitude, alter ecological regimes in sometimes subtle but drastic ways, and diminish opportunities for experiences dependent on wild and unaltered settings. The result would be the elimination of one extreme on the environmental modification spectrum and a loss of diversity of wildland settings.

To achieve the legal goals of the wilderness system, *management should emphasize the natural integrity of wilderness ecosystems.* This reflects a biocentric management philosophy. This position and its implications are most consistent with the legal mandate of the Wilder-

ness Act, with the intent of the legislative debate that fashioned the act, and with its historical-philosophical foundations that evolved over the past century. Consider the following arguments supporting a biocentric perspective.

First, understanding the diversity of recreationist's tastes would ensure that people who prefer a wild and pristine setting would not be displaced in favor of users whose tastes can be met in many other locations. Some users depend on a pristine wilderness for a satisfying experience. As the supply of pristine settings diminishes, management philosophies should strive to maintain diverse opportunities.

Second, recent research suggests that as people gain outdoor experience through such activities as car camping, they seek out more demanding kinds of experiences (Krutilla 1967). Some specific evidence shows that the demand for primitive styles of recreation directly correlates with the amount of childhood camping experience (Burch and Wenger 1967). Thus, many persons now using car-campground facilities might in the future opt for wilderness. Increased demands on wilderness are virtually certain. Biocentric management will help maintain opportunities to meet this increasing demand (fig. 1.4).

Third, management responses to increasing use can lead to unanticipated shifts in the kinds of recreational opportunity an area offers. Developments to protect a site can attract a different clientele. Campgrounds developed to protect natural qualities of the site (e.g., tent pads, tables, fireplaces, toilets) have attracted a new clientele drawn not by nature but by the facilities, socialization with other users, and other features (Clark and others 1971). Applying the biocentric criteria of naturalness and solitude would minimize such changes and limit the growth of inappropriate kinds of use and impacts. But by no means would this be an unpopular approach. Studies document that a large proportion of users favor minimal campsite development in wilderness, while other settings offer development.

Fourth, a biocentric approach would preserve the greatest range of future options. Management decisions that increase use through development can become irreversible, narrowing the range of opportunities by eliminating unmodified areas already in short supply. This could lead to the loss of important biological and scientific values.

Much debate has centered on certain sections of the Wilderness Act, particularly around the phrasing of Section 2(c), which defines wilderness as a place that "has outstanding opportunities for solitude *or a primitive and unconfined type of recreation*" (emphasis added). Clark (1976) has argued that the con-

Fig. 1.4. The need for wilderness management is growing, partly because of steadily increasing use and the impacts of that use. Management is necessary so future visitors can also experience naturalness and solitude. Here users congregate at Red Pass in the Glacier Peak Wilderness, Mount Baker-Snoqualmie National Forest, WA. Photo courtesy of Russ Koch.

junction "or" means that an area may provide either solitude or primitive and unconfined recreation as an acceptable type of wilderness experience that managers might attempt to provide. His point was that to consider the "or" as an "and," making both solitude *and* a primitive and unconfined type of recreation necessary qualities of wilderness, contradicts the intent of the act and reduces the range of feasible management alternatives.

An alternative view of this phrasing is that the descriptive terms are synonymous and were intended to clarify the nature of the experiences wilderness should offer (Worf and others 1972). That is, the "or" is intended to elaborate on the kind of experiences produced by wilderness. We endorse this latter interpretation because it aligns with both the legislative history of the act and ensuing legislation. For example, the late Pennsylvania Congressman John Saylor, a leading supporter of the Wilderness Act, described the wilderness experience as composed of various elements, including solitude (Saylor 1962).

Many others voiced similar views during debate on the Wilderness Act.

This interpretation is further supported by wording in the so-called Eastern Wilderness Act of 1975. Its statement of policy notes that wildernesses classified by the act become a part of the NWPS and that management shall "promote and perpetuate the wilderness character of the land and its specific values of solitude, physical and mental challenge, scientific study, inspiration and primitive recreation." Thus, management that provides a complex set of experiences, including solitude, seems appropriate.

Obviously, the levels of solitude to be found within and between areas will vary, perhaps substantially (Stankey and others 1976). The wilderness acts do not define a single standard for solitude that all areas must meet. The existing pattern of trails and campsites precludes such a standard anyway. Near trailheads and at popular locations use intensities will be higher, and it seems neither necessary nor possible to manage for some uniform level of interparty contact. The 1964 act calls for provision of *"outstanding opportunities* for solitude" (emphasis added), and we interpret that to mean exactly what it says; there should be places and times within the NWPS and within individual wildernesses where visitors find little or no contact with others.

We fully recognize that the wilderness experience is a product of human perception and cannot be precisely described and packaged. But managers do need some guidelines. To us, the Wilderness Act, in Section 2(c)1, provides them. In answering the question, "What distinguishes wilderness from other settings?" we have sought an answer that would be true to congressional intent and offer specific criteria for managers. According to the authors' definition: "Wilderness is an area (1) featuring substantially natural ecological conditions and (2) offering the visitor outstanding opportunities for solitude in pursuit of a primitive and unconfined type of recreation."

TWO QUALIFICATIONS

To repeat, the issue of what philosophy will underlie wilderness management is crucial to the future of the NWPS. The wilderness system we have in the next century will be a direct product of the philosophy that guides the many related policy and management decisions today. It is our judgment that a predominantly biocentric position is appropriate, necessary, and defensible. We are pleased that the policies and practices of federal agencies reflect such a perspective.

Our support for the biocentric approach is qualified in two important respects. First, because the biocentric philosophy, as we described it, represents an idealistic extreme, its implementation will be inhibited by practical constraints. For example, ideally biocentric management would allow fire to burn at will. But this is not practical. In many areas, as a result of several decades of fire suppression, unnaturally large supplies of highly combustible fuels have accumulated. Fires in these areas might become extraordinarily intense, causing catastrophic damage to the wilderness resource and/or to resources outside the wilderness boundary and danger to people and property (e.g., the Yellowstone Fires of 1988). Because the NWPS includes many relatively small tracts of land scattered throughout areas managed for other purposes, non-wilderness considerations will always influence what happens inside the wilderness boundary—and vice versa. Thus, we endorse the biocentric philosophy, with the recognition that its idealistic application would be unrealistic and impractical. A rule of reason must temper its application. Nevertheless, we feel that a management and policy orientation that judiciously strives toward the *intent* of biocentricity is proper and feasible.

Our second qualification is that biocentricity, and the entire wilderness preservation movement in a broader sense, are viable philosophies only so far as they are accompanied by (1) an equitable provision of alternative outdoor recreation opportunities, and (2) a comprehensive effort to humanize the places where we work and live. The elitist overtones of biocentricity concern us. Are we endorsing a philosophy that offers access only to a privileged few at the expense of the majority (Behan 1976; Hardin 1969; Julber 1972)? For example, when the Alpine Lakes of Washington were classified as wilderness, some recreational organizations saw this as another loss of opportunity (Popovich 1976). Whatever the specific merits of their claim, their concern over the failure of land management agencies to provide a broad spectrum of opportunities is one we cannot ignore if we hope to maintain support for wilderness over the long term. In a democratic society, we see little chance that a biocentric philosophy of wilderness management can survive unless an equitable range of outdoor recreation opportunities is provided.

The second point has even greater long-term significance. As de Grazia has noted, "only if you give the city a pleasant and healthful outdoor environment, can you slacken the expensive, wasteful and self-destroying drive for the wilderness. Only the city can save the wilderness" (de Grazia 1970, p. 96). Obviously, the citizens who press for wilderness

classification and the agencies that manage wilderness have only a limited capacity to change the poverty that plagues our inner cities, the social inequities that divide our people, the haphazard land use patterns and transportation systems that blight our landscapes, or the pollution that clouds our land, air, and water. But even though wilderness is our primary focus, we should not lose sight of these broader issues. This broadened perspective is apparent in the increasing interest of wilderness organizations in issues such as energy use and land use planning, and in federal programs to provide outdoor opportunities for people of the inner city. Unless we as a society are able to achieve a "humanizing" environment (Dubos 1968), wilderness can be only a short-term phenomenon.

A COMMON-SENSE POLICY

We lean toward a biocentric as opposed to an anthropocentric wilderness management philosophy, but we are not extremists. We are calling for a managment with a biocentric emphasis, but applied with common sense and sensitivity to local conditions. We reiterate the idea stated earlier that *wilderness management should not mold nature to suit people. Rather, it should manage human use and influences so as not to alter natural processes. Managers should do only what is necessary to meet wilderness objectives, and use only the minimum tools, regulation, and enforcement required to achieve those objectives.*

Reminding the reader that the details of management may vary among wildernesses, we support our broad notions by citing the late Senator Frank Church, floor manager of the Wilderness Act when it passed the Senate, and former chairman of the Interior Subcommittee on Public Lands. In a 1977 "Wilderness Resource Distinguised Lecture," at the University of Idaho, Senator Church (1977, p. 13) argued the following:

> it was *not* the intent of Congress that wilderness be administered in so pure a fashion as to needlessly restrict their customary public use and enjoyment. Quite to the contrary, Congress fully intended that wilderness should be managed to allow its use by a wide spectrum of Americans. There is a need for a rule of reason in interpreting the Act, of course, because wilderness values are to be protected. As I stated in 1972, while chairing an oversight hearing of the Subcommittee on Public Lands: ". . . The Wilderness Act was not deliberately contrived to hamstring reasonable and necessary management activities. We intend to permit the managing agencies . . . latitude . . . where the purpose is to protect the visitors within the area . . . [including, for example] minimum sanitation facilities . . . fire protection necessities . . . [and] the development of

potable water supplies. . . . The issue is not whether necessary management facilities are prohibited; they are not. The test is whether they are necessary."

Thus, the wilderness management framework intended by Congress was for the agencies to do only what is necessary. The facilities just mentioned may be required—and restrictions on use may sometimes be needed to protect especially fragile locations. But, in adopting regulations, common sense is required.

In summary, if purity is to be an issue in the management of wilderness, let it focus on preserving the natural integrity of the wilder-ness environment—and not needless restriction of facilities necessary to protect the area while providing for human use and enjoyment.

This statement helps reduce the range for debate on biocentric versus anthropocentric emphasis in wilderness management. While clearly calling for wilderness use by a wide spectrum of Americans, Senator Church cited elements of biocentric as well as anthropocentric philosophy. We expect that in the years ahead debate over wilderness management philosophy will continue, but will be argued between these much narrower extremes. Our hope is that the philosophy that ultimately prevails will emphasize the natural integrity of wilderness ecosystems, with common-sense applications that respond to the needs of individual areas.

SUMMARY

This chapter's objective has been to set the stage for systematic and progressively more detailed discussion of material related to management of the NWPS in the United States. So far we have focused on the broadest direction—the management philosophy.

More specifically, this chapter explored the meanings and definition of wilderness in light of some basic, albeit overlapping, themes and values espoused by historical wilderness spokesmen. We discussed briefly the difference between wilderness allocation and wilderness management. We argued the need for wilderness management from several vantage points. Finally, we described two alternative wilderness management philosophies, anthropocentric and biocentric, and evaluated their applicability in light of objectives of the Wilderness Act. We concluded that the judicious application of a biocentric philosophy would result in the most appropriate management of the NWPS—management that strives to maintain the historical natural process that formed the great American wildernesses inherited by our American forebears.

STUDY QUESTIONS

1. How did early European settlers of America view wilderness? How was that view changed in this century, and why?
2. Name three categories of wilderness values or themes recognized by the wilderness movement in this nation. Briefly explain each.
3. Why do managers need to understand people's values of wilderness?
4. How does wilderness allocation differ from wilderness management?
5. Who decides which lands shall be wilderness?
6. Why is wilderness management more necessary today than in the past?
7. Contrast the *anthropocentric* and *biocentric* philosophies of wilderness management.
8. Which of the two philosophies do you favor for managing wilderness in the United States? Why?
9. What does de Grazia mean by the statement, "Only the city can save the wilderness"? Do you agree?

REFERENCES

Alaska National Interest Lands Conservation Act. Act of December 2, 1980. Public Law 96-487. 94 Stat. 2371.

Allen, Durward. 1974. Of fire, moose, and wolves. Audubon. 76(6): 38-49.

Allin, Craig W. 1982. The politics of wilderness preservation. Westport, CT: Greenwood Press. 304 p.

Behan, R. W. 1972. Wilderness purism—here we go again. American Forests. 73(12): 8-11.

Behan, R. W. 1976. Rationing wilderness use: an example from Grand Canyon. Western Wildlands. 3(2): 23-26.

Browing, James A.; Hendee, John C.; Roggenbuck, Joe W. 1988. 103 Wilderness laws: Milestones and management direction in wilderness legislation, 1964-1987, Bulletin 51. Idaho Forest, Wildlife and Range Experiment Station, Moscos, ID. 73 pp.

Burch, William R., Jr. 1974. In democracy is the preservation of the wilderness. Appalachia. 40(2): 90-101.

Burch, William R., Jr.; Wenger, Wiley D., Jr. 1967. The social characteristics of participants in three styles of family camping. Res. Pap. PNW-48. Portland, OR: U.S. Department of Agriculture, Forest Service, Pacific Northwest Forest and Range Experiment Station. 30 p.

Cain, Stanley A. 1960. Ecological islands as natural laboratories. In: Brower, David, ed. The meaning of wilderness to science. San Francisco: The Sierra Club: 18-31.

Carhart, Arthur H. 1920. Recreation in the forests. American Forests. 26: 268-272.

Church, Frank. 1977. Wilderness in a balanced land use framework. First Annual Wilderness Resource Distinguished Lecture, University of Idaho Wilderness Research Center. March 21. [Reprinted as "Whither Wilderness," American Forests. 83(7): 10-12, 38-41.]

Clark, Roger N.; Hendee, John C.; Campbell, Frederick. 1971. Values, behavior, and conflict in modern camping culture. Journal of Leisure Research. 3: 143-159.

Clark, Roger N.; Stankey, George H. 1979. The Recreation Opportunity Spectrum: a framework for planning, management, and research. Gen. Tech. Rep. PNW-98. Portland, OR: U.S. Department of Agriculture, Forest Service,

Pacific Northwest Forest and Range Experiment Station. 32 p.

Clark, Roger W. 1976. Management alternatives for the Great Gulf Wilderness Area. In: Burch, William R., Jr.; Clark, Roger W., eds. Backcountry management in the White Mountains of New Hampshire. New Haven, CT: Yale University, School of Forestry and Environmental Studies: 2-27.

Cole, Glen F. 1974. Management involving grizzly bears and humans in Yellowstone National Park. BioScience. 24(1): 1-11.

Costley, Richard J. 1972. An enduring resource. American Forests. 78(6): 8-11.

Cowan, Ian McTaggert. 1968. Wilderness—concept, function, and management. The Horace M. Albright Conservation Lectureship, Vol. 8. Berkeley, CA: University of California, School of Forestry and Conservation. 36 p.

Craighead, John J.; Varney, Joel R.; Craighead, Frank D., Jr. 1974. A population analysis of the Yellowstone grizzly bears. Bulletin 40. Missoula, MT: University of Montana, School of Forestry, Montana Forest and Conservation Experiment Station. 20 p.

Davis, George D. 1988. Preservation of natural diversity: The role of ecosystem representation within wilderness. Paper presented at the National Wilderness Colloquium; 1988 January 13–14; Tampa, FL. Sponsored by U.S. Department of Agriculture, Forest Service, Southeastern Forest Experiment Station, Athens, GA.

Davis, Millard C. 1966-67. The influence of Emerson, Thoreau, and Whitman on the early American naturalists—John Muir and John Barrows. Living Wilderness. 39(95): 19-23.

DeFelice, Vincent N. 1975. Wilderness is for using. American Forests. 81(6): 24-26.

de Grazia, Sebastian. 1970. Some reflections on the history of outdoor recreation. In: Driver, B. L., ed. Elements of outdoor recreation planning. Ann Arbor, MI: University of Michigan Press: 89-97.

Dubos, Rene J. 1968. So human an animal. New York: Scribner. 267 p.

Eastern Wilderness Act. Act of January 3, 1975. Public Law 93-622. 88 Stat. 2096.

Edwards, Mike. 1985. A short hike with Bob Marshall. National Geographic. 167(5): 664-689.

Endangered American Wilderness Act. Act of February 24, 1978. Public Law 95-237. 92 Stat. 40.

Evans, Brock. 1981. The wilderness idea as a moving force in American cultural and political history. In: Congressional Record; 27 April 1981. Washington, DC: U.S. Senate: S4010-S4014.

Federal Land Policy and Management Act of 1976. Act of October 21, 1976. Public Law 94-579. 90 Stat. 2743.

Flader, Susan L. 1974. Thinking like a mountain: Aldo Leopold and the evolution of an ecological attitude toward deer, wolves, and forests. Columbia, MO: University of Missouri Press. 284 p.

Frome, Michael. 1974. Battle for the wilderness. New York: Praeger Publishing. 246 p.

Frome, Michael. 1985. Issues in wilderness management. Boulder, CO: Westview Press. 252 p.

Foote, Jeffrey. 1973. Wilderness—a question of purity. Environmental Law. 3(4): 255-260.

Ghiselin, Jon. 1973-74. Wilderness and the survival of species. Living Wilderness. 37(124): 22-36.

Glacken, Clarence. 1967. Traces on the Rhodian shore. Berkeley, CA: University of California Press. 763 p.

Hair, Jay. 1987. Wilderness: promises, poetry, and pragmatism. Wilderness Resource Distinguished Lecture; 1987 April 8; Moscow, ID: University of Idaho, Wilderness Research Center. 18 p.

Hardin, Garrett. 1969. The economics of wilderness. Natural History. 78(6): 20-27.

Heinselman, Miron L. 1973. Restoring fire to the Canoe Country. Naturalist. 24(4): 21-31.

Hendee, John C. 1974. A scientist's view on some current wilderness management issues. Western Wildlands. 1(2): 27-32.

Hendee, John C. 1985. Wilderness—the next twenty years. Distinguished Wilderness Lecture. Lander, WY: National Outdoor Leadership School Twentieth Anniversary Celebration. August 23-25.

Hendee, John C. 1986. Wilderness: important legal, social, philosophical, and management perspectives. In: Kulhavey, David; Conner, Richard, eds. Wilderness and natural areas in the East: a management challenge. Nacogdoches, TX: S. F. Austin State University, Center for Applied Studies. 416 p.

Hendee, John C. 1988. Introduction. p. 2-3. In: Hendee, John C., ed. The highest use of wilderness—wilderness experience programs to enhance human potential. Proceedings of a special plenary session, 4th World Wilderness Congress. Moscow, ID: University of Idaho, Wilderness Research Center.

Hendee, John C.; Stankey, George H. 1973. Biocentricity in wilderness management. BioScience. 23(9): 535-538.

Hornocker, Maurice. 1970. An analysis of mountain lion predation on mule deer and elk in the Idaho Primitive Area. Wildlife Monograph. No. 21. Washington, DC: The Wildlife Society. 39 p.

Houston, Douglas. 1971. Ecosystems of National Parks. Science. 172: 648-651.

Huth, Hans. 1957. Nature and the American. Berkeley, CA: Monograph. No. 21. Washington, DC: The Wildlife Society. 39 p. University of California Press. 250 p.

Ise, John. 1961. Our National Park policy: a critical history. Baltimore, MD: The Johns Hopkins Press. 701 p.

Julber, Eric. 1972. Let's open up our wilderness areas. Reader's Digest. 100(60): 125-128.

Krutilla, John V. 1967. Conservation reconsidered. American Economic Review. 57(4): 777-786.

Krutilla, John V.; Cicchetti, Charles J. 1972. Evaluating benefits of environmental resources, with special application to the Hell's Canyon. Natural Resources Journal. 12(1): 1-29.

Leopold, Aldo. 1921. The wilderness and its place in forest recreational policy. Journal of Forestry. 19(7): 718-721.

Leopold, Aldo. 1925. Wildernesses as a form of land use. Journal of Land and Public Utility Economics. 1(4): 398-404.

Leopold, Aldo. 1941. Wilderness as a land laboratory. Living Wilderness. 6(6): 3.

Leopold, Aldo. 1949. A Sand County almanac and sketches here and there. New York: Oxford University Press. 269 p.

Lotan, James E.; Kilgore, Bruce H.; Fischer, William C.; Mutch, Robert W., tech. coords. 1985. Proceedings—symposium and workshop on wilderness fire; 1983 November 15-18; Missoula, MT. Gen. Tech. Rep. INT-

182. Ogden, UT: U.S. Department of Agriculture, Forest Service, Intermountain Forest and Range Experiment Station. 434 p.

Lucas, Robert C. 1973. Wilderness: a management framework. Journal of Soil and Water Conservation. 28(4): 150-154.

Marshall, George. 1969. Introduction. In: McCloskey, Maxine E.; Gilligan, James P., eds. Wilderness and the quality of life. San Francisco: The Sierra Club: 13-15.

Marshall, Robert. 1930. The problem of the wilderness. Scientific Monthly. 30: 141-148.

McCloskey, Michael. 1966. The Wilderness Act: its background and meaning. Oregon Law Review. 45(4): 288-321.

Mech, L. David. 1970. The wolf. New York: The Natural History Press. 384 p.

Mihaley, Marc B. 1972. The Clean Air Act and the concept of nondegradation: Sierra Club vs. Ruckelhaus. Ecology Law Review. 2(4): 801-836.

Muir, John. 1938. John of the mountains: the unpublished journals of John Muir. Wolfe, Linnie Marsh, ed. Boston: Houghton Mifflin. 459 p.

Murdy, W. H. 1975. Anthropocentrism: a modern version. Science. 187(4182): 1168-1172.

Nash, Roderick, ed. 1976. The American environment: readings in the history of conservation. 2d ed. Reading, MA: Addison-Wesley Publishing Company. 236 p.

Nash, Roderick. 1982. Wilderness and the American mind. 3d ed. New Haven, CT: Yale University Press. 425 p.

Netboy, Anthony. 1974. Can we solve our high country needs like Europe? Yes. American Forests. 89(2): 34, 36, 55.

Ohman, Lewis F.; Ream, Robert R. 1971. Wilderness ecology: virgin plant communities of the Boundary Waters Canoe Area. Res. Pap. NC-63. St. Paul, MN: U.S. Department of Agriculture, Forest Service, North Central Forest Experiment Station. 55 p.

Olson, Sigurd F. 1957. The singing wilderness. New York: Alfred A. Knopf. 245 p.

Olson, Sigurd F. 1963. Runes of the North. New York: Alfred A. Knopf. 255 p.

Outdoor Recreation Resources Review Commission [ORRRC]. 1962. Wilderness and recreation—a report on resources, values, and problems. Study Report 3. Washington, DC: U.S. Government Printing Office. 352 p.

Popovich, Luke. 1976. Ah wilderness—an admiring look at Alpine Lakes. Journal of Forestry. 74(11): 763-766.

Saveland, James M. [n.d.]. Forecasting fire danger and fire occurrence for wilderness fire management. In: Proceedings, eighth national conference on fire and forest meteorology; 1985 April 29-May 2; Detroit, MI. [Place of publication unknown]: [Publisher unknown]: [Pages unknown].

Saveland, James M. 1985. Wilderness fire economics: the Frank Church—River of No Return Wilderness. In: Lucas, Robert C., compiler. Proceedings—national wilderness research conference: current research; 1985 July 23-26; Fort Collins, CO. Gen. Tech. Rep. INT-212. Ogden, UT: U.S. Department of Agriculture, Forest Service, Intermountain Research Station: 39-48.

Saveland, James; Hildner, Richard. 1985. Five-year review of fire in the Moose Creek Ranger District, Selway-Bitterroot Wilderness. In: Lotan, James E.; Kilgore, Bruce M.; Fischer, William C.; Mutch, Robert W., tech. coords. Proceedings—symposium and workshop on wilderness fire; 1983 November 15-18; Missoula, MT. Gen. Tech. Rep. INT-182. Ogden, UT: U.S. Department of Agriculture, Forest Service, Intermountain Forest and Range Experiment Station: 375.

Saylor, John. 1962. A report on wilderness. In: Congressional Record; May-June 1962. Washington, DC: House of Representatives.

Scott, Doug. 1984. Securing the wilderness: the visionary role of Howard Zahniser. Sierra Club Bulletin. 69(3): 40-42.

Scott, Neil R. 1974. Toward a psychology of wilderness experience. Natural Resources Journal. 14(2): 231-237.

Simmons, I. G. 1966. Wilderness in the mid-twentieth century. U.S.A. Town Planning Review. 36(4): 249-456.

Spurr, Stephen H. 1966. Wilderness management. The Horace M. Albright Conservation Lectureship, Vol. 6. Berkeley, CA: University of California, School of Forestry and Conservation. 17 p.

Stahl, C. J. 1921. Where forestry and recreation meet. Journal of Forestry. 19(5): 526-529.

Stankey, George H.; Lucas, Robert C.; Lime, David W. 1976. Crowding in parks and wilderness. Design and Environment. 7(3): 38-41.

Thompson, Donna; Bacon, Stephen Charles. 1988. Outward bound in America: past, present, and future. In: Hendee, John C., ed. The highest use of wilderness—wilderness experience programs to enhance human potential. Proceedings of a special plenary session, 4th World Wilderness Congress. Moscow, ID: University of Idaho, Wilderness Research Center: 23-27.

U.S. Department of the Interior, National Park Service. 1972. Natural history: part two of the National Park System plan. Washington, DC: U.S. Government Printing Office. 140 p.

Weaver, James W.; Cutler, Rupert. 1977. Wilderness policy: a colloquy between Congressman Weaver and Assistant Secretary Cutler. Journal of Forestry. 75(7): 392-394.

White, Lynn. 1967. The historical roots of our ecological crisis. Science. 155(3767): 1203-1207.

Wilderness Act. 1964. Act of September 3, 1964. Public Law 88-577. 78 Stat. 890.

The Wilderness Society. 1984. The Wilderness Act handbook. Washington, DC: The Wilderness Society. 64 p.

Wilson, Edward O. 1984. Million-year histories: species diversity as an ethical goal. Wilderness. 48(165): 12-17.

Worf, William A.; Jorgenson, Glen; Lucas, Robert. 1972. Wilderness policy review. Washington, DC: U.S. Department of Agriculture, Forest Service. 56 p.

Zivnuska, John A. 1973. The managed wilderness. American Forests. 79(8): 16-19.

Americans began to appreciate wilderness as it became scarce, especially after 1890, the year the U.S. Census reported that the nation no longer had a frontier. In the twentieth century, increasing numbers of Americans began to consider wilderness a resource to be appreciated, not an obstacle to be conquered. Early wilderness visitors, shown in the photo, did not have the advantages of lightweight equipment, portable gas stoves, or dehydrated food. Photo courtesy of the USFS.

2

HISTORICAL ROOTS OF WILDERNESS MANAGEMENT

This chapter was written by Roderick Frazier Nash, Professor of History and Environmental Studies, University of California, Santa Barbara.

INTRODUCTION

A designated, managed wilderness is, in a very important sense, a contradiction in terms. It could even be said that any area that is proclaimed wilderness and managed as such is not wilderness by these very acts. The problem is that *wilderness* traditionally means an environment that humans do *not* influence, a place they do *not* control.

Before the era of herding and agriculture, say 15,000 years ago, no distinction was possible between wilderness and civilization. In a hunting and gathering condition people did not control their environment; they simply lived in it—like buffalo or bears. But with the beginning of herding, and later of agriculture, *Homo sapiens* began to experiment with the Pandora's box of environmental modification—domesticating (controlling) animals and managing (controlling) plants, soil, and water. In time, totally humanized environments called towns and cities developed. In the process people created wilderness by drawing a physical and—even more important—a mental distinction between the places they controlled and the places they did not control (Nash 1975).

Etymologically, the word *wilderness* is derived from the Old English "wild-deor-ness," the place of untamed beasts (Nash 1970b). *Civilization*, conversely, was an environment under human control. Understandably, since the advent of the civilization that created the word wilderness, it has stood for the dark, the chaotic, the unknown and fearful, the back of beyond. It was defined by the absence of the controlling structures of modern institutions and technologies. Outlaws and brigands of ancient times, like today's revolutionary guerrillas and marijuana growers, sought wild country for the same reason it attracts some of today's backpackers—escape from civilization's nearly omnipresent cloak of control.

THE INTELLECTUAL DILEMMA

The only wilderness true to the etymological roots of the word is that which humans do not influence in any way whatsoever. The more people learn about wilderness, the more they visit it, map it, manage it, write about it—the less wild it becomes. From such a perspective, even knowledge about a region disqualifies it as wilderness in the true etymological sense. Further, management of any kind compro-

mises a region's wildness. Even maps, trails, and signs are a civilizing influence—steps toward ordering the environment in the interest of people, toward lessening the amount of the unknown. The association of rangers, wardens, and search-and-rescue teams with a given area obviously detracts from its wildness.

More subtle, but just as foreign to pure wilderness, are sophisticated management techniques. The notions of carrying capacity, use permits and quotas, regulations on behavior, prescribed fire, and fire control gradually erode the "wild" from "wilderness." For many visitors wilderness has been lost when recreational demand makes it necessary to wait seven years for an entrance permit (for trips on the Colorado River in Grand Canyon National Park, AZ) and, at the peril of arrest and fine, to maintain a rigid backcountry travel itinerary so other parties, following a day behind, have places to camp (in recreational use of the Middle Fork of the Salmon River, Challis National Forest, ID). For many users, this kind of intensive management transforms wilderness into an open-air motel complete with advance registration and checkout times. The resulting dissatisfaction underscores the need for less restrictive, *lighthanded management techniques* that emphasize visitor education, and voluntary rather than enforced restraint. And indeed, as this book describes, such techniques are evolving from experience and research.

The intellectual dilemma posed by a managed wilderness is compounded by the fact that, in the last analysis, wilderness is a state of mind. Like beauty, wilderness is defined by human perception. For some individuals, regulations will not be distracting. But for others, just the *knowledge* that they visit an area by the grace of, and under conditions established by, civilization is devastating to a wilderness experience. Ironically, the success of management in protecting the wilderness experience declines in proportion to its effectiveness. In this regard, it is relevant to remember that it is not wilderness that really needs management, it is people. Thus, a major theme of this book is that wilderness management is largely people management.

Still, as discussed in chapter 1, it is hard to deny the principle that management is essential today if wilderness is to have any meaning at all. The pure definition of wilderness (no maps, no knowledge, a totally blank space on the map) is, at least between the 60th parallels, a thing of the past. No one can ever again have the experience of a Lewis or a Clark, a Jim Bridger, or a John Wesley Powell. It is even wishful thinking to suppose one might today duplicate David Brower's 1930s experience of making a first ascent almost every time he climbed a Sierra peak. The best that can be hoped for, in the American West for instance, is a chance to be in beautiful and comparatively natural country, away from roads, relatively alone, and dependent, in the short run, on one's own resources for comfort and survival.

Another factor compelling acceptance of managed wilderness is awareness that, contradictory as it is, a controlled wilderness recreation brings the consequent certainty that without control what remains of wildness in wilderness would surely be loved to death (Nash 1978, 1982).

DESTRUCTION BY POPULARITY— THE ALTERNATIVE

The harbingers of wilderness destruction by popularity are certain spectacular areas to which the recreation-minded public flocks in increasing numbers. Mount Whitney, the highest peak in the United States outside Alaska, is a good example. It is part of an area of the Sierra Nevada that Sequoia National Park (CA) officials recommend for permanent wilderness status. The peak was scaled first in 1873; in 1973, approximately 14,000 persons made the climb. A dramatic illustration of the changes popularity has brought to Mount Whitney comes from a man who, on August 4, 1949, climbed the peak with his father. Proudly, they signed the summit register, the sixth and seventh individuals to have done so *that year*. On August 11, 1972, this same man climbed Mount Whitney with his son. Upon signing the register they noted with some shock that they were the 259th and 260th persons on record *that day*! Presumably there was less pride, and certainly less wilderness, in the experience.

Additional testimony comes from the Grand Canyon, where the 300-mile float trip of the Colorado River is perhaps the most intensively supervised wilderness activity in the United States today. Close control by national park officers is facilitated by severely limited access to the river and the expedition-level difficulty of the trip. As a result, an exceptionally complete set of visitation statistics has been compiled (table 2.1).

Reviewing these figures and realizing that almost all use occurs in the summer months, it is clear that the quality of wilderness experienced by the early Grand Canyon river runners has declined precipitously (Nash 1982). Some argue that, enjoyable as it is, the locale can no longer be considered wilderness. In disgust, they turn to the few remaining wild rivers, perhaps in Alaska and the Canadian northland. But many others comply, albeit reluctantly, with the strict management policies currently in effect for the

Grand Canyon. The logic that persuades them might be illustrated by comparing access to the Grand Canyon and other popular wildernesses with access to playing time on tennis courts.

Tennis players would obviously prefer to play when they wish, for as long as they wish. But the popularity of the game does not permit this luxury except on private courts, which can be compared to the game reserves of medieval nobility. On public, tax-supported courts (as in publicly supported wilderness areas) demand frequently exceeds available space. Hence management devices are instituted, such as sign-up sheets, time and frequency limitations, and rules for waiting players encouraging doubles games. Court monitors, like wilderness rangers, enforce the regulations.

An alternative response to the tennis problem would be to have no management. Everyone who wanted to play could squeeze onto a court. "Triples" would be common on the popular courts and, in peak-demand periods, a kind of volleyball-with-rackets, with as many as 25 on a side, could be played.

Acceptance, indeed preference, for management or self-restraint is understandable. Players recognize that tennis is a game that is played by two or four persons. Out of respect for the integrity of the game, and with their own self-interest in mind, players support management. They sign up, wait their turn, and vacate the court at the appointed hour.

Like tennis, wilderness recreation is also a game that cannot be played at any one time and place by more than a few persons. Moreover, it is a game that depends on the existence of a relatively unmodified natural and physical environment. These realiza-

tions prompt many to accept management. The resulting regulations may be distasteful, and are clear violations of the traditional sense of wilderness, but they are the best hope of salvaging an approximation of the wilderness experience from the pressures of popularity.

Of course another response to the increasing popularity of tennis is to call for the construction of more courts. Public agencies are sometimes able to accommodate this demand. But in the case of wilderness this is difficult if not impossible. A second Grand Canyon is not easily created, and the total amount of wilderness on the planet is shrinking rapidly. When Congress classifies additional wildernesses it doesn't really create more wilderness—it merely recognizes and establishes permanent protection for an already established use of the area.

Some tennis players have responded to the problems of obtaining court time on public facilities by joining private clubs. In a sense they have found an economic solution to the problem of scarcity. A few wilderness enthusiasts have followed suit, joining hiking and camping clubs located on private land. The national park and national forest ideas took a more democratic approach to land management, but its limitations are obvious as demand increases.

The basis for any historical discussion of wilderness management is the recognition that management is a newcomer to the wilderness movement. Preservation, allocation of land, existed long before there was positive management except for fire control and associated lookouts, trails, and guard cabins. For decades, few even thought about managing wilderness. Perhaps this tendency sprang from the con-

Table 2.1. Number of visitors floating the Colorado River through the Grand Canyon of Arizona.

Year	Visitors	Year	Visitors	Year	Visitors	Year	Visitors	Year	Visitors
1867	1[1]	1952	19	1962	372	1973	15,219[3]	1983	15,443
1869-1940	73	1953	31	1963–64	44[2]	1974	14,253	1984	15,952
1941	4	1954	21	1965	547	1975	14,305	1985	18,113
1942	8	1955	70	1966	1,067	1976	13,912	1986	21,168
1943-46	0	1956	55	1967	2,099	1977	11,830	1987	18,008
1947	4	1957	135	1968	3,609	1978	14,356	1988	22,088
1948	6	1958	80	1969	6,019	1979	14,678		
1949	12	1959	120	1970	9,935	1980	15,142		
1950	7	1960	205	1971	10,385	1981	17,038		
1951	29	1961	255	1972	16,432	1982	16,949		

1. Some contend that James White, a trapper fleeing Indians, floated the Grand Canyon on a log raft two years before the Powell expedition.
2. Travel curtailed by the completion of Glen Canyon Dam and the resultant disruption of canyon flow.
3. The downturn in visitation after 1972 resulted from a quota system instituted by Grand Canyon National Park. Numbers applying for noncommercial permits continued to rise sharply.

tradiction between the concepts of wilderness and management. Wilderness was not *supposed* to be managed. It was the region that began where management stopped. But certainly equal in importance was the fact that for years there were few significant management problems. The problems that existed seldom involved control of the number of recreational users, an aspect that now dominates discussion. As late as 1949, when only a dozen persons a season were climbing Mount Whitney and about the same number were running the Colorado River through the Grand Canyon, their control could hardly be regarded as a pressing issue. For a transitory, enchanted moment in American environmental history, wilderness preservation could exist without wilderness management.

ROOTS OF WILDERNESS APPRECIATION

To review the first accounts of wilderness pleasure trips is to realize just how spectacularly empty the country was. Consider, for example, the 625-mile hike that Joseph N. LeConte and three companions made in the southern section of the Sierra in 1890. The trip is interesting for its parallels—and its contrasts—with contemporary patterns of wilderness recreation. The four men, all in their early twenties, were students at the University of California, Berkeley. The trip was their summer vacation; they went into the mountains for fun. LeConte's excellent journal (LeConte 1972) permits comparisons between 1890 and our own time. One is struck, immediately, by the total lack of regulation. There were no permits in 1890, no regulations, no fish and game laws, not even clear maps. The students simply packed up (but they used burros rather than backpacks) and headed out. Much of the time they had only a general idea of where they were. A considerable part of their adventure stemmed from their recognition that no one was poised to bail them out of the trouble in which they regularly found themselves. In 1890, the wilderness was noteworthy for its emptiness. Except for a few miners on the lower Kings River and one of their geology professors conducting experiments above Yosemite Valley, they saw no people.

The Sierra was even emptier 20 years earlier when John Muir ranged through the mountains with a pocketful of bread and a little tea. Even the Sierra Club's organized "outings," begun under Muir's leadership in 1901, hardly compromised the Sierra's isolation. The use of pack animals restricted wilderness recreation to the easier routes and lower passes.

"Off the beaten track" had a meaning that has been transformed by contemporary backpacking. Few places are now beyond the reach of modern wilderness enthusiasts.

The state of the art in wilderness recreational equipment played a major role in restricting backcountry use until well into the twentieth century. Even today, oldtimers are astonished at what the outdoor equipment industry has wrought. In an earlier era, huge bedrolls, heavy tents, and the weight of canned foods sharply limited the places one could visit and the amount of time a party could spend in wilderness. So did the lack of portable, efficient gear for winter camping and rock climbing. Today's light, streamlined equipment has opened the most remote places (fig. 2.1). Then, too, in earlier years, the population of the United States was much smaller. And, compared to contemporary Americans, most of our grandparents had limited mobility (fewer cars, poor roads), less leisure, and greater dedication to the "work" ethic.

But the principal reason wild places were empty was that very few Americans cared to visit them. Even as late as World War II, wilderness appreciation was still in its infancy. The explanation lies in the heavy burden of suspicion and fear that wilderness carried as heritage from a pioneering past. Wilderness was not easy to appreciate something fought since the dawn of civilization. It was a matter of being too close to wilderness, of having too much of it. For appreciation to flourish, wilderness had to become a novelty, and this in turn depended on the rise of an urbanized, industrialized society. The United States was at the brink of the transition from a developing to a developed nation in the late nineteenth century. The frontier ended, according to the U.S. census, in 1890. Only then could large numbers of Americans begin to consider wilderness a resource to be enjoyed rather than an adversary to be conquered.[1]

EVOLUTION OF WILDERNESS IN THE NATIONAL PARKS

Understandably the first interest in wilderness for recreation was tentative, and only flirted with the wilderness experience. People wanted wilderness, but not too much. They preferred to be on its edge, to look at it, but also to have the security and comforts

---

1. For extensive discussion of this attitudinal change see Allin 1982, chap. 2; Nash 1982, chaps. 1, 2, and 9.

Fig. 2.1. Better access, light and efficient recreational equipment, population growth, and pressures of urban life are a few reasons for increased recreational use of wilderness. Here visitors contemplate Green Lake in North Cascades National Park, WA, after a tough cross-country hike. Photo courtesy of John C. Hendee.

of civilization. This was the context that generated the first wilderness management decisions. For example, the reservation of the world's first national park, Yellowstone, in 1872, had little to do with providing a true wilderness experience for vacationing Americans. The intent of Congress, as stated in the text of the act creating Yellowstone National Park, was to create a "public park or pleasuring ground for the benefit and enjoyment of the people" (Act of March 1, 1872). Study of the intent of Yellowstone's proponents indicates that they expected the "enjoyment" to be derived from viewing scenic wonders such as geysers, hot springs, and waterfalls from the civilized vantage point afforded by luxurious lodges. Even Nathaniel P. Langford, a leading explorer and publicizer of the first national park, enthusiastically predicted that it would not be long "before the march of civil improvements will reclaim this delightful solitude, and garnish it with all the attractions of cultivated taste and refinement" (Langford 1972, p. 97). This was entirely consistent with the established pattern of nature tourism of the nineteenth century, which emphasized the edge of wildness, convenient transportation (usually railroads), and lavish hotel accommodations (Runte 1979).

What did visitors to the early national parks expect? The brochures and literature distributed by park promoters invariably featured the attributes of civilization: comfortable coaches, grand lodges, el-

egantly dressed tourists. Far from enticing the visitor with visions of wilderness camping, the advertisements tried to convince the tourist that there was no need to "rough it." Wildness was to be enjoyed—but at a distance. Too wild a park, it was rightly assumed in the late nineteenth and early twentieth centuries, would be a deterrent to tourism. Interest in wilderness was growing, but it had not yet affected recreational desires enough for wilderness management to exist, even as a concept.

As for the roads and hotels that "opened up" Yellowstone and the other early parks and determined their dominant use, park personnel or Congress *did not decide* to feature this mode of enjoyment. It wasn't even an issue; people took conveniences for granted. The language used in the Yellowstone Act made such an interpretation easy. As long as the "timber, mineral deposits, natural curiosities, or wonders" were preserved "in their natural condition," there was no problem with developing the park for mass tourism. Specifically, Old Faithful and Yellowstone Falls were the objects of concern, not the wild backcountry of the park. As long as these "wonders" were kept in public ownership and free from vandalism, the nineteenth century purposes of the park were fulfilled.

Even the most ardent wilderness preservationists of the time, people like Sierra Club President John Muir, accepted this premise and its management implications. In 1913, Muir *supported* the admis-

sion of the first private automobiles into Yosemite Valley (Lillard 1968). His reasoning centered on the need to bring people into the parks in order to build citizen support for the park idea. Along with cars came civilized lifestyles. Hotels, like the posh Ahwahnee completed in 1926 in the scenic heart of Yosemite Valley, contributed to the people's outdoor pleasure as it was defined in the first decades of the twentieth century. And because the national parks were established by law to be "pleasuring grounds," who could object? Muir bitterly fought economic development of park wilderness. He opposed grazing, mining, logging, and, unsuccessfully, the 1913 decision in favor of hydropower development that inundated Hetch Hetchy Valley in northern Yosemite National Park. But Muir did not recognize development for recreation, for the public's pleasure, as a comparable threat to wilderness. He died in 1914 long before wilderness advocates understood that management was an unpleasant necessity.

The passage of the National Park Service Act on August 25, 1916, did nothing to change earlier conceptions of the meaning, purpose, and appropriate uses of national parks. Although the legislation stipulated that anything done in the parks must leave the scenery and wildlife "unimpaired," the whole reason for their existence was indisputably public enjoyment. But pleasure-seeking people could impair nature. The ambiguity inherent in the National Park Service Act has been the source of extensive commentary and still more extensive agony for subsequent park managers (Sax 1980). But for Americans in 1916, there was considerably less inconsistency in the act. Since wilderness protection and the provision of a wilderness experience were not recognized goals of park management, few questioned developments (such as roads and lodges) that eroded wildness. Why should they have, after all? Hardly anyone went into the park backcountry at this time. Dramatic assertions (probably true) that more than 90 percent of these early visitors saw only 3 percent of the park were not the result of any conscious management policy. They reflected quite accurately the tastes of recreation-minded Americans in the early twentieth century. Most people did not *want* to experience park wilderness. The practical implications for management of these conceptions of park means and purposes can be found in a letter of May 13, 1918, from Secretary of the Interior Franklin K. Lane to Stephen T. Mather, the first director of the National Park Service (NPS) (USDI NPS 1970). In all probability the letter was drafted for Lane's signature by Mather himself.

The letter opens with the standard insistence that the parks be kept in "absolutely unimpaired

form," but quickly makes compromises on behalf of public enjoyment. From the standpoint of wilderness preservation, the most damaging aspect of Lane's letter is the assumption that the public should be encouraged to enjoy the parks "in the manner that best satisfies the individual taste." There is, in other words, no attempt to define what kind of enjoyment is appropriate in a national park, no effort to distinguish uses that are consistent with the mandate to leave park land unimpaired. In effect, Lane is saying that the citizen will bring his preferences to the parks and the parks will fulfill them. The 1918 letter makes clear that "automobiles and motorcycles will be permitted in all of the national parks; in fact, the parks will be kept accessible by any means practicable." The implications of this statement are extraordinary and clearly work against wilderness. So does the secretary's directive to encourage a full range of accommodations from "luxurious hotels" to "free campsites." Nothing is said about low-density, off-road wilderness uses of the parks. Again, the point is that in the early 1900s wilderness recreation was not considered part of the statutory purpose of national parks. Americans of this period gave little evidence of being disappointed with such a definition and the resulting management policy.

Stephen T. Mather was the ideal director of the National Park System under the explicit and implicit mandates of the early twentieth century. His talent was public relations, and he recognized that national park survival and growth depended on skillful playing of the "number of visitors game" in the political arena. Immediately after passage of the 1916 legislation, Mather launched a vigorous program to boost national parks. It included a series of publications, the work of Robert Sterling Yard, and the initiation or continuation of management policies designed to attract and please visitors. Mather and Yard knew that wilderness would not "sell" to their contemporaries. Instead they cultivated a resort or circus image of parks. Drive-through sequoias, cut initially in the 1880s, continued to be a tourist "must" at Yosemite. At Yellowstone, soap was regularly dumped into the geysers to break their surface tension and cause eruptions at times convenient to tourists. At Old Faithful, the symbol of America's national park in this period, colored spotlights from adjacent hotels illuminated night eruptions. During the hour between eruptions, tourists were entertained by radio music.

Yellowstone's famous roadside bears shared top billing with Old Faithful. By explicit direction of Director Mather and his assistant and subsequent director, Horace M. Albright, the bears were regularly

fed with hotel garbage before grandstands of camera-wielding tourists. In the 1920s, it must be remembered, bear feedings and caged wildlife around hotels did not violate national park purpose—rather, they expressed it. Public enjoyment could easily be stretched to cover such activities.

At Yosemite National Park in the 1870s, the "firefall" replaced the "chicken fall" in which live chickens were tossed over the cliffs. It continued, under Mather and Albright, to dominate the park experience for most tourists. The firefall involved the construction of a huge wood fire on the lip of Glacier Point 3,000 feet above the floor of Yosemite Valley. As dusk fell, the crowds gathered. Music played ("Indian Love Call" was a favorite), and at a voice signal, "Let the fire fall!," the burning logs and embers were pushed over the cliff. The potential for forest fire was fully recognized and carefully avoided, but for decades no one even questioned whether the firefall was an appropriate activity for management to sponsor in a national park. No one asked if this was the *kind* of "enjoyment" parks were created to provide. It was not until the late 1960s that changing interpretations of the meaning and purpose of national parks led to the abolition of the firefall and the replacement of the *resort concept* with more wilderness orientation in national parks.

There had, however, been earlier indications of wilderness consciousness in national park circles. In 1929 the phrase "original wilderness character" was used in certain versions of the bill establishing Grand Teton National Park (WY). No hotels or new roads were to be permitted in the park. Although stricken from the final text of the bill (Act of February 26, 1929), the omitted phrase clearly indicated a desire to emphasize wilderness in the Teton reservation. The first explicit recognition of wilderness in national park legislation appeared five years later in the act establishing Everglades National Park. Section 4 specified that the Florida wetlands would be "permanently preserved as a wilderness." With an eye toward management, the bill went on to say that "no development of the project or plan for the entertainment of visitors shall be undertaken which will interfere with the preservation of the … essential primitive natural conditions now prevailing in this area" (Act of May 30, 1934). Another milestone in the development of the wilderness idea was the 1940 establishment of Kings Canyon National Park (CA), south of Yosemite, as a roadless and hotelless park. Providing a wilderness experience was, necessarily, its main objective. Indeed a preliminary version of the establishing legislation even used the name "Kings Canyon Wilderness National Park." The Sierra Club regarded Kings Canyon as compensation, in a sense, for the heavily developed character of Yosemite. To-

gether the two parks would serve a wide spectrum of recreational interests.

Other evidence shows some early awakening for the need to be concerned about management. In 1928 and 1929, George M. Wright of the NPS saw the need for an organizational unit to monitor impacts on wildlife in national park ecosystems. Wright organized a small group of individuals to begin a nation-wide systematic survey of the status of wildlife in the parks, with development of a well-defined wildlife policy as its goal. The work of this group (Wright and others 1932; Wright and Thompson 1934) provided a historic baseline of data concerning wildlife in the parks, including such wilderness-dependent species as the wolf and grizzly bear. Wright's work led to the establishment of the Division of Wildlife Research in the NPS, with Wright as its first head.

The expansion of thinking to include management as well as allocation was beginning. One of the first written examples of this transformation as it concerned national parks was a 1936 report of Lowell Sumner, a regional wildlife technician. In his policy recommendations for Sierra parks, Sumner wondered "how large a crowd can be turned loose in a wilderness without destroying its essential qualities." He realized that for wilderness to exist in the parks, the areas "cannot hope to accommodate unlimited numbers of people." Construction of tourist facilities would have to be restricted. And finally, Sumner's insights extended to the understanding that wilderness managers could also pose a threat to wilderness values. He urged that only "the very simplest maintenance activity" be undertaken in wilderness (Sumner 1936). Heavy management, in other words, could be a liability in dealing with an experience that featured solitude, self-reliance, and freedom from the controls normally present in civilization.

Sumner's thinking on these points matured so that six years later he could discuss the adverse effects of packstock grazing, fishing, and sheer numbers of visitors on the biological balances of wilderness areas. Then, in one of the first uses of the term, Sumner urged that use of wilderness be kept "within the carrying capacity or 'recreational saturation point.'" His 1942 definition described carrying capacity as "the maximum degree of the highest type of recreational use which a wilderness can receive, consistent with its long-term preservation." Wilderness managers should "determine in advance the probable maximum permissible use, short of impairment, of all wilderness areas." Here, in 1942, was the basic logic of modern wilderness recreation management (Sumner 1942, p. 20).

EVOLUTION OF WILDERNESS IN NATIONAL FORESTS

While the national parks of the early twentieth century were playing to crowds of people who had little interest beyond visiting pleasuring grounds, the U.S. Forest Service (USFS) took the first steps toward the explicit identification of wilderness as a specific recreational resource and the development of appropriate management techniques. While Gifford Pinchot headed the Division of Forestry (after 1905, the USFS), the emphasis was on production of commodities, consistent with the 1897 "Organic Act," which mentioned only timber, grazing, and watershed protection as uses of the forest reserves (Roth 1984). The forests were to be used, albeit carefully, as a constant source of valuable products. After Pinchot's departure from office in 1910, the meaning of "products" was expanded. Some people began to understand that forests were valuable for more than commodities. Henry Graves, the new chief of the USFS, began to conceive of the national forests as valuable for recreation. Of course, in these early years, *recreation* meant almost every imaginable outdoor activity, but wilderness had a small and growing significance. For instance, in 1910 Graves asked Treadwell Cleveland, Jr., to write an essay on public recreation facilities for the American Academy of Political and Social Science. The resulting discussion of the use of logging roads, bridges, and trails by the hunter, angler, and picnicker was unprecedented in the history of American forestry. And Cleveland (1910, p. 245) made a significant prediction:

> So great is the value of national forest area for recreation, and so certain is this value to increase with the growth of the country and the shrinkage of the wilderness, that even if the forest resources of food and water were not to be required by the civilization of the future, many of the forests ought certainly to be preserved ... for recreation use alone.

But the USFS, like the NPS, was constrained by the anti-wilderness bias of public opinion in this era. Few people wanted to rough it. Recreational development, therefore, consisted of the extension of forest roads and the leasing of sites for summer home and hotel construction. Chief Forester Graves was enthusiastic about progress in these areas in his 1912 report; and, three years later, he obtained permission from the secretary of agriculture to extend leases to 30 years. The result? More permanent structures were built. Wilderness suffered, but at the time few Americans really cared.

In 1918 landscape architect Frank A. Waugh prepared a report for the USFS entitled "Recreation Uses on the National Forests" (Waugh 1918). It marked the emergence of full awareness that recreation was an established rationale for national forests. William B. Greeley, who became chief forester in 1920, and his Associate Forester L. F. Kneipp gave increasing emphasis to this use and even secured budgetary appropriations for recreation beginning in 1922. Greeley, in particular, valued forest scenery, and on several occasions in the early 1920s vetoed tourist development plans. The most important decision of the era affecting wilderness affected the spectacular Trappers Lake in Colorado on national forest land. In 1919, a young USFS landscape architect named Arthur H. Carhart was assigned to survey the area for road access and several hundred vacation homes. The plan was entirely in keeping with USFS definitions of recreation, but Carhart was troubled. The beaver of Trappers Lake had been exploited in the 1850s, but otherwise the lake was untouched and reachable only by a tough 5-mile trail. Realizing the rarity of such wildernesses in the American West, Carhart had misgivings about developing Trappers Lake even for recreational purposes. So, after a summer spent not only surveying, but also developing a conviction that the area should be preserved in its pristine condition, Carhart had the courage to recommend doing nothing at all to Trappers Lake. Probably to his surprise, the Denver District Office of the USFS approved the idea. Trappers Lake was left without roads or summer homes. (Baldwin 1972; Allin 1982).

Arthur Carhart followed his pro-wilderness recommendation in Colorado with a similar one for the Superior National Forest in Minnesota. And late in 1919, he met with the young, nontraditional forester Aldo Leopold. The disappearance of large roadless areas in Arizona and New Mexico was evoking in Leopold misgivings similar to Carhart's. Leopold's efforts to retain large sections of country devoid of human influence included a call for a wilderness of at least 500,000 acres for each of the 11 states west of the Great Plains (Leopold 1921; Roth 1984). In 1924, Leopold had the satisfaction of seeing the USFS designate 574,000 acres of the Gila National Forest, New Mexico, as a reserve for wilderness recreation. The efforts of Carhart and Leopold produced the first allocation of public land specifically for wilderness values in America, and, indeed, in the world (fig. 2.2).

The management consequences of establishing the Gila Wilderness Reserve were minimal. A laissez-faire approach prevailed—prohibit building roads and hotels and then leave it alone. In the 1920s, no attempt was made to manage positively for wilde-

rness values, recreational or otherwise. Wilderness was simply set aside.

William B. Greeley, chief forester in the 1920s, exemplified this philosophy in action. He was enthusiastic about creating wilderness reserves on national forests, largely because he feared that the aggressive leadership Stephen T. Mather was giving the national parks threatened his own empire (Gilligan 1953). If the USFS did not move to protect its spectacular scenery and develop its recreational resources, there was a good chance that some of its land might be turned over to the NPS. Such considerations unquestionably supported the intentions of some foresters to preserve wilderness simply because it was a good thing to do. In 1926 Greeley formulated a policy for wilderness. Commercial use (grazing, even logging) of the areas could continue, but campsites, meadows for packstock forage, and special scenic "spots," as they were called (Gilligan 1953), would be protected. Greeley also instructed his Associate Forester, L. F. Kneipp, to make an inventory of national forest wilderness—the first roadless area review. The result showed 74 areas, each at least 360 square miles, in the 48 states. The chief forester's ideas of management stopped at this point. In a 1926 communication to his several districts, he explicitly disavowed any intention to regulate the numbers or the behavior of recreational users of wilderness. "I have no sympathy," he declared, "for the viewpoint that people should be kept out of wilderness areas in any large numbers because the presence of human beings destroys the wilderness aspect. ... Public use and enjoyment are the only justification for having wilderness reserves at all." As for the numbers of visitors, "the only limitation should be the natural one set up by the modes of travel possible" (Gilligan 1953, p. 104). Clearly, Greeley did not foresee the time when such limitations would be insufficient to keep wilderness from being destroyed, ironically, by those who loved it. In the third decade of the twentieth century there was little reason to worry about loving wilderness to death. The backcountry was still relatively empty.

At the 1926 session of the National Conference on Outdoor Recreation, Aldo Leopold made a strong plea for more systematic planning to protect wilderness (NCOR 1926). In Associate Forester Kneipp, Leopold found a supporter close to the center of power in Washington. Three years later, on July 12, 1929, Kneipp wrote Forest Service Regulation L-20, to order and consolidate what had until then been piecemeal preservation. The directive, which was not law but only an expression of agency policy, standardized the term "primitive area" for a decade.

(See chaps. 4 and 5.) Interestingly, the term *wilderness* was not used in L-20 because Kneipp and his colleagues thought the public would be repelled by its connotations (Pomeroy 1957). Kneipp also admitted that the term *wilderness* did not apply to regions that had been, and still were being, commercially used.

L-20, with the amendments and mimeographed instructions that followed it, required field staff to submit definite management plans for each primitive area. (Further discussion of the L-20 Regulation is found in chap. 4.) These first, extremely vague management instructions amounted to little more than a list of prohibited and permitted activities. Among those permitted were virtually the full range of commercial endeavors customarily pursued in national forests. A notable exception was a section of L-20 that established research reserves (after 1930, called experimental forests). These areas, usually small, embraced natural forest ecosystems of scientific importance. Commercial use of the research reserves was prohibited; even recreational use was discouraged. Here was at least implicit recognition that recreation could have an impact on the biological integrity of an area.

On the issue of recreational developments in the primitive areas, L-20 raised important management questions. Some USFS officials, with every good intention, responded to the instructions with an aggressive program of trail and shelter construction in order to compete with the civilized style of developments common in the national parks and attractive to the majority of vacationers in the 1930s. Kneipp had a different idea of wilderness management. On May 29, 1930, he wrote with some impatience to the field staff: "There should be no need for developing these areas to take care of the large numbers of people who are not capable of exploring wild country without considerable aid." Kneipp went on to direct his forest supervisors to stop plans for trail signs, latrines, corrals, and shelters in the wilderness. He recommended that "primitive simplicity" be used as a criterion for development decisions. "These primitive areas are for the class who seek almost absolute detachment from the evidences of civilization," he concluded (Gilligan 1953, p. 147).

Such sentiments must have cheered Robert Marshall. The New York-born son of a millionaire lawyer, Marshall devoted his entire life to wilderness. Professionally, he trained as a plant pathologist. For recreation, he penetrated the nation's wildest remaining corners, including the Brooks Range in northern Alaska. A prodigious hiker (He regularly covered 35 miles a day and occasionally logged more than 70!), Marshall resented any kind of convenience in wilderness, and his management ideas reflected this viewpoint. From his position after 1933 as director of the Forestry

Division of the U.S. Office of Indian Affairs, Marshall crusaded for the curtailment of road building in wild places. He was particularly offended by so-called fire roads. Easy to build, especially when the Great Depression brought thousands of job-hungry men under federal care in work programs like the Civilian Conservation Corps, dirt roads threatened to divide and conquer the last really large wildernesses in the West. Marshall's greatest achievement, really a memorial because he died two months later at 38, was the promulgation of the U Regulations by the USFS on September 19, 1939. Superseding the L-20 Regulation with respect to more than 14 million acres of wilderness on the national forests, the U rulings tightened protection. (See chap. 4 for additional details on the U Regulations.) In administratively des-

ignated *wilderness* and *wild areas* (the term *primitive* was no longer to be used in classifying areas), there would be "no roads or other provision for motorized transportion," no lumbering, and no hotels, lodges, or permanent camps (Baldwin 1972). Very little was said about management, either in the U Regulations or in the subsequent instructions for their implementation. To preserve wilderness it seemed enough to exercise a caretaker function with an emphasis on guarding against outside influences. Wilderness inventory and allocation, not management, were the preoccupations of the 1930s (fig. 2.3). Marshall's walls were covered with maps and lists—a circle drawn around an area was supposed to be sufficient to preserve it.

The USFS, through efforts by Carhart, Leopold,

Fig. 2.2. Arthur Carhart (upper left) and Aldo Leopold (upper right) were instrumental in setting aside 574,000 acres of the Gila National Forest, NM (left) in 1924 as the first designated wilderness in the United States. All photos courtesy of the USFS.

and Marshall, was in the forefront of the wilderness struggles. This was possible in large part because of the discretion accorded the USFS in deciding uses of the national forests. Later this was to change as the Wilderness Act, and especially its provision that only Congress could designate a wilderness, took land use discretion concerning wilderness away from the agency. As fights over what qualified as wilderness and the classification of many wilderness areas attest, the USFS, interest groups, and Congress have often disagreed over what areas, and what kinds of areas, should be designated as wilderness.

Still, a pride of authorship and leadership stemming from its early efforts to establish wilderness runs deep in the USFS. This legacy has complicated the agency's response to expanded proposals and liberalized definitions of wilderness thrust on it by the environmental movement of recent years.

THE WILDERNESS MANAGEMENT IDEA BEGINS

The same emphasis on circle-drawing and "let-alone" characterized citizen conservation groups in the 1930s. The Wilderness Society had its origins in 1934 and 1935 among a group of people, Marshall and Leopold included, whose declared objective was "holding wild areas *soundproof* as well as *sightproof* from our increasingly mechanized life" (Nash 1982, p. 206). The whole thrust of this effort was to keep adverse influences *out* of wilderness, not to understand and control what was happening *within* its borders.

The first recognition of a management dimension to wilderness preservation began in the 1930s. Marshall's contribution to "A National Plan for American Forestry" (1933), the so-called Copeland Report, contained sections on the overuse of backcountry campsites and the need to educate recreationists in outdoor etiquette, today called "minimum-impact camping." Further recognition that wilderness required management came in the summer of 1937 when Marshall, the new chief of the Division of Recreation and Lands in the USFS, toured the Sierra with members of the Sierra Club. On the trip the party visited high country severely damaged by the grazing of packstock and by campers. Discussions begun on the trip led to Marshall's requesting Professor Joel H. Hildebrand, president of the Sierra Club, to organize a committee to advise the USFS about wilderness management. Marshall provided the committee with key questions that revealed the direction of his thinking about wilderness. One question, for example, concerned the feasibility of distributing use—of zoning wilderness, in effect, to achieve certain ends. Specifically, Marshall was anxious that "certain areas may still be preserved in what might be termed a super wilderness condition, or, in other words, kept entirely free even from trails, in order that a traveler can have the feeling of being where no one has been before" (Hildebrand 1938, p. 90).

The Hildebrand Committee replied with a list of trails currently in the Sierra and a recommendation that construction of new trails be sharply limited

Fig. 2.3. Many people contributed to the wilderness movement in the United States. Robert Marshall (left), the chief of Division of Recreation and Lands in the USFS, led the establishment of the U Regulations in 1939 creating wilderness, wild, and roadless areas, the immediate forerunner of today's NWPS. Photo courtesy of The Wilderness Society. Lowell Sumner (right) of the NPS helped inventory wilderness conditions in the Sierra Nevada of CA in the 1930s and, at that early date, recognized that these fragile lands had a "saturation point" beyond which recreational use could lead to irreversible damage. Photo courtesy of the NPS.

and, if necessary, kept at a low (that is, primitive) standard. Responding to other questions from Marshall, the Sierra Club advised restricting trail signs, limiting the use and grazing of packstock, and prohibiting the cutting of pine boughs for beds. To manage the wilderness and enforce such regulations, the club suggested appointing high-country rangers or guards. Finally, in a significant forecast, both Marshall and the Sierra Club expressed concern that wilderness be made available to all the public by encouraging use by younger and poorer people. One idea discussed was making burros and camping equipment available on a rental basis.

The Marshall-Sierra Club interchange in 1937 began a new era in wilderness management. It recognized that recreation was only one value associated with wilderness and that, to maintain wild conditions, recreation should be regulated and restricted. Subsequently, a November 1940 article entitled "Certified Outdoorsmen" by J. V. K. Wagar observed that "nature once certified outdoorsmen." The weak, foolish, and careless just did not return from the wilderness they entered. "But now," he continued, "there is such ease of transportation and so much improvement in equipment that anyone can become a wilderness traveler" (Wagar 1940, p. 490). Wagar's point was that many people were in the wilderness who did not know how to care either for themselves or for the country. His suggested remedy was a program conducted by rangers from the NPS and the USFS to certify outdoorsmen. Those attaining the rank of "Expert Outdoorsman" would be safe to leave in the woods. Included in their knowledge would be the ability to respect and live gently on the land. In 1940, Wagar did not go so far as to suggest that *only* certified outdoorsmen be admitted to designated wilderness areas, but the implication was clearly present. If the NPS and USFS certified recreational users of the lands they administered, the next logical step was to require certification before admission to those lands in the interest of protecting the wilderness resource. More than 40 years later the author of this chapter proposed a mandatory "wilderness license" in *Backpacker* magazine (Nash 1981). Critics of the idea point out that such a license would further compromise the freedom of the wilderness. The counter argument is that educated (licensed) visitors could be permitted *more* freedom than visitors unfamiliar with minimum-impact wilderness skills. The same logic prevails in the current use by the agencies of "education of visitors" (but without licensing) as a major wilderness management tool.

Wilderness enthusiasts have long recognized that too many people, even too many qualified outdoor enthusiasts, can spoil a particular place. As early as August 15, 1926, the *New York Herald Tribune* featured a before-and-after cartoon of a mountain lake. In the first frame, a lone horseman approached the lake, which was surrounded with pines and full of leaping trout; in the second, a solid rank of fishermen surrounded the lake, and their camps obliterated the scenery. In this case the extension of a road to the lake was represented as the cause of the change. But by the 1930s, some Americans understood that, even without roads, wilderness values could be threatened by overuse. If that solitary horseman were joined by 50 other riders and 100 backpackers, the problem would be much the same.

As a prime consumer of wilderness recreation, the Sierra Club continued to take keen interest in developing techniques of wilderness management. In 1947 the *Sierra Club Bulletin* featured another article on recreational impact on wilderness. It was coauthored by Lowell Sumner of the NPS and Richard M. Leonard, the chairman of the Sierra Club's Outing Committee, which was by that year coordinating a number of large, high-country trips each year. Sumner and Leonard focused particularly on the mountain meadow of the Sierra, and their article included a photographic sequence depicting stages in the transformation of a lush grassland into a dustbowl. The cause was excessive recreational use. Discussing the problem under the heading "Saturation of the Wilderness," the authors declared, "We need more than just a concept. ... We need a comprehensive technique of use that will prevent oversaturation of wilderness and still enable people, in reasonable numbers, to enjoy wilderness" (Leonard and Sumner 1947, p. 60). Among the suggested management tools were rotation of camping and grazing sites, limitations on the length of permissible stay by one party in one area, and the use of transported oats rather than natural grasses for packstock food. According to Sumner and Leonard, 24-hour camping limits existed in 1947 in some meadows—the earliest such rules in wilderness management history.

In 1949, the Sierra Club sponsored a High Sierra Wilderness Conference, which grew into a biennial event that flourished for a quarter of a century. At the initial conference, about 100 federal and state administrators, outing club representatives, and professional outfitters and guides met to discuss a common concern: wilderness preservation. Attendants at the conference conceded that the allocation and permanent protection of wilderness from outside influences such as roads and commercial development addressed only part of the problem. The other

part was the impact of recreation users on wild country. The conferees, in other words, had the courage to recognize that they were part of the problem. By the Fourth Wilderness Conference in 1955, a full range of wilderness management concerns was being discussed. So was the idea, still a decade away from fruition, for a National Wilderness Preservation System (NWPS); but most commentators recognized that without proper management the allocation of wilderness could well be meaningless.

In the 1950s and 1960s, the related concerns of allocation and management continued to dominate the American discussion of wilderness. Inventory and designation of wild places progressed, as did the protection of established reserves. Notable here was the Echo Park Dam controversy involving Dinosaur National Monument (CO-UT) and, many felt, the integrity of all national parks (Nash 1982). Part of the price of a 1956 decision not to build a dam in Dinosaur was approval of one in Glen Canyon on the Colorado River. The completion of Glen Canyon Dam in 1963 intensified the efforts of both dam builders and wilderness protectors when the Grand Canyon itself became the subject of controversy three years later (Nash 1970a). The success of wilderness advocates in defending the Grand Canyon from dams, coming on top of the passage of the Wilderness Act and its establishment of the NWPS in 1964, constituted dramatic evidence of the new political muscle of preservation. But these successes were limited to the external dimension of wilderness preservation—allocation. The internal one—how an allocated wilderness was used—continued to generate problems. The fact was that the NPS had not substantially departed from the management assumptions of the Mather-Albright era.

Park management still emphasized visitor numbers, conveniences, and the viewing of scenic spectacles rather than the wilderness experience. This became clear in 1956, when the NPS launched Mission 66. The program responded to rapidly increasing park visitation, but some feared it was the wrong response because its major thrust was further development. More than a billion dollars were poured into it, mostly for the construction of roads, visitors' centers, and motel-type accommodations. No one thought of limiting visitation; the entire emphasis of Mission 66 was on improving the park's capability for handling *more* tourists, and little was said about wilderness values and wilderness management. The prevailing management philosophy was more appropriate to an amusement park or resort than to a wilderness. The NPS was not alone in this posture. Operation Outdoors, the USFS counterpart to Mis-

sion 66, similarly emphasized facilities and conveniences.

The facility and convenience orientation also appeared in backcountry management practices of the mid-1960s. Trail standards were improved in the interest of easier access. Picnic tables, bulletin boards, fireplace grates, latrines, and corrals for packstock were often placed at wilderness campsites. In some California areas, wilderness visitors even found rakes for use in tidying up their campsites (Snyder 1966).

But the tide was beginning to turn in the direction of visitor education, self-sufficiency, and lighthanded styles of management. A USFS employee who returned to the John Muir Wilderness in California in 1973 found stoves, latrines, and fences gone. Instead of concentrating visitors at designated campsites, management had opted to encourage dispersal. "You could find people," John Koen noted, "but they were just not as visible due to the lack of centralized, formal camp improvement" (Koen 1973). The year 1973 also marked the first use of permits to limit the number of visitors to some of the more heavily used wildernesses, for example the San Gorgonio Wilderness in California managed by the USFS, and the Colorado River in Grand Canyon National Park. Granted, wilderness permits had existed in Minnesota's Boundary Waters Canoe Area (USFS) since 1966, and were required in many wildernesses for record keeping, but they were freely given to every applicant. New to the early 1970s was the idea of using permits to limit use to a predetermined recreational "carrying capacity." Use of other wilderness rules and regulations, such as the banning of wood fires and a "pack-it-out" policy for litter, also increased. Grand Canyon National Park rules went so far as to require river runners to pack out solid human wastes. At a few heavily used wildernesses and backcountry areas, personnel were assigned to coordinate and disperse visitors.

WILDERNESS MANAGEMENT EVOLVES

The evolution of wilderness management direction from the heavyhanded visitor control of the late 1960s and early 1970s to the lighthanded visitor education emerging in the 1980s is only briefly mentioned here because it is thoroughly covered in chapters 15, 16, and 17. During the late 1970s and early 1980s, volunteer worker programs expanded considerably in national parks and forests (fig. 2.4), while at the same time recreation management budgets and personnel ceilings were being reduced.

Wilderness management research and field experience were revealing the power of education and appeals for cooperation as effective methods of managing visitor behavior (see chaps. 15 and 17). The professionalism of wilderness managers increased; managers eagerly exchanged views and experiences in regional and national wilderness workshops, sponsored by universities, the USFS, and other agencies, and including wilderness users, scientists, and university professors (fig. 2.5). A survey in 1982 found 23 wilderness-related courses in natural resource departments of universities, while hundreds of wilderness-related courses appeared in other academic departments, ranging from education and history to religion (Hendee and Roggenbuck 1985). Increasing public involvement, a trend spurred by the Wilderness Act, became a way of life for federal agencies, and as never before agencies were bound in partnership with wilderness-enthusiast clients. Under these conditions, lighthanded and educational approaches to wilderness management have evolved, with some tentative success. For example, in 1983 the Eagle Cap Wilderness on the Wallowa-Whitman National Forest, Oregon was the first unit of the NWPS to drop a permit system once instituted (Scholz 1983). This lighthanded management strategy rested on the premise that the number of wilderness visitors had reached something of a plateau, or that at least the near-exponential growth in visitation of the late 1960s and early 1970s had slowed. In addition, wilderness camping ethics and skills were improving, due in no small measure to an educational emphasis featuring contact by volunteer rangers. The new breed of wilderness users is concerned about protecting the wilderness resource and respecting the interests of other visitors in obtaining a wilderness experience. The hope is that the Eagle Cap Wilderness, in response to lighthanded management and user education, is healing, and that permits are no longer needed.

Books that confirm the presence of new attitudes and influence them include Laura and Guy Waterman's *Backwoods Ethics* (1979) and John Hart's *Walking Softly in Wilderness* (1977). Also important is the work of wilderness programs like those of Outward Bound, the National Outdoor Leadership School (NOLS), the Sierra Club, Boy Scouts, and 4-H, in addition to the college and university courses (fig. 2.6). Like good drivers, well-trained wilderness users may need fewer rules and less policing (Nash 1981). The emergence in the 1990s of a new generation of visitors who are sensitive to and respectful of the meaning and value of wilderness, and who know how to minimize their impacts on wilderness, would increase the possibility that lighthanded and educational approaches to wilderness management will be successful. This result could help diminish for future visitors the inherent contradictions of wilderness management.

Fig. 2.4. Increased professionalism of wilderness management in the late 1970s and early 1980s was marked by many workshops where agency managers, wilderness users, and scientists discussed alternative approaches to wilderness management. Dick Joy and Bill Worf of the USFS, and Al Samples of The Wilderness Society (left to right) talk policy at the 1982 wilderness workshop of the Eastern Region of the USFS in Gorham, NH. Photo courtesy of the USFS.

STUDY QUESTIONS

1. What is the "intellectual dilemma" of wilderness management?
2. Compare an expedition through the Grand Canyon today with what one would have experienced 100 years ago.
3. What accounts for the huge increases in wilderness recreation participants since the early twentieth century?
4. Compare and contrast the purposes for establishment of national parks and national forests. How did those purposes influence early notions of wilderness management in the two agencies?
5. How did Robert Marshall's contributions change ideas about wilderness use and management?
6. Who were Arthur Carhart and Aldo Leopold, and how did they contribute to early recognition of wilderness values by the USFS?
7. Explain the certified outdoorsman idea. How useful is it to wilderness today?
8. The Sierra Club is one of the oldest and most influential environmental groups interested in wilderness. How has the club's position on wilderness management changed over time? How do you think the Sierra Club and other groups will further evolve?

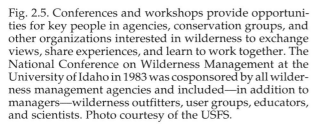

Fig. 2.5. Conferences and workshops provide opportunities for key people in agencies, conservation groups, and other organizations interested in wilderness to exchange views, share experiences, and learn to work together. The National Conference on Wilderness Management at the University of Idaho in 1983 was cosponsored by all wilderness management agencies and included—in addition to managers—wilderness outfitters, user groups, educators, and scientists. Photo courtesy of the USFS.

Fig. 2.6. Wilderness management has moved into schools and the community. Jim Bradley (holding halter), then wilderness management officer on the Eagle Cap Wilderness of the Wallowa-Whitman Forest, OR, organizes a skit designed to teach school children and wilderness visitors about minimum-impact camping. Photo courtesy of the USFS.

REFERENCES

Act establishing Grand Teton National Park, Wyoming, ch. 331, secs. 1-5, 45 Stat. 1314-1316 (1929), *repealed by* Grand Teton National Park Act, ch. 950, 64 Stat. 849 (1950) (codified at 16 U.S.C. 406d-1 through 406d-5, 431a, 451a, 482m, 673b, 673c).

Allin, Craig W. 1982. The politics of wilderness preservation. Westport, CT: Greenwood Press. 304 p.

Baldwin, Donald N. 1972. The quiet revolution: the grass roots of today's wilderness preservation movement. Boulder, CO: Pruett. 295 p.

Cleveland, Treadwell, Jr. 1910. National Forests as recreation grounds. Annals of the American Academy of Political and Social Science. 35(3): 241-247.

Everglades National Park Act. Act of May 30, 1934. Ch. 371, 48 Stat. 816 (codified at 16 U.S.C. secs. 410-410c).

Gilligan, James P. 1953. The development of policy and administration of Forest Service primitive and wilderness areas in the Western United States. Ann Arbor, MI: University of Michigan. 476 p. Dissertation.

Hart, John. 1977. Walking softly in wilderness: the Sierra Club guide to backpacking. San Francisco: Sierra Club. 448 p.

Hendee, John C.; Roggenbuck, Joseph W. 1985. Wilderness-related education as a factor increasing demand for wilderness. In: International forest congress 1984: forest resources management—the influence of policy and law; 1984 August 6-7; Quebec City, Quebec, Canada. Washington, DC: Society of American Foresters: 273-278.

Hildebrand, Joel H. 1938. Maintenance of recreation values in the High Sierra: a report to the United States Forest Service. Sierra Club Bulletin. 23(5): 85-96.

Koen, John. 1973. [Personal correspondence to John Hendee, George Stankey, and Robert Lucas]. On file at U.S. Department of Agriculture, Forest Service, Intermountain Research Station, Forestry Sciences Laboratory, Missoula, MT.

Langford, Nathaniel Pitt. 1972. Discovery of Yellowstone Park: journal of the Washburn expedition to the Yellowstone and Firehole Rivers in the year 1870. Haines, Aubrey L., ed. Lincoln, NE: University of Nebraska Press. 125 p.

LeConte, Joseph N. 1972. A summer of travel in the High Sierra. Sargent, Shirley, ed. Ashland, OR: Lewis Osborne. 144 p.

Leonard, Richard; Sumner, E. Lowell. 1947. Protecting mountain meadows. Sierra Club Bulletin. 32(5): 53-62.

Leopold, Aldo. 1921. Wilderness and its place in forest recreational policy. Journal of Forestry. 19(7): 718-721.

Lillard, Richard G. 1968. The siege and conquest of a National Park. American West. 5(1): 28-31, 67, 69-71.

Nash, Roderick. 1970a. Grand Canyon of the living Colorado. Ballantine, NY: Sierra Club. 143 p.

Nash, Roderick. 1970b. "Wild-deor-ness," the place of wild beasts. In: McCloskey, Maxine E., ed. Wilderness: the edge of knowledge. San Francisco: Sierra Club: 34-37.

Nash, Roderick. 1975. The "creation" of wilderness by herding and agriculture. In: Program/journal, 14th biennial wilderness conference; 1975 June 5-8; New York. Audubon, NY: Sierra Club: 51-55.

Nash, Roderick. 1978. Wilderness management: a contradiction in terms? Wilderness Resource Distinguished Lecture. Moscow, ID: University of Idaho Wilderness Research Center, April 18. [Also published as "Wilderness is all in your mind," Backpacker. 7(February-March): 39-41, 70, 72-75; 1979.]

Nash, Roderick. 1981. World view: protecting the wilderness from its friends. Backpacker. 9(February-March): 15-16.

Nash, Roderick. 1982. Wilderness and the American mind. Rev. New Haven, CT: Yale University Press. 425 p.

National Conference on Outdoor Recreation, 1926. 1926. S. Doc. 117, 69th Cong., 1st Sess.

National Plan for American Forestry. 1933. S. Doc. 12, 73rd Cong., 1st Sess.

Pomeroy, Earl. 1957. In search of the golden West: the tourist in western America. New York: Knopf. 233 p.

Roth, Dennis. 1984. The National Forests and the campaign for wilderness legislation. Journal of Forest History. 28(3): 112-125.

Runte, Alfred. 1979. National Parks: the American experience. Lincoln, NE: University of Nebraska Press. 240 p.

Sax, Joseph. 1980. Mountains without handrails: reflections on the National Parks. Ann Arbor, MI: University of Michigan Press. 160 p.

Scholz, Sue. 1983. The human approach: wilderness permits not required. Wallowa County [OR] Chieftain. July 7: 3 (col. 3).

Snyder, Arnold P. 1966. Wilderness management: a growing challenge. Journal of Forestry. 64(7): 441-446.

Sumner, E. Lowell. 1936. Special report on a wildlife study of the High Sierra in Sequoia and Yosemite National Parks and adjacent territory. Inservice report. Washington, DC: National Park Service Archives. [Unpaged.]

Sumner, E. Lowell. 1942. The biology of wilderness protection. Sierra Club Bulletin. 27(8): 14-22.

U.S. Department of the Interior, National Park Service. 1970. Administrative policies for natural areas of the National Park System. Washington, DC: 147 p.

Wagar, J. V. K. 1940. Certified outdoorsmen. American Forests. 46(11): 490-492, 524-525.

Waterman, Laura; Waterman, Guy. 1979. Backwoods ethics: environmental concerns for hikers and campers. Boston: Stone Wall Press. 192 p.

Waugh, Frank A. 1918. Recreation uses on the National Forests. Washington, DC: Government Printing Office. 43 p.

Wright, George M.; Dixon, Joseph S.; Thompson, Ben. H. 1932. Fauna of the National Parks of the United States. Fauna Series 1. Washington, DC: U.S. Department of the Interior, National Park.

Wright, George M.; Thompson, Ben H. 1934. Fauna of the National Parks of the United States. Fauna Series 2. Washington, DC: U.S. Department of the Interior, National Park Serice. 142 p.

Yellowstone National Park Establishment Act. An act dated March 1, 1872. Ch. 24, 17 Stat. 32 (1872) (codified at 16 U.S.C. secs. 21, 22).

Around the globe, many nations are following the American idea of maintaining certain lands in a wild state. In Australia, wilderness protection and management is especially popular with the general public. Here, a group of Australian "bush walkers" cross the Forbes River in Werrikimbe National Park in New South Wales. Photo courtesy of Rob Jung.

International Concepts of Wilderness Preservation and Management

This chapter was written by George H. Stankey; Vance G. Martin, President of the International Wilderness Leadership Foundation; and Roderick Frazier Nash, Professor of History and Environmental Studies, University of California, Santa Barbara.

INTRODUCTION

In 1872, with the designation of Yellowstone Park, the United States became the first nation in the world to establish a national park. The concept spread rapidly, however, through the remainder of the world, and today, more than 100 nations have joined the United States in creating national parks. In 1924, the first wilderness was established in the United States. Forty years later, this idea, too, became institutionalized as a form of land conservation with passage of the Wilderness Act of 1964 (see chaps. 2 and 4 for more detail on this history). The concept of wilderness—lands where natural ecological processes operate free of human influence to the maximum extent possible, yet where the provision of a primitive type of recreational opportunity characterized by solitude is offered—still remains largely an

Zealand, Canada, and South Africa for example— are beginning to consider the extent to which the concept of wilderness can be applied. The American experience in developing guidelines both for the establishment of such areas and in their management is an important model for the efforts of these other countries. Yet the very basis of the whole wilderness concept mandates that each country develop an approach founded in its own cultural experience and development needs.

In this chapter, we will examine and discuss how the cultural foundations of the wilderness idea affect its spread and adoption throughout the world. We will also review selected case studies of wilderness preservation programs that have been implemented elsewhere, comparing and contrasting these foreign

other than those formally designated as wilderness, we will examine the overall status of nature conservation programs around the world and identify the relationship between such programs and the concept of wilderness. Finally, we will look at some of the major problems confronting adoption of the wilderness idea in other countries, particularly the challenge of meeting basic human needs and winning support of local people while protecting wildlands in developing nations.

THE SCARCITY OF WILDERNESS

Compared to the spread of national parks, explicit preservation and management of wilderness has had only limited international acceptance. One reason is that in many countries there is no wilderness (even liberally defined) left to protect. Indeed, in many languages, Danish for instance, even the word for wilderness has disappeared. In France, a nation of long-settled, intensively managed countryside, wilderness is referred to by using the term *sauvage*, or savage, which would be considered anachronistic usage by many outdoor enthusiasts or professionals in America, Australia, and elsewhere where wilderness areas still exist. Switzerland is an example of a nation from which wilderness has long since vanished, despite its common conception as an area of rugged mountain landscapes. From border to border this small nation has been transformed by human activity into a thoroughly modified landscape.

Consider the experience of ecologist Raymond Dasmann when he moved to Geneva to assume a position with the International Union for the Conservation of Nature and Natural Resources (IUCN). In one of his first leisure moments, Dasmann opened maps of Switzerland and located the largest blank space, high up in an alpine valley, where, he assumed, he could find wilderness. A few weeks later he set off for the mountains with great expectations. After driving to the vicinity, he parked beside a country road and began to walk. His apprehension rose because the road never ended. Neither did the succession of cultivated fields, pastures, and dwellings. At last Dasmann reached the heart of his Swiss wilderness, the place he had planned to camp. He found himself in a barnyard. Cows stared curiously and children waved at the strange man with a pack on his back. Sadder but wiser, and with a deeper appreciation of the wilderness recreational opportunities in his own country, Dasmann drove back to Geneva and permanently retired his backpack to the closet.

Switzerland does have a national park. The 42,000-acre (16,900-ha) Swiss National Park is a scenically magnificent expanse of mountains and high valleys on the border of Switzerland and Austria at the headwaters of the Inn River. But, characteristic of many European national parks, the environment is not conducive to obtaining a wilderness experience, at least as would be commonly defined in the United States (fig. 3.1). In the first place, the region had been intensely used for economic purposes from the Middle Ages until the early part of the twentieth century. The land that became the park in 1914 supported mines, foundries, and chalk ovens. Today no such use is permitted; with the exception of region-ally extinct wildlife, the natural qualities of the environment are returning. Under proper management, and with sufficient time, wilderness conditions could be re-created in this area. But there is another problem. Rather than being managed for the joint purposes of preservation and enjoyment as U.S. national parks are, Swiss National Park was established as a biolog-ical sanctuary, and its charter insists that it be "protected from all human influence and interference." The concerns of science rather than recreation govern much of the park's management. Wilderness camping is prohibited; visitors wishing to remain in the park overnight must take accommodation in a lodge located in the center of the park where meals and rooms are provided. Visitors are permitted access only during daylight hours. They are further restricted to authorized paths, although many of these can be found. One can step off them, to sit down or eat lunch, for instance, only in areas a few yards square marked by yellow boundary posts. And when the chamois (a small European goat) become too numerous, park wardens drive them outside the park boundaries where they are shot by local hunters. Even if wilderness qualities do return to this part of Switzerland, obtaining a wilderness experience in the American sense will be extremely difficult (Reifsnyder 1974; Schloeth 1974).

For those who know only American wilderness criteria it is difficult to appreciate the pervasive presence of civilization in those parts of the world intensively used for agriculture and industry for thousands of years. China and India offer examples, as does the Matterhorn region on the Italian-Swiss border. Justly famous for its scenery, the Matterhorn area is almost totally devoid of wildness. The spectacular high valley leading to the picturesque resort town of Zermatt in Switzerland is laced with civilization. Roads and railroads work their way along the river, which is controlled by a chain of hydropower dams. Trams and lifts crisscross the narrow gorge. Tunnels pierce cliff faces. Clusters of buildings oc-

cupy every level nook, and farms extend upward on nearly impossible slopes. The grazing of cattle has lowered the timberline several hundred feet not only here but generally throughout the Alps.

Expensive chalets and climbers' huts perch on the highest outcrops. And, crossing the ridgetop divide, one finds the same paraphernalia of civilization extending up the other side. The civilizations of Switzerland and Italy meet at the Theodulepass, connected by ski lifts, just a few thousand feet below the Matterhorn. There is no possibility of a frontier in the American sense of that term—a dividing line between civilization and wilderness. People have been here a long time. Only the sheer rock faces of the peaks themselves are without human impact. Spectacular, yes; awesome, yes; dangerous, yes; wild, no. For technical rock climbing it is legendary, the birthplace of mountaineering. But it is not wilderness.

The experience of Great Britain furnishes additional evidence of why the American lead in wilderness preservation cannot be followed even if the culture would welcome islands of wildness in its midst. The British landscape has been settled continuously for more than 5,000 years. Everywhere the land has been shaped and altered by this long human occupancy. Thus, between the two World Wars, when a serious lobby to create national parks in Britain began to emerge, the goal of this effort was primarily to preserve the best of what had gone before rather than re-creating the natural environment (Blacksell 1982). National parks were seen as one option to achieve this end. The guiding principles for management of these parks were seen to be the preservation (retention) of landscape and the promotion of what the British call "informal recreation" for the public.

In 1949, the National Parks and Access to the Countryside Act created the statutory framework for a system of parks. Between 1951 and 1957, 10 parks— seven in England and three in Wales—were established. (A similar system had been recommended for Scotland, but fears about public takeover of private land thwarted any action.) Although these 10 areas are called national parks, the landscape they present is strikingly different from what an American would expect in such an area. More than a quarter of a million people live within the British national parks. These are not rangers and the employees of concessionaires, but ordinary citizens who live and make their livelihood there (Darby 1961). Only about 2 percent of the area of British national parks is owned by park authorities; the remainder is in private ownership or held by other government or public agencies. The ecology of the parks is dominated by centu-

Fig. 3.1. In Switzerland, humankind has so modified the landscape over the centuries, that wilderness, as Americans understand it, no longer exists. Photo courtesy of the Swiss National Tourist Office.

ries of commodity use, primarily agricultural; as a result, natural vegetative communities are rare and typically confined to isolated mountain crags and ungrazed ledges (Simmons 1978). British national parks, as contrasted to their American counterparts, serve primarily to preserve a rural lifestyle complete with traditional agricultural practices. There is, of course, nothing wrong with this, especially not to the English who value the human associations a landscape may contain (Lowenthal and Prince 1965). But the English situation demonstrates that by the time an old and intensely developed nation like Great Britain decides to establish a system of parks and reserves there may be little alternative but to include substantial amounts of civilization. The opportunity for modern England to preserve an extensive wilderness system akin to that of North America is simply not possible.

Yet, it is a mistake to presume that the differences in the conception of national parks between Britain and the United States imply a failure on the part of the British to appreciate or take steps to protect those environmental qualities typically found in American parks and wildernesses. The protection of nature has long been a concern in Britain. Concurrent with efforts to establish a system of parks in the

country was an effort to establish a statutory framework to create and maintain a system of nature reserves. Even before the end of World War II, plans were under way to promote the scientific management and protection of natural values throughout that nation (Sheail 1984). The result was establishment of The Nature Conservancy (not to be confused with the private organization of the same name in the United States; see chap. 6). But while The Nature Conservancy is responsible for establishment of an extensive system of reserves across Britain, most are small, isolated tracts, reserved to protect only one or a few selected species. Notwithstanding their value to nature conservation, they do not comprise a system in which the intricate web of relationships among wild species is preserved. They are not wilderness.

Later in this chapter we discuss activities in Europe which demonstrate movement towards wilderness protection. However, the European example, in general, demonstrates that the absolute scarcity of wilderness—the long-term absence of the natural environmental components of an area—and the occupancy of that area by the economic and developmental activities of people, mean that the option of setting aside wilderness is no longer available. The purposeful restoration of wilder-ness conditions can be attempted but is an extremely costly process and may not be possible where former occupants of the ecological web have been eliminated.

The irony here is that at least some scarcity is necessary for the concept of wilderness to be recognized and to develop the social desire to preserve it. McCloskey (1966) saw two conditions as necessary for developing a consensus that wilderness warranted preservation: (1) a society with highly educated leaders and with economic surpluses, and (2) an increasing scarcity of wilderness areas. In much of the world, the scarcity of wilderness exceeded the ability of nations to gain the economic and social stability required. Before countries like Switzerland and England had reached the point in their development where the level of civilization, including both economic status and cultural sophistication, permitted them to undertake efforts to preserve significant portions of the landscape, wilderness had vanished. It is a tough balancing act; all the economic surpluses and public consensus in the world cannot offset the fact that wilderness is gone. Equally unfortunate is an abundance of wilderness without interest and support for its preservation.

CULTURAL RELATIVITY AND THE WILDERNESS CONCEPT

Another factor limiting the spread of wilderness

preservation and management is the inability of some cultures that currently possess significant amounts of wilderness to recognize it. Such attitudes often are found in countries classified as "developing" and/or nontechnological. From the perspective of developed nations, the citizens of such developing countries live in wilderness. But the nontechnological societies find this point incomprehensible. Indeed, they have no conception at all of wilderness or its preservation.

Turning first to a historical example of this attitude, Chief Luther Standing Bear of the Oglala Sioux commented in the nineteenth century on the difference between his culture and that of the European settlers who were replacing it:

> We did not think of the great open plains, the beautiful rolling hills, and the winding streams with their tangled growth as "wild." Only to the white man was nature a "wilderness" and only to him was the land "infested" with "wild" animals and "savage" people. To us it was tame (McLuhan 1971).

As Standing Bear implies, only cultures that manipulate their environment distinguish between wilderness and civilization. The hunter-gatherer, on the other hand, did not transform wilderness into civilization and consequently saw no dichotomy between the two. For Standing Bear, every place was simply home.

Similarly, the Balinese Hindus of Indonesia perceive an inseparable unity between society and all other living creatures, a "oneness" between society and nature; and to treat them as separate and opposite (e.g., as civilization vs. wilderness) is beyond conception (Mantra 1984).

Often, only residents of highly developed societies can conceive of wilderness as different from civilization. Ironically, a culture must reach a point where its remaining wilderness is jeopardized before wilderness preservation becomes a social concern. What is necessary is to develop the pressure for preservation before all the wilderness has disappeared. As we noted earlier, this did not happen in countries like Switzerland and England. The United States was fortunate in this respect because the course of westward settlement, coupled with the vastness of the land, left large tracts of unappropriated, wild country in the West while the East became urbanized. When it came to creating wildernesses in the East after 1964, Americans experienced the kinds of difficulties familiar in the Old World (Nash 1970).

Chief Standing Bear represented a true hunting-gathering people that has few contemporary paral-

lels. But developing nations still exhibit many of the same attitudes toward wilderness and its preservation. Most of them have difficulty conceiving of *wilderness* in the way that term is used in the developed world. Evidence stems from the fact that developing societies commonly do not have the word "wilderness" or an equivalent in their languages. Among Malaysian tribes and many African peoples, there is no synonym for wilderness. Stares of incomprehension or laughter invariably meet the question: "What is your word for 'wilderness'?" After considerable explanation by the questioner, one might be offered a word equivalent to "forest" or "nature" but totally lacking the connotations of "wilderness." A Masai in East Africa, for example, offered "serenget" as in Serengeti Plains. It signifies an extended place. The concept that this place might be wild simply could not be communicated in Masai.

These differences in attitude between developed and less-developed (in the sense of less technological and less urban) people comprise one reason why wilderness preservation and management has no meaning in many parts of the world. And, frustratingly, this is particularly the case in the regions with the most wilderness. Many Africans, for instance, have lived with wild animals and in a wilderness environment for as long as they can remember. For them it is hard to understand the rationale for a wilderness reserve. It would be as if a proposal were made to a group of New Yorkers to create and manage an urban reserve between 32nd and 42nd streets in Manhattan. To the African, the restrictions on grazing, farming, and living that would invariably follow proclamation of a wilderness area would be perplexing. The New Yorker, to continue the analogy, would be similarly confused if, after the creation of the urban reserve, he or she were prohibited from driving and shopping there.

This difference in attitude and perception between the peoples of the developed and undeveloped parts of the world has led to serious conflicts. Since the 1930s, for instance, efforts have been under way throughout East Africa to establish national parks as a way of protecting the region's outstanding wildlife resource. The reasons cited for these reserves are the same as those commonly cited in support of wilderness, in both the United States and elsewhere: preservation of natural heritage, scientific and educational values, aesthetics, preservation of natural diversity, and so forth. The problem was that in many of these areas, native populations, such as the Masai, still pursued a nomadic lifestyle. In 1947, more than 1,150 mi^2 (3,000 km^2) had been set aside as the Amboseli National Reserve, along the border of present-day Tanzania and Kenya. Seeing the establishment of a national park as a threat to their lifestyle, the Masai resisted. The tribe sought exclusive tenure to the land and took every opportunity to spear wildlife, especially rhinos, that competed with domesticated livestock for scarce water and forage (Western 1984).

Not until 1974 was Amboseli declared a national park. This was accomplished by recognizing that the Masai could not be displaced from their traditional territories unless alternative water and forage supplies could be guaranteed. Such an exchange was achieved. Today, Amboseli National Park exists in a relatively stable, if uneasy, alliance with its former tribal occupants. Because of design deficiencies in the water scheme, the Masai have had to reenter the park to obtain water. But overall, the plan has been a success; wildlife numbers are increasing, poaching has declined, and tourism is projected to increase substantially (Western 1984).

But is Amboseli National Park a wilderness? As wilderness is understood in the United States, most people would probably conclude that it is not. Roads and structures are found throughout the area and it has been heavily impacted by prior occupancy. Indigenous peoples periodically reoccupy the area. Nevertheless, the area's ecological characteristics have been clearly revitalized and the future of a number of wildlife species given greater assurance. And while not a wilderness, at least in American terms, the area nonetheless provides and protects certain values normally associated with wilderness, such as ecological quality.

This difference in perceptions and attitudes has created a sort of "cultural blockage" to further adoption of the wilderness concept, especially in developing countries and, because wilderness is so heavily tied to relative cultural significance, this will always remain a major factor. However, a new paradigm has begun to emerge, and we are beginning to see wilderness management linked to economic planning and rural development. This integrated planning is the foundation of *sustainable development*, or meeting the needs of the present without compromising the ability of future generations to meet their own needs (WCED 1987). We will look into this more closely when we consider wilderness in Africa, Latin America, and other developing regions.

Despite the slow pace of adoption of the American style of wilderness protection elsewhere in the world, many of the ecological and social values secured in America through wilderness designation are protected elsewhere through other types of land use classifications. National parks and nature reserves are the more well-known types of such designations, but many others are used as well. In Austra-

lia, for instance, more than 40 different classification categories for conservation management are in use. Because so many classifications are used internationally, efforts have been made to standardize the terminology so as to permit comparisons between countries. It is important to discuss this, and we will do so in the context of a historical overview of international nature protection.

A HISTORY AND OVERVIEW OF INTERNATIONAL ACTIVITIES IN THE PROTECTION OF NATURE

The protection of nature has had a long history of international interest and involvement. This effort traces to near the turn of the century. As the twentieth century dawned, the great wilderness frontier of the United States was rapidly diminishing. With its closure, wilderness enthusiasts in America and Europe began to search out new opportunities to experience and enjoy vast expanses of wild country. Africa offered such an opportunity.

The impetus for the protection of Africa's outstanding natural qualities came largely from America and Europe. Even in 1900 there was already concern about the exploitation of wildlife. The American experience with the buffalo in which the apparently endless herds had been brought to the edge of extinction in only a short time was near to many people's minds. In 1900, seven European nations had signed draft articles proposing the close regulation of sport hunting in Africa, including license requirements, seasons, and limits. Nevertheless, inability to enforce these limitations and the unwillingness of one nation to let another tell it what to do spelled the doom of this effort (Nash 1982).

In Africa, the concept of a national park, given substance by the actions to preserve Yellowstone, found success. Kruger National Park in South Africa came into being largely because its head ranger demonstrated how the American national park idea applied to the African situation and how its attraction to tourists could contribute to the country's economy. Virunga National Park in what was then the Belgian Congo was created by King Albert of Belgium, who, having visited Yosemite in 1919, found there was no opportunity to set aside a comparable area in his homeland. Belgium did administer the Congo, however, so Albert turned there, proclaiming the park by royal decree in 1925 (Nash 1982). The park was first called Albert National Park.

THE EXPORTING AND IMPORTING OF WILDERNESS

The protection of wild nature in Africa by Americans and Europeans reflects what Nash (1982) describes as an "export-import" phenomenon. There is an inherent irony, he writes, "in the fact that the civilizing process which imperils wild nature is precisely that which creates the need for it. As a rule the nations that have wilderness do not want it, and those that want it do not have it" (Nash 1982, p. 343). What is being imported or exported here is the experience rather than the physical commodity. In the case of Africa, with abundant wild resources, the wilderness experience is exported to willing consumers, largely from industrialized, modern western societies. And it is an export with considerable economic value. Again quoting Nash (1982, p. 344):

> Less developed countries can afford to maintain wildness, while necessarily restraining development, if the exportation of nature pays sufficient dividends. A poster intended for natives in Africa makes the point explicitly: "Our national parks bring good money into Tanzania—preserve them." Local people are reminded . . . that an adult male lion in Amboseli National Park (can) generate $515,000 in tourist revenue over the course of its lifetime.

The tension between the nature exporters and the nature importers is historic and continuing. Exporters do not as a rule recognize the marketability of their product. Africans, for example, have lived with wild animals as long as they can remember. You cannot interest a Masai in seeing a giraffe any more than you can interest a New Yorker in seeing a taxicab. Similarly, the restrictions on grazing and farming in an African park or preserve are as perplexing to the natives as a law that prevents a New Yorker from living in and using 10 square blocks of midtown Manhattan would be. Not sharing the developed world's conception of the value of wild nature, the less-developed world sees no reason not to continue to exploit resources in the accustomed manner. But if incomprehensible foreign tourists want to travel thousands of miles just to *look* at wild animals, and especially if they spend money in the process, exporters will not protest.

Exporting and importing nature also has a regional or *intranational* significance. The urban segment of a population may support preservation of wilderness in hinterlands, the inhabitants of which are indifferent or actively hostile. In the United States, the East and urbanized places in the West, like San Francisco, reached the nature-importing stage several generations before the still-wild West. The first "nature"

tourists came from these areas. So did the first stirrings of the nature preservation movement. Henry David Thoreau and Theodore Roosevelt were Harvard men. John Muir came from Great Britain, and when he organized the Sierra Club in 1892 it was dominated by an elite group from Berkeley and San Francisco.

Parallels exist throughout the world. Concerned people in Tokyo protect what wildness remains on Japan's northernmost island, Hokkaido. Australia's outback is of primary interest to residents of Sydney and Melbourne. The Malaysian Nature Society has little support outside the nation's metropolis, Kuala Lumpur. The national parks of Norway and Sweden are the concerns of urban people in the southern portions of those countries. Nature preservation efforts in Alaska have been led by outsiders from the rest of the United States. Robert Marshall, for example, was a classic nature importer, amply endowed with the money and free time to indulge his passion for wilderness during the depths of the Great Depression.

In stating this thesis graphically, the economists' concept of marginal valuation is useful (see fig. 3.2). The vertical axis in figure 3.2 measures the value a society or nation attaches to an extra unit of the commodity or experience in question. The horizontal axis measures the degree of economic development in the society and is roughly equivalent to historical time. Reading from left to right, the graph shows what happens to the relative valuation of wild nature and civilization as a nation undergoes development. Initially the marginal valuation of civilization is much higher than that of wildness. Wildness at this stage is so abundant as to constitute a threat to the society. This condition favors nature exporting. With the passage of time, civilization be-

comes plentiful and nature scarce. The marginal valuation of each changes. After the curves cross, society values increasingly rare nature more than it values now plentiful civilization. Henceforth, it is civilization that constitutes the threat to people's mental and physical well-being. This situation encourages nature importing. The widening vertical distance between the curves to the right of the graph may be taken to represent the growing amount of nature appreciation.

The export-import metaphor helps us understand why the role of international collaboration and involvement is critical to worldwide protection of natural values. Many countries with relatively abundant wildland resources have the lowest levels of living and the highest ambitions for material improvement. A consensus among those involved in international wildland protection, as expressed at the 4th World Wilderness Congress (WWC), which met in the United States in 1987, is that protection of these resources will only succeed as part of an overall strategy for peace and development. It will be necessary to raise the living standards in the under-developed countries, so that individual nations will not be as likely to sacrifice natural resources to pay off foreign debt or to win a war (Brundtland 1987). If no integrated approach to development is implemented, the abundant wildland resources will still be under pressure from people who need those same resources for survival (Wallace and Eidsvik 1988).

For the developed countries of the world, such as the United States, to insist that developing countries give priority to the retention of their wildlands, thereby denying the legitimate aspirations of their citizens for an improved level of living, is not defensible. But if it can be demonstrated that retention of nature can also be a major source of income, then it becomes possible to have both preserved wildlands and economic progress.

It was an appreciation of the need for close cooperation between nations that helped promote some of the early international interest in nature conservation in Africa. In 1909 President Theodore Roosevelt and Gifford Pinchot hosted the North American Conservation Congress. Delegates at this congress resolved to work for a world conference the following year in the Netherlands. But Roosevelt's successor, William Howard Taft, dropped the project. Nevertheless, the idea of an international commission with the objective of worldwide nature protection was kept alive by a Swiss zoologist, Paul Sarasin. Sarasin was the founder of the Swiss National Park, and through his efforts a small international advisory committee was established in 1913 (IUCN 1964). At the invitation of the Swiss government, 16 countries (the United States did not attend) convened at the International Conference for

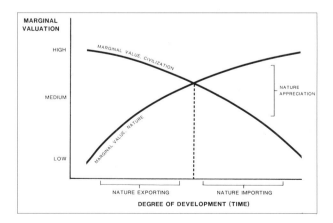

Fig. 3.2. How attitudes toward nature and civilization change with development. Reprinted with permission from Nash 1982.

the Protection of Nature. Conference attendants proposed that an information clearinghouse and a propaganda agency be established. But before any action could take place, World War I began.

Following the end of the war, a Netherlander, Paul G. van Tienhoven, assumed the leadership role from Sarasin. Van Tienhoven helped establish national committees for nature protection in France and Belgium as well as his own country between 1925 and 1926. In 1928, he established the International Office for the Protection of Nature, headquartered in Brussels, where it operated until 1940.

The protection of nature in Africa again surfaced as a major issue on the agenda of the fledgling international conservation community. In 1931, van Tienhoven organized an International Congress for the Protection of Nature. Delegates to this congress resolved that a major worldwide push should be instituted to save Africa's natural heritage. In 1933, the various colonial powers with interests in Africa convened to open the London Conference for the Protection of African Fauna and Flora. The conference proposed a number of articles, including regulations on hunting and trade in animal trophies. It also expressed strong support for the creation of more national parks as well as the creation of "strict natural reserves," areas reserved for use only by qualified scientists. The inability or unwillingness to provide enforcement weakened the positive results of the conference; the outbreak of World War II sealed its fate.

Following the end of World War II, the same favorable climate that prompted formation of the United Nations helped rekindle support for the international conservation movement. Again, it was the Swiss who took a leadership role. The Swiss League for the Protection of Nature hosted two conferences between 1946 and 1947, from which arose a new organization—the Provisional International Union for the Protection of Nature—administered by the Swiss League. In the following year, the league, along with the French Government and the United Nations Educational, Scientific, and Cultural Organization (UNESCO), sponsored yet another conference in Fontainebleau. Delegates from 33 nations attended. From this session, the International Union for the Protection of Nature was officially established. The goal of this new organization was anything but modest: "the preservation of the entire world biotic environment" (Nash 1982, p. 361). The underlying rationale for this objective was the dependence of human civilization on renewable natural resources. But amenity values also figured highly in the organization's concerns. Its preamble stressed the value of wildlife, wilderness areas, national parks, and the like. Later, in

1956, at its Fifth General Assembly in Edinburgh, the organization changed its name to the International Union for Conservation of Nature and Natural Resources (IUCN) to more clearly reflect the dynamic role of "conservation through rational use," which the union accepts as its responsibility in light of society's influence (Watterson 1964, p. 332).

THE INTERNATIONAL UNION FOR THE CONSERVATION OF NATURE AND NATURAL RESOURCES

IUCN is now often referred to as The World Conservation Union. The organization is composed of sovereign states, governmental agencies, and nongovernmental organizations (commonly referred to as NGOs such as the National Wildlife Federation and The Wilderness Society). Currently, IUCN has more than 540 members, including 58 states, 124 government agencies, and 349 NGOs with its headquarters in Gland, Switzerland. It is involved in monitoring conservation activities, planning and promoting conservation actions, and providing assistance and advice necessary to achieve progress in conservation on the ground. IUCN works with agencies in individual nations as well as various international bodies such as the United Nations Environmental Program (UNEP), Food and Agricultural Organization (FAO), and UNESCO.

Much of the work accomplished by IUCN is through the more than 3,000 members and consultants representing expert opinion in the natural resource sciences. It is organized into six subject area commissions: Ecology; Education; Environmental Planning; Environmental Policy, Law, and Administration; National Parks and Protected Areas; and Species Survival.

The Commission on National Parks and Protected Areas (CNPPA) is particularly concerned with the field of wilderness and natural area management. CNPPA undertakes a variety of responsibilities in aiding nations, particularly developing nations, in establishing and managing parks. The CNPPA also provides a service to the United Nations (UN) by publishing the United Nations List of National Parks and Protected Areas, a comprehensive listing of all conservation units managed by every UN member country. CNPPA supports the Protected Area Data Unit (PADU), located at Cambridge in the United Kingdom, which provides detailed computer-based analyses of the status of protected areas around the world. Finally, CNPPA takes primary responsibility for organizing the World National Parks Congress held about every 10 years. A proceedings has been

published from each of three congresses held to date (Seattle 1962; Yellowstone 1972; Bali, Indonesia 1982); the fourth conference is scheduled for early 1992 in Venezuela.

Another task assumed by CNPPA was to standardize the terminology of classification categories for conservation management. Since 1973, a series of discussion papers have attempted to define a set of conservation categories that would permit more useful assessment of progress in conservation management, both within and between countries. Because of the difference in terminology between countries, this system's effectiveness lies not in the labels given different areas, but rather on the management objectives for the areas. Presently, there are 10 categories (which are under revision): Scientific Reserve (Strict Nature Reserve); National Park; Natural Monument/Natural Landmark; Native Conservation Reserve/Managed Nature Reserve/Wildlife Sanctuary; Protected Landscape or Seascape; Resouce Reserve; Natural Biotic Area/Anthropological Reserve; Multiple Use Management Area/Managed Resource Area; Biosphere Reserve; World Heritage Site (National).

IUCN's conservation categories provide some commonality in the assessment of conservation progress internationally. At regional levels, more specific versions may be developed. For instance, IUCN and the Council of Europe have developed an eight-category system for application to the European community. This includes strict nature reserve, nature reserve, national park, protected natural or semi-natural landscape, protected cultivated landscape, protected cultural monument and natural features, specific protected areas, and green belt. For each category, the system describes the type of area and the reasons for protection, the form of protection and management, and the use of the area (Fairclough 1984).

Periodic assessments of world progress in conservation management are made by IUCN. At present, approximately 4 percent of the world's surface has been placed under some type of conservation management. Four percent equals an area approximately the size of the Indian subcontinent, including Sri Lanka, Pakistan, and Bangladesh.

The present IUCN list does not include wilderness as a category for conservation management, though it was included in earlier versions. A 1973 discussion paper by Dasmann for IUCN identified wilderness areas as one of three types of protected natural areas. Dasmann (1973, p. 12) defined wilderness as a type of area having two principal purposes: "that of protecting nature (defined as primary) and that of providing recreation for those capable of enduring the vicissitudes of wilderness travel by primitive means (without motorized transport, roads, improved trails and developed campgrounds, etc.)." Subsequent versions of the list, however, dropped wilderness as a separate category. Currently, wilderness is identified as a zone to be designated within areas classified as Category II (national parks) or Category VIII (multiple use management areas/managed resource areas—Category VIII areas would also include areas such as the national forests). In these latter areas, the IUCN guidelines note, the establishment of wilderness-type areas is consistent with the overall management objectives for such areas. But the guidelines contain no definition of wilderness other than stating that in such areas the protection of nature takes precedence.

The lack of explicit recognition of wilderness as a conservation category in the international terminology has been criticized. In 1984, a recommendation was passed at the IUCN General Assembly meeting in Madrid asking that a specific category of wilderness be added to the IUCN list. Part of the support for this request lies in the belief of individu-

Table 3.1. Protected areas of the world.

IUCN category	Units	Area (acres)	Area (hectares)
I - Scientific, Nature Reserves	526	94,160,000	38,106,074
II - National Parks or Equivalent	1,050	632,640,000	256,029,904
III - National Monuments	70	16,202,000	6,556,943
IV - Managed Nature Reserves and Wildlife Sanctuaries	1,488	255,758,000	103,504,852
V - Protected Land or Seascapes	380	48,400,000	19,586,625
Totals	**3,514**	**104,716,000**	**423,784,398**

Source: IUCN 1985.

als, in many countries where there is developing interest in wilderness protection, that formal international recognition of wilderness as a conservation category would lend important credibility to their efforts to gain recognition and support (Bainbridge 1984). A draft proposal has been prepared for presentation at the 1990 General Assembly, and it appears likely that wilderness will be included in a newly revised categories of protected areas.

One measure of the world's wildland areas comes from the data kept by IUCN's PADU, which was initiated in 1959 at the request of the UN. This data, which is kept at the Conservation Monitoring Center, registers the legally designated or privately owned protected areas found in 125 of the world's 160 countries. As of 1985, PADU describes the world's protected areas as presented in table 3.1. Of this total, about half, or more than 500 million acres (200 million ha), are of wilderness quality using U.S. standards (Eidsvik 1987). Further observation indicates that 250 million acres (100 million ha) are north of 60 degrees in the Northern Hemisphere. Wilderness areas in much of the world can be said to be wildland zones within national parks, nature reserves, and others of the IUCN's protected areas categories. The "core area" of the world's biosphere reserves are perhaps the best examples (Wallace and Eidsvik 1988).

BIOSPHERE RESERVES

The Biosphere Reserve program grew out of a recognition of the need for an international network of representative protected areas. This need was identified during a general conference of UNESCO in 1970 as that organization initiated the Man and Biosphere (MAB) Program. At its first meeting in 1971, the MAB Coordinating Council defined a variety of geographical and topical issues for investigation. MAB Project 8 was defined as the "conservation of natural areas and of the genetic material they contain" and had as its goal the establishment of a series of Biosphere Reserves that would provide, on a representative basis, samples of all major types of ecosystems for *in situ* conservation (conservation onsite as opposed to in zoos, botanical gardens, or laboratories) and provide sites for baseline research activities important to other MAB projects (IUCN 1979).

In 1974, a MAB Project 8 task force issued a report on Criteria and Guidelines for the Choice and Establishment of Biosphere Reserves (UNESCO 1974). The distinguishing characteristics of Biosphere Reserves, the task force concluded, would include (UNESCO 1974, pp. 15-16):

1. They will be protected areas of land and coastal environments and will constitute a worldwide network linked by international understanding on purposes, standards, and exchange of scientific information.
2. The network of Biosphere Reserves will include significant examples of biomes throughout the world.
3. Each Biosphere Reserve will include one or more of the following categories:
    a. Representative examples of natural biomes.
    b. Unique communities or areas with unusual natural features of exceptional interest.
    c. Examples of harmonious landscapes resulting from traditional patterns of land use.
    d. Examples of modified or degraded ecosystems capable of being restored to more natural condition.
4. Each Biosphere Reserve should be large enough to be an effective conservation unit and to accommodate different uses without conflict.
5. Biosphere Reserves should provide opportunities for ecological research, education, and training. They will have particular value as benchmarks or standards for long-term changes in the biosphere as a whole.
6. A Biosphere Reserve must have adequate long-term legal protection.
7. In some cases, Biosphere Reserves will coincide with, or incorporate, existing or proposed protected areas such as national parks or nature reserves.

As a category of conservation land use, Biosphere Reserves have two principal distinctive characteristics. First, they are representative examples of the world's major biomes; the emphasis in their selection is on the extent to which they help complete a portrait of the world's ecosystems rather than on their outstanding or unique qualities. Second, they often contain areas where natural conditions have been degraded by human activity. In general, most Biosphere Reserves are comprised of a natural or core zone where minimal human impact is present. Research and education could be undertaken in this zone, but only if they are nonmanipulative. In addition, a Biosphere Reserve would contain a buffer zone in which educational or research activities involving manipulation would be conducted. Traditional exploitive activities including timber harvesting, hunting, and fishing might also occur in a controlled manner. A reclamation or restoration zone would provide for the study and reclaiming of lands and natural processes disrupted by heavy human- or natural-caused alterations. Finally, a stable cultural zone would be managed to protect and study ongoing cultures and land use practices conducted in harmony with the environment (IUCN 1979).

The first Biosphere Reserves were designated in 1976. Subsequently, more than 283 areas in 72 coun-

tries have Biosphere Reserves. Such areas offer an important way to improve the scientific basis of resource management. For example, in the La Michilla Biosphere Reserve in Mexico, research has helped demonstrate how carefully regulated hunting could ensure a long-term source of meat while limiting competition with domestic cattle (zu Hulshoff 1984). In the United States, a number of national parks and wildernesses are also Biosphere Reserves. Because it is difficult to find a single area that satisfies all the criteria for Biosphere Reserve designation, multiple reserves have been established whereby experimentally oriented tracts are matched with large preserves similar in biologic and environmental features. For example, in the northern half of the Sierra Cascade Biotic Province, the J. J. Andrews Experimental Forest is linked to the nearby Three Sisters Wilderness (OR) to provide a "complete" Biosphere Reserve for this area (Franklin 1977). Although the designation of an area as a Biosphere Reserve might not result in many alterations in its objectives and management, it may nevertheless require area administrators to recognize that the resources under their management are of worldwide as well as national significance. Great Smoky Mountains National Park and Biosphere Reserve (NC-TN) thus becomes part of an international heritage, with its values to be shared among other countries.

WORLD HERITAGE SITES

At the Second World National Parks Conference in Yellowstone in 1972, Russell Train, then chairman of the President's Council on Environmental Quality (CEQ), proposed creation of a world heritage trust. The trust, he argued, was a disarmingly simple idea; it involved only an international extension of the concept of national parks. While national parks were based on the recognition that certain areas are of such national significance and value that they should receive national recognition and protection, so too, some areas possessed such universal natural, cultural, or historic value that they belonged to the heritage of the entire world (Train 1974).

Train's call for such a system was only the latest in a series of efforts he had spearheaded beginning in 1965 when he participated in a White House Conference on International Cooperation. A recommendation of that conference called for establishment of a trust for the world heritage, arguing that conservation of natural resources provided a significant opportunity for international cooperation. The heritage trust idea was discussed in subsequent meetings between 1966 and 1969. IUCN undertook the responsibility to develop an international convention to implement

such a trust and submitted a draft for consideration by interested parties in 1971. During this same period, a draft convention with similar objectives, primarily oriented to the conservation of cultural properties and historic sites, was under preparation by UNESCO. The IUCN draft included both cultural and natural sites. To avoid duplication, the United States proposed to UNESCO that both groups meet to consider combining their respective drafts into a single document. This was done during a meeting in Paris in 1972.

In late 1972, the Convention for the Protection of the World Cultural and Natural Heritage was adopted by the UNESCO General Conference. Under UNESCO procedures, a convention enters into force three months following ratification of that convention by 20 nations. Although Train had hoped the convention might be ratified and in force by early 1973, it was not until 1975 that the twentieth nation signed the convention. (The United States ratified the convention in 1973.) At present, 92 nations have ratified the convention (Hales 1984).

The convention includes both cultural and natural sites, but our attention here focuses on the latter. A natural property proposed for the World Heritage List must meet at least one of the following criteria:

1. Be an outstanding example representing the major stages of the earth's evolutionary history.
2. Be an outstanding example representing significant ongoing geological processes, biological evolution, and man's interaction with his natural environment.
3. Contain superlative natural phenomena, formations, or features, or areas of exceptional natural beauty.
4. Contain the foremost natural habitats where threatened species of animals or plants of outstanding universal value can survive.

As these criteria suggest, the distinguishing quality of a World Heritage Site, as opposed to a Biosphere Reserve, is the presence of outstanding or superlative qualities (fig. 3.3).

Representativeness is not a criterion for selection. As of July 1990, there were 322 World Heritage sites in 68 countries, 17 of which are in the United States, including areas such as Great Smoky Mountains National Park, which is also a Biosphere Reserve, and Yosemite (CA) and Yellowstone National Parks (WY-MT-ID). Some other locations are Chitwan National Park in Nepal, Australia's Great Barrier Reef, Plitvice Lakes National Park in Yugoslavia, and Serengeti National Park in Tanzania.

Designation as a World Heritage Site does not impose, at least directly, any new management requirements. But it does impose the symbolic requirement that the governing authority recognize the international quality of the site in question and implies that

the relevant constituency for its management surpasses that nation's boundaries. Designation does carry with it significant international prestige. The sovereign authority is obliged to protect the quality of the site having World Heritage Site status. Later in this chapter, we will discuss the dispute in Tasmania, Australia, over the construction of a dam on the Franklin River in the middle of an area nominated for the World Heritage List, which reflects the kind of leverage the listing can provide. A site whose condition deteriorates may be placed on a "List of World Heritage in Danger" and is eligible for technical and financial assistance from the World Heritage Fund for protection and restoration. IUCN and its CNPPA have the responsibility under the convention for advising UNESCO on natural areas nominated for inclusion on the World Heritage List.

RAMSAR SITES

Another international designation, in fact, the oldest international conservation treaty, is the "Ramsar Convention on Wetlands of International Importance, especially as Waterfowl Habitat." Named after the town in Iran where the convention was held in 1971, Ramsar currently has 55 member countries (formally called Contracting Parties). Each party must designate at least one of its wetlands to Ramsar's "List of Wetlands of International Importance." In practice, the Contracting Parties go beyond the minimum requirement and as of 1990, over 470 sites covering over 75 million acres (30 million ha) have been designated for the Ramsar list (West 1990). One of the best known in the United States is the Florida Everglades. Ramsar, long impeded through lack of funding, now has more stable financial support and is administered through a secretariat with offices at IUCN headquarters in Switzerland and at the headquarters of the International Waterfowl and Wetlands Research Bureau in the United Kingdom.

Wetlands are defined as "areas of arch, fen, peatland or water, whether natural or artificial, permanent or temporary, with water that is static or flowing, fresh, brackish or salt, including areas of marine water the depth of which at low tides do not exceed six meters" (Archibald 1988, p. 54). These areas are critical habitat for all waterfowl, and are the areas of highest biological diversity in temperate zones. As with Biosphere Reserves and World Heritage Sites, those areas on the Ramsar list have no sovereign rights as a result of their listing. However, such international importance often serves as an additional layer of protection for sensitive areas, as was the case when wetlands in Great Britain, Italy and Pakistan were saved

Fig. 3.3. World Heritage Site status is given to areas possessing outstanding natural qualities, exceptional natural beauty, or threatened species of plants or animals. The Daintrees area of Northern Queensland, Australia, typifies a rain forest setting. Photo courtesy of Ralph Lindsey.

from development by virtue of their Ramsar listing.

Wetlands have important wilderness values, but are usually not as high as other recreation areas on the priority list of the typical wilderness user because, by their very nature, they are difficult to traverse—one is generally on the outside looking in. In developed countries, the most frequent users of wetlands are duck hunters and bird watchers. However, it is important to note that, particularly in tropical areas, wetlands are the basis of livelihood (providing income, food, and materials) for millions of poor rural people who live nearby.

In the United States, pressure and funding for the protection of wetlands has long been championed by users groups such as Ducks Unlimited, and by The Nature Conservancy (TNC), both of which buy wetland areas and help in their management. Lately, the cause of wetlands has become increasingly a national issue because of their value as critical habitat and their important role in purifying water and replenishing

underground aquifers. This interest reached a new level of priority when President Bush made the commitment during his 1988 presidential campaign that there would be "no net loss of wetlands" under his administration. As a result, stringent regulations are enforced on farmers and developers who wish to alter wetlands.

Perhaps one of the most significant indications of the international recognition of the importance of wilderness can be found in a recent policy decision by the World Bank. In a 1986 policy decision, the bank noted that certain pristine areas yield more benefits to present and future generations if maintained in their natural state. To protect these long-term values, the World Bank announced that it will usually decline to finance projects in such areas. Where development in wildlands will occur, careful justifications are required, and compensation, in the form of financing to preserve an ecologically similar area, or some other mitigatory measure, must be undertaken (World Bank 1986).

International designations such as Biosphere Reserves, World Heritage Sites, and Ramsar Sites typically are imposed over some other type of protective area designation administered by a sovereign government, such as a national park or nature reserve. For example, although the guidelines for establishment of Biosphere Reserves indicate that they "may coincide with other protected areas," in fact almost 80 percent of them do. All the World Heritage Sites are areas already protected under national authority. But such designations add the protection of international recognition and prestige, thereby increasing the cumulative security of the area.

The Biosphere Reserve, the World Heritage Convention, and the Ramsar Convention do not specifically mention wilderness. Nevertheless, it is an important component of each system in at least an implicit sense. The key element of the Biosphere Reserve is the core area. The core is a primitive wilderness, strictly protected and maintained free of human disruption in order to conserve a representative example of a freely operating ecosystem in one of the world's major natural regions. The core contains an area where natural processes continue undisturbed and where the maximum biological diversity is included (zu Hulshoff and Gregg 1985). The linkage between the Biosphere Reserve designation and wilderness may be particularly important in developing countries. In such areas where public understanding and support for wilderness are limited, Biosphere Reserves may serve to demonstrate the kinds of benefits to society that can be realized through protection of a nation's natural heritage (Halffter 1985). This in turn may help build public and institutional support for the preservation of large tracts of undeveloped area, wilderness, as part of an overall comprehensive program of nature conservation. In the United States, where a number of Biosphere Reserves overlap wilderness (e.g., the Noatak National Arctic Range and Aleutian Islands Wildernesses in AK, Everglades National Park Wilderness in FL, and Three Sisters Wilderness), the wilderness core of these Biosphere Reserves will serve as the critical baseline for helping determine the extent of human influence on the biotic environment, and as a source for understanding how natural processes can accommodate human impacts. As public awareness grows about the critical role wilderness plays in improving our understanding of our environment, the security of such areas should increase.

THE PROTECTION OF WILDERNESS VALUES: A GLOBAL REVIEW

In the first part of this section, we will look at programs of wilderness preservation and management in several nations, which have developed some form of wilderness designation, including Australia, New Zealand, Canada, South Africa, and Zimbabwe. We will then examine resource management programs in other regions where the protection of wilderness values is a key component in the overall conservation effort.

AUSTRALIA

In some ways, the "land down under" resembles the United States in terms of the relationship between the nation's development and wilderness. Early settlement occurred along the eastern seaboard by immigrants from western Europe. To the west lay an immense region of wilderness—the United States (excluding AK) and Australia are roughly the same size. But a variety of physical and cultural differences have produced different responses to the concept of wilderness preservation between the two nations.

The Australian landscape can be described in a variety of ways—old, low, dry, remote. The continent is one of the oldest landmasses on earth and, as a result, has been substantially eroded over the eons. With the exception of The Great Dividing Range along the country's eastern shoreline, much of Australia is a flat, undistinguished plain. Average elevation is only about 1,000 feet (305 m) and the country's highest point, Mount Kosciusko, is only 7,200 feet (2,200 m). The dramatic mountain landscape of the western United States that inspired both fear and awe among early explorers is simply not found in Australia. Even more of a distinguishing hallmark is

Australia's aridity; the median rainfall over half the continent is less than 12 inches (30 cm), and nearly a third of the continent records less than 8 inches (20 cm). As a consequence, much of Australia's occupancy is limited to a relatively narrow band along the southeastern coastline. In a biblical sense, the bulk of Australia is wilderness—hostile and uninviting to human occupancy (see chap. 1).

Finally, Australia is remote. It is not without reason that the country is referred to as "the Antipodes"—poles apart from the rest of the world. And the quality of remoteness applies both to the relationship of Australia to the remainder of the world and to distances within the country, a fact that led Blainey (1966) to attribute "the tyranny of distance" as a major force affecting Australia's development.

While approximating the United States in size, Australia's population is less than one-tenth of that found in the United States; with a population of only 16 million people, the number of people in Australia is less than that of southern California. The population density of Australia is the lowest of any of the settled continents. But while it is the least densely populated continent, Australia is also the most urbanized; 80 percent of the population resides in a narrow crescent running from Brisbane to Adelaide along the southeastern coast of the nation. The small, but highly concentrated, population means that a large share of the country is unoccupied, although there are extensive areas that show the influence of agriculture and mining.

Australia shares with the United States a long history of concern with the protection of parks and natural values. The world's second national park was established here. Royal National Park, just south of Sydney in the State of New South Wales, was set aside in 1879—seven years after Yellowstone. But, like Yellowstone, Royal was established with motives other than wilderness preservation in mind. In particular, the park was seen as a way of thwarting the operations of a coal mining company along the city's southern boundary (Strom 1979). It was also seen as an area for public enjoyment. Ironically, the park proposal was criticized on the grounds that the area was "mere wilderness" and its proponents were quick to respond that while it might be so, it certainly should not remain so (Mosley 1978). Nevertheless, the action established the important precedent in Australia of a government-al action taken to set aside an area for nonexploitive purposes.

The course of the development of nature conservation and wilderness protection in Australia must be traced at the state rather than national level. Each of the country's six states holds principal authority over the management of its natural resources, including park and conservation management. Thus, the spread of the national parks idea and, later, that of wilderness, was driven by local rather than national issues and interests. As the 1800s ended and the twentieth century began to unfold, two important developments became evident with regard to park conservation in Australia. First, the park movement began to spread throughout the country. Other states began to follow the lead of New South Wales in establishing reserves, with each area typically referred to as "The National Park." Second, the legislation governing the establishment of these reserves began to give more emphasis to the protection of natural conditions. In 1906, the State of Queensland establish-ed the first statewide system of national parks, followed in 1915 by Tasmania, the small island state of Australia.

Many Australian conservationists were troubled by the tendency for roads to be built within parks to attract tourists—a familiar issue in the early history of American national parks. This concern led slowly to support for some type of classification that would ensure the long-term protection of an area's primitive roadless condition. The establishment of wilderness and primitive areas in the United States during the 1920s helped crystallize these concerns. In 1932, the term *primitive area* first appeared in an Australian park proposal (Mosley 1978). The primitive area concept was seen as both a type of zone established within national parks and as a separate reserve.

Through the 1930s and 1940s, the conservation community struggled to clarify the concept of primitive area. A major point of controversy was the extent to which a primitive area would protect an area's scientific and natural history values; there was strong support for a system of reserves closed to recreationists but open to naturalist and scientific uses. In 1944, the 3.2-million-acre (1.3- million-ha) Kosciusko National Park in southern New South Wales was designated with the provision that its governing body set aside no more than 10 percent of the area as a primitive area. But because grazing would be allowed to continue, under primitive area designation, scientists and naturalists opposed it, arguing instead that a smaller reserve, open only to scientific permit holders, be established. The controversy led to the deferral of any action to protect the area's primitive values until 1962, when primitive area designation was used as a means to halt the construction of hydroelectric power works in the higher portions of the Snowy Mountains.

Between the mid-1960s and 1970s, most states passed new national park legislation in response to growing demands and interests in park protection.

Because each state faced different issues and problems, different means of protecting wilderness values within the parks emerged. But the typical arrangement involved the designation and protection of wilderness through some means of administrative, as opposed to statutory, procedure. Creation of an area as wilderness in New South Wales, for example, can occur either through the identification of wilderness zones within a national park in the park management plan or by a declaration on the part of the director of the national park and wildlife service. At present, more than 630,000 acres (255,000 ha) have been classified as wilderness through the management planning process in Kosciusko National Park, about 37 percent of the park's present size. Draft legislation is under consideration that would make wilderness a legal classification and would also extend wilderness protection to lands other than those managed by the National Parks and Wildlife Service. In Victoria, a similar procedure is followed but, in addition, recommendations for wilderness protection can be made by the Land Conservation Council (LCC), a state government agency that can make recommendations to the government with respect to policies ensuring a program of balanced land use within the state. The LCC consists of the heads of several state natural resource agencies as well as representatives of primary industry and nature conservation interests (Davey 1980). One important feature of this process not present in other states is that lands outside the system of national parks can be recommended for wilderness protection.

Despite the steps taken by the various states to protect wilderness in Australia, concerns linger that the country's natural heritage is being eroded and that existing mechanisms to halt this loss are inadequate. A 1975 symposium sponsored by the Australian Academy of Science, promoting a national system of ecological reserves, concluded that the country's ecological features were under severe threat and that a greater emphasis to create a system of reserves was needed (Fenner 1975). For instance, Specht (1975) reported that in South Australia alone, 40 percent of the indigenous plant species were rare or endangered.

Such concerns helped give rise to an effort to appraise the nature and extent of the remaining wildlands in the nation (fig. 3.4). As part of this inventory effort, the question of definition also had to be addressed. Most existing definitions of wilderness were descriptive and qualitative. The New South Wales National Parks and Wildlife Service, for example, defined wilderness as "large tracts where man's disturbance has been minimal and the land-

scape and vegetation are essentially in a natural condition, supporting a harmonious balance of wildlife populations." The Australian Conservation Foundation, the country's largest and most active citizen conservation organization, defined wilderness as "a large tract of primitive country with its land and waters and its native plant and animal communities substantially unmodified by humans and their works. Large size and spaciousness are the essential characteristics of wilderness." And the Institute of Foresters of Australia (a professional foresters society) defined wilderness as "a large tract of primitive country with its land and waters and its natural plant and animal communities ideally unmodified by humans and their works." Although the definitions share concerns with an area's natural condition and its size, they all lack specificity in terms of how these qualities are to be measured.

A series of inventories of Australia's wilderness resource were begun in the mid-1970s. The initial effort by Helman and his associates developed a two-part definition to guide the inventory effort. A wilderness, they argued, was a large area of land perceived to be natural, where genetic diversity and natural cycles remain essentially unaltered. They also used the following dimensional criteria as a basis for mapping areas meeting this definition: (1) a minimum core area of 61,750 acres (25,000 ha); (2) a core area free of major indentations; (3) a core area of at least 6 miles (10 km) in width; and (4) a management (buffer) zone surrounding the core area, of about 61,750 acres (25,000 ha) or more (Helman and others 1976).

The area inventoried according to these criteria was limited to eastern New South Wales and southeastern Queensland. Twenty areas, totaling more than 2.5 million acres (1 million ha) in the core area were identified. Of this total, 16 were all or partly within an established national park while the remainder were in state forests or other public ownership.

The general criteria used in the Helman inventory were adopted in similar inventories conducted in Victoria and Tasmania. In Victoria, 12 areas covering 1.6 million acres (630,000 ha) were identified. But because several different landscape types were involved, the authors modified the Helman criteria somewhat; in semiarid areas, for instance, the core area had to have a minimum 185,000 acres (75,000 ha) and a minimum width of 12 miles (20 km) (Feller and others 1979). In Tasmania, the Helman criteria were used, with the exception that some smaller areas were also included. The inventory reported 13 areas, totaling 1.7 million acres (675,000 ha) (Russell and others 1979).

In contrast to the dimensional criteria approach of Helman, Lesslie, and Taylor (1983) used an alter-

Fig. 3.4. The Valley of the Monoliths, part of the 70,000-acre (28,000-ha) wilderness located within the Budawang Range, within Morton National Park, New South Wales, Australia. Although recreational use is permitted here, overnight camping is prohibited because of the highly erodible terrain. Photo courtesy of Rob Jung.

native inventory procedure in their study of wilderness in South Australia. They argued that wilderness is a condition existing along a continuum, characterized by two relative attributes—remoteness and primitiveness—and therefore has no absolute boundaries. Moreover, these two attributes cannot be measured by a single indicator. *Remoteness* is a function of how close an area is to settlement as well as to access points or routes. *Primitiveness* is both a perceptual as well as objective phenomenon. Consequently, these investigators assessed the extent of wilderness in South Australia according to ratings on four wilderness quality indicators: (1) remoteness from settlement, (2) remoteness from access, (3) esthetic primitiveness, and (4) biophysical primitiveness. For example, an area more than two and a quarter travel days from a settlement or access point was rated very high on the remoteness from settlement and remoteness from access indicators. On the other hand, areas less than one-fourth travel day from settlement or access were excluded from the inventory.

Because specific dimensional criteria were not used in the South Australia inventory, it is not possible to identify specifically how much land was included. Forty-seven areas were judged to meet the minimum standards of wilderness quality used

in the inventory. Most were located in the arid northern portion of the state, which has little settlement and is used primarily for low-intensity grazing.

The interest in inventorying the extent of the wilderness resource in Australia reflects the growing interest in its protection and management. Because of the political structure of Australia, where the states rather than the national government are the key actors in resource management, there is no equivalent to the U.S. NWPS. Nevertheless, there is great interest in protecting the nation's wilderness heritage. In 1983, the Council of Nature Conservation Ministers (CONCOM), a group composed of all commonwealth, state, and territory ministers having responsibility for national parks and wildlife, established a working group to examine the question of wilderness management throughout Australia. Among the objectives of the group was the preparation of guidelines for the establishment and management of wilderness throughout the country. Underlying this objective was a concern similar to that underlying support of the NWPS in the United States—a need for a consistent approach in wilderness protection.

In Australia today, three of the five states—New South Wales, Western Australia and Victoria—and the Northern Territory (plus the Australian Capital Territory, an area analogous to Washington, DC, in

Table 3.2. Summary of Australian statutory approaches to wilderness.

State or territory	Relevant act	Terminology used	No. of designated areas	Revocation Authority
Victoria	National Parks Act 1975	Wilderness Park or Wilderness Zone	2 (40,000 & 113,500 ha or 100,000 & 284,000 acres)	Parliament
Australian Capital Territory	Nature Conservation Ordinance 1980	Wilderness Zones	1 proposed (30,000 ha or 75,000 acres)	—
New South Wales	National Parks & Wildlife Act 1974	Wilderness Area	12 (2,400 to 92,400 ha or 6,000 to 231,000 acres)	Parliament
	Wilderness Act 1988	Wilderness Area	none	
Western Australia	Conservation of Land Management Act 1984	Wilderness Zones	1 (15,900 ha or 39,700 acres, others proposed)	Minister
Northern Territory	Territory Parks & Wildlife Conservation Act 1980	Wilderness Zones	none	Conservation Commission
Commonwealth of Australia	National Parks & Wildlife Act 1984	Wilderness Zone	2 proposed	Both Houses of Parliament
Queensland	No wilderness legislation, but does have one "primitive area."			
South Australia & Tasmania	No legislation currently exists, but it has either been foreshadowed or is in process.			

Source: Land Conservation Council 1990.

which the federal capital, Canberra, is located) have statutory recognition of wilderness as a land use. As shown in table 3.2, there are 15 designated areas ranging in size from 6,000 acres (2,400 ha) to 283,700 acres (113,500 ha) with numerous others proposed. The federal government has also agreed to fund a national wilderness inventory to be completed by 1993.

Even in the states that have wilderness statutes, designation imposes only the name of wilderness, not necessarily the management required to maintain or restore the conditions such a name implies. Moreover, the management of wilderness is largely limited to areas already within established reserves, such as national parks. With the exception of Victoria and the LCC, other resource management agencies,

such as forest commissions, do not have the responsibility or authority to establish and manage wilderness (Lesslie and Taylor 1985). Finally, although other states have the authority to set aside reserves that can achieve the protection of natural conditions and processes (e.g., primitive areas, conservation reserves), they nevertheless lack the specific designation of wilderness as a land use classification.

But the fact remains that Australia is a federation of separate states that prize and protect their autonomy. While little chance may exist for instituting a national program of wilderness protection, parallel to the U.S. system, The Wilderness Society of New South Wales is campaigning for a federal act. Two

important similarities exist between Australia and the United States. First, as the earlier discussion of inventories suggests, important areas with outstanding wilderness values still remain, despite more than two centuries of occupancy and development. Second, the protection of wilderness continues to remain an issue of major public importance. For example, McKenry (1975) found that nearly three-fourths of the persons surveyed in Victoria felt it desirable to maintain some wilderness areas in an undeveloped state. In summarizing the research on public opinion, the Australian Heritage Commission (1982, p. 17) concluded "the body of support for the conservation of the National Estate (both cultural and natural) is not only substantial; it is growing and likely to grow faster in the next decade."

These conditions have lent impetus to develop a more integrated approach to wilderness preservation across the nation. The CONCOM effort rests on a basic assumption that it is desirable that a consistent approach to the selection and management of wilderness areas be developed by all the agencies concerned. To encourage this consistency, they have recommended that areas satisfy the following characteristics: be large areas, preferably in excess of 61,750 acres (25,000 ha), where visitors may experience remoteness from roads and other facilities; and be areas where there is minimal evidence of alteration by modern technological society (CONCOM Working Group on Management of National Parks 1986).

The CONCOM report also clarifies the purpose of a program of wilderness preservation. The primary objective of management is to protect both physical and social aspects of wilderness quality. Wilderness quality, in turn, is defined as the extent to which land or water is remote from, and substantially undisturbed by, the influence of modern technological society. Under such an objective, use of wilderness is to be regulated so as to minimize impact and maintain the quality of the environment and the wilderness experience. Specifically, the following management recommendations are made (CONCOM Working Group on Management of National Parks 1986):

- Access for recreation should be restricted to nonmechanized methods only.
- Use of animals for transport should not be allowed because of adverse effects on the environment and on those using wilderness on its own terms.
- Access by mechanized means and transport animals for essential management purposes should be permitted only where no practical alternative means of access is available.
- The impact of self-reliant recreation on the ecological processes in the area should be monitored and, if nec-

essary, appropriate management action taken in accordance with these principles.
- The effects of interactions among visitors should also be monitored.
- In authorizing group or commercial activities, care should be exercised to eliminate the risk of downgrading wilderness values or spoiling the experience of other wilderness users.
- No permanent structures or developments should be retained except where they are of historical or archeological value, or where they are necessary to protect the environment. Where temporary structures are necessary for management purposes, they should be removed on completion of the work involved.
- Research should be restricted to that which is essential and which cannot be successfully conducted elsewhere.
- An awareness and understanding of the values of wilderness areas and the need to consider safety and minimization of human impact should be encouraged among visitors.
- Wilderness area fire management policies should take into account the above management principles, all available ecological knowledge, relevant fire history, recreation values, and the need to protect adjacent communities and property.

Nationwide adoption of these procedures and guidelines could help ensure a more coordinated approach to wilderness preservation and management in Australia. The management guidelines listed above are quite similar to those that guide the management of wilderness in the United States, in part because the American experience has been closely followed, but also because there is a growing consensus around the world as to the purpose and objectives underlying wilderness preservation.

As suggested, wilderness protection and management has become an increasingly important public policy issue in Australia. Public opinion polls have shown that the public is interested in the protection of the country's natural heritage and in the need for control of developmental activities that would jeopardize this heritage. In no place has this intense public interest been more evident than in the debate surrounding the proposed construction of a hydroelectric dam on the Gordon River in southwestern Tasmania. For many wilderness enthusiasts, it was Hetch Hetchy (Yosemite, CA) revisited, 1980 style.

Tasmania lies south of the Australian mainland. The southwestern portion of the island is an area of outstanding natural beauty and wildness. Rugged mountains, separated by deeply incised canyons, make travel through the region difficult. These mountains also stand against the prevailing southwesterly winds— the Roaring Forties—which produce annual rainfall totals upwards of 120 inches (305 cm), along with persistent cloud cover. As a result, the region is rich in water, and the deep canyons are the home of some

world-class white-water rivers.

This spectacularly wild country is no stranger to conflict and controversy, and it is the region's abundant water resources that lie at the core of the dispute. The same qualities that make it desirable for wilderness—its rugged topography and magnificent white water—also make it prime country for hydroelectric development. Early recognition of the area's outstanding natural qualities resulted in the establishment of the 58,000-acre (23,000-ha) Lake Pedder National Park in 1955. In the early 1960s, increasing recreational use of the area, coupled with concerns over damage by fire, led to the creation of the South West Committee, a group of concerned volunteers who sought increased protection for the area's scenic and ecological values. They were successful in obtaining designation of 1.6 million acres (646,000 ha) as a wildlife preserve (Gee 1978).

But, during this same period, steps to capture the region's vast water power were under way. A major road was constructed into the area, and studies for a dam site were initiated. Despite strong public protest, plans to construct a dam on the Gordon River, in the heart of the area, went ahead. In 1972, the impounded waters of the Gordon River inundated Lake Pedder. But, like the Hetch Hetchy controversy in the United States 60 years earlier, the Lake Pedder incident awakened many to the growing threats to wilderness and the virtual irreversibility of its loss.

The dam responsible for the flooding of Lake Pedder was only part of a larger scheme for development of the water resources of southwestern Tasmania. In 1979, the Tasmanian Hydro-Electric Commission (HEC) released a report recommending a nearly $1.4 billion development on the lower Gordon River. The dam, if developed, would have resulted in the flooding of the Franklin River gorge, a spectacular white water tributary of the Gordon. Not only would the dam have inundated much of the heartland of one of the three remaining temperate rainforests in the world, it also would have destroyed an area possessing significant archeological evidence of the use of the area by Aborigines more than 20,000 years ago (Jones 1982).

The stage was set for another major battle over the future of the South West. The issue was further confounded by the decision of the state government in 1982 to request the federal government to nominate the complex of three parks within the area—the South West National Park, the Franklin Lower Gordon Wild Rivers National Park, and the Cradle Mountain-Lake St. Clair National Park—for inclusion on the World Heritage List. The nomination was accepted in late 1982, but the World Heritage Committee expressed grave concern about the potentially adverse effects to the area if the dam were to be constructed (Cohen 1984).

In late 1981, a referendum was held on the question of constructing the dam. Two alternative locations were proposed, one placing the dam on the Gordon below its confluence with the Franklin, and the second farther upstream on the Gordon near another of its tributaries, the Olga. But the option of "no dam" was not canvassed. During the voting, one-third of the ballots had "no dams" written on them in response to a call by conservation organizations for citizens to express their dissatisfaction with the referendum. Although this rendered the ballot invalid, it provided a powerful measure of public opinion. The "no dams" movement spread; voters throughout Australia, in elections far removed from the Franklin dispute, gave evidence of their disapproval of the proposed dam; up to 40 percent of the ballots had "no dams" written on them.

Political power in Australia is substantially concentrated in the hands of the states. The land area involved in the Gordon Dam dispute was under state ownership. As a consequence, there was a tendency on the part of state officials to view the controversy as a straightforward issue involving states' rights. In early 1983, the Premier of Tasmania had rejected a $500 million grant from the commonwealth in exchange for the promise to halt plans to construct the dam. But in fact, the Gordon-below-Franklin Dam had become much more than a local issue. It had become a national concern, and was then launched into the international arena when the 2nd WWC convened in Australia (Brown 1980). The Australian Conservation Foundation ran an ad headlined, "Do people overseas care more about preserving Australia's treasures than our own government?" and signed by 25 eminent archeologists from New Zealand, the United Kingdom, Canada, and the United States. A major demonstration of civil disobedience occurred, with more than 2,500 people involved; the movement of machinery was blocked and nearly 1,300 people were arrested (The Blockaders 1983). The consideration of the South West for World Heritage listing also highlighted the national and international status of the issue. Nevertheless, the commonwealth government in power at the time (the Liberal Party, led by Prime Minister Malcolm Fraser) adamantly refused to take an active role in the issue, arguing it was solely a state matter. The opposition Australian Labour Party was actively opposed to the dam.

In early 1983, a federal election was called; the Liberal Party was replaced by the Labor Party, with

Bob Hawke as prime minister. Shortly thereafter, the Federal Parliament passed legislation specifically prohibiting the construction of any dam in the contested area. The federal government argued that inclusion of the South West on the World Heritage List imposed responsibilities on it to prevent any action jeopardizing this international status. The state countered, contending that the federal government had no jurisdiction in the matter and that the federal legislation was tantamount to a taking of property without just compensation (Cohen 1984).

In July 1983, the Australian High Court (equivalent to the U.S. Supreme Court) ruled in favor of the commonwealth. A variety of complex legal issues were involved that go beyond our concern here. Suffice it to say that the ruling clearly established that the federal government had an affirmative role to play in charting the nation's environmental future stemming from the international responsibility incurred as a signatory to the World Heritage Convention (Wilcox 1983). The international qualities of the area involved and the national significance of the dispute further supported involvement by the federal government.

The dam on the lower Gordon has been halted and the Franklin River still runs free. But threats to the environmental integrity of the region remain. Already other dams are under construction. Less than half of the area is secure within park boundaries; the location of some park boundaries is poorly chosen; along the lower Gordon, only about one-half mile (800 m) on each side of the river are protected from development (Heatley 1984). Much remains to be done. But this episode clearly demonstrates the powerful political nature of the wilderness preservation movement, a power that reaches far beyond the boundaries of the United States.

NEW ZEALAND

Twelve hundred miles (2,000 km) east of Australia, across the Tasman Sea, lie the islands first known as "the long white cloud." Some whiteness was snow on high peaks; some was clouds gathered by New Zealand's mountainous backbone. In contrast to the ancient and worn land mass of Australia, many peaks in the chain of mountains on the South Island known as the Southern Alps are more than 10,000 feet (3,050 m) high (fig. 3.5); Mount Cook towers to 12,350 feet (3,750 m), nearly twice the height of Australia's highest peak. Milford Sound, a fiord along New Zealand's west coast where more than 300 inches (760 cm) of rain a year may fall, winds between mile-high peaks. Nowhere else in the world does the land meet the sea so abruptly.

Although New Zealand has a land area equal only to that of Oregon State, its rugged topography, coupled with a small population (currently about 3 million), has meant that much of the nation's wild country has escaped the impacts of modern development. But the adverse effects of civilization are apparent nonetheless. Although about 10 percent of New Zealand has been set aside under some form of protective status for conservation, it is estimated that only about 0.5 percent of the land has been reserved where it also has productive potential for agriculture or forestry (Molloy 1984). In many remote parts of the country, the creeping effects of development and human presence are gradually eroding the wildness of the area; the control of introduced noxious species, the construction of huts and access facilities by mining companies, and even the extensive construction of recreational facilities, including trails and bridges, all combine to diminish the extent of lands of wilderness quality (Molloy 1976). In sum, perhaps only 6 percent of New Zealand remains suitable for wilderness status (Molloy 1979).

New Zealand's early settlers shared an ambivalence toward the wilderness with their counterparts in North America and Australia. To many early colonists, the scrublands, sandy coastal plains, and interior volcanic landscapes were "the bleakest, most barren, and uninteresting lands," yet, at the same time, others described the countryside as "wild, magnificent, fresh from the land of nature and inspiring thoughts of God" (cited in Molloy 1983). But there was general antipathy toward the conservation of nature in much of New Zealand's early history. An 1874 Forests Bill, designed to halt the widespread denuding of the country's forests, confronted a storm of opposition, rooted in charges that it smacked of governmental paternalism and an unfounded usurping of local power and privilege.

Slowly, however, specific Acts of Parliament led to the creation of a series of national parks. Tongariro and Egmont National Parks were established in 1894 and 1900, respectively. In 1905, a public reserve that would form the basis of the 3-million-acre (1.2-million-ha) Fiordland National Park was set aside. Other parks followed and, in 1952, Parliament enacted the National Parks Act to consolidate and coordinate previous *ad hoc* park legislation and to define the significance and purpose of national parks (Smith and others 1980). This legislation, burdened by the same ambiguities concerning preservation and public enjoyment that characterized the 1916 Organic Act of the National Park Service (NPS) of the United States, nevertheless did outline a procedure whereby wilderness could be established. But it only noted

that such areas "shall be kept and maintained in a state of nature," without any buildings, roads, or tracks allowed. Only foot access was permitted. Wilderness areas could be established by the recommendation of the Park Board (one board for each park), an appointed body typically composed of local interests, many of which were not inclined to favor preservation. As a result of this procedure, in the nearly 30 years that the 1952 National Parks Act remained in effect, only limited progress was made in preserving a system of wilderness zones within the national parks. By 1980, only seven areas containing 455,000 acres (184,000 ha) had been established as wilderness within the national parks; four additional areas, comprising approximately 620,000 acres (250,000 ha) had been proposed for wilderness.

An interesting history links New Zealand and the United States in the area of wilderness protection. In 1939, Lance McCaskill, a lecturer in agriculture at Christchurch Teachers' College, with an interest in soil conservation, had taken leave to visit the United States to study American approaches to conservation (Cumberland 1981). While in the United States, McCaskill met Aldo Leopold and, through his influence, introduced the concept of wilderness into New Zealand national park circles. Later, in 1949, the American conservationist Olaus Murie visited New Zealand and gave support to the idea of introducing some wilderness protection provisions into the pending national park legislation. McCaskill was instrumental in doing so and also played a major role in the establishment of New Zealand's first wilderness in 1955—the 29,640-acre (12,000-ha) Otahake Wilderness in Arthur's Pass National Park (Molloy 1983).

Wilderness could also be set aside on lands managed by the New Zealand Forest Service (NZFS) as well as on lands managed under the Reserves Act of 1977. Both the Reserves Act and the Forest Act of 1949 allow for the setting aside of portions of areas for wilderness purposes. In general, wilderness in these laws is considered as an area to be kept in "a state of nature"; structures and roads are prohibited, and access is by foot only (Lucas 1983). But little actual wilderness protection was achieved under either law, and in 1980, only eight areas totaling about 445,000 acres (180,000 ha) had been proposed for wilderness protection, all on NZFS lands, and none of these had received any formal protection.

Thus, in 1980, New Zealand found itself in a position similar to that in the United States in the 1950s. There were provisions for the protection of wilderness, but they were spread among different management agencies. Yet, with a general agreement about what wilderness was, no single unifying statement of consensus, nor a clearly agreed-on management philosophy existed. More important, because the mechanisms for wilderness protection were spread across three different laws, three different governmental agencies (NZFS, Department of Lands and Survey, and New Zealand National Park Authority), and two governmental ministries, it was difficult to promote the assessment and protection of wilderness in any systematic fashion.

Beginning in 1976, conservation groups, led by the Federated Mountain Clubs (FMC), the nation's largest mountain recreation organization, began to consider options to this situation. In addition to the *status quo*, two possibilities were considered: (1) a coordinated wilderness preservation system under existing legislation or (2) a separate wilderness preservation system under its own legislation (Molloy 1983). The latter option was modeled on NWPS in the United States. After considerable discussion, the FMC executive board chose the first option, a coordinated approach to wilderness preservation and management under existing legislation. Working with the three government agencies, the FMC helped produce a Joint Wilderness Policy in 1980. This document outlined the legislative status of wilderness in New Zealand and discussed the definition and identifying criteria for such areas. It then proposed a common definition with which each agency would work (a definition drawn nearly verbatim from that contained in the U.S. Wilderness Act) and identified the general guidelines for the establishment and management of wilderness.

Fig. 3.5. Wilderness treks, even in winter, are increasingly popular along the Southern Alps of New Zealand. The high peaks, coupled with abundant moisture, result in heavy snowfall and persistent clouds. Thus, the island came to be called "the long, white cloud." Photo courtesy of Rob Jung.

In 1981 the FMC sponsored New Zealand's first conference on wilderness. This focused national attention on wilderness in a way that had not been done before. The Joint Wilderness Policy served as a focus for much of the session, as well as the issue of a New Zealand wilderness preservation system (analogous to the U.S. NWPS) or a continuation of wilderness protection under existing laws, but guided by a jointly agreed-on policy. The relationship between wilderness protection and public awareness and support was recognized. As P. H. C. "Bing" Lucas, then Director-General of the Department of Lands and Survey, noted, "If the public and political climate is favorable, then New Zealand has the legislation to establish wilderness areas and the operating agencies to manage them. No single Wilderness Act, single Wilderness Authority, or single management agency is, in my view, likely to achieve more" (Lucas 1983, p. 52). Simply put, Lucas made the point that with public support, wilderness would be protected; without it, it wouldn't, regardless of the protective mechanisms in force.

The FMC also put up 10 proposals for wilderness areas spread throughout the nation. They were all large by New Zealand standards, ranging from 75,000 to 233,000 acres (30,000 to 94,000 ha). They also covered a range of natural landscapes, from coastal forest, steepland forest, and tussock grassland to rugged alpine and glaciated areas. These 10 areas represented perhaps the only options left, outside the national parks, for large, remote, undeveloped natural areas.

As a result of this conference, efforts increased to improve the coordination among the wilderness management agencies. In late 1981, the Minister of Lands and Forests appointed a six-person Wilderness Advisory Group to advise him on appropriate policies for wilderness establishment and use, on the identification and assessment of potential wilderness, and on priorities for action. The group was given two years to prepare their report.

The first task undertaken by WAG was to reach a consensus on a national wilderness policy. Following the work done to prepare the earlier drafted Joint Wilderness Policy, the group issued a draft wilderness policy statement for review by affected governmental agencies, organized recreation and conservation interests, and the general public. A final policy statement was released in 1985.

The purpose of this revised policy was to provide a succinct statement of the objectives of wilderness protection and the criteria for wilderness areas, while also allowing for flexibility in designation and management. Again, the general definition given

wilderness closely follows that used in the U.S. Wilderness Act. In addition, the policy calls for areas that are to be managed as wilderness to meet the following criteria: (1) large enough to take at least two days' foot travel to traverse (a condition reminiscent of early definitions of wilderness by Leopold and Marshall that characterized such areas as being able to absorb trips of one or two weeks; creeping development and civilization have greatly shrunken the standard); (2) have clearly defined topographic boundaries and be adequately buffered so as to be unaffected, except in minor ways, by human influences; and (3) not have developments such as huts, tracks (trails), bridges, signs, or mechanized access (Wilderness Advisory Group 1985).

A second major area of activity by WAG was specific recommendations for the classification of the 10 areas, totaling well in excess of 1.2 million acres (more than 500,000 ha) that had been presented at the FMC conference in 1981. WAG now reviewed these proposals and sought action on them by the management agencies. Results from WAG's efforts came slowly, and seemed to be as much a result of FMC and other conservation groups' direct pressure as it was of any new commitment to wilderness on the part of the land management agencies.

A process of departmental proposal and public comment was embarked upon for the two major proposals on NZFS land—the 230,000-acre (93,000-ha) Tasman Wilderness in the northern South Island and the 72,000-acre (29,000-ha) Raukumara Wilderness in the eastern North Island. For the Tasman Wilderness, the public's response rate was now much higher, with a very high proportion of submissions broadly sympathetic to wilderness designation for these areas. But major opposition from local NZFS staff, coupled with reluctance by politicians, saw all progress halted for three years. Final approval came in March 1987—23 years after the initial proposal had been made!

However, in Raukumara, progress was faster. This area is adjacent to the Motu River, the first wild and scenic river in New Zealand to gain legislative protection (in 1984). The major opponents to wilderness were recreational hunters who wanted the same rights to use helicopters for access, as granted to commercial operators involved in feral animal eradication. Soil erosion in the area, caused by introduced deer and goats, is a major threat, so in the short term, this desire can be accommodated as a control measure. Approval was recommended in June 1986.

Areas under the Lands and Survey Department's control have made slow progress. One, the 123,000-acre (50,000-ha) Adams, a remote glaciated mountainous area of the Southern Alps, was zoned "remote experi-

ence" in 1983, in spite of admirably fulfilling the wilderness criteria. Remote experience zoning is a second-best zoning to wilderness, and allows unspecified relaxation of wilderness conditions. The downgrading appeared to be due to departmental reluctance to be restrained by wilderness conditions, and because some climbers wanted helicopter access to a remote glacier area.

The weakness of departmental recognition of wilderness has since been highlighted. A tourist company has recently been granted a one-year license to ferry busloads of tourists for brief landings on the designated landing point. Heli-ski operations also impinged briefly on the northeastern part of this area and led to a rough airstrip being built on its eastern boundary. Part of the area has also been proposed for a managed hunting area for Himalayan Tahr by the hunting lobby. The zoning is to be reviewed regularly.

The 99,000-acre (40,000-ha) Hooker-Landsborough area, in similar glaciated country, achieved wilderness status in 1986, after another extended public submission process. The major delay was through conflict with commercial rafting companies who wanted to helicopter into the upper reaches of the Landsborough River for "wilderness rafting."

Progress on FMC's remaining areas has been slow for a number of reasons. The high-country tussock grassland area is public land under a grazing lease that gives the leasees trespass rights. This precludes any wilderness or even remote experience designation as the state does not effectively control the area. Two other areas have been in limbo because they are candidates for national park addition. In the southernmost coastal area, there is conflict with control huts and tracks (trails) for rare and endangered bird management, and with commercial fishing anchorages on the inhospitable coast. All these areas retain their *de facto* wilderness characteristics at the moment, but these qualities are jeopardized.

Another reason for the lack of progress has been the conversion of the multiple-purpose Lands and Survey Department and the NZFS into new commercial corporations, and a single-purpose Department of Conservation (DOC), to manage publicly owned protected and natural lands. DOC therefore takes over responsibility for all the lands included as potential wilderness. This unified management should be of major benefit to achieving wilder-ness protection in New Zealand.

However, recent progress has been made. At the end of 1989, six areas had been *gazetted* (designated) as wilderness, totaling 740,000 acres (300,000 ha), with a further five areas zoned as wilderness in management plans, totaling 394,000 acres (164,000 ha); see table 3.3.

Still, no formal moves have been made toward a national wilderness preservation system, but the formation of the DOC makes this a more easily obtained objective. Major opposition from mining, tourism, hydroelectric developers, some local communities, and even some recreational users is likely to remain.

An interesting issue facing wilderness enthusiasts in New Zealand is the extent to which wilderness is serving conservation as opposed to providing recreation. Much of the political support for wilderness has come from groups that traditionally have used alpine areas for hiking (or tramping, as New Zealanders call it) and who have been concerned that these favorite areas will be lost to timber harvesting, grazing, tourism, or other developmental activities. In much the same way as their American counterparts, New Zealanders see wilderness classification as a means of protecting these areas and preserving their recreation. At the same time, respondents to a survey by the FMC indicated, by a three to one margin, that the primary purpose of wilderness should be as a form of landscape preservation rather than as the source of high-quality recreation (Henson 1983). Still, less attention is given to wilderness protection as a means of preserving areas where natural ecological processes predominate; in fact, there is concern that such an orientation to wilderness protection might evoke pressures that restrict recreational use of favored mountain areas.

The focus of wilderness protection in New Zealand began with alpine areas. But it now includes two major forested areas (Raukumara and Tasman) as distinct from alpine areas. A desire exists to include other types of landscape, including tussock grassland, coastal areas, and the whole of New Zealand's claimed area in Antarctica (Ross Dependency). Inclusion of this range of less traditional wilderness landscapes and ecosystems is hindered, however, by lack of strong public pressure for preservation, and much stronger opposition to "locking up" because of potential value for development and private gain.

New Zealanders recognize and are concerned about the impacts that recreational use can bring to wilderness. "In our enthusiasm to share these outdoor experiences," says Les Molloy, a leader in New Zealand's wilderness movement, "we have gone overboard in exhorting urban populations to get out of their urban ruts and find that freedom at the end of the road" (Molloy 1976, p. 65). His view is shared by David Henson of the FMC: "One of the biggest threats to wilderness is we the users" (Henson 1983). The impacts caused by rising numbers of recreationists are of particular concern because of fears that, in response to

such problems, quotas and other use restrictions will be instituted, thereby affecting major users of these areas. A 1981 survey by the FMC found that the use of quotas and permits was the least preferred approach to management, while maintaining an area's remoteness and the use of buffer zones was most favored (Henson 1983).

Despite differences in the conception of wilderness between the United States and New Zealand, it is interesting to see many similar concerns about the future of such areas—the problems that arise from the growing popularity of such areas, their value in retaining some areas free of development, and their importance in protecting the nation's natural heritage for future generations. The New Zealand experience is further evidence of the growing international appreciation and concern with wilderness preservation.

CANADA

The Canadian experience furnishes added evidence for the paradox that the possession of wilderness is a disadvantage in the preservation of wilderness. In Canada's case it is the north country—unbelievably huge and empty (fig. 3.6), a continuing frontier that elicits frontier attitudes toward the land. The result of having this vast reservoir of wildness to the north is that the urgency for wilderness protection is lessened. "Wilderness preservation, because of a smaller population, large amounts of public land, and a perception of still relatively large unexploited forest wealth," says Canadian Professor Peter Dooling, "has scarcely raised a tremor in Canada compared with that in the United States" (Dooling 1985). Understandably, then, the wilderness preservation movement in Canada lags behind that in the United States, where the frontier vanished nearly a century ago.

In the beginning, the Canadian park movement was highly utilitarian, just as it is today in places like East Africa. The 1885 preservation of the hot springs at Banff, Alberta, and the 1887 enlargement of this area under the Rocky Mountain Park Act were directed at creating a resort, not a wilderness (Nelson and Scace 1968). The Dominion Forest Reserves and Parks Act of 1911 was no better in this respect; it did, however, establish the world's first National Park Administrative Service. The statute did not distinguish between wilderness preserves and commercially oriented forest reserves—it was an example of the same confusion that characterized American thinking in the 1890s. Canadian wilderness management in the subsequent decades consisted of advancing recreational development as fast as possible.

Although he had a strong personal commitment to wilderness, James B. Harkin, the first Commissioner of the Dominion (later "National") Parks set the tone in 1922, proudly declaring that "the mountain parks are worth $300,000,000 a year to the people of Canada in revenue from the visiting tourists." This fact was vitally important to the survival of the park system, Harkin continued, because "we have to show that the movement will pay for the efforts many times over" (Harkin 1922). This meant providing opportunities for tourists to spend money. Townsites inside the park (like Banff), hotels, swimming pools, tennis courts, golf courses, ski slopes, and campgrounds with laundries became standard features in the Canadian parks. Wilderness was forgotten in the drive to make the parks economically respectable, socially acceptable, and politically viable. If anyone was concerned about wilderness, they could always go north. Governmental concern with protecting Canada's northern wilderness is evident; six large parks and reserves have been established in the region, totaling more than 35 million acres (14 million ha). But although going north might sound attractive, it is too costly in time and money for the average Canadian. The far north, in other words, is wilderness that contributes little to the typical citizen's recreation.

Beginning in 1930, when the National Parks Act mandated the preservation of parks in an unimpaired condition, people with a concern for wilderness started to struggle against the dominant currents of Canadian thought and policy. It was an uphill fight. Even in existing wilderness preserves (notably those of Yoho and Wood Buffalo National Parks), mining and lumbering continued into the 1950s. At the provincial level, as important in Canada as the states are in Australia, Ontario passed a Wilderness Act in 1959. Although weak (it did not formally close the land to economic or recreational development), the Ontario law was a first step comparable to the USFS designations of the 1920s. Canadians concerned with wilderness organized the National and Provincial Parks Association in 1963. They took heart from a 1964 clarification of park purposes in the House of Commons: "National Parks cannot meet every recreational need; the most appropriate uses are those involving enjoyment of nature and activities and experience related to the natural scene" (Bryan 1973). One of the first crusades of the association was to have the highly developed townsites in Banff and Jasper National Parks removed from park status and reclassified as a mass-recreation area. The point was to rededicate national parks to preservation. As of January 1990, the town of Banff is a legally incorporated community, which carries out its own admin-

istration. Land ownership and planning control remain with the Canadian Park Service (CPS). Indeed, the Canadian parks continue to be perceived by society as the site for civilized holidays.

But the issue of wilderness remains a tenacious one on the public agenda. At both national and provincial levels, concern remains about establishing adequate, long-term protection for wilderness. The CPS, the national park management agency, currently administers 34 areas across the nation, totaling nearly 69,000 mi^2 (about 180,000 km^2). Commercial resource development is prohibited in the parks. The National Parks Act also requires that all land within the park be vested in the federal government; that is, it precludes any type of provincial or private land ownership within a national park boundary. One consequence of this requirement is that, with the exception of national parks in the Canadian northern territories, more than 90 percent of

the national park area existing today was established before 1930 (Dooling 1985). National park policy strives for a system of parks across the country that provides representation of the country's 39 terrestrial natural regions and 26 marine regions; however, the requirement of total federal ownership at a time of concern about provincial jurisdiction, coupled with the high costs of land acquisition, makes it difficult to achieve such representation. At present, only 42 percent of the natural regions are represented within the CPS holdings (Taschereau 1985).

Wilderness protection in the national parks is currently achieved through zoning. In such zones, the essential wilderness character of the area is to be maintained. Only those activities judged to be compatible with the natural setting are permitted; no motorized access is allowed, and only minimum primitive facilities for visitor use are provided. The

Table 3.3. Existing and proposed wilderness areas in New Zealand as of 1990.

Name	Area (acres)	Area (hectares)	Park/Locality
Gazetted (highest level of protection)			
North Island			
Te Tatau Pounamu	16,100	6,500	Tongariro National Park
Hauhungatahi	21,000	8,500	Tongariro National Park
Raukumara	98,800	40,000	Raukumara Forest Park
South Island			
Tasman	222,400	90,000	NW Nelson Forest Park
Otehake[1]	29,700	12,000	Arthurs Pass NationalPark
Pembroke	44,500	18,000	Fiordland National Park
Glaisnock	308,900	125,000	Fiordland National Park
Total Area	**741,400**	**300,000**	
Zoned in management plans			
Ruakituri	44,500	18,000	Urewera National Park
Paparoa	89,000	36,000	Paparoa Range
Hooker-Landsborough[2]	98,800	40,000	South Westland
Waialolo	74,100	30,000	Mt. Aspiring National Park
Olivine	98,800	40,000	Mt. Aspiring National Park
Total Area	**405,200**	**164,000**	
Zoned as remote experience zones (limited protection)			
Kaimanawa/Hangitikel	46,900	19,000	Kaimanawa Forest Park
Adams	123,600	50,000	Mid Southern Alps
Total Area	**170,500**	**69,000**	
Other potential areas			
Preservation	449,700	182,000	Fiordland National Park
Poteriteri	74,100	30,000	Fiordland National Park
Pegasus	155,700	63,000	Southern Stewart Island
Total Area	**679,500**	**275,000**	

Source: Barr 1990.
1. Under review; may be revoked.
2. Awaiting gazettal.

protection of wilderness in the national parks through a process of management planning and zoning has concerned many persons who feel that such administrative protection can be easily overturned by unsympathetic officials. (A similar concern in the United States helped lead to passage of the Wilderness Act; see chap. 4.) As a result, revisions to the National Parks Act in 1988 now require the boundaries of a wilderness zone to be designated through legislation.

This legislation passed in 1988 and transformed the policy-based wilderness zones into legislatively protected areas. A draft objective of such areas was given as:

> to protect natural areas of a size and configuration sufficient to provide for, or contribute significantly to, the perpetuation of natural ecosystems, features, and phenomena, which shall be maintained free of any activity likely to impair its wild character, and which will enable the visitor to experience a sense of remoteness, seclusion, and self-sufficiency.

Fig. 3.6. Much of Canada's far north holds outstanding opportunities for wilderness recreation. Here a kayaker enjoys the solitude and natural landscape of Pelly Bay. Photo courtesy of the Department of Economic Development and Tourism, Northwest Territories, Canada.

The 1988 revision of the National Parks Act imposed legal protection upon all areas in the parks designated as wilderness or special preservation areas. Additional areas may also be protected as such through a declaration by the Governor in Council. CPS has just begun the wilderness zoning process. Considering that there are 34 national parks covering 70,252 mi² (182,000 km²), of which 90 percent is wilderness quality, it is likely that large areas will be designated.

At the provincial level in Canada, we find a mixed picture in wilderness protection. Table 3.4 summarizes the current position. The Federal-Provincial Parks Conference established a minimum-size criterion for wilderness of 40,000 acres (16,200 ha); however, in practice, this has not always been followed. Only two of the nation's 10 provinces have legislation explicitly designed to protect wilderness: Alberta has the Wilderness Areas, Ecological Reserves and Natural Areas Act of 1981 and Newfoundland has the Wilderness and Ecological Reserves Act of 1980. In 1980, Ontario passed a Wilderness Areas Act, but it restricted the size of an area to only about 650 acres (260 ha), more closely resembling a nature reserve or research natural area. This legislation has since been subsumed under the province's parks act.

In Alberta, five large national parks, including Banff, Jasper, and Wood Buffalo, were designated in the late 1800s and early 1900s. But, as was the case with the early national parks in the United States, wilderness protection was not the reason for the establishment of these parks; Canadian national park legislation passed in 1930 contained the same "use and preserve" direction plaguing park legislation elsewhere in the world. And although lands with wilderness values were protected within the park, albeit without explicit recognition, most of the truly wild country was found in one park; nearly 70 percent of the estimated wilderness lands lay within Wood Buffalo National Park in Alberta's far north (Alberta Wilderness Association 1985).

In 1959, the Alberta Provincial Legislature passed the Wilderness Provincial Park Act, later (1962) renamed as the Willmore Wilderness Park Act. Willmore Wilderness Park, located 200 miles west of Edmonton in the Canadian Rockies, is an area of outstanding scenery, complex vegetation, and diverse wildlife. Many of the peaks in the area are more than 8,000 feet (2,470 m), and the area receives heavy recreational use. The enabling legislation permits recreational use within the area but does not limit coal and mineral exploration and, originally, did not prohibit motorized use, although such use was banned beginning in 1962 (Alberta Wilderness Association 1985). Since the area was established, its original size of more than 2,150 mi² (5,600 km²) has been reduced twice (1963 and 1965) to its present size of approximately 1,775 mi² (4,600 km²). Much of the loss in area can be attributed to pressures for coal exploration and development, mostly concentrated along the park's east side (Alberta Wilderness Association 1973). The loss of area has had a particularly

severe impact on winter range for mountain caribou; population numbers have dropped from more than 1,200 in the 1960s to less than 300 today (Alberta Wilderness Association 1985).

In 1961, a second attempt to provide legislative protection to wilderness in Alberta took place. In that year, the 484-mi² (1,259-km²) White Goat and the 157-mi² (412-km²) Siffleur Wilderness Areas were established under the Forest Reserves Act. Later, in 1965, both areas were transferred to the Public Lands Act. Then, in 1967, a fourth wilderness, the 58-mi² (152-km²) Ghost River Wilderness was declared under yet another piece of legislation—the Provincial Parks Act. Alberta now had four wilderness areas established through three separate pieces of legislation.

The potential confusion introduced by this maze of legislation, coupled with growing public interest in wilderness protection, particularly along Alberta's Eastern Slopes, meant that consideration of new legislation focusing specifically on wilderness was politically unavoidable. In 1970, a bill was introduced into the Alberta legislature proposing a revised Wilderness Areas Act. Its terms were hardly welcome to the wilderness community, however. It set a size limit of no more than 144 mi² (373 km²) (the presumption was that an area should be no more than one day's walk across, or about 12 miles [20 km]), and prohibited the use of horses, fishing, hunting, and the picking or removal of any natural object such as berries or mushrooms, and it requested a report as to which portions of the existing White Goat, Siffleur,

and Ghost River Wildernesses should be protected under the act. It did not require an annual meeting of the Advisory Committee on Wilderness Areas (an advisory group to the government), nor did the committee retain its power to call public hearings regarding proposals for wilderness areas. Despite strong public protest to these terms, the bill was passed in 1971.

In late 1971, the ruling party in Alberta politics was replaced. In the following year, the new government passed an amendment removing the size limit on wilderness areas covered by the act. But no changes were made to the prohibitions on recreational activities. Although the amendment did provide for the inclusion of the White Goat, Siffleur, and Ghost River Wilderness Areas under the new act, it approved a two-third's reduction in the size of the White Goat Wilderness Area.

The problem facing Alberta's wilderness proponents is that the existing wilderness legislation treats such areas as some type of ecological reserve where natural processes are to be protected from any disturbance, including those associated with traditional recreational activities such as horseback riding, fishing, and hunting. Because the Wilderness Areas Act is so restrictive, there has been little interest or pressure from groups such as The Alberta Wilderness Association to promote new areas for protection under it; in fact, no additional areas have been set aside under the act since the inclusion of the initial three areas in 1972. Instead, public interest groups

Table 3.4. Provincial/Territorial Wilderness areas in Canada through 1988.

Province/Territory	No. of areas	Total area miles²	km²
British Columbia[1]	1	800	1,300
Alberta	4	3,500	5,600
Ontario[1]	37	384	618
Newfoundland	1	664	1,070
Saskatchewan, Manitoba, Quebec, New Brunswick Nova Scotia, Prince Edward Island, Yukon Territory, Northwest Territory	—	—	—

Source: Hummel 1990.
1. Provincial wilderness in British Columbia and Ontario have been subsumed under the National Parks Act (amended 1988) for legal wilderness designation.

have lobbied for creation of a new type of protection that ensures opportunities for people to enjoy traditional wilderness recreation activities. Proposals for a "Wildland Recreation Areas" system or some other "recreational wilderness" system continue to receive support. In 1979, a new classification for Provincial Parks was created, establishing "wildland parks," defined as areas retained in their wild and primitive state and where participation in dispersed recreational activities compatible with the area's preservation was permitted. To date, however, only 49 mi² (129 km²) within Kananaskis Provincial Park has been set aside under this system.

In Ontario, wilderness protection is provided through the Provincial Parks Act. The act calls for the creation of wilderness parks. But the principal guidelines for the establishment and management of these parks were contained in a policy document issued by the Ontario Ministry of Natural Resources in 1978 entitled "Ontario Provincial Parks: Planning and Management Policies." This loose-leaf binder, commonly referred to as the "Blue Book," provided not only overall direction for the management of wilderness parks but also contained arguments for the size and scope of a wilderness park system. It defined wilderness parks as "substantial areas where the forces of nature are permitted to function freely and where visitors travel by non-mechanized means and experience expansive solitude, challenge, and personal integration with nature" (Hummel 1982). It also called for establishment of one wilderness park in each of Ontario's 13 ecological site regions. Wilderness parks, it argued, should average not less than 250,000 acres (100,000 ha), should not be less than 124,000 acres (50,000 ha) as an absolute minimum, and these smaller areas should be complemented by additional wilderness zones of up to 100,000 acres (40,000 ha) in natural areas and waterway parks (other park designations possible under the Provincial Parks Act).

Within areas designated as wilderness parks, four types of zones would be possible: wilderness, access, nature reserve, and historical. Typically, the major portion of a wilderness park would be in the wilderness zone. Development in this zone was limited to primitive campsites, portages, trails, and signs necessary for route identification. Mineral exploration and mining were prohibited, as were commercial forestry operations, agricultural activity, commercial fishing, and hunting. Motorized equipment was permitted only in the access zone. Three parks were set aside under these guidelines: Killarney (120,000 acres or 48,500 ha), Polar Bear (6 million acres or 2,408,700 ha), and Quetico (1,175,000 acres or 475,819 ha).

In 1983, the Blue Book guidelines were changed to much more lenient standards. Mineral exploration and mining, hunting, trapping, commercial fishing, and motorboat and aircraft access all were permitted in wilderness parks, although the three previously established parks remained under the earlier Blue Book guidelines. Commercial forestry operations were prohibited in the new wilderness parks, but the boundaries of the parks were carefully adjusted to minimize any impact on the forest industry. Some candidate areas under consideration for wilderness park designation were dropped because of impending conflicts with forestry and other resource uses. Five new parks were declared, totaling 2,950,000 acres (1,193,000 ha).

As a result of these changes, Ontario has what amounts to a dual system of wilderness parks managed under sharply different standards. Any sense of consistency and uniformity is seriously compromised. But the principal problem is that governmental policy has given special consideration to protection and support of the forest industry in the northern part of the province, ostensibly to protect and support the regional economy. The vast subsidies involved, however, almost certainly mean the loss of wild country in northern Ontario. As one author notes (Priddle 1982, p.49),

> The terrible irony of all of this is that this demise of our roadless areas is happening just at the time when a rich alternative future is just over the horizon . . . What is frustrating the European visitor is the difficulty of seeing the Canada of the coffee table books . . . The monuments, cathedrals, and art galleries of this country are our natural and unspoiled places.

Yet, the situation in Ontario is not without its bright spots. Wilderness and primitive forest protection emerged as a major political issue in Ontario following the placement of the Lady-Evelyn Smoothwater Provincial Park on IUCN's threatened areas list in 1986. Another outstanding example of wilderness preservation can be found in Quetico Provincial Wilderness Park, one of the original three wilderness parks established under the Blue Book guidelines. The wilderness zone comprises all but 630 acres (250 ha) of the park's 1,175,000-acre (476,000-ha) total. Quetico also lies directly adjacent to the Boundary Waters Canoe Area Wilderness (BWCAW) in the United States. The two areas form a nearly 2-million-acre (809,400-ha) tract of wilderness canoeing opportunities astride the international boundary.

Quetico Provincial Wilderness Park is managed to perpetuate the area's wilderness values. Many of

the specific policies are coordinated with those in the BWCAW. The overall objective of the resource management program is to ensure that natural processes are allowed to function freely, within the constraints of public safety and the need to protect values both within and outside the area. Water quality is an obvious concern; therefore, monitoring stations have been established within the area. In addition, air quality monitoring stations have been established near the park boundary in order to monitor possible acid precipitation problems in the park. As in the BWCAW, water levels in Quetico are not controlled and existing dams in the area have been removed or allowed to deteriorate. Prescribed fire is used as a means of restoring natural ecological conditions.

The objective of the visitor management program for Quetico is to minimize, through the control of use levels and user activities, the deterioration of both the park's biophysical environment and the quality of the user's wilderness experience. The general approach to visitor management is to minimize restrictions on the visitor once entry to the park's interior has occurred. Daily entry quotas have been established for each ranger station at the park's boundary to help ensure that the interior campsite capacities in selected areas are not exceeded. The visitor management program regulates party size, length of stay at selected high-use areas, and the importation of nonburnable, but disposable, food and beverage containers. Refuse must be carried out by the visitor.

The protection and management of wilderness in Canada varies greatly from province to province. As suggested earlier, the apparent abundance of wilderness has handicapped efforts to develop systematic programs of protection. Nevertheless, there appears to be a growing recognition that the nation's wildland is limited, that it is highly valued by both Canadians and foreigners, and that aggressive programs to ensure its survival are required. What responses will flow from this recognition remain to be seen.

In British Columbia, a major debate has centered on the status of the southern portion of Moresby Island, located about 60 miles (100 km) off the central coast of the province. Conservationists proposed a South Moresby Wilderness, encompassing nearly 360,000 acres (145,000 ha). The area contains a rich array of flora and fauna; upwelling ocean currents produce abundant food for a variety of birds (including the world's largest concentration of Peale's peregrine falcons) and fishes. Plants, ranging from the tiniest mosses to giant hemlocks and cedars, contribute to an extraordinary biological richness. More than 40

freshwater lakes contain a variety of unique plants, birds, fish, and mammals that evolved in response to the area's insular characteristics.

Moresby Island is a part of the larger Queen Charlotte Archipelago, an area that has been extensively logged. Local opposition to a proposed five-year logging plan has made the issue of wilderness preservation in the area a major concern, not only because of the environmental impacts associated with logging, but for its impact on a way of life as well. A proposal to preserve the southern portion of Moresby Island, along with adjacent waters and islands (an area comprising approximately 15 percent of the Queen Charlottes) was submitted to the provincial government. Logging operations were currently under way within this proposed reserve on Lyell Island, lying to the east of Moresby Island. Lyell Island is considered a key component of the overall wilderness proposal. Its east coast contains the world's largest ancient murrelet (a small sea bird) nesting ground, while along the west coast is found Canada's highest density of bald eagle nesting sites. Although a small area, the Windy Bay Ecological Reserve, has been recommended for protection by the government. Logging runs up to the boundary of the proposed reserve, resulting in blowdowns within the reserve and subsequent impacts on the area's wildlife habitat and watershed.

Protection of the area is further confounded by a dispute over unresolved aboriginal land claims by the Haida Indians. At the time of first European contact in the late 1700s, some 7,000 Haida occupied the Queen Charlottes; by the end of the 1800s, a century of exposure to European-introduced disease had left only about 600 Haida. The failure of the colonial government to recognize native land claims has left a bitter dispute between the Haida and the government (Strong 1987). In mid-1987, an agreement to protect South Moresby was finally negotiated between the federal and provincial governments.

This agreement provided for the investment of $106 million by the federal government and an additional $20 million by the provincial government to establish, in cooperation with the Haida people, a wilderness national park. Negotiations, planning, and management of this area are on-going, but there is little doubt that they will result in extensive wilderness protection.

Changing public attitudes are also reflected in the issuance in 1989 of a Wilderness Management Policy by the British Columbia Forest Service. This policy makes provision for the establishment of wilderness areas with a minimum limit of 1,000 ha. It is evident that a significant shift in policy has begun.

A recent comprehensive appraisal of wilderness protection in Canada (Hummel 1989) calls for a coordinated effort at provincial, territorial, and federal levels to secure legal protection of at least 12 percent of the nation's landscape by the turn of the century (this figure is adopted from recommendations contained within the Brundtland Report). The analysis points to the high level of public support for wilderness protection. As reflected in recent opinion polls, evidence of a national commitment to such a goal challenges the nation's political leaders to respond to the public's vision of a comprehensive program of wilderness protection. Clearly, the push for adequate wilderness protection in Canada is gaining strength and sophistication on the political agenda.

SOUTH AFRICA

South Africa has specific procedures to protect wilderness, along with a fairly long history of concern about nature protection and national parks. The 5-million-acre (2-million-ha) Kruger National Park was established in 1926 (from the Sabie Nature Reserve originally established in 1898) and the 2.5-million-acre (1-million-ha) Kalahari Gemsbok National Park was set aside in 1931. Much of the early concern with nature protection, particularly wildlife conservation, in Africa was expressed by Europeans and Americans concerned about the rapid loss of much of their own natural heritage. In early South Africa, the presence of a ruling white colonial government probably helped accelerate the adoption of programs establishing conservation reserves.

Though numerous dedicated professionals in both wildlife conservation and forestry have worked hard to strengthen the wilderness concept, much of the initial interest and success in preserving and popularizing wilderness in South Africa, beginning in the 1950s, can be traced to the efforts of Ian Player (fig. 3.7). Player began his career as a ranger with the Natal Parks Board in 1952. His duties kept him in close contact with both the wild country along the White and Black Umfolozi Rivers as well as with the Zulu game guards who aided the rangers in their battle with poachers in the Umfolozi Game Reserve. Nightly discussions around the campfire with his fellow workers had helped shape a deep concern on Player's part for the protection of the country's wild character and a deep appreciation for the keen understanding of the land held by the native people and others who had been raised there. It was during this period that he was first introduced to wilderness literature from the United States. Upon reading some of the basic principles underlying the wilderness concept, Player observed, "it was as though an atomic bomb had gone off in my mind. I realized that I had always understood physical wilderness but had never appreciated the intellectual concept" (Player 1979, p. 25).

Player immediately began to press for wilderness classification in a portion of the Umfolozi Game Reserve. The public and members of the reserve's governing board opposed the idea, concerned that such a designation would deny public access to the area's remoter reaches. But Player had maintained contact with Americans, including Howard Zahniser, who were involved in the efforts to secure passage of the Wilderness Bill in the United States (see chap. 4). Zahniser kept Player supplied with all the current literature about wilderness, including copies of the draft American legislation. Imbedded within this documentation was virtually every argument used against wilderness along with the appropriate rejoinder. Player used the material to great advantage and, despite continuing opposition, saw the eventual administrative designation of the southern portion of the Umfolozi Game Reserve as a wilderness in 1958, the first such area in Africa.

Player's long exposure to the African wilds had developed within him a deep sense of appreciation for the value of close contact with the natural environment. His contact with the Zulu natives of the area had also sharpened his appreciation for their intimate knowledge of nature and a lifestyle that harmonized with their environment. In 1957, he undertook a week-long trip (or trail, as wilderness treks are known in South Africa) along the east coast of the country, accompanied by six schoolboys, and introduced them to the wilderness. Later, the boys wrote to Player, each thanking him for the opportunity and commenting, "This experience changed my life" (Player 1979, p. 25). This trail experience led Player to begin an organization which had, as its purpose, the introduc-tion of people to the wilderness, guided by an individual who understood not only the secrets of nature but the role such settings played in gaining self- understanding. In 1963, the Wilderness Leadership School (WLS) was formally registered in South Africa. In 1974, Player found himself at a point in his life where he felt he could do more for the wilderness outside of the civil service than inside. As a result, he resigned to devote his full energies to the WLS, expanding its scope to an international foundation. More than 25,000 people, ranging from youth to corporate executives, have participated in the multiracial trails conducted by the WLS. The experience gained is not intended to create ecologists or naturalists out of participants, but rather to encourage an appreciation of natural processes and of the value of wilderness settings for personal growth and human understanding (Player 1987).

Fig. 3.7. Dr. Ian Player, noted South African and international wilderness advocate, and his friend, Magqubu Ntombela, famous game guard and Zulu tribal chief. Player was instrumental in establishing part of the Umfolozi Game Reserve as wilderness in 1958 and in founding the Wilderness Leadership School (WLS), a nonprofit group dedicated to introducing people to wilderness. The WLS takes people on walking treks in South Africa's wilderness. In 1988, Player, age 61, and Ntombela, age 88, continued to lead occasional four-day treks into the Umfolozi. Photo courtesy of Ian Player.

The idea of legal protection for wilderness on the national forests of South Africa evolved under the initial leadership of Danie Ackerman, a Yale forestry graduate, who returned periodically to America and was abreast of the wilderness movement in the United States. As a Chief Director of Forestry, Ackerman was well aware of the rapid disappearance of wilderness lands in South Africa and recognized that with less than 4 percent of the nation's land in public ownership, steps were badly needed to secure long-term protection. He was influential in the passage of the Forest Act in 1971, which authorized designation of wilderness areas on national forest land. The actual programs to select suitable wilderness areas and espouse their legal protection was left to regional teams. For example, in the extensive western Cape mountains, Dr. D. P. Bands played a significant role in the declaration of wilderness areas under the National Forest Act. Additionally, in 1973, Ackerman was successful in securing legislative authority to protect wilderness in the Drakensberg Mountains, along with the development of a wilderness management policy in the area. The designation of this area provided protection for the major portion of Afro-alpine vegetation in the nation. The area also contains an estimated 1,800 species, out of which about 300 are endemic (Bainbridge 1984). In total, three areas were given legal protection as wilderness in 1973— Cedarberg, Mdedelelo, and Mkhomazi—the first such legally declared wilderness in all of Africa.

A final, important element that has strengthened the professional wilderness expertise in South Africa was the establishment of a Nature Conservation chair at the University of Stellenbasch in Capetown. Wilderness conservation studies were included in this course, and Professor R. Bigalke trained many students who went into professional, wilderness-related careers.

Currently, wilderness in South Africa is established through legal declaration under the Forest Act. Wilderness was first recognized in 1971 in an amendment to the 1968 Forest Act. An area can be proclaimed as wilderness when the Council for the Environment, an appointed body, recommends such a proclamation to the Minister of Environment Affairs and Tourism. The minister in turn can then officially proclaim the wilderness area. The purpose of such a proclamation, in the words of the act, is "for the preservation of an ecosystem or the scenic beauty" (cited in Glavovic 1985, p. 166). Areas so declared can only be recinded by permission of parliament.

As table 3.5 indicates, 11 areas, totaling nearly 680,000 acres (276,000 ha), have been designated under the Forest Act as wilderness (fig. 3.8). An additional four areas are candidates for wilderness or for addition to existing wilderness, totaling more than 707,000 acres (286,000 ha). The largest of the new areas, Baviaanskloof Wilderness Area, will provide protection to approximately 163,000 acres (66,000 ha) in the Cape Fynbos region, an area containing more than 6,000 endemic species out of the 8,500 total species (Bainbridge 1984). It is also impor-tant to note that, among the wilderness zones (administrative protection only) is the Lake St. Lucia Wilderness, a unique achievement in that it is completely marine, demarcated by a fence barely protruding above the lake's surface.

A major controversy in South Africa concerns efforts to transfer control of the Cedarberg Wilderness, managed by the Directorate of Forestry, to the National Parks Board. In other words, the area would be declassified as a wilderness and reconstituted as a national park under the National Parks Act of 1976. The 175,000-acre (71,000-ha) area represents nearly one-third of the total wilderness currently set aside.

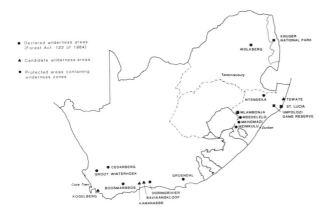

Fig. 3.8. Wilderness areas of South Africa consist of areas protected under the 1984 Forest Act, candidate areas for wilderness, and protected areas containing wilderness zones.

Those opposed to the transfer point out that, under national park administration, the area would be open to road construction and the development of structures, which are allowed in national parks for recreational purposes (Glavovic 1985).

Increasing attention is being given to the problems of wilderness management in South Africa by the relevant management authorities, which include the National Parks Board, the Natal (province) Parks Board, the Department of Nature and Environmental Conservation of the Cape province, and the Transvaal Nature Conservation Department. These organizations commonly manage wilderness by scientifically-based management systems and authorized management plans.

For example, management of wilderness areas in the Natal Drakensberg Mountains, formulated mostly under the team led by Bill Bainbridge, is intensive. This management is now under provincial authority, the Natal Parks Board, and is linked to the management of adjoining nature and game reserves. Management includes construction and maintenance of trails; visitor registration and user fees; elimination of exotic plants; and restoration of degraded areas through the use of indigenous and pioneer plant species. A prescribed burn system, principally employing biannual applied burns, is practiced throughout. Regular armed patrols are responsible for law enforcement, including the protection of rock art sites, control of trespass and poaching, and illegal smuggling into and out of the adjacent Kingdom of Lesotho (Bainbridge 1987).

Recent steps to upgrade the protection and management of South African wilderness include in-

creased public participation and the transfer of management responsibilities of forest conservation lands to provincial authority. In addition, the citizen-based Wilderness Action Group (WAG) has evolved to provide improved leadership in the movement for specific national wilderness legislation. As in other countries, efforts to secure long-term protection for wilderness in South Africa are characterized by increasing sophistication and maturity (fig. 3.9).

ZIMBABWE

Politically, Zimbabwe is a highly visible nation in the developing world and is the first truly developing country to proclaim a wilderness area (Martin 1990). The Mavuradonna Wilderness Area was designated early in 1989, unique in that it was implemented by a tribal authority (the Mzaribani District Council) on their own communal lands. Though not a precise analogy, the legal status is roughly equivalent to that of a state law in a federal system.

This designation was taken in conjunction with national policy direction established under the Communal Areas Management Programme for Indigenous Resources (CAMPFIRE), which develops economic, educational, and cultural linkages between natural resource management and tribal authorities. The minister of state for tourism officially opened the area, a further sign of national acknowledgement of the wilderness concept.

The Mavuradonna Wilderness Area is approximately 192 mi^2 (500 km^2) in the escarpment area of the Zambezi Valley, with one existing road bisecting the area. The area will be used for a combination of wilderness "trails" (hiking), sport hunting (primarily bow hunting), and wildlife cropping, with a primary purpose of generating economic benefit for the local villagers and farmers. The area will produce a projected minimum income of $225,000 (U.S. dollars) per year under the proposed uses, derived mostly from wildlife harvesting. As a result of this initial wilderness proclamation, two other areas in Zimbabwe are now under consideration for wilderness designation by other tribal authorities (Plum Tree and Tjolotjo), just south of Hwankie National Park.

There has been a perennial case in some sectors against designating wilderness in developing nations. The argument has been that the wilderness concept is too elitist, exclusionary and recreation-oriented to be of value in developing countries where the more basic issues of food, education, rising population, and poverty are higher priority. Therefore, the implications of the Mavuradonna Wilderness Area are significant. First, it signals a shift in attitude within the developing

world in favor of the wilderness concept. Secondly, with the management emphasis in this area being on *sustainable economic development* of the local people, wilderness designation is linked to rural development. Finally, under this economic emphasis, wilderness in Zimbabwe will require somewhat different management than U.S. wilderness, substantiating the concept that for wilderness to be an effective land use classification, it must be relative to the culture in which it resides (Martin 1990).

The Zimbabwean case has one other unique aspect. In all other case studies discussed thus far (the United States, Canada, Australia, New Zealand and South Africa) designation has been preceded by significant citizen activism and lobbying. The Mavuradonna Wilderness Area was established with little of this public agitation. Because Zimbabwe is the most recent, by far, of the countries to adopt some type of wilderness designation, this could mean that the concept is becoming more internationally established.

The five nations we have discussed, along with the United States, are the only ones where wilderness protection has achieved some type of formal status. Yet, it would be a mistake to presume that wilderness values are not recognized elsewhere or that they are not given some form of protection. The distinction here is subtle; formal and explicit protection of wilderness is relatively limited around the world, but if we broaden our perspective to look at programs designed for the protection of wilderness values, albeit without the explicit labeling of areas as wilderness, we find important evidence of other activity. The reasons for not describing such areas as wilderness vary widely; in some places, as we have noted, wilderness is simply not a part of the language. Elsewhere, there is the belief that other designations, such as national parks or nature reserves, adequately encompass the protection of wilderness.

The distinguishing quality of wilderness, as used in this book, is that it provides an area where natural ecological processes can operate, to the maximum extent possible, free of human influence and at the same time provide a particular type of experience, characterized by opportunities for solitude and primitive recreation. In the countries we have just reviewed, this general conception of wilderness prevails. Elsewhere, the similarity blurs. In particular, many of the other programs have a strong nature protection flavor to them. Yet, many other programs are experiencing strong pressures to accommodate a type of recreation similar to what we normally associate with wilderness.

Table 3.5. Wilderness areas in South Africa.

Name	Area (acres)	Area (hectares)	Province
Legally declared under Forest Act			
Mdedelelo	66,700	27,000	Natal
Mkhomazi	118,600	48,000	Natal
Ntendeka	12,900	5,200	Natal
Mlambonja	34,600	14,000	Natal
Mzimkulu	70,000	28,300	Natal
Wolkberg	43,000	17,400	Transvaal
Cedarberg	159,100	64,400	Cape
Groendal	53,900	21,800	Cape
Boosmansbos	35,100	14,200	Cape
Grootwinterhoek	58,400	23,600	Cape
Baviannskloof	165,000	66,000	Cape
Doringrivier	27,500	11,000	Cape
Total Area	**844,800**	**340,900**	
Wilderness Zones in National Parks or Game Reserves			
Umfolozi GR	61,800	25,000	Natal
Lake St. Lucia	44,300	17,700	Natal
Kruger NP (18 zones)	1,680,500	672,200	Transvaal
Proposed National Forest Wilderness Areas			
Tewate	50,600	20,500	Natal
Kammanassi	123,500	50,000	Cape
Kogelberg	39,500	16,000	Cape

Source: Bainbridge 1990.

LATIN AMERICA

When considering Central and South American wilderness, we must first consider terminology. As discussed earlier, many languages have no equivalent term for "wilderness." In Spanish, the generally accepted term is *area silvestre* (wild area). Despite the growing familiarity in Latin America with the North American concept of wilderness, Latin American managers more often feel this refers to specific, legally defined areas, and therefore, when speaking English, they prefer to use the term "wildlands" to refer to areas which may or may not have protection under designations other than wilderness.

Throughout Latin America, outside pressure on wildlands is currently viewed by natural resource managers as the major threat. National development projects for hydroelectric dams and transmission corridors, oil pipelines and refineries, and road construction can all rationalize their worth in terms of large economic return for the country in which they occur.

Commercial enterprises such as cattle ranching, agricultural plantations, logging, and mining also penetrate the ecosystems adjacent to and within the wildland areas. When the Inter-American Highway was built in the Darien Province of Panamá, the historical transport system which used the river was changed. The easy access by land stimulated lumber and mining exploitation and expanded cattle grazing because of the lowered economic cost of development. In Honduras, the government has obtained financing to continue construction of a forest extraction road into an area which is a short distance from the Río Plátano Biosphere Reserve. As a result, the area adjacent to the reserve is now open to lumber operations and colonization and, as of 1990, 30,000 squatters lived in Río Plátano.

Other pressures on wildlands come from subsistence farmers, refugees from war, and land speculators who have immigrated into many of the remaining wildlands of Latin America. Of these pressures, subsistence farming is by far the greatest threat to the integrity of tropical forest wildlands. These areas often serve as a type of escape valve for governments which can't cope with the overwhelming number of poor, landless people. These *shifting cultivators* clear land, grow subsistence food crops for a few years, until the soil is depleted, then repeat the cycle. While not condoning these practices, government officials can rarely do much to correct them because, without major economic and social restructuring, the only other place for these people is on the urban streets or in slums.

This difficult problem requires that wildland managers integrate wilderness priorities with those of rural development (e.g., agriculture extension, agroforestry, water quality, power, health and sanitation, and education). The best and most intensive rural development possible must occur next to wildland areas in order to stop the continual inward movement into the wilderness. Extensive and shifting practices must be converted to intensive and stabilized practices which improve the standard of living of the poor rural people.

Wildland Conservation and Integrated Development Planning

These pressures have prompted a new type of natural resource planning that is beginning to combine wildland protection with economic planning. This integrated planning features extractive resource management plans and rural development programs which can stabilize the economy by offering economic benefits from protected areas. Four of the important economic factors that influence this new

Fig. 3.9. District forester Graham Keet (top) represents the growing sophistication of wilderness management in South Africa. Keet, assisted by more than 100 administrators, laborers, and game guards, manages a district that includes the 115,000-acre (46,540-ha) Mkhomazi Wilderness. Regulations are enforced by armed patrols of game guards. Nick Steele (above), Director of the Kwazulu Bureau of Natural Resources, pioneered the use of horses in managing wilderness in southern Africa. Photos courtesy of Gordon Bailey.

type of wildland planning are discussed here.

The first is *sustainable use,* or using natural resources to meet present needs while ensuring that future needs can also be supplied from the same resource. Winning the support of subsistence people living in or near wildlands will require some allowance for well-managed use of the natural resources next to and even within portions of formally designated parks and reserves. This concept of sustainability is the key to acceptance of and support for protected areas in all developing countries.

One of the most prominent examples of sustainable use is being attempted in Brazil, where there are now four "extractive" reserves established to provide economic needs and sustain the lifestyle of *serinqueiros,* native rubber tappers. Through tapping the sap from wild rubber trees and harvesting brazil nuts and other products, these low-density users earn a living by bringing valuable products to market without destroying the wildland resources upon which their lives are based. Another type of such use is found throughout Central America, where some rural people still practice sustainable forms of agriculture and forestry which originated in the Mayan culture (Gomez-Pompa and others 1988). In addition to supporting an ecologically balance lifestyle for the native people and thereby lessening destruction of wildlands, these traditional practices are also being studied for sustainable, commercial adaptation and use.

A second economic factor which is increasingly seen as an important factor in Latin American wildland protection is one of *utility,* or supportive, indirect value in economic development projects. One example is that many protected areas serve as municipal watersheds. A major portion of the water used in Caracas, Venezuela comes from the Guatopo National Park. The park was established in 1958 to protect catchment areas which served four dam sites. Up to 20,000 liters of water per second can be supplied through this conservation plan made possible only through protecting the park's 250,000 acres (100,000 ha) of rain forest. Canaima National Park, Venezuela, is also an example of conservation for the purpose of development. The park's size was increased from 2.5 million to 7.5 million acres (1.0 to 3.0 million ha) in 1975 because it was a source of water for a scheduled hydroelectric plant. This area is also the location of Angel Falls and contains areas of forest and savanna ecosystems. This allocation of a large area provides protection for fragile habitats whose destruction would seriously alter the condition of the water, and the energy needs of the area outweigh any short-lived agricultural uses that may have been possible (MacKinnon and others 1986). Medical utility also exists in the management of wildland watersheds. In a region where intestinal parasitism is the leading cause of death, the management for the protection of water quality as well as the area's natural qualities is an excellent example of suitable, productive land use.

A third important factor is *ecotourism,* or tourism specifically attracted by and sensitive to wildland or natural areas, often with an environmental education component. As we discussed earlier in this chapter, in the paradigm of export-import, problems and resentment can easily arise if developing countries view preservation of wildlands as being solely for the benefit of developed-world tourists and scientists. Nature tourism, if recognized among a range of wildland benefits, can make a significant economic contribution to developing countries, as demonstrated in Costa Rica where citizens have come to recognize the value of wildlands for this type of use because of significant benefits. In 1988, tourism accounted for 13 percent of Costa Rica's exports ($170 million) and ranked third as foreign exchange generator, behind coffee and bananas (Budowski 1990). Not only do many tourists and scientists visit and make return trips to Costa Rica just to experience its wilderness, but several rural development projects are attempting to integrate ecotourism on a scale that can be controlled by local people who live near wildland areas (*The Asociacion de los Nuevos Alquimistas* [ANAI] 1990). As a result of this acknowledgement of wildland value, protective regulations are being enforced in Costa Rica, just one example of which was when the government of Costa Rica used its civil guard to remove illegal subsistence gold miners from primitive areas of Corcovada National Park. In many countries which do not yet recognize such a value of wildlands, these gold miners would have been ignored. In Costa Rica, the public accepted this action as necessary in order to support the tourism value of the park (Wallace and Eidsvik 1988).

One of the potentially most extensive tourist development projects in Central America is *La Ruta Maya,* the Maya Route (Sweatman 1990). This ambitious project involves five nations—Mexico, Guatemala, Honduras, El Salvador and Belize—collaborating to create a 1,500-mile (2,400-km) route connecting Mayan sites and providing access to remote wildland areas. *La Ruta Maya,* a $15 million project, will attempt to integrate environmental tourism (tropical forests, abundant bird life, and the largest barrier reef in the Americas) with cultural/historical tourism (more cities than in ancient Egypt, remote villages where traditional crafts have survived for over 3,000 years), and will use environmentally sensitive planning, technology, construc-

tion, and access. As presented succinctly in *National Geographic* magazine (October 1989, p. 422): "Only imaginative plans and quick action that provides alternative income can save (the tropical forest) . . . 'ecotourism' offers one hope."

A fourth economic factor which influences wildland conservation is the *debt-for-nature swap,* an innovative financial mechanism whereby a third party (usually a U.S. conservation organization) purchases the discounted debt of a developing nation from a major bank (debt which the bank wishes to close out due to various reasons) and then trades it to the debtor country for a plan to protect and manage important ecological areas. The first such swap occurred in July 1987, when Conservation International retired $650,000 of Bolivia's $4.5 billion foreign debt (purchased for $100,000) in return for creating and managing a 2.6-million-acre (100-million-ha) buffer zone around the Benai Biosphere Reserve in Bolivia. This first project proved controversial but useful in that it illustrated some of the difficulties of these debt-for-nature swaps, such as the potential inflationary effect, the need to work closely with a NGO within the developing country, and the potentially negative effect of change of government. However, despite the difficulties, this strategy to conserve wildlands has proven very popular and has now been performed successfully by numerous U.S. conservation groups in countries such as Ecuador, Costa Rica, the Philippines, and the Malagasy Republic, usually at the request of the country's government. Debt-for-nature swaps worldwide total roughly $100 million (Hale 1989) and are but a small percentage of the combined total of all types of debt conversion transactions of approximately $18 billion, but they are proving to be a valuable tool in wildland protection. Communication and cooperation between ecological groups, indigenous peoples, and involved governments appear to be the necessary components if such conservation plans are to succeed (Collett 1989).

In addition to these four economic factors, there are two other important elements which, when managed for, directly support wildland conservation. The first is *biodiversity,* or the range of different species—microbial, insect, plant and animal—which exists in any given area. Areas of high biodiversity contain many different genetic species. Areas of highest biodiversity typically occur in tropical forests.

Though it is difficult to explain the importance of biodiversity to people who live on a subsistence level, it is important for wildland managers and environmental educators to actually demonstrate this value within the context of locally relevant projects. The protection of entire biomes preserves the biodiversity of species needed to maintain the productive capacities of ecosystems. Protected areas provide nesting, calving, and spawning sites for species which local people rely on for food or other wildlife products. They also protect wildstock used to raise export products, as well as providing disease-resistant seedstock for improvement of cultivated crops. Wildlands are crucial for research and contain many unknown species—some of which can lead to major discoveries in medicine and agriculture, and so on (Wallace and Eidsvik 1988). The biodiversity of these areas is an economic tool which is necessary to ecologically sound, sustainable development.

To help conserve biological diversity, the World Wildlife Fund has established guidelines to be used in setting up a network of protected areas in the tropical Andes. This network encompasses over 666,667 mi^2 (1.6 million km^2) in Bolivia, Colombia, Ecuador, Peru, and Venezuela threatened by rapid deforestation and commercial interests. Guidelines include the prerequisite that the network should cover all altitudinal gradients from snow line to lowlands, and it should be large enough to support viable populations of species. As a result of this study, 16 priority protected areas, with 14 suggested additions, have been established.

The second element concerns protecting the rights and lifestyles of *traditional and/or indigenous peoples.* Until recently, the plight of these people went virtually unnoticed and they seemed doomed to perish. However, there are now new attitudes and regulations appearing that increase support for them. The Brazilian government has actually attempted to remove ecologically destructive gold miners from the Yanomami Indigenous Area, so that the Yanomamo Indians can retain their traditional lifestyle. The difficulty in this case, as in most developing countries, is one of enforcement—just as fast as the government destroys the gold miner's airstrips and forcibly removes some groups, new airstrips are built and other miners move in. This is a frontier, with all the attendant problems. But a new reality is trying to emerge.

A more successful example exists in Panamá where, because of colonization by outsiders and subsequent deforestation which posed a serious threat to the areas immediately adjacent to the Kuna Yala Reserve, the Kuna people of Panamá requested a Biosphere Reserve designation for their lands and have implemented their own protected area management project (Houseal and Weber 1987). Throughout Latin America there is an increasing mobilization of indigenous peoples, due in large part to worldwide assistance from a wide range of NGOs,

governments, and influential individuals, to the point where a union of tribal people, *União das Naçoes Indigenas* (UNI), now exists in Brazil.

Several of the largest remaining wildland areas are inhabited by longtime traditional residents. In Honduras it is the Paya, in Costa Rica the Bribri, and in Panamá the Chocos. As briefly mentioned earlier in the example of the Kuna, these populations may actually initiate and support the implementation of Biosphere Reserves. In the Río Plátano Biosphere Reserve of Honduras, which contains the Miskito Indian settlements, education programs struggle to interpret the reserve concept and ask for support. Costa Rica's and Panamá's La Amistad Biosphere Reserve is home to between 11,000 and 19,000 Cabecare, Bribri, and Guaymie people. Their native land use and culture is being studied in order to develop appropriate planning and management. When the Darien Reserve in Panamá was first designated, there were plans to relocate some villages. The strategy has changed to one of working with the village committees on management strategies which they can support.

Managing wildlands with indigenous people is extremely important for preserving wildland values. Most of these native people are wilderness dependent. In the short term, at least, protecting their lifestyles protects the wilderness.

International Conservation Cooperation in Latin America

As shown by the examples of *La Ruta Maya* and the debt-for-nature swaps, wildland conservation is increasingly a matter of international cooperation. While Antarctica probably provides the most complicated example, discussed later in this chapter, Latin America has been a virtual hive of such activity. Within the region itself, The Wildlands Unit at CATIE *(Centro Agronómico Tropical de Investigacion y Ensenanza)* in Turrialba, Costa Rica, developed a Protected Areas Mobile Seminar which takes place in several countries. Its purpose is to address the socioeconomic concerns in Central America as they apply to protected areas. Both NGO and agency specialists from outside as well as within Latin America provide support and technical assistance. Workshops of this sort promote sharing of ideas for conservation of resources and also build communication networks within the field (MacKinnon and others 1986).

North-south, or inter-regional, conservation cooperation is strategy involving all of the Americas. For example, Costa Rica (like many developing countries) has established many parks and reserves,

yet it has had difficulty in providing for maintenance and enforcement. Following the U.S. model of private philanthropy, which works with the federal and state land management agencies, the Costa Rican Foundation for National Parks was formed to assist the protection and development of the system and to provide environmental education. The foundation has raised money through substantial private donations from the United States and other countries. Being nongovernmental allows such foundations to react quickly to needs both on an emergency basis and for long term projects (MacKinnon and others 1986). Technical assistance and training has been the emphasis of international programs of TNC. TNC's international programs, begun in 1977, focus on establishing seven Conservation Data Centers in Latin America, for the purpose of creating inventories of biological diversity and for training local NGOs how to run and become self-sufficient (Boren 1988). Finally, regarding regional cooperation in the public sector, it must be remembered that the U.S. NPS is viewed as a role model for many national conservation plans. Through legislation, the NPS is required to provide different types of international assistance. It did this for many years through its International Seminar, as well as through technical support, supplemental field personnel, and management assistance. All four U.S. federal land management agencies (USFS, FWS, NPS, and BLM) are now providing assistance in a variety of areas (e.g., USFS Forestry Support Program).

Another good example of inter-regional cooperation for wildland conservation is the Programme for Belize, which involves both the public and private sectors. Administered by the Massachusetts Audubon Society and supported by other conservation groups within Belize, the program's goal is to buy 110,000 acres (44,500 ha), which will be added to the 42,000 acres (17,000 ha) already donated by Coca-Cola Foods in order to establish a preserve. The money is provided by private investments of $50 per acre, which "buy" the purchaser's the right to enjoy the tropical wilderness—no other rights are deeded. The program is only a start, as the group is also working with the Belize government to establish a multiple-use management plan for the entire country. The government supports the plan and the entire nation is being viewed as a conservation project which will devise ecologically appropriate plans to provide for sustained yields. Selective logging, tapping of chicle, cacao harvesting, sustainable development of iguana eggs, and careful development of tourism are included to provide economic benefit and support development of new skills and increased employment for the local populations (Tonge 1989).

To conclude this section on Latin America, we re-emphasize the importance of integrated, multi-use planning when conserving wildlands, which combines rural extension/assistance and local involvement with wildland management. A final example is in Mexico, where the usual activities of the Biosphere Reserve have been combined with the participation by local people and research for regional development. This is termed the "Mexican modality." The objective of these two new inclusions is to contribute to the development of alternatives which will result in better living standards for the people of less economically advantaged areas and to ensure the long term stability of the reserve through involvement of the people in the conservation of the flora and fauna. In the case of La Michilia and Mapimi Biosphere Reserves and *Sierra de Manatlán,* this "modality" has met with some success already. As typical with most Biosphere Reserves, management with such success also requires participation and resources of government agencies, NGOs, universities, commercial enterprises, and local people (Gilbert 1984, pp. 567-568).

UNION OF SOVIET SOCIALIST REPUBLICS

The hunting reserves of feudal lords marked the beginning of Russia's experience with wilderness preservation and management. After the 1917 revolution, all land was nationalized and remains so. This total public control creates, in theory, a promising political framework for all kinds of conservation, including that of wilderness. Though a concept in the Russian language analogous to wilderness exists—*dikaya mestnost*—a different word, more in keeping with their authoritarian style of government, has been used for designating such areas, *zapovedniki.*

After 1917, the U.S.S.R. began the creation of a nationwide system of *zapovedniki*—literally "forbidden areas." The *zapovedniki* constitute a system of nature reserves throughout the Soviet Union. One of the early calls for such reserved areas was made by V. P. Semenov-Tyan-Shanskiy in 1917, under the title "On the types of locales in which it is necessary to establish *zapovedniki* analogous to American National Parks" (Pryde 1972). The system expanded until 1951, when 128 areas totaled more than 31 million acres (12 million ha). But while the political system of the U.S.S.R. made the creation of *zapovedniki* easier than, say, the establishment of wildernesses under the 1964 Wilderness Act, that system also allows easy dissolution of *zapovedniki.* This very thing occurred in 1951, when about seven-eighths of the *zapovedniki*

system was abruptly eliminated, and again in 1961, when it was reduced by a third (Pryde 1977). Some areas were as large as Yellowstone National Park. Since that time the system has been slowly rebuilt; in the past 10 years, the U.S.S.R. has doubled the size of its wilderness reserves, to more than 105 million acres (43 million ha) (Pond 1987).

In the U.S.S.R., nature reserves are considered the highest form of nature conservation and are established for a variety of purposes related to such a value. Nature reserves serve to preserve habitats for rare or endangered plant or animal species, to preserve genetic diversity, and to support research (Gavva and others 1983). To serve these purposes, nature reserves are deemed to be permanent designations, isolated from the vagaries of changing land use.

Permanency of protection is as critical to the future of the *zapovedniki* as it is to wilderness in the United States. Clearly, an expanded system of reserves is needed. Many of the newer *zapovedniki* have been established along the southern borders of the U.S.S.R. where endangered wildlife species are most frequent-ly located. Problems with adequate funding and staffing, coupled with pressures from competing economic interests, limit the effectiveness of many of these reserves (Pryde 1987).

Despite the dominant role of nature conservation purposes for the *zapovedniki*, however, their value for recreation is also noteworthy. Growing pressures on several nature reserves, particularly those located in the Caucasus Range and near the Black Sea in the U.S.S.R. are forcing authorities to consider that these areas may have more value as settings for recreation than purely for science. The Kavkaz *zapovedniki* in the Caucasus near the Black Sea is open to camping, climbing, and hiking. This is wilderness by any standard, with virgin forests, wolves, and snow leopards. Management of the area is not well defined and, as a result, the resource is sometimes damaged by careless visitors. But because there is no single managing agency for the nature reserves, and the staffs that exist are composed of naturalists rather than social scientists and planners, reform is not likely (Pryde 1977). Some nature reserves such as Teberda and Issyk-Kul are acquiring the characteristics of national parks where tourism is allowed. Even in the national parks (there are only seven in the U.S.S.R.), large areas exist where strict nature conservation objectives prevail and visitor use is not allowed (Gavva and others 1983). But growing recreational demands will require closer attention to the effects of such use on natural values and, indeed, will command greater efforts to manage recreational use so as to not lose the valuable natural qualities of the land

(Mirimanian 1974). At present, a nationwide education program is under way to control what has been labeled "innocent vandalism," the destruction or removal of resources by people who simply do not realize the impact of their actions (Pryde 1977). The experience gained in wilderness management in North America, and elsewhere, may become a valuable resource in the management of these areas in the future.

NORDIC COUNTRIES

In the regions of Northern Europe known as the Nordic countries (Norway, Sweden, Finland, Denmark, and Iceland) significant wilderness values exist. Though the terminology used to designate areas of wilderness value differs from the U.S. system, the reasons behind protection are quite similar to the NWPS. Four basic designations for nature areas are used in the Nordic countries: national park, nature reserve, landscape protection areas, and special protected nature sites, such as monuments.

Sweden was the first European country to adopt the national park idea, setting aside eight parks in 1909, while other Nordic countries have done so more slowly. Although Norway proposed its first national park in 1902, the first park was not designated until 1962 (Holt-Jensen 1978), and it was the Norwe-gian Conservation Act of 1970 which provided more fully for nature protection under national park designation and also gave guidelines for the designation of areas outside of the national parks (Teigland 1989). The number of protected areas increased rapidly after 1945, similar to the trend in the United States. Also, in the late 1960s and 1970s, Norway's national parks experienced increased outdoor recrea-tion use, just as did national parks in the United States (Teigland 1989). Although nature protection through national parks increased in the post World War II era, it was still politically difficult until the 1960s to institute effective preservation measures for predatory animals considered to be threatened, such as the Scandinavian wolf, lynx, wolverine, and brown bear (Holt-Jensen 1978).

As of 1983, 58 national parks existed in the Nordic region, covering 8,900 mi^2 (23,000 km^2). This total does not include the arctic area of Greenland, in which one national park alone covers 270,000 mi^2 (700,000 km^2), or Svalbard, Norway, in which three national parks and two nature reserves total 13,500 mi^2 (34,910 km^2) (*Norges Offentlige Utredninger* [NOU] 1986). Although some differences exist among the Nordic countries in land management, they have many similarities. By looking at Norway in detail, and the other Nordic countries briefly, we can get a general understanding of the situation there.

The land mass of Norway covers an area of 143,000 mi^2 (370,000 km^2), about the size of Montana. The population is relatively sparse, approximately 4 million people. Seventy percent of the land is alpine, 30 percent is forested, and 3 percent is cultivated. Outdoor life has a very specific meaning to the Norwegian people: participation in nonmotorized leisure activities in natural settings.

In Norway, national parks are a form of protection for large, basically untouched areas characterized by a unique attribute or beauty. Generally, only government land can be designated as national parks, while other forms of protection are applied to private land. However, private properties adjacent to the park may be included in certain instances (NOU 1986). Use of motorized vehicles, including snowmobiles and landing of aircraft, is prohibited in the parks, with the exception of those areas used traditionally for reindeer herding, where the traditional people, Laplanders, are allowed to use snowmobiles for that purpose (Holt-Jensen 1978). Because others must walk, some resentment may occur, as most Norwegians support the wilderness tradition of using skis or dog-sledge, the traditional transportation forms, rather than snowmobiles.

As wilderness is defined in the United States, Norway has none. Yet the national parks, as described above, do promote a wilderness character (Kaltenborn 1989). Because of the difference in perspectives, it is important to distinguish between designated wilderness and *de facto* wilderness. *De facto* wilderness is found in Norway, and refers to areas which have the same environmental qualities as wilderness but are not designated as such. "Qualified" wilderness, borrowed from a 1970s article in a *Sierra Club Bulletin* refers to areas which were at least four hours travel from the nearest road and public transportation and were more than two hours from any tourist hut. This term was applied to the establishment of Norway's Hardangervidda National Park. Similar definitions have been attempted in other parks, but a legal definition for wilderness does not exist and the term is only applied as it relates to management practices. Similar management concerns exist for all types of wilderness lands, and focus primarily on land uses which conflict with the wilderness area's purpose or the user's experience, such as commerical tourism, industry and agriculture, new roads, hydropower plants, and housing developments (Teigland 1989).

In Norway, land is much more accessible to recreation than in the United States. The public in Norway has legal right of access to both private and

public land with the exception of cultivated land in the summer, gardens, and building sites. Motorized travel is limited to public roads, and visitors may travel by foot and camp anywhere except as noted in the exceptions above. Norwegian recreationists do perhaps have greater freedom than Americans to choose where and when they want to enjoy the outdoors (Vorkinn 1989).

A proposed plan for management of the Norwegian national parks was done from 1964 to 1967, and provided for: large, connecting areas of important conservation value, which held the opportunity for outdoor recreation/leisure use in an area of untouched nature; protection of areas of historical and aesthetic values, with a meaning for national identity, which would serve as a basis for tourism and travel; protection of untouched nature as a biological reserve for the enjoyment of future generations; and protec-tion of areas with great value for education and scientific research. In 1986, it was decided that the national parks did not fulfill their responsibility. This was because areas too small in size were being protected from development, the spectrum of nature types was too narrow, and some internationally endangered wildlife had inadequate habitats. For example, glacial areas, coastal areas, and lowland forests were nature types not protected. It was also felt that the wild reindeer habitat was not protected adequately (NOU 1986).

Protection in Norway has occurred in a piecemeal manner. Originally, hydropower developments threatened many of the rivers and lakes, so the protection of these river areas became the conservation goal. At present, there are 19 parks, three of which are in Svalbard. They cover 3 percent of mainland Norway and 25 more parks are planned. The fact that only one of the 19 parks currently has a written management plan accounts for a lack of consistent management policy (Kaltenborn 1989).

By considering one park, it is possible to get an appreciation of the wildland management challenges faced in Norway. The first national park designated was Rondane. The center of the area is characterized by dramatic peaks, sharp ridges, and narrow valleys. The surrounding area is more open with U-shaped valleys, plateaus, and plains resulting from glacial activity. Few fish live in the lakes because of the mineral content and low pH (see glossary), but fish are found in the rivers. In 1978, 294 plant species were registered, consisting mainly of lichens, although other vegetation is found in some isolated areas. About 2 percent of the area is birch forest. Eighty-one bird species and 29 animal species were recorded. The animals include wolf, arctic fox, bear, badger, otter, lynx, musk ox, and wild reindeer.

The reindeer are dependent on a larger area than the national park encompasses. These are the last of the wild European mountain reindeer, and, as mentioned above, it is generally felt that not enough of its habitat is protected. The Rondane area contains feeding and breeding areas which make it an important, but vulnerable, reindeer habitat. At present, the area is used for recreation, including hunting and fishing. There are some accom-modations, cabins, and marked trails. The main reason for the park is to conserve a distinctive area with geological features, plants, and wildlife in their natural habitat (Wagensteen and Claudius 1989).

Recently, a project has been implemented that is based on the Recreation Opportunity Spectrum (ROS) developed in the United States. Rondane is one of the parks which will be studied according to this type of zone management, which allows for different areas to be protected, serve as multi-use areas, or allows regulated traffic. Svalbard is the first area to actually implement this methodology.

The current management philosophy in Norway is mainly a biocentric one. While planners in the country see the need for further study of the social implications of protection of wild areas, they do feel the need for some sort of wilderness system. They also would like to see a stronger anthropocentric policy and intensified management in some of the more heavily used parks and recreation areas (Kaltenborn 1989).

The *Miljoverndepartementet* (Department of the Environment) has developed an interest in the management of wild areas. The secretariat for the ministry of the environment decides upon the goals and principles carried out in departmental policies and establishes priorities for itself and outside services. Management and research in the national parks are the responsibility of the *Direktoratet for Naturforvaltning* (Directorate for Nature Management). Along with the general protection of nature, recreation, wildlife, and freshwater fish, it also provides professional advice and reports to the Department of the Environment *(Handbok Kommunalt Miljovern 1988)*.

One project of the Directorate for Nature Management studies the effects of different management strategies for wilderness areas. The study includes areas on both sides of the Norway and Sweden border and is a cooperative project between the two countries. The different management strategies address the amount of service, control of camping, use of fire, and other aspects important for each area. The area of Femundsmarka, Rogen, and Langfjallet is intensively used for tourism, fishing, canoeing, and hiking, and strong public debate has occurred over vegetation damage, litter, and motor vehicle disturbance (Emmelin 1988).

Similarly, other Nordic countries have protected

wildland values, but under designations other than wilderness. As mentioned earlier, Sweden, the conservation pioneer in the Nordic countries, designated eight national parks in 1909. Today, 19 national parks exist in Sweden totaling 2,400 mi² (6,180 km²). Though the national parks are found in coastal regions, mountains and island groups known as skerries, many types of nature are still not represented. In Sweden, designation as a national park provides more protection than does that of a reserve. The areas chosen as parks are considered to be the finest examples of landscape and untouched ecosystems, and serve as scientific reference areas established to international standards (NOU 1986).

Finland also has areas designated as national park. The first park was established in 1938, and today 22 areas cover 2,500 mi² (6,530 km²). Sixteen of the parks are located in the south and are much smaller than those in the north. National parks in Finland are always established on government land, but regulations are decided by local interests. Reindeer herding is allowed, and fishing and hunting are allowed in some of the parks, as is free gathering of mushrooms and berries. Camping is more highly restricted than in Norway or Sweden. Finnish parks represent important biogeographical provinces and are administered by the Ministry of Environment (NOU 1986). Conservationists in Finland have begun to use the word "wilderness" with regularity, and some form of legal use of the word may eventually happen.

Though Denmark's mainland has no designated national parks, Greenland (which is under the Danish government) contains the world's largest park. The national park covers 270,300 mi² (700,000 km²). It is unique in that it is truly arctic and is a magnificent natural area covering a uniform and practically intact ecological system (NOU 1986).

Iceland designated its first national park in 1928. Today, there are three Icelandic parks which cover 270 mi² (700 km²). However, larger areas have been designated as reserves. The management of these parks and reserves is the responsibility of the Ministry of Culture and Education and the Nature Protection Council, an executive organization (NOU 1986).

The adaptation of wilderness concepts by Nordic countries has helped spur the protection of unique ecosystems found in northern regions. The growing movement toward recognition of wilderness values will likely insure continued wilderness protection.

NEPAL

Cultural stresses between natives and visitors are nowhere more apparent than in Nepal. Galen Rowell's intriguing book *Many People Come, Looking, Looking* (1980) traces the history of change in this tiny mountain country. Wedged between India and China, Nepal rests against some of the most spectacular mountain peaks in the world—the Himalayas. Trekkers and mountaineers from around the world come here to walk and climb. The region's rugged peaks present some of the most challenging opportunities in the world, centered on the world's highest peak—Mount Everest (designated as Sagarmatha National Park in 1976).

But the lure of this region is a relatively recent phenomenon. For generations, the culture of Nepal existed in a quiet symbiosis with its mountain environment, since the Sherpas (literally "people from the east") migrated into the area from Tibet about four centuries ago. The Sherpas occupy an area called the Khumbu Valley, lying at an average elevation of 13,000 feet (3,960 m). For years, they earned their livelihood from raising yak, cattle, and other livestock; agriculture; and trade with Tibet (Jefferies 1984). Then, in 1950, life for the Sherpas and their mountain wilderness began to change.

In that year, Nepal opened its borders to foreign visitors for the first time; up to that point, no westerners had traveled to the southern base of Mount Everest. Coupled with the Chinese invasion of Tibet, closing the northerly approaches, Nepal suddenly gained an important position to the mountaineering community. An American, Oscar Houston, received permission to travel to the Khumbu Valley where, along with his son and three other Americans, they were able to reconnoiter the possibilities of a southerly assault on Everest. Although they did not locate a safe route, they were taken by the character of the country and its people. As they hiked from the area along a well-maintained trail that showed no signs of overuse, Houston's son stated that he hoped that improvements in health and education would help the area progress. But Houston disagreed, telling his son, "After we tell the world about this place, it will never be the same, and if we don't, another party will come soon and they will tell what they found" (Rowell 1980, p. 43).

For a time it looked as though tourism would bypass Nepal. Although the area received much attention in 1953 when the New Zealand climber Edmund Hillary and his Sherpa guide Tenzing Norgay reached the summit of Mount Everest for the first time, little else occurred in the 1950s. Beginning in the 1960s, however, attention was slowly drawn to the area. A British military attache at Katmandu, Colonel James O. M. "Jimmy" Roberts, an enthusiastic mountaineer, left the army to promote trips to the area's

great peaks. His company, Mountain Travel, was registered as Nepal's first trekking agency. (*Trek* is a South African word used to describe a long migration by ox cart.) The initial response to his advertising efforts was modest, to say the least. An expensive advertisement in *Holiday* magazine netted only five responses (two from curious children). Yet it was the beginning, and once the flow of trekkers to Nepal began, it came in a rush. In 1966, only eight of more than 12,000 tourists to Nepal listed trekking or mountaineering as the purpose of their trip; in 1977, more than 17,000 applied for trekking permits (Rowell 1980). At Sagarmatha National Park, the number of trekkers rose from 1,400 in 1972 to nearly 4,000 in 1979 (Jefferies 1984).

The burgeoning numbers of trekkers and mountaineers were a mixed blessing. Nepal is a poor country; the UN lists it among the 25 least-developed nations in the world. Annual income of residents of the Himalayan region of Nepal is only about $65. The needs of the influx of tourists for food, shelter, firewood, and guide services thus represented a major source of income for area residents. But a rising standard of living carried with it a dark side. Farm workers who once earned two rupees (16 cents) a day now could earn 10 rupees (80 cents) a day in the tourist business. Now the farmers had to pay 10 rupees a day to have fields plowed. This in turn inflated the cost of food for everyone. A similar cycle affected the sale of firewood, but added the complicating factor of environmental impact. For example, one village was able to earn nearly $100,000 a year from the sale of firewood to expeditions and trekkers, a tremendous sum in this economy. This accelerated forest cutting, with little regard for the age, species, or location of the trees cut. The cutting is difficult to control, in part because people need the increased income to finance the purchase of high-cost food and petroleum fuels that are now essentials of their new lifestyle. Adding to this upward spiral of inflation and environmental impact, the Sherpas commonly convert wealth into large livestock herds, which increases grazing intensity on already hard-pressed forage (Jefferies 1984).

Other more subtle changes, as a result of the shifting lifestyle of the Sherpas, can be noted. Rowell (1980) cites the example of an anthropologist who visited the area in 1957 and again in 1971. He found that no new Buddhist inscriptions had been added to the city walls, whereas previously new work was always being done. The number of llamas at the monastery had declined by more than half. Those who remained told of the conflict between dealing with tourists and trying to live an exemplary religious life.

The once-wilderness mountain landscape of Nepal, maintained for countless generations, has changed rapidly, both culturally and ecologically, as tourism has grown. Although, from an American perspective, we might not call the area, even in its former condition, a wilderness, it was nonetheless an area where natural ecological processes had operated over a long period in a close association with indigenous populations, not unlike the situation in Alaska. But with the increased awareness of the area's superlative scenery and climbing opportunities, the delicate balance maintained for so long has quickly tumbled. Efforts to restore the balance are under way. The New Zealand government has maintained a close tie with the Nepalese since 1976 in attempting to establish a management program to improve resource management. This management plan involves not only nature conservation, but the protection of religious and historic values and controls on the use of renewable energy resources (Jefferies 1984). It also involves the training of Sherpas to take over administration of the management plan. Together, it is hoped that the wild qualities of the region can be managed in such a way that the area's unique culture and environment can be retained.

ANTARCTICA

The vast continent of Antarctica is, in many ways, the world's last wilderness. Vast (half again as large as the United States), forbidding, and arid (average annual snowfall at the South Pole is the equivalent of less than 1 inch [2.5 cm] of water), Antarctica, in an almost ironic sense, meets the Biblical definition of wildernesses of the Middle East (see chap. 1). And, except for the temporary residents of the various scientific bases established there, it is devoid of human habitation.

Until recently, the remoteness of the region, coupled with bitter cold, kept human exploration of Antarctica to a minimum. Captain Robert Scott, who, along with several others, reached the South Pole in 1912, wrote in his diary, "Great God This is an awful place." All on the expedition perished. But interest in Antarctica remained high. Between 1957 and 1958, the International Geophysical Year (IGY) was launched as an international effort to increase the understanding of the earth. A major component of this program saw the establishment of a series of scientific stations in the Antarctic. The IGY program helped create a period during which the previous conflict over sovereignty of the Antarctic was replaced by a greater spirit of cooperation. It became apparent, however, that a long-term solution was needed to help maintain and foster this spirit. In 1959, the Antarctic Treaty was signed by the repre-

sentatives of 12 nations, and has three main aspects. The central tenet of the treaty is that the region is to be used only for peaceful purposes, principally scientific research. The treaty is designed to regulate the impact of human intervention on Antarctica and to preserve and conserve its living resources. It prohibits the establishment of military bases as well as nuclear explosions and the disposal of nuclear wastes; it is the most comprehensive disarmament program in the world and the only treaty that provides for on-site inspection (Lucas 1984). The second aspect guarantees freedom of scientific investigation, and the third promotes international cooperation on the continent.

The Antarctic Treaty was followed by a series of conventions designed to provide additional protection for the area's unique qualities. In 1964, several of the parties to the treaty signed the agreed measures for the Conservation of Antarctic Flora and Fauna and provided the basis for the establishment of several types of protective designations for areas within the Antarctic requiring special status. In 1970, and again in 1977, other agreements were signed, among other things, to minimize the harmful effects of human activity on the environment, to assess the environmental impacts associated with any future developments, and to take steps to ensure that tourist activities will not have any adverse impacts on scientific activities. In 1972, the Convention for the Conservation of Antarctic Seals was agreed, thereby prohibiting the taking of certain species such as the southern fur seal and setting quotas for others, such as leopard seals (Lucas 1984).

Such activities suggest a growing international consciousness about the importance of protecting the pristine qualities of this unique landscape. During the 15th General Assembly of IUCN in Christchurch, New Zealand, in 1981, a resolution on the importance of adequate protection for the Antarctic was passed, citing "the paramount importance to mankind of its great wilderness qualities for science, education, and inspiration" (cited in Lucas 1984, p. 369). But, despite the remoteness of the region and its near pristine character, all is not well in the Antarctic. For example, radioactive fallout and heavy metals have been detected in Antarctica ecosystems (Tierney and Johnstone 1978). And, despite the generally harsh and desolate character of the Antarctic land mass, the continental shelf and the offshore waters are rich in resources. Much of the ocean life is already heavily exploited, and it is feared that krill may become so. Krill, an important link in the Antarctic food chain, provide the principal food for a number of key fish species, including five

species of whale. Found only in the Antarctic region, they are also especially vulnerable to heavy exploitation, given their tendency to swarm. Reports indicate that krill can be netted at a rate of up to 40 metric tons per hour (Lucas 1984).

In 1972, evidence of hydrocarbons was discovered along the continental shelf of the Ross Sea, attracting the interest of the off-shore oil industry. An informal moratorium on mineral development, instituted in 1977, remains in effect, but the prospect of such development also remains. A major oil leak from such an operation would have a catastrophic impact on the area's natural ecosystems. The remoteness of Antarctica and the hostility of the environment no longer provide "self-protection."

What of the future? Various proposals have been made to ensure protection of Antarctica's natural qualities. In 1972, the Second World National Parks Conference recommended that the nations party to the Antarctic Treaty declare the continent and the surrounding seas a world park, under the auspices of the United Nations. In 1975, the New Zealand government similarly proposed designating the area a world park and indicated its willingness to drop its own territorial claims (Mosley 1986). But other treaty members did not respond, and the New Zealand offer was withdrawn.

In 1988, a minerals agreement was reached among the Antarctic Treaty Consultative Parties to regulate mining in the world's last untapped continent. Beneath its frozen surface, Antarctica may harbor unknown quantities of oil, gold, platinum, and other mineral resources. However, it now appears that the Convention on the Regulation of Antarctic Minerals Resource Activities (CRAMRA) won't become enforceable as law. In order for it to be so, all seven nations with Antarctic territorial claims (Argentina, Australia, Britain, Chile, France, Norway, and New Zealand) must ratify CRAMRA. Australia and France have decided not to sign, proposing instead that Antarctica be protected as a "nature reserve/land of science" (referred to commonly as an "international wilderness park") wherein all mineral activities are banned, and that a Comprehensive Environmental Protection Convention be negotiated. The Australia/France proposals, among others, will be discussed at a Special Consultative Meeting on The Environment to be held in Chile, late in 1990.

Thus, the world park idea persists. Under the Agreed Measures for the Protection of Antarctica Fauna and Flora, the area is presently recognized as a "Special Conservation Area." Some see world park designation as a logical extension of this special recognition (Mosley 1986). The Antarctic is also seen

as deserving protection as a World Heritage Site. Such designations could ensure long-term protection of the area's natural, scientific, and recreational values. The presence of valuable resources, however, such as fisheries and minerals, coupled with concerns with national sovereignty, will likely continue to thwart such protective designations.

OTHER AREAS AND EFFORTS

Progress in the protection of wilderness values elsewhere in the world is variable and difficult to assess. One reason for this is that, even when wildland areas in developing countries are designated for some type of formal protection, they are often simply "paper parks," with no real management and no actual protection. Much attention has focused on the need for increased protection of the world's tropical, moist forests, which occur in a belt around the middle section of the globe. These lands, occupying only about 12 percent of the earth's total land area, contain an abundance and diversity of the world's species— 40 to 50 percent of the planet's total number of plant and animal species. In an area of only about 2 acres (1 ha) in the Brazilian rain forest, 235 different tree species were reported. A similarly sized area in a temperate forest would normally contain no more than 10 species (Myers 1979). Yet the impact of human occupancy and development on these rich reserves is enormous. Current estimates of tropical forest logging show that 28 acres (11 ha) to 117 acres (46 ha) are removed every minute! Reports in 1990 suggest that tropical deforestation may be damaging 50 percent more area than previously calculated. The need to protect tropical wildlands cannot be overemphasized and, as we discussed in the Latin American section, the beginning of concerted action can be seen. Increasing grassroots activity by local and international NGOs and the establishment of two major intergovernmental efforts—The Tropical Forestry Action Plan (TFAP) and the International Tropical Timber Organization (ITTO)—are signs of increasing commitment to protect tropical forests. The difficulties these intergovernmental organizations have faced are indicative of the complexity of the tropical deforestation issue.

As in Latin America, Southeast Asian countries confront similar issues concerning their tropical forests. Many examples of wildland protection, and its connection to the struggle of indigenous people to maintain their cultures, exist throughout Southeast Asia. Many developed country NGOs and institutions have come to assist in the region's environmental crisis but, as we have discussed, involvement by indigenous people is the key to lasting environmental reform. By indigenous people understanding their role in protecting local wildlands, environmental degradation of these wildlands can be stopped. Also, by promoting local processing of resources, affected countries can develop economic benefits, enhance employment opportunities for local people, and thereby sustain indigenous cultures.

Of the numerous countries in Southeast Asia, Malaysia and Indonesia provide good examples of both wildland deterioration and a burgeoning grassroots effort for their protection. In the east Malaysian state of Sarawak in Borneo, the rainforests are being logged to supply local markets and consumers in Europe, North America, and Japan. Extensive logging in Sarawak's wildlands has produced many deleterious side-effects: streams and rivers polluted with silt and milling wastes; heavy erosion; native people, such as the nomadic Penan, displaced from their homes; and depletion of endemic flora and fauna. Native people are fighting logging practices which are not sustainable, but complex issues surrounding deforestation—such as national debt, land ownership, corruption, and different concepts of development—make it difficult for natives, local governments, and international organizations to reach compromises of benefit to all parties.

In Indonesia, wildland watersheds are abundant and important to complex tropical ecosystems. Many indigenous people, such as the Dayaks, Irianese, and Javanese, depend on intact watersheds to support transportation and irrigation. Increased building of hydropower projects and dams, dumping of industrial wastes, and logging of forests degrade watersheds and lead to intensified flooding and erosion. Erosion destroys the soil's ability to hold water, so both sudden floods and drought are more likely to occur. In Indonesia, heavy erosion threatens almost half of the wildland watersheds, approximately 26 million acres (10.4 million ha) (Environesia 1989). Topsoil erosion makes agriculture outside of wildlands unproductive, and sedimentation creates organic run-off, which raises the biological oxygen demand (see glossary) of rivers and interferes with transportation and irrigation. Wildland destruction similar to that in Malaysia and Indonesia occurs throughout Southeast Asia.

Many indigenous people living in Southeast Asian forests have always used sustainable methods and have the best knowledge of these wildlands. A combination of local and international business, national debt, and domestic land distribution threaten the biological diversity of these unique wildlands and the indigenous people's economic and social autonomy.

In Europe, where wilderness as defined by the United States has ceased to exist, there has been increasing activity to protect *secondary wilderness,* areas which are recovering from former, extensive human exploitation. Recently, interest has been expressed in the formal protection of wilderness values in Scotland. Although the British government has not indicated a willingness to consider legislation, there nonetheless have been calls for them to recognize the wilderness values in the Cairngorms National Nature Reserve, an alpine tundra plateau in central Scotland. The area attracted considerable interest during the 3rd WWC held in Scotland in 1983, with a formal resolution passed asking the British government to preserve the area's wilderness values by nominating the area for World Heritage status. After review, it was determined that the Cairngorms did not meet World Heritage qualifications. However, calls persist for the protection of its wilderness values.

The increasing interest in, and appreciation of, wilderness in Scotland illustrates two different, yet related, reactions. First, virtually no area of Scotland (or in much of western Europe for that matter) could be considered pristine in the American sense. Scotland was once much more inhabited than today and virtually the entire ancient Caldeonian forest has been logged. To Scots traditionalists, these areas were wasted as a result of English occupation and changing land-use patterns (Watson 1984); therefore, such persons see the landscape as a wasteland rather than a pristine wilderness. But a second view sees the wide-ranging vistas of heath-covered moorland and extensive glens as providing the same quality wilder-ness experience to the visitor as do areas that still retain their pristine quality. In general, the wilderness experience offered by such settings is accessible and meaningful to thousands of enthusiastic hill walkers. Such a perspective offers additional support to the value of protection and careful management for those areas which, despite extensive human habitation and modification in the past, now offer high-quality wilderness experiences.

The conception of wilderness as land use versus experience remains a complex dilemma facing those charged with its protection and management (Hamilton-Smith 1980). This is evident in many international cases. Another recent and important example, in this regard, is Italy. Here, a small but determined effort—the *Wilderness Associazione Italiana,* founded by Franco Zunino—has succeeded in putting the wilderness concept on the agenda of two regional governing councils. The vice president of the Piedmont Regional Council reported at the 4th WWC in the United States (1987), that her council had proposed to the national government's Environment Department to establish a national park in the Val Grande area, "thereby taking a substantial first step toward the realization of the first wilderness area in Italy" (Vetrino 1988). In a typically European situation, the Val Grande area is what some people refer to as a "return-wilderness" because the area had been formerly inhabited and used for agricultural activities and was the scene of intense deforestation in the nineteenth century. Abandonment of the area by shepherds, and changing economic benefit of sheepherding, has made the Val Grande slowly reassume the characteristics of a wilderness area.

For the first time in Italy, another Italian regional government, *Regione Veneto,* has recognized the need for protection of wilderness and included it in its master landscape plan. The proposal calls for eight areas to be classified, totaling some 8,000 acres (20,000 ha), all of which are within previously established nature reserves or parks (Zunino 1990). While falling far short of the type of protection offered by national legislation, this proposed new direction in Italy shows divergent and important growth of the wilderness concept internationally.

Gradually, the international aspects of wilderness preservation are receiving more attention. Wilderness areas and values are the focus of an increasing number of organizations and programs throughout the world. NGOs such as the IUCN, World Wildlife Fund, TNC, Conservation International, and others are all doing important work internationally, especially by providing direct assistance for managing wildland areas in developing countries. They have developed increas-ingly sophisticated international programs with field staff, local training, and publications, which are devoted solely to wildland interests (Wallace 1990).

Another NGO effort, the World Wilderness Congress (WWC) (a project of the International Wilderness Leadership Foundation, IWLF), has met on four occasions (1977, 1980, 1983, and 1987) to explore a range of management, cultural, and scientific matters regarding wilderness protection. The WWC has provided a continuing, international forum for the wilderness concept. As a platform for all aspects of the need for and difficulties concerning wilderness, the WWC has been a focal point for the worldwide evolution of wilderness definition and legislation. In spite of the many cultural differences in the concept, as has been discussed in this chapter, each of the four WWCs has worked towards a definition of wilderness acceptable to the world community. The 4th WWC adopted the following revision of previous definitions for wilderness (Martin 1988):

- It is an enduring natural resource which provides opportunities to obtain those pristine elements which comprise the spiritual and physical wilderness experience.
- It is protected as an ecological preserve of natural, diverse processes and genetic resources. It is primarily affected by nature, with human impact substantially unnoticed, and where people are visitors, without mechanical transport or installation.
- It must enjoy the highest legislative protection. It should be of sufficient size to realize its essential nature. It should be managed so as to retain its wilderness qualities.

Following the 4th WWC, and recognizing the need for further work on this definition, the WWC Resolutions Committee and the IWLF requested that IUCN further revise the above definition in a way which accommodates indigenous peoples who live within wilderness. The following definition has been adopted (Eidsvik 1988):

> Wilderness is an enduring natural area, legislatively protected and of sufficient size to protect the pristine natural elements which may serve physical and spiritual well-being. It is an area where little or no persistent evidence of human intrusion is permitted, so that natural process may begin to evolve.

As is evident, there is a distinct difference between this evolving international definition and that contained in the U.S. Wilderness Act . . . "where the earth and its community of life are untrammeled by man, where man himself is a visitor who does not remain." In developing countries, virtually all wildland areas are either occupied by indigenous people or are under pressure from nearby, subsistence peoples who engage in shifting cultivation, grazing, or other potentially damaging practices.

Another specific project stimulated by the WWC has been a major effort to describe the status of the world's remaining wilderness lands. Presented for the first time at the 4th WWC, a "World Wilderness Inventory" was undertaken by the Sierra Club, with participation by the United Nation's Environment Program, the World Bank, and the World Resources Institute, and intended to provide an initial, reconnaissance-level survey of potential world wilderness areas (see fig. 3.10). Although the criteria used in the study's first phase are fairly crude (areas of 1 million acres [404,700 ha] or more, essentially roadless, and unaffected by permanent habitation or human structures), the survey revealed that approx-imately one-third of the earth still remains in a wilderness state. Table 3.6 shows that more than 40 percent of the total lies in the high latitudes, but even in Asia and Africa,

more than one-quarter of the land mass is still undeveloped (the figure for North America is 36 percent) (McCloskey and Spalding 1987).

The study has two significant aspects. First, it represents a significant collaboration between international, multilateral, and NGOs. For the first time, we have at least a preliminary measure of the global extent of wilderness lands, thereby providing us with an indication of the opportunities and challenges facing us. Second, it was meant to prompt further efforts to refine the initial data and to gain an increasing clarity on actual worldwide status of wilderness areas. This seems to now be well in motion, with surveys and questionaires being distributed internationally by the Sierra Club and others.

Finally, mention should be made of the effort to apply the wilderness concept to nonterrestrial areas. Initially, this was done by incorporating portions of aquatic areas in wilderness designation with surrounding terrestrial areas (BWCAW being the best example). Internationally, a significant example of this is the wilderness zone in Lake St. Lucia, in the Zululand area of South Africa. The low fence in the lake demarcates areas for nonmotorized use.

There has also been movement toward oceanic wilderness. The 2nd WWC saw discussions of a proposal for a wilderness zone in the Great Barrier Reef Marine Park (GBRMP). The GBRMP Authority was planning to designate zones with the Capricornia section of the GBRMP for wilderness type use only. Though small in terms of the overall size of the GBRMP, it should be emphasized that, in terrestrial terms, the zones are extensive (Kelleher 1989). An inquiry into the feasibility of oceanic wilderness was initiated at the 4th WWC by the National Oceanic and Atmospheric Administration (NOAA), through

Fig. 3.10. Circled areas represent wilderness of 1 million acres (404,700 ha) or more as identified in the first World Wilderness Inventory (courtesy of Sierra Club 1987).

Table 3.6. Wilderness area by continent.

Continent	Wilderness (mi²)	Wilderness (km²)	Percent wild	No. of Areas
Antarctica	5,098,700	13,209,000	100	2[1]
Asia	4,579,500	11,864,000	27	306
Africa	3,542,600	9,177,700	30	437
North America	3,476,600	9,006,700	36	89
South America	1,630,000	4,222,700	24	91
Oceania & Australia	1,029,200	2,666,300	30	94
Europe	286,000	741,000	7	31
World	**19,642,600**	**50,887,400**	**34**	**1,050**

Source: McCloskey 1987.
1. This is really one contiguous block divided in two only for purposes of biogeographical classification.

a symposium specifically dealing with this question. As a result of the symposium, the Natal Parks Board (which initiated the Lake St. Lucia wilderness zone) has proposed establishment of a St. Lucia Marine Reserve, on the Indian Ocean coast of the St. Lucia area, incorporating both terrestrial and oceanic/ marine wilderness.

International interest in wilderness is growing. Numerous countries around the world have begun to consider how wilderness might fit into their particular system of areas under conservation management. Even in countries where long-term occupancy and development have greatly modified the landscape, such as Taiwan, the possibility of restoring wilderness is being discussed. In many countries not discussed in this chapter, such as India, the wilderness idea has many advocates. It is likely a matter of time before this advocacy evolves into overt protection of wilderness areas. This growing interest reflects an increasing understanding both of the importance of wilderness settings as a repository of a country's natural heritage and as a symbol of that country's international responsibility to protect the environment.

SUMMARY

As we consider the global status of wilderness, we find the American experience pervasive. Like the national parks, wilderness as a category of land use is an idea largely formulated and refined in the United States. Today, we find the idea slowly gaining recognition and support around the world.

But American notions about wilderness should be seen as an influence, not a determinant, on the way other nations approach the idea. We see considerable similarity between the American definition and the general definition of wilderness as used in other countries. Wilderness as defined in New Zealand, for example, is reminiscent of our own Wilderness Act. But differences of geography, culture, and economics alter the specific ways in which other countries approach the designation and management of wilderness. The vast reaches of arid country in Australia; the debate over wilderness as an experience versus a land use in New Zealand; the question of whether wilderness should be a statutory process versus an administrative zone in many countries; the role of recreation versus ecological protection; and the matter of indigenous populations in wilderness in Australia and Scandinavia—and in our own Alaska, for that matter—all are questions that individual countries must confront and resolve in light of their own particular circumstances. In developing countries, the need for integrating wilderness and wildland protection into economic and rural development planning is a primary consideration.

One of the most significant contributions made by the American experiment in wilderness preservation has been to demonstrate the powerful influence of public opinion. As we look around the world, we find that much of the initiative for wilderness protection elsewhere has come from citizen advocacy groups—the Australian Conservation Foundation, the FMC of New Zealand, the Alberta Wilderness Association, and so on. As Lucas (1983) indicated to participants at New Zealand's first wilderness conference, wilderness protection is largely dependent on well-developed public will and support; the American example is often cited to confirm this.

The American experience in wilderness management is unique. Because our history of wilderness preservation is longer than elsewhere, so too is our experience in managing such areas. The growing

demands for recreational access to such areas, the conflicting objectives of preservation and use, and the relative scarcity of wilderness have combined to force attention on the question of management. And again, we find that this experience serves as a model, both good and bad, for the rest of the world to reflect on and consider. Specific management techniques must be adapted to local circumstances, U.S. wilderness management authorities have convincingly demonstrated this.

Wilderness in the United States is different from wilderness elsewhere. Given the cultural foundation of the term, this should be expected. The absence of native cultures in our wildernesses (Alaska being the last remaining major exception), the generally undeveloped quality of our wilderness lands, and the opportunities, in at least some places, for extended wilderness travel are characteristics of American wilderness largely absent elsewhere. But it is important to consider American wilderness as a part of a larger comprehensive world system of wild places, with each offering its own special kind of experience.

STUDY QUESTIONS

1. Identify and discuss some of the factors that account for the differences in progress in wilderness preservation between the United States and Europe.
2. The chapter proposes the paradox that the possession of wilderness is a disadvantage in the efforts to preserve wilderness. Discuss the meaning of such a statement and explain your agreement or disagreement with it.
3. Wilderness has not been one of IUCN's conservation categories. Discuss some of the pros and cons for wilderness being included on the IUCN list.
4. Identify some of the important relationships between wilderness and international conservation designations such as Biosphere Reserves, World Heritage Sites, and Ramsar Sites.
5. Describe some of the distinctive aspects of wilderness preservation and management in the United States as compared to elsewhere in the world.
6. How could the pressures for wilderness protection in lesser developed countries lead to undesirable changes in an area's ecological and cultural conditions? How might these changes be prevented or mitigated?
7. Explain sustainable development. What are implications for wilderness?

REFERENCES

Alberta Wilderness Association. 1973. Willmore Wilderness Park. Calgary, AB: Alberta Wilderness Association. 42 p.

Alberta Wilderness Association. 1985. Wilderness in Alberta: the need is now. Calgary, AB: Alberta Wilderness Association. 39 p.

The Asociacion de los Nuevos Alquimistas. [ANAI]. 1990. The committee for promotion and conservation of Talamanca. ANAI Bulletin. ANAI, Inc. Franklin, NC. April.

Archibald, George. 1988. The Ramsar convention and wetland protection. In: Martin, Vance G., ed. 1988. For the conservation of earth. Proceedings of the 4th World Wilderness Congress; 1987 September 11-88; Denver and Estes Park, CO. Fulcrum, Inc., Golden, CO 52-56 pp.

Australian Heritage Commission. 1982. The national estate in 1981. Canberra, Australia: Australian Government Publishing Service. 225 p.

Bainbridge, Bill. 1984. Management objectives and goals for wilderness areas: wilderness areas as a conservation category. In: Martin, Vance; Inglis, Mary, eds. Wilderness: the way ahead. Middleton, WI: Lorian Press: 114-124.

Bainbridge, W.R. 1987. The use of fire to maintain indigenous vegetation in the wilderness systems in southern Africa. In: Krumpe, E.E., & Weingart, P.D. eds. Management of national park and wilderness reserves: Proceedings of a symposium at the 4th World Wilderness Congress; September 14-18, 1987; Estes Park, Colorado, USA. In publication.

Bainridge, W.R. 1990. Private correspondence to Vance Martin.

Barr, Hugh. 1990. Federated Mountain Clubs of New Zealand. Private correspondence to Vance Martin.

Blacksell, Mark. 1982. The spirit and purpose of national parks in Britain. Parks. 6(4): 14-17.

Blainey, Geoffrey. 1966. The tyranny of distance. New York: St. Martin's Press. 365 p.

The Blockaders. 1983. The Franklin blockade. Hobart, Tasmania: The Wilderness Society. 124 p.

Boren, Frank D. 1988. Protecting biological diversity for the future. In: Martin, Vance G., ed. 1988. For the conservation of the earth. Proceedings of the 4th World Wilderness Congress; 1987 September 11-18; Denver and Estes Park, CO. Fulcrum, Inc., Golden, CO. 222-224 pp.

Brown, Bob. 1982. The use and misuse of wilderness in Southwest Tasmania. In: Martin, Vance G., ed. Wilderness. 1982. The Findhorn Press, Moray, Scotland. 81-86 pp.

Bryan, Rorke. 1973. Much is taken; much remains. North Scituate, MA: Wadsworth Publishing Company. 305 p.

Budowski, Tamara. 1990. Ecotourism. In Tecnitur; 5 (April-May): 28-30 pp.

Cohen, Barry. 1984. The Franklin saga. In: Martin, Vance; Inglis, Mary, eds. Wilderness: the way ahead. Middleton, WI: Lorian Press: 47-54.

Collett, Merrill. 1989. Bolivia blazes trail . . . to where? Conservation measures appear to have taken a back seat to commercial logging interests. The Christian Science Monitor, Monday, July 10, 1989, 4 p.

CONCOM Working Group on Management of National Parks. 1986. Guidelines for reservation and management of wilderness areas in Australia. Canberra, Australia: Department of Arts, Heritage and Environment. 11 p.

Conservation Monitoring Centre and Commission on National Parks and Protected Areas. 1985. 1985 United Nations list of national parks and protected areas. Gland, Switzerland: International Union for the Conservation of Nature and Natural Resources. 171 p.

Cumberland, Kenneth B. 1981. Landmarks. Surry Hills, New South Wales, Australia: Reader's Digest Proprietary Ltd. 304 p.

Darby, H. C. 1961. National parks in England and Wales. In: Jarrett, Henry, ed. Comparisons in resource management. Baltimore: The Johns Hopkins Press: 8-34.

Dasmann, R. F. 1973. A system for defining and classifying natural regions for purposes of conservation. IUCN Occas. Pap. 7. Morges, Switzerland: International Union for the Conservation of Nature and Natural Resources. 47 p.

Dasmann, R. F. 1984. The relationship between protected areas and indigenous peoples. In: McNeely, Jeffrey A.; Miller, Kenton R., eds. National parks, conservation, and development: the role of protected areas in sustaining society: Proceedings of the world congress on national parks; 1982 October 11-22; Bali, Indonesia. Washington, DC: Smithsonian Institution Press: 667-671.

Davey, A. 1980. Wilderness areas and the Land Conservation Council of Victoria. In: Robertson, R. W.; Helman, P.; Davey, A., eds. Wilderness management in Australia: Proceedings of a symposium; 1978 July 19-23; Canberra, Australia. Canberra, Australia: Canberra College of Advanced Education, School of Applied Science: 122-130.

Dooling, Peter J. 1985. Heritage landscapes: rethinking the Canadian experience. The Forestry Chronicle. 61(4): 319-322.

Dourojeanni, Marc J. 1984. Future directions for the neotropical realm. In: McNeely, Jeffrey A.; Miller, Kenton R., eds. National parks, conservation, and development: the role of protected areas in sustaining society: Proceedings of the world congress on national parks; 1982 October 11-22; Bali, Indonesia. Washington, DC: Smithsonian Institution Press: 621-627.

Eidsvik, Harold K. 1988. Wilderness sanctuaries. Forthcoming paper done for the IUCN commission on national parks and protected areas.

Emmelin, Lars. 1989. Femundsmarka, Rogen, Langfjallet Project—Effekter Av Olika Forvaltningsstrategeur. In Frilufsliv, Fritid og Natur, Report nr. 2-1989. Directorate for nature management. Trondheim. 112 p.

Environesia. 1989. Indonesia's watersheds struggle for survival. Newsletter for The Indonesian Environmental Forum. December. 3(4):1-7.

Esping, Lars-Erik. 1972. Sweden's national parks. National Parks and Conservation. 46(6): 18-22.

Fairclough, Anthony. 1984. Wilderness in the European community. In: Martin, Vance; Inglis, Mary, eds. Wilderness: the way ahead. Middleton, WI: Lorian Press: 66-73.

Feller, M.; Hooley, D.; Dreher, T.; East, I.; Jung, R. 1979. Wilderness in Victoria: an inventory. Melbourne, Australia: Monash University, Department of Geography. 84 p.

Fenner, Frank, ed. 1975. A national system of ecological reserves in Australia. Report 19. Canberra, Australia: Australian Academy of Science. 114 p.

Foster, Nancy; Lemay, Michele H. 1988. Ocean wilderness—Myth, challenge or opportunity? In: Martin, Vance G., ed. 1988. For the conservation of earth. Proceedings of the 4th World Wilderness Congress; 1987 September 11-18; Denver and Estes Park, CO. Fulcrum, Inc., Golden, CO. 171-174 pp.

Franklin, Jerry F. 1977. The biosphere reserve program in the United States. Science. 195: 262-267.

Garrett, Wilbur. 1989. La Ruta Maya. National Geographic. October. 176(4):422-479.

Gavva, I. A.; Krinitsky, V. V.; Yazan, Yu. P. 1983. Development of nature reserves and national parks in the USSR. Parks. 8(2): 1-3.

Gee, H. M. 1978. The evolving consciousness. In: Gee, Helen; Fenton, Janet, eds. The South West book: a Tasmanian wilderness. Melbourne, Australia: Australian Conservation Foundation: 239-250.

Gilbert, V. C. 1984. Cooperative regional demonstration projects: Environmental education in practice. UNESCO-UNEP, Conservation, science and society. 2:566-572. UNESCO, Paris. 1987. Evolution of the Biosphere Reserve concept.

Glavovic, P. D. 1985. The legal status of wilderness: aspects of the 1984 Forest Act. The South African Law Journal. 102: 162-171.

Gomez-Pompa, Arturo; Kaus, Andrea. Conservation by traditional cultures in the tropics. In: Martin, Vance G., ed. 1988. For the conservation of earth. Proceedings of the 4th World Wilderness Congress; 1987 September 11-18; Denver and Estes Park, CO. Fulcrum, Inc., Golden, CO. 183-189 pp.

Grainger, Alan. 1984. Forests and their role in the future of world civilisation. In: Martin, Vance; Inglis, Mary, eds. Wilderness: the way ahead. Middleton, WI: Lorian Press: 23-28.

Hale, Sandy. 1989. Debt conversion and natural resource management in Africa. Natural resource management services newsletter.

Hales, David F. 1984. The World Heritage Convention: status and directions. In: McNeely, Jeffrey A.; Miller, Kenton R., eds. National parks, conservation, and development: the role of protected areas in sustaining society: Proceedings of the world congress on national parks; 1982 October 11-22; Bali, Indonesia. Washington, DC: Smithsonian Institution Press: 744-750.

Halffter, Gonzalo. 1985. Biosphere reserves: conservation of nature for man. Parks. 10(3): 15-18.

Halffter, Gonzalo; Ezcurra, Exequiel. 1987. Evolution of the Biosphere Reserve concept. In: Proceedings of the symposium on Biosphere Reserves, 4th World Wilderness Congress; 1987 September 11-18, Estes Park, CO. 188-206 pp.

Hamilton-Smith, E. 1980. Wilderness: experience or land use? In: Robertson, R. W.; Helman, P.; Davey, A., eds. Wilderness/management in Australia: Proceedings of a symposium; 1978 July 19-23; Canberra, Australia. Canberra, Australia: Canberra College of Advanced Education, School of Applied Science: 72-81.

Handbok Kommunalt Miljovern. 1988. Norske Kommuners Sentralforbund og Miljoverndepartementet. 1988. Kommuneforlaget. Oslo, Norway.

Harkin, J. B. 1922. Conservation is the new patriotism. Ottawa, ON: Library of the Department of Indian Affairs and Northern Development. [Pages unknown].

Heatley, David. 1984. Western Tasmania—a wilderness still threatened. Habitat. 12(5): 7, 9.

Helman, Peter M.; Jones, Alan D.; Pigram, John J.; Smith, Jeremy M. B. 1976. Wilderness in Australia: eastern New South Wales and southeastern Queensland. Armidale, Australia: University of New England, De-

partment of Geography. 147 p.

Henson, Dave. 1983. FMC and wilderness preservation. In: Molloy, Leslie F., ed. Wilderness recreation in New Zealand: Proceedings of the FMC 50th jubilee conference on wilderness; 1981 August 22-24; Rotoiti Lodge, Nelson Lakes National Park, New Zealand. Wellington, New Zealand: Federated Mountain Clubs of New Zealand: 20-24.

Holt-Jensen, Arild. 1978. The Norwegian wilderness: national parks and protected areas. Oslo, Norway: Tanum-Norli. 78 p.

Houseal, Brian; Weber, Richard. 1987. Biosphere Reserves and the conservation of traditional land systems of indigenous populations in Central America. Proceedings of the symposium on Biosphere Reserves, 4th World Wilderness Congress; 1987 September 11-18; Estes Park, CO. 234 p.

Hummel, Monte. 1982. Whither wilderness in Ontario—a personal view. Environments. 14(1): 33-36.

Hummel, Monte. 1989. Endangered spaces: The future for Canada's wilderness. Key Porter Books Limited; Toronto, Canada. 288 p.

International Union for the Conservation of Nature and Natural Resources [IUCN]. History of IUCN. 1964. In: Adams, Alexander B., ed. First world conference on national parks: Proceedings of a conference; 1962 June 30-July 7; Seattle, WA. Washington, DC: U.S. Department of the Interior, National Park Service: 406-407.

International Union for the Conservation of Nature and Natural Resources [IUCN]. 1979. The biosphere reserve and its relationship to other protected areas. [Place of publication unknown]. 19 p.

Internation Union for the Conservation of Nature and Natural Resources [IUCN]. 1985. 1985 United Nations list of national parks and proected areas. IUCN, Gland, Switzerland and Cambridge, U.K. 171 p.

Jefferies, Bruce E. 1984. The Sherpas of Sagarmatha: the effects of a national park on the local people. In: McNeely, Jeffrey A.; Miller, Kenton R., eds. National parks, conservation, and development: the role of protected areas in sustaining society: Proceedings of the world congress on national parks; 1982 October 11-22; Bali, Indonesia. Washington, DC: Smithsonian Institution Press: 473-478.

Jones, Rhys. 1982. The world significance of archaeology on the Franklin. Habitat. 10(5): 7-9.

Kalterborn, Bjorn R. 1989. The Wilderness Act—Catalyst for international action: A Norwegian perspective. David W. Lime, ed. Managing America's enduring wilderness resource. Conference proceedings. Minnesota Extension Service, St. Paul, MN. 418-424 pp.

Kelleher, Graeme. 1982. Management of the Great Barrier Reef. In: Martin, Vance, ed. 1982. Wilderness. The Findhorn Press, Moray, Scotland. 136-141 pp.

Land Conservation Council. 1990. Wilderness special investigation descriptive report. Victorian Government Printing Office, Melbourne.

Lesslie, R. G.; Taylor, S. G. 1983. Wilderness in South Australia. Occas. Pap. 1. Adelaide, Australia: University of Adelaide, Centre for Environmental Studies. 87 p.

Lesslie, R. G.; Taylor, S. G. 1985. The wilderness continuum concept and its implications for Australian wilderness preservation policy. Biological Conservation. 32(4): 309-333.

Lowenthal, David; Prince, Hugh C. 1965. English landscape tastes. Geographical Review. 55 (2): 186-222.

Lucas, P. H. C. 1983. A New Zealand wilderness preservation system—or a joint wilderness policy? In: Molloy, Leslie F., ed. Wilderness recreation in New Zealand: Proceedings of the FMC 50th jubilee conference on wilderness; 1981 August 22-24; Rotoiti Lodge, Nelson Lakes National Park, New Zealand. Wellington, New Zealand: Federated Mountain Clubs of New Zealand: 46-52 .

Lucas, P. H. C. 1984. Finding ways and means of conserving Antarctica. In: McNeely, Jeffrey A.: Miller, Kenton R., eds. National parks, conservation, and development: the role of protected areas in sustaining society: Proceedings of the world congress on national parks; 1982 October 11-22; Bali, Indonesia. Washington, DC: Smithsonian Institution Press: 369-375.

Lutzenberger, Jose. 1984. Brazilian wilderness: A problem or a model for the world? In: Martin, Vance, ed. 1984. Wilderness, the way ahead. Proceedings of the 3rd World Wilderness Congress. Findhorn Press; Moray, Scotland; 38-46 pp.

Mantra, Ida Bagus. 1984. Keynote address: The Balinese view of nature. In: McNeely, Jeffrey A.; Miller, Kenton R., eds. National parks, conservation, and development: the role of protected areas in sustaining society: Proceedings of the world congress on national parks; 1982 October 11-22; Bali, Indonesia. Washington, DC: Smithsonian Institution Press: 212-213.

Martin, Vance G., ed. 1988. For the conservation of earth. Proceedings of the 4th World Wilderness Congress; 1987 September 11-18; Denver and Estes Park, CO. Fulcrum Publishing, Golden, CO.

Martin, Vance G. 1990. International wilderness: Adapting to developing nations. In: Lime, David, ed. 1989. Managing America's enduring wilderness resouce. Conference proceedings; 1989 September 11-17. Minnesota Extension Service, St. Paul, MN. 252-266 pp.

MacKinnon, John & Kathy; Child, Graham; Thorsell, Jim. 1986. Managing protected areas in the tropics. IUCN: Gland, Switzerland.

McCloskey, J. Michael; Spalding, Heather. 1987. A reconnaissance-level inventory of the wilderness remaining in the world. In: Martin, Vance, ed. 1988. For the conservation of earth. Proceedings of the 4th World Wilderness Congress; 1987 September 11-18; Denver and Estes Park, CO. Fulcrum, Inc., Golden, CO 18-41 pp.

McCloskey, Michael. 1966. The Wilderness Act of 1964: its background and meaning. Oregon Law Review. 45(4): 288-321.

McKenry, K. 1975. Recreation, wilderness and the public. Melbourne, Australia: Department of Youth, Sport and Recreation. 214 p.

McLuhan, T. C., ed. 1971. Touch the earth: a self-portrait of Indian existence. New York: Outerbridge and Dienstfrey. 185 p.

Mirimanian, Kh. P. 1974. Mountain national parks and nature reserves. In: Elliott, Hugh, ed. Second world conference on national parks: Proceedings of a conference; 1972 September 18-27; Yellowstone and Grand Teton National Parks, WY. Morges, Switzerland: International Union for the Conservation of Nature and Natural Resources: 209-212.

Molloy, L. F. 1976. Wilderness diminishing. New Zealand Alpine Journal. 29: 65-75.

Molloy, L. F. 1979. The role of state forests in a New Zealand wilderness system. New Zealand Journal of Forestry. 24(1): 101-107.

Molloy, Les. 1983. Wilderness recreation—the New Zealand experience. In: Molloy, Leslie F., ed. Wilderness recreation in New Zealand: Proceedings of the FMC 50th jubilee conference on wilderness; 1981 August 22-24; Rotoiti Lodge, Nelson Lakes National Park, New Zealand. Wellington, New Zealand: Federated Mountain Clubs of New Zealand: 4-19.

Molloy, L. F. 1984. The reservation of commercially important lowland forests in New Zealand. In: McNeely, Jeffrey A.; Miller, Kenton R., eds. National parks, conservation, and development: the role of protected areas in sustaining society: Proceedings of the world congress on national parks; 1982 October 11-22; Bali, Indonesia. Washington, DC: Smithsonian Institution Press: 394-401.

Mosley, Geoff. 1978. A history of the wilderness reserve idea in Australia. In: Mosley, Geoff, ed. Australia's wilderness: conservation progress and plans: Proceedings of the first national wilderness conference; 1977 October 21-23; Australian Academy of Science; Canberra, Australia. Melbourne, Australia: Australian Conservation Foundation: 27-33.

Mosley, Geoff. 1986. Antarctica: our last great wilderness. Melbourne, Australia: Australian Conservation Foundation. 56 p.

Myers, Norman. 1979. The sinking ark. Oxford: Pergamon Press. 307 p.

Nash, Roderick. 1970. The American invention of national parks. American Quarterly. 22(3): 726-735.

Nash, Roderick. 1982. Wilderness and the American mind. 3d ed. New Haven, CT: Yale University Press. 425 p.

Nelson, J. G.; Scace, R. C., eds. 1968. The Canadian national parks: today and tomorrow. Calgary, AB: The University of Calgary. 2 vol.

Norges Offentlige Utredninger [NOU]. 1986. New national plan for national parks. Norwegian University Press. Oslo, Norway.

Padua, Maria Tereza Jorge; Quintao, Angela Tresinari Bernardes. 1984. A system of national parks and biological reserves in the Brazilian Amazon. In: McNeely, Jeffrey A.; Miller, Kenton R., eds. National parks, conservation, and development: the role of protected areas in sustaining society: Proceedings of the world congress on national parks; 1982 October 11-22; Bali, Indonesia. Washington, DC: Smithsonian Institution Press: 565-571.

Player, Ian. 1979. Wilderness leadership school. In: Player, Ian, ed. Voices of the wilderness: Proceedings of the first world wilderness congress; 1977 October 24-28; Johannesburg, South Africa. Johannesburg, South Africa: Jonathan Ball Publishers: 24-28.

Player, Ian. 1987. South African passage: diaries of the wilderness leadership school. Golden, CO: Fulcrum, Inc. 195 p.

Pond, Elizabeth. 1987. Soviets send mixed signals on their concern about environment. The Christian Science Monitor. April 8: 11 (col. 1).

Priddle, George B. 1982. Parks and land use planning in northern Ontario. Environments. 14(1): 47-51.

Pryde, Philip R. 1972. Conservation in the Soviet Union. London: Cambridge University Press. 301 p.

Pryde, Philip R. 1977. Recent trends in preserved natural areas in the U.S.S.R. Environmental Conservation. 4(3): 173-178.

Pryde, Philip R. 1987. The distribution of endangered fauna in the USSR. Biological Conservation. 42(1): 19-37.

Reifsnyder, William. 1974. Foot-loose in the Swiss Alps. New York: Sierra Club. 443 p.

Rowell, Galen. 1980. Many people come, looking, looking. Seattle: The Mountaineers. 164 p.

Russell, J. A.; Matthews, J. H.; Jones, R. 1979. Wilderness in Tasmania. Occas. Pap. 10. Hobart, Australia: University of Tasmania, Centre for Environmental Studies. 103 p.

Schloeth, Robert F. 1974. Problems of wildlife and tourist management in the Swiss National Park. Biological Conservation. 6(10): 313-314.

Sheail, John. 1984. Nature reserves, national parks, and post-war reconstruction in Britain. Environmental Conservation. 11(1): 29-34.

Simmons, I. G. 1978. National parks in England and Wales. In: Nelson, J. G.; Needham, R. D.; Mann, D. L., eds. International experience with national parks and related reserves. Waterloo, Canada: University of Waterloo, Faculty of Environmental Studies, Department of Geography: 383-410.

Smith, Jaquetta; Davison, Jenny; Geden, Bruce. 1980. The public mountain land resource for recreation in New Zealand. Lincoln Pap. Resour. Manage. 7. Canterbury, New Zealand: Lincoln College, Tussock Grasslands and Mountain Lands Institute. 310 p.

Specht, R. L. 1975. The report and its recommendations. In: Fenner, Frank, ed. A national system of ecological reserves in Australia; 1974 October 31; Canberra, Australia. Rep. 19. Canberra, Australia: Australian Academy of Science: 11-21.

Strom, Allen A. 1979. Impressions of a developing conservation ethic, 1870-1930. In: Goldstein, Wendy, ed. Australia's 100 years of national parks. Sydney, Australia: New South Wales National Parks and Wildlife Service: 45-53.

Strong, Gregory. 1987. The South Moresby wilderness dilemma. Environmental Conservation. 14(1): 70-73.

Sweatland, Michael. 1990. Ecotourism. Unpublished paper.

Taschereau, P. M. 1985. The status of ecological reserves in Canada. Ottawa, Canada: The Canadian Council on Ecological Areas. 120 p.

Teigland, Jon. 1989. Strategies for managing land adjacent to wilderness: Norwegian perspectives. In: Lime, David W., ed. Managing America's enduring wilderness resource. Conference proceedings; 1989 September 11-17. Minnesota Extension Service, St. Paul, MN. 459-464 pp.

Tierney, Trevor; Johnstone, Gavin. 1978. Antarctica as wilderness. In: Mosley, Geoff, ed. Australia's wilderness: conservation progress and plans: Proceedings of the first national wilderness conference; 1977 October 21-23; Australian Academy of Science; Canberra, Australia. Melbourne, Australia: Australian Conservation Foundation: 118-126.

Tonge, Peter. 1989. Endow now, enjoy always. For $50 an acre, Belize's Central American beauty is being preserved. The Christian Science Monitor, Tuesday, May 30, 1989, 13 p.

Train, Russell E. 1974. An idea whose time has come: the World Heritage Trust, a world need and a world oppor-

tunity. In: Elliott, Hugh, ed. Second world conference on national parks: Proceedings of a conference; 1972 September 18-27; Yellowstone and Grand Teton National Parks, WY. Morges, Switzerland: International Union for the Conservation of Nature and Natural Resources: 377-381.

United Nations Educational, Scientific, and Cultural Organization [UNESCO]. 1974. Task force on: criteria and guidelines for the choice and establishment of biosphere reserves; 1974 May 20-24; Paris. MAB Rep. Ser. 22. [Place of publication unknown]: United Nations Educational, Scientific, and Cultural Organization and United Nations Environment Program. 59 p.

Vetrino, Blanca. 1988. In: Martin, Vance, ed. For the conservation of earth; Proceedings of the 4th world wilderness congress; 1987. September 11-18; Denver and Estes Park, CO. Fulcrum, Inc., Golden, CO. 131-133 pp.

Vorkinn, Marit. 1989. How is the interaction between recreational use of wilderness areas and adjacent lands?—A case study from Norway. Poster presented at the conference—Managing America's enduring wilderness resource. St. Paul, MN. 1989 September 11-17.

Wallace, George N.; Eidsvik, Harold K. 1988. The non-recreational use of wilderness in the international context. In: Wilderness benchmark 1988. Proceedings of the National wilderness colloquium; 1988 January 13-14; Tampa, FL; U.S. Department of Agriculture, Forest Service, Southeastern Forest Experiment Station: 66-75 pp.

Wangensteen, Torstein; Claudius, Dagfinn. 1989. Proposal for the management plan for Rondane National Park. Chief Administrative Office for Oppland Fylke. Department of the Environment. Oppland, Norway.

Watson, Adam. 1984. Wilderness values and threats to wilderness in the Cairngorms. In: Martin, Vance; Inglis, Mary, eds. Wilderness: the way ahead. Middleton, WI: Lorian Press: 262-268.

Watterson, Gerald G. 1964. Park programs and international agencies. In: Adams, Alexander B., ed. First world conference on national parks: Proceedings of a conference; 1962 June 30-July 7; Seattle. Washington, DC: U.S. Department of the Interior, National Park Service: 329-342.

West, Dana Luaren. 1990. 470 wetland sites under protection. WWF news—The international newspaper of WWF—World Wide Fund for Nature. May/June 8 p.

Western, David. 1984. Amboseli National Park: human values and the conservation of a savanna ecosystem. In: McNeely, Jeffrey A.; Miller, Kenton R., eds. National parks, conservation, and development: the role of protected areas in sustaining society: Proceedings of the world congress on national parks; 1982 October 11-22; Bali, Indonesia. Washington, DC: Smithsonian Institution Press: 93-100.

Wilcox, Murray. 1983. The 'dam case'—implications for the future. 18 Habitat. 11(5): 32-33.

Wilderness Advisory Group. 1985. Wilderness policy. Wellington, New Zealand: Department of Lands and Survey and New Zealand Forest Service. 6 p.

World Bank. 1986. The World Bank's operational policy on wildlands: their protection and management in economic development. [Place of publication unknown]: The World Bank. 12 p.

World Commission on Environment and Development (WCED). 1987. Our common future. Oxford University Press; Oxford, New York. 400 p.

zu Hulshoff, Bernd von Droste. 1984. How UNESCO's man and the biosphere programme is contributing to human welfare. In: McNeely, Jeffrey A.; Miller, Kenton R., eds. National parks, conservation, and development: the role of protected areas in sustaining society: Proceedings of the world congress on national parks; 1982 October 11-22; Bali, Indonesia. Washington, DC: Smithsonian Institution Press: 689-691.

zu Hulshoff, Bernd von Droste; Gregg, William P., Jr. 1985. Biosphere reserves: demonstrating the value of conservation in sustaining society. Parks. 10(3): 2-5.

Zunino, Franco. 1984. A wilderness concept for Europe. In: Martin, Vance; Inglis, Mary, eds. Wilderness: the way ahead. Middleton, WI: Lorian Press: 61-65.

Zunino, Franco. 1990. Personal correspondence to Vance Martin.

ACKNOWLEDGMENTS

Bill Bainbridge, Natal Parks Board, South Africa.

Hugh Barr, Past President, Federated Mountain Clubs of New Zealand.

Harold Eidsvik, Canadian Parks Service, International Union for the Conservation of Nature.

Peter Helman, private consultant, Sydney, Australia.

Evelyn Hurwich, The Antarctica Society, USA.

Kirsten and Jan Peter Ingebrigtsen, USA.

Brad Mills, Land Conservation Council of Victoria, British Columbia, Canada.

Pat Reed, visiting Research Scientist with the University of Georgia, USFS, Athens.

Margaret Robertson, Wilderness Society of New South Wales, Australia.

George Wallace, International School for Forestry and Natural Resources, Colorado State University, Fort Collins.

The Wilderness Act (P.L. 88–577) provides the basic framework governing the establishment and management of wilderness in the United States. Here, President Lyndon Johnson, surrounded by Cabinet and congressional officials, signs the act on September 3, 1964. Photo courtesy of the Lyndon Johnson Memorial Library.

THE WILDERNESS ACT: LEGAL BASIS FOR
WILDERNESS MANAGEMENT

George H. Stankey was lead author for this chapter.

INTRODUCTION

In the United States, wilderness has evolved from a general, ill-defined concept pervasively entwined in our history to a highly formal conception founded upon law. The precise nature of this evolution reflects both the history of concern for wilderness and its protection and the various actions taken by agencies in response to these concerns. To understand fully the basis of wilderness protection in the United States, one has to understand the history of the protection measures taken over the past 60 years and the reasons for these actions.

This chapter will examine the early actions taken by the resource management agencies to preserve wilderness. The reasons for these actions and the outcomes of their implementation will be discussed. This chapter also examines the growth of concern for the statutory wilderness protection that began following World War II and traces the way in which wilderness became a major item on the nation's political agenda. Finally, this chapter discusses the Wilderness Act, the basic legislation underlying wilderness preservation and management in the United States today. All ensuing designation legislation has its roots in this law. Some specific designation acts have contained special provisions that recognize or accommodate local situations, but they are typically accompanied by specific recognition that they do not constitute precedents for other areas; chapter 5 discusses these in more detail. In other cases, Congress has attempted to clarify the intent underlying the Wilderness Act, either through legislative language or through committee reports. In the final analysis, the Wilderness Act has remained a stable base from which decisions to protect and manage wilderness can be made.

THE L-20 REGULATION

The idea of wilderness protection has been with us for some time (see chap. 2). Although Yellowstone and Yosemite National Parks were not explicitly established to preserve wilderness, they nonetheless represented major steps in the protection of wilderness values. In the early 1900s, the individual efforts of Arthur Carhart and Aldo Leopold, both working within the U.S. Forest Service (USFS), brought specific recognition of wilderness as a land use. Yet there was much concern about the extent of the nation's remaining wilderness resource. Just how much roadless land remained after nearly five centuries of development? During the 1920s, the status of wilderness on the national forests began to receive increasing attention. For example, in 1927, the chief of the USFS announced plans to prohibit road building and other commercial development that would impair the character of an area that otherwise possessed wilderness quality (Roth 1984).

Also, in 1926, the USFS began to appraise the extent of wilderness remaining on the national forests. A national inventory was undertaken of all areas greater than 230,400 acres. This inventory reported that 74 tracts totaling 55 million acres still remained, with the largest tract about 7 million acres. Three years later, this inventory became a basis for the first systematic program of wilderness preservation—administrative regulation L-20 promulgated by the USFS in 1929.

From a wilderness viewpoint, the L-20 regulation was not very protective of the resource. It was primarily a list of permitted and prohibited uses. Timber harvesting was permitted in primitive areas in the belief that, if properly regulated, it would not be incompatible with the primitive area designation. For example, logging occurred in about 80,000 acres of the South Fork Primitive Area, one of the three primitive areas that originally comprised what is now the Bob Marshall Wilderness in Montana.

Many uses generally considered incompatible with contemporary notions of wilderness were allowed. Although there were 72 primitive areas with a gross area of 13,482,421 acres in 10 western states, the management plans for these areas allowed road construction in 15 areas, grazing in 62 areas, and logging in 59 areas. Only four primitive areas totaling 297,221 acres absolutely excluded logging, grazing, and roads (Gilligan 1954).

Nor was the L-20 Regulation strictly enforced. The broad latitude in L-20 management stemmed from a belief on the part of the USFS that primitive area status did not represent a long-term commitment of resources. Some historians have argued that one of the primary reasons for implementation of the L-20 Regulation was to prevent agency personnel from rushing into unnecessary development projects (Roth 1984). In this sense, the L-20 Regulation was to be used to prevent haphazard road building and commercial development in areas of scenic and recreational attraction until such time as detailed management plans might be prepared (ORRRC 1962). Primitive area designation was not viewed as a general measure for wilderness protection, but it was seen as an interim protective measure for certain key lands.

One contention suggested that the L-20 Regulation was a USFS strategy to combat the transfer of national forest lands to the National Park Service (NPS) (Allin 1982; Roth 1984). The primitive area classification was seen as one way of countering such losses, by giving the USFS a land use designation to compete with national park classification. Former USFS Chief Richard McArdle discounts this argument, pointing out that the creation of national forest wilderness has never prevented transfers of national forest land to the NPS. For example, the 226,000-acre Olympic Primitive Area, established by the USFS in 1938, was subsequently transferred to Olympic National Park in Washington (McArdle 1975). Allin (1987) argues persuasively that the interagency competition between the USFS and the NPS was a driving force in creating and sustaining the establishment of wilderness within the two organizations. For example, although the previously mentioned 1926 inventory involved units of at least 230,000 acres, a number of primitive areas were established that were smaller than this. This lends further credence to the idea that the USFS saw the L-20 Regulation as a way of precluding the creation of national parks from national forest lands.

The NPS was definitely concerned about the increasing awareness of recreation among some USFS officials. Director Stephen Mather of the NPS, frequently challenged the authority of the USFS to develop recreation programs, arguing that recreation was the sole responsibility of his agency (see Baldwin 1972, pp. 62-71).

The interagency rivalry was also reflected in the terminology used to identify wilderness. In the 1920s, the USFS called undeveloped areas *wilderness* while the NPS called such areas *primitive*. Following promulgation of the L-20 Regulation establishing primitive areas on the national forests, the NPS switched to wilderness.

THE U REGULATIONS

Dissatisfaction with the looseness of the L-20 Regulation led to its replacement with Regulations U-1, U-2, and U-3(a) in 1939 (Gilligan 1954) as a means of preserving unroaded lands on the national forests. These new regulations were formulated largely under the influence of Robert Marshall, then chief of the Division of Recreation and Lands in the USFS. Marshall was a dynamic proponent of wilderness, and much of his career centered on efforts to strengthen wilderness preservation programs both inside and outside the federal government. Earlier, as director of the Forestry Division of the U.S. Office of Indian Affairs, Marshall was responsible for the designation of 16 wilderness areas on Native American reservations (Nash 1982). Along with Aldo Leopold, Marshall was instrumental in the establishment of The Wilderness Society in 1935. Joining the USFS in 1937, Marshall pushed forcefully for expansion of wilderness reserves on the national forests. The U Regulations represented a culmination of his efforts. Although Marshall's role as an innovator and enthusiastic supporter of wilderness cannot be minimized, the role of his assistant in the Division of Recreation and Lands, John H. Sieker, has not been fully recognized or appreciated. Sieker, a forester educated at Yale and Princeton, enjoyed a close professional relationship with Marshall, endorsing his ideas about wilderness preservation. He also was well respected in the USFS. Marshall, while dynamic and energetic, was viewed by many as an eccentric. Politically, he was a liberal, advocating civil rights, civil liberties, and the redistribution of wealth, views that gained the enmity of conservative colleagues (Glover and Glover 1986). Moreover, he was not really a "member of the family," having only recently joined the USFS. As an insider, Sieker became an important force in efforts to implement and gain acceptance for the U Regulations (McArdle 1975). A recent biography of Marshall (Glover 1986) discusses his many contributions to wilderness preservation; also, see Mitchell (1985) for a sensitive description of Marshall.

The U Regulations broadened the purpose of wilderness as earlier defined by the L-20 Regulation. The USFS Manual noted:

> Wilderness areas provide the last frontier where the world of mechanization and of easy transportation has not yet penetrated. They have an important place historically, educationally, and for recreation. The National Forests provide by far the greatest opportunity for wilderness areas. Suitable provisions for them is an important part of National Forest land use planning.

Under the U Regulations, three land use designations were recognized. *Regulation U-1* established wilderness areas—tracts of land of not less than 100,000 acres. Acting on the recommendation of the chief of the USFS, the secretary of agriculture could designate such an area as wilderness. Only the secretary could authorize any modification or elimination of a wilderness area.

Regulation U-2 defined wild areas—tracts of land between 5,000 and 100,000 acres that could be established, modified, or eliminated by the chief of the USFS. Thus, in addition to their size, U-1 and U-2 areas were different in terms of who could establish, modify, or eliminate them; but they were managed identically.

Finally, *Regulation U-3(a)* established roadless areas. These areas were to be managed principally for recreational use "substantially in their natural condition." Roadless areas larger than 100,000 acres could be established or modified only by the secretary of agriculture; areas less than 100,000 acres could be established or modified by the chief of the USFS. Timber cutting, roads, and other modifications were permissible if provided for in area management plans. The only areas ever classified under this regulation were three separate tracts in the Superior National Forest in Minnesota that were consolidated in 1958 to form what is now the Boundary Waters Canoe Area Wilderness (BWCAW).

The U Regulations provided much more protection for wilderness than the L-20 Regulation they replaced. One thing was clear, the U Regulations were intended to be permanent, not just an interim measure to halt haphazard development (Allin 1982). They prohibited timber cutting, road construction, and special use permits for such things as summer homes and hunting camps. The use of mechanized access, except where well established or in emergencies, was banned. Grazing and water resource development were allowed. Mining was also allowed to continue, subject to existing mining and leasing laws. The USFS could insist that such developments take pains to minimize impact on the wilderness (Roth 1984).

Because many of the 76 primitive areas had been established without adequate surveys, each was to be reviewed and reclassified under the new guidelines. A 90-day public review period was called for. While under review, all primitive areas were to be managed according to the U Regulations requirements.

But progress in reviewing the primitive areas was very slow; between 1939 and the outbreak of World War II, three areas were reclassified as wilderness, six as wild, and three were consolidated into the Bob Marshall Wilderness in Montana. No reclassifications occurred during the war. After the war, reviews were begun again, but slow progress contin-

ued. By the late 1940s, only 2 million acres had become wilderness (Roth 1984). Sluggish progress troubled many conservationists. They were also concerned about the loss of acreage in the reclassification process. In some areas, they argued, timbered lower elevation areas within the old primitive area boundary had been lost when the area was reclassified. Although the USFS argued that total primitive area acreage had remained stable, critics countered that this was because high elevation areas, devoid of any timber, had been substituted, thus lowering the quality and variety of the wilderness (Roth 1984). For example, Oregon Senator Richard L. Neuberger strongly objected to the removal of more than 53,000 acres of timbered land in Oregon's Three Sisters Primitive Area during its reclassification (Hession 1967), and he later helped co-sponsor the wilderness bill. The concerns held by Neuberger and others helped lead to pressure for a new method of wilderness designation.

STATUTORY PROTECTION FOR WILDERNESS

Both the L-20 Regulation and the U Regulations were administrative designations; they were implemented at the discretion of the secretary of agriculture or the chief of the USFS. Responsible officials were free to protect wilderness within the limits of these regulations or to ignore it, if they chose.

Because of the discretionary nature of wilderness protection under an administrative system of designation, wilderness proponents were concerned that undeveloped lands would not necessarily receive appropriate safeguards; consequently, they sought additional protection for wilderness. This, however, was only one of several reasons for seeking more reliable protection for wilderness. Undeveloped areas in both parks and forests, as long as they were insufficiently protected, were attractive and vulnerable to a variety of uses. Also, wilderness backers worried that commodity producers would succeed in removing large blocks of acreage from primitive areas during their reclassifications under the U Regulations (McCloskey 1966). For example, at least 35 million acres of wilderness-quality lands not covered by the U Regulations were developed between the time of the Kneipp inventory in 1926 and 1960 (Roth 1984). Under a multiple-use system of resource management, some questioned whether it was even possible to preserve a system of large wilderness areas within the national forests (Gilligan 1954). Could overuse of wilderness-type areas in national parks be

stemmed and reversed? The answer to all these concerns seemed to lie in a legal, rather than an administrative, approach to wilderness protection in which the requirements and procedures for safeguarding wilderness values were prescribed by statute rather than left to the discretion of agency administrators.

Legal protection for wilderness was not a new idea. In the 1930s, Marshall supported the idea of establishing wilderness areas by congressional action (Nash 1982). At about the same time and nearly 30 years before passage of the Wilderness Act, H. H. Chapman, professor of forestry at Yale University, also argued that the precarious status of primitive areas, protected only by administrative regulation, pointed at the need for congressional protection (Chapman 1938). Interestingly, Chapman also argued that management responsibilities over these lands should remain in the hands of the administrative agency—an argument that prevails today in the Wilderness Act. Similarly, Secretary of the Interior Harold L. Ickes had argued in 1939 for congressional-level definition and standards for wilderness protection (Mackintosh 1985).

The need for a legislatively protected system received additional support from a report issued by the Legislative Reference Service of the Library of Congress in 1949 (Keyser 1949). The report was requested on behalf of Howard Zahniser of The Wilderness Society and was facilitated by the fact that the Director of the Reference Service (the research arm of Congress) Ernest Griffith, was another leader of The Wilderness Society (Scott 1976). The report, which highlighted the widely disjointed programs of wilderness preservation, included opinions from a survey of numerous federal, state, and nonpublic organizations. It reported substantial concern for the future of wilderness and widespread support for wilderness protection as secure as that of the national parks (McArdle 1975).

In 1954, a dissertation by James P. Gilligan at the University of Michigan provided an appraisal of the condition and quality of the existing system of wilderness and primitive areas. He noted that although 13 million acres had been set aside as wilderness, wild, or primitive areas, the conditions within them often left much to be desired. For example, he reported the existence of 200 miles of public roads, 145,000 acres of private inholdings, up to 500 mining claims, 60 mines, 24 airstrips, pasturage for 140,000 sheep and 25,000 cattle, and nearly 90 dams. He also reported, confirming the concerns of many conservationists, that wilderness boundaries frequently had been modified, shifting land suitable to economic development outside the preserved area (Allin 1982).

In 1962, the Wildland Research Center at the University of California, with Gilligan as project direc-

tor, in its report to the Outdoor Recreation Resources Review Commission (ORRRC), recommended the enactment of legislation creating a wilderness system protected by law. Otherwise, the center predicted that the wilderness resource would be gradually lost. This pessimistic conclusion was based on the following observations (ORRRC 1962):

1. Land-administering agencies could put wilderness to other uses.
2. Agencies lacked full jurisdiction over some land uses, such as mining, within wilderness.
3. There was a lack of coordinated control over wilderness uses.
4. There was a lack of distinctive management policy.

One of the strongest advocates of a national wilderness system was Howard Zahniser, executive director of The Wilderness Society (fig. 4.1). Zahniser's major theme was the need for a "persisting program" of wilderness preservation—a cohesive program that would eliminate the need for continual, fragmented holding actions against various threats. As early as 1949, he had outlined a wilderness system similar in structure to that eventually proposed in the first wilderness bill in 1956 (Hession 1967). At the Sierra Club's 1951 Biennial Wilderness Conference, he remarked (Zahniser 1951, published 1964):

> Let's try to be done with a wilderness preservation program made up of a sequence of overlapping emergencies, threats, and defense campaigns. Let's make a concerted effort for a positive program that will establish an enduring system of areas where we can be at peace and not forever feel that the wilderness is a battleground.

Zahniser and the others who supported legal protection for wilderness had three main concerns for the law that was to be written. First, they wanted a clear, unambiguous document. One of the oft-criticized features of the previous administrative approaches to wilderness protection was that they contained many loopholes through which protection could be contraverted. Wilderness proponents sought to reduce such ambiguity to the maximum extent possible. Second, they wanted to maintain the political coalition that had formed during the earlier efforts to protect Echo Park in Dinosaur National Monument (CO-UT) from flooding. This coalition of groups had effectively resisted efforts in 1955 by the Bureau of Reclamation and Army Corps of Engineers to construct a dam within the monument as part of an ambitious Upper Colorado River Storage Project. Zahniser recognized the importance of maintaining this tested coalition of allies and was careful to circulate early drafts of the wilder-

Fig. 4.1. Howard Zahniser, executive director of The Wilderness Society, made monumental contributions to establishment of a wilderness system and passage of the Wilderness Act. Zahniser died four months before the act was passed.[1] Photo courtesy of The Wilderness Society.

ness bill to the various organizations in order to maintain a uniform front of support. And third, they wanted to minimize opposition to the legislation. Zahniser and his colleagues sought to assure federal land-managing agencies that existing jurisdictions would be respected and that the proposed bill would not supersede the purposes for which the land was being administered, with the exception of preserving its wilderness character. To commodity interests, Zahniser reported that the bill would respect existing uses and the termination of any uses considered "nonconforming" (e.g., stock use) would be done in a manner "equitable" to them (Roth 1984).

Difficulties were encountered immediately. Both the USFS and the NPS opposed the legislation. The USFS argued that it was not urgently needed. Moreover, efforts to pass it might jeopardize agency efforts to expand and consolidate its existing program of wilderness protection by generating strong opposition to wilderness both from within as well as outside government (McArdle 1975). There was also concern that other special interests such as grazing might lobby to secure similar legislative guarantees

---

1. For reviews of Zahniser's work, see Scott 1976; Nash 1982; and Zahniser 1984.

for their uses of the national forests. Director Conrad L. Wirth of the NPS, also opposed it on the grounds that it was not necessary and that it might endanger national park wilderness areas by lumping them with those of other agencies (Allin 1982; Roth 1984).

Nevertheless, Zahniser persisted in his pursuit for improved wilderness protection. His goal was a congressionally established national wilderness system that would encompass areas of adequate size and numbers to meet future needs and provide legal protection to ensure the perpetuation of their primeval character. To meet this objective he and leaders from the Sierra Club, National Parks Association, National Wildlife Federation, and the Wildlife Management Institute prepared a draft bill in 1955 at the urging of Senator Hubert Humphrey (D-MN). In 1956, Senator Humphrey and nine other senators introduced the first wilderness bill. Representative John Saylor (R-PA) introduced similar legislation in the House. The long congressional struggle for establishment of a national wilderness preservation system was under way.

A BRIEF LEGISLATIVE HISTORY OF THE WILDERNESS ACT

It took eight years for the final Wilderness Act to emerge from Congress. During that time, 65 different wilderness bills were introduced. Eighteen hearings were held across the nation and many thousands of pages of testimony were printed (McCloskey 1966).[1]

The wilderness bill was substantially changed as it moved from the initial version drafted by Zahniser to the act signed into law by President Johnson (P.L. 88-577) on September 3, 1964. The next few pages discuss some of the issues that delayed passage as well as the major changes between the first draft and the final act.

The first wilderness bill would have set up a wilderness system that included lands from the National Forest System, National Park System, National Wildlife Refuges and Game Range System, and Bureau of Indian Affairs. Altogether, about 65 million acres would have been subject to study; as many as 35 to 45 million acres might actually have been classified (Hession 1967).

All 37 USFS areas classified as wilderness, wild, or roadless under the U Regulations were to be automatically included in the system under the 1956 bill. In addition, the 44 remaining primitive areas were to be temporarily included *within* the system,

and the secretary of agriculture was given nine years to review the status of each and recommend an appropriate classification. Congress would then decide whether to extend permanent protection to each primitive area or exclude it from the system.

The secretary of the interior was directed to review all the National Park System and the National Wildlife Refuges and Game Range System, also within nine years, and to recommend areas that should be included within the system. Unlike the USFS lands, no Department of the Interior holdings were automatically included in the system. Qualified areas under Bureau of Indian Affairs jurisdiction could be included, but only with the consent of the tribal councils. Moreover, protection would exist only so long as the appropriate Native American representatives concurred (Allin 1982). No time limit was placed on classifying Native American lands.

The original wilderness bill would have provided comprehensive protection from development. It would have prohibited lumbering, prospecting, dams, commercial enterprises, roads, motor vehicles, the landing of aircraft, the extension of motorboating to new areas, new mining, and new grazing. Some nonconforming but existing uses, such as grazing and motorboat and aircraft use, would have been respected (Allin 1982).

The first bill would also have established a National Wilderness Preservation Council composed of the heads of the USFS, NPS, Fish and Wildlife Service (FWS), Bureau of Indian Affairs, Smithsonian Institution, and six citizen preservationists. Its functions would have been to receive and review all wilderness reports and recommendations from the secretaries of agriculture and the interior, to transmit these reports to Congress, and to advise Congress and the president during ensuing deliberations on the agency recommendations. The wilderness council was viewed as one means of checking the broad executive discretion possessed by administrative agencies. The council, if it thought a secretarial report was unsatisfactory, would have been in a good position to influence congressional attitudes.

The function of Congress in this earliest version of the wilderness bill was to serve as a safeguard against any unwise and arbitrary action on the part of any secretary undertaking a measure that "disregarded conservation." This safeguard took the form of a legislative veto that could be enacted by either House of Congress. When any secretarial recommendation came before it, Congress had 120 days within which to register its objection. Otherwise, the secretary's recommendation to support or oppose wilderness classification would become effective

---

1. An excellent analysis of the legislative history of the Wilderness Act can be found in Allin 1982, pp. 102-136.

pursuant to the law. In other words, statutory protection of wilderness would come about in the absence of any *affirmative action* on the part of Congress.

It is important to note, in this first bill, the significant exchange of authority. Congressional authority to formulate and enact legislation was delegated to the secretaries of agriculture and the interior; that is, departmental recommendations became law if not vetoed. The idea of a legislative veto was dropped from the final version; in 1983, the U.S. Supreme Court ruled legislative vetoes unconstitutional. At the same time, the chief executive's veto power was transferred to Congress. Disagreement with this procedure (executive branch determination of wilderness classification) raised the more basic question, "Who should take the affirmative action in wilderness allocations?"

This question—one of the crucial issues during the evolution of the wilderness bill—assumed particular importance during consideration of the bill's provisions for granting temporary wilderness status to Interior Department holdings identified as suitable for wilderness designation and USFS primitive areas pending review and with regard to the procedures for recommending areas for classifications as outlined in the act. It should be noted that no one objected to the reviews. Argument centered on two questions: (1) Should these lands be included in the wilderness system initially (instead of remaining unclassified during their reviews), and (2) should affirmative congressional action—that is, a bill sponsored, debated, and passed like any other bill—be required before any addition to the wilderness system?

Representative Wayne Aspinall (D-CO), chairman of the House Committee on Interior and Insular Affairs, argued strongly that each new area should be the subject of a separate congressional evaluation and an individual bill. Aspinall and other conservative legislators argued, in this particular use of *affirmative congressional action*, that it represented one way of halting the erosion of congressional authority to the executive (Mercure and Ross 1970); however, the final bill allowed the executive branch power to *declassify* areas currently classified as primitive, subject in some cases to a congressional veto (Allin 1982). Wilderness proponents, on the other hand, were concerned that requiring congressional approval of each individual area would prove to be a cumbersome barrier to a rapid and equitable settlement of the wilderness allocation problem.

To force his position requiring affirmative congressional action on all wilderness proposals, Aspinall refused to allow hearings on the wilderness bill until

legislation calling for a general review of all federal land management policies was agreed upon. Aspinall believed that the debate over affirmative action centered on the rules governing the withdrawal of wilderness-quality lands from multiple-use status. With more than 5,000 land use statutes in place, he argued, an overhaul of the nation's land laws was necessary before making any extensive withdrawals for wilderness purposes (Baker 1985). As Chairman of the Interior and Insular Affairs Committee, Aspinall was able to make good on this threat. As a consequence, preservation groups agreed to support his proposed legislation to create a Public Land Law Review Commission on the condition that Aspinall report out a wilderness bill that could be debated and amended on the floor of the House. In addition, Senator Clinton Anderson (D-NM), a major figure in the drive to pass wilderness legislation, agreed to the affirmative congressional action provision, provided that Aspinall would release the wilderness bill from committee (Baker 1985).

As the wilderness bill neared the end of its long journey through Congress, final refinements were worked out. The San Gorgonio Wild Area in southern California, originally eliminated from the wilderness system in order to permit construction of a ski area, was restored to the system. USFS authority to declassify existing primitive areas by administrative directive was eliminated, thereby giving the legislative branch full authority to control wilderness declassification. While the Senate acceded to the House provision requiring affirmative congressional action, the House agreed to reduce the time period in which new mineral exploration would be allowed in wilderness from 25 years to 19 years. The House passed the final version by the vote of 373 to one; the Senate, by a margin of 73 to 12. The act was signed September 3, 1964, by President Lyndon Johnson, who said passage of the bill was "... in the highest tradition of our heritage as conservators as well as users of America's bountiful natural endowments."

Contrasting the Wilderness Act with the original 1956 bill reveals a number of changes—compromises made in order to secure congressional support. Major changes included the following:

1. Bureau of Indian Affairs lands were excluded from the bill. In 1937, nearly 5 million acres of Native American land had been administratively reserved for wilderness purposes, largely through the efforts of Robert Marshall. But during 1957-1958, the Department of the Interior eliminated this designation. Because the tribal councils, rather than the federal government, held title to these lands, wilderness designation could occur only so long as the appropriate Native American representatives

concurred. Consequently, the protection of wilderness on Native American land would have always been less substantial than on other areas. As a result, Zahniser dropped the areas from his wilderness bill.

2. The National Wilderness Advisory Council was eliminated. The USFS opposed the council from the beginning, arguing that it created an unnecessary step in the review process (McArdle 1975). Agency opposition, based partly on the six-to-five lay person-to-agency-head representation on the council, remained even after the suggested number of lay persons was reduced to three in 1958. Opposition to the advisory council was also founded on the belief that it might very well end up making most of the final classification decisions, given its influential advisory role to Congress and the president. Zahniser, who had initially insisted on the council, agreed to its removal and counted on the president to check secretarial recommendations (Hession 1967).

3. The USFS primitive areas were not included within the initial Wilderness System created in 1964, and their classification required affirmative action by Congress. Under the original bill, they would have been temporarily included within the system and a secretarial recommendation regarding their classification would have gone into effect in four months in the absence of congressional action to stop it. This provision appears to have been a direct result of discussions between President Kennedy and Congressman Aspinall in 1963 and between Senator Anderson and Congressman Aspinall in 1964. By agreeing to the affirmative action proposal, the president hoped to gain support from congressional leaders such as Aspinall to move more of his legislative programs through the Congress prior to the 1964 election (Hession 1967; Roth 1984). Senator Anderson was reluctant to concede on the issue of affirmative congressional action but had concluded that, without it, there would have been no wilderness bill at all (Baker 1985).

4. The prohibitions on uses of wilderness were less restrictive. As initially conceived, for instance, all new mining in wilderness would have been prohibited upon passage of the bill. Yet it became obvious that such a blanket restriction would mean no wilderness bill would pass. Senator Anderson argued that the compromise language contained in the act precluded large-scale mechanized activity that would be incompatible with wilderness values (Roth 1984). As passed, the act permitted prospecting to continue until December 31, 1983, and mining on claims established prior to this date would be allowed to continue indefinitely.

Many supporters of wilderness legislation were disappointed with the discrepancy between the act as passed and the original conception as proposed by Zahniser (Nash 1982). The Wilderness Act clearly was a compromise (Mercure and Ross 1970), yet unless it had been, it is unlikely the bill would have ever passed. The bill enjoyed the support of several senators and congressmen, without whose help it would probably have failed. Senators Clinton Anderson, Frank Church (D-ID), and Hubert Humphrey (D-MN) and Representatives John Saylor

(R-PA) and Lee Metcalf (D-MT) were key supporters (Baker 1985; McArdle 1975). The role of Zahniser as a committed citizen advocate was also crucial. Together, their efforts were rewarded with the passage of a piece of legislation unique in American as well as international conservation history—Public Law 88-577, the Wilderness Act.

THE WILDERNESS ACT

The Wilderness Act of 1964, in full, is in Appendix A. It has been our observation that many of the arguments and much of the confusion surrounding wilderness management stem from the lack of a careful reading and clear understanding of this important document. As the major piece of legislation guiding both wilderness classification and management, the Wilderness Act is the basic reference document for many questions regarding what can or cannot be done in wilderness.

Nevertheless, the Wilderness Act was not intended to be a comprehensive guide to management. As is the case with other landmark legislation, parts of the Wilderness Act are subject to widely differing interpretations, depending on one's particular wilderness philosophy.[1] As mentioned in chapter 1, much of the current debate over interpretation of the Wilderness Act centers on *classification* rather than management implications.

The following pages review the seven sections of the Wilderness Act in order to highlight important provisions. Ambiguities and contrasting interpretations will be noted. In some cases, subsequent legislation has clarified or elaborated on specific clauses of the Wilderness Act, such as grazing use and insect and disease control. The Wilderness Act provides only broad guidelines and directions; detailed guidelines are contained in special regulations issued by the secretaries of agriculture and the interior.

Because it is important that the reader understand the Wilderness Act, its areas of ambiguity, and its effects on the resource, the public, and the administering agencies, most of the remainder of the chapter is devoted to explaining the intent and meaning of the law. The Wilderness Act is organized into seven sections.

---

1. For contrasting perspectives, see Foote 1973; Worf 1980; and Allin 1985.

SECTION 1—TITLE

Section 1 states that this act shall be known as the "Wilderness Act."

SECTION 2—WILDERNESS SYSTEM ESTABLISHED

Section 2 provides a broad statement of policy, defines the term *wilderness*, and sets forth some of the conditions and implications of wilderness designation. Section 2(a) clearly states that the establishment and protection of wilderness is a policy of the U.S. Congress, reflecting a belief that because of population pressures, all areas of the nation will be occupied or modified—except those set aside in their natural condition.

Management is specifically referred to in this section, where the act states that wilderness areas

> shall be administered for the use and enjoyment of the American people in such manner as will leave them unimpaired for future use and enjoyment as wilderness, and so as to provide for the protection of these areas, the preservation of their wilderness character, and for the gathering and dissemination of information regarding their use and enjoyment as wilderness.

Note the phrase "as wilderness" appears several times. Although it is clear that Congress fully intended wilderness to be for people's use and enjoyment, it is also apparent that such "use and enjoyment" is to be contingent upon the maintenance of these areas "as wilderness," a condition the act later defines.

Section 2(a) also specifies that only federal lands will be included in the National Wilderness Preservation System (NWPS) and that no federal lands except those protected by the act or by a subsequent act shall be designated "wilderness." This provision was included to prevent the executive branch of government from designating wilderness, reserving that responsibility for Congress. Section 2(a) merely prohibits *official designation* as wilderness by agencies other than Congress. It does *not* prohibit administrative agencies from *managing* lands for wilderness purposes. The USFS, for example, had such authority based on the Multiple-Use, Sustained-Yield Act of 1960. The Wilderness Act specifically indicates that none of its provisions shall interfere with the purposes of the Multiple-Use, Sustained-Yield Act.

The Multiple-Use, Sustained-Yield Act was enacted largely at the urging of the USFS as a reaffirmation of the agency's traditional multiple-use philosophy regarding resource management. The act was intended to counter pressures for dominant-use legislation, but it did provide general statutory sanction of wilderness preservation in the national forests, incorporated in the following statement: "The establishment and maintenance of areas of wilderness are consistent with the purposes and provisions of this Act." Robinson (1975, p. 160) argues that inclusion of this provision helped lead to the withdrawal of USFS opposition to the proposed wilderness legislation (also, see discussion in Allin 1982, p. 122).

The Wilderness Act's provisions originally affected three federal agencies: the USFS in the Department of Agriculture, and the NPS and FWS, both in the Department of the Interior. Prior to 1964, the wilderness idea had been formally incorporated into USFS planning through the L-20 Regulation and U Regulations. The NPS had used a zoning system to protect wilderness values in undeveloped areas more than a half mile from roads (ORRRC 1962). Before the Wilderness Act, the FWS had not managed any areas specifically for wilderness purposes because habitat enhancement for wildlife often results in substantial modification of areas, thereby conflicting with wilderness values. Nevertheless, the FWS is charged with wilderness responsibilities under the 1964 act, and the first Department of the Interior area to be admitted to the NWPS was the Great Swamp Wildlife Refuge in New Jersey.

In late 1976, Congress passed the Federal Land Policy and Management Act (FLPMA), giving the Bureau of Land Management (BLM) in the Department of the Interior clear authority and direction for management of the public lands under its jurisdiction. FLPMA instructs the secretary of the interior to review those roadless lands of 5,000 acres or more as well as all roadless islands administered by BLM and to make recommendations regarding the suitability of these areas for wilderness designation. This inventory used the wilderness characteristics specified in the Wilderness Act. The results are described in chapters 5 and 6.

Although the BLM has only recently come under the terms of the Wilderness Act, the agency previously managed a system of areas for wilderness preservation purposes referred to as *primitive areas* (not to be confused with national forest areas of the same name designated under the L-20 Regulation) and natural areas. We will look at these areas in more detail in chapter 6. But under the terms of the FLPMA, any area formally designated as a primitive or natural area prior to November 1, 1975, was to be reviewed by the secretary of the interior for its suitability for wilderness classification and a recommendation made to the president by July 1, 1980.

In addition to specifying which federal lands shall constitute official wilderness, section 2(a) assigns management responsibilities. It specifies that each federal agency charged with jurisdiction of wilderness will continue to manage those areas originally under its jurisdiction, after they have been made part of the NWPS. This clause was included so that no new agency would be created. Additionally, appropriations to the wilderness system as a separate entity or appropriations based solely on the system's existence are prohibited.

The final subsection of section 2 defines wilderness, and it is this section that has probably led to more confusion and debate than any other. It first defines wilderness in an ideal, almost poetic, sense:

> A wilderness, in contrast with those areas where man and his own works dominate the landscape, is hereby recognized as an area where the earth and its community of life are untrammeled by man, where man himself is a visitor who does not remain.

The word *untrammeled* was specifically chosen by Zahniser, even though he was warned that it might confuse the definition. Not to be confused with *untrampled*, *untrammeled* means "not subject to human controls and manipulations that hamper the free play of natural forces."

Section 2(c) then goes on to define wilderness in a legal sense—an area of undeveloped federal land retaining its primeval character and influence, without permanent improvements or habitation, and which (1) generally appears to have been affected primarily by the forces of nature, with man's imprint substantially unnoticeable; (2) has outstanding opportunities for solitude or a primitive and unconfined type of recreation; (3) has at least 5,000 acres of land *or* is of sufficient size to make practicable its preservation; and (4) may also contain ecological, geological, or other features of scientific, educational, scenic, or historical value.

The definition of wilderness in section 2(c) gives important clues to the congressional view of wilderness. Recognizing that the ideal did not exist, they added a working definition based on reality. Wilderness was clearly intended to be an area where man's impact was minimal and which was predominantly natural and unmodified. At the same time, the act accommodates reality by stating these areas *"generally appear"* to be *"primarily* affected" by nature with man's imprint *"substantially* unnoticeable" (emphasis added).

In the effort to accommodate reality by express-ing the necessary conditions for wilderness in these more general terms, some difficult questions were created. For example, if a large tract of land were being considered for wilderness, with one portion in a pristine condition and another portion modified by previous developmental activity, would the criterion "substantially unnoticeable" be based on the aggregate area or on the modified portion? The answer obviously hinges on the spatial scale at which the criterion is applied. Some have argued that additions of modified areas, even to large contiguous tracts in pristine condition, compromise the quality of the entire system (Costley 1972). Yet others have argued that the entire unit of land must be considered and that small areas of modified land are "substantially unnoticeable" when viewed within the larger context. The principle of nondegradation, discussed in chapter 7, is useful in resolving this issue.

Remember that the intent of Congress was to establish a system of areas—an ideal—that embodied the values espoused by such early wilderness proponents as Muir, Leopold, and Marshall. Accordingly, the definition of wilderness in section 2(c) should not be subject to endless qualification. Yet, unreasonably rigid admission standards clearly were not the intent of Congress, either. As Congressman Saylor noted in 1963, the act first describes wilderness as an *ideal concept,* but then goes on to discuss wilderness *as it is to be considered* for the purposes of the act.

The definition of wilderness in section 2(c) cites the importance of "outstanding opportunities for solitude or a primitive and unconfined type of recreation." This phrase is variously interpreted to mean that opportunities for either solitude *or* a primitive kind of recreation are required (that is, either one would qualify an area) or that the phrases are similar and that both are included to help clarify congressional intent. As discussed in chapter 1, it is our belief that the latter interpretation is appropriate.

The 5,000-acre minimum is often cited as absolute, but a careful reading of the act clearly shows that it is a suggested guideline. The intent is that the area classified should be large enough to permit preservation objectives. In the conference committee that formulated the final wording of the Wilderness Act, the House recommended 5,000 acres as a minimum limit on the size of individual areas, but conferees decided that a statement of intent that a tract of "sufficient size to make practicable its preservation and use in an unimpaired condition" would be satisfactory (Baker 1985).

Finally, the definition says wilderness *may* include ecological, geological, scenic, and other features. The important point to note is that these values

are neither required for an area to be a wilderness nor are they by themselves sufficient criteria.

Our interpretation of this multifaceted definition of wilderness is that *the criteria of naturalness and solitude are the distinguishing qualities of classified wilderness.* They also serve as principal criteria to guide the management of wilderness and are used throughout this book in that context.

SECTION 3—NATIONAL WILDERNESS PRESERVATION SYSTEM— EXTENT OF SYSTEM

Section 3, a five-part section of the Wilderness Act, describes the NWPS and the procedures for admitting areas to the system.

Section 3(a) defines the areas that formed the core of the NWPS. These included all USFS areas previously classified as wilderness, wild, or canoe. Fifty-four areas were so classified, covering 9.1 million acres. It also instructed the secretary of agriculture to file accurate boundary descriptions of all these areas available to the public. No Department of the Interior lands were included in the initial wilderness system.

Section 3(b) instructs the secretary of agriculture, within 10 years of the passage of the act, to review all USFS primitive areas for their suitability as wilderness and to make a report on the findings to the president. In turn, the president is to send Congress recommendations to support, oppose, or modify the proposal. It also established a timetable for the review of the 34 primitive areas (a total of 5.4 million acres at the time the act passed), with one-third to be reviewed within the first three years after the act's passage, two-thirds after seven years, and the remaining areas within 10 years. Until Congress acts, primitive areas are to be administered as they were at the time of the act's passage.

This subsection also describes the president's latitude for enlarging an existing primitive area. At the time of his recommendation to Congress, he may make an addition to any existing primitive area of not more than 5,000 acres, as long as no single unit of added land exceeds 1,280 acres. Additions beyond the 5,000-acre limit require congressional approval (McCloskey 1966).

Section 3(c) is similar to 3(b) in that it instructs the secretary of the interior to review all roadless areas of at least 5,000 acres in the NPS and similar size holdings and *every* roadless island within the National Wildlife Refuges and Game Range System, and to submit a report regarding the suitability of these areas for wilderness classification. The islands were specifically cited because, in spite of the small size of many of them, their isolation makes preservation a practicable alternative. A 10-year review period, along with the timetable described in section 3(b), was established; that is, one-third in three years, two-thirds after seven years, and the remainder at the end of 10 years.

Section 3(d) provides guidelines for notifying public and local officials of recommendations that the secretaries of agriculture and the interior intend to submit to the president and provides for public hearings on these recommendations.

Finally, section 3(e) describes the procedures for modifying or adjusting any wilderness boundary. No modification of a wilderness boundary by an agency is permitted, even in cases where nonconforming or illegal uses are found. When exact boundary locations are not clear, the enabling legislation or conference or committee reports are used to establish legislative intent.

SECTION 4—USE OF WILDERNESS AREAS

Section 4(a) indicates that the purposes of the Wilderness Act are "within and supplemental" to the purposes for which national forests and units of the national park and wildlife refuge systems are established. It specifically states that the Wilderness Act in no way interferes with a number of specific acts such as the Multiple-Use, Sustained-Yield Act and the National Park Organic Act. By providing for wilderness preservation under the multiple-use umbrella, section 4(a) removes a major reason for conflict between these two potentially incompatible laws.

The responsibility of each managing agency to maintain the wilderness character of lands under its jurisdiction is reaffirmed in section 4(b). In addition, it states that, except as otherwise provided in the act, wilderness shall be devoted to the public purposes of recreational, scenic, scientific, educational, conservation, and historical use.

Section 4(c) is subtitled "Prohibition of Certain Uses" and describes facilities and activities that are not allowed in wildernesses designated by the act. This section must be carefully read, for it opens with the statement, "Except as specifically provided for in this Act, and subject to existing private rights ... " before going on to catalog prohibited uses. These exceptions are quite substantial.

Subject to the subsection's opening qualification, commercial enterprises and permanent roads are prohibited. Certain other uses (motorized vehicles and equipment, temporary roads, aircraft landings) are prohibited "except as necessary to meet minimum requirements for the administration of the

area for the purpose of this Act" (including measures required in emergencies involving the health and safety of persons within the area) (fig. 4.2).

Subsection 4(c) outlines illegal activities and administrative latitude. The section reads, in part, "Except as specifically provided for in this Act … and, except as necessary to meet minimum requirements for the administration of the area for the purpose of this Act …" and is followed by a list of prohibited activities such as temporary roads, motor vehicles, has pointed out that the phrase "minimum requirements" seems to mean "essential or necessary." Defined in this way, the clause "except as necessary to meet minimum requirements for the administration of the area for the purpose of this Act" becomes somewhat redundant. The clear intention of the act here is to permit administrators to carry out actions otherwise considered inappropriate in wilderness if it becomes apparent these actions are the minimum necessary to *manage the area as wilderness* (emphasis added).

Nevertheless, the basic interpretation of this section is that administrators must provide evidence that an action *is* the minimum necessary for managing the area as wilderness. Simple convenience or cost advantage is not sufficient reason to justify, for example, the use of mechanized equipment. Worf (1980) contends that nonmechanized wilderness maintenance is often cheaper than mechanized maintenance. If, however, the use of mechanized equipment clearly reduces the amount of impact on the wilderness and its use (e.g., by reducing the level and extent of resource impact), then administrators would have the flexibility to use such equipment.

McCloskey also points out a second ambiguity. Does the phrase "for the purpose of this Act" refer solely to the act's objective—"to secure for the American people of present and future generations the benefits of an enduring resource of wilderness"— an objective limited to preservation, or does it include a broader purpose—preservation *and* compatible human enjoyment? Differing interpretations of the phrase could lead to different administrative actions. The wording of the act indicates that both use of wilderness and its preservation were intended, but it also suggests that any construction to facilitate use, such as bridges or shelters, must satisfy the criterion of *necessity*. In general, facilities for the convenience and/or comfort of users do not meet this criterion and have not been provided.

Important exceptions to the prohibited uses are described in section 4(c). These exceptions, which are subject to existing private rights, are outlined in section 4(d) and constitute what we call allowable, but nonconforming uses; they are legal, but they are generally considered incompatible with the goal of the act. These nonconforming uses reflect some of the compromises in the original Wilderness Bill. Both subsections apply only to those areas of national forest land designated as wilderness by the 1964 act. But in the interests of consistency, subsequent legislation has called for the management of newly designated areas to follow the guidelines contained in the 1964 act, subject to any specific exceptions written into that subsequent legislation.

The following uses are expressly permitted in section 4(d):

1. Established uses of aircraft and motorboats.
2. Actions taken to control fire, insects, and disease outbreaks.

Fig. 4.2. The Wilderness Act allows agencies use of certain facilities and activities essential to management of a specific wilderness. Pictured on the left is a Remote Automated Weather Station, essential to fire management, sited in the Mount Logan Wilderness, Arizona Strip District, BLM. Photo courtesy of Tom Folks, BLM. Measuring snow (right) to predict water content in the Selway-Bitterroot Wilderness, MT. Photo courtesy of the USFS.

3. Any activity, including prospecting, for the purposes of gathering information about mineral or other resources, if carried out in a manner compatible with preservation of the wilderness environment.
4. Continued application of the U.S. mining and mineral leasing laws for national forest wilderness until December 31, 1983.
5. Water resource development (authorized by the president if determined that such use will better serve the national interest than would its denial).
6. Livestock grazing, where established prior to the act.
7. Management of the Boundary Waters Canoe Area under regulations laid down by the secretary of agriculture, which were generally less restrictive than those imposed by the Wilderness Act (resolved by subsequent legislation, as we shall discuss shortly).
8. Commercial enterprises necessary for activities that are appropriate in wilderness (e.g., outfitting and guiding) (fig. 4.3).

In summary, section 4(d) of the act recognized that certain existing uses—specifically aircraft and motorboats—could be permitted to continue in places where they were well established. It also noted that the secretary of agriculture may impose such restrictions as he deems necessary to protect the wilderness resource. So, while these uses are protected by the Wilderness Act, they can nonetheless be controlled by the administering agencies. For example, such administrative action might become necessary within the backcountry of Grand Canyon National Park in Arizona (the area has been proposed for wilderness classification) where it is estimated that more than 100,000 aircraft operations occur annually and aircraft are audible up to 95 percent of the time in some locations (Brownridge 1986). Current regulations permit aircraft to fly as low as 500 feet above the surface, but only in "sparsely populated" areas, yet concentrations of users in many backcountry areas probably require even higher minimum altitudes (Anon. 1985). Similarly, although the secretary of agriculture can undertake measures to control fire, insects, *and* disease, this authority is *discretionary*; for example, it is not mandatory that fires be controlled.

The provision of section 4(d) regarding actions to control fire, insects, and disease outbreaks has been elaborated on in subsequent legislative history. House Report 95-540, the committee report filed with the Endangered American Wilderness Act (P.L. 95-237) in 1978, emphasizes that any actions to control fire, insect, or disease outbreaks, such as the use of mechanized equipment, the building of fire roads, or the construction of firebreaks, are permissible, if judged necessary for the protection of public health or safety (The Wilderness Society 1984).

The discretionary latitude to control threats to wilderness values is exemplified in steps taken by the USFS to control outbreaks of the southern pine beetle in several wildernesses in Texas, Arkansas, Mississippi, and Louisiana. A major outbreak of the southern pine beetle coincided with the designation of several wildernesses in Texas in 1984; by 1985, more than 15,000 separate southern pine beetle spots (10 or more trees) had been located, many within wilderness. A variety of management actions have been proposed, including the use of synthetic attractants (pheromones), cutting buffer strips around infected areas, and reducing stand density (Billings 1986). Spread of the southern pine beetle can be rapid; in the Four Notch area in Texas (not presently a wilderness, but under further study), rates of 50 feet per day along a 3.5-mile front were reported (Billings and Varner 1986). The problem was confounded by the presence of several nesting sites of the red-cockaded woodpecker, an endangered species that nests only in mature, live pine trees. Buffer strips have proved successful in halting expansion of the beetle infestation, but controversy remains as to whether this is the most appropriate technique or the minimum tool necessary to control insect outbreaks.

The discussion of mining in wilderness occupies a substantial proportion of section 4(d). This clause of the Wilderness Act refers to national forest wilderness because most Department of the Interior lands are withdrawn from mineral entry. Until recently, however, six units of the NPS were open to mineral entry, including Death Valley National Monument (CA-NV), Crater Lake National Park (OR), Glacier Bay National Monument (AK), Coronado National Memorial (AZ), Mount McKinley National Park (AK), and Organ Pipe Cactus National Monument (AZ). In 1976, Congress passed legislation withdrawing these

Fig. 4.3. The Wilderness Act allowed continuance of established commercial activities. A wilderness outfitter leads a party of visitors along a pristine lake. Photo courtesy of the USFS.

units from further mineral entry and placed existing claims under stringent regulations issued by the secretary of the interior. (Details about this legislation are in chap. 14.)

Basically, the Wilderness Act specified that prospecting and mining could continue in national forest wilderness until December 31, 1983. After that date, mining could continue only on valid claims existing prior to that date (fig. 4.4). In other words, one could not file a claim for mining after December 31, 1983, but could continue mining a claim that existed prior to that date. A patent conveying both surface and mineral rights may be taken on a valid claim located prior to the Wilderness Act; for a valid claim located after the date of the Wilderness Act, the patent conveys title to mineral rights only.

A claim permits an individual to occupy a site and use it for the purposes of developing the mineral values it contains; however, uses beyond those necessary for development of the mineral values are not allowed and title to the land remains with the U.S. government. A patented claim conveys full ownership of the site, including surface and subsurface values, to the claimant. Both a claim and a patent are considered property rights.

The secretary of agriculture is instructed to issue *reasonable regulations* governing access to claims and related facilities such as transmission lines, roads, and buildings. Generally, these regulations impose more stringent standards for mineral operations in wilderness than on other national forest lands. Under current regulations (Title 36, Code of Federal Regulations, Part 252—Minerals), mining operators in national forests are required to prepare an operating plan that describes who is doing the work, where and when it will be done, the nature of the disturbance the work will create, and measures to be taken to protect other resources. Restoration is also called for at such time as the operation ceases. Surface resources, such as timber, may be used if needed for the mining operation and if founded on sound principles of forest management. After January 1, 1984, or the date of any wilderness established after this date, but subject to valid existing rights, minerals in wilderness were withdrawn from entry.

This portion of the act also instructs the secretary of the interior to develop, in consultation with the secretary of agriculture, a plan for recurrent surveys of the mineral values in any wilderness and to submit these findings to the public, Congress, and the president. A recent survey of 74 million acres of wilderness and wilderness study areas revealed that only 2.7 million acres had a high probability of containing significant oil and gas reserves; half of this total was in western

Montana (U.S. Geological Survey 1984).

Mining in wilderness is a paradox, and its presence can make sense only when viewed as a necessary political compromise (Matthews and others 1985). Nevertheless, many view its presence as an internal contradiction within the Wilderness Act. In Minnesota, in early 1973, U.S. District Judge Neville ruled that a proposed copper and nickel prospecting operation in the BWCAW should not be permitted. He observed (Sumner 1973):

> It is clear that wilderness and mining are incompatible. ... If the premise is accepted that mining activities and wilderness are opposing values and are anathema each to the other, then it would seem that in enacting the Wilderness Act Congress engaged in an exercise of futility if the court is to adopt the view that mineral rights prevail over wilderness objectives. ... Mineral development ... by its very definition cannot take place in a wilderness area ...
>
> There is an inherent inconsistency in the Congressional Act and it falls in the lap of the court to determine which purpose (mining or wilderness) Congress deemed most important and therefore intended. In this court's opinion, the wilderness objectives override the contrary mineral right provision of the statute.

An Appeals Court later ruled that because mining company officials had not made a final application to the USFS for entry into the BWCAW to explore for minerals, the decision-making process had not been completed by the administrative agency authorized to make the decision. Because no administrative action had been taken, there was no basis for judicial review. The case was returned to the lower court *without prejudice*, meaning it could be heard by the appeals court at a later time.

It is important to note that the action of the appeals court in returning the case to the lower court was related to a technical shortcoming rather than disagreement with the lower court's substantive analysis of the case. The appeals court ruling neither affirmed nor denied that analysis. The issue of mining in wilderness, then, remains unresolved. This particular case does not necessarily have widespread applicability. It was directed only at the BWCAW, an area whose management of the legal decision was covered by several special provisions in the Wilderness Act (Haight 1974). Moreover, many public mining laws do not apply in Minnesota. The key in Judge Neville's rationale was his resolution of two contradictory mandates (mining versus wilderness). The judge ruled that in cases where such apparent con-

tradictions exist, if "Congressional intent is plainly discernible in the legislative history, it will override the 'inconsistent' terms of the statutes" (Haight 1974).

Mining in wildernesses located in the eastern United States represents a further complication. The titles to most national forest lands in the East were acquired from private ownership, but mineral rights typically remained in private hands. Thus, the agency cannot prevent private mineral development. The scale of this problem is substantial; in 1984, 103 of the 192 designated and potential eastern wildernesses contained private mineral rights covering nearly 1 million acres (General Accounting Office 1984). Short of acquiring these mineral rights (estimated in the BWCAW alone as nearly $100 million), the USFS can protect the wilderness qualities of these areas only by the conditions it imposes on the mining operation. At the time the Wilderness Act passed, oil and gas

Fig. 4.4. Mining is permitted in wilderness, under certain restrictions. This mining operation is located on the western edge of the Cabinet Mountains Wilderness in western MT. Photo courtesy of the USFS.

development in wilderness was simply not an issue, but in recent years, concerns with developing domestic sources of supply have changed this situation. Much of the potential supply lies within classified wildernesses in the Rocky Mountains.

Requests for oil and gas development on national forest lands are approved or rejected by the BLM, acting for the Department of the Interior. It is Department of the Interior policy to request a USFS recommendation on any application and, to date, these recommendations typically have governed the Interior Department decision (Short 1980). No oil or gas permits have been issued in wilderness; in the event a permit is issued by BLM, the actual site development would be administered by the USFS.

Lands under the administration of the BLM were not addressed in the 1964 Wilderness Act. The FLPMA provided authority for the classification of wilderness on the public lands. The BLM review process is described in more detail in chapter 5. But during the review of potentially suitable wilderness lands under BLM jurisdiction, the FLPMA instructs the secretary of the interior to manage such lands so as to not impair their suitability for preservation as wilderness. This "nonimpairment" standard is subject, however, to the continuation of existing mining and mineral leasing "in the manner and degree in which the same was being conducted" at the time the FLPMA passed. A legal opinion issued in 1978 interprets the nonimpairment language of the FLPMA as being a paramount consideration applying to all areas under BLM administration identified as having wilderness characteristics, exempting from the nonimpairment standard only those uses actually taking place at the effective date of the FLPMA (Short 1980).

Section 4(d) grants authority to the president to authorize programs for the development of water resources within national forest wilderness, if it is determined that permission for such developments would better serve the interests of the United States than their denial. Actions involved here could include reservoir construction, power projects, and transmission lines. The act does not specifically refer to weather modification, a practice of questionable legality. In 1972, the Bonneville Power Administration (BPA) announced intent to seed clouds in western Montana. This might have affected precipitation levels and patterns in the Bob Marshall Wilderness. The plans were opposed by the USFS, the State of Montana, and the Montana Wilderness Association. Heavy natural precipitation that winter prompted the BPA to drop their plans and the case became moot. The BLM issued a position paper arguing that weather modification would not significantly alter natural pro-

2₄

cesses and therefore should be permitted in wilderness (see U.S. Department of the Interior 1974).

Grazing is allowed in national forest wilderness where it was established prior to the signing of the Wilderness Act (fig. 4.5). As with several other excepted uses, the secretary of agriculture is permitted to impose "such reasonable regulations as are deemed necessary." While the secretary of agriculture cannot prohibit grazing merely by reason of wilderness, he can restrict or eliminate such use based on principles of range management (McCloskey 1966).

Grazing in wilderness has led to some confusion. In 1980, Congress expressed the concern that certain national forest administrative policies and regulations were acting to discourage or unduly restrict on-the-ground activities necessary for proper grazing management. There was some pressure to amend the Wilderness Act in order to clarify the intent of Congress with regard to grazing in wilderness. In a House report on the Colorado Wilderness Act (P.L. 96-560), the committee observed that attempts to draft specific statutory language covering grazing in the entire NWPS would likely not be successful. Instead, the committee reaffirmed the existing language of the Wilderness Act and included a series of guidelines and specific statements of legislative policy (The Wilderness Society 1984). These included:

1. There shall be no curtailments of grazing in wilderness areas simply because an area is, or has been, designated as wilderness, nor should wilderness designations be used as an excuse by administrators to slowly "phase out" grazing.
2. The maintenance of supporting facilities, existing in an area prior to its classification as wilderness (including fences, line cabins, water wells and lines, and stock tanks), is permissible in wilderness.
3. The replacement or reconstruction of deteriorated facilities or improvements should not be required to be accomplished using "natural materials," unless the material and labor costs of using natural materials are such that their use would not impose unreasonable additional costs on grazing permittees.
4. The construction of new improvements or replacement of deteriorated facilities in wilderness is permissible if in accordance with these guidelines and management plans governing the area involved.
5. The use of motorized equipment for emergency purposes such as rescuing sick animals or the placement of feed in emergency situations is also permissible.

Later legislation establishing wildernesses in Arizona (P.L. 98-406), Utah (P.L. 98-428), and Wyoming (P.L. 98-550) contains a reference to the congressional guidelines on grazing contained in Public Law 96-560, incorporating them as statutory directives for these states. It is clear that Congress sees grazing as a continu-

ing, legitimate use in wilderness and the guidelines in Public Law 96-560 are intended to ensure appropriate treatment of grazing throughout the NWPS.

Another controversial portion of section 4(d) involved the management of the Boundary Waters Canoe Area. What is now the BWCAW was originally three roadless areas designated under the U-3(a) Regulation: the Superior, Little Indian Sioux, and Caribou Roadless Areas; they were renamed the BWCAW in 1958. Section 4(d) specified that the BWCAW was to continue to be managed in accordance with regulations established by the secretary of agriculture. In general, the primitive character of the area was to be maintained, but certain other uses, including timber harvesting, were permitted. In other words, the management of the area as prescribed under the earlier U-3(a) designation was to continue.

The BWCAW was divided into two zones for timber management purposes: the *Interior* or "no-cut" zone, and the *Portal*. The Interior zone was created in 1941, and all commercial timber harvesting was prohibited within it. But vegetation manipulation involving administratively required cutting or burning was permitted. In the Portal zone, commercial logging was allowed along with related developments such as road building.

In 1964, shortly before passage of the Wilderness Act, a select committee, headed by Dr. George Selke,

Fig. 4.5. Grazing of livestock, when established prior to passage of the Wilderness Act, is allowed to continue on the national forests. A band of sheep graze in the Bridger Wilderness, WY. Photo courtesy of the USFS.

was appointed by the secretary of agriculture to study the BWCAW and recommend appropriate management actions. Their report supported continuation of the two-zone management concept, but recommended changes in their relative size. The Interior zone was to be enlarged by 250,000 acres over a 10-year period, with the land being withdrawn from the Portal zone. Thus, by 1976, the Interior zone, originally the smaller of the two, had been enlarged to about 618,000 acres and the Portal zone had shrunk to about 412,000 acres.

Over a half-million acres in the area are still virgin forest (Heinselman 1973). It is the largest contiguous tract of virgin forest left in the eastern United States, and it is this uniqueness that led to much of the concern about the appropriateness of logging in the BWCAW. In 1973, the Minnesota Public Interest Research Group brought suit against the USFS and several logging companies, seeking an injunction against further logging. The suit was based, at least originally, on the contention that the USFS had failed to file an Environmental Impact Statement (EIS) before extending contractual deadlines for the logging of certain areas. Therefore, this suit was not directly based on the Wilderness Act (Haight 1974).

The judge handling the case based his ruling on reasoning similar to Judge Neville's in the mining case (Haight 1974):

> Logging and the various reforestation methods which follow it destroy the primitive character of the area involved ... the area loses forever its "primeval character and influence" and "natural conditions."

In response to the argument that the Wilderness Act permitted logging, the court noted, "Where there is a conflict between maintaining the primitive character of the BWCAW and allowing logging or some other uses, the former must be supreme" (Haight 1974). The court ruled that the logging under consideration by the USFS constituted a significant impact and, consequently, required the filing of an EIS. In later judicial action in 1975, an injunction was issued against logging in that portion of the BWCAW still considered virgin forest (about a half million acres). The injunction was based on the alleged conflict of logging with the Wilderness Act as well as on the inadequacy of the EIS prepared by the USFS. Ten existing timber sales and all future sales were halted by the injunction. But the Eighth Circuit Court of Appeals lifted the injunction in August 1976, ruling that the Wilderness Act did not prohibit logging in the Portal zone and that the EIS did meet the procedural requirements of the National Environmental Policy Act of 1969 (NEPA). The appeals court did rule that an environmental analysis of each of the 10 sales would have to be completed and that terms of how the sales were to be conducted were written into the contract. Future timber sales were enjoined, pending completion of a new timber management plan and EIS.

The Wilderness Act also legalized another otherwise prohibited use, specifically for the BWCAW, stating that nothing in its text "shall preclude the continuance within the area of any already established use of motor boats." The BWCAW's management plan recognized three zones: (1) a large-motor zone, where motors up to and including 25 horsepower could be used; (2) a small-motor zone where motors up to 10 horsepower were permitted; and (3) a no-motor zone. However, no limits were set on motor size for any lake that touched the periphery of the area. About 60 percent of the water acreage in the BWCAW was open to motor use, and motor use was permitted in both the Portal and Interior zones discussed earlier.

Thus, management of the BWCAW under terms of the Wilderness Act was significantly different from other areas. But continuing pressures for mining, logging, and mechanized access provoked increasing support for separate legislation for the area that would put it on a more equal footing with other wildernesses. Alternative legislation was proposed, ranging from a declassification of the area (designating it as a National Recreation Area) to full protection as wilderness. A citizen's advocacy group, Friends of the Boundary Waters Wilderness, was formed to push for the area's protection. Finally, in 1978, Congress passed Public Law 95-495 designating the BWCAW. The law constitutes the only amendment to the Wilderness Act as it repealed paragraph 5 of section 4(d) of the act, that portion dealing with the exceptions regarding management of the BWCAW.

The new law dealt with many of the special exceptions accorded the BWCAW in the Wilderness Act (fig. 4.6). It prohibited the use of motorboats within the area except for certain routes and lakes. Where motorboat use is permitted, the size of the motor permitted is specified. On some lakes, continued use was permitted until a termination date. Snowmobiles are generally prohibited, except for a few selected routes.

All timber sale contracts existing within the wilderness were terminated by the new law and all future logging in the virgin forest portions of the area was prohibited. The government agreed to pay compensation to those companies whose contracts were terminated or modified by the law.

The BWCAW was the only area in the NWPS that had an air-space reservation. An executive order signed by President Harry Truman in 1949 prohibited flights below 4,000 feet above sea level, except for emergencies and for official business of the federal, state, or county governments (Andrews 1953). The new law incorporates the terms of that executive order within it.

Public Law 95-495 added more than 45,000 acres to the BWCAW, bringing its total size to nearly 1.1 million acres, and also established within the wilderness a 222,000-acre Boundary Waters Canoe Area Mining Protection Area. Within this area, exploration for and mining of minerals owned by the United States is prohibited, as is exploration or mining that would in any way affect navigable waters. The act also authorized the secretary of agriculture to acquire any minerals or mineral rights owned by persons other than the federal or state government. If necessary to acquire mineral rights, the secretary is authorized to use his power of eminent domain; however, congressional appropriation of money to secure these private mineral rights would be necessary (Proescholdt 1984).

The BWCAW Act is the only legislation that has resulted in a modification of language in the Wilderness Act. But its general effect was to strengthen the wilderness provisions regarding the area and to eliminate some of the complex exceptions that applied to it. A 1981 court challenge of the act's constitutionality was rejected by the U.S. Court of Appeals.

Recognizing that certain commercial services might be necessary to realize fully the recreational values of wilderness, section 4(d) permits activities such as guiding and outfitting, despite the general prohibition of commercial enterprises cited in section 4(c).

After noting that the act does not touch upon the question of federal exemption from state water laws, section 4 concludes with a standard disclaimer that the federal government recognizes state jurisdiction over wildlife on federal lands.

Language in the House report on the Endangered American Wilderness Act offered further guidelines with regard to fishery management activities within wilderness. The report notes that fisheries enhancement activities and facilities are permissible, including fish traps, stream barriers, aerial stocking, and protection and propagation of rare species. These guidelines apply throughout the NWPS (The Wilderness Society 1984).

Congress has attempted, in passing subsequent wilderness legislation, to minimize the number of special exceptions to the Wilderness Act. The need for consistency in wilderness management, as discussed earlier, was a major rationale for the passage

of the act. In some areas, special circumstances have led to exceptions to the general prohibitions in the Wilderness Act. For example, in the Central Idaho Wilderness Act (P.L. 96-312) establishing the Frank Church-River of No Return Wilderness in 1980, aircraft use of landing strips "in regular use" shall be left open. This denies the USFS the discretion to close airstrips that is contained in the Wilderness Act, which reads "aircraft use may be permitted to continue where previously established." This exception applies only to the Frank Church-River of No Return Wilderness, where 19 such landing strips are located.

Major exceptions to the general management provisions of the Wilderness Act are contained in the Alaska National Interest Lands Conservation Act (ANILCA, P.L. 96-487). Prior to the passage of ANILCA in 1980, no classified wilderness existed in Alaska. At least one reason for this was the feeling that Alaska was different and that wilderness management there would have to be conducted differently than in the lower 48 states. When the legislation was drafted, Congress did include several special provisions regarding the management of Alaskan wilderness; however, it also explicitly stated that such provisions applied only to Alaskan wilderness. These exceptions included the use of snowmobiles, motorboats, and aircraft, temporary fishing and hunting camps, and subsistence uses by natives and nonnatives (The Wilderness Society 1984). The ANILCA even allows log salvage along coastlines within wilderness. The act also provided authority to the USFS, however, to regulate or limit the above uses in order to protect an area's wilderness character.

In summary, then, the direction contained in section 4 of the Wilderness Act primarily concerns the uses considered appropriate in such areas. It is, in other words, the criterion guiding wilderness management. As the preceding discussion suggests, these guidelines are fairly strict. Controversy continues over the application of these guidelines in the allocation of wilderness, as opposed to its management. This debate—the so-called purity argument—has centered on the extent to which previous human impacts can be accepted in wilderness. The USFS, in particular, took the position that evidence of previous human impact normally precluded the inclusion of an area from consideration as wilderness. This position was defended on the grounds that in order to justify the substantial opportunity costs associated with wilderness, it was important that any area selected be of highest quality; that is, the area must exhibit the highest degree of "environmental purity" (Costley 1972; Worf 1980). Current USFS policy,

however, distinguishes classification standards from management standards.

The purity doctrine has been rebutted by many authors (Behan 1971; Foote 1973). Former Senator Frank Church (D-ID), floor manager for the wilderness bill at the time of its passage, charged that neither the letter nor the intent of the Wilderness Act called for exclusion of areas once impacted by human use and that agency claims to the contrary were simply evidence of resistance to congressional will (Church 1977). Allin (1982) has further argued that USFS reliance on the "purity argument" derives from the organization's concern with preserving a greater degree of administrative control over forest lands. The increasing loss of administrative discretion over the management of the national forests led the agency to consider ways in which it could limit the impact of wilderness designation on commodity production. In considering ways to do this, Allin argues, the agency increasingly emphasized that areas being reviewed for wilderness designation must meet the standards specified in section 4 of the Wilderness Act.

The admission standards for wilderness are dealt with in section 2(c) of the Wilderness Act, not section 4. Reliance on section 4 to define wilderness has been viewed by preservationists as well as Congress as inappropriate at best and illegal at worst (Allin 1982). Congressional action in classifying wilderness also indicates that a rigid and stringently pure conception of wilderness is not necessary.

For example, in the Mission Mountains Wilderness in Montana and the Agua Tibia Wilderness in California, impacts judged by the USFS to preclude wilderness designation were ruled acceptable by Congress. In the Mission Mountains, about 2,000 acres of the old primitive area were salvage-logged in the 1950s after an insect outbreak. The USFS proposed excluding this area, managing it to restore wilderness values, and then proposing its inclusion in the wilderness system. Congress, however, included the impacted area. In the Agua Tibia Wilderness proposal, the USFS excluded an area containing a road used for fire protection purposes from an area recommended for wilderness. The road was closed to public use. But Congress approved a bill including the road, ruling that such a development was permissible under the administrative-exceptions clause of the Wilderness Act, section 4(c).

Not all impacts are acceptable to Congress, of course. A 6,000-acre area containing a 22-mile-long access road to a mining claim in the Emigrant Basin Primitive Area in California was excluded by Congress from the wilderness bill it approved for this area. Congress instructed the USFS to reexamine the area at a later date in conjunction with the review of

Fig. 4.6. Under the original terms of the Wilderness Act, many nonconforming uses, such as logging, mining, use of motorboats and snowmobiles, were permitted in the BWCAW. In 1978, the act was amended to drastically curtail or eliminate such exceptions, thus enhancing the wilderness environment. Photo courtesy of the USFS.

some roadless lands contiguous to the nearby Hoover Wilderness. The challenges and problems of wilderness management are closely tied to decisions regarding such questions as what constitutes a "substantially unnoticeable" impact; that is, the greater the latitude in admission standards, the more urgent will be the need for rigorous management guidelines to enhance restoration and protection of the wilderness resource.

Passage of the so-called Eastern Wilderness Act in 1975 provides perhaps the strongest statement of congressional intent with regard to the conditions needed to constitute wilderness. This act (discussed in more detail in chap. 5) explicitly accepted the notion that areas where previous human activity, such as logging and agriculture, had occurred could still be classified as wilderness (fig. 4.7). More recently, House Report 99-262 on a bill to designate new wilderness in Michigan, indicated that within areas proposed, two-thirds of the mineral rights were privately owned, motorboat and off-road vehicle use were present, developed camping facilities were located, and one area contained an experimental forest with structures located in it (Nelson 1985). Such congressional actions clearly repudiate the purity policy as applied to classification (Allin 1982). But such steps also reflect an evolving perception on the part of the public as to what constitutes wilderness. The criterion of naturalness will continue to be evaluated differently over time and in different parts of the country (Hendee 1986).

SECTION 5—STATE AND PRIVATE LANDS WITHIN WILDERNESS AREAS

Section 5 describes the rules and procedures for access to private or state-owned inholdings within national forest wilderness. It provides "such rights as may be necessary to assure adequate access" to such lands. The right of reasonable access is further endorsed in section 1110(b) of ANILCA: "the State or private owner or occupier shall be given by the Secretary such rights as may be necessary to assure adequate and feasible access." These rights are taken to apply to wilderness lands outside Alaska (The Wilderness Society 1984). It also indicates that such lands may be exchanged for federally owned property in the same state and of approximately equal value. Unless the state or private owner relinquishes the mineral interests in the surrounded land, however, the U.S. government will not transfer the mineral rights of any exchanged land.

The secretary of agriculture is permitted, subject to the appropriation of funds by Congress, to acquire private inholdings within wilderness if (1) the owner agrees to such acquisition and (2) the acquisition is

Fig. 4.7. Many eastern wildernesses are small and often adjoin private lands used for agriculture or for rural dwellings. Portions of Shenandoah National Park Wilderness, VA, border private farmlands. Photo courtesy of the Norfolk and Western Railway.

approved by Congress. Condemnation is not permitted by the Wilderness Act, an authority which was important to the development of legislation establishing eastern wilderness (see chap. 5). But even in the case of the Eastern Wilderness Act, the authority to condemn private land was limited to the 16 areas designated by that legislation.

SECTION 6—GIFTS, BEQUESTS, AND CONTRIBUTIONS

Both the secretary of agriculture and the secretary of the interior are authorized to accept gifts in furtherance of the purposes of the act. Such gifts might be land, money, or both. If the gift involves land adjacent to, rather than within, an existing wilderness, Congress must be notified 60 days before acceptance. Upon acceptance, the land becomes part of the wilderness. If they are consistent with the purposes of the act, a donor may attach stipulations to the gift.

SECTION 7—ANNUAL REPORTS

The last section of the Wilderness Act instructs the two secretaries to report jointly to the president at the opening of each session of Congress on the status of the NWPS. These reports are a valuable source of information on the number of areas and acres in the NWPS, changes in the system, regulations in effect, and the status of areas under consideration. They are available to the public from the Government Printing Office and from senators and representatives.

SOME EXCEPTIONS AND AMBIGUITIES IN WILDERNESS LEGISLATION

One additional aspect of the Wilderness Act deserves comment. The directives and guidelines for management of areas in the act pertain only to those areas classified by that legislation. Technically, the Wilderness Act imposes use restrictions only on the 54 national forest areas designated wilderness upon its passage. It also provides that, pending designation as wilderness, primitive areas were to be managed under regulations in effect at the time the Wilderness Act was passed. Left in some confusion, then, was the status of the Department of the Interior holdings, the wilderness study areas specified in other wilderness designation acts, and all other lands that might be added in the future to the NWPS.

Why Congress did not clearly specify the man-

agement direction for these other areas in the 1964 legislation is not entirely clear. The lack of definitiveness does allow Congress latitude for adding special management provisions to the legislation classifying each individual area, perhaps in response to an area's unique features, problems, or uses.

But wide use of special management provisions could also undermine one of the major reasons a wilderness bill was initially proposed—*consistency* (Aspinall 1964; Zahniser 1964). As a consequence, in all subsequent legislation designating wilderness, Congress has affirmed that these new areas shall be managed in accordance with the 1964 act's provisions. In other words, although the Wilderness Act did not specifically prescribe the management for areas subsequently classified, Congress has extended the 1964 act's provisions to them. Where exceptions have been included in subsequent legislation, they have been restricted to specific areas and not used as a precedent for changes elsewhere.

The Wilderness Act has many ambiguities, weaknesses, and omissions (permitting mining in wilderness; failure to describe procedures for the review of national forest roadless lands). The general vagueness of many procedures has placed substantial burden on administrative agencies, citizen advocates, and, especially, on the courts. At least one author has suggested that the contradictions and ambiguities may simply reflect political expediency. Congress avoided offending many competing interests, leaving the job of resolving these problems to others (Haight 1974).

Notwithstanding all the unresolved issues, the Wilderness Act represents the principal statutory foundation for wilderness preservation and management in the United States today. It defines the broad goals, objectives, policies, and procedures through which an enduring resource of wilderness is to be provided. Nevertheless, alternative interpretations of the legislation exist, each with its alternative implications for management. We think it important to make explicit our interpretation of the legislation as well as the rationale for our interpretation.

SOME FEATURES IN THE EVOLUTION OF WILDERNESS PROTECTION

Reviewing the progress in statutory wilderness protection reveals at least three major changes. First, the *permanency* attached to such efforts has been substantially enhanced. The L-20 Regulation afforded little if any permanency. In fact, as noted earlier, it was clear that the primitive area designation was viewed as an interim measure to halt haphazard development. Longevity of protection was improved by the U Regulations, but, as the history of the Wilderness Act demonstrates, administrative discretion to choose the level of protection was a major shortcoming. Similarly, although national park or wildlife refuge designation assured protection from many kinds of development, it did not necessarily guarantee permanent protection of wilderness values. The Wilderness Act brought increased assurance that such values would be protected.

Second, *permitted uses* of wilderness have been increasingly restricted. The L-20 Regulation contained little in the way of prohibited uses. Logging and other forms of resource development were permitted. The U Regulations were developed primarily to exclude some permitted uses—which they did. But because the U Regulations were instituted at the administrative rather than the legislative level, there remained the possibility that certain uses, inconsistent with wilderness, might be permitted.

Although national park or wildlife refuge designation prohibited certain uses, the prohibitions (and permitted uses) were not established with clear wilderness preservation objectives in mind. The Wilderness Act defined a more restrictive framework within which national park and wildlife refuge development plans were to take place.

Finally, the evolution from the L-20 Regulation and U Regulations to the Wilderness Act reflects a change in *purpose*. The L-20 Regulation was intended to establish a series of areas for the purposes of public education, inspiration, and recreation (ORRRC 1962). The U Regulations emphasized the importance of retaining the primitive quality of these lands, particularly with regard to the style of travel permitted. The major innovation was in regard to permitted use and procedures for establishment and modification of wilderness areas. It is clear from a review of some of Marshall's earlier writings (Marshall 1933) that protection of the natural environment was an important purpose of the U Regulations.

Similarly, the management guidelines for national parks and wildlife refuges prior to passage of the Wilderness Act did not explicitly define the purposes of wilderness preservation. Although a generally low level of development prevailed in many of these areas, the purposes which these areas were to serve lacked specificity and direction.

In the Wilderness Act, we find a new emphasis on the purpose for wilderness. Although public use and enjoyment are clearly provided for, there shall be constraints to preserve these areas as wilderness. Wilderness, as defined by the act, is a landscape

where the earth and its community of life are untrammeled by man. Thus, the Wilderness Act established a national policy and purpose of maintaining a system of areas where natural processes could operate as freely as possible. Recreational use was an appropriate use of these areas, *only so long as it was consistent with this purpose.* Over the period of formal protection for wilderness that we have reviewed, there appears to have been an evolution toward a more biocentric conception of wilderness, one focused on protection of the natural processes that created these settings.

This evolution of purpose in wilderness preservation is, in our opinion, a key development. Wilderness preservation has evolved from a holding strategy for minimizing unplanned development until more carefully thought-out plans could be formulated to a carefully defined and legally sanctioned national system for protecting the ecological integrity of selected areas. Our endorsement of a biocentric philosophy of wilderness management rests on the belief that framers of the Wilderness Act clearly intended to create a system of areas where nature's way was allowed, as far as possible, to continue unhampered by man. We share the lawmakers' recurring insistence that human use of these lands must not interfere with the preservation of the area as wilderness. It is from these assumptions regarding *purpose* that our interpretation of the Wilderness Act flows and that our management recommendations are founded.

STUDY QUESTIONS

1. Identify and discuss some of the factors leading to the pressure to create a congressionally established and protected wilderness system.
2. Discuss the relationship between the L-20, the U Regulations, and the Wilderness Act; how did these earlier administrative regulations affect the Wilderness Act? Consider both positive and negative influences.
3. What were some of the critical differences between the wilderness bill proposed in 1956 and the legislation passed in 1964? What were some of the reasons for these differences?
4. In your judgment, what are some of the major problems with the Wilderness Act in terms of how well it protects wilderness values? How can these problems be resolved?
5. What are some of the major changes that have occurred in the Wilderness Act since its passage in 1964? What forces have led to such changes? What future changes would you suspect might occur?

REFERENCES

Anon. 1985. Aerial tours over protected land: where and why low-flying aircraft are off limits. FAA General Aviation News. 24(4): 3-6.

Allin, Craig W. 1982. The politics of wilderness preservation. Westport, CT: Greenwood Press. 304 p.

Allin, Craig W. 1985. Hidden agendas in wilderness management. Parks and Recreation. 20(5): 62-65.

Allin, Craig W. 1987. Wilderness preservation as a bureaucratic tool. In: Foss, Philip O., ed. Federal lands policy. Westport, CT: Greenwood Press: 127-138.

Andrews, Russell P. 1953. Wilderness sanctuary. New York: Bobbs-Merrill. 10 p.

Aspinall, Wayne N. 1964. Underlying assumptions of wilderness legislation as I see them. Living Wilderness. 86: 6-9.

Baker, Richard A. 1985. The conservation congress of Anderson and Aspinall, 1963-64. Journal of Forest History. 29(3): 104-119.

Baldwin, Donald L. 1972. The quiet revolution: the grass roots of today's wilderness preservation movement. Boulder, CO: Pruett Publishing Co. 295 p.

Behan, R. W. 1971. Wilderness purism—here we go again. American Forests. 78(12): 8-11.

Billings, Ronald F. 1986 . Coping with forest insect pests in southern wilderness areas, with emphasis on the southern pine beetle. In: Kulhavy, David L.; Conner, Richard N., eds. Wilderness and natural areas in the Eastern United States: a management challenge; 1985 May 13-15; Nacogdoches, TX. Nacogdoches, TX: Stephen F. Austin University, School of Forestry: 120-129.

Billings, Ronald F.; Varner, Forest E. 1986. Why control southern pine beetle infestations in wilderness areas? The Four Notch and Huntsville State Park experiences. In: Kulhavy, David L.; Conner, Richard N., eds. Wilderness and natural areas in the Eastern United States: a management challenge; 1985 May 13-15; Nacogdoches, TX. Nacogdoches, TX: Stephen F. Austin University, School of Forestry: 130-135.

Brownridge, Dennis. 1986. In the Grand Canyon, the 'eternal silence' is shattered . High Country News. January 20: 1, 6.

Chapman, H. H. 1938. National Parks, National Forests, and wilderness areas. Journal of Forestry. 36(5):469-474.

Church, Frank. 1977. Wilderness in a balanced land use framework. Wilderness Resource Distinguished Lectureship. Moscow, ID: University of Idaho, Wilderness Research Center. 18 p .

Costley, Richard J. 1972. An enduring resource. American Forests. 78 (6): 8-11.

Foote, Jeffrey P. 1973. Wilderness—a question of purity. Environmental Law. 3(4): 255-260.

General Accounting Office. 1984. Private mineral rights complicate the management of eastern wilderness areas. RCED-84-101. Washington, DC: U.S. Government Printing Office. 48 p.

Gilligan, James P. 1954. The contradiction of wilderness preservation in a democracy. In: Proceedings, Society of American Foresters meeting; 1954 October 24-27; Milwaukee, WI. New York: Society of American Foresters: 119-122.

Glover, James M. 1986. A wilderness original: the life of Bob Marshall. Seattle, WA: The Mountaineers. 323 p.

Glover, James M.; Glover, Regina B. 1986. Robert Marshall-portrait of a liberal forester. Journal of Forest History. 30(3): 112-119.

Haight, Kevin. 1974. The Wilderness Act: ten years after. Environmental Affairs. 3(2): 275-326.

Heinselman, Miron L. 1973. Restoring fire to the canoe country. Naturalist. 24(4): 21-31.

Hendee, John C. 1986. Wilderness: important legal, social, philosophical and management perspectives. In: Kulhavy, David L.; Conner, Richard N., eds. Wilderness and natural areas in the Eastern United States: a management challenge; 1985 May 13-15; Nacogdoches, TX. Nacogdoches, TX: Stephen F. Austin University, School of Forestry: 5-1

Hession, Jack M. 1967. The legislative history of the Wilderness Act. San Diego, CA: San Diego State College. 228 p. Thesis.

Keyser, C. Frank. 1949. The preservation of wilderness areas—an analysis of opinion on the problem. Washington, DC: Library of Congress, Legislative Reference Service. 114 p.

Mackintosh, Barry. 1985. Harold L. Ickes and the National Park Service. Journal of Forest History. 29(2): 78-84.

Marshall, Robert. 1933. The forest for recreation. Senate Document 12. Washington, DC: U.S. Government Printing Office: 463-487.

Matthews, Olen Paul; Haak, Amy; Toffenetti, Kathryn. 1985. Mining and wilderness: incompatible uses or justifiable compromise? Environment. 27(3): 12-17, 30-36.

McArdle, Richard E. 1975. Wilderness politics: legislation and Forest Service policy. Forest History. 19(4): 166-179.

McCloskey, Michael. 1966. The Wilderness Act of 1964: its background and meaning. Oregon Law Review. 45(4): 288-321.

Mercure, Delbert V., Jr; Ross, William M. 1970. The Wilderness Act: a product of Congressional compromise. In: Cooley, Richard A.; Wandesforde-Smith, Geoffrey, eds. Congress and the environment. Seattle, WA: University of Washington Press: 47-64.

Mitchell, John G. 1985. In wildness was the preservation of a smile: an evocation of Robert Marshall. Wilderness. 48(169): 10-21.

Nash, Roderick. 1982. Wilderness and the American mind. 2d ed. New Haven, CT: Yale University Press. 425 p.

Nelson, Thomas C. 1985. Wilderness re-re-defined. Journal of Forestry. 83(12): 717-718.

Outdoor Recreation Resources Review Commission [ORRRC]. 1962. Wilderness and recreation: a report on resources, values, and problems. ORRRC Study Rep. 3. Washington, DC: U.S. Government Printing Office. 352 p.

Proescholdt, Kevin. 1984. Boundary Waters: more obstacles for a troubled law. Sierra. 69(4): 18-21.

Robinson, Glen O. 1975. The Forest Service. Baltimore: The Johns Hopkins University Press. 337 p.

Roth, Dennis. 1984. The National Forests and the campaign for wilderness legislation. Journal of Forest History. 28(3): 112-125.

Scott, Douglas. 1976. Howard Zahniser: architect of wilderness. Sierra Club Bulletin. 61(9): 16-17.

Short, L. Rex. 1980. Wilderness policies and mineral potential on the public lands. Rocky Mountain Mineral Law Institute. 26: 39-67.

Sumner, David. 1973. Wilderness and the mining law. Wilderness. 37(121): 8-18.

U.S. Department of the Interior, Bureau of Reclamation. 1974. Position paper on weather modification over wilderness areas and other conservation areas. Washington, DC: U.S. Department of the Interior, Bureau of Reclamation. 29 p.

U.S. Geological Survey. 1984. Wilderness mineral potential: assessment of mineral-resource potential in U.S. Forest Service lands studied, 1964-1984. Geol. Surv. Prof. Pap. 1300. Washington, DC: U.S. Department of the Interior, Geological Survey. 2 vol.

The Wilderness Society. 1984. The Wilderness Act handbook. Washington, DC: The Wilderness Society. 64 p.

Worf, William A. 1980. Two faces of wilderness—a time for choice. Idaho Law Review. 16: 423-437.

Zahniser, Edward. 1984. Howard Zahniser: father of the Wilderness Act. National Parks. 58(1-2): 12-14.

Zahniser, Howard. 1964. How much wilderness can we afford to lose? In: Brower, David R., ed. Wildlands in our civilization; 1951 March 30-31; Berkeley, CA. San Francisco, CA: Sierra Club: 46-51.

ACKNOWLEDGMENTS

Dennis M. Roth, Chief Historian, Public Affairs Office, USFS, Washington, DC.

The Wilderness Act of 1964 instructed the secretary of agriculture to review within 10 years all designated primitive areas to ascertain suitability as wilderness. Headwaters of the East Fork of the Boulder River, Absaroka-Beartooth Wilderness, MT. Photo courtesy of Richard Behan.

5

THE WILDERNESS CLASSIFICATION PROCESS

This chapter was written by Joseph W. Roggenbuck, Department of Forestry, Virginia Polytechnic Institute and State University, Blacksburg; George H. Stankey; and Dennis M. Roth, Chief Historian, Public Affairs Office, U. S. Forest Service, Washington, DC.

INTRODUCTION

Although this is primarily a text about wilderness management, it is difficult to ignore the wilderness allocation or classification process. In chapter 1, we briefly reviewed the relationship between allocation and management. In this chapter, we will focus on the allocation process. We will review how wilderness is classified under the Wilderness Act, how the classification process has been affected by various administrative and judicial decisions, and how these rulings bear upon wilderness management.

THE CLASSIFICATION PROCESS

Chapter 4 reviews the classification procedures outlined in section 3 of the Wilderness Act. First, the act provided for an "instant" wilderness system by proclaiming that all the lands administered by the U.S.

Forest Service (USFS) as wilderness, wild, or canoe areas prior to 1964 would be known henceforth as wilderness areas.

Second, the Wilderness Act instructed the secretaries of agriculture and the interior to review certain lands within their respective jurisdictions and to make recommendations to the president regarding the suitability of these lands for classification as wilderness. The USFS, through the secretary of agriculture, was instructed to review those lands previously designated as *primitive areas* (a total of 34 areas and 5.4 million acres) within 10 years of the passage of the act. According to the act's timetable, a third of the primitive areas were to be reviewed in the first three years, two-thirds by the end of seven years, and the remainder by the end of 10 years.

Similar instructions were addressed to the secretary of the interior. All roadless areas in the various

units of the National Park System and the National Wildlife Refuges and Game Ranges in excess of 5,000 acres, as well as all roadless islands, were to be reviewed by the respective agencies, and recommendations regarding their suitability for wilderness were to be forwarded to the president. The 10-year review period and timetable applied to both USFS lands and Department of the Interior holdings. The president would make his recommendations to Congress. Finally, Congress would propose and vote on legislation to classify each area as wilderness.

CONTROVERSY IN THE REVIEW OF ROADLESS LANDS

When the federal agencies began the task of implementing the Wilderness Act's directives regarding allocation, three problems immediately surfaced: (1) what criteria to use when making recommendations about the wilderness character of lands and the need for wilderness, (2) what lands to consider, and (3) who should be the primary force in the process to complete and "round out" the National Wilderness Preservation System (NWPS)—agencies or interest groups. These issues have permeated the wilderness review process until the present, and no agency demonstrates this debate more dramatically than the USFS.

REVIEW OF NATIONAL FOREST ROADLESS LANDS

The USFS's review of its roadless lands began with the establishment, in late 1964, of a special task force of experienced wilderness managers to write wilderness policy and guidelines in accordance with the act. Task force members, directed by Richard Costley, head of the agency's Recreation Division, thought they knew what wilderness was, and believed their work would conclude quickly. They soon learned that the Wilderness Act set only broad philosophical definitions, that little consensus had developed in their own agency on what wilderness was, and that ultimately the input of citizens and congressional action, as required by the act, would strongly influence the nature of the wilderness system (Worf 1980).

The task force took a "pure" or "strict constructionist" approach to wilderness policy. They did this for philosophical and administrative reasons. They were familiar with the vast and pristine wildernesses of the West, and believed that Congress had these kinds of areas in mind when it established the national system. They viewed exceptions to purity included in the act to be largely compromises made to accomplish the act's passage—and not as clear directives for future allocation and management. They knew of the many requests for commodity use of wilderness and decided that strict guidelines were needed to prevent the "cheapening" of the system.

From a more practical standpoint, they believed that wilderness and wilderness management would be expensive, both in terms of uses forgone and in terms of management to maintain primitive conditions and experiences. Expense would increase sharply if the agency had to remove evidence of previous human use (Costley 1972). The task force also worried that including areas with significant impacts in the system would be a dangerous precedent for permitting existing pristine areas to decline to a lower standard. Finally, the task force believed that consistent, clear, and precise guidelines were needed when developing administrative policies regarding a new resource value, especially one as subjective and emotional as wilderness. Only through such guidelines could a system of comparable, high-quality areas be achieved, and only through such guidelines could effective, coordinated management be maintained (Worf 1980).

The task force might have expected the environmental groups who had lobbied for the passage of the act to support its strict constructionist approach toward implementing the act. The environmentalists did so mainly with respect to wilderness management. Also, some evidence shows that early on they also supported the strict constructionist approach to allocation (Roth 1984). On the other hand, as the USFS developed its guidelines and conducted its review of the 34 primitive areas, environmental groups and the public began to demand a greater role in the wilderness allocation process, and their definition of wilderness was not always as pure as that of the USFS.

National Forest Primitive Areas
The USFS completed its review of the wilderness potential of its primitive areas within the 10-year period specified by the Wilderness Act. From a resource analysis standpoint, many of the reviews involved little controversy. But even at this early date, the USFS was conducting far more than a "strict constructionist" wilderness attribute *inventory* of its primitive areas. Instead, the agency was also *evaluating* whether or not lands should be recommended for wilderness given their potential for wilderness, other multiple use, *and* management considerations such as costs. For each primitive area, the agency took a strong advocacy stance for its position on whether an area should receive wilderness classifi-

cation within the existing primitive area boundaries, wilderness classification with larger or smaller boundaries, or alternative management because the area was deemed not suitable for wilderness.

The USFS review and defense of its recommendations appears prompted by its multiple-use mandate and two key provisions of the Wilderness Act. The first provision was that only a bill passed by both Houses of Congress and signed by the president (fig. 5.1) could create a wilderness. This made classification of areas in the wilderness system more difficult. It also made the allocation of wilderness a much more political process, and as Stewart Brandborg, executive director of The Wilderness Society at the time, noted, this was a giant liberating force for the conservation movement (Roth 1984). For the first time, Congress had given itself the power to determine how a piece of USFS land was to be used. In essence, the USFS became an advisor to Congress about wilderness decisions on its lands, as well as, grassroots citizens' groups throughout the land. Thus, the political process would be allowed to determine the ultimate size of the wilderness system.

The second provision, included in the Wilderness Act through the efforts of Congressman John Saylor (R-PA), permitted the president to recommend to Congress that undeveloped land contiguous to primitive areas also become part of the wilderness system. Thus, each primitive area review would include review of contiguous roadless lands for wilderness.

The review, debate, and final congressional decisions regarding the San Raphael and the Gore Range-Eagles Nest Primitive Areas illustrate the importance of the Saylor amendment, the political nature of the wilderness allocation process, and the influence and involvement of environmental groups.

THE SAN RAPHAEL PRIMITIVE AREA

The USFS began its review of primitive areas with the 74,990-acre San Raphael Primitive Area in California—an area with little timber or mineral value and known for its grassy balds, scenic rock outcrops, mountain lions, bears, eagles, condors, and Chumash Indian rock paintings. As directed by the Wilderness Act, the USFS examined contiguous roadless lands and proposed a wilderness area of 110,403 acres. Under the USFS proposal, 36,244 acres were to be added to the primitive area and 831 acres containing a fuelbreak and a lookout tower were to be withdrawn. Little controversy was expected.

At public meetings, environmentalists urged the inclusion of five other contiguous areas in the wilderness proposal. They also opposed deletion of the 831 acres because this area contained favorite camp-

ing spots for backpackers and resting sites for the California condor. This testimony advocated increasing the size of the wilderness proposal, by almost one-third, to about 158,000 acres.

In response to public testimony and management considerations, the USFS submitted a revised recommendation calling for classification of 142,722 acres as wilderness, an increase of 32,000 acres over its initial proposal and almost double the size of the original primitive area. Brandborg praised the USFS for its cooperation and constructive attitude. The president transmitted the recommendation, unmodified, to Congress on February 1, 1967, and strongly urged Congress to give it "early and favorable approval."

The temporary peace and goodwill between the USFS and the environmentalists began to unravel later in 1967. Disagreements centered on 4,700 acres—an area that environmentalists maintained should be

Fig. 5.1. Classifying an area as wilderness is a lengthy process requiring resource inventory, public involvement, formulation of alternatives, congressional and public debate, passage through both houses of Congress, and finally, the president's signature. Photo courtesy of the NPS.

included in the wilderness proposal because it had wilderness character, was a condor flyway, and contained Chumash Indian pictographs. The USFS reported that 2,500 acres of the area contained an administrative site and road and included areas that had been converted from brush to grass for wildlife habitat, livestock forage, and fire control. The remaining 2,200 acres contained the only suitable site for construction of a larger firebreak. In fact, in June of the preceding year, a fire that ignited from the crash of a small airplane burned more than 90,000 acres, 70,000 of which were in the proposed wilderness. The forest supervisor agreed to forgo immediate plans to expand already existing fuelbreaks, but USFS officials believed that even under the most liberal interpretation of the Wilderness Act, the existing fuelbreak with its bulldozer and plow marks could not be considered wilderness.

The local Santa Barbara Sierra Club had already convinced California Senator Thomas Kuchel to introduce a bill that was essentially an environmentalists' proposal. It called for a 158,000-acre wilderness and included the 2,200 acres that the USFS wanted to exclude for potential use as a firebreak. This action was early evidence that questions of wilderness allocation were not to be decided exclusively at high executive levels in Washington, DC. Grassroots organizations would help shape congressional decisions (Roth 1984).

In April 1967, the Public Lands Subcommittee of the Senate Committee on Interior and Insular Affairs held public hearings on the Senate bill. Conservationists indicated a willingness to accept a reduction of some 13,000 acres from their original proposal. At this point, the conservationists' altered request differed from the USFS proposal by only 2,200 acres—the area where the USFS wanted to retain the option of building a firebreak.

The 2,200 acres quickly assumed symbolic political importance far beyond their intrinsic worth as wilderness. They became a major stumbling block to final resolution of the proposal. The Senate accepted the USFS's recommendation and passed a bill that excluded the disputed area. House Interior committee member John Saylor was, however, able to restore the acreage in a House bill.

The House passed its Saylor-amended bill on October 1, 1967, requiring that the bill go to a House-Senate conference committee. Debate was vigorous. The environmentalists feared that if Congress accepted the USFS position, it would ever after simply "rubber stamp" USFS wilderness proposals (Roth 1984). The USFS believed its professionalism was at stake and was further distressed that its authoritative

recommendations about fire management were being questioned. Congressmen from the district where San Raphael was located supported the USFS proposal. They acknowledged that fire danger was still a serious matter and that fire management specialists in the USFS should have a free hand.

In December 1967, the conference committee published House Report No. 1029, along with a majority recommendation "that the House recede from its amendment"; that is, that the House delete the 2,200-acre addition from its proposed bill and adopt the Senate USFS version. Despite a full House debate on this recommendation, during which Congressmen Saylor and Morris Udall (D-AZ) attempted to have the bill recommitted to conference, the House passed the bill without the addition.

In a special White House ceremony in March 1968, President Johnson signed the San Raphael Wilderness bill into law. It was the first addition to the NWPS created in 1964. It had passed through the various steps and procedures prescribed by the Wilderness Act and received considerable debate in Congress:

1. A preliminary agency recommendation, resting on substantial review (including field surveys and a mineral assessment) was revised following citizen review.
2. The revised recommendation was submitted through the secretary of agriculture to the president.
3. The president submitted the proposal to Congress, recommending passage.
4. Congressional committees considered several draft bills and held public hearings.
5. When the House and Senate approved different versions of the bill, a joint conference committee studied the differences and recommended the Senate version.
6. Following defeat of a House motion to recommit the conference report, the committee-recommended bill was accepted by the House, and it was passed by Congress.
7. The president signed the legislation. More than three years passed between initial field investigation and final passage.

The San Raphael Primitive Area review provided three important insights into the wilderness classification process: (1) it began to define more precisely that kinds of lands Congress would accept for the NWPS; (2) it identified key players in the allocation process, with grassroots environmental groups wielding much more influence than anticipated; and (3) it demonstrated an intensity of debate over final provisions of wilderness legislation that had not been anticipated. With the study of the wilderness suitability of the Gore Range-Eagles Nest Primitive Area, another key player was introduced to the wilderness allocation process—the courts.

THE GORE RANGE-EAGLES NEST PRIMITIVE AREA

When the USFS began its review of the Gore Range-Eagles Nest Primitive Area in the White River National Forest in north-central Colorado, the contiguous undeveloped East Meadow Creek drainage quickly became the focus of attention. The area was rolling, timbered high country with small meadows and park-like stands of old-growth Engelmann spruce, lodgepole pine, and fir. It had high wildlife values, including an elk migration and nursing ground. Moreover, it had become a popular backpacking, horse packing, and big game hunting area for those who lived in or began their trips from nearby Vail, a wealthy ski resort town built in 1964.

A primitive truck-trail had been constructed through the area in the 1950s to combat a bark beetle infestation. In 1962, the USFS drew up a plan to log the area and in 1964 built an access road to the edge of the area. With the passage of the Wilderness Act, USFS officials at the district and forest levels evaluated the area's potential for wilderness. They recommended against such designation because of the "bug road," the existence of some private inholdings and unpatented mining claims, its location outside the drainage of the original primitive area, and because established sawmill operators in the area depended on USFS timber (Roth 1984).

The proposed timber sale provided a dilemma. The primitive area review process had not yet been completed. If the timber harvesting went forward, it would destroy the wilderness character of lands contiguous to a primitive area, effectively making a decision about wilderness classification—a judgment Congress reserved for itself. On the other hand, a decision against the timber sale would be seen as favoring the expansion of the wilderness system—something only Congress can do. Thus, a middle ground decision was offered that included timber cuts in only six of the proposed 14 timber harvesting blocks and left a large buffer zone between the primitive area and the timber sale.

The compromise did not work. Neither the environmental groups nor the forest products industry liked the decision. Both felt it was a decision that only Congress could make. A third group, the citizens of Vail, were especially upset. They argued that their town depended on recreation dollars, that the timber sale was planned in 1962 before their town even existed, and that timber harvesting in the East Meadow Creek would significantly reduce a valuable economic resource. They sought a court injunction to stop the timber sale.

Such an injunction was by no means a likely result of any legal action. The courts had long ad-hered to the principle of "sovereign immunity"; that is, the federal government could not be sued for its administrative actions unless it consented to be, and that private citizens or organizations could not gain standing to sue unless they could prove that they had or would suffer personal or economic injury. Given this, The Wilderness Society did not join the suit. Its Washington lawyers indicated that the plaintiffs would certainly lose, and it would be a waste of the organization's financial resources.

The citizens of Vail, the Sierra Club, and several Colorado conservation organizations nevertheless moved forward. Their attorney was aware of the implications of the landmark Scenic Hudson decision of 1965 where the judge gave local citizens' groups standing in court and eventually ruled in favor of their suit to halt the construction of a proposed hydroelectric plant. He also noted the language of the Wilderness Act which said, "Nothing herein contained shall limit the President in ... recommending the addition of any contiguous area of national forest lands predominantly of wilderness value."

The district court heard the case, and the judge accepted the plaintiffs' arguments. He granted them the right to sue the government and listened to the testimony of the environmental witnesses who vouched for the wilderness character of the area and the USFS's arguments that the bug road disqualified it. On February 17, 1970, the judge ruled in favor of the plaintiffs and permanently enjoined the timber sale. On October 1, 1971, the Tenth Circuit Court upheld the ruling. The USFS continued to believe that a bad interpretation of the Wilderness Act had been made. They believed that the law did not *require* the review of every single contiguous acre of land with wilderness character by the president and Congress, although, the act did not *prohibit* such consideration either. The Department of Justice, on behalf of the USFS, appealed to the Supreme Court, which refused to hear the case (Roth 1984).

Grassroots citizen groups had gained a major victory. The judicial decision in effect protected undeveloped lands contiguous to USFS primitive lands until Congress made the final decision; it demonstrated again that wilderness allocation decisions would be shaped by actions beyond the USFS and Washington, and it freed the environmentalists to turn their attention to *noncontiguous* undeveloped USFS lands.

Classification of Nonreserved National Forest Lands

One major block of lands potentially available for wilderness classification was not specifically men-

tioned at all in the Wilderness Act. These were the so-called *de facto wilderness* lands in the National Forest System, areas that are in fact wilderness in the general sense of the term—roadless and undeveloped—but which lack explicit classification as wilderness. Since 1964, the future of these lands and their relationship to the Wilderness Act have been the subject of considerable controversy.

During debate on the Wilderness Act, *de facto* wilderness lands in the national forests received very little attention. The act's primary intent was not to reform natural resource management but to redefine the way in which wildernesses were allocated and protected. Supporters of the act wanted congressional, rather than administrative, protection for wilderness. Consequently, they were concerned primarily with the existing wilderness and primitive area system, which generally represented the largest and most pristine areas of the National Forest System.

Although the act itself did not specifically direct the USFS to review lands other than those designated as primitive areas, the act did not preclude such review. For example, Section 3(b) states that "nothing herein contained shall limit the president in proposing, as part of his recommendations to Congress, the alteration of existing boundaries of primitive areas or recommending the addition of any contiguous area of national forest lands predominantly of wilderness value." Accordingly, the team of field personnel that convened in 1964 to draft guidelines for the agency's wilderness management called for forest supervisors to identify potential new wildernesses by December 1966.

The regional foresters and the chief of the USFS accepted the team's recommendation, but allowed more time for completion of the inventory—first until June 1970 and later until June 1972. This early inventory, actually begun in 1967, would set the stage for the first of the USFS Roadless Area Review and Evaluation (RARE) processes in the early 1970s.

The agency's decision to review its roadless lands, in addition to lands specifically designated in the Wilderness Act, represented a judgment of agency personnel that the act did not *prevent* such a review. The agency also recognized that conservationists would soon be demanding classification of additional wilderness lands not specified in the act. The agency wanted to seize the initiative—to act more than react and desired to approach wilderness review and evaluation from a multiple-use planning perspective.

U.S. FOREST SERVICE INVENTORY OF POTENTIAL WILDERNESS ADDITIONS

Three criteria were formulated to guide USFS man-

agers faced with the task of *identifying* potential additions to the wilderness system: (1) *suitability,* (2) *availability,* and (3) *need.* The USFS argued that no formula for reaching these important decisions existed, but that the objective in each case was to determine the predominant public value within the meaning of the Multiple-Use Sustained-Yield Act of 1960 (P.L. 86-517): "with consideration being given to the relative values of the various resources, and not necessarily the combination of uses that will give the greatest dollar return or the greatest unit output."

Suitability—Suitability was defined by minimum conditions set forth in the Wilderness Act *and* by conditions believed to enhance the opportunity for wilderness-dependent experiences. The criterion specified that an area recommended for wilderness designation should (1) have an absence of roads or other development; (2) be at least 5,000 acres if it did not adjoin existing wilderness or primitive areas (smaller, undeveloped contiguous areas were also to be inventoried); (3) be free of present or foreseeable nonconforming uses or activities; (4) possess a wide range of subjective values for helping people discover freedom and spiritual renewal; (5) offer outstanding opportunities for challenge and primitive recreation like camping, ski touring, and hiking; (6) include abundant and varied wildlife; and (7) possess outstanding opportunities for formal and informal education and scientific study.

Availability—The second criterion, availability, specified that wilderness designation must represent the highest and best use of the land over time. The tangible and intangible values of the wilderness resource had to offset the potential value of all resources that would be rendered inaccessible or unavailable if formal wilderness designation occurred. The availability measure, then, constituted an estimation of the opportunity costs incurred through wilderness classification; that is, the total economic and noneconomic values that would be forgone by wilderness designation. These would include the value of the timber and minerals in an area, the economic value of nonwilderness recreation that is not developed, and the costs of managing the area as wilderness.

Need—The third criterion, need, indicated that the requirement for wilderness must be measured and compared to that for other resources. It required clear evidence of current and future public need for additional, formally designated wilderness. Need was to be determined through a consideration of the location, size, type, and capacity of other wildernesses in the general vicinity, by local and national patterns and trends in wilderness use, and by the extent to

which nonwilderness lands were available to provide dispersed recreation opportunities not necessarily linked to wilderness.

The initial inventory identified 1,449 roadless areas with wilderness potential, containing 56 million acres (see table 5.1). The chief of the USFS planned to use this inventory, in combination with other data, to complete a list of study areas to receive more formal review and evaluation. During the study process the USFS held some 300 public meetings and received more than 50,000 written and oral comments—at the time the largest public involvement effort ever undertaken by the federal government (Hendee 1977). But of the 1,449 areas, only two were in the East and one was in Puerto Rico. The lack of areas in the East was a disappointment to environmentalists, and, as we shall soon see, quickly became a source of controversy.

The three criteria used for inventory suggest that the USFS decided early on that any review of its roadless lands would be more than a technical assessment of the wilderness character of such lands. Any review would certainly include an assessment of wilderness attributes required by the Wilderness Act and other related attributes like wildlife. More important, the review would be an *evaluation* of whether roadless areas that met the criteria defined in the act *should* be recommended for wilderness. This placed the agency solidly in the arena of value judgments regarding the range of public benefits to be gained or lost if a roadless area is or is not placed in the wilderness system. This position inevitably placed the agency in an advocacy role in its recommendations to Congress—a role it had long and legitimately performed in its resource planning and management, but one which was now shared with various public interest groups. This advocacy role in representing the judgments of the agency about the best possible mix of values to be gained from public lands would shape the wilderness classification process and outcome more than would technical assessments of wilderness attributes.

ROADLESS AREA REVIEW AND EVALUATION

Just how to go about the review and evaluation of the potential wilderness additions was at first an unanswered question. One alternative was to rely on the agency's normal land-use planning process, studying all management options, including wilderness, as each roadless tract was considered. But some officials feared that this would stall the final disposition of the roadless areas. Lengthy delays could mean that roadless lands could be developed in unplanned and, possibly, undesirable ways. Moreover, considering each roadless tract individually, over a long time, could polarize preservationists, who would seek wilderness designation for each tract, and the agency, which would consider a range of management alternatives for these lands. One such controversy in 1972 between the USFS and a citizen group involved a roadless area near Lincoln, Montana, and resulted in the designation of the 240,000-acre Scapegoat Wilderness—the first USFS area classified under the 1964 act that had not previously been a primitive area. The long and costly debate over this area demonstrated most clearly the need for an immediate and comprehensive review of roadless lands.

Millions of acres of federal land possessed wil-

Table 5.1. Summary of the USFS roadless area inventory (RARE I).

Region	Number of areas	Gross acres	Commercial forest land acres	Annual allowable timber harvest
		Thousands		MM bd ft
Northern	283	7,612	4,768	457
Rocky Mountain	248	5,757	2,474	134
Southwestern	89	1,430	189	8
Intermountain	433	11,942	3,805	182
California	131	3,098	716	209
Pacific Northwest	255	5,592	3,169	699
Southern	2	37	23	<1
Eastern	0	0	0	0
Alaska	7	20,698	3,712	586
Puerto Rico	1	8	<1	0
Total	**1,449**	**56,174**	**18,856**	**2,275**

Source: USDA Forest Service 1973, p. 16.

derness potential equivalent to that of the Lincoln-Scapegoat area. Thus, it seemed imperative to conduct a review of national forest roadless tracts as soon as possible to resolve some major allocation issues. Such a review would give the initiative to roadless area planning and management back to the USFS. It would serve as a first approximation of which roadless lands deserved careful, detailed study as to their potential for wilderness designation and which lands appeared to be more suited for alternative management. The agency also believed that a national review and evaluation of such areas would constitute a national Environmental Impact Statement (EIS) under the recently signed National Environmental Policy Act of 1969 (NEPA, P.L. 91-190), and thus avoid the need of writing an EIS for each roadless area.

The chief of the USFS assembled an interdisciplinary team to complete the national review and evaluation of the 1,449 potential wildernesses. The procedure developed and used by the team, called the Roadless Area Review and Evaluation (RARE), became the principal analytical tool used to recommend which of the inventoried areas should receive further intensive study for possible wilderness designation.

The RARE Process

Following are the principal objectives of the RARE selection process:

1. To obtain as much wilderness value as possible relative to the cost and value of the forgone opportunities to produce other goods and services for society.
2. To disperse the future wilderness system as widely as possible over the United States.
3. To represent as many ecosystems as possible so that the scientific and educational purposes of wilderness preservation are best served.
4. To obtain the most wilderness value with the least relative impact on the nation's wood product output.
5. To locate some new wilderness areas closer to densely populated areas so that more people can directly enjoy their benefits.

To evaluate undeveloped areas using the RARE technique, a number of quantitative and judgmental measures were obtained for each area. They included the following:

1. The total gross acres of roadless area.
2. A quality index (QI). Field personnel rated each area on three factors: (a) scenic quality (S), (b) isolation and likely dispersion of visitors within an area (I), and (c) variety of wilderness experiences and activities available (V). Each of these factors was weighted and used to calculate the QI by the formula: $QI = 4(S) + 3(I) + 3(V)$.
3. An effectiveness index (EI). To derive this measurement, total gross acres were multiplied by the quality index.

4. Total opportunity costs index. This index was composed of the sum of the following:
   a. Budget costs for studies, establishment, operation, and maintenance.
   b. Cost, if any, of acquiring private land.
   c. Cost of replacing special-use improvements.
   d. Mineral values.
   e. Potential water development values.
   f. Timber values.

The draft EIS called for the designation of 235 new areas covering 11 million acres (about one-fifth of the acreage inventoried) as new Wilderness Study Areas (WSA)—areas to receive intensive study and early consideration for inclusion in the NWPS (USDA FS 1973). Until the studies were completed, no management programs could be undertaken that would alter their undeveloped state. More than 7,000 letters and documents were received in response to the draft EIS (Hendee 1977). As public and official responses were analyzed, errors in the original data base were corrected and areas receiving particular interest were given special attention.

Following this analysis, 61 new study areas were included and 22 were deleted for a net gain of 39 new areas and a revised total (in the final EIS released in October 1973) of 274 areas and 12.3 million acres, an acreage gain of about 10 percent over the previously selected acreage in the draft EIS. Of this total, 46 areas and 4.4 million acres had already been officially committed for wilderness study prior to the announcement of the chief's list.

The *four principal variables*—the ones on which marginal cases were decided and which the chief and staff repeatedly used in making final decisions— were: (1) *public input*, including sentiment of involved citizens and organizations and the views of legislators and government agencies; (2) *potential wilderness quality of the roadless areas* as measured by the quality index; (3) *cost effectiveness*, reflecting the value of other resource uses forgone compared to relative wilderness values, and (4) an *overall judgment factor* resting heavily, but not entirely, on the recommendations of local, regional, and national decision makers (USDA FS 1973).

Many criticisms were leveled at the roadless area inventory and particularly at the RARE process (Milton 1975). Only eight months elapsed between the chief's initial inventory of new study areas and the final RARE list. Opportunities for careful field review by both agency personnel and concerned citizens were seriously limited. Many preservationists viewed the compressed timetable as a deliberate attempt to thwart detailed investigations of proposed areas as well as other roadless tracts, thereby limiting

the number of areas designated for wilderness study. The USFS argued that time was of the essence, that prolonged deliberation would unnecessarily delay orderly development of the national forests, and that uncertainties over resource development could seriously harm local economies.

Quite apart from the speed of the review, the designation of roadless lands revealed a number of serious deficiencies in the RARE methodology itself. Several criticisms centered on the calculation of the QI, which was based on an assessment of an area's scenic quality, potential for isolation and dispersion of recreation use, and variety of recreational experiences available. Critics claimed that each of these components measured the primitive recreation potential rather than the ecological condition of an area.

The indices of quality were also subjective and difficult to measure. Because no uniform guidelines or training existed for persons measuring the QI, the reliability of the judgments could not be determined. Judgments about the relative quality of individual areas were largely dependent on the values and perceptions of those performing the calculations.

The EI was calculated by multiplying the QI by area size. As a result, the value for the EI was almost wholly a function of size. Moreover, because size was also indirectly used in the QI, as a measure of isolation and dispersal potential, it was thus represented twice in the EI.

Size plagued the calculations in other ways. Although size tended to be emphasized in the calculations of the EI, it was often offset by the way in which roadless tracts were defined. Because the tracts were frequently defined along existing administrative boundaries, the aggregate size of large contiguous blocks of roadless lands that overlapped a number of administrative units (e.g., ranger districts) was diminished in importance because the area was treated as several separate smaller tracts.

The economic evaluation was made by *opportunity cost analysis,* the value of opportunities forgone by choosing one mutually exclusive alternative over another. But critics were quick to point out that many values associated with preservation were nonquantifiable and questioned the value of an analytical technique that rested on monetary measures of values assumed to be lost or gained.

Environmental groups were quick to seize upon these omissions and shortcomings. They believed worthy roadless areas—most notably in the East—were not included in the 1,449 areas, and therefore not adequately considered in the RARE process. Also, the 274 areas selected constituted only 19 percent of the total number of areas inventoried and 23 percent of the acreage. Disappointment in the wilderness recommendations led the Sierra Club and others to file a suit in federal court, charging that (1) the agency did not follow the appropriate procedures defined by NEPA and that (2) the procedures used in the inventory and selection of new WSAs were inadequate. Later that same year the chief of the USFS directed regional foresters to file an EIS before conducting activities that might alter the wilderness character of any roadless area. He added that wilderness must be considered one of the viable management alternatives for any inventoried roadless area. In light of this action, the court dismissed the first charge in the Sierra Club's suit, ruling that the filing of an EIS prior to any development would satisfy the requirements of NEPA. The second complaint was also dismissed because the procedures cited as inadequate were, in fact, not yet completed.

Dismissal of the complaints did not resolve the issue. The complaints were dismissed without prejudice; that is, the case could be heard by the court again. This might occur if, for example, local managers failed to follow the chief's instructions to meaningfully consider wilderness as a management alternative in a roadless area.

Both the Sierra Club and the USFS hailed the outcome of the lawsuit as a victory. The Sierra Club believed that the judge's ruling denied the USFS's highest priority goal in the RARE process: its attempt to regain and maintain primary leadership and control in allocation decisions regarding roadless lands in the national forests.

The USFS pointed to the chief's action in requiring an EIS as evidence of proper intent. Also, the judge's decision did not prevent the conversion of roadless areas to multiple-use management; it simply stated that a proper EIS must be filed for *each* area and that in the EIS, wilderness must be considered one of the viable management options (Allin 1982).

Regardless of who won or lost in this case, the RARE process had two important benefits for wilderness. First, the inventory provided a reasonably comprehensive list of remaining roadless lands in the National Forest System, and this highlighted the need for an increased emphasis on management guidelines and programs for these lands.

Second, the RARE process—for all its flaws—was an effort to systematically review and weigh the relative values of a variety of uses of existing roadless areas. In this, the review was able to take a regional and national perspective. The study set the stage for later more complete and defensible evaluations of the societal benefits of roadless lands.

WILDERNESS IN THE EAST

Even as the RARE process was reaching its culmination, the debate over what to do about national forest lands in the East (generally defined as east of the 100th meridian) was heating up. Environmentalists and many public interest groups were disappointed with the amount and kind of land that had been protected in the East under the Wilderness Act. They sought protection for tens of thousands of acres of land that, while not as pristine or as vast as areas in the West, still possessed a primitive character. Most of these acres had previously been logged or even farmed and roaded, but because of the regenerative capacity of ecosystems in the East, time was rapidly healing these wounds.

The USFS held steadfastly to its purity position that only areas that *retained* primeval conditions qualified for classification. Given that potential wildernesses in the East were small and marked by development, the USFS pressed for protection of these lands under an alternative system. At the same time, laws were being passed giving wilderness protection to Fish and Wildlife Service (FWS) lands in the East, and Shenandoah National Park (VA) had recently proposed a 75,000-acre wilderness in its backcountry—all lands which had previously been farmed and inhabited but which, with the passage of time, had returned to a wild state. When the congressional delegations from West Virginia and Alabama introduced bills in 1970 to protect lands under the Wilderness Act, the USFS recognized that time was short. In 1971, the regional foresters in Milwaukee and Atlanta proposed a "Wildwood Heritage System," distinct from the NWPS. The title of the proposed new land category was soon changed to "Wild Areas." Agency policy analysts described the proposed new land class (Roth 1984):

> Wild areas are distinct from wilderness areas because they are primarily for recreation enjoyment. Wildernesses are not primarily recreation areas, but are established primarily to ensure an enduring resource of wilderness for the nation as a whole. Wild areas would not qualify under the Wilderness Act. To include them would dilute the significance of the entire wilderness system. Grazing and mining would be prohibited in wild areas, whereas established uses are permitted in wilderness areas. Primitive recreation facilities and some hardening to protect the environment would be permitted in wild areas.

The wild areas would be protected from timber harvesting, but some tree cutting would be permitted to enhance wildlife habitat and recreation sites. Also, the USFS wanted the authority for prescribed burns in wild areas to clear out undergrowth and thus make foot travel through the areas more feasible.

In early 1972, President Nixon directed the Congress to make a greater effort to identify and protect wilderness recreation values in regions of the country where most of the public lives. Later that same year, Senators Herman Talmadge (D-GA and chairman of the Senate Agriculture Committee) and George Aiken (R-VT) introduced Senate bill 3973, recommending establishment of an Eastern National Forest Wild Areas System. The bill would have established a new system of eastern roadless areas, *separate* from the existing NWPS. In addition, it would have referred all wild area bills to Talmadge's Senate Agriculture Committee—rather than to Senator Jackson's (D-WA) Interior and Insular Affairs Committee which had received all previous wilderness bills. The rationale for this change was that national forest land in the East—having previously been private land rather than public domain—fell under the jurisdiction of the Senate Agriculture Committee. The Agriculture Committee, in contrast to the Interior and Insular Committee, was typically sympathetic to the timber industry and the USFS (Roth 1984).

The bill moved quickly through the Senate Agriculture Committee and was passed by the Senate in late 1972. It clearly stated that wild areas in the East could be restored to a primitive condition, but wilderness in the West had to be unspoiled by human contact. Thus, the bill was an affirmation of the USFS's purity doctrine (Strickland 1976).

The quick passage of Senate bill 3973 surprised environmental groups. Their response suggests the first real dissension about wilderness allocation within their ranks since the 1964 passage of the Wilderness Act. The Wilderness Society, with its strong central authority in Washington, was alarmed. Staff members Doug Scott and Ernie Dickerman argued that early leaders of the wilderness movement, like Harvey Broome and Howard Zahniser (both from the East), had first experienced wilderness in the East and had never meant primitive lands in the East to be excluded from the wilderness system. Also, they feared the purity language of Senate bill 3973; they could foresee only the purest of western lands qualifying for wilderness. The Wilderness Society had a large number of ecologists and naturalists in positions of power in their organization. A single, unified system was much more compatible with these members' scientific backgrounds. Finally,

they feared the Agriculture Committee with its leanings toward the timber industry and multiple use. They therefore quickly drew up an alternative bill that would place the eastern areas in the wilderness system. In January 1973, Senators Buckley (R-NY) and Jackson introduced Senate bill 316—a bill that bore great resemblance to the one written by The Wilderness Society (Roth 1984).

By this time, however, there was considerable grassroots support for the wild area concept among environmentalists in the East and Midwest. Joseph Penfold, conservation director of the powerful Izaak Walton League, felt that creating wilderness in the East would lower the standards of the system and threaten the integrity of all designated wilderness. Many Sierra Club chapters noted that the wild areas bill gave greater protection to primitive lands by prohibiting grazing and mining. They also believed that even if some areas in the East were placed in the wilderness system, other worthy areas would likely never qualify and these needed some sort of protection. Others felt that the USFS was the expert and was too powerful to be opposed. Finally, New Englanders had long ago developed their own philosophy of backcountry protection and use—a philosophy that included huts and shelters in the backcountry and high-standard trails. The wild area concept seemed a better fit.

The Wilderness Society launched a vigorous campaign of education and persuasion. The campaign illustrates an important tactic in the wilderness allocation process in particular and the American democratic process in general: accomplish one's own objective by constructing a means to permit the dissenter to change his position and still save face. The Wilderness Society created an organization called the "Citizens for Eastern Wilderness" whose primary purpose was to permit Sierra Club members to discretely align themselves with The Wilderness Society's position (Roth 1984). At the same time, the society hammered at the deficiencies of the two-system approach to wilderness protection.

By 1973, the environmental interests were together in support of the protection of areas in the East in the NWPS. The USFS dropped the idea of the two systems and proposed that 16 eastern areas be made instant wilderness and that another 37 be studied for possible inclusion. Senate bill 3433 was introduced into Congress—a bill which largely followed the philosophy of Senate bill 316. The bill called for 19 instant wildernesses to be established and 40 study areas to be reviewed by the secretary of agriculture within five years, according to the procedures outlined in the Wilderness Act. It contained two particularly important clauses: (1) The secretary of agriculture was given the power of condemnation when private landowners failed to use their land in a manner compatible with wilderness and were unwilling to sell voluntarily (This was an important authority, absent from the 1964 Wilderness Act, and included because of the large amounts of private inholdings in eastern national forests.); and (2) all lands classified as wildernesses or as Wilderness Study Areas (WSAs) were withdrawn from mineral entry.

The bill quickly passed the Senate and was sent to the House. In the House, progress was slowed by the death of Congressman John Saylor and preoccupation with the Watergate scandal. House Public Lands Subcommittee Chairman John Melcher (D-MT) required that Congressmen whose districts included the wilderness areas submit written statements of support. This represented a change from past protocol when only oral support was necessary. To the dismay of the environmental community, this resulted in reducing the number of wildernesses to 15 and study areas to 17. The bill then passed the House in December 1974 with only the change in numbers from the Senate bill. The bill was signed into law (P. L. 93-622) by President Ford on January 3, 1975 (Roth 1984).

This law (popularly called the "Eastern Wilderness Act" but in actuality it has no title) represents a major challenge for management. It represents a statement by Congress of its desire to locate wildernesses nearer population centers, and it included areas that are generally smaller in size and show more past evidence of human use than USFS lands previously placed in the system. Some claimed it was explicit repudiation of the USFS purity principle in allocation (Allin 1982).

THE ENDANGERED AMERICAN WILDERNESS ACT

The RARE process had been criticized by environmentalists for failing to select several undeveloped areas located near population centers for wilderness study. Indeed, the USFS had eliminated such areas as Lone Peak near Salt Lake City (UT), Sandia Mountains near Albuquerque (NM), and Pusch Ridge adjacent to Tucson (AZ) because they were in "sight and sound" of cities. Environmental groups claimed that Nixon administration messages to Congress in 1972 and 1973, the so-called 1975 "Eastern Act," and their own constituents supported the notion that accessibility to population centers enhanced rather than detracted from wilderness values. Also, while the RARE process was billed as an effort to address the

24

wilderness issue in a more rapid, unified, and comprehensive manner than would have occurred under the normal USFS unit planning process, environmentalists noted that the USFS prepared EISs on any proposed development or change in a roadless area on a unit (usually a ranger district) basis. At times, such a unit contained several roadless areas; in other cases one roadless area was much larger than a single planning unit. In both cases, environmentalists felt that the potential wilderness suitability of individual areas was being compromised.

Sierra Club leaders decided that the time was right for an omnibus wilderness bill that would place a variety of kinds of roadless areas from around the country in the NWPS. Such a bill would protect several areas that the RARE process had either excluded or had not recommended for future wilderness study. The bill would thus be symbolic of supposed defects in the USFS's RARE process, would help build grassroots support for wilderness throughout the country, and would demonstrate this support to every congressman and senator. The environmental groups convinced Senator Frank Church (D-ID) and Congressman Mo Udall (D-AZ) to introduce the Endangered American Wilderness bill in Congress in 1976. At first, congressional mail ran against the bill, but as the Sierra Club's campaign geared up, support began to build. It was also a stroke of good planning, or luck, that both of the bill's sponsors were presidential candidates. Their candidacy and sponsorship, the support of candidate Jimmy Carter, and his election greatly increased the likelihood of passage of the bill. Passage was further promised when the new Congress was formed and chairmanship of the House Interior Committee passed to Congressman Mo Udall. Ultimately, under the leadership of the new administration, including Rupert Cutler, the new assistant secretary of Agriculture for Conservation, Research, and Education (the former assistant executive director of The Wilderness Society), the USFS supported the bill. President Jimmy Carter signed the Endangered American Wilderness Act on February 24, 1978 (P.L. 95-237), creating 1.3 million acres of wilderness in 17 new wildernesses or additions to wilderness in Arizona, California, Colorado, Idaho, New Mexico, Oregon, Utah, Washington, and Wyoming. In number of acres, it was the largest addition to the national system accomplished by one act to that point. In one sense it repudiated the RARE since some of the areas that the RARE process had ignored in the inventory, or had not recommended for wilderness study, were now wilderness (Roth 1984).

RARE II—ANOTHER LOOK

RARE II—the second USFS Roadless Area Review and Evaluation—was a critical influence on the wilderness allocation process. Doug Scott of The Wilderness Society, an early supporter of RARE II, but later one of its most vocal critics, has conceded that it will do more to enlarge the national forest portion of the wilderness system than anything since "affirmative action" (Roth 1984, p. 61). RARE II also illustrates the key players, processes, and events that influence wilderness allocation decision: the tugs and strains between charismatic individuals and bureaucratic control; the role of reason and emotion—of rational planning and political horse trading; the struggle of the USFS as it attempted to advance its own philosophy of resource management and weigh multiple benefits and costs at national, regional, and local levels; the checks and balances of the legislative, executive, and judicial branches of government; and finally the pervasive influence of public interest groups.

As noted earlier, by the mid-1970s, there was considerable dissatisfaction with the first RARE process. From a list of USFS roadless areas, the RARE process recommended areas that were to be given further consideration for wilderness designation. When Jimmy Carter was elected President in 1976, controversies over the validity and reliability of the first RARE process had slowed the public land allocation process to a crawl.

RARE II was primarily the brainchild of Rupert Cutler. He thought RARE I was flawed. He had supported the Endangered American Wilderness Act and thereby had somewhat "liberalized" the USFS definition of wilderness; he wanted a study to help him better conceptualize the new minimum acceptability standard. He was also under pressure from commodity interests and the USFS to resolve future wilderness allocations. He was empathetic with the timber interests' demands and USFS requests for prompt decisions on roadless areas so that long-term planning and investments could move forward. Finally, he was aware of the commodity interests's apprehension about his nomination as assistant secretary of agriculture—given his past association with The Wilderness Society (Roth 1984).

The basic objective of RARE II was to accelerate the planning process mandated by the Forest and Rangeland Renewable Resources Planning Act of 1974 (RPA, P.L. 93-378) and the National Forest Management Act of 1976 (NFMA, P.L. 94-588). The act called for a comprehensive study to identify roadless and undeveloped lands in the National Forest

System and to determine their general uses both for wilderness and for resource management and development. The study would produce recommendations on which roadless lands should be designated wilderness, which should be released to uses other than wilderness, and which warranted further study for all uses, including wilderness. The study was to be a methodological rational approach to planning in a national context. It is important to note that the study was not so much a *wilderness study* as it was a *roadless area study*. The goal to identify roadless areas with important nonwilderness values was equal in importance to identifying areas which should be used to round out the *ideal* national forest portion of the wilderness system. The desired outcome was a balance of land uses that would best meet the nation's needs. The RARE II process was also to be done within the requirements of NEPA. Considerable public involvement would shape recommendations, and it was Cutler's dream that the study would serve as one large programmatic EIS; that is, the study would be the EIS for all areas recommended for wilderness, nonwilderness, or further wilderness study (Roth 1984).

The USFS asked Department of Agriculture lawyers to study the legality of RARE II and the acceptability of using such a study as a national EIS. Legal counsel indicated they were in "uncharted waters" (Roth 1984). The USFS doubted the likelihood that any national study would quickly resolve the wilderness issue. Its own analyses suggested there would be judicial challenges of the study's EIS. Congress had been slow to act on recommendations for primitive areas, and the USFS believed that eventually national forest roadless areas would be added to the NWPS on a state-by-state basis (USFS speculations came to pass on both issues) (Roth 1984).

When the USFS began RARE II, it pushed forward to improve on RARE I in two ways: first, to separate the identification, inventory, and evaluation of each roadless area; and second, to establish greater reliability and validity in the inventory process. In doing this, the USFS was striving to obtain greater public confidence in the RARE process by separating the assessment from the evaluation components. The assessment component—which included identification and inventory—had wilderness suitability as its primary criterion. The question was not whether a roadless area should or should not be wilderness, but rather whether it had attributes to meet minimum criteria for wilderness consideration. Judgments about which areas should be recommended for wilderness were left to the evaluation phase.

The RARE II Inventory

RARE I had reviewed 1,449 areas containing 56 million acres. The roadless status of most of these areas remained unchanged, and they became part of the RARE II inventory. The public was asked to comment and suggest additions and deletions for the RARE II study, and more than 50,000 provided comments. In response, the USFS raised the number of areas to 1,921 roadless areas and 65.7 million acres. Then the USFS decided to include 34 areas previously allocated to nonwilderness use and also portions of the Tongass National Forest in Alaska. Some areas which were not roadless were deleted.

Many more areas in the East were included in RARE II than had been previously studied. To accomplish this, somewhat less restrictive standards were used to select areas for the inventory process there. This responsed to the limited wilderness opportunities in the East, the need for wilderness close to people, and the faster regenerative capacity of ecosystems in the East. Areas were selected that did not exceed more than *one* of the following: one-half mile of improved road for each 1,000 acres, if road was under USFS jurisdiction; 15 percent of area in nonnatural planted vegetation; 20 percent of area with timber harvested in the past 10 years; and an area could contain a few dwellings if the dwellings and access were obscured by natural features. The final RARE II inventory list included 2,919 roadless areas and encompassed 62 million acres on national forests and national grasslands in 38 states and Puerto Rico (USDA FS 1979).

A variety of data were collected on the RARE II areas. Each area's renewable-resource potential was measured through a system called the Development-Opportunity Rating System (DORS). This system compared the benefits and costs of developing a roadless area for renewable multiple-use outputs, including sawtimber, grazing, developed recreation, hunting, and fishing. In addition, site-specific information on potential timber, programmed harvest, and grazing was reviewed. Each area's mineral potential was also assessed.

The USFS, in its RARE II process, also sought to increase ecological diversity within the NWPS, with the goal of obtaining two or more distinct examples of each of the nation's ecosystems (USDA FS 1978). Using a mapping system called the *Bailey-Küchler system*, a system using Bailey's (1976) ecoregion concept and Küchler's (1966) system of potential natural vegetation, the USFS identified 242 distinct ecosystems in the United States and Puerto Rico. The systems were distinct both in such physical environment factors as climate and soil and in factors of

Table 5.2. Wilderness attributes and their components.

Wilderness attributes	Components on which ratings are based
1. Natural integrity	Fourteen possible physical developments or human-caused impacts (e.g., roads, railroad rights-of-way, reservoirs, grazing, air pollution, etc.), scaled as to their presence, effect on natural integrity, size of area impacted, potential separability from rest of area, duration of impact if uncorrected, feasibility of correcting.
2. Apparent naturalness	Uses the same components as natural integrity, but the ratings differ.
3. Outstanding opportunity for solitude	Size of area, topographic screening, vegetative screening, distance from perimeter to core, human intrusions, scaled as to their degree of impact on opportunity for solitude.
4. Primitive recreation opportunities	Size of area, topographic screening, vegetative screening, distance from perimeter to core, diversity, challenge, absence of facilities, scaled as to their degree of impact on primitive recreation.
5. Supplementary attributes	
a. Ecological	Presence and abundance of endangered or threatened plants and animals or other special ecological features.
b. Geological	Presence and abundance of special geological features.
c. Scenic	Ratings based on visual management system.
d. Cultural features	Presence of any cultural-historical features.

the biological environment such as vegetation (Davis 1988). Later refinement of the mapping process indicated that the total number of ecosystems was actually 261. When studying individual roadless areas, the RARE II process gave preference for wilderness recommendation of those areas that contained an ecosystem not currently represented in the NWPS.

In late 1977, a USFS task force developed the RARE II Wilderness Attribute Rating System (WARS), a system to inventory the wilderness characteristics of the RARE II areas. WARS was constructed through a systematic process of review and testing by a group of resource managers, researchers, university professors, and environmentalists. It established a procedure for identifying the attributes of wilderness as defined by the Wilderness Act and for rating their condition. The purpose of WARS was to provide a measure of the area's wilderness quality in addition to the informaton about its potential commodity and developmental values.

Table 5.2 lists the critical and supplemental at-

tributes and their respective components that comprise the WARS. The *critical attributes used in WARS* are those mentioned in the Wilderness Act: natural integrity of area, apparent naturalness (amount and nature of perceptible impacts), solitude opportunity, and primitive recreation opportunity. The system also permits adjustment in ratings in natural integrity and apparent naturalness if area boundaries were adjusted to remove serious intrusion. Each of the four critical attributes was rated on a scale of one to seven, ranging from the outstanding presence of the attribute to its virtual absence. Composite wilderness attribute scores were determined by adding the ratings of each of the four critical attributes. Thus, each of the four attributes is weighted equally in the overall score.

There are two supplemental area ratings: a supplementary wilderness attribute rating and a scenic value rating. These ratings reflect Section 2(c)(4) of the Wilderness Act, which indicates that an area "may also contain ecological, geological, or other features of scientific, educational, scenic or historical

value." This suggests that these features are not necessary for wilderness suitability, but that their presence in an extraordinary degree enhances wilderness values. These two variables were not part of an area's overall composite wilderness attribute score, but instead were viewed as supplemental information to help make marginal decisions or to identify areas that might be placed in the USFS's Special Interest Areas System.

EVALUATION OF RARE II AREAS

The inventory process of RARE II resulted in a numerical wilderness attribute rating of each area ranging from four to 28, which indicated the extent to which the area contained wilderness attributes listed in the Wilderness Act. The question that remained was which of these areas should be recommended for wilderness designation, released for nonwilderness uses, or held for further study. For example, how far down the inventory rating list should the USFS go before the cutoff point between wilderness or nonwilderness is reached?

In the RARE II draft EIS published on June 15, 1978, the public was asked to comment on three things: (1) what individual areas should be allocated to wilderness, nonwilderness, or further planning, and why; (2) what approaches should be used by the department in reaching a decision on allocating the total roadless area inventory; and (3) what decision criteria should be used in developing a proposed course of action. Response was massive: 264,093 inputs carrying 359,414 signatures, seven times as many public comments as received in RARE I (Hendee 1986). Most responses expressed a preference for allocation of an individual area, but some also addressed the issue of alternative allocation strategies and final decision criteria.

Ten general alternative allocation strategies reflecting a range of mixes of wilderness and nonwilderness options were offered to the public. The potential physical, biological, social, and economic effects of each alternative were quantified and evaluated by the USFS to the extent feasible. Of primary concern were the benefits realized and benefits forgone (opportunity costs) if more or less wilderness were recommended. Each alternative would affect in drastically different ways the balance of commodity and noncommodity uses from the roadless areas, and this would affect employment, quality of life, and other factors at local, regional, and national levels. This analysis, along with public input, existing laws and regulations, identified public needs, and professional judgment by Department of Agriculture decision makers resulted in the USFS's pre-

ferred proposal. In essence, the proposal called for the allocation to nonwilderness of areas with high potential for commodity resource output and allocation to wilderness of those with high wilderness attributes. This responded to public input that expressed favor for economic values and jobs, timber production, accessibility, high scenery and diversity in the wilderness system, and high-quality additions to the system.

The preferred alternative became the philosophical base from which final decision criteria for recommendations about individual areas were developed. Several criteria were offered to the public, and on the basis of their response and agency evaluation of input, a 10-step procedure was selected (USDA FS 1979):

Step 1—The USFS's preferred alternative was modified by allocating to specific categories (wilderness, nonwilderness, further planning) those roadless areas supported by at least 71 percent of the public response for specific allocations.

Step 2—Regional foresters reviewed allocations to determine if they were appropriate, based on their perception of public agreement. Adjustments were made where compelling reasons for modifications existed and were fully documented.

Step 3—Adjustments were made to ensure that enough areas were included in the wilderness category to meet the predetermined mid-level RPA target for accessibility/distribution and low-level targets for landform, ecosystem, and wilderness-associated wildlife characteristics.

Step 4—National Grassland roadless areas were withdrawn from the wilderness category unless they were the only areas available to meet any of the four characteristic targets listed in Step 3.

Step 5—Adjustments were made to ensure roadless areas with high wilderness attribute ratings (based on application of the WARS) were proposed for wilderness or allocated to further planning.

Step 6—Roadless areas with proven, producing, or high-potential mineral and energy resources were moved to nonwilderness or further planning to ensure their potential was not foreclosed. Areas remaining in wilderness that would adversely impact local employment and community stability were moved to the nonwilderness category.

Step 7—Adjustments were made to ensure that mid-level program goals in the RPA Program for both wilderness and nonwilderness uses could be met.

Step 8—Six supplemental decision criteria suggested by the public response were then considered, along with judgment by USFS decision makers, to ensure that allocations resulting from the process to this point were appropriate. Local, regional, and national issues influenced this judgment. Any adjustments made were documented as to rationale.

Step 9—Thus adjusted by the eight previous steps, the preferred USFS alternative was evaluated, along with the 10 alternative approaches in the draft environmental statement, against the decision criteria. The purpose was to determine whether or not the adjusted alternative best met the criteria used in decision making.

Step 10—Regional foresters, the chief of the USFS and his staff, and Department of Agriculture representatives met as a group, assured quality control for all segments of the process results to date, and finalized the allocation of RARE II inventoried roadless areas, based on their perceptions of local, regional, and national needs and interests. The result of this decision-making step was the proposed action for the RARE II areas.

Recommendations of RARE II
The final RARE II EIS was published on January 4, 1979, approximately one and one-half years after the initiation of the study. It called for wilderness allocation of 624 areas totaling 15,008,838 acres, nonwilderness designation of 1,981 areas totaling 36,151,558 acres, and further planning for 314 areas totaling 10,796,508 acres. The document recommended the proposed wilderness areas to the Ninety-sixth Congress for legislative action and indicated that no activities would be permitted that might alter their wilderness qualities. Areas recommended for nonwilderness would be made available to multiple-use activities on April 15, 1979. Areas listed for further study would remain undeveloped until their status could be reviewed more thoroughly under routine USFS land and resource management planning process. Until a final recommendation was made on these areas, no commercial timber harvesting would be allowed, and exploration and leasing for oil, gas, and energy minerals would be permitted only under rigid stipulations.

When the RARE II results came forward, the environmentalists were disappointed. Only about one-

quarter of the national roadless areas were being recommended for wilderness; another one-sixth of the lands were allocated to further planning.

The environmentalists became even more critical about the distribution of proposed wildernesses. Of the approximately 15 million acres recommended for wilderness, 5 million were on the Tongass National Forest. The environmentalists had also expected a much larger recommendation for the further planning category. Indeed, as late as the final months of 1978, Cutler had stated that as much as half of the RARE II study acreage would be placed in the further study category. But pressure for prompt and decisive allocations led the USFS to recommend wilderness or nonwilderness designation for all but 11 million acres. Of this 11 million acres, much had just recently been committed to further study by the 1977 Montana Wilderness Study Act (Roth 1984).

Roth (1984) reported that the Carter administration was also troubled by RARE II. It had made a deal with timber industry not to change the RARE II recommendations in return for a promise of support for the president's proposed Department of Natural Resources. It had hoped to stay out of RARE II arguments, but in the end was drawn into the debate when its Department of Energy and Office of Management and Budget clashed with the Environmental Protection Agency and the Council of Environmental Quality (CEQ) over the final draft of the RARE II EIS. Three alternatives were drawn up for Carter's decision: a small amount of wilderness reflecting industry views, the more moderate USFS RARE II proposal, or the environmentalists' much larger wilderness proposal. Carter chose the middle ground: the final RARE II recommendations would stand virtually unchanged (Roth 1984).

THE COURT INTERVENES:
CALIFORNIA VS. BERGLAND
The final RARE II EIS called for the release to nonwilderness uses of those national forest roadless areas recommended for nonwildernesses during the first cycle of forest plans mandated by the NFMA. These "released" areas became the center of controversy in 1979 and into the 1980s.

In California, the general sense was that the wilderness issue should not be settled quickly, and RARE II recommendations for the state reflected this feeling. Of the approximately 6 million acres in California considered by RARE II, about 1 million were recommended for wilderness, 2.4 for nonwilderness, and 2.6 million were placed in the further study category. Still, there was controversy. For example, the Trinity County Board of Supervisors

created a philosophically mixed committee to study the RARE II recommendations for the Shasta-Trinity National Forest. This committee recommended that 48 percent of the roadless acreage become wilderness, whereas the initial RARE II recommendations called for only 17,000 acres out of the total of 449,000 acres, or about 4 percent. The USFS informed the board of supervisors that the RARE II recommendations responded to the larger picture—to a variety of national, regional, and local issues. It could not and would not take a county position. This position did not sit well, either with the board or with many influential Congressmen (Roth 1984).

The Shasta-Trinity controversy soon became a test of the entire RARE II process. Against the wishes of both The Wilderness Society and the Sierra Club, Huey Johnson, director of the California Resources Agency, sued the USFS and sought a court injunction against the release of 46 California study areas to nonwilderness uses. Once again, the institution of last resort was the courts. Johnson, in *California vs. Bergland,* contended that the programmatic RARE II analysis did not meet the requirements of NEPA, and on January 8, 1980, the district court agreed. The court enjoined the 46 areas from development, and indicated that before there could be any change on status of these areas, an EIS for each area would have to be prepared. In October 1982, the Ninth Circuit Court of Appeals upheld the lower court ruling (Roth 1984).

As a result, Assistant Secretary of Agriculture for Natural Resources and Environment, John Crowell, in the new Reagan administration, directed the USFS to reevaluate all RARE II recommendations within the ongoing land use planning process. His inclusion of *all* areas caused environmental groups to fidget; the further analyses might cause areas recommended *for* wilderness by RARE II to be dropped. Congressmen and the USFS squirmed at the thought of another time-consuming and expensive study. Also, Crowell called for proceeding with any activities currently planned in areas recommended for nonwilderness uses unless there was a specific court injunction against it. To many environmentalists, this seemed to violate the implications of the California court injunction.

RARE II Summary

By the early 1980s, RARE II had accomplished much. A comprehensive and careful inventory of USFS roadless areas had been completed, including maps, lists of wilderness attributes, ecosystem representation, extent and content of public involvement, and descriptions of commodity tradeoffs. The USFS,

Carter administration, and general Reagan administration supported wilderness designation for about 15 million acres of national forest lands and further study for 11 million acres. Just how legislation to protect these areas would come forward was unclear, and there was uncertainty over the final resolution of the areas released for nonwilderness uses. Suggestions for a third RARE study had little support. At the same time, the Crowell directive to study these lands under the normal USFS land management planning process seemed to acknowledge that the RARE II process had failed to achieve a prompt resolution of the wilderness allocation issue and a coordinated national evaluation of roadless lands.

A recent analysis of the effect of the data collected during RARE II on the eventual decisions regarding wilderness designation in Arizona, Idaho, and Utah reported that information about the renewable and nonrenewable resource potential of areas was relatively unimportant in explaining designation of an area for wilderness, nonwilderness, or further planning. Mohai and Verbyla (1987, p. 21) conclude that "wilderness signatures and WARS were consistently among the best predictors of designation." But many areas that were designated as nonwilderness did not have high resource potential, while many areas with high resource development opportunity were recommended for wilderness. Their analysis confirms the fact that rational and empirical analyses based on hard data play only a limited role in the highly politicized environment surrounding decisions about wilderness.

U.S. FOREST SERVICE WILDERNESS ALLOCATIONS IN THE 1980s

Three issues have dominated national forest wilderness allocations in the 1980s, and they reflect important consequences stemming from RARE II. A question faced early in the decade concerned the adequacy of the RARE II analysis as a programmatic EIS. The *California vs. Bergland* court decision indicated that the final RARE II recommendations did not constitute an acceptable EIS for certain areas in California, but no one—not the USFS, commodity interests, or environmentalists—wanted another extensive roadless area study to develop site-specific EISs. A second major controversy involved the permanence of release of areas recommended for multiple uses other than wilderness by RARE II. The timber industry and the USFS preferred permanent or long-term release, *hard release;* this would permit long-term planning for management of commodity

or nonwilderness recreational use of these lands. The environmental community favored short-term release, *soft release*—a situation that would likely provide them opportunities in the future to gain wilderness protection for some of the released land. Finally, the question of how to add areas to the NWPS was asked. Should legislation be drawn up to add single areas or a few areas at a time to the system? Should one omnibus bill be passed that included all or most areas recommended by RARE II? Or should each state involved in RARE II resolve the proposal by means of a legislative bill?

The Statewide Wilderness Bill— The Prototype of the 1980s

The final months of the RARE II study were a time of intense pressure to make final decisions about RARE II lands. As indicated earlier, this pressure resulted in far fewer acres being placed in the further study category than the environmental community had

Fig. 5.2. RARE II was a second effort to break the deadlock on identifying and recommending undeveloped areas in the national forests for wilderness designation. Although RARE II had many criticisms and concerns, it did provide recognition of areas where important wilderness values were found, such as Blodgett Canyon in the Bitterroot National Forest, MT. Photo courtesy of Don Dodge.

expected. The timber industry also lobbied intensely for an *omnibus bill*—a bill that would establish RARE II wilderness areas and permanently release the nonwilderness areas for commodity use. By this time, the commodity interests were acutely aware of the popularity of the wilderness idea among the general public. As long as areas were added to the system on an area or a few-areas basis, a vote for wilderness was a cheap environmental vote for congressmen and senators. The wilderness areas represented environmental protection and involved little controversy for congressmen, typically far from their constituencies. The commodity interests developed a strategy of packaging the RARE II proposals together in comprehensive legislation. This would cause congressmen and senators from 38 states to have to think about how wilderness allocations would affect jobs and quality of life in their own states when they voted on wilderness in other states (Meads 1979).

At the same time, congressmen, too, were more prepared to look at the big picture. As a result of RARE II, politicians were much more aware of the wilderness potential of national forest lands throughout the country. With the data from RARE II, they had a much firmer grasp of where existing and potential areas were, the quality and characteristics of those areas, locations where need was the greatest, and tradeoffs that could be made to meet commodity and wilderness needs (fig. 5.2). Thus, they were prepared to deflect the emotional appeals of single-interest, grassroots commodity or environmental groups.

The environmental community opposed the omnibus bill approach from the beginning. These groups had a 15-year history of successful influence on the wilderness allocation process, and their strategy had been largely based on grassroots organizations. These groups influenced local forest supervisors and congressmen. To move the locus of power to arbitrators of one comprehensive bill in Washington, DC, could have a devastating effect on the membership. Second, with an omnibus bill, many favorite areas of local environmental groups or their congressmen inevitably would be lost in compromise. Many would not even be considered because they were not on the RARE II list. Finally, most discussion of an omnibus bill included some sort of permanent release to commodity use of areas not recommended by RARE II for wilderness or wilderness study. The environmental groups feared this most of all, for it would forever prevent them from lobbying for wilderness protection for many areas which they felt were still deserving wilderness candidates.

By this time, individual state delegations, tired of inactivity on the omnibus bill, feeling pressure

from their own constituencies, and wanting to seize the initiative, began to put forward statewide bills—bills that responded to the RARE II recommendations for their state. This approach was a logical extension of the way Congress had done business in the past, when a local congressman typically sponsored a bill to designate areas in his district. With the more comprehensive data contained in RARE II, the state delegation members would negotiate among themselves to submit a bill that was acceptable to them. Such statewide bills rapidly became the norm in the 1980s; virtually all national forest wilderness added to the system in this decade has been included in state bills.

Sufficiency Language

The *California vs. Bergland* decision was, on the face of it, a clear victory for environmentalists. The decision, however, raised questions about the sufficiency of the entire RARE II process; if confirmed, this could have set the stage for another national review (Allin 1982). Yet, the mood of Congress in the late 1970s and early 1980s was not in favor of further delay, study, and expense with respect to wilderness evaluation. National leaders of the environmental groups feared a legislative backlash and perhaps a permanent release of nonwilderness RARE II lands. Congressman Tom Foley (D-WA) had introduced legislation in late 1979 that would have mandated immediate nonwilderness management for the 36 million acres recommended for nonwilderness on RARE II by the administration. It also would have required nonwilderness management by January 1, 1985, for any area in the national forests not given statutory wilderness protection by that time. This would have effectively fixed the size of the National Forest Wilderness System at the level set aside at that date (Allin 1982).

The California wilderness bill provided an opportunity for compromise. Congressmen Phil Burton (D-CA), "Bizz" Johnson (D-CA), and John Seiberling (D-OH), chairman of the House Public Lands Subcommittee, convened a meeting of representatives of industry, environmental groups, and the USFS to settle the issues of "sufficiency" and "release." The eventual agreement was to place within each statewide wilderness bill a *sufficiency clause*—a statement which said that the RARE II study was sufficient for NEPA purposes. This was to protect against RARE II lawsuits. Implementation of the group's recommendation regarding release language, however, has been fraught with controversy.

Soft or Hard Release

The compromise worked out by the Burton-Johnson-Seiberling meetings called for the release of lands not recommended for wilderness or wilderness study

for one cycle (10 to 15 years) of the planning process required by the NFMA of 1976. When the next generation of plans was prepared, the USFS could study any of these lands remaining roadless for their wilderness potential. This type of release became known as "soft release," or later as "Colorado release" when the terminology was included in the 1980 Colorado wilderness bill. Permanent release became known as "hard release."

The compromise began to unravel with the election of Ronald Reagan in 1980. The leaders of the National Forest Products Association had never been happy with the "soft release" compromise. With the Reagan administration in the White House, they once again lobbied vigorously for permanent release. In early 1981, Senator Hayakawa, with cosponsorship by Senator James McClure (R-ID), the new chairman of the Energy Committee, and Senator Jesse Helms (R-NC), new chairman of the Agriculture Committee, introduced a bill that would not create any wilderness, but listed deadlines after which RARE II roadless lands would be forever off limits to wilderness recommendation. This bill at first appeared likely to pass, for it had the support of a popular administration and powerful members of the Republican-controlled Senate. For the next three years, the environmental lobbyists worked hard to stop this and similar bills in committees.

With the passage of the years, all sides were becoming impatient for a settlement. Grassroots environmental organizations could not understand why release language should hold up the addition of lands that all parties involved had agreed should be placed in the wilderness system. Many felt that the released lands would have been developed by the end of the first generation of management plans anyway, so the negotiations between hard and soft release proponents were largely moot.

With the approach of December 31, 1983—marking the end of new mineral exploration and leasing in wilderness—mining companies mounted a campaign to get the Department of the Interior to lift its administrative moratorium on the processing of claims in existing wilderness. As indicated in chapter 4, such mineral exploration and leasing are legal within wilderness, but because of costs, negative public opinion, and strict USFS regulations, no leases had been issued. Secretary of the Interior James Watt broke from this tradition, considered mineral leasing requests in the Bob Marshall Wilderness of Montana and Washakie Wilderness in Wyoming and actually approved a mineral lease in the Capitan Wilderness of New Mexico. The public outcry to this action was loud and reverberated through Congress. Congressional

committees passed resolutions condemning the proposed mining activity and ordering it to be stopped, and bills were introduced into Congress to permanently ban wilderness leasing.

The environmental groups acted quickly to take advantage of the revived interest in wilderness. They pointed out that even the Bob Marshall Wilderness, crown jewel of the wilderness system, was vulnerable to the commodity interest groups. They then mounted a campaign for passage of a big western state wilderness bill with soft release language—a bill that would act as a precedent for other western states.

The tide for the first time in years was running in the environmentalists' favor. In 1983, the timber industry was in a severe recession, had fewer lobbyists in Washington, and was preoccupied with obtaining relief from money-losing federal timber contracts. The Reagan administration signaled some softening of its position when it testified it would be willing to accept "permanent or long-term release."

The final break occurred when Senator Hatfield (R-OR) began to move his bill forward in the summer of 1983. His pace quickened in 1984 when the Oregon Natural Resources Council, a grassroots environmental group, filed a lawsuit to stop development of any RARE II lands in Oregon based on Judge Karlton's 1980 *California vs. Bergland* decision. Such a lawsuit, if successful, would have a serious negative impact on the troubled timber industry. The Hatfield bill, when introduced in Congress in 1984, contained "Colorado" or "soft" release language.

Meanwhile, the House had passed New Hampshire, Vermont, Wisconsin, and North Carolina bills that included the soft release language. USFS officials expressed concern that an amendment to a forest management plan might, with "soft release" terminology, be considered a revised plan. Thus, a second-generation plan might occur much before the anticipated 10 to 15 years. Senators Helms and Melcher of the Senate Agriculture Committee shared this concern, and Senator Melcher and Congressman Seiberling worked with the USFS to correct this unclear terminology in the bills. This having been accomplished, the bills passed out of the Senate Agriculture Committee.

The final negotiations of the release issue were feverish, with USFS Chief Peterson working closely with Senate and House leaders. Future state bills would have no fixed time period for release, but would simply refer to the forest plans typically lasting 10 to 15 years. During this period, the USFS was not categorically prohibited from managing released land to preserve its wilderness character. It just was not required to do so. Commodity interests had gained

in the final solution by tightening up the definition of a plan revision; this was to ensure that a plan would really run the expected 10 to 15 years. Also, the agreement stipulated that roadless areas less than 5,000 acres, and those areas examined in USFS unit plans before the RARE II study and recommended for nonwilderness use, were released during the first generation of forest plans.

Agreement on the release issue opened the door to rapid wilderness allocation. In the summer of 1984, 18 national forest wilderness bills were passed, adding 6.6 million acres to the NWPS. This was the largest national forest addition in a single session of Congress since passage of the Wilderness Act. About 13.6 million acres were released to USFS multiple-use management.

CLASSIFICATION OF DEPARTMENT OF THE INTERIOR ROADLESS LANDS

Unlike the national forest *de facto* wilderness lands, the Wilderness Act of 1964 provided clear descriptions of National Park Service (NPS) and FWS lands subject to wilderness classification. All roadless lands in excess of 5,000 acres and all roadless islands were to be studied (fig. 5.3). For those areas considered suitable for wilderness designation following agency study, wilderness proposals were to be developed for submission to Congress through the Department of the Interior, the Office of Management and Budget, and the president.

Operating with these guidelines, the Department of the Interior did not have to decide what lands to consider or how to propose them for wilderness classification. But it did have to struggle with the problem of establishing criteria: among its available candidates, which ones should be recommended as wilderness? On what basis? It was eight years after the act passed before official selection guidelines were established in the Interior Department. In the meantime, a beginning had to be made.

Soon after passage of the act, the Interior Department estimated that 22.5 million acres of NPS land and 24.1 million acres of FWS holdings were subject to wilderness study—which increased as new units were added to the National Park and Wildlife Refuge Systems. Eventually, during the 10-year period following the passage of the Wilderness Act, the NPS identified for review 63 units covering more than 28 million acres, while FWS identified 113 units totaling 29 million acres (U.S. Congress 1973).

The review was very slow in reaching Congress. Only one area, the Great Swamp National Wildlife

Fig. 5.3 The secretary of the interior was instructed to review all roadless areas 5,000 acres or larger in the NPS and was to recommend which should become wilderness. Hidden Valley, viewed from a ridge above Avalanche Lake, Glacier National Park, MT, was recommended for wilderness classification. Photo courtesy of Richard Behan.

Refuge in New Jersey, was submitted and classified during the first five years of the act. The first NPS areas, Crater of the Moon National Monument in Idaho (43,000 acres) and Petrified Forest National Park in Arizona (50,000 acres), were not added to the NWPS until eight years after passage of the act.

Just why the process moved so slowly is not completely clear. Allin (1982) contends that the NPS had little enthusiasm for wilderness because such land use designation would limit its management discretion and prohibit future development for its primary clientele, the touring motorist. Also, early on, the NPS seemed to take a very strict stance on wilderness resource requirements. For example, Director Hartzog made it clear that lands designated as Class III, natural environment areas, would not meet the criteria for wilderness, but instead would be viewed as transition or buffer zones between developed and wilderness lands. Preservationists complained that the sights and sounds of civilization that might be found in these threshold zones were acceptable in wilderness, and that the NPS really was simply trying to retain the option of development of

these zones. Subsequent statements by Director Hartzog confirmed these suspicions (Allin 1982). Also, the NPS developed a policy to exclude any private inholdings within a roadless area from a wilderness recommendation unless federal acquisition of the area was assured. Other nonconforming but legally permitted uses like water-monitoring devices and motorboat patrol zones were also eliminated from wilderness.

The absence of an explicit allocation procedure likely explains some of the delay and difficulty encountered by the NPS and FWS. Traditionally, the NPS had zoned roadless and undeveloped tracts in the individual parks' Master Plans. For example, much of Yellowstone's 2.2 million acres is *de facto* wilderness, zoned roadless in the area's Master Plan. The problem the department faced in meeting the obligations of the Wilderness Act was much the same as that faced by the USFS in its roadless area reviews—determining specific boundaries for wilderness study.

REVIEW CRITERIA

In June 1972, Assistant Secretary of the Interior for Fish and Wildlife and Parks, Nathaniel Reed, issued a memo to the directors of the NPS and the FWS defining criteria to be followed in determining an area's suitability for wilderness designation. These criteria suggest Assistant Secretary Reed had begun to note the shift in public opinion away from "purity" in wilderness allocation decisions. In particular, the memo specified that roadless areas should not be excluded from wilderness consideration by the existence of the following conditions:

1. Existing or proposed use of tools, equipment, structures, or facilities if these are necessary for the health and safety of wilderness users, or the protection of the resource.
2. Prior rights or privileges such as grazing or limited commercial services that are proper for realizing recreational or other wilderness purposes.
3. The existence of unimproved roads, structures, installations, or utility lines, which can and should be removed upon designation as wilderness.
4. Use of the area for research unless it requires permanent structures or facilities not needed for management.

In addition, the following nonconforming uses or facilities should not, by themselves, exclude an area from a wilderness recommendation so long as subsequent legislation designating the area specifically allows them: small structures like primitive boat docks or shelters, controlled burning, natural-appearing lakes created by water development projects, hydrologic devices for monitoring water resources, underground utilities such as gas pipelines and transmission lines, and minimum tools and equipment necessary to maintain the water developments and utilities.

Special provisions should also be included in the wilderness legislative proposals of those areas that are currently surrounded by nonqualifying federal lands, but which in the foreseeable future will qualify, to permit the secretary of the interior to designate such lands as wilderness at the appropriate time. Finally, no portion of a national park or wildlife refuge should be designated as wilderness unless the wilderness designation is compatible with the purposes for which the park or refuge were established.

STUDY PROCESS

The NPS and FWS began their wilderness review with the roadless lands that were under their jurisdiction in 1964. To the extent possible, wilderness study proceeded concurrently with the preparation

of park or refuge General Management Plans (GMP). The process typically had four phases: preliminary study phase, public meetings, final recommendations, and legislative process. The *preliminary phase* included the collection and analysis of basic and field data, preliminary recommendations of wilderness boundaries (if wilderness is recommended), preparation of first draft of the preliminary wilderness suitability study and draft EIS, and briefing of higher agency and departmental officials and the appropriate congressional delegation on the proposal.

Changes in the proposal sometimes result from agency, departmental, and the CEQ review. The *public hearing(s)* provide citizens and organizations an opportunity to comment on the draft proposal. Appropriate notices are listed in advance of the hearing(s) in the Federal Register and local newspapers, and appropriate notification of hearings is sent to the governor of the state and governing board of each affected county. Typically, an informational packet on the issues and concerns regarding the draft wilderness proposal is prepared for distribution. Comments are then recorded and analyzed to aid in subsequent decision making.

The final recommendation phase involves preparation of the final wilderness recommendation given public input, review and approval of final report by agency at regional and Washington offices, submittal of wilderness recommendation and final EIS to the assistant secretary for Fish, Wildlife and Parks for approval, and then to the secretary of the interior. The approved proposal with its final impact statement then goes to Office of Management and Budget and to the CEQ for review and approval. The approved proposal is submitted by the secretary to the president. During the final legislative phase, the president submits his recommendation regarding the proposal to Congress; typically the Washington Office of the agency prepares draft legislation and the transmittal letters from the secretary to the president and from the president to each branch of Congress. A bill or bills including the actual or modified wilderness proposal is then introduced in Congress by a House or Senate member. The process of debate, negotiation, compromise, and eventual passage by committees and the full Congress resembles closely the wilderness bills including USFS lands.

On the face of it, this appears reasonably straightforward. Indeed, NPS and FWS wilderness proposals typically have not involved as much controversy as those on national forests. The prospect of commodity development does not exist on these lands so environmental advocacy groups have focused their attention on the USFS and, more recently,

the BLM. Still, there have been controversies regarding Assistant Secretary Reed's guidelines, agency implementation of those guidelines, and frequent reluctance by a state congressional delegation to carry a legislative proposal forward. As an example, The Wilderness Society (1974-75) argues that the Interior Department's classification guidelines confuse the stringent management criteria in Section 4 of the Wilderness Act with the flexible entry criteria in Section 2. As a result, they contend, Interior Department officials interpret wilderness classification as a decision to cease virtually all management activity unless specific authorization is given in the wilderness legislation for an area. Based on this interpretation, wilderness designation would be rejected in many areas because it would end management activities needed to accomplish objectives of the legislation originally establishing the park or refuge. The Wilderness Society suggests that a management activity needs to meet only a minimum necessity test. Administrators need to demonstrate only that a management activity is the minimum necessary for proper administration of the area both for the purposes for which the park or refuge was originally established and as wilderness. If the activity meets this test, it does not constitute a sufficient reason to disqualify an area for classification as wilderness.

The relationship between the original legislation establishing a park or refuge and subsequent wilderness designation within these areas has also created problems, particularly on National Wildlife Refuges and Game Ranges. Many of the proposals submitted by the FWS following review of their roadless areas recommend against wilderness designation. For example, about 29,000 acres of the 40,000-acre Red Rock Lakes National Wildlife Refuge in Montana was recommended for wilderness (USDI FWS n.d.). The remaining 11,000 acres were judged not suitable because of existing and planned developments to manage waterfowl, especially the trumpeter swan. Field studies of the 45,000-acre Laguna Atascosa National Wildlife Refuge in Texas revealed that, although a portion of the area did qualify as wilderness, such designation would conflict with the primary objective of the refuge, which is to provide habitat for waterfowl. Wilderness designation was not recommended (USDI FWS 1970). Congress concurred in substance with both recommendations, designating 32,350 acres of the Red Rocks Refuge as wilderness and concurring with the FWS recommendation against designation at Laguna Atascosa.

Conflicts between legislative objectives exist despite the declaration in Section 4(a) of the Wilderness Act that wilderness designation is "within and supplemental to" the purposes for which national forests, national parks, wildlife refuges, and game ranges were established. Where a legitimate conflict exists between the goals of wilderness and those of the basic enabling legislation, the organic legislation is generally predominant. For example, where wilderness classification might restrict necessary wildlife management practices on a game range, wilderness designation is limited, rejected, or made with special recognition of the intrusion.

The Department of the Interior also recognizes what are called "potential wilderness additions." This was originally conceived as a designation for areas where clearly nonconforming uses were present (e.g., structures), but which would qualify for wilderness designation once the nonconforming use was removed. In omnibus legislation passed in late 1976, eight national park units, containing 53,506 acres, were identified as potential wilderness additions. Most of these areas were so labeled because of grazing, and it is not altogether clear why they could not have been included in the wilderness because grazing is allowed in wilderness when it is a preexisting right. But under this designation, the secretary of the interior will have authority to establish them as formal wilderness at such time as the nonconforming use ceases.

By 1974, the end of the 10-year study period, the NPS had completed review and submitted wilderness proposals on 56 areas. But controversy, an apparent lack of broad-based public support, lack of a concerted push by environmental groups, or a reluctant state congressional delegation has caused almost 9 million acres of NPS-recommended wilderness to languish before Congress as of April 1985. Yellowstone National Park had a 2-million-acre wilderness proposal, submitted to Congress in 1972, still awaiting congressional action. In 1974, the NPS recommended wilderness designation for 1.9 million acres in Death Valley National Park (CA) and 860,000 acres in Olympic National Park (WA), but these proposals were still not acted on as of February 1988.

Olympic National Park Wilderness Review— A Case Study

A summary of the wilderness study in Olympic National Park will help illustrate the review procedure prescribed by the Wilderness Act for roadless areas 5,000 acres or larger in the national parks, wildlife refuges, and game ranges.

It has been the policy of the NPS to prepare a GMP (formerly called Master Plan) for each area of the NPS to provide the framework for its overall management, public use, and physical development.

To help determine future use, a land classification plan based on area resources is included in the GMP.

In classifying land, the NPS uses the six land classes developed by the Outdoor Recreation Resources Review Commission (ORRRC). These six classes, modified for applicability to the NPS, include:

Class I	High-density recreation areas
Class II	General recreation areas
Class III	Natural environment areas
Class IV	Outstanding natural areas
Class V	Primitive areas
Class VI	Historic and cultural areas

Roadless areas within a park, typically Class V, but sometimes Class III, IV, and VI lands, have usually been managed and preserved in a roadless, natural condition prior to review and proposal for classification as wilderness. Because of the close relationship between national park GMPs and wilderness areas within a park, the review of park lands to develop a recommendation for wilderness designation has usually been carried out in conjunction with a major public review and updating of the park GMP. Such was the case in Olympic National Park. Along with the review and updating of the park GMP, roadless portions of the 870,200-acre park were formally reviewed in a wilderness study. The chain of events leading to a wilderness recommendation for Olympic National Park proceeded as follows.

During 1972 and early 1973, with the help of a NPS planning team comprised of members from the local park staff, the regional office, and the planning division in the NPS Denver Service Center, a new GMP and a preliminary wilderness proposal were prepared for Olympic National Park. The initial draft called for 93 percent of the park to be classified as wilderness. The park contained four roadless units 5,000 acres or larger, and most of the acreage in three of them was proposed for wilderness classification. One unit included the majority of the park (816,650 acres); the other two units were elongated strips of land along the Pacific Ocean comprising 13,160 and 5,080 acres. A fourth unit, the 26,800-acre Mount Angeles Roadless Area, was not proposed for wilderness classification in order to retain long-range options for alternate access development. Also excluded from the preliminary proposal were two 20-acre enclaves in the roadless interior intended for permanent hostels furnishing both food and lodging to future visitors.

In August 1973, this preliminary proposal (along with the new management plan and accompanying draft EIS) was released to other agencies and the public. Public meetings on the GMP and wilderness proposal held in October and November were attended by 500 people. Altogether, nearly 6,000 agencies, persons, and organizations responded to the NPS's preliminary wilderness proposal. From November 1973 through early spring 1974, the NPS analyzed and evaluated their responses and prepared both a final wilderness recommendation and an altered GMP. The final wilderness recommendation eliminated the small areas intended for hostels and recommended the addition not only of these two enclaves but also most of the Mount Angeles unit for wilderness classification. With other minor boundary adjustments, the final wilderness recommendation included 862,139 acres, about 96 percent of the park.

This recommendation was submitted to the Washington office in June 1974 and was transmitted from the NPS to the Department of the Interior and the Office of Management and Budget. A recommendation for wilderness classification of the four units in Olympic National Park, along with 15 other parks and wildlife refuges, was included in a White House message to Congress. Early in 1975, Senate bill 1091 called for designation of an Olympic National Park Wilderness identical to that proposed in the NPS recommendation. About the same time, a bill calling for designation of a slightly larger wilderness (H.R. 5823) was introduced in the House. But no congressional action was taken on either version.

By 1987, the wilderness proposal for the Olympic National Park backcountry still had not been acted on by Congress. This decade of inactivity is instructive for students of the wilderness allocation process. It demonstrates clearly a point that we and others (e.g., Mohai and Verbyla 1987) have made throughout this chapter: the wilderness allocation process is much more than a rational planning process carried out by agency bureaucrats. In this case, the NPS met its legal requirement for wilderness review and submitted a proposal through the White House to Congress. But the wilderness classification process in the final analysis is also a political process, fueled by interested parties and pressure groups who move when they see their values threatened. Allin (1982) has noted that the NPS has often failed to aggressively seek support for wilderness designation, in part because the agency believed its backcountry areas were already being adequately protected by its management practices and because it did not want its management discretion limited. Also, the environmental community in the late 1970s and 1980s has focused its attention and wilderness lobbying efforts at preserving areas threatened the most—the multiple-use lands of the USFS (Allin 1982).

Late in 1987, the political and environmental

climate in Washington, DC had evolved enough to nudge the NPS wilderness proposal forward. In 1984, Congress passed the state's national forest wilderness bill emanating from the RARE II process. Thus, the state's environmental lobby was free to turn its attention to the NPS. More importantly, Senator Dan Evans, a frequent visitor and long time supporter of the Olympic National Park backcountry, decided to retire at the end of the 100th Congress. He wanted to leave a legacy of wilderness protection to the wild country of the national parks he loved. In November of 1987, he asked the NPS to help him draft a wilderness proposal for Olympic, Mount Ranier, and the North Cascades National Parks.

With this opportunity, the NPS worked quickly. On March 15, 1988, the State of Washington's Senators, Dan Evans and Brock Adams, introduced the Washington Park Wilderness Act of 1988 (S. 2165), proposing 871,730 acres in Olympic National Park and large acreages in Mount Ranier and the North Cascades complex for wilderness. A House companion measure (H.R. 4146) was introduced at the same time by Congressman Rod Chandler of Washington. The Olympic wilderness proposals were similar to the NPS recommendation of 862,139 acres back in 1974. The increase in size of about 9,000 acres was made possible by park boundary adjustments and land acquisition during the intervening 14 years, most notably the acquisition of land at Lake Ozette and the extension of park ownership of the Pacific beach to lowest tide line.

Hearings were held on both the Senate and House bills during the summer of 1988, and there was general support for wilderness designation from affected agencies, the city of Seattle, the environmental community, and many public interest groups. The environmental lobby did, however, recommend a slightly larger wilderness proposal by calling for inclusion of the roadless portions of the park's strip of land along the Queets River, the surface area of Lake Ozette, the north shore of Lake Crescent, and an addition of a small, isolated stretch of wild beach along the pacific. Compromises were quickly reached. The Congress accepted the Queets River and wild beach proposal, but rejected the Lake Crescent addition because of inholdings and the Lake Ozette surface due to motorized access across the lake to private dwellings. On November 16, 1988, during the waning days of the 100th Congress, the Congress passed Public Law 100-668, creating 876,669 acres of Olympic National Park as wilderness (fig. 5.4). The long process of review, study, debate, and wilderness designation of a national park backcountry was complete.

Fig. 5.4. A large part of Olympic National Park was designated wilderness in 1988, 14 years after the initial NPS proposal. Photo courtesy of the NPS.

THE BUREAU OF LAND MANAGEMENT

As we have seen, the Wilderness Act of 1964 gave the USFS, the NPS, and the FWS the authority to study, protect, and manage "legal" wilderness on lands under their jurisdiction. The act failed to give comparable authority to the BLM, even though this agency managed 473 million acres of federal land, far more than the other agencies. These lands were the "forgotten lands," vast acreages of the public domain that were never disposed of through the various federal programs to place land in private ownership or never designated for special purposes like national parks or national forests. About 174 million acres were in the conterminus United States, virtually all in the West. Although many of these lands had been impacted by grazing, mining, and primitive low-quality roads, their wilderness values seemed immense. Estimates in the early 1970s of BLM lands in the lower 48 states with wilderness qualities ranged from about 50 million acres to as high as 90 million acres. These lands, along with the BLM lands in Alaska, represent by far the largest block of potential additions to the NWPS.

The Federal Land Policy and Management Act of 1976 (FLPMA, P.L. 94-579) gave the BLM an organic act, a long-needed statement of direction and purpose for the agency. Two sections of the act called on the BLM to study, make recommendations to the president, and ultimately, to manage legally classified wilderness. section 603 instructed the agency to review its roadless lands of 5,000 acres or more and its roadless islands and make recommendations regarding their acceptability or nonsuitability for wilderness desig-

nation within 15 years of passage of the act. The same was to be done for the BLM primitive or natural areas that existed prior to November 1, 1975, with recommendations regarding these areas to go to the president by June 1, 1980. In 10 western states, 53 such areas existed which, with their contiguous roadless lands, amount to 1.2 million acres. They had been established by administrative edict, possessed qualities comparable to those of legally defined wilderness, and were being managed for wilderness values.

Section 202 of the FLPMA mandated the development, maintenance, and revision of land use plans, which among other things gave priority to the designation and protection of areas of critical environmental concern. Under this authority, the BLM is currently studying and developing recommendations for wilderness designation. These lands include roadless parcels less than 5,000 acres in size (and thus not qualifying for study under section 603), but which lie adjacent to existing or proposed wilderness or park areas.

The final legal directive assigning wilderness study initiatives to the BLM was the Alaska National Interest Lands Conservation Act of 1980 (ANILCA, P. L. 96-487). This law withdrew BLM roadless lands in Alaska from wilderness review, but stated that the secretary of the interior at his discretion could periodically study and make wilderness recommendations to Congress. Secretary of the Interior James Watt issued a memorandum on March 12, 1981, directing that no further wilderness inventory and review be done in Alaska, and this memorandum remains in effect. The one exception to this is a wilderness review of the Central Arctic Management Area specifically mandated by the ANILCA legislation.

The Review Process

INVENTORY
The BLM's wilderness review process has three major phases: inventory, study, and reporting. The inventory phase sought to identify lands with wilderness attributes—lands that met the minimum standards for wilderness as defined in the Wilderness Act. The BLM attempted to accomplish this task quickly and anticipated spending more time in the study and evaluation of areas that made the "first cut." The task was enormous, and the BLM selected a two-step approach. During the first step, called the *initial inventory* and conducted between 1978 and 1979, areas identified by the BLM staff and the public as not having wilderness attributes were eliminated from further review. This was done largely by using resource data and maps available in the BLM district

offices, and this process reduced the acreages under consideration to about 50 million acres.

The remaining lands then became the focus of the *intensive inventory.* BLM resource professionals conducted on-the-ground inspections of each area to assess the presence or absence of wilderness characteristics. The public was invited to participate in the field inspections and to review the agency's assessment procedures and recommendations regarding each area. Public response was considerable, more than 10,000 comments were received from across the country. The intensive inventory was essentially completed by the end of 1980, and areas found to possess the basic characteristics of wilderness were designated WSAs. Such areas amounted to 861 areas containing about 25 million acres.

At the time the BLM was doing its inventory, the focus of the interests and efforts of the environmental advocacy groups was on the USFS's RARE II study. As a result, there were fewer challenges of the BLM process than might otherwise have been the case. Still, the 25 million acres were far fewer than the environmental community expected, and there were accusations that the BLM was applying wilderness attribute standards too strictly. For example, debate raged over what constituted a road and whether worn tire tracks across the desert should disqualify an area from wilderness consideration. The displeasure intensified in late 1982 and early 1983 when Secretary of the Interior James Watt removed approximately 85 WSAs, or about 1.5 million acres, from further wilderness study. These WSAs contained *split-estate lands,* (where the federal government owned the surface and someone else owned the subsurface estate, were areas of less than 5,000 acres, or contained more than 5,000 acres, but received a high wilderness rating because of adjacent existing or proposed park or wilderness lands. The Sierra Club, having learned valuable lessons from its legal action against the USFS, sued. The U.S. District Court for the Eastern District of California, in the case of the *Sierra Club vs. Watt,* ruled in favor of the Sierra Club. The court, among other statements, noted that Watt had failed to use good judgment, and it restored the deleted areas to wilderness study.

STUDY
In February 1982, the BLM published its "Wilderness Study Policy: Policies, Criterion and Guidelines for Conducting Wilderness Studies on Public Lands" (USDI BLM 1982). This document specified the BLM's national wilderness program policy, listed and described planning criteria to use in the evaluation of the WSAs, prescribed quality standards for analysis and docu-

mentation, and recommended a framework for integrating the wilderness study process into the agency's multiple-resource planning system. Through this process, the BLM hoped to complete a high-quality study of its WSAs, including full public involvement, by the end of 1987. This would allow four years for mineral review of those areas recommended for wilderness and for making reports to the president. But when additional areas had to be reviewed as a result of the *Sierra Club vs. Watt* decision, this schedule proved to be overly optimistic. Additionally, the secretary of the interior, following the lead of the secretary of agriculture and the USFS, decided to submit all recommendations on a *statewide* basis, rather than on an individual area basis. The revised schedule called for completion of studies for submission starting in 1989 and continuing on into 1991, with all studies being submitted before the 1991 due date.

The overall goal of the WSA study was to determine whether each area, or a portion thereof, was more suitable or for other uses. The BLM's wilderness program policy provided the philosophical underpinnings for the review. Basically, this philosophy is that wilderness is one of the multiple uses of public lands, and therefore the study should be more than just a review of the wilderness potential of the WSAs. The inventory phase had already established that these areas possessed wilderness attributes. The study then should assess the values, resources, and existing and potential uses of the WSAs for wilderness *and* for other commodity or recreational outputs. Also, any recommendation for a WSA should reflect the mix of resource uses and benefits currently provided in the area. The BLM recognizes that wilderness itself is multiple use, providing such benefits as primitive recreational use, wildlife habitat protection, watershed protection, and protection of cultural and archeological resources. The agency also views wilderness as a long-term allocation *and* management commitment. Thus, the capability of the agency to protect wilderness values in the long run is to be a primary consideration in recommendations for a given WSA.

CRITERIA FOR WILDERNESS
RECOMMENDATIONS
From this underlying philosophy of wilderness two criteria were used to direct and justify all BLM wilderness recommendations—both for those judged suitable and those nonsuitable. The first criterion was the amount and quality of an area's wilderness values and the second was manageability. The first criterion acknowledged that although all WSAs had at least minimum wilderness attributes, some were of higher quality than others. Four components or

kinds of wilderness values were measured and recorded: (l) quality of the area's mandatory wilderness characteristics; (2) special features, or quality of the area's optional wilderness characteristics; (3) multiple resource benefits—the benefits to other multiple resource values and uses that wilderness designation could ensure; and (4) diversity in the NWPS.

QUALITY OF WILDERNESS VALUES—The Wilderness Act of 1964 provided the BLM with a list of mandatory attributes—size, naturalness, and solitude or primitive recreation—to be evaluated. Objective information was gathered and fully documented on these and other criteria components for each study area. This information was summarized in matrix classifications and other descriptive methods, but arbitrary and subjective weighting or ranking was not done. The BLM had watched with interest and learned from the problems of the RARE I study.

The BLM recognized that a WSA needed only to "generally appear" natural and have human imprints "substantially unnoticeable" for it to receive a wilderness recommendation. Yet areas with fewer such impacts seemed to have higher wilderness potential than those with more. Thus, during the field study, a general description, the location, the size of the area, and the overall influence of human imprints in the WSA were documented. In addition, whether the imprint was the result of activities occurring inside or outside of the area was noted, and the potential of separating the imprinted portions from the rest of the area and recommending the remainder for wilderness designation was recorded. The BLM recognized that sights and sounds of humans outside a WSA do not necessarily preempt its wilderness classification, and thereby acknowledged the will of Congress expressed in House Report 95-546 accompanying the previously discussed Endangered American Wilderness Act of 1978.

The BLM used a slightly different interpretation of the Wilderness Act's call for the provision of outstanding opportunities for solitude *or* primitive and unconfined recreation than did the USFS. It defined these two attributes—solitude and primitive recreation—differently and directed that if an area had one or the other, it qualified for wilderness. If an area had both attributes, it would possess greater wilderness potential. *Solitude* was defined as the state of being alone or remote from habitation; isolation; or in a lonely, unfrequented, or secluded place. Environmental features can enhance opportunities for solitude. Size and configuration of area, topographic screening, vegetative screening, presence of outside

sights and sounds that enhance or diminish wilderness values, and opportunities for users to find a secluded spot were measured and recorded for each study area. *Primitive* and unconfined types of recreation were activities that provided dispersed, undeveloped recreation which do not require facilities or motorized equipment. A WSA received higher consideration if it either provided for a diversity of such activities or if it offered one activity of outstanding quality.

The Wilderness Act indicates that a wilderness area "*may* also contain ecological, geological, or other features of scientific, educational, scenic or historical value" (emphasis added). The BLM recognized that these attributes are supplemental and not mandatory for an area to be recommended for wilderness. Still, the agency recognized that their preservation enhances wilderness values and, in marginal areas, may alter the final recommendation. Thus, the study guidelines provide for the recording of the abundance of these attributes and the importance of each to the overall value of the area.

The BLM responded to previous direction and actions affecting wilderness classification by giving special consideration to multiple-resource values and uses, such as wildlife habitat and archeological sites, that would be threatened if the area were not given the protective status of wilderness. Also, those WSAs were given greater wilderness value which, if protected in a natural state, had a high likelihood of fostering the return of animals and fishes that were formerly found in the area, or of improving water quality or visual resources within and beyond the boundaries of the WSA.

The final wilderness value component considered was diversity—diversity in ecosystems and landforms represented in the NWPS, balancing the distribution of wilderness areas throughout the country, and, to the extent possible, giving greater consideration to areas located closer to population centers. These initiatives reflect the will of Congress in its efforts to locate wilderness areas closer to the people and a long-standing goal of the federal wilderness resource agencies to preserve examples of all of the nation's ecosystems (fig. 5.5). As USFS had done in its RARE II process discussed earlier, the BLM used the Bailey-Küchler system to map ecosystems, and if an area under study contributed to the diversity of natural systems and features in the NWPS, it received additional wilderness value. On the other

Fig. 5.5. Although not involved in the 1964 Wilderness Act, the BLM subsequently reviewed lands under its management to identify areas for consideration as wilderness. Adding BLM lands to the wilderness system would increase representation of desert ecosystems, as depicted by Cottonwood Point Wilderness in the Arizona Strip District. Photo courtesy of Tom Folks, BLM.

hand, if its ecosystem or landform duplicated that of existing or proposed areas, it was given a lower ranking. The same was true for geographical distribution; areas located in regions with fewer wilderness areas received higher consideration. Finally, areas located within a five-hour drive of population centers of 100,000 people or more were given special consideration.

MANAGEABILITY—In its evaluation of WSAs, the BLM carefully considered whether it could *manage* and *protect* wilderness attributes over the long term. If current or projected resource conditions or uses would make wilderness protection of an area difficult or impossible, its wilderness potential was believed to be substantially lessened. Five factors or assumptions were used in making judgments about management feasibility. First, management problems anticipated from nonconforming but allowable uses were considered. Such uses included mining and grazing. If it was reasonably certain that the nature or intensity of such uses would substantially destroy wilderness values, the study recommendation would be for nonwilderness allocation. Second, the status of the land in the WSA was considered. If someone other than the BLM owned the surface or subsurface rights to the land, the BLM believed that wilderness management would be a problem. Thus, if the WSA contained private inholdings, state lands, valid existing mineral leases or claims, the wilderness rating of the area was lowered. The same was true if a private individual or corporation owned subsurface mineral rights. Third, the BLM evaluated the impact of the guaranteed right of access to any private inholding. Such access generally included the existence or further development of roads through the WSA, over which the BLM had little control. Fourth, the agency adopted a policy of no buffer zones around a WSA, a policy that reflected the view of Congress. Thus, an area would stand alone, and appropriate use and development of commodity resources could occur up to the boundaries of a wilderness area. If such existing or proposed uses would make the management of the wilderness infeasible, the wilderness potential of the area was lowered. Finally, the BLM acknowledged that there would be no change in air quality recommendations as a result of a wilderness recommendation. If existing or proposed uses of land adjacent to a WSA caused or might cause air quality of the area to drop below Class II status, the area would less likely be recommended as wilderness. These judgment criteria indicate that the BLM, like the USFS before it, subscribes to purity in management and recognizes

an integral link between allocation decisions and ease and quality of management. The USFS experience, as we have seen, suggests that the BLM's position on allocation purity might be challenged by public opinion and environmental advocacy groups.

QUALITY STANDARDS FOR WILDERNESS STUDY—In addition to the wilderness attribute and manageability criteria, the BLM also published standards to be used in analysis and documentation of WSAs. The purposes of the standards were fourfold: (1) to ensure consistency in analysis and reporting across the WSAs, (2) to ensure consideration of wilderness value within the agency's multiple-use mandate, (3) to place the wilderness review within the agency's land management planning process, and (4) to ensure that resource analyses and recommendations in study reports meet the requirements of necessary EIS or Environmental Assessments (EA).

The first standard required careful study of the WSA's energy and mineral values, with a view of reducing the nation's dependence on foreign resources vital to our economy and security. Thus, the presence or potential presence of vital metals or fuels in a WSA figured prominently in its wilderness recommendation. Even after a study recommendation was made favoring wilderness allocation, a formal evaluation of the mineral values contained in the WSA would be made by the U.S. Geological Survey/Bureau of Mines before the study report was forwarded to the president.

The next two standards called for consideration and reporting of a range of alternative uses of all or part of the WSA, followed by the reviewing of the impact on other resource values if the area was recommended for wilderness, or upon wilderness values if the area was not recommended for wilderness. In making these analyses, BLM planners reviewed the existence of wilderness and commodity resources within the WSA, and outside the WSA on public or private lands but within the same region. Consideration was given to the impact of land use recommendations on local and regional economies and whether use and development of nonwilderness resources in the area are compatible with management of the area as wilderness.

Standard 4 describes the public involvement process to be used in the analyses, evaluations, and recommendations regarding the WSAs. This process, which includes the general public and state and local governments, seeks to identify issues that the public believes should be considered with respect to a particular WSA, and any values and resources in the WSA that would augment BLM's current information

base. It is also intended to tap public opinions on whether an area is suitable for wilderness designation or more suitable for other resource uses. Wilderness recommendations will not be based exclusively on a vote-counting majority-rule system, but BLM district managers and state directors will consider public input along with the WSA's multiple resources and social and economic values and uses.

The fifth standard requires that consideration be given to any adverse or favorable social and economic effects which designation of wilderness areas would have on local areas. This is a standard planning requirement of all BLM unit analyses, and is accomplished through guidance contained in the BLM's Social and Economic Policy and Action Plan. Finally, FLPMA and BLM planning regulations require that wilderness study teams document the extent to which any recommendation is consistent with fully approved and adopted resource-related plans of state and local governments. If a state or local government informs the BLM that all or part of a WSA report is inconsistent with that government's policies, the BLM will respond to this comment, explaining how the inconsistency was resolved and why. If the current state or local plan is generally consistent with the BLM policies and programs, every effort is to be made to mitigate the impacts of inconsistencies caused by a wilderness study report.

REPORTING

The wilderness *study* process ends with the state director's decision adopting a preliminary wilderness recommendation for the WSAs in his state. The wilderness *reporting* process represents the roles of the director, the secretary of the interior, and the president in acting on the state director's preliminary recommendation. A somewhat different process is used for those areas found suitable by the BLM director for wilderness versus those he decides are unsuitable. For those areas with a wilderness recommendation, the director requests a formal mineral survey by the U.S. Geological Survey/Bureau of Mines. Upon completion of the survey, the state director reviews the initial WSA recommendation in light of the mineral survey result. If no change is called for, he submits the initial recommendation along with the mineral report to the BLM director for final acceptance. With the BLM director's concurrence, the recommendation is submitted to the assistant secretary for Land and Water Resources, then to the secretary of the interior, and ultimately to the president.

But if the findings of the mineral survey suggest that the initial recommendation is inappropriate, then the state director returns the proposal to the appropriate district manager for a revised recommendation. His new recommendation with appropriate supporting information then proceeds up through the agency and departmental decision hierarchy as described above. If the BLM director, on the initial finding of the state director, makes a recommendation against wilderness, the recommendation proceeds directly to the assistant secretary. With his concurrence, the "nonsuitable" proposal moves on to the secretary of the interior and then to the president.

**Congressional Action on
BLM Wilderness Recommendations**
The BLM appears to be the motherlode of wilderness activity. Literally millions of acres of roadless lands have been inventoried and evaluated with relatively little controversy. Millions of acres appear to have high wilderness value, but many of these lands also contain valuable nonwilderness resources. At this time the final reporting process has not been completed for most states, and little congressional action has been taken. As of March 1989, only 466,949 acres of BLM land had been classified as wilderness.

Over the next 10 years, as the process of debate and passage of state bills involving national forest land nears completion, we anticipate that the attention of the environmental groups, commodity groups, and the general public will turn to the "forgotten lands." At that time such issues as wilderness inventory criteria, the requirement of allocation purity to ensure quality management, and the relative value assigned to the multiple resources of the WSAs in the wilderness recommendations are certain to generate controversy, debate, and compromise. The final outcome, yet to be determined, could add up to 25 million acres, and strongly influence the character and quality of the NWPS.

ALASKA—A SPECIAL CASE?

About 90 percent of Alaska is *de facto* wilderness and the epitome of the last frontier. This vast area (375 million acres) is worth special attention if only because it appears to be a cornucopia of natural resources, including wilderness. It is also a study in special problems related to the disposition of public lands to Alaskan natives and state and federal land management agencies.

DISPOSITION OF THE
ALASKAN PUBLIC DOMAIN

Since its acquisition from Russia in 1867, most of Alaska has remained in federal ownership. But with the impending passage of the Alaskan Statehood Act in 1958, pressures for the transfer of much of this land to the state to facilitate economic development began to grow. Congress responded by granting the state a generous package of land rights. It was given full title to the submerged lands of the continental shelf, estimated at 35 to 45 million acres. It was allowed to select 104 million acres from the federal domain along with full title to all mineral rights on these state-selected lands. Moreover, Alaska was to receive 90 percent of the revenues from mineral leasing on all those lands remaining under federal jurisdiction, twice the percentage other states received (Allin 1982).

A major omission in the disposal of lands to the state was any mention of claims by Alaskan natives. A 1961 Supreme Court decision ruled that native claims against selections made by the state could continue, but it also ruled that because the federal government had clearly given the state the right to select, such selections could continue. The potential legal nightmare such rulings created was headed off by the decision of then Secretary of the Interior Stewart Udall to freeze all further land transactions until such time that Congress could settle the native claims issue. Udall's temporary freeze was replaced by Public Land Order Number 4582 halting the selection process until the end of 1970. Alaska Governor Walter J. Hickel, arguing that the state's economic future was stymied because 95 percent of Alaska remained in federal ownership, attempted to have the Land Order set aside, but was unsuccessful (Allin 1982).

The issue was further confounded in 1968 with the discovery of vast oil reserves on Alaska's North Slope. In order to capitalize on these vast reserves, it became immediately apparent that a pipeline from the oil fields to an ice-free port on Alaska's southern coast would need to be constructed. The pipeline, estimated to be 800 miles long, would cross federal land subject to the Public Land Order. The pipeline also represented an intrusion on wilderness comparable to the construction of the railroads across the western United States a century earlier (Allin 1982). A legal resolution of the native claims was badly needed.

After extensive debate in Congress, the Alaska Native Claims Settlement Act (ANCSA) was passed in 1971. ANCSA terminated the land freeze imposed by the Land Order. The secretary of the interior was directed to withdraw up to 80 million acres suitable for addition to the four existing conservation systems; that is, national forests, national parks, fish and wildlife refuges, and wild and scenic rivers (these were the so-called [d][2] lands, referring to the section of ANCSA where the instructions for withdrawal were contained). This was to be completed within nine months and lands withdrawn by the secretary would generally not be available for selection by the state or by the natives. The legislation also contained language that allowed the secretary to withdraw an unspecified amount of land "to insure that the public interest in these lands is properly protected" (Allin 1982, p. 217; these were referred to as the [d][l] lands). This led some conservationists to recommend that as much as 50 million acres be set aside in addition to the 80 million acres specifically called for.

ANCSA authorized the passage of 40 million acres to the ownership of native villages or newly formed native corporations. Each Alaskan village was permitted to withdraw 23,040 acres (36 square miles). In addition, each of the 12 native corporations was allowed to withdraw an amount of land prescribed by formula in the law.

In late 1972, Interior Secretary Rogers C. B. Morton announced his plans for Alaskan land withdrawal. More than 240 million acres were involved; a little more than 80 million acres were withdrawn for addition to existing conservation systems, including nearly 19 million acres in three new national forests, 32 million acres in new national parks, and 32 million acres in new national wildlife refuges. In addition, 20 new units in the National Wild and Scenic River System were recommended. Also, 47 million acres were withdrawn under the (d)(l) authority. In addition, 4.5 million acres were tied up in pipeline corridors mandated by ANCSA and another 112 million acres were withdrawn as a pool from which the natives could select their 40 million acres. His recommendations drew fire from almost every quarter. The state was alarmed by the large withdrawal (47 million acres) under the (d)(l) provisions. Wilderness groups were opposed to the recommendation to establish three new national forests in Alaska; they contended that commodity exploitation under multiple-use management would continue on BLM lands remaining after selections were completed and therefore no national forest lands were needed. They were also concerned that although the USFS had committed itself to the designation of WSAs on these new forests, there was no guarantee of large-scale wilderness protection for them (Allin 1982).

Thus, after the passage of two major laws regarding the disposition of the public domain in Alaska,

there still remained sharp disagreements over the future management direction of the land and resources in the state. The continuing dispute triggered yet another effort to arrive at a legislative solution to the dilemma. Beginning in 1973 and extending until 1980, probably the most significant congressional and public debate over natural resource allocation raged. On the one side, the State of Alaska and its allies argued for the assertion of states rights and the opportunity for economic development. On the other side, conservation organizations argued that the last great opportunity to preserve a major portion of the nation's wild heritage was at hand and that we could not afford to lose it.

Given the large stakes, it is not surprising that Congress found it difficult to reach a satisfactory resolution over the future of the Alaskan lands.[1] Conservationists were highly organized. The heart of this group was the Alaska Coalition, a diverse collection of state and national organizations ranging from the Sierra Club and The Wilderness Society to the United Auto Workers and National Council of Senior Citizens. The State of Alaska led the opposition, along with local developmental and commodity interests.

The inability of Congress to reach a satisfactory compromise on the issue eventually led to an unusual series of events. In 1978, Secretary of the Interior Cecil Andrus announced that the Carter administration was losing patience over the lack of progress and that it was exploring ways in which it might take action on its own behalf to solve the problem. When Congress failed to respond with any positive proposal, the Carter administration made good on its promise. In late 1978, Secretary Andrus withdrew 110 million acres for three years under the authority of the FLPMA. Two weeks later, President Carter invoked the Antiquities Act of 1906 to create 17 new national monuments covering 56 million acres of the 110 million withdrawn by Andrus. In one stroke, President Carter had more than doubled the size of the NPS. In addition, under presidential direction, Secretary Andrus began the process of creating 40 million acres of new national wildlife refuges in Alaska, and Secretary of Agriculture Bob Bergland withdrew 11 million acres of existing national forests to prevent mineral entry and state selection (Allin 1982). The executive branch had seized the initiative from the legislative branch in a dramatic fashion.

But a legislative solution to the future of resource management in Alaska was still required. After two more years of congressional debate, it became apparent that some form of compromise had to be reached. The issue came to a head with the national elections in 1980. Not only was the Carter administration voted out of office, but a number of key congressional supporters of conservation legislation in Alaska were also defeated. As a consequence, conservation interest groups agreed to accept legislation that, despite some provisions which they did not favor, was nevertheless acceptable. On December 2, 1980, in the closing days of his administration, President Carter signed the ANILCA into law. The new law had profound implications for the future of wilderness.

1. See pp. 222-256 in Allin 1982 for a detailed discussion of the congressional debate on the issue.

THE ALASKA NATIONAL INTEREST LANDS CONSERVATION ACT

The ANILCA set aside 104.3 million acres of national parks, wildlife refuges, wilderness areas, and other conservation units in Alaska. Of these acres, approximately 56 million were placed in the NWPS. Wilderness acreage breakdown by agency was 32.4 million for the NPS, 18.6 million for the FWS, and 5.4 million for the USFS. ANILCA stated that designated wilderness shall generally be managed according to the provisions of the Wilderness Act of 1964, but it made several exceptions to the letter or the spirit of the 1964 act (fig. 5.6). This was to minimize impacts on existing use or users of the wilderness lands and to permit some economic expansion. A few of these exceptions were similar to special provisions made for certain wilderness areas in the lower 48 states, but many were new to the system. Exceptions such as

Fig. 5.6. With the passage of ANILCA in 1980, wilderness in AK was ensured. Certain uses, such as cabins and floatplanes, shown at Admiralty Island National Monument Wilderness, were permitted so visitors could cope with adverse weather and bears. Photo courtesy of the USFS.

providing public cabins recognized the unusual severity of Alaska weather and the danger of being attacked by bears; provisions made for subsistence hunting and gathering recognized the special relationship between the rural Alaska residents and the wild resources on which they depend. ANILCA did state that its special provisions apply *only* to Alaska wilderness; they are not to be viewed as precedents to alter wilderness management and future wilderness legislation in the lower 48 states (The Wilderness Society 1984). Further discussion of the management implications of ANILCA is included in chapter 4.

ANILCA upheld the sufficiency of the RARE II EIS in Alaska. But it did specifically require an investigation of a 2.1-million-acre tract called the Nellie Juan-College Fiord WSA in the Chugach National Forest. In addition, the Chugach National Forest was to proceed with recommendations regarding the wilderness suitability of 14 areas identified during RARE II for further study. The final EIS prepared by the forest recommends 1.7 million acres (29 percent of the total forest area) for wilderness. No further study areas are located on the Tongass National Forest; 30 percent of the Tongass is presently classified wilderness. ANILCA also specifies that unless Congress expressly authorizes it, the USFS shall not conduct any further statewide roadless review and evaluation, thereby precluding the possibility of a RARE III in Alaska.

SUMMARY

The Wilderness Act of 1964 established instant wildernesses, described a general procedure for adding additional areas to the system, and gave only broad guidelines on the kinds of lands most suitable for wilderness designation. In this chapter, we have traced the process of the growth and evolution of the system. The system is today far larger, with a greater diversity of areas distributed more evenly throughout the country than any of the supporters of the wilderness idea could have anticipated. This evolution represents a classic example of the forces that shape natural resource policy in the country.

There have been stresses and strains as the four federal resource agencies with wilderness jurisdiction have responded to the evolving cultural meanings of wilderness. Important lessons have been learned. Although the allocation process requires a sound technical basis in identification and inventory of wilderness attributes, it is largely a political process. As such, the American public has been the ultimate judge of the disposition of roadless lands.

Environmental groups learned this early on, and they have had a far greater influence on land allocation than initially expected. With open access to wilderness review processes, ordinary citizens can have a profound influence on congressional wilderness allocations. Agency planners and policy makers struggled to understand and institutionalize the wilderness ideal, to integrate wilderness within their traditional resource programs, and to retain a position of leadership regarding wilderness. At first there were frequent problems, controversies, and even impasses. When this occurred, the courts were at times the final arbitrator. Gradually, the agencies have found a more even and defensible course. This they have done by taking a comprehensive planning approach; integrating wilderness into long-standing planning processes, recognizing that wilderness study involves two very different issues, assessment and evaluation; anchoring assessment in wilderness attributes defined in law; keeping in touch with public values when making evaluative judgments; and working closely with individual members of Congress and congressional committees who make the final allocation decisions.

The most difficult task facing the wilderness resource agencies remains keeping in touch with the slowly but inevitably evolving cultural definition of wilderness in the United States and applying it to the management of the remaining roadless areas. Such sensitivity seems necessary when recommending which lands should be wilderness, when integrating wilderness and the other multiple uses of public lands, and ultimately when making individual wilderness management decisions. We have seen the drift of public opinion away from rigidly applied wilderness attribute standards when making allocation judgments. This drift may continue, or the pendulum may shift back again. In the final analysis, this evolving process leads to diversity in the NWPS, a diversity which can lead to stability in a broad base of political support and a resource capable of providing for a variety of human needs.

STUDY QUESTIONS

1. Discuss the factors that led to the RARE I process. What were some of the deficiencies of RARE I and how might they have been corrected? What were some of the benefits of RARE I?
2. In your judgment, how well did RARE II correct the deficiencies of RARE I? What problems still remain?
3. What were some of the factors that led to the increasing use of "omnibus" state wilderness legislation?
4. Describe the concepts of sufficiency, hard release, and

soft release as they apply to the wilderness classification process. How have they been employed in the state where you live?

5. Discuss the problems in obtaining wilderness designation of areas like Yellowstone, Yosemite, and Olympic National Parks. What are some of the reasons underlying the lack of progress?

6. Describe the various opportunities and problems facing the wilderness classification of lands under the administration of the BLM.

7. Describe the relative roles and importance of environmental advocacy groups versus the agencies' wilderness study processes in generating and fueling the wilderness allocation process.

8. How have decisions by the courts influenced the wilderness allocation process, and the size and nature of the NWPS?

REFERENCES

Allin, Craig W. 1982. The politics of wilderness preservation. Westport, CT: Greenwood Press. 304 p.

Bailey, Robert G. 1976. Ecoregions of the United States. Ogden, UT: U.S. Department of Agriculture, Forest Service, Intermountain Region. Map.

Costley, Richard J. 1972. An enduring resource. American Forests. 78(6): 8-11.

Davis, George D. 1988. Preservation of natural diversity: the role of ecosystem representation within wilderness. Paper presented at the National Wilderness Colloquium; 1988 January 13-14; Tampa, FL. Sponsored by U.S. Department of Agriculture, Forest Service, Southeastern Forest Experiment Station, Athens, GA.

Hendee, John C. 1977. Public involvement in the United States Forest Service roadless area review: lessons from a case study. In: Coppock, Rerrance; Sewell, Dennis, eds. Public participation in planning. New York: Wiley: 89-103. (Reprinted from paper delivered at Seminar on Public Participation; July 1974 Edinburgh, Scotland; University of Edinburgh.)

Hendee, John C. 1986. Wilderness: important legal, social, philosophical and management perspectives. In: Kulhavy, David L.; Conner, Richard N., eds. Wilderness and natural areas in the Eastern United States: a management challenge; 1985 May 13-15; Nacogdoches, TX. Nacogdoches, TX: Stephen F. Austin University, School of Forestry: 5-11.

Küchler, A. W. 1966. Potential natural vegetation (map). Natural Atlas of the United States. Washington, DC: U.S. Department of the Interior, Geological Survey: 89-92.

Meads, Lloyd. 1979. Speech before the Western State Legislative Forestry Task Force, 8/1/79. Sierra Club records, Forest Service History Section.

Milton, William John, Jr. 1975. National Forest roadless and undeveloped areas: develop or preserve? Land Economics. 51(2): 139-143.

Mohai, Paul; Verbyla, David L. 1987. The RARE II wilderness decisions. Journal of Forestry. 85(1): 17-23.

Roth, Dennis M. 1984. The wilderness movement and the National Forest: 1964-1980. FS-391. Washington, DC: U.S. Department of Agriculture, Forest Service. 70 p.

Strickland, Ronald Gibson. 1976. Ten years of congressional review under the Wilderness Act of 1964: wilderness classification through affirmative action. Washington, DC: Georgetown University. [Pages unknown]. Dissertation.

U.S. Congress. 1973. Ninth annual wilderness report. House Document No. 93-194. Washington, DC: U.S. Government Printing Office. [Total pages unknown].

U.S. Department of Agriculture, Forest Service. 1973. Final environmental statement: roadless and undeveloped areas. Washington, DC. 690 p.

U.S. Department of Agriculture, Forest Service. 1978. Roadless area review and evaluation (RARE II). Draft environmental impact statement 78-04. Washington, DC. 112 p.

U.S. Department of Agriculture, Forest Service. 1979. Final RARE II environmental impact statement. Washington, DC. 113 p. plus appendices.

U.S. Department of the Interior, Bureau of Land Management. 1982. Wilderness study policy: policies, criteria and guidelines for conducting wilderness studies on public lands. Federal Register. 47(23): 5098-5122.

U.S. Department of the Interior, Fish and Wildlife Service. [n.d.]. Red Rock Lakes Wilderness proposal. [Place of publication unknown]. 16 p.

U.S. Department of the Interior, Fish and Wildlife Service. 1970. Laguna Atascosa Wilderness study area. [Place of publication unknown]. 12 p.

The Wilderness Society. 1974-75. The wilderness system: a report covering every existing or proposed wilderness. The Living Wilderness. 38(128): 38-47.

The Wilderness Society. 1984. The Wilderness Act handbook. Washington, DC: The Wilderness Society. 64 p.

Worf, William A. 1980. Two faces of wilderness—a time for choice. Idaho Law Review. 16: 423-437.

ACKNOWLEDGMENTS

Craig W. Allin, Professor of Political Science, Department of Politics, Cornell College, Mt. Vernon, IA.

Upon passage of the Wilderness Act of 1964, 54 areas managed by the USFS became "instant wilderness." Among these was the Three Sisters Wilderness in OR, consisting of (from left) South, Middle, and North Sister Peaks. Photo courtesy of the USFS.

6

The National Wilderness Preservation
System and
Complementary Conservation Areas

George H. Stankey was lead author for this chapter.

INTRODUCTION

This chapter examines the extent of the National Wilderness Preservation System (NWPS)—how much there is, where it is, and who manages it. We also discuss the early origins and possibilities for growth of the NWPS as well as complemental federal, state, and private programs of wilderness protection.

WILDERNESS AND THE ENVIRONMENTAL MODIFICATION SPECTRUM

In chapter 1, we described the concept of the *environmental modification spectrum*, the notion that a continuum of environmental conditions exists, ranging, as Nash (1982) has succinctly described, from "the paved to the primeval." At one end, cities and urbanized landscapes dominate; at the other, primeval conditions characterize the setting. Passage of the Wilderness Act led to the creation of a formal system of protected natural areas at the primeval end of this spectrum. But protection of areas with outstanding natural quality is not limited to the NWPS. Through a series of laws and administrative actions, other types of areas also have been preserved and managed because they possess unique natural qualities. For example, rivers designated as "wild" within the Wild and Scenic Rivers System (P.L. 90-542) are assured protection against dams and other developments along their shorelines. Several states have implemented programs of wilderness protection to complement the federal program. Numerous areas of outstanding scientific value have been preserved under Research Natural Area (RNA) designations, frequently with the support of private organizations. Because these other areas also lie at the primeval end of

the spectrum, it is important to understand the ways in which they compliment or conflict with the NWPS.

THE NATIONAL WILDERNESS PRESERVATION SYSTEM

In chapter 4, we discussed the directives contained within the Wilderness Act with regard to the NWPS. Upon passage of the act, a core of 54 areas, totaling 9.1 million acres and administered by the U.S. Forest Service (USFS) in the Department of Agriculture, was brought into the system as "instant wilderness." No Department of the Interior areas were included at the outset.

The act directed the secretary of agriculture to initiate reviews of the 34 primitive areas (a total of 5.4 million acres) and to submit recommendations regarding their future management to Congress within 10 years of the act's passage. These were the areas that underlaid the requirement of affirmative action on the part of Congress in adding any new areas to the NWPS. Similarly, the secretary of the interior was instructed to review lands of the National Park System and Fish and Wildlife Refuge System, also within 10 years, and make recommendations to Congress regarding their suitability as wilderness. As discussed in chapter 5, the act allows additional undeveloped and unroaded lands to be added to the NWPS. For example, in 1975, the so-called Eastern Wilderness Act provided for inclusion of areas east of the 100th meridian, areas which did not qualify for inclusion in the NWPS under the prevailing interpretation of the Wilderness Act. In 1976, Congress passed the Federal Land Policy and Management Act (FLPMA, P.L. 94-579) giving the Bureau of Land Management (BLM) responsibility and authority to study and recommend areas for wilderness designation. From these and other subsequent laws, then, the NWPS is being built.

Where do we stand two decades later? Appendix C presents the NWPS by state and administrative agency as of March 1989; distribution and relative size of the units are shown on the fold-out map, Appendix B (The Wilderness Society 1989). From the original 54 areas and 9.1 million acres, the NWPS has grown to 474 areas covering about 90.8 million acres, a ninefold and tenfold increase in areas and acres, respectively. The average size per area is slightly more than 200,000 acres, more than double the average in 1976 when data for this book were first assembled. This is largely a reflection of the addition of some very large areas in Alaska, such as the Wrangell-Saint Elias Wilderness, covering 8.7 million acres; the

Arctic Wilderness, totaling 8 million acres; and the Gates of the Arctic Wilderness at nearly 7.1 million acres. In all, nearly two-thirds of the wilderness system acreage is in Alaska. Only 67 areas in the system exceed the 200,000-acre average, however, and in the lower 48 states, the average wilderness is approximately 81,000 acres.

The total area of the NWPS is equal to an area approximately the size of Montana and comprises about 4.6 percent of the lower 48 states. The bulk of the areas and acreage is located in Alaska and the western United States, but wildernesses are now located in all but six states: Connecticut, Delaware, Iowa, Kansas, Maryland, and Rhode Island.

The smallest wilderness is the Pelican Island Wilderness in Florida, administered by the Fish and Wildlife Service (FWS) and covering only 6 acres. As discussed in chapter 4, the Wilderness Act defines a wilderness as containing at least 5,000 acres, but qualifies this by stating "or is of sufficient size as to make practicable its preservation and use in an unimpaired condition." In all, 81 areas less than 5,000 acres have been added to the NWPS and many, like Pelican Island, are islands where protection of their wilderness character is possible, despite their size.

Table 6.1 shows the distribution of the NWPS relative to the percentage of the U.S. population and area found in each of the 10 regions of the Census Bureau. The figures in table 6.1 confirm the pattern revealed on the map insert, Appendix B; the NWPS is located predominantly in the western United States. It is also located away from the nation's population; less than 5 percent of the NWPS is located in the eastern United States, where more than one-half of the population resides. Conversely, the western United States has only about 20 percent of the population, but 95 percent of the NWPS. The disparity between population and wilderness is dramatic in Alaska; less than one-tenth of 1 percent of the population is there, but the state contains nearly two-thirds of the entire NWPS, reflecting the relatively limited development that has occurred there.

Figure 6.1 shows the growth of the NWPS, in total and for each of the managing agencies. The system grew slowly during the first few years following passage of the act. As discussed in chapter 5, this was largely because of the time it took the agencies to develop procedures to carry out reviews of potentially suitable areas. During the first decade after passage of the Wilderness Act, the number of areas grew from 54 to 89 and the acreage from 9.1 million to slightly more than 11 million. By the end of the 1970s, the number of areas had doubled, to 118, as had the acreage, to 18.5 million.

Table 6.1. Distribution of NWPS relative to regional population and area.

Region	Percentage of U.S. population	Percentage of U. S. area	Percentage of NWPS
New England (ME, NH, VT, MA, RI, CT)	5	2	<1
Mid-Atlantic (NY, NJ, PA)	16	3	<1
E. No. Central (OH, IN, IL, MI, WI)	18	7	<1
W. No. Central (MN, IA, MO, ND, SD, NE, KS)	7	14	1.5
South Atlantic (DE, MD, DC, VA, WV, NC, SC, GA, FL)	17	8	2.5
E. So. Central (KY, TN, AL, MS)	6	5	<1
W. So. Central (AR, LA, OK, TX)	11	12	<1
Mountain (MT, ID, WY, CO, NM, AZ, UT, NV)	5	24	19.7
Pacific (WA, OR, CA, AK, HI)	14	25	75.6
Other (PR, GU, etc.)	1	<1	0

Source: Statistical Abstracts 1986.

In 1980, the NWPS experienced tremendous growth. Several state omnibus bills were enacted that year, but the growth was fueled primarily by passage of the Alaska National Interest Land Conservation Act (ANILCA, P.L. 96-487). In that single year, 83 units, covering more than 61 million acres, were added; 35 of these, totaling more than 56 million acres, were in Alaska. In one year, the number of areas in the NWPS grew more than fourfold while acreage grew to nearly nine times that of the instant system created in 1964.

The second major growth period occurred in 1984, when 223 units totaling 8.3 million acres were added. Many of these additions were in the eastern and southern United States; average size is small, about 37,000 acres. Only one area was added in 1985—the 13,300-acre Clifty Wilderness in Kentucky. With these additions the NWPS reached a total only 30,000 acres shy of 89 million acres, approximately 4.4 percent of the conterminous 48 states.

As originally passed, the Wilderness Act discussed only the USFS, National Park Service (NPS), and FWS. Passage of the FLPMA in 1976 added the BLM to the list of wilderness management agencies. Appendix C (summary data) shows the distribution of the NWPS among the four agencies.

Almost three-fourths of the *areas* are managed by the USFS, but the NPS manages more of the *acreage*. At present, the BLM manages only a very small percentage of the NWPS (0.5 percent of the acreage), but as the discussion in chapter 5 suggests, its role will almost certainly expand over the next decade. "The FLPMA authorized BLM, which manages more acreage (300 million acres) than any other federal agency, to inventory its lands for wilderness characteristics and make recommendations" (Dorrington

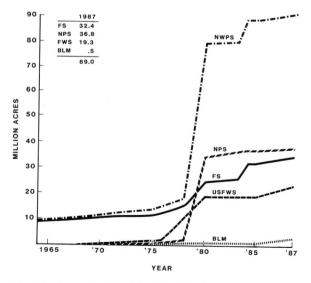

Fig. 6.1. Growth of the NWPS, 1964-86.

1990, p. 4). For each Wilderness Study Area (WSA), the BLM must investigate possible uses for the area, such as, developing resources—oil and gas, minerals, and lumber. The BLM's decisions about wilderness designation of its lands will be the last major addition to the NWPS. "From a biologic diversity standpoint, BLM's holdings are quite significant. Most existing federal wilderness spans moderate to high elevation terrain while BLM lands contain many low elevation ecosystems not currently in the NWPS" (Dorrington 1990, p. 4).

The NWPS should be examined in terms of the kinds of lands that it contains. A major goal, albeit implied, of the Wilderness Act was to help ensure diversity within the nation's wildlands. Many supporters of wilderness have cited the preservation of a diverse, representative sample of ecological variety in the United States as a major reason for having the NWPS. Ecological diversity has never been an explicit criterion driving the wilderness allocation process. As a result, the diversity contained within the system is largely accidental; little systematic effort has been made toward broadening the NWPS's ecological coverage. One exception to this general neglect can be found in the USFS's second Roadless Area Review and Evaluation (RARE II), as discussed in chapter 5.

Ecological variety or *biodiversity* includes an amalgamation of species, genes, communities, ecosystems, landscapes, regions, and biomes. Large wildernesses are more capable of representing native biodiversity at several levels of organization. The following briefly describes the intricacies of biodiversity (Noss 1990 draft). Big wilderness supports complex genetic systems.

> At the species level, viable populations are more likely to be maintained in big wilderness than in smaller areas. At the ecosystem level, the variety of habitats within big wilderness supports many different associations of species. Although each association might be protected separately in a system of smaller reserves, their functional combination at a higher level of organization is not. Only in large wilderness areas can native biodiversity be maintained at the landscape level, i.e., with the full spectrum of environmental gradients and habitats overlaid by mosaics of disturbance-recovery patches in approximate steady-state proportions. Today, only 5 (2 percent) of 261 Bailey-Küchler ecosystem types in the United States and Puerto Rico are represented in designated wilderness in units of 1 million ha or more, all of these in Alaska. Only 50 (19 percent) of these ecosystem types are represented in units of at least 100,000 ha.

Nevertheless, some efforts have been made to assess the extent to which the NWPS achieves coverage of the nation's ecological diversity. The most complete analysis reveals major shortcomings (Davis 1984). By merging Bailey's ecoregion concept and Küchler's mapping of potential natural vegetation, the United States can be divided into 261 distinct ecosystems (Davis 1988). At present, 157 of the nation's 261 ecosystems (60 percent) are adequately represented within the NWPS. Representation is especially poor within the grasslands, deserts, eastern hardwoods, and coastal lowland ecosystems.

It is estimated that an additional 60 ecosystems could be included within the NWPS, primarily through additions of BLM holdings. Even with these additions, if the four federal wilderness management agencies recommend representative examples of each basic ecosystem under their jurisdiction, and if Congress concurs with these recommendations, there would still remain 50 basic ecosystems not represented in the NWPS or in any equivalent state wilderness system (Davis 1984); see table 6.2. These 50 ecosystems are not found within any areas suitable for wilderness designation and under the management of appropriate federal or state authorities. Protection of these areas, if possible at all, would need to occur through different conservation classifications as well as under different jurisdictions.

WILDERNESS IN THE NATIONAL FOREST SYSTEM

As discussed in chapter 4, the first official USFS system of wilderness reservations was created by the L-20 Regulation, implemented in 1929 and creating a system of *primitive areas*. Earlier, some areas had been set aside and called *wilderness areas* by the district forester, the forerunner of today's regional forester. With establishment of the L-20 Regulation, however, these were renamed primitive areas; for example, the Gila Wilderness, New Mexico, established at the prompting of Aldo Leopold in 1924, became the Gila Primitive Area in 1933.

The L-20 Regulation remained in effect for 10 years. During this time, the number of acres set aside in primitive areas grew rapidly. Between 1930 and 1939, the primitive area system grew from 360,444 acres in three areas to 14.2 million acres in 75 areas. This acreage, in fact, was the core from which the "instant wilderness system" established in section 3(a) of the Wilderness Act was derived.

In 1939, the L-20 was replaced by the more rigorous U Regulations, and a gradual process of

Table 6.2. Ecosystems for which no agencies appear to have candidate areas for wilderness classification.

Ecoregion and potential natural vegetation

Laurentian Mixed Forest
  Elm ash forest

Eastern Deciduous Forest
  Oak savanna
  Mosaic bluestem prairie and oak hickory
    forest
  Northern floodplain forest
  Maple basswood forest
  Beech maple forest

Outer Coastal Plain
  Bluestem sacahuista prairie
  Palmetto prairie
  Oak hickory forest

Southeastern Mixed Forest
  Oak hickory forest
  Northeastern oak pine forest
  Southern mixed forest

Willamette Puget Forest
  Cedar hemlock Douglas-fir forest
  Mosaic Oregon oakwoods

Pacific Forest
  Oregon oakwoods
  Coastal sage

Prairie Parkland
  Bluestem prairie
  Blackland prairie
  Bluestem-sacahuista prairie
  Southern cordgrass prairie
  Mosaic of bluestem prairie and oak hickory
  Cross timber
  Fayette prairie
  Oak hickory forest
  Southern floodplain forest

Puerto Rico
  Subtropical dry forest

Prairie Brushland
  Mesquite acacia savanna
  Mesquite live oak savanna
  Mesquite buffalo grassland
  Juniper oak savanna
  Mesquite oak savanna

Tall Grass Prairie
  Bluestem grama prairie
  Sandsage bluestem prairie
  Bluestem prairie
  Northern floodplain forest
  Oak hickory forest

California Grassland
  Saltbush greasewood
  California steppe
  Tule marshes

California Chaparral
  Fescue oatgrass

Great Plains Shortgrass Prairie
  Bluestem grama prairie
  Sandsage bluestem prairie
  Shinnery

Palouse Grassland
  Fescue wheatgrass

Chicuahuan Desert
  Caniza shrub

American Desert
  Mesquite bosques

Everglades
  Cypress savanna

Hawaiian Islands
  Guava mixed forest
  Lama manele forest
  Koa forest

Source: Davis 1984, p. 151.

review and reclassification under the new guidelines was begun. It is interesting to note that between 1939 and 1964 (when the Wilderness Act passed), the system of reserved land grew by only 382,000 acres and 13 areas, or less than 3 percent. Many citizens were frustrated with this slow growth, and some credit that as having brought about a congressionally designated wilderness system.

Table 6.3 outlines the progress of primitive area reclassification between 1939 and 1964, at five-year intervals. Under the U Regulations, three types of areas could be designated: wilderness areas, defined as areas in excess of 100,000 acres; wild areas, defined as areas between 5,000 and 100,000 acres; and roadless areas, defined as areas managed principally for recreational use and maintained in a natural condition.

In the 25 years between establishment of the U Regulations and the passage of the Wilderness Act (1939-1964), slightly more than half of the primitive areas were reviewed. Typically, areas that met the

Table 6.3. Reclassification of USFS primitive areas to wilderness, wild, or roadless status, 1939–64.

Year	Primitive areas		Wilderness areas		Wild areas		Roadless	
	Number	Acres[1]	Number	Acres[1]	Number	Acres[1]	Number	Acres[1]
1939	75	14.2	—	—	—	—	—	—
1944	60	11.3	4	1.4	9	0.3	2	0.8
1949	58	11.2	4	1.4	12	0.5	3	0.8
1954	53	9.5	8	2.9	15	0.5	3	0.8
1959	42	8.2	12	3.9	26	0.9	1[2]	0.8
1964	34	5.4	54	9.1		[3]		[3]

1. Acres in millions.
2. In 1958, the three Superior Roadless Areas were collectively renamed the Boundary Waters Canoe Area.
3. Under terms of the Wilderness Act, all areas designated under the U Regulations were automatically made units of the NWPS and called wilderness.

criteria of the more stringent U Regulations were reclassified, with only a change in name from primitive area to wilderness or wild area. Some areas were not reclassified because of developments that had taken place under the more permissive guidelines contained in the L-20 Regulation. For example, the USFS established the 1.8-million-acre Selway-Bitterroot Primitive Area in 1936. In 1963, 1.2 million acres were redesignated as wilderness under the U-1 Regulation, approximately 216,000 acres were redesignated as the Salmon River Breaks Primitive Area, and the remaining 411,000 acres were declassified either because they were not suitable for wilderness or because other resource values were judged to exceed the wilderness values. In addition, the USFS noted that the deleted areas had been originally designated under the "less exacting standards for Primitive Areas" (Cunningham and Scott 1969). In other cases, several small primitive areas were consolidated into one large wilderness unit. For example, the present Bob Marshall Wilderness in Montana was established in 1940 from three primitive areas: the South Fork, the Pentagon, and the Sun River.

World War II slowed progress on the reviews considerably. Twelve areas had been studied between 1939 and 1941; only five were completed between 1941 and 1949. Progress through the early 1950s was also slow and, as discussed in chapter 4, concern over both the delays in completing the reviews as well as the declassification of portions of the existing primitive areas served to promote interest in establishment of a legally protected system of wilderness protection. When the Wilderness Act passed, 34 primitive areas totaling about 5.4 million acres still had not been reviewed.

The Wilderness Act instructed the secretary of agriculture to review these 34 primitive areas within 10 years and to make recommendations to the Congress regarding their suitability for designation as wilderness. This review process was completed on time, but many of the recommendations faced intense scrutiny and debate within Congress as well as by citizens. As a result, it took a long time for some primitive areas to be reclassified under terms of the Wilderness Act. In fact, one primitive area still remains unclassified—the 174,000-acre Blue Range Primitive Area in Arizona. Typically, most primitive area reclassifications have either involved the addition of the area to an existing wilderness—for example, the 12,000-acre High Sierra Primitive Area in California was added to the existing John Muir Wilderness—or they have been added to adjacent areas under wilderness study to create an altogether new wilderness—for example, the 50,000-acre Spanish Peaks Primitive Area in Montana was combined with adjacent undeveloped lands to form the 255,000-acre Lee Metcalf Wilderness.

Since passage of the Wilderness Act, the number of wilderness areas under USFS administration has grown from 54 to 354 and the acreage from 9.1 million acres to nearly 32.5 million. Today, 17 percent or about one acre in six on the national forests is wilderness. Of the 354 units, the USFS shares jurisdiction on 13—10 with the BLM, two with the FWS, and one with the NPS.

WILDERNESS IN THE NATIONAL PARK SYSTEM

Although wilderness was not an administrative classification used in the national parks prior to the Wilderness Act, it was an important concept underlying the establishment of many parks. It was infor-

mally defined as land beyond one-half mile of roads (ORRRC 1962); many parks were predominantly *de facto* wilderness despite the lack of any formal administrative designation. Because no formal system of wilderness reservation akin to the USFS's primitive area program existed in the national parks, no NPS lands were included in the "instant" wilderness system created in 1964. The act instructed the secretary of the interior to undertake reviews of all areas larger than 5,000 acres in the NPS and make recommendations to the Congress regarding the suitability of these areas for wilderness designation. As discussed in chapter 5, this review process began slowly, and only near the end of the 10-year period were the reviews completed. The first national park wilderness was not designated until 1970; by the end of 1976, there were still only 17 areas totaling 1.1 million acres.

Over the past decade, however, a major expansion in national park representation in the NWPS has occurred. Today, there are 43 national park units in the NWPS covering over 38.5 million acres. On the face of it, the average NPS wilderness unit is nearly 1 million acres. In reality, only seven are that large and all but one of these are in Alaska.

Several large additions of national park land to the NWPS are still possible. For example, the wilderness proposals for Glacier National Park in Montana, Yellowstone National Park in Wyoming, Montana, and Idaho, North Cascades National Park in Washington, Rocky Mountain National Park in Colorado, and Great Smoky Mountains National Park in North Carolina and Tennessee all have yet to be acted upon. Congressional action on these proposals likely will result in the addition of several million acres of national park land.

WILDERNESS IN THE
NATIONAL WILDLIFE REFUGE SYSTEM

The FWS had little experience with wilderness to guide it upon passage of the Wilderness Act, yet it was the first of the Department of the Interior agencies to have an area classified—the 3,700-acre Great Swamp Wilderness in New Jersey. Still, the first decade after passage of the act saw limited action in the classification of FWS lands.

The secretary of the interior was instructed to review all lands within the Fish and Wildlife Refuge System larger than 5,000 acres, as well as all roadless islands, and to make recommendations to Congress regarding the suitability of these lands for wilderness. Of the 81 areas in the NWPS that are less than 5,000 acres, half are managed by the FWS, and many of these are on islands.

Passage of the ANILCA legislation in 1980 resulted in a vast expansion of the FWS component of the NWPS. Under that legislation, more than 18 million acres of FWS land were added to the NWPS. Today, the agency manages 66 units in the NWPS totaling slightly more than 19.3 million acres, 96 percent of it in Alaska (fig. 6.2). The FWS is similar to the NPS in that there remain several large refuges where wilderness proposals have not yet been acted upon, including the Cabeza Prieta and Kofa Refuges in Arizona and the Desert Refuge in Nevada.

WILDERNESS IN THE
BUREAU OF LAND MANAGEMENT

The BLM was not covered by the Wilderness Act when it was passed in 1964. At that time, the BLM had no basic authority to manage the public lands; rather, it was primarily a custodial agency, charged with disposal of the public domain. The national review of public land laws that Congressman Aspinall wanted in exchange for releasing the wilderness bill for debate helped lead to the development of organic legislation giving BLM a mandate to manage the public lands. This took the form of the FLPMA.

FLPMA required the secretary of the interior to review areas of the public lands determined to have wilderness characteristics and to report to the president his recommendations as to their suitability or nonsuitability for preservation as wilderness. This review is to be completed by October 21, 1991. In turn, the president is to report his recommendations to Congress by October 21, 1993. Until a final congressional decision is made, such lands will be managed so as to not impair their suitability for wilderness designation. Nearly 25 million acres located in 869 areas have been identified as having these basic wilderness characteristics. At present, the BLM administers 25 wildernesses, 11 managed in conjunction with another agency. A total of 466,949 acres are involved.

Prior to passage of FLPMA, the BLM had managed an administrative system of reserves for wilderness purposes. Under this system, both primitive areas and natural areas were set aside. The BLM primitive areas are not to be confused with national forest areas similarly labeled under the 1929 L-20 Regulation. BLM use of *primitive area* was, in part, a response to the clause in the Wilderness Act restricting the use of *wilderness* to only those areas covered by the act. BLM primitive areas were, nevertheless, intended to be equivalent to units of the NWPS; the BLM manual indicated that primitive areas were to be managed to maintain the same quality as lands in

Fig. 6.2. About 96 percent of the 19.3 million acres of wilderness managed by the FWS is located in Alaska. Pictured is False Pass in the Unimak Island Wilderness, AK. Photo courtesy of the FWS.

the NWPS (Foster 1976). Criteria used to define primitive areas were the same as those used in the Wilderness Act.

The BLM established 11 primitive areas, totaling 234,131 acres in five states, and 44 natural areas, totaling 271,616 acres in 10 states. FLPMA instructed the secretary of the interior to review these areas by July 1, 1980, with regard to their wilderness suitability. Several of these primitive and natural areas form the core of BLM wildernesses designated at this time, such as the Paria Canyon-Vermilion Cliffs Wilderness in Arizona and Utah, formed from the old Paria Canyon Primitive Area and Vermilion Cliffs Natural Area. The new wilderness encompasses 110,000 acres although the two former areas only totaled about 78,000 acres. The remaining 46 primitive areas and natural areas were designated Instant Study Areas, covering a total of nearly 1.1 million acres. Proposals recommending more than 380,000 acres for wilderness classification in four areas have been sent to Congress, while 26 other areas have been recommended as not being suitable for wilderness designation.

FUTURE GROWTH OF THE NWPS

In the nearly 25 years since passage of the Wilderness Act, the NWPS has grown considerably. In fact, it is unlikely that even the most ardent supporters of the act envisioned a system of areas as large as that

Table 6.4. Status of National Wilderness Preservation System, March 1989.

| | | *National Wilderness Preservation System* | |
Agency	*Units*[1]	*Federal acreage*[2]	*Percent*
NWPS (EXCLUDING ALASKA)			
Forest Service, USDA	340	27,004,280	79
National Park Service, USDI	35	6,147,565	18
Fish and Wildlife Service, USDI	45	656,656	2
Bureau of Land Management, USDI	27	466,949	1
Total	**447**	**34,275,450**	**100**
NWPS (ALASKA)			
Forest Service, USDA	14	5,453,336	10
National Park Service, USDI	8	32,355,000	57
Fish and Wildlife Service, USDI	21	18,676,320	33
Total	**43**	**56,484,656**	**100**
NWPS (INCLUDING ALASKA)			
Forest Service, USDA	354	32,457,616	36
National Park Service, USDI	43	38,502,565	42
Fish and Wildlife Service, USDI	66	19,332,976	21
Bureau of Land Management, USDI	27	466,949	1
Grand total	**490**	**90,760,106**	**100**

Sources: The Wilderness Society,1989; the National Wilderness Preservation System, 1964-89.
1. Totals are not additive due to overlapping agencies' responsibilities. Includes 14 areas with joint management.
2. Some acreages are estimates pending establishment of final boundaries.

THE NWPS AT A GLANCE

1. As of March 1989, the NWPS contained nearly 90.8 million acres—an area representing about 3.9 percent of the 50 states and 4.6 percent of the lower 48 states, an area approximately the size of Montana.
2. The average size of a wilderness is 200,000 acres; however, in the 48 states, the average drops to 81,000 acres.
3. The largest area is the 8.7-million-acre Wrangell-Saint Elias Wilderness in Alaska, managed by the NPS; the smallest is the Pelican Island Wilderness in Florida, only 6 acres, managed by the FWS.
4. The NPS manages 42 percent of the NWPS acreage, but only 9 percent of the areas. The USFS manages 36 percent of the acreage and 73 percent of the areas.
5. Six states have no wilderness: Connecticut, Delaware, Iowa, Kansas, Maryland, and Rhode Island.
6. The western United States, with only 20 percent of the population, contains 95 percent of the NWPS.

established today. For example, McCloskey (1966) estimated the NWPS might reach 48 million acres, but he did not include lands from the BLM. Stankey (1971) forecast a NWPS of slightly more than 70 million acres, but underestimated the amount of *de facto* wilderness present. A similar estimate was made by the Sierra Club (Gillette 1972). On the other hand, Fredsall (1974) predicted the NWPS might reach 240 million acres with about half under BLM management in Alaska.

What does the future hold for further growth in the NWPS? Although an uncertain matter, some general observations can be made. First, future growth has considerable potential. Several large wilderness proposals in national parks remain to be acted upon. Much BLM land similarly must be acted upon. Approximately 57 million acres have been identified as wilderness study areas in the conterminous United States, and many millions more will likely undergo careful study for wilderness classification in Alaska. Thus, it appears likely that major additions will be made to the NWPS, leading to a system in excess of 100 million acres.

Second, while the growth of the NWPS may start to slow in the future, it is not likely that we will be able to say that enough wilderness has been designated or that the system has been rounded out. For one reason, our conceptions of wilderness will undoubtedly change, resulting in new areas becoming qualified for designation, or possibly resulting in the declassification of existing areas. Also, as noted earlier, there are many

types of areas that apparently are unavailable for wilderness designation; however, the situation might change in the future, and opportunities to protect these areas might become available. Thus, we will likely see the system reach a point where the addition of new areas becomes very slow, but the newly added areas will represent especially valuable additions from various perspectives, for example, ecological diversity.

Finally, growth of the NWPS will be affected by decisions regarding the management of other lands. We believe it would be unfortunate if provisions are not made to maintain some areas as roadless while not classifying them as wilderness.

Many people seek recreation in areas that are roadless but that are not wilderness. Unless we provide for such demands, wilderness will eventually receive much of this activity, as it will be perceived as the only place such recreation can be accommodated. This in turn could lead to increased impact on wilderness and to more intensive wilderness management. Illegal wilderness use will probably increase as those pursuing activities such as driving off-road vehicles attempt to find places to enjoy these activities.

In addition to wilderness, roadless recreation areas are also needed. A variety of names have been suggested for such areas, including backcountry and frontier areas. These relatively unmodified settings would enhance a variety of opportunities such as camping, fishing, and hiking. They would be distinguished from wilderness by the great latitude provided management to increase recreational capacity, the kinds of permitted recreational activities, and the relatively lower priority assigned to the maintenance of natural ecological processes. Such areas could reduce the level of impact on classified wilderness while meeting the needs of many users.

New units and acreage are continuously being added to the NWPS. Table 6.4 shows the status of the system in March 1989. A variety of means exist for providing a system of roadless areas. One alternative is the creation of a formal system, protected by law, analogous to the NWPS. Many favor this option because classification without a legal basis does not guarantee long-term protection. Another alternative would be to develop a formal administrative system of roadless recreation areas. Finally, such opportunities could be offered through an improved land-use planning program in which a full range of recreation settings is provided through coordinated planning by federal, state, local, and private suppliers. Although much more effort is needed to make this last alternative a reality, there have been some major advances in developing a framework to help achieve it. The concept of the Recreation Opportunity Spec-

trum (ROS) is gaining application throughout the USFS and BLM as well as other state and federal agencies (Buist and Hoots 1982). Application of this concept could do much to help ensure the provision of a system of roadless recreation areas to complement classified wilderness.

The idea of a system of roadless recreation areas, however established, has failed to attract much support. Commodity interests see it as only another lockup of resources on the public lands, while wilderness proponents see it being used as a substitute for wilderness protection rather than as a complement to it.

COMPLEMENTARY CONSERVATION AREAS

In addition to formally classified wilderness, a variety of other areas complement or supplement the purposes of the NWPS. Although some areas serve purposes similar to wilderness, others are quite different. Nevertheless, at least a portion of these other systems is located at the primitive end of the environmental modification spectrum, and their relationship to designated wilderness merits attention.

THE NATIONAL TRAILS SYSTEM

In 1968, Congress established a National Trails System (P.L. 90-543):

> In order to provide for the ever-increasing outdoor recreation needs of an expanding population and in order to promote public access to travel within, and enjoyment and appreciation of the open-air, outdoor areas of the nation.

The system includes three different types of trails: (1) national recreation trails, (2) national scenic trails, and (3) connecting or side trails. Some of these trails overlap with wilderness or areas proposed for wilderness designation. Such overlapping designations pose at least a potential conflict to the extent that they attract use inappropriate to wilderness.

NATIONAL RECREATION TRAILS

National recreation trails are intended to provide a variety of outdoor recreation uses near urban areas. The secretary of the interior or the secretary of agriculture may establish a national recreation trail with the consent of any other jurisdiction whose lands would also be involved (such as a state or local government). Trails on state lands may also be designated as national recreation trails by the secretary of the interior with consent of the state.

Criteria for designating national recreation trails have been adopted by the secretaries of the interior and agriculture. Such trails may be relatively short (perhaps one-half mile), but must be continuous. Some trails may be exclusively for the handicapped. National recreation trails are to be available to large numbers of people; consequently, locations such as stream valleys, utility rights-of-way, abandoned railroad rights-of-way, and levees or dikes are likely candidates. They may be designed solely for one use, such as hiking or recreational vehicle use, but opportunities for multiple use are to be explored. Before designation of a trail, the administering agency must provide the appropriate secretary (interior or agriculture) assurance that the trail will be available to the public for at least 10 consecutive years. At present, 374 national recreation trails have been established, totaling 1,300 miles.

NATIONAL SCENIC TRAILS

National scenic trails differ from recreation trails in several respects. First, they can be designated only by an act of Congress. Public Law 90-543 established two such trails: the 2,000-mile Appalachian Trail (fig. 6.3) and the 2,350-mile Pacific Crest Trail. In addition, 14 other trails totaling more than 15,000 miles were identified in the law for review as potential additions to the system; most recently, the Continental Divide National Scenic Trail, which follows the crest of the Rocky Mountains, was established.

National scenic trails must possess superior scenic, historic, natural, or cultural qualities in combination with maximum outdoor recreation potential. They should avoid contact with developments such as transmission lines, highways, and industrial facilities; have adequate public access; and follow principal historic routes. Generally, they will be several hundred miles in length. Use of motorized vehicles on these trails is prohibited.

Portions of the National Trail System pass through some units of the NWPS. For instance, the Pacific Crest Trail runs through several wildernesses in the Cascade and Sierra Nevada Mountains. Managers of these areas are faced with conflicting objectives when wilderness and national scenic trails overlap. Wilderness is managed for naturalness and solitude; national scenic trails can attract many users whose primary interest is not in wilderness-related values. Generally, the more restrictive management standards for wilderness will prevail, but the con-

Fig. 6.3. Many areas set aside for ecological protection offer recreational opportunities comparable to designated wilderness. Here, hikers enjoy an afternoon on the Appalachian National Scenic Trail. Photo courtesy of the NPS.

Fig. 6.4. Originally intended to prevent the damming of some of the nation's free-flowing streams, the Wild and Scenic Rivers Act became an instrument for limiting development along river corridors and protecting the quality of water-oriented recreation. Rafters on Idaho's Selway River ride heavy white water. Photo courtesy of the USFS.

flicting objectives and the heavier use attracted to national trails does create management problems. For example, where the Pacific Crest Trail passes high mountain lakes, these attractive spots can become overused by hikers. Wilderness managers have encouraged rerouting of the Crest Trail away from fragile wilderness settings where possible, but it has been impossible to eliminate all the potential conflicts. Similarly, the presence of huts along the Appalachian Trail poses management problems when the trail crosses wilderness.

THE WILD AND SCENIC RIVERS SYSTEM

The Wild and Scenic Rivers Act of 1968 (P.L. 90-542) protected certain rivers throughout the nation in order to assure their free and unimpaired flow and preserve their outstanding scenic, recreational, geological, fish and wildlife, historic, and cultural values. Originally promoted as a means of countering federal dam construction programs, the act evolved into an effort to limit development in general along rivers and their banks in the name of recreation Tarlock and Tippy 1970; see figure 6.4.

The act designated portions of eight rivers and

adjacent lands as immediate members of the system. Another 27 rivers were identified for study within 10 years for possible inclusion in the system; 18 to be studied by the Department of the Interior and nine by the Department of Agriculture. At present, 119 river segments have been added to the National Wild and Scenic Rivers System. More than 9,000 miles are involved, with more than 4,000 classified as wild, 1,500 as scenic, and 2,500 as recreational. A number of bills proposing further additions are pending before Congress.

Designation of rivers under the Wild and Scenic Rivers Act can occur in two ways. First, specific congressional legislation can be enacted to protect a river. Second, a river can be added to the system by the secretary of the interior, provided certain nomination procedures are followed by the state in which the river is located, and provided there is no administrative cost to be borne by the federal government (Peters 1975). The Klamath River in California is an example of a river added under secretarial designation. Five agencies, including the BLM, NPS, USFS, State of California, and Hoopa Valley Indian Reservation, are responsible for the river's management.

The act recognizes three classes of rivers:

1. *Wild Rivers*—Those rivers or sections of rivers that are free of impoundments, and generally inaccessible except by trail, with watersheds or shorelines essentially primitive, and waters unpolluted. These represent vestiges of primitive America.
2. *Scenic Rivers*—Those rivers or sections of rivers that are free of impoundments, with shorelines or watersheds still largely primitive and shorelines largely undeveloped, but accessible in places by roads.
3. *Recreational Rivers*—Those rivers or sections of rivers that are readily accessible by road or railroad, that may have some development along their shorelines, and that may have undergone some impoundment or diversion in the past.

Designation of a river under the Wild and Scenic Rivers Act, combined with wilderness designation of the river and adjacent lands, could have very important complementary benefits. Wilderness designation generally affects broad reaches of land and would protect the broader watershed of which the river is a part. Wild and Scenic River designation, on the other hand, provides some important protection not afforded by the Wilderness Act. First, designation of a river segment as *wild* provides complete protection against dam construction and other water development projects. Such facilities can be developed in classified wilderness if judged by the president to be in the public interest (see chap. 4). Second, the Wild and Scenic Rivers Act prohibits construction of power transmission lines; such facilities can be developed in wilderness. Third, although the Wilderness Act does not allow for the condemnation of private inholdings, the Wild and Scenic Rivers Act permits administering agencies to condemn private land, if less than 50 percent of the entire river is owned by federal, state, or local government. Land within a city, village, or borough cannot be condemned if valid zoning ordinances protecting the river areas are in effect. Finally, while lands in the NWPS were open to mineral entry until 1984, there was complete withdrawal from mineral entry of lands within one-fourth mile of the bank of any river designated for management under the *wild* category of the Wild and Scenic Rivers System (Tarlock and Tippy 1970). In general, the Wild and Scenic Rivers Act is more restrictive than the Wilderness Act, and in cases where the two laws overlap the more restrictive provisions prevail.

Classification of rivers as wild, scenic, recreational, or a varying combination of the three classification types plays an important role in preserving diverse wild river communities. As of November 1988, 119 rivers had been designated under the Wild and Scenic Rivers Act with 9,260 total miles of river

sections designated. Of this total mileage, 4,693 miles were designated wild, 1,586 miles were designated scenic and 2,571 miles were designated recreational. The type of classification—wild, scenic, or recreational—on some rivers had not yet been determined in November 1988, so the total mileage of these three types is 410 miles short of the total mileage (9,260 mi) pending classification of Horsepasture (NC), Merced (CA), Kings (CA), Kern (CA) and Sipsey Fork (AL) rivers (American Rivers 1988).

Congress continually adds new river sections to the National Wild and Scenic Rivers System. For example, on May 11, 1989, Secretary of the Interior Manuel Lujan added a 17.1-mile segment of the Middle Fork of the Vermilion River in eastern Illinois to the National Wild and Scenic Rivers System. "The Vermilion is considered to be the state's best remaining example of a prairie river—a type once prevalent in the midwest" (American Rivers 1989, p. 12). In June 1990, President Bush signed into law legislation protecting parts ot the Pecos and Jemez rivers in New Mexico from pumice mining. Eleven miles of the East Fork of the Jemez near the Santa Fe National Forest's Battleship Rock and 20.5 miles of the Pecos in the Pecos Wilderness expanded the National Wild and Scenic Rivers System (Journal North 1990). Continued support and interest in protecting free-flowing wild rivers will insure their preservation.

In addition to the National Wild and Scenic Rivers System, 23 state systems have also been established; one state, Wisconsin, predates the federal system. Nearly 200 rivers are protected under state legislation involving more than 5,800 miles, with another 400 miles under study for possible future designation. Nearly one river in five under some form of protective management is protected through state legislation (Anderson and Morck 1984). Most state programs are fairly restrictive; they typically prohibit instream modification, establish land use controls, and provide for the management of river use and users (Leatherberry and others 1980).

STATE WILDERNESS

The 1964 Wilderness Act pertains only to federal lands. Many states have also undertaken actions to preserve lands possessing wilderness qualities. This is an important step, for it represents another way to increase the range of areas given wilderness protection. Many types of ecosystems simply are not found on federal lands; thus, even the most lenient approach to wilderness designation would fail to protect them. Where the states are important landowners, such as in the Midwest and in the East, state wilderness

Table 6.5. State wilderness preservation programs, 1984.

State	Type of program
Alaska	Provides for designation of wilderness zones within five of the eight types of units managed as state parks. Wilderness is designated through the park management plan.
California	Under state law, the California Wilderness Preservation System provides for designation of state-owned lands as "wilderness areas" by the legislature, and units of the state park system as "state wildernesses" by the State Park and Recreation Commission. The law is closely modeled after the federal legislation.
Florida	The State Wilderness System Act proclaims legislative intent to establish a state wilderness system. Recommended areas are set aside in perpetuity through a resolution by the Department of Natural Resources.
Maryland	The Maryland General Assembly has passed legislation creating a State Wildlands Preservation System. The system is modeled after the federal law.
Michigan	The Wilderness and Natural Areas Act of 1972 provides for designation of both wilderness and wild areas, size being the principal distinction. This distinction closely resembles earlier procedures of the USFS. The legislation is modeled after the federal law.
Minnesota	State wilderness areas are defined as one type of unit comprising the Outdoor Recreation System of Minnesota. Areas are designated by the commissioner of the Department of Natural Resources (DNR) upon the recommendation of a DNR Planning and Environmental Review Team. The legislation is modeled after the federal law.
Missouri	The Missouri Wild Areas System has been established within state parks. A statewide survey of potentially suitable areas provides the basis for recommendations for additions to the system, with the director of the Department of Natural Resources possessing the authority for establishment. The definition of a wild area follows closely that of a federal wilderness.
New York	The state claims one of the oldest preservation programs in the United States. The New York Forest Preserve, established in 1885, provided the impetus for language in the state constitution in 1894 that the Forest Preserve "shall be forever kept as wild forest land." A wilderness classification program has been established for both the 6-million-acre Adirondack Park and the 255,000-acre Catskill Park. Designation is accomplished through the master plan for each park. The wilderness definition closely follows the federal language.
Wisconsin	Wilderness areas are a component of a Wild Resources System administered by the Wisconsin Natural Resources Board. The designation is implemented by the board and the Department of Natural Resources, with the advice of a Wild Resources Advisory Council. Management plans are prepared for each unit. The criteria defining wilderness resemble those of the federal act.

protection could help expand the extent of coverage. Moreover, by preserving areas as wilderness, state programs could also help ensure provision of a kind of primitive recreation opportunity that would otherwise not be available (Stankey 1984).

A national survey undertaken in 1983 examined state-level activity in wilderness preservation (Stankey 1984). Eighty-nine agencies in the 50 states plus Puerto Rico, Guam, and the Virgin Islands were queried. Only three states, Guam, and the Virgin Islands did not reply.

To qualify for recognition as state wilderness, programs had to satisfy these criteria: (1) statutory or administrative recognition of the program; (2) provision for preserving natural qualities and for providing primitive recreational opportunities; (3) prohibition of resource development activities; (4) establishment of area size, either as specific acreage qualitative descrip-

tion (how large an area must be to meet objectives); and (5) recognition of other values, such as features of historic or scientific interest, considered consistent with management as wilderness.

Nine states were found to have wilderness preservation programs meeting these criteria. In addition, three states have established areas for wilderness purposes, but did not meet all the criteria. These latter programs will be discussed shortly. Table 6.5 lists the nine state programs and their general structure.

Most states have modeled their wilderness programs on the federal legislation. However, some significant differences exist. For example, in some states, such as Alaska, wilderness is a zoning classification applied to units of the state park system. In California, the state legislature can designate wilderness but, in lieu of action by that body, proposals can be brought before the California Park and Recreation Commission; to date, the legislature has established two areas while the commission has designated four (Trumbly and Gray 1984). In Florida, the state legislature provided a legal pronouncement of its intent to see a state wilderness system established, but delegated classification authority to the Department of Natural Resources. The department, in turn, establishes areas by "proper resolution," with dedication of the area in perpetuity.

Most states also closely follow the definition of wilderness given in the federal legislation. In six of the nine states, the basic wilderness definition contained in the federal act has been adopted with only minor

rewording. The most common variation is with regard to the desired size of a wilderness. This reflects the typically smaller areas found in state ownership: in Missouri the standard is 1,000 acres; in Minnesota, 2,500 acres; and in Michigan and Wisconsin, 3,000 acres. California has a 5,000-acre suggested minimum, the same as the federal act, and New York recommends a minimum of 10,000 acres.

The states typically provide greater leniency toward the admission of previous human impacts than the federal act. Minnesota, for example, indicates that no unit shall be authorized as a state wilderness unless it satisfies the following criteria: appears to have been primarily affected by the forces of nature, with the evidence of man being substantially unnoticeable or *where the evidence of man may be eliminated by restoration.* Similarly, in Alaska, resource modification within a wilderness zone of a state park can be permitted if undertaken to restore the area to a natural condition. In Florida, timber removal and other environmental modifications in wilderness can be permitted in order to restore and maintain natural conditions; Michigan has a similar provision. The California legislation, on the other hand, appears to provide for the admission of areas where previous impacts have been already remedied: "A wilderness is further defined to mean an area . . . which . . . has been substantially restored to a near natural appearance."

Wisconsin has established a system that recognizes not only wilderness areas but also wilderness lakes. Wilderness areas are defined under guidelines that resemble those of the federal legislation. *Wilderness lakes,* on the other hand, are lakes 5 acres or larger with no access roads or developments within one-fourth mile of the shoreline. Only foot access is allowed and camping is prohibited. To date, 3,660 acres have been set aside as wilderness lakes (Germain 1984).

Earlier, we suggested that state wilderness systems might be especially valuable in helping to "fill in" settings not represented under federal ownership. Little explicit attention has been given to this idea in the enabling legislation governing the state systems. In Minnesota, an objective of the program is to preserve an accurate representation of the state's natural heritage; however, only one area has been classified by the act; this lies within the existing federally managed Boundary Waters Canoe Area Wilderness (BWCAW) and it is unlikely that it expands biological representation beyond what already occurs. In Florida, a legislatively based set of priorities has been established to govern the selection and establishment of wilderness areas. Priority is to be given those areas that (1) are in proximity to urban or rapidly developing areas, (2) are in imminent danger from some other source, (3) are designed

Table 6.6. Number of areas and acres in state wilderness preservation programs, 1984.

State	Number of areas	Number of acres
Alaska	n.g.	n.g.
California	6	419,410
Florida	10	56,864
Maryland	4	8,870
Michigan[1]	2	46,492
Minnesota[2]	n.g.	106,360
Missouri	10	16,159
New York[3]	20	1,156,935
Wisconsin	n.g.	29,772
Total	**52**	**1,840,862**

n.g. = not given
1. Includes only those areas designated as wilderness or wild under the Michigan Wilderness and Natural Areas Act of 1972.
2. Includes only state lands lying within the federally protected BWCAW.
3. Information from December 1989, courtesy of the Adirondack Park Agency.

to protect rare or endangered species or other unique natural features, and (4) constitute the last vestiges of natural conditions within a given region.

At least 50 areas and nearly 2 million acres have been established in the nine states (see table 6.6). About 60 percent of the acreage is in New York, but important progress also has been made elsewhere as, for example, in Maryland which has no federal wilderness. To see how state programs function, let us examine the California system in more detail.

In 1974, the California legislature established the California Wilderness Preservation System. Three basic criteria govern admission to the system: (1) the land must be state owned; (2) the area must remain in, or have been returned to, or have substantially reestablished its principal, natural character and influence; and (3) the area must be of sufficient size to make its preservation practicable.

Although the system is legislatively founded, new areas can be added either administratively or legislatively. Legislatively established areas are called *wilderness areas* and are fully protected by law. *State wildernesses* also can be administratively designated on lands in the state park system by the California Park and Recreation Commission, a body appointed by the governor and overseeing management of the state park system. Although both types of areas are subject to the protective management requirements of the act, those established by administrative designation can be reclassified and thus removed from the state wilderness system without approval of the legislature (Trumbly and Gray 1984).

The 1974, legislation created two wilderness areas: the Santa Rosa Mountains Wilderness Area of about 87,000 acres and the 10,000-acre Mount San Jacinto Wilderness Area abutting the federally designated San Jacinto Wilderness. Since passage of the act, more than 322,000 acres of wilderness have been added, all through administrative designation; currently, the California State Wilderness System contains more than 420,000 acres. And although more than three-fourths of the system is administratively designated, no area has been declassified. The largest unit in the system is the 294,000-acre Anza-Borrego Desert State Wilderness.

Although the California act closely parallels the federal legislation, there are some important differences. The state legislation explicitly states that wilderness areas need not be "pristine" but only "substantially restored to a near natural appearance." It also contains language prohibiting aircraft flights below 2,000 feet above ground level; no such prohibition is contained in the federal law. Special provisions permit the unobtrusive use of equipment for the collection of hydrometeorological data and the conduct of weather modification activities; this latter activity in particular is one that has raised concerns with regard to its potential impact on wilderness (see chap. 4). Finally, the California law prohibits any vehicle use within wilderness except for emergencies involving the health and safety of individuals. The Wilderness Act of 1964 is more permissive in this regard, permitting permanent roads if they are determined to be necessary for the minimum requirements for administration of the area as wilderness.

Although the California Wilderness System is small compared to the federal wilderness acreage in the state (420,000 acres in state ownership as compared to more than 5.9 million acres administered by federal agencies), the types of areas contained in the state system are an important complement to that in the NWPS. Much of the land in the state system is in the Anza-Borrego Desert State Park; other areas are along the coastline and nearby coast ranges. Federal ownership is concentrated in the northern portion of the state and in the Sierra Nevada Mountains. Thus, the state wilderness system leads to a broader diversity of ecosystems under wilderness protection than would be the case solely under federal management (Trumbly and Gray 1984).

In addition to these nine states, three others have established individual wilderness areas. Although these were isolated designations, not part of a broader formal program of wilderness designation, they are further evidence of state-level protection for *wilderness values*.

Hawaii—The Hawaii Department of Land and Natural Resources has established on the Island of Kauai the Alakai Wilderness Preserve. The area was established in 1964 "for the purposes of preserving, protecting, and conserving all manner of flora and fauna." The area covers 9,939 acres. Mining, livestock grazing, structures, and roads are prohibited. Day-use recreation is permitted, but overnight camping is restricted to two cabins in the area.

Maine—In 1931, former Governor of Maine Percival P. Baxter donated nearly 6,000 acres of land to the state for use as a park. The land, he specified, "shall forever be kept and remain in the natural state." Over a period of 30 years, additional donations by the governor brought the total size of the area, known as Baxter State Park, to 200,000 acres.

The area is surrounded by a perimeter road system, with short branching roads leading to nearby destinations in the interior. Most of the area is accessible only by trail, and under the existing management plan, no further expansion or improvement of the road system, except for reasons of safety, will be permitted. Camping is carefully regulated. During the winter, camping, mountain hiking, and climbing are allowed only with a special use permit issued by park officials.

The park is intended to provide a special set of recreational experiences linked to enjoyment of the natural, undeveloped environment. Uses not dependent upon such a setting are to be accommodated elsewhere. For example, 50,000 acres within the area have been set aside as a scientific research management unit, and some activities in support of research activity but inconsistent with wilderness are conducted. Although named a state park and supported by state funds, it is not a unit of the existing state park system and is managed according to the directives outlined by Governor Baxter more than 50 years ago. Along with the Adirondack Preserve to the south, it represents one of the relatively few remaining areas in the Northeast where natural conditions still prevail.

Oklahoma—The Oklahoma Department of Wildlife Conservation manages a 14,000-acre unit called the McCurtain County Wilderness Area. The objective is to retain the area in a natural condition, with only nature operating to alter existing conditions. Motor-driven vehicles, commercial operations, and the removal of wildlife and plants are all prohibited. Entry to the area is only by permit or by persons involved in its management; scientific research is recognized as a permitted use.

State activity in wilderness preservation represents an important complementary activity to federal efforts. Although the federal legislation has set the general direction in defining wilderness and setting management guidelines, the states have adopted and modified these notions to apply to their situation. In addition, many states are actively engaged in programs designed to protect the quality of their natural heritage through a variety of activities other than wilderness designation. For example, a 1977 national survey of state nature conservation activity undertaken by The Nature Conservancy (TNC) found that 25 states had a total of 436 areas and nearly 182,000 acres of land in areas managed according to strict nature protection guidelines (TNC 1977). The results significantly strengthen the application of the wilderness concept around the country.

RESEARCH NATURAL AREAS

In 1966, the Department of the Interior, as part of the United States' participation in the International Biological Program (IBP), established the Federal Committee on Research Natural Areas. The committee was composed of representatives of the major federal land management agencies along with liaison representatives from the Department of Defense, Atomic Energy Commission, and Tennessee Valley Authority. Its purpose was to inventory and prepare a directory of natural areas on federal lands.

Research Natural Areas (RNAs) are related to wilderness because one of their key objectives is the maintenance of natural processes and because they serve an important research and education role. Their specific objectives include the following:

1. To assist in the preservation of examples of all significant natural ecosystems for comparison with those influenced by humans.
2. To provide educational and research areas for scientists to study the ecology, successional trends, and other aspects of the natural environment.
3. To serve as gene pools and preserves for rare and endangered species of plants and animals (Federal Committee on Research Natural Areas 1968).

In general, six basic characteristics of research natural areas can be identified (Moir 1972):

1. They are examples of the natural environment.
2. Their natural features have been disturbed as little as possible by man.
3. They are defined by ecological criteria.
4. They are assured the greatest possible degree of preservation and permanency.
5. Their withdrawal is for scientific and educational purposes.
6. They harbor genetic stock of possible value to society.

At present, approximately 440 RNAs in the United States are administered by eight federal land managing agencies. They range in size from less than 1 acre to more than 100,000 acres and total nearly 5 million acres. But given that one purpose of the RNA system is to preserve a representative array of the nation's ecosystems, much remains to be done. For example, within the USFS component of the system, 148 areas have been set aside, totaling more than 172,000 acres. But of the 145 forest types in the nation, 62 are not represented; and among the 83 that are found within RNAs, 28 have only one example (Burns 1984). Thus, the goal of representativeness could be easily lost in the event of some catastrophe.

Most RNAs are surrounded or buffered by federal land. Research conducted on these areas must be essentially nondestructive and consistent with the purpose and character of the surrounding land. Studies involving manipulation of the environment are generally not permitted.

Recreational use of RNAs is, by definition, limited and subordinate to the scientific and educational objectives for these areas. They nevertheless do serve as important recreational settings for activities that focus on learning and environmental awareness. More importantly, they supplement the scientific and educational objectives of the NWPS.

BIOSPHERE RESERVES AND WORLD HERITAGE SITES

In chapter 3, we discussed international progress in protecting wilderness values and noted that Biosphere Reserves and World Heritage Sites were two important sources of such protection. In the United States, both designations have been used in conjunction with other conservation classifications, such as national parks, in order to further recognize and protect important natural values. Like the other types of designations we have discussed, Biosphere Reserves and World Heritage Sites represent another mechanism through which wilderness values can be protected.

The Biosphere Reserve Project was established in 1973 under the auspices of the United Nations Educational, Scientific, and Cultural Organization (UNESCO). The basic objective of the program is to foster development of an international network of representative ecosystems for use in research and education and to promote improved land management practices. *Biosphere Reserves* typically include portions where little or no human impact has occurred, the Core Zone, as well as areas of human use and impact, Multiple Functions Zone and Cultural Zone. Worldwide, 283 Biosphere Reserves have been established in 72 countries.

In the United States, the Biosphere Reserve Project is jointly coordinated by the NPS and the USFS. The first areas established were in 1976: Great Smoky Mountains National Park, Everglades National Park in Florida, and Virgin Islands National Park; along with the Coweeta Experimental Forest in North Carolina, Hubbard Brook Experimental Forest in New Hampshire, and Luquillo Experimental Forest in Puerto Rico. At present, 38 areas in the United States have received recognition as Biosphere Reserves, with the total acreage in excess of 7 million acres. Portions of several reserves are also classified as wilderness as, for example, in the Noatak National Arctic Range in Alaska where more than half of the nearly 6-million-acre wilderness is classified as a Biosphere Reserve. Nearly 81,000 acres of the 285,000-acre Three Sisters Wilderness in Oregon is similarly classified. Most recently, the nearly l-million-acre Admiralty Island Wilderness and the 2.7-million-acre Glacier Bay Wilderness have been classified as part of the Glacier Bay-Admiralty Island Biosphere Reserve.

World Heritage Sites, on the other hand, are a product of the International Convention for the Protection of the World Cultural and Natural Heritage (World Heritage Convention) adopted by the UNESCO Geneva Convention in 1972. Rather than focusing on "representative ecosystems" as the Biosphere Reserve program does, areas qualifying for World Heritage Site listing must contain outstanding or superlative qualities of the natural environment. Management of World Heritage Sites focuses on protection of these outstanding qualities. In some cases, areas may be protected by both designations; however, both of these international-level conservation classifications are typically applied in conjunction with an existing designation in the country where the area is located (e.g., national forest, national park).

World Heritage status has been recognized for 19 sites in the United States plus one area jointly administered by Canada and the United States, the Kluane National Park/Wrangell-Saint Elias National Park. Six sites overlap areas where wilderness designations are also in effect: the Arctic National Wildlife Refuge and Wrangell-Saint Elias National Park in Alaska, Organ Pipe Cactus National Monument in Arizona, and Point Reyes National Seashore and Sequoia/Kings Canyon and Yosemite National Parks in California.

Eight areas in the United States are both Biosphere Reserves and World Heritage Sites: Big Bend National Park (TX), Everglades National Park, Great Smoky Mountains National Park, Olympic National Park (WA), Organ Pipe Cactus National Monument/Caneza Prieta National Wildlife Refuge (AZ), Sequoia/Kings Canyon National Park, Virginia Coast Reserve (VA), and Yellowstone National Park.

Selection of these areas as Biosphere Reserves, World Heritage Sites, or both, reflects international recognition of their value as repositories of natural values, as the source of knowledge and understanding about natural processes, and their contribution to society as a source of pleasure and inspiration. Such designations represent another complementary form of recognition and protection of wilderness values.

SPECIALLY DESIGNATED NATIONAL FOREST LANDS

National forest lands can be set aside for special purposes under a variety of administrative designations. These areas are broadly labeled *Special Interest Areas*. Originally, they were designated by authority of the U-3 Regulations of 1939 (see chap. 4), which established roadless areas, managed primarily for their recreational values. Such authority is now contained in regulations issued by the secretary of agriculture.

The six different kinds of areas that can be established by such administrative designations and the number of areas so managed include: scenic areas (82), geological areas (14), archeological areas (8), historical

areas (8), botanical areas (12), and other special interest areas (14). Each designation gives added protection for an area possessing certain special qualities. Designation occurs under the authority of the forest supervisor. Areas established under these regulations can be managed at least as restrictively as wilderness. For example, management guidelines for the Jewell Basin Hiking Area in western Montana prohibit the use of stock, and all travel must be by foot.

A major concern about such administrative designations centers on the permanence of protection they provide. Because they are established administratively at local or regional levels, they can also be eliminated at those levels. This was also the situation with wilderness under the U Regulations and a compelling reason conservationists sought congressional protection for wilderness.

PRIVATE EFFORTS—
THE NATURE CONSERVANCY

The Nature Conservancy (TNC) is a private organization that undertakes efforts to protect and preserve ecosystems that would otherwise be lost to development. Its origins trace from 1917 when a group of scientists, under the auspices of the newly established Ecological Society of America, formed a committee for the preservation of natural environments. The early work of this group led to publication of *The Naturalists Guide to the Americas*, detailing the known outstanding and unprotected natural areas of North and South America. Later, in 1950, the Ecologists Union, one of the organizations arising from the Ecological Society, took the name of "The Nature Conservancy" (a name borrowed from a national organization in Great Britain) and launched a program to achieve better protection of wildlife and plants, including an effort to attain nonprofessional participation (Blair 1986).

Through the use of a program of revolving funds—using grants and other monies to acquire land followed by fund-raising efforts to replenish the fund—TNC has become an important force in protecting natural environments. Because a major objective of TNC is to preserve natural diversity, the organization has developed four major tasks to achieve this goal: (1) *identification*, determining which endangered natural systems and species have not been preserved; (2) *protection*, preserving the best areas where they are found; (3) *stewardship*, managing the protected sites; and (4) *funding*, repaying the amount spent from the revolving fund.

Inventories of endangered locations have been initiated in 38 states plus several multi-state projects. Since the early 1950s, TNC has been involved in the protection of more than 2.4 million acres; in 1984 alone, some 338 projects totaling nearly 312,000 acres were acted upon. In most cases, TNC has acquired critical habitats—about half through outright gifts and the remainder through partial gifts and purchases. Today, the organization manages 873 units, the largest privately owned group of nature sanctuaries in the world, 24 of which have professional managers, assisted by volunteers. In Iowa, for example, the Fern Ridge Preserve provides habitat for balsam firs and an endangered species of snail; the area is managed by the local Conservancy chapter. In Florida, on the other hand, TNC has acquired more than 1,700 acres for addition to the federally managed Crocodile Lake National Wildlife Refuge to assist in the protection of the endangered crocodile (Blair 1986). Nationally, approximately half a million acres, valued at nearly half a billion dollars, are controlled by TNC (Gilbert 1986).

Several private companies have contributed major areas of undeveloped land to TNC. In 1969, Georgia-Pacific gave the Conservancy $6 million worth of redwood forests in northern California. Union Camp Corporation gave 50,000 acres of wetlands, lakes, and forests in Virginia's Great Dismal Swamp in 1973. Over the years, a conservative estimate of corporate gifts of conservation land to TNC is placed at $72 million (Blair 1986).

Areas under TNC management are managed primarily to protect natural values. Nevertheless, certain uses are allowed, including recreation. However, great care is taken to ensure that such use and supporting facilities such as trails do not conflict with critical species or natural communities.

SUMMARY

After a period of relatively slow growth following passage of the Wilderness Act, the NWPS has grown rapidly. In the first edition of this book, we indicated that it seemed reasonable that the NWPS might expand beyond its 14 million acres (1978) to something between 50 and 70 million acres. So much for expert opinion; today, the system stands at approximately 90.8 million acres and considerable growth potential still remains.

In the first edition, the question of what was "enough" wilderness was raised. Then, as now, we concluded that the question was not a particularly useful one. Enough for what purposes? As the discussion in this chapter indicates, key ecosystems still lie outside wilderness boundaries, thereby reducing the goal of ensuring widespread protection of eco-

logical diversity in the United States. Moreover, new conceptions of wilderness have evolved and will continue to evolve. Wilderness areas in caves or under the sea are ideas still only partially developed. The idea that we will someday reach a point where we "round out" the wilderness system is probably akin to looking for the end of the rainbow—but working toward equal representation of all ecosystems is nevertheless a worthwhile goal.

It remains clear, however, that wilderness alone cannot supply all the environmental values and recreational opportunities the public seeks at the primitive end of the environmental modification spectrum. Other roadless, nonwilderness settings must also be provided to more adequately meet public desires. Expansion of the National Trails System, the Wild and Scenic Rivers System, state wilderness systems, and the provision of roadless recreation areas managed intensively for recreation are needed to adequately cope with growing public interest and demand. The quality of tomorrow's wilderness will depend as much on our success in fully developing these alternative opportunities as on our achievements in developing and implementing innovative wilderness allocation and management programs.

STUDY QUESTIONS

1. In what important ways does wilderness classified by the states complement the federal wilderness system?
2. Discuss the various factors that will likely influence the future growth of the NWPS.
3. In what ways do programs such as the National Trails System and the Wild and Scenic Rivers System complement the NWPS? In what ways do they conflict with the NWPS? How might some of these conflicts be resolved?
4. In what ways are the goals of the research natural area program similar to those of the NWPS? In what ways do they differ?
5. Compare and contrast the Biosphere Reserve and World Heritage Site programs. What similarities do they share; how do they differ? Discuss the relationship between both programs and the goals of the NWPS.

REFERENCES

American Rivers Newsletter. 1989. Vermilion river designated wild and scenic. American Rivers, 801 Pennsylvania Avenue, S.E., Suite 303, Washington, DC 20003. 16:12-13.

American Rivers. 1988. River mileage classifications for components of the National Wild and Scenic Rivers System. Table published in November by American Rivers, 801 Pennsylvania Avenue, S.E., Suite 303, Washington, DC 20003.

Anderson, Dorothy H.; Morck, Victoria L. 1984. The state of Federal river recreation management. In: Popadic, Joseph S.; Butterfield, Dorothy I.; Anderson, Dorothy H.; Popadic, Mary R., eds. 1984 national river recreation symposium proceedings; 1984 October 31-November 3; Baton Rouge, LA. Baton Rouge, LA: Louisiana State University, School of Landscape Architecture: 466-473.

Blair, William D., Jr. 1986. The Nature Conservancy: conservation through cooperation. Journal of Forest History. 30: 37-41.

Buist, Leon J.; Hoots, Thomas A. 1982. Recreation Opportunity Spectrum approach to resource planning. Journal of Forestry. 80(2): 84-86.

Burns, Russell M. 1984. Importance of baseline information to the research natural area program. In: Johnson, Janet L.; Franklin, Jerry F.; Krebill, Richard G., coords. Research natural areas: baseline monitoring and management; Proceedings of a symposium; 1984 March 21; Missoula, MT. Gen. Tech. Rep. INT-173. Ogden, UT: U.S. Department of Agriculture, Forest Service, Intermountain Forest and Range Experiment Station: 50-52.

Cunningham, William P.; Scott, Douglas W. 1969. The Magruder Corridor controversy. Living Wilderness. 33(107): 36-39.

Davis, George D. 1984. Natural diversity for future generations: the role of wilderness. In: Cooley, James L.; Cooley, June H., eds. Natural diversity in forest ecosystems: Proceedings of the workshop; 1982 November 29-December 1; Athens, GA. Athens, GA: University of Georgia, Institute of Ecology: 141-154.

Davis, George D. 1988. Preservation of natural diversity: The role of ecosystem representation within wilderness. In: Wilderness benchmark 1988: proceedings of the national wilderness colloquium; 1988 January 13-14; Tampa, FL: U.S. Department of Agriculture, Forest Service, Southeastern Forest Experiment Station: 76-82.

Dorrington, Michael. 1990. Biological diversity, wilderness, and the public lands. U.S. Department of the Interior. Bureau of Land Management. 1-6.

Federal Committee on Research Natural Areas. 1968. A directory of research natural areas. Washington, DC: U.S. Government Printing Office. 129 p.

Foster, John D. 1976. Bureau of Land Management primitive areas—are they counterfeit wilderness? Natural Resources Journal. 16(3): 621-663.

Fredsall, R. M. 1974. Land withdrawal situation report. Unpublished paper on file at: Western Wood Products Association, Portland, OR.

Germain, Cliff. 1984. Wisconsin's Wild Resources System. Natural Areas Journal. 4(4): 36-41.

Gilbert, Bil. 1986. The nature conservancy game. Sports Illustrated. 65(17): 86-100.

Gillette, Elizabeth R. 1972. Action for wilderness. San Francisco: Sierra Club. 222 p.

Journal North. June 8. 1990. Bush signs legislation to protect Jemez, Pecos areas from mining. Santa Fe, New Mexico.

Leatherberry, Earl C.; Lime, David W.; Thompson, Jerrilyn LaVarre. 1980. Trends in river recreation. In: The 1980 national outdoor recreation trends symposium; 1980 April 20-23; Durham, NH. Gen. Tech. Rep. NE-57. Broomall, PA: U.S. Department of Agriculture, Forest Service, Northeastern Forest Experiment Station: 147-164.

McCloskey, Michael. 1966. The Wilderness Act: its background and meaning. Oregon Law Review. 45(4): 288-321.

Moir, William H. 1972. Natural areas. Science. 177(4047): 396-400.

Nash, Roderick. 1982. Wilderness and the American mind. 3d ed. New Haven, CT: Yale University Press. 425 p.

Noss, Reed F. 1990 Draft. What can wilderness do for biodiversity? Unpublished paper.

The Nature Conservancy. 1977. Preserving our natural heritage: State activities. Washington, DC: U.S. Government Printing Office. 2 vol.

Outdoor Recreation Resources Review Commission [ORRRC]. 1962. Wilderness and recreation: a report on resources, values, and problems. ORRRC Study Rep. 3. Washington, DC: U.S. Government Printing Office. 352 p.

Peters, Clay E. 1975. A national system of wild and scenic rivers. Naturalist. 26(1): 28-31.

Stankey, George H. 1971. Myths in wilderness decisionmaking. Journal of Soil and Water Conservation. 26(5): 183-188.

Stankey, George H. 1984. Wilderness preservation activity at the State level: a national review. Natural Areas Journal. 4(4): 20-28.

Tarlock, A. Dan; Tippy, Roger. 1970. The Wild and Scenic Rivers Act of 1968. Cornell Law Review. 55(5): 707-739.

Trumbly, James M.; Gray, Kenneth L. 1984. The California Wilderness Preservation System. Natural Areas Journal. 4(4): 29-35.

The Wilderness Society. 1989. The National Wilderness Preservation System, 1964-1989. Colored. For sale by The Wilderness Society, 1400 Eye Street, NW, Washington, DC 20005.

ACKNOWLEDGMENTS

American Rivers, Washington, DC.

Thirteen wilderness management principles serve as concepts from which more specific direction and policy can be derived. A first principle is that wilderness is one extreme of the land use spectrum, where naturalness and outstanding opportunities for solitude are legally mandated. Wolf Peak in the Absaroka-Beartooth Wilderness, MT, looking south. Photo courtesy of Richard Behan.

7

PRINCIPLES OF WILDERNESS MANAGEMENT

John C. Hendee was lead author for this chapter.

INTRODUCTION

Wilderness management is complex. When a problem arises, many solutions might be possible; seldom are there single, unequivocal answers at hand. Instead, managers must devise and choose from alternative solutions. It is important that the manager's decision-making rationale produce solutions that are compatible with the wilderness idea. This chapter offers a set of principles—fundamental assumptions—that will help managers make decisions with a high degree of consistency. These principles will guide managers in solving day-to-day problems and in writing long-term policy. The principles offer perspectives on the nature of the wilderness resource, its use, and its place in the spectrum of land uses. The list may not cover every situation, and managers may want to add a principle or two of their own. Nevertheless, application of these principles will usually result in appropriate action. The principles will be cited and often applied to specific management situations throughout this book.

PRINCIPLE 1: MANAGE WILDERNESS AS ONE EXTREME ON THE ENVIRONMENTAL MODIFICATION SPECTRUM

The concept of the environmental modification spectrum describes a continuum of settings that range from the "paved to the primeval" (Nash 1982); that is, from the totally modified landscape of a modern city to those remote and pristine reaches of the nation. Our society has decided, through the Wilderness Act, to preserve selected areas at the undeveloped end of this spectrum as part of the National Wilderness Preservation System (NWPS)

> to assure that an increasing population, accompanied by expanding settlement and growing mechanization, does not occupy and modify all areas within the United States ... leaving no lands designated for preservation and protection in their natural condition.

Principle 1 recognizes the existence of a wide range of environments that are not designated wilderness. These lands are successively more modified than wilderness: roadless but nonwilderness lands; roaded wildlands set aside for park, recreation, or scenic purposes; multiple-use lands serving resource production goals as well as public recreation; and so on.

In this spectrum, wilderness is distinguished by its relatively undisturbed condition, naturalness, and solitude. Uses that alter these qualities reduce the range of environmental conditions available to meet public interests and desires. Such uses also threaten to erode the threshold along this spectrum that separates wilderness from other land. Thus, a fundamental objective of wilderness management is to maintain and perpetuate the distinctive qualities that define and separate wilderness from other land uses.

To achieve this fundamental objective, we need to resist pressures that would increase the level of environmental modification in wilderness. Wilderness simply cannot, and should not, meet all of the demands that might be placed on it. To do so would directly violate provisions of the Wilderness Act, as well as lead to a loss of those environmental qualities that prompted passage of the act in the first place; that is, the naturalness and solitude such areas offer. Yet it is impossible to protect these distinguishing qualities in the long run unless other opportunities along the environmental modification spectrum are also provided, where both commodity and recreation demands not requiring wilderness qualities can be met.

PRINCIPLE 2: MANAGE WILDERNESS AS A COMPOSITE RESOURCE, NOT AS SEPARATE PARTS

To label something as a *resource* is to say that it normally is useful to society, that it meets a vital need, and that it has a specific monetary value. Most of our wildland resources—timber, forage, water—can be appraised in this fashion, but a few, especially wilderness, cannot.

Wilderness has only recently acquired value in our culture. To the early settlers, the abundant wilderness was something to be eliminated; it served only to hide hostile natives and dangerous animals and to hinder progress. In the past two or three generations, however, the growing scarcity of wilderness has highlighted its unique qualities and prompted efforts to ensure its preservation. It was not the physical presence of flora and fauna that made wilderness a valuable resource, it was the recognition of its unique worth when preserved in its natural condition.

Wilderness has clearly achieved the status of a resource in our society by virtue of its cultural values. The Wilderness Act refers to "an enduring resource of wilderness." From a management standpoint, one important attribute of the wilderness resource is the natural relationship among all its ecosystem parts: vegetation, water, forage, wildlife, and geology. *Wilderness is a composite resource with interrelated parts, and its management must be focused on the whole, not on those component parts.* For wilderness, therefore, one should not develop separate management plans for vegetation, wildlife, and recreation. Rather, one plan must deal simultaneously with the interrelationships between these and all other component parts of the resource. Likewise, criteria controlling the use of wilderness should be based on the maintenance of natural relationships. For instance, fishing regulations might be guided by effects of anglers on shoreline vegetation and soil and the solitude afforded visitors, as well as by the impact on the fish populations. Other wilderness recreation use might be managed or controlled not only by site capacity, but also by tolerance of vegetation, wildlife distribution and behavior, and water quality.

If wilderness is viewed as a resource, what can be said about its renewability? Clearly, commercial exploitation—logging, mining, hydrocarbon development—would destroy what we define as the wilderness resource. But just as clearly, the passage of time, coupled with a restriction on further disturbance, eventually would lead to a reestablishment of primi-

tive, naturally appearing conditions—although perhaps without some plant or animal that was a part of the original ecosystem. In this sense, then, wilderness is renewable only to a degree. Depending on the type of environment, renewal could require many human generations or centuries. Interestingly, Americans are now beginning to believe that wildlands, especially in the East, have renewability as wilderness. Whereas in the West, wilderness is usually designated on lands not yet impacted by settlement, in the East, numerous areas have been classified as wilderness that were once homesteaded, roaded, and logged, but are now reverting to wildness. Thus, for some of these lands under today's conditions, wilderness is judged as their highest and best use (Hendee 1986). In Chapter 10, Wilderness Ecosystems, Jerry Franklin asks which are more unnatural or permanently changed—wildernesses in the West that have had fire protection for 70 years, or wildernesses in the East that have been extensively homesteaded and logged.

Renewability of the wilderness resource was a major theme in debate over the Wilderness Act. Many proponents have pointed to the importance of the act as a mechanism that might allow the wilderness characteristics of disturbed sites to recover. One of the great promises of the Wilderness Act is that we can dedicate formerly abused areas where the primeval scene can be restored by natural forces. Thus, it is not easy to describe precise status of wilderness on the renewable-to-nonrenewable continuum. As criteria for the degree of naturalness and solitude required for wilderness designation have broadened during the roadless area reviews of the 1970s and 1980s, so has acceptance of the idea that lands can revert to a wilder state to once again become wilderness. But even when management seeks to restore wilderness conditions, the focus must be on allowing natural processes to operate, thus protecting natural relationships between parts of ecosystems.

PRINCIPLE 3: MANAGE WILDERNESS AND SITES WITHIN, UNDER A NONDEGRADATION CONCEPT

We have described wilderness as part of an environmental modification spectrum that ranges from the paved to the primeval. But even within the part of the spectrum that includes wilderness, a range of settings exist. Not all areas classified as wilderness are identical in their primeval qualities. Areas vary in the degree to which naturalness has remained unspoiled, or to

which opportunities for solitude remain undiminished by current, established uses. Such variations also occur within each wilderness. Expectations and definitions of wilderness change with the condition of the areas surrounding them. The relativity of wilderness was reflected in debates over the so-called Eastern Wilderness Act of 1975 (P.L. 93-622) and the subsequent classification as wilderness of areas in the East that perhaps did not meet the early criteria of the Wilderness Act of 1964 (P.L. 88-577).

How are managers to work to a reasonably uniform standard for the NWPS when qualities such as naturalness and solitude vary so widely, not only by region but also among and within individual wilderness? Wilderness managers have found the answer in the concept of nondegradation, which has been generally applied to management of air and water quality. Basically, the *nondegradation* concept calls for the maintenance of existing environmental conditions if they equal or exceed minimum standards, and for the restoration of conditions which are below minimum levels. For example, where air quality is currently higher than required by legislation, the higher level should be preserved and not be allowed to deteriorate to minimum legal standards. Thus, the minimum legal standards of air quality do not constitute an acceptable level to which air quality everywhere will be allowed to deteriorate; rather, the objective is to maintain currently high standards, to prevent further degradation, and to restore below-minimum conditions to acceptable levels (Meyers and Tarlock 1971; Mihaley 1972).

As applied to wilderness, the nondegradation principle recognizes that naturalness and solitude vary between individual wildernesses. The objective is to prevent degradation of current naturalness and solitude in each wilderness and restore substandard settings to minimum levels, rather than letting all areas in the NWPS deteriorate to a minimum standard. For example, certain wildernesses that possess only minimum levels of naturalness and solitude need not set a standard to which areas of higher quality will be allowed to descend. The near-pristine areas in the Intermountain West should not be allowed to decline to the substantial level of impact found in some southern California wildernesses. Likewise, wilderness classification of heavily impacted areas in the eastern United States does not mean that the level of naturalness and solitude found in those areas should constitute an acceptable level for areas in the West. To a degree, under the nondegradation principle, the conditions prevailing in each area when it is classified establish the benchmark of naturalness to be sought by management—

unless conditions are deemed below standard and the objective is to restore naturalness.

The nondegradation concept also allows the opportunity to upgrade or to restore quality. Where existing conditions are judged to be below minimum acceptable levels, an appropriate priority of management is to promote restoration of the wilderness to minimum quality levels. This does not imply that wilderness restoration will involve activities such as planting grass and shrubs, fertilizing, and watering. Numerous management activities can promote natural restoration by controlling visitor numbers, timing of use, and other measures. How purely to manage each wilderness has been a longstanding issue; adoption of the nondegradation concept may help resolve this in principle.

PRINCIPLE 4: MANAGE HUMAN INFLUENCES, A KEY TO WILDERNESS PROTECTION

The need for managing wilderness users hardly has to be argued (see chap. 1). Wilderness visitation has grown steadily, and many new areas that already sustain substantial roadless recreation have been added to the NWPS. Specific examples of site impacts and deterioration can be found in virtually any area. Human influence extends even to the most remote wilderness environments. Indirect influence is evident, for example, in the unnatural vegetation patterns resulting from fire prevention and suppression, which in turn contribute to an unnatural distribution of wildlife. The fragile, sometimes irreplaceable, qualities of these areas are easily lost unless thoughtful, deliberate management protects against the direct impacts of use and the indirect but pervasive influences of civilization. Increasing the size of the NWPS offers only short-term protection. Ultimately the preservation of wilderness, and the values and benefits it offers people, will depend on the management of wilderness areas after they have been classified.

The principal goal of wilderness preservation is the maintenance of long-term ecological processes. *Thus, wilderness management is basically concerned with management of human use and influences to preserve natural processes.* Recreational impacts are currently among the most critical unnatural influences in wilderness. Therefore, managers are challenged to guide, modify, and, if necessary as a last resort, to directly control use to minimize its impact. This has become an accepted tenet of wilderness management, although specific controls on visitation are usually controversial.

Some resource managers believe that once land becomes wilderness, their responsibility for managing it virtually ends. Nothing could be more wrong. Wilderness areas provide for many uses and produce important human values, and must be managed to protect and increase those benefits.

Currently, wilderness management emphasizes management of people. But ecological problems are also becoming important; wilderness managers are increasingly challenged to monitor the naturalness of wilderness and provide counterinfluences to human impacts. Fire and wildlife, for example, need to be restored to a closer approximation of their historical roles and status in many areas (see chaps. 11 and 12). The growing number of site impacts in wilderness, our increasing knowledge about how they occur, and skill in controlling or correcting them, are also extending wilderness management activity to deal directly with these ecological and physical impacts (see chap. 17). Furthermore, the NWPS has grown rapidly and is approaching 100 million acres, and now includes areas previously impacted and in need of protection so that natural qualities can return.

PRINCIPLE 5: MANAGE WILDERNESS TO PRODUCE HUMAN VALUES AND BENEFITS

Wilderness is classified not just to protect its flora and fauna, but for enjoyment (as wilderness) by people. The purpose of preservation goals established for wilderness areas is clear. As the act notes: "It is ... the policy of the Congress to secure for the American people of present and future generations the benefits of an enduring resource of wilderness." Thus, wilderness managers are legally mandated to produce the important and—in the judgment of some—necessary benefits that wilderness yields to people.

Just what are the benefits derived from wilderness? Wilderness visitors may directly benefit from the enjoyment, education, therapy, or spiritual renewal coincident to their wilderness recreation. Others might vicariously appreciate or indirectly benefit from wilderness, simply by seeing it on television or by reading about it. Other indirect benefits can accrue to society from increased scientific knowledge derived from research in wilderness. These benefits are not easily measured, nor is there evidence that they are optimally or exclusively produced in wilderness. Nevertheless, realization of human benefits to be derived from wilderness preservation and use is implicit in the wilder-

ness ideology and philosophy that led to passage of the wilderness acts and the allocation of federal resources. This also reflects one of the central beliefs of the founding fathers of our wilderness system: that the character-building values of wilderness are vital to our society (Scott 1984). The continued protection of these human values and benefits must be a fundamental goal of wilderness management.

Two widely differing wilderness management philosophies exist, both aimed at enhancing the human benefits of wilderness. The biocentric perspective emphasizes environmental integrity as the basis for human benefits. The anthropocentric perspective promotes management of natural processes to increase aesthetic pleasure and facilitate wilderness use (see discussion in chap. 1).

The federal wilderness management agencies—the National Park Service (NPS), U.S. Forest Service (USFS), Fish and Wildlife Service (FWS), and Bureau of Land Management (BLM)—all follow management guidelines that reflect a commitment to maintain high standards of naturalness and opportunities for solitude (USDA FS 1976; USDI BLM 1984; USDI F&WS 1982; USDI NPS 1975). These guidelines provide direction for handling specific wilderness issues and call for deliberate efforts to preserve wilderness to protect its contrasts to environments already modified by human activity. (The summary of agency wilderness wildlife policies at the end of chap. 11 illustrates the similar direction, with some specific organizational differences.)

As discussed in detail in chapter 1, it is from the primeval attributes of wilderness that human benefits are derived; attempts to facilitate wilderness enjoyment by improving access to make visitation easier, more convenient, or simultaneously accessible to an unacceptable number of people can ultimately diminish its unique benefits. This reality calls for a biocentric emphasis in wilderness management policy, but applied with common sense—a rule of reason. "Purity in the extreme" can and has triggered a backlash, as illustrated in the discussions of Church (1977) and Weaver and Cutler (1977). The biocentric-anthropocentric concepts are abstractions that facilitate discussion of management alternatives to keep the wild in wilderness, but allowing as much use as is consistent with that goal so people can directly benefit from the wilderness experience.

PRINCIPLE 6: FAVOR WILDERNESS-DEPENDENT ACTIVITIES

Wilderness is the setting for activities ranging from scientific study to recreational pursuits such as fishing, backpacking, and picnicking, some of which depend significantly on a primeval setting. For example, some types of scientific study are dependent on the availability of a substantially unaltered ecosystem, perhaps covering a large area. Conversely, other activities, such as certain kinds of hunting and fishing, are not dependent on a wilderness situation at all, although they can be enhanced by such a setting. Whenever one or more uses conflict, the principle of *wilderness dependency*, which calls for favoring activities most dependent on wilderness conditions, is used to resolve use conflicts and prevent overuse. This principle is intended to assure optimum use of wilderness resources.

Activities that are not wilderness dependent can be enjoyed in many alternative settings, but wilderness-dependent ones cannot. Thus, most conflicts should be resolved in favor of wilderness-dependent uses. Such policy avoids displacing those seeking wilderness experiences, whose opportunities are in short supply compared to those satisfied with nonwilderness experiences. This point of view was championed by Robert Marshall (1930, 1937) and more recently by Bryan as "A Sociological Criterion" (Bryan 1979). Providing an adequate range of nonwilderness recreation is important, as discussed under principle 1, so persons not dependent on wilderness can find alternative areas.

Defining an activity as wilderness dependent can be difficult. Often, it is not the activity itself that is dependent, but the particular style in which it is pursued. For example, hunting is not necessarily wilderness dependent. But certain styles of hunting, such as pursuing game under the most natural conditions away from roads, or stalking a dall sheep, are highly dependent on wilderness settings. The importance of naturalness and solitude to the experience, not the mere quest for game, defines certain kinds of hunting as wilderness dependent (see chap. 12).

Likewise, although people can fish in a wide variety of settings, certain styles of fishing may be wilderness dependent. Those who desire remote, difficult-to-reach lakes where one can fish under natural conditions without meeting other people may rely on wilderness for such opportunities. Many visitors report that fishing is an important part of their wilderness experience, enhancing other satisfactions such as ob-

Fig. 7.1. An important principle of management is to favor wilderness-dependent recreational activities—those that require naturalness and solitude. (left) Rider in the Sycamore Canyon Wilderness, AZ. Photo courtesy of Starr Jenkins, USFS. (right) Angler at Lower Aero Lake in the Absaroka-Beartooth Wilderness, MT. Photo courtesy of Richard Behan.

servation of aquatic life, photography, and so on.

Thus, favoring wilderness-dependent activities might call for reducing or discouraging—rather than eliminating—certain *forms* of some activities (fig. 7.1). One is reminded again of the interdependency of wilderness with the rest of the Recreation Opportunity Spectrum (ROS). The key to maintaining wilderness-dependent activities in classified wilderness is to provide alternative nonwilderness lands to which inappropriate activity can be diverted.

PRINCIPLE 7: GUIDE MANAGEMENT WITH WRITTEN PLANS THAT STATE OBJECTIVES FOR SPECIFIC AREAS

Wilderness management actions must be guided by formal plans that state goals and objectives and explain in detail how they will be achieved. Without such clear prescriptions, management can become uncoordinated and even counterproductive to the goals of the Wilderness Act. Local managers and the public need wilderness management plans to consider whether qualities and strategies are appropriate for specific areas and are consistent with legislative goals and national policy. Public involvement is an important educational process for both managers and citizens.

As will be explained in chapter 8, wilderness management plans focus increasingly refined guide-

lines on the management of individual areas. The general goals of the Wilderness Act are translated into narrower departmental regulations, then to more explicit agency policy, and finally to specific objectives for a given area and the policies and management actions prescribed to achieve them. This planning process permits local agency officials and citizens to review the varying situations of individual areas and to develop management strategies consistent with broad legislative goals. Departmental regulations and agency policy provide some direction, yet must remain responsive to specific local conditions.

Wilderness management plans must include specific objectives—clear statements of desired wilderness conditions. Every proposed management action must be evaluated for its potential contribution to a specific objective. Clear objectives and the commitment to be guided by them are important because management actions can have enduring— even irreversible—results. Philosophies, perceptions, and definitions of wilderness can vary widely among managers. Plans with clear, formally stated objectives are needed to guide judgments about what management actions are necessary; to provide continuity when managers are replaced; and to prevent damage from ill-conceived plans, no matter how well intended. Excessive or poorly conceived management actions can be as damaging to wilderness values as the absence of management. For example, a series of relatively minor decisions outside an

overall plan might result in too many trails built to unnecessarily high standards, an excessive number of signs, or unnecessary restrictions on user activities. The combined impact of these uncoordinated actions can depreciate wilderness values. Only actions necessary to achieve objectives should be implemented.

Objectives are also essential to monitoring progress and evaluating the success of wilderness management. If an objective is not reached, an evaluator needs to know why: lack of feasibility? the need for different policies or implementing actions? the need for a different or more conscientious administration? Because the goals of the Wilderness Act are so broad, it is difficult to write clear objectives for the various aspects of wilderness management. But it is crucial to develop, through an orderly planning process, the clearest and most specific objectives possible and to use them as constant guides to management.

PRINCIPLE 8: SET CARRYING CAPACITIES AS NECESSARY TO PREVENT UNNATURAL CHANGE

Wilderness has limited capacity to absorb the impacts of use and still retain its wilderness qualities. As use increases or as damaging patterns of use develop at specific places or during particular times, wilderness qualities may disappear, either gradually or with startling swiftness. *Carrying capacity*—the use an area can tolerate without unacceptable change—offers a framework for managing use to preserve wilderness qualities.

Change due to natural ecological processes inevitabily occurs in wilderness. The purpose of management is not to freeze ecosystems in any point of succession—a vignette of earlier times—but to allow *natural* change to occur, with an absolute minimum of human manipulation. Both ecological conditions and available wilderness experiences are subject to such change. The standards of ecological integrity and human solitude that are established for an area—and the specific area management objectives that express these standards—help define the carrying capacity of an individual wilderness (fig. 7.2).

Applied to wilderness, the concept of carrying capacity has two important parameters: (1) physical-biological and (2) social-psychological. *Physical and biological dimensions* describe the amount and kind of use an ecosystem can sustain without undue evidence of unnatural impact. Campsite deterioration and expanding impact resulting from soil compaction, the denuding and proliferation of paths near locations of concentrated human use, exposed and protruding tree roots, and the unnatural behavior and distribution of wildlife are all signs of unnatural change from the physical impact of use. *Social or psychological dimensions* refer to the levels and concentrations of human use an area can accommodate before the solitude so vital to wilderness experiences is diminished. "Outstanding opportunities for solitude" are specified in the Wilderness Act. Several studies document that solitude—privacy from persons in other parties, particularly from large parties, and other users camping near one's campsite—is the most important attribute of the wilderness experience (Stankey 1973; Graefe and others 1986). Concentrations of visitors at popular attractions such as hot springs, lakes, or shelters might indicate that the social carrying capacity is being approached or exceeded.

Carrying capacity is discussed in more detail in chapter 9, but here four major points are stressed:

1. Carrying capacity is a relative term, not an absolute number to be discovered by managers and researchers. Its range depends on specific objectives established for an area.
2. Capacity must be established and identified in the field by managerial judgments—no magic yardstick can tell when it will be or when it has been exceeded.
3. Capacity is tied to (a) the qualities of the physical-biological environment and (b) the qualities of the human experience available in wilderness.
4. The development of capacity limits is a necessary part of the planning process for those areas and locations where unacceptable change may occur. To achieve the long-term goals of wilderness preservation, time and space aspects of wilderness use must be managed to avoid unnatural changes.

Fig. 7.2. Wilderness managers must sometimes set constraints on carrying capacity. Too many visitors can depreciate the quality of the wilderness environment and solitude. Trail riders east of Cloudy Pass near Lyman Lake, Glacier Peak Wilderness, WA. Photo courtesy of Robert DeWitz, USFS.

PRINCIPLE 9: FOCUS MANAGEMENT ON THREATENED SITES AND DAMAGING ACTIVITIES

Wilderness management is mainly concerned with specific physical impacts of use on the wilderness environment and on the social-psychological experience of visitors. It calls for selective, site-specific orientation rather than an across-the-board approach that would impose restrictions everywhere in a wilderness to solve problems that might be only local or temporary in nature.

Controls on use are already being implemented in some of the more heavily used wildernesses and at certain popular locations in many others (Washburne and Cole 1983). Whenever such restrictions are contemplated, several difficult questions must be asked: Who should be restricted? under what conditions and criteria? how should restrictions be implemented?

Obviously, not all uses produce equal impacts. All types of wilderness use and activities can be ranked according to their relative physical and social-psychological impacts. When restrictions are necessary, those activities having the greatest impact can be the first ones controlled. For example, various types of wilderness use might be ranked, in the absence of an actual study, in the following order of decreasing environmental and social-psychological impact: large parties of horse users, small parties of overnight campers, small parties of overnight campers not building fires, small parties of day hikers. Additional criteria—such as visitors' skill levels—might be used to establish or modify priorities among users (Behan 1976).

The unacceptable impact from various users might require regulation in only a few locations in a wilderness, which avoids shifting the problems to other sites. Furthermore, the vulnerability of the resource is greater at different times, such as in early spring when vegetation is lush and easily damaged or on peak weekends when use is heavier. Thus, to minimize excessive environmental and social-psychological impacts, restrictions should be selective—to times, places, and users having the greatest potential for damage.

This principle of selective restriction strives to promote equity by specifying those conditions under which uses will be regulated. Discrimination against certain types of use, such as packstock or large, organized groups of hikers, is based on their respective impacts on the wilderness environment. It relieves wilderness managers of deciding arbitrarily on a certain mix of horse users, organized groups, hikers, and so forth; or alternatively, from deciding that because they cannot make such choices, everyone or no one must be restricted.

PRINCIPLE 10: APPLY ONLY THE MINIMUM REGULATIONS OR TOOLS NECESSARY TO ACHIEVE WILDERNESS AREA OBJECTIVES

Freedom, spontaniety, and escape are recognized as important qualities of the wilderness experience. But as discussed elsewhere in this book, restrictions must sometimes be imposed to prevent these fragile attributes from being destroyed by overuse. Ironically, regulation itself can diminish the quality of the wilderness experience unless it is carefully implemented. *The guiding principle is that only the minimum regimentation necessary to achieve established wilderness management objectives is justified.* This principle is sometimes called the *minimum tool rule*—apply only the minimum tools, equipment, device, force, regulation, or practice that will bring the desired result.

As will be explained in chapters 15 and 16, management actions may be either direct or indirect. Which approach is appropriate depends on a manager's judgment about the degree of regulation necessary to achieve objectives and the likely effectiveness of various regulatory and nonregulatory actions in a certain situation (Lucas 1983). Actually, it is helpful to think of management actions as a continuum, ranging from subtle, lighthanded, and indirect options, to direct and authoritarian options—such as telling visitors where they can travel and camp, and how long they can stay.

The challenge of wilderness management lies in the developing, testing, and implementing of *indirect controls* that delay and minimize the imposition of direct controls. The more subtle controls include visitor education, appeals for self-regulated and low-impact camping practices, and the locating of trailheads and trails to minimize impact on fragile areas. *Direct controls* might begin with the management of specific, overused sites, where efforts would be made to educate and disperse users. Only as a last resort, when an array of specific and successively more restrictive measures have been exhausted, would direct control of visitation to an entire wilderness be considered.

If, for example, managers wish to more evenly distribute visitors, they might first use the educational approach—provide information about cur-

Fig. 7.3. Public education is one of the wilderness manager's most important tools. Visitor guidance can help prevent many undesirable impacts, thus postponing more stringent regulations. This follows the principle of using only the minimum level of regulation necessary to achieve wilderness management objectives. Here, a wilderness ranger contacts users to seek their help in preserving the area. Photo courtesy of the USFS.

rent visitor distribution, alternative trailheads and routes, times when use is low, and so on (fig. 7.3). But if and when this approach appears to be inadequate to deal with impacts, or it fails to redistribute use as desired, then a more restrictive, direct-action approach might be in order. A manager might then limit camping at heavily impacted sites, set entry quotas at each trailhead, or even assign campsites. Ultimately, for every wilderness area there is a point beyond which the wilderness experience becomes so diluted by restrictions that the feelings of freedom, spontaniety, and escape are in danger of being lost. It is at this point—which must be subjectively determined by managers—that rationing of entry must begin.

PRINCIPLE 11: INVOLVE THE PUBLIC AS A KEY TO THE ACCEPTANCE AND SUCCESS OF WILDERNESS MANAGEMENT

The Wilderness Act was one of the first major laws mandating *public involvement* in natural resources management—in the selection and designation of areas to be classified as wilderness. Nevertheless, for the first decade following passage of the Wilderness Act, many wilderness managers thought that the public did not have enough expertise to participate in wilderness management decisions. They thought that only professional resource managers could un-

derstand the legal and ecological complexities involved. During the second decade of wilderness management the public rapidly learned how to participate in public land management. Wilderness managers became more adept at working with people and providing for public involvement as an essential step in planning wilderness allocation and management. Today, public involvement is recognized as perhaps the most important tool for the successful development and implementation of wilderness management plans and actions. In fact, most resource managers today consider public involvement essential to the development and implementation of any management of public lands, and increasingly it is required by law. Clearly, any proposed wilderness management action needs public involvement as a source of wisdom and essential public support, without which its implementation will fail.

Public involvement is also extending beyond decision making to the work itself. Volunteerism in national park and national forest management is mushrooming. Wilderness duty is a favorite with volunteers—so much so that managing volunteers was one of the important "Issues in Wilderness Management" addressed at a 1983 national conference (Frome 1985). Trends involving volunteer rangers; wilderness information specialists; HOST programs; wilderness "cleanup" and "adopt-a-trail" projects; private contracting of trail construction and maintenance; and wilderness field management help increase citizen involvement in wilderness work.

These volunteer efforts supplement diminishing budgets, but their greatest value goes beyond that. Public involvement in the day-to-day management of wilderness increases recognition and appreciation of wilderness values—and that is one of the ultimate purposes of the NWPS (Hendee 1986).

Public involvement in wilderness management is firmly established and growing in importance. This has serious implications. It is turning wilderness managers into public facilitators. No longer will most future wilderness managers apprentice as seasonal employees, developing field skills for subsequent career positions. Apprenticeships now are more likely to be filled by volunteers. Career positions will largely deal with managing volunteer projects, coordinating cooperative work with conservation and service organizations, contracting with private firms, and educating the public. This scenario reflects the rapid change that is affecting all public resource management. Wilderness management is in fact the cutting edge of changes that may affect all resource management, with growing public involvement in decisions and with carrying out management tasks.

PRINCIPLE 12: MONITOR WILDERNESS CONDITIONS AND EXPERIENCE OPPORTUNITIES AS A KEY TO LONG-TERM WILDERNESS MANAGEMENT

Any management plan or program needs a monitoring system to evaluate progress toward stated objectives, and to guide the long-term revision, adjustment, and refinement of the plan. Devising monitoring systems remains one of the major challenges for advancing wilderness management. All planning approaches described in chapter 8 require monitoring to assess success. A good plan describes as objectives the wilderness conditions to be achieved. Only through *monitoring*—the systematic gathering, comparing, and evaluation of data—can one tell whether those objectives are being realized. For example, under the Limits of Acceptable Change (LAC) planning approach, data are needed to establish baseline conditions and determine the degree of change occurring in various opportunity zones (Stankey and others 1985).

Just what data should be collected and by what methods is an important topic for research. The challenge is to measure and evaluate certain indicators that reflect important attributes of *biological*, *physical*, and *social* conditions in wilderness (Merigliano and Krumpe 1986). A major study at the University of Idaho Wilderness Research Center identified a set of candidate indicators and ranked their importance as seen by selected groups of wilderness scientists and managers (Krumpe 1985). The approach categorized *biological* conditions into vegetation, mammals, and fish, considering a total of 86 potential indicators which might singly or in combination reveal change. Categories of *physical* conditions were soil, water, and air, with 75 potential indicators. Categories of *social conditions* were descriptions of visitors and their level of experience, with 50 indicators considered. Fieldwork has yet to test most of the proposed indicators in wilderness—especially as they relate to planned wilderness management—which illustrates that monitoring is a new concept in wilderness management.

Wilderness monitoring is important for realizing the ultimate values of the NWPS for science and environmental assessment. Significant questions facing humanity concern how human activity has modified natural processes globally as well as regionally and locally. Acid rain and related air pollution impacts, the effects of human activity on water quality and volume, climatic variation, heating and cooling of the earth, and other subtle changes are all areas of concern. Such impacts may be reflected first in changes in vegetation and fish and wildlife habitats, and, subsequently, in loss of species. Wilderness provides enclaves of the most natural remaining areas and is thus a source of information on the degree of distortion of natural processes elsewhere—but only if sufficiently detailed information is collected and made available for use as environmental baselines. Monitoring and assessment systems could partially provide such data, supplementing more detailed scientific studies of wilderness conditions.

PRINCIPLE 13: MANAGE WILDERNESS IN COORDINATION WITH MANAGEMENT OF ADJACENT LANDS

The principle—that management of wilderness must consider the management of adjacent lands—is also related to the environmental modification spectrum. Here, however, the concern broadens from outdoor recreation opportunities to a variety of other resource uses and management practices. Simply put, wilderness does not exist in a vacuum—what goes on outside of, but adjacent to, a wilderness can have substantial

impacts inside its boundary. Conversely, the designation of a tract of land as a wilderness can substantially affect the management of adjacent areas.

This interrelationship is probably best illustrated by the impacts resulting from timber harvesting. The building of logging roads to the edge of a wilderness boundary can dramatically affect the amount and character of its recreational use by providing easy access. Impacts resulting from increased use can compromise the goal of maintaining natural conditions. Such impacts might be attenuated by reducing the number of roads, lowering road standards, and closing roads after timber harvesting.

Similarly, the development of high-density recreational facilities (youth camps, picnic areas, paved roads, and parking lots) immediately adjacent to wilderness or undeveloped backcountry can bring serious management problems as users of these facilities penetrate the wilderness for hiking, fishing, or other activities. For example, one of the most heavily used entrances into the San Gorgonio Wilderness in southern California is the South Fork Meadows trail. Formerly, access to the wilderness boundary was over a route called "Poopout Hill" an appropriate name for a climb that required considerable effort. Today, the hill is topped by a paved road and lined by numerous summer camps. Because of this improved access and the added visitation from the youth camps, use impacts in the area reached such a level that entry at that trailhead had to be rationed beginning in 1973 (Hay 1974). This rationing program, an extraordinary management step necessitated by the improved road and development, has been successful in that it has allowed numerous youths to experience wilderness, yet it has maintained the wilderness threshold.

Impacts can also move from wilderness to nearby nonwilderness areas. For example, programs to reestablish natural fire regimes in wilderness can result in smoke pollution and some risk of fire losses in adjacent areas managed for commodity production. Wildlife that thrive on summer range in high wilderness meadows may compete with domestic stock for forage in the lower valleys during winter. In the Southeast, where the southern pine beetle is a constant threat to the region's pine forests, there is concern that wilderness areas may harbor infestations that might spread to adjacent lands (Warren 1985).

Relating the management of wilderness to that of adjacent lands is complex and controversial. One commonly suggested possibility is creation of a *buffer zone*—a band of land around the periphery of wilderness that would absorb impacts and help avert conflicts. Some managers and some commercial interests oppose this solution, however, arguing that the buffer zone should fall within the wilderness. Congress has spoken against buffer zones. In any case, wilderness can be protected from impacts originating on surrounding lands only through comprehensive land use planning that anticipates potential conflicts and addresses the complimentary and competitive relationships between wilderness and adjacent lands (Stankey 1974).

Managers planning the allocation of various forest resources should carefully define activities that are compatible with wilderness and take steps to keep incompatibilities at a minimum (Clawson 1975). A concentric circle concept, with high-density, facility-oriented sites located around the periphery of a planning region, and environment-oriented and primitive-style opportunities such as wilderness, located in the core, can help integrate the various recreational resources. This gradation of uses would protect the environmental quality of the interior wilderness, while keeping the development-oriented opportunities accessible (Carhart 1961; Gould 1961; Hart 1966). To do otherwise invites problems, particularly when the most intensive uses impinge on the least developed areas.

Explicitly defined use zones also help protect against the phenomena of invasion, succession, and displacement of primitive-site recreation users by new and more numerous developed-site recreationists. The displaced users move on to more primitive sites and can start a new wave of invasion, succession, and displacement. Eventually, large areas suffer from excessive use and impacts.[1]

Managers may inadvertently aggravate undesirable impacts from this "recreational succession" by responding to every increase in use with development to accommodate it—for example, by encouraging campgrounds, large parking lots, or resort developments at the edge of wilderness. Furthermore, naturalness and solitude of the most remote sections of a wilderness can be impaired if wilderness managers are not aware of use interrelationships. Actions such as building trails to areas that are currently visited only by cross-country travelers seeking the greatest possible isolation may ultimately eliminate the most remote part of the recreation spectrum.

---

1. This process is described in Burch and Wenger 1967; Hendee and Campbell 1969; Clark and others 1971; and Stankey 1974.

SUMMARY

These 13 principles provide the foundation for much of our discussion about wilderness management. Two principles—11, public involvement, and 12, monitoring—have been added in this revised edition. As suggested, the principles are still evolving. By themselves, they do not ensure quality wilderness management, but they do provide basic concepts to guide that management. At the very least, for those in search of consistent policies and actions, they provide a basis for reviewing and evaluating solutions to problems.

STUDY QUESTIONS

1. How does the availability of recreational opportunities on nonwilderness lands affect nearby wilderness?
2. What is the environmental modification spectrum as it relates to planning forest resource uses? How can it help protect wilderness values?
3. In what sense is wilderness a renewable resource? What are the implications of the concept of renewability for wilderness management?
4. What are the two major parameters of carrying capacity that wilderness managers must consider in establishing the carrying capacity of a specific wilderness area? Explain each briefly.
5. What are wilderness-dependent uses? How can favoring them help protect wilderness from excessive impacts and at the same time protect users from unnecessary restrictions?
6. What is the *minimum tool rule*? What would be a lighthanded or minimum-tool approach to reducing damage to vegetation at a popular wilderness campsite?
7. How does the concept of nondegradation affect management of eastern wildernesses being integrated into the NWPS?
8. How has increased public involvement affected the job of professional wilderness managers? Overall, do you think the effects have been positive or negative? Why?

REFERENCES

Behan, R. W. 1976. Rationing wilderness use: an example from the Grand Canyon. Western Wildlands. 3(2): 23-26.

Bryan, Hobson. 1979. Conflict in the great outdoors: toward understanding and managing for diverse sportsmen preferences. Sociological Studies No. 4. Tuscaloosa, AL: University of Alabama, Bureau of Public Administration. 98 p.

Burch, William R.; Wenger, Wiley D. 1967. The social characteristics of participants in three styles of family camping. Res. Pap. PNW-48. Portland, OR: U.S. Department of Agriculture, Forest Service, Pacific Northwest Forest and Range Experiment Station. 30 p.

Carhart, Arthur. 1961. Planning for America's wildlands. Harrisburg, PA: The Telegraph Press. 97 p.

Church, Frank. 1977. Wilderness in a balanced land use framework. First Annual Wilderness Resource Distinguished Lecture. University of Idaho Wilderness Research Center, 1977 March 21. 18 p. [Reprinted as "Whither wilderness" American Forester. 83(7): 11-2, 38-41; 1977.]

Clark, Roger N.; Hendee, John C.; Campbell, Frederick. 1971. Values, behavior, and conflict in modern camping culture. Journal of Leisure Research. 3(3): 143-149.

Clawson, Marion. 1975. Conflicts and strategies in forest land management. Journal of Soil and Water Conservation. 39(2): 63-67.

Eastern Wilderness Act. Act of Jan. 3, 1975. Public Law 93-622, 88 Stat. 2096.

Frome, Michael, ed. 1985. Issues in wilderness management. Boulder, CO: Westview Press. 252 p.

Gould, Ernest M., Jr. 1961. Planning a recreational complex. American Forests. 67(8): 30-34.

Graefe, Alan R.; Donnelly, Maureen, P.; Vaske, Jenny. 1986. Crowding and specialization: a reexamination of the crowding model. In: Lucas, Robert C., comp. Proceedings—national wilderness research conference: current research; 1985 July 23-26; Fort Collins, CO. Gen. Tech. Rep. INT-212. Ogden, UT: U.S. Department of Agriculture, Forest Service, Intermountain Research Station: 333-338.

Hart, William J. 1966. A systems approach to park planning. IUCN Publ., New Series: Suppl. Pap. No. 4. Morges, Switzerland; International Union for Conservation of Nature. 118 p.

Hay, Edward. 1974. Wilderness experiment: it's working. American Forests. 80(12): 26-29.

Hendee, John C. 1986. Wilderness: important legal, social, philosophical, and management perspectives. In: Kulhavy, David L.; Connor, Richard H., eds. Wilderness and natural areas in the Eastern United States: a management challenge. Symposium; 1985 May 13-15; Nacogdoches, TX: Stephen F. Austin State University, School of Forestry: 5-11.

Hendee, John C.; Campbell, Frederick. 1969. Social aspects of outdoor recreation—the developed campground. Trends in Parks and Recreation. 6(4): 13-16.

Krumpe, Edward. 1985. Wilderness monitoring. Moscow, ID: University of Idaho, Wilderness Research Center. 33 p.

Lucas, Robert C. 1983. The role of regulations in recreation management. Western Wildlands. 9(2): 6-10; Summer.

Marshall, Robert. 1930. The problem of the wilderness. Science Monographs. 30(2): 141-148.

Marshall, Robert. 1937. The universe of the wilderness is vanishing. Nature. 29(4): 235-240.

Merigliano, Linda; Krumpe, Ed. 1986. Scientists identify, evaluate indicators to monitor wilderness conditions. Park Science. 6(3): 19-20.

Meyers, Charles J.; Tarlock, A. Dan. 1971. Water pollution. In: Meyers, Charles J.; Tarlock, A. Dan, eds. Water resource management. Mineola, NY: Foundation Press: 677-708.

Mihaley, Marc B. 1972. The Clean Air Act and the concept of nondegradation. Sierra Club vs. Rukelhaus. Ecological Law Review. 2(4): 801-836.

Nash, Roderick. 1982. Wilderness and the American mind. Rev. New Haven, CT: Yale University Press. 425 p.

Scott, D. W. 1984. The visionary role of Howard Zahniser. Sierra. 69(13): 40.

Stankey, George H. 1973. Visitor perception of wilderness recreation carrying capacity. Res. Pap. INT-142. Ogden, UT: U.S. Department of Agriculture, Forest Service, Intermountain Forest and Range Experiment Station. 61 p., illus.

Stankey, George H. 1974. Criteria for the determination of recreational carrying capacity in the Colorado River Basin. In: Crawford, A. Berry; Peterson, Dean F., eds. Environmental management in the Colorado River Basin. Logan, UT: Utah State University Press: 82-101.

Stankey, George H.; Cole, David N.; Lucas, Robert C.; [and others]. 1985. The limits of acceptable change (LAC) system for wilderness planning. Gen. Tech. Rep. INT-176. Ogden, UT: U.S. Department of Agriculture, Forest Service, Intermountain Forest and Range Experiment Station. 37 p.

U.S. Department of Agriculture, Forest Service. 1976. Chapter 2320: Wildernesses, primitive areas, and wilderness study area. In: Forest Service Manual. Washington, DC.

U.S. Department of the Interior, Bureau of Land Management. 1984. Bureau of Land Management manual.

U.S. Department of the Interior, Fish and Wildlife Service. 1982. Wilderness area management. In: Refuge manual. 6 RM 8. Washington, DC.

U.S. Department of the Interior, National Park Service. 1975. Chapter VI: Wilderness and preservation and management. In: Management policies. Washington, DC.

Warren, B. Jack. 1985. Why we need to control pine beetles in wilderness areas. Forest Farmer. 44(4): 6-8.

Washburne, Randel F.; Cole, David N. 1983. Problems and practices in wilderness management. A survey of 19 managers. Res. Pap. INT-304. Ogden, UT: U.S. Department of Agriculture, Forest Service, Intermountain Forest and Range Experiment Station. 56 p.

Weaver, James W.; Cutler, Rupert. 1977. Wilderness policy: a colloquy between Congressman Weaver and Assistant Secretary Cutler. Journal of Forestry. 75(7): 392-394.

Wilderness Act. An act of Sept. 3, 1964. Public Law 88-577, 78 Stat. 890.

The management direction for individual wildernesses, under constraints of the Wilderness Act and agency direction, are set forth in wilderness area management plans or contained in parts of Resources Management Plans covering large areas, including wilderness and non-wilderness lands. Wilderness management, to preserve an area's distinctive qualities of naturalness and solitude, can be no better than the underlying planning process. A horseman adjusts his saddle overlooking Big Creek Lake, Selway-Bitterroot Wilderness, on the MT-ID border. Photo courtesy of the USFS.

8

WILDERNESS MANAGEMENT PLANNING

*This chapter was written by John C. Hendee and Russell von Koch,
Recreation Planner, Bureau of Land Management, Moab, Utah.*

INTRODUCTION

The management of wilderness needs to be guided by formal plans that prescribe specific actions necessary to meet objectives. A wilderness management plan translates the general direction of legislation, departmental regulations, and agency policy to in-the-field management actions. The authors are grateful to agency officials who provided copies of the management plans referenced in this chapter.

THE NEED FOR PLANNING

Without management plans derived from an orderly planning process, wilderness management may be no more than a series of uncoordinated reactions to immediate problems. Consider the changes that have occurred over the years at Lake Kachess in Washington State, a nonwilderness setting that illustrates creeping development (Clark and Stankey 1979, p. 19):

> In the early 1900s, the Lake Kachess campground was a primitive setting. Access was difficult and use was light. But over the ensuing three-quarters of a century, a number of changes altered Lake Kachess. Improved access made it possible for greater numbers of people to reach the area. Management concerns with overuse (both resource impacts and crowding) led to development of various facilities (tent pads, vault toilets, parking ar-

eas) and other onsite modifications. Each action at Lake Kachess changed the nature of the opportunity the area provided. Yet visitors still filled the campground. Clearly there was no optimum environment for recreation at the lake; nor is it possible to say that current conditions are either better or worse than they once were. But they certainly are different.

That kind of "management by reaction" may work against wilderness preservation goals because management direction can easily be shaped by a succession of minor decisions. The cumulative results of such decisions may be undesirable and hard to reverse in wilderness. Unplanned management can be recognized by a shifting of focus from problem to problem; inconsistent, conflicting actions; and a loss of overall direction toward wilderness preservation goals.

Through planning, managers can reconcile differences in management philosophy and ideas before taking actions that have long-range effects on the wilderness resource.[1] Good plans have a stabilizing influence on management, despite changes in personnel or the influence of multiple administrative units in a wilderness where several managers may have different philosophies, perceptions, and definitions of wilderness. Plans that establish clear, attainable, measurable, and acceptable objectives for an area, and the policies and actions by which such objectives will be pursued, are essential for guiding wilderness management toward consistent outcomes.

In the coming decades, successful wilderness management will depend a great deal on the quality of plans that guide management actions for individual areas. In an era of heightened concern about cost effectiveness and competition for scarce federal dollars, the potential for obtaining the personnel and money essential for wilderness management will be increased by plans that identify clear objectives and the management actions necessary to achieve them.

Furthermore, involving the public in the planning process will attract and focus the volunteer efforts to help accomplish essential tasks. More important now than ever before, the planning process gives the interested public an opportunity to learn about, evaluate, provide input, and become involved in a wilderness area's management. Effectiveness and consistency of wilderness management, as well as the public's acceptance of that management and its implementation, are highly dependent on plans and the planning process.

In this chapter we: (1) review the wilderness man-

agement planning processes of the National Park Service (NPS), U.S. Forest Service (USFS), Fish and Wildlife Service (FWS), and Bureau of Land Management (BLM); (2) suggest terminology for developing plans; (3) suggest a framework and format for preparing wilderness management plans; (4) provide excerpts from actual plans to show how the suggested framework is applied; and (5) discuss problems that can arise in preparing wilderness management plans.

Because wilderness management plans are developed under the larger land use planning organization of the different management agencies, there are differences in agency format and process for wilderness management planning. The framework and format we suggest is generic and basic, and is intended for adaptation and application. Regardless of the agency process, wilderness management needs to be guided by clear definitions of goals and objectives, and by prescribed management actions necessary to achieve the goals and objectives.

PLANNING FLEXIBILITY AND EFFECTIVENESS

Wilderness management planning processes are still in a formative stage. Several approaches and styles of plans have been developed. One, called a goal-achievement framework, is described later in the chapter. Another approach that is appropriate where carrying capacity is an issue, the Limits of Acceptable Change (LAC) approach, is described briefly in this chapter and discussed more fully in chapter 9. A diversity of approaches is useful because it provides alternative methods for addressing management issues in different areas. There is room for flexibility in the format and level of detail of wilderness plans as long as they effectively translate overall management direction—laws, regulations, and policy—into specific objectives and necessary management actions. Whatever the format, well-reasoned plans are necessary to guide public discussion, to achieve public understanding of necessary management actions, and to help implement the plans within the constraints of the Wilderness Act.

WILDERNESS PLANNING UNDER THE NATIONAL ENVIRONMENTAL POLICY ACT

Following the passage of the National Environmental Policy Act (NEPA, P.L. 91-190) in 1969, the federal wilderness-managing agencies incorporated envi-

---

1. Additional background on planning is found in Culhane and Friesma 1979; McCool and others 1986; McLaughlin and Harris 1987; and Schomaker 1984.

ronmental analysis procedures into their planning processes. Under the guidelines for implementing NEPA, issued by the Council on Environmental Quality (CEQ), agencies must assess the environmental and social impacts of alternative management actions before implementation.

These alternatives must include a range of actions, including taking no action at all. The analysis of alternatives begins with an Environmental Assessment (EA) to document whether or not an Environmental Impact Statement (EIS) is needed. Following the EA, either a statement of "No Significant Impact" is prepared or the preparation of an EIS begins if the action will result in a significant impact. If it is apparent in the beginning that significant impacts would result from the proposal (or plan), the EA can be bypassed and an EIS prepared directly. Following the EIS, a record is prepared to document the decision. During this NEPA analysis process, managers have an opportunity to consider prospects for the type of wilderness environment described in Section 2(c) of the Wilderness Act of 1964 (P.L. 88-577)—one featuring naturalness and outstanding opportunities for solitude and primitive recreation—in light of conditions in the area under consideration and the impacts of actions proposed in the plan or proposed project.

WILDERNESS MANAGEMENT PLANNING IN THE U.S. FEDERAL AGENCIES

Recent congressional legislation provided planning directives to be included in the different management activities of the four federal natural resource managing agencies (Randolph 1987). Wilderness management planning is an integral part of the overall management approaches for the natural resource units managed by these agencies.

The following discussion of planning procedures used by the federal agencies assumes the completion of the environmental analysis requirements mandated by NEPA. Readers interested in the CEQ's guidelines may wish either to review 40 Code of Federal Regulations Part 1500 or to refer to literature describing NEPA as applied to land management planning (Dana and Fairfax 1980). NEPA processes can be confusing to persons unfamiliar with its provisions. Briefly stated, *NEPA requires that environmental impacts be considered through an analysis of a proposed action and its alternatives, and that the public be allowed to comment on the actions under consideration.* Most agencies have now combined environmental analysis and planning procedures.

NATIONAL PARK SERVICE

Management direction for wilderness in the National Park System comes from the Wilderness Act, the National Park Service Act of 1916, legislation establishing individual national park units, and wilderness classification acts designating wilderness areas within particular parks. Interpretation of this legislation is found in the Management Policies of the NPS (USDI NPS 1978). The congressional intent reflected in these laws is implemented predominantly through two levels of planning applicable to all national park units, including national recreation areas, and national monuments administered by the NPS: (1) General Management Plans and (2) Implementation Plans both of which include public involvement in their formulation.

1. *General Management Plans* (GMP) are required for each national park under the National Parks and Recreation Act of 1978 (P.L. 95-625). Before the GMP for each park is developed, a Statement for Management is prepared to establish management objectives. These documents set out conditions to be achieved to realize the park's purpose. They provide the basis for all management actions taken to perpetuate park resources, facilitate appropriate public use, and deal with the many influences that affect the park and its management.

The GMP describes the basic management philosophy for the entire national park and provides the strategies for addressing issues and achieving identified management objectives over a five- to ten-year period and sometimes longer. The plan presents two types of strategies: those required to manage the park's resources properly, and those required to provide for appropriate visitor use and interpretation of the resources. Based on these two strategies, managers identify the programs, actions, and support facilities necessary for efficient park operation and visitor use. Interdisciplinary teams provide various perspectives and are used to develop GMPs.

The National Parks and Recreation Act requires each GMP to include: (1) measures for the preservation of the area's resources; (2) indications of types and general intensities of development; (3) identification of and implementation commitments for visitor carrying capacities; and (4) potential modifications to the external boundaries of the unit. The GMP should include sufficient detail to direct subsequent planning and implement the desired actions.

2. *Implementation Plans*, sometimes called *action plans*, are the NPS's second level of planning. They deal with portions of a park, such as a wilderness or backcountry area, and are prepared for topics not adequately covered in the GMP or for topics ad-

dressed later (USDI NPS 1982). Implementation Plans describe methods for achieving the objectives in the Statement for Management and the GMP.

NPS policy requires each administrative unit of the National Park System containing backcountry, classified wilderness, or proposed wilderness to prepare a management plan for each of those areas (USDI NPS 1982). The purpose is to give management direction for achieving the specific purposes of backcountry and wilderness and for realizing the desired public benefits. Each plan identifies and offers mitigating actions for problems, such as: overcrowding; stock damage to trails and tundra; disposal of human waste; threats to visitor safety; or danger from or to grizzly bears.

Management plans for an entire park, for wilderness, and for backcountry are developed as follows: managers and staff assistants, with public involvement, prepare a plan under the direction of the park superintendent. When satisfied, the superintendent forwards the plan to the regional office with a recommendation for approval. Following a policy review by the regional staff and the Washington Office, the regional director grants final approval.

U. S. FOREST SERVICE

Management direction for wilderness in the National Forest System comes from the Multiple-Use Sustained-Yield Act of 1960 (P.L. 86-517), the Wilderness Act, the Forest and Rangeland Renewable Resources Planning Act of 1974 (RPA, P.L. 93-378), the National Forest Management Act of 1976 (NFMA, P.L. 94-588), and sometimes the wilderness classification acts establishing individual wilderness areas on national forests. The U.S. Department of Agriculture Regulations 36 CFR 261 and 36 CFR 293 and USFS policy guidelines for wilderness management and for land use planning (chap. 2320 of the USFS Manual) contain further direction (USDA FS 1985).

The USFS has three levels of land and resource planning that relate to wilderness: (1) Renewable Resources Assessment and Program, which guides the overall management of the National Forest System; (2) Regional Plans; and (3) Forest Land and Resource Management Plans, usually called Land Management Plans or Forest Plans.

1. *The Renewable Resources Assessment and Program* is required by the RPA, as amended by the NFMA. Together, these laws provide a comprehensive framework for planning management of the National Forest System. The RPA calls for (1) preparation of an assessment of the supply and demand for the nation's forest and rangeland resources, and (2) development of a management program for national forests that considers alternative management directions and the role of the national forests. The RPA program proposes (subject to annual appropriations by Congress) national direction and output levels for the National Forest System. These proposals and associated management implications are based on an assessment of supply, demand, fiscal, and political considerations. Wilderness is one of the resources analyzed.

2. *Regional Plans* apply RPA-related program goals and objectives to the national forests within each region and coordinate national forest planning with the planning of other agencies. Regional Plans also address and resolve regionally significant public issues and concerns. For example, they set land and resource management standards and guidelines for National Forest System lands in the region, specify necessary data exchange, provide long-term planning from which regional program and budget plans can be developed, and establish a basis for monitoring national forest programs.

3. *The Forest Land and Resource Management Plan,* commonly known as the Land Management Plan (LMP) or Forest Plan, translates national and regional direction into forest and wilderness goals, a description of the lands where prescriptions apply, a statement of the desired future condition, and a set of standards and guidelines for meeting the goals. The LMP addresses local, regional, and national issues related to national forest management; defines a mix of management activities that will promote the sustained use and protection of forest resources; guides development of implementation programs; and identifies activities and expenditures necessary to achieve practical results. For example, the proposed LMP for the Pisgah-Nantahala National Forests in North Carolina provides direction for management of these two national forests, including their several wildernesses and wilderness study areas (WSAs).

Each Forest Plan contains the overall management direction and describes the activities necessary to achieve desired future conditions. Overall management direction includes broad goals, measurable standards, and management requirements that must be maintained during plan implementation. The management activities described are both forestwide and area specific and may include specific prescriptions for wilderness areas and other management areas. Management prescriptions are a blend of measurable standards and management actions. Appendix D shows an example of the Wilderness section of the Land and Resource Management Plan for the Mt. Baker-Snoqualmie National Forest in Washington State (June 1990).

Before NFMA and its regulations were implemented, a Wilderness Resource Operating Plan guided the management of each wilderness. The recent change in national forest planning brought about by NFMA has raised the focus of planning to a higher level—the national forest. Wilderness areas are covered in the management direction chapter of the forest plan. To implement the Forest Plan, field level documents are prepared. These include yearly operating plans, capital investment proposals as for trail construction, for example, and overall budget needs projected for three years.

FISH AND WILDLIFE SERVICE

Management direction for wilderness in the National Wildlife Refuge System comes from the Wilderness Act, from the National Wildlife Refuge System Administration Act of 1966 (P.L. 89-669) and its supplemental amendments, from the Alaskan National Interest Lands Conservation Act of 1980 (ANILCA, P.L. 96-487), and from legislation establishing individual units of the refuge system—except where the areas were purchased or withdrawn from public lands under executive order. Further national direction comes from published regulations for Wilderness Preservation and Management (50 CFR, part 35), Department of the Interior guides, and agency national policy for wilderness management (USDI FWS 1982).

Congressional direction—in the form of laws and their interpretation in federal departmental guides and national agency policy—is implemented through two levels of planning. These two levels include: (1) Refuge Management Plans for each refuge unit, which can include separate plans for management of hunting and fishing, grazing, public use, fire control, and other important activities; and (2) Individual Wilderness Management Plans for each refuge wilderness in the National Wildlife Refuge System if such is deemed necessary. If individual wilderness management plans are completed, they become part of the Refuge Management Plan guiding each area (USDI FWS 1982).

A major function of the FWS's wilderness management plan is to describe the relationship between wilderness management objectives and the wildlife management objectives established for a particular refuge. Each wilderness management plan contains a description of the area and a detailed account of the management activities permitted within it. These plans also address public use, public facilities and improvements, public health and safety concerns, research needs, and the funding and staff required to administer the area.

BUREAU OF LAND MANAGEMENT

As explained in chapter 6, the Federal Land Policy and Management Act of 1976 (FLPMA, P.L. 94-579) calls for the review of all roadless areas and roadless islands by 1991 to determine their suitability for wilderness designation. At the end of the review, the secretary of the interior will make his recommendations to the president as to which roadless areas are suitable and unsuitable for wilderness designation. Under FLPMA, the president has until 1993 to forward his recommendations to Congress. Congress then decides which areas should be classified as wilderness and added to the NWPS.

The BLM wilderness review is being conducted in three phases: (1) inventory, (2) study, and (3) reporting. During the *inventory phase,* the BLM conducted field surveys of the lands under its administration and identified areas meeting the definition of wilderness contained in Section 2(c) of the Wilderness Act of 1964. BLM WSAs in the western states were identified by the end of 1980 with the exception of some areas under appeal. The function of the *study phase* is to determine if these WSAs are better suited to management for wilderness values or for nonwilderness purposes. During the *reporting phase* of the BLM wilderness review process, the Department of the Interior will transmit its recommendations to the president (USDI BLM 1978). WSAs are managed under the BLM's Interim Management Policy and Guidelines to protect their wilderness values until Congress either drops them from further wilderness consideration or incorporates them into the NWPS (USDI BLM 1979).

Wilderness areas administered by the BLM are managed under direction contained in BLM's wilderness management regulations (43 CFR, part 8560), BLM's wilderness management policy (BLM Manual, section 8560), and BLM Manual, Section 8561-Wilderness Management Plans (USDI BLM 1984). The regulations explain procedures for the management of wilderness areas. The wilderness management policy addresses a wide range of potential uses and management actions within wilderness areas and provides guidance for the preparation of wilderness management plans. Both the regulations and the management policy provide guidance for BLM planning activities. The Wilderness Management Plans Manual section directly addresses the preparation and implementation of wilderness management plans. The BLM's approach to writing wilderness management plans is based on concepts of the goal-achievement planning framework described later in this chapter.

BLM wilderness management plans are developed within the context of the bureau's overall planning system. The BLM has two types of planning documents that guide management of wilderness areas: Resource Management Plans (RMP) and activity plans. Wilderness management plans are one kind of activity plan. Activity plans are also prepared for other BLM-managed resources such as livestock grazing allotments, wildlife habitats, and recreation.

1. *The Resource Management Plan* (RMP) is a type of land-use plan designed to guide the management of an entire resource area. Resource areas are subunits of BLM districts and may include several million acres of public land. RMPs developed during the course of the wilderness study (in resource areas that include WSAs) address wilderness as a planning issue. At this point, the RMP is primarily concerned with making wilderness suitability recommendations. Each alternative considered in the RMP contains a description of how the various resources and uses of WSAs would be managed. Planning decisions inconsistent with WSA protection requirements may not be implemented unless Congress determines that an area should not be designated a unit of the NWPS. In the case of areas that are eventually classified as wilderness, RMP decisions would be included in a wilderness management plan where they are consistent with the Wilderness Act.

Fig. 8.1. The most important elements of good management plans are clearly stated objectives. Objectives serve as criteria both for determining necessary management actions and for evaluating how well they were achieved. Here NPS and USFS wilderness managers discuss a planning problem involving coordination between the agencies. Photo courtesy of the NPS.

2. *An activity plan*—specifically a wilderness management plan—is prepared for a specific wilderness area or two or more closely related areas. The plan may also apply in some cases to areas adjacent to wilderness areas, such as trailheads. Wilderness management plans help to implement the bureau's wilderness management policy. They show clearly the actions that will be taken to preserve the wilderness resource and the connection between these actions and wilderness management objectives. BLM wilderness management plans have three functions: (1) to explain the goals, objectives, policies, and specific actions for management of the wilderness resource and all associated resources; (2) to establish the general sequence for implementing necessary management actions; and (3) to establish timeframes and procedures for monitoring and revising plans.

As the preceding descriptions of agency planning processes illustrate, each agency has integrated wilderness planning into its overall planning procedures. These all use basic planning concepts, but differ in their details and terminology.

PLANNING TERMINOLOGY AND LOGIC

Regardless of the particular organization or format used in a wilderness management plan, it should include certain basic planning concepts. When labeled, these concepts provide a terminology for discussing management direction, ranging from general goals to specific actions. It is not critical whether a particular statement is classified as a goal or as an objective. The relationship among the components of the framework—the planning logic—is important.

Goals are general portraits of ideal ends or effects. They limit the range of potential objectives by providing direction and purpose. Goals are often lofty statements of intent. One example from the Wilderness Act is "to secure for the American people the benefits of an enduring resource of wilderness." Sometimes there is confusion about whether a particular statement is a goal or an objective. Distinction should rest on specificity and attainability. Objectives are attainable in the short term and are more specific than goals. Broad goals for the NWPS are found in the Wilderness Act, although, as explained earlier, other legislation can shape goals and influence direction for specific agencies and particular areas.

Objectives are statements of specific conditions to be achieved—reference points, which, if attained,

will assure progress in the direction of established goals (Young 1974). In the suggested planning framework that follows, objectives are used to describe wilderness conditions to be achieved and/or maintained through management.

Objectives are shaped by the goals they serve. They are descriptions of the field conditions sought through management and serve as criteria for identifying necessary management policies and actions. Clearly stated objectives are the key to effective management plans. Managers may need to develop objectives for all important aspects of the wilderness resource and its use: for example, visitor access, wildlife, fire management, and recreation (fig. 8.1).

Situation and assumption statements define local conditions and expectations about particular aspects of the wilderness area covered by the plan. Important information about the current situation and assumptions about how things will change in the future should be identified because wilderness areas have different physical characteristics, attractions, and levels of use. This information can be helpful both in setting feasible objectives and in identifying measures necessary to achieve them. For example, current floatboating in a portion of a wilderness, combined with expectations about future use, might influence objectives as well as the policies and management actions needed to achieve them.

Management direction is expressed by mechanisms such as policies, programs, and actions; and by standards against which attainment can be monitored. These are the manager's arsenal of tools, which can be applied to achieve objectives.

1. *Policies* are explicit expressions of intent describing what will be done in order to attain objectives. Sometimes a policy describes what will not be done or otherwise prescribes constraints on management activity.
2. *Programs* are sets of related actions that are combined to help achieve particular objectives within the constraints of established policy.
3. *Actions* are specific practices applied to achieve objectives within the constraints of established policy and programs.
4. *Standards* serve as performance criteria, indicating acceptable norms or specifications defining desired conditions of achievement.

Following is an example of how goals, objectives, current situation statements, assumptions, and management mechanisms may be organized into a logical framework for wilderness management planning.

To assure progress toward the *goal* of preserving "outstanding opportunities for solitude or a primitive and unconfined type of recreation," specific objectives must be established and met. An *objective* for recreational use, one particular aspect of wilderness that would usually be covered explicitly in a management plan, might be to "provide opportunities for experiencing recreation that features a natural setting, solitude, and physical and mental challenge." This objective is a statement of a condition to be achieved through management. Although the achievement of such a condition might not be directly measurable or apparent to a layman, it is attainable. Theoretically, a team of experts could study the situation and judge whether the objective had been reached to a sufficient standard. Ideally, wilderness monitoring systems using several indicators of biological, physical, and human use conditions will determine the degree to which objectives are being reached (see chap. 7, principle 12).

One *current situation* statement describing conditions in the wilderness might point to a large number of group encounters at several heavy-use locations, and an *assumption* might be that recreational use at these locations will increase. An excessive amount of group encounters could degrade the natural environment and diminish the wilderness experience for users. A *policy* could direct management to take necessary action to ensure that group encounters do not exceed a maximum standard. *Programs* aimed at reducing the number of group encounters could encourage wilderness users to select lesser-used trails and campsites. The redistributing program might include a number of *actions* such as posting signs at wilderness entrances and having wilderness rangers inform visitors of lesser used trails and campsites. *Standards* define acceptable results to be achieved through management. In this case, pertinent standards might define acceptable levels of cleanliness and impacts in the wilderness.

The internal logic reflected in the planning framework is important. Managers develop feasible *objectives* consistent with wilderness goals, suited to local conditions in specific areas, and acceptable under agency management guidelines that interpret the Wilderness Act. The *objectives* established in the plan, considering current *situations* and *assumptions* about the future, lead to *policies, programs,* and *actions* which are designed to achieve conditions described under *standards* of quality.

A FRAMEWORK FOR WRITING WILDERNESS MANAGEMENT PLANS

The planning framework described in this chapter adapts basic planning principles to wilderness management. It emphasizes planning as a decision-making process that seeks to attain clearly stated

Table 8.1. Outline of the goal-achievement framework applied to wilderness management planning.

Goals	Broad statements of intent, direction, and purpose, found in: (1) legislation, for example the Wilderness Act; (2) departmental regulations; and (3) agency national policy and philosophy that interprets legislation and establishes management direction.
Objectives	Statements that describe specific conditions sought in a particular wilderness, serve as criteria for deciding what management mechanisms are needed, and are used as the basis for later evaluation of the effectiveness of management.
Current situation and assumptions	Statements of local conditions and situations, situation and predictions about changes, that help determine the need for specific management mechanisms.
Management mechanisms	Policies, programs, and actions through which objectives for a given wilderness are achieved, and standards by which their attainment can be measured through monitoring.

management goals and objectives (Alston 1972; Webber 1969; Wheaton and Wheaton 1970). Goals and objectives stated in plans serve two purposes: (1) they are *criteria* for determining what management policies and actions are necessary, and (2) they are the targets against which the effectiveness of wilderness management is judged.

Table 8.1 shows a *goal-achievement framework* for organizing and writing wilderness management plans using the previously described concepts and terminology (Koch 1974). The approach is a type of management-by-objectives framework. It features straightforward statements of goals and objectives followed by prescriptions of the management mechanisms needed to achieve them.

A variety of plan formats can adapt the logic of this framework. Table 8.2 is a suggested outline showing how the framework could be applied to a wilderness management plan. Plan organization and format are normally dictated by agency guidelines. This outline is merely one format for focusing wilderness management direction through a management plan.

APPLYING THE FRAMEWORK— EXAMPLES FROM PLANS USING THE FRAMEWORK

The following examples are from existing management plans that use concepts described in the framework. The overall goals (see box, right) and the table of contents (see box, p. 204) are from the plan for the BLM's Bear Trap Canyon unit of the Lee Metcalf Wilderness in Montana (USDI BLM 1984). This plan was prepared as a prototype for future BLM wilderness management plans using the goal-achievement planning framework. Other examples of objectives and

management actions are taken from wilderness management plans for the USFS's Alpine Lakes (WA) and Frank Church-River of No Return (ID) Wildernesses.

Readers are cautioned to view the examples as illustrative of format rather than of content. The content includes management direction developed by local

OVERALL GOALS—BEAR TRAP CANYON UNIT, LEE METCALF WILDERNESS, BLM

The first goal is to provide for the long-term protection and preservation of the area's wilderness character under a principle of nondegradation. The area's natural condition, opportunities for solitude, opportunities for primitive and unconfined types of recreation; and any ecological, geological, or other features of scientific, educational, scenic or historical value will be managed so that they will remain unimpaired.

The second goal is to manage the wilderness area for the use and enjoyment of visitors in a manner that will leave the area unimpaired for future use and enjoyment as wilderness. The wilderness resource will be dominant in all management decisions where a choice must be made between preservation of wilderness character and visitor use.

The third goal is to manage the area using a minimum of tools, equipment, or structures to successfully, safely, and economically accomplish the objective. The chosen tool, equipment, or structure should be the one that least degrades wilderness values temporarily or permanently. Management will seek to preserve spontaneity of use and as much freedom from regulation as possible.

The fourth goal is to manage nonconforming but accepted uses permitted by the Wilderness Act and subsequent laws so as to prevent unnecessary or undue degradation of the area's wilderness character. Nonconforming uses are the exception rather than the rule, therefore, emphasis is placed on maintaining wilderness character.

Source: USDI BLM 1984.

Table 8.2. A goal-achievement framework for wilderness management planning—expanded outline for organizing and writing a plan.

Plan framework	Section of plan	Content
	Introduction	Brief description of the area, purpose, and organization of the plan.
	Summary and overview of overall situation and management strategy	An overview or summary of current conditions affecting management such as use levels and patterns, special situations, personnel, and general management strategy.
Goals	National direction	Concise summary of legislative requirements, and departmental guidelines, and national agency policy and philosophy.
	Overall[1] area goals	A statement of goals for the management of the particular wilderness.
Objectives	Objectives for all important aspects of wilderness management	Specific wilderness conditions sought for all important aspects of the wilderness such as vegetation, recreation, wildlife, fire, trails, and travel. (Topics may vary by agency or area.)
Current situation and assumptions	A. Current situation	A. Summary of trends, conditions, and assumptions pertinent to each objective.
	B. Assumptions	B. Judgments about future trends, pressures, and problems pertinent to each objective.
Management direction mechanisms[2]	C. Management policies	C. Guiding policies that—considering current situation and assumptions about the future—are necessary to guide actions toward established objectives.
	D. Management actions	D. Programs and actions that are judged necessary to achieve established objectives to an acceptable standard.

1. See example from the BLM Bear Trap Canyon unit plan, Lee Metcalf Wilderness, MT.
2. A separate section in the plan covers each important aspect of the wilderness and includes related current situations, assumptions about the future, policies, and actions. Examples from actual plans appear later in this chapter.

managers in response to specific situations as well as to national direction. Alternative management direction can appear in a plan using the framework when different goals and objectives—and of course different policies and actions—are specified.

The table of contents for the Bear Trap Canyon Wilderness Management Plan, as shown below, has been abbreviated to conserve space. In the actual plan, the subtitles given in the Recreation section (objectives, current situation and assumptions, and management direction) are repeated for each topic. The Bear Trap plan is a good example of how the management direction of an area can be fully described in a brief document. Parts I through IV include 27 pages of maps and narrative. The appendices and tables account for another 11 pages (USDI BLM 1984).

PLANNING GUIDANCE—ALPINE LAKES WILDERNESS, USFS

The Alpine Lakes Wilderness, located on national forest land in the Cascade Mountains of central Washington State, is part of the larger Alpine Lakes Management Unit established by Congress in 1976. An LMP for this complex 940,515-acre area was prepared and completed in 1981, with a wilderness management plan developed as a separate yet integrated subpart of the larger Alpine Lakes Area Management Plan. The wilderness management plan contains a goal statement and a management analysis that establishes four "wilderness use zones," including a transition zone found near trailheads, trailed zone, general trailless, and dedicated trailless zones. It establishes a carrying capacity for each zone, in-

Table of Contents, Bear Trap Canyon Wilderness Management Plan.

I. INTRODUCTION (4 pages)
- A. Purpose of Plan
- B. Plan's Organization
- C. Wilderness Area Overview
  - 1. Location
  - 2. Unique Attributes of the Area
  - 3. Significant History
  - 4. General Management Situation

II. OVERALL GOALS FOR THE WILDERNESS AREA (1 page)

III. OBJECTIVES FOR MANAGEMENT OF WILDERNESS ELEMENTS (18 pages)
- A. Recreation
  - 1. Management Objectives
  - 2. Current Situation and Assumptions
    - a. Current Situation
    - b. Assumptions
  - 3. Management Direction
    - a. Management Policies
    - b. Management Actions
- B. Commercial Use
- C. Administration
- D. Signs
- E. Water
- F. Trails
- G. Cultural Resources
- H. Insections, Noxious Plants, and Forest Diseases
- I. Fire
- J. Scientific Study
- K. Vegetation
- L. Fish and Wildlife
- M. Information and Education

APPENDIX I	Bear Trap Canyon Wilderness Management Action Outline
APPENDIX II	Excerpts from 1981 Bear Trap Canyon Recreation Management Plan
APPENDIX III	Public Involvement Process for the Bear Trap Canyon Wilderness Management Plan
APPENDIX IV	Environmental Assessment
APPENDIX V	List of Plan Participants
APPENDIX VI	Plan Monitoring and Revision Procedures
APPENDIX VII	Bibliography
APPENDIX VIII	Text of Legislation Establishing the Wilderness

Table 1	Estimated Recreation Visits to Bear Trap Canyon
Table 2	Estimated Peak Season Use (May 15-Sept. 7)
Table 3	Comparison of Alternatives
Table 4	Comparison of Impacts

Source: BLM 1984.

Sample section on soils from Alpine Lakes Wilderness Management Plan, USFS.

Management Objective
To insure that the rate of soil erosion will not noticeably exceed naturally occurring levels and to allow processes of soil formation to operate unaltered by human activity.

Current Situation
The extreme variability of parent materials and the effects of extensive glaciation has produced a complex distribution of soil types. Over 200 different soils have been identified in the area. Residual rock is frequently covered by or intimately mixed with glacial materials. Soils developed from glacial materials differ considerably, depending on whether they are derived from indurated till, loose outwash, morainal materials or from fine-textured lacustrine deposits. Soil temperature classes range from mesic to frigid. Soil resource inventory maps and general interpretations are available for the entire area. Most of the material is considered geologically recent and mountain slopes are long and very steep, so erosion and soil mantle creep are active over much of the area. Also, portions of the area are covered by a layer of coarse pumice that is highly erosive by wind and water.

Human activity adds to this background erosion by exposing soil along trails. Erosion rates are also increased in and around campsites and shelters by compaction and trampling of vegetation. The use of pack and saddle stock compounds the problem, especially in wet soil and meadows. Trail location and design techniques that reduce the impact of trails are available but have not always been used.

Management Direction
1. Trail location will avoid areas with high erosion potential such as steep slopes, wet soils and meadows where alternatives exist. Highly susceptible areas are shown on the Wilderness Visual Absorption Capacity map.
2. Camp areas will be located, relocated or closed to prevent erosion in excess of Forest Service Region 6 standards.
3. Areas where accelerated soil erosion is occurring due to human activity will be rehabilitated wherever possible. Native species will be used for revegetation.
4. Surface water runoff that collects on trails, in campsites or on other human-created alterations will be controlled to prevent accelerated erosion.
5. Abandoned trails will be rehabilitated if needed to prevent soil erosion or shorten recovery time.

Source: USDA FS 1981.

cludes management standards, current situation statements, and management direction for 17 resources and uses. As an example, the soils section of the plan is shown in the box above (USDA FS 1981). The Alpine Lakes plan proceeds to apply other wilderness objectives, for example, recreation, fish and wildlife. Direction established by the Alpine Lakes Area Management Plan has been incorporated, unchanged, into Forest Plans.

PLANNING GUIDANCE—BEAR TRAP CANYON UNIT, LEE METCALF WILDERNESS, BLM

The BLM's Bear Trap Canyon Unit wilderness management plan has a section on fire management; see box on page 206. (USDI BLM 1984). Note how this section of the plan presents an objective (part A) followed by current situation and assumptions statements (part B). Part C, Management Direction, is limited to three policy statements and one management action, which, with one exception, refer to other documents or actions to be planned in the future. This example illustrates the concept of *tiered planning* of documents and actions. Planning decisions are said to be tiered when one document provides overall guidance, and a following subordinate plan provides the more detailed guidance. In this example, the wilderness management plan provides general guidance about suppressing fires and the use of prescribed fires and leaves the details of implementing such actions to detailed fire management plans.

OBJECTIVES—FRANK CHURCH-RIVER OF NO RETURN WILDERNESS, USFS

The following two objectives were taken from the USFS's plan for the 2.3-million-acre Frank Church-River of No Return Wilderness (USDA FS 1984):

Sample section from Bear Trap Canyon Unit, Lee Metcalf Wilderness, BLM.

FIRE

A. Management Objectives
Fire will be used to reestablish and maintain a diversity of vegetative types and wildlife habitats in the area without endangering public safety or values outside the wilderness. Suppression techniques will be employed which result in the least amount of surface disturbance. The fire protection strategy will compliment the resource management objectives in the most cost effective manner.

B. Current Situation and Assumptions
1. Current Situation
    Wildfires have occurred infrequently in the canyon, although fire scars are noticeable, including those of a 1953 fire about three miles from the take-out point. There have been two person-caused fires in the Bear Trap in the last ten years.
    To date, fire suppression actions have been based on manual requirements to dispatch sufficient equipment and manpower to control the fire within the first burning period.
2. Assumptions
    Prescribed fire is needed to reestablish and/or maintain the mosaic of ecological and successional vegetative types in the area.
    As wilderness visitations increases, prevention actions will be designed to maintain or reduce the current level of person-caused fires.

C. Management Direction
1. Management Policy
    Unscheduled ignitions will be managed according to the guidelines established in the Dillon Resource Area fire management plan and environmental assessment.
    Prescribed fire will be planned through normal resource specialist activity programming.
    Suppression actions will be accomplished with minimum use of motorized equipment.
2. Management Action
    The Dillon Resource Area fire management plan and environmental assessment will be used to guide all fire actions within the Wilderness boundaries.

Source: USDI BLM 1984.

Recreation Objective: Provide a broad range of opportunities for primitive and unconfined recreation in a manner which protects and preserves the wilderness.
Wildlife and Fish Objective: Provide habitat conducive to maintaining the natural distribution and abundance of native species of wildlife and fish by allowing only natural processes to shape habitat and affect interactions among species.

Although the recreation objective is more general than the objective for wildlife and fish, the preparers of this plan were able to develop detailed guidance for both sections. This was possible because both objectives are clearly stated. For example, under the recreation objective, the plan proceeds to discuss the existing situation, including such topics as areas of concentrated use, conflicts between recreation uses, degradation of other resource values, and condition of campsites. The assumptions section predicts recreation use in specific areas and ties visitor use to the population of the region. Other actions under the recreation objective pertain to the management of facilities, pack and saddle stock, visitor restrictions, boating restrictions, and the adoption of the *Limits of Acceptable Change* process to monitor the impacts of recreation use on the wilderness environment.

THE LIMITS OF ACCEPTABLE CHANGE

The goal-achievement framework for wilderness management planning presented in this chapter appeared in the first edition of *Wilderness Management.* Subsequently, recreation researchers and planners developed a related approach to wilderness management planning known as the *Limits of Acceptable Change* (LAC). Now being implemented in several areas, including the Bob Marshall Wilderness Complex (BMWC) in Montana, the LAC method is becoming a useful wilderness management planning tool, especially in areas with conflicts between uses (Stankey and others 1985). The LAC approach is discussed in detail in chapter 9 on carrying capacity.

The goal-achievement framework for wilderness management planning and the LAC method both focus on the developing of wilderness management actions, which achieve desired conditions. Thus, both approaches follow a management-by-objectives approach. The two planning strategies differ mainly in their specific approaches and levels of detail. Both approaches incorporate public involvement into their processes.

Under the *goal-achievement framework,* using the Wilderness Act's section 2(c) and other sources, objectives are developed that describe the conditions desired for a particular wilderness area. After assessing the current management situation and assumptions about the future, management actions necessary to move toward the conditions described in the objectives are then designed.

By following the steps of the *LAC process,* managers (with help from the public) identify the issues and concerns that need to be resolved through the planning process. They then define wilderness opportunity classes (a form of zoning), select indicators of resource and social conditions (Merigliano 1986; Merigliano and Krumpe 1986), and inventory the wilderness to determine the current status of the indicators. After completing this inventory, the next step is to specify standards for the indicators within each opportunity class—for example, the amount of bare soil allowable at campsites. Management planning under LAC essentially begins by identifying alternative mixes of the opportunity classes for the wilderness. Under one such alternative, most of the wilderness could be managed to maintain the most pristine class, while another alternative might emphasize a less pristine class. After identifying potential alternatives, managers must evaluate them and (again with the help of the public) select a desired mix of opportunity classes for the wilderness area. Then, management actions necessary to maintain resource and social indicators within the standards set for each opportunity class are written as prescriptions. The final step is monitoring the indicators to see if objectives are being achieved—are the opportunity classes being maintained to the desired standard?

Both the goal-achievement framework and the LAC method incorporate monitoring and revision procedures. Management actions are not fixed but can be revised if monitoring shows that desired wilderness conditions are not being achieved.

The wide array of wilderness environments, with their differing types and intensities of wilderness management concerns, leads us to conclude that no single management planning approach will be suitable for all situations. Both the goal-achievement framework and the LAC approach are flexible enough to adapt to various situations.

PREPARING WILDERNESS MANAGEMENT PLANS: PROBLEMS AND SUGGESTIONS

WRITING THE PLAN

The actual writing of a wilderness management plan has some pitfalls, one of which is the potential for investing too much effort both in stating current situations and assumptions about the future. Some of each are needed, but if they are too detailed, they can become the focus of the plan. In extreme situations, a plan can attain a problem-solution focus, with current situation statements and assumptions describing problems in detail and presenting dire forecasts of worsening situations. This orientation can lead to severe management prescriptions to fulfill assumptions, whether or not the assumptions are well founded. In many cases, accurate data are lacking, so that assumptions about the future are no better than guesses. A good plan needs to balance clear descriptions of current situations against explicit assumptions.

Situation and assumption statements are easy to dwell on because they are easier to write than management objectives. But a plan that focuses on situation and assumption statements lacks objectives as criteria for prescribing management policies and actions, and standards for judging their attainment. For example, a current situation statement describing heavy use, combined with assumptions predicting substantial increases in use, could lead indirectly to very restrictive policies and actions. Although these might ultimately be necessary, a recreational use objective that describes *intended* conditions would provide a better basis for prescribing policies and actions (where, when, and how use must be restricted) aimed at achieving or maintaining the desired conditions. This approach is also easier to explain and to justify to critics, because debate and disagreement over wilderness management may be focused on the stated objectives and actions necessary to achieve them, rather than on the accuracy of situation and assumption statements or on individual policies or actions that, considered in isolation, might not appear necessary.

Clearly stated objectives are the key to good wilderness management plans, whatever the planning

approach, framework, or format. Objectives are particularly difficult to write for wilderness because of the subjective nature of the resource and the experiences it offers. Nevertheless, it is important to have clear objectives so that they can guide policies and actions and set standards for measuring attainment. It is helpful to think of objectives as statements of wilderness conditions or as experience opportunities that management seeks to preserve or provide.

Not all objectives can be described with the same level of specificity. The precision of individual objectives varies with the aspect of wilderness under consideration. An objective for interpretive signs might be more specific than an objective for wildlife, vegetation, or water. Objectives ranging from *general* to *specific* can still suggest management direction. But *vague* objectives give few clues to management direction. Compare the following examples that focus on planning:

A Specific Objective: To maintain lakes and watercourses in their current natural condition, subject to natural forces and free of human-caused contaminants.

A General Objective: To maintain lakes and watercourses free of human-caused contaminants.

A Vague Objective: To protect lakes, watercourses, and water quality.

Understanding the distinction between general and vague objectives is important. Objectives can be stated in broad, general terms, and still retain fairly definite implications about the kinds of policies and actions needed to achieve them. Vague objectives, on the other hand, are abstract and lack clear implications for management direction, policy, programs, or actions. While an acceptable objective might be general, its management implications should be clear.

It is also important to recognize that *the specificity of goals and objectives is directly related to their location in the planning hierarchy or framework. The closer to the field-action level an objective is, the more specific it should be.* Compared to the lofty goals of the Wilderness Act ("to preserve, unimpaired, a wilderness resource"), management objectives for one particular aspect of wilderness will seem quite specific—for example, "to provide for primitive recreation only to the extent that naturalness, outstanding opportunities for solitude, physical and mental challenge are preserved." Farther down the hierarchy, a field manager's objectives may be to implement very specific actions derived from goals, objectives, and policies formulated higher up in the planning process. For example, one field manager indicated that the objectives he was interested in were the number of signs to be posted that summer, the number of campsites to be

relocated, and the miles of trail to be cleared or maintained. To him, the objectives stated in the plan for the entire wilderness were so general they appeared to be goals rather than attainable objectives. Perspective varies in the framework. At lower levels in the planning and management process, field objectives *are* statements of actions to be carried out— but actions derived from goals, objectives, and policies set forth in the planning process. *If the plan has internal logic, it should be possible to trace any field actions to higher levels of the planning process by asking why the activity is being carried out.*

The level of detail that wilderness management plans should contain is an important consideration. A plan containing 200 pages of single-spaced typing might be so overwhelming that managers may never read it. On the other hand, except for the simplest circumstances, a plan of only eight pages will not contain enough detail, even though it might give general direction. Again, balance of generality and detail is needed, depending on the size, complexity, levels of visitation, and problem situations in the particular wilderness. The plan should contain sufficient detail to describe all objectives, policies, and the what and where of particular actions; but the when,

Fig. 8.2. Wilderness management plans may identify particular locations where special management is needed, such as travel corridors, heavy-use locations, unusual attractions, or vegetation zones where special restrictions apply. For example, a no-campfire regulation in high alpine zones may help preserve aesthetic features such as this ancient whitebark pine snag in the John Muir Wilderness, CA. The tree might otherwise be used as firewood. Photo courtesy of the USFS.

how, and by whom level of detail is more appropriately included in action, operating, or work plans.

Management plans will be useful if they are straightforward, well-organized, and readable. They should clearly inform managers and users of the management direction for the wilderness, what this entails in policies that govern field actions, and the kind of major actions that will be carried out at particular locations. The plan should not be so long and detailed that only its authors or the affected managers are willing to read it. A few of the current wilderness management plans are quite complex and reflect the growing sophistication of wilderness management and the diversity of management approaches. But if plans are so complex that their internal logic is not apparent to the public, the advantages they gain through complexity will be lost.

ZONING—A WILDERNESS OPPORTUNITY SPECTRUM

During the past decade, managers and researchers have made a concerted effort to classify the spectrum of outdoor recreation opportunities and the kinds of facilities, management practices, and visitor behavior appropriate to each type of opportunity (Clark and Stankey 1979). This *Recreation Opportunity Spectrum (ROS)* idea is, in effect, zoning on a macroscale. It classifies *opportunity* from primitive, semiprimitive nonmotorized, semiprimitive motorized, roaded and natural, rural, and urban zones. Not surprisingly, as managers began to address increasingly complex wilderness management situations, the idea of a *Wilderness Opportunity Spectrum (WOS)* emerged as part of the management strategy to address finer gradations of primitive and semiprimitive classes. The WOS includes, for example, pristine, primitive, and portal designations, indicating decreasing degrees of naturalness and solitude. Other designations are still evolving (Stankey and others 1985). *The WOS, like the ROS, is a kind of zoning—delineating particular areas where different management prescriptions or restrictions on visitor behavior apply.* Other examples include: no-camping zones; trailless zones, where only cross-country travel and special minimum-impact camping practices are allowed; and special management zones having particular problems, high-use sites, impacted locations, or perhaps sensitive wildlife areas (fig. 8.2). Areas characterized by relatively dense concentrations of visitors and use impacts are also a kind of zoning.

The WOS and other zoning approaches are appropriate in certain situations. We offer three criteria for judging their utility and appropriateness. *First,*

remember the cardinal rule of wilderness management—*do only what is necessary.* Implement zoning restrictions only when required to protect the wilderness resource and consider the impact that the zoning would have on visitor perceptions and use. *Second, make zoning clear to users.* To be effective, any zone that requires different visitor behavior must be indicated by some reliable means such as a use permit or map. *Third, zoning should not be used to justify nonwilderness conditions that presently exist;* when such conditions exist, they should be corrected, *not* assigned to a "special management zone." Congress established wilderness as a land classification and agencies should not try to change its status through zoning.

Identifying zones where special management will be needed may often be necessary. But minimum wilderness standards, at least, need to be maintained. As the Lake Kachess example at the beginning of this chapter illustrates, the invasion, succession, and displacement of wild conditions by less wild ones is a well-established phenomenon in recreation use and management (Clark and Stankey 1979). In fact, it is one of the factors that triggered the establishment of the NWPS. A major goal of wilderness managers is to try to keep the wilderness threshold at the wilderness area boundary.

PUBLIC INVOLVEMENT AND PLAN REVIEW PROCESS

Public participation is especially important for the management of wilderness. *The public must have an opportunity to help formulate wilderness management plans if these documents are to have credibility and acceptance.* Plans not supported by the public will be difficult to implement.

Involving the public is an accepted part of the decision-making process in the federal agencies with wilderness management responsibilities. The 1964 Wilderness Act was one of the first resource management laws that required public involvement in decision making (P.L. 88-577, Sec. 3[d][1]d) and was followed five years later by NEPA, which mandated public involvement in natural resource management.

Today it seems unthinkable to consider any kind of planning in natural resources without public participation. The public is a source of ideas, a sounding board for the acceptability of proposed management direction and policy, and a potential partner in its formation and implementation. Study of public participation in resource decision making indicates that managers who hesitate to involve the public are often those who have not tried it or who doomed

their public involvement efforts to failure by their own anxiety or negative attitude about it. Most managers who have successfully used public involvement are impressed with its helpfulness in making better and more acceptable decisions. Many user groups are affected by wilderness management: hiking and climbing clubs, conservation groups, hunters and anglers, horse riders, photographers, youth organizations, and outfitters. They deserve to be involved in planning. Without the understanding and support of the involved public, wilderness management will fall short of its goals. In recent years, public involvement in wilderness matters has extended beyond planning wilderness allocations and management to include involvement in wilderness work as well (Hendee 1985). Volunteers, conservation group work parties, "adopt-a-trail" efforts, even private contracting of wilderness work projects, all increase the involvement of the public in wilderness management.

As mandated by the NEPA, the four federal wilderness management agencies have adopted procedures that integrate public involvement with the planning process. Agency staff now routinely prepare EAs and EISs before making land use decisions. Such documents, with their sections detailing potential alternatives and environmental consequences, are made available to the public for comment.

Many different strategies may be successful for securing public involvement. Some may have widespread applicability. Two public involvement approaches used in connection with the BLM's Bear Trap Canyon plan and the Canyonlands National Park backcountry management plan, are described below. Either procedure could be amended to fit different circumstances. Both managers and the public must be prepared for the large amount of time required to get public input, incorporate it into new drafts, and then get agency staff and the public response to the revisions. A full year or more may be required to complete public involvement in a wilderness management plan.

Example: Bear Trap Canyon, BLM

The public involvement process used during development of the Bear Trap Canyon Unit's wilderness management plan began with the establishment of a five-member advisory group. This Bear Trap Canyon Wilderness Committee, representing a variety of interests both private and commercial, met as a group in January 1984. BLM staff provided the group with a list of management issues and requested comments. These issues were to be addressed in the management plan.

In March, members of the committee, key individuals, and agency officials were sent a copy of an inhouse draft of the plan to review. Committee members were asked to disseminate pertinent portions of the document for comment to their constituencies. Next, individuals on the BLM's district office wilderness mailing list were sent postcards and asked to return them if they wanted copies of the draft Bear Trap plan for review.

A printed draft, revised in response to concerns of reviewers, was sent to members of the public who had indicated an interest in reviewing the plan, to the advisory group, and to agencies. Public notices in local newspapers informed the public that copies of the draft were available. The document sent to the public consisted of a draft plan and draft EA.

Due to public interest, the BLM extended the closing date of the original 45-day comment period from August 31 until October 12, 1984. During the comment period, the agency hosted two public open houses in local communities. A total of 27 written comments were received. In general, they supported continuation of existing management of the area. Most respondents supported long-term protection and preservation of wilderness values, and they believed that existing use levels did not warrant restrictive measures.

A standard procedure for managers is to print the public comments on a draft environmental analysis document and their response to such comments as part of the final version of the environmental analysis. In the Bear Trap plan, the planning team organized its response to public comment issue by issue. The following issues illustrate the variety of concerns that can emerge from public comment: management for long-term protection of wilderness values versus maximizing visitor enjoyment, prohibition of overnight camping for rafting parties, trail closures and maintenance, prohibition of horse use, application of a let-fires-burn policy, construction of backcountry toilets, the number of commercial outfitters, use of paddle boats, and Air Force overflights.

In response to public comment and additional in-agency review, the BLM revised portions of the draft document before printing the final draft of the plan. The final plan and environmental assessment were published and distributed to the public in January 1985, one year after the first public involvement efforts began.

Example: Arches and Canyonlands National Parks

Development of the backcountry management plan for Arches and Canyonlands National Parks (USDI NPS 1985) used a workbook approach to help identify and develop issues and alternatives. NPS managers used the workbook at seven public meetings

and mailed over 900 copies to the interested public. The workbook contained introductory material describing the purpose of the backcountry management plan, the existing conditions within each park, and the existing backcountry management program in each park. Participants in the planning process were asked to respond to a series of questions on potential management options.

The workbook started with basic questions—such as which areas of the parks should be managed as backcountry—and continued with questions about management of visitor use and resources. Each question was preceded by background that described the current situation and the management concerns of the NPS. For example, a chart showing backcountry visitation figures for the past several years preceded one of the questions about visitor management. Participants could respond to each question by either selecting one of the management options presented by the NPS or by writing in their own suggestions. NPS managers, after reviewing the public's workbook responses, prepared the first draft of the backcountry management plan and a draft EA, which were then mailed to interested members of the public and requested additional comment.

These examples are only two of the many strategies that could be followed to involve the public in the preparation of wilderness management plans. Each of the federal land management agencies has developed its own procedures based on its own experience. *In summary: (l) public involvement in wilderness management is essential and valuable; (2) many approaches are possible; and (3) adequate time (a year or more) is required for public involvement.*

While this discussion focuses on how the public may assist with the review of draft plans, considerable technical and policy review of plans takes place at different levels within the agency and within other public agencies. It is essential that any other governmental units such as fish and wildlife, forestry, environmental, or other resource protection and management agencies have a chance to review and provide input to plans. From both the public and agencies, the challenge is to secure the optimum review and input to afford managers the benefit of several opinions and to better represent the public and wilderness users in plan development.

The time required for agency review and public and other agencies involvement will vary with the situation, but we suggest that planners ask themselves, "In what ways should the public be involved throughout the planning process?" Addressing these questions can help the management planning process remain feasible, effective, and not an end in itself.

CRITERIA FOR EVALUATING WILDERNESS MANAGEMENT PLANS

Growing public involvement assures that wilderness management plans will come under increasing public scrutiny; additionally, the growth of wilderness management as a resource specialty means that plans will be reviewed by other managers. What criteria are appropriate for evaluating plans regardless of their format, specific agency requirements, or type of public involvement? We suggest the following questions to guide the review and evaluation of wilderness management plans:

1. Does the plan display management goals by summarizing key provisions of the Wilderness Act, legislation designating the area, departmental guidelines, and national agency policy that guide and direct management of the area? Inclusion of such goals will help relate management of the individual wilderness to the entire NWPS, of which it is a part.

2. Are the local conditions relevant to management of the wilderness described concisely and explained?

3. Is the general management strategy concisely explained? This might include differing methods of administration by various units of the agency, the numbers of managers and their responsibilities; a description of user requirements such as a permit system, use of the WOS or other zoning scheme, and other details essential to an overview of the management strategy.

4. Does the plan have an internal logic that links objectives to prescribed management direction, such as policies and actions? It is essential that some kind of framework guide prescription of management policies and actions on the basis of their necessity to achieve objectives or some desired condition in the area.

5. How well does the plan consider alternative actions for meeting management objectives? The NEPA requires managers to analyze alternatives. Such analysis is especially useful if it focuses on how each alternative would attain desired conditions.

6. Does the plan address the need for coordination of its resource management activities and nonconforming uses? A National Scenic Trail crossing a wilderness is one example; grazing might be another. Coordination with other affected parties, such as adjacent landowners, is essential. For example, NPS and USFS wildernesses are often adjacent. There is also need to coordinate plans with other organizations, such as the state wildlife departments responsible for managing wildlife populations.

7. Does the plan specify when and by whom the

plan will be reviewed and updated? Does it identify what conditions or situations might prompt an earlier review? This information will help keep a plan from becoming obsolete.

8. Were the managers who administered the wilderness area directly involved in the preparation of the plan? It is our experience that such involvement builds commitment to implementing the plan. The best plan is of little value if it is not fully understood by managers and used to guide everyday wilderness management.

9. Is the guidance contained in the plan designed to resolve the issues and management concerns facing field managers? Does the plan respond to the important issues, concerns, and opportunities raised during public involvement efforts? To be effective and useful, plans need to provide site-specific application of national wilderness management guidance. Generic planning documents, those that are so general that they could apply to any wilderness area, cannot provide the guidance field managers need to resolve their everyday challenges.

10. Does the plan provide for a monitoring system, using field measures of indicators of wilderness conditions—biological, physical, and human use— to determine if objectives are being attained to desired standard? How often is monitoring to be done and how will the data be used? Planning is an organized approach to setting objectives and deciding what needs to be done to meet them. The plan is not complete unless it includes provisions for objective data collection to see if the plan's implementation is working to an acceptable standard.

SUMMARY

Good planning is essential to good management. *Planning is a formal process of thinking ahead about what conditions are desired and how to achieve them, the management problems likely to be encountered, and alternative methods for resolving them.* This chapter described how wilderness management plans fit into agency planning processes and suggested some elements of good planning and a framework for developing plans. A planning process should try to apply the principles of wilderness management proposed in chapter 7. The remaining chapters discuss substantive wilderness topics, information that must be focused on wilderness management through planning. These topics include visitor carrying capacity; ecosystems; wildlife, fire, visitor, and site management; and managing impacts.

STUDY QUESTIONS

1. Why is it important to have management plans for a wilderness area?
2. How does the NEPA affect wilderness management plans?
3. Each of the four federal wilderness managing agencies (BLM, FWS, USFS, and NPS) has two or more levels of planning applicable to its wilderness areas. Briefly describe them.
4. Define the following basic planning concepts: goals, objectives, situation and assumption statements, and management mechanisms.
5. How can too strong a focus on describing current situations and assumptions about the future cause problems in preparing and implementing a wilderness management plan?
6. What are three criteria for deciding whether zoning restrictions are useful and appropriate in a particular wilderness area?
7. Why is it important to involve the public in the development of a wilderness management plan?
8. What are some questions to consider in evaluating wilderness management plans?
9. How are the goal-achievement framework and the LAC process alike? How do they differ?

REFERENCES

Alston, Richard M. 1972. FOREST: goals and decisionmaking in the Forest Service. Res. Pap. INT-128. Ogden, UT: U.S. Department of Agriculture, Forest Service, Intermountain Forest and Range Experiment Station. 84 p.

Clark, Roger N.; Stankey, George H. 1979. The Recreation Opportunity Spectrum: a framework for planning, management, and research. Gen. Tech. Rep. PNW-98. Portland, OR: U.S. Department of Agriculture, Forest Service, Pacific Northwest Forest and Range Experiment Station. 32 p.

Culhane, Paul F.; Friesma, H. Paul. 1979. Land use planning for the public lands. Natural Resources Journal. 19: 43-74.

Dana, Samuel T.; Fairfax, Sally K. 1980. Forest and range policy, its development in the United States. 2d ed. New York: McGraw-Hill. 458 p.

Federal Land Policy and Management Act of 1976. Act of October 21, 1976. Public Law 94-579. 90 Stat. 2743, as amended.

Forest and Rangeland Renewable Resources Planning Act of 1974. Act of August 17, 1974. Public Law 93-378. 88 Stat. 476, as amended.

Hendee, John C. 1985. Important legal, social, philosophical, and management perspectives. In: Proceedings, wilderness and natural areas in the East: a management challenge; 1985 May 13; Nacogdoches, TX.

Koch, Russell W. 1974. A goal achievement framework to guide wilderness management planning. Seattle: University of Washington. 30 p. M.F. Professional paper.

McCool, Stephen F.; Ashor, Joseph L.; Stokes, Gerald L. 1986. An alternative to rational-comprehensive planning: transactive planning. In: Lucas, Robert C., compiler. Proceedings—national wilderness research con-

⟪complete⟫

ference: current research; 1985 July 23-26; Fort Collins, CO. Gen. Tech. Rep. INT-212. Ogden, UT: U.S. Department of Agriculture, Forest Service, Intermountain Research Station: 544-545.

McLaughlin, William J.; Harris, Charles C. 1986. Regional resource recreation planning. In: A literature review. Washington, DC: President's Commission on Americans Outdoors: Management-105—Management-120.

Merigliano, Linda L. 1989. Indicators to monitor the wilderness recreation experience. In: Lime, D.W., ed. Managing America's enduring wilderness resource. Conference proceedings, Minneapolis, MN, Sept. 11-17, 1989: 156-162.

Merigliano, Linda and Krumpe, Edwin. 1986. Scientists identify, evaluate indicators to monitor wilderness conditions. Park Science. 6 (3): 18-19.

Multiple-Use Sustained-Yield Act of 1960. Act of June 12, 1960. Pub. L. No. 86-517, 74 Stat. 215.

National Environmental Policy Act of 1969. Act of January 1, 1970. Public Law 91-190. 83 Stat. 852-856. (1970).

National Forest Management Act of 1976. Act of October 22, 1976. Public Law 94-588. 90 Stat. 2949, as amended.

National Park Service Act. Act of August 25, 1916. Ch. 137, 45 Stat. 235 (codified at 16 U.S.C. sec. 1-18f).

National Parks and Recreation Act of 1978. Act of November 10, 1978. Public Law 95-625. 92 Stat. 3467.

National Wildlife Refuge System Administration Act. Act of October 15, 1966. Public Law 89-669. 80 Stat. 926. (1966).

Randolph, John. 1987. Comparison of approaches to public lands planning: U.S. Forest Service, National Park Service, U.S. Fish and Wildlife Service, Bureau of Land Management. USDI, National Park Service and National Recreation and Park Association. Trends. 24(2): 36-45.

Schomaker, J. H. 1984. Writing quantifiable river recreation objectives. In: Popadic, Joseph S.; Butterfield, Dorothy I.; Anderson, Dorothy H.; Popodic, Mary R., eds. Proceedings; 1984 river recreation symposium; 1984 October 31-November 3; Baton Rough, LA. Baton Rouge, LA: Louisiana State University: 249-253.

Stankey, George H.; Cole, David N.; Lucas, Robert C.; [and others]. 1985. The Limits of Acceptable Change (LAC) system for wilderness planning. Gen. Tech. Rep. INT-176. Ogden, UT: U.S. Department of Agriculture, Forest Service, Intermountain Forest and Range Experiment Station. 37 p.

U.S. Department of Agriculture, Forest Service. 1981. Alpine Lakes Area land management plan, selected alternative from the final environmental impact statement, Mt. Baker-Snoqualmie and Wenatchee National Forests. Seattle: U.S. Department of Agriculture, Forest Service. 220 p.

U.S. Department of Agriculture, Forest Service. 1984. Frank Church-River of No Return Wilderness management plan. Ogden, UT: U.S. Department of Agriculture, Forest Service, Intermountain Region. 118 p.

U.S. Department of Agriculture, Forest Service. 1985. Wildernesses, primitive areas, and wilderness study areas. In: Forest Service Manual, chapter 2320. Washington, DC: U.S. Department of Agriculture, Forest: [Pages unknown].

U.S. Department of Agriculture. June 1990. Land and resource management plan. Pacific Northwest Region. Mt. Baker-Snoqualmie National Forest. pp. 4:207-213, 217.

U.S. Department of the Interior, Bureau of Land Management. 1978. Wilderness inventory handbook. Washington, DC: U.S. Department of the Interior, Bureau of Land Management. 30 p.

U.S. Department of the Interior, Bureau of Land Management. 1979. Interim management policy and guidelines for lands under wilderness review. Washington, DC: U.S. Department of the Interior, Bureau of Land Management. 32 p.

U.S. Department of the Interior, Bureau of Land Management. 1984. Manual Section 8561. Wilderness Management Plans. Washington, DC: Department of the Interior, Bureau of Land Management. 27 pp.

U.S. Department of the Interior, Bureau of Land Management. 1985. Wilderness management plan for the Bear Trap Canyon Unit of the Lee Metcalf Wilderness. BLM-MT-ES PS-003-4332. Billings, MT: U.S. Department of the Interior, Bureau of Land Management. 60 p.

U.S. Department of the Interior, Fish and Wildlife Service. 1986. Wilderness area management. In: Refuge Manual. Washington, DC: U.S. Department of the Interior, Fish and Wildlife Serive: 6 RM 8.

U.S. Department of the Interior, National Park Service. 1978. Wilderness preservation and management. Management policies, chapter 2. Washington, DC: U.S. Department of the Interior, National Park Service. [Pages unknown].

U.S. Department of the Interior, National Park Service. 1982. Planning process guideline NPS-2. Washington, DC: U.S. Department of the Interior, National Park Service. [Pages unknown].

U.S. Department of the Interior, National Park Service. 1985. Wilderness management plan. In: Arches and Canyonlands National Parks management plan. Denver, CO: U.S. Department of the Interior, National Park Service: [Pages unknown].

Webber, Melvin. 1969. Planning in an environment of change: part 2: permissive planning. Town Planning Review. 38(4): 277-295.

Wheaton, L. C.; Wheaton, Margaret F. 1970. Identifying the public interest: values and goals. In: Erber, Ernest, ed. Urban planning in transition. New York: Grossman Publishers: 152-164.

Wilderness Act. Act of September 3, 1964. Public Law 88-577. 78 Stat. 890.

Young, Robert C. 1974. Establishment of goals and definitions of objectives. In: Driver, B. L., ed. Elements of outdoor recreation. Ann Arbor, MI: University of Michigan Press: 261-272.

ACKNOWLEDGMENTS

James Browning, graduate student, College of Forestry, Wildlife and Range Sciences, University of Idaho, Moscow.

Dave Heffernan, Wilderness Coordinator, FWS, Arlington, VA.

David Porter, BLM, Colorado State University, Fort Collins.

Dale Potter, Assistant Recreation Staff Officer, USFS, Mt. Baker-Snoqualmie National Forest, WA.

Pat Reed, visiting Research Scientist with the University of Georgia, USFS, Athens.

Roland Wauer, Chief, Resource Management (retired), NPS.

The carrying capacity of wilderness is the amount, kind, and distribution of use that can occur without leading to unacceptable impacts on either the physical-biological resource or the available wilderness experience. By establishing use limits, the experiences unique to wilderness, enjoyed by these campers in Shenandoah National Park, VA, can be protected. Photo courtesy of the NPS.

9

Managing for Appropriate Wilderness Conditions: The Carrying Capacity Issue

This chapter was written by George H. Stankey; Stephen F. McCool, School of Forestry, University of Montana, Missoula; and Gerald L. Stokes, Chesapeake Bay Foundation, Virginia Land Conservation Office, Tappahannock.

INTRODUCTION

Although many qualities are associated with wilderness, two of them, naturalness and solitude, are most frequently prescribed in popular literature and the law. Both qualities are potentially sensitive to the use an area receives, and an excessive number of users can impact the quality of the natural setting as well as the sense of solitude that one experiences. As use levels rise, these qualities can be jeopardized to the point that the area no longer constitutes wilderness in either a conventional or legal sense.

Concern with overuse is by no means a recent phenomenon. As Nash relates in chapter 2, there was concern with overuse and its associated impacts in the high country of California's Sierras as early as the mid-1930s. Sumner's call in 1942 for the restriction of use within an area's "carrying capacity or 'recreational saturation point'" reflects both a concern as well as a recognition that continued increases in use could destroy the area's wilderness qualities (Sumner 1942).

Such concerns still remain. Most wilderness visitors and managers can relate personal experiences with undesirable conditions: steady streams of traffic along trails, badly eroded campsites devoid of vegetation, and in some cases, seas of mud and horse manure on trails. By anyone's definition, wilderness has been lost when such conditions prevail. Yet, while such conditions do exist in some areas, pristine settings still are found elsewhere and "outstanding opportunities" for solitude are available.

The enormous variability of use and its impacts can be seen by comparing traffic within selected wildernesses. For example, in 1985, the Tebenkof Bay Wilderness in Alaska received only 0.04 visitor-day per acre of use while the Desolation Wilderness in California, only slightly smaller than the Tebenkof Bay Wilderness, received about 3.5 visitor-days per acre of use—nearly 100 times that of the Alaskan area. Similarly, the 14,000-acre Joyce Kilmer-Slickrock Wilderness in North Carolina and Tennessee received about 3.7 visitor-days per acre of use while the 14,600-acre Lye Brook Wilderness in Vermont received only 0.31 visitor-day per acre—a tenth of that in the Joyce Kilmer-Slickrock.

All these areas are classified as wilderness, yet, use intensity differs among them. Is Tebenkof Bay vastly underutilized? Or is the Desolation overutilized? Clearly, there is great concern among users and managers alike about overuse and resource damage, but in the face of such extraordinary variations in use conditions, how does one approach the matter of deciding what is an appropriate use level in wilderness?

The establishment of appropriate use levels in wilderness typically has been addressed through the concept of carrying capacity. In chapter 7, we argue that the preservation of qualities essential to wilderness required a carrying capacity constraint as a fundamental principle of wilderness management. Our concern is with determining at what point social and environmental conditions within wilderness become inconsistent with the qualities required by the Wilderness Act. Theoretically and practically, each set of wilderness conditions and experiences sought as management objectives implicitly carry

Fig. 9.1. A quality wilderness environment, shown here in the Three Sisters Wilderness, OR, can be protected where use limits have been established. Excessive use, however, can lead to resource damage and to a degraded wilderness experience. Photo courtesy of the USFS.

with them some limit in the kinds and amounts of recreational use that can be considered acceptable; they also imply the need for various policies and actions to see that these acceptable limits are not exceeded (fig. 9.1). In this chapter, we explore the origins of the carrying capacity concept, consider how the concept can be applied in wilderness settings, and propose a reformulated conception of the carrying capacity model designed to help citizens and managers establish guidelines for acceptable wilderness conditions. A brief case study examining how such guidelines have been developed for the Bob Marshall Wilderness Complex (BMWC) in Montana is also described.

THE CARRYING CAPACITY CONCEPT

Carrying capacity is a fundamental concept in natural resource and environmental management (Dasmann 1964; Godschalk and Parker 1975). It can be defined as the maximum level of use an area can sustain as set by natural factors of environmental resistance such as food, shelter, or water. Beyond this natural limit, no major increases in the dependent population can occur (Odum 1959). In the field of wildlife management, for instance, carrying capacity describes the number of animals of a particular species that can use the range on a sustained basis, given available food, shelter, and water. If the balance between animals and the range's capacity is upset, either by an increase in the number of animals or through loss of the range's productive capacity (e.g., drought), problems will occur. Food resources become depleted as animals search for nutrition. Even though animal numbers might increase in the short term, loss of range productivity means that, in the long term, fewer animals can be supported; in extreme cases, irreversible environmental impacts can occur.

This description may seem to imply that carrying capacity is an uncomplicated, straightforward notion. In fact, it is not. The capacity of the range would be quite different if populated by elk or sheep rather than deer; if it was a mix of species it would be even more complicated. The dynamic nature of ecosystems makes a static determination of carrying capacity difficult, if not impossible, to calculate. Furthermore, the natural factors of environmental resistance can be influenced by land managers; food crops can be planted, water storage reservoirs created, and so forth. Thus, carrying capacity can be increased or decreased by management actions; it is not an inherent, fixed value of the land. It can be diminished by unregulated overuse or enhanced by thoughtful management.

As a concept that identified limits to the amount of use a resource could sustain, it is not surprising that carrying capacity was adopted early as a guide to decisions in recreation management in general and wilderness management in particular. Determining how many people could use a given recreational setting before unacceptable impact occurred, could be critical information for managers. In the early 1960s, Wagar (1964) published one of the first substantive discussions of the carrying capacity concept in recreational management. A major contribution of this analysis was the inclusion of the impacts of use on social or experiential considerations in addition to the typical environmental concerns (Manning 1986). As Wagar noted, "The study … was initiated with the view that the carrying capacity of recreation lands could be determined primarily in terms of ecology and the deterioration of areas.… It soon became obvious that the resource-oriented point of view must be augmented by consideration of human values" (Wagar 1964, preface).

Under this broadened concept of carrying capacity, recreational areas had not only an *ecological capacity* but a *social capacity* as well. Use could impact not only an area's physical-biological resources, such as soils and vegetation, but also the character of the recreational experience. The recognition of a *social dimension* of carrying capacity implies that determination of carrying capacity is a sociopolitical process as well as a biophysical one (Burch 1984).

Wagar's monograph marked the beginning of a major effort of both researchers and managers to define the carrying capacity of recreational areas. This effort was driven, in part, by the great surge in recreational use following the end of World War II. Wilderness in the United States, once remote and little used, began to receive increasing amounts of use as what Clawson (1985) called the *four fueling factors*—leisure time, income, access, and population—grew substantially. Between 1955 and 1964, for instance, the average annual growth of recreational use on national forest wilderness exceeded 10 percent (Stankey and Lucas 1986). With this surge in use came increasing concerns about ecological and social impacts that might jeopardize the essential wilderness qualities of naturalness and solitude.

Such concerns prompted continuing interest in the use of carrying capacity as a framework within which decisions could be made to control impacts that would otherwise erode the special qualities of wilderness. A recent analysis of references dealing with carrying capacity revealed that more than 2,000 papers have been published, with 40 percent of them appearing between 1975 and 1979 (Drogin and others 1986). With this literature and the associated management experience in applying the concept of carrying capacity, our understanding has grown considerably.

But there was limited progress in developing a well-understood procedure for applying the carrying capacity concept in the field. Some authors even argued that the concept should be abandoned (Bury 1976; Wagar 1974). Many reasons underlie the reservations about the utility of the carrying capacity concept. For instance, recreation lands are used by many different people seeking many different, often conflicting, experiences. Some want solitude, others look for companionship; what are appropriate encounter levels for one, represent congestion or loneliness for another. Theoretically, then, every experience results in a different carrying capacity. Brown and Haas (1980) distinguished five different types of users in Colorado's Rawah Wilderness and reported that the psychological domain of "meeting/observing other people" showed the most discrimination among the five types. When there is agreement as to the type of experience that an area is to provide, there is generally agreement about what constitutes appropriate use of an area. Shelby, for instance, found "remarkable similarity" in the definitions of appropriate encounter levels in three study areas when the general management direction (wilderness, semiwilderness, undeveloped recreation) was specified (Shelby 1981, p. 133).

Impacts on physical-biological resources do not help establish obvious capacity limits. Any recreational use of an area produces some change; typically, much of the total impact found in an area occurs with only light recreational use (Cole 1985). Thus, if a manager elects to allow a level of use producing little or no change, it will be necessary to restrict use very stringently (Wagar 1968).

Finally, carrying capacity implies a strong cause-and-effect relationship between the amount of use an area receives and subsequent impact. However, many studies of this relationship point out that use intensity is a poor predictor of total impact. The season and type of use involved, for instance, frequently are more important in explaining impact than the amount of use (Cole 1985; Kuss 1986).

Perhaps the most serious problem, however, was that many people considered the carrying capacity of an area as an inherent value of the resource base, one that could be determined through careful observation and research. As Wagar (1968) notes, this idea seems to have been borrowed from range management, where resource capacity is defined largely by natural factors such as soils and precipitation. This conception of carrying capacity promoted the idea that

if this inherent value could be determined, management of the area would be made easier.

Such a conception had no real foundation and was probably motivated by a desire to make complex, controversial decisions about recreational use easier to formulate. But more significantly, such a conception obscured the important distinction between carrying capacity as the product of a technical assessment as opposed to its establishment through value judgments that weighed resource and social impacts, along with human needs and values. Carrying capacity, in other words, was seen as a scientific idea whose identification was only constrained by the level of effort and ingenuity exerted by managers and researchers, rather than the result of a judgmental process.

Perhaps one of the most important developments in our understanding of the carrying capacity concept over the past 30 years is that *carrying capacities are the product of value judgments as well as science.* It follows that if carrying capacity is not primarily a product of technical assessment (a scientific question) but rather of value judgments, the question then becomes, "Whose value judgments?" This moves the determination of carrying capacity out of the realm of solely scientific assessment and into the political arena through public involvement. As a result, carrying capacity determination becomes a process by which biophysical and social research is integrated with agency policies and the values of managers and users to reach a collective judgment about carrying capacity.

In developing a wilderness management program, managers and the public must recognize that what wilderness is and therefore how it should be managed, is based on value judgments. These value judgments reflect philosophical, emotional, spiritual, experiential, and economic responses of those making the judgments. Obviously, few people will have identical responses, and therefore few will make identical value judgments. Thus, the task facing agency managers is one of determining consensus value judgments regarding what constitutes desired wilderness conditions and how those conditions should be maintained within the constraints imposed by the Wilderness Act and the establishment of a particular area. Inherent in this collective value judgment is the recognition that management of wilderness is actually management of wilderness users and their impacts (Lucas 1973). Decisions that reflect value judgments must, in a pluralistic society, be made with the support, consent, and/or agreement of the managed (the users). This implies that wilderness planning and management is essentially a political process incorporating biophysical and social data and agency policies. It is constrained by the parent Wilderness Act, by relevant, enabling legislation and is subject to planning and management activities. The management program developed for a wilderness can be viewed as a social contract between managers and the public, framed by enabling legislative mandates and agency policy.

Research input is important in the formulation of these judgments, but as an aid, not a determinant (Burch 1984). This role involves (Stankey 1979)

> describing the social and ecological consequences of alternative use levels, thus providing the opportunity for managers to judge whether these consequences are consistent with area management objectives. With each change in objective, the acceptable and appropriate social-ecological milieu also changes ... while research can help managers who are concerned with carrying capacity, it cannot supply answers about what the carrying capacity of a site *is* or *should be.*

The evolving recognition of carrying capacity as a *normative idea, derived from social judgments about appropriate conditions,* has led to increasing attention to the factors that shape and influence these judgments. It has also spawned a series of independent yet parallel efforts to develop a more adequate framework for managing recreational use and its associated impacts. The concept of Visitor Impact Management (VIM), proposed by Graefe and others (1986), the text *Carrying Capacity in Recreation Settings* by Shelby and Heberlein (1986), and the concept of the Limits of Acceptable Change (LAC) (Stankey and others 1985) all represent efforts to correct deficiencies in the traditional carrying capacity model of recreation management. They share a common focus on the identification of measurable objectives regarding desired conditions and on the distinction between steps involving objective description and analysis and those involving judgmental evaluations.

In this chapter, we will describe how the LAC concept can be used as a framework for contending with what is commonly described as the carrying capacity problem. The LAC and VIM systems are similar in structure and both draw heavily on the ideas about evaluative standards called for by Shelby and Heberlein (1986).

CONSIDERATIONS IN MANAGING USE AND IMPACT

Several basic considerations must be taken into account in managing recreational use and its impact. First, to determine the kinds of impacts that will occur and their possible implications, three factors must be considered (Manning 1986):

- *Natural resource factors.* The physical and biological characteristics of the natural resource base greatly influence the degree of change in the environment resulting from recreational use. Although recreational use inevitably causes change in the environment, some resource bases are inherently more fragile than others.
- *Sociopolitical factors.* The needs and wants of people are important in determining appropriate uses of natural resources. User perceptions and opinions of what types and level of use are preferred are an essential element in developing prescriptions of appropriate use.
- *Managerial factors.* Legal directives and agency missions play a major role in determining appropriate and feasible resource, social, and management conditions. Managerial factors help identify what conditions should be maintained and what actions might be employed to achieve those conditions.

Second, any recreational use of an area leads to change in the character of the above factors. *The inevitability of change is a critical consideration* that managers must take into account in prescribing carrying capacities. For example, virtually all studies of ecological impact caused by recreation point to the fact that most of the total impact recorded occurs under fairly low use levels (Cole 1985). In order to control ecological impact by restricting the number of visitors in an area, it would be necessary to establish extremely low use limitations, possibly beyond what is acceptable to the public. Rather than attempting to define how much use is too much, the LAC focuses attention on deciding the amount of change that will be allowed to occur.

Third, determining the amount of change that will be considered acceptable involves a *subjective value judgment,* but such judgments are derived from the management objectives prescribed for the area (see chap. 8). These objectives provide the framework within which the judgments regarding desired conditions for the area—resource, social, and managerial—can be defined. These desired conditions need to be expressed explicitly and quantitatively so as to reduce disputes over interpretation, a common problem with many objectives. In other words, area management objectives contain explicit standards that define the extent to which conditions will be allowed to change, if at all.

In the case of wilderness, the Wilderness Act provides at least general guidelines as to what management objectives are to be achieved. For instance, environmental conditions must be highly natural while use conditions provide opportunities for low-density recreation. Yet, the exact meaning of these conditions remains unclear; people will have different ideas about what they mean and their implications for management. Specifying standards helps

give objective meaning to them. Within the framework of the Wilderness Act and other relevant enabling legislation, the specific conditions to be achieved through management actions are a function of consensus value judgments derived through public involvement specific to each area.

Finally, although the traditional focus of concern in use and impact management has been the number of users, the impacts of use—on resources and other users—are often related to aspects other than amount. This includes things such as the type of use, timing and location of use, and visitor behavior. This has two important implications. It means the traditional management response of regulating use numbers might have little to do with controlling impact which, as we discussed in chapter 7, is really what we are concerned about. And it suggests that more attention needs to focus on other management strategies that more directly prevent or mitigate impacts defined as unacceptable.

These basic considerations underlie much of the discussion in this chapter. The goal of management is to identify the desired resource, social, and managerial conditions to be maintained or restored in wilderness, with these desired conditions expressed as explicit, measurable standards. Thus, the focus of management attention shifts from defining maximum use to identifying desired conditions and managing use levels and/or other management parameters so that impacts do not exceed these conditions (Shelby and Heberlein 1986). The LAC concept represents a reformulated view of the traditional model of carrying capacity; a detailed discussion of how it can be applied follows.

THE LIMITS OF ACCEPTABLE CHANGE (LAC) CONCEPT

Establishing appropriate use levels in wilderness is a major concern. For instance, a recent survey of wilderness managers nationwide reported that more than one-fourth of the areas regularly experienced use in excess of capacity in at least some portions and another 40 percent said use exceeded capacity occasionally (Washburne and Cole 1983). Such problems stimulated the development of regulations to implement the National Forest Management Act of 1976 (NFMA, P.L. 94-588) that "provide for limiting and distributing visitor use of specific portions in accord with periodic estimates of the maximum levels of use that allow natural processes to operate freely and that do not impair the values for which wilderness areas were created" (Federal Register 1982).

The concept of the *Limits of Acceptable Change* (LAC) represents a major alternative approach for resolving the carrying capacity issue. The general idea underlying the LAC is neither new nor does it represent a radical change in how planning is conducted. The recognition that change in response to use is inevitable and that decisions have to be made with regard to how much change will be permitted to occur has long been recognized. Lime (1970), for instance, called for establishment of standards in the Boundary Waters Canoe Area (MN) that defined acceptable limits to the impacts that would be permitted to occur on both the various resource elements and users. Frissell and Stankey (1972) outlined the basic framework for the LAC concept. They focused attention on the control of human-induced change. The goal of management, they argued, is to halt the character and rate of change that would lead to conditions judged as unacceptable in *de jure* wilderness (as defined by law).

The LAC concept recognizes, and seeks to enhance and protect, diversity in wilderness conditions. Our intent here is not to suggest that nonwilderness conditions should be tolerated or accepted in wilderness, as it is inevitable that any wilderness will contain a variety of conditions. Some of these are related to physical-biological differences. Others are related to the inevitable variations in use patterns as a result of the area's trail system, location of lakes, streams, attractions, and entry points (Stankey and others 1976). This inherent variability produces differences in the conditions found within the area. In some areas, pristine physical-biological conditions and outstanding opportunities for solitude are found. Elsewhere, the evidence of use is more apparent and contact with others more common.

Variability is not only inevitable but desirable, up to a point, because it enables the variable tastes and desires of recreational visitors to be met. No single condition constitutes wilderness; rather, a range exists, from the absolutely pristine to more modified states. The point of debate, of course, is just how modified a situation can be before it no longer represents wilderness. Because there are few, explicit standards describing unacceptable wilderness conditions, it is not surprising that conditions in many areas have evolved to where they represent local horror stories—ankle-deep mud on miles of trails, tent cities around popular lakes, and so on. Establishing a clear measure of what constitutes acceptable wilderness conditions in the form of explicit, measurable standards is the intent of the LAC process.

The focus of our discussion about the LAC concept in this chapter is on the impacts associated with recreational use. Recreation is a major concern in

many wildernesses and the impacts it causes can adversely affect both the integrity of natural ecosystems and the quality of the experience for other visitors. A national survey of wilderness managers reported that recreation-related problems occurred in 25 to 75 percent of the areas, while nonrecreational uses led to problems in only about 10 percent of the areas (Washburne and Cole 1983).

Nevertheless, the LAC concept is applicable to any problem which concerns the control of nonnatural change, for example, grazing, mining, or impacts on air quality. As with the management of recreation impacts, the LAC concept provides a framework within which the appropriate amount and extent of change can be identified. It also can alert managers to the need for action when changes exceed standards, for example, excessive impacts on wilderness forage from recreational packstock (fig. 9.2).

THE LAC PROCESS

The traditional model of carrying capacity focused principally on identifying how much use an area could tolerate before unacceptable impacts occurred. In order for such an approach to be effective, it was necessary to know the relationship between use and impact; if so much use occurs, what type of impact will result? Since use was not a constant or predictable measure, it was a difficult issue to evaluate. The level of impact resulting from a given number of users can vary considerably, depending on the specific characteristics of those users.

Consider this example: imagine we determine that an area can tolerate 100 users before unacceptable impact occurs. What happens if 50 of these users are backpackers and 50 are using packstock? Or if the use occurs in the early spring, when soils are wet and soft, as opposed to midsummer when soils are dry and hard? Or if some of the users follow minimum-impact camping procedures carefully while the remainder are novices? As the characteristics of the user group or their specific behavior change, the associated impact will change as well, perhaps substantially so, even though the number of users remains constant. To set a capacity based on numbers of users would require a different capacity for each possible combination, an impossibility in practical terms.

The real concern in the above example is not the number of users involved, but the impacts on the conditions of the area that result from use. It is these conditions that the LAC process focuses on. Given that any use produces at least some impact, the

Fig. 9.2. Horses typically have more impact on wilderness ecosystems than an equal number of hikers, especially on fragile sites such as lakeshores. To prevent irreversible damage, horses are now prohibited at Reflection Pond in the Glacier Peak Wilderness, WA. Photo courtesy of the USFS.

process requires managers to identify where, and to what extent, varying degrees of change are appropriate and acceptable. Once the appropriate and acceptable degree of change has been identified, managers can select from an array of management techniques to ensure that desired conditions are maintained or restored. These techniques range from light-handed measures such as providing information to visitors on appropriate camping methods to restricting the number of visitors to the area. The conditions that characterize a particular subunit of a wilderness and distinguish it from others are specified by measurable objectives which define LAC (Frissell and Stankey 1972; Lime 1970).

The LAC process consists of four major components: (1) the specification of acceptable and achievable resource and social conditions, defined by a series of measurable parameters; (2) an analysis of the relationship between existing conditions and those judged acceptable; (3) identification of management actions judged to best achieve these desired conditions; and (4) a program of monitoring and evaluating management effectiveness. These four components, in turn, are broken down into nine steps to facilitate application.

Figure 9.3 shows the nine-step LAC process. The circular form of the figure suggests a dynamic and iterative process. Problems and issues change over time; new technologies and information alter our definition of effective management. Any planning

process must be able to account for these changes; the LAC provides continuous feedback on conditions in the planning system that might warrant changes in management.[1]

Each of the nine steps of the LAC is designed to achieve a particular task and provides the basis for later activities. In the following discussion, we will review the rationale for each step and the specific activities involved in completing it.

Step 1: Identify Area Issues and Concerns
The purpose of step 1 is to identify those public issues and managerial concerns that relate to (1) distinctive features and characteristics of the wilderness area and (2) the relationship of the individual area to other units of the wilderness system and to nonwilderness areas offering primitive recreation opportunities. General management direction for every wilderness is based on the Wilderness Act, area-specific enabling legislation, and organizational policy. This step builds on that foundation, refining management direction to deal with the specific situation in each area.

In step 1, managers could consider matters such as:

1. Does the area contain outstanding ecological, scientific, recreational, educational, historic, or conservation values that warrant special attention?
2. Does the area provide critical habitat for threatened or endangered species?
3. Has public input identified areas or issues that merit special attention?
4. Do land uses on contiguous areas represent situations requiring special management attention; for example, are timber harvests planned, or are changes in access likely?
5. Are there existing or potential nonconforming uses in the area that will require special attention?
6. Are there regional and/or national issues that need consideration? For example:
    a. What is the availability of wilderness and dispersed recreation opportunities in the planning region?
    b. What is the regional demand for wilderness and dispersed recreation?
    c. Are the physical-biological features of the area found elsewhere in the region or does it possess unique features?
    d. Are the types of recreation opportunities offered by the area available in other wildernesses or does the area offer unique opportunities; for example, are opportunities for long-distance backcountry horse riding available in many other areas or just this one?
7. Are there sociopolitical factors specific to the area that will influence the planning process and its possible outcomes; for example, is there established outfitter use and historical patterns of stock use?

---

1. Further details on the LAC process can be found in Stankey and others 1984 and 1985.

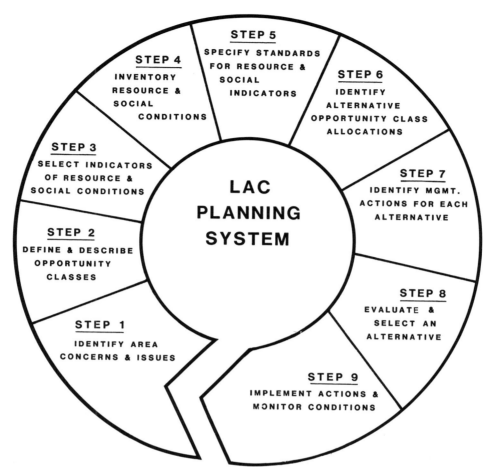

Fig. 9.3. The LAC process provides a framework for prescribing and maintaining acceptable wilderness conditions.

Answers to such questions help managers identify the values of the area and its role in the region and in the National Wilderness Preservation System (NWPS). For example, in some areas, primary management attention might focus on the preservation or restoration of a very high level of environmental protection. This might be based on the presence of an endangered species such as the grizzly bear or on the basis that the area contains ecosystems otherwise nonexistent in the NWPS (Davis 1984). In such a case, primary management emphasis would be on environmental protection, with wilderness recreation given relatively less attention. In another area, more attention might be directed at maintenance or restoration of outstanding opportunities for solitude or for specific forms of primitive recreation, such as extended cross-country travel. In either example, only *relative* emphases are involved. The need to preserve environmental conditions and to provide opportunities for solitude and primitive recreation must be accommodated in all areas.

The purpose in step 1 is to gain a better understanding of the role of the area in a larger regional setting; the inability to perform a comprehensive analysis should not hold up completion of the step.

Some issues and concerns identified in step 1 might be incompatible. For example, managers might identify solitude as a major value in the area, while the public supports increased access. No simple solution exists for resolving such conflicts. The inevitable diversity of tastes and preferences highlights the importance of examining individual wildernesses within a regional framework. In step 6, managers can accommodate these diverse concerns as they allocate the area to different opportunity classes.

Step 2: Define and Describe Opportunity Classes
In step 2, a series of opportunity classes are developed for the wilderness. An *opportunity class* defines the resource, social, and managerial conditions considered desirable and appropriate within the wil-

derness. The designation of opportunity classes follows the basic Recreation Opportunity Spectrum (ROS) system (Buist and Hoots 1982; Clark and Stankey 1979; Driver and Brown 1978; USDA FS 1982) and represents the range of wilderness recreation settings for which to manage within any given area. This range or diversity of conditions may be divided into two or more classes, which implies that opportunity classes represents a continuum of social, resource, or managerial variables. The underlying variables or dimensions used should be carefully identified and developed prior to determining the number and description of opportunity classes. For example, a wilderness may vary in the level of contact among visitors and the amount of visible human-induced impact. These two dimensions would constitute the underlying continuum that would be divided into two or more opportunity classes. Each dimension included should be addressed in each opportunity class description. Often, the dimensions selected will directly relate to the issues identified in step 1. Thus, each opportunity class is defined relative to one another; more (or less) impact on the environment is considered acceptable, more (or less) contact with others is acceptable, and so on.

Through opportunity classes, we formally protect and maintain a diverse range of wilderness conditions. At this stage in the LAC process, opportunity classes are not allocated to the wilderness in the field. The opportunity class description represents the varied wilderness setting conditions that are considered to be desirable and appropriate. Actual mapping of opportunity class allocations occurs in step 6. The outcome of this step, the opportunity class descriptions, provides a basis for identifying indicators (step 3), developing standards (step 4), and suggesting management actions (step 7).

At present, the *ROS defines six classes*: Primitive, Semiprimitive Nonmotorized, Semiprimitive Motorized, Roaded Natural, Rural, and Urban. Typically within wilderness areas, the Primitive and Semiprimitive Nonmotorized classes would apply. In general terms, these two classes can be characterized as follows:

Primitive
- An area characterized by an essentially unmodified natural environment.
- Fairly large in size.
- Interaction between users is very low.
- Evidence of other users is minimal.
- Area is managed to be essentially free from evidence of human-induced restrictions and controls.
- Motorized use within the area is not permitted.

Semiprimitive Nonmotorized
- An area is characterized by a predominantly natural or natural-appearing environment.
- Moderate-to-large size.
- Interaction between users is low.
- Often evidence of other users is present.
- Area is managed in such a way that minimum onsite controls and restrictions may be present, but are subtle.
- Motorized use is not permitted.

These setting descriptions are broad, and within each it is possible to describe several subclasses. For example, at major entry points, use levels may be relatively high, with fairly frequent contact among parties. Similarly, resource impacts can be moderately visible in these areas. Elsewhere in the same wilderness, there are areas where few visit and where ecological conditions are almost undisturbed. Between these extremes a continuum of conditions exist, all within the wilderness. Eliminating this internal variability would be difficult and could only be attained with a highly regulated system of entry and use dispersal. Managers may also explicitly consider maintaining this variability. This decision would be reflected in the opportunity class descriptions.

During this step, managers will decide not only how each opportunity class is defined, but also how many opportunity classes are appropriate for the wilderness. For example, smaller wildernesses may have only one or two classes, while larger areas may have as many as four to six. The question of how many classes to designate can be answered only after analysis of the issues, the current range of conditions, the demands for wilderness recreation, and regional supply of different wilderness settings.

Descriptions of resource conditions will be influenced by issues identified in step 1, but typically include the type and extent of recreational visitor impacts. In writing statements regarding acceptable resource conditions for each opportunity class, managers should address the following considerations:

1. Type of impact.
2. Severity of impact.
3. Prevalence and extent of impact.
4. Apparentness of impact, extent to which impact is noticeable to visitors.

To contrast the kinds of resource conditions judged appropriate for different opportunity classes, consider the following statements written for an opportunity class preserving the most pristine condition in an area, *class I*, and one representing a situation where more resource and social impacts are judged acceptable, *class IV*. These two opportunity classes represent the extremes of a four-class spectrum.

Class I

- Resource impacts are minimal; restricted to minor temporary loss of vegetation where camping occurs and along some travel routes.
- Impacts typically recover on an annual basis and are subtle in nature.
- Impacts generally not apparent to most visitors.

Class IV

- Resource impacts found in many locations and some can be substantial in a few places, such as near major entry points.
- Impacts may persist from year to year, possibly substantial loss of vegetation and soil at some sites.
- Impacts are readily apparent to most visitors.

Social conditions must also be covered in the description. Hence, managers should consider levels and types of encounters occurring in the opportunity class. Specifically, the description should address:

1. Extent of interparty contact
2. Location of interparty contact.

In some cases, the description could also include contacts among different types of users.

Again, to compare conditions in a class I opportunity class with those in a class IV opportunity class, consider the following:

Class I

- Few, if any, contacts with other groups.
- Contact limited to trails.
- Camping out of sight and sound of others almost always possible.

Class IV

- Contact with others moderately frequent.
- Fairly high level of interparty contact can occur on the trail.
- Camping has fairly high level of interparty contact.

Such descriptions describe very different kinds of social settings for these two opportunity classes. They indicate that class I will provide high levels of solitude while class IV is an area of use concentration and relatively frequent contact.

Finally, managers need to develop descriptive statements of managerial conditions. The desired managerial condition is an especially important part of the description because it establishes a framework for what will be done to achieve the defined resource and social conditions. A clear description of appropriate management conditions is important because standards will not be prescribed in step 5 as they are for desired resource and social conditions. Why? Because management conditions deal primarily with the means by which the resource and social conditions, as expressed in the standards, will be achieved.

A carefully developed description addresses the following kinds of management issues:

1. Presence of management personnel.
2. Onsite versus offsite management strategies.
3. Site modification.
4. Rules and regulations on behavior.
5. Facilities and trail construction standards.

Comparing the managerial settings in class I with those in class IV, the descriptors might read as follows:

Class I

- Direct onsite management of visitors not practiced. Little or no evidence of site management.
- Rules and regulations communicated to visitors outside the area. Little evidence of management personnel.

Class IV

- Extensive use of onsite management and site modification.
- Rules and regulations enforced with signs and management personnel in the area. Substantial use of regulations to influence visitor behavior.

Although the descriptive statements of managerial conditions indicate the desired intensity and intrusiveness of action, situations will exist where these actions differ considerably from what is desired. For example, an area may be designated as class I—low use density, few encounters, minimal impacts, and little evidence of management personnel. But current conditions may be far worse than those defined as acceptable by the standards adopted for this area. In order to achieve these standards, managers would have to adopt fairly intrusive actions—such as designation of campsites and consequent enforcement—in order to restore wilderness conditions to the acceptable level. Once such conditions are achieved, management direction may then be "relaxed" to what is described in the opportunity class description.

Collectively, these narrative descriptions of the resource, social, and managerial conditions for each opportunity class constitute the *management objectives* for the area. They describe the conditions sought in the wilderness and serve as criteria for identifying what and where specific management actions are needed (see chap. 8). These objectives serve throughout the process to determine what types of information are needed, what standards need to be developed, the appropriateness of various activities, and what management actions need to be instituted.

Step 3: Select Indicators of Resource and Social Conditions

The preceding two steps provide managers with generalized descriptors of the desired condition. In step 3, we move on to identify *indicators*—specific variables—that, singly or in combination, are taken as indicative of the condition of the overall opportunity class. Such measures allow managers to unambiguously define desired conditions and to assess the effectiveness of various management practices.

To develop these more specific statements, managers need to first review the broadly defined issues and concerns in step 1 that require attention. In fact, *indicators are largely issue driven*. For example, there might be concern with issues such as excessive use levels along trails in the area or with the amount of biophysical impact at campsites. These broad categories of issues or concerns are *factors*. The following list covers likely topics:

Suggested Resource and Social Factors

Resource	*Social*
1. Trail conditions	1. Solitude while traveling
2. Campsite conditions	2. Campsite solitude
3. Water quality	3. Conflicts between visitors with different travel methods
4. Air quality	
5. Wildlife populations	
6. Threatened and endangered species	4. Conflicts regarding party size
7. Range condition	5. Noise

Within these broad categories, however, managers need to identify one or more indicators that reflect the overall condition of the factor. For example, campsite condition encompasses a number of concerns; what specific indicators should be selected for measurement? Criteria that can help guide selection of indicators would include:

1. The indicator should be suited to being measured in a cost-effective fashion at acceptable levels of accuracy.
2. The condition of the indicator should reflect some relationship to the amount and/or type of use occurring.
3. Social indicators should be related to user concerns.
4. The condition of the indicator should be at least potentially responsive to management control.

Thus, indicators that could be used to measure campsite condition might include total area of bare ground, number of damaged trees in the campsite area, soil compaction, or a composite index reflecting overall campsite condition. For a factor such as campsite encounters, indicators might include the number of other persons camped within sight or sound or the total number of sites located within some unit area.

No single indicator constitutes a comprehensive measure; it will reflect only a portion of what the objective seeks to achieve. For example, if provision of outstanding opportunities for solitude is the objective, managers might use indicators such as the number of interparty contacts while on the trail or while at the campsite. If, for example, interparty contacts can be held to two or less per day while traveling, the objective of providing outstanding opportunities for solitude presumably has been attained. Other factors, such as whether contact is with a horse or hiker party, also influence whether or not the objective is achieved. Thus, two or more indicators can be used as a way of comprehensively measuring performance in terms of the objectives.

It is important to select indicators that relate as directly as possible to the objective. For example, managers might select use density (visitor-days per 1,000 acres) as the indicator for a solitude objective. Varying density levels would be specified as standards for the different opportunity classes. The linkage between density and subsequent interparty contact levels is indirect and weak, especially for dispersed recreation opportunities. Thus, the choice of density as an indicator would be less useful than a contact indicator directly related to solitude.

A recent study at the University of Idaho, using the expert opinion of physical, biological, and social scientists, identified 32 specific indicators that might be used by managers to monitor wilderness conditions (Merigliano 1987). But because indicators are driven largely by the issues that are identified in a planning effort, it is important that managers select only those that relate to their situation. Additionally, as the authors note, definitions as to what are the most important or useful indicators will often change over time; thus, the list of selected indicators should be reviewed periodically as to its appropriateness.

Step 4: Inventory Existing Resource and Social Conditions

The inventory is guided by the indicators selected in step 3. The indicators specify the variable(s) inventoried; they also identify the unit of analysis. For example, managers might be concerned about water quality. In selecting indicators that will define water quality standards, they might select coliform counts in lakes or streams adjacent to campsites. Thus, the resulting water quality inventory has a specific focus that defines what data are to be collected and where. During the inventory, data need to be collected that provide information on the coliform counts throughout the area. The inventory must be conducted in an objective and systematic fashion. If not, the data will be of limited value.

Inventory data provide managers with the range of conditions of the indicators. Such information can be recorded directly onto base maps, which provide easy analysis of its spatial patterns. This will be helpful when, in step 6, managers consider different allocations of opportunity classes across the area, because it facilitates comparison between existing conditions and those defined as acceptable for an opportunity class.

Some other data might be inventoried, including variables that could affect how the area is to be managed (e.g., the location of administrative facilities). Managers might also be concerned with the distribution of opportunity classes over different landscape types within the wilderness and, therefore, would need to consider the inventory of such types at this point in the process.

Resource inventories can be conducted at different levels of detail. Often, managers will have inventory data from previous fieldwork or they might have partially completed inventory data. Although it is most desirable to have an up-to-date comprehensive inventory of the condition of the indicators, managers often have to work with incomplete or noncurrent data. Where this is the case, the limits of the data should be carefully documented and an improved data base should be a priority in scheduling the monitoring phase in step 9.

Step 5: Specify Standards For Resource and Social Indicators For Each Opportunity Class

In step 5, the task is to assign quantitative or highly specific measures to the indicators. This greater specificity is obtained by establishing *standards*—measurable aspects of the indicators defined in step 3. These standards provide a basis for judging whether a particular condition is acceptable or not.

By using data collected in step 4, it is possible to specify standards that describe the acceptable and appropriate conditions for each indicator in each opportunity class. Setting standards is a judgmental process; however, the process is explicit, traceable, and subject to public involvement and review. Standards relative to appropriate use conditions are often best derived with the input of the visitors themselves; suggestions for obtaining such information can be found in chapter 5 in Shelby and Heberlein (1986).

Standards are not just idealistic goals; they are conditions that managers feel can be achieved over a reasonable time. In some cases, standards might be merely statements of current conditions. In other cases, standards can be written to purposively direct modification of wilderness conditions, typically, but not necessarily, toward a more natural state.

Basically, then, standards should be stringent enough to be meaningful, but not so stringent that they cannot be attained. Three general guidelines apply to the process of establishing standards:

STANDARDS FOLLOW DESCRIPTORS

The qualitative descriptions developed in step 2 provide clues as to the kinds of conditions characterizing each opportunity class. For example, if a description written for a class IV area suggests that "contacts are fairly frequent while traveling" managers could use the inventory data to help specify how "fairly frequent" might be quantitatively defined. The inventory data might show that contact levels on trails near major entry points average 10 to 15 parties per day. These data could be used to help set the standard for the "average contacts with others per day" indicator to define the class IV area. If inventory data showing average contact levels are not available, data on visitor preferences for contact might be used instead.

Normally, it is important that the standards are not established for existing conditions. For example, there will be places where existing conditions have deteriorated to the point that they no longer represent acceptable wilderness conditions, irrespective of the area's legal classification. In such cases, managers are legally bound to restore these areas to a condition that is, *at the minimum*, acceptable in wilderness. In no way is the LAC process designed to condone maintenance of unacceptable wilderness conditions. And, even if existing conditions are judged as minimally acceptable, managers should seek opportunities to improve them by establishing more stringent standards. In formulating standards, there needs to be a balance between using existing conditions to lend realism to the specific standards and using professional judgment along with public input to set the standards at levels that can lead to an improvement in conditions.

STANDARDS DESCRIBE A RANGE OF CONDITIONS

When looking at the opportunity classes for any given indicator, the standards should describe a logical progression or gradation of conditions. For example, managers might select "other parties camped within sight or sound at night" as an indicator for solitude. In a class I opportunity class, the description might read "very high chances for solitude." For this class, a standard of "no other parties camped within sight or sound" might be prescribed. Then, moving on to the other opportunity classes and remembering that the intent is to provide a

logical progression or gradation of conditions relative to this particular indicator, managers might set standards of "no more than 1," "no more than 2," and so on for the remaining opportunity classes.

On occasions, the standards set for an indicator might be shared by two or more opportunity classes. In such cases, the opportunity classes would be distinguished by the standards set for other indicators. Shared standards are appropriate where the range of conditions is low, where the desired state is equal across opportunity classes, or where the indicator has limited relationship to recreation, such as water quality. Again, the descriptors will help managers decide when shared standards should be adopted. In some instances, an indicator might apply only to a single opportunity class, for example, an indicator related to a threatened and endangered species whose range is limited.

Although a progression of standards across opportunity classes will be typical, there might be certain conditions that apply areawide and that do not discriminate between classes. Examples include air quality and water quality. Also, baseline standards might prescribe conditions that must be met in all areas; namely, under no situation could a condition in a wilderness fall below this baseline standard. Baseline standards do not preclude more stringent standards within individual areas.

STANDARDS EXPRESS THE TYPICAL
SITUATION
Standards are often best expressed in terms of probabilities. For example, a standard for daily contacts while traveling in the primitive opportunity class might be expressed as: "Interparty contact levels on the trail will not exceed two per day on at least 90 percent of the days during the summer use period." This recognizes the fact that the high degree of resource and social variability in a complex wilderness system often makes specific, absolute standards unrealistic.

Choosing indicators and writing standards are crucial steps because they determine, to a great extent, the future character of the wilderness. Public input, research information, and managerial experience will be helpful guides. There is no need, however, to be paralyzed by concerns as to whether the "right" indicators have been chosen or whether the standards are "correct." As noted earlier, the process is judgmental and state of the art (Clark 1982). Because monitoring and evaluation are an integral part of this procedure, management will be able to revise indicators and standards in response to improved information. Moreover, the judgments are made in a visible fashion so that they can be reviewed by others.

Step 6: Identify Alternative Opportunity Class Allocations Reflecting Area Issues and Concerns and Existing Resource and Social Conditions
The objective in step 6 is to decide what resource and social conditions (in the form of specific standards) are to be maintained or achieved in specific areas of the wilderness. This is a *prescriptive step*, concerned with establishing what *should be*, and input from both managers and the public should be used to make these decisions. Step 6 initially involves an analysis of the inventory data collected in step 4, along with the area issues and concerns identified in step 1. These issues and concerns, however, do not prescribe what should be done. They have to be balanced against the realities of what exists, as revealed by the maps of existing condition for each indicator, as well as what is possible in terms of agency resources.

Maps of alternative opportunity classes, reflecting both area issues and concerns and existing resource and social conditions, result from step 6. Some issues might prove contradictory ("increase opportunities for easier access into most portions of the wilderness" and "provide greater opportunities for solitude"). Managers could respond in a variety of ways. They might attempt to provide the full range of opportunity classes in sufficient amounts to satisfy the varying demands. Or, they might elect to manage primarily for only a couple of the opportunity classes, on the grounds that the other classes are adequately represented elsewhere in the region. Finally, they might propose a variety of management alternatives that reflect a range of opportunity class mixes. Through such variations, it would be possible to offer a diverse range of conditions for public review and consideration.

Step 7: Identify Management Actions For Each Alternative
After alternative opportunity classes have been formulated, managers need to identify the differences, if any, that exist between current conditions (inventoried in step 4) and the standards (identified in step 5). This will help identify problems and management actions that are needed. Then managers need to consider what actions will be instituted to achieve the conditions specified by each alternative and to evaluate the costs and appropriateness of implementing these actions. If an alternative calls for a set of opportunity areas that closely match the current situation, the management actions needed to achieve this might not be too costly. On the other hand, if a major change is proposed, considerable costs may be incurred.

Where existing conditions are better than standards, we would generally assume there is little need for change in management, although there might be a need to evaluate whether existing actions should be changed or eliminated. For example, if existing conditions are better than desired, but there is evidence that the trend in conditions is worsening, managers might want to initiate at least some preliminary actions in order to prevent this trend from continuing and eventually violating the standard. Where conditions are close to or substantially worse than standards, managers must consider new actions.

For any given alternative, a number of possible management actions could be undertaken to achieve the standards. The qualitative descriptions for each opportunity class developed in step 2 serve as guidelines as to whether or not a particular management action is appropriate. But, these descriptions are not iron-clad rules—they are guidelines, not standards. As a general rule, apply the "principle of minimum regulation" (see chap. 7); use only that level of control necessary to achieve a specific objective.

If existing resource and social conditions are consistent with the opportunity class designation, so should the management actions. If, on the other hand, the existing resource and social conditions differ from those desired, the management actions needed to achieve those standards (consistent with the necessity and minimum regulation provision), should be employed, even if they are not consistent with the management condition descriptor written in step 2.

For example, if a heavily impacted area were to be converted to a pristine condition, intensive management would be needed. Such a program might include: restrictions on where and how long visitors could camp; restriction of recreational stock; and closures of certain areas. Normally, such actions would be inappropriate in that opportunity class, but without such measures, achieving management objectives in a reasonable time span would be difficult. Hence, more restrictive management is imposed until progress is made toward achieving the standards.

Managers should remember that *standards define minimally acceptable conditions sought in an area.* Nevertheless, such standards do not preclude providing protection in part of an opportunity class above that specified by the standards. Many areas consist of frequently visited valley-bottom trail corridors bounded by trailless, relatively pristine valley walls. By maintaining conditions better than the standard requires, further diversity in wilderness conditions is achieved.

Step 8: Evaluate and Select a Preferred Alternative

The selection of a preferred alternative will reflect the evaluation of both managers and concerned citizens. No simple formula exists for making such a decision. Some questions to guide this selection include:

1. Which user groups are affected and how (does it facilitate or restrict use by certain groups)?
2. Which values are promoted and which are diminished?
3. How does a particular alternative fit into the regional and/or national supply and demand considerations? Does the alternative contribute a unique kind of wilderness setting to the system?
4. What is the feasibility of managing the areas as prescribed, given constraints of personnel, budgets, etc?

In the analysis of the alternatives, a variety of costs need to be considered. These would include: the financial costs (personnel, materials); information costs (costs for acquiring information needed to implement actions); opportunity costs for not carrying out a proposed action; and other resource and social costs. These latter costs are difficult to quantify, particularly in monetary terms, but they are extremely important (Lucas 1982).

Although it is difficult to measure the costs and benefits of the various alternatives, their presence or absence usually can be identified. Managers usually can identify the kinds of costs (e.g., increased impacts on vegetation) and benefits (e.g., increased opportunities for solitude) associated with a management action. Even though it is difficult to measure their extent, recognition of their existence will improve the ability of managers and citizens to evaluate the alternative.

Deciding what constitutes the "best" alternative is obviously not easy. Information on the issues identified above should clarify the costs and benefits associated with each alternative. In addition, public participation plays an important role in selecting a final alternative, as it ensures that important issues in the area have been identified and dealt with. Because the LAC focuses on conditions, and because the costs and benefits associated with achieving the different alternatives have been identified, public groups will be able to focus their comments on specific assumptions, actions, or areas in the alternatives. It will also enable different groups to better understand how different alternatives affect their own interests.

Step 9: Implement Actions and Monitor Conditions

With selection of an alternative and its associated management program, the program must be imple-

mented and its performance assessed. Monitoring provides systematic feedback on how well management actions are working and identifies trends in condition that require new actions.

A major concern is the appropriate frequency of monitoring. Ideally, all indicators addressed by standards would be frequently monitored throughout an area. Given budgetary constraints, however, certain indicators will be monitored less frequently than others and certain areas will be monitored less closely than others.

Generally, priorities for monitoring should consider situations where: (1) conditions were very close to standards at the time of the last assessment; (2) rates of resource or social change are judged to be the highest; (3) the quality of the data base is poorest; (4) the understanding of management action effects is poorest; or (5) unanticipated changes in factors have occurred such as access, adjacent land uses, and so on.

Monitoring could reveal a number of possible outcomes. Not only the condition existing at the time of monitoring, but the trend in that condition as well is important. For instance, existing conditions might be better than the standards call for, but are nevertheless worsening over time. Or, existing conditions might be worse than those called for by the standards, but their trend could be improving, worsening, or stable. The point is, monitoring *alerts managers to the trend in relation to the standards.* Depending on the specific circumstances, managers might want to implement actions to prevent changes in conditions, even when standards have not been violated. For example, when the trend clearly indicates that conditions are worsening, even though within the standard, managers might begin implementing steps to halt this trend. Just as we do not wait until the gas gauge in the car indicates empty before we take action, monitoring provides managers with information needed to initiate actions before standards are exceeded.

The results of monitoring help evaluate program effectiveness and improve future programs. If monitoring shows that previously acceptable conditions have deteriorated and are now worse than the standards, new or additional actions are called for. If conditions had previously violated standards, and monitoring shows they still do, the actions can be judged ineffective, at least within the time since being initiated.

An action might prove ineffective for various reasons. Perhaps the action was appropriate, but its implementation was not effective or the programs have not had enough time to work. Trends reflected in the monitoring data should indicate where the problem lies. *Monitoring provides feedback regarding the effectiveness of certain management actions in solving particular kinds of problems.* For example, use rationing might have been prescribed to solve a problem of too many sites impacted by camping. If monitoring shows no decrease in the number of sites, very likely the problem and its causes have not been adequately defined. On the other hand, if conditions are improving, perhaps the action just needs more time. The next round of monitoring will tell.

Managers need to be alert to changes in external circumstances that could affect the resource and social conditions within the wilderness. These could include: external access systems; adjacent land uses; population growth; or the relative availability of alternative types of recreational opportunities. In some cases, impacts stemming from such alterations can be coped with through different management actions. In the case of major changes, fundamental alterations in area management objectives might need to be considered.

The LAC process provides a general framework within which acceptable wilderness conditions can be prescribed and the management actions to maintain or restore these conditions are identified. But like any planning framework, the value of the LAC lies in its ability to help shape planning and management in the real world. In the following discussion, we examine how the LAC has been applied in the development of a plan to guide the management of the Bob Marshall Wilderness Complex (BMWC) in western Montana.

IMPLEMENTING LAC IN THE BOB MARSHALL WILDERNESS COMPLEX

The BMWC is composed of three wildernesses lying astride the Continental Divide in Montana: the Bob Marshall Wilderness, designated in 1964 as one of the "instant" wildernesses created by the Wilderness Act, although originally set aside in the late 1920s; the Scapegoat, established in 1972; and the Great Bear, designated in 1978 (fig. 9.4). Together they comprise 1,535,352 acres, one of the largest unroaded areas in the lower 48 states. The BMWC is large enough to contain complete ecosystems and contains watersheds for three major drainages: the Middle and South Forks of the Flathead River and the Sun River. The area preserved includes major riparian zones and grasslands, as well as the "ice and rocks" typical of many wildernesses.

The BMWC contains nearly all large game and nongame wildlife resident in the area when the Europeans arrived, including grizzly bear, elk, black bear,

Fig. 9.4. The BMWC is composed of three separate but contiguous wildernesses, covering about 1.5 million acres in western Montana. Conditions range from pristine to heavily impacted, presenting a difficult challenge to managers. This photograph shows Woodward Lake in the Bob Marshall Wilderness. Photo courtesy of the USFS.

deer, and reported sightings of the gray wolf. Vegetation has been significantly influenced by the occurrence of fire, with the major fire type composed of low-frequency, high-intensity stand replacement fires.

More than 50 outfitters, with about 55 base camps, provide hunting and summer-oriented horseback and rafting recreation opportunities. More hunters hire outfitters than do nonhunters. About 14 percent of all visitors in the summer and 24 percent of the fall visitors use outfitters. Compared to 1970, the number of outfitted guests has remained about the same or declined slightly (Lucas 1985). In 1970, about 32 percent of all visitors hunted, contrasted to 1982 when 16 percent hunted.

Like many other wildernesses, use is not dispersed evenly over the complex. More than 70 trailheads and one active airstrip provide access to about 1,500 miles of trails; however, only seven trailheads account for about 50 percent of the total use. From 1970 to 1982, the average number of parties encountered increased from 1.3 per day to 1.6, yet this is still relatively small when compared to other wildernesses.

Recreation use of the complex totals approximately 250,000 visitor-days annually. Most of the visits to the complex are hikers, comprising approximately 57 percent of the people, with horseback riders totaling about 36 percent of the visitors (Lucas 1985). This is a change from 1970 when horseback

riders outnumbered hikers about two to one. Horseback riders tend to come in larger group sizes and stay longer than hikers, however, so the majority of total use in visitor-days comes from horseback riders. Between 1970 and 1982, party sizes and lengths of stay tended to drop for both groups.

The Bob Marshall Wilderness is often considered the "flagship" of the NWPS; as such, its management is viewed with great interest not only across the nation, but from around the world. Four national forests (Flathead, Helena, Lewis and Clark, and Lolo) within the complex are administered through five ranger districts. A wilderness management plan for the Bob Marshall Wilderness was developed in 1972, but much of it was never really actually implemented because of the lack of public support.

The limited implementation of the 1972 Bob Marshall management plan, the designation of the Scapegoat and Great Bear Wildernesses comprised of contiguous components of the same ecosystem, and the need for updated comprehensive management direction for the BMWC prompted the four national forests to develop a coordinated approach to all three wildernesses through their respective Forest Land and Resource Management Plans.

LAC was selected to provide the technical framework for developing common wilderness management direction for the entire wilderness complex. A comprehensive management document for the BMWC would then be appended to each forest's respective Forest Land and Resource Management Plan. A major concern to managers was the lack of ownership in and support for the 1972 Bob Marshall Wilderness plan by wilderness users and interest groups. Thus, the public involvement process was considered a critical element to ensure success of the LAC.

A major decision facing managers of the BMWC was whether or not to develop LAC following the traditional rational-comprehensive planning model. Under the *rational-comprehensive approach*, the managers/planners develop a plan based on voluminous information, develop alternatives including a preferred alternative, and then solicit public comment and review through a formal public involvement process.

There have been a number of criticisms about how the rational-comprehensive planning approach has been implemented. These criticisms include: the large data requirements of the model; its highly centralized character; and the limitations of available knowledge (Braybrooke and Lindblom 1963; McLaughlin 1977). One of its major shortcomings is the manner in which public input is sought and handled. Typically, public input is sought only in-

termittently throughout the process, often during preliminary "scoping" sessions when issues and concerns are initially identified and in response to formal alternatives conceived and presented by the technical planning staff.

Forest planners were aware of an alternative style in which planning for the BMWC could be undertaken. Transactive planning was developed by Friedmann (1973) as a response to the deficiencies and problems posed by traditional rational planning. In particular, Friedmann argued that alternatives to solving social problems by centralized decision making must be developed, and that such alternative processes should include those impacted by the decisions contained in the plan. *Transactive planning* incorporates the concept of societal guidance (Etzioni 1968), wherein people are willing and able to construct and guide their future if given the opportunity to do so. Hudson (1979), in a comparison of different planning theories, noted that a key element of transactive planning was its recognition of the importance of social interaction among those affected by a decision. Friedmann suggested that small working groups of citizens form the basis of a transactive planning process. Such working groups, because of their relatively small size, encouraged face-to-face communication and dialogue and provided a setting where participants could acquire and use technical knowledge.

In these working groups, participants share their intimate knowledge and experiences with the planner, who, in turn, shares the technical and organizational planning models and systematic ways of data manipulation with the citizens. The dialogue that develops between citizen and planner leads to mutual learning. Through the dialogue and learning processes, the working group, using its accumulated knowledge, makes an informed decision about a course of action (McCool and others 1986; Stokes 1982).

These working groups, if adequately represented by a cross-section of involved individuals and interest groups, can comprise a political marketplace; that is, a forum that has the legitimate representation necessary to conduct the bargaining required for a consensus approach (plan). Such a group has the potential to form a viable political coalition that can ensure the plan has adequate political support to achieve implementation (Caulfield 1975; Stokes 1982).

Issues confronting the BMWC are similar to those in other wildernesses: visitors are concerned about campsite impact and opportunities for solitude; trail conditions are frequently identified by both managers and visitors as unacceptable; conflict between hikers and horseback riders has increased; flights into the Schafer Meadows airstrip, an area included within the Great Bear Wilderness with its designation in 1978, produce noise which disturbs nearby wilderness visitors; forage for horses is relatively scarce, and recreational stock and wildlife compete for it; the entire complex is occupied grizzly bear habitat; and a natural fire management program, while accepted by most visitors (Lucas 1985), may have negative impacts on specific trails and campsites.

In response to these issues, as well as to regulations promulgated as a result of the NFMA to provide for "limiting and distributing visitor use" in wilderness, the U.S. Forest Service (USFS), with the Flathead National Forest serving as the lead forest, initiated a planning effort in 1982 to develop more specific and additional direction than established in the 1972 plan.

A *task force* consisting of managers, researchers, and citizen representatives was assembled. An interforest core team was formalized under the auspices of a LAC Action Plan, signed by all four forest supervisors in August 1983, to develop a draft plan. Both managerial and research components were intensively involved in the planning effort. The core team, along with its research support, operated as the technical arm of the LAC Task Force as a whole.

The task force public participation format was based on the following assumptions that reflected the underlying transactive planning model (Stokes 1986):

1. The scientific/technical data available, although not all-inclusive, are adequate for this first-generation LAC planning effort and can be refined over time.
2. The collective knowledge of users, managers, and researchers is sufficient to complement, validate, or refine conclusions based on the data.
3. Managers, citizens' representatives, and researchers are willing to participate within the task force to develop a sense of ownership in the BMWC management challenges and solutions to those challenges.
4. The citizens component includes a sufficiently broad spectrum of interest groups to constitute a microcosm of local, regional, and national interest in the BMWC. The task force is not, however, necessarily representative of all wilderness interest groups. The formal public review process provides the opportunity for groups or individuals not included in the task force to make their views known.
5. The citizens component provides an adequate political marketplace wherein the bargaining and tradeoffs necessary to develop a consensus can be conducted.
6. Managers will ensure that all solutions/directions are consistent with the Wilderness Act and organizational policies.
7. The composition of the citizens component represents a viable political coalition that will ensure the LAC management direction is carried out.
8. Solutions developed under the umbrella of the LAC Task Force will be within the constraints imposed by the Wilderness Act and subsequent policies and regulations.

Fig. 9.5. An LAC task force held numerous meetings over a four-year period before formulating a management plan to control unacceptable human impacts in the BMWC. Citizen participation was critically important throughout the process. Photo courtesy of Steve McCool.

9. What is acceptable and supportable by the citizens component will be acceptable and supportable by the population at large.

The task force functioned as an *ad hoc* umbrella group composed of managerial, research, and citizens components (fig. 9.5). This composition of representatives allowed the opportunity for sharing technical/scientific knowledge and personal knowledge among participants. Most citizens' representatives had personal knowledge of the BMWC based on their experience as users. Many of them also had technical knowledge to share with others.

The managers had both personal knowledge of the area and scientific/technical background and knowledge; the researchers provided concepts such as LAC and the best scientific data and analysis that were available. Through discussions and dialogue at general task force meetings and smaller subgroup meetings, the personal knowledge of all representatives became integrated with the collective scientific/technical knowledge of the group.

The LAC Task Force consisted of up to 50 persons. Over a period of nearly four years, with an independent facilitator helping in the last two years, the recreation management direction for the BMWC was established. Nine meetings of the full task force were held, along with numerous other meetings of geographical or problem-based subgroups. A major public information and involvement program was also initiated. In total, more than 80 formal and informal meetings and information and working sessions occurred in the four-year period. A seven-member Agency Core Team, composed of ranger district representatives, the Flathead National Forest recreation staff officer, and the independent facilita-

tor, provided the task force with information and tentative proposals from which to work.

The technical component of the planning effort followed the LAC process, although the last three steps were modified somewhat because of the size and complexity of the BMWC. For example, identifying individual management actions for all areas violating proposed standards for several different alternatives, called for in step 7, would have resulted in an unwieldy document.

The LAC steps were used to focus task force input. For example, the task force developed the preliminary list of issues and indicators, identified alternative standards, mapped alternative opportunity class allocations, and identified potential management actions. Much of the core team and researcher effort was focused on: educating the task force about the LAC process; interpreting research data; and resolving other administrative issues. Also, because the LAC process was new and to some extent still being developed, the continuous core team was continuously being educated. Task force members contributed by validating or pointing out weaknesses in data and in the LAC process itself. On many occasions debate broke out among members of the task force about the appropriateness of management actions, validity of the data, conflicts between outfitters and nonoutfitted public, and other issues. For example, a major issue was whether the standard for the barren soil core of campsites was to be applied to authorized horse-handling facilities in outfitter base camps.

Following development of a proposed alternative and subsequent review by the task force, a draft management plan was developed and made available for formal public comment. Comments to the draft

were considered and responses developed. Where appropriate, changes in the draft were included. An environmental assessment was developed to document the potential consequences of three alternative opportunity class allocations: (1) one emphasizing management for wilderness-dependent recreation opportunities; (2) one focusing on preserving and enhancing pristine environmental conditions; and (3) the preferred alternative. Alternative one is similar to alternative two, but allows more impact along heavily used travel corridors. A biological evaluation of the preferred alternative was conducted to determine if it would adversely affect the well being of endemic threatened and endangered species. The evaluation concluded with a "no effect" decision, but recommended that biologists be consulted about campsite closures and other similar actions to ensure that threatened and endangered species would not be adversely affected. Finally, the draft was rewrit-

ten and formally amended to the respective forest plans through a supervisor's decision.

The LAC process resulted in four wilderness recreation opportunity classes. Names for the opportunity classes were dropped early in the process when it became evident that such terms as *transition* did not describe the intent of the class, were value-laden, and were subject to controversy. Class I, the most pristine, permits almost no evidence of human occupancy and use, while class IV allows somewhat more change to occur. For example, signs indicating trail name or number and administrative signs and signing for use dispersal and resource protection are permitted in class IV areas; but in class I, no signs are permitted. Mapping of the opportunity classes centered around identifying heavily used travel corridors that were mapped as either class III or IV. These corridors were generally mapped at about 1 mile in width. The remaining area was then mapped as class

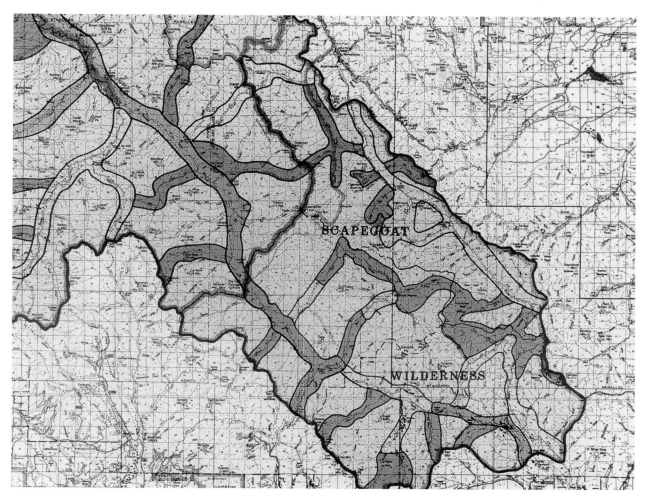

Fig. 9.6. Portion of map displaying recreational opportunity classes in Scapegoat Wilderness, part of the BMWC, MT. Various shadings indicate levels of naturalness ranging from pristine to heavily impacted.

Table 9.1. Proposed standards for resource and social indicators for each opportunity class in the BMWC.

Indicators	Opportunity class I	Opportunity class II	Opportunity class III	Opportunity class IV
SOCIAL				
1. Number of trail encounters with other parties	80 percent probablility of 0 encounters per day	80 percent probablility of 1 or fewer encounters per day	80 percent probability of 3 or fewer encounters per day	80 percent probablility of 5 or fewer encounters per day
2. Number of other partis camped within sight or continuous sound	80 percent probablility of 0 parties per day	80 percent probablility of 0 parties per day	80 percent probablility of 1 or 0 parties per day	80 percent probablility of 3 or fewer parties per day
HUMAN-IMPACTED SITES				
3. Area of barren core (square feet)[1]	100	500	1,000	2,000
4. Number of human-impacted sites per 640-acre area[2]	1 permitted	2 permitted	3 permitted	6 permitted
5. Number of human-impacted sites above a particular conditioned class index per 640 acres	No moderately or highly impacted campsites/section	No more than 1 moderately impacted site and 0 highly impacted sites/section	No more than 2 moderately impacted sites and 0 highly impacted sites/section	No more than 3 moderately impacted sites and 1 highly impacted site/section
RANGE				
6. Degree of forage used	No more than 20 percent forage used	No more than 20 percent forage used	No more than 40 percent forage used	No more than 40 percent forage used
7. General range trend	Static or improving	Static or improving	Static or improving	Improving
8. Overall range condition	Excellent	Excellent	Generally good or better	Generally good

1. Excludes authorized horse handling facilities. A variance will be given to outfitter base camps not currently in compliance and a timetable for compliance will be developed and administered through the outfitter operation plans.
2. Human-impacted sites defined as any site with evidence of human impact, normally centered around a firering, regardless of its prior use for camping.

I or II, depending on existing resource and social conditions as well as task force preferences. A portion of the map is shown in figure 9.6.

The final opportunity class allocation for the Bob Marshall, Great Bear, and Scapegoat Wildernesses, as of March 1987, is shown in the box below. The total acreage for the BMWC is 1,535,352 acres. As the tabulation in the box shows, only 6 percent of the entire BMWC was allocated to the *least* pristine opportunity class.

Percentage of the BMWC in each opportunity class.

Most pristine			Least pristine
Class I	*Class II*	*Class III*	*Class IV*
60	18	16	6

Source: USDA FS 1987.

Because the corridors were mapped with a 1-mile width, but the trails themselves are very narrow, only a very small proportion of the complex is in the least pristine opportunity class. Although this alternative is greatly influenced by the realities of existing use patterns and influences, it does represent the consensus of the task force as to how recreational use of the BMWC should be managed. It is important to note that during the task force deliberations concerning opportunity class allocations, most representatives agreed initially on more than 75 percent of the area. In the final meeting, only two small areas, outfitter base camp locations, were debated.

Indicators, and their standards, were also developed through task force participation. Various small group techniques were used to develop and validate these. The indicators and standards are shown in table 9.1. The

standards were developed, with the exception of the encounter standards, by examining the inventory data available. Encounter standards were developed with the help of visitor preference data generated by Lucas (1985). Using these data allowed realistic and attainable standards, but do not legitimize existing unacceptable conditions in the wilderness. The task force thoroughly discussed the standards, their meaning, and application. This discussion was helpful to managers because it extended their knowledge of LAC and its implications, and it also helped in developing standards that were consistent with preserving the character of the BMWC.

These discussions also helped user representatives understand LAC and its implications, and it facilitated their sharing of the responsibility for developing standards. Participation of user representatives was important to future defense of the plan when difficult, unpopular decisions are required.

Management actions were developed to address potential or existing unacceptable resource and social conditions. This again was done with the help of the task force. Task force members appeared to have the greatest difficulty with this step, primarily because it placed the citizen and the researcher in the role of manager. Several exercises were developed to generate a list of potential management actions. Because of the size of the complex and the numerous places where current conditions violate proposed standards, actions for specific locations were not developed, with the exception of the Schafer Meadows area. Instead, a list of actions identified by type of problem and by opportunity class was developed. Actions are listed in order of their preference by task force members, generally from the least restrictive to the most restrictive. The information below in the box contrasts the actions preferred for dealing with campsite impact problems in opportunity classes I

Class I	**Class IV**
•Information and education	•Information and education
•Contact repeat users	•Ranger contact
•Limit group size	•Campsite restoration
•Limit number of stock per group	•Enforcement
•Campsite closure	•Contact repeat users
•Enforcement	•Temporary corrals
•Prohibit stock in campsite	•Limit group size
•Seasonal campsite closure	•Limit number of stock per group
•Remove existing facilities	•Permanent hitch racks
•Campsite restoration	•Seasonal campsite closure
•Equipment requirements	•Campsite closure
•Close campsite to certain users only	•Prohibit stock in campsite
•Ranger contact	•Equipment requirements
•Temporary corrals	•Campsite permit
•Campsite permit	•Pit toilets
	•Close campsite to certain users only

and IV (the most and least pristine classes). Similar information is included in the plan to address campsite density, range condition, and encounter problems.

In both classes, information and education is favored as the most acceptable action to control campsite impacts. This is based, in part, on a general concern to follow the principle of minimum regimentation. But, the acceptability or appropriateness of the remaining actions is tied to the kinds of conditions defined as consistent with the opportunity class definition outlined in step 2 of the LAC process. For example, minimizing the presence of management personnel in opportunity class I areas led to placing "ranger contact" far down the list of acceptable actions for that class, whereas it is consistent with opportunity class IV areas.

The LAC process now drives the annual workplan for managing recreation in the BMWC. Each year an operating plan is developed that identifies the problem areas where management action, such as campsite rehabilitation or closure, will be directed. Monitoring of indicators is also included in the operating plan. The LAC process also drives trail maintenance and construction standards, such as clearing width, as well as annual trail maintenance and construction projects. In class I areas, visitors can expect a somewhat challenging experience. While the trail may be visible, visitors may have to climb over occasional logs. In class IV areas, trails are frequently maintained and widely cleared.

The continuing involvement of the task force is an integral component of the plan. Each year the task force meets to discuss the past year's monitoring and management actions. Proposed actions of a controversial nature are also presented to the task force for their input.

The BMWC is the first place where LAC was attempted in full, although elements of LAC have been applied in other wildernesses. Use of the task force format allowed a number of issues to surface and be addressed early in the planning process, thus avoiding unnecessary conflict later. Involving the task force also

resulted in a highly educated group of citizens and managers who now can speak authoritatively about wilderness management issues. Compared to traditional rational-comprehensive planning processes, task force members have favorably reacted to this type of planning (Ashor 1985; McCool and Ashor 1984). The task force reinforced important wilderness values as expressed in the Wilderness Act by identifying unacceptable resource and social conditions.

The LAC process and transactive planning worked well together in a situation that had the potential of being extremely controversial. The LAC process focused public involvement on specific issues where input was needed, and did so in a systematic manner. The public contributed in a positive way in this process. The principles of transactive planning allowed managers to incorporate public input in an innovative way and address many issues before they escalated into major conflicts, yet within the context of LAC. The intimate public involvement required in transactive planning also created a level of understanding about the LAC process that would not have resulted with traditional methods of involving the public in USFS decision making.

USFS officials were clear in their instructions to the task force that the agency retained the authority, responsibility, and accountability for making decisions, but that such decisions would be made in an open and trackable way. A goal was to develop a consensus in the task force about different issues, which the USFS would then adopt. If the task force could not come to a consensus, then the USFS would make the decision using task force input (Stokes 1986).

The concern of the LAC process is to help develop a strategy for management that will ensure long-term preservation of the wilderness resource by controlling human-induced impacts that lead to unnatural changes. Application of the LAC process to planning of the BMWC has focused on managing the area's recreational use because much of the impact on the area's quality stems from such use.

But managers must be concerned about many issues other than recreation. For example, wildlife

Table 9.2. Percentage of important wildlife habitat components in each opportunity class by alternative.

	Most pristine			Least Pristine
Alternative	*Class I*	*Class II*	*Class III*	*Class IV*
1. Wilderness recreation	50	25	14	11
2. Pristine conditions	66	17	15	2
3. Preferred	62	17	17	4

values are very important. The BMWC contains both diverse wildlife populations and key threatened and endangered species such as the grizzly bear and, though unconfirmed, the gray wolf. Although the LAC process did not directly address wildlife concerns, nonetheless, it was possible to examine how the alternative opportunity class allocations would affect the wildlife values contained within them. Wildlife biologists helped map important wildlife habitat components within the wilderness areas, such as riparian zones, meadows, parks, sidehill grasslands, and avalanche chutes. Altogether, these areas comprised about 20 percent of the total wilderness. Table 9.2 shows the percentage of these critical habitat areas in each opportunity class for the three proposed alternatives. Nearly two-thirds of the critical habitat is in the most pristine opportunity class in the preferred alternative. If it was judged important to place even more of this habitat in areas managed as class I opportunity classes, it would be possible to do so by extending the spatial extent of this class.

LIMIT USE WHEN STANDARDS ARE EXCEEDED

The LAC process does not consider a use limit policy as an action to avoid in all circumstances; rather, a use limit is viewed as one of a number of management actions that can be taken in response to problems. Monitoring serves as feedback to the rangers, indicating when previously implemented actions have failed or succeeded in maintaining acceptable conditions. When previous actions have proven ineffective, a use limit may remain the only alternative available. Because of projected increases in use levels or negative changes in conditions, managers may decide to implement a use limit prior to standards being violated, rather than waiting until the LAC has been reached.

Instead of focusing on identifying how many people can use an area without generating unacceptable impacts, the LAC seeks to define the desired conditions for an area. As long as these desired conditions are present, the logic of the system leads us to conclude that the use levels occurring within the area are acceptable or within the area's capacity. Those use levels are not producing impacts judged unacceptable according to the standards of resource and social conditions defined for that area.

But as conditions begin to approach those defined as acceptable, managers must give thought to how area standards can be protected. In chapters 15, 16, and 17, specific techniques to accomplish this are

discussed. In general, *the concept of minimum regimentation should govern management* (see chap. 7). But at some point and in some areas, it will become necessary to limit the number of users. To do so, it will be necessary to identify a specific numerical capacity. The LAC process facilitates this; the area's numerical capacity is defined as being the current use level or a figure close to it. As Washburne (1982, p. 728) notes, "the approximate capacity is determined by actual experience. If, for the given combination of area conditions, use patterns, and management program, some standards are exceeded, the numerical capacity figure must be near current use, and capacity can be determined by some relatively modest adjustments of current use figures."

SUMMARY

Three key ideas form the theme of this chapter. First, the challenge facing wilderness managers in dealing with the issue of *carrying capacity* is not a matter of developing "magic numbers" that describe how much use is too much. Rather, it is a matter of prescribing what kind of social and resource conditions are desired, comparing these desired states against existing conditions, and identifying the kinds of policies and actions needed to maintain or restore the desired conditions. *Managerial judgment* is the key element in this process. Judgment is a product of experience, research data, basic inventory information, public input, careful analysis, and common sense. Computers and other sophisticated analytical tools can help managers do a better job of acquiring, reviewing, and evaluating information, but they do not make decisions—people do.

Judgments can still be arbitrary and capricious, particularly if made in the absence of any substantive information. Thus, the second basic idea is that establishing appropriate conditions is dependent on the formulation of explicit *management objectives* that provide precise measures, standards, of desired conditions. These objectives and their associated policies define the LAC for the resource and social elements identified as critical indicators. A key factor in the success or failure of a wilderness management plan is the process by which the *public participates* in the development of consensus value judgments on which the plan is based; that is, in the determination of what are or are not appropriate wilderness conditions.

Third, either *resource or social indicators* can lead to the determination that an area has reached its capacity. As area conditions change and the standards for an indicator are approached, managers will begin to employ different management actions to control impacts.

Some of these will be more effective than others and it might be possible to avoid any direct use restrictions. At some point, however, it may become necessary to restrict further increases in the number of users in order to protect desired conditions. But it is the condition of the area, not the number of visitors, that is the focus of management attention. As Washburne (1982, p. 728) concludes:

> The search for capacity numbers may well distract from the critical task of wilderness management: deciding what is acceptable and what is not, and writing standards that clearly describe such conditions. Rather than focusing primarily on numbers of users, it seems better to concentrate on the underlying conditions desired, and to take corrective action where necessary—which may or may not involve reductions in recreation use.

STUDY QUESTIONS

1. Discuss the various factors that might influence the establishment of carrying capacity for a local recreation area. Identify ways in which managers of that area might alter its carrying capacity.
2. Identify at least five considerations that influence the level of impact on an area other than the level of use that area receives. Describe how these other considerations affect impact and how management might control them.
3. What information would you consider useful in selecting indicators to measure impact? Use a local recreation area as an example.
4. What information and criteria would you use in specifying standards to identify acceptable levels of resource or social impact for an area?
5. The idea of a carrying capacity implies that at some point no further increases in recreation use will be allowed. Some argue that restrictions are necessary in order to protect area resources and the nature of the recreation experience. Others, however, argue that restricting the use of recreation areas is inappropriate and inequitable. Discuss some of the pros and cons underlying these respective positions.

REFERENCES

Ashor, Joseph L. 1985. Recreation management in the Bob Marshall Wilderness Complex: an application of the Limits of Acceptable Change concept and transactive planning theory. Missoula, MT: University of Montana. 224 p. Thesis.

Braybrooke, D.; Lindblom, C. E. 1963. A strategy of decision. New York: The Free Press. 268 p.

Brown, Perry J.; Haas, Glenn E. 1980. Wilderness recreation experiences: the Rawah case. Journal of Leisure Research. 12(3): 229-241.

Buist, Leon J.; Hoots, Thomas A. 1982. Recreation Opportunity Spectrum approach to resource planning. Journal of Forestry. 80: 84-86.

Burch, William R., Jr. 1984. Much ado about nothing—some reflections on the wider and wilder implications of social carrying capacity. Leisure Sciences. 6(4): 487-496.

Bury, Richard L. 1976. Recreation carrying capacity—hypothesis or reality? Parks and Recreation. 11(1): 22-25, 56-57.

Caulfield, Henry P., Jr. 1975. Politics of multiple objective planning. In: Proceedings of the multiple objective planning and decision making conference; 1975 January 15; Boise, ID. [Moscow, ID: Idaho Research Foundation, Inc.]. 29 p.

Clark, Roger N. 1982. Promises and pitfalls of the ROS in resource management. Australian Parks and Recreation. May: 9-13.

Clark, Roger N.; Stankey, George H. 1979. The Recreation Opportunity Spectrum: a framework for planning, management, and research. Gen. Tech. Rep. PNW-98. Portland, OR: U.S. Department of Agriculture, Forest Service, Pacific Northwest Forest and Range Experiment Station. 32 p.

Clawson, Marion. 1985. Outdoor recreation: twenty-five years of history, twenty-five years of projection. Leisure Sciences. 7(1): 73-100.

Cole, David N. 1985. Management of ecological impacts in wilderness areas in the United States. In: Bayfield, N. G.; Barrow, G. C., eds. The ecological impacts of outdoor recreation on mountain areas in Europe and North America. R.E.R.G. Report No. 9. Wye, England: Recreation Ecology Research Group: 138-154.

Dasmann, Raymond F. 1964. Wildlife biology. New York: John Wiley and Sons. 231 p.

Davis, George D. 1984. Natural diversity for future generations: the role of wilderness. In: Cooley, James L.; Cooley, June H., eds. Natural diversity in forest ecosystems: Proceedings of the workshop; 1982 November 29-December 1; Athens, GA. Athens, GA: University of Georgia, Institute of Ecology: 141-154.

Driver, Beverly L.; Brown, Perry J. 1978. The opportunity spectrum concept and behavioral information in outdoor recreation resource supply inventories: a rationale. In: Lund, G. H.; LaBau, V. J.; Ffolliott, P. F.; Robinson, D. W., tech. coords. Integrated inventories of renewable natural resources. Gen. Tech. Rep. RM-55. Fort Collins, CO: U.S. Department of Agriculture, Forest Service, Rocky Mountain Forest and Range Experiment Station: 24-31.

Drogin, Ellen B.; Graefe, Alan R.; Vaske, Jerry J. 1986. A citation index for the recreation impact/carrying capacity literature: a descriptive analysis and demonstration. Unpublished paper on file at: University of Maryland, Department of Recreation, College Park, MD.

Etzioni, Amitai. 1968. The active society: a theory of societal and political processes. New York: The Free Press. 698 p.

Federal Register. 1982. Rules and regulations: National Forest system and resource management planning. Federal Register. 47: 7690.

Friedmann, John. 1973. Retracking America: a theory of transactive planning. Garden City, NY: Anchor Press/Doubleday. 289 p.

Frissell, Sidney S., Jr.; Stankey, George H. 1972. Wilderness environmental quality: search for social and ecological harmony. In: Proceedings of the 1972 national conven-

tion; 1972 October 1-5; Hot Springs, AR. Washington, DC: Society of American Foresters: 170-183.

Godschalk, David R.; Parker, Francis H. 1975. Carrying capacity: a key to environmental planning? Journal of Soil and Water Conservation. 30(4): 160-165.

Graefe, Alan R.; Kuss, Fred R.; Loomis, Laura. 1986. Visitor impact management in wildland settings. In: Lucas, Robert C., compiler. Proceedings—national wilderness research conference: current research; 1985 July 23-26; Fort Collins, CO. Gen. Tech. Rep. INT-212. Ogden, UT: U.S. Department of Agriculture, Forest Service, Intermountain Research Station: 432-439.

Hudson, Barclay M. 1979. Comparison of current planning theories: counterparts and contradictions. American Planning Association Journal. 45(4): 387-398.

Kuss, Fred R. 1986. Impact ecology knowledge is basic. In: Lucas, Robert C., compiler. Proceedings—national wilderness research conference: current research; 1985 July 23-26; Fort Collins, CO. Gen. Tech. Rep. INT-212. Ogden, UT: U.S. Department of Agriculture, Forest Service, Intermountain Research Station: 92-93.

Lime, David W. 1970. Research for determining use capacities of the Boundary Waters Canoe Area. Naturalist. 21: 8-13.

Lucas, Robert C. 1973. Wilderness: a management framework. Journal of Soil and Water Conservation. 28(4): 150-154.

Lucas, Robert C. 1982. Recreation regulations—when are they needed? Journal of Forestry. 80(3): 148-151.

Lucas, Robert C. 1985. Visitor characteristics, attitudes, and use patterns in the Bob Marshall Wilderness Complex, 1970-82. Res. Pap. INT-345. Ogden, UT: U.S. Department of Agriculture, Forest Service, Intermountain Research Station. 32 p.

Manning, Robert E. 1986. Studies in outdoor recreation: search and research for satisfaction. Corvallis, OR: Oregon State University Press. 184 p.

McCool, Stephen F.; Ashor, Joseph. 1984. Politics and rivers: creating effective citizen involvement in management decisions. In: Popadic, Joseph S.; Butterfield, Dorothy I.; Anderson, Dorothy H.; Popadic, Mary R., eds. Proceedings of the 1984 national river recreation symposium; 1984 October 31-November 3; Baton Rouge, LA. Baton Rouge, LA: Louisiana State University, School of Landscape Architecture: 136-151.

McCool, Stephen F.; Ashor, Joseph L.; Stokes, Gerald L. 1986. An alternative to rational-comprehensive planning: transactive planning. In: Lucas, Robert C., compiler. Proceedings—national wilderness research conference: current research; 1985 July 23-26; Fort Collins, CO. Gen. Tech. Rep. INT-212. Ogden, UT: U.S. Department of Agriculture, Forest Service, Intermountain Research Station: 544-545.

McLaughlin, William J. 1977. The Indian Hills experiment—a case study in transactive planning theory. Fort Collins, CO: Colorado State University, College of Forestry and Natural Resources. 306 p. Dissertation.

Merigliano, Linda L. 1987. The identification and evaluation of indicators to monitor wilderness conditions. Moscow, ID: University of Idaho, College of Forestry, Wildlife and Range Sciences. 273 p. Thesis.

Odum, Eugene P. 1959. Fundamentals of biology. Philadelphia: W. B. Saunders Co. 546 p.

Shelby, Bo. 1981. Encounter norms in backcountry settings. Journal of Leisure Research. 13(2): 129-138.

Shelby, Bo; Heberlein, Thomas A. 1986. Carrying capacity in recreation settings. Corvallis, OR: Oregon State University Press. 164 p.

Stankey, George H.; Lucas, Robert C.; Lime, David W. 1976. Crowding in parks and wilderness. Design and Environment. 7(3): 38-41.

Stankey, George H. 1979. A framework for social-behavioral research: applied issues. In: Burch, William R., Jr., ed. Long-distance trails: the Appalachian Trail as a guide to future research and management needs. New Haven, CT: Yale University, School of Forestry and Environmental Studies: 43-53.

Stankey, George H.; McCool, Stephen F.; Stokes, Gerald L. 1984. Limits of Acceptable Change: a new framework for managing the Bob Marshall Wilderness Complex. Western Wildlands. 10(3): 33-37.

Stankey, George H.; Cole, David N.; Lucas, Robert C.; Petersen, Margaret E.; Frissell, Sidney S. 1985. The Limits of Acceptable Change (LAC) system for wilderness planning. Gen. Tech. Rep. INT-176. Ogden, UT: U.S. Department of Agriculture, Forest Service, Intermountain Forest and Range Experiment Station. 37 p.

Stankey, George H.; Lucas, Robert C. 1986. Shifting trends in backcountry and wilderness use. Unpublished paper on file at: U.S. Department of Agriculture, Forest Service, Intermountain Research Station, Forestry Sciences Laboratory, Missoula, MT.

Stokes, Gerald L. 1982. Conservation of the Blackfoot River corridor: an application of the transactive planning theory. Fort Collins, CO: Colorado State University. 229 p. Dissertation.

Stokes, Gerald L. 1986. LAC task force role. In: Lucas, Robert C., compiler. Proceedings—national wilderness research conference: current research; 1985 July 23-26; Fort Collins, CO. Gen. Tech. Rep. INT-212. Ogden, UT: U.S. Department of Agriculture, Forest Service, Intermountain Research Station: 546-547.

Sumner, E. Lowell. 1942. The biology of wilderness protection. Sierra Club Bulletin. 27(8): 14-22.

U.S. Department of Agriculture, Forest Service. 1982. ROS users guide. Washington, DC: U.S. Department of Agriculture, Forest Service. 38 p.

U.S. Department of Agriculture, Forest Service. 1987. Opportunity class allocation for the Bob Marshall, Great Bear, and Scapegoat Wildernesses. Map. Forest Service, Flathead, Lolo, Helena, Lewis and Clark National Forests.

Wagar, J. Alan. 1964. The carrying capacity of wild lands for recreation. Forest Science Monograph 7. Washington, DC: Society of American Foresters. 23 p.

Wagar, J. Alan. 1968. The place of carrying capacity in the management of recreation lands. Rocky Mt.-High Plains Parks and Recreation Journal. 3(1): 37-45.

Wagar, J. Alan. 1974. Recreational carrying capacity reconsidered. Journal of Forestry. 72: 274-278.

Washburne, Randel F. 1982. Wilderness recreational carrying capacity: are numbers necessary? Journal of Forestry. 80(11): 726-728.

Washburne, Randel F.; Cole, David N. 1983. Problems and practices in wilderness management: a survey of managers. Res. Pap. INT-304. Ogden, UT: U.S. Department of Agriculture, Forest Service, Intermountain Forest and Range Experiment Station. 56 p.

Wilderness ecosystems are constantly changing as a result of normal successional processes and patterns of periodic disruptions. Wilderness management should ensure that natural processes proceed with minimal disruption. Here, clusters of subalpine fir invade a meadow near Big Agnes Mountain in the Mount Zirkel Wilderness, CO. Photo courtesy of Jay Higgins.

10

WILDERNESS ECOSYSTEMS

This chapter was written by Jerry F. Franklin, Chief Plant Ecologist,
Pacific Northwest Research Station, Portland, Washington, and Ed
Bloedel, Professor of Ecosystems Analysis, College of Forest Resources,
University of Washington, Seattle.

INTRODUCTION

This chapter considers major features of wilderness ecosystems of concern to managers and contrasts them with ecosystems significantly altered by modern man. The emphasis is on the dynamic nature of ecosystems, their strong internal linkages, and the ways various human activities have affected and continue to affect the "naturalness" of wilderness ecosystems. Only when ecosystem dynamics, including interrelationships with humans, are fully understood can the consequences of alternative management strategies be assessed.

Some readers may think that ecosystem concepts are only marginally related to wilderness management because so much of the previous material concerns people management. But a large body of literature reminds us that ignorance of ecosystem concepts—internal linkages among environment, plant, and animal, and successional dynamics—lies at the root of many wilderness and park management problems. Concern about fire management

policies throughout much of the West (Habeck 1970; Habeck and Mutch 1973; Kilgore 1973) and in the lake states (states bordering the Great Lakes) (Frissell 1973; Heinselman 1973; Wright 1974) is based on ecosystem considerations (see chap. 12). Management of large ungulates, bighorn sheep, elk, and caribou, or carnivores, such as grizzly bears, inevitably must be based on ecosystem concepts (see chap. 11). Even the limits of human use under the naturalness constraint of the Wilderness Act—physical carrying capacity—rest on ecosystem concepts (see chap. 8). Finally, the entire notion of regulated human use and management of wilderness so as to not distort naturalness, the idea of humans as an integral but not dominant part of wilderness, is an ecosystem concept.

Some readers without natural science backgrounds may find this chapter difficult reading, since it is a quick review in ecology. The basic ecological concepts discussed are essential for understanding the implications of the subsequent chapters on fire and wildlife.

HUMANKIND'S HISTORIC ROLE IN WILDERNESS

29

One question should be addressed at the outset: Are humans an integral component of the wilderness and are their influences natural or unnatural? The answer is relative rather than absolute. Primitive humans unquestionably played a role in shaping the wilderness landscapes of North America, including those formally recognized today as components of the National Wilderness Preservation System (NWPS) (fig. 10.1). Humans burned and hunted, raised crops, and built settlements. With rare exceptions, (The human role in the extinction of Pleistocene mammals may be one of these.), however, aboriginal humans did not exist in sufficient numbers nor did they have the technology to control and direct the forces of nature. Humankind was an influencing factor, but only one of many, and negative feedback mechanisms kept human populations and impacts in check. For example, when resources were depleted or when climatic changes occurred, primitive humans died or moved on. They could not dominate their environment nor could they delay or alter negative feedbacks.

This situation has changed with the rise of technological civilization. Current human technology has grown extremely powerful and in the short term can buffer humans from strong negative feedback.

Fig. l0.1. Ecosystems represented in the NWPS range from the semiarid lands of the Gila Wilderness, NM (left), the deciduous forests of the Presidential Range-Dry River Wilderness, NH (right), to the moonlike landscape of Craters of the Moon National Monument, ID (above). Left and right photos courtesy of the USFS. Above photo courtesy of the NPS.

"Natural" human influences might be considered those that have been elements in the long-term evolution of the presettlement ecosystems—present for hundreds, thousands, and even tens of thousands of years. The impacts of modern humankind are *not* this type. The wilderness ecosystems we are concerned with here—those in designated wilderness—did not evolve under the influence of these forces and are not adapted to them. Uncontrolled, modern humankind's influences alter the historical direction and rate of ecosystem evolution. The contrast between primitive and modern humans in their ability to control and alter natural forces and ecosystems does not require elaboration. Modern technology has allowed us to impact every point on the globe and influence even basic and powerful natural forces such as climate. Finally, our technology allows us to avoid, delay, or control negative feedback mechanisms that kept the primitive human's numbers in check. Nature will probably exact a large price for our violations on ecosystems, but typically the feedback will be neither as direct nor as rapid as it was for the primitive human. In most instances, we have overcome the negative feedback of nature with modern technology, at least in the short term.

To sum up, humans are a natural part of wilderness, but, because of their recent origin, strength, pervasiveness, and ability to buffer rapid feedback, their technological forces are *not*. We cannot accept modern humans—or more specifically their technology—as a natural component of wilderness. In a historical context, their technology is not natural. Legally, exposure to this technology is restricted by the Wilderness Act. Nevertheless, modern technology is impacting the wilderness and will increasingly do so. We will use technology to manage wilderness—to perpetuate or create desired conditions, sometimes to substitute for a natural process such as wildfire or predation. Because of the pervasive and powerful nature of the forces we generate (and sometimes command), it is critical that we understand their effects as a guide to minimizing impacts and, in the case of management, use these forces to mimic natural forces or processes no longer present.

ECOSYSTEMS AND THEIR CHARACTERISTICS

An *ecosystem* includes all the organisms of an area, their environment, and a series of linkages or interactions between them. As Odum (1971) summarizes, "The ecosystem is the basic fundamental unit in ecology, because it includes both organisms … and abiotic environments, each influencing the properties of the other and both necessary for the maintenance of life."

The *abiotic environment* includes climatic conditions such as temperature and moisture regimes, and inorganic substances supplied by mineral soil. The *biotic* community contains all living organisms within our ecosystem. The *organisms* include *autotrophs* and *heterotrophs*. *Autotrophic organisms* are the green plants that provide the ecosystem's entire energy base by fixing solar energy and using simple inorganic substances to build up complex organic substances. *Heterotrophic organisms* (e.g., animals, microbes, and fungi) use the complex substances produced by autotrophs as a food base and rearrange or decompose them. Heterotrophs can be divided into (1) *ingestors* (macroconsumers, biophages) that feed on live materials—bear, deer, squirrels, butterflies, and slugs, for example, and (2) *decomposers* (microconsumers, saprophages) such as bacteria, fungi, and some insects that feed on dead material such as leaf litter, fallen logs, and feces.

A wilderness ecosystem has a series of attributes that are fundamentally the same as those in any other ecosystem. First, at a given time there is a particular *composition* and *structure*. That is, an array of plant and animal species in various proportions. Each biological component contains given amounts of biomass or energy, nutrients, and other materials—the compartments or states recognized in computer models of ecosystems (fig. 10.2). The elements are spatially arranged to produce an ecosystem we recognize as forest, meadow, or savanna.

Within ecosystems, various *processes*—photo-

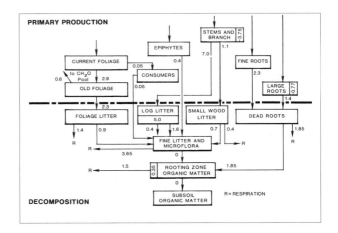

Fig. 10.2. Any ecosystem, such as forest or meadow, contains many linked components, each possessing given amounts of biomass, energy, nutrients, or other material.

synthesis, transpiration, consumption (by ingesters), decomposition—are going on. These processes are driven by *environmental factors* (the *driving forces* of ecosystem models) such as moisture supply, temperature, and sunlight. Not all processes are carried out exclusively by organisms, however; weathering of parent materials, erosion, and evaporation are examples of essentially physical processes. Likewise, not all environmental or abiotic factors are the classical climatic influences of light, temperature, and moisture. Fire and flood are examples of periodic driving forces.

The *linkages* or *flows* (fig. 10.2) between parts of an ecosystem are characteristics of special importance to resource managers. Energy, water, nutrients, and other substances do not remain indefinitely in any one place or state. They are transferred through the ecosystem along a series of flow pathways. Organic materials are generally degraded or broken down into simpler substances as they flow from primary producers to consumers and decomposers. Materials are ultimately recycled within the system or lost from it by leaching, volatilization, or other processes. Environmental factors are important in controlling the rates at which the flows take place; biologic composition and spatial arrangement largely determine the flow paths. These fundamentals are extremely important, for it is by altering paths and rates of flows that humans most profoundly influence ecosystems. As an example, imagine what would happen to a forest ecosystem if decomposition rates (breakdown of dead organic matter with the release of energy and nutrients) were significantly reduced.

Short-term fluctuations—diurnal, seasonal, and annual—occur in the linkages through processes such as photosynthesis, herbivory (ingestion of plant materials by animals), or water runoff. Ecosystem science has progressed further in simulating these relatively short-term dynamics than it has in approximating longer term changes (see, for example, U.S. National Committee for the International Biological Program 1974). But long-term changes in ecosystem states, processes, flow paths, and rates also occur. These are changes associated with successional development of the ecosystems.[1]

To summarize and relate these ecosystem characteristics to the real world, let us look at them in the context of a lodgepole pine stand. This stand has a complement of plant and animal species of varying abundance that define its *biological composition:*

lodgepole pine, dwarf huckleberry, fungus, squirrel, Steller's jay. These organisms and their parts have a spatial arrangement defining the *stand structure:* an overstory canopy, shrub layer, litter layer, rooting zone. By combining elements of composition and structure we can define the major boxes or *compartments:* leaves, stems, roots, primary or plant consumers, secondary and tertiary consumers or predators. Each compartment contains a certain amount of biomass energy, nutrients, and water. Flows or transfers of energy or materials take place from one compartment to another—for example, from the leaves and branches to animals by grazing or from live green plants to the decomposing organisms by litter fall. Processes and transfer rates are largely controlled or driven by *environmental or abiotic factors* such as temperature and moisture availability. All of the elements of the lodgepole pine stand are linked together by the paths of energy and material flow— tree, bird, deer, nematode, bacterium. Changes in composition, structure, climate, and so forth will alter the rates and/or paths of energy and material flow. Therefore, the basic functions carried out by the ecosystem are expressed in terms of production of organic matter (energy fixation) and use and conservation of water and nutrients.

One attribute of ecosystems we have not considered is the size, or, more generally, how the boundaries of an ecosystem are defined. Basically, an ecosystem can be as large or as small as we want it to be, depending on our perspectives. It can be an aquarium, forest stand, watershed, an entire park or wilderness, a biome, or the entire world. It is necessary only that the area have the characteristics defined by Odum—constituent organisms interacting with their environment, energy flow, and material cycles. Scientists often find a watershed a useful unit for ecosystem study because it is relatively easy to define the physical boundaries and to measure many of the flows into and out of the ecosystem; it also incorporates both terrestrial and aquatic elements and allows study of their interaction. In summary, an ecosystem can be of widely varying size, depending on the objectives of the work.

In wilderness management, the size of the ecosystem unit of interest will also vary. In some cases, it might be an individual stand, or community, such as a meadow. When locating camping areas or determining carrying capacity, it might be a small lake basin or watershed—or the "heavy use areas," "trail corridors," or "subalpine zone" as described for planning purposes in chapter 8. Management of habitat for large ungulates such as elk might necessitate that the relevant ecosystem be defined as a large

---

1. For a concise, theoretical analysis of successionally related changes in ecosystem, see Odum 1971.

river basin. A viable ecosystem for grizzly bears may be even larger as is suggested in proposals for a "greater Yellowstone ecosystem." And of course, the entire wilderness can be the ecosystem unit for many planning and management activities. Determining the size of the ecosystem unit or the number of units to be recognized in a wilderness will depend on management's objectives (see chap. 8) and the kinds of problems, both biological and social, facing the manager.

DYNAMICS OF ECOSYSTEMS

A land manager must continually keep in mind two basic concepts about ecosystems. First, *all parts of an ecosystem are interrelated;* any given action reverberates throughout the whole ecosystem. Such linkages are typically responsible for extensive, unexpected, and sometimes undesirable effects of a given activity. For example, pesticides accumulating in food chains lead ultimately not to the demise of the target pest, but rather to declines in organisms high in the trophic chain, such as brown pelicans, peregrine falcons, and bald eagles. Another example is the subtle and complex interactions of red alder with a forest soil that lead to changes in total soil nitrogen, nitrates, soil acidity, actinomycete populations, and ultimately the ability of a root rot such as *Phellinus* to survive (Trappe 1972).

The second basic concept is *the dynamic character of an ecosystem over long time periods*—as opposed to short-term cyclical changes. The long-term trends are often referred to as *successional changes.* Odum (1971) defines succession as an orderly process of community development involving changes in species structure and community processes with time. Succession is directional and predictable, and results from modification of the physical environment by the community. Succession culminates in a stabilized ecosystem with maximum biomass and linkages between organisms per unit of energy flow. Daubenmire (1968) describes succession as any unidirectional change that can be detected in changes in proportions of species in a stand or the complete replacement of one community by another. Long-term plant succession is a familiar concept for land managers and particularly important for those who propose to manage or maintain natural landscapes. It suggests there is no one answer to the question, "What should a wilderness look like?" The ecosystem of any given wilderness, if allowed to remain natural, is continually changing.

The classical successional sequences are described as either primary or secondary (Daubenmire 1968) (fig. 10.3). *Primary succession* is normally considered a much slower process than *secondary succession* be-

cause it involves amelioration (preparation, improvement) of extreme site conditions by gradual alterations brought about by the organisms. An example of primary succession is a lake filling in and being replaced consecutively with marshes, shrubfields, and finally forests. Another illustration is colonization and development of vegetation on bare rock surfaces, sand, talus or volcanic ash, and lava fields. Secondary succession can be seen in the fairly rapid changes following cutting or burning of a forest or removal of grazing animals from a depleted range.

Secondary succession has been described extensively (Daubenmire 1968). For example, following fire or clearcutting, forest lands are dominated by opportunistic, shade-intolerant herbaceous species (fireweed), which are replaced in turn by shrubs and ultimately a stand of shade-intolerant pioneer tree species. In time, the more shade-tolerant tree species seed in under the canopy, and intolerant trees fail to reproduce in the shaded environment. Over several centuries the stand proceeds through a gradual compositional change to a stable climax forest composed of shade-tolerant species capable of perpetuating themselves indefinitely.

This is a useful concept based on the assumptions of: orderly progression toward a stable climax following a disturbance, gradual elimination of less shade-tolerant competitors by more tolerant species, and, sometimes, the necessity for a hardy pioneer species to prepare the way for less hardy species. This classical view of forest succession may then be viewed as being largely dependent on *intrinsic processes*—amelioration or preparation of severe sites by pioneering species and their eventual elimination by the less hardy climax species through competition.

As a concept, *forest succession* is based largely on inferences drawn from size- or age-class distributions, however, and many situations do not fit classical concepts when examined closely. For example, the assumption that pioneer trees *must* precede climax tree species, making the environment more suitable for the latter, simply does not hold in many situations. Given an adequate seed source, both types of tree species can often invade a bare area simultaneously, and the stand structure 100 years later reflects differing growth or competitive abilities, not necessarily later arrival of the smaller tolerant species or its dependence on site amelioration by the pioneer species (Oliver 1981). Age structure analyses are showing more and more that inferences drawn from size structure analyses can lead to erroneous conclusions about successional developments.

Likewise, we encounter some forests where there is no change in the composition of the tree species over

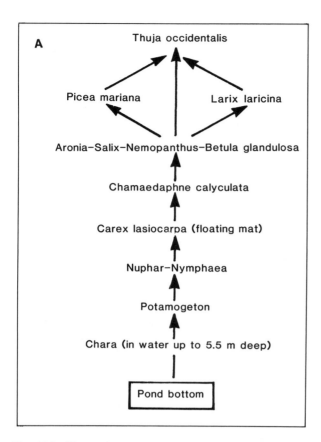

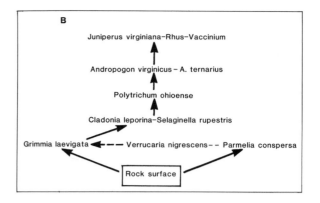

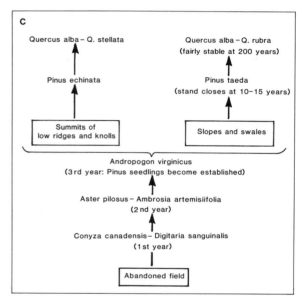

Fig. 10.3. Classical successional sequences are either primary or secondary: (above) succession of dominants in a MI pond; (top right) succession in shallow depressions in granite in NC; (right) successional trends in the Piedmont plateau. From Daubenmire 1968.

time. Some ponderosa or lodgepole pine forests are of this type. In these situations, only one tree species is capable of surviving, and if it happens to be intolerant, regeneration of the species must await openings in the canopy as the stand grows older. For example, even in the renowned Douglas-fir region of the Pacific Northwest, there are dry habitats where Douglas-fir is both the main pioneer and climax tree.

The important things to remember include: (1) a variety of processes are involved in forest succession including opportunity (seed source), site amelioration, and competition; and (2) a climax species can be tolerant or intolerant, depending on the site. Keeping these qualifications in mind, it is still useful to think of successional change as a reasonably ordered sequence of plant species culminating in a stable or climax (self-perpetuating) type over much of our wildland. Such changes occur regardless of the causes. Thus, an ecosystem can be considered to have a trajectory, or general direction, of change over time. If the system is

destroyed or set back in the sequence by a disturbance, presumably it will begin evolving again toward the same end point or climax state provided the climate has not changed, the site has not been significantly degraded, and the same organisms are available to reinvade the site.

The fact is, of course, that because of periodic disturbances—fire, flood, storm, avalanche, pathogens, or geomorphological processes (such as mass soil movements)—very few of our natural ecosystems ever reach a stable climax state. Therefore, an important corollary to the dynamic successional nature of ecosystems is that periodic disturbances of some type almost inevitably intercede before an end point or climax state is reached. In the lake states, in most of the West's ecosystems, and in interior Alaska, fire is the primary disrupter, and it occurs at fairly frequent intervals, thereby initiating new successional sequences (explained more fully in chap. 12). In the redwood region, both flood and fire have been intrinsic environmental

elements that periodically altered the ecosystem, which does not imply that they are essential for perpetuating redwood itself. Hurricanes function as periodic disrupters or rejuvenators of forest ecosystems in much of the eastern temperate forest, as do typhoons in Japan and strong winter winds along the northern Pacific Coast. Pathogens (e.g., mountain pine beetle, lodgepole needleminer, dwarf mistletoe, and stem cankers) are the periodic disturbers of some wildland ecosystems such as some lodgepole pine forests that escape fire. What is important is the realization that ecosystems are adapted to a particular set of disruptions. The patterns of disturbance are as much a part of the wild landscape as a successional sequence or trajectory.

To summarize, long-term ecosystem dynamics are the consequence of normal successional processes (colonization, competition, site alterations by organisms, etc.) and patterns of periodic disruption (caused, e.g., by fire, insect, disease, storm, and avalanche). Through knowledge of these successional forces and relevant ecosystem characteristics, the general direction of natural change over time is apparent to the wilderness manager. The job of wilderness management is often to ensure that the dynamics of the ecosystem and the resulting successional change—the natural trajectory of the ecosystem—proceed without disruption or distortion by humans. If the trajectory is to be altered by human intervention, it should be done as a conscious choice and with full understanding of the consequences.

HUMAN INFLUENCES ON ECOSYSTEM DYNAMICS IN WILDERNESS

The mosaic of ecosystems in a wilderness reflects the basic environmental conditions (soil, macroclimate, and microclimate), the array of organisms available for occupying the sites, and the pattern of disturbances—types, time, and areal extent. If modern humans alter *any* of these, the mosaic will be altered to an unnatural state to a greater or lesser degree. Ecosystems vary in their capability to sustain human impacts (fig. 10.4).

What are some of the changes that modern humans have brought about in wilderness areas? A visible and well-known example is *fire control*. Fires at some interval are a natural feature of almost all of

Fig. 10.4. Wildland ecosystems can be ranked according to their ability to sustain use impacts. Examples of fragile ecosystems are: (top left) San Juan Islands Wilderness, WA; photo courtesy of George Devan, FWS; (top right) alpine Absaroka-Beartooth Wilderness, WY; photo courtesy of L.J. Prater, USFS; (left) arid Desert Game Range, NV; photo courtesy of David B. Marshall, FWS; (right) Highly resilient are several wildernesses located in the eastern hardwoods of the Monongahela National Forest, WV; photo courtesy of the USFS.

our forest ecosystems. It has been argued that western coniferous forests have actually evolved in such a way as to increase flammability and ensure periodic burning. Certainly many of the species of great interest to us depend on fire for their perpetuation—giant sequoia (Kilgore 1973), Douglas-fir and ponderosa pine on some sites (Cooper 1960; Habeck and Mutch 1973), red pine and white pine in the lake states (Frissell 1973), and the closed-cone pines (Vogl 1973) (see chap. 12).

Elimination of fire, when periodic low-intensity fires are naturally part of an ecosystem's environment, can have catastrophic consequences. First, a successful fire suppression program will change the composition of the forests in many cases. Succession will proceed further before disruption than it would under natural conditions. Not only will the plant composition of the forest change, but the habitat for many animal species will also be altered with consequent changes in the animal composition of an area. Within a forest community, changes will also take place in stand structure and in paths and rates of material flow. Organic matter and nutrients accumulate in slowly decomposed woody plant material on the forest floor. Continuity develops between the crown and ground fuels as the density of saplings and poles increases. One result is likely to be not just a loss of earlier successional communities and less tolerant tree species, but ultimately a catastrophic fire to which the ecosystems in the area are *not* adapted.

The coniferous forests on the northwestern coast of North America offer an interesting contrast with most other coniferous forest regions. Here, fire appears *not* to have been primarily a chronic or frequent disturber of the forests; *rather*, infrequent catastrophic fires, often affecting large areas, seem to have been the rule. For example, the natural fire rotation calculated for forests in Mount Rainier National Park is 434 years (Hemstrom and Franklin 1982).

Grazing by domestic animals is another influence in wilderness ecosystems introduced by modern humans. Concentrated grazing by sheep or cattle (or even large wild ungulates such as elk or mountain goats, introduced to regions where they are not native) is not part of the natural regimen under which many of our wilderness meadows and savannas have evolved. Consequently, they may be poorly adapted to it. When large-scale grazing is introduced, changes in the composition of the meadows occur due to preferential feedings on, and/or sensitivity of, some plant species. The site may be physically altered due to compaction and accelerated erosion, and changes in water table level can also occur. Exotic plant species, introduced with livestock

and horsefeed, may take advantage of the altered conditions to establish themselves. Animal pathogens may be introduced into native ungulate populations (just as Europeans brought measles to the Native American) with catastrophic results—such as when scabies, a disease of native sheep, was introduced into bighorn sheep populations.

Some of the changes, addition of exotic species and site degradation, can be particularly significant because they can permanently alter the potential of the site—its ability to return to its original natural state. An outstanding example of the effects of grazing on the ecosystem is found in the sagebrush-bunchgrass and Palouse prairie types of eastern Washington and Oregon (Daubenmire 1970). Heavy grazing by large herbivores reduces the vigor of and can eliminate the bunchgrass dominants such as bluebunch wheatgrass and Idaho fescue. Exotic cheatgrass or Kentucky bluegrass invades, and, once established, native species can never recolonize the sites. Grazing can thus bring about permanent changes in ecosystems even in the absence of site degradation.

Modern humans have altered, and continue to alter, wilderness ecosystems by eliminating or reducing populations of specific species. The best known examples are the elimination of predatory animals—for example, wolverine, grizzly bear, cougar, and various raptors. Populations of such species have been eliminated from some wildernesses, reduced in others. In any case, the composition of these ecosystems is not what it was originally. In terms of *some* ecosystem functions—their ability to fix energy and conserve nutrients—the loss of such organisms may not be particularly significant. But in terms of a human's perception of a tract as a pristine landscape, the loss is very significant. Further, loss of some predators, such as the wolf, can have significant ecological impacts when they, as natural controls on large herbivore populations, are lost. Historically, the relative importance of the ecological role of the wolf to overall ecosystem function probably varied. In ecosystems with large populations of large ungulates such as moose or caribou, the role of the wolf has been considered critical. In many other areas it probably was not. Current ecological theory suggests that predator populations are not usually the major factor controlling prey population levels. The report "Wildlife Management in the National Parks" concludes that "predation alone can seldom be relied upon to control ungulate numbers" (Leopold and others 1969).

Because predators high on the trophic chain are strongly affected by human activities and are often the first affected, they are usually good indicators of

the degree of naturalness of a particular area. But this is not always the case. Chronic pollution by such gases as sulphur dioxide and by ozone can effect compositional changes in plants or animals or even rates of productivity or decomposition. Nevertheless, large predators remain excellent indicators of wilderness quality.

Losses of species are not confined to higher animals, however. Plant species have also been eliminated or drastically reduced in some areas. These losses significantly alter the ecosystem's structure and its basic functions of energy fixation and nutrient conservation. Disregarding grazing and fire, losses in plant species are most frequently caused by human introduction of *exotic pathogens.* Outstanding examples that affect designated wildernesses include the nearly complete loss of American chestnut to chestnut blight and substantial losses of whitebark and other five-needled pines to white pine blister rust. Exotic pathogens of this type can have extremely profound effects on otherwise pristine landscapes. Once introduced, exotic pathogens are uncontrollable, and, if the host species lack significant genetic or other mechanisms for resistance, effects (alterations) are essentially permanent.

Consider the effects of balsam woolly aphid on true firs, *Phytopthora* root rot on Port-Orford cedar, and white pine blister rust on western white pine. Balsam woolly aphid, an insect introduced from Europe, is threatening the survival of Fraser fir in southern Appalachian wilderness, and, in the West, it has reduced the vigor and attractiveness of subalpine fir and Pacific silver fir in many parts of their range, as well as eliminating them in some areas. *Phytopthora lateralis,* a root rot introduced on horticultural stock, is easily spread by spores transported along roads, trails, and streams. Port-Orford cedar has no resistance to this pathogen, and infected stands are suffering 100-percent mortality. Only the isolation of some stands and the fact that the spores may possibly be short lived (viable for only a few years) offer any hope of survival of the species in its natural habitat (Zobel and others 1985); certainly it will never again have the importance it once did in the virgin stands of the Klamath Mountains. The effects of white pine blister rust, another introduced pathogen, are well known to the forest managers of the northern Rocky Mountains. The blister rust probably causes relatively little mortality in large mature trees but can be devastating in young stands and will greatly reduce the importance of western white pine in future forests. Whitebark pine is extremely susceptible to this pathogen (the most susceptible of all five-needled pines), and both young and old trees may be eliminated in infected areas (Arno 1986).

Besides introducing pathogens, humans have purposely added specific organisms to pristine landscapes in order to make them more attractive recreationally. The introduction of sport fish to originally barren lakes and streams is an outstanding example. There can be no question that when fish introductions of this type are successful the affected aquatic ecosystem is significantly changed. An entirely new component may be added (if a fish at the same trophic level was not previously present). Native fish may be displaced or eliminated entirely; hence, the native brook trout in the Great Smoky Mountains is now found only in high, isolated streams. In any case, alterations in the composition of other organisms, and paths and rates of energy and nutrient flows, are to be expected. There are many other examples mostly involving exotic game or fish species. Managers' attitudes toward exotic pests as opposed to introduced fish and game species are often philosophically inconsistent.

Many other human impacts have altered the dynamics and states of wilderness ecosystems. Hunting and trapping clearly fall into this category and are a major reason why national park wildernesses are of greater value for research on natural ecosystems than are wildernesses administered by other agencies. There are the direct effects of human use, although these tend to be concentrated in relatively small areas, such as, compaction of soil and destruction or alteration of vegetation at camping sites. Although heavily impacted locations may be small relative to the total area, they may be among the most popular, aesthetic, and frequently visited. Clearly, in local areas, input of human wastes can reach levels sufficient to cause significant pollution. In such cases, the threat to human health probably becomes a management concern before the threat of eutrophication.

In wilderness in the East, past human activities have sometimes included logging, road building, and clearing of land for agriculture. Modern humans are introducing a variety of substances (plastic and other refuse; petroleum products in the Boundary Waters Canoe Area Wilderness [BWCAW] where motors are allowed) by their activities in wilderness, and, on a far larger scale, by activities outside of the wilderness. Pollutants present in the atmosphere may be deposited in rain or as dust or brought in by migrant organisms. Pesticides and sulfurous gases are such materials. Atmospheric pollution, including acid rain and ozone, is of increasing concern, even in western wilderness, and is the subject of major research and monitoring programs. In at least some cases, such pollution is clearly affecting the ecosystem and producing pathological effects on organisms (damage to trees in the Los Angeles basin and several southern California wil-

dernesses). For example, Miller (1973) describes accelerated mortality of ponderosa pine in the San Bernardino Mountains. More broadly, acid precipitation has been blamed for accelerated mortality of spruce stands throughout the northeastern United States.

NATURAL VERSUS HUMAN-INFLUENCED ECOSYSTEMS

A key feature of wilderness ecosystems and a focal point of the Wilderness Act is *naturalness*—freedom from significant influences of modern technological humans. Can the ecologist define naturalness or is it a quality, like solitude, which is largely in the eye of the beholder?

At the outset we must recognize that no completely unaltered ecosystems are left on this planet. The effects of modern humans and their products are pervasive. This is as true in the Antarctic, where DDT is found in the tissues of penguins, as it is in Central Park in New York City. None of the world remains unaltered. The examples given in the previous section should make it clear that even in areas we perceive as pristine, modern humans have already had a significant impact.

 Human activities can affect several key attributes of ecosystems. First, they can affect the *functional ability* of the ecosystem, the capacity to perform key actions—to fix and cycle energy, conserve and cycle nutrients, and provide suitable habitat for an array of inhabiting species. Second, they can affect the *structure,* or spatial arrangement of the parts, of the ecosystem—whether it is a savanna, meadow, even-aged or uneven-aged forest, or some other type. Third, they can affect the *composition* and *population structure,* that is, the number of species and their relative abundance as well as the densities and age- and size-class distributions of individual species. Finally, human actions can alter the basic *successional patterns,* or trajectories, characteristic of a given site.

The ecological significance of human activity is based on the magnitude and permanence of its effects. In assessing its importance, one needs to know if the change in one of the four attributes (function, structure, composition, dynamics) is very large or small and if it is transient or essentially permanent. As will be seen, it is the changes in structure and composition that are most easily perceived by the manager and visitor. Although changes in function and dynamics may be more important in the long run, they are often very difficult to identify until they have progressed beyond correction.

Human activities that bring about changes in ecosystem attributes can be categorized as follows:

1. Introduction of an exotic organism such as chestnut blight, a sport fish, or cheatgrass;
2. Elimination of a native organism such as grizzly bear, American chestnut, or wolf;
3. Addition of materials, especially foreign substances such as a pesticide or sulfur dioxide;
4. Removal of materials, especially energy-rich or nutrient-rich substances, as in grazing and logging or by erosion;
5. Physical alteration of site; for example, trail or road construction and compaction of soil from recreation use;
6. Alteration of the natural patterns and level of disturbance; for example, control of natural fires or insect epidemics;
7. Alteration of the basic environmental regime of the site; for example, by weather modification projects, reduction of the ozone layer, or addition of noise, none of which has its origin within the wilderness itself.

Any of the activities included in these seven categories can have profound effects on ecosystem function, structure, composition, and dynamics. But the significance of the alteration, as measured by its magnitude and permanence, may be far different from the degree to which it is sensed as unnatural by the layman. Some examples follow.

Introduction of the chestnut blight resulted in permanent elimination of the American chestnut (Shugart and West 1977). The hardwood ecosystems of which it was a part underwent a permanent change in composition and population structure, not only as a result of the loss of a dominant tree but also because of adjustments in animal species dependent on it for food. Rates of energy and nutrient cycling, forest structure, and successional sequences were also altered as the ecosystems adjusted and other species filled the gaps. Despite these changes, visitors to forests from which chestnuts have been eliminated do not typically perceive these as unnatural or human-altered ecosystems. Likewise, presence of planted sport fish is rarely perceived as an unnatural influence, although the effects on the structure and function of the largely unseen lake, pond, or stream ecosystem may be significant and permanent.

On the other hand, visitors are more likely to be aware of the elimination of grizzly bears and wolves from many wildernesses. Composition (the diversity of these ecosystems) has been changed permanently, but the effect on their structure and function is probably relatively minor in many, but not all, cases. But because visitors are much more aware of large animals of this type, their absence is more likely to be perceived as unnatural.

Logging has been a factor in some wildernesses, quite aside from the roads that were required for access. This is particularly common in wildernesses

in the eastern United States. Composition and ecosystem functioning were drastically altered. However, many aspects of system function, such as conservation of nutrients, have quickly recovered to near prelogging levels. These ecosystems are returning to approximations of their former structure and composition at a slower rate, but, barring site degradation, will generally recover. This is not to say that such logged areas will ever have exactly the same composition and species population structure; conditions (environmental and biological) are never exactly the same at the initiation of a successional sequence as they were before disturbance. It is probable that the duration of the logging impacts on structure and composition are substantially less in the moderate, summer-wet forest environments of the Appalachian Mountains with their rapid vegetative regrowth than in the more arid western coniferous forest environments.

Logging disturbance, especially clearcutting, is perceived by all visitors as highly unnatural, and, of course, it is. Nonetheless, in many habitats, while effects are long-term, they are not necessarily permanent in terms of composition, ecosystem functions, structure, or successional trajectory.

Interferences in patterns of natural disturbances (e.g., fire control programs) are much more subtle in their effects. Yet they are equally unnatural, leading to permanent alteration in ecosystem function (e.g., paths and rates of nutrient cycling), composition, and successional trajectory. Effects are gradual, and, initially, are not as drastic and noticeable as logging impacts. Yet they may be much more profound.

Seemingly, the ecologist can provide some measurements of the naturalness of the landscape. These measurements are based on the degree to which modern man has altered the functional abilities (energy fixation and nutrient conservation) of the ecosystems, their composition and structure, the successional trajectories, and the historic pattern of natural disturbances. The larger and more permanent the alteration, the greater its significance as an unnatural influence.

This also suggests that recreationists, managers, and ecologists will not necessarily see eye-to-eye on an area's degree of naturalness or, more likely, unnaturalness. Ecologically, a dramatic but transient disturbance, such as a road, might be judged less of an unnatural influence than the permanent loss of plant or animal species, which might not be apparent to the untrained eye.

Thus, *ecological and sociological perceptions* of the naturalness of wilderness can differ widely. In ecological terms, there is not as sharp a difference in naturalness as many have assumed between the wildernesses in the East and in the West. Exotic species have been introduced and native dominants have been lost in both areas. And it is an open question whether the wilderness areas in the West have been more permanently changed and are more

Fig. 10.5. The above photos (left, 1916; right, 1976) record 60 years of ecological change at Red Buttes WSA, near Maroon Bells-Snowmass Wilderness, CO. Left photo courtesy of W. Hutchinson, USFS. Right photo courtesy of the USFS.

unnatural after nearly 70 years of fire control programs and extensive grazing than the forest sites of the Appalachian Mountains that were logged 50 or more years ago.

Ecologically, the most significant human alterations of natural ecosystems are not necessarily the most obvious. What a visitor perceives as natural may have been profoundly and permanently altered (fig. 10.5). The degree of naturalness in ecological terms is a function of knowledge about ecosystem factors and, if quantified, will often differ from the lay visitor's perception of naturalness. Here, both managers and users need to broaden their perspectives so they can distinguish between cosmetic and profound ecologic impacts (see Franklin 1987).

Despite the varying perception of naturalness, we have selected as our wildernesses those tracts of land that both ecologists and wilderness advocates view as among the most natural and unaltered. Such lands are extremely valuable for determining environmental and ecological baselines in each biotic region in which they occur. Not only is there more naturalness to be lost in wilderness than elsewhere, but also there are greater opportunities to maintain and learn from this environment. Because these are our most natural environments, we need to minimize both broad, external impacts (such as atmospheric pollutants) and specific impacts within the area (such as predator reduction, fire control, and grazing of domestic livestock) (Franklin 1987). Because wildernesses are the most unaltered landscapes in each biotic region, it seems important to at least maintain the level of naturalness present in each area and to actually enhance the naturalness of some others.

ECOLOGICAL KNOWLEDGE IN INTERPRETING AND MANAGING WILDERNESS

Knowledge of ecosystems and ecosystem dynamics is important for wilderness managers; the key question is what information is needed and how does the manager go about obtaining and using it. General principles are as follows:

1. In developing a management plan for a wilderness, key ecological data are essential, although the detail needed may vary with management objectives and problems. These data include at least a general knowledge of the ecosystems and their properties:
   a. What kinds of ecosystems are present? (classification)
   b. Where are they located? (distribution, mapping)
   c. What are their biological and physical characteristics? (characterizations of biotic composition, climate,)

d. What are their dynamic properties? (rates and directions of change or successional trends)
   e. What are the key factors affecting the dynamics?
2. Periodic monitoring of changes within, and at the *ecotones* (a transitional zone between two adjacent communities, containing species characteristic of both as well as others occuring only within one), of key ecosystems is essential to assessing their naturalness. Inventories that provide essential descriptive data at one point in time must be supplemented by repeated measures over time to *monitor* change. A number of ecological monitoring methods are available, and Merigliano (1987) outlines a wide range of indicators to be measured to assess wilderness conditions.
3. The levels of ecological inventory and the needed monitoring will vary with the ecosystem. The most important considerations are the rate at which the ecosystem is likely to change and its importance in the total wilderness landscape. In addition, each ecosystem must be considered in terms of the specific objectives for management of that wilderness and the current conditions and assumptions about the future, which combine to identify problems (see chap. 8). Features requiring intensive inventory and monitoring may include: meadows, lakes, streams, and some animal components. These are ecosystems or elements that can change relatively rapidly and are focal points of visitor interest and use. Forest ecosystems, on the other hand, often provide a landscape background and usually undergo relatively slow changes.
4. Ecological expertise and ecological data are not a substitute for clear management objectives. The wilderness manager must decide what the ecological objectives of the management will be—the degree of naturalness desired. Many alternatives are available, such as maintenance of *status quo;* return to presettlement condition; and perpetuation of a particular species, ecosystem, or community mosaic. Ecological information can tell the manager what is present, how it is changing, and, possibly, why. Such information can also indicate biologically feasible options or potentials, constraints and dangers, and alternative management strategies. But the manager must decide what is desired in types and distribution of ecosystems. Ecological information will then indicate if that is attainable, and if so, the necessary management actions to achieve it. Chapter 8 on planning emphasizes the importance of objectives and offers a planning approach to outlining them.

Recent advances in technology make it much easier for the wilderness manager to inventory and monitor ecosystem condition. Foremost are remote-sensing technology, geographic information systems (GIS), and portable microcomputers. These developments dramatically expand information gathering, storage, and manipulation capabilities. All managers should be familiar with them. These tools can supply current information on the state of wilderness ecosystems, something seriously deficient in the past.

IDENTIFYING WILDERNESS ECOSYSTEMS

An ecological inventory is absolutely essential to writing and implementing a wilderness management plan. The manager must know what ecosystems are present, where they are, and the direction and rate at which they are changing. Level of detail will vary with management objectives and problems, and available personnel, money, and technology. There will also be professional differences about the appropriate techniques and emphasis.

Wilderness inventories will have certain things in common. In a given wilderness, knowing the vegetation types or communities and their locations is necessary. The timber and range type maps of the forester and range manager are examples. General classifications and maps of this type can be created with relatively simple standard procedures, such as mapping on aerial photographs, with appropriate ground checking; or by more sophisticated approaches such as remote sensing, again with ground checking (Agee and Kertis 1986). Some form of mapping is essential. The best statistically designed point-sample inventory of a wilderness can identify the vegetation types present and their extent, with quantitative error terms, but nothing about where they are or how they are spatially oriented to each other. GIS should make the mapping requirements readily manageable.

Knowledge of the existing vegetative communities or cover types is essential, but is inadequate to assess the rate and naturalness of change. The wilderness manager needs a stratification of the landscape into basic environmental or habitat units. Existing vegetation may or may not provide a good index to areas that vary in basic environmental and ecosystem characteristics. Perhaps an example will make the contrast between habitat type and cover type (or existing vegetation) clearer. Many types of ponderosa pine forest exist in western North America. A survey of existing communities may establish that there is a ponderosa pine/shrub community. In fact, this community may occur in several habitats distinctive in their environmental conditions. As a consequence, on one the pine forest is climax, while on another it is subject to replacement by more tolerant species due to better moisture conditions.

Wilderness managers need to know both the kinds and distribution of existing communities and the basic habitat types. Approaches to identifying and classifying the basic habitat types or environmental mosaic of a landscape are many and diverse, however, and here is where ecologists often part company—among themselves and from other specialists.

Remember, at this point the objective is to identify natural landscape units that are relatively homogeneous in biological and physical characteristics. This allows the manager to categorize the lands according to use potential, management problems, and response to various natural or artificial perturbations or treatments. To do this, knowledge of both the *existing communities* and the *basic environmental mosaic* (habitat types) are needed.

In the western United States, major emphasis is on the use of stable or near-climax vegetation to identify *habitat types*—the collective area presently or potentially occupied by the same plant association or climax community. Pfister and Arno (1980) have outlined the philosophy, potential use, and current progress of this approach, which is based on the concepts developed and demonstrated by R. Daubenmire in the northern Rocky Mountains (Daubenmire and Daubenmire 1968). The self-perpetuating tree species and selected understory species are used to stratify the landscape into basic habitat types. Using potential natural vegetation helps identify the environmental mosaic. Obviously, when a wilderness is occupied mainly by successionally advanced communities, a map of existing vegetation provides a good index to the environmental mosaic. But where communities are mainly early successional types, maps of existing community types may look very different from those of habitat type or potential natural vegetation.

The habitat-type approach works well for stratifying broad areas into relatively homogeneous units. This approach quickly and accurately creates inferences about environmental conditions, and about the potential limitations of the habitat types for various uses. These inferences can then be easily extrapolated across the landscape. Nevertheless, drawbacks exist. The current or existing vegetative cover may not receive sufficient attention. In addition, it is necessary to integrate the habitat-type classification with soils and landform data for a complete ecosystem classification. Also, in the classification process some information about an individual stand is lost as it is lumped into a type with other similar, but not identical, stands. Mapping must follow the classification to make it useful in land planning; it cannot be carried out until the initial classification is completed.

An *alternative approach*—vegetation gradient modeling—has been developed by Kessell (1979) in Glacier National Park (MT), in which gradient models of the vegetation and fire fuels are combined with a hectare-by-hectare resource inventory using aerial photographs and topographic maps in a computerized storage and retrieval system. By using sampling, community characteristics (composition and structure of the vegetation, nature of the fire fuels, etc.) are related to *six gradients: elevation, topographic-*

moisture, time since last burn, primary succession, alpine wind exposure, and *specific subdrainage.* Once the gradient models are constructed, the inventory process proceeds. Topographic maps, fire history maps, and aerial photographs are used to determine the location of each hectare of ground on the six gradients. This information is stored in a computer, and, when combined with the gradient models, predicts community characteristics within that hectare. Depending on the data collected in the field survey, a wide range of information—from fire fuel loadings to number of trees per hectare by species—can be generated. This approach was developed specifically to produce real-time fire behavior models on which managers could base fire control decisions.

An important concern in this approach, which was the first direct application of vegetation gradient models to management inventory and decision making, is the accuracy of the gradient models on which the predictions of stand conditions are highly dependent. The successional gradient, which in the broadest application must relate current stand condition to time since last disturbance, is a particularly difficult problem. Factors of history (chance), availability of seed source, and intensity of disturbance can play major roles in providing for different successional patterns under similar environmental conditions. Nevertheless, as a flexible and comprehensive inventory system, Kessell's approach offers an alternative to the habitat-type approach.

In the eastern United States the emphasis has been on using data on existing vegetation, combined with data on soils, landform, slope, and aspect, to provide the basic landscape classification (Leak 1982; Ohmann and Ream 1971; Spies and Barnes 1985). Reasons for using this approach in the East include: the early successional nature of many of the communities (i.e., the difficulty of identifying climax types and relating seral types to them); the tendencies toward broader, more gradual ecotones between types (less discrete communities, more gradual gradients in moisture and temperature); and tradition (philosophy and sampling methods). Apparently, the classification and mapping of soils in biologically meaningful ways is more possible in the East than in the rugged mountains of the West.

Experience suggests that an *ecosystem classification* ultimately should be *based on vegetation, soils, and landform.* The vegetation component should consider both the dominant and less conspicuous species because the dominants define the existing community while less conspicuous species are often more sensitive indicators of environmental conditions. The relative emphasis on each component—vegetation, soils, and landform—in developing the environmental or habitat type classification will vary from area to area depending on the relative contribution each can make in a particular landscape.

In many cases, wilderness managers will find that the landscape is the ecosystem unit of interest, since, for example, many resources have to be dealt with at the level of river basins. *Landscape ecology* is now a major subdiscipline of ecology (see Forman and Godron 1986). While landscape ecology has derived many of its concepts from European traditions (i.e., domesticated and stable landscapes), perspectives relevant to more natural and dynamic landscapes are emerging rapidly.

Landscape concepts are clearly relevant to the wilderness manager. Concepts such as patch types; effects of patch size, shape, and context; and types and roles of corridors need to be understood and applied by managers in their interpretation and management of wilderness areas. Typical landscape-level issues will include management of habitat for large ungulates such as elk. Very large areas of diverse habitat may be required for top carnivores such as the grizzly bear, as is suggested by proposals for a "greater Yellowstone ecosystem" to provide for viable populations of this wide-ranging species. Management of aquatic habitat and organisms, such as anadromous fish (e.g., salmon), also requires a landscape perspective. The movement of materials along the continuum from headwater stream to river and considerations of terrestrial and aquatic ecosystem interactions force such a perspective (Swanson and others 1982). A study of aquatic habitats in the Hoh River in Olympic National Park (WA) illustrates some of the interactions that occur at larger scales, which are essential to aquatic productivity, as well as the critical importance of some spatially limited "biological hotspots" (Franklin and others 1982).

CHARACTERIZING WILDERNESS ECOSYSTEMS

The inventory of the ecosystem in a wilderness is only the beginning. Each ecosystem type must, to some degree, be characterized biologically and physically. A good deal of information, but probably not enough, will have been gathered while sampling for the classification. The types of data valuable for management interpretations of the ecosystem units include:

1. *Floristic composition,* including measures of importance (frequency and cover of understory and density of trees by size classes) rather than simply presence and absence.

2. *Faunistic composition,* such as permanent and transient vertebrates, and information on how each uses and depends on the particular ecosystem. Numerous studies (e.g., by Thomas and others 1976) have shown the value of relating faunistic composition and utilization to major vegetation types; in this way, the character and potential of animal habitation and utilization can be rapidly extrapolated over broad areas. In any case, because of large fluxes in populations, absolute data on densities are probably of a much lower order of priority than relative abundance and thorough species lists.

3. *Environmental features and controls* such as temperature, moisture, and snow regimes. These indices of nutrient status range from very crude approximations (extrapolations from climatic situations or inferences from vegetative composition) to detailed analyses. Some characterization of the environmental regime of an ecosystem unit is essential to understanding its behavior and management potential. An example of one approach to environmental characterization is offered by Zobel and others (1976). Physical and chemical characterizations of the soil may be included here if not separately handled as part of a soil survey (mapping unit characterization) effort.

4. *Rates of key processes* such as productivity and decomposition. The objective here is to obtain a measure of the "metabolic rate" of each ecosystem unit. Again, very crude indices may be applied because definitive data on processes such as productivity and decomposition are difficult and expensive to obtain. *A site index measurement,* tree height at an index age such as 100 years, is sometimes a useful index for a forest ecosystem. Clipping can be used in herbaceous communities to obtain some estimate of productivity. In any case, it is desirable to get some feeling for rates of energy fixation and nutrient cycling in major ecosystems because this information provides insights into the rapidity with which areas will recover from various disturbances. Site productivity or growth potential is a key element in recovery.

SUCCESSIONAL CHARACTERIZATION OF ECOSYSTEMS

Characterizing the rate and direction of change in the ecosystem units is particularly important. The objective is to be able to forecast expected changes in composition and structure of an ecosystem type over a unit of time and with alternative patterns of disturbance (none, frequent fire, heavy grazing).

A variety of techniques can be used to characterize successional status. In forests, one of the simplest techniques is *size-class analysis* of the tree species present. For example, the tree species well represented in reproduction size classes are considered likely candidates for late successional or climax status (Daubenmire 1968). Dominants that are failing to reproduce are, on the other hand, typically considered to be pioneer or seral species. The contrasting interpretations are illustrated in table 10.1.

Age-class analyses can add considerably to size-class analyses in interpreting successional trends.

Size and age are by no means perfectly correlated; the small incense-cedar saplings and large dominant Douglas-firs in a southern Oregon stand may be the same age. Differential growth rates in even-aged stands often lead to such structures. The increasing numbers of stand-age structure data are greatly improving our interpretations of stand development. For example, a study of two Engelmann spruce/subalpine fir stands on southern Utah plateaus (Hanley and others 1975) showed that both species are climax, with Engelmann spruce essentially an all-aged species and subalpine fir uneven-aged species (wavelike pattern of reproduction) (fig. 10.6). Similarly, Viers (1982) has demonstrated the all-aged characteristic of coast redwood on the northern California coast which is due to limited but regular establishment of reproduction; associated Douglas-fir typically reproduces in pulses following major stand disturbances.

Historical analyses, such as reconstruction of the fire history of a wilderness from stand ages and records, can provide major insights into rates of successional change and the disturbance factors that formed and controlled the landscape mosaic (Heinselman 1973). *Fire-scar analysis* can be a particularly useful part of such a study. Old journals, books, newspapers, photographs, and interviews with longtime residents of regions also can be useful. But fire management programs based on historical fire regimes may not always produce the desired results. Ahlgren (1976) concludes that, in the lake states, red pine and eastern white pine cannot be restored to their previous positions by natural means, including reintroduction of fire.

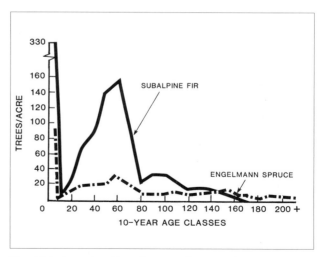

Fig. 10.6. Age-class distribution of an Engelmann spruce and subalpine fir stand, Deer Hollow study location, UT. From Hanley and others 1975.

Table l0.1. Examples of size-class distributions (stand tables) and their interpretation.

A: Numbers of trees by size class and species in 15- by 25-m plot at Santiam Pass in central Oregon Cascade Range[1]

| Species | <5 | | Size class (diameter in cm) | | | |
	<1 m tall	>1 m tall	5-10	10-30	30-50	50-70
Subalpine fir (dead)				4	2	
Lodgepole pine (dead)				2	1	
Pacific silver fir	3,720	15	4	9	1	
Mountain hemlock	8	2	3	19	6	1
Western white pine					1	

B: Populatlon of trees on 1 hectare near Lake Itasca, Minnesota.[2]

| Species | Size class (diameter in cm) | | | | |
	0-10	10-20	20-30	30-40	>40
Sugar maple	220	86	35	6	—
Basswood	175	81	7	11	3
Eastern hophornbeam	460	20	3[3]	—	—
American elm	47	16	55	—	—
Northern red oak	14	7	3	-3	—
White ash	100	10	3	—	—
Bur oak	17	7	—	—	—
Quaking aspen	39[4]	94	55	43	—
Paper birch	53[4]	50	7	3	—
Eastern white pine	260	—	—	3	3
Balsam poplar	—	—	7	—	—
Yellow birch	—	4	—	—	—
White spruce	3	—	—	—	—
Bigtooth aspen	2	—	—	—	—
Slippery elm	30	—	—	—	—

1. Two early successional species (subalpine fir and lodgepole pine) have been eliminated while the longer lived western white pine is still present, but failing to reproduce. Mountain hemlock currently dominates, but is reproducing very poorly and will be replaced by abundantly reproducing Pacific silver fir (from Franklin and Mitchell 1967).
2. The first seven species are interpreted as climax species or permanent occupants, the next five as serial species or disappearing relics of an earlier successional stage, and the last three as unsuccessful invaders (from Daubenmire 1968).
3. Approximate maximum size of the species in this region.
4. Root or stem-base suckers, no seedlings.

Existing computer models allow simulation of successional changes over decades or even centuries and with different types and intensities of disturbance. These models are undergoing continual improvement. The potential for this methodology in wilderness management is substantial, particularly when linked to GIS. Forest-stand simulators predict changes in composition, biomass, and structure, due either to the dynamics of the ecosystem or to disturbances of various types (a fire of specific intensity or destruction of selected portions of the stand by an insect, disease, or wind). They are analogous to the various stand simulation and management alternative models such as FORPLAN, which currently is used on the national forests.

Two general types of *simulation models* are available: the *regional landscape model*, which simulates probable changes in the relative proportions of various community types over time and under alternative disturbance patterns; and the *stand simulation model*, which simulates changes in environmental conditions, composition, and biomass within an individual stand.

Regional models (which could apply to a wilderness) require (l) a *classification scheme* that separates ecosystems into important and definable categories; (2) *tabular data* that define the initial conditions for the area of interest, for example acreages by the defined ecosystem categories; and (3) *data on the rate* at which an ecosystem is changing from one category

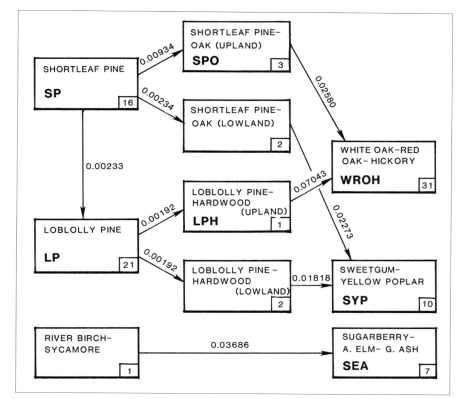

Fig. 10.7. Compartment model and simulation of change in forest type in GA. (right) Annual natural succession, with coefficients indicating percentage of land area in donor compartment transferred to recipient department. Number in each compartment is percentage of undisturbed plots. (below left) The change in forest type in north-central GA simulated for the period 1961-2002. Species abbreviations are along right margin. Adapted from Burgess and O'Neill 1975.

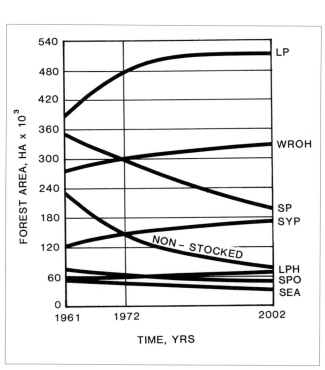

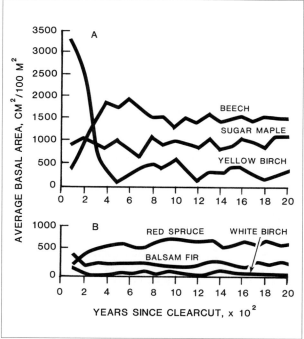

Fig. 10.8. Long-term prediction of average basal area for six species under constant climate and fertile, well-drained soils. (A) Includes species typical at low elevations; and (B) species typical at high elevations. Each line represents the average of 100 plots. From Botkin and others 1972.

Fig. l0.9. Fragile vegetation renders alpine meadows and lake shorelines sensitive to heavy use. Short growing seasons hamper recovery of damaged areas. Grassy Lake in the John Muir Wilderness, CA, shows impacts of human use, including pronounced trampling on right. Photo courtesy of the USFS.

to another. Such models have been developed for the western Great Lakes and Georgia Piedmont regions (Burgess and O'Neill 1975). The *compartment model* and results of a 40-year simulation are illustrated in figure 10.7.

A broad array of *stand level models* are available (Shugart 1984). The most broadly applied appear to be the *gap models,* which use the approach first used in the Hubbard Brook Parent simulator or JABOWA (Botkin and others 1972) ecosystems (Shugart 1984). Gap models match the environmental conditions on a site with the known environmental tolerances and optima of potentially inhabiting species to introduce (reproduce), grow, and remove (as mortality) trees in the stand. The basis for the growth prediction is an optimum growth curve for each species. Appropriate reductions from this curve are made when the sunlight, soil, and temperature conditions experienced by each tree are less than optimum. Growth is also limited by maximal diameters and heights. Reproduction is a probabalistic (stochastic) process of introducing seedlings based on environmental conditions (especially sunlight) within the stand. Death is typically conditioned by occurrence of both minimal growth and maximal species age although often approaches have been used (Franklin and Hemstrom 1981). The long-term successional patterns simulated by this model typically fit very well with those developed by experienced ecologists in areas in which it is applied (fig. 10.8). One particular advantage of the stand-level model is the opportunity to simulate

ecosystem behavior if only a part of a stand (e.g., a single species) is disturbed with the remainder left intact. The effect of a loss of an individual species, such as in an insect or disease epidemic, can therefore be simulated (Shugart and West 1977).

The *PROGNOSIS model,* which was developed in the northern Rocky Mountains, offers another approach to stand-level simulations for long periods of time (Stage 1973). This basic model is being expanded continually to incorporate a wider array of resource concerns.

These models are mentioned here because they illustrate a type of tool that will allow the wilderness manager to integrate large amounts of ecological data and simulate successional trends in stands and landscapes under a variety of natural disturbances and management regimes. As tools, they are comparable to the wilderness use simulation model described in chapter 17 for developing information on acceptable levels of visitor use under different criteria. A challenging step in formulating such models is collection of data on transfer rates—birth and death rates in stand and rates of change from one community to another in regional models. Data on the frequency and intensity of natural disturbances (fire or windthrow) are also difficult to obtain but essential to realistic simulations of various management alternatives.

LEVELS OF DETAIL FOR INVENTORYING AND MONITORING

As mentioned earlier, the level of resolution or detail appropriate in inventorying and monitoring wilderness ecosystems will vary. The manager needs at least a crude understanding of the ecosystems over the general landscape and their characteristics. But he needs much more detailed knowledge of initial conditions and frequent updating on changes in certain locations, particularly where human activities concentrate and/or when rapid biologic or physical changes occur, either from human or natural causes.

Subalpine meadows are the classic example of ecosystems for which detailed information might be needed, particularly in heavily used areas. Documented instances of compositional change and rapid tree invasion of meadows are abundant. Some of these have been ascribed to natural causes such as tree invasion in the suablpine meadows of the Pacific Northwest (Franklin and others 1971) resulting from climatic change. More often, humans and domestic livestock are responsible. Lodgepole pine has invaded Sierran and Rocky Mountain meadows as a result of reduced wildfire, livestock grazing, changes in soil

moisture (due to erosion and / or trail trenching), and climatic change. Grazing, trampling, and compaction have altered meadow composition in many wildernesses.

Meadows, margins of lakes and ponds, and timberline forests are examples of fragile ecosystems particularly likely to be heavily impacted by visitors (fig. 10.9). They should receive special attention in inventory and, especially, in monitoring programs. The initial state (composition) of these ecosystems needs to be known in greater detail. Greater numbers of permanent sample plots and photo points are appropriate and they should be remeasured more frequently than heavily forested and lightly used ecosystems.

An example of a pioneering effort in monitoring such sensitive areas (and the value of such an effort) is Thornburgh's (1962) study of the Image Lake area in the Glacier Peak Wilderness (WA). Significant deterioration of the vegetation was apparent at that time. Thornburgh provided lists of use-susceptible and use-resistant species and recommended exclusion of livestock from the area. Remeasurements of 25 permanent transects made in 1966 and 1971 have served as a basis for management programs to rehabilitate damaged sites and to control types and intensity of use in the lake basin. Shifts in impact areas from the vicinity of the lakeshore to higher benches (use of the immediate lakeshore area was restricted) were detected by continuous monitoring. Similar studies at other locations in the North Cascades National Park (WA) and research on techniques for rehabilitating damaged sites (such as seeding native plants or using plug transplants) have been a major spinoff from the Image Lake study.

Depending on the objectives, many possible techniques for monitoring ecosystems are vailable. This discussion has focused on monitoring biological changes, such as changes in vegetation composition and structure, on permanent plots or transects. Inferences drawn from the initial inventory on rates and directions of change are useful, but they are no substitute for observing actual changes on permanent, long-term samples.

We will not attempt to outline the many possible strategies for setting up a series of permanent plots, points, and photo points for monitoring. Some general principles follow:

1   Sample more intensively and remeasure plots more frequently in areas where changes are likely.
2. When sampling areas are likely to be heavily impacted, set up control plots in comparable areas where you expect little change in use.

3. Ecotones between different types of vegetation, such as forest and meadow, are sensitive locations for monitoring biological changes.
4. Permanently locate or reference monitoring sites on the ground; document in detail their location and the techniques used.

With the great emphasis on meadows and similar areas of special visitor attraction, the need for monitoring of changes in forest ecosystems is often overlooked. It is important that at least some monitoring be carried out in forested areas over long periods to identify actual, not inferred, trends in forest structure and composition. Representative sites for major forest ecosystem types are obvious choices for permanent plots. Careful documentation and referencing of plot location are critical because of the long time spans and difficulty of relocating plots in forested landscapes. Frequency of remeasurement will depend on objectives and likely rate of change. Seral forests of short-lived species (aspen and alder) and fire types where fire intervals are (or were) frequent obviously require more frequent attention than the conifer forests in wetter parts of the Pacific Northwest, which are composed of long-lived species and have long return intervals for fire. When dealing with forest (or even shrub-dominated) ecosystems, it is extremely important to pay close attention to entries or "births" of new individuals.

Special interest species, such as those which are known to be rare or endangered, may be another focus of wilderness monitoring programs. Such programs may be mandatory in the case of species having legal standing as threatened or endangered. Since wilderness, as large natural tracts, sometimes provides major reservoirs of such species, wilderness managers can expect increased emphasis on monitoring and management of selected flora and fauna in the future.

Sound data management programs are absolutely critical to the success of any long-term research and monitoring program (Michener 1986). Past failures of such efforts are often attributable to failures in data documentation and archiving. Guidelines are available on methods of managing such data sets (Michener 1986).

Currently, the monitoring, or collecting of baseline data in wilderness, is woefully inadequate. In most areas it is essentially absent. What little monitoring is being done is generally not part of a systematic, comprehensive plan. Documentation is poor. Most work is focused on "sores," which are immediate problem areas. Such sites merit high priority but tend to overshadow needs for monitoring and gathering baseline data over the wilderness as a whole.

No other natural resource managers would ever tolerate such an inadequate inventory base in their programs. In timber management programs, for example, there are extensive systems of continuous inventory plots, comprehensive stand examinations, simulation models, and complex data storage and retrieval systems. Certainly this type and intensity of inventory and monitoring are not advocated for wilderness. But it should make the wilderness manager aware of the total inadequacy of past efforts and the imperative for improving a data base in the future. Even providing for periodic high-quality aerial photography of wilderness tracts, something sorely lacking for many areas, would be a major improvement.

STUDY QUESTIONS

1. To what extent are humans and their influences natural to wilderness ecosystems?
2. Define the term ecosystem. What are the three main components of an ecosystem?
3. What are two qualities of ecosystems that wilderness managers must continually bear in mind?
4. Describe the classic concept of forest succession. Describe several situations where succession may not follow the concept.
5. What is an important corollary to the concept of ecosystem successional dynamism? How should the wilderness manager deal with ecosystem succession?
6. How should a wilderness manager proceed with formulating a wilderness management plan? What is the foundation of the plan? What general provisions should it contain?

REFERENCES

Agee, James K.; Kertis, Jane. 1986. Vegetation cover types of the North Cascades. Report CPSU/UW 86-2. Seattle, WA: National Park Service Cooperative Park Studies Unit/College of Forest Resources, University of Washington. 64 p.

Ahlgren, Clifford E. 1976. Regeneration of red and white pine following wildfire and logging in northeastern Minnesota. Journal of Forestry. 74(3): 135-140.

Arno, Stephen F. 1986. Whitebark pine cone crops—a diminishing source of wildlife food. Western Journal of Applied Forestry. 1: 92-94.

Botkin, Daniel B.; Janak, James F.; Wallis, James R. 1972. Some ecological consequences of a computer model of forest growth. Journal of Ecology. 60(3): 849-872.

Burgess, Robert L.; O'Neill, Robert V., eds. 1975. Eastern deciduous forest biome progress report September 1, 1973 to August 31, 1974. Publ. 751 (EDFB-IBP 75-11). Oak Ridge, TN: Oak Ridge National Laboratory, Environmental Sciences Division. 252 p.

Cooper, C. F. 1960. Changes in vegetation, structure, and growth of southwestern pine forests since white settlement. Ecological Monographs. 30(2): 120-164.

Daubenmire, R. 1968. Plant communities. Evanston, NY: Harper and Row. 300 p.

Daubenmire, R. 1970. Steppe vegetation of Washington. Tech. Bull. 62. Pullman, WA: Washington State University, College of Agriculture, Washington Agricultural Experiment Station. 131 p.

Daubenmire, R.; Daubenmire, Jean B. 1968. Forest vegetation of eastern Washington and northern Idaho. Tech. Bull. 60. Pullman, WA: Washington State University, College of Agriculture, Washington Agricultural Experiment Station. 104 p.

Forman, Richard T.; Godron, Michel. 1986. Landscape ecology. New York: John Wiley and Sons. 619 p.

Franklin, Jerry F. 1987. Scientific use of wilderness. In: Lucas, Robert C., compiler. Proceedings—national wilderness research conference: issues, state-of-knowledge, future directions; 1985 July 23-26; Fort Collins, CO. Gen. Tech. Rep. INT-220. Ogden, UT: U.S. Department of Agriculture, Forest Service, Intermountain Research Station: 42-46.

Franklin, Jerry F.; Mitchell, Russell G. 1967. Successional status of subalpine fir in the Cascade Range. Res. Pap. PNW-46. Portland, OR: U.S. Department of Agriculture, Forest Service, Pacific Northwest Forest and Range Experiment Station. 16 p.

Franklin, Jerry F.; Moir, William H.; Douglas, George W.; Wiberg, Curt. 1971. Invasion of subalpine meadows by trees in the Cascade Range, Washington and Oregon. Arctic and Alpine Research. 3(3): 215-224.

Franklin, Jerry F.; Hemstrom, Miles A. 1981. Aspects of succession in the coniferous forests of the Pacific Northwest. In: West, Darrell C.; Shugart, Herman H.; Botkin, Daniel B., eds. Forest succession concepts and application. New York: Springer-Verlag: 212-229.

Franklin, Jerry F.; Swanson, Frederick J.; Sedell, J. R. 1982. Relationships within the valley floor ecosystems in western Olympic National Park: a summary. In: Starkey, Edward E.; Franklin, Jerry F.; Matthews, Jean W., eds. Ecological research in National Parks of the Pacific Northwest. Corvallis, OR: Oregon State University, Forest Research Laboratory: 43-45.

Frissell, Sidney S., Jr. 1973. The importance of fire as a natural ecological factor in Itasca State Park, Minnesota. Quaternary Research. 3(3): 397-407.

Habeck, James R. 1970. Fire ecology investigations in Glacier National Park. Missoula, MT: University of Montana, Department of Botany. 80 p.

Habeck, James R.; Mutch, Robert W. 1973. Fire-dependent forests in the Northern Rocky Mountains. Quaternary Research. 3(3): 408-424.

Hanley, Donald P.; Schmidt, Wyman C.; Blake, George M. 1975. Stand structure and successional status of two spruce-fir forests in southern Utah. Res. Pap. INT-176. Ogden, UT: U.S. Department of Agriculture, Forest Service, Intermountain Forest and Range Experiment Station. 16 p.

Heinselman, Miron L. 1973. Fire in the virgin forests of the Boundary Waters Canoe Area, Minnesota. Quaternary Research. 3(3): 329-383.

Hemstrom, Miles A.; Franklin, Jerry F. 1982. Fire and other disturbances of the forests in Mount Rainier National Park. Quaternary Research. 18: 32-51.

Kessell, Stephen R. 1979. Gradient modeling resource and fire management. New York: Springer-Verlag. 432 p.

Kilgore, Bruce M. 1973. The ecological role of fire in Sierran conifer forests. Quaternary Research. 3(3): 496-513.

Leak, William B. 1982. Habitat mapping and interpretation in New England. Res. Pap. NE-496. Broomall, PA: U.S. Department of Agriculture, Forest Service, Northeastern Forest Experiment Station. 28 p.

Leopold, A. Starker; Cain, Stanley A.; Cottam, Clarence M. 1969. Wildlife management in the National Parks: Reports of the special advisory board on wildlife management for the Secretary of the Interior, 1963-1968. Washington, DC: Wildlife Management Institute. [no pagination].

Merigliano, Linda L. 1987. The identification and evaluation of indicators to monitor wilderness conditions. Moscow, ID: University of Idaho, College of Forestry, Wildlife and Range Sciences. 273 p. Thesis.

Michener, William K., ed. 1986. Research data management in the ecological sciences. No. 16. Columbia, SC: University of South Carolina, Belle W. Baruch Library in Marine Science, University of South Carolina Press. 426 p.

Miller, Paul L. 1973. Exidant-introduced community change in a mixed conifer forest. American Chemistry Society Advances in Chemistry No. 122. Washington, DC: American Chemistry Society: 101-117.

Odum, Eugene P. 1971. Fundamentals of ecology. 3d ed. Philadelphia: W. B. Saunders Company. 574 p.

Ohmann, Lewis F.; Ream, R. R. 1971. Wilderness ecology: virgin plant communities of the Boundary Waters Canoe Area. Res. Pap. NC-63. St. Paul, MN: U.S. Department of Agriculture, Forest Service, North Central Forest Experiment Station. 55 p.

Oliver, C. D. 1981. Forest development in North America following major disturbances. Forest Ecology and Management. 3: 153-168.

Pfister, R. D.; Arno, S. F. 1980. Classifying forest habitat types based on potential climax vegetation. Forest Science. 26: 52-70.

Shugart, Herman H. 1984. A theory of forest dynamics. New York: Springer-Verlag. 278 p.

Shugart, Herman H., Jr.: West, D. C. 1977. Development of an Appalachian deciduous forest succession model and its application to assessment of the impact of chestnut blight. Journal of Environmental Management. 5: 161-179.

Spies, Thomas A.; Barnes, Burton V. 1985. A multifactor ecological classification of the northern hardwood and conifer ecosystems of Sylvania Recreation Area, Upper Peninsula, Michigan. Canadian Journal of Forest Research. 15: 949-960.

Stage, A. R. 1973. PROGNOSIS model for stand development. Res. Pap. INT-137. Ogden, UT: U.S. Department of Agriculture, Forest Service, Intermountain Forest and Range Experiment Station. 32 p.

Swanson, F. J.; Gregory, S. G.; Sedell, J. R.; Campbell, A. G. 1982. Land-water interactions: the riparian zone. In: Edmonds, Robert L., ed. Analysis of coniferous forest ecosystems in the Western United States. Stroudsburg, PA: Hutchinson Ross Publishing Co.: 292-332.

Thomas, Jack Ward; Miller, Rodney J.; Black, Hugh; Rodick, Jon E.; Maser, Chris. 1976. Guidelines for maintaining and enhancing wildlife habitat in forest management in the Blue Mountains of Oregon and Washington. In: Sabel, Kenneth, ed. Transactions, forty-first North American wildlife and natural resources conference; 1976 March 21-25; Washington, DC. Washington, DC: Wildlife Management Institute: 452-476.

Thornburgh, Dale. 1962. Image Lake report. Berkeley, CA: University of California, Berkeley. 51 p. Thesis.

Trappe, James M. 1972. Regulation of soil organisms by red alder: a potential biological system for control of *Poria weirii*. In: Managing young forests in the Douglas-fir region. Vol. 3. Corvallis, OR: Oregon State University: 35-51.

U.S. National Committee for the International Biological Program. 1974. U.S. participation in the International Biological Program. Washington, DC: National Academy of Sciences. 166 p.

Viers, Stephen D., Jr. 1982. Coast redwood forest: stand dynamics, successional status, and the role of fire. In: Means, Joseph E., ed. Forest succession and stand development research in the Northwest. Corvallis, OR: Oregon State University, Forest Research Laboratory: 119-141.

Vogl, Richard J. 1973. Ecology of knobcone pine in the Santa Anna Mountains of California. Ecological Monographs. 43(2): 125-143.

Wright, H. E., Jr. 1974. Landscape development, forest fires, and wilderness management. Science. 186(4163): 487-495.

Zobel, D. B.; McKee, W. A.; Hawk, G. M.; Dyrness, C. T. 1976. Relationships of environment to composition, structure, and diversity of forest communities of the central Western Cascades of Oregon. Ecological Monographs. 46(2): 135-156.

Zobel, Donald B.; Roth, Lewis F.; Hawk, Glenn M. 1985. Ecology, pathology, and management of Port-Orford cedar (*Chamaecyparis lawsoniana*). Gen. Tech. Rep. PNW-184. Portland, OR: U.S. Department of Agriculture, Forest Service, Pacific Northwest Forest and Range Experiment Station. 161 p.

Wildlife is a part of all wilderness ecosystems; its distribution, abundance, and behavior reflects the naturalness of a wilderness. Seeing rare species such as this wild sheep can be the high point of a visitor's trek. Photo courtesy of Richard Behan.

11

WILDLIFE IN WILDERNESS

*This chapter was written by John C. Hendee and Clay Schoenfeld,
Professor, retired, Wildlife and Journalism, University of Wisconsin,
Madison.*

*"Great wilderness has two characteristics: Remoteness and the presence of wild
animals in something like pristine variety and numbers " (Crisler 1958).*

INTRODUCTION

The character of a wilderness is often represented by its resident wildlife: the Bob Marshall Wilderness in is grizzly country, the canyon lands evoke images of the cougar, the caribou symbolizes the vastness of Alaskan wilderness. Without wilderness, many species of wildlife could not survive or function as truly wild. Wilderness without wildlife and wildlife without the freedom of wilderness are virtually unthinkable, their interdependency is so firmly established in our minds. But as pointed out in chapter 7, wilderness management must be comprehensive and not focused on any one aspect of the wilderness resource at the expense of the others. It is the holistic comprehension of the complexity, diversity, and oneness of wilderness that needs to be understood in order to preserve it (Craighead 1982). Thus, wildlife is only one component of the wilderness resource and must be managed as such—one consideration in an overall management scheme.

This chapter discusses wilderness wildlife and the important relationships between wildlife and wilderness. The chapter also explores the many wilderness management concerns that involve wildlife, and the various legal, administrative, and cultural restraints that influence the management of wildlife. Finally, the chapter proposes some objectives for managing wildlife in wilderness and guidelines for attaining them.

Throughout this chapter, the authors stress that wildlife and wilderness are interdependent and that the basic principles of wilderness management (see chap. 7) should prevail. That is, when management actions are necessary, only the minimum tools, methods, and regulations should be used to meet objectives. In classified wilderness, we should allow natural forces to shape wildlife habitat and populations to the fullest possible extent.

THE WILDERNESS WILDLIFE RESOURCE

A literal definition of "wilderness" would be "place of the wild beasts" (Bourassa 1978; Nash 1970). But what wild beasts?

From ecological and economic perspectives, a number of definitions of wilderness wildlife have been suggested. Aldo Leopold (1933) considered wilderness wildlife as species harmful to or harmed by economic land uses. He named seven species that met this criterion—wapiti (elk), caribou, bison, grizzly, moose, mountain (bighorn) sheep, and mountain goat. Starker Leopold (1966) identified the following North American ungulates as associated primarily with wilderness climax forage types: caribou, bighorn sheep, mountain goat, muskox, and bison. Dasmann defined wilderness species as those that are obligate members of a climax community or wilderness area (Dasmann 1966). Among his illustrations were the passenger pigeon, caribou, muskox, bighorn sheep, and grizzly bear. Allen (1966) labeled the cougar, grizzly, and wolf as the true wilderness animals because they are capable, wide ranging, and at odds with the livestock industry. Hochbaum (1970) would include many species of migratory waterfowl, like swans and geese, which seek undisturbed (wilderness) wetlands for nesting purposes.

Frome (1974) argues that any wilderness wildlife list should not be limited to large birds and mammals because other wildlife forms such as insects and snails are also indispensable in the wilderness cycle of life. He points out that our proper concern is all creatures great and small, not just the grizzly, wolf, sea turtle, whale, and eagle.

Salamanders and butterflies are as important in wilderness as mountain lions and eagles. Even smaller and less familiar creatures—what E. O. Wilson calls "the miniature wilderness that can take almost forever to explore" (Wilson 1984, p. 12)—may hold the keys to the preservation of whole ecosystems. But as a practical matter, the ungulates and carnivores at or near the top of their food chains serve as indicators of the health of lower trophic levels.

CATEGORIES OF WILDERNESS WILDLIFE

Wilderness wildlife may be categorized as (1) wilderness-dependent wildlife, (2) wilderness-associated wildlife, and (3) common wildlife found in wilderness. We recognize the difficulty of placing a particular species into any single category—at least for the entire National Wilderness Preservation System (NWPS)—because of overlap, regional and local variation, and exceptions that do not fit neatly into compartments. These categories are useful, however, for discussion at least, because they suggest something about the relationship of the species to the habitat currently found in wilderness.

Wilderness-dependent wildlife includes species vulnerable to human influence, whose continued existence is dependent on and/or reflective of the relatively wild habitat characteristics of wilderness. The wolf, grizzly bear, mountain sheep, pine marten, and wolverine are examples, although sometimes even these species are found in modified environments. Inspecting lists of threatened and endangered species suggests that more than a hundred species of mammals, birds, fishes, reptiles, and amphibians appear—at least seasonally—in classified or proposed areas of the NWPS. In any particular area, locally or regionally rare species are dependent on the continued naturalness of their habitats and thus can be placed in the wilderness-dependent category. For example, in northern Rocky Mountain wilderness are such locally or regionally rare species as grizzly bear, mountain caribou, native "westslope" cutthroat trout, Canada lynx, wolverine, mountain goat, Richardson's blue grouse, fisher, marten, peregrine falcon, bald and golden eagles, osprey, mountain sheep, and northern white-tailed ptarmigan.

Wilderness-associated wildlife includes species commonly associated with wild habitat characteristic of wilderness. This category includes wildlife common in the high-elevation wilderness habitat of the western United States and species associated with conditions characteristic of wilderness in the East, including southern swamps and hardwood forests. A list of wilderness-associated species would be illustrative, not exhaustive, and would identify species linked with wilderness by both human perception and ecological reality.

Regional variation in the public's perception of wilderness-associated species may exist and may be based on the relative wildness of the surrounding territory. For example, while black bears and bobcats are not strongly associated with wilderness in the West, they are more impressive indicators of wild conditions in the minds of easterners. Some other species commonly perceived as wilderness-associated might also appear in the wilderness-dependent category, such as mountain sheep, pine martens, fishers, wolves, southern bald eagles, grizzly and polar bears, Florida panthers, eastern cougars, and others.

Common wildlife found in wilderness includes species that happen to be found in wilderness but that also live in many other more modified environ-

ments. Their relationship to wilderness is incidental. They are not necessarily associated in fact or in human perception with especially wild places. Some examples include: deer, coyotes, bobcats, raccoons, rabbits, muskrats, minks; a host of rodents like squirrels, field mice, and rats; and many kinds of birds, such as raptors, grouse, woodpeckers, sparrows, juncos, and thrushes.

Unlike the other two categories, the common wildlife species do not have specific relationships to wilderness. They are neither dependent on such areas, nor do they have any real or perceived association with wilderness. But when found in wilderness, they are no less important in their natural roles. In fact, these common species, because they are adapted to more modified environments (and may even be benefited by them) may reveal through their natural place in the wilderness scheme an important comparison with nonwilderness conditions.

Unfortunately, a fourth category, *exotic or nonnative species*, is increasingly relevant to wilderness. This category would include those introduced species that have adapted to wilderness ecosystems and compete with resident native wildlife species. This would include such species as wild hogs, horses and burros, feral goats, and nutria. The ecological impacts of many exotic species have been well documented in proposed or designated wilderness areas. Wilderness wildlife managers are often involved in conceiving, implementing, and evaluating alternatives for their management, impact mitigation, or control.

These categories are useful guides to inventories of wilderness wildlife and the characteristics of natural habitat on which they depend. Such information is essential for management as well as useful in assessing some of the values dependent on an area's wilderness designation.

WILDERNESS-WILDLIFE RELATIONSHIPS

Many of the relationships of wilderness and certain species of wildlife are strong enough to constitute a framework to guide management direction. In this section, we review some of these special relationships and their influence on wilderness management.

Wildlife as a Measure of Wilderness Character

The distribution, numbers, and diversity of wildlife species can be a measure of the naturalness of a wilderness. Wildlife reflect ecological conditions and their changes over time, so wildlife can serve as a monitor of wilderness character and quality—in fact, as well as in human perception.

Culturally, for many people, the concept of wilderness is linked to some form of wildlife. For example, when Margaret and Olaus Murie (1966) wrote of their American elk studies in Wyoming, they called their book *Wapiti Wilderness*. Writing about his "Wilderness Observations and Experiences of a Professional Outdoorsman," John Crawford (1980) called his book *Wolves, Bears, and Bighorns*. Andy Russell (1971) entitled his book on Canadian wilderness *Grizzly Country*. The presence of particular kinds of wildlife always suggests the relative absence of human influence and the existence of primitive harmonies. For example, we are learning that grizzlies, wolves, and humans are not compatible in any concentration. Simply knowing that such wildlife is present is important to the meaning of wilderness. For if key wildlife is removed, although everything else remains visibly the same, the intensity of the sense of wilderness may be diminished (Nash 1970).

The emerging land ethic of Aldo Leopold, an early spokesperson for wilderness protection, expanded from wildlife to wilderness on to the total environment. He dates the moment that evolution began quite precisely in *A Sand County Almanac, and Sketches Here and There*. The incident occurred about 1920 during Leopold's U.S. Forest Service (USFS) days in the Southwest. Shots rang out from the rimrock, and, Leopold writes (Leopold 1949, p. 130):

> We reached the old wolf in time to watch a fierce green fire dying in her eyes. I realized then, and have known ever since, that there was something new to me in those eyes—something known only to her and to the mountain. I was young then, and full of trigger-itch; I thought that because fewer wolves meant more deer, that no wolves would mean hunter's paradise. But after seeing the green fire die, I sensed that neither the wolf nor the mountain agreed with such a view.

Leopold experienced the same feeling—that eliminating wildlife diminishes wilderness—after the demise of an old grizzly, the last of its kind roaming the Arizona high country. When a government hunter shot the bear for bounty, Leopold wrote a eulogy: "(Mount) Escudilla still hangs on the horizon but when you see it you no longer think of bear. It's only a mountain now" (Leopold 1949, p. 137).

The extent to which wildlife is used as a perceived wilderness criterion is striking. Asked to describe the Alaskan wilderness, John Milton described wildlife species, especially caribou, as carrying the soul of the Alaskan wilderness because they require freedom and vast space in which to range. Milton also referred to the wolf, wolverine, and the migratory waterfowl on the Yukon Flats and Delta as illustrating wilder-

ness under human pressure. To Milton, Alaska's wildlife symbolize its wilderness—the space, the openness, and the silence of the North (Milton 1972).

Sigurd Olson (1963) wrote of the wild laughing choruses of the common loon as the sound that more than any other typifies the rocks and waters and forests of wilderness.

A 1984 Associated Press dispatch out of Anchorage, Alaska, started out like this: "Wolves are among the last symbols of American wilderness. They are spirits of the wind, the last wild shadows in a nation sanitized and tamed by concrete and street lights."

These examples suggest the importance of wildlife as a reflection of wilderness values and quality. The presence and health of wilderness indicator species are used to monitor wilderness conditions, cases in point being wolves in Alaska and the northern Midwest, grizzly bears and mountain caribou in the northern Rocky Mountains, and desert bighorn sheep in the Southwest.

Wildlife's Role in Wilderness

Wildlife is an inseparable part of the wilderness resource. It plays a vital role in the development, maintenance, and modification of soil and vegetation that cover wilderness topography; in dispersal, planting, and germination of seeds; in pollination; in fertilization; and in conversion of dead plants into organic matter more usable by living plants (Talbot 1970).

An example from the Everglades Wilderness (FL) is the alligator and its relentless search for water in the dry season. Alligators seek low places where the water table lies just below the surface and work either to deepen the existing waterholes or to excavate new ones, breaking the caked earth with their powerful tails and shoveling away the debris with their broad snouts. During the worst droughts, alligators have been known to dig their way down through 4 feet of compacted mud and peat before coaxing water from the porous substrate. Such gator holes, found throughout the parched glades, attract many thirsty creatures ranging from otters to herons, and soon become biological microcosms of the whole region. The alligators, conserving energy and living on their own fat, largely ignore the boarders; the refugees sustain life on the gator holes' remaining fish, insect life, and vegetation, and live side by side in a relative state of truce. When the rains finally return, it is from these gator-made oases that the various species go forth to repopulate the Everglades (Carr 1973). Other species also play vital roles in natural processes—and the essence of wilderness management is preserving those processes.

The Wilderness Role in Wildlife Preservation

Wilderness may be crucial to the survival of some wildlife species, particularly those with highly specialized habitat needs. While many species with an affinity for wilderness conditions may in fact survive in less pristine habitats, they live most naturally in wilderness.

The Alaskan brown bear requires all of the ingredients of the Alaskan wilderness to survive (Troyer 1973). The wild flamingo requires remote stretches of undisturbed country during the breeding season (Buchheister 1963). In the Great Smokies, black bears may den 30, 40, or even 60 feet above the ground, requiring mature trees whose existence is guaranteed in very few places not given wilderness protection. Increasing evidence shows that the spotted owl cannot survive in the Pacific Northwest in the absence of old-growth forests (Forsman and others 1982; Thomas and others 1990). Luman and Neitro (1980) believe old-growth forest in the Northwest is also important, if not necessary, for the pine marten, fisher, and mountain lion. Probably dozens of species of birds and mammals and thousands of lesser plant and animal forms are dependent on old-growth forests associated with wilderness. Preservation of these old-growth remnants is critical. So little is known about many of the lesser forms (some microscopic in size) that we run substantial risks of losing yet unrecognized life elements of value to future human needs (Meyers 1983).

Bailey (1980) believes the fate of the desert bighorn depends on maintaining large blocks of suitable habitat immune from competition with livestock, feral burros and horses (fig. 11.1)—and on careful, rigid control of harvests. Gionfriddo and Krausman (1986) identify urban encroachment on desert bighorn

Fig. 11.1. Feral horses, roaming adjacent to a BLM roadless area in Nevada, compete for forage with native wilderness wildlife. Photo courtesy of the BLM.

sheep habitat to the boundary of the Pusch Ridge Wilderness adjacent to Tucson. Mammals identified as endangered in New Mexico—notably black-tailed prairie dog, Mexican wolf, marten, black-footed ferret, mink, river otter, and jaguar—are frequently associated with wilderness (Conway 1978).

Wilderness can serve as essential seasonal habitat. For instance, the extensive Arctic wilderness provides summer breeding grounds for much of the continental population of tundra swans, white-fronted geese, snow geese, brant, eiders, and scaup (Pimlott 1974). Wilderness in the West is summer host to herds of big game seeking high meadows for secure calving areas and for escape from heat and insects.

Such wilderness can function as a wildlife bank. For example, between 1892 and 1962 many of the elk ranges of the West were restocked with more than 10,000 surplus elk live-trapped in the wilderness-like backcountry of Yellowstone National Park (WY–MT–ID) (Leopold and others 1968). Mech and Rogers (1977) believe the recent marten population expansion in Minnesota originated in the virgin conifer stands in the Boundary Waters Canoe Area Wilderness (BWCAW). Similar evidence suggests that central Idaho's Frank Church-River of No Return Wilderness has been a reservoir for cougar population expansion (Hornocker 1971).

Even more significant, though less obvious, may be the role of wilderness as a hidden trove of recessive genes necessary for genetic adaptability to environmental change. Advances in genetic engineering make their recessive traits increasingly accessible. Who is to say what obscure wilderness species harbors the genes humans will ultimately call on for their survival? We already have a vaccine for leprosy distilled from the armadillo, quinine and cortisone derived from certain jungle plants, a type of rubber from the quayule plant, potential help for hemophilia gleaned from the blood of the manatee, and protein from the beefalo, a cross between the domestic cow and the buffalo.

Legally classified wilderness protects habitats that have been least modified from conditions under which their biotic communities evolved. No ecologist can yet judge all the consequences of destroying the habitat of a single species, and hence of destroying that species. We simply do not know enough. *The function of wilderness as a reservoir of genetic variability is crucial.*

For example, the extinction of the tule elk would result in the irreversible disappearance of a valuable gene pool. The tule is a dwarf subspecies that has adapted itself to a semiarid environment with great variations in climate and topography. There may be a strong demand in the future for genetic qualities of such an animal to convert forage in large areas of the world which have similar habitats (Ciriacy-Wantrup and Phillips 1970). Because much of the tule's natural range has been converted to agriculture, the population was reduced by the mid-1970s to about 400 animals in three areas of California. But by 1985, a California Department of Fish and Game program to reintroduce the elk to undeveloped areas had rebuilt the population to an estimated 1,550 in 15 herds (CA Dept. of Fish and Game 1985).

Even when legally classified wilderness is not essential for the survival of the species, it may be extremely beneficial. In classified wilderness, species can work out their destinies under the most natural conditions remaining. Based on experiences with grizzly/human conflicts in national parks and forests, a dispersed system of legislatively designated sanctuaries may be emerging as the focal point for conservation of wilderness wildlife (Martinka 1982). To help establish priorities for preserving rare, threatened, or endangered species within wilderness, given the wilderness framework of constraints, Adamus and Clough (1978) have offered a set of 13 useful criteria. Four relate to *suitability*, whether a protection program is likely to succeed; and nine reflect *desirability*, the extent to which the species needs or deserves protection.

The wilderness acts, by limiting intensive habitat management practices, may reduce conditions beneficial to some species. But wilderness areas may protect vegetative conditions missing or limited on private and other public lands, islands of habitat that otherwise would not be available, particularly for wildlife species dependent on old-growth vegetation.

In spite of the obvious benefits wilderness provides many species, wilderness alone is not enough. Environmental conditions favorable to one species may be highly unfavorable to another. David Smith, in "Report of the President's Advisory Panel on Timber and the Environment," explained it this way (Smith 1973, p. 382):

> Animal populations are ultimately controlled by the vegetation on which they most directly or indirectly feed. The larger herbivorous mammals and birds which include most game species thrive best feeding on low vegetation. Therefore, low, young forests actually have far more game than tall, old, and magnificent ones. This observation is sometimes extended to statements that old forests are biological deserts, but it might be more correct to call them game deserts. Old forests probably support as much or more animal life as young ones, but there may be a higher proportion of

small birds, squirrels, insects, and other organisms that inhabit the high foliage canopy or the soil. The old forest usually has a more diverse fauna than the young, thus it is more intriguing for the birdwatcher but less so for the hunter.

Hay and Posewitz (1978, pp. 5, 6) explain:

> The statement that wilderness is good for wildlife is no more true or false than is the statement that timber harvest is good for wildlife. Because the habitat requirements of the multitude of animals termed "wildlife" are so diverse, there is no question that some species will benefit and some species will be injured by either option . . . A mosaic of vegetation conditions supports the greatest variety of wildlife.

In short, the key to diverse wildlife is diversity of habitat. The NWPS offers the possibility of preserving most of the nation's 261 ecosystems, as defined by the Bailey-Küchler method, which reflects physical and biological factors. But traditional emphasis on areas with dramatic high country appeal at the expense of less scenic areas will need to be changed if the NWPS is to fulfill its potential in providing that diversity. By 1987, 157 ecosystems were adequately represented in designated wilderness (Davis 1988).

Wilderness Wildlife as an Environmental Baseline and Laboratory

Cutler summarized the crucial roles of wilderness areas as permanent and natural laboratories: (1) invaluable reservoirs of genetic germ plasm that preserve resource options and serve as storehouses of potential new products, (2) as biological standards of comparison with ecological communities more heavily affected by human activities, and (3) as sites for integrated studies of the structure and function of natural ecosystems (Cutler 1980).

Aldo Leopold promoted the theme in his writings that wilderness provides a standard against which the alteration of developed lands can be measured—that wild places reveal what the land was, what it is, and what it ought to be. He emphasized the importance of areas where evolution operates without hindrance from humans, thereby providing standards against which to measure the effects of development. Each biotic province, said Leopold, "needs its own wilderness for comparative studies of used and unused land" (Leopold 1949, p. 196).

Key scientific reports, based on the population dynamics of wilderness wildlife, would be impossible without designated wilderness to serve as natural laboratories. Long-term study of the habitat and behavior of the moose and timber wolf also requires large natural areas. Durward Allen, citing his experiences studying moose-wolf relationships in the Isle Royale Wilderness, Michigan, makes the case that some aspects of biological learning will inevitably depend on the setting aside and full protection of such areas (Allen 1978). Natural systems in some areas have matured through ages beyond our reckoning. If we are to learn how natural communities really work and survive, we must continue ongoing research and establish many more long-range studies in undisturbed wilderness laboratories.

Recreational, Economic, and Aesthetic Values

As will be pointed out in chapter 14, recreational use of wilderness has increased rapidly during the past four decades. The presence of wildlife is surely part of the wilderness lure. Many people come to view or photograph native species in natural settings. In season, others come to hunt or fish under primitive conditions. Millions of Americans enjoy wilderness wildlife vicariously by appreciating it through friends, stories, photos, and art; through television and movies; or simply by knowing that it is there. Even those who have never been within sight of real wilderness have some vision of its enchantment due in part to the rich profusion of books celebrating its beauty in pictures and poetry and to a strong instinct for maintaining some connection to a more primitive life (Robinson 1975).

The value of incidental contact with wildlife in outdoor recreation experiences is indicated by a study in which 96 percent of all campers interviewed said that the opportunity to see wildlife in their natural setting added to their outdoor experience (Lime and Cushwa 1969). The fact that many people are not deliberately seeking contact with wildlife in wilderness makes little difference; the incidental contact—the chance observation under natural conditions—can enrich immeasurably the many satisfactions that accrue from the overall wilderness experience. For some, even *danger* can be an important positive aspect of the wilderness experience, either by direct confrontation with dangerous wildlife and the elements, or simply by knowing that the possibility exists. Close encounters with grizzlies or even their sighting, for instance, make impressive stories around future campfires.

Can we quantify this lure of wilderness wildlife? Wildlife is a powerful focus for outdoor recreation activity by millions. A 1980 national survey of hunting, fishing, and other wildlife-associated recreation (USDI FWS 1982a) indicates the popularity of wildlife recreation. More than 42 million people fish and

more than 17 million people hunt in the United States. More than 93 million people, 55 percent of all Americans 16 years and older, engaged in some form of wildlife appreciation in 1980—and that does not count the millions who enjoy wildlife-related programs on television. Wildlife-related recreation is something of a national pastime associated with the expenditure of billions of dollars. Much of it is related, if only symbolically, to wilderness wildlife.

Methods of quantifying the economic value of outdoor recreation opportunities are developing, but factoring out the value of one element, such as wildlife, in the recreation equation is difficult. One approach, the *contingent valuation method* based on survey responses depicting a hypothetical increase or decrease in bighorn populations, estimated the value of the desert bighorn sheep herd in the Pusch Ridge Wilderness to be $2.2 million to $3.9 million (King and others 1986). Wildlife is also an important base for many outfitters and guides—and supports a multimillion-dollar-a-year industry in western states such as Idaho and Montana.

Even less measurable, yet no less real, is the value of wilderness wildlife as a reminder of the need for balance in a complex world dominated by unnatural forces and intense social pressures. The existence of wilderness and its associated wildlife, even if they are not visited, adds to the quality of life for millions of Americans.

Political Values of Wilderness Wildlife
Wildlife is the most powerful focus for environmental protection in the world. Two of the largest citizen environmental organizations in the United States are wildlife oriented (Hendee 1984). The largest, the National Wildlife Federation, with 5.8 million members (including its affiliates), increased nearly threefold between 1970 and the mid-1980s. The Audubon Society, with more than 500,000 members, grew more than threefold in membership during the same period. While wildlife is a common thread of these organizations, their interests go beyond wildlife and certainly include wilderness protection. They are a strong political force.

The USFS's 1977 public opinion survey in connection with the Roadless Area Review and Evaluation II (RARE II) asked the public what factors should be considered in proposing additional wilderness. The presence of *wilderness-associated wildlife*—that is, wildlife associated with wilderness in people's minds even if not in ecological fact—was a major factor suggested. In subsequent public comment, four of the 10 most frequent reasons for supporting wilderness designation for individual areas

were wildlife related (Hendee and others 1980).

Kellert's studies of Americans' attitudes toward wildlife indicate strong public support—especially by younger, more highly educated and urban-dwelling Americans—for protecting many wilderness wildlife species such as wolves, eagles, and grizzly bears. Kellert argues that wildlife makes direct and vicarious contributions to the American quality of life, especially where contact with and awareness of such wildlife are inextricably woven into the fabric of a region's heritage. For example, findings from his study of Minnesota residents' attitudes toward timber wolves revealed that people have *seen* and *heard* a timber wolf in the wild, and a majority reported having read an article about wolves within the previous year. The study revealed a strong "existence value" for wolves, and a majority of all publics except farmers agreed that (1) it was important to them to "know that wolves exist in Minnesota"; (2) "timber wolves are essential to maintaining the balance of nature"; and (3) they "would very much like to see a timber wolf in the wild" and "hear a wolf howl." A majority of all but farmers and trappers opposed the idea of "giving preference to people who derive a living from the land over protection of the timber wolf." On the other hand, relatively few residents were willing to protect timber wolves if it meant excluding people from northern areas of Minnesota (Kellert 1984).

Other findings complicate the wolf picture. A national population survey (Kellert 1985) indicated that wolves were among the least liked animals. Only 42 percent nationwide said they did not dislike wolves, but that figure jumped to 74 percent among Alaskans. Again, younger age, higher education, and especially knowledge of animals were correlated with a favorable disposition toward wolves. Kellert observes that affection for wolves has increased, and that this trend can be expected to continue, especially among residents of regions containing wolves that are not potentially impacted by them. Just as much of the public has grown to cherish the wilderness it once feared, it has also learned to value even those animals considered in earlier days as fair game for bounty hunters (Wauer and Supernaugh 1983).

In our participatory society, wilderness preservation could not have come to pass in the absence of a viable political constituency. While this constituency has been composed of many groups, for 100 years, wildlife supporters, including hunters and anglers, have played an important role, spurred by their recognition of wilderness as a fish and wildlife refuge.

It was the hunters of the Northwood Walton Club, and the outdoor magazine, *Forest and Stream*,

who took the lead in the pioneer New York State campaign that succeeded in setting aside the Adirondacks Forest Preserve in 1885. The major 132-million-acre expansion of U.S. national forests came during the presidency of Teddy Roosevelt, a founder of the Boone and Crockett Club—a big-game hunting club—who believed forest conservation and game conservation to be synonomous. It was the Boone and Crockett Club that urged the passage of the Yellowstone Park Act of 1894 which was designed in part to protect Yellowstone wildlife from poachers and thus established the precedent of the national parks as game preserves (Reiger 1975; Trefethen 1975). Preservation of wildlife and wildlands was not born in universities, legislative halls, or urban coffee shops, but around hunters' campfires and the potbellied stoves of fishing cabins. Teddy Roosevelt gave the conservation movement its first real life, and he did it while oiling his rifle (Posewitz 1981). When a wilderness bill was first introduced in Congress in 1956, among its charter supporters were the National Wildlife Federation and the Wildlife Management Institute (Mercure and Ross 1970).

To be sure, sports enthusiasts are not always supportive of a particular classified wilderness. They exhibit considerable concern about the ultimate levels of hunting and fishing to be allowed in wilderness, and there is concern that classification of wilderness may restrict wildlife management for game production. These concerns demonstrate the need for a basic philosophy incorporating wildlife into a wilderness framework—a philosophy emphasizing wildlife uses carried out in a manner consistent with wilderness values.

WILDLIFE-RELATED PROBLEMS IN WILDERNESS MANAGEMENT

The need to manage *human uses and influences* to maintain wilderness naturalness and solitude extends to wilderness wildlife, as the Wildlife Management Institute stressed (1975, pp. 6, 24):

> Man and his activities can so interrupt wilderness wildlife's natural cycles and systems that only through deliberate intervention can mankind assure the survival of key species of wildlife. America can retain and expand its rich Wilderness wildlife heritage only if it applies scientifically sound facts to the management of all species and if its citizens harmonize their activities with the systems of Wilderness.

Some of the most difficult wilderness management issues involve wildlife, because classified wilderness is always part of a larger federal agency jurisdiction—and these agencies all have wildlife-management missions and traditions that predate the wilderness acts. The situation is further complicated by the legal tradition dating back to the Magna Carta that puts most fish and wildlife under state authority; that authority is also recognized by the wilderness acts. There are differences of opinion about how far a state's legal authority extends to federal lands, but a 1976 Supreme Court decision (*Kleppe vs. State of New Mexico*) upheld the right of Congress to legislate control of wild horses and burros on federal lands. In 1990 in Alaska, the federal government claimed control of all wildlife on federal public lands (Muth and Glass 1989).

Management of wilderness wildlife is affected by a variety of constraints that have the potential to conflict with the goals of naturalness and solitude set forth in the wilderness acts. For example, hunting and fishing are established activities in all national forest and Bureau of Land Management (BLM) wildernesses and in some national wildlife refuges and national parks. Legislation following the 1964 Wilderness Act requires preservation of certain threatened or endangered species in some wildernesses, even using artificial devices and alterations if necessary. Furthermore, ecological trends stimulated by previous management, such as the unnatural influence on vegetation resulting from the exclusion of fire, may be reflected dramatically in current wilderness wildlife populations.

MULTIPLE AGENCIES AND MISSIONS

In keeping with its refuge tradition, the Fish and Wildlife Service (FWS) wilderness management guidelines allow wilderness areas to be closed to all public use if such use has been determined to be incompatible with refuge objectives. In keeping with its multiple-use mission, the USFS wilderness management guidelines require that national forest lands adjacent to wilderness be administered in accordance with multiple-use guidelines. Buffer strips of undeveloped wildland, for instance, will not be maintained to provide a *de facto* extension of wilderness. In keeping with its long-time practice, the National Park Service (NPS) wilderness management policies encourage wildlife population control through natural predation; public hunting is generally not permitted, but fishing is allowed. The discrepancies between different agencies' policies concerning wildlife are extensive.

The differences in wilderness management policy and approaches among agencies are shaped and guided by their ideological biases, historical experiences, and underlying missions (Alston 1983). Perhaps most administrative practices in wilderness will never be universally understood, agreed upon, nor endorsed by all sectors of the general public or federal land managers. Nevertheless, the growing professionalization of wilderness management, reflected by completion of wilderness management plans, academic training, the effects of training workshops, and contact with the "wilderness" publics, is narrowing the differences among agency policies and management approaches.

Recognition of the varying legal missions of the four wilderness management agencies is basic to understanding wilderness wildlife management possibilities and constraints. Each of the four federal wilderness managing agencies—the USFS, the NPS, the FWS, and the BLM—owes its existence and derives its missions from particular national needs and trade-offs expressed through various congressional acts. Each agency responds to a different set of interest groups. Each has different philosophical traditions, a particular management legacy, and a different balance of disciplines among its professional personnel. These are important influences that directly and subtly shape management policy for wilderness within each agency. However, wilderness and wilderness wildlife management are subordinate to other pressing concerns in all agencies. Money is scarce for wilderness management and in even shorter supply for wilderness wildlife management.

U.S. Forest Service
The USFS, while legally committed to multiple use, which includes wilderness, has important timber production responsibilities that are a central mission of the agency and shape its staffing, budgeting, and management priorities. Under its resource use legacy, the USFS supports wilderness preservation, but has been more cautious about it than many wilderness enthusiasts have desired (Robinson 1975). However, recent changes and a "new perspectives" movement in the agency suggest more support for the future. Wilderness management on the national forests is also complicated by geographic and administrative dispersal. A wilderness may also abut other wilderness, a national park, and state and private lands. A designated USFS wilderness may encompass multiple ranger districts and two or more national forests, each of which has nonwilderness lands that absorb much of the management's attention. For example, the Frank Church-River of No Return Wilderness is

administered by USFS administrative regions, six different national forests, and 12 ranger districts. Such dispersal presents a communication and management challenge. The boundaries may signify different local philosophies affecting management policy, including wilderness wildlife management.

National Park Service
The NPS, created in 1916, has focused on preservation of native animal life as one of the specific purposes of the parks. This intention is expressed in a frequently quoted passage of the NPS Act of August 25, 1916:

> which purpose is to conserve the scenery and the natural historic objects and the *wildlife* [emphasis added] therein and to provide for the enjoyment of the same in such manner and by such means as will leave them unimpaired for the enjoyment of future generations.

The newly formed NPS developed a philosophy of wildlife protection, which in that era was indeed the most obvious and immediate need in wildlife conservation. Thus, the parks became refuges, the animal populations were protected from hunting, and their habitats were protected from fire, which in some areas turned out to be detrimental to some species. For a time, predators were controlled to protect the "good" animals from the "bad" ones (Leopold and others 1968). The net preservationist policy frequently produced gross overpopulation problems in browsing species such as deer and elk (fig. 11.2).

NPS policy has evolved to emphasize the protection of natural *processes*, with purposeful management of plant and animal communities as an

Fig. 11.2. Some animals, such as elk and deer, may migrate seasonally in and out of wilderness, which can lead to insoluable management problems. These elk graze on summer range in the upper Madison River drainage on the Gallatin National Forest near Yellowstone National Park, MT. Photo courtesy of W. E. Steuerwald, USFS.

essential step in preserving wildlife resources, but without bias in favor of particular species or climax vegetation. Wildlife are now managed to keep them wild, a change from earlier times in many locations. Recreational use poses problems, however, and determining the tolerance levels of wildlife species to people is critical in managing wildlife as a visual resource in wilderness areas (Cooper and Shaw 1979).

Fish and Wildlife Service
The FWS manages several different types of areas; most of the agency's wilderness and Wilderness Study Areas (WSAs) are in the National Wildlife Refuge System. There are many different views of what that system is or should be. This was illustrated in the Leopold Committee report (Leopold and others 1969, p. 32):

> Most duck hunters view the (waterfowl) refuges as an essential cog in the perpetuation of their sport. Some see the associated public shooting grounds as the actual site of their sport. A few resent the concentration of birds in the refuges and propose general hunting to drive the birds out. Bird watchers and protectionists look upon the refuges as places to enjoy the spectacle of masses of water birds, without disturbance by hunters or by private landowners; they resent any hunting at all. State fish and game departments are pleased to have the Federal budget support wildlife areas in the states but want maximum public hunting and fishing on these areas. The General Accounting Office in Washington seems to view the refuges as units of a duck factory that should produce a fixed quota of ducks per acre or a bird-days per duck stamp dollar. The Fish and Wildlife Service recognizes the primary importance of protecting and perpetuating migratory waterfowl, as subjects of hunting and as objects of great public interest.

National wildlife refuges usually have been developed from areas misused in the past through draining, lumbering, burning, or overgrazing. They often need restoration to become first-class wildlife habitat. Such refurbishing is accomplished mainly with dams, dikes, and fences, and through farming programs to produce special and supplemental wildlife foods. Management may employ a wide variety of practices, including irrigation systems, regulated livestock grazing (to provide habitat for more successful wildlife use), soil conservation, forestry, and rough-fish control. Most of these practices obviously conflict with the natural processes sought for wilderness. By 1985, about 22 percent of the land administered by the FWS was classified as wilderness, ensuring that wilderness management would be a major activity for the agency in the future. Neverthe-

less, the wildlife protection legacy of the FWS will likely continue to shape a fairly restrictive view of human activity in wildernesses under their management.

Bureau of Land Management
The BLM administers more acreage of public lands than all the national parks, wildlife refuges, and national forests combined. The Federal Land Policy and Management Act of 1976 (FLPMA, P.L. 94-579) gave wilderness management authority to BLM and called for (1) an inventory, within 15 years, of roadless areas 5,000 acres or larger and roadless islands, and (2) recommendations as to their suitability for wilderness classification. Congress has already established 25 wildernesses, totaling more than 360,000 acres, and will undoubtedly classify many millions of acres of BLM land as wilderness in the 1990s (see chaps. 5 and 6). In the interim, the agency is committed to managing such lands to preserve their wilderness character until Congress takes final action (see chap. 8). Thus, the BLM is assured of major wilderness management responsibilities.

Reconciling wilderness wildlife problems will be a large part of this challenge for an agency with vast range resources and their associated traditional emphasis on commercial livestock grazing, an accommodating view of predator control to support grazing uses, and a receptive posture toward use of minerals and timber. In particular, BLM wilderness managers may face difficult conflicts arising from competition for forage between domestic livestock and wilderness wildlife.

All this is not meant as criticism of the four federal wilderness managing agencies. It merely helps to explain the different influences in the "culture" of each agency that will be reflected in its wilderness management emphasis and directions for wildlife. That there are divergent wilderness wildlife management policies and practices may be good. A practice possible to introduce only under existing USFS traditions later may prove acceptable in national park wilderness, while the BLM may borrow a technique from an adjacent wildlife refuge. Conversely, a form of wilderness management tolerated by one agency on one area may seem unacceptable to another and will not automatically be copied throughout the NWPS. The NWPS, like any ecosystem, can profit from this diversity, if it is within the overall framework of the Wilderness Act. Wilderness wildlife management must make the best of the diversity inherent in multiple-agency responsibilities, while at the same time continuing to search for consistency in wilderness wildlife management standards.

Wilderness wildlife management policies of the

four wilderness management agencies are summarized in Appendix E, which illustrates specific differences as well as the general similarities in overall management direction.

FUNDING CONSTRAINTS

Wilderness management is not adequately funded to meet its goals of preserving naturalness and solitude in the face of demands for public use. The result has been an attitude in all wilderness agencies that wilderness management is low priority, since it is concerned with relatively inaccessible areas getting light use compared to other lands. That has meant that, in times of scarce federal money, such management may be postponed. Money for wilderness wildlife management is particularly scarce—and fiscal realities dictate possibilities. In some cases, too, using the "minimum tool" approach to management in wilderness may be more expensive than a mechanized approach routinely applied outside of wilderness. The FWS requires that wilderness management plans include a brief description of the annual cost in funds and manpower to administer the wilderness area over and above normal refuge operations (USDI FWS 1982b).

CONTRADICTORY LEGISLATION

Wilderness management operates under a number of constraints, including some directly related to wildlife. The hierarchy of wilderness management direction includes: the Wilderness Act of 1964 (P.L. 88-577); the Code of Federal Regulations that interpret and clarify that act; national wilderness management policies of the administering agencies; plans for jurisdictions (such as regions or forests) that include wilderness; and individual wilderness management plans that specify how national direction will be applied on the ground. Other laws, such as the Endangered Species Act of 1973 (P.L. 93-205) and the Clean Air Act Amendments of 1977 (P.L. 95-95) further constrain management. In some cases, laws classifying individual areas into the NWPS specify how particularly controversial wilderness management issues will be handled (see chap. 4), and these issues often affect fish and wildlife.

For example, mining, legally allowed in USFS, BLM, and some NPS and FWS wildernesses, could have a substantial impact on wilderness wildlife. Unavoidable sedimentation in streams would affect fish, and the legally allowed means of access could disturb wildlife. Minimizing these impacts requires careful regulation and monitoring of legal mineral

extraction within a wilderness management framework supported by strict environmental standards.

Grazing by horses, goats, sheep, and cattle is allowed by the Wilderness Act in some national forest and potential BLM wilderness. Likewise, the Colorado Wilderness Act of 1980 (P.L. 96-560) mandated guidelines for grazing of livestock in new wilderness areas in that state, and those guidelines have been adopted in several subsequent state bills (Browning and others 1988). Grazing can have substantial impact on wildlife in those areas. This commodity use also brings pressures for predator control in the affected areas. Water impoundments exist in some wilderness areas and can be established by presidential order in others—with obvious local impact on the naturalness of fish and wildlife distributions.

Endangered species protection illustrates the problem of conflicting legislative direction. The Wilderness Act limits managerial freedom to manipulate vegetative cover to perpetuate, improve, or alter an area's value to wildlife. On the other hand, the Endangered Species Act directs agencies to make sure no actions are taken that would "jeopardize the continued existence of any endangered species or threatened species or result in the destruction or adverse modification of habitat of such species which is determined by the Secretary . . . to be critical" (P.L. 93-205, 7a), no matter where they are, including in wilderness. Thus, conforming to the Endangered Species Act may require management techniques (e.g., vegetative manipulation) that would otherwise be restricted in wilderness. For example, in wilderness on the Cape Romain National Wildlife Refuge off the coast of South Carolina, raccoons prey on the eggs of the endangered sea turtle. A raccoon trapping program to protect the sea turtle, an unnatural alteration of raccoon numbers, requires periodic motorized access to tend traps.

Endangered species protection in wilderness may require actions beyond the usual approach of allowing natural processes to work their slow pace. For example, the taking of condor eggs to be hatched and raised in captivity is not a natural solution, but it has been applied as a necessary approach to save the condor (Campbell 1984). One of the most difficult philosophical questions surrounding a species unable to compete, and thus facing imminent extinction, is whether this is a result of natural processes which, in wilderness, should continue. Such philosophy is moot, however, because the Endangered Species Act requires actions to protect and encourage the recovery of threatened and endangered species. Such efforts may, at times, require practices normally not allowed in wilderness. For example, when tanks to provide

water for desert bighorn sheep dry up and the only means of supplying water is by trucking it, then such motorized access is used.

The Historic Preservation Act of 1966 (P.L. 89-665) and related executive orders also result in activities that may be contrary to NWPS intent—such as preserving or refurbishing historic structures that would otherwise be removed or allowed to deteriorate. Examples are cabins in some western wildernesses and lighthouses in wilderness on East Coast wildlife refuge islands and capes. If such attractions draw excessive recreational use, wilderness wildlife may be impacted in the surrounding locality.

Wilderness in Alaska represents a special case because of special provisions in the Alaska National Interest Lands Conservation Act of 1980 (ANILCA, P.L. 96-487). Following years of debate on ANILCA, Congress established special provisions that make wilderness areas in Alaska different in some ways from those in the lower 48 states. In general, the units are open to most "customary" uses unless specifically closed following public hearings. Motorized access by plane, motorboat, or snowmobile is guaranteed to private inholdings such as homesteads, mining claims, trade centers, management cabins, and native lands. Hunting, trapping, and fishing may continue in wilderness, even in some designated national park units, and temporary facilities, equipment, and sometimes motorized access directly related to such activities are allowed.

The extent to which wilderness in Alaska will be different depends on the evolution of wilderness management policies and practices as agencies begin developing management plans. It will take many years to develop a coherent set of administrative practices consistent with all the federal and state statutes, regulations, and policies to apply to wilderness and subsistence uses in Alaska. The USFS established a special cooperative research effort to clarify the costs, benefits, and social and resource impacts associated with subsistence uses (Muth 1985). Two key issues are who should qualify as a subsistence taker, and how the *need* for subsistence taking should be established—questions of pressing interest to sports enthusiasts already concerned about impacts on goose (and other wildlife) populations (Williamson 1985).

SPACE FACTORS

Few wilderness areas are big and diverse enough to meet the year-round needs of all the fish and wildlife populations that use a wilderness. Larger wilderness wildlife species, such as elk and grizzly bears (fig. 11.3),

require vast areas to which wilderness boundaries may not be related. Certainly most of the wilderness areas in the East are too small to contain the ranges of many wilderness species (Hendee 1986). Can adjacent habitat be managed, in such cases, to develop natural boundaries that will contain and protect the animals? If so, what is the carrying capacity of the core area?

The FWS's Grizzly Bear Recovery Plan recognizes that grizzly conservation cannot be accomplished on a wilderness-by-wilderness basis because a bear can cover 1,000 square miles in a lifetime of normal activity. Hence, the plan attempts to coordinate management efforts in the two remaining viable grizzly habitats in the lower 48 states—the Yellowstone ecosystem in Wyoming, Idaho, and Montana, and the Northern Continental Divide ecosystem in Montana, Idaho, and Washington (Servheen 1982). The plan requires coordinated management in the wilderness areas and adjacent wildlands with roads that serve other purposes as well.

Fig.11.3. The grizzly bear is one of several species of wildlife that require large tracts of undisturbed habitat. Most wildernesses are too small, or boundaries do not coincide with the natural movements of such animals, thus complicating effective management. Photo courtesy of the FWS.

INTERDEPENDENCIES

Most wildernesses are ecological enclaves subject to direct or indirect modification by activities and conditions in the surrounding area (Leopold and others 1968). *No wilderness exists in a vacuum.* It is always surrounded by and/or abuts something that can markedly affect wilderness management for wildlife within the area. The controversy about management of elk in northwestern Wyoming illustrates how complex these interrelationships can become.

Adding fuel to the controversy is a supplemental feeding program on the refuge. Begun in 1912 to offset loss of winter habitat, the feeding program became a fixed ritual. Elk jostled to be first in line at the daily arrival of the hay sled. Tourists rode among them on sleighs. The elk's independence and fear of humans, their wildness, may have been compromised according to some observers. Opponents say the feeding program interferes with the elk's natural behavior and question whether it is subsidizing the public hunt (Wood 1984). Supporters say reduction

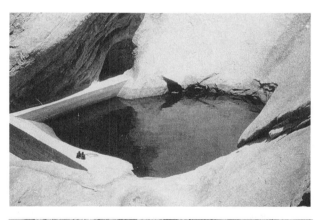

of the elk's traditional winter range and disruption of traditional migration patterns make the feeding a necessary evil, without which it would be impossible to maintain the total elk population at numbers half the historical level. The refuge which provides only 25 percent of the historical winter range that once supported elk numbers as high as 25,000, today is managed for a third as many. Sometimes external pressures on wilderness result from established rights and uses that predate an area's classification and are thus continued under provisions of the Wilderness Act.

The National Elk Range was created in Jackson Hole, Wyoming, in 1912 to perpetuate an elk population whose winter range was largely expropriated for cattle ranching. Elk herds wintering at the refuge come from summer range, much of it wilderness, in three locations: Grand Teton and Yellowstone National Parks and Bridger-Teton National Forest. Those migrating from Yellowstone and Bridger-Teton moved to the refuge through the forest, where they were heavily hunted, resulting in a decline in the populations. But the elk population in Grand Teton began to grow after the park was enlarged in 1950.

To restore the balance among the herds, a cooperative agreement among the relevant federal agencies and the State of Wyoming provides for a hunting season in part of the Grand Teton Park designed to reduce the herd to former levels. The policy made Grand Teton the only national park in the lower 48 states where hunting was permitted, and it continues to draw heated opposition.

For example, although the Cabeza Prieta Wildlife Refuge in Arizona is relatively free of human disturbance, a variety of impacts that compromise its wilderness character was retained when the area was classified as wilderness. Water developments

Fig.11.4. In some national wildlife refuge wilderness, legislation establishing the refuge or game range (and superseding wilderness designation within it) may call for management measures to ensure the survival of particular species. A charco rock tank catchment (top) in the proposed Cabeza Prieta Game Range Wilderness, AZ, helps ensure the survival of desert bighorn. A "guzzler" (left) and a water flue (right), both in the Desert National Wildlife Range, NV, provide vital water for wildlife. Photos courtesy of the FWS.

(fig. 11.4), including wells with windmills and rock tank catchments, are considered necessary for the conservation of desert bighorn sheep and Sonoran pronghorn antelope. Military operations at the Williams Bombing and Gunnery Range include air-to-air gunnery and missile firing over the refuge. The Border Patrol and the Agricultural Research Service both require road access on occasion. A program of coyote poisoning was implemented, ostensibly to protect the native bighorn. The area would not seem very wild to the conquistadors who named it, but it is some of the wildest land left in the Southwest. Such compromises with external influences were necessary to honor overriding legal commitments to obtain legal wilderness classification for this area.

In other cases, pressure to protect adjacent areas has caused suppression of natural processes in wilderness areas. Windstorms, wildfire, outbreaks of disease and insects, floods, droughts, avalanches, volcanic activity, and the activities of predators are among nature's tools for creating and maintaining diverse wilderness habitats and wildlife populations. Wilderness wildlife species are particularly responsive to changes following fire, insects, disease, and predator controls. The absence of fire has impacts on those species that require early stages of plant succession. For example, both structural and floristic characteristics of the vegetation are changing in Oregon's Eagle Cap Wilderness in response to the effects of prolonged fire suppression (Cole 1981). Wildlife species are inevitably affected by such changes. Even in desert ecosystems, where the role of fire has not been studied as intensively, it is likely that fire benefits bighorn sheep habitat as it benefits the habitat of other wildlife species (Krausman and others 1979). An area's wildlife populations reflect the successional stages of its habitat. Sometimes natural forces may need to be simulated to maintain the historic diversity of habitat—and thus the wildlife that once prevailed—which is still a very controversial idea.

Wilderness may host insects and diseases intolerable in surrounding lands, and the introduction or control of pests and diseases in adjacent areas can disturb the naturalness of nearby wilderness. For example, white pine blister rust, an introduced pest, has seriously reduced wilderness stands of whitebark pine that provide food for grizzly bears. DDT spraying to inhibit spruce budworm in areas adjacent to what is now the proposed Yellowstone Wilderness produced widespread mortality among mountain whitefish, trout, and longnose suckers in the Yellowstone River (Cape 1969). The fish kills provided data that were noticeable and measurable, but they may have reflected damage to the ecosystem ultimately far more serious and widespread.

Predator control not only suppresses the targeted species, but can also lead to an irruption in the prey population. On the other hand, predator control on public and private lands outside wilderness can push target animals (such as wolves) into the preserved area, where they may make a larger impact on their prey. For example, if cougar are more prevalent in western wilderness because of harassment on surrounding lands and a preference for solitude, they will have a bigger impact on deer populations in the wilderness.

PEOPLE-WILDLIFE CONFLICTS

Recreational use of wilderness has increased faster than most other kinds of outdoor recreation during the past few decades, and, although declining in recent years, visitation is unevenly distributed and usually concentrated in summer seasons and along trails at particularly popular locations (see chap. 14). In a national survey of wilderness managers representing 269 separate units, the majority said their most significant problem was local resource degradation and lack of solitude resulting from concentrated use (Washburne and Cole 1983). Overuse in particular areas is an increasing problem in wilderness, even where total use is not an issue. At heavily used locations, conflicts can occur among users pursuing different activities, many of which involve wildlife.

Other human impacts on wilderness wildlife are more direct. One study revealed that on 23 million acres of wilderness in the national parks and national forests of the lower 48 states, nearly 20,000 miles of trails sustained an annual average of 468 visitor-days per trail mile, with use twice that high in the more crowded Northeast and South (Washburne 1981). Such intrusions, while essential to much wilderness use, pose a threat of wildlife disturbance.

Those fishing at a high lake may resent the intrusion of hikers swimming or skipping stones along the shore. Human impacts on naturalness of wildlife can be highly visible. In wilderness where people habitually camp, such species as chipmunks, jays, mice, and bears may become habitual scroungers of food and garbage. On the other hand, the presence of people is likely to reduce opportunities to see truly wild animals. For example, in the Gallatin Range of Yellowstone National Park, an inverse relationship between intensity of human use and the frequency of wildlife observation has been reported (Chester 1976).

Washburne and Cole (1983) investigated the extent to which wilderness managers perceived the impact of recreation on wildlife as a problem. Effects

on large nonpredatory mammals and birds are most common, especially in NPS areas, although managers believed impacts were frequent on birds in FWS areas, and on large mammals in BLM areas. Though little direct information is available on wildlife impacts of human use (Ream 1980), the frequently reported human impacts on vegetation and soil that lead to erosion, compaction, and bog formation may ultimately impinge on wildlife. Just how such impacts occur and how serious they are offer good topics for research.

Whatever their form, wilderness uses have the potential to degrade wildlife habitat and affect wildlife habits. Harassment of wildlife, intentional or not, can seriously disrupt feeding, breeding, and rearing and lead to wildlife displacement. In turn, wilderness wildlife can threaten human safety, as indicated by the people-grizzly conflict in U.S. and Canadian national parks (Craighead and Craighead 1971; Gilbert 1976; Herrero 1985). In Alaskan wilderness, the presence of the brown bear will deter many potential users. How to—and even whether to—make wilderness safe for both native wildlife species and human visitors is a topic often discussed in wilderness management. Confrontations between humans and grizzlies—even the possibility of confrontations—frequently result in bear disposal or relocation. Because wild bears are less confrontational than bears habituated to humans, keeping bears wild is a priority in the interest of both. Current strategies include restricted visitor travel or access near known hazards, such as a grizzly feeding on carrion, a backcountry campsite recently visited by a bear, or a family of bears spending considerable time near a trail (Martinka 1982). For example, in 1984, nearly one-half million acres of Yellowstone National Park and many wilderness and backcountry campsites were temporarily closed or restricted under new regulations to protect the grizzly population. Those restrictions have been controversial and only partially successful, and officials are experimenting with other solutions.

Human pressure on wildlife can be subtle. In the case of the mountain sheep, for example, Geist (1975) theorizes that knowledge of home range is passed on from generation to generation through the dominant rams. Thus, if human pressure forces a sheep population out of its range, and especially if the big rams are lost, knowledge of the home range will be lost and the sheep population will be adversely affected. Even merely startling a wild animal repeatedly causes it to expend additional energy, which it then must replace by consuming more food, if available. In a rigorous northern environment, where

neither the animals nor the range can afford the extra stress, the effects may be very harmful indeed (Geist 1971a, 1971b). In the Sangre de Cristo Range in Colorado, human pressures have forced mountain sheep into lambing ranges at higher elevations, where extended bad weather can lead to an 80-percent incidence of pneumonia in lambs and a steady decline in the population of the herd (Woodward and others 1974). Likewise, human disturbance is suspected as a limiting factor for bighorns in the Sierra Nevadas (Dunaway 1971) and in Arizona (Etchberger and others 1989; Krausman and others 1979). Krausman's studies (Krausman and Leopold 1983; Krausman and others 1989) are increasingly documenting the ways in which bighorns are impacted by human activity and settlement.

Few studies have looked at the effects of unintentional harassment of wild animals, the major source of the problem being outdoor recreationists who innocently produce stressful situations for wildlife. As examples of such harassment, Ream (1980) lists (1) the birdwatcher who pulls down a tree limb to look in a nest, or photographers who cut the surrounding vegetation so they can get an unobstructed photograph of a bird nest; (2) backpackers who camp near a critical waterhole or mineral lick, unknowingly inhibiting wildlife use of the area; and (3) cross-country skiers who ski too closely to deer or elk restricted by deep snow and exhausted by lack of food, causing the animals stress and unnecessary expenditure of vital energy. These and many other situations may result in excitement, disruption of essential activities, severe exertion, displacement, and possibly death. Often impacts are not recognized until the damage is irreversible. To complicate matters, habitat areas heavily used by wildlife are often also choice locations for human trails and campsites. For example, pellet counts indicate that few animals defecate on steep, north-facing slopes with prodigious quantities of down timber, or in "dog-hair" lodgepole stands; however, at the first open flat spot, the ground is invariably liberally sprinkled with pellets, indicating where the animals spend most of their time (Ream 1980).

Hunting

Hunting regulations vary widely within the current NWPS. Hunting is not allowed in national park wilderness outside of Alaska, except for some in Grand Teton National Park, nor in some national wildlife refuge wilderness. But the same wildlife that use such wilderness part of the year may be hunted when they migrate seasonally outside the protected areas. Hunting is allowed in USFS and BLM wil-

derness and in some national wildlife refuge wilderness—a questionable practice to people who fear its impact on naturalness, but not to hunters and organizations that supported the Wilderness Act because of this provision.

Disagreement exists about whether recreational hunting is consistent with the wilderness concept, or even with the "naturalness" required by the Wilderness Act. Proponents argue that wilderness hunting is a traditional, ecologically pure experience, in which humans can perceive themselves as predators under the most natural conditions. Large numbers of hunters and wildlife managers feel that the finest quality hunting experiences are found in the opportunities to track and stalk game in wilderness without artificial diversions such as roads, clearcuts, or cultivated crops, and to blend with the wildest setting possible on a quiet vigil during the hunt. For them, hunting is a wilderness-dependent activity.

On the other hand, outspoken antipathy to hunting, anywhere, is common (Applegate 1973; Hendee and Potter 1976). This attitude regards nearly any killing of wild creatures as destructive and inhumane. For example, a vast majority of Illinois adults answering a recent survey favored wilderness concepts and policies, even agreeing that cattle grazing should be permitted. But, 80 percent said "hunting should be prevented" in wilderness areas (Young 1980).

Some of the issues are value based and are unlikely ever to be resolved to everyone's satisfaction. Proponents say hunting and fishing are more than a quest for game; they provide a variety of human satisfactions (Hendee 1974). In the wilderness, many of these satisfactions may be strongly tied to an overall wilderness experience. For the hunter, wilderness provides a certain perception of quality hunting, a place where wildland challenges the hunter and provides the hunted some advantage, enhancing the concept of sportsmanship along the way (Posewitz 1981).

But the same appeals of solitude and an unaltered environment that attract hunters to wilderness also draw nonhunters, and for many of them, the sights and sounds of hunting, or even the knowledge that animals are being hunted in the area part of the year, may detract from the wilderness experience. Other points of contention can be argued scientifically, but both sides have mobilized enough data to continue the controversy indefinitely. Among the issues:

1. *Is hunting needed to help regulate game populations?* Proponents believe hunting is needed to help keep game species from destroying habitat for themselves and other species in the absence of natural controls, and point out that healthy habitat is the key to healthy wildlife populations. Ungulates (deer, elk, moose), particularly, can eat the vegetation to the point where they reduce the habitat's capacity to support them. In some cases, herds have withstood heavy increases in hunting without population decline—elk in the Cache National Forest, for instance (Kimball and Wolfe 1974). In other cases, however, hunting pressure can cause significant population declines—the caribou in North America (Bergerud 1974) and the Pahsimeroi mountain goat herd in Idaho (Kuck 1977) are examples.

2. *Do human hunters take the place of predators that were part of primitive ecosystems but are frequently missing from modern wilderness?* The vertebrates most commonly absent, and which are difficult if not impossible to provide for, are the large carnivores—cougars, grizzlies, and wolves (Allen 1966). Proponents say human hunters can substitute for these natural predators. Opponents point out that natural predators tend to cull calves and old animals from herds, while human hunters often seek prime males. This poses important long-range questions about true naturalness in wilderness and the genetic integrity of game species and populations.

Geist (1971a, 1971b) has observed that prolonged and extensive ungulate hunting will alter the biology of the species affected. A four-year study in the Big Creek drainage of Idaho, in what is now the Frank Church-River of No Return Wilderness, showed that deer and elk killed by cougars were much more likely to be in poor condition than those killed by human hunters. The old and the young, not the prime specimens, were selected in natural predation (Hornocker 1970).

The key question is whether human predators apply a strong enough selective force to bring about genetic changes in the surviving population. And if so, to what end? Do the bighorn hunters harvest only the slow-witted, or do they kill the sentinel rams who are the custodians of the herds' traditions?

3. *Is hunting in wilderness consistent with the mandate to maintain wilderness areas in as natural a state as possible?* Unquestionably, heavy hunting affects animal behavior patterns and makes it more difficult to study natural behavior. Peek (1980) reports that hunting has influenced elk movement patterns in wilderness situations. Proponents, however, see hunting in wilderness as part of the natural state for which wilderness areas are established. The North American Wildlife Policy Committee noted (Allen 1973):

Traditionally, hunting as a total experience involves environmental satisfactions: room to roam, quiet, solitude. Hunting at its best can cultivate an increasing outdoor sophistication in the individual. He improves his knowledge and enjoyment of nature in all its aspects. He refines his sporting standards, including recognition that quality is poorly measured by the size of the bag.

Even among hunters themselves, there is disagreement about what *types of hunting experiences* are consistent with wilderness naturalness. Several western wildernesses permit temporary yet lavish camps, where outfitters can add a little comfort and convenience for clients who pay well for a wilderness hunt. Although this can facilitate wilderness opportunities for some, it dilutes the wilderness experience for others. Many wilderness managers are working with progressive outfitters to reduce the impacts of hunting camps and increase the overall "integrity" of wilderness hunting experiences.

There is also debate about the *level of hunting compatible with wilderness conditions.* The optimum level, one which would minimize disruption of population dynamics and behavior patterns, may be lower than the level allowed in nonwilderness (Peek 1986).

In conclusion, we must avoid the assumption that wildlife management policies for environments modified by people are all directly applicable to wilderness. Wilderness is unique as a relatively unaltered environment, and management that allows excessive

Fig. 11.5. Wilderness wildlife guidelines proposed in this book emphasize hunting and fishing as important wilderness recreation activities where they are biologically sound, legal, and carried out in the spirit of a wilderness experience. A proud hunter poses with a pack mule loaded with the meat and antlers of a bull elk. Photo courtesy of Robert C. Lucas, USFS.

human influences, no matter how well intended, is potentially irreversible. In wilderness, the goal is to allow natural processes and forces to work on animal populations, and provide for wildlife experiences featuring naturalness and solitude for humans.

At its best, in wilderness where it is legal, hunting can offer a popular and healthy outdoor recreational activity under quality conditions, *if* it is carried out under regulations that protect wilderness from overuse, perpetuate wildlife populations, and insure wilderness-dependent experiences (fig. 11.5).

Fishing

Wilderness fisheries are an important issue for resource managers because most recreational use of roadless areas centers on lakes and streams, particularly high lakes in western mountains (Brown and Schomaker 1974). At lakes in heavily used areas, the physical impact of human use is obvious and managers may try to manipulate the high lake fisheries to manage human use and impact. But studies of use at seven lakes in Washington's Alpine Lakes Wilderness (Hendee and others 1977) indicated that only about 40 percent of the visitors to the lakes actually fished; only 40 percent of the parties contained anglers and they fished an average of less than two hours per day; and 40 percent of them caught no fish. An equally important finding: nonanglers spent just as much time at the lakeshore as anglers. Other studies (Carpenter and Bowhis 1976; Hoagland 1973) and baseline data presented in chapter 13 confirm that, on the average, only about half the visitors to wilderness high lakes actually fish. Thus, any policy designed to relocate western wilderness visitors by regulating fishing can affect only a portion of total use. Of course, redistributing even part of the use may go a long way toward solving an overuse problem. In a wilderness such as the BWCAW, where fishing is a central attraction, fishing regulations could help to lessen substantially the impact from large motorboats that are traditional in the portions of the BWCAW open to motorized boating (Lucas 1965).

Clearly, fishing on wilderness waters is an important activity for many visitors (fig. 11.6). And for many, fishing, like hunting, can achieve its finest quality in wilderness. But fish management in wilderness is controversial, and may involve nonindigenous species (such as eastern brook trout that have been widely introduced to western high lakes), periodic aerial stocking of wilderness lakes, dams to keep streams flowing all summer, fish-spawning facilities, and heavy use of some wilderness sites by anglers. For example, the Desolation Wilderness in California has many small dams built to provide

Fig.11.6. Carried out in an appropriate style, fishing can be an important part of an overall wilderness experience. An angler tries his luck at Johnson Lake in the Anaconda-Pintler Wilderness, MT. Photo courtesy of W.E. Steuerwald, USFS.

flow in streams in late summer to sustain fishery.

Artificial stocking of wilderness lakes distorts the naturalness of the affected aquatic ecosystems, and the use of aircraft for stocking can invade the solitude of users. But fish stocking is strongly supported by many sports groups, and in the past, organizations such as the American Fisheries Society and the National Wildlife Federation have urged aerial stocking in national forest wilderness and stocking in national parks to restore fishing opportunities (Wallis 1976). Agency fish-stocking policies vary somewhat, as Appendix E indicates. USFS policy allows stocking native fish aimed at achieving quality fishing, under guidance of the area's wilderness management plan and using primitive transport; it permits aerial stocking only where it was an established practice before the area was added to the NWPS. The NPS policy allows fish stocking in wilderness only to reestablish native species, but not in naturally barren lakes; the FWS stocks only to restore native fish populations following human impact, not to increase recreational opportunities; BLM policy calls for stocking only where it was established before wilderness designation, with barren lakes considered case by case.

Research Needs and Opportunities

Because wilderness provides protected enclaves of wildlife and habitat, it offers outstanding opportunities for wildlife-related research. A major problem, however, is that wilderness classification imposes limitations on scientific research, as on any other activity, so as to limit impacts on the wilderness environment. All four wilderness agencies permit "collection of plants and animals for research purposes by qualified persons." The methods to be allowed for such collections may be restricted and approval granted on a case-by-case basis. One recent report stated that "virtually no basic biological research is being conducted in USFS wilderness because in its regulations the agency gives a rigid interpretation to the restrictions of the Wilderness Act" (Drabelle 1984, p. 26). Impositions on the wilderness environment for scientific investigations must be well justified, for they may be no less intrusive than impositions for other purposes. Hornocker (1978) has proposed an amendment to the Wilderness Act that would emphasize the importance of wildlife to the integrity of wilderness ecosystems and provide funding for using wilderness as a natural laboratory.

Other Human Impacts on Wildlife

Despite dedication to a natural condition, the main threats to designated wildernesses and their wildlife stem from humankind's direct and indirect intrusions and the scarcity of unaffected reserves.

Some *indirect human influences* are nearly global, affecting wilderness and nonwilderness alike. Atmospheric depositions, including acid rain, have impacted fisheries; air pollution has damaged vegetation and increased cloud cover with yet-to-be-defined impacts on vegetation regimes. Noise from airplane traffic, especially at low altitudes, may affect wildlife distributions and behavior when used to study animals such as mountain sheep (Krausman and Hervert 1983). Some chemical pollutants from pesticides and industry have accumulated in food chains, affecting wildlife even in designated wilderness.

Ecological influences of previous management practices, particularly fire protection, affect wilderness wildlife habitats and populations. Recreational uses and nonconforming but allowed uses, such as grazing and mining, can impact natural habitats and disturb wildlife populations (Ream 1980). In many areas, nonnative plants have been introduced, often from seeds found in feed used for recreational livestock.

Even the agencies' wilderness management efforts lead to intrusions, as managers make necessary compromises with naturalness to comply with requirements of the Wilderness Act (such as for mining and grazing), to balance competing uses (such as hunting, fishing, and recreation), and with administrative use to protect the wilderness resource. For example, a 1980 survey of 127 designated wilderness areas totaling about 15 million acres in the national forests, where wilderness management is generally the most restrictive, revealed the following human

impacts and activities: 50 shelters; 118 administrative sites (although 28 such sites had been eliminated since 1964); 806 outfitter camps, 76 of them with permanent facilities; 1,160 miles of new trail constructed in the previous five years; 729 grazing allotments to provide almost 400,000 animal-unit months of grazing for cattle, sheep, horses, and recreational livestock; 1,787 structural range improvements (such as fences, corrals, and water developments), 17 with motorized access permitted; 177 water controls or use structures; 1,242 helispots and 15 airfields open to public use; 561 mineral-leasing projects and 76 prospecting or operating plans, 29 with mechanized access pending (although 16 areas have been removed from mineral entry); and 308 approved projects using motorized or mechanical equipment for trail construction, administrative purposes, or other agency use during the previous three years.

In the preceding 10 years, 68 fish or wildlife habitat projects had also existed, 33 involving threatened or endangered species; 40 wildlife transplant projects; and 93 fish-stocking projects, 65 of them by aerial means. Most areas were open to hunting and fishing, with 110 known trapping operations and nine approved predator-control projects during the previous five years. Potentially serious in their impact on wilderness ecology were 12 weather modification projects, nine of them outside wilderness, but affecting it. Potentially beneficial to naturalness and wildlife was restoration of a more natural role for fire in 24 approved fire management areas—the remaining areas at that time had "suppression by 10 a.m." as the intended treatment of fire (Washburne and Cole 1983).

No wilderness exists in a vacuum; each wilderness is surrounded by or adjoins something that affects naturalness within the area. Perhaps the most pervasive influence is simply the kaleidoscope of human activity on the periphery that collectively can impact adjacent wilderness ecosystems. New highways or logging roads increase wilderness access; dams and irrigation developments change water regimes; winter resorts, subdivisions, control of pests and disease, predator control, agricultural crops, and weather modification will create subtle impacts on the adjacent wilderness.

These intrusions are why we have a NWPS—to ensure that the permeating influences of civilization are controlled short of displacing naturalness and solitude everywhere. Yet, these many influences remind us that even designated wilderness areas are not free from human disturbance. *It is only an illusion that we have stopped dilution of naturalness and solitude in designated wilderness areas; the challenge of the future is to manage these areas to minimize such loss.* The degree

of impact on wilderness naturalness probably varies with the size of each wilderness area, and the degree to which entire natural systems are included so as to insulate them from civilization by distance. Most wilderness areas are too small to encompass the annual movements of wide-ranging wildlife species such as the grizzly bear, wolf, and elk. Only a few designated wilderness areas or contiguous groups of areas outside Alaska contain a million acres or more, and most recent additions to the NWPS are small.

WILDERNESS MANAGEMENT OBJECTIVES FOR WILDLIFE

The purpose of this concluding section is to recommend objectives for wildlife in the NWPS and suggest guidelines for the wilderness wildlife management we see as necessary to meet those objectives. This is consistent with a basic theme of this book, that wilderness management must be directed at establishing clear management objectives for all aspects of wilderness—including fish and wildlife—spelled out in plans at all levels to guide management actions (see chap. 8).

Although details of wilderness management for wildlife will vary according to location and agency, the following broad objectives are applicable to the entire NWPS regardless of agency jurisdiction. These objectives are statements of conditions sought with respect to wildlife in wilderness; they serve as criteria for choosing and evaluating management policies and actions.

PROPOSED WILDERNESS MANAGEMENT OBJECTIVES FOR WILDLIFE

1. To seek natural distribution, numbers, population composition, and interaction of indigenous species of wildlife.
2. To allow natural processes, as far as possible, to control wilderness ecosystems and their wildlife.
3. To keep wildlife wild, with its behavior altered as little as possible by human influence.
4. To permit viewing, hunting, and fishing where such activities are (1) biologically sound, (2) legal, and (3) carried out in the spirit of a wilderness experience.
5. To favor the protection and restoration of threatened and endangered species dependent on wilderness conditions whenever appropriate.
6. To seek the least possible degradation of the qualities that make for wilderness—naturalness, solitude, and absence of permanent visible evidence of human activity—within the constraints of all overriding legislation applicable to wildlife in a particular wilderness.

WILDERNESS WILDLIFE MANAGEMENT GUIDELINES

To achieve these proposed objectives, a number of management guidelines are recommended. In some cases, the proposed direction merely applies the wilderness management principles set forth in chapter 7. Although the following guidelines suggest direction for wildlife management in wilderness, they do not displace the book's overriding theme that a wilderness philosophy or ethic, based on an appreciation of all affected values, is the criterion for all wilderness management actions. Only *necessary actions* to achieve objectives set forth in wilderness management plans are justified, and they must employ the *minimum methods* and techniques required.

1. *Respect overriding legislation.* An obvious requirement of wilderness management for wildlife is to comply with the different laws that apply in classified wilderness under the jurisdiction of different agencies. The Wilderness Act states (P.L. 88-577, Secs. 4a and b):

> The purposes of this Act are hereby declared to be *within and supplemental to the purposes for which national forests and units of the national park and national wildlife refuge systems are established and administered.* Except as otherwise provided in this Act, each agency administering any area designated as wilderness shall be responsible for preserving the wilderness character of the area *and shall so administer such area for such other purposes for which it may have been established as also to preserve its wilderness character* (emphasis added).

The only direct reference to wildlife in the Act states that "Nothing in this Act shall be construed as affecting the jurisdiction or responsibilities of the several states with respect to wildlife and fish in the national forests" (P.L. 88-577, Sec. 4d).

The most obvious examples of such jurisdiction and responsibilities are those that permit hunting in national forest, BLM, and some national wildlife refuge wildernesses, but not as a general rule in national park wildernesses. In certain situations, hunting has been allowed in individual national parks to control excessive animal populations that threaten their own habitat and that of other animals.

Within some units of the National Wildlife Refuge System classified or proposed as wilderness, superseding legal rights also override specific wilderness purposes. These refuges were specifically established to preserve habitat for particular wildlife species, and some management activities that seem inappropriate in wilderness may be necessary to protect those species and their habitats. For example, the Red Rock Lakes National Wildlife Refuge in Montana, much of which is wilderness, was established mainly for trumpeter swans, and dams and floating nest platforms are used to manage the swans. As mentioned before, in the Cabeza Prieta National Wildlife Refuge, specific and prior rights granted for other purposes (such as Border Patrol and Williams Gunnery Range) must be honored. Similarly, state wildlife agencies pursuing their legal right to manage the fishery resource have stocked national forest wilderness lakes.

Overriding legal requirements impinges on wildlife more than on any other aspect of wilderness. For example, the ANILCA, Sec. 1315(6), allows for fisheries development, including hatcheries, in USFS wilderness in Alaska. Wilderness management for wildlife must be tailored to the unavoidable constraints placed by laws on the administrative agency concerned, while embracing the broad principles of the Wilderness Act. It is extremely important that communication prevail among the wilderness managing agencies, state fish and wildlife agencies, and wildlife conservation groups, so that all concerned can at least acknowledge where they disagree on wilderness wildlife management issues, interpretations of the law, and advisable policy. This is a continuing challenge, particularly critical as it relates to different purposes, philosophies, and perspectives of state fish and wildlife agencies, as compared to those of the federal wilderness management agencies.

2. *Allow natural processes to shape wilderness habitat.* Classified wilderness is a place where nature rolls the dice, and the resulting naturalness, whatever its characteristics, is wilderness. Artificial habitat manipulations that are desirable for fish and wildlife management on nonwilderness lands and waters are not consistent with either the Wilderness Act or the wilderness ethic that should guide its implementation. When there are legal exceptions to the natural process criterion, the most *natural practices and tools* should be used in a manner exerting the *minimum impact* on wilderness naturalness and solitude.

Wilderness means *natural.* Vegetation should reflect natural conditions, substantially unaltered by people and their influence. Lakes and streams should reflect undisturbed watersheds and channels. Animal life should approach natural numbers and species; at some times and places this will mean reduction or loss of some wildlife populations. The principal task facing wilderness managers is to assure the conditions that permit natural processes to operate freely. Where it is clear that human actions have compromised natural processes, the manager may have to

mimic or simulate natural processes, for example, by eliminating exotic species or introducing fire where it has been unnaturally suppressed. But this should be done as briefly and naturally as possible. The often-expressed concept that wilderness should be a "vignette of primitive America" should not suggest a static picture of a pre-European settlement landscape, maintained in suspended animation by whatever techniques are needed. Wilderness, rather, should be *a vignette of natural dynamic forces* characteristic of early America, operating as freely as possible. Ecological change will be inevitable and constant, its velocity dependent on the ecosystem involved. There may be times in its succession when a wilderness will not be a particularly good habitat for some wildlife species nor particularly appealing to visitors.

The committee on North American Wildlife Policy pointed out that by encouraging natural processes (Allen 1973, p. 167):

> It will often be possible even to restore a "damaged" wilderness to a high standard. Native animals that have disappeared may be reintroduced. The effects of minor grazing or forest cutting can be erased, over time, by plant succession. Fire and other natural disturbances should be allowed to initiate new cycles of plant and animal life, as they did before the coming of modern man. The capacity of life communities to regenerate enlarges the possibilities for wilderness in a wide diversity of environments that should be included in the system.

Consider the example of recovery of natural conditions in the BWCAW. In 1948, about 14 percent of this area was privately owned, and there were about 45 resorts plus some 100 individual cabins in what was to be designated in 1964 as wilderness (Lucas 1972). Now the private properties are gone, except for a few cabins whose owners have life estates, and the canoeist paddling Basswood Lake today cannot discern the shores where the Peterson Lodge entertained 50 guests at a time in 1955. But the loons know things have changed; they have returned to Hoist Bay in response to restored naturalness and solitude. In some ways at least. You *can* turn back the clock.

It will not always be so easy to restore wildlife species to wilderness. Habitat regeneration is very slow in alpine or desert regions, and buildup of depleted populations can take many years. Studies indicate, for example, that the social structure of cougars is such that pioneering into new habitat is slow if minimum cougar populations are not present

nearby (Seidenstricker and others 1973). Likewise, for hereditary reasons, the North American mountain sheep appear incapable of dispersing into new or restored habitat (Geist 1971b).

A natural processes criterion would seem to preclude artificial control of native predatory animals, insects, or plant diseases with exceptions only when resources are threatened outside the wilderness. Where and when insect or disease blights strike, they should simply run their course as a contribution to a constantly changing natural ecosystem. Of course, massive infestations originating outside wilderness can threaten particular areas, such as, the introduced gypsy moth in Shenandoah National Park, Virginia, and the balsam woolly aphid in declining stands of native Fraser fir in Great Smoky Mountains National Park (NC-TN). The southern pine beetle has infested wilderness in Texas prompting removal of infested trees by the USFS amid great controversy (Warren 1985). Where predators are present, they should be permitted their natural role. Where the predators are absent, however, prey populations may irrupt and unnaturally threaten the continued existence of a natural environment. In such a case, native predatory species might be imported, their prey cropped, or both. The major barrier to such a strategy may be political as well as technical—as managers of Rocky Mountain National Park, Colorado, can attest after press and popular opinion lambasted the unofficially suggested reintroduction of wolves to control deer and elk populations. A similar controversy appears likely in wilderness areas of the Yellowstone ecosystem during the 1990s. The fear is that wolves might find easier pickings on sheep ranches outside the wilderness, and that may be true. Loss of the predator influence is only one disruption of game ecosystems. Disruption of natural migratory patterns and population distributions may be more disturbing to the system (Craighead and others 1973).

It is not always easy to decide what is natural. Consider moose in northern wilderness. It is likely that logging long ago helped to create the lingering high-quality natural moose habitat by providing those early stages in plant succession preferred by large ungulates. It is ironic that this natural habitat (and the habitat-dependent moose) would decline greatly with the cessation of logging to satisfy the Wilderness Act. The moose could probably be saved by introducing manager-ignited (unnatural) fires, in lieu of logging, to create seral plant communities (Peek and others 1976). In the future, such a case may be resolved in favor of the moose because fire management policies for wilderness are evolving toward permitting prescribed fire ignitions by managers

where needed in wilderness (see chap. 12), as well as permitting natural lightning-started fires to burn where resources outside wilderness are not threatened. (The NPS has used managed ignitions in some places since the late 1960s.)

Fire has been the great renewer of forest areas, the creator of cover-type variety on a large scale in most wildernesses. On a smaller scale, habitat diversity has been affected by insects, disease, windthrow, and stagnation. Where fire has been traditionally suppressed, diversity and numbers of wildlife are reduced. In such cases, to achieve the goal of natural distributions and numbers of native wildlife, fire must play a more prevalent and thus a more natural role in wilderness ecosystems.

And, again, we must not be too quick to define natural. An Adirondack forest, by virtue of natural plant succession, may have recovered from logging 100 years ago, and in some ways be more natural today than a Rocky Mountain forest never logged but held for the past 75 years in suspended plant succession by efficient fire prevention and control programs. Because wilderness fire may be the most effective and appropriate habitat management tool, fire management and wilderness wildlife management must go hand in hand.

As a practical matter, of course, natural processes may sometimes have insufficient time and opportunity to influence the character of wilderness, particularly in the East where areas typically are smaller and scattered. Fire and insect control actions can be expected on surrounding lands to protect economic values there, and few wilderness administrators will risk the public relations problems involved if a wilderness burn escapes or an exploding insect population moves out to commercial forest. But some judgment is needed about what natural events will be acceptable or unacceptable in the long run. As resource management technology advances, greater latitude will be available to managers in making such choices.

3. *Use minimum impact tools where natural processes must be supplemented or simulated.* Wilderness managers may at times have to mimic natural processes by prescribed burning, substituting human hunters for natural predators, or even, in very special cases, using handtools to disturb vegetation as a substitute for natural features—for example the bison-built prairie wallows that hosted native flowers and forbs that fed antelope and prairie chicken (Leopold and others 1968). Otherwise, the wilderness manager may merely preside over unnatural monotypes.

Any management tool or practice selected must represent the *minimum* departure from the natural process for which it substitutes. This is the essence of wilderness management—*doing only what is necessary and using minimum tools*—so that human influence on the wilderness is substantially unnoticed.

What constitutes the minimum tool will, of course, vary with the situation. To provide a dependable water supply where special legal requirements dictate such unnatural features, the choice may be between a windmill with a rock catchment (Leslie and Douglas 1979) or trucking water to established tanks (USDI FWS 1982b). Management efforts do not need to be widespread to be effective. Critical areas that may determine bird or animal survival, numbers, and distribution are often a small fraction of the total range.

Restoring once-indigenous species by transplanting, however, is a controversial wilderness management option, since it can affect the entire wilderness vegetation-ungulate-carnivore complex. Durward Allen recommends that available ranges should be stocked if there are breeders to spare, and he cites successful transplants of trumpeter swans, pronghorn antelope, sage grouse, turkeys, and bighorn sheep (Allen 1966). On the other hand, he acknowledges that some wood bison in Canada have been rendered genetically impure by the introduction of plains bison. Populations should not be transplanted without adequate knowledge about the various subspecies. Otherwise, forage, disease, and predation problems may make the program counterproductive. If subspecies or strains of animals are delicately attuned to life in specific environments, natural evolutionary balance may be upset by trapping and shifting populations in an effort to restock underpopulated habitat (Leopold 1966). If wilderness is to feature natural, indigenous populations, it is no place to experiment without caution, and thorough scientific evaluations prior to transplanting the animals are a necessity.

In at least one instance where man intentionally introduced a nonindigenous species into wilderness, it led to adverse effects on a delicate ecosystem. Between 1925 and 1929, approximately 12 mountain goats were transplanted from western Canada and Alaska into what is now Olympic National Park in northwestern Washington State. The goat population flourished, grew to about 1,000 goats, and led to damage of fragile alpine vegetation from the physical impact of goats and the local flora's inability to withstand grazing pressure. Park personnel were forced to live trapping, and transplanting goats to native ranges was necessary to reduce goat numbers within the park. Now, the elimination of the goats as a

non-indigenous species is being seriously considered.

The opposite problem, that of exotics invading wilderness, is a knotty one, particularly in the case of such vigorous species as starling, tamarisk, eastern brook trout in western lakes and streams, Japanese honeysuckle, and knapweed. The problem is critical when the invading species has displaced an indigenous but endangered one. For example, the greenback trout in Rocky Mountain National Park was forced out in part by the introduction of the aggressive eastern brook trout. Feral goats live in wilderness in Hawaii where they threaten rare and endangered plants and birds. Feral burros in Grand Canyon and Death Valley displace native bighorn sheep. Populations of wild boars and feral pigs inhabit 13 areas of the National Park System, including some designated as wilderness. Since a NPS aim is to come as close as possible to achieving natural ecosystems, ambitious boar-pig reduction programs have been undertaken in the most severely affected areas, but they have been largely unsuccessful (Singer 1984).

An ongoing control program in Hawaii Volcanoes National Park, on the other hand, has succeeded in reducing the feral goat population from an estimated 15,000 in 1970 to about 200 in 1980. The program uses fencing to protect some areas—even some in wilderness—as well as helicopter hunts and radio-collared "Judas" goats for locating herds (personal communication, Chief Dan Taylor, Division of Resources Management, Hawaii Volcanoes National Park). In some places, native vegetation is now coming back; in others, aggressive nonnative species have apparently become well established and threaten the integrity of the native ecosystem. Such extreme measures have been supported because of the severe damage the goats do to native vegetation, which they apparently prefer to exotic plants, and because in some cases they are destroying native habitat on which rare and endangered birds depend (Baker and Reeser 1972).

As the Hawaii Volcanoes situation illustrates, there is probably no satisfactory way of completely eliminating some introduced plant and animal species once they are established. The elimination procedures might be worse than the presence of the species from a wilderness perspective. From another perspective, at some point such species may be considered virtually indigenous—especially if one views wilderness as "natural processes operating freely now"—rather than a historical vignette of past naturalness.

4. *Favor wilderness-dependent endangered species.* The coordination of the Endangered Species Act with wilderness may require the wilderness manager to subvert natural processes. For example, restoring a breeding population of eagles to a wilderness may require installing artificial nest platforms. (The eagles will rapidly camouflage rough, wooden platforms.) Actions necessary to save endangered species should include only what is necessary and should follow the minimum tool rule, as called for earlier. But even management actions may not provide adequate help for endangered species, and determining what to do and how to do it may be difficult.

For example, in the original Gila Wilderness, New Mexico, the rare native Gila trout survived in a few streams only because dams outside the wilderness or natural stream barriers inside prevented competing species or interbreeding trout from contaminating the Gila's habitat. Question: In a species-contaminated stream in the Gila, do you construct stream barriers and poison existing introduced fish populations in order to restock Gila trout and thus protect an endangered species as the law requires? And if you decide this much manipulation is necessary, do you blast a cliff into the streambed to form a natural-appearing barrier that can fool visitors, or do you make the barrier out of rock masonry that appears as unnatural? Clearly, such decisions have an aesthetic overtone. Sensitivity and case-by-case judgment are needed.

Where necessary, managers can give diminishing species special protection by designating areas where entry is excluded—such as for coastal sea mammals and birds needing inviolate areas as feeding and breeding grounds. Precedents for such management are evolving. For example, in the California Bighorn Sheep Zoological Area in the Inyo National Forest, California, there is no entrance or passage without permission, no discharge of firearms, and no grazing of any kind—all in the interests of preventing stress on an endangered species during such critical periods in its life cycle as breeding, lambing, and winter foraging. And, as mentioned earlier, some areas of wilderness and backcountry in grizzly habitat of the Yellowstone ecosystem may be temporarily closed to human entry to provide solitude required by the wilderness-dependent and endangered grizzly.

5. *Manage for wild indigenous species.* Certainly wilderness wildlife management should be limited to native plants and animals. In classified wilderness, for example, Gambel's quail in a desert wash should be observed in the shade of mesquite, not tamarisk—a plant native to Asia. A visitor to wilderness in the crater of Haleakala National Park (HI) should see native mamane trees and silver swords, not feral goats. Wilderness wildlife should be native and wild. Forage relationships in wild animals should be

natural. No artificial feeding practices are fitting in designated wilderness, and their tolerance in adjacent areas must take into account the possible impact of "subsidized" species on naturalness in the adjacent wilderness; for example, winterfed elk that migrate to wilderness in summer. The naturalness criterion of wilderness calls for indigenous species that have exceptional opportunities to keep their wildness.

6. *Encourage angling styles that are part of and compatible with wilderness experiences.* Fishing is a traditional recreation activity in most wildernesses and is allowed by the Wilderness Act under the direction of state fish and wildlife agencies. Fishing can achieve its finest quality in wilderness, can be a scarce wilderness-dependent experience, and can be a means to realize wilderness values. Wilderness is a place where one can indulge in a primitive myth of living off the land. Catching a few fish and eating them in camp with family or friends contributes to the overall quality of a wilderness experience for many and is a goal of many users. Our view is that fishing, if carried out in a manner consistent with wilderness values, is an acceptable wilderness activity. We think fishing is best as *part* of a wilderness experience, rather than the *reason* for a wilderness visit.

Managers should encourage the use of techniques and equipment that do not degrade the environment—for example, the use of artificial lures that simulate naturally occurring foods. The use of natural bait itself may cause too much worm-digging, overturning of rocks, destroying logs and stumps. Fishing regulations for wilderness should encourage a focus on the overall wilderness experience rather than on the size of the catch. Regulations might include catch-and-release requirements, the use of barbless hooks, or perhaps a requirement that all fish taken must be cooked and eaten at the site—not hauled home to fill the freezer. Naturalness of the experience, not the bulging creel, should be emphasized.

Stocking of certain high lakes in many western states was begun years ago to transport to suitable waters those species prevented from entering by natural barriers. Some of these lakes are now in classified wilderness and their stocking, and the methods used, are among the most controversial wilderness management issues. There is no question that artificial stocking compromises the naturalness of wilderness, particularly the specific aquatic ecosystems that are affected.

At a minimum, management of each individual wilderness should strive to retain most of its waters the way nature willed them, whether as naturally barren waters or with naturally reproducing fisheries, without stocking. Stocked fisheries would seem tolerable in classified wilderness only where the practice is clearly established and carried out in a manner to minimize its impact on wilderness qualities and the experiences of visitors. Further, any stocking of wilderness lakes should be based on comprehensive wilderness management planning that takes into account overall wilderness use and the capability of individual lakes to sustain human impact. Where stocking is allowed, only indigenous species and low-impact methods seem consistent with wilderness. Fishery management objectives can often be met in wilderness without the intensive management practices applied elsewhere. The presence of fish in wilderness waters must be related first to their natural role in the ecosystem. When we manage a fishery for maximum sustained yield to anglers, we may deprive certain wild animals of their natural level of food. A wilderness lake that is unusually productive for fish may have to be that way to support the osprey, loons, and eagle pairs that nest along its shores, or the bears that feed on fish runs in feeder streams.

Wilderness managers and the interested public should fully participate with state fisheries managers in developing wilderness fisheries management programs. The planning and management of wilderness fisheries should include the development of a full range of alternative fishing opportunities outside of wilderness to relieve pressures and allow a focus in wilderness on forms of fishing dependent on the wilderness setting. The most defensible rationale for manipulating fish populations in some high-altitude lakes may be the usefulness of the practice as a diversionary management tool. Managers might continue to stock a previously stocked lake to divert anglers from other more natural lakes or drainages less able to withstand human impact, but such decoy tactics might best be emphasized in recreation areas adjacent to classified wilderness. The long-range policy question is whether any artificial stocking in designated wilderness is too harsh a conflict with naturalness.

We support a restrictive posture on further expansion of fish stocking in wilderness—but acknowledge opposing views such as written to us by Richard Stroud, then executive vice president of the Sport Fishing Institute:

> As the mountain lacking the grizzly becomes just a pile of rocks, so, too, a high elevation lake without fish life becomes just a big puddle. Perhaps in no other aquatic ecosystem—owing to extreme water clarity and sharpened human perception—is the visual impact of fish life as important as in high mountain

lakes. The naturalness of the aquatic ecosystem is only an illusion, lacking representativeness of all trophic levels. Introduction of fish life corrects an error of nature—overcomes an unnaturalness, if you will . . . I strongly disagree with the "let nature roll the dice" philosophy. Strictly followed, it would preclude introduction of any fish into any barren lakes. . . . I do not believe that discriminate stocking of selected fishless waters compromises Wilderness values. On the contrary, I contend the results enhance these values.

This view, backed by a strong political constituency, assures that fish stocking in wilderness will continue to some degree. This makes it all the more important that fish-stocking programs be a part of—and not apart from—overall wilderness management plans so an optimum balance can be struck between that practice and all the affected wilderness values.

7. *Favor hunting and trapping methods and conventions that foster wilderness-dependent experiences.* Ideally, wilderness hunting and trapping should be scientifically managed to ensure that the natural ecosystem is not impaired; just intensive and selective enough (with regard to age and sex) to protect the natural behavior and dynamics of game populations; mimicking as closely as possible the pattern of kill by natural predators; with very little or no hunting of predators near the top of the food chain, such as wolves and grizzlies; and with no hunting where either a lack of knowledge or lack of regulatory staff makes the consequences on naturalness uncertain. In reality, the lack of control and knowledge about predation effects makes it impossible to predict with certainty just how hunting affects wildlife naturalness. The need for a conservative approach is thus imperative.

Protection against unwanted influences of hunting and other human disturbance is especially critical for sensitive, threatened, or endangered species. For example, to protect the genetic spark of the bighorn sheep, perhaps hunting regulations should encourage the taking of females and yearling males, rather than prime male breeders with trophy horns (Morgan 1973). The commercialization of certain animal parts such as teeth, claws, antlers, horns, and even gallbladders may lead to illegal commercial hunting that can further increase negative impacts of harvest.

Plinking (shooting at random targets) can be especially damaging in wilderness where there may be few witnesses to dissuade an armed visitor from yielding to the temptation of live targets such as whistling marmots in a timberline boulder field.

Enforcement in remote wilderness is difficult and when such actions occur, and where other visitors have been disturbed by nonhunting gunfire, managers may want to consider limiting guns in wilderness except during hunting season. Plinking is definitely not a wilderness-dependent activity. It causes noise pollution and anxiety to wilderness animals and users alike, and can inflame antihunting sentiment. Nevertheless, particularly in the frontier-oriented West, guns are associated with wilderness, and restrictions would be controversial.

Where hunting is allowed in wilderness, it must be of such a quality that it does not degrade the wilderness resource or the experience of other users. Hunters should be allowed to experience those aspects of their sport which are uniquely wilderness dependent. Wilderness-quality hunting may mean different things to different people, but we define it as the opportunity to pursue the recreation under biologically sound and ethical rules, in a manner pleasing to oneself and one's fellow hunters, acceptable to most nonhunters, and in keeping with wilderness criteria of naturalness, solitude, and contrast with civilization. It is not realistic to expect that all wilderness hunters would voluntarily restrict themselves to muzzle loaders or bow and arrows. But conforming to a wilderness ethic implies restrictions on extravagant base camps or walkie-talkies to crackle messages from canyon to canyon. Wilderness is the one place the hunter can confront game on its terms, and this opportunity should be encouraged for those who can appreciate the unique values of such an experience.

8. *Promote wilderness wildlife research using appropriate methods.* The need for management, the feasibility of management methods, and evaluation of results must be based on continuing scientific research. Applied research is needed in all phases of wilderness wildlife and fisheries management. This challenge calls for a concerted endeavor by federal, state, and university scientists.

Much research is needed on wildlife-related human behavior. As the North American Policy Committee stated: "Our most neglected and crucial research needs are those concerning human social behavior. The biologist alone, the social scientist alone, the economist alone cannot deal with these questions. Their combined effort is required, and it must do great things" (Allen 1973, p. 176). Thus, the need for wildlife-related wilderness research is based on both ecological and human behavior issues.

In using wilderness as a wildlife research laboratory, however, the scientist is under the same constraints as everyone else not to degrade its natural-

ness or solitude. While some instrumentation may be necessary to record accurately the scientific parameters of wilderness, physical structures as a general rule are not in keeping with wilderness criteria, nor are such techniques as painting big markings of live-trapped animals for later observation from an obtrusive helicopter.

We must recognize, however, that radio telemetry and aircraft, used with discretion, are invaluable means—sometimes the only means—of obtaining data on the natural distributions and behavior patterns of large wilderness wildlife species. These resources deserve the understanding that can be gained only through judicious programs of marking and observation. One reviewer of this chapter told us: "If we allow radio communications by wilderness managers, and modern cameras, canoes, and camping gear on the part of visitors, why should the wildlife researcher have to revert to outmoded techniques, so long as he leaves no lasting imprint on either the landscape or the wildlife resource?" (Peek 1989). But temperance is needed. For example, radio collars are an intrusion on the wilderness and may constitute a form of harassment that threatened species such as grizzlies do not need (Craighead 1982). Some also feel that such methods distort natural behavior. At the very least, radio collars can be color matched to the animal to minimize visual impact. Marking with paint or dye, colored tags, and streamers should be discouraged and methods such as radioactive tagging and tracing with nucleotides should not be tolerated.

Investigations have only begun on the relationships and the natural mechanisms that work within natural ecosystems. Many wildlife research opportunities are essentially wilderness dependent; they require vast natural areas that may ultimately exist only in wilderness. It would be foolhardy to deny competent scientists the opportunity to learn from those processes that have developed through millions of years and that have proven their durability by surviving. We need to understand the strategies of coexistence among life forms in natural ecosystems that have survived longer than any others on earth (Batten 1983).

Nonetheless, the scientific community should be sure that investigations in wilderness seek essential data, that wilderness is not open to casual inquiry with intruding mechanization, and that the scholar above all is governed by a wilderness ethic. Can it be done? For 20 years an uninterrupted study of wolf-moose relationships was conducted in what is now the Isle Royale Wilderness using observations from aircraft: no trapping, no tranquilizing, no radio collars, no marking (McNamee 1982). And some modern tech-

nology well-suited for habitat studies, such as satellite imagery, can be applied to wilderness ecosystems without intrusion (Craighead and others 1982).

Wilderness wildlife research should, in short, be restricted by overriding principles of wilderness management: do only what is necessary and use the minimum methods, approaches, or tools (fig. 11.7). Wilderness wildlife research proposals need to be strongly justified as sources of information about natural processes that

Fig. 11.7. Wildlife research in wilderness using high technology, such as radio telemetry, is allowed with agency approval. Most wilderness wildlife is studied using simple means and methods, such as observation, that are compatible with wilderness conditions. Here Dr. Paul Krausman, University of Arizona, studies desert bighorn sheep in the Pusch Ridge Wilderness near Tucson, AZ. Photo courtesy of John C. Hendee.

are necessary to wilderness protection, to improved understanding of global human impacts on nature, and thus to the continued well being of humans on the planet. If sophisticated mechanization is allowed in wilderness for scientific purposes that are not so justified, it could set a precedent, opening the door to excessive development for other purposes such as radar installations for monitoring air traffic, telecommunication installations, instrumentation of headwaters for water yield information for commercial irrigation, climatological data gathering for weather forecasting, and so forth.

The International Association of Fish and Wildlife Agencies' guidelines for wildlife management in wilderness stated: "Research on wildlife . . . is a legitimate activity when conducted in a manner compatible with preservation of the wilderness environment. Methods that temporarily infringe on the wilderness environment may be approved if alternative methods or other locations are not available"

(FS, BLM, and IAFWA 1983). Currently, agency policies sometimes permit sophisticated instrumentation and mechanization for wilderness wildlife research, usually on a case-by-case basis. The overall research effort must be consistent with wilderness locations, and suitable opportunities must be unavailable in nonwilderness locations.

RESEARCH PRIORITIES

Three wilderness wildlife research topics deserve high priority because they focus on the wilderness conditions of naturalness and solitude: (1) response of both habitat and native animals to massive natural disturbance (such as fire), (2) normal predator-prey relationships, and (3) natural baselines for comparison with managed conditions. Inevitably, these topics overlap, and they cannot be neatly separated.

We need to expand our knowledge of wildlife ecology, including population dynamics and habitat species relationships in relatively undisturbed environments, and to design and evaluate management elsewhere. Such baseline work at the *autecological* (single species), *synecological* (natural communities), and *ecosystem levels* is especially needed for game, predatory, and threatened and endangered species. For example, the coyote and bobcat, which have been extensively controlled and studied where they cause problems, have not been adequately investigated in undisturbed environments. Increased knowledge about how these species space themselves and are naturally regulated without human interference could help management of their prey to reduce predation on domestic livestock.

Research comparing grizzly bear behavior in wilderness and in the national parks where they pose a serious human safety problem might help management reduce human injuries from encounters with bears. Efforts to manage wolves in Alaska and elsewhere could be enhanced by comparative data from undisturbed populations of wolves and their effects on similarly undisturbed big game.

Longstanding questions about what factors control population levels of ungulates and the larger carnivores require study in large, undisturbed areas. Research to test the competing hypotheses about how ungulate populations are naturally regulated (ungulate habitat vs. predator interactions), in addition to other important hypotheses, will require relatively intact ecosystems found only in large designated wilderness areas (Peek 1980, 1981). This work has important ramifications for management

of native ungulates outside and inside wilderness.

Hunting may alter population structure and behavior, but we do not know exactly how or how much. Populations of big game such as elk and deer are heavily hunted in some USFS and BLM wilderness areas. Comparative studies with the unhunted wilderness areas of the national parks are needed to increase understanding of population dynamics, behavior, and habitat interactions, and thus improve wildlife management capabilities.

Interactions between large mammals are often artificial or a result of human influences in managed areas—for example, artificially enhanced populations of large ungulates such as elk and deer. These synecological relationships may be affecting habitat selection, behavior, and dynamics.

The special interaction between predator and prey is in particular need of investigation in undisturbed settings. Studies of the moose-wolf interaction in Isle Royale National Park (Allen 1979), and cougar-ungulate interaction in the Frank Church-River of No Return Wilderness (Hornocker 1970), should be extended and replicated in other systems and with other species. Such work requires large wilderness areas.

Programs to restore threatened or endangered species include assessment of minimum breeding populations that contain an adequate gene pool to allow evolutionary adaptations to continue. While we currently know a little about how to generate numbers of animals, we know almost nothing about what is needed in gene pool variability to perpetuate a species. In special need of investigation is population response to dramatic natural change in undisturbed environments—wildfire, hurricanes, land slumps, and volcanic eruptions. The resulting knowledge will increase understanding of response to artificial change and the limits of wildlife adaptability.

In summary, the greatest scientific values of wilderness are based on the opportunity to study, over long periods of time, large ecosystems that are relatively undisturbed. Wilderness wildlife is an integral part of these ecosystems, sometimes dependent on and reflective of their degree of naturalness and solitude. Study of wilderness-wildlife ecosystems can reveal natural processes, providing management and baseline information for assessing human influence on the area, especially the vegetation. Such information is increasingly important as resource management becomes more complex and human use and influence expand. At the same time, wildlife research methods in wilderness must be balanced against the need to maintain wilderness values.

SUMMARY

We recommend the foregoing guidelines as necessary to achieve the proposed wilderness wildlife management objectives. We emphasize, however, that these guidelines are intended to supplement, not substitute for, wilderness management principles suggested in chapter 7 and elsewhere in the book. But it seems unrealistic to seek one monolithic wilderness wildlife management pattern; wilderness management needs to be tailored to the unavoidable constraints of the administrative agency concerned and focused on needs of individual areas. For this reason, a wilderness ethic is always needed as a guiding policy. This chapter has sought to set the stage for such a process. It has also sought to remind readers of the interdependency of wilderness and wildlife.

Wildlife is only one component of the wilderness-wildlife resource and cannot be managed separately. Wildlife uses, such as recreational fishing or hunting, must be governed not just by the surplus population capacity of fish and game but by the impact of such uses on the naturalness of relationships among all components of the wilderness resource. A particular lake may have the capacity to support a certain level of fishing pressure, but the acceptable level must also be measured against the aggregate impact of anglers and other users on the vegetation and soil around the lake or along the stream, and on the solitude of visitors' experiences.

The case for a comprehensive approach does not downgrade wilderness management for wildlife; indeed we believe that wildlife should receive much more consideration in wilderness planning and management. But wildlife in wilderness is an ingredient of the natural ecosystem whose integrity hinges on and contributes to the wildlife resource. The wildlife manager must recognize that relationship in order to contribute to and enhance wilderness.

Finally, we wish to emphasize the importance of wildlife in the wilderness web. Wilderness lets us view the natural processes by which the land and the living things on it have achieved their characteristic forms and by which they maintain their existence. It makes us aware of the incredible intricacies of plant and animal communities and their intrinsic beauty, and of contrasts with creeping degradation in many nonwilderness settings. These things add up to the great lesson of human-environment interdependency: that air, waters, soils, trees, plants, insects, birds, fishes, mammals, and people are all part of the same scheme—an intricately woven landscape fabric. Snip one thread and the entire cloth begins to unravel; stitch up one tear and you begin to repair the whole. Exposure to wilderness and wildlife, even indirectly, can be a doorway to the ecological understanding of our complete interdependence with our environment and with life everywhere. The ultimate wilderness and wildlife value may be its contribution to the development of a culture that will secure the future of an environment fit for life and fit for living, and to an appreciation of all those amenities that are inexorably linked to the prosperity of the human spirit.

STUDY QUESTIONS

1. What are four categories of wilderness wildlife? How important is wilderness to each?
2. What are three ways in which wilderness contributes to the preservation of wildlife?
3. What are some traditions and overall missions of the four federal wilderness management agencies that affect their management of wildlife within their jurisdictions? Discuss some advantages and disadvantages of the diversity these different outlooks provide.
4. What are some wilderness uses allowed under the Wilderness Act, and some mandates under other legislation, that have the potential to complicate wilderness wildlife management?
5. What are some effects on wildlife of human activities in wilderness, on adjacent nonwilderness lands, and elsewhere?
6. What are six broad objectives for wilderness wildlife management that may be used as criteria for choosing and judging management policies and actions?
7. What are some of the problems wilderness managers face as they attempt to allow "natural processes" to shape wilderness wildlife habitat?
8. How can wilderness wildlife research benefit wildlife and humankind? How can wilderness managers and researchers preserve other wilderness values while conducting necessary research?

REFERENCES

Adamus, Paul R.; Clough, Garret C. 1978. Evaluating species for protection in natural areas. Biological Conservation. 13(3): 165-179.

Alaska National Interest Lands Conservation Act, Public Law 96-487, 94 Stat. 2371 (1980).

Allen, D. L. 1979. Wolves of Minong. Barton, MA: Houghton-Mifflin Co. 466 p.

Allen, Durward. 1966. The preservation of endangered habitats and vertebrates of North America. In: Darling, F. Fraser; Milton, John, eds. Future environments of North America. Garden City, NY: The Natural History Press: 22-37.

Allen, Durward, chairman. 1973. Report of the committee on North American wildlife policy. In: Transactions: 38th American wildlife and natural resource conference; 1973 March 18-21; Washington, DC. Washington, DC: Wildlife Management Institute: 152-181.

Allen, Durward L. 1978. Wolf-moose studies demonstrate scientific value of wilderness. Illinois State Academy of Science. 71(4): 436-438.

Alston, Richard M. 1983. The individual vs. the public interest: political ideology and National Forest policy. Boulder, CO: Eastview Press. 250 p.

Applegate, James. 1973. Some factors associated with deer hunting by New Jersey residents. In: Hendee, John C.; Schoenfeld, Clay, eds. Human dimensions in wildlife programs. Washington, DC: Wildlife Management Institute: 111-117.

Bailey, J. A. 1980. Desert bighorn, forage competition, and zoogeography. Wildlife Society Bulletin. 8(3): 208-216.

Baker, James K.; Reeser, Donald W. 1972. Goal management problems in Hawaii Volcanoes National Park. Natural Resources Rep. No. 2. Washington, DC: U.S. Department of the Interior, National Park Service. 21 p.

Batten, Mary. 1983. Jungles. International Wildlife. 13(6): 17-21.

Bergerud, Arthur T. 1974. Decline of caribou in North America following settlement. Journal of Wildlife Management. 38(4): 757-770.

Bourassa, Connie M. 1978. Clarifying 'wilderness.' Western Wildlands. 5(1): 4-7.

Brown, Perry J.; Schomaker, John H. 1974. Final report on criteria for potential campsites. Suppl. 32 to Project 12-11-204-3. Ogden, UT: Utah State University Institute for Study of Outdoor Recreation and Tourism. 50 p.

Browning, James A.; Hendee, John C.; Roggenbuck, Joe W. 1988. 103 wilderness laws: milestones and management direction in wilderness legislation, 1964-1987. Station Bulletin 51. Moscow, ID: University of Idaho, College of Forestry, Wildlife and Range Sciences, Idaho Forest, Wildlife and Range Experiment Station. 73 p.

Buchheister, Carl W. 1963. Wilderness and wildlife. In: Leydet, Francois, ed. Tomorrow's wilderness. San Francisco: Sierra Club: 76-83.

California Department of Fish and Game. 1985. Tule elk in California: a report to the legislature. [Available from the California Department of Fish and Game, Sacramento, CA.] 7 p.

Campbell, Sheldon. 1984. Restocking the wilderness with captive-bred animals: the California condor story. In: Martin, Vance; Inglis, Mary, eds. Wilderness: the way ahead. Middleton, WI: Lorian Press: 108-113.

Cape, Oliver B. 1969. Effect of DDT spraying on the Yellowstone River system. In: Cox, George W., ed. Readings in conservation ecology. New York: Appleton-Century-Crofts: 325-343.

Carpenter, M. Ralph; Bowhis, Donald R. 1976. Attitudes toward fishing and fisheries management of users in Desolation Wilderness. California Fish and Game. 62(3): 168-178.

Carr, Archie. 1973. The everglades. New York: Time-Life Books. 184 p.

Chester, James. 1976. Human-wildlife relationships in the Gallatin Range, Yellowstone National Park: 11-40.

Ciriacy-Wantrup, S. V.; Phillips, William E. 1970. Conservation of the California tule elk. Biological Conservation. 3(1): 23-32.

Clean Air Act Amendments of 1977, Public Law 95-95, 91 Stat. 685, as amended.

Cole, David N. 1981. Vegetational changes associated with recreational use and fire suppression in the Eagle Cap Wilderness. Biological Conservation. 20(4): 247-270.

Colorado Wilderness Act, Public Law 96-560, 94 Stat. 3265 (1980).

Conway, M. C. 1978. Handbook of species endangered in New Mexico: mammals. Non-Game Wildlife Studies. Albuquerque, NM: New Mexico Department of Fish and Game: A1-A21.

Cooper, Tamise; Shaw, William W. 1979. Wildlands management for wildlife viewing. In: Proceedings of a conference on our national landscape. Gen. Tech. Rep. PSW-35. Berkeley, CA: U.S. Department of Agriculture, Forest Service, Pacific Southwest Forest and Range Experiment Station: 700-705.

Craighead, John. 1982. Satellite imagery: an alternative future. Western Wildlands. 8(1): 18-27.

Craighead, John J.; Craighead, Frank C. 1971. Grizzly bear-man relationships in Yellowstone National Park. Bioscience. 21(16): 845-857.

Craighead, John J.; Craighead, Frank C., Jr.; Ruff, Robert L.; [and others]. 1973. Home range and activity patterns of nonmigratory elk of the Madison drainage herd as determined by radiotelemetry. Wildlife Monograph No. 33. Washington, DC: The Wildlife Society. 50 p.

Craighead, John; Sumner, Jay S.; Scaggs, Gordon B. 1982. A definitive system for analysis of grizzly bear habitat and other wilderness resources. Missoula, MT: Wildlife-Wildlands Institute. 279 p.

Crawford, John S. 1980. Wolves, bears, and bighorns. Anchorage: Alaska Northwest Publishing Co. 175 p.

Crisler, Lois. 1958. Arctic wild. New York: Harper and Row. 301 p.

Cutler, M. Rupert. 1980. Wilderness decisions: values and challenges to science. Journal of Forestry. 78(2): 74-77.

Dasmann, Raymond F. 1966. Wildlife biology. New York: Wiley. 231 p.

Davis, George D. 1988. Preservation of natural diversity: the role of ecosystem representation within wilderness. In: Wilderness benchmark 1988: proceedings of the national wilderness colloquium; 1988 January 13-14; Tampa, FL: U.S. Department of Agriculture, Forest Service, Southeastern Forest Experiment Station: 76-82.

Drabelle, Dennis. 1984. Feral explorations: wilderness as the landscape of science. Wilderness. 48(165): 24-26.

Dunaway, David J. 1971. Human disturbance as a limiting factor of Sierra Nevada bighorn sheep. 15 p. mimeo. [Paper presented at First North American Wild Sheep Conference, 1971 April 14-15; Colorado State University, Fort Collins, CO.]

Endangered Species Act, Public Law 93-205, 87 Stat. 884 (1973).

Etchberger, Richard C.; Krausman, Paul R.; Mazaika, Rosemary. 1989. Mountain sheep habitat characteristics in the Pusch Ridge Wilderness, Arizona. Journal of Wildlife Management. 53(4): 902-907.

Federal Land Policy and Management Act of 1976, Public Law 94-579, 90 Stat. 2743, as amended.

Forsman, Eric D.; Horn, Kirk M.; Nettro, William A. 1982. Spotted owl research and management in the Pacific Northwest. Transactions of the 47th North American Wildlife and Natural Resources Conference. Washington, DC: Wildlife Management Institute: 323-331.

Frome, Michael A. 1974. A place for wild animals, wild plants. Defenders of Wildlife News. 49(3): 194-200.

Geist, Valerius. 1971a. Is big game harassment harmful? Oilweek. 22(17): 12-13.

Geist, Valerius. 1971b. Mountain sheep. Chicago: University of Chicago Press. 383 p.

Geist, Valerius. 1975. Mountain sheep and man in the northern wilds. Ithaca, NY: Cornell University Press. 248 p.

Gilbert, Bil. 1976. The great grizzly controversy. Audubon. 78(1): 62-69 .

Gionfriddo, James P.; Krausman, Paul R. 1986. Summer habitat use by mountain sheep. Journal of Wildlife Management. 50(2): 331-336 .

Hay, Tom; Posewitz, Jim. 1978. Wilderness and wildlife. Montana Outdoors. 9(1): 2-7.

Hendee, John C. 1974. A multiple satisfactions approach to game management. Wildlife Society Bulletin. 2(3): 104-112.

Hendee, John C. 1984. Public opinion and what foresters should do about it. Journal of Forestry. 82(6): 340-344.

Hendee, John C. 1986. Wilderness: important legal, social, philosophical and management perspectives. In: Proceedings, Wilderness and natural areas in the East, a management challenge; 1985 May 13; Nacogdoches, TX: 5-11.

Hendee, John C.; Potter, Dale. 1976. Hunters and hunting: management implications of research. In: Proceedings, recreation research applications workshop; 1975 September 15-18; Asheville, NC. Misc. Publ. 28802. Asheville, NC: U.S. Department of Agriculture, Forest Service, Southeastern Forest Experiment Station: 137-161.

Hendee, John C.; Clark, Roger N.; Dailey, Thomas E. 1977. Fishing and other recreation behavior at roadless high lakes: some management implications. Res. Note PNW-304. Portland, OR: U.S. Department of Agriculture, Forest Service, Pacific Northwest Forest and Range Experiment Station. 27 p.

Hendee, John C.; Smith, Zane G.; Lake, Robert. 1980. Public involvement in resource decisions: RARE I and II and their implications for the future. In: Proceedings, Symposium on multiple-use management of forest resources. Clemson, SC: Clemson University: 217-232.

Herrero, Stephen. 1985. Bear attacks: their causes and avoidance. Piscataway, NJ: Winchester Press. 287 p.

Historic Preservation Act, Public Law 89-665, 80 Stat. 915 (1966).

Hoagland, John F. 1973. A description of anglers and angling in two use areas of the Uinta Mountains. Logan, UT: Utah State University. 99 p. M.S. thesis.

Hochbaum, H. Albert. 1970. Wilderness wildlife in Canada. In: McCloskey, Maxine E., ed. Wilderness: the edge of knowledge. San Francisco: Sierra Club: 23-33.

Hornocker, Maurice. 1970. An analysis of mountain lion predation on mule deer and elk in the Idaho Primitive Area. Wildlife Monographs. 21. 39 p.

Hornocker, Maurice 1971. Suggestions for the management of mountain lions as trophy species in the Intermountain region. 51st annual conference. Proceedings: western association of state game and fish commissioners; 1971 July 19-23; Snowmass-at-Aspen, CO. Boise, ID: Idaho Fish and Game Department. 51: 399-402.

Hornocker, Maurice. 1978. Interactions between threatened and endangered species and wilderness. In: Transactions of the 43rd Wildlife and Natural Resources Conference. Washington, DC: Wildlife Management Institute: 334-350.

International Association of Fish and Wildlife Agencies. 1983. Guidelines for fish and wildlife conservation in wilderness. Washington, DC: IAFWA. 3 p.

Kellert, Stephen R. 1984. The public and the timber wolf in Minnesota. [New Haven, CT]: Yale University, School of Forestry and Environmental Studies. 155 p. mimeo.

Kellert, Stephen R. 1985. Public perceptions of predators, particularly the wolf and coyote. Biological Conservation. 31: 167-189.

Kimball, John F., Jr.; Wolfe, 1974. Michael L. Population analysis of a northern elk herd. Journal of Wildlife Management. 38(2): 161-174.

King, David A.; Bugarsky, Deborah J.; Shaw, William W. 1986. Contingent valuation: an application to wildlife. Paper presented at the 18th international union of forestry research organizations world congress; 1986 September 7-21. Ljubljana, Yugoslavia. 11 p.

Krausman, Paul R.; Shaw, William W.; Stair, John L. 1979. Bighorn sheep in the Pusch Ridge Wilderness Area, Arizona Desert Bighorn Council Transactions. 23: 40-45.

Krausman, Paul R.; Hervert, John J. 1983. Mountain sheep responses to aerial surveys. Wildlife Society Bulletin. 11(4): 372-375.

Krausman, Paul R.; Leopold, Bruce D. 1983. The importance of small populations of desert bighorn sheep. In: McCabe, R. E., ed. Transactions of the fifty-first North American wildlife and natural resources conference. Washington, DC: Wildlife Management Institute: 52-61.

Krausman, Paul R.; Leopold, Bruce D.; Seegmiller, Rick F.; Torres, Steven G. 1989. Relationships between desert bighorn sheep and habitat in western Arizona. Wildlife Monographs. 102. 66 p.

Kuck, Lonn. 1977. The impacts of hunting on Idaho's Pahsimeroi mountain goat herd. In: Proceedings of the 1st International Mountain Goat Symposium; 1977 February 19; Kalispell, MT. Vancouver, BC: British Columbia Ministry of Recreation and Conservation: 114-125.

Leopold, A. Starker. 1966. Adaptability of animals to habitat change. In: Darling, F. Fraser; Milton, John, eds. Future environments of North America. Garden City, NY: The Natural History Press: 66-75.

Leopold, A. Starker; Cain, Stanley, A.; Cottam, Clarence M.; and the special advisory committee on wildlife management for the Secretary of the Interior. 1968. The National Wildlife Refuge system. In: Trefethen, James B., ed. Transactions: 33d North American wildlife management and national resource conference; 1968 March 11-13; Houston, TX. Washington, DC: Wildlife Management Institute: 30-54.

Leopold, Aldo. 1933. Wildlife management. C. Scribner's Sons, New York. 481 p.

Leopold, Aldo. 1949. A Sand County almanac, and sketches here and there. New York: Oxford University Press. 269 p.

Leslie, D. M., Jr.; Douglas, C. L. 1979. Desert bighorn sheep of the River Mountains, Nevada. Wildlife Monographs. 66. Washington, DC: Wildlife Society. 56 p.

Lime, David W.; Cushwa, Charles T. 1969. Wildlife aesthetics and auto campers in the Superior National Forest. Res. Pap. NC-32. St. Paul, MN: U.S. Department of Agriculture, Forest Service, North Central Forest and Range Experiment Station. 8 p.

Lucas, Robert C. 1965. The importance of fishing as an attraction and activity in the Quetico-Superior area.

Res. Note LS-61. St. Paul, MN: U.S. Department of Agriculture, Forest Service, Lake States Experiment Station. 3 p.

Lucas, Robert C. 1972. Wilderness perception and use. In: Thompson, Dennis L., ed. Politics, policy, and natural resources. New York: McMillan; 1972: 309-323.

Luman, Ira D.; Neitro, William A. 1980. Preservation of mature forest seral stages to provide wildlife habitat diversity. In: Transactions of the 45th North American Wildlife and Natural Resources Conference. Washington, DC: Wildlife Management Institute: 271-287.

Martinka, C. J. 1982. Keeping people and bears apart. Western Wildlands. 8(1): 8-11.

McNamee, Thomas. 1982. Trouble in Wolf Haven. Audubon. 84(1): 84-96.

Mech, L. David; Rogers, L. L. 1977. Status, distribution, and movements of martens in northeastern Minnesota. Res. Pap. NC-143. St. Paul, MN: U.S. Department of Agriculture, Forest Service, North Central Forest Experiment Station. 7 p.

Mercure, Delbert V., Jr.; Ross, William M. 1970. The Wilderness Act: a product of Congressional compromise. In: Cooley, Richard; Wandesforde-Smith, Geoffry, eds. Congress and the environment. Seattle: University of Washington Press: 47-64.

Meyers, Norman. 1983. A wealth of wild species: storehouse for human welfare. Boulder, CO: Westview Press. 272 p.

Milton, John P. 1972. The web of wilderness. Living Wilderness. 35(16): 14-19.

Morgan, James K. 1973. Slamming the ram into oblivion. Audubon. 75(6): 16-19.

Murie, Margaret E.; Murie, Olaus. 1966. Wapiti wilderness. New York: Knopf. 302 p.

Muth, Robert M. 1985. Subsistence use of fish, game, and other renewable natural resources in southeast Alaska: a problem analysis. Juneau, AK: U.S. Department of Agriculture, Forest Service, Forestry Sciences Laboratory. 51 p.

Muth, Robert M. 1990. Community stability as social structure: The role of subsistence uses of natural resources in southeast Alaska. In: Robert G. Lee, Donald R. Birch, Jr., eds. Community and forestry, Boulder, CO: Westview Press.

Muth, Robert M.; Glass, Ronald J. 1989. Wilderness and subsistence-use opportunities: Benefits and limitations. Pages unknown. In: Helen R. Freilich, Compiler. Wilderness benchmark 1988. Proceedings of the national wilderness colloquium. USDA Forest Service, Southeastern Forest Experiment Station, General Technical Report SE-51. Asheville, NC.

Nash, Roderick. 1970. Wild-deer-ness. In: McCloskey, Maxine E., ed. Wilderness: the edge of knowledge. San Francisco: Sierra Club: 36.

National Park Service Act, chapter 137, 45 Stat. 235 (1916) (codified at 16 U.S.C. Sec. 1-18f).

Olson, Sigurd. 1963. Listening point. New York: Knopf. 242 p.

Peek, James M. 1980. Natural regulation of ungulates: what constitutes a real wilderness? Wildlife Society Bulletin. 8(3): 217-227.

Peek, James M. 1981. Thoughts on preservation. Western Wildlands. Winter: 13-15.

Peek, James. 1986. A review of wildlife management.

Englewood Cliffs, NJ: Prentice Hall. 486 p.

Peek, James. 1989. [Personal communication]. October 17. Moscow, ID: University of Idaho, College of Forestry, Wildlife, and Range Sciences.

Peek, James M.; Ulrich, David L.; Mackie, Richard J. 1976. Moose habitat selection and relationships to forest management in northeastern Minnesota. Wildlife Monograph No. 48. Washington, DC: Wildlife Society. 65 p.

Pimlott, Douglas. 1974. The Arctic offshore gamble. Living Wilderness. 33(172): 16-24.

Posewitz, James A. 1981. For wildlife managers, a chance to preserve future choices. Wild America. September 9-11.

Ream, Catherine H. 1980. Impact of backcountry recreationists on wildlife: an annotated bibliography. Gen. Tech. Rep. INT-84. Ogden, UT: U.S. Department of Agriculture, Forest Service, Intermountain Forest and Range Experiment Station. 62 p.

Reiger, John F. 1975. American sportsmen and the origins of conservation. New York: Winchester Press. 39 p.

Robinson, Gleo O. 1975. The Forest Service. Baltimore: Johns Hopkins. 337 p.

Russell, Andy. 1971. Grizzly country. New York: Knopf. 302 p.

Seidenstricker, John C., IV; Hornocker, Maurice G.; Wiles, Wilbur V.; [and others]. 1973. Mountain lion social organization in the Idaho Primitive Area. Wildlife Monograph No. 35. Washington, DC: Wildlife Society. 60 p.

Servheen, Christopher. 1982. A national recovery plan. Western Wildlands. 8(1): 12-15.

Singer, Francis J. 1984. Effects of wild pig rooting in a deciduous forest. Journal of Wildlife Management. 48(2): 466-473.

Smith, David. 1973. Appendix L: Maintaining timber supply in a sound environment. In: Report of the President's advisory panel on timber and the environment. Washington, DC: U.S. Government Printing Office: 396-426.

Talbot, Lee M. 1970. An international view of wilderness. In: McCloskey, Maxine E., ed. Wilderness: the edge of knowledge. San Francisco: Sierra Club: 16-22.

Thomas, Jack Ward; Forsman, Eric D.; Lint, Joseph B.; Meslow, E. Charles; Noon, Barry R.; and Verner, Jared. 1990. A conservation strategy for the northern spotted owl. A report to the Inter-Agency Scientific Committee to address the conservation of the northern spotted owl. U.S. Department of Fish and Wildlife Service, Washington, D.C.

Trefethen, James B. 1975. An American crusade for wildlife. New York: Boone and Crockett Club. 409 p.

Troyer, Will. 1973. Alaska's brown bear. Living Wilderness. 73(126): 32-37.

U.S. Department of Agriculture and U.S. Department of the Interior. 1989. Final report and recommendations of the Fire Management Policy Review Team and summary of public comments. Federal Register. 54(115): 25660-25678.

U.S. Department of Agriculture and U.S. Department of the Interior. 1990. Temporary subsistence management regulations for public lands in Alaska; Final temporary rule. USDA Forest Service, 36CFR part 242, and USDI Fish and Wildlife Service, 50CFR part 100, Federal Register 55(126):27114-27170.

U.S. Department of the Interior, Fish and Wildlife Service.

1982a. The 1980 national survey of fishing, hunting and wildlife associated recreation. Washington, DC. 156 p.

U.S. Department of the Interior, Fish and Wildlife Service. 1982b. Wilderness area management. In: Refuge manual. Washington, DC: 6 RM 8.

Wallis, Orthello L. 1976. Management of high country lakes in the National Parks of California. [Paper presented to High Mountain Lakes Symposium by California/Nevada Chapter American Fisheries Society and California Trout; 1976 January 29; Fresno, CA]. 17 p. mimeo.

Warren, B. Jack. 1985. Why we need to control pine beetles in wilderness areas. Forest Farmer. 44(4): 6-8.

Washburne, Randel F. 1981. Carrying capacity assessment and recreational use in the National Wilderness Preservation System. Journal of Soil and Water Conservation. 36(3): 162-166.

Washburne, Randel F.; Cole, David N. 1983. Problems and practices in wilderness management: a survey of managers. Res. Pap. INT-304. Ogden, UT: U.S. Department of Agriculture, Forest Service, Intermountain Forest and Range Experiment Station. 56 p.

Wauer, Roland H.; Supernaugh, William R. 1983. Wildlife management in the National Parks. National Parks. 57(7-8): 12-16.

Wilderness Act, Public Law 88-577, 78 Stat. 890 (1964).

Wildlife Management Institute. 1975. Placing American wildlife management in perspective. Washington, DC: Wildlife Management Institute. 24 p.

Williamson, Lonnie L. 1985. Hunting: an American tradition. American Hunting. January: 18-19.

Wilson, Edward O. 1984. Million-year histories: species diversity as an ethical goal. Wilderness. 48(165): 12-17.

Wood, Pinckney. 1984. The elk hunt goes on at Grand Teton. National Parks. 58(9-10): 29-31; 1984.

Woodward, Thomas N.; Gutierrez, R. J.; Rutherford, William H. 1974. Bighorn ram production, survival, and mortality in south-central Colorado. Journal of Wildlife Management. 38(4): 771-774.

Young, R. A. 1980. The relationships between information levels and environmental approval: the wilderness issue. Journal of Environmental Education. 11(3): 25-30.

Fire has been a historic force shaping the character of the wilderness. Restoring fire to its natural role is a major challenge to wilderness managers. Here a fire burns in the Scapegoat Wilderness, part of the BMWC, MT, in the summer of 1988. Photo courtesy of Bert Lindler, *Great Falls Tribune*.

12

FIRE IN WILDERNESS ECOSYSTEMS

This chapter was written by Bruce M. Kilgore, Chief, Division of Natural Resources and Research, Western Region, National Park Service, San Francisco, California, and Miron L. Heinselman, retired Adjunct Professor, Department of Ecology and Behavioral Biology, University of Minnesota, St. Paul, and retired Principal Plant Ecologist, U.S. Department of Agriculture, U. S. Forest Service, North Central Forest Experimental Station, St. Paul.

INTRODUCTION

Periodic fires are part of the natural forest, chaparral, grassland, and tundra environment in primeval wilderness. In these lands where the earth and its community of life are untrammeled by man, fire is as natural and vital a process as rain, snow, or wind. From jack pine and aspen in the Boundary Waters Canoe Area Wilderness (BWCAW) of Minnesota, through lodgepole pine in Yellowstone National Park, Wyoming, to the giant sequoia of California's Sequoia, Kings Canyon, and Yosemite National Parks, fire has clearly played an essential role in the distinc-

tive functioning of each of these ecosystems.

Evidence for the past role of fire is found in charred wood and cones in glacial deposits, in charcoal stratigraphy of laminated lake bottom sediments, and in fire-scarred cross sections or wedges from both recent and ancient trees (McBride 1983; Swain 1973). Such fires were ignited by lightning or by aborigines. To a great extent the ignition source was unimportant; when fuels and weather conditions were right, the vegetation would burn. The kind of fire activity that characterizes a specific re-

gion is known as its "fire regime." Such regimes vary from ponderosa pine forests where frequent low-intensity surface fires were the pattern, through true fir forests where very long-interval (more than 300 years) stand-replacement fires occurred.

The goal of wilderness fire management, be it in national forest wilderness or in a national park, is to restore fire as nearly as possible to its natural role. Before 1970, our western, urban-based society perceived fire as a destroyer and attempted to ban it from wilderness. The past two decades have brought an enlightened biocentric approach to wilderness management (as contrasted to the previous anthropocentric approach) that allows fire to play its natural role to the maximum possible extent—consistent with the safety of people and adjacent nonwilderness resources. This chapter explores our current knowledge of fire ecology and alternatives for restoring this important force to wilderness. We also examine needs for future research to better understand the role and function of fire in national parks and wildernesses and how we can best provide for that role.

FIRE OCCURRENCE AND BEHAVIOR

In the past 10 years we have developed the capability to predict with fair accuracy the behavior of wildland fire (Albini 1976; Andrews 1986; Burgan and Rothermel 1984; Keown 1985b; Rothermel 1983). Nevertheless, knowledge of fire behavior and actual fire experience are still required to ensure valid input of data and interpretation of the output (Keown 1985b). Before we consider the place of fire in wilderness management, let us review the key factors that determine whether a fire will be ignited, namely fuel, weather, topography, and ignition source, and how it will behave thereafter.

Fuels

The accumulation of some minimum level of smaller fuels, sufficiently dried, and properly arranged is critical to ignition and spread of fire. Even heavy fuel loads may not burn when exposed to a moving, self-perpetuating fire if they are discontinuous, poorly arranged in terms of heat transfer, or too moist. The chemistry of certain fuels such as chaparral, however, renders them more flammable when living than when dead and dry. In forests, unlike chaparral, crown fires usually require adequate surface fuels beneath the stand and some ladder fuels to carry fire up into the tree crowns (Van Wagner 1977).

Fig. 12.1. Lightning is the primary source of ignition in wilderness ecosystems. Photo courtesy of John Cossett, USFS.

Weather

Suitable burning weather is characterized by one or more factors that promote drying of available fuels: (1) a precipitation-free period long enough to reduce the moisture content of fine- to medium-sized fuels to the critical level; (2) sufficiently high temperatures; and (3) low relative humidity (often less than 30 percent). In level terrain, some wind is generally required to make wildfires spread rapidly. In mountainous terrain, fires create their own drafts uphill. In certain chaparral areas, like southern California, dry, warm Santa Ana or Foehn winds are important contributors to fire weather.

Ignition Source

The major natural ignition source is lightning (fig. 12.1). If thunderstorms are not accompanied by heavy rains, fires can result from strikes in snags, trees with dry rot, flammable crowns, or ignition of surface fuels. On many wilderness travel routes, humans are also an ignition source; in historic times, Native Americans commonly burned much of what is wilderness today (Arno 1985; Gruell 1985). Aborigines burned for many reasons, including: signaling, hunting, managing forage and animal populations, man-

aging vegetation, maintaining habitat diversity, and waging war (Dennis and Wauer 1985).

Topography/Landscape Features

Fire movements are strongly related to slope, soil, and geology of local landforms. Fires tend to move upslope. Their movements are particularly influenced by aspect and steepness of slopes. The steeper south- and southwest-facing slopes and infertile or dry landforms are particularly fire prone. Heavy forest stands or moist and fertile sites will burn only after long drying periods. Other landscape features that limit fire spread include nonflammable vegetation types, lakes, rivers, swamps, barren rock areas, snowfields, timberlines, and fresh burns where fuels are lacking.

SEASONAL AND CLIMATIC FACTORS

The annual climatic regime also has much to do with the expected occurrence of wildland fires and, therefore, the recommended timing of prescribed burning. Many North American wildernesses have snowcover from early fall through late spring or early summer. Except for this common element, seasonal patterns, which vary significantly from one area to another, fall into one of three major types (see Schroeder and Buck 1970; USDA 1941):

1. Wet winters and dry summers characterize the maritime climates of the Pacific coast, and the Cascade and Sierra Nevada ranges from Washington to Baja California. Much of the total annual precipitation in the mountains is snow. Winters are not very cold; summers are clear, warm, and dry. Occasional summer thunderstorms occur and they carry little rainfall; hence mid-to-late summer is the fire season here.
2. Dry winters and wet summers are typical of the Northeast, the Great Lakes, the Midwest, most of the Canadian boreal forest region, and the eastern ranges of the Rocky Mountains from Alberta to New Mexico. Summers have frequent frontal rainstorms, and thunderstorms are common from spring through fall, but particularly in midsummer. Most storms are accompanied by enough rain to extinguish lightning ignitions. Some dry storms, however, occur in most years; and prolonged summer droughts occur at intervals of five to 30 years.
3. More complex patterns are found in the Intermountain West and the Southeast. Characteristics of both the Pacific maritime and continental climates are found from interior British Columbia south through eastern Washington and Oregon, all of Idaho, and extreme western Montana to Utah, Nevada, and Arizona. Winter snowfall and snowpacks are moderate to heavy, and occasional periods of frontal summer rainfall occur. Extended summer dry periods are frequent, however, and dry thunderstorms are common. Lightning occurrence decreases northward.

The southeastern states and the Gulf Coast have considerable maritime precipitation derived from the Gulf of Mexico and the Atlantic Ocean. Annual precipitation is heavy and well distributed over the year, but temperatures are high, and even short droughts create conditions conducive to burning. Winter fires are possible in most areas because vegetation is cured and snowcover is usually lacking. Although thunderstorms are frequent, most (but not all) lightning ignitions are extinguished by rainfall. The vegetation of many areas is not very flammable except for the southern pine regions of the Coastal Plain and Piedmont.

MAJOR DROUGHT EPISODES

In the northern United States and Canada, "fire weather" is much drier than average weather. In primeval times, stand-replacing fires evidently occurred during infrequent major regional or subcontinental droughts. The extensive Greater Yellowstone Area fires of 1988 seem to fall in this category (Christensen and others 1989; Trenberth and others 1988). Elsewhere, it is clear from studies of fire-scarred pines, Douglas-fir, and giant sequoia that surface fires burned at closely spaced intervals (Frissell 1973; Fritz 1932; Heinselman 1973; Houston 1973; Kilgore and Taylor 1979; Loope and Gruell 1973; Mastroguiseppe and others 1983; Spurr 1954). Certainly not all these fires occurred in major drought years. Some studies seem to indicate, however, that more intense fires in these areas may have coincided with such droughts (Parsons and others in press).

**FIRE SIZE AND INTENSITY
AS ECOLOGICAL VARIABLES**

Most lightning-caused fires are small and soon go out. But some develop into surface fires that burn over hundreds or even thousands of acres—scarring trees, significantly changing the understory vegetation, killing occasional trees or groups of trees, recycling nutrients, and reducing surface fuels. An occasional blaze develops into a major crown fire, killing whole forests over large areas as occurred in the Greater Yellowstone Area in 1988 (Christensen and others 1989; Schullery 1989). But even in crown fires usually some areas remain unburned—protected by the vagaries of wind, topography, and fuel. Such sites are commonly found on north slopes, near lakes or streams, and in draws, canyons, or swamps. Bypassed areas are important as sources of plant propagules for recolonization of the burn. It is commonly supposed that small, relatively undamaging

fires are best for the wilderness. But in some ecosystems, including Yellowstone Park's lodgepole pine forests, infrequent but large crown fires covering thousands of acres are responsible for an area's distinctive character and typical vegetational mosaic (Christensen and others 1989; Knight 1987; Romme and Despain 1989). Wilderness managers need to try to provide—safely—for some burns of this character, or such ecosystems cannot be maintained in an approximation of their natural state (Kilgore in press).

FIRE REGIMES

Although chance also plays a role, how a given ignition subsequently develops is mainly determined by *fire regime,* defined by Heinselman (1985) as "the kind of fire activity that characterizes a specific region." We classify ecosystems into varying fire regimes made up of factors such as (1) fire type and intensity, (distinguishing crown fires or severe surface fires from low-intensity surface fires); (2) frequency or return intervals typical for the vegetational type or geographic unit; and (3) size of area burned in a typical ecologically significant fire. For this discussion, we have established the following regimes:

1. Frequent low-intensity surface fires—1- to 25-year return intervals.
2. Infrequent low-intensity surface fires—more than 25-year return intervals.
3. Infrequent high-intensity surface fires—more than 25-year return intervals.
4. Short-interval, stand-replacement, crown, fires—25- to 100-year return intervals.
5. Variable regime: frequent low-intensity surface fires and long-interval, stand-replacement fires—100- to 300-year return intervals.
6. Very long-interval stand-replacement fires—more than 300-year return intervals.

Combinations of regimes are typical of many regions; we have included one mixed regime to illustrate such variation. While the concept of fire regime may be an "intuitive rather than rigorous ... concept" (Pyne 1984), it is nevertheless useful in that it lends a semblance of order to an otherwise confusing, contradictory, and voluminous literature of fire ecology that tends to be highly specific and descriptive only of a particular fire at a particular time and site (Pyne 1984).

ECOLOGICAL BASIS FOR WILDERNESS FIRE MANAGEMENT PROGRAMS

Early plant ecologists such as Clements, Cowles, Hall, Ramaley, and Cooper, recognized the important effects of fire on many native vegetation types (Bock 1976). In addition, a group of fire scientists in the South known as the "Dixie Pioneers" (Komarek 1973) challenged the concept that all fires are bad. This group included a forester (Chapman 1912), a botanist (Harper 1913), an animal farmer (Greene 1931), a wildlife scientist (Stoddard 1935), and several U. S. Forest Service (USFS) scientists from southern experiment stations (Heyward and Barnette 1934). In combination, the work of these southern fire scientists showed that—depending on a variety of factors, including fire intensity—prescribed burning could be beneficial to longleaf pine, cattle, and quail without adversely affecting the chemistry of forest soils in the region.

In the western United States, two foresters with the Bureau of Indian Affairs and a forestry professor in California were studying the relationship of fire and ponderosa pine. Harold Weaver (1943), working in Washington, Oregon, and Arizona; Harry Kallander, working in Arizona; and Harold Biswell of the University of California, Berkeley, came to three conclusions: (1) that ponderosa pine forests had developed in nature with frequent low-intensity fires; (2) that fire exclusion had resulted in extreme fire hazards; and (3) that low-intensity prescribed burns can reduce fuels while simulating other ecological impacts of natural burning (Biswell 1967). Early research on the role of fire in Everglades National Park in Florida (Robertson 1953) and the BWCAW (Heinselman 1973) illustrated the importance of natural fire far beyond western wilderness. More recently, natural fire management programs implemented in National Parks Service (NPS) and USFS wildernesses in the West have led to a much better understanding of the role of fire in natural ecosystems (Despain and Sellers 1977; Kilgore 1973a, 1987; Kilgore and Briggs 1972; Mutch 1974; Parsons and DeBenedetti 1979; van Wagtendonk 1978).

THE NATURAL (HISTORICAL) ROLE OF FIRE IN WILDERNESS ECOSYSTEMS

One of the most fundamental concepts, on which all wilderness fire programs are based, is that many natural ecosystems are *fire dependent.* An ecosystem can be called fire dependent if periodic perturbations by fire significantly influence the functioning of the

system. A full recognition of fire's role is only now pervading ecological theory, but it seems clear that many of the forest, grassland, and savanna ecosystems of the primeval American wilderness were fire dependent (Ahlgren and Ahlgren 1960; Baumgartner and others 1985; Conrad and Oechel 1982; Kozlowski and Ahlgren 1974; Lotan and others 1985b; Mooney and others 1981).

Mutch (1970) hypothesized that

> plant communities may be ignited accidentally or randomly, but the character of burning is not random. . . . Fire-dependent plant communities burn more readily than nonfire-dependent communities because natural selection has favored development of characteristics that make them more flammable.

This hypothesis has tremendous significance. Because they drop highly flammable dry needles annually, ponderosa pine stands are frequently swept by fire and thus the pine gains a competitive advantage over other species that occur in mixed conifer communities (Mutch 1970).

Fire performs many roles in most ecosystems or plant communities. It plays these roles in concert with other important environmental factors such as topography, elevation, soils, and climate. The most important roles are:

1. Influences plant community composition.
2. Interrupts and alters succession.
3. Influences scale of the vegetational mosaic.
4. Regulates fuel accumulations.

5. Influences nutrient cycles and energy flows.
6. Affects wildlife habitat.
7. Interacts with insects and diseases.
8. Influences ecosystem productivity, diversity, and stability.

Influences Plant Community Composition

Fire influences species composition of plant communities by: (1) triggering release of seeds (jack pine, lodgepole pine, and others); (2) stimulating flowering and fruiting; (3) altering seedbeds by reducing litter and humus and exposing bare soil, ash, or thin humus, thus favoring germination and survival (pines, Douglas-fir, giant sequoia, larch, and many other trees, shrubs, and herbs—including some exotic species in certain systems); (4) stimulating vegetative reproduction of many species when the overstory is killed; (5) reducing competition for moisture, nutrients, heat, and light; (6) selectively eliminating parts of a plant community; and (7) controlling species and age composition for types reproduced by crown fires only (jack pine, lodgepole pine, and chaparral).

Interrupts and Alters Succession

More than any other factor, fire in the original North American wilderness periodically killed old chaparral and forests, burned grasslands, prairies, and desert vegetation, and altered the course of succession. The nature of such disturbances depended on the fire regime typical of the vegetation, topography, and region. For example, the giant sequoia-mixed conifer forests of the Sierra Nevada are thought to have typically experienced light or moderate intensity

Fig. 12.2. Two photos, taken 80 years apart, in the Mariposa Grove, Yosemite National Park, CA, illustrate plant succession in absence of fire. The 1890 photo (left) shows few understory trees. Photo courtesy of Mrs. Dorothy Whitener and Mary and Bill Hood. By 1970 (right), a dense thicket of white fir has grown. Such thickets provide a fuel ladder that could result in a fire intense enough to kill mature giant sequoias. Photo courtesy of Dan Taylor, NPS.

Fig. 12.3. Natural fire in red fir forests at Crater Lake National Park, OR, creates a mosaic of fire effects. (A) The Goodbye Fire of 1978 during a period of rapid spread. (B) The Goodbye Fire eight years later, showing the variable severity from a distance. (C) A low-severity patch in the fire, where even some of the small understory trees survived. (D) A moderate-severity patch, where many of the understory trees were killed. The white line marks approximate scorch height (4 feet) of the fire. A sheltering overstory of trees remains at this site. (E) A high-severity patch after eight years, where all trees have been killed. Photos courtesy of the NPS.

surface fires at short intervals (five to 18 years). These fires suppressed invading shrubs, true firs, and incense-cedar (fig. 12.2). They scarred, but seldom killed, the giant sequoias. At long intervals—perhaps every 500 to 1,000 years—fuel and weather would permit more intense burning, perhaps including crowning out or torching of individual giant sequoias (Parsons and others in press), and created openings that favored sequoia reproduction (Hartesveldt 1964; Harvey and others 1980; Kilgore 1973b). This pattern contrasts sharply with that of jack pine and lodgepole pine in the boreal and Rocky Mountain forests, where the primeval regime was primarily crown fire or severe surface fires covering thousands of acres at intervals of 50 to 200 years. Such fires killed most or all of the trees and opened the closed cones of the pines to reseed the area (Clements 1910; Heinselman 1973; Loope and Gruell 1973; Rowe and Scotter 1973).

Studies during recent decades have challenged the basic tenets of the Clementsian model of succession (Christensen 1988, 1989; Connell and others 1987). Postfire changes in vegetation may follow various pathways, depending on species-specific attributes related to reproduction and survival (Cattelino and others 1979). For example, a Rocky Mountain community made up of aspen, lodgepole pine, and western larch may develop in several directions, depending on the intervals between fires and the life history traits of the three species. Aspen has a 130-year lifespan and is capable of vegetative reproduction; lodgepole pine has a 200-year lifespan and needs 20 years to produce mature cones; and larch has a 300- to 400-year lifespan and it can become established from seeds dispersed at a considerable distance. If a stand is reburned in less than 20 years, lodgepole pine may be lost if it is not also present in surrounding communities. If the community burns

between 20 and 130 years after the last fire, all three species will be present. If the community burns after 200 years, only larch may remain. Chance conditions soon after disturbance, as well as long-term climate changes, play an important role in successional change and contribute to heterogeneity in wilderness (Christensen and others 1989; Sousa 1984).

Influences Scale of the Vegetational Mosaic
Periodic fire occurrence often results in a vegetational mosaic on the landscape. The scale of the patches of contrasting age classes, species compositions, successional stages, or vegetation types created depends on past fire size and the kind of fire regime involved (fig. 12.3). Scale is also heavily influenced by the physiographic base on which fire works. Steep and broken terrain often shows more complex patterns than level, gently rolling, or uniformly graded terrain, because fire and other important environmental factors are more varied in behavior and effects on complex slopes. In regions such as the boreal forest, where large crown fires or severe surface fires are common, individual patches of the mosaic may cover many thousands of acres in dynamic patterns. While there are basic principles at work, the patches—like the pieces in a kaleidoscope—are periodically rearranged by fire and succession (Wright 1974; Wright and Heinselman 1973), and a variety of configurations are possible (Knight 1987).

Regulates Fuel Accumulations
In most coniferous forest ecosystems, the production of plant biomass exceeds decomposition for many years following initiation of a new succession. Although production of all plant biomass increases with temperature, precipitation, and fertility, so does rate of decomposition. The overall result is that plant materials accumulate throughout the ecosystem in

both living and dead trees, shrubs, and grasses, and in rotting organic debris comprising the ground litter and humus.

All of these materials are potential fuel; but Brown (1985) noted that it is important to recognize that at any one time, some biomass, like living tree boles, simply will not burn. Brown (1985) also pointed out that even buildup of downed dead biomass occurs in an irregular manner as branches and tree boles accumulate on the ground in response to natural causes of mortality and downfall. Nevertheless, complex though it is, the general trend is toward an increase in fuels with elapsed time following fire.[1] Then when fire does occur again, all materials combustible under the prevailing weather and fuel moisture conditions may be reduced to ash or volatilized, and the fuel cycle starts again. Some living trees and shrubs are killed but not burned by a given fire; such snags (standing dead tree trunks) and dead shrub skeletons gradually fall and become part of a new ground fuel buildup for a subsequent fire.

Influences Nutrient Cycles and Energy Flows
In fire-dependent ecosystems, fire is a major factor influencing nutrient cycling and energy flow. The immediate effect of fire is the conversion of organic matter stored in litter, twigs, leaves, branches, and dead and down tree trunks to ash and charred materials, with some loss to the atmosphere by volatilization and some material remaining incompletely burned.[2] Available phosphorus, potassium, calcium, and magnesium levels generally increase following burning; while total nitrogen decreases, available nitrogen often increases (Wells and others 1979). Rates and pathways are influenced by fire frequency and intensity. Overall, low-intensity surface fires facilitate cycling of nutrients and generally do not increase soil erosion, while high-intensity fires volatilize large amounts of nitrogen, disrupt soil structure, and may induce water repellancy and erosion (Wells and others 1979).

Affects Wildlife Habitat
With the great differences in fire frequencies and intensities found in various fire regimes, one would expect fire to have various impacts on the broad array of wildlife species and habitats found in different ecosystems (Kilgore 1976). The influence of fires

1. See, for example, Agee and Huff 1987; Biswell 1974; Dodge 1972; Heinselman 1973; Kilgore and Sando 1975; Rowe and Scotter 1973; and Weaver 1974.
2. See, for example, Boerner 1982; Foster and Morrison 1976; Grigal and McColl 1975; and Vitousek and Reiners 1975.

on wildlife habitat can be summarized with several broad principles (Kramp and others 1983): (1) quantity and quality of browse is often increased immediately after fires; (2) fires increase quantity or availability of berries and seeds; (3) in boreal forests, fires tend to eliminate some forage plants associated with older stands of timber, such as arboreal lichens; (4) fires may increase populations of surface and wood-boring insects that are important to quail, woodpeckers, and other insectivorous birds, but may decrease populations of other insects and animal parasites; (5) fires impact "cover" by changing the scale and pattern of vegetational mosaics, as impact "edge" and diversity of related wildlife habitat through frequency, intensity, and size of burn, and may also temporarily destroy habitat for many small mammals; and (6) fires interrupt succession and alter plant species composition and vegetational structure in ways that favor some wildlife species and do not adversely affect others.

Considerable variation in wildlife population response to habitat changes caused by fire may be related to differences in (1) intensity, severity, and duration of the fire; (2) the season of burning; (3) the vegetational type and animal species involved; and (4) whether we are considering short-term effects or longer term effects. In a state-of-knowledge review of the effects of fire on fauna, Lyon and others (1978) concluded that although fire may temporarily displace species dependent on late stages of plant community development, such as caribou, marten, wolverine, and fisher, there is a remarkable stability of species numbers and populations of smaller birds and animals following fire; and in general, grouse and larger animals such as moose, deer, elk, and black bear increase in numbers after fire.

Interacts with Insects and Diseases
Relatively little quantitative research has been devoted to interactions between fire, insects, and diseases, although there is much general knowledge about ecological relationships (Alexander and Hawksworth 1976; Barrett 1985; Miller and Keen 1960; Parmeter 1977; Roe and Amman 1970). One of the first concentrated efforts at a more detailed understanding of fire-insect-disease interactions is in climax lodgepole pine stands with sparse fuels in south-central Oregon (Gara and others 1985). Many complex and interesting interactions are being investigated in what appears to be a highly productive line of study for future understanding of fire-insect-disease relationships in wilderness ecosystems.

Broadly, fire, or the lack of it, regulates the total vegetative mosaic and the age structure of individual

forest stands (Wright and Heinselman 1973) which, in turn, influence insect populations. When extensive stands of balsam fir or lodgepole pine reach maturity, outbreaks of the spruce budworm or mountain pine beetle can kill trees and create fuel concentrations that make large-scale fires possible. Such fires then terminate the outbreak by eliminating the host trees until new stands attain susceptible ages. Stand-replacing fires may thus temporarily remove such plant parasites as dwarf mistletoe on black spruce, lodgepole pine, and other species (Alexander and Hawksworth 1975; Irving and French 1971). As noted in Waring and Schlesinger (1985), attempts to reduce the frequency of disturbance by fire or insects may lead to situations where large areas of otherwise unmanaged forests are more susceptible than normal to catastrophic disturbances by insects, fire, or other factors.

Influences Ecosystem Productivity, Diversity, and Stability

Production of vegetation is heavily linked to complete nutrient cycling. Fire speeds up the recycling of nutrients that might otherwise move very slowly. Periodic light surface fires or severe fires at long intervals prevent the accumulation of nutrients, dry matter, and energy in organic soil layers, reduce peat formation, and prevent permafrost encroachment (Heinselman 1974). Recurrent burns might be necessary to maintain long-term system productivity in many ecosystems.[1]

Because there is considerable disagreement about how to measure diversity and stability, it is difficult to compare the effects of fire on these factors in wilderness ecosystems. Vogl (1970) noted, "if stability is defined as the ability to resist change, then ... vegetative cycles maintained and driven by fire must be considered to be stable." As such, grasslands, chaparral shrub fields, and lodgepole pine communities would be considered very stable, because fires in such seral communities result in replacement vegetation similar to that originally found there, while fire in a climax spruce-fir forest results in extreme changes (Brown 1975). In vegetation where large crown fires are typical, individual patches of a mosaic may cover thousands of acres in dynamic patterns, yet the mosaic as a whole changes little over time.

Early ecological concepts held that climax communities were inherently more diverse and stable than pioneer communities that follow fire. But "undisturbed" natural systems apparently did not exist in the real world. Fire interrupts successional trends

1. See, for example, Loucks 1970; Vitousek and Reiners 1975; and Wright and Heinselman 1973.

at intervals related to the operational fire regime. Thus, the ever-changing, fire-created mix of successional stages, communities, and stand ages in the vegetation mosaic of most wilderness ecosystems stabilizes the system as a whole (Heinselman 1978; Loucks 1970; Wright and Heinselman 1973).

HOW HAS THE HISTORICAL ROLE OF FIRE BEEN MODIFIED BY FIRE SUPPRESSION?

Since the early part of the century, fire has been systematically suppressed in national forests, national parks, and other public and private lands. Early suppression efforts were sometimes feeble, but by the 1930s and 1940s had dramatically improved. Thus, most season-long fires that had burned forests, shrublands, and grasslands periodically for thousands of years were suppressed. This disrupted the mosaics of vegetation described in the discussion of fire regimes. As such, many lightning fires that may have covered large acreages in the Sierra Nevada or the forests or grasslands of Florida or Washington have instead been suppressed at less than the size they would have attained. This has been particularly true since aerial detection systems, smokejumpers, and aerially delivered fire retardants have been used to suppress lightning ignitions while still small.

In addition, Europeans gradually put an end to the burning done by Native Americans in many parts of North America. Such burning had been virtually eliminated by the 1700s in eastern America and as late as the 1870s in the Sierra Nevada of California. Removal of such fires, together with the advent of fire suppression, resulted in major changes in frequency of fires in certain areas, such as the giant sequoia-mixed conifer forests of Kings Canyon National Park (Kilgore and Taylor 1979). Native American-set fires were fairly widespread in the West (Arno 1985; Gruell 1985; Lewis 1985), but at the same time were often localized in distribution. Much Native American burning would have been in lower elevation areas not involved in present day wildernesses. Hence, removal of this ignition source had varied and not totally understood impacts on different fire regimes in present park and wilderness lands.

HOW HAS THE HISTORICAL ROLE OF FIRE BEEN MODIFIED BY CIVILIZATION?

Not only suppression of aboriginal and lightning fires, but developments adjacent to and downslope from wilderness and national parks have made major changes in the role that fires can now play in these near-natural zones. Many wilderness units and parks

are now surrounded by commercial forests, farms, homesites and towns, or even paved parking lots and condominiums. Vegetation has often been subjected to unnatural forces—pinyon-juniper stands removed by chaining, grasslands invaded by chaparral, and plant densities reduced by grazing livestock. Fires that historically would have been ignited in lower elevation zones and moved up into the present wilderness and park units will no longer play a role in maintaining the historical fire frequency. Moreover, any management plans to allow natural lightning ignitions to burn within such parks and wilderness units are seriously compromised by having high-value developments and private lands adjacent to the wilderness boundaries. Serious consideration must be given to alternatives, including use of agency-ignited prescribed burns under conditions subject to complete management control (Kilgore 1982). Of course, because these fires are restricted to "safe" burning periods, they often fall short of mimicking natural fire effects.

THE IMPACTS OF ATTEMPTED FIRE EXCLUSION ON WILDERNESS ECOSYSTEMS

The reduction in the presence of fire for the past 50 to 80 years in certain western wildernesses may have resulted in two primary changes that should be of concern to the wilderness manager: (1) it may have resulted in the increased incidence of unnatural fuel accumulations, and (2) it may have caused some modifications of vegetation structure beyond the range found in presettlement ecosystems (Bonnicksen and Stone 1981, 1982b; Parsons and others 1986).

In short fire-interval ecosystems, where fires occur every 10 years or so, on the average, lack of fire for a 50- to 80-year suppression period could allow accumulation of fuels to an unnatural level (van Wagtendonk 1985). By contrast, in long fire-interval ecosystems, where natural fire cycles range from 100 to 500 years or more, fire suppression for the past 50 to 80 years has probably not affected these ecosystems greatly (Habeck 1985).

Forest structure is often divided into four conceptual aspects: *age structure, species composition, horizontal structure* or *mosaic pattern*, and *vertical structure* or *fuel ladders* (Kilgore 1981). Each of these aspects can be modified by fire exclusion. In the frequent, low-intensity fire regime, lack of fire has allowed shifts in species composition from sun-loving pine to more shade-tolerant true fir and related changes in mosaic patterns and vertical fuel ladders as well as changes in age composition of the various mixed conifer species (Bonnicksen and Stone 1982b; Kilgore and Sando 1975;

Kilgore and Taylor 1979; Parsons and DeBenedetti 1979; van Wagtendonk 1985).

Fire suppression has brought the following structural changes to ponderosa pine and sequoia-mixed conifer forests: (1) a large increase in the younger age classes of pine (in climax ponderosa pine types) and shade-tolerant white fir (in sequoia-mixed conifer forests); (2) survival of saplings beneath mature trees (in ponderosa pine forests) and one or more vertical layers of white fir beneath the overstory canopy of sequoia and pine (in sequoia-mixed conifer forests) providing ladder fuels (fig. 12.2) that can lead to high-intensity crown fires; (3) many more trees per acre, particularly of young shade-tolerant saplings; (4) a blending of what had been discrete patchy units into a more uniform forest, with more uniform burning intensities, gradually destroying the identity of individual even-aged groups or aggregations found in presettlement times (Bonnicksen and Stone 1982b; Cooper 1960; Kilgore 1973a; Kilgore and Taylor 1979; Lunan and Habeck 1973; Parsons and DeBenedetti 1979; Vankat and Major 1978; Weaver 1943, 1974; West 1969).

Brown (1985) suggests that "mosaics of successional stages offer a more fundamental and reliable basis for determining naturalness than do fuel build-ups." Work is continuing on the impact of fire suppression on other vegetational types (Davis and others 1980), particularly those Rocky Mountain forests involving mixtures of lodgepole pine, Douglas-fir, ponderosa pine, and larch in which a variable regime of frequent low-intensity surface fires alternates with long-interval stand-replacement fires.

OBJECTIVES OF WILDERNESS FIRE MANAGEMENT

In view of the important natural roles played by fire in various wilderness ecosystems and the impacts of fire suppression/exclusion on short fire-interval systems during the past 50 to 80 years, it is not surprising that some form of restoration of the fire process is the objective of most wilderness fire management programs. The basic objective can usually be stated as follows: "To restore fire to its natural role in the ecosystem to the maximum extent consistent with safety of persons, property, and other resources." Note that the goal is *not* to produce any specific mix of vegetational types, to create desirable wildlife habitat, to reduce fuels, to improve aesthetics, or to attain related specific benefits. Some of these benefits might accrue from a successful program, but the

objective is to "restore the naturalness of the environment and let natural processes take over" to the maximum extent possible.

In large national parks and wildernesses, the objectives are also to try to perpetuate landscapes and landscape processes. Said another way, managers want to aim for a moving-picture vignette made up of a range of the kinds of spatial patches that would have existed in our time had we not interfered with the processes responsible for creating and maintaining such patches. The range of patches and relative importance of different disturbance processes should be regarded as variables likely to change in the future (Kilgore in press).

AGENCY WILDERNESS FIRE POLICY/OBJECTIVES

Although the national wilderness management program is shared by many state and federal agencies, the most important wildernesses are managed by the USFS and the NPS. The objectives and programs for wilderness fire management in these two agencies have changed tremendously in the past two decades. In 1968, largely based on recent ecological research findings, the NPS modified its policy of immediate suppression of all fires, which had been standard practice since the late 1800s. The USFS also began allowing lightning-caused fires to play a more natural role in wilderness in 1970, and in 1971, exceptions to the policy of suppressing all fires by 10 a.m. the following day were authorized when approved by the chief of the USFS. This gradual modification of policy (see Kilgore 1976, 1982) culminated in early 1985 in a policy revision whereby the USFS may ignite fires in wilderness under certain conditions.

One of the important aspects of the new USFS policy is the use of prescribed fire to reduce unnatural buildups of fuels when this is necessary to meet the two objectives of fire management in wilderness. These two objectives are: (1) to "permit lightning-caused fires to play, as nearly as possible, their natural ecological role within wilderness" and (2) to "reduce, to an acceptable level, the risks and consequences of wildfire within wilderness or escaping from wilderness" (USDA FS 1985). USFS personnel will ignite fires only where—because of past fire suppression—"acceptable" lightning-caused fires alone cannot achieve wilderness management objectives. Thus before using prescribed fire, wilderness managers need to be sure the fire danger in a given area, as a result of fire suppression, is greater than would have existed had fire been allowed to occur naturally during the past 50 to 80 years (Kilgore 1987).

In the NPS, the objectives for wilderness fire management, as well as most other resource management objectives for the natural areas of the national parks, are grounded in principles laid down by the Leopold Report of 1963. Despite the fact that the original document can be interpreted as seeing park ecosystems as static rather than dynamic entities (Graber 1983), the Leopold Report (1963) was the first document to explicitly call for an ecologically based management philosophy and "it remains to this day the most concise statement of park principles" (Kenner 1985). The report stated:

> As a primary goal, we would recommend that the biotic associations within each park be maintained, or where necessary recreated, as nearly as possible in the condition that prevailed when the area was first visited by white man. A national park should represent a vignette of primitive America. . . . A reasonable illusion of primitive America could be recreated, using the utmost skill, judgment, and ecologic sensitivity. This in our opinion should be the objective of every national park and monument. . . . Above all other policies, the maintenance of naturalness should prevail.

Several NPS researchers proposed that the "principal aim of National Park Service resource management in natural areas should be the unimpeded interaction of native ecosystem processes and structural elements" (Parsons and others 1986). Any need for intervention in such natural ecosystem operations would be reduced to a limited set of cases, such as: (1) to reverse or mitigate anthropogenic factors where knowledge and tools exist to do so; (2) to protect a featured resource; and (3) to protect human life and property (Graber 1985). Included in that limited set of cases requiring intervention— meaning the use of prescribed fire—would be the situation where a fire would now burn with greater intensity than would have occurred under natural conditions, "for example, an unnaturally intense crown fire caused by unnatural fuel buildup that drastically changes a community type adapted only to frequent low-intensity surface fires" (Parsons and others 1986).

Differing points of view have been expressed by several scientists who particularly criticized NPS fire management policy (Bonnicksen 1989) or implementation (Wakimoto 1989). Bonnicksen (1989) supported management actions grounded in science rather than dependence on "letting nature take its course." Specifically he suggested scheduled prescribed burns and mechanical treatments to break up blocks of forest into mosaic patterns determined by managers.

Wakimoto (1989) urged greater emphasis on written prescriptions, better trained fire staff, and uniform terminology. The Society of American Foresters (SAF) has taken a position supporting the important role fire plays in forest and range ecosystems—a role which varies from "a gentle surface fire to a volatile inferno." The SAF position supports managed natural fires (prescribed natural fires) "when contained within predetermined prescriptions ... as important ecological components of natural systems" as well as human-ignited prescribed burning and suppression when executed by qualified professionals (Society of American Foresters 1989).

Agee and Huff (1986) believed that neither structure nor process alone can be defended as the appropriate vegetation management goal for wilderness. "Both can be interpreted as being mandated by the Wilderness Act; conversely, both can be criticized for not producing truly natural vegetation. The issue becomes which is most appropriate in a certain situation" (Agee and Huff 1986). After analysis of a wilderness situation having frequent fire (Crater Lake, OR), they concluded that the natural fire regime, size of the area, and degree of past human intervention all influence the setting of goals. They indicated that a more reasonable approach at Crater Lake may be "to integrate both types of goals into a hybrid structure/process goal" in which fire is reintroduced in a low-intensity mosaic pattern as the restorative tool, but with attention paid to maintaining structural elements (mature pine) that are not easily replaced if removed by fire (Agee and Huff 1986).

In the sequoia-mixed conifer forest, some researchers advocate fairly tight quantitative standards for restoration of vegetative aggregations found as part of that ecosystem (scene management) before fire is restored (Bonnicksen 1985). On the other hand, some managers feel that simply allowing natural fires (lightning-caused) to burn again in all ecosystems is best (Worf 1985). We tend to see a middle ground similar to that noted by Agee and Huff (1986) where prescribed fire could be used to reduce unnatural fuels and to ameliorate major changes in forest structure (Kilgore 1985b), but without the precision suggested by Bonnicksen and Stone (1982b). Clearly some situations, such as Crater Lake forests where logging has reduced pine/white fir ratios, require special care in restoring fire if managers are to replicate natural conditions in the sites (Thomas and Agee 1986). Managers are wrestling with these concepts and tend toward a conservative management strategy of "minimum intervention" (Bancroft and others 1985; Parsons 1989). These are difficult decisions, and research in the very near future could play an important role in clarifying the best way to go

in achieving the broad common goal. That goal is to let "natural processes operate as freely as possible while minimizing the impacts of human actions—past and present—on wilderness ecosystems" (Kilgore 1985a). As Knight (in preparation) pointed out, one of the primary values of large natural areas is the "near-natural disturbance regime and the biological diversity that it engenders, relatively free from human interference." Such a passive or semipassive approach to wildland management has been both supported (Knight in preparation) and criticized (Bonnicksen 1989; Chase 1986) by various scientists.

Following high-intensity fires in the Greater Yellowstone Area in 1988, an Interagency Fire Management Policy Review Team appointed by the secretaries of agriculture and interior recommended modifications to agencies' fire management policies for national parks and federally designated wilderness areas (USDA, USDI 1989). Although the review team confirmed that the objectives of prescribed natural fire programs in national parks and wildernesses are sound, it suggested that implementation of these policies needed to be refined, strengthened, and reaffirmed.

Policy changes were made to even more carefully screen prescribed natural fires to allow only legitimate prescribed fire programs and to encourage use of management-ignited prescribed burns to complement prescribed natural fire programs. All fire management plans are now reviewed to ensure that current policy requirements are met and that they include interagency planning, stronger weather and fuel prescriptions, and additional decision criteria. In addition, line officers must now certify daily that adequate resources are available to ensure that prescribed fires will remain within prescription, given reasonably foreseeable weather conditions and fire behavior. Agencies are also developing contingency plans to constrain use of prescribed fire in the event of unfavorable weather or fire conditions, or when needed to balance competing demands for scarce fire suppression resources (USDA, USDI 1989).

WHAT IS "NATURAL" IN WILDERNESS FIRE MANAGEMENT?

The term "natural" does not yet have a common meaning in wilderness fire management or fire ecology. It can mean (1) fire occurring during the pre-European, pretechnological, or presettlement periods; (2) fire occurring without human intervention or influence; (3) the attributes of the fire process known or presumed to be an intrinsic part of a given

vegetative type; or (4) the role fire played in the evolution of an ecosystem.

Managers of national parks and wilderness units are still seeking to clarify whether Native Americans should be considered as sources of "natural" or "primeval" fire. During the 1983 Wilderness Fire Symposium, workshop participants addressing the role of Native American burning recommended against adopting a policy that would override site-specific characteristics and needs of individual areas.

The working definition developed for the 1983 Wilderness Fire Symposium, involving both the fire process and the resulting effects, was that (Kilgore 1985a):

> A natural fire for any given ecosystem (1) burns within the range (and frequency distribution) of fire intensities, frequencies, seasons, and sizes found in that ecosystem before arrival of western technological man, and (2) yields the range of fire effects results found in that ecosystem before the arrival of technological man.

Even with this definition in mind, philosophical and policy questions remain about the appropriateness of restoration efforts. Should wilderness and park managers (1) simply allow natural fires to burn; (2) reduce obvious fuel accumulations in certain zones with prescribed fires and then allow natural fires to burn; or (3) carefully restore natural stand structure to estimated presettlement conditions before allowing natural fires to burn (Bancroft and others 1985; Bonnicksen 1985; Bonnicksen and Stone 1985; Kilgore 1985a; Lucas 1985; Parsons and others 1986; Worf 1985)? Allowing natural fires to burn has a broad appeal, but it has drawbacks, too. In presettlement times, many lightning fires originated outside of and spread into areas now classified as wilderness. In addition, some lightning fires currently ignited in wilderness will be suppressed. Hence, an array of options needs to be carefully evaluated (Kilgore 1987). These options include allowing natural fires to burn where possible and using prescribed fire where natural fires cannot be allowed to burn, where ignitions from outside wilderness are no longer possible, and where unnatural fuel accumulations must be reduced.

As we learn more about how fire operates, the definition of "naturalness" becomes more complex. As Johnson and Agee (1988) point out, "components of these [national park and wilderness] ecosystems cannot be defined at a particular level that will unequivocally be perceived as 'natural,'" because the word *natural* involved individual value judgments.

"Park and wilderness preservation goals will have to be stated in more precise system-component terms, depending on the values represented by the individual area" (Johnson and Agee 1988).

Although it may be difficult to define such concepts as "wilderness," "wildness," and "natural," the management objectives for parks and wilderness require that we try. If not, we will have lost contact with the philosophy behind the original establishment of national parks and wilderness. In our approach to such objectives, we need to realize that whatever we thought we knew from the research of the past may be supplanted by newer knowledge. We need to be continually open to the best and latest thinking about the more complex role fire and fire suppression have had on the given ecosystem we deal with. The lofty concept of "maintenance of naturalness" can serve as a basis for evaluating the results of our detailed technical prescriptions. This will be a major challenge for both scientists and managers in the next decade.

FIRE POLICY ALTERNATIVES AND THEIR CONSEQUENCES

Five broad policy alternatives are available: (1) attempt to suppress all fires; (2) allow all fires to burn; (3) manage lightning-caused fires; (4) use prescribed fires; and (5) manipulate vegetation and fuels without fire. Although these options can be combined, it is useful to describe each separately. Failure to pursue a specific policy will still result in the unintended or haphazard implementation of one or more options.

Attempt to Suppress All Fires

A fire-exclusion policy requires an immediate, aggressive attempt to suppress all fires, regardless of cause, location, or expected damage. It might fail in application, but if the policy requires prompt suppression, without exceptions, then the objective is to exclude fire from the ecosystem. Until the early 1970s, this had been the standard policy in most wildernesses and national parks, and it remains the policy in many. At the very least, it is often defensible as a holding action until the expertise and equipment to implement a more desirable option are available, or until a rational judgment concerning the best alternative can be made. But if it is known that an ecosystem was strongly fire dependent, managers must recognize that fire exclusion is really a powerful form of vegetational manipulation. It requires personnel, machines, and large inputs of management funds. In most areas, fire exclusion is really a large-scale ecological experiment because, if the natural system was

fire dependent, we have no way of foretelling the ultimate consequences of excluding fire. If the policy succeeds, there will probably be major changes in both vegetation and wildlife populations and perhaps also major changes in the productivity, diversity, and stability of the ecosystem.

As noted earlier, accumulation of fuels and changes in vegetational structure may occur. In the kinds of ecosystems we are discussing here, fire was one of nature's ways of reducing fuels and recycling biomass and nutrients. With both lightning and humans as sources of ignition, one wonders if fire exclusion is really a viable option in such ecosystems. By following a policy of exclusion, we may be setting the stage for major crown fires that could not only endanger human life and property, but could also disrupt the very ecosystems we are purportedly protecting. Fire exclusion often requires the use of bulldozers or other heavy line-building equipment, aircraft, smokejumpers, and retardants. When major fires in wilderness threaten lives or property outside the wilderness, managers are tempted to use all available techniques, regardless of the consequences to natural resources. Fire exclusion, if practiced too long, can therefore force managers to inflict major damage on the landscape in the name of saving the wilderness from fire. The erosion of tractor-built firelines in Alaska illustrates the kind of lasting environmental damage that can occur from fire suppression (Viereck 1973). Unless it is not a significant factor in the ecosystem, fire should not be excluded except as an interim measure.

More reasonable variations of this aggressive attack policy in wilderness are the USFS's "confine, contain, and control" tactics. As noted by Fischer (1984), *confine* means to restrict a fire within predetermined boundaries, *contain* means to surround the fire with a fireline to check its spread, while *control* means to put it out, involving fireline construction, burning out, and otherwise removing any threat of subsequent escape. Some fairly creative efforts at minimizing impacts on wilderness resources can be developed under the "confine" tactic, including careful observation and monitoring of the fire's progress to assure that it stops at reasonable natural boundaries. In some cases, this may require little more than the monitoring tactic involved in the NPS's prescribed natural fire program.

Allow All Fires to Burn

Allowing all fires to burn is the opposite of fire exclusion. It is even less acceptable than exclusion unless the ecosystem is essentially fireproof. Such a program may endanger human life and property—

including lives and property beyond wilderness boundaries. Responsible management must provide for the safety of persons and property—both outside the wilderness and for visitors and agency personnel within the area. Therefore, this option usually must be rejected.

Manage Lightning-caused Fires

A policy of managing lightning-caused fires rests on the belief that they are natural and desirable in wilderness ecosystems (fig. 12.4). This policy attempts to restore such fires to their natural status while protecting lives and property and coping with unnatural fuel accumulations that if ignited might damage wilderness resources. The approach avoids direct manipulation as much as possible by allowing

Fig. 12.4. Between 1968 and 1986, about 1,200 lightning-caused fires were allowed to burn about 190,000 acres on specially designated zones in national parks and national forest wildernesses. Most of these fires were small, low-intensity fires, which burned less than one-fourth of an acre (top), but a few covered thousands of acres over several months, usually closely monitored by fire specialists (above). Photos courtesy of Bruce Kilgore, NPS.

Fig. 12.5. Prescribed burns (left) are used in certain wildernesses and parks when lightning fires cannot be allowed to burn because of hazardous accumulations of fuel and changes in forest structure induced by fire suppression. Such prescribed burning is also appropriate in small-sized wildernesses and near wilderness boundaries, where natural fire might threaten commercial developments and private lands (right). Photos courtesy of Bruce Kilgore and William Jones, NPS.

nature to select the time, place, vegetation, and fuels for fires through lightning ignitions. The management involves selective fire control based on both safety and ecological considerations.[1] For many areas, this is a viable approach to the fire problem, and we will be discussing it further.

Use Prescribed Fires
The goal of a prescribed-fire policy is to restore the natural fire regime by substituting deliberate ignitions for lightning-caused or Native American-caused fires (fig. 12.5).

The commonly held assumption that the ecological effects of fire will be the same, whether human or lightning caused, is not totally valid. Although it might be possible through skillful firing to create significant burns that closely resemble lightning-caused fires, it might also be possible to burn in seasons when lightning never occurs, or at closer than natural intervals. These circumstances should not alone preclude the use of prescribed fire. The main advantage of this option is that fires can be managed best if the time and place of ignition are selected in advance, thus allowing time to ready personnel and equipment, monitor weather forecasts, assess fuels, and prepare control lines (Agee 1974; Heinselman 1971, 1973; Lotan and others 1985b). Many situations exist—such as small management unit size and proximity to wilderness boundaries—where lightning fires cannot be allowed to burn.

Prescribed fire then becomes a reasonable substitute. This option will also be explored in greater detail.

Manipulate Vegetation and Fuels Without Fire
Another policy rejects fire, both lightning-caused and prescribed, as an unacceptable or unsafe agent of change, and substitutes mechanical manipulations such as harvest of the forest, soil disturbance, or planting for the periodic natural perturbations caused by fire. Safety is usually given as the reason for favoring this option (Kaufert 1964). Vegetation removal need not be commercially motivated, and no product must necessarily be moved from the site. In fact, it would be illegal to sell the timber in either a wilderness or national park under present U.S. statutes.

There are many ecological problems with this approach. An important criticism of such widespread control is that the scientific values associated with natural vegetation would be lost when virgin forests or natural vegetation of any type are heavily manipulated. As a method of restoring vegetation already altered by commercial logging, the method might have some merit. But once a little manipulation is begun, it is easy to conclude that more would be better. At some point the whole concept of natural ecosystems is sacrificed, and a managed forest is substituted. If carried very far, this alternative becomes silviculture, not perpetuation of wilderness. Silviculture has its place—but not in wilderness.

Combined Alternatives
Various combinations of the above fire alternatives would be possible, but the most practical combina-

---

1. See Agee 1974; Daniels 1974; Habeck and Mutch 1973; Kilgore 1987; and Mutch and Davis 1985.

tion—one now being used in various parks and wildernesses—involves (1) allowing lightning-caused fires to assume their natural role as much as possible, (2) using prescribed burns where it is impractical to allow lightning fires to burn or where past suppression requires a reduction in unnatural fuel accumulations, and (3) suppressing fires in developed areas and near boundaries. The "confine" tactic from the suppression strategy may also prove highly useful in managing a wilderness fire program.

FUTURE TRENDS AND IMPORTANT POLICY DECISIONS

The panel of scientists assessing the ecological consequences of the 1988 fires in the Greater Yellowstone Area pointed out that administration of national parks and wildernesses is becoming more complex (Christensen and others 1989). They note that it was relatively easy to set broad objectives to protect a particular national park or wilderness scene; but it is far more difficult to develop objectives to preserve and protect particular natural processes. The next generation of managers will need to rewrite ideals into management objectives and answer the questions "what kind of manipulation is acceptable? by what means? for what purposes? on what scale? according to what social and political processes?" (Christensen and others 1989).

In the next decade, four policies related to manipulation of wilderness fire must be decided: (1) Under what conditions are scheduled prescribed burns or human-ignited burns appropriate in parks and wildernesses? (2) Do we need to simulate the historic role of Native American burning in certain wilderness units? (3) How do we deal with the natural role of high-intensity, stand-replacing fires characteristic of many northern wilderness ecosystems? (4) If natural-ignition fires are part of a given unit's fire plan, what scale of fire (patch size) is acceptable?

Lacking evidence on the importance of Native American burning and recognizing the difficulties of mimicking it, the NPS has minimized such activity in management plans for parks in the Sierra Nevada (Parsons and others 1986). The 1983 Missoula wilderness fire workshop concluded that the role of Native American burning would need to be decided on a site-by-site basis. No overall policy decision could be given for California, Minnesota, and Florida parks and forest wilderness units (Dennis and Wauer 1985). A review panel, convened to evaluate the fire management programs in Sequoia-Kings Canyon and Yosemite National Parks in California, proposed that "considerable additional research is needed on role

and patterns of burning by Native Americans in these ecosystems so that an informal decision can be made as to whether fire management policy should incorporate those activities" (Christensen and others 1987).

At the same time, through a combination of research and experimental management, the NPS is seeking to determine how much change in vegetational structure and fuel accumulation is needed as a basis for using prescribed burns to restore more natural conditions before allowing lightning fires to burn (van Wagtendonk 1985). Sequoia-Kings Canyon and Yosemite National Parks are gathering additional data on fire history and effects, including: (1) paleoecological studies of the importance of fire over the past 10,000 years; (2) a detailed fire history extending back more than 2,000 years, using fire scar data from giant sequoias; (3) studies of fire-pathogen interactions to provide better understanding of the effects of fire suppression and prescribed burning on forest pathogens; (4) studies of the effects of prescribed fire on roots and cambium; and (5) studies of long-term climate variation in the Sierra as it relates to sequoia establishment and fire occurrence. The USFS is moving cautiously to determine whether there has been substantial change in the fire danger in a given wilderness area, because of fire suppression, before allowing agency personnel to use prescribed burning in wilderness.

High-intensity fires in wilderness pose one of the most difficult policy and program dilemmas of the 1990s (Heinselman 1985; Kilgore 1982). Various reports on the Greater Yellowstone Area fires of 1988 emphasize this point (Brown in press; Christensen and others 1989). Based on his experience with the BWCAW, Heinselman believes that "you simply cannot duplicate the ecological effects of [such] stand-replacing crown fires with gentle and manageable prescribed surface burns." It seems important, therefore, that we develop either the capability to allow such fires to burn or to substitute higher intensity prescribed burns that produce the ecological effects of such stand-replacing fires. In either case, burning conditions and precautions to safeguard human life and property would exceed those found with many lightning-ignited fires in these zones. Although a number of such fires have been allowed to burn in large wilderness units in Idaho and Montana between 1979 and 1986, none covered the acreage or reached the intensity of the Greater Yellowstone fires of 1988 (Jeffery 1989; Schullery 1989; Williams 1989). Hence, the issue of how to handle large-scale, high-intensity fires will continue to be a major challenge for fire managers in the 1990s.

WILDERNESS FIRE MANAGEMENT PLANNING AND CONSTRAINTS

Wilderness fire management planning aims to provide a guide for all fire management actions within the wilderness portion of a park, wilderness, or other natural area (Fischer 1985). Such planning involves (1) determining the appropriate response to lightning fires, and (2) use of manager-ignited fires to accomplish wilderness management objectives (Fischer 1984). Wilderness fire management planning has been separated by Fischer (1985) into six essential elements: (1) describing fire and ecosystems interactions—including fire history, potential, and effects; (2) describing special resource and use considerations—such as archeology, rare and endangered species, administrative sites, grazing allotments, and so forth; (3) defining fire management objectives; (4) delineating fire management units and zones; (5) developing fire management prescriptions; and (6) devising a fire management plan.

Managers need a clear understanding of the natural fire regime in an area of concern. Recent minimum-impact techniques have been developed—relying heavily on increment boring—to determine fire history in wilderness and park ecosystems (Barrett and Arno 1988). Ideally, managers would use such techniques to describe "quantitative and unambiguous standards of naturalness" for developing and evaluating a park and wilderness fire management plan (Bonnicksen 1985). Yet such standards do not now exist and would be extremely difficult to develop with any precision for the many ecosystems and fire regimes discussed earlier that are found throughout wildernesses. There is even some question about whether a given "natural" standard from the past would be appropriate in the future without allowance for the considerable chance variations that would occur against a backdrop of long-term climate changes (Christensen and others 1989).

In places like Sequoia and Kings Canyon National Parks, fire management is now focused primarily on restoring fire as an ecological process rather than restoring precise vegetational structure. Given our limited and imperfect knowledge about vegetational structure, fire regimes, the role of Native American burning, and possible shifts in long-term climate, the NPS has decided it can best recreate and maintain an ecosystem in which fire can function fairly naturally, by using a strategy of minimum intervention (Bancroft and others 1985).

At the same time, every effort is being made to further define "natural," to carefully monitor behavior and impact of both lightning fires and prescribed burns carried out in these areas, and to continually reevaluate both objectives and methods as these programs continue (Parsons and others 1985). Computer simulation of historical fire patterns, intensities, and frequencies can be used along with additional fire history studies to obtain a better understanding of the range of predictable fire intensities found in natural fires. Based on their review of the large, high-intensity fires in the Greater Yellowstone Area in 1988, Christensen and others (1989) maintain that "we cannot escape the need to articulate clearly the range of landscape configurations that is acceptable within the constraints of the design and intent of particular wilderness preserves."

ECONOMIC CONSIDERATIONS

Wilderness fire management programs have been planned and evaluated largely on an ecological basis rather than on cost effectiveness (Agee 1985). Yet one of the arguments for allowing lightning fires to burn in parks and wildernesses is that society will save costs of suppressing fires as well as gaining positive net values by perpetuating wilderness character. Identifying dollar value returned for dollar value spent in various wilderness fire programs is difficult (Towle 1985). In a survey of 12 national parks with significant fire management programs, Agee (1985) found that few generalizations could be made about the cost effectiveness of complex fire management plans. None of the plans compared the costs of the current plan with costs of total suppression. Average costs of lightning-caused or agency-ignited prescribed fires were from $7 to $19 per acre, while suppression costs averaged $1,830 per acre.

Using an existing fire simulation model for Olympic National Park, Washington, Agee (1985) compared cost effectiveness of several fire management scenarios. He found that allowing lightning fires to burn unsuppressed in prescribed natural fires zones, and allowing such ignitions to burn in both natural and conditional zones, with occasional suppression in the conditional zone, was less costly than full suppression. Moreover, he concluded that, even in the natural zone, up to 40 percent of the fires could escape and the plan would still be more cost effective than a full suppression plan. Using another method of cost analysis, Condon (1985) determined that the prescribed fire alternative had considerable economic advantage over the suppression alternative in a specific 20,000-acre wilderness in California.

NPS managers in Alaska feel that fire management plans have reduced suppression costs. As an example, suppression of a 13,000-acre fire in 1981 at

Wrangell-St. Elias National Park and Preserve cost $2.1 million. The limited action response identified for that zone in the subsequently completed fire plan would have called for monitoring the fire—at an estimated cost of $25,000. Another 20-acre fire was allowed to burn, with monitoring costs of $600; estimated suppression costs were $20,000 (Taylor and others 1985).

INTERAGENCY PLANNING

One of the most significant advances in wilderness fire planning has been the movement toward joint efforts across agency boundaries. This began in 1976 with the Interagency Wilderness Fire Management Program involving one-half million acres of the Teton Wilderness in Wyoming (Bridger-Teton National Forest) adjacent to Yellowstone National Park. For the first time, fire on national park lands would be allowed to cross the boundary onto national forest lands, by plan, and fires from the Teton Wilderness would be allowed to cross into Yellowstone National Park (Kilgore 1982). Cooperative agreements were in effect in 1982 that involved more than 4 million acres on five national forests and two national parks in the Greater Yellowstone region.

The 1988 Greater Yellowstone Area fires were the first test of this concept. In its report on these fires, the Interagency Fire Management Policy Review Team urged that fire management planning be further strengthened by developing joint agency fire management plans, agreements, or addendums to existing plans for those areas where fires could cross administrative boundaries (USDA, USDI 1989). They also suggested that periodic joint review of these plans should occur which would include agreement on processes and criteria to be used to make decisions on prescribed vs. wildfire and suppression strategies and tactics. The report also urged development of regional and national contingency plans and procedures, with program monitoring, to provide curtailment of prescribed fire activities when necessary because of competition for national and regional fire suppression resources.

More recent interagency fire planning efforts have involved Lassen National Forest and Lassen Volcanic National Park in California (Swanson and Denniston 1985) and an extensive interagency effort in Alaska (Taylor and others 1985). Experience with the Lassen plan indicated the importance of both the informal as well as the formal aspects of the planning process. This included laying good groundwork with line officers in the administrative hierarchies to foster commitment, and involving the grassroots levels of the organization to promote a feeling of ownership

(Swanson and Denniston 1985). Getting the public involved early in the planning process was an important phase of the process. In addition, the planning team integrated among agencies so that differences in procedures and terminology did not interfere with the overall objective, namely, to prepare a plan that would allow fire to burn in the combined park and forest ecosystems in a prescribed, rational pattern.

In Alaska, land managers and wildfire protection organizations have begun planning for fire management on more than 220 million acres of fire-prone wildland. Thirteen plans are being prepared by teams of federal, state, and private organizations to cover the major fire-prone areas of the state (Taylor and others 1985). The purpose of this planning is to accomplish fire-related land-use objectives in the most cost-efficient manner. Management options considered are: (1) full suppression for sites where human life or habitation are present and for areas of high natural resource value; (2) modified action where fires that escape initial attack will be evaluated to determine further control stategy; and (3) limited action where fire activity is desirable or where resource values do not warrant suppression costs, except to limit escape from the designated area.

This important planning effort has replaced the previous policy of total suppression with a comprehensive fire management program. The State of Alaska is in transition from simple fire suppression to planning for complex fire management, involving six federal and three state agencies and more than a dozen regional native corporations (Taylor and others 1985).

CONSTRAINTS ON PLANNING

Constraints that need to be considered in the wilderness fire management planning process include the following: (1) air quality impacts; (2) unnatural buildup of fuels and changes in vegetational structure following extensive and extended suppression activities; (3) wilderness user safety; (4) impacts of fire management on cultural resources, and particularly on archeological resources; and (5) the limitations imposed by relatively small-sized wilderness units as well as fires starting near boundaries in any wilderness unit.

Air Quality
All planning for use of prescribed fire must take into consideration the Clean Air Act (P.L. 95-95) and the public interest (Ferry and others 1985). Prescribed fires—including those ignited by lightning—produce varying quantities of smoke; such smoke is an integral part of many ecosystems and cannot be

Fig. 12.6. Smoke is natural to many forest ecosystems and cannot be eliminated without consequences. Yet when fires are deliberately set as part of a wilderness management program, the impacts of smoke on visitors and nearby communities must be carefully considered and controlled. Photo courtesy of the NPS.

separated from ecosystems without some consequence (fig. 12.6). Yet when manager-ignited fires are used as part of a wilderness management program, smoke management objectives and techniques must be carefully considered.[1]

Unnatural Fuels and Forest Structure

We have already discussed the possible impacts that fire exclusion may have had on certain short fire-interval ecosystems in terms of an unnatural increase in fuels or a change in the vegetational structure. Additional research is needed to better understand whether the changes that have occurred require management action. Nevertheless, the possibility that such changes could in time result in high-intensity crown fires influences managers to favor prescribed burning initially over lightning ignitions, particularly where suppression may have had significant impacts.

1. See the Prescribed Fire Smoke Management Guide produced by the Prescribed Fire and Fire Effects Working Team of the National Wildfire Coordinating Group, Ferry and others 1985.

Wilderness User Safety

As numbers of visitors increase in parks and wildernesses where fires are allowed to burn for long periods of time (months in some cases), the likelihood of human contact with prescribed fires also increases (Mutch and Davis 1985). Although public safety has not been directly threatened to date, the potential exists. Managers need to prepare visitors and agency personnel to avoid both accidents and disasters. A more detailed discussion of this subject will follow in the operational section.

Impacts on Cultural Resources

Although wildernesses are dedicated to perpetuation of wild natural resources, land managers must be concerned about cultural resources, too. Wilderness fire management programs may conflict with cultural programs. Fire may damage cultural resources, and suppression may do even greater damage (Anderson 1985). Most information on fire damage is based on observation and speculation rather than tested results (Kelly and Mayberry 1979; Switzer 1974). Although fire intensity and duration of heat are potentially damaging to cultural resources, heavy equipment used during suppression is the most significant threat to archeological resources (Traylor and others 1979). During the 1977 wildfire at Bandelier National Monument, New Mexico, archeologists guided fireline construction to prevent needless destruction (Anderson 1985). Managers of both park and forest wildernesses that hold significant cultural resources should consider this factor.

Limitations in Small-sized Wildernesses

Allowing lightning fires to burn is often not practical in smaller wilderness units where distance from the ignition point to the boundary may be less than a mile or where topography would allow the fire to move quickly to outside lands. This same limitation, of course, can apply to ignitions near boundaries of even larger wilderness units, as was seen in the Greater Yellowstone Area fires of 1988. Particularly where developments and private lands abut parks or wilderness boundaries, agency-ignited prescribed burns must be used to create a buffer zone of reduced fuels. Near certain small wildernesses like Pinnacles National Monument, California (Agee and others 1980)—and to some extent in larger units like Sequoia-Kings Canyon and Yosemite National Parks—neighboring landowners suppress all lightning-caused fires. Thus, a major source of natural ignitions outside the park boundary is no longer operative. Agency-ignited prescribed burns must now be substituted for natural ignitions to maintain near-natural fuel levels and forest structure.

OPERATIONAL ASPECTS OF WILDERNESS FIRE PROGRAMS

Following planning, the most important step in a wilderness fire management program is implementation (Kilgore 1982). It is here that objectives will be accomplished. It is here that the need for professional competence is greatest. The planning culminates in the operational aspects carried out by the fire management personnel of the USFS, the NPS, and other agency staff. A number of these aspects are worthy of special comment here.

Fire Behavior Prediction

In the 1980s, fire behavior prediction technology advanced rapidly (Andrews 1986; Burgan and Rothermel 1984; Rothermel 1983) and has been frequently applied to wilderness and parks (Keown 1985b). Predictions of fire intensities, potential for crowning, and effects on air quality and visitor safety are important outputs from those techniques. Fire behavior predictions are useful for understanding historical fire behavior in a wilderness, and "gaming" techniques can be used to compare predictions of fire size, intensity, and rates of spread with the actual results. Knowledge of

long-term climatic cycles and fluctuations (e.g., see Finklin 1983) are essential to adequately "game" such fire behavior. Wilderness managers can use these results to ensure that fires allowed to burn will meet management objectives or to modify prescriptions in wilderness fire plans, if necessary. All the research tools available to land managers, however, can only supplement—not replace—basic fire behavior knowledge and experience (Keown 1985b).

Fire Suppression Techniques

The special characteristics of parks and wildernesses require that routine wildfire suppression actions be adjusted to minimize signs of human activities (fig. 12.7). Tractor firelines, felled snags, helispots, and areas clearcut of standing trees and snags can cause longer lasting adverse impacts on the wilderness resource than the wildfire itself (Mangan 1985). Decisions must be made about what equipment will be allowed in wilderness and under what circumstances. Although general guidelines and special concern for impacts on wilderness resources are not new to most land managers and agencies, special guidelines need to be developed (e.g., Moody and Mohr 1988) and followed during suppression actions in each wilderness—including suppression priorities beyond protection of human life, such as property, threatened and endangered species, historical or archeological sites, and Native American religious sites. Both prefire training in special suppression techniques and postfire monitoring and

Fig. 12.7. Efficient fire control, using helicopters (above left) and fire-retardant bombing (left) has contributed to less than natural incidence of fire in some wildernesses. Photos courtesy of the USFS. Lately, light-hand tactics are being used in areas such as the Eagle Cap Wilderness, Wallowa-Whitman National Forest, OR (above), whereby fire is allowed to burn into low-fuel areas—either to go out or to be extinguished with minimal effort and disturbance of the natural setting. Photo courtesy of Francis Mohr, USFS.

evaluation of the results can help improve our efforts to "lay a light hand on the land" in wilderness fire suppression efforts (Mangan 1985).

Visitor Safety and Wilderness Fires

As noted earlier, both accidents and disasters are possible as the number of visitors to parks and wildernesses increase in areas where fires are allowed to burn. An *accident* is "an unwanted event caused by an individual who does not adequately use established safeguards to cope with a hazardous situation" (Mutch and Davis 1985). A *disaster,* on the other hand, has been defined as "an event, concentrated in time and space, that threatens people with major unwanted consequences as a result of collapse of precautions that previously had been culturally accepted as adequate" (Mutch and Davis 1985; Turner 1976).

Safety procedures that can help prevent prescribed fire accidents include: (1) interpretative contacts made with visitors near ongoing fires; (2) consistent, accurate monitoring and evaluation of fire behavior as a basis for effective briefings and contingency plans; (3) informing nearby residents and visitors about fire occurrences, status, and actions; (4) caution signs on roads and trails to warn travelers that a fire is in progress; and (5) maps and brochures that instruct/inform about safety hazards and precautions.

Mutch and Davis (1985) describe the possibility of a disaster resulting from prescribed fire programs in wilderness. Ten to twenty small lightning fires have gradually been allowed to burn under prescription during June and July in a large wilderness where numerous visitors, traveling on foot and on horseback, are scattered at unknown locations. Over a period of weeks, the weather turns hot and dry until one day in mid-August, "red flag" weather is forecast: strong afternoon winds (gusts to 50 mi/h), temperatures of 95 to 100°F, and humidities below 15 percent (Mutch and Davis 1985). A wilderness manager who has not followed these developing circumstances may be overtaken by a disaster. A disaster requires an incubation period in which events accumulate unnoticed. Perhaps these events were widespread fuel accumulation over time plus new policies/procedures allowing lightning ignitions to burn under certain conditions. A precipitating event such as the extreme winds, which could not be forecast in June or July, triggered a reaction unexpected by someone observing only one or two elements in the scenario. Wilderness managers must understand the stages by which a disaster develops, must recognize subtle warning signals during the early stages, and must adjust wilderness fire programs to ensure

the safety of both recreationists and agency personnel (Mutch and Davis 1985). As a result of the 1989 Interagency Fire Management Policy Review Team's recommendations, agencies have developed regional and national contingency plans to curtail or constrain prescribed natural fires under extreme conditions (USDA, USDI 1989).

Archeology and Wilderness Fires

In national park and wilderness units where archeological resources are significant, archeologists working in cooperation with firefighters can prevent needless site destruction (Anderson 1985). Work at the 1977 Bandelier National Monument fire indicated that: (1) resource base maps showing archeological site locations need to be given to archeologists and fire bosses on the firelines; (2) special priority should be given to monitoring any heavy equipment through all aspects of the suppression effort; (3) when numerous cultural resources are threatened by a fire, archeologists should be present to help mitigate fire suppression and to rehabilitate impacts on the resources; and (4) all archeologists serving on the fire should have completed certified courses in fire behavior and hold a current "red card" confirming their experience with fire suppression (Anderson 1985). Cultural resource managers and fire managers must work together to protect these valuable nonrenewable resources.

Air Quality and Wilderness Fires

Although prescribed fire appears essential to meet wilderness management objectives, the short-term effects of fire on air quality may violate certain air quality standards, either inside or outside the wilderness itself. The Environmental Protection Agency (EPA) has developed National Ambient Air Quality Standards (NAAQS) for six air pollutants, including particulate matter. The Clean Air Act requires all federal agencies to comply with all federal, state, and local air quality regulations (Haddow 1985).

Proposed standards for particulates will include both inhalable and respirable particulates, much smaller sized particles than previous standards have addressed. Most smoke particulates emitted from prescribed burning are in these small size classes. Land managers need to work closely with EPA and state air regulatory personnel to explain the importance of uses and control methods available for wilderness fire. Tools must be developed to predict and monitor air quality impacts and to coordinate policy making with federal and state regulatory agencies (Haddow 1985). In this way, both wilderness fire and air quality objectives can be achieved.

Training Programs and Wilderness Fires

The NPS, USFS, and state agencies managing wilderness fire programs recognize that well-trained professionals are essential to direct and implement the complex fire management programs involved in wilderness fire management. These agencies have inhouse and intraagency training programs for managers, professionals, and technicians in fire behavior, fire effects, fire monitoring, and fire suppression concepts and techniques. Specialists are trained at centers located in Grand Canyon National Park and Marana, Arizona, and through state programs such as those in California (Gaidula 1985). The programs supplement college and university fire ecology and fire management courses. Thus, the best current information is being shared among personnel responsible for planning and carrying out day-to-day fire management activities in our national parks and wildernesses.

Monitoring and Evaluating Wilderness Fires

As in most planning systems, wilderness fire planning calls for monitoring and evaluation as a final step (Parsons and others 1985). Operational monitoring of prescribed fire is the process of collecting and recording data on fire behavior, weather, fuels, topography, air quality, and fire effects to provide a basis for (1) immediate evaluation of whether the fire is still in prescription or (2) later evaluation of whether objectives were achieved (Ferry 1985). The primary purposes for monitoring fire behavior and weather on wilderness fires are to ensure the fire remains in prescription and inside boundaries and that human life and property are not threatened (Ferry 1985). The main reasons for gathering data on fuels, fire effects, and air quality are: (1) to ensure that resource management objectives are met; and (2) to minimize impacts on resources—such as air and water—outside the wilderness or park. The resource objective in wilderness and parks usually involves the restoration of natural processes, including intensities and frequencies of fire, and consequently a natural range of conditions.

Techniques for monitoring wilderness fires are outlined by van Wagtendonk and others (1982), Nichols (1983), Ewell and Nichols (1985), Ryan and Noste (1985), Ewell and Haggerty (1986), and Gavin and others (1990). Major deficiencies in current monitoring programs were the failure to monitor the program at the broad interagency level and the lack of emphasis on smoke management (Ferry and others 1985). Failure to take a broad look at the combined programs of the NPS, USFS, and BLM could result in the type of disaster described under visitor safety and wilderness fires.

Learning From Past Mistakes

Although the use of prescribed fire will always incur some risk, we can and must learn from ongoing programs, particularly where fires have not gone as planned. Such situations may be the result of mistakes in judgment or lack of knowledge and training. Between 1976 and 1980, three agencies had prescribed burns that went awry, two in wilderness and one in nonwilderness: the Mack Lake Burn (USFS), the Ouzel Fire (NPS), and the Walsh Ditch Fire (Fish and Wildlife Service [FWS]).

The Mack Lake Burn in Michigan was ignited on May 5, 1980, by foresters of the Huron-Manistee National Forest in what was intended to be a 210-acre prescribed burn in cutover jack pine. The objective was to provide critical nesting habitat for an endangered species, the Kirtland's warbler. Yet, by 7 p.m., one firefighter was dead and 20,000 acres of jack pine had burned along with 41 homes and summer cottages (Simard 1981).

The Ouzel and Walsh Ditch fires, by contrast, were wilderness fires ignited by lightning, and in each case the managing agency personnel decided to allow the fire to burn. Ouzel began on August 9, 1978, in a fire management unit above 10,000 feet elevation in spruce-fir forest of the Rocky Mountain National Park in Colorado. Although it initially smoldered and crept along, by early September high winds caused crowning and spotting (Butts 1985). On September 15 and 16, it made substantial runs outside the prescribed fire zone in the direction of Allens Park, a small community near the park's boundary. The fire had to be suppressed.

The Walsh Ditch fire started on July 30, 1976, on the Seney National Wildlife Refuge, in a marshy peat bog on Michigan's Upper Peninsula that had been recently designated as wilderness. No suppression action was taken until August 18, at which time the fire had reached 1,000 acres and was headed for state lands (Popovich 1977). By the time it was controlled, it covered 55,000 acres of the Seney Refuge, 15,800 acres of adjacent forest, and 1,500 acres of private lands. It took more than 1,000 people two months at a cost of $8 million to suppress the fire.

Certain aspects of each fire were not well managed—and we need to learn from these experiences (see more detailed analysis in Kilgore 1982). Several principles that we can learn from all three burns are:

- Complete a realistic fire management plan and prescriptions before burning or allowing a fire to burn (see Fischer 1984).
- In developing the plan, consider fire history and historic vegetation patterns, fire weather forecasts, and burning indices.

- Rigorously follow the plan! Do not gamble by modifying prescriptions specified in the plan.
- Use only well-trained and experienced personnel. Managers must assure that their prescribed burning staff gets actual burning experience (under supervision) before assuming the responsibility for prescribed fires.

EXAMPLES OF WILDERNESS FIRE MANAGEMENT PROGRAMS AND SUPPORTING RESEARCH

Wilderness fire management and research programs have been under way in a number of national parks, wildernesses, and related reserves for several years. A few examples will help identify the state of the art, as well as provide contacts and literature sources. The beginnings can be traced in part to the so-called Leopold Committee's 1963 report on "Wildlife Management in the National Parks" (Leopold and others 1963). Although not aimed directly at fire problems, it identified the ecosystem changes resulting from the elimination of natural fire as a key element influencing national park wildlife habitat. In 1965, a NPS directive called for implementing the Leopold Report, particularly for areas in the natural category in several of the large parks (Baker 1965) and expressly encouraged the use of fire, including prescribed fire, as an appropriate natural agent in ecosystem restoration programs. Fire management programs were not long in appearing.

Sequoia-Kings Canyon and Yosemite National Parks, California

The first designation of a *Natural Fire Management Zone* in forested western wilderness and the first breakthrough in prescribed burning in the West came in Sequoia and Kings Canyon National Parks in 1968. Beginning then, lightning-caused fires were allowed to burn under surveillance unless safety problems or resource damage was anticipated, in a special management zone above 8,000 feet in the Middle Fork Kings River drainage. This zone was gradually expanded and now encompasses about 740,000 acres or roughly 86 percent of these parks. The forests are generally open and subalpine, and much of the terrain is extremely rocky or above timberline. Some 305 fires were allowed to burn within this zone up to 1986, burning about 29,000 acres. Partial suppression was needed for only a few fires, and no serious problems developed (Agee 1974; Bancroft and Partin 1987; Kilgore 1982; Kilgore and Briggs 1972; Parsons 1981; van Wagtendonk 1978).

In 1969, starting in the Redwood Mountain Area

of Kings Canyon National Park, prescribed burning to reduce unnatural fuels and invading shade-tolerant understory trees began in the lower elevation mixed-conifer forests, including some giant sequoia groves (Kilgore 1972, 1973a, 1975; Kilgore and Biswell 1971; Kilgore and Sando 1975). Initially, some cutting and piling of small trees and litter was used to avoid control problems and unnatural overstory damage. Similar work was done later on a 20-acre unit of the Mariposa Grove of giant sequoias in nearby Yosemite National Park. Later, more extensive understory prescribed burning in mixed conifers was carried out without significant modification of fuels in both the Yosemite and Sequoia-Kings Canyon areas. This type of burning is now part of a large-scale operational program (Bancroft and Partin 1987; Bancroft and others 1985; Parsons 1981; van Wagtendonk 1978). In 1972, a natural fire zone was also established in Yosemite. By 1982, it included 594,000 acres or about 78 percent of the park. Essentially, any fire within this zone can safely be allowed to burn because of prevailing fuel, vegetation, and physiographic factors *if* specified weather and fuel prescriptions are met.

An additional 57,000 acres were in a *Conditional Fire Zone,* an area of restricted burning because of the fuel accumulations generated by previous fire exclusion. As these fuels are reduced, parts of the conditional zone become areas in the natural fire zone. In the remainder of the park, which includes most of the park's developments, a full-scale fire suppression program is in effect, but prescribed burning is being used to reduce fuels in critical areas (van Wagtendonk 1978). Certainly some of the success of the Sequoia-Kings Canyon and Yosemite fire management programs can be credited to the extensive research available when these programs began and to the continued cooperation of research and management.[1]

Selway-Bitterroot Wilderness, Idaho and Montana

The Selway-Bitterroot Wilderness, managed by the USFS, is one of the largest units (1,337,910 acres) of the National Wilderness Preservation System (NWPS)

---

1. See Agee 1973, 1974; Agee and others 1978; Biswell 1961; Biswell and others 1966, 1968; Bonnicksen and Stone 1981, 1982a, 1982b; Cotton and Biswell 1973; Hartesveldt 1964; Hartesveldt and Harvey 1967; Harvey and others 1980; Kilgore 1970, 1971a, 1971b, 1972, 1973a, 1973b; Kilgore and Biswell 1971; Kilgore and Briggs 1972; Kilgore and Sando 1975; Kilgore and Taylor 1979; Parsons 1978, 1981; Parsons and DeBenedetti 1979; Parsons and others in press; Rundel 1971, 1972; Stark 1968; Vankat and Major 1978; van Wagtendonk 1974, 1978, 1985; van Wagtendonk and Botti 1984; and Weaver and Biswell 1969.

and it is the first unit having operational experience with a sizable Wilderness Fire Management program.

The White Cap Fire Management Area in the Selway-Bitterroot was the first approved exception to the USFS 10 a.m. (total suppression) policy. This exception was approved in 1972. In a pioneering joint research and management effort, fire management prescriptions were written for each vegetational management zone of the 100-square-mile area (Mutch 1974). Special guidelines were developed by USFS researchers and managers for planning and inventory procedures (Aldrich and Mutch 1973). Other research support came from Habeck's studies of fire history, vegetation, and fuels in the Selway-Bitterroot (Habeck 1972, 1976).

The first major test of the White Cap plan was the 1,200-acre Fitz Creek Fire in 1973 (Mutch 1974). Although the fire had to be suppressed in one area where it had escaped the approved fire management area, the experiment was successful and presaged the incorporation of fire management considerations into wilderness planning throughout the USFS. Between 1974 and 1979, additional fire management plans were developed for various units of the Selway-Bitterroot Wilderness. The Independence Fire of 1979 burned more than 16,300 acres during a three-month period, the largest pre-1988 fire allowed to burn under a natural fire program by any agency (Keown 1980, 1985b). By 1982, more than 1 million acres in the Selway-Bitterroot Wilderness were covered by plans that allow lightning-caused fires to play a more natural role. During the first 10 years of the program, 76 lightning fires were allowed to burn nearly 39,000 acres (Kilgore 1982). Again, cooperation between managers and research people helped provide a solid technical base for this effort.[1]

Grand Teton and Yellowstone National Parks and the Surrounding Forest Wildernesses, Wyoming and Montana

Natural fire management programs in Grand Teton and Yellowstone National Parks in Wyoming began in 1972. During the first 14 years of this program, more than 177 lightning fires were allowed to burn more than 33,000 acres (Renkin and Despain 1987). Among these were 13 larger fires, ranging from 160 to 7,400 acres (Kilgore 1982). This early history, however, was dwarfed by the 1988 fires, which burned some 1.4 million acres in the Greater Yellowstone Area, including about 793,880 acres in Yellowstone National Park (fig. 12.8). These included both prescribed natural fires and wildfires (Christensen and others 1989). A series of four fires that started as prescribed natural fires covered more than 450,000 acres in Yellowstone National Park, including two fires (or fire complexes) of nearly 200,000 acres each (Greater Yellowstone Coordinating Committee 1989).

Studies of fire history and fire effects on various aspects of different ecosystems by Taylor (1969), Houston (1973), Loope and Gruell (1973), Sellers and Despain (1976), Despain (1982), and Romme (1982) served as the site-specific data base to support early fire management plans for these areas. This basic information was important to NPS managers in 1974 when the Waterfall Canyon Fire attracted much public attention to the concept of allowing lightning fires to burn in parks and wildernesses.

Considerable public support for the fire was received, but this fire illustrated the initial difficulty

1. See Aldrich and Mutch 1972, 1973; Daniels 1974; Habeck 1972, 1973, 1976; Habeck and Mutch 1973; Keown 1980, 1985a; Moore 1974; and Mutch 1970, 1974.

Fig. 12.8. In the summer of 1988—a period of extreme drought—a series of lightning-caused fires and human-caused fires burned some 793,880 acres in Yellowstone National Park. The Clover Fire in the background and the Mist Fire in the foreground joined several other fires that eventually covered about 1.4 million acres in Yellowstone Park and adjacent national forests. Photo courtesy of Jim Peaco, NPS.

in gaining support for natural fires, particularly where they were visible in residential, commercial, or aesthetically important areas. Initial public reluctance to accept natural burns was a legacy of 50 years of fire prevention campaigns that condemned all fires (Stankey 1976). Subsequent studies, however, found growing public knowledge about the natural effects of fire and growing public acceptance of fire management in wilderness (McCool and Stankey 1986).

This 3,500-acre fire also stimulated controversy about impacts of smoke on visitors to national parks and on nearby communities. Air quality concerns must be met through smoke management criteria in current fire management plans; past and future research and monitoring can also play important roles in meeting this need (Ferry and others 1985).

One of the largest natural fire areas in the United States became operational in 1982 with approval of the revised Teton Wilderness Plan. Wilderness segments of Yellowstone and Grand Teton National Parks were coordinated in a more than 4-million-acre prescribed natural fire program that included designated natural fire areas in the adjacent USFS Teton, Washakie, North Absaroka, and Absaroka-Beartooth Wildernesses (Kilgore 1987). As noted earlier under interagency planning, fire on national park lands would be allowed to cross the boundary onto national forest lands, and fires on any of the national forest wildernesses would be allowed to cross into Yellowstone and Grand Teton National Parks. This interagency fire management concept was tested in 1988, and the Interagency Fire Management Policy Review Team recommended that interagency planning needed further strengthening (USDA, USDI 1989). Agency researchers would do well to monitor the biological and sociological results of any additional fires that burn under these interagency programs.

FIRE-DEPENDENT ECOSYSTEMS IN THE AMERICAN WILDERNESS

A review of the role of fire in ecosystems of various wilderness regions—including differences in fire history and fire effects—will help explain the need for active fire management programs.

The Sierra Nevada Region of California
This high mountain country contains some of the world's best known national parks and wilderness units and some of the most magnificent conifer for-

ests on earth, including Sequoia, Kings Canyon, and Yosemite National Parks and the surrounding national forest wildernesses. The climate is winter-wet/summer-dry, with snow remaining into June in higher elevations. Dry lightning storms occur infrequently, but ignitions are common because of the dry summers (21 to 40 lightning-caused fires per million acres per year according to Schroeder and Buck [1970]). Episodes of dry thunderstorms combined with unusual dryness cause widespread fires at intervals of several years; low-intensity surface fires occur at five- to 20-year intervals in giant sequoia and ponderosa pine-sugar pine stands (Biswell 1959, 1961; Hartesveldt 1964; Kilgore and Taylor 1979; Wagener 1961).

Many giant sequoias bear impressive multiple fire scars, some of them more than a thousand years old. Most individual fires were probably small because the terrain is broken and the vegetation varied. Intensity has traditionally been thought to have been generally low, with local hotspots, depending on fuel and topography. Lightning-caused fires are also common in the high country, but seldom become large or intense because of the open character of the forest and fuel discontinuities caused by exposed bedrock, boulder fields, wet meadows, lakes, and snowfields (Kilgore and Briggs 1972). The giant sequoia and midelevation pine forests were kept open and structured by frequent periodic surface fires in primeval times, with some evidence of patchy, higher intensity burning (Parsons and others in press). Fire suppression over the last 70 years has caused unnatural fuel accumulations and invasions of true firs and incense-cedar beneath the pines and sequoias. These conditions set the stage for unnatural conflagrations that could kill even the fire-resistant pines and sequoias (Biswell 1959, 1961; Dodge 1972; Hartesveldt 1964; Kilgore 1970, 1972, 1973a; Kilgore and Sando 1975; Parsons and others in press; Weaver 1974).

The California-Oregon Coast Ranges Region
The string of wildernesses in the coastal mountains, from southern Oregon to southern California, contain chaparral or oak-madrone at lower elevations and ponderosa and lodgepole pine and other species at higher elevations. The climate is similar to the Sierra Nevada, but with fewer lightning ignitions (five to 20 fires per million acres per year). The vegetation of the chaparral-oak-madrone-digger pine zones is extremely flammable, and in nature was probably subject to periodic high-intensity fires that killed most of the vegetation. Attempted fire exclusion has created very difficult fire control problems

in the chaparral and related vegetation zones (Biswell 1974; Dodge 1972; Vogl 1967; Weaver 1974). The natural fire regime in the ponderosa-Jeffrey pine zones was probably similar to that in the Sierra Nevada.

The Coast Redwoods Region

Several small *de facto* wildernesses occur within Redwoods National Park and in some of the larger California redwoods parks. This region is within the coastal fog belt of northern California—a winter-wet/summer-dry climate, mitigated by fog drip. Elevations are slight, and snow, when it does fall, soon melts. Lightning-caused ignitions occur, although summer thunderstorms are not common. The redwoods were clearly subject to intermittent fires—many of the largest veterans bear deep fire scars hundreds of years old. The natural fire regime was probably one of long-interval, severe surface fires (Veirs 1980, 1982). Redwood sprouts from the root crown, and some groups of trees are sprouts from fire-killed individuals (Fritz 1932; Stone and Vasey 1968).

The Cascades Range of Oregon and Washington

The Cascades are dominated by a series of spectacular geologically recent volcanic peaks, many now included in wildernesses or national parks. Climate and fire history vary greatly from west to east; while summer weather is mostly clear and dry, thunderstorms do occur and lightning ignitions result in 11 to 40 lightning fires per million acres per year.

On well-watered west slopes, the natural fire regime seems to have been mostly one of large-scale but very long-interval crown fires or severe ground fires. Return intervals were perhaps 150 to 500 years or more for various sites. Extensive even-aged stands of Douglas-fir attest to past fires, and many fire boundaries are still evident (Franklin and Hemstrom 1981). The lower elevation eastside ponderosa pine forests probably had a regime of frequent light surface fires. East of the Cascade Crest, Fahnestock (1976) documented a lightning-caused fire occurrence rate of 13 fires per million acres per year in the Pasayten Wilderness (WA) from 1910 to 1969. Two fires, each exceeding 20,000 acres, accounted for 59 percent of the lightning-caused burn area. This history suggests a long-interval crown fire or severe surface fire regime for the Pasayten. Fire control has not yet significantly affected fuels or disrupted the age structure of the forest.

The Intermountain Region and the Southwest

Between the Cascade-Sierra system and the main Rocky Mountain system there is a discontinuous series of more isolated ranges from Washington and western Montana south to Arizona and New Mexico having a vegetation and fire history somewhat different from either system. The climate retains some Pacific maritime influence, with heavy snow in the winters and dry summers in the north, but with late summer rains in Arizona and New Mexico. Summer thunderstorms are frequent, with 20 to 60 lightning fires per million acres per year, especially during periods of prolonged drought (70 per million acres in the White Cap drainage of the Selway-Bitterroot Wilderness). June through September is the fire season in the north; May and June are the fire months in New Mexico and Arizona.

Throughout the region, light to moderate small fires occurred every six to 15 years in ponderosa pine and Douglas-fir stands. These fires, mainly burning on the forest floor, were severe enough to kill back most of the Douglas-fir regeneration, thin out overdense ponderosa pine saplings, and occasionally kill out individuals, clumps, or small groves of aged ponderosa pine or Douglas-fir. Such a history maintained the open ponderosa pine stands originally characteristic of lower elevations thoughout the region (Cooper 1961; Habeck and Mutch 1973; Weaver 1961, 1974). Frequent fires kept juniper woodland restricted to shallow, rocky soils and rough topography in many parts of the West. Minimum fire frequency in sagebrush-scrub communities has been reported at 32 to 70 years (Houston 1973).

At higher elevations, on some north slopes, and farther north on slopes with more maritime climates, the fire regime has often been one of long-interval (150 to 300 years), severe surface fires or crown fires that killed whole stands on individual slopes or drainages and regenerated relatively even-aged stands of western white pine, western larch, and lodgepole pine (Aldrich and Mutch 1972; Wellner 1970). In some areas, these stands also contain mixtures of western redcedar, western hemlock, and grand fir. Fire suppression in the last 60 years has probably altered fuels and vegetation most in areas that were subject to periodic light surface fires. The heavy-fuel, long-interval crown-fire regime areas and higher elevation forests have probably not been affected so much because many areas would not have burned in the period in any case (Habeck 1985; van Wagtendonk 1985).

The Rocky Mountain Region

The Rocky Mountain system, as discussed here, includes all of the eastern front ranges and the secondary western ranges extending from Jasper National Park in the Canadian Rockies south to Colorado. It

includes such widely known park and wilderness units as Glacier and Yellowstone National Parks and surrounding forest wilderness units, the Bob Marshall Wilderness of Montana, and many lesser known wilderness units in Montana, Wyoming, Utah, and Colorado.

This region holds a broad cross section of vegetation, ranging from whitebark pine, alpine larch, and extensive meadows and alpine tundra in the north and at timberline to local areas of western hemlock, western redcedar, western white pine, western larch, Douglas-fir, and ponderosa pine; but the primary species at middle to upper elevations are lodgepole pine, Engelmann spruce, subalpine fir, and quaking aspen (Daubenmire 1943; Day 1972; Habeck 1968; Horton 1956; Loope and Gruell 1973; Marr 1961; Oosting and Reed 1952; Rowe 1959; Stringer and LaRoi 1970). The climate is more continental than preceding regions, with long, very cold winters at high elevations and warm summers with considerable rainfall, much of it as thunderstorms. Most lightning fires are extinguished by rains, as such occurrence is only two to 15 fires per million acres per year; summer droughts increase northward, with highest fire occurrences in Montana and parts of Colorado.

Fire regimes in the Rockies are extremely complex, reflecting the great variation in climate, topography, vegetation, and productivity of mountainous regions (Heinselman 1985). One aspect of the vegetative complexity is the wide ecological amplitude of lodgepole pine. Lodgepole is an extremely adaptable species. In some areas it occurs in even-aged stands resulting from periodic stand-replacing fires, while in other sites it occurs with multiple ages, sizes, densities, and height classes, interspersed with small even-aged stands.

The major vegetation pattern found in lodgepole pine today was caused by stand-replacement fires, although many uneven-aged lodgepole pine stands result from lower intensity surface fires (Brown 1975; Tande 1979). Most individual fires were low-intensity, creeping, surface fires, but most acreage was burned by the occasional high-intensity crown fires that occurred during severely dry and windy weather (Lotan and others 1985a).

Prior to 1988 in Yellowstone National Park and adjacent wilderness, Despain and Sellers (1977), Romme (1980, 1982), and Romme and Knight (1981) had concluded that most stands would not sustain crown fires until they developed a significant understory component of Engelmann spruce and subalpine fir 300 years or more after the previous fire. Until 1988, such fires had ranged from 1,000 to 8,000 acres (Heinselman 1985). Despain (1983) reported large

areas of lodgepole pine with almost no spruce-fir component. He concluded that these were essentially self-perpetuating "climax" lodgepole pine stands that often exceeded 300 to 400 years of age, with no evidence of fire since establishment.

The extensive fires of 1988 in the Greater Yellowstone Area increased our understanding of the variable role of large high-intensity fires in lodgepole pine in the Rocky Mountain region (Romme and Despain 1989). The extremely dry fuel conditions combined with repeated episodes of high winds resulted in 1.4 million acres burned in the Greater Yellowstone Area, 68 percent of this in Yellowstone National Park. Of this acreage, 60 percent was burned by canopy fire and 33 percent by surface fire (Christensen and others 1989). Because of the dryness of fuels and severity of winds, a number of younger-age forests adjacent to older forests did in fact burn. But the heterogeneous behavior of the fires led to a complex mosaic of burned and unburned areas (fig. 12.9) that will be a dominant feature of the Yellowstone landscape (Christensen and others 1989; Romme and Despain 1989).

Engelmann spruce and subalpine fir stands often occur in valleys, coves, and around lakes and streams where they escape most fires, but many stands are also clearly of fire origin (Day 1972; Loope and Gruell 1973). Most quaking aspen stands were fire maintained through root suckering, but fire exclusion has prevented their renewal for 60 years, and many stands that might have burned are now in decline (Gruell and Loope 1974).

Fire has also been a factor in maintaining meadow and grassland communities in the parks of river valleys and flats. Ancient, fire-scarred Douglas-firs occurring in groves or as scattered individuals along the margins of these local grasslands tell of their fire history from Jasper Park in the north to the Yellowstone-Grand Teton region in the south (Houston 1973; Loope and Gruell 1973; Stringer and LaRoi 1970; Tande 1979). Fires apparently burned these grassland, meadow, and sagebrush areas, and crept into the Douglas-fir groves around their margins, at intervals of six to 60 years over at least the past 400 years. Both lightning and Native American ignitions were probably involved, but lightning alone is clearly a major ignition factor.

In summary, the two dominant regimes in most presettlement Rocky Mountain wilderness were: (1) long-interval crown fires (perhaps 100 to 300 years) in the continuous forests of lodgepole pine mixed with spruce and fir; and (2) short-interval (five to 60 years), low- to moderate-intensity surface fires in the lower elevation Douglas-fir, aspen, and ponderosa

Fig. 12.9. The 1988 fire season in Yellowstone Park was characterized by unusually dry fuels and periods of high wind. Once a fire was ignited, burning embers might be lofted several miles, starting numerous spot fires. Some spot fires grew to thousands of acres, some burned out at comparatively small size. The landscape of Yellowstone thus became a mosaic of burned and unburned forest, as shown in aerial views of (left) the Madison River near Madison Junction, and (below) the Old Faithful Complex (background), which was overrun by the North Fork Fire on September 7. Photos courtesy of Jim Peaco, NPS.

pine stands, grassy parklands, and in adjacent open lodgepole pine stands (Heinselman 1978).

The Lake Superior Region

The ancient Laurentian highlands surrounding Lake Superior contain several reserves that include the last major remnants of the old "Northwoods:" Isle Royale and Voyageur's National Parks; Quetico Provincial Park in Ontario; the adjacent BWCAW; and Porcupine Mountains State Park in Michigan. This is spectacular lake country, and together these areas contain several thousand small- to medium-sized lakes, largely in glacially dammed bedrock basins.

All areas have had some logging, but more than a million acres of virgin country still remain, largely in the BWCAW-Quetico area and on Isle Royale.

The climate is continental, with long, cold winters and short, warm summers. More than half of the annual 28 inches of precipitation falls during May through September, when thunderstorms are common. The frequent lightning ignitions are usually extinguished by rains but some dry storms occur. Lightning fires occur at the rate of about one to five fires per million acres per year. Fast-moving crown fires tend to occur in spring and fall (Haines and Sando 1969; Sando and Haines 1972).

Heinselman (1973, 1978, 1981, 1985) has noted that the presettlement Great Lakes forests had three distinct fire regimes: (1) jack pine and spruce-fir forests with very large stand-replacement crown fires or severe surface fires every 50 to 100 years in the west and 150 to 200 years in the east (Such fires in the BWCAW sometimes exceeded 250,000 acres in size.);

(2) red pine and white pine forests with combinations of moderate intensity surface fires at 20- to 40-year intervals, and more intense crown fires at 150- to 300-year intervals; and (3) mixed aspen-birch-conifer forests with high-intensity surface or crown fires. (While intervals are less sure here, spruce budworm outbreaks occurred every 40 to 70 years, creating tremendous fuel loads at those intervals.)

In summary, the natural fire regime of most coniferous forests in this region was one of long-interval crown fires or severe surface fires. As an example, in the well-studied BWCAW, most of the area burned and most stand origins in the last 300 years can be accounted for in about a dozen fire years (fig. 12.10) (Heinselman 1973). This history suggests that most of the ecologically significant fires occurred during infrequent periods of severe drought. There were many other fires, but they account for only small areas. The natural fire rotation for the BWCAW as a whole is about 100 years. This is the

Fig. 12.10. Fire—a natural component of many wilderness ecosystems—has a pronounced influence on the composition of plant and animal populations. This map shows the fire history of a portion of the BWCAW, noting the origin of existing forest stands. Fires dating back to the 1600s have been mapped. Map courtesy of Miron Heinselman.

gion. Jack pine and balsam fir cover the land from Quebec to Alberta; lodgepole pine and subalpine fir reach from Alberta to the Yukon. White spruce and black spruce, tamarack, plus quaking aspen, balsam poplar, and paper birch cross the continent. The climate is characterized by long, very cold winters and a winter-dry/summer-wet pattern, with occasional extended droughts when periods of warm, clear weather occur. The long days at northern latitudes permit severe drying during June and July; thunderstorms are infrequent, with lightning-fire occurrence less than one fire per million acres per year (Schroeder and Buck 1970).

During presettlement times, the dominant fire regime in the main boreal forest regions of Canada and interior Alaska was apparently one of high-intensity short- to long-interval crown fires (or severe surface fires). These were large to very large in size (Heinselman 1981), often covering more than 25,000 acres and sometimes more than a million acres (Heinselman 1985). In the drier regions of northwestern Canada and interior Alaska, fire cycles probably averaged 50 to 100 years; by contrast, cycles of 100 to 300 years were found in eastern Canada, with its wetter climate, and near treeline in the open subarctic spruce-lichen woodlands. The fire regimes of some jack pine and lodgepole pine forests in western Canada include medium-intensity surface fires that do not kill whole stands at 25-year intervals.

In summary, the typical natural fire regime in this region is one of long-interval crown fires or severe surface fires, killing most of the stands in given areas (Heinselman 1978). Most of the area burned in given subregions probably burned during major droughts at intervals of 10 to 40 years (MacLean and Bedell 1955; Rowe and others 1974).

only region where studies of charcoal stratigraphy in annually laminated lake sediments have been combined with pollen analysis to document the pre-Columbian fire regime (Swain 1973; Wright 1974). This work shows that periodic forest fires have occurred in the region for at least 9,300 years.

The Boreal Forest Region

This vast region stretches from Quebec and Labrador across northern Canada to interior Alaska (Helmers 1974; Rowe 1959). Only a few forested nature reserves having wilderness qualities have yet been designated, but great areas are still *de facto* wilderness, and more reserves may be established. Present reserves include Riding Mountain, Prince Albert, Wood Buffalo, and South Nahanni River National Parks in Canada and Denali National Park and several newer national parks and wildernesses in Alaska.

The forests are relatively simple for so vast a re-

The Eastern Deciduous Forest, Appalachian, and Gulf Coast Region

Many small- to medium-sized wilderness units have been designated or are under study in this region, including Baxter State Park in Maine, Adirondack State Park in New York, and the Great Smoky Mountains National Park in North Carolina and Tennessee. The vegetation of this large region is too diverse and complex to treat here, but in general, it is largely a mixture of broadleaf hardwoods, several pines, and some fir, spruce, and northern white cedar. The climate varies from north to south, but in general, precipitation is abundant throughout the seasons, temperatures are relatively high, and severe and short-term droughts do occur. Thunderstorms are frequent, but include rain, and forest fuels decompose rapidly. These climatic patterns result in a fire regime of infrequent surface fires during the dormant season in the hardwood forests and slightly

more frequent, but long-interval fires in conifer forests. The southern coastal plain pine region and the Everglades were clearly the exception; here frequent light surface fires were the rule (Komarek 1974; Robertson 1962).

Wetlands, Prairies, and Deserts

Wilderness units have been established or proposed for a wide spectrum of chiefly nonforested wetland, prairie, or desert grass and shrub ecosystems. Fire was vital to many of these ecosystems (Humphrey 1974; Robertson 1962; Vogl 1974). A review of these units is beyond the scope of this chapter. Managers must carefully study the natural role of fire in each area, and where evidence indicates important effects, a fire management program is needed.

TRENDS AND FUTURE NEEDS

Wilderness fire managment is complex and demanding work, requiring professional competence and intimate knowledge of the specific ecosystem and land unit to be managed. More people trained in ecology, botany, and forestry, with understanding of fire behavior and an interest in preservation management, are needed to manage these programs.

The need for natural fire programs in wilderness is generally understood by informed supporters of parks and wilderness but not among people who have been indoctrinated since childhood with the negative aspects of fire. To many such people *all* fire is bad, all smoke is pollution, and most fires kill wildlife. Stankey (1976) has described the nature and extent of the problem. This legacy from fire prevention campaigns that told an incomplete story can be overcome only by new and innovative educational work with the media and schools. Stankey's (1976) findings and more recent studies by McCool and Stankey (1986) suggest that wilderness users respond positively as they learn more about fire.

NEEDS FOR FUTURE RESEARCH

Kilgore (1987) suggests that future research and policy decisions should respond to four key questions:

1. *Have past attempts at fire exclusion affected fire regimes and the functioning of ecosystems?* To what extent has fire control resulted in unnatural changes in fuel accumulation, species composition, age structure, or horizontal or vertical structure of vegetation?

In response to these changes, to what extent should lightning fires be allowed to burn (Brown 1985; Habeck 1985; van Wagtendonk 1985)?

2. *How important was aboriginal burning?* Should we restore lightning ignitions but not Native American ignitions? Can we and should we mimic Native American burning (Arno 1985; Dennis and Wauer 1985; Gruell 1985; Lewis 1985; Phillips 1985).

3. *What is "natural" in wilderness fire management?* Our objective is usually to maintain or restore naturalness to a wilderness ecosystem. What is "natural" and how do we achieve this objective? Are we concerned about the process or structure of the vegetation/ecosystem or both (Agee and Huff 1986; Bonnicksen 1985; Kilgore 1985a; Parsons and others 1986)? Should some historical period be used to determine natural? Park and wilderness preservation goals must be stated more precisely and on an individual area basis (Johnson and Agee 1988). A great deal of variation due to chance and to change in climate may need to be accepted as "natural." The next generation of managers will need to answer these questions: What kind of manipulation is acceptable? for what purposes? by what means? on what scale? (Christensen and others 1989).

4. *How do we respond to large, high-intensity stand-replacement fires in wilderness?* Ideally, where these fires are part of the natural fire regime, we would try to allow them to burn. This has been done in several instances, namely the sizable fires in the Selway-Bitterroot Wilderness in 1979 (Independence and Barefoot Peach), the Bob Marshall Wilderness (Charlotte Peak) in 1985, and the Frank Church-River of No Return Wilderness of Idaho in 1986. This was also done in the Greater Yellowstone Area in 1988; while the ecological effects may have been acceptable, the social and economic effects, by and large, were not acceptable (Christensen and others 1989; USDA, USDI 1989). The continual challenge to wilderness managers is whether we *can* safely allow a given fire to burn and whether we *should* do so with the known conditions at the time. Fire researchers are trying to develop the capability to predict August behavior of natural fires ignited in June or July in wilderness areas; these predictions would probably be in the form of climatological probabilities to aid managers in making decisions about long-duration lightning-caused fires (Kilgore 1987). On smaller wilderness areas, or fragmented larger areas like the BWCAW, the questions still remain: can we allow some of these crown fires to burn and should we do so? If not, can we somehow simulate the role of such fires using prescribed fires without losing control of such fires (Bird and Lucas 1985; Heinselman 1985).

These questions should be answered soon, for if Pyne (1985) is correct, we are nearing the close of the era in which wilderness fire policy and programs are being developed. By the 1990s, most fire plans will have been completed, management decisions will have been made, and natural fires in wilderness will be an accepted practice.

WILDERNESS FIRE PROGRAMS AND ECOLOGICAL KNOWLEDGE

Wilderness fire management is important not only because it can maintain the natural landscapes and biota of wilderness as a cultural and recreational resource, but also because it can maintain large-scale functioning ecosystems that will contribute to basic scientific knowledge (fig. 12.11). Our understanding of natural ecosystems as systems is still in its infancy. "In such natural areas, imperfect though they may be, opportunities still exist to learn about the kinds of changes that have occurred for millenia" (Knight in preparation). Future scientists will require whole, functioning, natural ecosystems as laboratories to probe the questions just raised and perhaps many more important ones we do not yet know how to ask. The answers are certain to be vital to the future of humans, and fire is certain to emerge as a crucial element. Many of the most widespread natural ecosystems of the earth—including most coniferous forests, savannas, glades, and grasslands—are fire dependent. And many of our most important domestic plants and animals and useful forest trees evolved in such ecosystems. It is chiefly in our larger wildernesses and national parks that some of these ecosystem questions can be studied and answered (Wright 1974) because people are rapidly converting the rest of our planet to farms, pastures, commercial forests, mines, highways, and urban areas. The value of natural wilderness will surely increase in the next few decades. And we might soon discover that it holds many secrets important to our future on this planet.

STUDY QUESTIONS

1. What three factors determine fire regimes? Name four typical regimes.
2. List six roles that fire plays in most ecosystems or plant communities. Explain the importance of each.
3. What impact has the attempted exclusion of fire had on fuels and forest structure of wilderness ecosystems? How does this vary from short fire-interval to long fire-interval ecosystems?

Fig. 12.11. In the future, scientists will require whole, functioning, natural ecosystems, both to complete current investigations and to launch new ones. Fire is a natural force in many wildland ecosystems. Photo courtesy of Bruce Kilgore, NPS.

4. What is the main objective of wilderness fire management in national parks and forests?
5. Describe and contrast the current wilderness fire policies of the NPS and the USFS.
6. List four wilderness fire policy alternatives and the advantages and disadvantages of each. Which alternatives can or should be combined in a wilderness fire program?
7. Name four constraints on planning for wilderness fire management. Indicate how each impacts developments of wilderness fire plans.
8. What are accidents and disasters, as defined by Mutch and Davis (1985)? How can wilderness managers work to prevent either from happening?
9. How has research supported development of wilderness fire management programs? Give three examples.
10. Describe and contrast the fire history and fire effects found in two very different wilderness regions of North America—the Sierra Nevada and the Rocky Mountains.

REFERENCES

Agee, James K. 1973. Prescribed fire effects on physical and hydrologic properties of mixed-conifer forest floor and soil. Contrib. Rep. 143. Davis, CA: University of California, Water Resources Center. 57 p.

Agee, James K. 1974. Fire management in the National

Parks. Western Wildlands. 1(3): 27-33.

Agee, James K. 1985. Cost-effective fire management in National Parks. In: Lotan, James E.; [and others], tech. coords. Proceedings—symposium and workshop on wilderness fire; 1983 November 15-18; Missoula, MT. Gen. Tech. Rep. INT-182. Ogden, UT: U.S. Department of Agriculture, Forest Service, Intermountain Forest and Range Experiment Station: 193-198.

Agee, James K.; Wakimoto, R. H.; Biswell, H. H. 1978. Fire and fuel dynamics of Sierra Nevada conifers. Forest Ecology and Management. 1: 255-265.

Agee, James K.; Clark, L. D.; Broyles, R. P.; Rose, L. 1980. Wilderness fire management at Pinnacles National Monument. Fire Management Notes. 42(1): 10-12.

Agee, James K.; Huff, Mark H. 1986. Structure and process goals for vegetation in wilderness areas. In: Lucas, Robert C., comp. Proceedings—national wilderness research conference: current research; 1985 July 23-26; Fort Collins, CO. Gen. Tech. Rep. INT-212. Ogden, UT: U.S. Department of Agriculture, Forest Service, Intermountain Research Station: 17-25.

Agee, James K.; Huff, Mark H. 1987. Fuel succession in a western hemlock/Douglas-fir forest. Canadian Journal of Forest Research. 17(7): 697-704.

Ahlgren, I. F.; Ahlgren, C. E. 1960. Ecological effects of forest fires. Botanical Review. 26: 483-533.

Albini, Frank A. 1976. Estimating wildfire behavior and effects. Gen. Tech. Rep. INT-30. Ogden, UT: U.S. Department of Agriculture, Forest Service, Intermountain Forest and Range Experiment Station. 92 p.

Aldrich, D. F.; Mutch, R. W. 1972. Ecological interpretations of the White Cap drainage: a basis for wilderness fire management. Draft Fire Management Plan. Hamilton, MT: U.S. Department of Agriculture, Forest Service, Bitterroot National Forest. 84 p.

Aldrich, D. F.; Mutch, R. W. 1973. Wilderness fire management guidelines and inventory procedures. Unpublished paper on file at: U.S. Department of Agriculture, Forest Service, Northern Region, Missoula, MT. 36 p.

Alexander, M. E.; Hawksworth, F. G. 1975. Wildland fires and dwarf mistletoes: a literature review of ecology and prescribed burning. Gen. Tech. Rep. RM-14. Fort Collins, CO: U.S. Department of Agriculture, Forest Service, Rocky Mountain Forest and Range Experiment Station. 12 p.

Alexander, Martin E.; Hawksworth, F. G. 1976. Fire and dwarf mistletoes in North American coniferous forest. Journal of Forestry. 74(7): 446-449.

Anderson, Bruce A. 1985. Archeological considerations for park and wilderness fire management planning. In: Lotan, James E.; [and others], tech. coords. Proceedings—symposium and workshop on wilderness fire; 1983 November 15-18; Missoula, MT. Gen. Tech. Rep. INT-182. Ogden, UT: U.S. Department of Agriculture, Forest Service, Intermountain Forest and Range Experiment Station: 145-148.

Andrews, Patricia L. 1986. BEHAVE: fire behavior prediction and fuel modeling system - BURN subsystem, Part I. Gen. Tech. Rep. INT-194. Ogden, UT: U.S. Department of Agriculture, Forest Service, Intermountain Research Station. 130 p.

Arno, Stephen F. 1985. Ecological effects and management implications of Indian fires. In: Lotan, James E.; [and others], tech. coords. Proceedings—symposium and workshop on wilderness fire; 1983 November 15-18; Missoula, MT. Gen. Tech. Rep. INT-182. Ogden, UT: U.S. Department of Agriculture, Forest Service, Intermountain Forest and Range Experiment Station: 81-86.

Baker, H. W. 1965. Guidelines for resource management in the areas in the natural category of the National Park System. Memorandum on the implementation of the Leopold Report. 1965 October 14. Washington, DC: U.S. Department of the Interior, National Park Service. 9 p. [Processed.]

Bancroft, Larry; Nichols, Thomas; Parsons, David; Graber, David; Evison, Boyd; van Wagtendonk, Jan. 1985. Evolution of the natural fire management program at Sequoia and Kings Canyon National Parks. In: Lotan, James E.; [and others], tech. coords. Proceedings—symposium and workshop on wilderness fire; 1983 November 15-18; Missoula, MT. Gen. Tech. Rep. INT-182. Ogden, UT: U.S. Department of Agriculture, Forest Service, Intermountain Forest and Range Experiment Station: 174-180.

Bancroft, William L.; Partin, W. A. 1987. Fire management plan, Sequoia and Kings Canyon National Parks. Three Rivers, CA: U.S. Department of the Interior, National Park Service, Sequoia and Kings Canyon National Parks, Resources Management Office. 219 p.

Barrett, S. W. 1985. Fire effects on insects/diseases: bibliographic data base. Final Report, Cooperative Agreement 22-C-3-INT-30. Missoula, MT: U.S. Department of Agriculture, Forest Service, Intermountain Research Station, Intermountain Fire Sciences Laboratory. 30 p.

Barrett, Stephen W.; Arno, Stephen F. 1988. Increment-borer methods for determining fire history in coniferous forests. Gen. Tech. Rep. INT-244. Ogden, UT: U.S. Department of Agriculture, Forest Service, Intermountain Research Station: 15 p.

Baumgartner, David M.; Krebill, Richard G.; Arnott, James T.; Weetman, Gordon F., eds. 1985. Lodgepole pine: the species and its management: Symposium proceedings; 1984 May 8-10; Spokane, WA. Pullman, WA: Washington State University, Cooperative Extension. 381 p.

Bird, Douglas; Lucas, Robert C. 1985. The high-intensity and large-fire issue in wilderness. In: Lotan, James E.; [and others], tech. coords. Proceedings—symposium and workshop on wilderness fire; 1983 November 15-18; Missoula, MT. Gen. Tech. Rep. INT-182. Ogden, UT: U.S. Department of Agriculture, Forest Service, Intermountain Forest and Range Experiment Station: 302-303.

Biswell, H. H. 1959. Man and fire in ponderosa pine in the Sierra Nevada of California. Sierra Club Bulletin. 44(7): 44-53.

Biswell, H. H. 1961. The bigtrees and fire. National Parks. 35(163): 11-14.

Biswell, H. H. 1967. The use of fire in wildland management in California. In: Natural resoures: quality and quantity. Berkeley, CA: University of California Press: 71-87.

Biswell, H. H. 1974. Effects of fire on chaparral. In: Kozlowski, T. T.; Ahlgren, C. E., eds. Fire and ecosystems. New York: Academic Press: 321-364.

Biswell, H. H.; Gibbens, R. P.; Buchanan, H. 1966. Litter production by bigtrees and associated species. California Agriculture. 20(9): 5-7.

Biswell, H. H.; Gibbens, R. P.; Buchanan, H. 1968. Fuel conditions and fire hazard reduction costs in giant sequoia forests. California Agriculture. 22: 2-4.

Bock, J. H. 1976. Introductory remarks: communication between ecologists and managers. In: Proceedings, Tall Timbers Fire Ecology Conference No. 14; 1974 October 8-10; Missoula, MT. Tallahassee, FL: Tall Timbers Research Station: 193.

Boerner, Ralph E. J. 1982. Fire and nutrient cycling in temperate ecosystems. Bioscience. 32(3): 187-192.

Bonnicksen, Thomas M. 1985. Ecological information base for park and wilderness fire management planning. In: Lotan, James E.; [and others], tech. coords. Proceedings—symposium and workshop on wilderness fire; 1983 November 15-18; Missoula, MT. Gen. Tech. Rep. INT-182. Ogden, UT: U.S. Department of Agriculture, Forest Service, Intermountain Forest and Range Experiment Station: 168-173.

Bonnicksen, Thomas M. 1989. Fire gods and federal policy. American Forests. 95: 14-16, 66-68.

Bonnicksen, Thomas M.; Stone, Edward C. 1981. The giant sequoia-mixed conifer forest community characterized through pattern analysis as a mosaic of aggregations. Forest Ecology and Management. 3(4): 307-328.

Bonnicksen, Thomas M.; Stone, Edward C. 1982a. Managing vegetation within U.S. National Parks: a policy analysis. Environmental Management. 6(2): 109-122.

Bonnicksen, Thomas M.; Stone, Edward C. 1982b. Reconstruction of a presettlement giant sequoia-mixed conifer forest community using the aggregation approach. Ecology. 64(3): 1134-1148.

Bonnicksen, Thomas M.; Stone, Edward C. 1985. Restoring naturalness to National Parks. Environmental Management. 9(6): 479-486.

Brown, James K. 1975. Fire cycles and community dynamics in lodgepole pine forest. In: Baumgartner, D. J., ed. Management of lodgepole pine ecosystems: Proceedings of the symposium; Pullman, WA: Washington State University, Cooperative Extension Service: 429-456.

Brown, James K. 1985. The "unnatural fuel buildup" issue. In: Lotan, James E.; [and others], tech. coords. Proceedings—symposium and workshop on wilderness fire; 1983 November 15-18; Missoula, MT. Gen. Tech. Rep. INT-182. Ogden, UT: U.S. Department of Agriculture, Forest Service, Intermountain Forest and Range Experiment Station: 127-128.

Brown, James K. [In press]. Should planned ignition be used to manage fire in Yellowstone National Park? Yale Bulletin.

Burgan, Robert E.; Rothermel, Richard C. 1984. Fire behavior prediction and fuel modeling system - FUEL subsystem. Gen. Tech. Rep. INT-167. Ogden, UT: U.S. Department of Agriculture, Forest Service, Intermountain Forest and Range Experiment Station. 126 p.

Butts, David B. 1985. Case study: the Ouzel Fire, Rocky Mountain National Park. In: Lotan, James E.; [and others], tech. coords. Proceedings—symposium and workshop on wilderness fire; 1983 November 15-18; Missoula, MT. Gen. Tech. Rep. INT-182. Ogden, UT: U.S. Department of Agriculture, Forest Service, Intermountain Forest and Range Experiment Station: 248-251.

Cattelino, Peter J.; Noble, I. R.; Slatyer, R. O.; Kessell, 5. R.

1979. Predicting the multiple pathways of plant succession. Environmental Management. 3(1): 41-50.

Chapman, H. H. 1912. Forest fires and forestry in the Southern States. American Forests. 18: 510-517.

Chase, Alston. 1986. Playing God in Yellowstone. New York: Atlantic Monthly Press. 446 p.

Christensen, Norman L. 1988. Succession and natural disturbance: paradigm, problems, and preservation of natural ecosystems. In: Agee, James K.; Johnson, Darryll B., eds. Ecosystem management for parks and wilderness. Seattle: University of Washington Press: 62-86.

Christensen, Norman L. [In press]. Wilderness and high intensity fire: how much is enough? In: Proceedings, 17th Tall Timbers Fire Ecology Conference. Tallahassee, FL: Tall Timbers Research Station.

Christensen, Norman L.; Cotton, Lin; Harvey, Thomas; Martin, Robert; McBride, Joe; Rundel, Phillip; Wakimoto, Ronald. 1987. Review of fire management program for sequoia-mixed conifer forests of Yosemite, Sequoia, and Kings Canyon National Parks. Final Report. Three Rivers, CA: U.S. Department of the Interior, National Park Service, Sequoia and Kings Canyon National Parks. 37 p.

Christensen, Norman L.; Agee, James K.; Brussard, Peter F.; Hughes, Jay: Knight, Dennis H.; Minshall, G. Wayne; Peek, James M.; Pyne, Stephen J.; Swanson, Frederick J.; Wells, Stephen; Thomas, Jack Ward; Williams, Stephen E.; Wright, Henry A. 1989. Ecological consequences of the 1988 fires in the Greater Yellowstone Area. Final Report, The Greater Yellowstone Postfire Fcological Assessment Workshop. [Yellowstone National Park, WY: U.S. Department of the Interior, National Park Service]. 58 p.

Clements, F. E. 1910. The life history of lodgepole burn forests. Bull. 79. Washington, DC: U.S. Department of Agriculture, Forest Service. 56 p.

Condon, Michael K. 1985. Economic analysis for wilderness fire management: a case study. In: Lotan, James E.; [and others], tech. coords. Proceedings—symposium and workshop on wilderness fire; 1983 November 15-18; Missoula, MT. Gen. Tech. Rep. INT-182. Ogden, UT: U.S. Department of Agriculture, Forest Service, Intermountain Forest and Range Experiment Station: 199-205

Connell, J. H.; Noble, I. R.; Slatyer, R. O. 1987. On the mechanisms producing successional change. Oikos. 50: 136-137.

Conrad, C. Eugene; Oechel, Walter, eds. 1982. Proceedings of the symposium on dynamics and management of Mediterranean-type ecosystems; 1981 June 22-26; San Diego, CA. Gen. Tech. Rep. PSW-58. Berkeley, CA: U.S. Department of Agriculture, Forest Service, Pacific Southwest Forest and Range Experiment Station. 637 p.

Cooper, Charles F. 1960. Changes in vegetation, structure, and growth of southwestern pine forests since white settlement. Ecological Monographs. 30: 129-164.

Cooper, Charles F. 1961. Pattern in ponderosa pine forest. Ecology. 42: 493-499.

Cotton, L.; Biswell, H. 1973. Forestscape and fire restoration at Whitaker's Forest. National Parks and Conservation. 47(2): 10-15.

Daniels, O. L. 1974. Test of a new land management concept: Fritz Creek 1973. Western Wildlands. 1(3): 23-26.

Daubenmire, R. F. 1943. Vegetation zonation in the Rocky Mountains. Botanical Review. 9(6): 325-393.

Davis, K. M.; Clayton, B. D.; Fischer, W. C. 1980. Fire ecology of Lolo National Forest habitat types. Gen. Tech. Rep. INT-79. Ogden, UT: U.S. Department of Agriculture, Forest Service, Intermountain Forest and Range Experiment Station. 77 p.

Day, R. J. 1972. Stand structure, succession, and use of southern Alberta's Rocky Mountain forest. Ecology. 53(3): 472-478.

Dennis, John G; Wauer, Roland H. 1985. Role of Indian burning in wilderness fire planning. In: Lotan, James E.; [and others], tech. coords. Proceedings—symposium and workshop on wilderness fire; 1983 November 15-18; Missoula, MT. Gen. Tech. Rep. INT-182. Ogden, UT: U.S. Department of Agriculture, Forest Service, Intermountain Forest and Range Experiment Station: 296-298.

Despain, D. G. 1982. Some effects of free-burning fires in Yellowstone National Park. In: Lotan, James E., ed. Fire—its field effects: Proceedings of the symposium; 1982 October 19-21; Jackson, WY. Missoula MT: Intermountain Fire Council; Pierre, SD: Rocky Mountain Fire Council: 93-101.

Despain, D. G. 1983. Nonpyrogenous climax lodgepole pine communities in Yellowstone National Park. Ecology. 64(2): 231-234.

Despain, D. G.; Sellers, R. E. 1977. Natural fire in Yellowstone National Park. Western Wildlands. 4(1): 20-24.

Dodge, M. 1972. Forest fuel accumulation—A growing problem. Science. 177(4044): 139-142.

Ewell, Diane M.; Haggerty, Patti. 1986. Fire monitoring guide-long term. Three Rivers, CA: U.S. Department of the Interior, National Park Service, Sequoia and Kings Canyon National Parks, Resources Management Office. 50 p.

Ewell, Diane M.; Nichols, H. Thomas. 1985. Prescribed fire monitoring in Sequoia and Kings Canyon National Parks. In: Lotan, James E.; [and others], tech. coords. Proceedings—symposium and workshop on wilderness fire; 1983 November 15-18; Missoula, MT. Gen. Tech. Rep. INT-182. Ogden, UT: U.S. Department of Agriculture, Forest Service, Intermountain Forest and Range Experiment Station: 327-330.

Fahnestock, George F. 1976. Fire, fuels, and flora as factors in wilderness management: the Pasayten Case. In: Proceedings, Tall Timbers Fire Ecology Conference No. 15; 1974 October 16-17; Portland, OR. Tallahassee, FL: Tall Timbers Research Station: 33-69.

Ferry, Gardner; [and others]. 1985. Prescribed fire smoke management guide. No. 420-1. Washington, DC: Prescribed Fire and Fire Effects Working Team, National Wildfire Coordinating Group. 28 p.

Ferry, Gardner W. 1985. Monitoring and evaluating wilderness prescribed fires. In: Lotan, James E.; [and others], tech. coords. Proceedings—symposium and workshop on wilderness fire; 1983 November 15-18; Missoula, MT. Gen. Tech. Rep. INT-182. Ogden, UT: U.S. Department of Agriculture, Forest Service, Intermountain Forest and Range Experiment Station: 225-229.

Finklin, A. I. 1983. Weather and climate of the Selway-Bitterroot Wilderness. Moscow, ID: University of Idaho Press. 144 p.

Fischer, William C. 1984. Wilderness fire management planning guide. Gen. Tech. Rep. INT-171. Ogden, UT: U.S. Department of Agriculture, Forest Service, Intermountain Forest and Range Experiment Station. 56 p.

Fischer, William C. 1985. Elements of wilderness fire management planning. In: Lotan, James E.; [and others], tech. coords. Proceedings—symposium and workshop on wilderness fire; 1983 November 15-18; Missoula, MT. Gen. Tech. Rep. INT-182. Ogden, UT: U.S. Department of Agriculture, Forest Service, Intermountain Forest and Range Experiment Station: 138-144.

Foster, N. W.; Morrison, I. K. 1976. Distribution and cycling of nutrients in a natural *Pinus banksiana* ecosystem. Ecology. 57(1): 110-120.

Franklin, J. F.; Hemstrom, M. A. 1981. Aspects of succession in the coniferous forests of the Pacific Northwest. In: West, D. C.; Shugart, H. H.; Botkin, D. B., eds. Forest succession, concepts, and application. New York: Springer-Verlag; 212-229.

Frissell, S. S., Jr. 1973. The importance of fire as a natural ecological factor in Itasca State Park, Minnesota. Quaternary Research. 3(3): 397-407.

Fritz, Emanuel. 1932. The role of fire in the redwood region. Circ. 323. Berkeley, CA: University of California. 23 p.

Gaidula, Peter. 1985. Training in support of park and wilderness fire management programs. In: Lotan, James E.; [and others], tech. coords. Proceedings—symposium and workshop on wilderness fire; 1983 November 15-18; Missoula, MT. Gen. Tech. Rep. INT-182. Ogden, UT: U.S. Department of Agriculture, Forest Service, Intermountain Forest and Range Experiment Station: 220-224.

Gara, R. J.; Littke, W. R.; Agee, J. K.; Geiszler, D. R.; Stuart, J. D.; Driver, C. H. 1985. Influence of fires, fungi, and mountain pine beetles on development of a lodgepole pine forest in south-central Oregon. In: Baumgartner, David M.; Krebill, Richard G.; Arnott, James T.; Weetman, Gordon F., eds. Lodgepole pine: the species and its management: Symposium proceedings; 1984 May 8-10; Spokane, WA. Pullman, WA: Washington State University, Cooperative Extension: 153-162.

Gavin, Thomas; Sydoriak, Charisse A.; Botti, Stephen J. [and others]. 1990. Western Region fire monitoring handbook. San Francisco, CA: National Park Service, Prescribed and Natural Fire Monitoring Task Force. 134 p. + supplements.

Graber, David M. 1983. Rationalizing management of natural areas in National Parks. The George Wright Forum. 3(4): 48-56.

Graber, David M. 1985. Managing for uncertainty: National Parks as ecological reserves. The George Wright Forum. 4(3): 4-7.

Greater Yellowstone Coordinating Committee. 1989. The Greater Yellowstone postfire assessment. Yellowstone National Park, WY: U.S. Department of Agriculture, Forest Service, and U.S. Department of the Interior, National Park Service. 147 p.

Greene, S. W. 1931. The forest that fire made. American Forests. 37(10): 583-584, 618.

Grigal, D. F.; McColl, J. G. 1975. Litterfall after a wildfire in virgin forests of northeastern Minnesota. Canadian Journal of Forest Research. 5(4): 655-661.

Gruell, George E. 1985. Indian fires in the Interior West: a widespread influence. In: Lotan, James E.; [and others], tech. coords. Proceedings—symposium and workshop on wilderness fire; 1983 November 15-18; Missoula,

MT. Gen. Tech. Rep. INT-182. Ogden, UT: U.S. Department of Agriculture, Forest Service, Intermountain Forest and Range Experiment Station: 68-74.

Gruell, George E.; Loope, L. L. 1974. Relationships among aspen, fire, and ungulate browsing in Jackson Hole, Wyoming. Ogden, UT: U.S. Department of Agriculture, Forest Service, Intermountain Region. 33 p.

Habeck, J. R. 1968. Forest succession in the Glacier Park cedar-hemlock forests. Ecology. 49(5): 872-880.

Habeck, J. R. 1972. Fire ecology investigations in Selway-Bitterroot Wilderness: historical considerations and current observations. Publ. R1-72-001. Missoula, MT: University of Montana and U.S. Department of Agriculture, Forest Service, Northern Region. 118 p.

Habeck, J. R. 1973. A phytosociological analysis of forests, fuels, and fire in the Moose Creek Drainage, Selway-Bitterroot Wilderness. Missoula, MT: University of Montana and U.S. Department of Agriculture, Forest Service. 113 p.

Habeck, J. R. 1976. Forests, fuels and fire in the Selway-Bitterroot Wilderness, Idaho. In: Proceedings, Tall Timbers Fire Ecology Conference No. 14; 1974 October 8-10; Missoula, MT. Tallahassee, FL: Tall Timbers Research Station: 305-353.

Habeck, J. R. 1985. Impact of fire suppression on forest succession and fuel accumulations in long-fire-interval wilderness habitat types. In: Lotan, James E.; [and others], tech. coords. Proceedings—symposium and workshop on wilderness fire; 1983 November 15-18; Missoula, MT. Gen. Tech. Rep. INT-182. Ogden, UT: U.S. Department of Agriculture, Forest Service, Intermountain Forest and Range Experiment Station: 110-118.

Habeck, J. R.; Mutch, R. W. 1973. Fire-dependent forests in the Northern Rocky Mountains. Quaternary Research. 3: 408-424.

Haddow, Dennis V. 1985. Wilderness fire management and air quality. In: Lotan, James E.; [and others], tech. coords. Proceedings—symposium and workshop on wilderness fire; 1983 November 15-18; Missoula, MT. Gen. Tech. Rep. INT-182. Ogden, UT: U.S. Department of Agriculture, Forest Service, Intermountain Forest and Range Experiment Station: 129-131.

Haines, D. A.; Sando, R. W. 1969. Climatic conditions preceding historically great fires in the North Central Region. Res. Pap. NC-34. St. Paul, MN: U.S. Department of Agriculture, Forest Service, North Central Forest Experiment Station. 19 p.

Harper, R. M. 1913. A defense of forest fires. Literary Digest. 47: 208.

Hartesveldt, Richard J. 1964. Fire ecology of the giant sequoias: controlled fire may be one solution to survival of the species. Natural History Magazine. 73(10): 12-19.

Hartesveldt, Richard J.; Harvey, H. T. 1967. The fire ecology of sequoia regeneration. In: Proceedings, Tall Timbers Fire Ecology Conference No. 7; 1967 November 9-10; Lake County, CA. Tallahassee, FL: Tall Timbers Research Station: 65-77.

Harvey, H. Thomas; Shellhammer, Howard 5.; Stecker, Ronald E. 1980. Giant sequoia ecology: fire and reproduction. Sci. Monogr. Ser. No. 12. Washington, DC: U.S. Department of the Interior, National Park Service. 182 p.

Heinselman, M. L. 1971. Restoring fire to the ecosystems of the Boundary Waters Canoe Area, Minnesota. In: Pro-

ceedings, Tall Timbers Fire Ecology Conference No. 10; 1970 August 20-21; Fredericton, NB. Tallahassee, FL: Tall Timbers Research Station: 9-23.

Heinselman, M. L. 1973. Fire in the virgin forests of the Boundary Waters Canoe Area, Minnesota. Quaternary Research. 3(3): 329-382.

Heinselman, M. L. 1974. Restoring fire to the canoe country. Naturalist. 24(4): 21-31.

Heinselman, M. L. 1978. Fire in wilderness ecosystems. In: Hendee, John C.; Stankey, George H.; Lucas, Robert C., eds. Wilderness management. Misc. Publ. 1365. Washington, DC: U.S. Department of Agriculture, Forest Service: 249-278.

Heinselman, M. L. 1981. Fire intensity and frequency as factors in the distribution and structure of northern ecosystems. In: Mooney, H. A.; [and others], eds. Proceedings of the conference fire regimes and ecosystem properties; 1978 December 11-15; Honolulu, HI. Gen. Tech. Rep. W0-26. Washington, DC: U.S. Department of Agriculture, Forest Service: 7-57.

Heinselman, M. L. 1985. Fire regimes and management options in ecosystems with large high-intensity fires. In: Lotan, James E.; [and others], tech. coords. Proceedings—symposium and workshop on wilderness fire; 1983 November 15-18; Missoula, MT. Gen. Tech. Rep. INT-182. Ogden, UT: U.S. Department of Agriculture, Forest Service, Intermountain Forest and Range Experiment Station: 101-109.

Helmers, A. E. 1974. Interior Alaska (includes reprinting of map "Major Ecosystems of Alaska"). Naturalist. 25(1): 16-23.

Heyward, F.; Barnette, R. M. 1934. Effect of frequent fires on chemical composition of forest soils in the longleaf pine region. Tech. Bull. 265. Gainesville, FL: Florida Agricultural Experiment Station. 39 p.

Horton, K. W. 1956. The ecology of lodgepole pine in Alberta and its role in forest succession. Tech. Note 45. Ottawa, ON: Canadian Department of Northern Affairs and Natural Resources, Forestry Branch. 29 p.

Houston, D. B. 1973. Wildfire in northern Yellowstone National Park. Ecology. 54(5): 1111-1117.

Humphrey, R. R. 1974. Fire in the deserts and desert grassland of North America. In: Kozlowski, T. T.; Ahlgren, C. E., eds. Fire and ecosystems. New York: Academic Press: 365-400.

Irving, F. D.; French, D. W. 1971. Control by fire of dwarf mistletoe in black spruce. Journal of Forestry. 69(1): 28-30.

Jeffery, David. 1989. Yellowstone: the great fires of 1988. National Geographic. 175(2): 255-273.

Johnson, Darryll R.; Agee, James K. 1988. Introduction to ecosystem management. In: Agee, James K.; Johnson, Darryll R., eds. Ecosystem management for parks and wilderness. Seattle: University of Washington Press: 3-14.

Kaufert, F. H. 1964. Controversy in canoeland. American Forester. 70(10): 24-27, 78-82.

Kelly, Roger E.; Mayberry, Jim. 1979. Trial by fire: effects of NPS burn programs upon archeological resources. In: Proceedings, second conference on scientific research in National Parks; 1979 November. San Francisco, CA: U.S. Department of the Interior, National Park Service, Western Regional Office: 603-610.

Kenner, Brian. 1985. The philosophical basis for National

Park management. The George Wright Forum. 4(3): 22-37.

Keown, Larry D. 1980. Fire management in the Selway-Bitterroot Wilderness. Grangeville, ID: U.S. Department of Agriculture, Forest Service, Nezperce National Forest, Moose Creek Ranger District. 67 p.

Keown, Larry D. 1985a. Fire behavior prediction techniques for park and wilderness fire planning. In: Lotan, James E.; [and others], tech. coords. Proceedings—symposium and workshop on wilderness fire; 1983 November 15-18; Missoula, MT. Gen. Tech. Rep. INT-182. Ogden, UT: U.S. Department of Agriculture, Forest Service, Intermountain Forest and Range Experiment Station: 162-167.

Keown, Larry D. 1985b. Case study: the Independence Fire, Selway-Bitterroot Wilderness. In: Lotan, James E.; [and others], tech. coords. Proceedings—symposium and workshop on wilderness fire; 1983 November 15-18; Missoula, MT. Gen. Tech. Rep. INT-182. Ogden, UT: U.S. Department of Agriculture, Forest Service, Intermountain Forest and Range Experiment Station: 239-247.

Kilgore, B. M. 1970. Restoring fire to the Sequoias. National Parks and Conservation. 44(277): 16-22.

Kilgore, B. M. 1971a. Response of breeding bird populations to habitat changes in a giant sequoia forest. American Midland Naturalist. 85(1): 135-152.

Kilgore, B. M. 1971b. The role of fire in managing red fir forests. In: Transactions of the 36th North American wildlife and natural resources conference; 1971 March 7-10; Portland, OR. Washington, DC: The Wildlife Management Institute: 405-416.

Kilgore, B. M. 1972. Fire's role in a sequoia forest. Naturalist. 23(1): 26-37.

Kilgore, B. M. 1973a. Impact of prescribed burning on a sequoia-mixed conifer forest. In: Proceedings, Tall Timbers Fire Ecology Conference No. 12; 1972 June 8-9; Lubbock, TX. Tallahassee, FL: Tall Timbers Research Station: 345-375.

Kilgore, B. M. 1973b. The ecological role of fire in Sierra conifer forests: its application to National Park management. Quaternary Research. 3(3): 496-513.

Kilgore, B. M. 1975. Restoring fire to National Park wilderness. American Forester. 81(3): 16-19.

Kilgore, B. M. 1976. From fire control to fire management: an ecological basis for policies. In: Transactions of 41st North American wildlife and natural resources conference; 1976 March; Washington, DC. Washington, DC: Wildlife Management Institute: 477-493.

Kilgore, B. M. 1981. Fire in ecosystem distribution and structure: western forest and shrublands. In: Mooney, H. A.; [and others], eds. Proceedings of the conference fire regimes and ecosystem properties; 1978 December 11-15; Honolulu, HI. Gen. Tech. Rep. W0-26. Washington, DC: U.S. Department of Agriculture, Forest Service: 58-89.

Kilgore, B. M. 1982. Fire management programs in parks and wilderness. In: Lotan, James E., ed. Fire—its field effects: Proceedings of the symposium; 1982 October 19-21; Jackson, WY. Missoula, MT: Intermountain Fire Council; Pierre, SD: Rocky Mountain Fire Council: 61-91.

Kilgore, B. M. 1985a. Human-ignited prescribed fires in wilderness: a response to Bill Worf. In: Lotan, James E.;

[and others], tech. coords. Proceedings—symposium and workshop on wilderness fire; 1983 November 15-18; Missoula, MT. Gen. Tech. Rep. INT-182. Ogden, UT: U.S. Department of Agriculture, Forest Service, Intermountain Forest and Range Experiment Station: 283-285.

Kilgore, B. M. 1985b. What is "natural" in wilderness fire management? In: Lotan, James E.; [and others], tech. coords. Proceedings—symposium and workshop on wilderness fire; 1983 November 15-18; Missoula, MT. Gen. Tech. Rep. INT-182. Ogden, UT: U.S. Department of Agriculture, Forest Service, Intermountain Forest and Range Experiment Station: 57-67.

Kilgore, B. M. 1987. The role of fire in wilderness: a state-of-knowledge review. In: Lucas, Robert C., comp. Proceedings—national wilderness research conference: issues, state-of-knowledge, future directions; 1985 July 23-26; Fort Collins, CO. Gen. Tech. Rep. INT-220. Ogden, UT: U.S. Department of Agriculture, Forest Service, Intermountain Research Station: 70-103.

Kilgore, B. M. [In press]. Management options and policy directions concerning high intensity fire: a fire policy panel. In: Proceedings, 17th Tall Timbers Fire Ecology Conference. Tallahassee, FL: Tall Timbers Research Station.

Kilgore, B. M.; Biswell, H. H. 1971. Seedling germination following fire in a giant sequoia forest. California Agriculture. 25(2): 8-10.

Kilgore, B. M.; Briggs, G. S. 1972. Restoring fire to high elevation forests in California. Journal of Forestry. 70(5): 266-271.

Kilgore, B. M.; Sando, R. W. 1975. Crown-fire potential in a sequoia forest after prescribed burning. Forest Science. 21(1): 83-87.

Kilgore, B. M.; Taylor, D. 1979. Fire history of a sequoia-mixed conifer forest. Ecology. 60: 129-142.

Knight, D. H. 1987. Parasites, lightning, and the vegetation mosaic in wilderness landscapes. In: Turner, M. G., ed. Landscape heterogeneity and disturbance. New York: Springer-Verlag: 59-83.

Knight, Dennis H. [In preparation]. The Yellowstone fire controversy. In: [a book].

Komarek, E. V. 1973. Comments on the history of controlled burning in the southern United States. In: Proceedings, 17th Annual Watershed Symposium. 17: 11-17.

Komarek, E. V. 1974. Effects of fire on temperate forests and related ecosystems: southeastern United States. In: Kozlowski, T. T.; Ahlgren, C. E., eds. Fire and ecosystems. New York: Academic Press: 251-277.

Kozlowski, T. T.; Ahlgren, C. E., eds. 1974. Fire and ecosystems. New York: Academic Press. 542 p.

Kramp, Betty A.; Patton, David R.; Brady, Ward W. 1983. The effects of fire on wildlife habitat and species. RUN WILD Wildlife/Habitat Relationships Tech. Rep. Albuquerque, NM: U.S. Department of Agriculture, Forest Service, Southwestern Region. 29 p.

Leopold, A. S.; Cain, S. A.; Cottam, C. M.; Gabrielson, I. N.; Kimball, T. 1963. I. Study of wildlife problems in National Parks: wildlife management in National Parks. In: Transactions of the North American Wildlife and Natural Resources Conference. 28: 28-45.

Lewis, Henry T. 1985. Why Indians burned: specific versus general reasons. In: Lotan, James E.; [and others], tech.

coords. Proceedings—symposium and workshop on wilderness fire; 1983 November 15-18; Missoula, MT. Gen. Tech. Rep. INT-182. Ogden, UT: U.S. Department of Agriculture, Forest Service, Intermountain Forest and Range Experiment Station: 75-80.

Loope, L. L.; Gruell, G. E. 1973. The ecological role of fire in the Jackson Hole area, northwestern Wyoming. Quaternary Research. 3(3): 425-443.

Lotan, James E.; Brown, James K.; Neuenschwander, Leon F. 1985a. Role of fire in lodgepole pine forests. In: Lodgepole pine: the species and its management: Proceedings of a symposium; 1984 May 8-10; Spokane, WA. Pullman, WA: Washington State University, Cooperative Extension: 133-152.

Lotan, James E.; Kilgore, Bruce M.; Fischer, William C.; Mutch, Robert W., tech. coords. 1985b. Proceedings—symposium and workshop on wilderness fire; 1983 November 15-18; Missoula, MT. Gen. Tech. Rep. INT-182. Ogden, UT: U.S. Department of Agriculture, Forest Service, Intermountain Forest and Range Experiment Station. 434 p.

Loucks, Orie L. 1970. Evolution of diversity, efficiency, and community stability. American Zoology. 10: 17-25.

Lucas, Robert C. 1985. Planned ignitions in wilderness: response to paper by William A. Worf. In: Lotan, James E.; [and others], tech. coords. Proceedings—symposium and workshop on wilderness fire; 1983 November 15-18; Missoula, MT. Gen. Tech. Rep. INT-182. Ogden, UT: U.S. Department of Agriculture, Forest Service, Intermountain Forest and Range Experiment Station: 286-290.

Lunan, J. S.; Habeck, J. R. 1973. The effects of fire exclusion on ponderosa pine communities in Glacier National Park. Canadian Journal of Forest Research. 3: 574-579.

Lyon, L. Jack; Crawford, Hewlette S.; Czuhai, Eugene; [and others]. 1978. Effects of fire on fauna: a state-of-knowledge review. Gen. Tech. Rep. W0-6. Washington, DC: U.S. Department of Agriculture, Forest Service. 22 p.

MacLean, D. W.; Bedell, G. H. D. 1955. Northern clay belt growth and yield survey. Tech. Note 20. Ottawa, ON: Canadian Department of Northern Affairs and Natural Resources, Forestry Branch.

Mangan, Richard J. 1985. Fire suppression for wilderness and parks: planning considerations. In: Lotan, James E.; [and others], tech. coords. Proceedings—symposium and workshop on wilderness fire; 1983 November 15-18; Missoula, MT. Gen. Tech. Rep. INT-182. Ogden, UT: U.S. Department of Agriculture, Forest Service, Intermountain Forest and Range Experiment Station: 159-161.

Marr, J. W. 1961. Ecosystems of the east slope of the Front Range in Colorado. Study Ser. in Biol. No. 8. Denver, CO: University of Colorado. 134 p.

Mastroguiseppe, M. E.; Alexander, M. E.; Romme, W. H. 1983. Forest and rangeland fire history bibliography. Missoula, MT: U.S. Department of Agriculture, Forest Service, Intermountain Forest and Range Experiment Station, Northern Forest Fire Laboratory. 49 p. [Mimeo.]

McBride, Joe R. 1983. Analysis of tree rings and fire scars to establish fire history. Tree-Ring Bulletin. 43: 51-67.

McCool, Stephen F.; Stankey, George H. 1986. Visitor attitudes toward wilderness fire management policy—1971-84. Res. Pap. INT-357. Ogden, UT: U.S. Department of Agriculture, Forest Service, Intermountain Research Station. 7 p.

Miller, J. M.; Keen, F. P. 1960. Biology and control of the western pine beetle: a summary of the first fifty years of research. Misc. Publ. 800. Washington, DC: U.S. Department of Agriculture, Forest Service. 381 p.

Moody, Bill; Mohr, Francis. 1988. Light hand tactics guide. Portland, OR: U.S. Department of Agriculture, Forest Service, Region Six. 10 p. [Mimeo.]

Mooney, H. A.; Bonnicksen, T. N.; Christensen, N. L.; Lotan, J. E.; Reiners, W. A., eds. 1981. Proceedings of the conference fire regimes and ecosystem properties; 1978 December 11-15; Honolulu, HI. Gen. Tech. Rep. W0-26. Washington, DC: U.S. Department of Agriculture, Forest Servce. 594 p.

Moore, W. R. 1974. From fire control to fire management. Western Wildlands. 1(3): 11-15.

Mutch, R. W. 1970. Wildland fires and ecosystems—a hypothesis. Ecology. 51(6): 1046-1051.

Mutch, Robert W. 1974. "I thought forest fires were black!" Western Wildlands. 1(3): 16-22.

Mutch, Robert W.; Davis, Kathleen M. 1985. Visitor protection in parks and wildernesses: preventing fire-related accidents and disasters. In: Lotan, James E.; [and others], tech. coords. Proceedings—symposium and workshop on wilderness fire; 1983 November 15-18; Missoula, MT. Gen. Tech. Rep. INT-182. Ogden, UT: U.S. Department of Agriculture, Forest Service, Intermountain Forest and Range Experiment Station: 149-158.

Nichols, Howard T. 1983. Fire monitoring guide—short term. Three Rivers, CA: U.S. Department of the Interior, National Park Service, Sequoia and Kings Canyon National Parks, Resources Management Office. 100 p.

Oosting, H. J.; Reed, J. F. 1952. Virgin spruce-fir forest in the Medicine Bow Mountains, Wyoming. Ecological Monographs. 22(2): 69-91.

Parmeter, John R., Jr. 1977. Effects of fire on pathogens. In: Mooney, Harold A.; Conrad, C. Eugene, eds. Proceedings of the symposium on the environmental consequences of fire and fuel management in mediterranean ecosystems; 1977 August 1-5; Palo Alto, CA. Gen. Tech. Rep. W0-3. Washington, DC: U.S. Department of Agriculture, Forest Service: 58-64.

Parsons, D. J. 1978. Fire and fuel accumulation in a giant sequoia forest. Journal of Forestry. 76(2): 104-105.

Parsons, D. J. 1981. The role of fire management in maintaining natural ecosystems. In: Mooney, H. A.; [and others], eds. Proceedings of the conference fire regimes and ecosystem properties: Proceedings of the conference; 1978 December 11-15; Honolulu, HI. Gen. Tech. Rep. W0-26. Washington, DC: U.S. Department of Agriculture, Forest Service: 469-488.

Parsons, D. J. 1989. Restoring fire to the Sierra Nevada mixed conifer forest: reconciling science, policy and practicality. Paper presented at the Society for Ecological Restoration and Management Annual Meeting; 1989 January 16-20; Oakland, CA.

Parsons, D. J.; DeBenedetti, S. H. 1979. Impact of fire suppression on mixed-conifer forest. Forest Ecology and Management. 2: 21-33.

Parsons, D. J.; Bancroft, Larry; Nichols, Thomas; Stohlgren, Thomas. 1985. Information needs for natural fire management planning. In: Lotan, James E.; [and others], tech. coords. Proceedings—symposium and workshop on wilderness fire; 1983 November 15-18; Missoula, MT. Gen. Tech. Rep. INT-182. Ogden, UT: U.S. Depart-

ment of Agriculture, Forest Service, Intermountain Forest and Range Experiment Station: 356-359.

Parsons, D. J.; Graber, D. M.; Agee, J. K.; van Wagtendonk, J. W. 1986. Natural fire management in National Parks. Environmental Management. 10(1): 21-24.

Parsons, D. J.; Stephenson, Nathan L.; Swetnam, Thomas W. [In press]. Restoring fire to the sequoia-mixed conifer forest: should intense fire play a role? In: Proceedings, 17th Tall Timbers Fire Ecology Conference. Tallahassee, FL: Tall Timbers Research Station.

Phillips, Clinton B. 1985. The relevance of past Indian fires to current fire management programs. In: Lotan, James E.; [and others], tech. coords. Proceedings—symposium and workshop on wilderness fire; 1983 November 15-18; Missoula, MT. Gen. Tech. Rep. INT-182. Ogden, UT: U.S. Department of Agriculture, Forest Service, Intermountain Forest and Range Experiment Station: 87-92.

Popevich, L. 1977. Up in flames—taking heat on the Seney. Journal of Forestry. 75(3): 147-150.

Pyne, Stephen J. 1984. Introduction to wildland fire: fire management in the United States. New York: John Wiley and Sons. 455 p.

Pyne, Stephen J. 1985. Vestal fires and virgin lands: a historical perspective on fire and wilderness. In: Lotan, James E.; [and others], tech. coords. Proceedings—symposium and workshop on wilderness fire; 1983 November 15-18; Missoula, MT. Gen. Tech. Rep. INT-182. Ogden, UT: U.S. Department of Agriculture, Forest Service, Intermountain Forest and Range Experiment Station: 254-262.

Renkin, Roy A.; Despain, Don G. 1990. Occurrence and activity of lightning-caused fires relative to weather and forest type in Yellowstone National Park. Mammoth, WY: National Park Service, Yellowstone National Park. [In preparation].

Robertson, W. B. 1953. A survey of the effects of fire in Everglades National Park. Everglades National Park, FL: U.S. Department of the Interior, National Park Service. 169 p. [Mimeo.]

Robertson, W. B. 1962. Fire and vegetation in the Everglades. In: Proceedings, Tall Timbers Fire Ecology Conference No. 1; 1962 March 1-2; Tallahassee, FL. Tallahassee, FL: Tall Timbers Research Station: 67-80.

Roe, Arthur L.; Amman, G. D. 1970. The mountain pine beetle in lodgepole pine forests. Res. Pap. INT-71. Ogden, UT: U.S. Department of Agriculture, Forest Service, Intermountain Forest and Range Experiment Station. 23 p.

Romme, W. H. 1980. Fire frequency in subalpine forests of Yellowstone National Park. In: Proceedings of the fire history workshop; 1980 October 20-24; Tucson, AZ. Gen. Tech. Rep. RM-81. Fort Collins, CO: U.S. Department of Agriculture, Forest Service, Rocky Mountain Forest and Range Experiment Station: 27-30.

Romme, W. H.; Knight, D. H. 1981. Fire frequency and subalpine forest succession along a topographic gradient in Wyoming. Ecology. 62(2): 319-326.

Romme, W. H. 1982. Fire and landscape diversity in subalpine forests of Yellowstone National Park. Ecological Monographs. 52: 199-221.

Romme, W. H.; Despain, D. G. 1989. Historical perspective on the Yellowstone fires of 1988. BioScience. 39(10): 695-699.

Rothermel, R. C. 1983. How to predict the behavior of forest and range fires. Gen. Tech. Rep. INT-143. Ogden, UT: U.S. Department of Agriculture, Forest Service, Intermountain Forest and Range Experiment Station. 161 p.

Rowe, J. S. 1959. Forest regions of Canada. Bull. 123. Canadian Department of Northern Affairs and Natural Resources, Forestry Branch. 71 p.

Rowe, J. S.; Scotter, G. W. 1973. Fire in the boreal forest. Quaternary Research. 3(3): 444-464.

Rowe, J. S.; Bergsteinsson, J. L.; Padbury, G. A.; Hermesh, R. 1974. Fire studies in the Mackenzie Valley. INA Publ. QS-1567-000-EE-Al. Canadian Department of Indian and Northern Affairs. 123 p.

Rundel, P. W. 1971. Community structures and stability in the giant sequoia groves of the Sierra Nevada, California. American Midland Naturalist. 85(2): 478-492.

Rundel, P. W. 1972. Habitat restriction in giant sequoia: the environmental control of grove boundaries. American Midland Naturalist. 87(1): 81-99.

Ryan, Kevin C.; Noste, Nonan V. 1985. Evaluating prescribed fires. In: Lotan, James E.; [and others], tech. coords. Proceedings—symposium and workshop on wilderness fire; 1983 November 15-18; Missoula, MT. Gen. Tech. Rep. INT-182. Ogden, UT: U.S. Department of Agriculture, Forest Service, Intermountain Forest and Range Experiment Station: 230-238.

Sando, R. W.; Haines, D. A. 1972. Fire weather and behavior of the Little Sioux fire. Res. Pap. NC-76. St. Paul, MN: U.S. Department of Agriculture, Forest Service, North Central Forest Experiment Station. 6 p.

Schroeder, M. J.; Buck, C. C. 1970. Fire weather - a guide for application of meteorological information to forest fire control operations. Agric. Handb. 360. Washington, DC: U.S. Department of Agriculture, Forest Service. 229 p.

Schullery, Paul. 1989. Yellowstone fires: a preliminary report. Northwest Science. 63(1): 44-54.

Sellers, Robert E.; Despain, Don G. 1976. Fire management in Yellowstone National Park. In: Proceedings, Tall Timbers Fire Ecology Conference No. 14; 1974 October 8-10; Missoula, MT. Tallahassee, FL: Tall Timbers Research Station: 99-113.

Simard, A. J. 1981. The Mack Lake Fire. Fire Management Notes. 42(2): 5-6.

Society of American Foresters. 1989. Fire management in the forest and range environment: a position of the Society of American Foresters. Journal of Forestry. 87(5): 56-58.

Sousa, W. P. 1984. The role of disturbance in natural communities. Annual Review of Ecology and Systematics. 15: 353-391.

Spurr, S. H. 1954. The forests of Itasca in the nineteenth century as related to fire. Ecology. 35(1): 21-25.

Stankey, George H. 1976. Wilderness fire policy: an investigation of visitor knowledge and beliefs. Res. Pap. INT-180. Ogden, UT: U.S. Department of Agriculture, Forest Service, Intermountain Forest and Range Experiment Station. 17 p.

Stark, N. 1968. Seed ecology of *Sequoiadendron giganteum*. Madrono. 19: 267-277.

Stoddard, H. L. 1935. Use of controlled fire in southeastern upland game management. Journal of Forestry. 33(3): 346-351.

Stone, E. C.; Vasey, R. B. 1968. Preservation of coast redwood on alluvial flats. Science. 159(3811): 157-161.

Stringer, P. W., LaRoi, G. H. 1970. The Douglas-fir forests of Banff and Jasper National Parks, Canada. Canadian Journal of Botany. 48(10): 1703-1726.

Swain, A. M. 1973. A history of fire and vegetation in northeastern Minnesota as recorded in lake sediments. Quaternary Research. 3(3): 383-396.

Swanson, John R.; Denniston, Alan E. 1985. The Park-Caribou Plan: an example of integrated planning. In: Lotan, James E.; [and others], tech. coords. Proceedings—symposium and workshop on wilderness fire; 1983 November 15-18; Missoula, MT. Gen. Tech. Rep. INT-182. Ogden, UT: U.S. Department of Agriculture, Forest Service, Intermountain Forest and Range Experiment Station: 215-219.

Switzer, Ronald R. 1974. The effects of forest fire on archeological sites in Mesa Verde National Park, Colorado. Artifact. 12(3): 1-8.

Tande, G. F. 1979. Fire history and vegetation pattern of coniferous forest in Jasper National Park, Alberta. Canadian Journal of Botany. 57: 1912-1931.

Taylor, Dale L. 1969. Biotic succession of lodgepole pine forests of fire origin in Yellowstone National Park. Laramie, WY: University of Wyoming. 320 p. Dissertation.

Taylor, Dale L.; Malotte, Frenchie; Erskine, Douglas. 1985. Cooperative fire planning for large areas: a Federal, private, and State of Alaska example. In: Lotan, James E.; [and others], tech. coords. Proceedings—symposium and workshop on wilderness fire; 1983 November 15-18; Missoula, MT. Gen. Tech. Rep. INT-182. Ogden, UT: U.S. Department of Agriculture, Forest Service, Intermountain Forest and Range Experiment Station: 206-214.

Thomas, Terri L.; Agee, James K. 1986. Prescribed fire effects on mixed conifer forest structure at Crater Lake, Oregon. Canadian Journal of Forest Research. 16(5): 1082-1087.

Towle, Everett L. 1985. Management considerations for a cost-effective fire management program in National Forest wilderness. In: Lotan, James E.; [and others], tech. coords. Proceedings—symposium and workshop on wilderness fire; 1983 November 15-18; Missoula, MT. Gen. Tech. Rep. INT-182. Ogden, UT: U.S. Department of Agriculture, Forest Service, Intermountain Forest and Range Experiment Station: 191-192.

Traylor, Diane; Hubbell, Lyndi; Wood, Nancy; Fiedler, Barbara. 1979. The La Mesa fire study: investigation of fire and fire suppression on cultural resources in Bandelier National Monument. Santa Fe, NM: U.S. Department of the Interior, National Park Service, Southwest Cultural Resources Center. 159 p.

Trenberth, K. E.; Branstator, G. W.; Arkin, P. A. 1988. Origins of the 1988 North American drought. Science. 242: 1640-1645.

Turner, B. A. 1976. The development of disasters - a sequence model for the origin of disasters. Sociological Review. 24: 753-774.

U.S. Department of Agriculture. 1941. Climate and man. U.S. Department of Agriculture Yearbook, 1941. Washington, DC. 1248 p.

U.S. Department of Agriculture, Forest Service. 1985. Chapter 2320. Wilderness and Primitive Areas. Forest Service Manual, Amendment 93. Washington, DC: U.S. Department of Agriculture, Forest Service.

U.S. Department of Agriculture and U.S. Department of the Interior. 1989. Final report and recommendations of the Fire Management Policy Review Team and summary of public comments. Federal Register. 54(115): 25660-25678.

Vankat, John L.; Major, Jack. 1978. Vegetation changes in Sequoia National Park, California. Journal of Biogeography. 5: 377-402.

Van Wagner, C. E. 1977. Conditions for the start and spread of crown fire. Canadian Journal of Forest Research. 7: 23-34.

van Wagtendonk, J. W. 1974. Refined burning prescriptions for Yosemite National Park. Occas. Pap. 2. Washington, DC: U.S. Department of the Interior, National Park Service. 21 p.

van Wagtendonk, J. W. 1978. Wilderness fire management in Yosemite National Park. In: Proceedings of the 14th biennial wilderness conference, New York. Sierra Club and National Audubon Society; Boulder, CO: Westview Press: 324-335.

van Wagtendonk, Jan W. 1985. Fire suppression effects on fuels and succession in short-fire-interval wilderness ecosystems. In: Lotan, James E.; [and others], tech. coords. Proceedings—symposium and workshop on wilderness fire; 1983 November 15-18; Missoula, MT. Gen. Tech. Rep. INT-182. Ogden, UT: U.S. Department of Agriculture, Forest Service, Intermountain Forest and Range Experiment Station: 119-126.

van Wagtendonk, J. W.; Bancroft, L.; Ferry, G.; [and others]. 1982. Prescribed fire monitoring and evaluation guide. Washington, DC: National Wildfire Coordinating Group, Prescribed Fire and Fire Effects Working Team. 16 p. [Mimeo.]

van Wagtendonk, Jan W.; Botti, Stephen J. 1984. Modeling behavior of prescribed fires in Yosemite National Park. Journal of Forestry. 82(8): 479-484.

Veirs, Stephen D., Jr. 1980. The influence of fire in coast redwood forests. In: Proceedings of the fire history workshop; 1980 October 20-24; Tucson, AZ. Gen. Tech. Rep. RM-81. Fort Collins, CO: U.S. Department of Agriculture, Forest Service, Rocky Mountain Forest and Range Experiment Station: 93-95.

Veirs, Stephen D., Jr. 1982. Coast redwood forest: stand dynamics, successional status, and the role of fire. In: Forest succession and stand development research in the Northwest: Proceedings of the symposium; 1981 March 26; Corvallis, OR. Corvallis, OR: Oregon State University, Forest Research Laboratory: 119-141.

Viereck, L. A. 1973. Wildfire in the taiga of Alaska. Quaternary Research. 3: 465-495.

Vitousek, P. M.; Reiners, W. A. 1975. Ecosystem succession and nutrient retention: a hypothesis. BioScience. 25(6): 376-381.

Vogl, Richard J. 1967. Fire adaptations of some southern California plants. In: Proceedings, Tall Timbers Fire Ecology Conference No. 7; 1966 November 9-10; Hoberg, CA. Tallahassee, FL: Tall Timbers Research Station: 79-109.

Vogl, Richard J. 1970. Fire and plant succession. In: Role of fire in the Intermountain West. Missoula, MT: Intermountain Fire Research Council: 65-75.

Vogl, Richard J. 1974. Effects of fire on grasslands. In:

Kozlowski, T. T.; Ahlgren, C. E., eds. Fire and ecosystems. New York: Academic Press: 139-194.

Wagener, Willis W. 1961. Past fire incidence in Sierra Nevada forest. Journal of Forestry. 59: 739-748.

Wakimoto, Ronald H. 1989. National fire management policy: a look at the need for change. Western Wildlands. 15(2): 35-39.

Waring, Richard H.; Schlesinger, William H. 1985. Forest ecosystems—concepts and management. Orlando, FL: Academic Press. 340 p.

Weaver, Harold. 1943. Fire as an ecological and silvicultural factor in the ponderosa pine region of the Pacific slope. Journal of Forestry. 41: 7-15.

Weaver, Harold. 1961. Ecological changes in the ponderosa pine forest of Cedar Valley in southern Washington. Ecology. 57(2): 416-420.

Weaver, Harold. 1974. Effects of fire on temperate forests: western United States. In: Kozlowski, T. T.; Ahlgren, C. E., eds. Fire and ecosystems. New York: Academic Press: 279-319.

Weaver, Harold; Biswell, H. 1969. How fire helps the big trees. National Parks. 43(262): 16-19.

Wellner, Charles A. 1970. Fire history in the Northern Rocky Mountains. In: Role of fire in the Intermountain West. Missoula, MT: Intermountain Fire Research Council: 42-64.

Wells, C. G.; Campbell, R. E.; DeBano, L. F.; [and others]. 1979. Effects of fire on soil: a state-of-knowledge review. Gen. Tech. Rep. W0-7. Washington, DC: U.S. Department of Agriculture, Forest Service. 34 p.

West, Neil E. 1969. Successional changes in the montane forest of the central Oregon Cascades. American Midland Naturalist. 81: 265-271.

Williams, Ted. 1989. Incineration of Yellowstone. Audubon. 91(1): 38-85.

Worf, William A. 1985. Wilderness management: a historical perspective on the implications of human-ignited fire. In: Lotan, James E.; [and others], tech. coords. Proceedings—symposium and workshop on wilderness fire; 1983 November 15-18; Missoula, MT. Gen. Tech. Rep. INT-182. Ogden, UT: U.S. Department of Agriculture, Forest Service, Intermountain Forest and Range Experiment Station: 276-282.

Wright, H. E. 1974. Landscape development, forest fires, and wilderness management. Science. 186(4163): 487-495.

Wright, H. E.; Heinselman, M. L. 1973. The ecological role of fire in natural conifer forests of western and northern North America: introduction. Quaternary Research. 3: 317-328.

ACKNOWLEDGMENTS

Dr. James K. Agee, Professor and Chair of the Forest Resources Management Division, University of Washington, Seattle.

Dr. Stephen F. Arno, Fire Effects Research Work Unit, Intermountain Fire Sciences Laboratory, Missoula, MT.

Dr. Harold H. Biswell, Professor Emeritus, University of California, Berkeley.

Kathleen M. Davis, Resources Management Specialist, Southern Arizona Group, NPS, Phoenix.

William C. Fischer, Fire Effects Research Work Unit, Intermountain Fire Sciences Laboratory, Missoula, MT.

Dr. David J. Parsons, Research Scientist, Sequoia-Kings Canyon National Parks, CA.

Dr. Jan W. van Wagtendonk, Research Scientist, Yosemite National Park, CA.

Unless closely controlled, toxic emissions from industrial plants, such as this smelter, can be lofted long distances into wilderness and damage vegetation, wildlife, and scenic quality. Photo courtesy of Clint Carlson, USFS.

13

WILDERNESS AIR RESOURCE MANAGEMENT

This chapter was written by James O. Blankenship, retired Air Resource Management Specialist, U. S. Forest Service, Department of Agriculture.

INTRODUCTION

Historically, people have been repelled by air pollution because it presents a danger to health and is offensive to human senses. Evidence of air pollution episodes and people's reaction to them date back to at least the 1200s. As early as the beginning of the nineteenth century, residents of the United States were calling for abatement of air pollution; however, the first federal air pollution legislation was not passed until 1955. Regulations were subsequently renewed and made more restrictive through six major legislative acts.

Not until recent legislation, the 1977 Clean Air Act Amendments, did Congress include authority for protecting air quality in wilderness. Extending protection to wilderness and other natural areas was mainly brought about by heightened concern during the 1970s for the growing impact of air pollution on major national parks such as Shenandoah (VA) and Grand Canyon (AZ). Growth of metropolitan areas and development of electric power generating plants and other industrial operations near national parks and wildernesses were beginning to influence visibility and other air quality-related values of these areas. Since 1977, evidence of air

pollution damage to visibility and other wilderness values has been accumulating. Air pollutants from the Los Angeles area affect the Grand Canyon. Pollution from southern Arizona smelters affects the Grand Canyon and the Chiricahua Wilderness and is believed to affect the Superstition, Mazatzal, Galiuro, and Gila Wildernesses in Arizona and New Mexico. Agricultural burning affects visibility in the Three Sisters and other wildernesses in Washington and Oregon, and fertilizer plants and natural gas desulferization ("sweetening") operations threaten air quality in Wyoming's Bridger Wilderness. Documented evidence shows ozone damage to trees and gradual visibility reduction in Shenandoah National Park caused by industrial and automobile-generated air pollution. Nearly every wilderness in the eastern United States may be currently affected by some form of human-caused air pollution.

LEGAL FRAMEWORK

The legal basis for protecting wilderness air quality is established in two major pieces of legislation and their

Table 13.1. Allowable PSD increments (μ/m^3).

Pollutant	Averaging time for measurements	Class I	Class II	Class III
Sulfur dioxide	annual	2	20	40
	24 hours	5[1]	91[1]	182[1]
	3 hours	25[1]	512[1]	700[1]
Total suspended particulate matter	annual	5	19	37
	24 hours	10[1]	37[1]	75[1]

1. Not to be exceeded more than once a year.

implementing regulations: the Wilderness Act and the Clean Air Act of 1977 (P.L. 95-95). The National Forest Management Act of 1976 (NFMA, P.L. 94-588) also provides for protection of air quality on national forest lands as a policy decision. The legal framework seems complex and the abundance of alphabetical labels commonly used for various concepts (PSD, AQRV, FLM, and others) can be a bit overwhelming. But the topic is very important and worth careful study.

THE WILDERNESS ACT

The Wilderness Act, discussed in detail in chapter 4, provides broad guidelines and directions for the management and preservation of wilderness. Although the act does not mention air quality, it contains an implicit mandate to protect wilderness from the effects of civilization's impacts, including air pollution.

THE FOREST AND RANGELAND RENEWABLE RESOURCES PLANNING ACT OF 1974

This act, as amended by the NFMA, directs the secretary of agriculture to recognize the fundamental need to protect, and where appropriate, improve the quality of soil, water, and air resources.

THE CLEAN AIR ACT

The Clean Air Act is the most important specific source of direction for protection of wilderness air resources. The act includes a program to prevent degradation of air that is cleaner than the national standards established by the act. This program is referred to as the Prevention of Significant Deterioration (PSD) program. Under the PSD program, the act

designated certain areas for special protection. These areas, designated as Class I areas in the legislation, include wildernesses more than 5,000 acres in size and national parks more than 6,000 acres in size that were in existence prior to August 7, 1977 (see table 13.4 at the end of this chapter).

There are now 158 Class I areas, most of which are wildernesses, including 88 national forest wildernesses (see table 13.4). The PSD program established limits for the additional amounts of air pollution, referred to as "PSD increments," that can be allowed in these Class I areas (table 13.1). All other parts of the nation, including other wildernesses, were designated Class II, with more added air pollution allowed. The program also provides for future designation of Class III areas in which even greater levels of additional air pollution may be allowed, but no Class III areas have been established. All wildernesses designated since August 7, 1977, are currently Class II areas under the PSD scheme. Some wildernesses, those established prior to the 1977 date but enlarged by subsequent legislation, now contain both Class I and Class II segments. The act provides for redesignation of areas from Class II to Class I, and this has occurred in three Montana Native American reservations.

Redesignations must be requested by states (or tribal governments for Native American reservations) and granted by the Environmental Protection Agency (EPA). Oregon has begun a process to redesignate additional wildernesses as Class I areas. The procedure for redesignating an area to Class I requires an analysis of effects of redesignation on health, environment, the economy, society, and energy. Consultation with any federal land manager (FLM) whose lands the redesignation would encompass and invitation for public comment are also

required. EPA must approve the request after public notice and comment periods.

Protection of the air resource in Class II wilderness requires a somewhat different approach than in Class I areas. With respect to Class I areas, the Clean Air Act states:

> The Federal Land Manager and the Federal official charged with direct responsibility for management of such lands shall have an affirmative responsibility to protect the air quality related values (including visibility) of such lands within a Class I area and to consider ... whether a proposed major emitting facility will have an adverse impact on such values.

The framers of the Clean Air Act used the word "affirmative" to stress the importance of the role being assigned to managers of Class I areas. This "affirmative responsibility" goes beyond the customary management activity. The Senate Report (1977) emphasizes this point by stating:

> While the general scope of the Federal Government's activities in preventing significant deterioration has been carefully limited, the Federal Land Manager should assume an aggressive role in protecting the air quality values of land areas under his jurisdiction. ... in the case of doubt, the land manager should err on the side of protecting the air quality related values for future generations.

This affirmative responsibility is implemented, in part, through a preconstruction review procedure known as the PSD New Source Review process. The PSD program has special requirements for all major industrial activities, which are included in a list of 28 named PSD source categories in the regulations. Examples of such sources are coal-fired powerplants, gas sweetening plants (which remove hydrogen sulfide from "sour" natural gas), smelters, pulp mills, and cement plants. When a new or expanded facility of the type in the list is proposed in a clean air area (one currently cleaner than the maximum pollution levels allowed by the national ambient air quality standards), it and other PSD sources, cannot cause the pollution level to exceed the applicable Class I and Class II increments established by the act.

The facility must also pass the Air Quality-Related Values (AQRV) impact analysis. The *AQRV analysis* is essentially a determination, by the manager of a Class I area, that the additional air pollution caused by the proposed new industrial activity will not cause unacceptable adverse impact on the air quality-related values of the area. FLMs of an area are responsible for establishing which components of the area are AQRVs and determining what level of impact is unacceptable.

The PSD program and the AQRV analysis (for Class I wilderness only) are the primary vehicles for protection of wilderness under the Clean Air Act. An applicant for an industrial permit submits plans to the permitting authority, usually the State Air Quality Bureau, which has been delegated this authority by the EPA. In a few states, the EPA has retained the authority, and in a few instances the EPA has delegated this authority below the state level. The permitting authority then examines the potential impacts and, if the proposed emissions may affect a Class I wilderness, alerts the FLM. The FLM evaluates the effects of the projected emissions on the area's AQRVs, then determines the acceptability of these effects and, finally, recommends to the permitting authority whether the project should be permitted as planned. This recommendation is based on the effects of the project's emissions on the AQRVs of the area, hence it is referred to as the "air quality-related values test." In at least one state, the permitting authority considers similar recommendations for Class II areas.

In an air quality-permitting case involving the Flat Tops Wilderness in Colorado, a proposed oil shale production plant was offered a PSD permit with stringent air pollution control requirements. The company decided not to accept the permit. The state imposed these requirements after the FLM (the regional forester in Denver) provided data about the potential effect of sulfur dioxide and nitrogen oxides on visibility, acidity of lakes, and destruction of lichens, which supported the need for controls. The FLM was successful in requiring strict permit conditions in this case because national forest staff people had explained the importance of Class I areas to state officials several years before the permitting decision and had obtained field data about wilderness AQRVs in the area before the permit application (Fox and others 1982).

Protection of Class II wilderness calls for the proponent of a new or expanding industrial operation to conduct an air quality impacts analysis. The applicant must consider the "Best Available Control Technology" (BACT) to keep the air pollution impacts to an acceptable level. BACT is also required for Class I areas. Using this provision, wilderness managers can request that the permitting authority require more effective control technology in those instances where the proposed new emissions are expected to cause an unacceptable impact on the wilderness resource. The procedures for arriving at such a recommendation would be the same as for a Class I area, involving presentation of an analysis of the AQRVs

at risk and the predicted effects of the proposed new air pollution on them. In the case of a Class I area recommendation, the wilderness manager has greater leverage through direct application of the Class I provisions; in the Class II situation, the manager must convince the permitting authority to require a more stringent control technology to protect the special values of a wilderness not covered by the Class I requirements. In Wyoming, the manager of the Popo Agie, a Class II wilderness, convinced the state to consider AQRV data in permitting actions that could affect the wilderness.

The wilderness manager and the air regulatory authority have different roles: the state or EPA air regulatory authority enforces the air quality standards and emission limitations established by the Clean Air Act and state and federal regulations. In contrast, the wilderness manager is concerned with effects of air pollution on natural resources and makes recommendations to protect them. The wilderness manager's recommendation can be a major factor in protecting wilderness values that may be affected by air pollution, but it is only a recommendation. Effective participation requires early involvement and an understanding by both sides of the programs, capabilities, constraints, and policies of the air regulatory agency and the wilderness management agency.

LAND MANAGEMENT AGENCY REGULATIONS

Air resource management authority, objectives, policy, and responsibilities are spelled out in the policy manuals and regulations of the various agencies that have wilderness management responsibility. For example, chapters 2320 and 2580 of the Forest Service Manual provide objectives for the protection of AQRVs in wildernesses designated as Class I. In addition, the Forest Service Air Resource Management Handbook 2509.19 (1987) covers all national forest lands, including wildernesses designated Class II. Similar guidance is provided by the National Park Service (NPS) and other Department of the Interior wilderness-managing agencies (Ross and others 1986).

EFFECTS OF AIR QUALITY ON WILDERNESS VALUES

The purpose of the Wilderness Act is to provide future generations with an opportunity to enjoy the wilderness experience while at the same time perpetuating naturally functioning ecosystems. As far-

fetched as it may seem, polluted air, a condition that many wilderness visitors hope to escape, may follow them into otherwise remote areas and spoil both the wilderness experience and the wilderness environment.

ECOSYSTEMS

The effects of air pollution on wildland ecosystems are not currently well understood (McConnell 1986; Schreiber and Newman 1987). Most studies have been directed at effects on crops and farm animals, where knowledge was sought for economic reasons. Studies motivated by purely environmental or aesthetic concerns are a relatively recent occurrence. Many designated wildernesses contain alpine or subalpine ecosystems. Little has been published on the effects of air pollution on these ecosystems. Much of the wildlands ecosystems work has been done at lower elevations, using species not usually found in higher elevation ecosystems. Even in those instances where lower elevation studies have included the species found in higher elevation systems, it is uncertain whether the data can be transferred without regard to the elevational differences.

Vegetation
Effects of air pollution on vegetation vary widely, based on sensitivity of the particular species to the specific pollutant, the concentration and exposure time of the pollutant, the general health of the individual plant, and sometimes on the time of year or stage of growth at the time of exposure. Wilderness vegetation is often susceptible to air pollution damage because many wildernesses are situated at higher elevations where natural environmental stress to plants is great (Roberts 1987).

Common pollutants most likely to adversely affect wilderness vegetation are sulfur dioxide, nitrogen oxides, photochemical oxidants (such as ozone, which is a secondary pollutant, produced from nitrogen oxides and hydrocarbons by photochemical reactions in the atmosphere), and acidic deposition, commonly referred to as acid rain. The *acid rain* phenomenon occurs when sulfur dioxide and nitrogen oxides are chemically transformed into acidic sulfates and nitrates during atmospheric transport and are subsequently deposited downwind as acid precipitation (either rain or snow), acid fog, or as acidic particles. These acidic compounds or acid precipitation may be incorporated into the soil or water on which they fall.

Vegetative damage in wilderness is generally *chronic* (constant, prolonged) rather than *acute* (sud-

den) and is often masked by or is accompanied by attack of the weakened plant by insects or disease. Similarly, plants stressed by insects or disease are often more susceptible to air pollution damage. Some sensitive plants, such as certain lichens, will eventually disappear under continued low-level exposure to pollutants like sulfur dioxide (Hale 1982; Smith 1981).

Lethal effects of air pollutants, manifested by reproductive failure or sudden death, may develop after chronic injury. Nonlethal effects often exhibited are changes in physiology, behavior, or pathology. Other common nonlethal effects are decrease in growth rate and reproduction and altered progeny.

Large areas of wildland vegetation have been damaged by air pollution. In addition to the recently publicized acid rain damage in Europe, southeastern Canada, and the northeastern United States, about 100,000 acres of coniferous forest in southern Oregon have been affected by photochemical oxidants and, in Montana, 52,000 acres of coniferous forest were killed or injured by fluoride emissions from an aluminum-processing plant (Miller 1980). In Shenandoah National Park, symptoms of foliar injury caused by ozone can be observed in the park each year (Bennett 1985). Ninety percent of the most sensitive species (milkweed) and 8 percent of the least sensitive species (black locust) showed air pollution damage.

Studies primarily using crop species indicate that effects include morphological and physiological responses, added insect and disease stresses, nutrient cycle alterations, and changes in biomass production. Examination of all available facts regarding the large-scale forest dieback in the Black Forest of Germany and of red spruce in the northeastern United States led McFee and others (1984) to conclude:

> At present we have no direct evidence that acidic deposition currently limits forest growth in either North America or Europe, but we do have indications that tree growth reductions are occurring, principally in coniferous species that have been examined to date, that these reductions are rather widespread, and that they occur in regions where rainfall acidity is generally quite high, or pH is low (about 4.3 pH) for an annual average.

The term *pH* is derived from "potential of Hydrogen." It is a measure of acidity or alkalinity. It is measured on a logarithmic scale in which 7 is neutral; lower values are acidic and higher values are alkaline. Because of the logarithmic nature of the pH scale, a pH of 6 is 10 times more acidic than pH 7, pH 5 is 100 times more acidic than pH 7, and pH 4 is 1,000 times more acidic than pH 7.

In summary, the effects of chronic levels of air pollution on vegetation are loss of vigor, visible physical damage to plant parts, interference with reproductive processes, and eventual loss of sensitive species, resulting in a reduction of floristic diversity. Acute doses of air pollutants rarely occur in wilderness, but when they do occur they can cause severe damage or death to sensitive species. The effect of acid rain or atmospheric deposition on wilderness vegetation is a controversial but poorly understood issue.

Wildlife

Mammals and birds generally are not known to be directly affected by the levels of air pollution currently found in most American wildernesses. Injuries to wildlife from air emissions were reported as early as the 1880s in Germany and England, however. More than 100 air pollution episodes involving animals have been reported since the early 1900s, with 75 percent of these recorded in the last 25 years (Newman 1980). Direct effects of air pollutants on wildlife can be acute, causing sudden dieoffs, or chronic, causing symptoms such as deterioration of bone and teeth from fluoride pollution (fluorosis). The nature of the effect depends on the pollutant and its concentration, the duration of exposure, and the health of the wildlife at the time of exposure. *Acid shock,* caused when acidifying substances accumulate in the snowpack and are released during spring snowmelt, is known to cause reproductive failure in sensitive fish, frogs, and salamanders (Schreiber and Newman 1987). Three categories of air pollutants are known to affect wildlife: (1) photochemical oxidants, (2) particulates, and (3) acidifying air pollutants. Air pollutants most commonly affect the respiratory and pulmonary systems, followed by the central nervous and gastrointestinal systems.

Responses of wildlife to air pollutants can be both ecological and physiological. *Ecological effects,* such as a genetic change in sensitivity to ozone in California deer mice as a result of ozone exposure, reduced populations of small mammals in California as a result of exposure to oxidants, and reduced populations of larks in Japan from several air pollutants, have been recorded. *Physiological responses* such as blindness (from oxidant exposure) in bighorn sheep in California and fluorosis of white-tailed deer in Canada have been recorded (Schreiber 1984). Low-level releases of toxic pollutants such as hydrogen sulfide have caused animal mortality in the vicinity of oil and gas well operations in the United States and Canada.

Indirect effects of air pollution on wildlife include food and habitat degradation, synergistic effects,

and effects on trophic dynamics, such as food-chain interruptions, and biological accumulation of pollutants. Vegetation that provides food, cover, and reproductive habitat can be altered by air pollution, reducing habitat diversity and placing indirect stress on species. Quality of wildlife may be reduced, as in Poland where the size and trophy value of roe deer antlers declined significantly in a pine forest receiving sulfur dioxide and particulate emissions (Richkind and Hacker 1980). The acidification of soils and water is known to adversely affect fish and amphibians as well as soil and water microorganisms. Substantial declines in fish populations from acidification in Norway, Canada, and the United States are documented (Altshuller and Linthurst 1984; Haines 1981).

Soils

Although little is known about effects of air pollution on wilderness soils specifically, soil responses would probably be very slow and immeasurable until long after impacts are apparent for more sensitive indicators such as vegetation and water. Soils collect atmospheric pollutants. The effects of these pollutants are a function of the pollutant concentration, the time over which the exposure occurs, and the inherent *buffering capacity* of the soil—ability to neutralize acids without a change in pH. The buffering capacity of a soil depends primarily on the nature of the parent material from which the soil is formed. Sedimentary soils, derived from limestone and shale, and soils with high clay content and high organic matter content generally have high buffering capacity. Granitic-based soils, often found in high mountain wildernesses, have inherently low buffering capacity.

Air pollution is not believed to induce drastic changes in the soil itself, but rather in nutrient cycling. Air pollution effects, including those of acid deposition, may include increased rate of weathering (the decomposition of bedrock), resulting in accelerated release of trace elements. Increased acidification of the soil may cause increased leaching of cations, which tends to remove essential nutrients such as calcium, magnesium, and phosphorus from the plant root zone. This may cause plants to become nutrient deficient. Acidification may also result in increased solubility of potentially toxic elements such as aluminum, zinc, manganese, and copper. Nitrate and sulfate additions to the soil may have a fertilizing effect on plants. Microbes in the soil tend to react quickly to changes in their soil habitat. Large-scale changes in microbial activity may be induced by air pollution and could have serious nutrient cycling ramifications (Linthurst 1984; McFee and others 1984).

Water

Air pollution effects on water occur principally from acidification of surface waters through the acid rain and deposition process described in the section on vegetation. Wilderness watersheds situated at high elevations are at particular risk. As air masses move up over such elevated terrain, acid-laden moisture is wrung out of the atmosphere and deposited as *orographic precipitation.* If these elevated watersheds lie on granitic-based soils, damage potential rises because the buffering capacity of such soils is low.

Lake surveys conducted by the EPA in 1984 and in 1985 reveal that lakes in the East have a higher incidence of acidification (as measured by low pH values) than western lakes (fig. 13.1). In the West, 719 lakes were sampled that statistically represented 10,393 lakes in the area. Of these, 455 were in designated wilderness. Only one lake sampled (Fern Lake, fed by a sulfur hot spring in Yellowstone National Park) had a pH equal to or lower than 5. In the East, about 10 percent of the lakes in the Adirondacks of New York, in the upper peninsula of Michigan, and in Florida had pH 5 or less. Sulfate concentrations in lakes in the northeastern United States were six times higher than those of western lakes. This is not a surprising result because ambient air pollution levels in the East are usually much higher than in the West, and soils in the East typically have a low sulfate absorption capacity.

A more important finding involves the buffering capacity of wilderness lakes and watersheds. The EPA surveys show that western lakes have much lower *acid-neutralizing capacity* (ANC) than eastern lakes. ANC is the scientific indicator of buffering capacity. Although not currently acidified, these western lakes are susceptible to long-term damage because of their low buffering capacity (Marshall 1987). Many of the lakes sampled in the West were at high elevations, particularly in the Sierra Nevada, the central Rockies, and the southern Rockies. A moderately strong inverse relationship existed between elevation and ANC (the higher the elevation, the lower the ANC) in the Sierras and central Rockies, but there was little or no relationship elsewhere. In the East, a strong relationship between elevation and ANC was found only in the Adirondacks (where the inverse relationship was also found), although few eastern areas were much higher in elevation than surrounding lands.

The conclusions of the survey are that more than 27 percent of the western lakes have *low conductivity* (a measure of the amount of chemical material dissolved in water), low concentrations of base cations, and many have solute concentrations among the lowest reported anywhere in the world. (In other words, they are

Fig. 13.1. A device used for collecting water samples from beneath the surface of lakes to detect effects of air pollution, especially acidification. Photo courtesy of Jim Blankenship, USFS.

extremely pure, almost like distilled water.) These attributes are directly related to lake and stream alkalinity and ANC. The data suggest that these watersheds would provide little buffering against acidic deposition (Landers and others 1986).

In summary, air pollution affects water primarily through deposition of acidifying substances. Acidification of water in turn affects the functioning of organisms living in or dependent upon the water, such as reproduction of fish, salamanders, and frogs, as well as macroinvertebrates important in the food web of higher order animals.

VISITOR EXPERIENCE

Two effects of air quality that directly affect the wilderness visitor and are most likely to cause dissatisfaction with the wilderness experience are *visibility impairment* and the presence of *unpleasant or unnatural odors*. Either condition has great impact because the visitor normally does not expect to see or smell air pollution in wilderness. Air pollution also can indirectly affect visitors by damaging the natural ecosystems that wilderness experiences depend on.

Visibility

Visibility is the one air quality-related value Congress has singled out for protection in the Clean Air Act. The act provides special protection for visibility in Class I wildernesses and establishes a national goal "to protect air quality related values (including visibility) on any such lands within a class I area ... and the remedying of any existing impairment of visibility in mandatory class I Federal areas." Visibility impairment is caused by the scattering of light by particles or gases, or by the extinction of light by particles, between the viewer and the scene being viewed. Visible smoke and other pollution plumes, as well as general haze caused by particulate matter, nitrogen oxides, and sulfates, can invade wilderness and cause visibility impairment sufficient to reduce a visitor's enjoyment of the area. Wildernesses near industrial plants or large metropolitan areas are particularly subject to reduced visibility. Several wildernesses near these air pollution sources are currently suffering gradual visibility reductions as regional haze continues to spread from these sources (fig. 13.2). Some examples include: the Superstition Wilderness near Phoenix, Arizona; the San Gorgonio Wilderness near Los Angeles, California; wilderness in Shenandoah National Park, Virginia, near Washington, DC; and Lye Brook Wilderness, Vermont, near Albany, New York.

The importance of clean air and good visibility to wilderness visitors has been documented in a number of studies (Ross and others 1986). Visitor awareness of air quality and visibility-reducing pollutants has been studied by the NPS for several years. Results to date show that visitor awareness of haze increases as visibility decreases, as would be expected. The visitor's enjoyment of the recreational experience also decreases as the awareness of haze increases (Ross and others 1984). Studies also show that a given amount of air pollution in an area with relatively clean air, such as in most wildernesses, is much more perceptible to humans than the same amount of air pollution in an area with dirtier air. This means that a small amount of air pollution, which may go unnoticed in or near urban areas, is likely to be noticed if it occurs in a wilderness.

Visibility impairment caused by smoke from prescribed fire is a matter of growing concern to the public, state air regulatory agencies, and the EPA. This includes smoke from prescribed burns ignited by lightning or by fire specialists, both inside and outside wilderness (see chap. 12). Policy for dealing with prescribed burning is currently being developed by the regulatory agencies and by wilderness management agencies. More intensive management of prescribed fire in and near wilderness to reduce intensity and duration of smoke emissions, as well as use of slash treatment methods other than burning, are being utilized to reduce this conflict. Public concern over the issue is likely to exert continuing pressure on all parties to reduce the occurrence of smoke in wildernesses, at least during periods of visitor use. This could hamper efforts to restore fire as an important natural element in wilderness ecosystems.

Fig. 13.2. Visibility in the Kalmiopsis Wilderness (OR) on a clear day (left), and a polluted day (right). Visibility is a key air quality value, and the only one specifically mentioned in the Clean Air Act. Photos courtesy of Jim Blankenship, USFS.

Odor

Odors transported into wilderness are usually caused by hydrogen sulfide from natural gas wells or gas sweetening plants, and by emissions from other industrial operations such as pulp and paper mills, metal-smelting plants, and gas and oil refineries. Currently, such operations are located near enough to several wildernesses to cause occasional odor problems. Odor control technology, applied at the time such facilities are constructed, offers the best opportunity for eliminating or reducing the occurrence of offensive odors in nearby wilderness. For this reason, wilderness managers need to be involved with air regulatory agencies during the development of air quality permits for all industrial operations that produce strong odors, if these operations are to be located near wilderness areas.

MONITORING PROGRAMS AND TECHNIQUES

Although scientists have been studying the effects of air pollution on plants for several decades, efforts have centered on crops and greenhouse specimens. Knowledge about wilderness ecosystems is hampered by the nature of wilderness: study areas which are usually isolated, remote, and without electric power or other facilities sometimes essential to the task of collecting scientific data about air pollution and its effects. Physical and environmental factors in many wildernesses add to the difficulty and expense of collecting scientific data.

Only recently have wilderness managers recognized the need for scientific data about wilderness ecosystems. Facilities and equipment commonly used to collect such data sometimes violate wilderness policies, so research is often conducted elsewhere. As a result, we know little about effects of pollution on natural ecosystems or techniques for collecting such data in wilderness. Concern about air pollution effects from natural gas treatment in western Wyoming stimulated a monitoring program in the Bridger Wilderness. The procedures and techniques employed, and the coordination efforts involved, are detailed in a USFS workshop proceedings (1984).

It can be argued that better information about wilderness resources can be collected at lower cost by methods that require special exemptions from the general prohibition against motorized travel and mechanized equipment in wilderness. Nevertheless, wilderness monitoring must be done in accordance with the Wilderness Act and the regulations of wilderness management agencies. Requests for exceptions for the collection of air quality-related values data have not been considered until all alternatives have been examined. State-of-the-art methods and optimum data, no matter how desirable, may not be necessary for the protection of wilderness resources. As was learned in the 1985 EPA western lakes survey, adequate data may be obtained by methods that are compatible with wilderness. Crews usually hiked or rode horses to collect samples instead of using helicopters (fig. 13.3). The methods and procedures described and recommended for use in the following sections of this chapter are expected to be implemented within the spirit and rules for wilderness.

Developing standardized tools and procedures for monitoring AQRVs will be necessary if wilderness managers are to convince authorities to institute the regulations necessary to protect pollution-sensitive

wilderness values. Development of such tools and procedures will provide comparability between similar permitting decisions and provide the credibility needed to influence permitting authorities to make decisions that support wilderness protection. The use of standardized procedures also reduces the cost of data collection. Procedures for measuring baseline air quality in wilderness have been recently defined (Fox 1986; Fox and others 1987). Although these procedures have undergone scientific review, they are as yet untested in the political and legal arena.

Vegetation

Monitoring vegetation for pollution damage is particularly difficult because environmental stress, diseases, and other factors often produce effects quite similar to those of air pollution. Recommended procedures involve long-term sampling using permanent plots and individually identified plants. *Sampling areas should be located parallel to prevailing wind direction.* Such sampling, where gradients of pollution might be expected, provides evidence for cause and effect.

Several equivalent landscape units (areas with similar vegetation, aspect, and elevation) should be sampled in this manner. Data collected from each plot should include: species composition; site factors such as slope, aspect, and elevation; soils; and geology. Growth forms to be monitored in these plots include lichens, evergreen plants, and trees. Lichen plots should include photographic records, species lists, and plant chemistry. Data from evergreen plants should include leaf death and chlorosis (deficiency of green pigment), chemical elemental analysis, and leaf retention by age class. Attributes monitored for trees are tree ring growth and historic records of pollutant deposition. Procedures for such sampling are described by Fox and others (1987).

Wildlife

Air pollution effects on wildlife from acute doses of pollutants are essentially nonexistent in wilderness situations. Chronic doses, more likely to be experienced in wilderness, are more readily reflected in effects on vegetation and aquatic macroinvertebrates, fish, and amphibians. Monitoring these wilderness biological components is believed to provide effective protection to wildlife. Therefore, direct monitoring of wildlife seems unnecessary (see the following section on aquatic biology).

Aquatic Biology

The primary objective of monitoring aquatic biology in wilderness areas is to provide information on the status of air-pollution-sensitive communities and to determine whether change is occurring in such communities. A minimal set of elements to be monitored include: chlorophyll; trout, salmon, or other sensitive fisheries; and macroinvertebrates. Chlorophyll is the best readily measurable indication of phytoplankton (minute aquatic plant) production, which is directly related to the nutritive status of surface waters. Macroinvertebrates and trout or salmon are selected because of their sensitivity to air-pollution-induced changes in aquatic systems. *Aquatic macroinvertebrates* are animals without backbones that live in streams and lakes and are big enough to be seen without a microscope when in advanced stages of their development. Because some are more tolerant to acid conditions than others, they offer a graduated barometer that indicates the severity of the problem and, when correlated with chemical and physical data, can provide early detection of environmental degradation.

Sampling of chlorophyll is conducted as part of the aquatic chemistry monitoring, using an acetone extraction/fluorescence method (Fox and others 1987). Waters selected for fisheries monitoring should also be selected for aquatic chemistry monitoring.

When monitoring fisheries, examine the following attributes: the abundance of the selected species; population age structure, age distribution, as determined by fish scale analysis; condition factors, the relative health of individuals, as determined by weight and length; growth and mortality rates; and missing or weak year classes, to determine if reproduction patterns of selected species have been interrupted. Procedures for such monitoring are explained in detail in Fox and others (1987).

Fig. 13.3. In keeping with wilderness ethics, USFS crews usually hiked or rode horses while collecting water samples from wilderness lakes as part of a national acidic precipitation study. Photo courtesy of Jim Blankenship, USFS.

Three biotic analysis elements for macroinvertebrate monitoring are recommended. The first of these, the *Biotic Condition Index* (BCI), measures a stream against its own potential and not that of other streams. It is a measure of the tolerance of individual species to disturbances in the ecosystem. The BCI has several particularly useful characteristics:

- It is sensitive to all types of environmental stress.
- It is applicable to various types of streams.
- It gives a linear assessment from unstressed to highly stressed conditions.
- It is independent of sample size providing the sample contains a representative assemblage of species.
- It is based on data readily available or easily acquired.

The second analysis element for macroinvertebrates is a *diversity index* that combines a measure of dominance of species in the community and the number of species present. Subsequent changes in the diversity index give early warning of environmental changes that may be destructive of higher order animals in the wilderness.

The third analysis element is *macroinvertebrate standing crop,* as measured by the weight of the organisms from each sample. It is used to indicate whether a stream is reaching its potential and shows its potential for supporting a resident fishery.

Soils and Geology

Soils perform an important role in the productivity and diversity of the terrestrial and aquatic biota. Soils also serve as an effective collection system for many atmospheric contaminants. Responses of soil and geology to changes in air quality are usually very slow and difficult to measure over short time periods. Estimating the sensitivity or stability of the ecosystem and its response to atmospheric input requires a careful description and quantitative measurements of the soil.

Monitoring programs and techniques should: (1) characterize the soil-geologic resource and evaluate its sensitivity to internal change and its ability to buffer the aquatic system and (2) determine the soil's present condition in terms of pH, nutrient ions, and metal load as a baseline against which to measure future changes. These procedures are recommended for achieving two purposes: first, to acquire information for evaluating the susceptibility or vulnerability of the soils due to changes in air quality; and second, to detect change by repeated measurements.

A geological reconnaissance survey is necessary to focus sampling on sites most likely to be susceptible to change. Data collected should include: *soil descriptions,* horizons, depth, field pH, texture, structure, color, and consistency; *mineralogy,* sand, silt, clay,

and so forth; and *laboratory analysis* of exchangeable ions and acidity, extractable sulfate, nitrogen and sulfur in the 0 horizon, metal content, and other attributes (Fox and others 1987). Sites for more intensive characterization and long-term monitoring should be coordinated with vegetation and aquatic monitoring sites so these data can be coordinated.

Aquatic Chemistry

Procedures for data collection and monitoring of wilderness aquatic systems will vary according to the specific information needs, time and funding available, and constraints of the particular wilderness. Sampling strategies and procedures will vary according to whether the purpose is to identify the most sensitive system, to establish a baseline, or to predict future effects of air pollution. A general two-stage strategy for determining baseline chemical characteristics of surface waters is recommended. The first stage is used to determine the presence and spatial distribution of sensitive surface water systems. The second phase is used to select sensitive systems for more intensive examination and longer term monitoring. The recommended procedures focus on the measurement of acid deposition.

The initial characterization of baseline chemistry of lakes and streams in the first phase involves measuring major ions and trace metals in the water and trace elements in sediments. The specific attributes and methods recommended for measuring each are listed in table 13.2; complete details and references for the methods are provided in Fox and others (1987). These procedures represent a practical approach for collecting data, using equipment, transportating, and employing specimen and sample preservation techniques compatible with wilderness use.

The second phase, the selection and monitoring of sensitive systems identified through the first stage, requires definition of the specific objectives of monitoring, establishing more rigorous sampling and analysis procedures, and the integration of data collected on aquatic chemistry and biology, vegetation, soils, and atmosphere.

Cultural and Archeological Features

Identification and evaluation of air pollution effects on these features involve two separate disciplines, social science and archeology. Personnel from these two disciplines must work together to identify significant features, such as pictographs, that might be damaged by air pollution. When these steps are completed, it may be necessary to have a chemist or geologist evaluate the probability of damage that may result from the proposed change in air quality.

Table 13.2. Measurements required for characterizing baseline water quality.

Attributes	Methods
Alkalinity	Gran's method
Aluminum (labile and total)	Atomic absorption spectrophotometry (graphite furnace)
Ammonium	Standard indophenol blue technique
Calcium	Atomic absorption spectrophotometry or ICP (inductively coupled plasma)
Chloride	Ion chromatography
Chlorophyll a	Acetone extraction/fluorescence
Dissolved organic carbon	Infrared spectrophotometry
Fluoride	Ion-selective electrode and meter
Magnesium	Atomic absorption spectrophotometry or ICP
Nitrate	Ion chromatography
pH	pH electrode with expanded-range pH meter (closed system)
Phosphate	Standard molybdenum blue technique
Potassium	Atomic absorption spectrophotometry
Silica	Standard molybdenum blue technique or ICP
Sodium	Atomic absorption spectrophotometry
Sulfate	Ion chromatography
Conductance	Conductivity cell and meter
Dissolved oxygen	Dissolved-oxygen meter
Transparency	Secchi disk

Source: Fox and others 1987.

Visibility

A national Class I area visibility monitoring network is currently being established by EPA, in cooperation with federal land managers. This network consists of approximately 30 fully instrumented visibility monitoring sites, located in or near Class I national parks and wildernesses throughout the United States. The purpose of this network is to characterize current visibility over wide areas of the nation and monitor visibility trends on a regional basis. Because this network will be very sparse, even when completed, it will be desirable to establish visibility monitoring for individual wildernesses in addition to the national network.

A fully instrumented visibility monitoring station contains equipment to collect optical and photographic data, particle data, and local meteorological data. *Optical data* are specific values derived from measuring the loss or scattering of light between the instrument (which represents the human viewer) and the target (which represents the scene being viewed). *Photographic data* are color slides taken at timed, regular intervals to record the scene under various pollution levels. The optical data are collected with a teleradiometer or a transmissometer.

The photographic data are collected with a 35 mm camera with a telescopic lens, operated by an automatic timer (fig. 13.4).

Particle data are needed to determine whether impairment of visibility is natural or human-caused. Such data are also useful for pinpointing the specific source of human-caused impairment. These data are collected by pulling air through a sampling device that separates particles by sizes and collects them on filters. Specific information about the characteristics and probable origin of the particles can be derived by laboratory analysis. A particle sampler capable of distinguishing particles less than 2.5 microns and particles between 2.5 and 10 to 15 microns is recommended because these are important size ranges in determining the cause of visibility impairment. *Local meteorological data* are also important in determining if visibility impairment is natural or human-caused and in determining the likely source of human-caused impairment. Such data are most often collected with remote automated weather stations that measure windspeed and direction, temperature, relative humidity, and precipitation. Visibility monitoring stations are further described in the Forest Service Air Resource Management Handbook 2509.19 (1987).

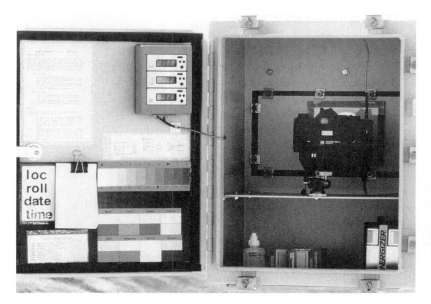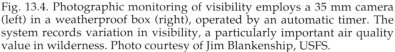

Fig. 13.4. Photographic monitoring of visibility employs a 35 mm camera (left) in a weatherproof box (right), operated by an automatic timer. The system records variation in visibility, a particularly important air quality value in wilderness. Photo courtesy of Jim Blankenship, USFS.

A fully instrumented visibility monitoring station is costly, both in terms of initial equipment and annual operating and data handling. Operating such a station inside wilderness is difficult because of power requirements and the need for frequent servicing, and it conflicts with the policy of minimizing modern technology in wilderness. Wilderness management agencies have established monitoring stations near wilderness boundaries in order to overcome some of these difficulties. An alternative that provides useful data at much lower cost is an automatic camera station. It is often possible to obtain data by locating the station at the wilderness boundary and photographing scenes inside the wilderness. In instances where data must be collected from stations inside the boundary, automatic camera stations offer the best alternative. They can operate on battery power and can be located and concealed to reduce conflict with wilderness users. Such systems have been used in national forest and national park wildernesses. Decisions to locate such equipment inside a wilderness should be made only after fully considering all alternatives as well as weighing the value of the data to be collected.

The adequacy of photographic data alone depends on the purpose for which the information is needed and the design of the data collection procedures. Camera data are the least expensive repetitive visibility data that can be collected at remote monitoring stations, and may be adequate for some infor-

mation needs, such as determining visibility trends or the impact of prescribed fire on visibility. Photographic data can provide the following:

- The general conditions of the sky and terrain features at the time of exposure.
- The visual range (how far you can see) under best conditions.
- The light scattering coefficient (a measure of the amount of light scattered by pollutants, derived from analysis of the photograph).

Camera stations should provide views of important scenic vistas inside the wilderness and at varying distances (usually between 10 and 45 miles). The view must contain at least one visibility target, such as a mountain peak, which is on the horizon and has the following characteristics:

- Large (at least 20 percent of the size of the full moon).
- Identifiable (easily identified on topographic maps).
- Dark, preferably covered with coniferous or other dark vegetation and as free of snow as possible.
- Distant, preferably 10 to 45 miles from the camera, but within the wilderness.
- Elevation about the same as that of the camera.

The use of photographic visibility data is further described by Johnson and others (1985). Costs and detailed procedures for establishing and operating camera visibility monitoring stations are provided by Fox and others (1987).

Odor

The threshold levels at which certain odors are detectable by humans have been determined, and a list of these levels is available in the Forest Service Air Resource Management Handbook (see table 13.3). These values can be compared to the predicted concentrations from a proposed source to determine if an air pollutant odor will be present in a wilderness.

SUMMARY

Air quality has the potential to seriously affect wilderness ecosystems and visitor enjoyment. Managers of wilderness have responsibility under the Wilderness Act and the Clean Air Act to manage the wilderness air resource and to protect the air quality-related values of Class I wilderness. Carrying out this responsibility requires that wilderness managers become involved early in the regulatory process through which permits are issued for air-polluting industries proposing to locate near wildernesses. Successful involvement requires that wilderness managers obtain data about the air quality-related values of each Class I wilderness.

Management decisions are based on available information. Information about wilderness air quality is currently very limited. Techniques and procedures for remedying the situation are emerging but are hampered by the character of wilderness and the policies established to protect wilderness from civilization's influence. It is necessary that those collecting data in wilderness use the minimum tools necessary (see chap. 7). Exceptions should be sought and granted only when it can be clearly shown that there is no other feasible way to gather information essential for protecting the wilderness resource.

As human activities continue to encroach on wilderness air quality, the information derived from monitoring the effects of wilderness air pollution will take on new importance. Although data are likely to remain less than optimum, this is preferable to inadequate data, which could result in irretrievable loss of wilderness values.

STUDY QUESTIONS

1. What laws form the legal framework for protecting wilderness from air pollution?
2. What are the differences between Class I and Class II areas? How is wilderness treated in each class?
3. Who makes the final decision to permit construction or expansion of a facility that may emit pollution that will affect a wilderness? How is the federal land manager involved?
4. What does AQRV mean? What are some examples?
5. What does pH measure? What does a pH of 7 indicate? A pH of 4?
6. What are several types of plants highly sensitive to air pollution?
7. What are the two main direct effects of air pollution on wilderness visitors' experiences?
8. What are the arguments for and against use of the most sophisticated modern equipment for monitoring wilderness air quality?

Table 13.3. Thresholds for human detection of some common air pollutant chemicals.

Chemical	Odor threshold (parts per million)	Odor description
Acetic acid	1.0	sour
Acetone	100.0	chemically sweet
Amine monomethyl	0.021	fishy, pungent
Amine trimethyl	0.0021	fishy, pungent
Ammonia	46.8	pungent
Carbon disulfide	0.21	vegetable sulfide
Chlorine	0.314	bleach, pungent
Diphenyl sulfide	0.00047	burnt, rubbery
Formaldehyde	1.0	hay, strawlike
Hydrogen sulfide	0.00047	rotten eggs
Methanol	100.0	sweet
Metheline chloride	214.0	—
Phenol	0.047	medicinal

Source: Forest Service Handbook 2509.19 - Air Resource Management Handbook (August 26, 1987), Exhibit 2, p. 49—4.

Table 13.4. Class I areas designated by the Clean Air Act.

State and area	Federal Land Manager	

Alabama		
Sipsey Wilderness		USFS
Alaska		
Bering Sea Wilderness		FWS
Mount McKinley National Park[1]		NPS
Simeonof Wilderness		FWS
Tuxedni Wilderness		FWS
Arizona		
Chiricahua National Monument Wilderness		NPS
Chiricahua Wilderness		USFS
Galiuro Wilderness		USFS
Grand Canyon National Park		NPS
Mazatzal Wilderness		USFS
Mount Baldy Wilderness		USFS
Petrified Forest National Park		NPS
Pine Mountain Wilderness		USFS
Saquaro Wilderness		NPS
Sierra Ancha Wilderness		USFS
Superstition Wilderness		USFS
Sycamore Canyon Wilderness		USFS
Arkansas		
Caney Creek Wilderness		USFS
Upper Buffalo Wilderness		USFS
California		
Agua Tibia Wilderness		USFS
Caribou Wilderness		USFS
Cucamonga Wilderness		USFS
Desolation Wilderness		USFS
Dome Land Wilderness		USFS
Emigrant Wilderness		USFS
Hoover Wilderness		USFS
John Muir Wilderness		USFS
Joshua Tree Wilderness		NPS
Kaiser Wilderness		USFS
Kings Canyon National Park		NPS
Lassen Volcanic National Park		NPS
Lava Beds Wilderness		NPS
Marble Mountain Wilderness		USFS
Minarets Wilderness[2]		USFS
Mokelumne Wilderness		USFS
Pinnacles Wilderness		NPS
Point Reyes Wilderness		NPS
Redwood National Park		NPS
San Gabriel Wilderness		USFS
San Gorgonio Wilderness		USFS
San Jacinto Wilderness		USFS
San Rafael Wilderness		USFS
Sequoia National Park		NPS
South Warner Wilderness		USFS
Thousand Lakes Wilderness		USFS
Ventana Wilderness		USFS
Yolla Bolly-Middle Eel Wilderness		USFS
Yosemite National Park		NPS

Colorado		
Black Canyon of the Gunnison Wilderness		NPS
Eagles Nest Wilderness		USFS
Flat Tops Wilderness		USFS
Great Sand Dunes Wilderness		NPS
La Garita Wilderness		USFS
Maroon Bells-Snowmass Wilderness		USFS
Mesa Verde National Park		NPS
Mount Zirkel Wilderness		USFS
Rawah Wilderness		USFS
Rocky Mountain National Park		NPS
Weminuche Wilderness		USFS
West Elk Wilderness		USFS
Florida		
Bradwell Bay Wilderness		USFS
Chassahowitzka Wilderness		FWS
Everglades National Park		NPS
Saint Marks Wilderness		FWS
Georgia		
Cohutta Wilderness		USFS
Okefenokee Wilderness		FWS
Wolf Island Wilderness		FWS
Hawaii		
Haleakala National Park		NPS
Hawaii Volcanoes National Park		NPS
Idaho		
Craters of the Moon Wilderness		NPS
Sawtooth Wilderness		USFS
Idaho-Montana		
Selway-Bitterroot Wilderness		USFS
Idaho-Oregon		
Hells Canyon Wilderness		USFS
Kentucky		
Mammoth Cave National Park		NPS
Louisiana		
Breton Wilderness		FWS
Maine		
Acadia National Park		NPS
Moosehorn Wilderness		FWS
Michigan		
Isle Royale National Park		NPS
Seney Wilderness		FWS
Minnesota		
Boundary Waters Canoe Area Wilderness		USFS
Voyageurs National Park		NPS
Missouri		
Hercules-Glades Wilderness		USFS
Mingo Wilderness		FWS

1. Now named Denali National Park.
2. Now named Ansel Adams Wilderness.

Table 13.4. cont.

State and area	Federal Land Manager		State and area	Federal Land Manager	
Montana			**South Carolina**		
Anaconda-Pintler Wilderness	USFS		Cape Romain Wilderness	FWS	
Bob Marshall Wilderness	USFS		**South Dakota**		
Cabinet Mountains Wilderness	USFS		Badlands Wilderness	NPS	
Gates of the Mountains Wilderness	USFS		Wind Cave National Park	NPS	
Glacier National Park	NPS		**Texas**		
Medicine Lake Wilderness	FWS		Big Bend National Park	NPS	
Mission Mountains Wilderness	USFS		Guadalupe Mountains National Park	NPS	
Red Rock Lakes Wilderness	FWS		**Utah**		
Scapegoat Wilderness	USFS		Arches National Park	NPS	
UL Bend Wilderness	FWS		Bryce Canyon National Park	NPS	
Nevada			Canyonlands National Park	NPS	
Jarbidge Wilderness	USFS		Capitol Reef National Park	NPS	
New Hampshire			Zion National Park	NPS	
Great Gulf Wilderness	USFS		**Vermont**		
Presidential Range-Dry River Wilderness	USFS		Lye Brook Wilderness	USFS	
New Jersey			**Virgin Islands**		
Brigantine Wilderness	FWS		Virgin Islands National Park	NPS	
New Mexico			**Virginia**		
Bandelier Wilderness	NPS		James River Face Wilderness	USFS	
Bosque del Apache	FWS		Shenandoah National Park	NPS	
Carlsbad Caverns National Park	NPS		**Washington**		
Gila Wilderness	USFS		Alpine Lakes Wilderness	USFS	
Pecos Wilderness	USFS		Glacier Peak Wilderness	USFS	
Salt Creek Wilderness	FWS		Goat Rocks Wilderness	USFS	
San Pedro Parks Wilderness	USFS		Mount Adams Wilderness	USFS	
Wheeler Peak Wilderness	USFS		Mount Rainier National Park	NPS	
White Mountain Wilderness	USFS		North Cascades National Park	NPS	
North Carolina			Olympic National Park	NPS	
Linville Gorge Wilderness	USFS		Pasayten Wilderness	USFS	
Shining Rock Wilderness	USFS		**West Virginia**		
Swanquarter Wilderness	FWS		Dolly Sods Wilderness	USFS	
North Carolina-Tennessee			Otter Creek Wilderness	USFS	
Great Smoky Mountains National Park	NPS		**Wisconsin**		
Joyce Kilmer-Slickrock Wilderness	USFS		Rainbow Lake Wilderness	USFS	
North Dakota			**Wyoming**		
Lostwood Wilderness	FWS		Bridger Wilderness	USFS	
Theodore Roosevelt National Memorial Park	NPS		Fitzpatrick Wilderness	USFS	
Oklahoma			Grand Teton National Park	NPS	
Wichita Mountains Wilderness	FWS		North Absaroka Wilderness	USFS	
Oregon			Teton Wilderness	USFS	
Crater Lake National Park	NPS		Washakie Wilderness	USFS	
Diamond Peak Wilderness	USFS		Yellowstone National Park	NPS	
Eagle Cap Wilderness	USFS		**New Brunswick, Canada**		
Gearhart Mountain Wilderness	USFS		Roosevelt Campobello International Park[1]	—	
Kalmiopsis Wilderness	USFS				
Mountain Lakes Wilderness	USFS				
Mount Hood Wilderness	USFS				
Mount Jefferson Wilderness	USFS				
Mount Washington Wilderness	USFS				
Strawberry Mountain Wilderness	USFS				
Three Sisters Wilderness	USFS				

1. Although outside the U.S., located on an island off the coast of Maine, this park is managed by an International Commission representing Canada and the U.S.

REFERENCES

Altshuller, Aubrey P.; Linthurst, Rick A., eds. 1984. The acidic deposition phenomenon and its effects: critical assessment review papers. Vol. I. EPA-600/8-83-016-AF. Washington, DC: U.S. Environmental Protection Agency, Office of Research and Development. 728 p.

Bennett, James P. 1985. Overview of air pollution effects on national parks vegetation in 1985. Park Science. 5(4): 8-9.

Clean Air Act of 1977. 42 U.S.C. 7401 et seq.

Forest and Rangeland Renewable Resources Planning Act of 1974. Act of August 17, 1974. Public Law 93-378. 88 Stat. 476, as amended.

Fox, Douglas G. 1986. Establishing a baseline/protocols for measuring air quality effects in wilderness. In: Lucas, Robert C., compiler. Proceedings—national wilderness research conference: current research; 1985 July 23-26; Fort Collins, CO. Gen. Tech. Rep. INT-212. Ogden, UT: Intermountain Research Station: 85-91.

Fox, Douglas G.; Murphy, Dennis J.; Haddow, Dennis, tech. coords. 1982. Air quality, oil shale, and wilderness—a workshop to identify and protect air quality related values of the Flat Tops. 1981 January 13-15; Glenwood Springs, CO. Gen. Tech. Rep. RM-91. Fort Collins, CO: U.S. Department of Agriculture, Forest Service, Rocky Mountain Forest and Range Experiment Station. 32 p.

Fox, Douglas G.; Bernabo, J. Christopher; Hood, Betsy. 1987. Guidelines for measuring the physical, chemical, and biological condition of wilderness ecosystems. Gen. Tech. Rep. RM-146. Fort Collins, CO: U.S. Department of Agriculture, Forest Service, Rocky Mountain Forest and Range Experiment Station. 48 p.

Haines, Terry A. 1981. Acidic precipitation and its consequences for aquatic ecosystems: a review. Transactions of the American Fisheries Society. 110(6): 669-707.

Hale, M. E., Jr. 1982. Lichens as bioindicators and monitors of air pollution in the Flat Tops Wilderness Area, Colorado. Final Report, U.S. Forest Service Contract No. OM RFP R2-81-SP35. Fort Collins, CO: U.S. Department of Agriculture, Forest Service, Rocky Mountain Forest and Range Experiment Station. 42 p.

Johnson, Christopher E.; Malm, William C.; Persha, Gerald; Molenar, John V.; Hein, James R. 1985. Statistical comparisons between teleradiometer-derived and slide-derived visibility parameters. Journal of the Air Pollution Control Association. 35(12): 1261-1265.

Landers, D. H.; Eilers, J. M.; Brakke, D. F.; Overton, W. S.; Schonbrod, R. D.; Crowe, R. E.; Linthurst, R. A.; Omernik, J. M.; Teague, S. A.; Meier, E. P. 1986. Characteristics of lakes in the Western United States. Vol. I: Population descriptions and physico-chemical relationships. EP 1.23/9:600/8-83-016 AF. Washington, DC: U.S. Environmental Protection Agency. 425 p.

Linthurst, Rick A. 1984. Soils. Presentation made at Air Resource Management Course; 1984 February 26-March 2; Marana, AZ. Marana, AZ: National Advanced Resource Technology Center.

Marshall, Eliot. 1987. EPA finds western lakes free of acid pollution, but vulnerable. Science. 235 (4787): 423.

McConnell, Charles. 1986. The Wilderness Act and the Clean Air Act. Presentation made at Air Resources Training for Managers; 1986 April; Marana, AZ. Marana, AZ: National Advanced Resource Technology Center.

McFee, William W.; Adams, Fred; Cronan, Christopher S.; Firestone, Mary K.; Foy, Charles D.; Harter, Robert D.; Johnston, Dale W. 1984. Effects on soil systems. In: Altshuller, Aubrey P.; Linthurst, Rick A., eds. The acidic deposition phenomenon and its effects: critical assessment review papers. Vol. I. EPA-600/8-83-016-AF. Washington, DC: U.S. Environmental Protection Agency, Office of Research and Development: Chapter E-2.

Miller, Paul R., tech. coord. 1980. Proceedings of symposium on effects of air pollutants on Mediterranean and temperate forest ecosystems; 1980 June 22-27; Riverside, CA. Gen. Tech. Rep. PSW-43. Berkeley, CA: U.S. Department of Agriculture, Pacific Southwest Forest and Range Experiment Station. 256 p.

National Forest Management Act of 1976. 16 U.S.C. 1601-1614.

Newman, James R. 1980. Effects of air emissions on wildlife resources. FWS/OBS 80/40. Washington, DC: U.S. Department of the Interior, Fish and Wildlife Service, Office of Biological Services. 32 p.

Richkind, K. E.; Hacker, A. D. 1980. Responses of natural wildlife populations to air pollution. Journal of Toxicology and Environmental Health. 6: 1-10.

Roberts, Leslie. 1987. Federal report on acid rain draws criticism. Science. 237(4281): 1404-1406.

Ross, David M.; Haas, Glenn E.; Loomis, Ross J.; Malm, William C. 1984. Visibility impairment and visitor enjoyment. Paper presented at the Air Pollution Control Association 74th annual meeting; 1984 June; Atlanta, GA.

Ross, David M.; Malm, William C.; Loomis, Ross J. 1986. An examination of the relative importance of park attributes at several National Parks. Paper presented at the Air Pollution Control Association international specialty conference "Visibility Protection—Research and Policy Aspects"; 1986 September 7-10; Teton National Park, WY.

Schreiber, R. Kent. 1984. Fauna. Presentation made at Air Resource Management Course; 1984 February; Marana, AZ. Marana, AZ: National Advanced Resource Training Center.

Schreiber, R. Kent; Newman, James R. 1987. Air quality and wilderness: a state-of-knowledge review. In: Lucas, Robert C., compiler. Proceedings—national wilderness research conference: issues, state-of-knowledge, future directions; 1985 July 23-26; Fort Collins, CO. Gen. Tech. Rep. INT-220. Ogden, UT: U.S. Department of Agriculture, Forest Service, Intermountain Research Station: 104-134.

Senate Report No. 95-127, 95th Cong., 1st session (1977).

Smith, William H. 1981. Air pollution and forests: interactions between air contaminants and forest ecosystems. New York: Springer-Verlag. 379 p.

U. S. Department of Agriculture, Forest Service. 1984. Air quality and acid deposition potential in the Bridger and Fitzpatrick Wildernesses: Workshop proceedings; 1984 March; [location of workshop unknown]. Ogden, UT: U.S. Department of Agriculture, Forest Service, Intermountain Region, Air Quality Group. 292 p.

U. S. Department of Agriculture, Forest Service. 1987. Air Resource Management Handbook 2509.19. Washington, DC.

Most estimates of wilderness use by recreationists are based on permits, trail registrations, or guesses. The most accurate wilderness use data probably come from mandatory visitor permit systems. Here, a wilderness ranger checks a permit displayed on a backpack in Rocky Mountain National Park, CO. Photo courtesy of the NPS.

14

WILDERNESS USE AND USERS: TRENDS AND PROJECTIONS

Robert C. Lucas was lead author for this chapter.

INTRODUCTION

Wilderness has been preserved because society believes it has values that justify not developing it. Many of these values are based on some kind of use. This is clear in the Wilderness Act, which states that wilderness is to be preserved for "use and enjoyment as wilderness" by "the American people of present and future generations."

THE IMPORTANCE OF UNDERSTANDING WILDERNESS USE

Understanding wilderness use is an essential foundation for any consideration of wilderness management. Not only do many wilderness values stem from a range of wilderness uses, but so do most threats to wilderness, and, as a result, most management problems as well. In chapter 15, where recreational management is discussed, we will develop the idea that most wilderness management is use management (which also applies to uses other than recreation). Wilderness-use management is inherently complex. Without knowledge of the character of use, its management is extremely difficult. This is particularly true for recreational use if management seeks to minimize visitor regimentation and rely instead on light-handed, subtle approaches.

Many kinds of wilderness use exist (fig. 14.1) which

Fig. 14.1. Wilderness is valued for many reasons. The most prominent use is recreational, but the Wilderness Act provides for certain commercial uses, such as outfitter camps (upper left); photo courtesy of Richard Walker; scientific use (upper right); water development in the Mount Zirkel Wilderness, CO (lower left); and livestock grazing, such as this sheep band in the Bridger Wilderness, WY (lower right). Photos courtesy of the USFS.

reflect a variety of values (Driver and others 1987). First, we will identify the uses of wilderness and discuss the amount of each use. Because information is scarce for all uses except recreation, and because recreation is an important use of most wildernesses, we will devote a special section of this chapter to a review of the amount, character, and distribution of wilderness recreational use and of the characteristics of users. Trends in use and projections and speculation about future use will complete the chapter.

WILDERNESS USE: AN OVERVIEW

Different kinds of wilderness use vary in their dependency on wilderness conditions. Commodity uses, such as grazing or mining, take place in some wildernesses but do not depend on or require wilderness conditions. This is true of certain recreational uses,

also. Some recreation—for example, campers playing volleyball in a wilderness meadow—just takes place in a wilderness, without depending on the wilderness qualities of the environment. Other activities—for example, observing the results of natural ecological processes on the landscape, experiencing solitude and isolation, and facing the challenges of traveling and living in an undeveloped area—clearly depend on wilderness settings. Other activities, such as observing wildlife, are intermediate and for some people can be enhanced by the wilderness setting, even if not dependent on it. The theory of *outdoor recreation specialization* (Bryan 1979) describes the greatest degree of specialization as involving a particular activity within a specific setting—for example, the contrast between general, unspecialized fishing and highly specialized fly fishing primarily on spring-fed creeks. From this viewpoint, the more wilderness-dependent uses are more specialized.

This concept of wilderness dependency is basic to managing wilderness use. Chapter 7 sets forth a management principle that wilderness-dependent activities should be favored over those that can be carried on outside wilderness. This chapter attempts to evaluate the degree of wilderness dependency of different uses; but, with present knowledge, this must be a largely subjective, impressionistic, and debatable evaluation.

PUBLIC RECREATIONAL USE

Recreation is the most obvious wilderness use. In 1985, wilderness recreation totaled more than 16 million visitor-days. Wilderness use and recreational visitation are usually treated as synonyms. It is so prominent that often it is the only use people think of. *Onsite recreational use* certainly involves the largest numbers of direct wilderness users, has great impacts, and poses major management challenges.

Recreational use includes many diverse activities. People take all sorts of hikes—short day hikes, long backpacking trips, and everything in between. Some ride horses. Others walk, leading pack animals. They float rivers in boats, canoes, and rafts. In a few places, where regulations permit, some visitors use motorboats, snowmobiles, or airplanes for access. This is most common in Alaska, although wilderness airstrips open to public use are numerous in Idaho and are found in a few other wildernesses outside Alaska. People travel in all sorts of groups— family, friends, or groups sponsored by varied organizations—and a few travel alone.

COMMERCIAL RECREATIONAL USE

In addition to public visitor use, the Wilderness Act also authorizes *commercial recreational use* of wilderness. Outfitters and guides accompany some visitors, adding to and facilitating the use of wilderness. This use usually involves travel by horse or boat. Other types of outfitting businesses involve only equipment rental—the visitors travel without guides. This is common in canoeing areas where rentals vary from only a canoe on up to all camping equipment. In parts of the California Sierras one can rent burros. In contrast, few businesses rent horses for do-it-yourself wilderness travel. A few outfitters also rent backpacking equipment and ski-touring gear.

The types of commercial recreation occurring in wilderness certainly depend on roadless land, and probably on large blocks of it. Outfitters provide camping and food, but specialized transportation (horses, rafts, etc.) is the key service provided. Roads would eliminate the need for such specialized transportation. Outfitted use is traditional, as well as permitted by the Wilderness Act. It can be carried out compatibly with wilderness conditions and be wilderness dependent. On the other hand, some styles of outfitting that stress comfort and convenience and provide an abundance of facilities have raised concerns of conflict with wilderness qualities.

Overall figures on the extent of commercial recreation in wilderness are not available. Outfitter use varies from none in some wildernesses (most eastern areas and some smaller western areas) to a majority of the use in others (particularly on dangerous whitewater rivers such as the Colorado, Middle Fork of the Salmon, and Selway where special equipment and skill are essential). In general, outfitters and guides play a more important role in larger wildernesses where horse travel is common. But even in two of the largest wildernesses, the Bob Marshall Wilderness in Montana and the Selway-Bitterroot in Montana and Idaho, studies show only a minority of the visitors employ outfitters—about one-fifth in the Bob Marshall Wilderness and one-sixth in the Selway-Bitterroot (Lucas 1980, 1985). Still, outfitting is a sizable industry. In 1986, 57 outfitters were licensed to take parties into the Bob Marshall Wilderness, 38 outfitters were licensed in the Selway-Bitterroot.

INDIRECT RECREATIONAL USE

Besides direct, onsite recreational use of wilderness, there are several important types of *indirect use* (Haas and others 1986). Millions of people who never set foot in wilderness nevertheless derive satisfaction from experiencing wilderness indirectly through the experiences of others. This *vicarious* use can come about through reading; viewing television, photos, and films; listening to lectures and accounts by others of their experiences; or by staying at resorts or recreation areas that are near wilderness. Vicarious use is not usually thought of as a use of wilderness, and yet it is a major use. Without wilderness, the source of these vicarious experiences would disappear. Historical accounts of wilderness encounters would remain, but would provide only a weak substitute. They lack the possibility that one could actually visit the area. Indirect use produces three types of values.

Option Value—Many people value keeping open the option to visit wilderness and, in a sense, are indirect users. Whether or not they ever actually visit a wilderness, it is worth something to them to know they could (Haas and others 1986).

Existence Value—For many other people, the

simple fact that wilderness exists has value even without the visitation option (Haas and others 1986). As Krutilla (1967) pointed out, some people who derive satisfaction from the knowledge that wilderness still exists "would be appalled by the prospect of being exposed to it." Option and existence values have been defined and measured (Cicchetti and Freeman 1971; Fisher and Krutilla 1972; Tombaugh 1971; Walsh and others 1986).

Bequest Value—Many people also want to leave wilderness as an inheritance to later generations (Krutilla 1967). Walsh and others (1986) surveyed the general public in Colorado and estimated that bequest values were in excess of $5 million, were about $5 million for existence value, and a little more than $4 million for option value. Together, these three types of preservation values were greater than the estimated value of direct recreational use. All of these indirect uses seem to be dependent on wilderness to a high degree.

Clawson (1963) pointed out that a recreation experience has not only an onsite phase, but also four offsite phases: anticipation, travel to, travel from, and recollection. It seems likely that compared to most other types of recreation, wilderness visits have particularly long and well-developed offsite anticipation and recollection phases. Planning frequently starts well in advance, and experiences are often relived afterwards.

Some wildernesses are closed to all direct, onsite recreational use. Specifically, this is true of some Fish and Wildlife Service (FWS) wilderness, especially some small islands. In addition to the indirect, vicarious use these areas provide, they also provide breeding grounds that produce many birds and, in some cases, other wildlife that are observed and enjoyed outside the wilderness.

Any estimate of the amount of indirect use clearly would be very difficult to make, and none is available. Sales of wilderness-related books are substantial, and films with nature-wilderness themes draw crowds. Several popular television programs are based on nature and wilderness. We could speculate that the number of vicarious and other indirect users is probably much greater than the number of actual visitors.

SCIENTIFIC USE

One of the major values of wilderness is its potential for *scientific use*. Wilderness serves as a laboratory, particularly for the study of ecology and other biological sciences by offering relatively natural, unmodified conditions, and processes operating in large areas. Aldo Leopold (1941) wrote of wilderness as a land laboratory, valuable for learning how healthy ecosystems function and how to heal abused lands. As the rest of the world becomes more developed and modified by man, the contrast between wilderness and nonwilderness increases and the value of wilderness laboratories is enhanced. This is a substantially wilderness-dependent activity.

Research Natural Areas (RNAs) serve some of the same purposes (Dyrness and others 1975; Johnson and others 1984; Schmidt and Dufour 1975), but, because of their smaller size, they are often exposed to outside influences, and large-scale, long-term ecological processes are usually better represented in wilderness (see chap. 6 for further discussion on these topics). Research on some mammals with large home ranges, such as grizzly bears, wolves, and mountain lions, is often dependent on wilderness because these animals have only limited ranges elsewhere.

Certain types of environments—particularly high mountains—are well represented in classified wilderness; therefore subjects for certain kinds of research often are located in wilderness. Studies of glaciers are a notable example. Such scientific use is not dependent on wilderness; the subject just happens to be there. Other scientific use also depends on objects that happen to be located in wilderness, such as, archeological sites (prehistoric campsites, dwellings, and artifacts) and paleontological resources (e.g., dinosaur fossils). Scientific activities at such sites often pose management dilemmas because research often requires removal of fossils, artifacts, and so on. These resources are also vulnerable to removal by visitors. Seeing fossils and artifacts in their natural wilderness setting is also valuable, and the experience is diminished by their removal. These problems are prominent in the Bisti Wilderness, managed by the Bureau of Land Management (BLM) in northwestern New Mexico (USDI BLM 1986) where important dinosaur fossils are common.

Wilderness can also provide a good setting for some kinds of *social and psychological research*. The isolation of small groups of people and their close interdependence in the face of the challenges of wilderness travel provide unusual and valuable research opportunities. Sociologist William Burch (1974) believes, "Questions concerning the structure and function of small groups and their relation to larger wholes seem naturally adapted to wildland situations."

No one keeps a record of scientific use of wilderness, and there is some difference of opinion as to its extent (Franklin 1987). A study of 53 long-estab-

lished national forest wildernesses and 22 national park wildernesses identified more than 800 research projects. National parks had far more studies than national forests, (an average of 29 studies per national park, compared to 4 per national forest wilderness). National forest research was much more likely to focus on recreation than national park studies, which were largely biological (Butler and Roberts 1986). *A central register of wilderness research projects is needed to document scientific use and trends.* This register would facilitate research by increasing scientists' awareness of similar or related studies and improve communication between investigators.

One of the main scientific assets and potential uses of wilderness is its function as a gene pool. In wilderness, the natural genetic diversity of native plants and animals is preserved (Ghiselin 1973-74; Seagrave 1976). Outside wilderness this diversity is often reduced as species become extinct and as domestic species are selectively bred for greater uniformity, increased yield, and other characteristics. It must be pointed out, however, that the wilderness system is very short on representation of many types of environments and ecosystems—such as grasslands and low-elevation forests—and this reduces the gene pool value. Both the BLM and the U.S. Forest Service (USFS) use the Bailey-Küchler system to classify ecosystem/landform regions (Davis 1980). Only 157 of 261 ecosystems were represented in the wilderness system in 1987 (Davis 1987). As a result, much scientific use will continue to depend on nonwilderness lands that are vulnerable to various forms of development.

EDUCATIONAL USE

Wilderness is also used for *educational purposes*—as a site for field trips; as a study area for theses, dissertations, and research; and as a source of instructional examples. Some educational uses based on large-scale, long-term ecological processes may be dependent on wilderness, but, for many topics, other lands probably are available.

The second educational use is more akin to recreational use: wilderness as a setting for teaching woodsmanship and survival skills. Many universities have field trips that teach wilderness skill courses. Some youth-serving organizations, such as the Boy Scouts, have taught outdoor living skills with their application in wilderness as the pinnacle of achievement. Whether this use is really dependent on wilderness has been questioned. What does seem to be needed is a large, unroaded area. Some courses also teach wilderness values as well as low-impact use

techniques, which are considered more wilderness dependent. The National Outdoor Leadership School (NOLS), headquartered in Lander, Wyoming, is an example. Several thousand students take NOLS courses each year.

Educational use is not measured, but some indication of its magnitude can be gained from data on wilderness-related courses in colleges and universities. Hendee and Roggenbuck (n.d.) reported that each year nearly 8,000 students take wilderness courses. Most courses focus on wilderness appreciation, use, enjoyment, and skills. Almost 60 percent of the instructors take their classes to wilderness. In 1971, educational institutions accounted for about 5 percent of total use of several wildernesses in Washington and Oregon (Dick and others 1972).

THERAPEUTIC USE

Wilderness also provides a setting for *therapeutic programs* designed primarily to alleviate abnormal behavior or psychological problems. Delinquent and mentally disturbed people are taken on wilderness canoe trips, river float trips, and backpacking trips. The participants often seem to benefit from the isolation from outside pressures, close contact with staff, the challenges and the need for group support in meeting them, and perhaps from qualities of the wilderness (Gibson 1979).

PERSONAL DEVELOPMENT

Other programs, combining elements of therapy and education, aim at *personal development* and *self-discovery* for healthy people. Working in a wilderness setting, these programs are designed to build self-reliance, personal understanding, awareness of other persons, persistence, and similar traits. Outward Bound Schools are one well-known example of this type of program, but there are many others (Hanson 1977; Kaplan 1984). It is difficult to say whether such programs really depend on wilderness or just roadless, challenging country. The numbers of such users are probably a fairly small part of the total use of wilderness, but a few areas receive substantial personal development use. Visits are often long, resulting in more visitor-days of use then numbers of visits would suggest. Some other uses have religious and spiritual purposes that draw on the wilderness setting.

COMMODITY USE

Several *onsite commodity uses* take place in, but do not depend on, the particular qualities of wilderness.

Mining

The 1964 Wilderness Act permits mining, but agency regulations are designed to minimize adverse impacts on the wilderness (see chap. 4 for more details). Almost all wilderness mining claims exist in national forest wilderness. Most national parks are closed to all mining, but six were established with special provisions permitting mining: Crater Lake National Park (OR); Glacier Bay National Monument (AK); Denali National Park (AK); Organ Pipe Cactus National Monument (AZ); Death Valley National Monument (CA-NV); and Coronado National Memorial, (AZ). Glacier Bay, Denali, and Organ Pipe contain wilderness. Crater Lake and Death Valley have wilderness proposals pending. Coronado National Memorial has been dropped from possible wilderness classification. Mining is going on in Death Valley and Denali, and there has been mineral exploration, but no mining has occurred in Glacier Bay and Organ Pipe. In 1976, Congress passed a law (P.L. 94-429) closing these six national parks to new mining claims and placed all existing claims under strict new regulations. The 1964 Wilderness Act permitted the continued staking of claims, in national forest wilderness only, until the end of 1983. But because claims could be staked only on public domain lands, prospecting was limited to western wildernesses, which are part of the public domain, and was excluded from eastern wildernesses, which are not. In the East, almost all the land in wildernesses was private land before it was acquired by the federal government. But in many cases the mineral rights were not acquired by the government and therefore mining is a possible use, subject to restrictions to protect the wilderness. But private mineral rights in eastern wilderness could be acquired by condemnation (P.L. 93-622) if funds were available to compensate owners.

Actual onsite commodity uses of national forest wilderness appear rather limited, despite the controversy that surrounds them. Mining claims are numerous—just how numerous is hard to determine because, until recently, there was no requirement to notify the USFS when claims were filed on national forest land. Claims were recorded in the county courthouse, along with many other claims on other lands. In 1985, there were at least 10,000 mining claims (Wilkinson and Anderson 1985). In 1984, one area, the Cabinet Mountains Wilderness in Montana, reported more than 700 claims. We can find no reported mineral extraction from any national forest wilderness or primitive area in the last 25 years. This low level of mining is consistent with mineral surveys of wilderness and primitive areas (mentioned in chap. 5), which have failed to turn up major mineral deposits. Restrictions on mining activity to protect the wilderness make mining more difficult and costly and probably have discouraged development. Nevertheless, exploratory drilling to plan a copper-silver mine has recently been completed in the Cabinet Mountains Wilderness, and a mine (probably with an entrance at lower elevation outside the wilderness boundary but extending under it) seems likely.

Oil and gas production are under lease inside the USFS Indian Mounds Wilderness in east Texas (Evans 1986). Such use, which operates under different laws than hard-rock mining, is a possibility in many places and is very controversial. Oil and gas leasing procedures are explained in chapter 4.

The BLM policy for primitive areas generally prohibited mining and mineral leasing except for valid existing rights established before the area was classified as a primitive area. Under the provisions of the Federal Land Policy and Management Act of 1976 (FLPMA, P.L. 94-579), mining claims can continue to be filed on lands included in wilderness study areas, providing the mining operations do not impair the suitability of such areas for preservation as wilderness. Mining in effect on the date of FLPMA can continue, providing it does not cause unnecessary or undue degradation. Since 1982, the secretary of the interior has maintained an administrative prohibition on new mineral leasing in Wilderness Study Areas (WSAs).

When BLM lands are legislatively designated as wilderness they are withdrawn from all new mining and mineral leasing. BLM regulations for designated wilderness areas require holders of existing mining claims to file a plan of operations outlining how mining is to be undertaken. Before such plans are approved, the BLM must determine if the mining claim is valid. If it is not, actions are taken to invalidate the claim. Thousands of mining claims exist in BLM wilderness study areas. In future years they will pose a significant management problem for the BLM.

Logging

Except for limited timber cutting necessary for mine timbers, logging was allowed in just one wilderness, the Boundary Waters Canoe Area Wilderness (BWCAW) in Minnesota—an area which has been an exception within the National Wilderness Preservation System (NWPS) in a number of ways. The Boundary Waters Canoe Area Wilderness Act of 1978 (P.L. 95-495) amended the Wilderness Act for

the first time and ended logging inside the area. Before logging was ruled out in 1978, the area in which it was permitted had been progressively reduced over the years, with about two-thirds available for cutting before the 1964 Wilderness Act and about 40 percent thereafter. Roughly half of the area was logged over about a century before the 1978 amendment brought the BWCAW into line with the rest of the NWPS. Another possible exception is cutting of trees for control of insects or disease, especially if they threaten areas outside the wilderness. This was done in several national forest wildernesses in Texas for control of southern pine beetles (Billings 1986), but this has been questioned and may not continue.

Water

Facilities for water storage are also permitted by the 1964 Wilderness Act. New water storage projects require presidential approval, but many small reservoirs built before enactment of the Wilderness Act continue to be used and maintained.

Not all water usage depends on dams inside wilderness. Many wildernesses store vast amounts of water in the form of snow and provide a large proportion of the streamflow in the West. This has stimulated controversial attempts to increase precipitation. In a few places, weather modification has been attempted in an effort to increase snowfalls and the resulting summer streamflows. Proposals have been made to manipulate precipitation in other wildernesses (Montana DNRC 1973; USDI BR 1974). Changing the weather inevitably changes the ecosystem—and wilderness exists primarily to allow natural processes to operate without modern human influence. This issue seems less prominent in the 1980s than it was in the 1960s and early 1970s.

Measuring snowpacks to forecast streamflow also poses conflicts with wilderness qualities. Sometimes snow is measured with the aid of helicopters, snowmobiles, or snow pillows (automatic snow-weight recording devices connected to radio transmitting stations). Such methods are questionable within wilderness. Wilderness-managing agencies have responded somewhat differently to this conflict. In the national forest wildernesses, except where helicopter use was well established before the Wilderness Act, snow measurements are made without mechanized equipment, usually by crews traveling on cross-country skis. Electronic devices that measure and transmit snow data are not permitted. The Department of the Interior policy for national park wilderness is to permit existing water-resource monitoring devices to be retained in wilderness.

New devices will be placed in wilderness only if the secretary of the interior decides that essential information cannot be obtained from locations outside the wilderness and that the proposed device is the minimum necessary to successfully and safely accomplish the objective.

Most irrigation water impoundments in wilderness were built long before the Wilderness Act. Typically, the dams are low and constructed of local rock and timber, and shoreline vegetation has had many years to adjust to the higher water level. Thus, many of the reservoirs are not conspicuously unnatural unless water levels fluctuate greatly. In 1987, about 100 dams existed in national forest wilderness. There are others in national park wilderness and backcountry (ORRRC 1962). Reservoirs are concentrated in a few wildernesses; most wildernesses do not have any such developments. Many of the reservoirs are in the Montana portion of the Selway-Bitterroot Wilderness, which has low dams on 30 to 40 lakes, some built in the 1880s and 1890s before the area was even a national forest, let alone a wilderness. A few dams in the BWCAW, built to facilitate log drives, are still in place and maintain lake levels. Many more have been abandoned. Some wildernesses in the California Sierras have small dams to control streamflows; otherwise, streams would go dry in late summer, with a resulting loss of fish. In the Sierras, a few high, concrete hydroelectric dams, built before the Wilderness Act, are found in wildernesses. The last such dam was constructed on the Rubicon River in the Desolation Wilderness (CA) in 1963, only one year before the Wilderness Act became law.

Grazing

Grazing by domestic livestock—sheep, cattle, and a few horse herds—is also allowed by the Wilderness Act. Grazing probably is less common now than it once was. Changes in the livestock business generally have reduced the economic attractiveness of such extensive grazing. Higher costs for herders and transportation to distant wilderness, emphasis on intensive production of forage on better lands, and more use of feedlots have all reduced demand for wilderness grazing. The fact that fees for grazing public land are low probably contributes to maintaining wilderness grazing demand. In 1986, about 14 percent of all cattle and sheep grazing in the National Forest System grazed in wilderness at least part of the year. Because grazing seasons are short in many wildernesses, the percentage of *Animal Unit Months* (AUMs) in wilderness is lower, only about 2 percent in 1974, the most recent for AUM figures. One

AUM equals one cow or five sheep for one month. Figures on grazing in BLM primitive areas and potential wilderness are unavailable, but grazing of these lands is substantial; more than 80 percent of BLM land in the western states (excluding Alaska) is subject to grazing (Foster 1976). Grazing often generates pressures for mechanized access and for predator control that pose difficult policy challenges for wilderness managers.

WILDERNESS RECREATIONAL USE: A CLOSER LOOK

Much more is known about recreational use than the other wilderness uses. As an important use, recreation is the object of a large part of all wilderness management, and thus warrants a detailed discussion. However, wilderness is *not* a type of primitive recreation area. Wilderness is established for many purposes, as discussed in chapter 4 and elsewhere, of which recreation is only one.

The discussion of recreational use will cover three main points: (1) amount, (2) character, and (3) distribution (fig. 14.2). Roggenbuck and Lucas (1987) present a more detailed discussion of wilderness recreation use and users than is found in this chapter.

Recreational use has been reported for many types of areas, including wilderness, for many years. But use data are of very uneven quality, and some review of the methods used to measure wilderness use and their shortcomings is necessary background.

Fig. 14.2. Bald Knob Lake in the Absaroka-Beartooth Wilderness, MT. Data on the amount, character, and distribution of recreational use are important information for managers. Lakes and streams are often favorite camping spots. Photo courtesy of the USFS.

USE ESTIMATION AND MEASUREMENT METHODS

Wilderness recreational use is one of the most difficult types of recreational use to measure. The typical wilderness has many access points. Some larger ones (e.g., the BWCAW and the Selway-Bitterroot Wilderness) have 70 or 80 entries, and even some of the smaller areas have 15 or 20 accesses, usually distant from ranger stations and difficult to check. Compared to developed sites, use is light and variable (wilderness recreation is, by definition, low density). This makes it prohibitively expensive to observe all entry points—some would have no use at all to observe on some days. Use is dispersed over such a wide area that it is nearly impossible to make any sort of direct head count, as can be done in developed auto-access campgrounds. Therefore, a variety of indirect ways of estimating or measuring wilderness use have been devised: sample observations, electronic counters, automatic cameras, estimates based on data from trail registers or mandatory permits, or finally, just guessing (Roggenbuck and Lucas 1987).

Systematically *observing visitors at a sample of trailheads* on sample days has been tried (Lucas and Oltman 1971; Lucas and others 1971), but the highly variable use makes reliable sampling difficult and costly. Large samples are difficult to obtain. For example, the 74,000-acre Mission Mountains Wilderness in Montana has 19 access points. If the main use season is about 100 days, this results in 1,900 date/place combinations from which to sample. One person working full time could sample about 4 percent of these, and then only for about six or seven hours per day because of travel time. Stratified sampling that would concentrate on more used times and places could increase the efficiency of sampling somewhat. But this would require some reasonably accurate information on use patterns to plan the stratification of the sample.

In addition to entry-point sampling, traffic has been sampled at roadblocks on access roads, commonly referred to as cordon line sampling (Lucas 1964). In many areas, one road serves many entry points and results in much more use being sampled for the same effort than trailhead sampling.

Automatic electronic trail traffic counters have been tried with varying success (Lucas and others 1971). An improved model projects an infrared beam onto a reflector and registers a count whenever there is an interruption by something moving through the beam, much like automatic door openers in stores. When carefully installed, the counters work well. At best, the counters can indicate the number of large moving

objects passing since the last time the counter was read. They cannot indicate whether the objects were hikers, packhorses, elk, or cows; when they passed; or how they clustered into parties or groups. Length of stay or information about activities cannot be obtained from the counters. Neither can direction (entry or exit) nor route of travel. Nevertheless, automatic counters are being used in a number of wildernesses and provide useful information, especially on trends in use.

Automatic movie cameras, set to expose one frame at preset intervals, say every 30 seconds, have been used by the National Park Service (NPS) (Marnell 1977) to estimate use of several wild rivers. Some of these cameras photograph a calendar clock in a corner of each frame to record the date and time of each observation. Other use-recording systems used in some wildernesses employ a movie camera triggered by an electronic traffic counter to film a few frames. Group size and method of travel can be determined. Day-use groups can be distinguished from campers. Direction of travel is apparent. Virtually everything an employee could observe is recorded on film. For protection of visitors' privacy, no identification of individuals is ever made, and only public areas through which visitors pass are filmed, not campsites or swimming areas. After traffic has been classified and tallied, the film is destroyed so no permanent record is kept. This system has worked well for managers and researchers (Lucas and Kovalicky 1981; Petersen 1985).

Many estimates of wilderness use are based on *voluntary self-registration at trail registers*. Trail registers provide much more complete information than traffic counters. Party size, method of travel, date of entry, length of stay, some data on destination (or itinerary), and visitor residence are usually obtained. The problem, of course, is that some (or even many) visitors do not register (Lucas 1975, 1983; Lucas and others 1971; Wenger and Gregersen 1964). Some kinds of visitors—especially horsemen, hunters, people making very short visits, and lone individuals—are less likely to register than others. Thus, the resulting registration data not only underestimate use, but also provide biased estimates of its composition.

Efforts have been made to develop systems for basing use estimates on the trail register data (Lucas

Fig. 14.3. This experimental trail register sign resulted in higher rates of registration among visitors. Photo courtesy of the USFS.

and others 1971). In effect, adjustment factors are applied to raw data from the trail register cards to compensate for nonregistration. It is necessary to observe a sample of registration behavior to develop the adjustment factors. In some areas, volunteers have been used for checking registration rates (Huppuch and Pellerin 1985).

It appears that registration rates may be highly variable among wildernesses and over time (Lucas 1975, 1983). It is therefore essential to carefully check registration rates employed as a basis for use estimates. Field checking registration is difficult and expensive, however, and is rarely done. Electronic traffic counters or, better, automatic cameras are a less costly means for measuring true total use, for comparison with registered use.

Currently, use estimates based on trail registers have a large, but usually unknown, margin of error. If registration rates could be raised, trail registers could still be a usable basis for use estimates. Low rates require large expansion factors and yield undependable estimates. A study of ways of raising registration rates (Petersen 1985) showed that location and sign message could raise rates substantially, especially for types of visitors with poor compliance. Locating trail registers 1 to 3 miles from the trailhead raised rates the most. Providing a new sign (fig. 14.3) that explained briefly the importance of registering also helped raise registration rates.

The most accurate, useful wilderness use data probably come from *mandatory visitor-permit systems* (Hendee and Lucas 1973; Lime and Buchman 1974). In 1980, about 70 percent of NPS wildernesses and about 50 percent of USFS wildernesses required visitors to obtain permits, a practice also common in Canadian wilderness-type areas (Washburne and Cole 1983). In almost all cases, permits must be obtained from the managing agency. In a very few wildernesses, permits are issued by cooperators, such as resort employees. In a few USFS wildernesses in Oregon, permits were required until the early 1980s and were self-issued by visitors at trailheads. The visitor deposited one copy of the permit and carried another while in the wilderness. Permits provide all of the information obtained from trail registers, in addition to greater detail on planned routes of travel.

Some visitors fail to get permits (Lime and

Lorence 1974), just as some visitors do not register at trail registers. Compliance varies, although it is usually higher than for trail registers. It is high in most national parks and in the BWCAW where the system has been in effect almost 20 years and visitor awareness is high, but it might be lower in areas with newer permit systems. In North Cascades National Park in Washington, permits were required for overnight backcountry visitors beginning in 1973 (Hays 1974). The first year, about 65 percent of all parties obtained permits, but this rose to 86 percent in 1974. All but 2 percent of the visitors accepted the concept of a permit system. Most noncompliers said they were unaware of the requirement. Availability of permits at times and places convenient for visitors undoubtedly increases compliance, and enforcement is necessary.

DeGraff (1983) describes how administration of a wilderness permit system on the Inyo National Forest in California developed from its start in 1971. Trailhead quotas were established, integrated with adjacent national parks. To restrict use only when necessary, permits were limited to peak use seasons, which vary for different areas. Trial and error resulted in many changes over the years. Telephone reservations were tried and dropped. Mail application procedures were refined and computerized. Office hours were extended. Some permits were held for first-come, first-served distribution on the day of entry. After much experimentation, personal permit pickup was instituted to fairly redistribute permits reserved by no-shows. Permits can be obtained from a pickup box after office hours. Fairness and convenience have been guiding principles, and enforcement is consistent, resulting in more than 95 percent cooperation by visitors.

As with signing trail registers, some types of visitors are less likely to comply with permit requirements than others. Data from the BWCAW show that people on short visits, staying in resorts or campgrounds, or using motorboats, were low in compliance (Lime and Lorence 1974). In the North Cascades, compliance was low for young adults, visitors in one- or two-person parties, rural and small-town residents, groups made up of friends (rather than families), and anglers. Permit data could be adjusted (this is done with BWCAW permit data), but usually the emphasis has focused instead on raising compliance.

In most areas, commercial outfitters are required to report numbers of guests served, often as a basis for the fees they pay for their special-use permits. This provides a good measure of this use, although it is a small proportion of the total in most cases.

Finally, wilderness use can be estimated by means of an *educated guess* based on last year's report and an assumed rate of change. Estimates might be modified according to various observations—how many cars were parked at a particular access this year compared to previous years (but probably at different times of the season and on different days of the week), changes in the number of guests reported by outfitters, wilderness rangers' impressions, unusual weather, and so on. Some wildernesses show wide fluctuations in use from year to year. Often this comes from the use of guessing, which is sensitive to changes in who does the guessing or in which observations are used from year to year.

Individual wildernesses use a wide variety of techniques to estimate use (Washburne and Cole 1983). Most areas report using a combination of techniques. Accuracy varies from good to very poor. Unfortunately, the methods used and the expected accuracy level are not reported in annual use estimates. Adjustments made for noncompliance on permits or trail registers, if made at all, are often essentially guesswork based on unsystematic spot checks.

Estimates of the use of the overall wilderness system are a mixture of all types of estimates, and the resulting level of accuracy is uncertain, but probably only fair to poor. Whether errors compensate more than they accumulate is unknown.

Comparisons of visitor use over time are particularly unreliable. Older estimates were mainly guesses, and as more accurate methods were adopted, large changes in reported use often developed. Therefore, historical records of trends in use must be treated cautiously.

Certainly, use data need not be perfect to be useful, and any improvement adds to the management value of the information. The need for accuracy in use data is greater in heavily used wildernesses than in lightly used areas. The issue of use data will reappear in chapter 15 on visitor management. Chapter 15 also discusses systems for summarizing data from permits or trail registers.

UNITS OF MEASUREMENT

Several units of measurement can be used to measure recreational use (most are explained in USDI BOR 1975). The main units of measure are listed in table 14.1. The standard unit used by the NPS, the overnight-stay, and the USFS visitor-day are not directly comparable. For an individual party, *overnight stays* could be converted approximately into *visitor-days* by multiplying by two, and perhaps adding one

(or one-half) on the assumption that each night usually is matched by a large part of the first day and the last day:

Day 1	Night 1	Day 2	Night 2	Day 3	Night 3
:	:	:	:	:	:	:
:	:	:	:	:	:	:
8	8	8	8	8	8
a.m.	p. m.	a.m.	p.m.	a.m.	p.m.

This hypothetical visit from 8 a.m. on day one to 8 p.m. on day three equals two overnight stays or five 12-hour visitor-days.

VALUE OF DIFFERENT UNITS

This array of units is confusing. Which of the units is best? As is so often the case, the answer is "that depends." Specifically, it depends on the purpose for which the data are to be used. Often, several different units are relevant to a particular purpose.

For indicating potential impact on camping areas and camper congestion, the overnight stay or the group-night provides the most relevant information as a direct measure of camping. For an overall measure of solitude, the visitor-day, which reflects how many people are present over time, is generally useful, and people at one time (PAOT) is particularly appropriate. For a measure of the proportion of society using wilderness, the number of visitors is most useful. Visits are a partial substitute for visitors, much easier to obtain, and give a general idea of total use and certain types of managerial workloads such as visitor contact and permit issuance. But the great variation in the kinds of use labeled visits makes this a difficult unit of measure to interpret. A brief visit of an hour or so counts the same as a two-week stay. Visits can be used with visitor-days, if both are reported, to gain an idea of length of stay.

Different wilderness-management agencies do not now use comparable terms to report use. We would suggest that at least visits and visitor-days be regularly reported annually for all wildernesses. Actually, *for clarity, visitor-hours would be preferable to visitor-days.* The term "day" is subject to differing interpretations. In contrast, a visitor-hour is unambiguous, and can be converted easily to any sort of day desired. We also recommend the overnight stay as a useful supplemental unit, although calling it a visitor-night would clarify its meaning.

CURRENT LEVELS OF USE

How much is wilderness used? The USFS is the only agency to report recreational use separately for wildernesses. The NPS in 1986 reported more than 1.6 million overnight stays for backcountry camping, defined as camping in minimally developed areas not reached by roads. Even in parks with classified wilderness, these figures may include other lands not within the wilderness. For some parks, these overnight stay figures reflect wilderness camping use. They do not include wilderness day use, which is often substantial in national parks. But the heaviest backcountry camping is in areas with large reservoirs, such as Lake Mead (AZ-NV) and Glen Canyon (AZ-UT), where motorboat camping—rather than wilderness types of recreation—is common. Reported backcountry overnight stays at all areas which include wilderness or have parts included in wilderness proposals totaled 900,000 in 1986 (table 14.2). This would equal about 2 million visitor-days of camper use of national park wilderness and perhaps half a million visits.

In 1986, the 329 national forest wildernesses and one remaining primitive area reported about 11.2 million visitor-days of recreational use. Table 14.3 (Table 14.3 is at the end of the chapter.) shows estimated use for each area. Use varies widely among the different areas. (Use distributions will be covered in a later section.) Visits have not been reported since 1969, but length-of-stay information indicates about 4 million visits in 1986. The number of visitors would be less, because some people make several wilderness visits each year. For example, visitors to the Desolation Wilderness averaged about three trips a year to wilderness areas (not just the Desolation), and northern Rockies wilderness visitors averaged about three and one-half trips (Lucas 1980). Thus, the 4 million or so USFS wilderness visits in 1986 were probably made by less than 2 million individuals.

Use figures for FWS wildernesses are available for 1978 from a survey of wilderness managers by Washburne and Cole (1983), who report 279,000 visitor-days. Some FWS refuges are closed to use, and use is light in most areas. Washburne and Cole's survey also reported 51,000 visitor-days of use of 11 BLM primitive areas in 1978.

It is difficult to compare use of NPS wilderness and backcountry with USFS wilderness for several reasons: use of different units of measure, different types of reporting areas, and lack of information on day use of national park backcountry. Unpublished use figures for Yellowstone National Park (WY-MT-ID) showed about 100,000 backcountry day-use vis-

its in 1975, and 65,000 overnight stays. This means that visitor-days of day use were less than half of the total visitor-days accounted for by overnight visitors (assuming about 150,000 12-hour visitor-days for 65,000 overnight stays, and around 60,000 12-hour visitor-days for 100,000 day users). If Yellowstone is typical, all national parks were used at a level of about 3 million visitor-days in their wilderness or backcountry portions during 1986. This is close to Washburne and Cole's (1983) estimate of 3,065,000. If day use equaled overnight use, the estimate would be about 4 million total visitor-days.

Total wilderness recreation use was probably about 15 million 12-hour visitor-days in 1986 and close to 5 million visits. A large majority of this use takes place in USFS wilderness, almost all of the remainder is in NPS wilderness. The other two wilderness-managing agencies, the FWS and the BLM, receive much less use.

CHARACTER OF USE

Length of Stay
Most wilderness visits are short. Many small- or medium-sized wildernesses are predominantly day-use areas. Average length of stay, in calendar days, and percentage of visits that were day use are available for some areas (table 14.4).

Table 14.1. Units of measure for wilderness recreational use.

Unit	Definition	Use and comments
Visitor-day (Recreation Visitor-day or RVD)	1 person present for 12 hours, or equivalent (2 for 6 hours, etc.)	USFS standard unit since 1965
Visitor-hour	1 person present for 1 hour	NPS occasionally
Group- (or party-) days	1 group (party) for 12 hours	Some research
Man-day	1 person for 1 calendar day (7 hours or more; 5-7 hours = 0.75; 3 to 5 hours = 0.5; 15 minutes to 3 hours = 0.25; less than 15 minutes = 0)	USFS standard before 1965 (non-comparable to visitor-days, but 1.5 visitor-days per man-day is a rough conversion for wilderness use)
Recreation-day	1 person present for any part of a calendar day	Rarely used
Visit (or occasion)	The entry of 1 person into an area, regardless of length of stay (Repeat visits counted)	NPS; USFS before late 1960s
Group (or party) visits	The entry of 1 group (party) into an area	Some research
Visitor	1 person who makes 1 or more visits, usually during 1 year	Rarely used (sometimes inaccurately used as a synonym for *visit*)
Group (or party) visitor	As above for 1 group (party)	Rarely used
Overnight stay	1 person passing 1 night within an area (could also be called a visitor-night)	NPS standard unit; for relation to USFS visitor-days, see text
Group (or party) nights	As above for 1 group (party)	Some research
People at one time (PAOT)	Total number of people present at one time, usually a day	Some USFS reports, some research

Table 14.2. NPS backcountry overnight stays for parks with wilderness or potential wilderness, 1986, by states.

National Park (NP), National Monument (NM), National Preserve (NPres), or other category	1986 overnight stays in backcountry
Alaska	
Denali (Mount McKinley) NP & NPres	27,999
Gates of the Arctic NP & NPres	1,989
Glacier Bay NP & NPres	5,564
Katmai NP & NPres	2,564
Kobuk Valley NP	185
Lake Clark NP & NPres	1,967
Noatak NPres	4,140
Wrangell-Saint Elias NP & NPres	2,757
State total	**47,165**
Arizona	
Chiricahua NM	0
Organ Pipe Cactus NM	2,861
Petrified Forest NP	586
Saguaro NM	1,796
Grand Canyon NP[1]	73,185
State total	**78,428**
Arkansas	
Buffalo National River	16,050
California	
Joshua Tree NM	2,641
Lassen Volcanic NP	7,599
Lava Beds NM	8
Pinnacles NM	0
Point Reyes National Seashore	17,611
Sequoia-Kings Canyon NP	155,250
Yosemite NP	105,614
State total	**288,723**
Colorado	
Black Canyon of the Gunnison NM	405
Great Sand Dunes NM	758
Mesa Verde NM	0
Rocky Mountain NP[1]	35,056
State total	**36,219**
Florida	
Everglades NP	13,814
Gulf Islands National Seashore	0
State total	**13,814**
Georgia	
Cumberland Island National Seashore	0
Hawaii	
Haleakala NP	3,150
Hawaii Volcanoes NP	4,056
State total	**7,206**
Idaho	
Craters of the Moon NM	130
Michigan	
Isle Royale NP	33,228
Minnesota	
Voyageurs NP[1]	8,784
Montana	
Glacier NP[1]	14,771
New Mexico	
Bandelier NM	4,116
Carlsbad Caverns	159
State total	**4,275**
New York	
Fire Island National Seashore	51
North Dakota	
Theodore Roosevelt NP	782
South Dakota	
Badlands NP	188
Tennessee (and North Carolina)	
Great Smoky Mountains NP[1]	68,375
Texas	
Guadalupe Mountains NP	2,687
Big Bend NP[1]	41,886
State total	**44,573**
Virginia	
Shenandoah NP	38,134
Washington	
Olympic NP[1]	72,961
Mount Rainier NP[1]	27,948
North Cascades NP[1]	25,764
State total	**126,673**
Wyoming	
Grand Teton NP[1]	22,047
Yellowstone NP[1]	31,627
State total	**53,674**
Grand total	**881,243**

1. Not yet classified as wilderness in 1986.

Table 14.4 Characteristics of use of NPS backcountry and USFS wilderness and primitive areas.

Area	Year	Average[1]	Percent day-use	1	2-4	5-10	Over 10	Hike	Horseback	Hike with stock	Other	Fish	Hunt	Photography	Swim	Nature study	Mountain climbing	Family	Family with friends	Friends	Club organization	Alone
		Length of stay (percent of total)		Party size (percent of total)				Method of travel (percent of total)				Activities (percent of total)						Type of group (percent of total)				
Boundary Waters Canoe	1961	5.1	—	(Average 5.0)				0	0	0	100	—	—	—	—	—						
Area W (MN)	1974	4.2	41	3	70	27	0	3	0	0	97	—	—	—	—	—		61	61	27	11	1
	1984	—	—	—	—	—	—	4	0	0	96	—	—	—	—	—						
Bob Marshall W (MT)	1970	5.9	14	6	50	42	2	31	59	6	4	61	34	58	11	28	0	45	15	32	2	6
	1982	5.3	10	6	61	25	8	48	43	3	6	59	19	64	18	28	1	26	29	34	5	6
Scapegoat W (MT)	1970	2.9	41	6	60	20	14	69	18	12	1	62	11	53	20	27	2	36	21	29	8	7
	1982	4.2	34	8	54	30	8	66	30	3	1	43	20	56	14	28	1	30	27	34	1	8
Great Bear W (MT)	1970	4.9	25	0	66	27	7	46	42	0	13	62	43	53	4	15	0	24	14	62	0	0
	1982	3.2	37	3	73	22	2	69	24	1	6	70	5	60	18	31	0	31	36	30	0	3
Bob Marshall W Complex	1970	5.1	20	5	54	36	5	40	49	6	5	61	32	56	11	26	0	55	55	36	3	6
(MT)	1982	4.7	22	8	63	23	6	57	36	3	4	57	16	61	17	28	1	28	30	33	3	6
Eagle Cap W (OR)	1965	3.0	—	—	—	—	—	67	33	0	0											
Glacier Peak (WA)	1965	2.2	—	—	—	—	—	82	18	0	0	—	—	—	—	—		47	47	38	8	7
Three Sisters (OR)	1965	2.2	—	—	—	—	—	85	15	0	0											
Cabinet Mountains W (MT)	1970	1.6	67	5	72	18	4	90	7	2	1	61	6	45	15	25	2	40	15	33	5	5
Spanish Peaks PA (MT)	1970	1.8	63	8	57	27	6	72	20	7	1	41	16	53	9	29	4	38	13	35	4	10
Mission Mountains PA (MT)	1970	1.7	62	5	57	32	5	97	2	1	0	74	2	56	18	31	2	46	17	29	2	5
S. Appalachian Trail (VA-TN-NC-GA)	1970-71	2.5	53	—	—	—	—															
Selway-Bitterroot W (ID-MT)	1971	3.0	48	5	66	22	6	70	20	6	4	42	16	58	17	35	2	40	14	37	3	6
John Muir W (CA)	1972	—	—	9	72	12	7	—	—	—	—	—	—	—	—	—		—	—	—	—	—
San Gorgonio W (CA)	1972	—	—	7	53	15	25	—	—	—	—	—	—	—	—	—		—	—	—	—	—
Yosemite NP (CA)	1972	2.9	—	14	71	12	3	—	—	—	—	—	—	—	—	—		—	—	—	—	—
	1973	3.0	—	(Average 3.1)				—	—	—	—	—	—	—	—	—		—	—	—	—	—
	1974	2.7	—	(Average 3.0)				—	—	—	—	—	—	—	—	—		—	—	—	—	—
	1975	2.8	—	(Average 3.0)				—	—	—	—	—	—	—	—	—		—	—	—	—	—
	1976	2.6	—	(Average 2.8)				—	—	—	—	—	—	—	—	—		—	—	—	—	—
	1977	2.6	—	(Average 3.0)				—	—	—	—	—	—	—	—	—		—	—	—	—	—
	1978	2.4	—	(Average 3.0)				—	—	—	—	—	—	—	—	—		—	—	—	—	—
	1979	2.8	—	(Average 2.7)				—	—	—	—	—	—	—	—	—		—	—	—	—	—
Sequoia-Kings Canyon NP (CA)	1972	—	—	13	75	7	5	—	—	—	—	—	—	—	—	—		—	—	—	—	—
Grand Teton NP (WY)	1974	—	62	—	—	—	—															
North Cascades NP (WA)	1974	3.5[2]	—	13	63	18	6	—	—	—	—	—	—	—	—	—		—	—	—	—	—
Olympic NP (WA)	1974	2.8[2]	—	14	72	9	5	—	—	—	—	—	—	—	—	—		—	—	—	—	—
Mount Rainier NP (WA)	1974	1.9[2]	—	13	71	14	2	—	—	—	—	—	—	—	—	—		—	—	—	—	—
Desolation W (CA)	1974	3.2	40	9	69	18	5	99	1	0	0	48	1	54	46	52	4	33	16	34	7	10
Great Smoky Mountains NP	1976	2.5[2]	—	16	73	10	10	97	3	—	—	—	—	—	—	—		—	—	—	—	—
(NC-TN)	1979	3.0[2,3]	—	15	74	11	0	97	3	—	—	—	—	—	—	—		—	—	—	—	—
	1983	4.5	18	16	66	19	0	—	—	—	—	—	—	—	—	—		40	40	44	—	16
Weminuche (CO)	1977	3.4	16	9	64	21	7	—	—	—	—	52	3	73	n/a	42	8	44	13	27	11	5
Eagles Nest (CO)	1977	1.4	36	7	74	16	5	—	—	—	—	46	3	65	n/a	31	4	34[4]	9	39	3	15
Rawah (CO)	1977	2.3	12	6	72	18	6	—	—	—	—	54	3	73	n/a	7	3	47	5	37	3	7
Linville Gorge (NC)	1978	2.7	37	73	73	19	8	—	—	—	—	15	3	48	39	41	26	—	—	—	—	—
Shining Rock (NC)	1978	2.8	29	76	76	17	7	—	—	—	—	5	5	48	25	43	3	—	—	—	—	—
Joyce Kilmer-Slickrock (NC)	1978	2.9	24	85	85	11	3	—	—	—	—	12	6	46	35	47	3	—	—	—	—	—
Popo Agie (WY)	1978	—	7	16	69	14	1	—	—	—	—	—	—	—	—	—	—	25	14	47	n/a	15
Bridger (WY)	1978	—	11	16	62	21	1	—	—	—	—	—	—	—	—	—	—	27	7	49	n/a	16
Fitzpatrick (WY)	1978	—	12	20	58	19	3	—	—	—	—	—	—	—	—	—	—	19	7	53	n/a	20
Maroon Bells-Snowmass (CO)	1978	—	38	(Average 3.3)				—	—	—	—	—	—	—	—	—	—	—	—	—	—	—
Pusch Ridge (AZ)	1979-80	—	78	74	74	26	26	—	—	—	—	—	—	—	—	—	—	—	—	—	—	—

Source: Roggenbuck and Lucas 1987; W = Wilderness; PA = Primitive Area; NP = National Park; n/a = not asked.

l. Consists of the Bob Marshall, Great Bear, and Scapegoat Wildernesses.

2. Includes campers only (no day users). 3. Summer only. 4. Average of two ranger districts.

Among the areas for which visitor surveys are available, only the Bob Marshall Wilderness, Weminuche and Rawah in Colorado, and all three Wyoming wildernesses have little day use. Many of these areas are large, and the location of the wilderness boundary well beyond the trailhead in many places screens out day users. Most are remote from large population concentrations, making them more often destinations for vacations rather than weekend hiking areas. Managers of more than 15 percent of wildernesses surveyed by Washburne and Cole (1983) reported that day use accounted for only one-tenth or less of visitors to the area they managed. Surveys have consistently shown that managers underestimate day use, so some skepticism may be justified. Many other managers reported 80 to 100 percent day use. Trips of a week or more account for less than one-tenth of all visits even in the very large areas such as the BWCAW, the Bob Marshall Wilderness, .and the Selway-Bitterroot Wilderness. Visits in many areas, especially small- to medium-sized wildernesses, averaged 2 days (table 14.4; Washburne and Cole 1983). The wildernesses in the eastern United States had average stays of two to three days and 25 to 50 percent day use, not much different from most wildernesses in the West. Lengths of stay in most areas with more than one survey have become a little shorter in more recent years.

Party Size

Parties of wilderness visitors are generally small; from one-half to three-fourths of the parties at all areas for which we have data are in the two- to four-person size range (table 14.4). Lone individuals usually are infrequent visitors, although NPS backcountry campers are more likely to be alone than people making visits to USFS wildernesses. In most areas, parties of more than 10 people account for only about 5 percent of all groups.

There are a few unusual cases among these examples: the BWCAW has a 10-person-per-party limit and the San Gorgonio Wilderness (CA) is used heavily by parties of 10 to 15 young people from nearby summer camps. But the overall pattern is quite consistent.

Party size is declining at every area with data for more than one year; more places have restricted party size; and the larger, organized groups have generally become smaller as both managers and organization leaders have become concerned about the impact of large groups on the environment and on other visitors. The proportion of small, independent groups has increased while the proportion of large, organized groups has declined.

Method of Travel

The most common method of travel in almost all areas is hiking (table 14.4), with a few exceptions. Most visits to the BWCAW are made in paddled canoes (in 1986, 89 percent of all overnight groups). Some BWCAW visitors use outboard-motor-powered canoes or motorboats, and a few hike, snowshoe, or ski. Snowmobile use was permitted in the BWCAW for a time—in 1974, 4 percent of all visits were made by snowmobile—but their use was terminated by the chief of the USFS in 1976. Use of motors is limited to specific zones in the BWCAW, and outboard motors are restricted to 10 or 25 horsepower on almost all waters open to motors.

The BWCAW is one of the few areas where mechanized travel is permitted within a wilderness. Many wilderness landing fields have remained open to airplanes under the act, especially in the Great Bear Wilderness in Montana, and the Selway-Bitterroot Wilderness and Frank Church-River of No Return Wilderness, both in Idaho, where airstrips are often the starting point of horseback or float trips. The BWCAW has a policy not found elsewhere not only prohibiting air access but also banning low-elevation flights as a result of Executive Order 10092 signed by President Truman in 1949.

About half of the BMWC visitors ride horses, which may also be the case in the Teton Wilderness in Wyoming—a large area with a reputation as horse country (fig. 14.4). Managers of the Teton Wilderness estimated that 95 percent of the visitors used horses in 1978, and managers of six other areas estimated that more than half of the visitors rode horses (Washburne and Cole 1983). Hikers predominate, however, in the very large Selway-Bitterroot Wilderness. Most wildernesses in the eastern United States are almost entirely hiker-use areas. Horses are rare or absent in most of these wildernesses.

Hiking and nonmotorized boating (canoeing, kayaking, or rafting) in wildernesses have grown more rapidly than other travel methods in recent years. This trend is strong, apparently in all areas. The only area studied where horse users were in the majority, the Bob Marshall Wilderness, now is visited by more hikers than horseback riders, although longer stays by horse users result in their accounting for more than half of all visitor-days of use.

Activities

Typically, wilderness visitors participate in a variety of activities. Surveys of visitors to seven wilderness-type areas indicated that, on the average, respondents participated in three major activities (table

Fig. 14.4. Horseback travel is a traditional way of visiting wilderness. However, in a few large western wildernesses, hiking is a much more common method of travel. Photo courtesy of the USFS.

14.4). In western areas, about one-half or more of the visitors fish, but fishing is less common in eastern wildernesses. For many, the fishing is somewhat incidental, rather than central, as pointed out in chapter 11. Visitors often spend a limited amount of time fishing, and pursue it as only one of a number of activities (Carpenter and Bowhis 1976; Hendee others 1977; Lucas 1965).

Photography and nature study are also major activities in most places, and swimming is common in many areas. These are all low-impact, nonconsumptive uses that fit well into wilderness management objectives. Hunting varies from minor to fairly common in the USFS wildernesses. (It is generally prohibited in the NPS.) Mountain climbing is an infrequent use in most areas, including all those in table 14.4, but common in a few areas.

Season of Use

Summer is the big use season in most places. Some areas have nationwide reputations as big-game hunting areas, but in the only two such areas studied (the Bob Marshall and the Selway-Bitterroot), summer visitors still substantially outnumbered fall hunters. Many areas in the South, southwest, and at low elevations in California have winter or spring peaks in use (Washburne and Cole 1983). In the North and at higher elevations in the mountains, winter use is light, but much more common than a decade or two earlier and growing (fig. 14.5).

Many areas experience weekend peaks in use, especially in the smaller, more accessible wildernesses, where it can produce serious congestion and overuse. An example of moderate weekend peaking

at the Desolation Wilderness is shown in figure 14.6. Other smaller, more accessible areas, such as the San Gorgonio and San Jacinto near Los Angeles, show more severe weekend peaks. Many of the small, eastern wildernesses, however, do not show sharp weekend peaks (Roggenbuck and Lucas 1987).

Social Groups and Organization Sponsorship

In almost all areas, a large majority of the visitors are part of family groups (which sometimes also include friends), and about one-third to one-half of the groups in the areas studied include children under 16. Most other visitors come with small groups of friends. Organization-sponsored groups are not common, ranging from almost none in some areas to about one-tenth elsewhere. Organizations include conservation and outdoor recreation clubs such as the American Wilderness Alliance and Sierra Club; youth groups such as Boy and Girl Scouts (fig. 14.7), young people's camps of all sorts, church and school groups. The Sierra Club sponsored about 300 hiking, hiking-with-packstock, horseback, and boat trips (almost two-thirds of which involved wilderness or similar areas); and local chapters of the club sponsored many more outings.

Fig.14.5. Winter use of wilderness is increasing and has minimal impact on wilderness qualities. Ski touring in the Selway-Bitterroot Wilderness, ID. Photo courtesy of Richard Walker.

Table 14.4 shows the types of groups visiting some wildernesses for which we have data. Family means related or married people, not necessarily an entire family, for example, a father and son. Family groups have been a large, stable segment of the wilderness visitor population for many years.

Visitor Residence

Many wilderness areas draw visitors from all over the nation. The John Muir Wilderness in California, for example, had visitors from all 50 states and several foreign countries in 1976, the last year residence data were tabulated. Sequoia and Kings Canyon National Parks (CA) had backcountry visitors from 39 states in 1972. But for every area for which data are available, the overwhelming majority of visitors are from the region near the wilderness. Almost 85 percent of the 76,000 visits to the John Muir Wilderness in 1976, and 93 percent of the visits to Sequoia-Kings Canyon backcountry in 1986 were made by Californians. Residents of Washington accounted for 74 to 78 percent of all visits to North Cascades, Olympic, and Mount Rainier National Parks in Washington in 1974. From 58 to 85 percent of the 1970-1971 visits to seven USFS wilderness and similar areas in Montana were made by Montanans. More recent figures are unavailable, but changes are probably small. About two-thirds of 1986 BWCAW visits were made by

Fig. 14.7. Most wilderness visitors travel in small parties composed of family or close friends, but fraternal and professional organizations also use wilderness. A patrol of Boy Scouts hike into the Desolation Wilderness, CA. Photo courtesy of L. J. Prater, USFS.

residents of Minnesota. In a sense, people, like wildlife, have "home ranges" within which they concentrate most activities. Some NPS wilderness or backcountry, and some eastern wildernesses draw more out-of-state visitors (Roggenbuck and Lucas 1987). One conclusion suggested by visitor-residence data is that energy shortages and higher travel costs are unlikely to reduce wilderness use significantly. Residence data also indicate that, although wilderness *is* a national resource, from a recreational use viewpoint, wilderness use typically takes place near home and therefore wilderness is needed fairly close to population centers.

DISTRIBUTION OF USE

The geographical distribution of wilderness use is very uneven—there are many people in a few places and only a few in many other locations. Unevenness is evident among wildernesses as well as within individual wildernesses, whether we look at numbers of visits by trailheads, flows of visitors through the area, or visitor use of camping areas.

There is general agreement that such extremely uneven use is undesirable. There is no agreement, however, as to what constitutes optimum distribution. We will discuss the problem of comparing use between areas; briefly, wildernesses vary greatly in their ability to absorb use, and equal use of every area would be disastrous.

The problem of determining optimum distribution within a wilderness is more complicated. It is clear that an even distribution—the same amount of

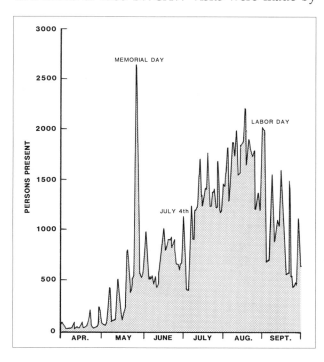

Fig. 14.6. Daily distribution of use in the backcountry of Yosemite National Park, CA, April through September, 1978. From van Wagtendonk 1981.

use on every acre, or of every mile of the trail system and of every campsite—is neither possible nor desirable. It is impossible—barring total regimentation—for several reasons. Trips vary in length; thus, the interior is not as heavily visited as the periphery. Also, most use is on trails or water routes, which typically branch and diverge, so the main trunks inevitably carry more people than the branches.

Evenly dispersed use is undesirable for two reasons. First, different parts of a wilderness vary in their ability to absorb use. Some places are fragile; others are more durable. Second, "outstanding opportunities for solitude" (the Wilderness Act's words) would be lost. The solitude experience would be homogenized. It would be essentially the same everywhere for everyone. But definitions of solitude and its value vary from person to person. With completely even use, persons who really prize solitude would be frustrated. At the same time, persons not strongly motivated to seek solitude would encounter fewer visitors than they would willingly accept—in a sense, solitude would be wasted on them. The Limits of Acceptable Change (LAC) system (chap. 9) recognizes the desirability of diversity in visitor experiences and provides a mechanism to plan for it.

No neat formula calculates an optimum distribution of use within a wilderness. We suspect that in some areas present use is too unevenly distributed and that some redistribution to reduce the extremes is desirable. Badly overused trouble spots are a common problem. This issue of optimum use distributions is considered in many sections of this book—in discussions of principles of management (chap. 7), carrying capacity (chap. 9), and use management (chaps. 15, 16, and 17).

Area-to-area Distribution of Use

Reported visitor use shows substantial variation among individual wildernesses in the national parks (table 14.2) and national forests (table 14.3). The reasons for such different drawing power are poorly understood, but the most heavily used USFS wildernesses are almost all located relatively close to large population concentrations. This is also true for NPS areas. California, Minnesota, southern Appalachian, and New England wildernesses receive the most intense recreational-use pressure (tables 14.2 and 14.3), but other wildernesses in these same regions are lightly used.

Location near many people makes heavy use possible, but a reputation as an attractive area is also necessary if heavy use is to actually occur. This reputation must be based to some extent on actual

attractions and recreational opportunities, but these are not the only factors determining an area's appeal. Personalities and historical accidents probably play an important role. Publicity in national magazines and guidebooks has contributed to the popularity of some wildernesses and some particular trails in specific wildernesses.

Some people have speculated that merely classifying an area as wilderness attracts extra use. Assigning an area a name and identifying it as wilderness may stimulate use. This is often called the "designation effect." But there is scant evidence that designation results in a spurt in use. The only area studied both before and after designation, the Rattlesnake Wilderness in Montana, showed almost no change in use over four years (McCool 1985). An analysis of changes in use in newly designated wildernesses showed that use of the new area usually increased more rapidly recently. Reported use in 1986 than long-established wilderness, but the differences were variable and probably less than believers in the "designation effect" would have predicted (Petersen 1981).

By themselves, visitor totals indicate little regarding pressure on the resource. For one thing, areas vary in size. For example, although total use in the Collegiate Peaks Wilderness in Colorado and the Bob Marshall Wilderness is about the same, the Bob Marshall is about six times as large as the Collegiate Peaks.

To aid in comparing areas and indicating pressure, acreage and use figures for all national forest areas have been expressed in terms of visitor-days per acre (table 14.3). As table 14.3 suggests, among different areas there are large differences in the degree of visitor congestion as well as in pressure on the soil, vegetation, water, and wildlife. Some of this variation is acceptable and desirable, but the extremes may be questioned.

Although table 14.3 helps us understand interarea differences in use pressure, it still does not present a complete picture of existing congestion nor of opportunities for solitude. In addition to size, at least two additional *factors* should be considered in *describing levels of wilderness congestion*. The first factor is *length of season*. In the northern Rocky Mountains or Cascades, the main use season might be only two or three months (because of trails blocked by snow or streams too high to ford). In the milder regions, the season is much longer. For instance, the Salmon River in Idaho, only about 2,000 feet above sea level, is used year round. Therefore, for most areas, adding a length-of-season variable to the measure of annual use per unit of area would produce even higher use levels during the main season than table 14.2 suggests. For in-

stance, more than 1 million visitor-days of use in 1986 in the BWCAW were not distributed evenly over an entire year—about 90 percent of the visitor-days came during the three summer months and the latter part of May.

Second, *the proportion of usable or effective acreage is not the same in all wildernesses*. Although all wilderness acreage is available in the sense that it provides at least a backdrop for the recreationist and space for isolation (and, of course, is a vital part of a natural ecosystem), only a portion is used directly by the visitor. The amount of land available for distribution of use is affected by steepness of slope; type of vegetation; and area of lakes, streams, and wet, boggy soils. In the San Jacinto Wilderness, for example, it was estimated that of the 690 acres in one travel zone (management area), approximately 400 acres were unavailable for use because of excessive steepness, type of vegetation, and the presence of excessively wet meadows. Other areas are even more rugged, and the proportion of the area usable might be much smaller. For example, we would estimate that considerably less than 10 percent of the area in the Mission Mountains Wilderness is potentially usable because of steepness. Managers of the John Muir Wilderness estimated only 2 percent of the area was actually used directly, and many other areas are probably similar.

Usable acreage also is influenced by the degree of development of access and travel routes. Most wilderness travel is restricted to the existing trail systems or areas directly adjacent to trails. (Trail and cross-country travel will be discussed further in the next section.) Some areas are well supplied with an extensive trail network while other areas have only sketchy, sparse trail systems. Miles of trail and numbers of entry points (which relate more closely to capacity than does gross area) on a per-thousand-acre basis, vary considerably among the sample of areas included in table 14.5. For example, the Great Gulf Wilderness (NH), has about 60 times as many entry points per 1,000 acres and more than 8 times as dense a trail network as does the Teton Wilderness.

Intrawilderness Use Distribution

Use within any particular wilderness is likely to vary as much as use between wilderness areas. For in-

Table 14.5. Trail and entry-point density in selected USFS and NPS wildernesses.

Wilderness (State)	Acres	Entry points[1]		Trail miles	
		Number	Number per 1,000 acres	Number	Number per 1,000 acres
Great Gulf (NH)	5,400	13	2.41	25	4.63
Rainbow Lake (WI)	6,600	10	1.52	21	3.11
Hercules Glades (MO)	12,315	22	1.79	34	2.72
Linville Gorge (NC)	7,655	12	1.57	19	2.48
Shining Rock (NC)	13,400	4	0.30	30	2.21
Lye Brook (VT)	14,300	9	0.63	31	2.17
Pecos (NM)	165,000	38	0.23	267	1.62
Desolation (CA)	63,479	22	0.35	99	1.56
Anaconda-Pintler (MT)	159,086	30	0.19	207	1.30
Dolly Sods (WV)	10,215	8	0.78	12	1.17
Yosemite National Park (CA)	681,150	67	0.09	650	0.95
Glacier National Park (MT)	927,500[2]	81	0.09	801	0.86
Shenandoah National Park (VA)	79,019	104	1.32	68	0.86
Frank Church-River of No Return (ID)	2,239,720	—	—	—	—
Bob Marshall (MT)	950,000	47	0.05	818	0.86
High Uintas (UT)	237,177	21	0.09	199	0.84
Bridger (WY)	383,300	41	0.11	315	0.82
Selway-Bitterroot (ID-MT)	1,243,659	87	0.07	916	0.74
Sawtooth (ID)	216,383	26	0.12	152	0.70
Mission Mountains (MT)	73,945	23	0.31	48	0.65
Teton (WY)	563,500	24	0.04	318	0.56

1. Entry points are defined as trails crossing the wilderness boundary.
2. Acreage figures for Glacier and Yosemite National Parks refer to areas proposed for classification as wilderness.

stance, in the BWCAW in 1986, about 61 percent of the user groups entered through only 10 of the area's 87 entry points. In fact, two entry points accounted for almost one-fourth of all groups entering the area. In the Mission Mountains, more than 90 percent of the groups entered at only two of the area's 19 trailheads (Lucas and others 1971). Just 4 percent of Yosemite National Park's (CA) trailheads received 68 percent of total use in 1979 (van Wagtendonk 1981). Figure 14.8, which shows the use pattern in the Spanish Peaks Primitive Area in Montana (now part of the Lee Metcalf Wilderness), is representative of the spatial distribution of use in most wildernesses. Most trail use is heavily concentrated along short segments of the trail system—for instance, on the 2 miles of trail leading to Lava Lake near the eastern edge of the area. Nearly two-thirds of the area's use is day use, which accounts for the concentration on trails such as the one to Lava Lake. But most of the trail system has only a trickle of use, an average of less than one party every two days of the use season. Campsite use is also uneven, with heaviest use at some larger lakes that are reasonably accessible.

The heavy concentration of use along only a few trail miles is shown in figure 14.9. Trail segments are ranked from the most to the least used. Total travel, in cumulative visitor-miles, is graphed against cumulative trail miles. For the entire trail system, the 10 percent of trail miles with the heaviest use accounted for about half of all visitor-miles. From the graph, one can determine the percentage of total use concentrated on any proportion of the trail network—30 percent of the trail miles get a little more than 70

percent of all use, and 92 percent of the trail system accounts for all use. The index number expresses how much the curve rises above the 45-degree diagonal, which represents an even use distribution. The higher the index number, the more concentrated the use. The index's value can vary from zero (the 45-degree diagonal) to 100, the number which would describe a situation in which one short segment had *all* the use. In the Spanish Peaks, the use is relatively concentrated (index number 53), but two larger areas that have been studied—the Bob Marshall and Selway-Bitterroot—showed even more concentrated use (index numbers 85 and 67, respectively). Horse use tends to be more concentrated than hiking use. Horse parties go farther, but they tend to stay on main trails. As a result, areas with heavy horse use generally have more concentrated total-use patterns. The Bob Marshall, the only area studied where a majority of visitors traveled by horse, also shows the most concentrated use. The Desolation Wilderness (index number 60), an area about the same size as the Spanish Peaks but with about 20 times as much use, shows slightly more concentrated use distribution than the Spanish Peaks. One might expect that users, in an attempt to avoid crowds, would disperse more evenly. But this does not seem to happen often. The dense trail network in the Desolation might also lead one to expect use to disperse more evenly, but this has not happened either. Uneven use seems universal, but those areas for which data for several years are available all show a trend toward more even distribution of use at access points in more recent years, perhaps partly because more visitors are seek-

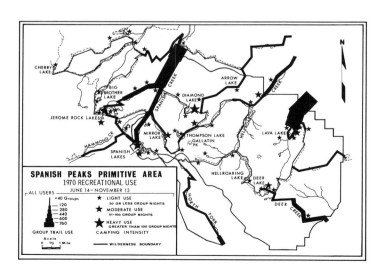

Fig. 14.8. Distribution of recreational use, Spanish Peaks Primitive Area, MT, 1970.

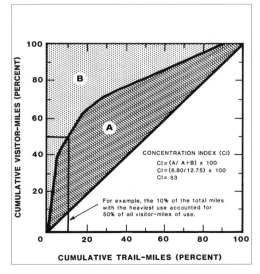

Fig. 14.9. Trail use concentration, Spanish Peaks Primitive Area, MT, 1970.

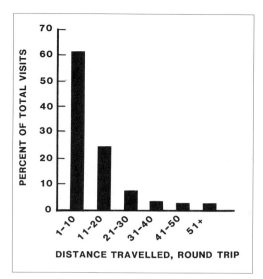

Fig. 14.10. Distance traveled per trip. Information from eight MT and ID wildernesses.

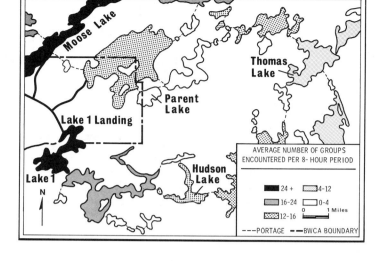

Fig. 14.11. Average number of groups encountered per eight-hour period in part of the BWCAW, MN, 1971.

ing less-crowded, less-impacted areas, and partly because managers have taken actions to shift use.

The pattern of short trips, both spatially and temporally, is characteristic for most wildernesses. This conclusion is illustrated in figure 14.10, which summarizes visitor trail travel for eight Montana and Idaho wildernesses and backcountry areas. Only about 14 percent of the visitors traveled more than 20 miles round trip in the wilderness—a statistic which refutes the notion that wilderness trips are typically long safaris. Only about 2 percent of the visitors traveled more than 50 miles.

An effective way of describing wilderness congestion resulting from use concentration is to measure the number of other parties a group could be expected to meet per hour or day in a given portion of the wilderness. In the BWCAW, data from trip diaries during the summer use season in 1971 (Lime 1975) revealed wide variation in frequency of encounters at different lakes. Groups reported the number of other parties they saw on individual lakes each day and the number of hours spent on the lake. Visitors to some lakes encountered more than 40 times as many groups as did visitors to other lakes. Often, only one or two portages separated heavily and lightly congested lakes. This distribution of encounter levels is illustrated, for a small portion of the area, in figure 14.11.

Use patterns in most wildernesses are strongly trail related. The only exceptions are areas where water access predominates, as in coastal southeastern Alaska and the BWCAW. From studies of USFS

wilderness areas, it is estimated that fewer than 20 percent of the visitors to most areas travel cross-country. And an even smaller percentage of the total distance covered in the wilderness is off-trail travel. The specific amount of cross-country travel depends on the motives, interests, and experience of the visitors, as well as on the terrain and vegetation in the area. Visitors are almost locked into trails in steep, heavily forested country, especially in areas characterized by abundant downed trees. This describes most areas in the northern Rockies and much of the Cascades and the East. Alpine, plateaulike areas and open desert country, on the other hand, open up cross-country opportunities.

Campsite use is also usually uneven. In the BWCAW, Merriam and others (1973) reported 23 campsites varied from 28 to 1,138 total visitor-days of use over five years. Six sites totaled less than 200 visitor-days each, and 11 totaled more than 600 visitor-days. Western wilderness shows similarly uneven campsite use. Many *potential* campsites—a majority, in fact, in some areas—show no evidence of ever having been used at all (Brown and Schomaker 1974). In the Desolation Wilderness, the most popular 16 percent of the campsites accounted for one-half of all use. The least-used half accounted for only 18 percent of all use. When the same type of analysis shown in figure 14.8 for trail use is applied to campsite use concentration, it appears that campsite use is less concentrated than trail use.

The most frequently used campsites in the Spanish Peaks Primitive Area and the Bridger Wilderness

(WY) shared the same characteristics: (1) proximity to both water and fishing opportunities; (2) scenic and water views (usually of a lake, not a stream); (3) location within 700 feet of a trail; (4) availability of at least 500 square feet of level land (4 percent or less slope); and (5) availability of firewood within 300 feet (Brown and Schomaker 1974). The development of highly efficient backpacker stoves, and the growing proportion of visitors who use them, should reduce the importance of proximity to firewood in the future. About half of the campsites were within 50 feet of the shoreline of a lake or stream, almost two-thirds were within 100 feet, and 85 percent were within 200 feet (fig. 14.12). Camping so close to water causes problems, which is discussed in other chapters, but it is also obvious that sites close to water are highly attractive, and getting people to change their selection of campsites may not be easy. Very few campsites freely selected by visitors are far from water.

USER CHARACTERISTICS

The Stereotype

A common stereotype of wilderness visitors pictures them as young, attractive, athletic, wealthy, leisured, citified. This stereotype is common in discussions as diverse as congressional testimony on wilderness classification proposals and barroom arguments in small towns near wilderness. The stereotype is largely untrue (Norgaard and others 1979; Stankey 1971), which we will attempt to show by presenting results of scientific surveys of wilderness visitors.

Understanding who the wilderness visitors really are is important for both policy and management decisions. Policy is influenced by knowledge of who receives the benefits gained from wilderness use. Management, especially the use of information and education, requires knowledge of user characteristics and values. Just as businesses conduct market research to understand their customers, so do wilderness managers need to understand their customers, the visitors.

Age

Wilderness visitors tend to be younger than the general population, yet all age groups are fairly well represented (table 14.6). Data from areas studied show large proportions of children and young adults (from 30 to 57 percent are 25 or younger). There are almost as many older adults (30 to 50 percent are 26 to 45 years of age), especially in some of the areas with above-average proportions of visitors traveling by horse. Age distribution for the general American

population is also included in table 14.6 for comparison.

All of these age figures refer to individual visitors, but a number of studies have been based on party leaders or persons registering for the entire party. A study comparing party leaders and other party members (Jubenville 1971) concluded that, although attitudes were similar, socioeconomic characteristics differed significantly. For example, party leaders tend to be older (Hendee and others 1968).

The age structure of wilderness visitors did not change over time in the Bob Marshall Wilderness Complex (BMWC), the only place where data on trends in visitor ages are available (Lucas 1985). Changes in birth rates, the degree to which individual wilderness visitors continue to visit wilderness as they age, and the age groups from which most new visitors are recruited will interact in complex ways over the years to determine how age structures change in the future.

Physical Ability

The only study of physical condition as related to wilderness use (Wiesner and Sharkey 1973) concluded that college men who visited wilderness were neither stronger nor more fit than those who did not, but that they had, in comparison with other college men, more favorable attitudes about exercise and parents who were more physically active. As a barrier to participation, lack of *interest* was more critical than lack of *ability*.

Gender

Wilderness has sometimes been viewed as a male sanctuary. Perhaps at one time it was, but now about one-fourth of the visitors are female. The larger, horse-oriented wildernesses average less female visitation; the smaller hiking areas average a little more. The trend is toward more women visitors.

Residence

Most wilderness visitors are from urban areas, as are most Americans. But because visitors do not typically travel long distances to visit wilderness, the proportion from urban places depends largely on the degree of urbanization in that region. Thus, about 60 percent of the 1982 visitors to Montana wilderness come from urban areas, and 51 percent of the Montana population lived in urban areas in 1980. In southern California, with much larger cities within the region, more than 90 percent of wilderness visitors come from cities with more than a million people.

Although current residence is overwhelmingly urban, several studies (Burch and Wenger 1967;

Fig. 14.12. Lakes are attractive to wilderness visitors, but camping close to the shoreline is often prohibited. This campsite near Mirror Lake in the Lee Metcalf Wilderness, MT, has been closed to camping. Photo courtesy of the USFS.

Hendee and others 1968; Lucas 1980, 1985; ORRRC 1962) show more rural background for wilderness visitors during childhood. Some people may be attracted to wilderness by the contrast between rural surroundings in childhood and the pressures of city living in adulthood, which could be described as a "nostalgia theory" of wilderness attraction (Lucas 1980). Wilderness visits may thus fulfill a longing for open spaces and contact with nature for people who have not entirely adapted to city living. At an earlier stage in America's history, a major migration from rural to urban areas took place. In 1970, in the BMWC there were 21 percent more visitors who had grown up in rural areas or small towns than who currently lived there—about twice the magnitude of the shift in the general population. This lends some support to the nostalgia theory. In 1982, the difference was only 7 percent for visitors, but again about twice as large as the shift for the general population.

Thus, there still is support for the theory in the 1982 figures, but its effect is weakening as fewer people experience rural-to-urban migration, and in the future its effect may likely disappear. This could lead to some slight dampening of the future rate of growth of wilderness visitation.

Income

Wilderness visitors are above average in income (so are almost all types of outdoor recreationists), but only moderately so in most places. Income data from recent studies are given along with U.S. averages for 1970 and 1980 in table 14.6.

Income comparison, unfortunately, cannot be simple, as is indicated by the inclusion of two sets of national income averages for each year in table 14.6. The first set of figures, reported for 1970 by Vaux (1975), includes both families and single persons who constitute an economic unit, while the second set for each year is for families. Wilderness visitors look affluent compared to Vaux's data for individuals and families combined, but appear quite similar when compared to data for families. In fact, most wilderness visitors are part of a family economic unit, and the questions in most surveys have asked about family income. Therefore, it seems most appropriate to compare the income distribution of wilderness visitors to families, rather than to Vaux's families and individuals, which includes large numbers of single people in the comparison.

Earlier studies of wilderness visitors' income (Norgaard and others 1979; Stankey 1971) show the same moderate overrepresentation of higher incomes in a wide variety of areas. High incomes are *not necessary* to visit wilderness. Typical expenditures for wilderness visits are low, usually under $10 per person per day in the late 1960s and early 1970s (Lucas 1980; Stankey 1971).

Occupation

Persons in professional-technical occupations and students form the majority of visitors to most wildernesses (table 14.6). Generally, from 20 to 40 percent of the visitors of working age are in professional or technical work. The professions most often encountered are in the fields of education, research, social service, and religion, rather than law, medicine, and engineering. Usually about one-fourth of adults and young adults are students, although a few areas have reported low figures for students—down to 4 percent in the Great Bear Wilderness in 1970, while it was still an unclassified, roadless wilderness study area where many visitors entered at a central airstrip (which is still open).

Homemakers and skilled laborers usually are the next most common occupations, each comprising about one-tenth of the total in most areas. Studies based on group leaders tend to underestimate numbers of homemakers. Other occupational categories are not well represented. Blue-collar workers, other than skilled craftsmen, account for only about 5

Table 14. 6. Characteristics of wilderness visitors.

Area	Year	Age (percent of total)						Income (percent of total)					Occupation[1] (percent of total)				Education (yrs)[2] (percent of total)			
		1 to 15	16 to 25	26 to 35	36 to 45	46 to 55	56 and over	Under $5,000	$5,000 to $9,999	$10,000 to $14,999	$15,000 to $24,999	$25,000 and over	Professional/Technical	Student	Homemaker	Skilled labor	0 to 8	9 to 12	13 to 16	17 and over
Boundary Waters Canoe Area W (MN)	1960	30	42	13	13	13	2	—	—	—	—	—	—	—	—	—	0	21	54	25
Three Sisters (OR)	1965	3	21	24	23	21	7	—	—	—	—	—	—	—	—	—	36	36	36	28
Bob Marshall W (MT)	1970	13	17	21	25	13	10	6	30	23	29	14	30	16	9	9	4	36	29	31
	1982	13	18	47	47	22	22	—	—	—	—	—	40	12	2	14	2	26	44	28
Scapegoat W (MT)	1970	4	29	25	24	11	8	11	42	29	14	7	22	25	8	5	4	43	33	18
	1982	14	18	44	44	24	24	—	—	—	—	—	35	10	3	17	4	29	43	26
Great Bear W (MT)	1970	5	7	28	31	18	9	11	19	22	30	20	33	4	9	14	3	35	39	24
	1982	9	26	45	45	19	19	—	—	—	—	—	35	10	5	15	1	31	46	23
Cabinet Mountains W (MT)	1970	8	40	22	12	12	6	12	45	28	12	4	19	30	9	9	3	48	32	15
Spanish Peaks PA (MT)	1970	26	29	17	17	8	3	17	29	26	17	11	30	33	7	8	2	31	35	29
Mission Mountains PA (MT)	1970	9	24	25	20	14	9	15	32	26	16	11	40	20	9	12	4	29	28	35
Selway-Bitterroot W (ID-MT)	1971	4	27	24	19	14	11	12	37	25	17	10	26	22	9	9	3	38	33	26
Desolation W (CA)	1972	29	28	18	12	10	2	11	16	23	28	21	39	26	9	7	0	18	40	42
S. Appalachian Trail (VA-TN-NC-GA)	1970-71	—	—	—	—	—	—	10	24	23	44	44	38	38	7	3	20	20	44	36
Cranberry (WY)	1972	—	—	—	—	—	—	12	32	35	21	21	—	—	—	—	63	63	37	37
Four California Wildernesses	1973	—	—	—	—	—	—	27	15	18	26	14	—	—	—	—	—	—	—	—
Great Smoky Mountains NP (NC-TN)	1973	n/a	34	31	19	16	16	—	—	—	—	—	—	—	—	—	—	—	—	—
	1983	n/a	34	38	15	9	4	—	—	—	—	—	—	—	—	—	—	—	—	—
Eagles Nest (CO)	1977	62	62	62	38	38	38	—	—	—	—	—	—	—	—	—	0	12	53	33
Rawah (CO)	1977	76	76	76	22	22	22	—	—	—	—	—	—	—	—	—	0	17	49	34
Weminuche (CO)	1977	61	61	61	37	37	37	—	—	—	—	—	—	—	—	—	7	20	42	39
Popo Agie (WY)	1978	7	78	78	14	14	1	—	—	—	—	—	—	—	—	—	—	—	—	—
Bridger (WY)	1978	17	71	71	10	10	3	—	—	—	—	—	—	—	—	—	—	—	—	—
Fitzpatrick (WY)	1978	1	74	74	20	20	5	—	—	—	—	—	—	—	—	—	—	—	—	—
Linville Gorge (NC)	1978	11	31	37	13	7	7	—	—	—	—	—	47	17	1	5	1	15	47	37
Shining Rock (NC)	1978	12	27	32	16	13	13	—	—	—	—	—	29	10	2	9	2	21	47	31
Joyce Kilmer-Slickrock (NC-TN)	1978	10	34	36	12	8	8	—	—	—	—	—	42	14	3	8	0	14	44	41
Visitors																				
U.S families and individuals	1970	—	—	—	—	—	—	34	29	21	12	4	—	—	—	—	—	—	—	—
	1980	—	—	—	—	—	—	12	16	15	25	32	—	—	—	—	—	—	—	—
U.S. families	1970	—	—	—	—	—	—	19	32	27	22	22	—	—	—	—	—	—	—	—
	1980	—	—	—	—	—	—	6	13	14	28	39	—	—	—	—	—	—	—	—
U.S. individuals[3]	1970	30	17	12	12	11	18	—	—	—	—	—	8	5	25	20	25	54	21	21
	1980	24	19	16	12	10	19	—	—	—	—	—	9	4	21	21	18	50	32	32

Sources: Lucas 1964, 1980, 1985; Murray 1974; Roggenbuck and Lucas 1987; and Vaux 1975.
W = Wilderness.
PA = Preserve Area.
NP = National Park.
l. Only the four most common types of occupations are shown. Others are usually 10 percent or less.
2. Based on years of schooling completed to date for visitors 16 years old or over, except for the BWCAW
  which is based on data from people who had completed their educations, and only
  for paddle canoeists, the most common type of user, and the most comparable to visitors to other wildernesses.
3. Estimated from U.S. Census data in which age is defined slightly different.

percent of all visitors, and farmers are usually well under 5 percent.

The occupational breakdown of wilderness visitors is strikingly different from that of the general population. Most wilderness visitors are in occupations that emphasize working with people, ideas, or abstractions rather than working with things. The contrast between their working environment and the wilderness is strong, and this could be one important appeal of wilderness. It has been termed the escape or compensatory hypothesis. Familiarity and the social setting of friends and family also probably play a role in shaping preferences for wilderness recreation (Burch 1969).

Education
The most distinguishing characteristic of wilderness visitors is high educational levels (table 14.6). All studies agree on this (Roggenbuck and Lucas 1987). With few exceptions, 60 to 85 percent of the visitors to most wildernesses have attended college, and 20 to 40 percent have done graduate study.

Does advanced education somehow help develop an interest in the natural world and primitive recreation? Or are certain types of people drawn to both university education and wilderness? One can only speculate, but the association suggests that leveling off or declining college enrollments could slow growth in wilderness recreational use in the future if education is, in fact, an important source of interest in wilderness.

Conservation Organization Membership
Between 20 and 30 percent of the visitors to areas studied belong to a conservation group or outdoor recreation activity club (Hendee and others 1968; Roggenbuck and Lucas 1987). This compares to less than 10 percent of car campers (Hendee and others 1969). About 40 percent of the club members (about one-tenth of all visitors) belong to a wilderness–oriented organization such as the Sierra Club, The Wilderness Society, or the National Parks and Conservation Association. This is far higher than for the total adult population, probably no more than 1 percent of whom belong to these organizations. Available data show a small decline in club membership, mainly in clubs not strongly linked to wilderness (Lucas 1985).

The Stereotype Reconsidered
Characteristics of wilderness users are well known. In fact, the profile of the wilderness visitor is clearer than that of most other recreationists. The characteristics are quite similar from area to area, even in different parts of the nation. The stereotype of the young, rich, idle, city dweller has little basis in fact and should be discarded once and for all.

Typical wilderness visitors tend to be young, but not to the exclusion of older people; mostly male but with a trend to more females; from nearby areas, only slightly more likely to be from urban areas than the general population; only moderately high income; in professional-technical occupations; and highly educated.

USE TRENDS

Wilderness recreational use has increased greatly over the last 40 years, but recently use has leveled off and even declined in some areas.

WILDERNESS USE DATA SOURCES

USFS wilderness use data are most complete and cover the longest period. Total use, including both overnight and day use, has been estimated for each wilderness and primitive area since 1946, and some data go back to 1941 (Elsner 1985).

NPS data are more limited and available for a shorter period. Data are not available for designated wildernesses at all, but since 1971 overnight stays in backcountry have been reported. Most NPS backcountry areas are used similarly to USFS wilderness. Although day use is a common use of many wildernesses, often including a majority of visits (Roggenbuck and Lucas 1987), it is not reported for NPS wilderness. Finally, NPS and USFS wilderness recreation data also differ in accuracy, as discussed earlier. NPS figures probably are more accurate than USFS data.

As use figures are aggregated for large regions or for the nation, errors might be partially canceled. Particularly at the national level, we think wilderness use data for the national forests are good enough to be worth analyzing, but with some caution. NPS data are probably good at the national level and worth analyzing for most individual parks, again with caution. Trends are most reliable if considered over a period of years, rather than from year to year.

TRENDS IN NATIONAL FOREST WILDERNESS USE

Table 14.7 shows the growth in USFS wilderness use between 1946 and 1986, roughly by decades. Changes in the way use was measured in 1965 mean it is not possible to compare directly the growth rates over the 40 years. During the 18 years between 1946 and 1964, however, use grew sevenfold, at an average annual growth rate of 11.5 percent. In the two decades following passage of the Wilderness Act, use has increased more than 2.5 times, averaging 4.4 percent per year. In recent years, part of the increase in use stems from the addition of new wildernesses.

Table 14.7. Growth in USFS wilderness use, 1946-86.

Year	Use	Average annual percentage growth
	(thousand man-days)	
1946	406	—
1955	1,175	12.5
1964	2,872	10.4
	(thousand visitor-days)	
1965	4,522	—
1975	7,802	5.6
1986	11,233	3.4

When the Wilderness Act passed in 1964, the national forests contained 88 units reporting wilderness use. This included 54 areas designated as wilderness by the Wilderness Act, and 34 primitive areas managed as wilderness pending review for possible wilderness classification. Over the years, all but one of these primitive areas have been reclassified, usually becoming a wilderness, but sometimes being added to an existing wilderness. Many new areas also have been added to the NWPS; at present there are 354 national forest units in the NWPS. In order to analyze basic trends in wilderness use, it is necessary to consider this major expansion in the number of units reporting use.

In our analysis we trace the growth of recreational use in the original 88 units, the "core system." Since 1965, annual growth in use of the core system declined steadily:

Annual percentage change in use of USFS wilderness.

Period	Percent
1965-70	5.3
1970-75	4.5
1975-80	2.3
1980-86	-2.4

Since 1965, use of the core system has grown at an average annual rate of 2 percent, about half that reported for the total national forest wilderness system, and since 1980 its use has declined. The peak year of use of the core system occurred in 1979; in 1986, use of the core system was 87 percent of the 1979 use. Still, in absolute terms, the growth in national forest wilderness use is impressive. It actually exceeds growth for many other forms of recreation taking place in the national forests. As a percentage of total national forest recreational use and of national forest campground use, wilderness use has grown steadily and only recently has shown a decline:

USFS wilderness use as a percent of total and campground use.

Year	Total use	Campground use
	(Man-days base)	
1941	0.4	2.2
1946	1.2	5.1
1951	1.8	—
1956	2.0	—
1961	1.9	7.2
1964	2.1	9.0
	(Visitor-days base)	
1965	2.8	13.3
1970	3.4	16.9
1975	3.7	19.9
1980	4.0	23.0
1985	5.6	37.0
1986	5.3	34.4

Wilderness use has increased its share of national forest recreation in most of this period, despite slower growth recently. Other types of recreation have also leveled off or declined since 1980.

TRENDS IN NATIONAL PARK WILDERNESS USE

Growth in NPS backcountry use is shown in table 14.8. During the first five years following 1971, use grew rapidly, more than doubling from 1.1 million overnight stays to a peak of 2.6 million in 1976, and remained there for three years. This was followed by a decline, slowly at first, more rapidly recently. Reported use in 1986 was less than in 1973, despite a 20-percent growth in the number of units reporting backcountry use. Between 1976 and 1986, NPS backcountry use declined about 37 percent, while in the same period USFS wilderness use (including new areas) grew nearly 65 percent. Little association be-

tween the patterns of annual use exists for the two agencies; between 1971 and 1986, there are only five years when the changes reported by the two agencies were even in the same direction, up or down.

Table 14.8. Changes in overnight stays in NPS backcountry, 1971-86.

Period	Overnight stays (thousands)	Average annual percentage change
1971	1,096	—
1976	2,609	18.9
1981	2,330	-2.3
1986	1,645	-6.7

The decline in NPS backcountry use is further confirmed by examining the year of peak use and contrasting it with 1986. As table 14.9 indicates, in 17 national parks with significant backcountry or wilderness portions, the peak year of use in 12 instances was prior to 1980 and in only one case was it as recent as 1982. In Shenandoah National Park, for example, 1986 use was only 32 percent of the 1973 peak. No park reported peak backcountry use after 1982. The decline in national park use is not limited to the backcountry. All recreational overnight stays in the national parks declined 8 percent from a peak in 1977 to 1986, but backcountry stays declined more.

For comparative purposes, data for more than 20 national forest core system wildernesses (excluding those with extreme fluctuations from year to year) are also shown (table 14.10). Three wildernesses show 1986 as the peak year, but many are similar to the national parks, with most reporting their peak year as 1982 or earlier.

TRENDS IN RELATED ACTIVITIES

Growth in activities associated with wilderness does not always parallel trends in wilderness recreational use. For example, membership in the Sierra Club grew from 84,000 in 1970 to 344,000 in 1983, a growth of nearly 12 percent annually, and other environmental organizations also grew rapidly (Hendee 1984). Between 1979 and 1980, sales of backpacks rose 11 percent and sales of tents increased 20 percent. Yet, other data can be interpreted as reflecting declining activity; sales of other wilderness recreation-related equipment such as sleeping bags declined 30 percent and hiking boots declined 10 percent between 1979 and 1980 (Cordell and Hendee 1982). The National Sporting Goods Association described the traditional outdoors market as "a mature and, perhaps, a declining market."

We must conclude, therefore, that wilderness use, like participation in many other recreational activities, has begun to stabilize. Much of the apparent growth is accounted for by the rapid expansion in the number of units that report wilderness use, primarily under national forest administration. This growth, however, results largely from bookkeeping, as new areas with a history of recreational use are tabulated as wilderness, whereas previously their use was included within some other recording category.

POSSIBLE REASONS FOR SLOWING GROWTH OF WILDERNESS RECREATION PARTICIPATION

Many factors can be considered as potential causes of slower growth. We will examine the most prominent ones and try to judge their roles.

Changing Age Structure

Virtually all studies of recreation participation point to age as one of the most powerful predictive measures of future participation (Marcin and Lime 1977). But English and Cordell (1985) found that participation rates among different age cohorts have risen steadily since 1960, a fact that suggests that the normal dampening effects of increased age on recreation participation might be less in the future than in the past. One of the most fundamental changes in American society today is the increasing age of the population. As the following tabulation shows, the increase, especially since 1970, has been steady:

The ages of the American population, 1960-85.

Age group	1960	1970	1980	1985
	(U.S. population in millions)			
Under 18	64	70	63	63
18-24	16	24	30	28
25-34	23	25	37	42
35-44	24	23	26	32
45-54	20	23	23	23
55 and over	32	39	47	51

Although the population is aging, changes are not striking in those age classes who visit wilderness the most. The number of people in the 18-24 age class has declined slightly since 1980, but the 25-34 class, the most inclined to visit wilderness of any age class in many areas, increased throughout the period (especially in the 1970s when use grew rapidly). The 35-44 category, also common wilderness visitors, in-

creased, especially in the 1980s as the "baby boomers" moved up a step. Decreases in the under 18 and increases in the 55 and over classes should have had little effect on wilderness use because neither age class is a major wilderness user. The decrease among children and teenagers is likely to reduce potential wilderness use in future decades. Population age trends are probably a partial explanation of slower growth in wilderness use, but clearly not the whole story. One analysis concluded that about half of the slowdown in use of several USFS wildernesses in Montana could be accounted for by shifts in the age structure of the Montana population (Polzin 1987).

Changes in Population Distribution

Although changes in age structure might affect trends in overall wilderness use, spatial changes in population distribution have the potential to affect trends in specific regions. Changes in population distribution, however, show limited relationship to changes in wilderness use; at times, the relationship is backwards. For example, between 1975 and 1985, the population of California grew 22 percent and classified USFS wilderness acreage about doubled, with most of the additions in 1984. Use of USFS wilderness during this same period, however, fell 29 percent, and NPS backcountry use in California also declined sharply.

Population growth, then, appears to have little effect on changes in wilderness use. The large migrations to the South and West during the 1970s are not matched by significant growth in wilderness use in those areas.

Constraints on Leisure Time

Contrary to previous notions that leisure time would expand, making it possible for people to enjoy more recreation, recent trends are quite the opposite. The workweek increased from a median of 43 hours in 1975 to 47 hours in 1984, and median leisure time dropped from 24 to 18 hours per week (President's Commission on Americans Outdoors 1986). Also, both spouses often hold jobs. These dual-income households are on the rise. Although the discretionary income of such households increases, it may be difficult to coordinate vacations and free time between spouses. These factors may contribute to the drop in wilderness visitations.

Effects of System Expansion

One possible explanation for the declining use of long-established wildernesses in both national forests and national parks might be the large increase in the size of the NWPS. A prospective wilderness visitor now has more than 450 established wildernesses to choose from, more than 300 of which were added from 1980 on. Although some of the decline is likely attributable to system expansion, there are many reasons why this factor has probably had little effect.

First, the market population is not fixed. If a new area is classified as wilderness, many of its visitors are the same people who visited the area before it was so designated. The wilderness is new, but the land and its recreational attractions were always there; it is "new" only in an official sense. New visitors might indeed show up, perhaps nearby residents attracted by the publicity generated by wilderness designation. This last group would exemplify the "designation effect," the stimulation of demand purported to result from labeling an area "wilderness" (McCool 1985). Although new areas might attract use from older areas, they would be expected to add to total use of the system, thus accelerating the rate of growth in use, not causing it to slow down, as has been happening.

Second, growth of wilderness recreation opportunities also is less impressive if acreage, not numbers of areas, is considered. The 56 million acres of new wilderness in Alaska are best omitted from discussion because of their great distance from most of the U.S. population. The wilderness system in the conterminous 48 states now includes 34.3 million acres, double the pre-1980 total. But most of the acreage growth outside Alaska occurred in one year, 1984—too recently to help explain the use peaks in the 1970s and early 1980s.

Third, some of the growth in acres and numbers of areas in the NWPS results from shifts of national forest primitive areas to wilderness, or official designation of portions of a national park as wilderness. In both cases, the recreational use was already being counted. There is little basis for any designation effect because these areas have long been specially designated and widely perceived as wilderness even though not technically so classified. This type of growth appears insignificant in relation to dilution of demand.

Fourth, the new areas are usually smaller and less scenic than the older wildernesses. Although the Wilderness Act clearly indicates that wilderness has many purposes besides recreation, the original national forest wildernesses and the national parks were established mainly because of scenic quality, natural attractions, and recreation potential. They commonly are perceived as the crown jewels of the wilderness system, and many of the new areas are not strong competitors for visitors.

Table 14.9. Peak year of wilderness use, NPS areas.

National Park	Peak year of overnight backcountry use	Percentage of peak year use occurring in 1986
Yosemite (CA)	1971	48
Everglades (FL)	1973	61
Olympic (WA)	1973	39
Shenandoah (VA)	1973	32
Denali (AK)	1976	91
Grand Canyon (AZ)	1976	45
Great Smoky Mountains (NC-TN)	1976	55
Grand Teton (WY)	1976	44
Glacier (MT)	1977	49
Rocky Mountain (CO)	1977	56
Mount Rainier (WA)	1979	76
Voyageurs (MN)	1979	76
King's Canyon (CA)	1980	54
Sequoia (CA)	1980	56
North Cascades (WA)	1981	65
Yellowstone (WY-MT-ID)	1981	57
Big Bend (TX)	1982	89
Total	**1976**	**62**
(overnight backcountry use, all national parks)		

Table 14.10. Peak year of wilderness use, selected USFS core system wildernesses.

Wilderness	Peak year of wilderness use	Percentage of peak year use occurring in 1986
San Gorgonio (CA)	1966	49
Three Sisters (OR)	1973	76
Desolation (CA)	1974	74
Hoover (CA)	1975	26
John Muir (CA)	1975	33
Pecos (NM)	1978	91
Mazatzal (AZ)	1978	64
Bridger (WY)	1979	38
Sawtooth (ID)	1979	71
Great Gulf (NH)	1980	53
San Jacinto (CA)	1980	26
Selway-Bitterroot (ID-MT)	1981	65
Mount Jefferson (OR)	1981	93
Jarbridge (NV)	1981	69
Bob Marshall (MT)	1982	82
Absaroka-Beartooth (MT)	1982	77
Boundary Waters Canoe Area (MN)	1982	74
Eagles Nest (CO)	1983	71
Linville Gorge (NC)	1984	47
Teton (WY)	1985	80
Cloud Peak (WY)	1986	100
High Uintas (UT)	1986	100
Glacier Peak (WA)	1986	100

Finally, whatever effect major expansion of the wilderness system may have had on past use of older areas, its future effect probably will be less. The recent large expansion of the system (more than 300 areas and 71 million acres added between 1980 and 1985) is not likely to be duplicated in years to come.

Effects of Changing Educational Levels

The most distinguishing socioeconomic characteristic of wilderness users is their high educational level, as described before. Trends in number of Americans enrolled in colleges and universities suggest lessening impetus for growth in wilderness recreation. Enrollment grew rapidly in the 1960s, increasing 126 percent from 1960 to 1970. Growth slowed to 32 percent from 1970 to 1980. From 1980 to 1984, enrollment grew only 1 percent, another reflection of the aging postwar "baby boomers." This likely has contributed to slower growth in wilderness use.

Changing Gasoline Cost and Supply

The impact of rising gasoline prices on travel for wilderness recreation does not appear great. First, during the 1973-1974 embargo, use of national forest wilderness continued to grow, although the rate of growth slowed. Second, in recent years, increases in the price of gasoline have not kept up with inflation;

despite this, the use trend has been downward.

Availability of gasoline has been a problem from time to time, but typically this has been a local and temporary situation that took place before the recent slowdown in growth of use. Most wilderness visitors live relatively close to the wilderness visited, and it seems unlikely that either energy cost or availability would significantly affect overall use.

Changing Interests and Preferences

The socioeconomic variables examined above appear to explain only part of the declining rate of wilderness recreation participation. Thus, the question is whether public interest in wilderness is beginning to wane. Was the rapid growth witnessed in the 1960s and early 1970s simply a function of the heightened interest in the environment that characterized that period? Could declining rates of participation be a reflection of increasing dissatisfaction among users?

Wilderness does not seem to be losing broad public support. A national survey by Opinion Research Corporation in 1977 found strong public support (Cordell and Hendee 1982). A statewide poll

conducted in Montana (Utter 1983) also found strong support—almost 85 percent of the respondents favored designation of wilderness. Although these cross-sectional studies do not permit an assessment of the trends in public attitudes toward wilderness, they nevertheless suggest that there is a high and continuing interest in wilderness preservation. Perhaps the upper-middle class American lifestyle supports the *concept* of wilderness, but not the actual *use*.

We can examine general population surveys of recreation participation to see if wilderness-related recreation activities are changing. The mixture of activity definitions and methodologies makes it difficult to interpret these results. But it appears that in recent decades the percentage of U.S. citizens participating in wilderness-related activities has remained relatively close to 5 percent. Thus, the proportion of the population whose recreational interests might likely be met in wilderness settings does not appear to be changing greatly.

Likewise, there appears to be little likelihood that rising dissatisfaction is leading to declining use levels in wilderness. Most studies of wilderness users report high levels of satisfaction (Van Horne and others 1985). Lucas (1985) found Bob Marshall Wilderness visitors surveyed in 1970 and 1982 about equally satisfied. Furthermore, he found that, whereas in 1970 more than one-third of the experienced visitors found conditions worse than on earlier trips, in 1982 only 16 percent felt this way.

It is possible that the declining rates of wilderness participation that we have noted might be a function of the increasing levels of diverse recreation activity by many people. Van Horne and others (1985) report that since 1960 per capita participation rates in many activities have risen. At the same time, data from the National Recreation Survey also indicate that although 18 percent of the respondents said they were spending more

time at present in outdoor recreation, 33 percent said they were spending less (Van Horne and others 1985). What these data may suggest is that there is simply not enough time to do all people might wish to do, including wilderness recreation.

Changing Wilderness Images
Perhaps the image of wilderness recreation has so changed that it might contribute to slackening use. Many visitors may feel obligated to minimize their impact. Although this is a positive development, it may create anxiety about how to behave and guilt about mistakes and shortcomings as to diminish the free and easy pleasures of an earlier, more innocent era.

Most wilderness areas also now have more regulations. In addition, *Giardia* infection has become widely recognized as a problem in wilderness waters. A decade or two ago, visitors might have relaxed with clear consciences around a roaring campfire next to a high mountain lake, maybe sipping clear, cold water dipped from the lake. Now they might get a ticket from a wilderness ranger, perhaps for camping too close to the lake, perhaps for the campfire, and in addition, suffer diarrhea from drinking the water. This sort of shift in perception might help explain recent trends. Some visitors might even restrain their use of wilderness as their contribution to wilderness protection.

Questionable Use Data
The more we have worked with agency wilderness use estimates, the more we have become aware of serious shortcomings. The leveling off and declines in reported use are so widespread that there seems little doubt about the direction of change, but its magnitude, especially for individual areas, is questionable.

Wild swings in reported use from year to year

Table 14.11. Projections of USFS wilderness use, thousands of man-days and percentage change.

	1959 (actual)	1976	Change	2000	Change
National Forest Recreation Survey (1961)	1,950[1]	5,804	+198	16,183	+730
Outdoor Recreation Resources Review Commission (1962)	1,399[1]	4,948	+254	12,053	+762

1. The National Forest Recreation Survey included data for all areas; the ORRRC study excluded areas smaller than 100,000 acres, then called "Wild Areas."

are common. Many of these fluctuations are so large that it seems impossible that they represent real changes; estimation errors must be large and common. This hampers research, but more important, it devastates professional management, reducing it almost to blindfolded guessing. Should managers relax because use of a particular wilderness is plummeting or gear up for a crisis because use is exploding? For some areas, a decision is impossible because the use trend is up one year and down the next. *Improvement in the accuracy of use estimates seems essential.* This will require commitment to development and careful application of reliable technology for measuring use.

Reasons for Slowing Growth Unclear
Trends in wilderness use present a complex pattern, but our overall conclusion is that use is leveling or declining. The reasons are not clear, but probably include a combination of changes in socio-demographic structure and in social preferences and tastes.

This slowing trend corresponds with forecasts for other outdoor recreation. Clawson (1985), for example, speculates that for the next 25 years outdoor recreation will increase about 4 percent annually, as opposed to the 10 percent of the past 25 years. Jungst and Countryman (1982) project wilderness use to the year 2020 to grow at a rate between 2 and 7 percent, depending on the prediction model used and the assumptions about the independent variables used in the models.

Wilderness use will undoubtedly remain an important form of recreation use in the national forests and national parks. Despite the apparent decline in NPS wilderness use, it remains about 7 percent of total NPS overnight use. As noted earlier, wilderness use in the national forests has increased its share of the total recreation pie, now accounting for more than 5 percent.

IMPLICATIONS OF SLOWING GROWTH IN USE

A Chance to Catch Up
If the changes in wilderness use are real, and if they continue, they suggest some important management implications. Lower rates of use might represent an opportunity for managers to "catch up" with problems that a few years ago looked overwhelming. Not only are growth rates slowing, but trends in the character of use and users also hold promise for reducing impact levels. This includes a shift toward activities having lower impacts (e.g., a shift from horse use to hiking), greater visitor knowledge on how to minimize impact, and a reduction in littering.

The Wilderness Allocation Debate
For years many people have cited rapidly growing recreational use as a reason to designate more wilderness. This reason now appears to be less important. Wilderness has many important values besides recreation: ecosystem protection, scientific research, and vicarious enjoyment. These values will need to be more central in future debates over whether certain lands should be wilderness.

Reconsider Management Policies
Many wilderness management policies were adopted when use was growing rapidly and in anticipation of massive future growth. Use rationing, assigned campsites, length of stay limits, camping setbacks from water, and other policies often adopted in order to head off serious problems before use got out of hand may now merit reconsideration in light of reduced use and possible future declines. Perhaps visitor freedom can be increased and the quality of visitors' experiences thus enhanced.

USE PROJECTIONS

Projections of wilderness recreational use have been limited by poor and noncomparable basic use data, and also by scanty knowledge of the relationship of wilderness use to causal factors. Projections should be viewed with caution and skepticism.

Probably the earliest projection of wilderness use was made in 1961 as part of the USFS National Forest Recreation Survey project (USDA FS 1961). That unpublished projection foresaw a tripling of man-days by 1976 and more than eightfold growth by the year 2000 (table 14.11). This is about a 5-percent average annual rate of increase. The actual reported figure for 1976 was 7,105,600 12-hour visitor-days, compared to a projection of 5,804,000 man-days—a different unit of measure. Although one cannot convert from one unit to the other with precision, the projected 1976 use amounts to roughly 8,500,000 visitor-days. Thus, in 1976 projected use was about 20 percent higher than reported use.

The projection technique was based on simple assumptions, with no supporting research (there was almost no recreation research at the time). The procedure required projections of population, income, leisure, and travel, variables that are almost as hard to project as recreation use itself. The "independent variables" also are obviously not independent of one another, which creates problems for common multivariate statistical procedures.

At almost the same time, wilderness use was

projected as part of the Outdoor Recreation Resources Review Commission (ORRRC 1962) studies. The commission also worked only with USFS data (no wildernesses were managed by any other agency before 1964). These projected rates of increase were similar to those of the USFS study (table 14.10). This is surprising because the projection procedures were quite different. Using a regression model, per capita use was related to income, based on man-days reported for USFS wildernesses and primitive areas from 1947 to 1959. These predictions of per capita use were multiplied by projected population.

Almost 20 years elapsed before other wilderness use projections were developed in response to Resource Planning Act (RPA) requirements. Three projection studies were published in 1982 and 1983, all of them using more advanced statistical techniques than the early studies. Jungst and Countryman (1982) developed several models, with resulting projected average annual rates of increase of 2.6 percent to 7.2 percent to the year 2020. This wide range reflects the uncertainty of projections. Although the difference between 2.6 and 7.2 may not seem large, in a 40-year period, 2.6 percent results in less than a tripling of use, while 7.2 percent results in about a sixteenfold increase.

Hof and Kaiser (1983) did not project wilderness use itself, but included several activities that probably parallel wilderness use, particularly dispersed primitive camping. Their approach involved estimating per capita participation, using various socioeconomic and supply variables in a regression model, and applying the equation using high, medium, and low projected values for the independent variables. Primitive camping was projected to increase from a 1977 base of 100 to 155, 205, and 311 by the year 2030 in the low, medium, and high scenarios, respectively. These indices translate to annual average rates of growth ranging from less than 1 percent to slightly more than 2 percent.

It is clear that we have limited capabilities to project wilderness use. The handful of studies agree that use will increase but do not agree on rates of increase. None predicted the slowing or declines seen in recent years.

That wilderness use grows slowly or declines moderately does not imply a decline in the value of wilderness. Although many people have used past increases in use as an easy argument for more wilderness or larger budgets for management, slackening use can help solve crowding and impact problems and increase the effectiveness of improved management. Good results from management are less likely to be buried by ever-increasing use and proliferation of problems. This respite should motivate us to increase our efforts to manage and protect wilderness.

SUMMARY

Managing wilderness depends upon understanding all of the varied uses it receives because most wilderness management is use management. Some uses depend on wilderness, but others just take place there. Probably recreation is the most obvious use, but other uses include: commercial recreation; indirect, offsite uses; scientific uses; education uses; therapeutic uses; personal development uses; and a variety of commodity uses such as mining, oil and gas production, logging in a few special cases, water storage, and grazing.

Recreation use presents major challenges to wilderness managers. Although more is known about recreational use than most other wilderness uses, even basic measures of how much use occurs often are low in accuracy. Many use measurement methods are used: use counts at a sample of access points and days; electronic trail traffic counters; automatic movie cameras; self-registration; visitor permits; and more or less educated guesses. Recreational use is reported in many units, but visitor-days (USFS) and overnight stays (NPS) are most common. Unfortunately, they are not comparable or convertible with much accuracy. The 329 USFS wildernesses report about 11 million visitor-days and NPS wilderness probably receives about 3 million visitor-days. BLM and FWS wilderness are much less used.

Most wilderness visits are short, with day-use predominating in many areas. In recent years, visits have tended to become a little shorter. Parties visiting wilderness usually are small, most often two to four people, and have become smaller over the years. The most common method of travel in almost all areas is hiking, with a few exceptions. Activities are varied. Fishing, photography, nature study, and swimming are common in many areas. Summer is the main use season, with exceptions mainly in the south and southwest, at low elevations. Winter use in the north and at high elevations is growing. Many areas have sharp weekend peaks in use. Most visitors are in family groups, with groups of friends usually the next most common. Organized groups (clubs, etc.) are scarce. Visitors to typical wildernesses come from all over the country, but most live relatively close to the area visited. Wilderness recreational use is distributed very unevenly. Some wildernesses, entry points, trails and campsites are heavily used, while many others have little use. A completely even

distribution is not possible and not desirable, but, in many areas, use probably is too uneven.

Although there is a common stereotype of wilderness visitors as young, wealthy, athletic, out-of-state, big city residents, the facts are largely different. An accurate picture of wilderness visitors, or "customers," is much like market research, and it is needed for both policy and management decisions.

Visitors are younger than the general population, but many are older. Age patterns have changed little in recent years. Limited data suggest little difference in physical condition. About one-fourth of wilderness visitors are female, but this proportion has increased over time. Visitors are only slightly more likely to be urban residents than are nonvisitors. Urban resident visitors often grew up in more rural settings, however. Wilderness visitors are moderately above average in income, as are most types of outdoor recreationists. Professional-technical occupations are very common. The single most distinguishing socio-economic characteristic of wilderness visitors is a high level of education. Membership in wilderness–oriented clubs is low.

Trends in amount of use have changed greatly over the years. In the 1940s, 1950s, and most of the 1960s, use increased rapidly, but, in later years, the rate of growth, while still high, has gradually slowed. In the 1980s, use finally levelled off and even declined in many places, more in NPS areas than USFS wildernesses. Many factors may account for the shift, but changing age structure and changing interests and preferences probably are the main causes. Projections of future use are scarce and vary widely. Slow growth or declines in wilderness recreational use do not mean wilderness is less valuable or that wilderness management is becoming less important.

STUDY QUESTIONS

1. Why is understanding wilderness use important for wilderness management?
2. What are the important *non*recreational uses of wilderness? Which ones are substantially wilderness dependent?
3. What are the different methods employed to measure recreation use of wilderness? What strengths and weaknesses does each method have?
4. In what ways is wilderness recreational use unevenly distributed? What are the major management implications of this uneven use?
5. What are the main characteristics of wilderness recreational use in terms of lengths of stay, party size, method of travel, activities, social groups, and visitor residence?

6. What are the major characteristics of wilderness visitors? What is the single most distinguishing socioeconomic characteristic?
7. How are trends in wilderness recreational use shifting? How should managers respond to these trends?

REFERENCES

Billings, Ronald F. 1986. Coping with forest insect pests in southern wilderness areas, with emphasis on the southern pine beetle. In: Kulhavy, David L.; Conner, Richard N., eds. Wilderness and natural areas in the Eastern United States: a management challenge. Nacogdoches, TX: Stephen F. Austin University, School of Forestry, Center for Applied Studies: 120-125.

Brown, Perry J.; Schomaker, John H. 1974. Final report on criteria for potential wilderness campsites. Unpublished paper on file at: U.S. Department of Agriculture, Forest Service, Intermountain Research Station, Forestry Sciences Laboratory, Missoula, MT.

Bryan, Hobson. 1979. Conflicts in the great outdoors: toward understanding and managing for diverse sportsmen preferences. Social Study No. 4. University, AL: University of Alabama, Bureau of Public Administration. 98 p.

Burch, William R., Jr. 1969. The social circles of leisure: competing explanations. Journal of Leisure Research. 1(2): 125-147.

Burch, William R., Jr. 1974. In democracy is the preservation of wilderness. Appalachia. 40(2): 90-101.

Burch, William R., Jr.; Wenger, Wiley D., Jr. 1967. The social characteristics of participants in three styles of family camping. Res. Pap. PNW-48. Portland, OR: U.S. Department of Agriculture, Forest Service, Pacific Northwest Forest and Range Experiment Station. 29 p.

Butler, Lisa Mathis; Roberts, Rebecca S. 1986. Use of wilderness areas for research. In: Lucas, Robert C., compiler. Proceedings—national wilderness research conference: current research; 1985 July 23-26; Fort Collins, CO. Gen. Tech. Rep. INT-212. Ogden, UT: U.S. Department of Agriculture, Forest Service, Intermountain Research Station: 398-405.

Carpenter, M. Ralph; Bowhis, Donald R. 1976. Attitudes toward fishing and fisheries management of users in Desolation Wilderness, California. California Fish and Game. 62(3): 168-178.

Cicchetti, Charles J.; Freeman, A. Myrick, III. 1971. Option demand and consumer surplus: further comment. Quarterly Journal of Economics. 85(8): 528-539.

Clawson, Marion. 1963. Land and water for recreation: opportunities, problems, and policies. Chicago: Rand McNally. 144 p.

Clawson, Marion. 1985. Outdoor recreation: twenty-five years of history, twenty-five years of projection. Leisure Sciences. 7(1): 73-100.

Cordell, H. Ken; Hendee, John C. 1982. Renewable resources recreation in the United States: supply, demand, and critical policy issues. Washington, DC: American Forestry Association. 88 p.

Davis, George D. 1980. The case for wilderness diversity. American Forests. 86(8): 25-27, 60-63.

Davis, George D. 1987. Ecosystem representation as criterion for world wilderness designation. Paper prepared

for the Wild Wings Foundation and presented at the World Wilderness Congress; 1987 September 12-18; Denver and Estes Park, CO.

DeGraff, Ernest P., Jr. 1983. An analysis of wilderness permit administration for rationing use on the Inyo National Forest. Unpublished paper prepared for the Recreation Short Course, Department of Recreation and Park Administration, Clemson University, SC. On file at: Clemson University; Inyo National Forest, Bishop, CA; and U.S. Department of Agriculture, Forest Service, Intermountain Research Station, Forestry Sciences Laboratory, Missoula, MT.

Dick, R.; Oltremari, J.; Sheppard, D.; Wilcox, A. 1972. Wilderness as a classroom—a preliminary report. Unpublished paper prepared for class, Forest Resources 456, University of Washington. On file at: U.S. Department of Agriculture, Forest Service, Intermountain Research Station, Forestry Sciences Laboratory, Missoula, MT.

Driver, B. L.; Nash, Roderick; Haas, Glenn. 1987. Wilderness benefits: a state-of-knowledge review. In: Lucas, Robert C., compiler. Proceedings—national wilderness research conference: issues, state-of-knowledge, future directions; 1985 July 23-26; Fort Collins, CO. Gen. Tech. Rep. INT-220. Ogden, UT: U.S. Department of Agriculture, Forest Service, Intermountain Research Station: 294-319.

Dyrness, C. T.; Franklin, Jerry F.; Maser, Chris; Stanton, A. Cook; Hall, James D.; Faxon, Glenda. 1975. Research natural area needs in the Pacific Northwest: a contribution to land-use planning. Gen. Tech. Rep. PNW-38. Portland, OR: U.S. Department of Agriculture, Forest Service, Pacific Northwest Forest and Range Experiment Station. 231 p.

Elsner, Gary H. 1985. Recreation use trends: a Forest Service perspective. In: Wood, James D., Jr., ed. Proceedings—national outdoor recreation trends symposium II; 1985 February 25-27; Myrtle Beach, SC. Atlanta, GA: U.S. Department of the Interior, National Park Service, Southeast Regional Office: 143-154. Vol. II.

English, Donald B. K.; Cordell, H. Ken. 1985. A cohort-centric analysis of outdoor recreation participation changes. In: Watson, Alan E., ed. Proceedings: southeastern recreation research conference; 1985 February 28-March 1; Myrtle Beach, SC. Statesboro, GA: Georgia Southern College, Department of Recreation and Leisure Services: 93-110.

Evans, Kent E. 1986. Indian Mounds Wilderness Area: perceived wilderness qualities and impacts of oil and gas development. In: Kulhavy, David L.; Conner, Richard N., eds. Wilderness and natural areas in the Eastern United States: a management challenge. Nacogdoches, TX: Stephen F. Austin University, School of Forestry, Center for Applied Studies: 156-165.

Fisher, Anthony; Krutilla, John V. 1972. Determination of optimal capacity of resource-based recreation facilities. Natural Resources Journal. 12(3): 417-444.

Foster, John D. 1976. Bureau of Land Management primitive areas—are they counterfeit wilderness? Natural Resources Journal. 16(3): 621-663.

Franklin, Jerry F. 1987. Wilderness ecosystem research—a scientific perspective. In: Lucas, Robert C., compiler. 1987. Proceedings—national wilderness research conference: issues, state-of-knowledge, future directions;

1985 July 23-26; Fort Collins, CO. Gen. Tech. Rep. INT-220. Ogden, UT: U.S. Department of Agriculture, Forest Service, Intermountain Research Station: 42-46.

Ghiselin, John. 1973-74. Wilderness and the survival of species. Living Wilderness. 37(124): 22-27.

Gibson, Peter M. 1979. Therapeutic aspects of wilderness programs: a comprehensive literature review. Therapeutic Recreation Journal. 13(2): 21-33.

Haas, Glenn E.; Herman, Eric; Walsh, Richard. 1986. Wilderness values. Natural Areas Journal. 6(2): 37-43.

Hanson, Robert A. 1977. An outdoor challenge program as a means of enhancing mental health. In: Children, nature and the urban environment: Proceedings of a symposium-fair; 1975 May 19-23; Washington, DC. Gen. Tech. Rep. NE-30. Upper Darby, PA: U.S. Department of Agriculture, Forest Service, Northeastern Forest Experiment Station: 171-173.

Hays, John. 1974. Mandatory backcountry permits—an investigation into noncompliance in North Cascades National Park—summer 1974. Unpublished paper on file at: North Cascades National Park, Sedro Wooley, WA.

Hendee, John C. 1984. Public opinion and what foresters should do about it. Journal of Forestry. 82(6): 340-344.

Hendee, John C.; Lucas, Robert C. 1973. Mandatory wilderness permits: a necessary management tool. Journal of Forestry. 71(4): 206-209.

Hendee, John C.; Roggenbuck, Joseph W. [n.d.]. Wilderness-related education as a factor increasing demand for wilderness. In: International forest congress 1984: forest resources management—the influence of policy and law; 1984 August 6-7; Quebec City, Quebec, Canada. [Place of publication unknown: publisher unknown]: 273-278.

Hendee, John C.; Catton, William R., Jr.; Marlow, Larry D.; Brockman, C. Frank. 1968. Wilderness users in the Pacific Northwest—their characteristics, values, and management preferences. Res. Pap. PNW-61. Portland, OR: U.S. Department of Agriculture, Forest Service, Pacific Northwest Forest and Range Experiment Station. 92 p.

Hendee, John C.; Gale, Richard P.; Harry, Joseph. 1969. Conservation, politics, and democracy. Journal of Soil and Water Conservation. 24(6): 212-215.

Hendee, John C.; Clark, Roger N.; Dailey, Thomas E. 1977. Fishing and other recreational behavior at high-mountain lakes in Washington State. Res. Note PNW-304. Portland, OR: U.S. Department of Agriculture, Forest Service, Pacific Northwest Forest and Range Experiment Station. 27 p.

Hof, John G.; Kaiser, H. Fred. 1983. Projections of future forest recreation use. Resour. Bull. WO-2. Washington, DC: U.S. Department of Agriculture, Forest Service. 12 p.

Huppuch, Charles; Pellerin, Michael. 1985. Validation of trailside registration stations by volunteers. In: Anderson, L. M., ed. Proceedings: southeastern recreation research conference: 1984 presented papers; 1984 February 16-17; Asheville, NC. Athens, GA: University of Georgia, Institute for Behavioral Research: 23-28.

Johnson, Janet L.; Franklin, Jerry F.; Krebill, Richard G., coords. 1984. Research natural areas: baseline monitoring and management: proceedings of a symposium; 1984 March 21; Missoula, MT. Gen. Tech. Rep. INT-173.

Ogden, UT: U.S. Department of Agriculture, Forest Service, Intermountain Forest and Range Experiment Station. 84 p.

Jubenville, Alan. 1971. A test of differences between wilderness recreation party leaders and party members. Journal of Leisure Research. 3(2): 116-119.

Jungst, Steven E.; Countryman, David W. 1982. Two regression models for projecting future wilderness use. Iowa State Journal of Research. 57(1): 33-41.

Kaplan, Rachel. 1984. Wilderness perception and psychological benefits: an analysis of a continuing program. Leisure Sciences. 6(3): 271-290.

Krutilla, John V. 1967. Conservation reconsidered. American Economic Review. 57(4): 777-786.

Leopold, Aldo. 1941. Wilderness as a land laboratory. The Living Wilderness. 6(3): 3.

Lime, David W. 1975. Sources of congestion and visitor dissatisfaction in the Boundary Waters Canoe Area. In: Third Boundary Waters Canoe Institute proceedings; 1975 May 9; Duluth, MN. Minneapolis, MN: Quetico-Superior Foundation: 68-82.

Lime, David W.; Buchman, Roland G. 1974. Putting wilderness permit information to work. Journal of Forestry. 72(10): 622-626.

Lime, David W.; Lorence, Grace A. 1974. Improving estimates of wilderness use from mandatory travel permits. Res. Pap. NC-101. St. Paul, MN: U.S. Department of Agriculture, Forest Service, North Central Forest Experiment Station. 7 p.

Lucas, Robert C. 1964. Recreational use of the Quetico-Superior Area. Res. Pap. LS-8. St. Paul, MN: U.S. Department of Agriculture, Forest Service, Lake States Forest Experiment Station. 49 p.

Lucas, Robert C. 1965. The importance of fishing as an attraction and activity in the Quetico-Superior Area. Res. Note LS-61. St. Paul, MN: U.S. Department of Agriculture, Forest Service, Lake States Forest Experiment Station. 3 p.

Lucas, Robert C. 1975. Low compliance rates at unmanned trail registers. Res. Note INT-200. Ogden, UT: U.S. Department of Agriculture, Forest Service, Intermountain Forest and Range Experiment Station. 6 p.

Lucas, Robert C. 1980. Use patterns and visitor characteristics, attitudes, and preferences in nine wilderness and other roadless areas. Res. Pap. INT-253. Ogden, UT: U.S. Department of Agriculture, Forest Service, Intermountain Forest and Range Experiment Station. 89 p.

Lucas, Robert C. 1983. Low and variable visitor compliance rates at voluntary trail registers. Res. Note INT-326. Ogden, UT: U.S. Department of Agriculture, Forest Service, Intermountain Forest and Range Experiment Station. 5 p.

Lucas, Robert C. 1985. Visitor characteristics, attitudes, and use patterns in the Bob Marshall Wilderness Complex, 1970-82. Res. Pap. INT-345. Ogden, UT: U.S. Department of Agriculture, Forest Service, Intermountain Research Station. 32 p.

Lucas, Robert C.; Oltman, Jerry L. 1971. Survey sampling wilderness visitors. Journal of Leisure Research. 3(1): 28-43.

Lucas, Robert C.; Schreuder, Hans T.; James, George A. 1971. Wilderness use estimation: a pilot test of sampling

procedures on the Mission Mountains Primitive Area. Res. Pap. INT-109. Ogden, UT: U.S. Department of Agriculture, Forest Service, Intermountain Forest and Range Experiment Station. 44 p.

Lucas, Robert C.; Kovalicky, Thomas J. 1981. Self-issued wilderness permits as a use measurement system. Res. Pap. INT-270. Ogden, UT: U.S. Department of Agriculture, Forest Service, Intermountain Forest and Range Experiment Station. 18 p.

Marcin, Thomas C.; Lime, David W. 1977. Our changing population structure: what will it mean for future outdoor recreation use? In: Hughes, Jay M.; Lloyd, R. Duane, compilers. Outdoor recreation: advances in application of economics—proceedings of a national symposium; 1974 November; New Orleans, LA. Gen. Tech. Rep. W0-2. Washington, DC: U.S. Department of Agriculture, Forest Service: 42-53.

Marnell, Leo F. 1977. Methods for counting river recreation users. In: Proceedings—river recreation management and research symposium; 1977 January 24-27; Minneapolis, MN. Gen. Tech. Rep. NC-28. St. Paul, MN: U.S. Department of Agriculture, Forest Service, North Central Forest Experiment Station: 77-82.

McCool, Stephen F. 1985. Does wilderness designation lead to increased recreational use? Journal of Forestry. 83(1): 39-41.

Merriam, L. C., Jr.; [and others]. 1973. Newly developed campsites in the Boundary Waters Canoe Area: a study of five years' use. Station Bulletin 511. For. Ser. 14. St. Paul, MN: University of Minnesota, Agricultural Experiment Station. 27 p.

Montana Department of Natural Resources and Conservation. 1973. Final environmental impact statement: Hungry Horse weather modification project. Helena, MT; November 12. 46 p.

Murray, Judith Buckley. 1974. Appalachian Trail users in the southern National Forests: their characteristics, attitudes, and management preferences. Res. Pap. SE-116. Asheville, NC: U.S. Department of Agriculture, Forest Service, Southeast Forest Experiment Station. 19 p.

Norgaard, Judith King: Kovalicky, Tom; Stankey, George H. 1979. Wilderness myths: some falsehoods are put to rest. Montana Magazine. 9(6): 53-56.

Outdoor Recreation Resources Review Commission [ORRRC]. 1962. Wilderness recreation—a report on resources, values, and problems. ORRRC Study Rep. 3. Washington, DC: U.S. Government Printing Office. 352 p.

Petersen, Margaret E. 1981. Trends in recreational use of National Forest wilderness. Res. Note INT-319. Ogden, UT: U.S. Department of Agriculture, Forest Service, Intermountain Forest and Range Experiment Station. 3 p.

Petersen, Margaret E. 1985. Improving voluntary registration through location and design of trail registration stations. Res. Pap. INT-336. Ogden, UT: U.S. Department of Agriculture, Forest Service, Intermountain Forest and Range Experiment Station. 8 p.

Polzin, Paul. 1987. [Personal communication]. August. Missoula, MT: University of Montana, Bureau of Business and Economic Research.

President's Commission on Americans Outdoors. 1986. Report and recommendations to the President of the United States. Washington, DC: U.S. Government

Printing Office. 210 p.

Roggenbuck, Joseph W.; Lucas, Robert C. 1987. Wilderness use and user characteristics: a state-of-knowledge review. In: Lucas, Robert C., compiler. Proceedings—national wilderness research conference: issues, state-of-knowledge, future directions; 1985 July 23-26; Fort Collins, CO. Gen. Tech. Rep. INT-220. Ogden, UT: U.S. Department of Agriculture, Forest Service, Intermountain Research Station: 204-245.

Schmidt, Wyman C.; Dufour, W. P. "Buster." 1975. Building a natural area system for Montana. Western Wildlands. 2(1): 20-29.

Seagrave, Sterling. 1976. Scientists learn from wild plants. BioScience. 26(2): 153-154, 156.

Stankey, George H. 1971. Myths in wilderness decision making. Journal of Soil and Water Conservation. 25(5): 183-188.

Tombaugh, Larry W. 1971. External benefits of natural environments. In: Larson, E. H., ed. Recreation: symposium proceedings; 1971 October 12-14; Syracuse, NY. Upper Darby, PA: U.S. Department of Agriculture, Forest Service, Northeastern Forest Experiment Station: 73-77.

U.S. Department of Agriculture, Forest Service. 1961. Table G, summary of NFRS, Forest Service summary, NFRS Form No. 10, in appendix 18, National Forest Recreation Survey (NFRS). Unpublished report on file at: U.S. Department of Agriculture, Forest Service, Intermountain Research Station, Forestry Sciences Laboratory, Missoula, MT.

U.S. Department of the Interior, Bureau of Land Management. 1986. Wilderness management plan: Bisti Wilderness, New Mexico. BLM-NM-PT-86-010-4332. Albuquerque, NM. 76 p.

U.S. Department of the Interior, Bureau of Outdoor Recreation. 1975. A glossary of terms used by the Bureau of Outdoor Recreation. Washington, DC. 32 p.

U.S. Department of the Interior, Bureau of Reclamation, Division of Atmospheric Water Resources Management. 1974. Position paper on weather modification over wilderness area and other conservation areas. Denver, CO. 29 p.

Utter, Jack. 1983. Opinions of Montanans on wilderness and resource development. Journal of Forestry. 81(7): 435-437.

Van Horne, Merle J.; Szwak, Laura B.; Randall, Sharon A. 1985. Outdoor recreation activity trends—insights from the 1982-83 nationwide recreation survey. In: Wood, James D., Jr., ed. Proceedings—national outdoor recreation trends symposium II; 1985 February 25-27; Myrtle Beach, SC. Atlanta, GA: U.S. Department of the Interior, National Park Service, Southeast Regional Office: 109-130.

van Wagtendonk, Jan W. 1981. The effect of use limits on backcountry visitation trends in Yosemite National Park. Leisure Sciences. 4(3): 311-323.

Vaux, H. J., Jr. 1975. The distribution of income among wilderness users. Journal of Leisure Research. 7(1): 29-37.

Walsh, Richard G.; Loomis, John B.; Gillman, Richard A. 1986. How much wilderness to protect? In: Lucas, Robert C., compiler. Proceedings—national wilderness research conference: current research; 1985 July 23-26; Fort Collins, CO. Gen. Tech. Rep. INT-212. Ogden, UT: U.S. Department of Agriculture, Forest Service, Intermountain Research Station: 370-376.

Washburne, Randel F.; Cole, David N. 1983. Problems and practices in wilderness management: a survey of managers. Res. Pap. INT-304. Ogden, UT: U.S. Department of Agriculture, Forest Service, Intermountain Forest and Range Experiment Station. 56 p.

Wenger, Wiley D., Jr.; Gregersen, Hans M. 1964. The effect of nonresponse on representativeness of wilderness-trail register information. Res. Pap. PNW-17. Portland, OR: U.S. Department of Agriculture, Forest Service, Pacific Northwest Forest and Range Experiment Station. 20 p.

Wiesner, Robert R.; Sharkey, Brian J. 1973. Some characteristics of wilderness backpackers. Perceptual Motor Skills. 36(3): 876-878.

Wilkinson, Charles F.; Anderson, H. Michael. 1985. Wilderness. Oregon Law Review. 64(1&2): 334-370.

ACKNOWLEDGMENTS

Edward Bloedel, Division of Recreation, USFS, Washington, DC (at the time of review—now recreation staff, Sawtooth National Forest, ID).

Keith H. Corrigall, Chief, Branch of Wilderness Resources, BLM, Washington, DC.

Dr. Glenn Haas, Professor, Department of Recreation Resources and Landscape Architecture, Colorado State University, Fort Collins.

Robert Jacobsen, Superintendent (retired), Shenandoah National Park, VA.

Dr. David Lime, Professor, College of Natural Resources, University of Minnesota, St. Paul.

Margaret Petersen, USFS Regional Wilderness and Recreation staff, Portland, OR.

Dr. Joseph Roggenbuck, Professor, Department of Forestry, Virginia Polytechnic Institute and State University, Blacksburg.

Dr. George Stankey, Professor, College of Forestry, Oregon State University, Corvalis.

Table 14.3. Use intensities in USFS wilderness and primitive areas, 1986, by states.

Wilderness	Visitor-days	Gross acres	Visitor-days per acre
Alabama			
Cheaha	5,600	6,780	0.83
Sipsey	15,000	12,726	1.18
State totals	**20,600**	**19,506**	**1.06**
Alaska			
Admiralty Island National Monument	150,700	969,564	0.16
Coronation Island	600	19,232	0.03
Endicott River	500	98,729	0.01
Maurille Islands	500	4,937	0.10
Misty Fjords National Monument	188,100	2,142,907	0.09
Petersburg Creek-Duncan Salt Chuck	3,200	46,849	0.07
Russell Fjord	2,900	348,701	0.01
South Baranof	40,800	319,568	0.13
South Prince of Wales	1,300	91,018	0.01
Stikine-LeConte	14,800	449,951	0.03
Tebenkof Bay	3,300	66,839	0.05
Tracy Arm-Fords Terror	35,600	653,179	0.05
Warren Island	500	11,181	0.04
West Chichagof-Yakobi	144,600	265,529	0.54
State totals	**587,400**	**5,488,184**	**0.11**
Arizona			
Apache Creek	1,000	5,420	0.18
Bear Wallow	3,000	11,080	0.27
Blue Range (Primitive Area)	13,200	175,112	0.08
Castle Creek	1,300	26,030	0.05
Cedar Bench	1,600	14,950	0.11
Chiricahua	11,700	87,700	0.13
Escudilla	2,200	5,200	0.42
Fossil Springs	NR[1]	11,550	—
Four Peaks	6,600	53,500	0.12
Galiuro	9,300	76,317	0.12
Granite Mountain	2,400	9,800	0.24
Hellsgate	3,400	36,780	0.09
Juniper Mesa	1,700	7,600	0.22
Kachina Peaks	NR	18,200	—
Kanab Creek	NR	68,250	—
Kendrick Mountain	NR	6,510	—
Mazatzal	34,600	252,016	0.14
Miller Peak	6,100	20,190	0.30
Mount Baldy	12,300	7,079	1.74
Mount Wrightson	45,500	25,260	1.80
Munds Mountain	NR	18,150	—
Pajarita	8,400	7,420	1.13
Pine Mountain	7,800	20,061	0.39
Pusch Ridge	88,900	56,933	1.56
Red Rock-Secret Mountain	NR	43,950	—
Rincon Mountain	37,500	38,590	0.97
Saddle Mountain	NR	40,600	—
Salome	3,000	18,950	0.16
Salt River Canyon	13,300	32,800	0.41
Santa Teresa	5,300	26,780	0.20
Sierra Ancha	6,200	20,850	0.30
Strawberry Crater	NR	10,140	—
Superstition	98,200	159,780	0.61
Sycamore Canyon	33,700	55,942	0.60
West Clear Creek	NR	13,600	—

Table 14.3. (cont.)

Wilderness	Visitor-days	Gross acres	Visitor-days per acre
Wet Beaver	NR	6,700	—
Woodchute	2,100	5,600	0.38
State totals	**460,300**	**1,257,740²**	**0.37**
Arkansas			
Black Fork Mountain	800	7,568	0.11
Caney Creek	11,500	14,460	0.80
Dry Creek	2,700	6,310	0.43
East Fork	1,500	10,777	0.14
Flatside	3,600	10,105	0.36
Hurricane Creek	1,100	15,177	0.07
Leatherwood	1,500	16,956	0.09
Poteau Mountain	3,400	10,884	0.31
Richland Creek	1,600	11,822	0.14
Upper Buffalo	1,300	12,046	0.11
State totals	**29,000**	**116,105**	**0.25**
California			
Agua Tibia	7,000	15,933	0.44
Ansel Adams (originally Minarets)	159,800	228,671	0.70
Bucks Lake	11,600	21,000	0.55
Caribou	10,000	20,625	0.48
Carson-Iceberg	33,900	160,000	0.21
Castle Crags	7,400	7,300	1.01
Chanchelulla	4,700	8,200	0.57
Cucamonga	34,600	12,781	2.71
Desolation	227,500	63,475	3.58
Dick Smith	10,700	65,130	0.16
Dinkey Lakes	24,700	30,000	0.82
Domeland	4,300	94,686	0.05
Emigrant	59,900	112,180	0.53
Golden Trout	69,600	305,464	0.23
Granite Chief	54,600	25,000	2.18
Hauser	1,000	8,000	0.13
Hoover	49,000	48,622	1.01
Ishi	8,400	41,600	0.20
Jennie Lakes	30,800	10,500	2.93
John Muir	451,400	581,053	0.78
Kaiser	14,400	22,700	0.63
Machesna Mountain	1,800	19,880	0.09
Marble Mountain	67,500	242,464	0.28
Mokelumne	25,400	104,461	0.24
Monarch	1,300	45,000	0.03
Mount Shasta	28,800	37,000	0.78
North Fork	2,800	8,100	0.35
Pine Creek	1,000	13,100	0.08
Red Buttes[3]	1,100	16,150	0.07
Russian	13,400	12,000	1.12
San Gabriel	23,500	36,118	0.65
San Gorgonio	190,600	56,749	3.36
San Jacinto	33,400	32,850	1.02
San Mateo Canyon	20,000	39,540	0.51
San Rafael	97,900	150,740	0.65
Santa Lucia	30,300	21,704	1.40
Santa Rosa	5,300	20,160	0.26
Sheep Mountain	6,400	43,377	0.15
Siskiyou	41,200	153,000	0.27

Table 14.3. (cont.)

Wilderness	Visitor-days	Gross acres	Visitor-days per acre
Snow Mountain	16,100	37,000	0.44
South Sierra	2,100	63,000	0.03
South Warner	15,300	70,500	0.22
Thousand Lakes	18,200	16,335	1.11
Trinity Alps	248,800	495,377	0.50
Ventana	29,600	167,325	0.18
Yolla Bolly-Middle Eel	33,400	146,528	0.23
State totals	**2,230,500**	**3,931,378**	**0.57**
Colorado			
Big Blue	29,500	98,585	0.30
Cache La Poudre	3,700	9,308	0.40
Collegiate Peaks	144,900	167,994	0.86
Comanche Peak	20,100	66,901	0.30
Eagles Nest	89,900	133,915	0.67
Flat Tops	121,300	235,230	0.52
Holy Cross	124,600	123,410	1.01
Hunter-Fryingpan	10,400	74,450	0.14
Indian Peaks	62,700	70,894	0.88
La Garita	13,000	103,986	0.13
Lizard Head	12,700	41,496	0.31
Lost Creek	49,600	105,451	0.47
Maroon Bells-Snowmass	40,600	183,871	0.22
Mount Evans	75,800	74,401	1.02
Mount Massive	35,000	28,047	1.25
Mount Sneffels	6,600	16,527	0.40
Mount Zirkel	73,300	139,898	0.52
Neota	3,900	9,924	0.39
Never Summer	56,600	14,100	4.01
Platte River[3]	NR	770	—
Raggeds	9,300	59,930	0.16
Rawah	7,700	73,886	0.10
South San Juan	4,600	127,690	0.04
Weminuche	175,000	463,678	0.38
West Elk	89,400	176,412	0.51
State totals	**1,260,200**	**2,599,984**[2]	**0.48**
Florida			
Alexander Springs	3,600	7,700	0.47
Big Gum Swamp	10,200	13,600	0.75
Billies Bay	2,200	3,120	0.71
Bradwell Bay	1,600	24,602	0.07
Juniper Prairie	6,800	13,260	0.51
Little Lake George	200	2,500	0.08
Mud Swamp/New River	700	7,800	0.09
State totals	**25,300**	**72,582**	**0.35**
Georgia			
Big Frog[3]	300	83	3.61
Cohutta[3]	73,800	32,307	2.28
Ellicott Rock[3]	400	2,181	0.18
Southern Nantahala[3]	3,000	12,439	0.24
State totals	**77,500**	**47,010**	**1.65**
Idaho			
Frank Church-River of No Return	411,500	2,370,676	0.17
Gospel Hump	26,300	206,000	0.13

Table 14.3. (cont.)

Wilderness	Visitor-days	Gross acres	Visitor-days per acre
Gospel Hump	411,500	2,370,676	0.17
Hills Canyon[3]	26,300	206,000	0.13
Sawtooth	44,900	217,088	0.21
Selway-Bitterroot[2]	98,200	1,089,238	0.09
State totals	**601,300**	**3,967,102**	**0.15**
Indiana			
Charles C. Deam	30,100	12,953	2.32
Kentucky			
Beaver Creek	2,800	4,791	0.58
Clifty	NR	13,300	—
State totals	**2,800**	**4,791[2]**	**0.58**
Louisiana			
Kisatchie Hills	2,900	8,700	0.33
Minnesota			
Boundary Waters Canoe Area	1,031,100	1,086,954	0.95
Mississippi			
Black Creek	4,000	4,560	0.88
Leaf	1,800	940	1.91
State totals	**5,800**	**5,500**	**1.05**
Missouri			
Bell Mountain	1,200	9,027	0.13
Devils Backbone	79,500	6,595	12.05
Hercules-Glades	11,200	12,315	0.91
Irish	3,000	16,500	0.18
Paddy Creek	NR	6,888	—
Piney Creek	8,400	8,142	1.03
Rockpile Mountain	1,100	4,131	0.27
State totals	**104,400**	**56,710[2]**	**1.84**
Montana			
Absaroka-Beartooth[3]	304,300	921,465	0.33
Anaconda-Pintler	40,100	158,516	0.25
Bob Marshall	146,200	1,009,356	0.14
Cabinet Mountains[4]	30,800	94,272	0.33
Gates of the Mountain[4]	3,300	28,562	0.12
Great Bear	37,800	286,700	0.13
Lee Metcalf	35,400	250,297	0.14
Mission Mountains	11,000	73,877	0.15
Rattlesnake	3,700	33,000	0.11
Scapegoat	23,400	239,936	0.10
Selway-Bitterroot[3]	64,900	251,443	0.26
Welcome Creek	1,900	28,135	0.07
State totals	**702,800**	**3,375,559**	**0.21**
Nevada			
Jarbidge	11,300	64,827	0.17
New Hampshire			
Great Gulf	23,500	5,552	4.23
Pemigewasset	22,600	45,000	0.50
Presidential Range-Dry River	11,100	27,380	0.41
Sandwich Range	3,400	25,000	0.14
State totals	**60,600**	**102,932**	**0.59**

Table 14.3 (cont.)

Wilderness	Visitor-days	Gross acres	Visitor-days per acre
New Mexico			
Aldo Leopold	12,600	202,016	0.06
Apache Kid	3,400	44,650	0.08
Blue Range	3,900	29,304	0.13
Capitan Mountains	7,500	35,822	0.21
Chama River Canyon	16,400	50,300	0.33
Cruces Basin	2,400	18,000	0.13
Dome	9,600	5,200	1.85
Gila	61,400	558,065	0.11
Latir Peak	2,600	20,000	0.13
Manzano Mountain	10,800	37,195	0.29
Pecos	220,500	223,333	0.99
San Pedro Parks	15,900	41,132	0.39
Sandia Mountain	50,700	38,386	1.32
Wheeler Peak	5,800	19,663	0.29
White Mountain	12,400	48,873	0.25
Withington	900	19,000	0.05
State totals	**436,800**	**1,390,939**	**0.31**
North Carolina			
Birkhead Mountains	11,400	4,790	2.38
Catfish Lake South	800	7,600	0.11
Ellicott Rock[3]	3,000	4,022	0.75
Joyce Kilmer-Slickrock[3]	55,800	13,181	4.23
Linville Gorge	34,100	10,975	3.11
Middle Prong	8,600	7,900	1.09
Pocosin	400	11,000	0.04
Pond Pine	600	1,860	0.32
Sheep Ridge	1,200	9,540	0.13
Shining Rock	68,300	18,450	3.70
Southern Nantahala[3]	4,500	10,900	0.41
State totals	**188,700**	**100,218**	**1.88**
Oregon			
Badger Creek	3,000	24,000	0.13
Black Canyon	1,200	13,400	0.09
Boulder Creek	2,800	19,100	0.15
Bridge Creek	500	5,400	0.09
Bull of the Woods	9,300	34,900	0.27
Columbia	3,500	39,000	0.09
Cummins Creek	500	9,300	0.05
Diamond Peak	8,900	52,337	0.17
Drift Creek	6,600	5,800	1.14
Eagle Cap	176,300	360,275	0.49
Gearhart Mountain	7,400	22,809	0.32
Grassy Knob	500	17,200	0.03
Hells Canyon[3]	5,000	130,095	0.04
Kalmiopsis	12,700	179,700	0.07
Menagerie	2,800	4,800	0.58
Middle Santiam	2,300	7,500	0.31
Mill Creek	4,300	17,400	0.25
Monument Rock	5,200	19,800	0.26
Mount Hood	46,400	47,160	0.98
Mount Jefferson	103,500	107,008	0.97
Mount Thielsen	5,500	55,100	0.10
Mount Washington	13,100	52,516	0.25
Mountain Lakes	1,500	23,071	0.07
North Fork John Day	58,500	121,400	0.48

Table 14.3 (cont.)

Wilderness	Visitor-days	Gross acres	Visitor-days per acre
North Fork Umatilla	7,000	20,200	0.35
Red Buttes[3]	7,500	3,750	2.00
Rock Creek	300	7,400	0.04
Rogue-Umpqua Divide	7,800	33,200	0.23
Salmon-Huckleberry	34,600	44,600	0.78
Sky Lakes	13,300	116,300	0.11
Strawberry Mountain	17,500	69,350	0.25
Three Sisters	178,400	285,202	0.63
Waldo Lake	8,400	39,200	0.21
Wenaha-Tucannon[3]	29,300	66,417	0.44
Wild Rogue	48,500	36,500	1.33
State totals	**833,900**	**2,091,190**	**0.40**
Pennsylvania			
Allegheny Islands	800	368	2.17
Hickory Creek	1,900	9,337	0.20
State totals	**2,700**	**9,705**	**0.28**
South Carolina			
Ellicott Rock[3]	8,100	2,809	2.88
Hell Hole Bay	100	1,980	0.05
Little Wambaw Swamp	700	5,000	0.14
Wambaw Creek	1,800	1,640	1.10
Wambaw Swamp	700	5,100	0.14
State totals	**11,400**	**16,529**	**0.69**
South Dakota			
Black Elk	36,200	9,824	3.68
Tennessee			
Bald River Gorge	17,400	3,887	4.48
Big Frog[3]	2,700	4,972	0.54
Citico Creek	15,700	16,000	0.98
Cohutta[3]	3,500	1,795	1.95
Gee Creek	4,800	2,493	1.93
Joyce Kilmer-Slickrock[3]	6,400	3,832	1.67
State totals	**50,500**	**32,979**	**1.53**
Texas			
Big Slough	1,600	3,000	0.53
Indian Mounds	1,100	9,946	0.11
Little Lake Creek	1,100	4,000	0.28
Turkey Hill	2,100	5,400	0.39
Upland Island	2,700	12,000	0.23
State totals	**8,600**	**34,346**	**0.25**
Utah			
Ashdown Gorge	600	7,000	0.09
Box-Death Hollow	900	26,000	0.03
Dark Canyon	8,200	45,000	0.18
Deseret Peak	2,400	25,500	0.09
High Uintas	296,100	460,000	0.64
Lone Peak	53,200	30,088	1.77
Mount Naomi	8,000	44,350	0.18
Mount Nebo	34,500	28,000	1.23
Mount Olympus	7,600	16,000	0.48
Mount Timpanogos	47,800	10,750	4.45

Table 14.3 (cont.)

Wilderness	Visitor-days	Gross acres	Visitor-days per acre
Pine Valley Mountain	6,200	50,000	0.12
Twin Peaks	11,800	13,100	0.90
Wellsville Mountain	2,300	23,850	0.10
State totals	**479,600**	**779,638**	**0.62**
Vermont			
Big Branch	2,700	6,720	0.40
Breadloaf	10,500	21,480	0.49
Bristol Cliffs	800	3,738	0.21
George D. Aiken	1,100	5,060	0.22
Lye Brook	5,200	15,680	0.33
Peru Peak	1,600	6,920	0.23
State totals	**21,900**	**59,598**	**0.37**
Virginia			
Beartown	1,600	6,375	0.25
James River Face	3,300	8,903	0.37
Kimberling Creek	1,500	5,580	0.27
Lewis Fork	23,200	5,730	4.05
Little Dry Run	3,100	3,400	0.91
Little Wilson Creek	8,600	3,855	2.23
Mountain Lake	16,900	8,253	2.05
Peters Mountain	9,200	3,326	2.77
Ramseys Draft	5,300	6,725	0.79
Saint Mary's	2,400	10,090	0.24
Thunder Ridge	1,400	2,450	0.57
State totals	**76,500**	**64,687**	**1.18**
Washington			
Alpine Lakes	319,200	306,934	1.04
Boulder River	21,500	49,000	0.44
Buckhorn	18,000	45,817	0.39
Clearwater	4,100	14,300	0.29
Colonel Bob	2,900	12,120	0.24
Glacier Peak	187,700	577,048	0.33
Glacier View	27,900	3,050	9.15
Goat Rocks	123,100	105,023	1.17
Henry M. Jackson	75,700	103,591	0.73
Indian Heaven	11,900	20,650	0.58
Lake Chelan-Sawtooth	59,000	151,564	0.39
Mount Adams	18,900	56,831	0.33
Mount Baker	14,600	117,900	0.12
Mount Skokomish	31,800	15,686	2.03
Noisy-Diobsud	5,500	14,300	0.38
Norse Peak	52,100	50,923	1.02
Pasayten	62,700	530,031	0.12
Salmo-Priest	9,100	41,335	0.22
Tatoosh	21,100	15,720	1.34
The Brothers	32,200	17,239	1.87
Trapper Creek	2,700	6,050	0.45
Wenaha-Tucannon[3]	46,400	111,048	0.42
William O. Douglas	87,100	166,603	0.52
Wonder Mountain	800	2,320	0.34
State totals	**1,236,000**	**2,535,083**	**0.49**

Table 14.3. (cont.)

Wilderness	Visitor-days	Gross acres	Visitor-days per acre
West Virginia			
Cranberry	34,200	35,864	0.95
Dolly Sods	17,000	10,215	1.66
Laurel Fork North	2,400	6,055	0.40
Laurel Fork South	1,800	5,997	0.30
Otter Creek	13,000	20,000	0.65
State totals	**68,400**	**78,131**	**0.88**
Wisconsin			
Blackjack Springs	2,700	5,886	0.46
Headwaters	4,500	20,104	0.22
Porcupine Lake	700	4,235	0.17
Rainbow Lake	1,600	6,583	0.24
Whisker Lake	4,700	7,428	0.63
State totals	**14,200**	**44,236**	**0.32**
Wyoming			
Absaroka-Beartooth[3]	2,700	23,750	0.11
Bridger	198,400	428,169	0.46
Cloud Peak	102,000	195,500	0.52
Encampment River	1,900	10,400	0.18
Fitzpatrick	30,500	198,838	0.15
Gros Ventre	NR	287,000	—
Huston Park	2,200	31,300	0.07
Jedediah Smith	NR	116,535	—
North Absaroka	22,200	350,538	0.06
Platte River[3]	2,000	22,230	0.09
Popo Agie	30,900	101,991	0.30
Savage Run	3,400	14,940	0.23
Teton	98,500	585,468	0.17
Washakie (originally S. Absaroka)	56,300	704,822	0.08
Winegar Hole	NR	14,000	—
State totals	**551,000**	**2,667,946[2]**	**0.21**
Grand totals	**11,249,000[5]**	**32,133,566[2]**	**0.35**

1. NR = Use figure not reported for 1986, often the first year after establishment.
2. Acreage total only includes those areas that reported their use.
3. Areas located in more than one state (figures for entire wilderness), **see information below.**
4. 1985 use; 1986 was not reported.
5. 16 areas did not report their use in 1986.
6. Use in Colorado was not reported for the 770 acres there. Therefore, the visitor-days-per-acre figure probably is somewhat higher than given here.

Absaroka-Beartooth (MT-WY)	307,000	945,215	0.32
Big Frog (GA-TN)	3,000	5,055	0.59
Cohutta (GA-TN)	77,300	34,102	2.27
Ellicott Rock (GA-NC-SC)	11,500	9,012	1.28
Hells Canyon (ID-OR)	25,400	214,195	0.12
Joyce Kilmer-Slickrock (NC-TN)	62,200	17,013	3.66
Platte River (CO-WY)	2,000	23,000	0.09[6]
Red Buttes (CA-OR)	8,600	19,900	0.43
Selway-Bitterroot (ID-MT)	163,100	1,340,681	0.12
Southern Nantahala (GA-NC)	7,500	23,339	0.32
Wenaha-Tucannon (OR-WA)	75,700	117,465	0.64

Managing recreational use of wilderness requires a range of activities—laying out and maintaining trails, providing wilderness rangers, conducting information and education programs, and writing regulations. The most effective management combines an array of activities. A trail crew repairs a wilderness trail. Photo courtesy of John C. Hendee.

15

Wilderness Recreation Management: A General Overview

Robert C. Lucas was lead author for this chapter.

INTRODUCTION

The Wilderness Act (chap. 4) stresses two objectives: maintaining a natural setting and providing a special wilderness experience involving "outstanding opportunities for solitude or a primitive and unconfined type of recreation." But allowing recreational use of a relatively pristine area is in itself a threat to the natural setting, and, if visitor contacts diminish solitude or cause conflicts, use also can be a threat to the wilderness experience. *These objectives—maintaining a natural setting and the wilderness experience—must be achieved without diminishing the wilderness character of the area.* Development, such as paving trails, introducing trample-resistant vegetation around campsites, or providing picnic tables, is inappropriate. Legal constraints within the act, and the spirit of the wilderness idea, limit the use of such improvements and facilities because they reduce naturalness and interfere with primitive experiences. Trail systems are the main exception. Without recourse to a development-oriented approach, wilderness managers must rely primarily on managing visitor use to control unwanted impacts. In fact, most wilderness management is management of recreational use (The Wilderness Society 1984). If trail development and maintenance are considered part of recreational use management, this statement is particularly true.

Chapters 15, 16, and 17 discuss visitor management in reference to the two objectives. Chapter 15 provides a general overview of wilderness recreation management concerns that relate both to managing experiences and ecological impacts from recreational use. It includes the legal context for management, types of use-related problems, managers' and visitors' perceptions of problems, the aspects of use that can be managed, recreation information needs and information gathering, issues related to recreation, and general management approaches. This chapter is meant to set the stage for the next two chapters. Chapter 16 discusses visitor impacts on the environment and suggests methods to prevent or mitigate deterioration. Chapter 17 explores the factors affecting the quality of the wilderness experience and what managers can do to reduce impacts on its quality.

LEGAL CONTEXT FOR RECREATION MANAGEMENT

The Wilderness Act sets constraints for recreation management, as well as the two main objectives just discussed. Constraints affecting recreation management need to be considered in the overall context of Wilderness Act prohibitions and exceptions, briefly reviewed below and discussed further in chapter 4 and by The Wilderness Society (1984). The act also allows some uses in addition to recreation with which managers must deal.

The Wilderness Act prohibits structures or installations, commercial enterprises, permanent or temporary roads, motorboats, motorized equipment, aircraft, or mechanical transport (such as bicycles). The 1975 act establishing 16 wildernesses in the East calls for management in accordance with the 1964 Wilderness Act. All later wilderness designations require management based on the 1964 act, with a few specific exceptions.

The Wilderness Act also contains some specific and limited exceptions to these constraints including: existing private rights; emergencies involving the health and safety of people within a wilderness; fire, insect, and disease control; mineral exploration before 1985; water control structures; access to private inholdings, valid mining claims, and occupancies; commercial operations by outfitters and guides; continuation of established motorboat and aircraft use; and livestock grazing. Many of these exceptions do not apply to the national parks.

Legislation designating individual wildernesses has sometimes modified these exceptions (Browning and others 1988). Established uses, such as mechanized access to operate and maintain an existing dam, have been authorized in certain areas.

The Alaska National Interest Lands Conservation Act of 1980 (ANILCA, P.L. 96-487), discussed in detail in chapter 4, added 56 million acres to the wilderness system. ANILCA specifically incorporates the original Wilderness Act's direction, "except as otherwise expressly provided for." But, because of special conditions in Alaska, ANILCA provides for a number of activities and facilities not permitted in wilderness elsewhere, including continued traditional access by airplanes (fig. 15.1), motorboats, and snowmobiles; continued use of public and private cabins and possible construction of new public cabins; continued subsistence use of fish, wildlife, and plants; and provision of fish production facilities such as fish ladders and hatcheries.

Critically important for wilderness recreation management, the Wilderness Act grants exceptions to most of the prohibitions (except commercial enterprises and permanent roads) for administrative activities. The exceptions are limited to management action "necessary to meet minimum requirements for the administration of the area for the purpose of this Act." This does not give managers a free hand. Any management exception to the act's restrictions must pass a series of stringent tests: the action must be *necessary* to meet just the *minimum requirements* to manage the area for the *purpose of the Wilderness Act.* This purpose is to "assure that an increasing population, accompanied by expanding settlement and growing mechanization, does not occupy and modify all areas within the United States ... to secure ... an enduring resource of wilderness" and to "preserve its wilderness character" while devoting areas to recreational, scenic, scientific, educational, conservation, and historical use of types consistent with wilderness.

This means that management actions, however well intended, cannot be justified just because they are convenient or economical, or because they achieve nonwilderness goals, such as increasing streamflows, increasing numbers of elk, or stopping natural erosion. This is a difficult but critically important challenge for wilderness managers, and many have agonized over decisions whether or not specific actions qualify for the exception (Worf 1987).

DIMENSIONS OF RECREATION MANAGEMENT

The two dimensions, (1) management to *provide visitors opportunities for quality wilderness experiences* and (2) management to *limit the resource site impacts* caused by visitor use, are not separate and distinct. They are intertwined in an intricate web, much like an ecosystem. The interrelations between these two aspects are sometimes subtle and easily overlooked. For example, many resource impacts also affect visitor

Fig. 15.1. Legislation establishing wilderness in Alaska permits activities and facilities usually prohibited elsewhere. Access by airplane is one of the Alaskan exceptions. Photo courtesy of Robert C. Lucas, USFS.

Table 15.1. Five types of problem visitor actions, examples, and general management response.

Type of visitor action	Example	Management response
1. Illegal actions	Motorcycle violation	Law enforcement
2. Careless actions	Littering, nuisance activity (e.g., shouting)	Persuasion, education about impacts, rule enforcement
3. Unskilled actions	Ditching tent	Primarily education about low-impact use practices, some rule enforcement
4. Uninformed actions	Concentrated use	Education-information
5. Unavoidable impacts	Physical impact of even careful use	Reduction of use levels to limit unavoidable impacts; relocation of use to more durable site

experiences, and reducing impacts could improve visitor experiences. But management to control impacts sometimes restricts visitors in ways that adversely affect visitor experiences. Managers will rarely find simple solutions to single problems. Usually a management solution to one problem affects other problems, sometimes with unwanted, negative side effects. Sometimes the cure may be worse than the problem. A careful balancing act by managers is always required.

TYPES OF RECREATIONAL USE PROBLEMS

Solutions to problems of wilderness use management are aided by considering a *typology*, or classification, of undesirable visitor actions and their associated impacts, and the managerial responses that are needed and justified (table 15.1). The basis of this typology is the visitors' awareness and motivation for behavior, and how it relates to laws and regulations. Five categories cover the range of visitor actions:

1. *Illegal actions.* Examples are the illegal use of chainsaws or motorbikes in wilderness, with the resulting disruption of other visitors' experiences, and damage to wildlife, soil, and vegetation. The managerial response would be law enforcement based on clear communication of legal restrictions. Managers need to remember that some illegal actions may result from ignorance of laws, and therefore could be treated much like types 3 and 4, unskilled and uninformed behaviors. Mechanized recreation, for example, can be handled by providing areas managed for semiprimitive, motorized recreation, and letting such recreationists know where the areas are and what they offer.

2. *Careless or thoughtless violations of regulations.* Examples are littering, shortcutting trail switchbacks, parties larger than specified in regulations, camping in closed areas, and building wood fires where prohibited. The manager can try to motivate visitors to alter such behavior by persuasion, by making it easier to do the right thing, or by discouraging the wrong thing. For example, managers might provide litterbags or encourage litter pickup through the use of incentives or direct appeals by rangers, or physically block trail shortcuts and enforce rules and regulations against these acts.

3. *Unskilled actions.* Digging a drainage ditch around a tent is an example of an impact resulting from a lack of skills or knowledge. Many once-recommended woodsman practices—such as building bough beds and pole shelters (fig. 15.2) and burying garbage—are now inappropriate in wilder-

Fig. 15.2. Camping practices such as bough beds, ditching around tents, and building pole shelters are unnecessary and spoil the wilderness setting. Education can help eliminate such damaging practices. Photo courtesy of the USFS.

ness because of accumulated impacts stemming from heavy use. Most are unnecessary with modern camping equipment. Some practices acceptable in other areas are out of place within wilderness. The manager's main response is to educate visitors about desirable practices, and, when clearly necessary, to establish and enforce rules against such actions while always trying to educate visitors about why such rules are necessary.

4. *Uninformed behavior.* This kind of behavior can intensify some types of use impacts. It is illustrated by large numbers of visitors who enter a wilderness at a few well-known access points when they might have visited attractive nonwilderness lands or used other access points if they had been better informed about alternative places. Concentrating or dispersing use is a complex issue, and the appropriate policy depends on several factors, discussed later, particularly in chapter 15. But use is often poorly distributed. In such cases, no matter how skilled and careful the visitors are, problems are created. The manager's main response is to provide visitors with prior information about alternatives available or set use quotas for each entry point.

5. *Unavoidable minimum impacts.* Every party that visits a wilderness causes some minimum, unavoidable impacts by its mere presence. The party is *there;* other parties will see it and their solitude will be reduced. Visitors must step on plants, defecate, and urinate. Although, on some rivers, human waste is carried out by visitors. Vegetation under a tent or sleeping bag is compressed and damaged to some extent. Even with all the skill and knowledge possible, there remains a minimum, unavoidable level of impact. The term "no trace camping" used in some areas is a misnomer; "minimum impact" is more accurate (explained in chap. 16). Managers can shift use to other areas better able to support it. Trails, for example, can be relocated to more durable sites (also discussed in chap. 16). If, after all actions to reduce visitor impacts have been taken (education, regulation, relocation), the accumulation of unavoidable impacts is excessive, the manager can only reduce or eliminate use; all other options have been used up.

MANAGERS' AND VISITORS' PERCEPTIONS OF PROBLEMS

Visitors often see wilderness problems differently than managers (Hendee and Harris 1970; Peterson 1974). Managers need to be aware of this when defining problems and seeking solutions; trying to change visitor behavior is difficult enough anytime,

Fig. 15.3. Most wilderness managers regard damage to campsite vegetation, as seen here in the Eagle Cap Wilderness, OR, as a serious problem. Many visitors, however, are bothered more by crowding and conflicts with other visitors. Photo courtesy of the USFS.

but it becomes almost impossible if visitors do not consider some condition undesirable, no matter how inappropriate managers may believe it to be.

Managers' Perceptions
In 1980, Washburne and Cole surveyed managers of 269 areas either classified as wilderness or likely to be classified about perceived management problems and about use patterns and management practices (Washburne and Cole 1983). They found that managers of different areas reported similar problems, and usually saw these problems as localized rather than widespread. Managers considered human impacts on campsite vegetation (fig. 15.3) to be the most serious problem (table 15.2). Human impacts on lakeshore vegetation rated second. Littering was the third most serious problem. Human impacts on trails, packstock impacts on vegetation at campsites, and visitor crowding came next, all with similar ratings. Most other problems, except disposal of human feces, were not generally considered serious. Typically, managers who reported these problems in their area described them as affecting "a few places." Visitor impacts to campsite vegetation was the only problem perceived as affecting "many places" in much more than one-tenth of the wildernesses studied.

Managers perceived ecological impacts as a problem more often than visitor crowding or conflicts. But those who managed a wilderness where they believed use exceeded capacity cited crowding slightly more often than environmental impacts as

Table 15.2. Wilderness managers' perceptions of problems in areas they manage.

Type of problem	Seen as:		
	not a problem	a problem in a few places	a problem in many places
	Percent of areas		
Visitor crowding	53	37	10
Visitor conflict	71	27	2
Human impacts on vegetation:			
Trails	56	35	9
Campsites	29	44	27
Lakeshores	40	42	18
Packstock impacts on vegetation:			
Trails	71	24	5
Campsites	55	34	11
Lakeshores	68	28	4
Litter	38	50	12
Water pollution	82	16	2

Source: Washburne and Cole 1983.

the limiting factor Both the "people problems" of crowding and conflict and the impact problems need to be viewed in light of the extreme unevenness of recreational use (chap. 14). This helps explain why problems are usually perceived as localized.

Visitors' Perceptions

Most surveys of wilderness visitors indicate more concern with social conditions such as crowding, conflict among visitors, and littering, than with resource conditions such as campsite and trail impacts (Lucas 1979).

Visitors react particularly negatively to littering (Lee 1975; Stankey 1973). Even small amounts of litter evoke strong responses. Littering may be viewed as a violation of strongly held norms and, thus, as evidence of abuse rather than normal use.

Conflict among visitors is often a greater problem in the visitors' opinions than sheer numbers of other visitors or crowding, and conflict often follows littering as a problem in visitors' perceptions (Lucas 1964; Manning 1985; Stankey 1973). Conflict is usually among different types of visitors, but sometimes is caused by objectionable behavior by similar types of visitors. Large parties are a source of conflict to most visitors. Some conflict stems from different methods of travel, particularly where mechanized use is permitted as an exception; for example, outboard motors in parts of the Boundary Waters Canoe Area Wilderness (BWCAW), Minnesota (Manning 1985). Horse-hiker conflicts are usually less severe,

but may be intensifying (Lucas 1985).

Most visitors do not seem to be very aware of campsite impacts. Both campsite choice and visitor satisfaction appear to be little affected by campsite impacts. Rock firerings and ashes, unless extreme, seem to be acceptable to most visitors (Shelby and Harris 1985), while managers often react very negatively to campfire impacts (fig. 15.4).

Trail conditions usually have not been of particular concern to visitors. But a study of trends from 1970 to 1982 in the Bob Marshall Wilderness Complex (BMWC) showed a sharp increase in complaints

Fig. 15.4. Most visitors tolerate firerings and campfire remains; many managers find such impacts unacceptable. Photo courtesy of the USFS.

about trails (Lucas 1985). In the BMWC, trail conditions can make travel particularly difficult, especially large mudholes, and are probably the source of visitor dissatisfaction, rather than ecological implications of such conditions. Lee (1975) found very low association between visitors' ratings of trail conditions and "expert" judgments by managers in Yosemite National Park (CA). He speculated that ease of travel accounted for most of the visitors' ratings.

Usually, visitors show little concern about lack of facilities other than trails and bridges. Some potential rules and regulations produce strong negative reactions, but established regulations in areas where visitor surveys have been conducted usually have been fairly well accepted, possibly because to some people such regulations are reason enough to have stopped visiting the area. We will discuss visitor attitudes about various management actions in more detail in the next two chapters.

Where managers' and visitors' perceptions of problems diverge widely, managers need to reconsider their ideas about the nature and importance of the condition they see differently from visitors. If they are convinced it is an important problem, they need to educate visitors to share this view. Widely divergent perceptions will reduce both compliance with regulations and desired responses to education and information intended to change behavior.

ASPECTS OF VISITOR USE SUBJECT TO MANAGEMENT

Management cannot control or influence all the many aspects of wilderness visitors' use. Those aspects that can be controlled or influenced are what Shelby and Heberlein (1984) term *management parameters.* These are what managers can work on. How and to what extent can these different aspects of use and their impacts be modified? How does management of each one relate to reducing ecological impacts and improving experience quality? What general issues should managers consider in dealing with each aspect of use? We will review these factors for a variety of use characteristics.

Amount of Use
Clearly, managers can restrict numbers of visitors if managers believe visitors' *unavoidable minimum impacts* (type 5) exceed the physical or social carrying capacity, or if uninformed, unskilled, or careless actions cannot be reduced sufficiently in other ways. Use can be restricted indirectly, for example, by closing roads and lengthening trails or by changing

signs; or directly, by limiting the number of use permits issued (in other words, rationing use). As we noted in chapter 9, however, the direct rationing of use should be a last resort after every other appropriate approach has been exhausted. Nevertheless, rationing the number of visitors entering may be preferable to tight regulation of movements inside the wilderness, which can reduce the quality of visitor experiences.

Distribution of Use
Wilderness use distributions are typically uneven, some of which result from *uninformed actions* (type 4) by users who possess limited knowledge of alternative opportunities. But sometimes concentrated use reflects available trails and access to them (which can be changed in the long run), differences in attractiveness of locations, or proximity to population centers. Here, the impacts fall into our type 5 category—unavoidable minimum impacts. In either case, managers' main technique for altering the distribution of use is by providing information to users, or, in more extreme cases, by rationing use by entry points or travel zones.

Any efforts to redistribute use need to be linked to well-defined objectives to avoid simply spreading problems more widely. Wilderness managers may have at least four objectives for seeking to shift some use:

1. *Shift some use from wilderness to alternative nonwilderness locations.* Several studies suggest that many wilderness visitors probably would be as well or better satisfied in areas with more facilities and managed more intensively for dispersed recreation than wilderness can be (Hendee and others 1968; Lucas 1973, 1980; Stankey 1973). These users are seeking relatively primitive, roadless recreation experiences but do not require or necessarily want the completely undeveloped conditions provided in classified wilderness. Managers, by providing information about roadless, but nonwilderness, locations might steer users to desired experiences. This might relieve pressures on legally classified wilderness as well as better meet some visitors' desires.

Schomaker and Glassford (1982) point out that visitors to some nonwildernesses may be seeking experiences similar to wilderness visitors and could be adversely affected by increased development and use, so caution is needed. The Recreation Opportunity Spectrum (ROS) system provides a particularly useful framework for identifying and managing nonwilderness primitive and nonmotorized semi-primitive settings in a balanced, comprehensive way (Clark and Stankey 1979; Driver and Brown 1978).

At the same time, information about wilderness needs to stress its special character and deemphasize recreation opportunities that are not wilderness dependent. Rather than photographs of fishermen displaying dozens of fish caught, hunters kneeling by trophy elk, or very large groups of visitors, isolation, solitude, and challenge could be portrayed with photographs of small parties in natural, typical surroundings (not necessarily in uniquely beautiful, scenic spots).

2. *Shift some use from heavily used wildernesses to other less-used wildernesses.* Use per acre varies greatly from wilderness to wilderness (see chap. 14). Sometimes a lightly used wilderness capable of absorbing more use is located near a heavily used area. Most visitors have only sketchy, word-of-mouth information about use levels from one wilderness to another. Managers might provide such information to enable those visitors particularly concerned with solitude and relatively undisturbed conditions to more readily find them, while at the same time reducing some impacts by diverting use from heavily used areas. If this approach does not shift use as much as desired, it might need to be supplemented by more direct controls. Shifting visitors among wildernesses needs to be a carefully planned program. Uncoordinated efforts could result in exporting problems.

3. *Reduce the contrasts between lightly and heavily used sections within a wilderness by shifting some use to less-used entry points, trails, and campsites.* Several accesses, a few miles of trail, and a few campsites usually account for a large proportion of all wilderness recreational use. Information about less-used locations might help direct users to them. More direct controls could be imposed through wilderness permits or onsite dispersal by wilderness rangers, although these measures should be viewed as last-resort actions. As will be discussed further in chapters 16 and 17, dispersal of use is not necessarily a good idea because of variation in both the ecosystem's capability and the visitors' desired levels of contact with others. Nevertheless, managers and probably most other people familiar with use conditions in many wildernesses would agree that use is excessively concentrated.

4. *Shift some use to specific locations better able to accommodate the use.* For example, horse users might be encouraged to go to places with more abundant forage on durable sites, or to places where hikers do not usually go to reduce conflict. Users might be diverted at times from areas where sensitive wildlife could be adversely affected by disturbance or where the presence of dangerous wildlife, especially griz-

zly bears, presents a serious threat to visitors. Guidelines for effective redistribution of use are presented in chapter 17.

Timing of Use
Most wildernesses have short use seasons and many have sharp weekend and holiday peaks in use (chap. 14). Managers might shift use from peak times to low use periods, first by providing information about peak period and off-season use levels and use on weekdays compared to weekends, and finally by regulation, if necessary.

Method of Travel
In some wildernesses all visitors hike, but in many others, visitors travel by several means (chap. 14). Horse travel is the most common method of travel other than hiking, but in several areas various types of boats are used, some with motors. Means of travel may provoke conflicts and increase environmental impacts (see chap. 16 and Stankey 1973). Managers can use education to influence behavior to reduce impacts and conflicts, but where problems are serious, they will usually regulate use. Some types of travel may be limited to certain portions of a wilderness or prohibited. It would be possible to zone in order to separate different travel methods, giving each type of travel its exclusive use zone.

Party Size
Large parties are not common in most wildernesses (chap. 14), but the few that occur seriously diminish other visitors' experiences (Stankey 1973) and, almost inevitably, impact a larger area than smaller parties (Cole 1986). Managers can limit party size, and they have in many places (Washburne and Cole 1983), but this technique needs to be supplemented with education and persuasion. Frequently, large parties are sponsored by organizations that are easier to contact than independent users and they may be anxious to cooperate with wilderness managers. The average size of parties sponsored by such groups as the American Forestry Association and the Sierra Club has declined in recent years, partly in response to concerns about the adverse impacts of large parties.

Length of Stay
Length of stay can be regulated; but generally it does not contribute much to overuse because few parties stay in the wilderness very long (chap. 14). Nevertheless, when a party stays for a long time at a popular campsite, it unfairly monopolizes the site and increases impacts. For these reasons, some limit on

length of stay at any one campsite seems desirable, and some areas have limits, usually 14 days. In some situations, where use is rationed and typical stays are long, some reasonable limit on total stay may permit more people to visit the area. This is the reasoning behind a seven-day limit for backpackers in the most popular part of Grand Canyon National Park (AZ).

Behavior

Behavior includes many visitor actions: staying on trails or shortcutting them; choosing a spot to camp; whether a campfire is built, and, if so, how; how wastes are handled; how noisy a group is; actions toward other visitors; littering; and so on. Influencing behavior of wilderness visitors is a key to visitor management. It can reduce or eliminate the need to regulate and control visitor use. All undesirable behavior is not inevitable; people can adopt new practices and, in fact, many are doing so (Lucas 1985). Two aspects of visitor behavior are particularly relevant: (1) effects on the resource and (2) effects on the experiences of others. They are discussed briefly here, and more fully in the next two chapters.

Effects on the Resource

Resource impacts can be dramatically increased or reduced, depending on visitor behavior. Illegal and careless behaviors (types 1 and 2) may be more serious than inappropriate behavior by well-meaning but unskilled visitors (type 3), but unskilled behavior probably is most common.

Several kinds of behavior determine resource impacts. First, self-sufficient camping (the opposite of living off the land) has low impact. Proper equipment is important; for example, tents with aluminum or fiberglass poles eliminate the need to cut trees for tent poles (fig. 15.5). Second, through education, camping and traveling skills can be upgraded to reduce impacts. For example, visitors can learn to use campfires only where wood is abundant, keep them small, and leave little evidence of the fire.

Horse use requires special skill and knowledge because of its potential for damaging soils and vegetation. Most horses weigh more than 1,000 pounds, and their weight is supported on small hooves with iron shoes. They are often tied up, which concentrates their impacts. A horse can eat 20, 30, or more pounds of grass and other forage each day in a wilderness. Several booklets (Back Country Horsemen n.d.; Miller 1973; USDA FS 1981) and some agency brochures discuss how to minimize impacts while using horses. In addition, use of new, light equipment reduces the number of animals needed to transport camper gear, thereby further reducing the

Fig. 15.5. Availability of aluminum and fiberglass tent poles makes it unnecessary to cut trees in order to erect tents or lean-to shelters. Photo courtesy of the USFS.

level of ecological impact (and also probably reducing visitor conflict). In some areas, a few visitors are using llamas as pack animals. Llamas may cause fewer impacts than horses or mules because they are lighter, have feet somewhat like an elk rather than shod hooves, and usually can be turned loose near camp rather than tied in one place, but llama use is still new and information on their impacts is scarce. Managing resource impacts will be discussed in detail in chapter 16.

Effects on the Experiences of Others

Visitor behavior also affects other visitors' experiences. Acceptable wilderness behavior is based on respect for other visitors' desires for privacy, solitude, and limited evidence of visitor use in terms of litter and severe impacts. Appropriate behavior requires knowledge of a largely unwritten set of rules or norms for wilderness use. Noise, littering, and campsite improvements, such as shelves, stools, shelters, and rock fireplaces, are all examples of behavior that can reduce the quality of wilderness experiences for others. Managing for quality visitor experiences is treated at length in chapter 17.

GATHERING VISITOR MANAGEMENT INFORMATION

Professional management of visitors requires base data and monitoring just as much as managing timber, water, or any other type of resource. Much past management of wilderness recreation has been based on the manager's personal experiences, opinions, and intuition rather than on systematically collected

information. Professional judgment must always be a major part of wilderness management; but judgment should be based on reliable information about use, about its effects on resources and experiences, about likely user responses to management actions, and about probable responses of the ecosystem to management decisions.

Guesswork will not meet the challenge of wilderness management now and in the future. Research and managers' experiences both indicate that estimates of use levels and patterns and users' attitudes are often very inaccurate. For example, when wilderness permits have been instituted and tallied, managers often have found that their previous estimates of use were often far off—sometimes too high, sometimes too low. Field surveys have generally shown that use is less evenly distributed than managers estimated, length of stay is shorter than thought, and there is less horse use and more hiker use than believed. Similarly, managers have commonly held assumptions about visitors' attitudes on solitude, on facilities, and on use controls that have often turned out to be wide of the mark (Hendee and Harris 1970). Even campsite impacts—a seemingly objective, readily observed condition—have proved to be less severe than managers thought (see the discussion of campsite inventories in chap. 16). Unsystematic observation and subjective recall are neither reliable nor accurate.

To support professional wilderness management, data must meet certain general standards: data must be (1) systematic, (2) valid, (3) reliable, and (4) reasonably accurate.

Systematic refers to a planned, standardized way of collecting and handling data, including a schedule for data collection. It is the opposite of casual, catch-as-catch-can measurements.

Valid data measure what is actually intended, not something that may be more convenient but which is only loosely linked to the real object of concern. For example, if numbers of camp encounters (how many other camper groups can be detected from a party's camp) are needed, observations at noon when many people are not yet camped would not be valid.

Reliable data will vary little no matter who collects them. Objective, measurable units are more likely to be reliable than subjective ratings.

Reasonably accurate data reflect the same qualities essential for a systematic, reliable approach, plus sample size. Measuring only one campsite every five years, for example, would yield estimates on campsite condition trends with very low accuracy. Measuring every campsite every year would be extremely

accurate but very expensive. Thus, reasonable accuracy is the goal—accuracy which is good enough to detect changes that are significant for management decisions. (This again is the principle of doing only what is necessary.)

Data should be measured and recorded for specific, individual parameters, rather than just combined ratings. For example, for campsites, recording square feet devegetated, number of trees cut, and so on, is more useful than just a "class 2 or 3," or "fair or poor" rating. Individual measures identify specific problems, help suggest appropriate corrective actions, and always can be combined in one or more ways to form composite ratings.

Collecting recreation management data is costly, and the benefits of better information must be compared to these costs (Herfindahl 1969). Poor decisions based on inadequate information also can be costly and can result in irreversible damage. Managers need to guard against collecting information for information's sake. *Complete, precise information is rarely a realistic goal; adequate information at an acceptable cost, geared to important management needs, is the goal.* Adequate basic data about wilderness use and its effects are the essential first step to improved management. The Limits of Acceptable Change (LAC) system described in chapter 9 is one means for identifying information needs. The choice of indicators establishes the types of information that will be essential for management. This information is needed to develop management plans and actions, to monitor the reactions of visitors and the ecosystem to managerial actions, and to revise plans. Without this data base, the manager cannot tell whether management is achieving its objectives and can learn little from experience. Employee turnover compounds the uncertainty.

Effective collection of management data was illustrated in chapter 8, under the Anaconda-Pintler (previously Pintlar) Wilderness plan wherein specific objectives, policies, and management actions were spelled out. Two categories of data are relevant to visitor management: visitor data and resource data.

VISITOR DATA

A variety of *visitor data* are needed in management. First, *use data*—basic information on amount of use, patterns of use, and characteristics of use. Usually this information has been collected by area managers and occasionally by research scientists. Second, *user data*—characteristics and behavior of visitors; specific aspects of their experiences in the area; their knowledge of appropriate ways of doing things;

their desires and preferences; the satisfactions they get from use; their attitudes about conditions in the area and about other uses; and their feelings about and probable reactions to management actions, policies, or regulations. Such information generally has been gathered as part of studies by research scientists rather than by managers, but it should be done regularly by managers. Often less than full-scale scientific surveys will be adequate; systematic recording of observations and results of conversations with visitors can be useful. Data on encounters with other visitors (or solitude) may be needed if the LAC system is being used. Such data also have been collected by scientists, but a technique for systematically estimating encounters needs to be developed for use by managers. All of these data change over time and need to be measured periodically. Basic use data are collected annually; other visitor information needs to be updated at longer intervals.

Amount and Characteristics of Use

Methods for gathering basic use data were discussed in chapter 14 and are briefly reviewed here. Direct observation of a sample of times and places is one approach, but costly and not precise. Automatic counters, if carefully installed and maintained, are reliable but provide limited information. Automatic cameras provide essentially all the information an observer could gather without interviewing visitors, and probably provide the most complete and accurate information. Photographic data must be collected in conformity with privacy laws and ethics, as described in chapter 14. Trail registers provide incomplete data that can be adjusted for nonregistrants if registration behavior is checked, but again this is costly. Mandatory permits also can provide quite reliable and complete data on use, although compliance varies among types of visitors (Lime and Lorence 1974). Permit systems merit further discussion because they are widely used to control use to try to reduce impacts and crowding (Washburne and Cole 1983) but are controversial.

Permit Systems

A permit system is costly to operate in terms of managers' salaries and visitor effort. But the benefits, in addition to obtaining use data, can be substantial (Hendee and Lucas 1973). Contact between managers and visitors has the potential for communicating information about where and when to go that could improve visitors' experiences and reduce excessive impacts on the wilderness (fig. 15.6). Such contact also offers the potential for improving visitors' knowledge of regulations, desirable behavior and

Fig. 15.6. Permit systems can bring visitors and managers together, thus providing opportunities for education and mutual exchange of information. Photo courtesy of the USFS.

practices, and hazards. The benefits of communication are lost, however, if the agency representatives who issue permits are not well informed and skilled in public contacts or if written material used with mail or self-issued permits is not well done and up to date. Also, use of a permit system to force contact results in a "captive audience" and might be less effective than other types of contact. If it is not practical for managers to make contact with visitors at trailheads or in the wilderness, however, issuing permits at ranger stations or visitor centers will provide an opportunity for personal contacts.

A permit system has other advantages. A record of visitor itineraries can add a dimension of safety to wilderness travel. The permit is necessary, of course, when use must be directly regulated. The costs of administering a permit system and the costs of visitor inconvenience need to be weighed carefully against benefits. Unless an area needs or is on the verge of needing to limit use, adopting a permit system just to measure use seems questionable. If a permit requirement facilitates communication of important, site-specific information (e.g., places to go or to avoid, campfire restrictions), this may forestall the need to regulate or ration use. However, other alternatives both for measuring use and communicating with visitors exist and need to be evaluated in the process of considering a permit system.

For some areas where use levels and environmental impacts are not high enough to warrant rationing, the self-issued, mandatory permit might be a useful compromise. In this system, the standard U.S. Forest Service (USFS) wilderness permit is available from a box near trailheads. Visitors fill out a permit, take one copy, and deposit one copy. This appears to be a good way to gather accurate use information. Field checks by wilderness rangers have showed 90 to 95 percent compliance, better than reported for agency-issued permits. Self-issued permits are also better than trail registers, as shown by a study of mandatory permits in Montana (Lucas and Kovalicky 1981).

The self-issued permit is most convenient for visitors; it eliminates any need to drive out of the way to an issuing office or to schedule travel so as to obtain a permit during office hours. Most managers also find that it reduces administrative costs considerably. Although personal contact is lost, a well-designed map-brochure can present regulations and suggested practices, perhaps even better than busy clerks with little wilderness background.

With self-issued permits, it is difficult to divert visitors from overused areas. With agency-issued permits, this is possible; but, unfortunately, it often is not done because of a lack of well-informed, skilled people to issue permits. Contacts with wilderness rangers at trailheads or in the field may be more effective in communicating suggestions on wilderness behavior and reminders of regulations.

If managers seek to redistribute use to achieve management goals for solitude and impacts, all persons registering or obtaining permits might be sent information on use-problem areas during the off season. Many of them will make future trips, or know people who will. This approach was used successfully in 1975 with some BWCAW visitors, as is described in more detail later. The good compliance with self-issued permit requirements would provide an excellent mailing list for such information.

Despite the advantages of self-issued permits, they have been employed only by managers of a few USFS wildernesses, most of them in Oregon. Some managers believe that regular trail registers are adequate in situations where agency-issued permits are not required, and that they have less impact on visitors' and managers' workloads.

Use Summaries
The permits or trail register cards provide raw data on each party: size of the group, party leader's place of residence, main method of travel, number of stock (horses, mules, or other), date of entry, and either exit

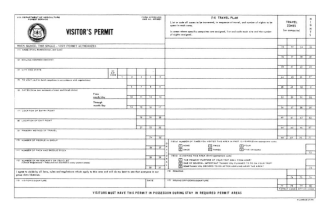

Fig. 15.7. The standard wilderness permit used in all national forest wilderness and national park backcountry in CA in 1985. A similar form is widely used by the USFS.

date or length of stay (fig. 15.7). Permits also usually contain information on entry and exit locations, travel itinerary, and camping locations by travel zones. Trail register cards can also include some information on itinerary and, at least, entry point.

For management purposes, raw data can be organized in many different ways, and selectivity is essential. Wildernesses are diverse and data needs vary among them. Basic units for measuring recreational use were defined and discussed in chapter 14. No single measure is best; different units are useful for different purposes. Number of group visits, individual visits, visitor-days, and group-nights are particularly useful for many important visitor management decisions.

How data are tabulated depends on the management purpose being served (Elsner 1972; Frayer and Butts 1974; Lime and Buchman 1974). Data can be tabulated on the basis of *location variables* (such as entry points or travel zones), by *visitor characteristics* (such as residence of leader, length of stay, group size, or method of visitor travel), or by *time variables* (such as day of week, weeks of the season, or months). These variables can also be combined into more complex tables—for example, entry points used by visitors from a nearby large urban area during the peak month, perhaps to guide a visitor information program. Tabulating groups by travel method at each trailhead might be particularly useful.

Both the National Park Service (NPS) and the USFS have done extensive analyses of wilderness permit data. The NPS generally collects, analyzes, and stores data in individual parks while the USFS has used centralized computer capabilities, although this is changing as local computer systems develop. The computer programs at the USFS, Fort Collins, Colorado, Computer Center (FCCC) are part of the

USFS Recreation Information Management (RIM) system. The original programs, developed by Elsner (1972), have been expanded and modified. Some of the information in standard tables includes: group visits, individual visits, and visitor-days by primary mode of travel; group leader's residence, both by state of residence and by three-digit ZIP Code sectional centers for the state or states within which the wilderness is located; persons present on each day for the whole wilderness; numbers of groups by group-size classes; both groups and visits ranked by length of stay; both groups and visits ranked by entry point; and use by travel zones.

Visitor Characteristics, Attitudes, and Satisfaction

Automatic cameras or permits are the best source of data on amount of use and its characteristics, but they cannot provide certain useful information—particularly visitors' behavior, attitudes, knowledge, and satisfaction. Also, permits reflect user plans before the trip, rather than actual outcomes. For example, itineraries can shift and trip lengths often change (van Wagtendonk and Benedict 1980). A variety of information collection approaches are possible, and deciding which is best depends on the questions and the setting. Only important managerial questions justify data collection, and managers will have different needs than research scientists. Clark (1977) described the three main information collection methods—surveys, observation, and diaries—and their application to different situations.

Surveys generally involve questionnaires that collect self-reported information. Visitors are asked via a mailed questionnaire or a face-to-face or telephone interview to describe themselves, their behavior and activities, their values, attitudes, ideas, and so on. Some factors, for example, satisfactions and dissatisfactions, seem impossible to measure any other way. Of course, problems can occur. Questions can be misunderstood, interviewers can influence responses, memories can falter, social pressure can color answers, and samples can be poorly selected and unrepresentative. Former visitors who have gone elsewhere because of dissatisfaction will be missed in surveys of current visitors, and this can be particularly important information.

The survey technique is valuable, but its proper use requires special skill and training. The design and conduct of social surveys are described in Dillman (1978) and Potter and others (1972). Surveys by federal agencies must be approved by the Office of Management and Budget under the terms of the Paper-

work Reduction Act of 1980 (44 U.S.C., Chap. 35, P. L. 96-511). Approval is granted only for studies passing review of the need for the information and the scientific validity of the research plan. Planning for surveys must begin early enough to provide time for this approval process.

Observation can be a systematic, scientific tool (Burch 1964; Campbell 1970). Checklists of items to observe can be prepared and used to structure the process. For things readily observed, the technique is more objective and accurate than verbal recall. For example, if one were interested in how much time visitors actually spend fishing while camped at lakes (Hendee and others 1977), or whether they register at trail registers (Lucas 1983), observation would be the most effective technique. Observation is usually done by an employee such as a wilderness ranger, but photographic techniques are an alternative.

Diaries or other self-reporting forms are a third useful technique. Before entering the wilderness, visitors are given a log book or form in which to record certain facts, such as travel times, numbers of encounters, or the highlight of each day (Lime 1970). For detailed information, where memory recall in later surveys could be a problem, this is a useful technique. Using this self-reporting technique, a larger sample can be obtained and the data gathered without an observer intruding on visitor solitude. Reporting inaccuracies are possible. Some visitors will not fill out the diary, and those who do have to make a serious effort.

Informal interviews are commonly used by managers, for example, by wilderness rangers when they meet visitors, and is discussed again in chapter 17. With some thought to organization and record-keeping, the standards for data described before, being (1) systematic, (2) valid, (3) reliable, and (4) reasonably accurate, can at least be approached. Data collected in this way can be useful if their limitations are recognized.

In some cases, a combination of data-gathering techniques is both possible and advantageous. For example, if the activity or issue being studied can be observed, at least partly, and people also are asked about what they do and why they do it, then the two approaches can strengthen each other and ensure against drawing unwarranted conclusions.

Special studies need to be conducted with sensitivity to the experience of the wilderness visitor. Conspicuous observation or interviews within the wilderness seem generally inappropriate to us, although determining visitors' evaluations of onsite conditions must use such techniques; for example, Shelby and Harris (1985) justifiably interviewed

campers in the Mount Jefferson Wilderness (OR) about acceptability of specific campsite conditions. Contacts inside the wilderness also sometimes may have several scientific weaknesses. Observation or interviews could modify the behavior they seek to describe, thus diminishing validity. Sampling people inside an area ordinarily cannot yield a sample with definable statistical properties—the probability of any visitor being sampled is usually unequal and unknown. This is a problem if describing the user population is an objective. Interviews at entry or exit points or later at home usually are more considerate of visitors and scientifically more sound. Completing a questionnaire sometime after the trip may even contribute to visitors' enjoyment of the *recollection phase* of the trip. This might partly explain the high rates of return of mail questionnaires.

RESOURCE DATA

Much of the visitor information is useful for managing not only visitor experiences, but also ecological impacts, because it documents characteristics of use and users related to their potential to cause impacts.

Basic information and monitoring of resource

Fig. 15.8. Systematic monitoring of wilderness conditions, such as campsite impacts, is essential to effective management. Photo courtesy of the USFS.

conditions affected by visitor use also are essential in management of wilderness recreation site impacts. For example, how good or bad are physical-biological conditions at each camping area? How are conditions changing? How does impact relate to use? Has grazing damaged meadows? Is water quality deteriorating? Are trails eroding? This information is essential for identifying sites where use or visitor behavior must be modified, sites to which use might be diverted, and sites where new facilities (such as trails) or maintenance and repair of existing facilities are needed.

A number of basic resource inventory and monitoring techniques derived from the fields of range management, wildlife management, forestry, and ecology are available (chap. 16). Depending on money available and the need for the information to meet objectives for the wilderness, a variety of information could be collected—data about the condition of trails and travel routes, campsites, forage areas, water quality near use areas, and so forth. This would help identify critical spots that should be checked regularly. At some interval, maybe five or 10 years, a complete reinventory would probably be desirable. Without some systematic observation of resource conditions, it will not be possible to say with any confidence whether conditions are improving or deteriorating (fig. 15.8). It would also be impossible to judge the effectiveness of managerial actions designed to protect or improve conditions. Without such monitoring, decisions to continue an action, to change it, intensify it, or drop it cannot be made in a professional manner.

Because information is costly, it should be collected systematically, should be related to specific objectives, and should be in a form that is easily used and that permits comparisons between places and times. The Code-A-Site system (Hendee and others 1976), and improved variations derived from it, is an example of systematic, readily retrieved information collection. Photographic techniques provide other examples. Some techniques require actual measurement of conditions, while others are based mainly on estimates. Measurement is more precise and objective; estimation is quicker. These and other inventory and monitoring techniques are presented in detail in chapter 16.

GENERAL RECREATION MANAGEMENT APPROACHES

Several important issues are involved in choosing appropriate recreation management approaches: direct-indirect management, the role of regulations,

location of management, and multiple combinations of management methods.

DIRECT-INDIRECT VISITOR MANAGEMENT

The important distinction between direct and indirect visitor management (Gilbert and others 1972) is presented in table 15.3. (Specific management techniques will be discussed in the next two chapters.) *Direct management* emphasizes regulation of behavior. Individual choice is restricted and managers try to exert considerable control over visitors. *Indirect management* emphasizes influencing or modifying behavior by managing factors that influence visitors' decisions. Individual visitors retain freedom to choose. Managers try to control visitors less completely, thus allowing more variation in use and behavior.

Indirect management generally should be the first choice, with direct management used only when indirect means cannot achieve management objectives, although the opposite view has been expressed (McAvoy and Dustin 1983). Most wilderness users prefer indirect management (Stankey 1973), and the concept of wilderness as an undeveloped, free, open, and unconfined place accentuates the desirability of a management philosophy that is as indirect, unobtrusive, and subtle as possible. Trying indirect management first is in accordance with the principle of minimum regimentation, which was presented in chapter 7.

Education is the key to much indirect management, and it is the main managerial response to careless, unskilled, and uninformed actions (types 2, 3, and 4 in table 15.1). Specific education techniques are discussed in the next two chapters.

Direct controls are necessary at specific problem areas at some times, but they should be applied in ways that permit as much visitor freedom as possible. Respecting visitor freedom is an essential element in wilderness visitor management, and all planned management actions should be tested in terms of their effect on freedom. Controls should be applied with restraint and only when and where they are clearly justified. Visitor regulation is a common and important tool for managing both ecological impacts and visitor experiences, but because it is controversial, it deserves a thorough discussion at this point.

REGULATION—COSTS AND BENEFITS

Regulations can help solve some problems, but solutions are not free. For managers, regulation costs are in terms of the employees' time needed to explain and enforce them, while, for visitors, costs are in terms of lost opportunities and diminished enjoyment.

Costs to Visitors

Costs to visitors stem in part from the differences between the basic definitions of "recreation" and "regulation." *Recreation* is usually defined in concepts similar to those employed by Driver and Tocher (1970): It is a particular type of human experience that results from self-rewarding physical or mental engagements, based on personal free choice during nonobligated time. This definition stresses internal control and free choice for personal reasons that vary as much as people do. *Regulation,* in contrast, is defined by Webster's Second Edition as: "To govern according to rule, to reduce to order or uniformity." Thus, instead of the self-direction and diversity inherent in recreation, regulation involves external direction and uniformity.

The tension between recreation and regulation is intensified in wilderness management. We have pointed out that the Wilderness Act defines wilderness as an area that provides "outstanding opportunities for solitude or a primitive and *unconfined* type of recreation" (emphasis added). On the other hand, the act also requires managers to protect and manage wilderness "so as to preserve its natural conditions"—an almost impossible mandate if uncontrolled recreational use is allowed.

The appropriateness of recreation regulations depends largely on the benefits and costs of implementing a specific regulation as compared to a nonregulatory action for solving a particular problem. Lucas (1982) presents a method for analyzing such costs and benefits. A problem can be defined and its significance judged only by comparing field conditions to an area's objectives.

Psychological research suggests that regulations can diminish the quality of recreational experiences. Visitors to the Rawah Wilderness in Colorado said autonomy added strongly to their satisfaction (Brown and Haas 1980). Some specific expressions of autonomy in the psychological scales used in the study were "doing things your own way," "feeling free from society's restrictions," "freedom of choice," and "traveling where you desire." These notions of autonomy have also been found to be highly valued in other studies of wilderness visitors (Haas and others 1980; Roggenbuck 1980).

The criteria for the primitive setting within the ROS system (USDA FS 1982) include minimal "evidence of human-induced restrictions and controls." Semiprimitive settings have a few more controls and restrictions; more highly developed settings have

Table 15.3. Direct and indirect techniques for managing the character and intensity of wilderness use.

Type of management	Method	Specific techniques
INDIRECT Emphasis on influencing or modifying behavior. Individual retains freedom to choose. Control less complete, more variation in use possible.	Physical alterations	Improve, maintain, or neglect access roads. Improve, maintain, or neglect campsites. Make trails more or less difficult. Build trails or leave areas trailless. Improve fish or wildlife populations or take no action (stock, or allow depletion or elimination).
	Information dispersal	Advertise attributes of the wilderness. Advertise recreation opportunities in surrounding area, outside wilderness. Educate users to basic concepts of ecology and care of ecosystems. Advertise underused areas and general patterns of use.
	Eligibility requirements	Charge constant entrance fee. Charge differential fees by trail zones, season, etc. Require proof of camping and ecological knowledge and/or skills.
DIRECT Emphasis on regulation of behavior. Individual choice restricted. High degree of control.	Increased enforcement	Impose fines. Increase surveillance of area.
	Zoning	Separate incompatible uses (hiker-only zones in areas with horse use). Prohibit uses at times of high damage potential (no horse use in high meadows until soil moisture declines, say July 1). Limit camping in some campsites to one night, or some other limit.
	Rationing use intensity	Rotate use (open or close access points, trails, campsites). Require reservations. Assign campsites and/or travel routes to each camper group. Limit usage via access point. Limit size of groups, number of horses. Limit camping to designated campsites only. Limit length of stay in area (max./min.).
	Restrictions on activities	Restrict building campfires. Restrict horse use, hunting, or fishing.

Source: modified from Gilbert and others 1972.

Wilderness Recreation Management: A General Overview

even more. Clearly, the particularly strong tension between wilderness experiences and regulations implied by the Wilderness Act, as discussed earlier, is widely perceived to be real and important.

Benefits to Visitors

Regulation can be beneficial, and, of course, recreation in many sports and games requires rules. Eliminating some freedoms in outdoor recreation can create other, perhaps more valuable, freedoms (Dustin and McAvoy 1984). Safety is a case in point. For example, removing powerboaters' freedom to operate in swimming areas greatly increases swimmers' freedom to swim safely. Even the benefits of safety can have costs when safety regulations detract from high adventure or risk recreation such as kayaking in difficult rapids, rock and ice climbing, cave exploring, and so on. In other cases, where safety is not an issue, regulations remove the freedom to behave in ways that interfere with others' freedom to enjoy an area—for example, regulations requiring quiet in campgrounds after 10 p.m.

Regulations also can prevent the "tragedy of the commons" described by Hardin (1968); that is, the loss to all caused by the natural tendency of individuals to overuse a resource owned by all, such as common pastures in medieval England. For example, game laws, especially bag or catch limits, prevent overexploitation of resources on which recreation depends. Closely related are regulations designed to protect the environment by banning high-impact activities such as picking flowers, cutting live trees, and shortcutting switchbacks on trails.

Another major positive role for regulation is the allocation of opportunities. Thus, managers can determine who will benefit from a recreation area (Jacob and Schreyer 1980) and can separate conflicting types of recreation such as snowmobiling and skiing. Basically, regulations can establish objectives for places based on their position on the ROS (USDA FS 1982).

Considerable evidence suggests that recreationists often accept regulations fairly well, particularly if their necessity is explained. For example, 82 percent of the applicants for the limited number of permits to visit California's San Gorgonio and San Jacinto Wildernesses supported restricted use of the area (Stankey 1979). Even those turned away without a permit supported rationing through permits by 3 to 1. High acceptance of use rationing was also reported in Colorado's Rocky Mountain National Park (Fazio and Gilbert 1974). Only 10 to 12 percent of the sampled visitors to nine wilderness and backcountry areas believed that restricting use was undesirable when an area was being used beyond

capacity (Lucas 1980). Similar acceptance of use limitations also has been reported for whitewater rivers (McCool and Utter 1982).

Acceptance Does Not Equal Preference

Acceptance of restrictive regulations, as described above, should not be misinterpreted as an indication that visitors like such regulations. Surveys of visitor attitudes toward regulations show a strong preference for less authoritarian styles of management. Stankey (1973) found that 81 percent of visitors to four wildernesses were opposed to a system of permits that "assigned where people can visit and camp." Two-thirds of the campers in eight wildernesses studied in Idaho and Montana opposed the idea of a regulation prohibiting wood fires, and horse users rejected by 3 to 1 a possible requirement that they carry in all feed for their stock (Lucas 1980). A majority of 1982 visitors to the BMWC indicated that a regulation prohibiting camping within 200 feet of water was undesirable (Lucas 1985). Hendee and others (1968) found that 58 percent of visitors to three wildernesses in Washington and Oregon agreed with the statement, "One should camp wherever he pleases in remote backcountry." The same study found general rejection of restrictions on visitor numbers and even more opposition to elimination of horse use.

In many cases, conscientious visitors accept restrictions because they see them as the lesser of two evils. On the other hand, some people *do* object to regulations. For example, Behan (1974) strenuously protested what he called "police state wilderness," referring to mandatory permits and visitor regulation. An editorial in the *High Country News* (1975) lamented wilderness recreation regulation, while recognizing the need for some regulation, applied with restraint.

Visitor acceptance also can be a false indicator that all is well if people avoid an area because of what they view as restrictive regulations. These displaced visitors are succeeded or replaced by those who accept the regulation. This can give managers a false sense of success. Research on this succession and displacement process is difficult and therefore scarce, but one of the few studies done found that "too many use controls" was one of the top three reasons given by boaters who had stopped using the lower St. Croix and Upper Mississippi Rivers (Denburg 1982).

One possible example of displacement of visitors related to regulations involves a national forest wilderness and a neighboring national park. It has been suggested that heavy regulation of backpackers in Montana's Glacier National Park (for example, no dogs, assigned campsites, following preestablished itineraries) may have contributed to a sharp drop in

Fig. 15.9. Camping close to water, as in the Selway-Bitterroot Wilderness in ID, is often prohibited. Nevertheless, campers often claim they are unaware of the regulations or that they were unable to find an alternative campsite farther from shorelines. Photo courtesy of Richard Behan.

use compared to the large USFS-managed Bob Marshall Wilderness nearby where regulation is less strict (Missoulian 1984). Use of Glacier Park's backcountry dropped 53 percent since 1977, while use of the Bob Marshall Wilderness declined 5 percent over the same period, with all of the decline since 1982. Other possible explanations for different use trends might be fear of grizzly bears. Although grizzlies inhabit both Glacier National Park and the Bob Marshall, all bear attacks have occurred in the national park.

Use of Regulations by Managers

Several surveys of wilderness management practices show more reliance on regulations than on nonregulatory alternatives. A study of all wildernesses under all agencies showed that managers of 54 percent of these areas regulated camping, half had mandatory use permits, 15 percent rationed use, and 69 percent of the areas with significant horse use had regulations affecting such use (Washburne and Cole 1983). When asked what they considered the most effective management technique, the majority listed educational contacts; but a large minority also listed regulations such as designated campsites and lakeshore camp restrictions as the most effective techniques. Another study of the entire National Wilderness Preservation System (NWPS) showed that regulatory controls were used more often than nonregulatory, "manipulative" actions (such as education), especially by the NPS (Fish and Bury 1981). The study's authors also reported that most managers felt that regulatory controls could more effectively reduce problems of overuse, although they

indicated wilderness users reacted more favorably to nonregulatory actions (Bury and Fish 1980).

Guidelines for Regulation

Some general guidelines seem reasonable for managers trying to fit regulation into its appropriate place in recreation management, whether related to managing impacts or visitor experiences, or both.

1. *Do not regulate if effective nonregulatory alternatives exist.* Establishing a regulation, by itself, achieves nothing out in the real world, although it may provide a sense of satisfaction that *something* is being done. This may be an illusion: effectiveness depends on a sequence of events, each of which is as essential as each link in a chain, and which can be expressed in a series of three questions.

First, is it possible to inform visitors of each regulation? Managers have a responsibility to inform visitors—guests might be a better word—before citing them for a violation. The old principle, "ignorance of the law is no excuse," seems out of place in recreation management. Limited knowledge of recreation regulations is common. For example, campers in a developed campground in Pennsylvania were aware of just under half of the regulations in effect there (Ross and Moeller 1974). Only 20 percent of off-road vehicle recreationists in Michigan could correctly describe *any* of the regulations in the area they were visiting (Dorman and Fridgen 1982). The main reason given by violators of a regulation prohibiting camping too close to water (fig. 15.9) in Colorado USFS wildernesses was unawareness of the regulation (Swain 1986).

Second, if visitors are informed about a regulation and understand it, will their behavior change enough to solve the problem? The main underlying question here is whether visitors' motives, knowledge, attitudes, and behavior are understood well enough to estimate their response to a regulation. Visitor behavior can be changed by regulations, but drastic changes in behavior are usually difficult to achieve. For example, Brown and Schomaker (1974) found that 85 percent of campsites in the Spanish Peaks Primitive Area, Montana (now part of the Lee Metcalf Wilderness), were within 200 feet of water. Only 44 percent of the sites were within 50 feet, indicating that a 50-foot setback would require much less change in behavior than a 200-foot regulation,

and almost certainly be more completely achieved. Swain (1986) found the main reason Colorado wilderness visitors violated a regulation requiring dogs to be kept on a leash was rejection of the need for such a regulation. Many said they intended to continue to violate the regulation, even if it meant paying a fine, an example of divergent perceptions of problems.

Finally, if the regulation changes visitor behavior as intended, will this really help achieve management objectives? The underlying question is whether managers understand the causal process that creates the management problem. For example, if visitors do not camp on three existing campsites within 200 feet of Granite Lake, six new campsites may develop beyond 200 feet, and parties eating lunch or resting at the old campsites may trample the vegetation enough to prevent substantial recovery, resulting in nine impacted sites where there were only three.

2. *Try to develop effective nonregulatory visitor management.* Maybe wilderness managers are too quick to assume that regulations are the only or the most effective way to achieve objectives. They may sell indirect, nonregulatory approaches short. A wilderness ranger reported that about half of the campers in his area were camping within 200 feet of shorelines even after several years of intensive efforts to enforce a regulation prohibiting camping within 200 feet of lakes and streams. An information program that described the problem and explained the impacts of campsite location on the environment, on other visitors, and on sanitation might have changed specific campsite selection by visitors at least as much as the regulation with its poor compliance.

There are *two main types of indirect, nonregulatory actions that managers can employ—design and education.* Both will be discussed in detail in the next chapter. Design can modify ease of access and trail systems to affect amount and type of use. Information, education, and persuasion are subtle, nonauthoritarian, and potentially powerful management tools.

Wilderness visitors seem particularly well-suited for management programs based on education and information. The most distinguishing socioeconomic characteristic of wilderness visitors is a high level of education (chap. 14). Furthermore, wilderness visitors usually attach high personal importance to wilderness (Lucas 1980), a fact that suggests many would respond to information about how to protect these areas.

3. *Explain regulations.* An explanation of necessary regulations should improve compliance, especially in ways that relate to the most important aspects of the problem. Good explanations could also reduce the costs to visitors by reducing perceptions

of regulations as arbitrary hassles and also help make enforcement more reasonable and selective without being capricious. Trying to develop an explanation of a regulation may also identify weaknesses in the rationale linking the regulation to a management problem.

4. *Regulate at the minimal level needed to solve the problem.* Regulations span a continuum from severe to relatively mild. Avoid regulations that are stricter or more sweeping than needed or that restrict visitor behavior that is not part of the problem. Target the specific problem as precisely as possible. For example, if campfires are causing unacceptable impacts at some locations, prohibiting fires would deal with the problem more precisely than banning camping.

5. *Regulate at the entry level rather than at the activity level within an area.* In many cases, especially in wilderness and backcountry recreation, freedom and spontaneity can be preserved if most regulations are applied outside the area at the time of entry; those admitted to an area would be substantially free to travel and camp where the mood moved them, with little regulation. Limits on number of visitors admitted, party size, and method of travel are examples of "outside" regulations; assigned campsites or prescheduled travel itineraries are examples of "inside" regulations.

6. *Monitor the problem and the effects of the management action.* Monitoring of some sort is essential because most management actions are taken with only a limited understanding of their likely consequences; monitoring is the only way to determine what the actions really accomplish. If managers are to use their day-to-day experience to minimize regulations, to make necessary regulations more effective through progressive fine-tuning, and to develop other approaches to solving problems, they must monitor effectively. Without monitoring, managers are engaged in a huge, unorganized, and unrecognized experiment that yields very little new knowledge because what is done is not documented and results are not objectively observed and tallied. Intuitive hunches that something is working are not enough, especially when the person judging was also involved in the decision about the management action.

7. *Finally, when considering recreation regulations, managers need to remember that visitors are one reason wildernesses exist.* Wilderness, of course, exists primarily to preserve natural ecosystems while also offering opportunities for wilderness experiences. The visitors are the owners of wilderness, not intruders, and should not be viewed as problems (although

some of them sometimes are). This is recognized in the USFS's "Good Host" program, which is intended to promote agency employees' sensitivity to visitors' needs and desires, but all of its implications for recreation management may not have been fully recognized.

LOCATION OF MANAGEMENT

We have just referred to the advantages of applying regulations outside a wilderness instead of inside. This is part of a more general wilderness visitor management issue. Contact with visitors, in person, through signs, and with printed materials, to present information about suggested practices, regulations, closures, or alternative places to visit, are usually best delivered outside the wilderness. To do otherwise could detract from certain dimensions of the wilderness experience: the sense of isolation, solitude, freedom, and of being in an undeveloped setting. Pretrip contact usually is also more effective in achieving the desired change in behavior because the information comes early enough in the decision process to be used (Lucas 1981). This is not to say that wilderness rangers are out of place in the backcountry. (Most visitors react positively to them.) But, when working inside wilderness, they should be concentrating on tasks that cannot be done outside the wilderness: monitoring conditions, dealing with violations of regulations, educating visitors engaging in inappropriate behavior, and correcting specific onsite problems such as litter cleanup or maintaining trails. Of course, many of their duties also are performed outside wilderness: for example, educational contacts, planning, and data analysis.

MULTIPLE MANAGEMENT APPROACHES

Employing several techniques in a balanced, coordinated manner is needed when developing wilderness recreation management approaches. Relying on only one approach is sure to be less effective than an integrated combination of approaches—neither regulations, education, design, nor wilderness rangers are the whole answer. No single approach is so powerful, versatile, or acceptable in terms of costs to visitors or managers that it constitutes a panacea.

SUMMARY

Recreation management is a vital part of wilderness management. It is guided by two principal objectives: providing a natural setting and a special type of visitor experience. Both objectives are important, but sometimes achieving them results in conflict. A facility-oriented engineering approach is largely inappropriate. Other approaches, based on management of use and visitor behavior, must be stressed. Five types of undesirable visitor actions exist, ranging in severity, each with different kinds of appropriate management responses. Managers and visitors differ in their perceptions of problems; managers perceive impact problems as more important than social problems, whereas visitors take the opposite point of view. Divergent perceptions reduce compliance with regulations and acceptance of recommendations. Managers need to be aware of visitor perceptions and work to narrow gaps between visitors and their own perceptions of problem conditions. Many aspects of recreational use are subject to management: amount of use, distribution of use, timing of use, party size, length of stay, and visitor behavior. Professional management of these aspects of wilderness recreation to protect natural conditions and opportunities for wilderness experiences requires adequate data about visitors and resources, much of which currently is of poor quality or is completely lacking.

Some management approaches are direct, imposing control on visitors' actions, while other approaches are indirect, altering factors that influence visitors' choices. In general, indirect approaches are preferable, being more consistent with wilderness concepts. Regulation is the prime example of a direct approach, and should be used with restraint, after careful consideration of objectives of alternative techniques, and with recognition of the limitations on effectiveness of regulations. Monitoring of the results of management actions is essential to improve future management, and much improvement is needed. Management from outside a wilderness generally is preferable to management inside, especially in regulations and educational contacts. No single management approach is effective enough or acceptable enough to be the sole choice; a blend of approaches is essential.

STUDY QUESTIONS

1. What two objectives are stressed in the Wilderness Act? How do these objectives relate to recreational use and management?
2. Under what conditions are administrative activities granted an exception to Wilderness Act prohibitions?
3. How can recreational use problems in wilderness be classified? How does this relate to appropriate management responses to problems?

4. How do managers' and visitors' perceptions of problems in wilderness compare?
5. What aspects of wilderness recreation use can managers control or influence?
6. What objectives might guide managers' efforts to redistribute wilderness recreation use?
7. What sort of information do managers need? Why? What standards should information meet? How can it be gathered?
8. What characterizes direct and indirect visitor management? What are the strengths and weaknesses of each?
9. How should visitor regulations be used? What should be considered in adopting regulations?

REFERENCES

Back Country Horsemen. [n.d.] Back country horsemen's guidebook. 2d ed. Columbia Falls, MT: Back Country Horsemen. 60 p.

Behan, R. W. 1974. Police state wilderness: a comment on mandatory wilderness permits. Journal of Forestry. 72(2): 98-99.

Brown, Perry J.; Schomaker, John H. 1974. Final report on criteria for potential wilderness campsites. Report submitted to the Intermountain Forest and Range Experiment Station under cooperative agreement supplement No. 32 to 12-11-204-3, conducted through the Institute for the Study of Outdoor Recreation and Tourism, Utah State University, Logan, UT; June. 50 p.

Brown, Perry J.; Haas, Glenn E. 1980. Wilderness recreation experiences: the Rawah case. Journal of Leisure Research. 12(3): 229-241.

Browning, James A.; Hendee, John C.; Roggenbuck, Joe W. 1988. 103 wilderness laws: milestones and management direction in wilderness legislation, 1964-1987. Stn. Bull. 51. Moscow, ID: University of Idaho, Idaho Forest, Wildlife and Range Experiment Station, College of Forestry, Wildlife and Range Sciences. 73 p.

Burch, William R., Jr. 1964. A new look at an old friend—observation as a technique for recreation research. Portland, OR: U.S. Department of Agriculture, Forest Service, Pacific Northwest Forest and Range Experiment Station. 19 p.

Bury, Richard L.; Fish, C. Ben. 1980. Controlling wilderness recreation: what managers think and do. Journal of Soil and Water Conservation. 35(2): 90-93.

Campbell, Frederick L. 1970. Participant observation in outdoor recreation. Journal of Leisure Research. 2(4): 226-236.

Clark, Roger N. 1977. Alternative strategies for studying river recreationists. In: Proceedings, river recreation management and research symposium; 1977 January 24-27; Minneapolis, MN. Gen. Tech. Rep. NC-28. St. Paul, MN: U.S. Department of Agriculture, Forest Service, North Central Forest Experiment Station: 91-100.

Clark, Roger N.; Stankey, George H. 1979. The Recreation Opportunity Spectrum: a framework for planning, management, and research. Gen. Tech. Rep. PNW-98. Portland, OR: U.S. Department of Agriculture, Forest Service, Pacific Northwest Forest and Range Experiment Station. 32 p.

Cole, David N. 1986. Ecological changes on campsites in the Eagle Cap Wilderness, 1979 to 1984. Res. Pap. INT-368. Ogden, UT: U.S. Department of Agriculture, Forest Service, Intermountain Research Station. 15 p.

Denburg, Ronald F. 1982. Crowding and social displacement on the lower St. Croix and upper Mississippi Rivers. Madison, WI: University of Wisconsin. 380 p. M.S. thesis.

Dillman, Don A. 1978. Mail and telephone surveys: the total design method. New York: John Wiley & Sons. 325 p.

Dorman, Phyllis; Fridgen, Joseph. 1982. Evaluation of an off-road vehicle information and education program. In: Forest and river recreation: research update. Misc. Publ. 18. St. Paul, MN: University of Minnesota, Agricultural Experiment Station: 33-37.

Driver, B. L.; Tocher, S. Ross. 1970. Toward a behavioral interpretation of recreational engagements, with implications for planning. In: Driver, B. L., ed. Elements of outdoor recreation planning. Ann Arbor, MI: university Microfilms, for School of Natural Resources, University of Michigan: 9-31.

Driver, B. L.; Brown, Perry J. 1978. The opportunity spectrum concept and behavior information in outdoor recreation resource supply inventories: a rationale. In: Lund, Gyde H.; LaBau, Vernon J.; Ffolliott, Peter F.; Robinson, David W., tech. coords. Integrated inventories of renewable natural resources: Proceedings of the workshop; 1978 January 8-12; Tucson, AZ. Gen. Tech. Rep. RM-55. Fort Collins, CO: U.S. Department of Agriculture, Forest Service, Rocky Mountain Forest and Range Experiment Station: 24-31.

Dustin, Daniel L.; McAvoy, Leo H. 1984. The limitation of the traffic light. Journal of Park and Recreation Administration. 2(3): 28-32.

Elsner, Gary H. 1972. Wilderness management . . . a computerized system for summarizing permit information. Gen. Tech. Rep. PSW-2. Berkeley, CA: U.S. Department of Agriculture, Forest Service, Pacific Southwest Forest and Range Experiment Station. 8 p.

Fazio, James R.; Gilbert, Douglas L. 1974. Mandatory wilderness permits: some indications of success. Journal of Forestry. 72(12): 753-756.

Fish, C. Ben; Bury, Richard L. 1981. Wilderness visitor management: diversity and agency policies. Journal of Forestry. 79(9): 608-612.

Frayer, W. E.; Butts, D. B. 1974. BUS: a processing system for records of back country camper use. Journal of Leisure Research. 6(4): 305-311.

Gilbert, Gorman C.; Peterson, George L.; Lime, David W. 1972. Toward a model of travel behavior in the Boundary Waters Canoe Area. Environment and Behavior. 4(2): 131-157.

Haas, Glenn E.; Driver, B. L.; Brown, Perry J. 1980. Measuring wilderness recreation experiences. In: Proceedings, Wilderness Psychology Group annual conference; 1980 August 14-15; Durham, NH. Durham, NH: University of New Hampshire: 20-40.

Hardin, Garrett. 1968. The tragedy of the commons. Science. 162(3859): 1243-1248.

Hendee, John C.; Catton, William R., Jr.; Marlow, Larry D.; Brockman, C. Frank. 1968. Wilderness users in the Pacific Northwest—their characteristics, values, and management preferences. Res. Pap. PNW-61. Portland,

OR: U.S. Department of Agriculture, Forest Service, Pacific Northwest Forest and Range Experiment Station. 92 p.

Hendee, John C.; Harris, Robert W. 1970. Foresters' perception of wilderness-user attitudes and preferences. Journal of Forestry. 68(12): 759-762.

Hendee, John C.; Lucas, Robert C. 1973. Mandatory wilderness permits: a necessary management tool. Journal of Forestry. 71(4): 206-209.

Hendee, John C.; Clark, Roger N.; Hogans, Mack L.; Wood, Dan; Koch, Russel W. 1976. Code-A-Site: a system for inventory of dispersed recreational sites in roaded areas, back country, and wilderness. Res. Pap. PNW-209. Portland, OR: U.S. Department of Agriculture, Forest Service, Pacific Northwest Forest and Range Experiment Station. 33 p.

Hendee, John C.; Clark, Roger N.; Dailey, Thomas E. 1977. Fishing and other recreation behavior at high-mountain lakes in Washington State. Res. Note PNW-304. Portland, OR: U.S. Department of Agriculture, Forest Service, Pacific Northwest Forest and Range Experiment Station. 26 p.

Herfindahl, Orris C. 1969. Natural resource information for economic development. Baltimore, MD: Johns Hopkins University Press for Resources for the Future. 212 p.

High Country News [Lander, WY]. 1975. Editorials: rules needed and lamented. July 18: 3 (col. 1).

Jacob, Gerald R.; Schreyer, Richard. 1980. Conflict in outdoor recreation: a theoretical perspective. Journal of Leisure Research. 12(4): 368-380.

Lee, Robert G. 1975. The management of human components in the Yosemite National Park ecosystem. Berkeley, CA: Department of Forestry and Conservation, College of Natural Resources, University of California. 134 p. [Final Res. Rep., prepared for the Yosemite Institute, Yosemite National Park, Yosemite, CA.]

Lime, David W. 1970. Research for determining use capacities of the Boundary Waters Canoe Area. Naturalist. 21(4): 8-13.

Lime, David W.; Buchman, Roland G. 1974. Putting wilderness permit information to work. Journal of Forestry. 72(10): 622-626.

Lime, David W.; Lorence, Grace A. 1974. Improving estimates of wilderness use from mandatory travel permits. Res. Pap. NC-101. St. Paul, MN: U.S. Department of Agriculture, Forest Service, North Central Forest Experiment Station. 7 p.

Lucas, Robert C. 1964. Wilderness perception and use: the example of the Boundary Waters Canoe Area. Natural Resources Journal. 3: 394-411.

Lucas, Robert C. 1973. Wilderness: a management framework. Journal of Soil and Water Conservation. 28(4): 150-154.

Lucas, Robert C. 1979. Perceptions of non-motorized recreational impacts: a review of research findings. In: Ittner, Ruth; Potter, Dale R.; Agee, James K.; Anschell, Susie, eds. Recreational impacts on wildlands; Conference proceedings; 1978 October 27-29; Seattle, WA. Portland, OR: U.S. Department of Agriculture, Forest Service, Pacific Northwest Region: 24-31.

Lucas, Robert C. 1980. Use patterns and visitor characteristics, attitudes, and preferences in nine wilderness and other roadless areas. Res. Pap. INT-253. Ogden, UT:

U.S. Department of Agriculture, Forest Service, Intermountain Forest and Range Experiment Station. 89 p.

Lucas, Robert C. 1981. Redistributing wilderness use through information supplied to visitors. Res. Pap. INT-277. Ogden, UT: U.S. Department of Agriculture, Forest Service, Intermountain Forest and Range Experiment Station. 15 p.

Lucas, Robert C. 1982. Recreation regulations—when are they needed? Journal of Forestry. 80(3): 148-151.

Lucas, Robert C. 1983. Low and variable visitor compliance rates at voluntary trail registers. Res. Note INT-326. Ogden, UT: U.S. Department of Agriculture, Forest Service, Intermountain Forest and Range Experiment Station. 5 p.

Lucas, Robert C. 1985. Visitor characteristics, attitudes, and use patterns in the Bob Marshall Wilderness Complex, 1970-1982. Res. Pap. INT-345. Ogden, UT: U.S. Department of Agriculture, Forest Service, Intermountain Forest and Range Experiment Station. 32 p.

Lucas, Robert C.; Kovalicky, Thomas J. 1981. Self-issued wilderness permits as a use measurement system. Res. Pap. INT-270. Ogden, UT: U.S. Department of Agriculture, Forest Service, Intermountain Forest and Range Experiment Station. 18 p.

Manning, Robert E. 1985. Crowding norms in backcountry settings: a review and synthesis. Journal of Leisure Research. 17(2): 75-89.

McAvoy, Leo H.; Dustin, Daniel L. 1983. Indirect versus direct regulation of recreation behavior. Journal of Park and Recreation Administration. 1(3): 12-17.

McCool, Stephen F.; Utter, Jack. 1982. Recreation use lotteries: outcomes and preferences. Journal of Forestry. 80(1): 10-11, 29.

Miller, Bob. 1973. Suggestions for using horses in the mountain country. Bozeman, MT: [No publisher listed]. 13 p. [Sponsored by The Wilderness Society, Montana Wilderness Association, Wilderness Guides, Treasure State Outfitters, Montana Outfitters and Dude Ranchers, Montana Fish and Game Department.]

Missoulian. 1984. Number of visits to park's backcountry declines. August 24: 13 (cols. 1-5).

Peterson, George L. 1974. A comparison of the sentiments and perceptions of wilderness managers and canoeists in the Boundary Waters Canoe Area. Journal of Leisure Research. 6(3): 194-206.

Potter, Dale R.; Sharpe, Kathryn M.; Hendee, John C.; Clark, Roger N. 1972. Questionnaires for research: an annotated bibliography on design, construction and use. Res. Pap. PNW-140. Portland, OR: U.S. Department of Agriculture, Forest Service, Pacific Northwest Forest and Range Experiment Station. 80 p.

Roggenbuck, Joseph W. 1980. Wilderness user preferences: eastern and western areas. In: Proceedings, wilderness management symposium; 1980 November 13-15; Knoxville, TN. Atlanta: U.S. Department of Agriculture, Southern Region: 103-146.

Ross, Terence L.; Moeller, George H. 1974. Communicating rules in recreation areas. Res. Pap. NE-297. Upper Darby, PA: U.S. Department of Agriculture, Forest Service, Northeastern Forest Experiment Station. 12 p.

Schomaker, John H.; Glassford, Thomas R. 1982. Backcountry as an alternative to wilderness? Journal of Forestry. 80(6): 358-360, 364.

Shelby, Bo; Heberlein, Thomas A. 1984. A conceptual framework for carrying capacity determination. Leisure Sciences. 6(4): 433-451.

Shelby, Bo; Harris, Richard. 1985. Comparing methods for determining visitor evaluations of ecological impacts: site visits, photographs, and written descriptions. Journal of Leisure Research. 17(1): 57-67.

Stankey, George H. 1973. Visitor perception of wilderness recreation carrying capacity. Res. Pap. INT-142. Ogden, UT: U.S. Department of Agriculture, Forest Service, Intermountain Forest and Range Experiment Station. 61 p.

Stankey, George H. 1979. Use rationing in two southern California wildernesses. Journal of Forestry. 77(6): 347-349.

Swain, Ralph W. 1986. Colorado Wilderness violators: who they are and why they violate. Fort Collins, CO: Colorado State University. 107 p. M.S. thesis.

U.S. Department of Agriculture, Forest Service. 1981. Techniques and equipment for wilderness horse travel. Missoula, MT: U.S. Department of Agriculture, Forest Service, Missoula Equipment Development Center; Report 2300-Recreation; 8123 2403. 42 p.

U.S. Department of Agriculture, Forest Service. 1982. ROS users guide. Washington, DC. 38 p.

van Wagtendonk, Jan W.; Benedict, James M. 1980. Wilderness permit compliance and validity. Journal of Forestry. 78(7): 399-401.

Washburne, Randel F.; Cole, David N. 1983. Problems and practices in wilderness management: a survey of managers. Res. Pap. INT-304. Ogden, UT: U.S. Department of Agriculture, Forest Service, Intermountain Forest and Range Experiment Station. 56 p.

The Wilderness Society. 1984. The Wilderness Act handbook. Washington, DC: The Wilderness Society. 64 p.

Worf, William A. 1987. Introduction to wilderness research needs panel discussion. In: Lucas, Robert C., compiler. Proceedings—national wilderness research conference: issues, state-of-knowledge, future directions; 1985 July 23-26; Fort Collins, CO. Gen. Tech. Rep. INT-220. Ogden, UT: U.S. Department of Agriculture, Forest Service, Intermountain Research Station: 351-352.

ACKNOWLEDGMENTS

Edward Bloedel, Division of Recreation, USFS, Washington, DC (at the time of review—now recreation staff, Sawtooth National Forest, ID).

Dr. David Cole, USFS, Intermountain Research Station, Wilderness Research Unit, Missoula, MT.

Dr. William Hammitt, Professor of Forest Recreation, Department of Forestry, Wildlife, and Fisheries, University of Tennessee, Knoxville.

Dr. David Lime, Professor, College of Natural Resources, University of Minnesota, St. Paul.

Dr. Stephen McCool, Professor, School of Forestry, University of Montana, Missoula.

Gret Warren, Recreation and Wilderness staff, USFS Regional Office, Portland, OR.

Recreational activities are highly concentrated at campsites and frequently result in severe ecological impacts. This site in the Lee Metcalf Wilderness, MT, has lost a substantial amount of vegetation, organic matter has eroded away, and mineral soil has been compacted. The "imprint of man's work"—stacked wood and log seats—is quite evident, contrary to the mandate of Wilderness Act of 1964. Photo courtesy of Robert C. Lucas, USFS.

16

ECOLOGICAL IMPACTS OF WILDERNESS RECREATION AND THEIR MANAGEMENT

*This chapter was written by David N. Cole, research biologist and project
leader of the U.S. Forest Service's Wilderness Management Research Work
Unit, Intermountain Research Station, Missoula, MT.*

INTRODUCTION

Eight parallel trails gouged into an alpine meadow, denuded campsites with severe soil erosion, numerous trees battered and scarred by tethered livestock. Such examples of recreational impact are common in the wilderness these days. In many places, managing such impacts presents at least as difficult a challenge as managing for quality wilderness experiences, the subject of the next chapter.

This chapter begins with a discussion of the significance of recreational impacts, its purpose being to bring recreation impacts into perspective with other wilderness management problems. This discussion is followed by a description of important types of recreational impact, those caused by trampling, campfires, construction and maintenance of

trails, pack animals, wildlife disturbance, and water pollution and disposal of human waste. Most of the chapter deals with management of campsites, trails, and pack and saddle stock.

The examples used in this chapter are largely drawn from large wildernesses in the West. This reflects the fact that very little research has been published on eastern wildernesses. Some examples are taken from developed recreation areas with vehicular access. The general dearth of research on the ecological effects of wilderness recreation leaves many of the interpretations offered open to debate. Study locations are noted in the text; caution should be exercised when extrapolating the results of a single study to distant areas.

SIGNIFICANCE OF RECREATIONAL IMPACTS

To evaluate the significance of recreational impacts in wilderness areas, it is important to reexamine the goals of wilderness management. The relevant phrases in the Wilderness Act state that wilderness is an area "which is protected and managed so as to preserve its natural conditions and which *generally* appears to have been affected *primarily* by the forces of nature, with the imprint of man's work *substantially* unnoticeable" (emphasis added). This implies that some recreational impact will be tolerated, but (1) the integrity of largely undisturbed wilderness ecosystems should not be substantially compromised and (2) the evidence of impact should not be conspicuous. The first of these objectives is concerned with protecting wilderness ecology; the second, with protecting quality of the visitor's experience. Both are important. But now the question of what constitutes a substantial compromise of ecosystem integrity arises. Here we suggest that those impacts that seriously disrupt ecosystem function and that either occur over very large areas or that affect rare ecosystems are most significant. Impacts that alter a large proportion of a relatively rare ecosystem type are particularly detrimental. Irreversible changes are most undesirable, and, as long as impact continues, even easily reversible changes are significant.

Despite the ecological impact evident in most wilderness areas, in few cases is recreational use substantially compromising the integrity of large wilderness ecosystems. As we saw in chapter 13, recreational use is highly concentrated along a few major trails and at a few popular destinations. This leaves the vast majority of most wildernesses essentially unvisited and, therefore, undisturbed by recreational use. For example, even in the most heavily used part of the Eagle Cap Wilderness, Oregon, less than 2 percent of the area has been significantly altered by recreational use (Cole 1981a). Far more potent threats to the integrity of wilderness ecosystems exist. Acid rain is altering the basic ecology of lakes throughout uncommon ecosystems in certain areas. A New York State "wilderness" in the Adirondack Mountains, is perhaps the best current example of an area substantially affected by acid rain. In addition to external threats, such as acid rain, internal threats can also be potent. Fire suppression and livestock grazing have significantly altered the vegetation of vast wilderness acreages (see Vale 1977; Vankat and Major 1978; and chap. 12 in this book).

The generalization that recreational use is not

Fig. 16.1. While generally accepted in wilderness, fishing and the planting of fish in naturally barren waters can substantially alter aquatic ecosystems. Photo courtesy of the USFS.

substantially compromising wilderness ecosystems has several important exceptions. The first exception is the introduction of fish, often exotic species, into formerly barren lakes and streams and the subsequent removal of fish through angling. In such cases adding a new component to the food chain has significantly affected entire aquatic ecosystems. It has reduced, displaced, or eliminated competitors or prey organisms and has stimulated the invasion or expansion of predatory populations. Angling, while partially negating the effect of introductions, has altered the population structure of fisheries and, in extreme cases, has nearly eliminated a major consumer and link in the food chain (fig. 16.1).

Generally, fishing is allowed throughout wilderness. In a few cases, the angling pressure is attenuated by "catch-and-release" regulations. Such regulations are in effect in parts of the Frank Church-River of No Return Wilderness, Idaho, and the Golden Trout Wilderness, California, for example. But wilderness designation seldom brings such restrictions. A more common action is discontinuing of artificial stocking of fish. This will allow some formerly barren areas, where reproduction is poor, to revert to a more natural state.

A second significant recreational impact is disturbance of wildlife as a result of hunting or unintentional harassment. Hunting is generally allowed in wildernesses, outside of the national parks. Although effects are difficult to document, disturbance has undoubtedly altered the distribution, population structure, and behavior of many wildlife species. (This is discussed in more detail in chap. 11.)

Finally, less common, but also significant, is physical alteration or pollution of uncommon ecosystems or sites inhabited by rare plants or animals.

Disturbance of such places can lead to the elimination of rare species or the alteration of most examples of certain ecosystem types. Pollution of lakes, disturbance of meadows by packstock, and camping impacts along desert riparian strips are examples of such impacts that occur in certain wildernesses.

Recreational use more commonly compromises the goal of avoiding conspicuous evidence of human impact. The importance of such impacts depends on the visitor's sense of aesthetics and sensitivity to change, and whether or not the change is recreationally desirable, and the magnitude of the change. Thus, trail impacts in meadows are more troublesome than impacts in forests because they are more obvious and aesthetically displeasing, even though the amount of change in meadows may be less than in forests. Felling of trees and cutting of brush may be desirable and appropriate on trails where it makes travel easier but undesirable and inappropriate elsewhere.

The few studies of visitor perceptions of impact show little relationship between visitor satisfaction and amount of impact (Lucas 1979). Many visitors do not notice ecological change; of those who do, many do not conceive of change as "damage"—or undesirable change. Finally, most visitors do not change their behavior or have less satisfactory experiences even when confronted by impacts that they consider undesirable. For example, even those who dislike the heavy evidence of horse use in the Bob Marshall Wilderness are likely to continue to camp in the same places and travel the same trails and, on the whole, enjoy it.

In dramatic contrast, site impacts are the foremost concern of many managers (Godin and Leonard 1979). Managers are often well aware of such impacts and are charged, as managers, to effectively deal with them. Most of the discussion that follows deals more with management to avoid conspicuous evidence of human use than with management to maintain ecosystem integrity.

RECREATIONAL ACTIVITIES AND ASSOCIATED IMPACTS

Now that we have examined the significance of recreational impacts in light of wilderness management goals, we will take a more detailed look at the effects of various recreational activities on the wilderness resource.[1]

TRAMPLING

The old adage to "take nothing but pictures and leave nothing but footprints" is outdated. In many places, too many footprints have left an unwanted legacy. The effects of human trampling have been investigated for more than 50 years, and we now have a clear understanding of many of the general effects of trampling. These can be conveniently displayed in a conceptual model (fig. 16.2).

Trampling has three initial effects: abrasion of vegetation, abrasion of surface soil organic layers, and compaction of soils. Plants can be crushed, sheared off, bruised, and even uprooted by recreational trampling. Although several studies have shown that very light amounts of trampling can stimulate growth (e.g., Bayfield 1971), any consistent trampling is likely to reduce the vigor and reproductive capacity of all but the most resistant species.

Studies have revealed a variety of physiological and morphological changes that occur when vegetation is trampled. Changes include reductions in plant height, stem length, and leaf area, as well as in number of plants that flower, number of flower heads per plant, and seed production (Liddle 1975; Speight 1973). In Glacier National Park, Montana, Hartley (1976) found reduced carbohydrate reserves in the roots of trampled glacier lilies, presumably a response to a reduction in the ability to photosynthesize after trampling. All of these changes are manifested in

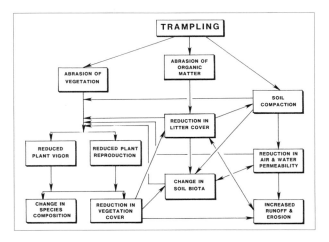

Fig. 16.2. A conceptual model of trampling effects partly based on Liddle 1975 and Manning 1979. Note the numerous reciprocal and cyclic relationships between soil and vegetational impacts.

---

1. For further information, the reader is referred to two excellent review articles (Manning 1979; McEwen and Tocher 1976), several longer reviews (Hart 1982; Kuss and others 1985; Liddle 1975; Speight 1973; Wall and Wright 1977), and a book (Hammitt and Cole 1987).

reduced vigor and reproduction, leading to less plant biomass and cover. Thus, most recreation sites exhibit a gradient in which the cover of vegetation decreases from undisturbed vegetation to places where trampling stress is concentrated and no cover survives. The sharpness of this gradient depends on both the fragility of the vegetation and whether the trampling is concentrated or dispersed. For example, the gradient from no vegetation to normal cover levels is very narrow along trails, where trampling is concentrated, particularly those through fragile vegetation, and quite wide on campsites, where trampling is dispersed, particularly those in resistant vegetation.

Plants vary in their ability to tolerate trampling. Some plants are even favored by trampling—not as a direct response to abrasion, but in response to reduced competition with other plants and favorable changes in microclimate that result from trampling. For example, trampling often increases light levels and temperature ranges—changes that favor certain species. Many, if not most, of these favored species are introduced plants that are brought into the wilderness by humans and packstock.

The vegetation that grows in areas of moderate disturbance, then, is very different in composition from undisturbed vegetation. It consists of trampling-tolerant survivors as well as either native or nonnative invaders capable of growing in the local environment and dispersing to the site. Which of these types of plants dominates is highly variable. In the Eagle Cap Wilderness, dandelion, a Eurasian weed, is the most common plant on lower elevation campsites (Cole 1982a). Apparently it cannot tolerate conditions on campsites in subalpine forests, where the most common plants are rushes and sedges that were originally on the site and that survive trampling, although at reduced densities (Cole 1982b).

The tendency for the original site occupants to decrease in density, creating more favorable conditions for new invaders, explains the observation that *species richness*—the number of different species occupying the site—often increases with low to moderate levels of trampling before declining to zero as trampling intensifies.

Knowledge of which species and types of plants are most tolerant of trampling can be useful in locating sites with resistant vegetation types. Growth forms that tolerate trampling have been identified by Speight (1973) and Holmes and Dobson (1976) and include:

1. A procumbent or trailing, rather than erect, growth form.
2. A tufted growth form.
3. Possession of thorns or prickles.
4. Stems that are flexible rather than brittle and rigid.
5. Leaves in a basal rosette or cluster.
6. Small, thick leaves.
7. Flexible leaves that can fold under pressure.
8. The ability to initiate growth from intercalary meristems, located at the base of leaves, as well as from apical meristems at the tips of stems and branches, where they are likely to be damaged.
9. The ability for perennials to initiate seasonal regrowth from buds concealed below the soil surface.
10. The ability to reproduce vegetatively from suckers, stolons, rhizomes, or corms, as well as through seeding.
11. A rapid rate of growth.
12. The ability to reproduce when recreational use is low.

Generally, broad-leaved herbs, lichens, and tree seedlings have little tolerance and are quickly eliminated on recreation sites. Elimination of tree seedlings on forested recreation sites portends major, undesirable changes on these sites once the overstory dies. Established trees, because of their size, are little affected by trampling except in the few cases where studies have found reduced growth rates (Brown and others 1977), increased water stress (Settergren and Cole 1970), and damage to root systems and increased windthrow as a result of erosion (Frissell and Duncan 1965). Grasslike plants, as well as certain other low-growing herbs, are most tolerant of trampling. Plants growing in shade are less able to tolerate trampling because *adaptations to shading*—possession of large, thin leaves and tall stems—make these plants vulnerable when trampled. This explains the common finding that trampling of forested sites generally results in more rapid loss of vegetation than trampling of open woodlands or meadows (McEwen and Tocher 1976).

Although their size spares them from most trampling damage, large shrubs and trees are affected by a number of associated recreational activities. Vegetation removal during trail construction and for firewood will be discussed below. Trees may be felled for tentpoles, hitch rails, or other structures, and shrubs and trees may be removed to create additional tent space. They are also subjected to *deliberate mutilation*—carved initials and ax scars. In contrast to most species, aspen usually dies from these surface injuries, suggesting that aspen groves make poor recreation sites (Hinds 1976).

Normally, less than half of a given volume of soil is solid matter; the rest is pore space that contains air and water. Trampling *compacts the soil*—presses together the solid soil particles, filling or compressing many of the pores. Larger pores—those that permit rapid percolation of water after precipitation and are normally occupied by air—are severely reduced by trampling (Monti and Mackintosh 1979). This can

indirectly affect vegetation and soil microbiota (fig. 16.3). It can cause oxygen shortages and reduce water availability. Along with the greater difficulty plant roots have in moving through compacted soils, these changes generally reduce plant vigor and retard reproduction and establishment of seedlings.

Increases in *bulk density*—the weight of soil packed into a given volume—as high as 170 percent have been recorded on backcountry campsites in Sequoia National Park, California (Stohlgren 1982). But increases are more commonly 30 percent or less. A loss of 60 percent of the larger soil pores was recorded on developed campsites in Ontario (Monti and Mackintosh 1979). Compaction is generally most pronounced in the upper 6 inches of soil. Generally, susceptibility to compaction is least where soils are sandy or have a narrow range of particle sizes, and where trampling occurs when soils are dry (Lull 1959).

In addition to effects on aboveground vegetation, compaction will also affect soil biota. Larger organisms, such as earthworms, that help rejuvenate the soil find it more difficult to penetrate dense soils. Microbiota are likely to be adversely affected by lower oxygen concentrations. Of particular concern are adverse effects on mycorrhizal fungi, which improve nutrient uptake and water absorption in plants and thus often are a limiting factor in revegetating disturbed areas (Reeves and others 1979)-

Perhaps of even more importance, compaction drastically reduces the rate at which water filters into the soil. Several studies have reported infiltration rates cut by more than 95 percent on developed campsites (Brown and others 1977; James and others 1979). Water

that does not filter into the soil runs off across the surface. Greater runoff increases erosion potential and decreases the supply of soil water. Although this reduced water supply is unlikely to be a problem in areas with plentiful rainfall, it is likely to increase water stress in arid environments or during dry periods of the year (Settergren and Cole 1970).

Erosion is likely to be a more common and significant problem. Deeply eroded trails are unsightly and difficult to use. Erosion on campsites and other sites of concentrated use, by removing the most productive soils on the site, diminishes the potential for vegetational growth on the site. Moreover, the formation of soil is such a slow process that erosion can be considered an irreversible process.

Abrasion and loss of organic matter exacerbates many of these same problems. Normally, thick organic horizons protect the mineral soil from much of the direct impact of trampling and decrease surface water runoff. Loss of these layers facilitates increased compaction and runoff. This leads to further loss of organic litter carried off by running water, completing what Manning (1979) has called the "*vicious circle*" of soil impact.

Loss of litter directly affects plant and animal populations, both above and below the soil surface. For example, vegetation composition is likely to shift as plants that germinate best on organic media give way to those that are more successful on bare mineral soil. Seeds of most species are unlikely to germinate on a smooth, compacted soil surface devoid of litter without a variety of microenvironments.

Fig. 16.3. A heavily impacted campsite in the subalpine forest of the Eagle Cap Wilderness, OR, illustrates many of the effects of trampling. Note loss of vegetation and exposure of mineral soil and tree roots. Photo courtesy of David Cole, USFS.

Fig. 16.4. The impacts associated with campfires have both aesthetic and ecological consequences. Photo courtesy of Robert Lucas, USFS.

CAMPFIRES

Collection and burning of wood in campfires results in its own special impacts (fig. 16.4). As with trampling, these impacts are both aesthetic (firerings, blackened rocks, and charcoal) and ecologic (felled trees and sterilized soils). Ecological impacts result from both the removal of wood, either live or dead, standing or on the ground, from large areas around the campsite, and the burning of this wood in campfires (Cole and Dalle-Molle 1982).

The removal of firewood and associated trampling greatly enlarge the area affected by camping activities. In Great Smoky Mountains National Park in Tennessee and North Carolina, the area disturbed by firewood collection was typically more than nine times the size of the devegetated area around campsites. In this much larger area, number of live and dead trees, usually the smaller size classes, were reduced, as were woody fuels. Pieces of wood 1 to 3 inches in diameter were barely one-third as abundant as on neighboring undisturbed sites (Bratton and others 1982). Saunders (1979) has also documented shifts in understory composition—presumably caused by trampling—in areas disturbed primarily by firewood collection.

Because leaves, needles, and twigs—the tree components most critical to nutrient cycling—are little affected by firewood collection, removing downed wood need not adversely affect long-term site productivity. The major source of damage is likely to be the elimination of large (more than three-inch diameter) woody debris. Decaying wood of this size plays an important role in the ecosystem that has only recently been appreciated (Harvey and others 1979). It has an unusually high water-holding capacity, accumulates nitrogen, phosphorus, and sometimes calcium and magnesium, and is a significant site for nitrogen-fixing microorganisms. It is the preferred substrate for seedling establishment and subsequent growth of certain species. Of particular importance, *ectomycorrhizal fungi*—organisms that develop a symbiotic association with the roots of most higher plants, improving the plants' ability to extract water, nitrogen, and phosphate from less fertile soils—are also concentrated in decayed wood. Consequently, although collection of smaller pieces of wood is unlikely to cause adverse impacts, elimination of large woody debris is likely to reduce site productivity, particularly on droughty and infertile soils.

Loss of large woody debris is likely to adversely affect the populations of invertebrates, small mammals, and birds that use the wood as a food source or

living place. It eliminates sites protected from trampling where seedlings can regenerate and removes natural dams that decrease the potential for soil erosion. Clearly, loss of large woody debris due to firewood collection is a serious impact where a sizable area is affected; recovery rates, moreover, are likely to be lengthy. Collection of wood that can be broken by hand is likely to have little effect.

A wood campfire severely affects the area burned. Fenn and others (1976) found that a single intense campfire burned 90 percent of the organic matter in the upper inch of soil. Fires cause pronounced changes in soil chemistry. Reported fire effects include the loss of nitrogen, sulfur, and phosphorus, increases in pH and many cations, and reductions in the moisture-holding capacity, infiltration rates, and mycorrhizal fungi populations of soil. Overall, these changes constitute a sterilization of the soil, likely to render the site less hospitable for the growth of vegetation and likely to require at least 10 to 15 years to recover, particularly if the site has been used for some time (Cole and Dalle-Molle 1982). Such impacts are particularly pronounced where fires have been built in several places on a single campsite.

Other problems result from carelessness with campfires. Escaped campfires have burned thousands of acres. More common is the destruction of small vegetational coppices by creeping root fires. This has been a serious problem in subalpine tree clumps in the mountains of the Southwest. Here, such clumps are very beautiful, are valued highly as campsites, and regenerate very slowly, if at all.

Although more research will be necessary before we understand the significance of firewood collection and burning, the preceding review suggests some important means of minimizing impact. *With firewood collection, the key is not disturbing woody debris larger than 3 inches in diameter.* The firewood collection problem can be minimized by teaching visitors to collect only wood they can break by hand. In fact, if campers would leave their axes and saws at home many impacts—loss of large woody debris, scarring, and felling of trees—would be eliminated. It may also be necessary to prohibit or discourage campfires, or to promote the use of small stoves in areas where wood production is low. If use in such areas is high, firewood will quickly disappear, tempting visitors to use the larger pieces. In fact, campfires should probably be discouraged or prohibited wherever use is very high—regardless of site productivity—to avoid adverse impacts. As of 1980, regulations in 15 percent of all classified and proposed wildernesses prohibited campfires (Washburne and Cole 1983). This prohibition was most common in areas with

little firewood—arid, arctic, and alpine regions. Other areas prohibit fires in zones of low productivity, above 9,600 feet in Yosemite National Park, California, for example. Such a prohibition at high elevations would also reduce the destruction of tree coppices by escaped campfires.

Minimizing campfire impacts is more complex, involving *a choice between either confining impacts to a small total area of concentrated use or dispersing and covering up evidence of use.* Generally, in heavily used areas, campers should be encouraged to use established firerings so that only a small amount of ground is severely altered. This requires leaving a firering at well-used sites, encouraging campers to use these sites, and keeping them clean and attractive. In areas that are not used frequently, it might be better to persuade visitors to use undamaged sites, to build small, less-damaging fires, and to camouflage the site when they leave to discourage repeated use of the site and, through the addition of organic matter, initiate recovery of the site. In this case campers must be willing to select undisturbed sites and be able to leave the site looking undisturbed. The worst situation is allowing firerings to move around a site, continually being rebuilt after being removed by rangers or earlier campers, and allowing many fire sites to proliferate at popular destinations. Unfortunately, this situation is all too common. Further discussion of the pros and cons of dispersal and concentration can be found in the section on campsite management in this chapter and in Cole and Dalle-Molle (1982).

TRAIL CONSTRUCTION AND MAINTENANCE

The construction and maintenance of trails have pronounced effects on vegetation and soil. Although these impacts are usually deliberate and considered necessary to provide recreational opportunities and to manage visitor traffic, their impacts, as with all others, should be kept to a minimum.

The major impacts of trail construction and maintenance stem from the opening up of tree and brush canopies, the building of a barren, compacted trail tread that may alter drainage patterns, and the creation of a variety of new habitats in the process. U.S. Forest Service (USFS) standards for maximum clearing widths and heights range from 4 by 8 feet on hiker trails to 8 by 10 feet on trails for stock. This clearance increases light intensity considerably and reduces competition for species that can survive along the trail. These changes can alter the composition of vegetation substantially (Dale and Weaver 1974). Composition along trails also shifts in

response to increased trampling and grazing, increased nitrogen from manure and urine, and increased moisture, the result of having fewer trees to intercept precipitation, fewer plants to transpire, and more watershed along the sides of the compacted trail tread.

The creation of a bare, compacted trail tread and a narrow zone of disturbed vegetation on either side is a dramatic change, but is usually accepted by visitors. The dramatic changes are confined to a zone usually no more than 8 feet wide, although in meadows compositional changes have been noted more than 20 feet from the center of the trail (Cole 1979; Foin and others 1977). Probably more disturbing are sites, usually boggy areas, where the disturbed, barren tread widens, greatly exceeding the USFS maximum tread width standard of 24 inches. This change is caused by use—not construction—although poor location and design during construction may have initiated the problem.

Trail construction can also create new habitat by other means. Examples include creation or elimination of rock faces where trails traverse rock outcrops; creation of debris slopes where boulders are pushed downslope to build the trail; creation of flat, soil-covered surfaces where trails traverse steep talus slopes; and creation of boggy areas where trails impede normal drainages. Again, these changes do not affect large areas and are generally considered to be acceptable; however, they should be recognized as undesirable and kept to a minimum.

Perhaps the two most serious changes are disruptions of drainage systems and aesthetic problems resulting from obtrusive engineering of trails. Unfortunately, the solution to one of these problems is likely to aggravate the other. That is, designs to solve drainage problems may be perceived as overengineering, while lack of engineering may lead to drainage problems. This trade-off will be discussed in more detail in the trail management section of this chapter. The solution demands a careful balance—enough engineering to avoid disturbing drainage while remaining sensitive to user preferences for trails that blend into the natural environment (fig. 16.5). In each situation, those who construct trails will have to evaluate which is more "natural" and appropriate—a high-standard trail that avoids off-trail disturbance or a low-standard trail that risks the possibility of more resource damage and a less comfortable walking surface. When extensive engineering is required, obtrusiveness can be minimized by using native materials.

GRAZING OF RECREATIONAL STOCK

Pack and saddle stock trample vegetation and soil along trails and on campsites, as hikers do, leading to

the changes noted in the section on trampling impact. Differences between stock and hiker impact will be summarized in the section of this chapter on packstock management. Here we will outline changes occurring on areas grazed by recreational packstock—meadows and grasslands that are generally unaffected by hikers.

Grazing areas are affected primarily by trampling and grazing, although defecation may also cause minor changes (fig. 16-6). Grazing, by removing leaves, disrupts the ability of plants to manufacture food. Excessive and repetitive defoliation depletes food reserves, reducing plant vigor and reproductive capacity. Numerous studies have illustrated that grazing can reduce current growth; stem, leaf, and seed stalk heights; reproductive activity; basal and foliar cover; and root growth (see Stoddart and others 1975). Loss of vigor, in turn, makes vegetation more susceptible to trampling damage, particularly penetration of the vegetative mat by stock hooves, and results in a reduction in cover.

Trampling causes changes in vegetation and soil conditions, as described earlier. Of particular concern in grazing areas is disturbance of wet meadows. Wet soils, thick organic deposits, and vegetation mats are all susceptible to deformation and disintegration when trampled. Heavy trampling of such sites can lead to a surface of broken sod and hummocks, increased erosion, and even lowering of water tables. In Kings Canyon National Park, California, disturbance by recreational stock, superimposed on the earlier effects of sheep and cattle grazing, led to accelerated rill, channel, and gully erosion of meadows. Gullies up to 14 feet deep lowered water tables and dried out meadows, promoting invasion of lodgepole pine, before being stabilized through improved meadow management and grazing programs (DeBenedetti and Parsons 1979).

Plants differ in their susceptibility to grazing, much as they differ in susceptibility to trampling. Those capable of growing from buds close to or under the ground are more likely to survive close grazing than those with buds located where they can be removed by grazing. Of even more importance, plants are preferentially grazed so that the least palatable species are most likely to survive grazing. All of these selective forces, along with the introduction of exotic species in manure, coats, hooves, and supplemental feed, contribute to pronounced changes in species composition and reductions in forage. In the Eagle Cap Wilderness, montane valley-bottom meadows grazed by stock had only about two-thirds the vegetational cover of nearby ungrazed

Fig. 16.5. Where trail construction and use is likely to disrupt drainage, bridges are often required; however, such structures should be kept to the minimum required to avoid resource damage. Photo courtesy of the USFS.

meadows. The grazed meadows were dominated by forbs and had a sizable component of annual and exotic species, while the ungrazed meadows were dominated by native grasses and sedges (Cole 1981a).

Because it reduces available forage, stock grazing may adversely affect wildlife populations that use the same forage resource. For such competition to occur, there must be overlap in the diets of the stock and wildlife species and they must be using the same meadows (Fardoe 1980). Of the important ungulates in wilderness areas, competition with elk is most likely. Elk and horses have similar diets (Hansen and Clark 1977), and elk commonly use popular grazing areas as winter range. Unpublished range studies in the Bob Marshall Wilderness, found that recreational stock grazing has caused deterioration of forage areas that are used by elk in winter. Competition with bighorn sheep and mountain goats is also possible, but winter range of these species is probably less accessible to livestock.

WILDLIFE DISTURBANCE

Firewood collection can affect small mammal and bird populations by altering food sources and living places and eliminating protected sites. Similar modifications of habitat are also likely to affect reptile and amphibian populations. Organic trash around campsites also attracts animals, ranging from invertebrates to small rodents, certain birds, and large mammals, such as bears.

Although such changes in habitat are the major source of impact for smaller wildlife species, most of these changes are highly localized and, with the exception of the attraction of "pest" species to campsites, not evident to most users. Change be-

Fig. 16.6. Grazing by pack and saddle stock has altered vegetation and soil conditions over large proportions of many wildernesses. Photo courtesy of the USFS.

comes highly significant only where all of a species' habitat is disturbed or where the "pest" is a bear. Of more significance to the achievement of wilderness management goals are the changes resulting from stocking fish, angling, hunting, and unintentionally harassing wildlife. As noted earlier, hunting outside of national parks and angling are accepted practices that are likely to continue in wilderness, despite their considerable alteration of natural conditions. Fish stocking occurred in more than 40 percent of all wildernesses according to a survey conducted in 1980 (Washburne and Cole 1983). Some wilderness managers are beginning to discontinue this practice, however.

Although poorly understood due to the difficulty of designing studies unintentional harassment, particularly of birds and large mammals, has undoubtedly altered the distribution, structure, and behavior of animal populations (Ream 1980). Where harassment affects an entire population (as is likely to be the case with grizzly bear or hunted, localized populations of bighorn sheep and mountain goat) or affects most of a species' habitat, this disturbance is probably much more disruptive to wilderness ecosystems than many of the impacts we have been discussing, such as effects of trampling on trails and campsites. Admittedly, minimal evidence of human use is highly compromised by trail and campsite impacts.

Harassment of wildlife by recreationists produces excitement or stress in animals. This may lead to panic, exertion, disruption of essential functions such as breeding or nesting, displacement to other areas,

and sometimes death. Animals that are healthy and have ample food and places to escape to are more capable of withstanding harassment than animals that are underfed, highly parasitized, experiencing severe weather, giving birth or nesting, or lacking secure areas for escape (Ream 1979). Damage to animals—in terms of increased energy expenditures or radical changes in behavior or distribution—also increases as disturbance becomes more frequent and more unpredictable (Geist 1970).

Generalizing about harassment is made more difficult by the considerable variability between and within species. Effects on wolves, which are relatively intolerant of disturbance, are much more serious than effects on coyotes. Similarly, effects on eagles, which may not return to feeding sites for several hours after disturbance (Stalmaster and Newman 1978), are more serious than effects on jays. Within species, prior experience with humans strongly tempers responses. Some individuals can learn to tolerate at least predictable disturbances. Differences between hunted and nonhunted populations can also be profound, because hunted animals have experienced a need to escape. Individuals giving birth or with young are more readily disturbed than others.

Disturbance of several subspecies of bighorn sheep has been widely studied, primarily in California and Canada. Although a number of these studies have implicated harassment as a cause of declining sheep populations, most recent work suggests that sheep can habituate to human intrusion. One recent Canadian study monitored heart rates and behavioral responses to disturbance. While largely unaffected by foot traffic approaching from a road below, sheep responded dramatically to the presence of dogs and foot traffic approaching from upslope (an unexpected action that blocks their preferred escape route). The authors conclude that recreational disturbance can be minimized by confining use to established trail systems and discouraging people from taking dogs (MacArthur and others 1982).

This Canadian study appears to validate management actions taken to protect the rare California bighorn sheep in the Sierra Nevada. An apparent correlation between increasing numbers of recreationists and a decline in bighorn numbers led to use restrictions in the early 1970s. Use of the major trails through the bighorn range was limited to 25 hikers per day, and off-trail hiking and grazing of packstock were prohibited. The trail was also no longer signed or maintained. More recent research (Hicks and Elder 1979) indicated that bighorn-human encounters were rare and generally not highly

Fig. 16.7. Use of wilderness during winter is increasing in popularity. Such use can stress wildlife populations at a time when they have little tolerance of increased stress. Photo courtesy of the USFS.

stressful, except where hikers got above the sheep. Consequently, current management emphasis is on keeping hikers on the trail.

Several recent trends may greatly increase wildlife disturbance. First is the recent popularity of attempting to disperse visitors from popular parts of the wilderness to less visited places. In 1980, 50 percent of all managers of wildernesses and proposed wildernesses were attempting to disperse use (Washburne and Cole 1983). This action, if successful, is likely to dramatically increase the frequency of wildlife harassment and reduce the size of secure areas where harassed animals can escape. Any attempt to alter visitor use distributions should consider the consequences to wildlife.

The second trend is toward increased off-season use. Cross-country skiing, in particular, can stress populations at a time of year when they are least able to tolerate it (fig. 16.7). Ferguson and Keith (1982) have documented a tendency for elk and moose to move away from ski trails. Significantly they found that a single skier usually caused the animals to flee; the passage of additional skiers was irrelevant. Therefore, a few large parties are likely to cause less disturbance than many widely dispersed small parties. Although little is known about the consequences of such disturbance to reproduction or survival, we do know that flight increases the necessary caloric intake of these animals. Some ungulates adapt to winter conditions by decreasing activity to conserve energy (Moen 1976), therefore disturbance interferes with this adaptation and may increase food demand beyond the supply provided by winter range. Clearly the severity of such an effect would vary

from year to year and from place to place; only through increased monitoring of wildlife populations in relation to disturbance will we be able to ascertain how serious problems are. Nevertheless, many managers are currently educating winter users about the threats posed by harassment and the need to avoid animals.

Other significant problems occur when use is concentrated on limited critical habitat. Use does not need to coincide with the presence of animals, such as where summer grazing by packstock reduces available food sources on critical elk winter range. Recreational use around desert waterholes and salt licks can also cause more substantial problems than one would expect from total use Fig.s. Managers should identify habitat critical to wildlife at various seasons and develop plans for minimizing disturbance.

Ream (1979) discusses three general approaches to m*inimizing problems with wildlife disturbance.* Of foremost importance in wilderness is *management of people.* Management can range from prohibiting overnight use and closing sensitive places to visitation—actions that currently are almost entirely confined to Fish and Wildlife Service (FWS) and National Park Service (NPS) wildernesses—to educating users about avoiding wildlife conflict.

The other potential strategies involve modification of wildlife behavior and habitats. *Behavioral modification*—habituation to predictable, harmless human activity—is useful where hunting is not allowed (Ream 1979). This can be used to attenuate reactions to human disturbance. Finally, *habitats can be modified* to change population distributions or to mitigate disturbance, although the appropriateness of such actions in wilderness must be questioned. Further discussion of wildlife management can be found in chapter 12.

WATER POLLUTION AND DISPOSAL OF HUMAN WASTE

Most management concern with water pollution has centered on the potential for transmission of disease. *Three prominent sources of contamination are: (1) the recreational user, his dogs, and packstock; (2) domestic livestock; and (3) wildlife.* Even where animal contamination is absent, bacteria can be found in the soil, forest floor, and stream sediment (Silsbee and Larson 1982). Therefore, even so-called pristine areas receiving almost no recreational use at all can harbor bacteria harmful to humans.

Water quality studies in mountainous wilderness in the West have generally found very low levels of bacterial contamination, even in areas of concen-

trated use. For example, at Rae Lakes, one of the most popular alpine lake basins in Kings Canyon National Park, coliform bacteria counts were usually low enough to allow drinking (Silverman and Erman 1979). Along the Colorado River, in Grand Canyon National Park, Arizona, water was unfit for drinking but coliform levels were generally low except when major tributary streams were in flood (Brickler and others 1983). Here the source of contamination appeared to be domestic livestock or wildlife. Springs and streams in Great Smoky Mountains National Park also exceeded maximum permissible levels of coliform bacteria. Again, contamination did not appear related to recreational use (Silsbee and Larson 1982).

Even where contamination is not evident, transmission of disease does occur. Most common is giardiasis, an intestinal disease caused by the protozoan pathogen, *Giardia lamblia*. Although it is not clear whether contamination is spreading or whether the disease is being more frequently and accurately diagnosed, it is clear that surface waters in many, if not most, wildernesses are contaminated with *Giardia*. As with bacterial contamination, humans, domestic animals, and wildlife all act as hosts capable of spreading the organism. Beaver have most frequently been implicated as the major source of *Giardia* contamination.

Where level of bacterial contamination has been related to amount of recreational use, no evidence shows that areas receiving more recreational use present higher health hazards than lightly used areas do. In fact, one study of used and unused watersheds in Montana found less contamination in the watershed open to recreational use and a decrease in contamination after the closed watershed was opened to use (Stuart and others 1971). The authors concluded that the primary source of contamination was wildlife and wildlife populations and, therefore, contamination was reduced by recreational use. In an unpublished study in the Anaconda-Pintler Wilderness, Montana, elevated bacterial counts were most often found just downstream from trail crossings used by horses and pack animals. In the Eagle Cap Wilderness, contamination levels were higher in streams, particularly at midelevations in meadows, than in lakes; and coliform counts generally peaked along with runoff after a storm (McDowell 1979).

All of this suggests, that management of recreational use is likely to do little to reduce health hazards. The most important management action is informing visitors about the prevalence of contamination and the need to treat water. In Great Smoky Mountains National Park, the NPS removed more than 100 spigot pipes at backcountry springs, to erase the impression that such water was safe to drink.

Instead, through trail signs, brochures, and direct visitor contact (Silsbee and Larson 1982) visitors are advised to treat water. Treatment is particularly important when using turbid water after a storm; water should be taken above rather than below trail crossings.

Proper control of waste, both from humans and recreational stock, is also important, although this will not eliminate health hazards. Toilets may be necessary at sites that receive heavy, consistent use throughout the season (Leonard and Plumley 1979), but they should be installed only where the individual shallow burial ("cat-hole") method results in frequent surface exposure of feces. In 1980, 19 percent of wildernesses had open-pit toilets, 15 percent had enclosed outhouses, 4 percent had vault toilets, and one area used a composting toilet (Washburne and Cole 1983). Where provided, toilets must be sensitively located by managers, because their presence—especially when accompanied by a direction sign saying toilet—is a reminder of civilization and may not be consistent with the spirit of wilderness.

Even conscientious disposal in individual "cat-holes" poses problems. Recent research in Montana's Bridger Range has shown that significant numbers of intestinal pathogens in feces survived an entire year of burial (Temple and others 1982). Statements that nature will take care of wastes "in a few days" are misleading and may promote careless disposal. This research shows that the possibility of disease transmission persists for a considerable time. Moreover, depth of burial (2 to 8 inches) made no difference in survival of pathogens; neither did it matter whether disposal occurred at high or low elevations, in forest or in meadow. This emphasizes the need to promote burial at sufficient depth and far enough away from campsites and water bodies to minimize the chance of direct contact by other users. Although education campaigns in proper human waste disposal are common, greater emphasis on the potential hazard and the need for careful disposal seems in order. Horses and mules should be kept away from surface water as much as possible and they should never be confined where manure is likely to contaminate water sources.

Other types of water pollution appear to be more prevalent and also more subject to management control. In the Kings Canyon National Park study, where the health hazard was minimal (Silverman and Erman 1979), recreational use was associated with a number of changes in the basic ecology of lakes. The most heavily used lakes had less nitrate and more iron, and more aquatic plants than other lakes (Taylor and Erman 1979). The authors suggest that recreational use—through erosion of trails and

campsites, improper waste disposal, destruction of vegetation, and campfires—may cause an increase in trace elements, such as iron, the absence of which formerly limited plant growth. Stimulated plant growth results in increased nitrogen uptake and, therefore, decreased nitrate levels. Insects, aquatic worms, and small clams were also more abundant on the bottom of more heavily used lakes (Taylor and Erman 1980). At a lake in a semiwilderness area in Canada, Dickman and Dorais (1977) found unusually high phosphorus levels and increases in phytoplankton that they attributed to increased erosion of phosphorus-rich substrate, triggered by human trampling.

Although we do not know how common lake eutrophication has become, its effects are felt throughout the food chain. Moreover, such changes are long-lasting. In the Kings Canyon National Park study, changes were still prevalent at Bullfrog Lake, a formerly heavily used lake, 16 years after it had been closed to camping and grazing. Such changes are highly significant because they are likely to affect the entire lake ecosystem. This can be a serious problem in wilderness areas having a small number of heavily used lakes. In this situation, recreational use can dramatically alter the structure and functioning of all representatives of that type of ecosystem. This would clearly constitute a serious failure to achieve the goal of preserving natural conditions. This suggests that aquatic ecosystems may be the wilderness ecosystems most prone to significant disruption by recreation use (fig. 16.8).

MANAGING CAMPSITE IMPACTS

The most common and profound recreational impacts are associated with campsites and trails, and with the management of packstock (Washburne and Cole 1983). The rest of this chapter is therefore devoted to a discussion of these problems and their management.

CAMPSITE IMPACTS

Visitors spend more time on the campsite than anywhere else in wilderness. Unfortunately, this focuses impacts on the very places where they spend most of their time. Although natural conditions are desirable, some amount of impact can actually make a site more habitable. Some clearing of brush and trees, for example, provides better tent sites, causing many visitors to select sites with some vegetation loss. Problems arise when damage to the sites becomes extreme or where sites proliferate over entire destination areas, providing constant reminders of the large numbers of people using the area.

Vegetation Change

Many studies have examined changes in vegetation on wilderness campsites. In most cases trees are mechanically damaged and reproduction is suppressed. Generally, there is little evidence that vigor of large trees is reduced, and aside from outright felling of trees and girdling as a result of tethering stock, tree mortality is uncommon. An exception to this generalization was documented in the Boundary Waters Canoe Area Wilderness (BWCAW), Minnesota, where severe erosion of shallow soil around tree roots has caused high mortality (Frissell and Duncan 1965). Ground-level vegetation is more profoundly affected. Plant cover is reduced, usually to bare ground in the central part of the campsite, and species composition changes. Diversity is usually reduced, and exotic plants often become a significant component of the flora.

Fig. 16.8. In many wildernesses, aquatic ecosystems are particularly prone to significant disruption by recreational use. Photo courtesy of Robert C. Lucas, USFS.

To illustrate the magnitude of campsite changes, consider the median change on 22 campsites located in subalpine forests in the Eagle Cap Wilderness. On the median campsite, more than 2,000 square feet had been obviously disturbed by camping. Almost 90 percent of the ground cover had been lost on the site—as inferred by comparing campsite conditions to those of an undisturbed control site close by. Half of the site, the central area around the firering, was entirely devoid of vegetation. The surviving vegetation was very different in composition from undisturbed vegetation. The two species most common in undisturbed areas, a huckleberry and a heather, contributed almost 40 percent of the cover on controls but only 6 percent of the surviving cover on campsites. In contrast, a sedge and a rush that contributed only 8 percent of the cover on controls contributed almost 30 percent of the cover on the campsites. Overall, low shrubs and mosses were greatly reduced in cover. Grasses and grasslike plants, while losing some coverage, were less drastically affected, so they became the most abundant type of plant on the campsites.

Essentially all of the trees growing on these sites, 96 percent, had been damaged, although much of the damage was minor, consisting of broken lower branches and nails driven into the trunk. Nevertheless, one-fourth of the trees bore trunk scars from chopping and another one-fourth had been felled. About one-third of the trees had exposed roots, usually a result of tying stock to tree trunks. Some 90 percent of the tree seedlings had been eliminated by trampling, which does not bode well for perpetuating forested campsites. Along with the felling of most of the saplings on the site, death of seedlings suggests that overstory trees will not be replaced when they die.

These values are probably fairly typical for established wilderness campsites. The Eagle Cap is a moderately popular wilderness—less frequently used than wildernesses closer to population centers, but more frequently used than many other areas. Moreover, the 22 sites studied ranged from the most popular sites in the wilderness to sites probably used less than one night per year (Cole 1982b).

Changes in Soil Condition

The changes in soil condition most frequently noted are loss of the organic litter horizon, exposure of bare mineral soil, and compaction of the soil. Various measures of compaction have been employed, the two most common being bulk density and resistance to penetration. A few studies have also documented decreases in water infiltration rates and changes in organic matter content and soil chemistry.

On the Eagle Cap campsites, the depth of the organic horizons was cut in half. In some places all litter was lost; exposure of bare mineral soil increased from 1 percent on control plots to 31 percent on campsites. Although some of the surface organic matter pulverized by trampling is probably removed by erosion, some evidently moves downward and accumulates in the uppermost mineral horizons because soil organic matter content increased 20 percent on campsites. Similar studies have found both increases (Legg and Schneider 1977; Marion and Merriam 1985) and decreases (Stohlgren 1982) on campsites.

Bulk density increased 15 percent on the Eagle Cap sites, considerably less than has been observed elsewhere. Infiltration rates were reduced by about one-third on the Eagle Cap sites. In similar studies they were reduced by two-thirds in the Bob Marshall Wilderness (Cole 1983a) and three-fourths in Grand Canyon National Park (Cole 1986). Finally, several changes in soil chemistry were found. Values of pH increased, soils became less acidic, and there were sizable increases in the concentrations of magnesium, calcium, and sodium. These chemical changes probably reflect input from campfire ashes, excess food, soap, and other substances scattered about the site.

In sum, almost every parameter examined on the Eagle Cap campsites had been substantially altered by camping (see fig. 16.3). By no definition of the phrase can we conclude that "natural conditions" are being preserved on these wilderness campsites. And remember, these are typical sites—not worst cases or atypical examples.

Campsite impacts are highly concentrated. For the Eagle Cap Wilderness as a whole, less than 0.2 percent of the area has been affected by camping (Cole 1981a). In most places, only occasional campsites are encountered. But large numbers of campsites are concentrated in a few popular destination areas. For example, camping has impacted more than 220 sites in one 325-acre area around two popular lakes in the Eagle Cap (Cole 1982c). Over half of these sites had lost more than 25 percent of their vegetation, and most were in sight of the trail. Nevertheless this represents a disturbance of only 1.3 percent of this most popular part of the wilderness. Although this disturbance represents little threat to the ecological integrity of the Eagle Cap Wilderness, it does provide conspicuous evidence of human use. Not only is there scant opportunity to camp on an undisturbed site, but pronounced impacts are found around almost every corner and behind every tree clump.

FACTORS THAT INFLUENCE AMOUNT OF IMPACT

In order to better understand how to minimize camping impacts, it is important to understand why some sites are more seriously damaged than others. *The major factors that influence how much change occurs on an individual site are (1) the amount and frequency of use the site receives, (2) the type and behavior of its users, and (3) the environmental conditions of the site itself.* Season of use would be an important factor, except that campsites are seldom used when soils are wet and, therefore, particularly fragile.

Of the factors that influence amount of impact, the usual assumption has been that the amount of use a site receives is most important. Research results suggest, however, that this assumption is misleading at best. In the Eagle Cap (Cole 1982b), for example, even campsites used no more than a few nights per year (light-use sites) have been severely altered (table 16.1). Most overstory trees have been damaged, most seedlings have been eliminated, most of the vegetation has been lost, soil has been compacted, and soil chemistry has been changed. Sites used five to 10 times more frequently, about one night per week during the main use season (moderate-use sites), differed in the following ways: the disturbed area was usually much larger, as was the devegetated area; exposure of tree roots was pronounced; organic horizons were thinner; and changes in undergrowth species (indicated by the floristic dissimilarity value) were more extreme. Compared with these sites, the only major difference on the most heavily used sites—those used several nights per week—was that organic horizons were even thinner.

These and similar results from the Rattlesnake (MT), Mission Mountain Tribal (MT) (Cole and Fichtler 1983), and Boundary Waters Canoe Area Wildernesses (Frissell and Duncan 1965; Marion and Merriam 1985) suggest a general relationship between use and impact similar to that in Fig. 16.9. Only when comparing sites receiving very low levels of use do differences in amount of use make any sizable difference in amount of impact.

Certain types of impact on campsites are determined almost entirely by the behavior of campers. The best examples are damage to trees and "pollution" of the site with campfire ashes, charcoal, food, and so on. Not all parties build campfires or damage trees. A campsite could be heavily used and yet not suffer tree damage or changes in soil chemistry caused by building campfires or discarding wastes. Other types of impact are little affected by behavior, however. Even campers who carefully practice low-impact use will still trample vegetation and compact soil.

Three other characteristics of user groups also influence campsite impact—size of the party, length of stay, and whether or not they use packstock. The effect of party size on campsite impact has never been formally studied. One can assume that large parties will increase the disturbed area of individual campsites. Campsite area and size of the devegetated area are therefore likely to be much larger than on sites used by small parties (fig. 16.10). But there is little reason to believe that party size should affect any other characteristic of established campsites. On undisturbed sites, however, large parties will cause impact more rapidly than small parties. Therefore it is con-

Table 16.1. Relationship between selected campsite impact parameters and the amount of use a site receives.

Impact parameter		Light-use sites (N = b)	Moderate-use sites (N = 6)	Heavey-use sites (N = 10)	Kendall's tau (∞ = 0.05)
			Median		
Camp area	(m²)	48	224	205	NS
Devegetated area	(m²)	19	122	93	0.30
Trees with exposed roots	(%)	3	33	39	0.41
Damaged trees	(%)	74	85	97	NS
Seedling loss	(%)	73	92	89	NS
Surviving vegetation cover	(%)	9	6	4	- 0.41
Decrease in depth of organic horizons	(%)	3	21	68	0.36
Floristic dissimilarity	(%)	31	60	64	0.33
pH increase	(%)	3	5	11	NS
Decrease in infilration rates	(%)	8	57	12	NS
Increase in soil organic matter	(%)	19	26	20	NS
Increase in bulk density	(%)	16	11	16	NS

Source: Cole 1982b.

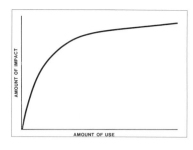

Fig. 16.9. Generalized relationship between amount of use and amount of impact. Only at low-use levels are site impacts likely to reflect different amounts of use.

siderably more difficult for a large party to cause minimal impact when visiting relatively undisturbed places.

Campsites used for long periods of time by the same party tend to be more heavily impacted than other sites. Two factors seem to be at work here. First, use patterns on the site are repeated day after day, leading to severe disturbance of certain parts of the site. For example, places where tents are set up and used for a week or more are likely to be highly altered. This factor may be of little importance on a site where impact levels are already high. The second factor—and this applies even to well-impacted sites— is the natural tendency for people to "improve" and "develop" their campsite the longer they stay.

The effect of packstock will be discussed in more detail later. Parties with packstock disturb a larger area than hikers because the campsite includes an area where stock are tethered. Such camps usually show more soil disturbance, a result of trampling by heavy, shod animals, and more tree damage, a result of tying horses to trees for extended periods.

The final factor determining amount of impact is the durability of the site used for camping. Trail condition provides a useful illustration of the importance of location. It is common to find badly eroded or boggy sections of trail alternating with sections that are in good shape, despite the fact that the very same number and type of people are using both good and bad trail segments. Environmental differences such as steepness of slope, soil texture, and moisture content account for most of these differences in condition. On campsites, soil characteristics, depth of surface organic horizons, and vegetation type can greatly influence amount of impact.

A number of studies have examined, through experimentation, the effects of increasing amounts of trampling on different types of vegetation.

Trampling disturbance, particularly loss of vegetation, varies widely between vegetation types. In a review of all previous experimental trampling studies, Cole (1985) found the loss of vegetation resulting from 100 passes—one person walking at a normal gait 100 times along the same path—to range from less than 5 percent in a mountain grassland in Montana to almost 90 percent in a lodgepole pine forest in Alberta.

When five forest types and one grassland in western Montana were experimentally trampled, Cole (1985) found the grassland to be much more resistant to loss of vegetation than the five forest types. The grassland lost less than 5 percent of its cover even after 1,200 passes; the forest types, in contrast, lost 63 to 96 percent cover, depending on the type, after 1,200 passes. If a management objective was to maintain at least 50 percent cover on campsites, the grassland could be used about 40 times more frequently, and the most resistant forest types 10 times more frequently than the least resistant forest type. Clearly, where people camp is critical in determining loss of vegetation.

The general conclusion is that, with the exception of sites devoid of ground cover, nonforested sites are most resistant to vegetational damage (Cole 1981a; McEwen and Tocher 1976). Where use is sufficient to eliminate most vegetation, regardless of its resistance, sites with thick organic horizons are usually most durable. Thick organic horizons decrease the likelihood of exposing mineral soil and cushion the underlying soil from the compacting effects of trampling.

Fig. 16.10. A large party is likely to alter a larger area, and more rapidly disrupt undisturbed places, than a small party. Photo courtesy of the USFS.

It is commonly believed that sites located close to lakes and streams are more fragile than sites away from water bodies. When examined in the Eagle Cap Wilderness, this did not prove to be the case (Cole 1982b). Campsites close to lakes were no more highly impacted than sites located away from lakes.

MANAGEMENT STRATEGIES AND TECHNIQUES

Each of the factors that influence amount of impact offers a strategy for reducing site impacts. For example, three primary strategies for minimizing impacts involve: *(1) reducing amount of use on campsites, (2) changing type of use and behavior in such a way that per capita impact is reduced, and (3) shifting use to more durable sites or actively increasing site resistance* through hardening and provision of facilities. A fourth management strategy is containment—recognizing situations where impacts are inevitable and can best be minimized by limiting their areal spread. A fifth strategy—site cleanup and rehabilitation—treats symptoms rather than causes (table 16.2). These strategies can be implemented by various techniques or actions. Effective campsite management programs call for an evaluation of objectives, problems, and all potential solutions before selecting a series of coordinated actions, often using several different strategies.

Limiting Amount of Use
As of 1980, overnight use was limited in 16 classified and 15 potential wildernesses (Washburne and Cole 1983). Managing campsite impact is just one of many reasons for limiting use. Since then this number has increased substantially. What we know about the relationship between amount of use and amount of impact—that a little use causes most of the impact—

suggests that limiting use is likely to do very little to improve the condition of well-established campsites. In most cases, unless all visitation is curtailed on a site, there is little chance for recovery (Cole 1981b). The only exception to this rule is where use levels are kept very low and dispersal is practiced (see next technique).

In places where use levels are high—the usual case where rationing has been implemented—use limits are likely to be more effective in limiting the *number* of campsites than the *severity* of impacts on individual sites. To limit the number of campsites, however, it is necessary to simultaneously employ the containment strategy (discussion follows) and get campers to use existing or designated sites, rather than make new sites. In general, then, use limits are likely to be effective only when supporting containment or when they maintain extremely low use levels. Use limits can, however, be highly effective in dealing with other management problems, particularly crowding.

Dispersal of Use
As with use limitations, use dispersal is undertaken for a variety of reasons. In 1980, managers were attempting to disperse use in 50 percent of all wildernesses and likely additions to the wilderness system (Washburne and Cole 1983). Goals ranged from shifting use to less frequently visited areas, to discouraging camping on impacted campsites. Any dispersal of use will affect the number, distribution, and condition of campsites.

As in the case of use limitation, use dispersal is unlikely to improve the condition of individual sites unless use levels are very low. Studies in wilderness areas in the West suggest that even a night or two of use per year usually inflicts persistent damage. We also know that only a slight increase in use will

Table 16.2. Factors that influence impact on campsites. Each factor defines a strategy and set of specific techniques (of which only one example is provided here) for managing impacts.

Factor	Strategy	Technique (example)
Amount/frequency of use	Reduce use	Institute quotas
Type/behavior of use	Change type/behavior of use	Party size limits
Environmental/site conditions	Increase site resistance	Bridge unavoidable bogs along trails
Use distribution	Contain use	Camping in designated sites only
Maintenance input	Rehabilitate sites	Clean up litter

significantly alter previously unused or seldom-used sites. In the Eagle Cap, even the lightly used sites away from trails had lost more than 70 percent of their vegetation. Therefore, increased use of little-used areas or sites will increase both the number of impacted sites and their level of impact. The more than 220 campsites around Mirror and Moccasin Lakes in the Eagle Cap (where the average number of parties probably does not exceed 10 per night) is partially a result of a management decision to remove existing rock firerings and to request visitors not to camp on heavily used sites. At such popular destinations, directing use away from heavily used sites actually spreads campsite damage. Encouraging more use of less popular parts of the wilderness will also increase campsite impacts in these places, with little compensatory improvement in the condition of popular locations.

Dispersal is likely to improve campsite conditions in lightly used remote parts of wildernesses, where visitors can be encouraged to spread out and camp on undisturbed sites. In this vast majority of wilderness acreage, dispersal can help perpetuate the "ideal" wilderness situation where no sites become heavily impacted. But if use increases significantly, it may be necessary to impose limits. Limits can be effective in this rather unorthodox situation. The dispersal strategy must be supported with an intensive educational program wherein campers are taught minimum impact camping techniques and how to select apparently unimpacted and resistant sites. The deal is to allow sites to fully recover before being used again; otherwise sites will deteriorate and dispersal will merely spread lasting impacts. Because of this possibility, the monitoring of campsites and their condition is particularly important to a dispersal program.

Temporary Campsite Closures

In about 15 percent of wildernesses and likely additions (Washburne and Cole 1983), certain heavily impacted campsites are temporarily closed to allow recovery before being used again. Such a rest-rotation system is likely to be effective only if required recovery periods are short in relation to periods of use and deterioration. Several studies have found that near-maximum levels of deterioration occur within the first few years after a site is opened for use (LaPage 1967; Merriam and Smith 1974). Recovery, however, takes decades or centuries, particularly in mountain and arid environments (Parsons 1979; Willard and Marr 1971). In the more resilient East, recovery is probably more rapid, making temporary campsite closures more feasible. This is just a supposition,

however, because recovery rates there have never been documented.

The effectiveness of a temporary campsite closure program was monitored around Big Creek Lake in the Selway-Bitterroot Wilderness, Montana, where seven out of 15 campsites were closed to allow recovery. Eight years after closure, vegetation on closed sites was still only one-third as extensive as that on controls, and mineral soil exposure was 25 percent, compared with only 0.1 percent on controls (Cole and Ranz 1983). The most profound change since initiation of the closures was the creation of seven new campsites, close to the closed sites, on which conditions have rapidly deteriorated. Within eight years of their creation, loss of vegetation and soil exposure were as high on new sites as on long-established sites. The likely effect of a rest-rotation system, then, is an increase in the number and area of impacted sites without any significant improvement in the condition of sites in use.

Limitations on Length of Stay

Limits have been placed both on the maximum number of nights allowed in the wilderness (29 percent of all areas) and at individual campsites (17 percent). For both campsite and areawide limits, the most common maximum length of stay is 14 days (Washburne and Cole 1983).

The imposition of areawide length-of-stay limits is unlikely to have any effect on site impacts. The major benefit of such a regulation is to allow more people to use an area in which total use is limited. Length-of-stay limits for campsites are also likely to do little to improve campsite conditions in popular parts of wildernesses or on popular campsites because new parties are likely to occupy sites shortly after they are vacated. Such a limit is likely to prevent "homesteading," although this is more a social than an ecological problem. It can also prevent serious deterioration of sites that had not been heavily impacted previously and avoid the tendency for sites used for long periods to become developed or improved. But in these cases the common 14-day limit is too long. To avoid damaging little-used areas, sites should never be used more than a night or two in succession.

Reducing length of stay to a minimum, by sleeping and eating in different places, can significantly reduce per capita impact in little-disturbed areas. Using this technique, a party traveling through the wilderness will prepare and eat supper in one location, clean up, and travel farther to a good bed site. In the morning, the party gets up and moves on to a good breakfast site. A typical camp is never established.

Generally, the most valuable use of length-of-stay limits is minimizing time spent at little-used sites. This goal is most effectively accomplished through education, particularly when such limits are not imposed on heavily used sites. For social reasons it may also be beneficial to prohibit occupancy of one site for more than 14 days as a means of dealing with "homesteading."

Party Size Limits

Almost one-half of all wildernesses limit the number of people per party. Limits range from five to 60 persons, the most common being 25 (Washburne and Cole 1983). As noted earlier, larger parties are likely to disturb larger areas, but in the most highly disturbed part of the campsite severity of impact is unlikely to be much greater than with small parties. This follows from the finding that even the central part of the campsite, where use levels are low, experiences near-maximum levels of impact. Establishing lower party size limits could reduce the size of campsites and devegetated zones; however, current limits are usually so high as to be ineffectual. To be effective, limits probably should be 10 or fewer and users should be educated to not spread out on campsites. Excessively large sites may require partial revegetation and some means of keeping visitors off the periphery. Mount Rainier National Park, Washington, limits party size, teaches minimum impact camping, monitors all campsites, and where site expansion is occurring, "plants" rocks and logs to keep people off the periphery.

Party size limits are of most value in lightly used parts of wilderness where dispersal is being practiced. Rate of impact tends to increase with party size, so a small party will find it much easier to leave little trace of their visit than a large party. Again, limits must be quite low and might be most effectively implemented as part of a program to foster appropriate use of places off the beaten track.

Minimum-Impact Education

As much of the foregoing suggests, education is one of the keys to reducing campsite impacts. More than one-half of wildernesses have an educational program (Washburne and Cole 1983). The success of the "pack-it-in, pack-it-out" litter control program shows what can be done through education. It should also be possible, through education, to eliminate damage to trees and greatly reduce pollution of the site with campfire ashes, food remains, soap, and so on. But there are limits to what education can accomplish. Vegetation will still be trampled and soils will be compacted. Therefore, education is not a panacea;

instead, it is a foundation on which to build a program of other actions such as dispersal or use limits.

The main purpose of educational programs is to teach appropriate behavior. Appropriate behavior varies both between and within wildernesses—particularly between heavily and lightly used areas, between western and eastern wildernesses, and between managing agencies. In most heavily used areas, site impacts are most effectively minimized by containment of impacts—encouraging repetitive use of a small number of sites. Consequently, educational programs should stress not damaging new sites and keeping existing sites pleasant, to encourage repeat use. Lightly used areas usually call for dispersal and the discouragement of repetitive use of sites—the exact opposite of the educational message in heavily used places. Site selection and minimum-impact camping are particularly important in lightly used areas.

Like any tool, educational programs must be used with care. Most educational programs have never been properly evaluated, yet are often taken as gospel—too sensible to be questioned. But when improperly implemented or when dispensing erroneous information, educational programs can do great damage. We must be concerned about *how* to educate visitors and even more so with *what* we teach visitors. Monitoring, again, will prove invaluable in determining the consequences, positive or negative, of an educational program.

Many potentially worthwhile *minimum-impact techniques* exist. Of those applicable to campsites (others applicable to trail use, stock handling, and impacts on other visitors are discussed elsewhere), the more generally useful and noncontroversial techniques include the following:

1. *Use proper equipment.* Tents with aluminum or fiberglass poles eliminate the need to cut poles or to build lean-tos. Air mattresses and foam pads replace bough beds. Waterproof tent floors make drainage ditches unnecessary. Stoves either eliminate or reduce firewood gathering and campfire impact.

2. *Keep party size small.* Ideally, groups should be no larger than four to six people. This will make it easier to fit existing campsites. A small party size is particularly important in low-use areas and when camping on unimpacted sites.

3. *Select resistant and appropriate campsites.* The use of resistant sites will be discussed in more detail below. The appropriateness of sites varies with how much use the area receives, a party's potential to cause damage, and a party's ability to minimize and cover up damage. Large parties, parties with packstock, and parties knowing little about mini-

mum-impact camping should choose existing, well-used campsites in acceptable condition that are unlikely to deteriorate further. This is particularly important in heavily used areas. In lightly used areas, it is better to select pristine sites *if* a party knows how to minimize impact. Lightly impacted campsites should always be avoided because they are on the threshold of rapid deterioration if used further, but are likely to quickly recover if left unused (Cole and Benedict 1983).

Fig: 16.11. A small fire built on mineral soil, without a ring of rocks, can have little impact. Photo courtesy of John Dalle-Molle.

4. *Be careful with fire.* It is always best to forgo a campfire, thus eliminating collection of firewood and the resultant charcoal and blackened rocks. On relatively undisturbed sites, fire evidence encourages repeat use and, eventually, results in excessive damage. If planning to have wood fires, select a route where wood is plentiful and use existing firerings. If no firering exists, build the fire on a site with no vegetation and, if possible, no humus or litter. Dig a shallow pit down to mineral soil, away from rocks that might be blackened. Burn only dead and down wood that can be broken by hand. Larger pieces are critical to healthy ecosystems, and they do not burn readily to ash. Leave saws and axes at home. Keep fires small (fig. 16.11) and avoid burning large quantities of waste food, which requires large amounts of wood. Burn all wood to ash by adding small twigs and heaping stubborn charcoal and unburned pieces in the center of the pit where the heat is greatest. After all wood is burned to ash, fill in and camouflage the pit.

5. *Avoid all site improvement.* Never flatten a site, trench a tent, or build rock walls as windbreaks.

6. *Minimize site pollution.* Pack out all garbage and use only biodegradable soaps, in small quantities and away from water sources.

7. *Properly dispose of human waste.* Use toilets where available. Where toilets are unavailable, use the "cathole" method in which individuals bury their waste in a shallow hole (4 to 8 inches deep) located well away from campsites and water.

8. *Stay only a short time at individual campsites.* This is most important in little-used areas where a night or two of use is generally all a site can take before substantial trampling damage occurs. Be aware of damage and move accordingly. Highly resistant sites (e.g., a gravel bar) could be used continuously for a long period of time, while a fragile site in lush vegetation is likely to be damaged almost immediately.

Concern for tent and fire sites and where you walk (particularly avoiding tree seedlings) can also be extremely helpful in minimizing damage.

9. *Leave a clean campsite.* It is particularly important to leave well-established sites attractive to encourage subsequent visitors to camp there rather than on a new site. Clean up litter and leave but one small firering free of trash and charcoal. Dispose of excess charcoal, ash, and blackened rocks well away from the site. When using an undisturbed site, camouflage the fire site with organic matter and soil. Scatter any excess firewood and, if a firering was built, replace rocks in their original locations, charcoal side down. If a tent site was cleared of ground litter, return it to its "natural state" as well.

As a final note, many of these techniques can be *required* rather than *suggested* through an educational program. Regulations, for example, limit party size and length of stay, where camping is and is not allowed, and prohibit campfires, cutting of live vegetation, pollution of water, and littering. Both regulation and education can be obtrusive management techniques that make the visitor feel pressured into behaving a certain way. The main difference is that with education the visitor retains the freedom of deciding exactly what to do in particular situations and the threat of punishment is absent. Ideally, managers, rather than telling visitors what to do, should be gradually sensitizing visitors to the resource and its capabilities so they can adapt their behavior in such a way that impact is minimized.

When establishing a *minimum-impact educational program* consider the following points:

1. *Focus the message*, providing clear rationale for recommended behavior. Clearly explain the problem, the type of behavior that aggravates the problem, and the change in behavior that will improve the situation. Educate visitors so they can vary their behavior in response to differences in use levels and ecosystem fragility. Suggested techniques should be practiced and explained in enough detail so that visitors can easily master them and understand their rationale.

2. *Identify the audience.* Learn enough about user groups in the area to tailor your message to them. Identify any "problem users," specific types of users that are the primary causes of certain impacts. Aim slightly different messages to each user group, appealing to interests most important to that group,

rather than sending everybody the same message. For example, there is no reason to belabor backpackers with the details of low-impact stock use.

3. *Select communication methods.* A variety of media can be useful for educating visitors. But many have not been tried and few have been evaluated. Personal contact by trained staff and audiovisual programs have been found to be effective in one test (Fazio 1979). Brochures can also be effective (Roggenbuck and Berrier 1981), but are most useful if people have them in the planning stages of outings (Lime and Lucas 1977). Minimum-impact information is being included more frequently in published guidebooks and how-to-do-it manuals, but managing agencies have had little influence on the content. Mass media such as television, radio, and newspapers have occasionally been used, but in one test failed to reach the right audience (Fazio 1979). Minimum-impact techniques have been demonstrated in town, at schools and universities, club meetings, and at trailheads. Outfitters and guides should be encouraged to act as role models in low-impact wilderness use. The most effective programs will use a variety of media, each tailored for a particular user group and message (Bradley 1979).

4. *Decide where to contact the audience.* Where to contact the audience depends on the targeted user group and the communication medium selected. An effective program will carefully tailor the medium to the target audience. Visitors who write for information or a permit can be contacted at home. This has worked particularly well on whitewater rivers such as the Middle Fork of the Salmon River and the Colorado River through Grand Canyon. Local residents, the most frequent users of many areas, can be reached with special programs in the community, on radio and television, or through the newspaper. College students, another major user group, can be reached on campus. Horse users, Boy Scouts, and other groups can be contacted directly. It can also be useful to educate future wilderness users while they are young and receptive. Managers of the Eagle Cap Wilderness have prepared an educational program for sixth graders (Bradley 1979). Additional sources of information include Bradley (1979) and Fazio (1979).

Encouraging Use of Resistant Sites

Because certain sites are much more durable than others, managers can minimize impact by directing use either to resistant sites or away from fragile sites. This can be done through regulation or through education. Currently 8 percent of areas prohibit camping in certain ecosystems, usually meadows; another 14 percent allow camping only on desig-

Fig. 16.12. Dry meadows make durable campsites, provided stays are short and campfires are not built here. Photo courtesy of David Cole, USFS.

nated sites, hopefully located in resistant places (Washburne and Cole 1983). Many more areas discourage use of "fragile" ecosystems, particularly meadows, through education.

Camping in meadows is often discouraged or prohibited. Such campsites—both when occupied and after use—are much more obvious and aesthetically displeasing than sites set back in forests. Most research suggests, however, that grassland and meadow vegetation, particularly if it is dry, is much more resistant to damage than the forest undergrowth (Cole 1981a, 1985; McEwen and Tocher 1976). Therefore, in lightly used areas, where the dispersal strategy is being practiced, visitors should be encouraged to camp on meadows and grasslands (fig. 16.12). Here, encounters with other parties are unlikely and it is most important to minimize trampling damage. In heavily used areas, where even resistant vegetation will be lost, one should encourage camping in the forest so impacts and other campers will be screened by trees.

Setbacks From Water

One of the most common management actions is to discourage camping close to streams and lakes. Thirty percent of all wildernesses prohibit such camping (Washburne and Cole 1983) and many more discourage it through educational programs. Camping setbacks range from 20 feet to as much as one-half

mile; the most common distance is 100 feet (Washburne and Cole 1983).

Such setbacks have social and ecological justifications as well as repercussions. Three conditions that might make lakeshores particularly vulnerable are (1) moist soil with great potential for vegetational damage and soil compaction (Liddle 1975), (2) steeply sloping shores prone to erosion, and (3) potential for water pollution. Soil moisture and slope steepness do not necessarily decrease with distance from water, however. Flat rock outcrops close to shores are undoubtedly much more tolerant of use than moist or sloping sites a considerable distance from the lake.

Most water quality studies suggest that even in high-use areas pollution from human sources does not present a significant health problem (McDowell 1979, Silverman and Erman 1979). But in at least one case heavy use appears to have altered benthic plant populations and the concentration of certain ions (Taylor and Erman 1979). More monitoring is necessary to determine whether or not this is a common problem. Around heavily used lakes, particularly in areas where lakes are rare, setbacks may be justified as a means of reducing pollution.

Another justification for setbacks is the tendency of visitors to develop trails from campsites to the lake. Social reasons—maintenance of public access and the aesthetic qualities of the lakeshore, plus reducing the visibility of campers—may also justify setbacks. This action will keep visitors from camping where they most like to camp. It will also increase the area of alteration, at least for the short-term, because visitors will develop a second set of campsites away from the lake. Moreover, a setback will often eliminate most of the potential places to camp. In the Spanish Peaks Primitive Area (now part of the Lee Metcalf Wilderness), Montana, for example, a 200-foot setback would preclude use of 85 percent of the area's existing campsites (Brown and Schomaker 1974).

Setbacks should be instituted not because it is a faddish management action but because it will solve a specific problem. Often much could be accomplished by persuading visitors to prevent water pollution; this would avoid imposition of rigid setbacks. Elsewhere, setbacks may be necessary only in a few heavily used places. Where setbacks are established, the old sites should be actively rehabilitated.

Site Hardening and Facilities

True site hardening, wherein a site's durability is increased through manipulation, such as planting hardy grasses, is almost nonexistent in wilderness. More common is the provision of facilities that absorb or concentrate impact: fireplaces, tent pads, shelters, stock-holding facilities, toilets, and trash cans. Providing such items is a controversial action. We support the installation of such facilities to protect resources or for visitor safety, but not for visitor comfort and convenience. The most common facilities in wilderness are open-pit toilets (19 percent), enclosed outhouses (15 percent), shelters (12 percent), constructed fireplaces (10 percent), tables (8 percent), and a drinkable water supply (7 percent) (Washburne and Cole 1983).

Facilities should be the exception rather than the rule—a means of dealing with concentrated use, particularly by novices, in a few places in the wilderness. In Great Smoky Mountains National Park, for example, shelters receive 35 percent of the backcountry use, but because they concentrate impact, they account for only 7 percent of the bare soil on camp areas in the park (Bratton and others 1978). Although this may seem inappropriate in wilderness, we feel that wilderness offers a range of recreational opportunities that realistically must accommodate a few focal points of use. The provision of facilities may help prevent excessive deterioration of these places, while their judicious use preserves quality experiences for those who choose to visit such popular locations.

The facilities that can be most readily defended as necessary are constructed fireplaces, stock facilities, and toilets. Stock facilities will be discussed in the section on packstock management. Fireplaces are most appropriate in areas of high fire hazard, for example, wildernesses in southern California. But in a number of other places they are used to confine campfire damage and to designate an acceptable campsite. Generally, we feel that this is unfortunate, although perhaps necessary if visitors will otherwise build new firerings or disturb new sites.

Toilets are also an undesirable but sometimes necessary facility, particularly where use is so high that the likelihood of visitors digging up fecal material becomes substantial. Much can be accomplished by teaching people to defecate far from high-use camps. But in some situations toilets become a necessity. The most common toilet is a box a few feet high. In some areas, however, outhouses are enclosed, and in at least one wilderness, Alpine Lakes, Washington, composting toilets have been installed.

Containment of Use

Containing use is a well-developed principle of site management outside of wilderness and, while many consider it to be inappropriate—labeling it the sacrifice concept—it is being consciously and uncon-

sciously applied within wilderness. For example, a trail contains and concentrates use. Exhorting visitors to stay on trails, and not to shortcut switchbacks, are examples of appropriate containment. Applied to campsites, the same concept would encourage use of existing sites to avoid rapid deterioration of new sites. Currently 14 percent of wildernesses allow camping only on designated sites, at least in certain parts of the wilderness. Another 13 percent encourage the use of existing campsites (Washburne and Cole 1983).

Most sites deteriorate substantially even when used only a few nights per year. Therefore, at a heavily used destination area the choice is between a few deteriorated sites—the result of containment— or many deteriorated sites—the result of dispersal. Containment is a better strategy for minimizing impacts, unless management is willing to reduce use to extremely low levels and actively rehabilitate deteriorated sites. Generally, this is neither practical nor desirable. Wilderness can and should accommodate a range of opportunities; having a few popular locations with a handful of well-impacted campsites seems appropriate as long as the vast majority of the area remains largely undisturbed.

While this conclusion may be disturbing to those who want pristine wilderness, we find it a sensible compromise that allows generous opportunities for recreational use. The finding that heavily used sites show little more impact than sites used a few times per year has its positive side; concentrating use on a few sites will not result in ever-increasing deterioration, provided that sites are well-located and inappropriate visitor behavior is discouraged. Moreover, as long as most people want to visit popular areas and use the most heavily impacted sites—as most currently do (Cole 1982c; Heberlein and Dunwiddie 1979)—natural conditions will be preserved throughout most of the wilderness; opportunities for solitude will be preserved for those who seek it; and the need to manipulate visitor distributions and behavior, which results in loss of freedom, will be minimized.

Containment can be accomplished either through regulation, by allowing camping only on designated sites; or through education, by encouraging the use of existing campsites. Sites can be either clustered or dispersed. Although easier to administer and patrol, we feel that clustered sites are usually undesirable because they reduce campsite solitude and exacerbate problems such as bear encounters, waste disposal, and depletion of firewood supplies. Where use is so high that unacceptably large numbers of campsites are required, use limits may have to be established.

Where use limits are established, managers often set up a reservation and fixed itinerary system, too. Visitors are required to stay at sites they reserve before entry. With such a system, the number of sites necessary to accommodate a given number of parties is minimized because the need for overflow sites is eliminated. Reservations and a fixed itinerary greatly reduce freedom and spontaneity, however, and are among the most unpopular actions taken in wilderness (Lucas 1980). Such regulations should be written only if absolutely necessary. Visitor freedom is maintained by limiting use at trailheads and then allowing free movement within the area. This approach has been successful in a number of wildernesses, including both NPS and USFS areas in the Sierra Nevada of California. Based on historic use patterns, trailhead quotas can be set to keep use levels in destination areas within acceptable limits most of the time (Parsons and others 1981).

Containment need not—and usually should not—be practiced throughout an entire wilderness. For example, a new backcountry management plan implemented by Grand Canyon National Park divides the backcountry into a number of use areas. In the most heavily used areas, camping is allowed only at designated sites. Elsewhere, visitors can camp wherever they choose. Alternatively, a guide to campsite selection and use, shown in table 16.3, could be incorporated into an educational program.

Both dispersal and containment can be practiced in the same use area. Visitors who are properly equipped, skilled, and sensitized to low-impact use can be dispersed, while those who are novices or poorly equipped for low-impact use can be contained on certain sites. This could be accomplished through a two-level permit system.

Once a containment strategy is established, with or without use limits, it may be possible to actually reduce the existing number of campsites. If so, it will be necessary to keep people off these sites and to actively rehabilitate them. Closed sites might be identified through signing or a string exclosure. Open sites can also be signed, but a less obtrusive tactic might be leaving firerings only on open sites. It is important to leave a few more sites open than the maximum number of parties anticipated at any time.

Site Rehabilitation

As we noted, temporary closures as part of a campsite rest-rotation system are unlikely to succeed. Campsites may be permanently closed to enforce setbacks from lakes, to close poorly located sites, or to reduce the number of sites in places where containment is being tried. Closed campsites can be

Table 16.3. Campsite conditions and recommended user responses.

Condition class	Visible indicators	Recommended user responses
1. Pristine	The site appears never to have been used before.	USE WITH CAUTION IN CERTAIN SITUATIONS Ideal sites in low-use areas if parties are careful to minimize impacts. Parties should be small, without packstock and experienced in low-impact camping. Moderately impacted sites preferable for other parties and in high-use areas. Select resistant sites away from attractions and popular locations. Keep stays short.
2. Semi-pristine	Sites are barely recognizable as campsites. Vegetation has been flattened, but bare soil is not evident.	DO NOT USE Sites will rapidly deteriorate if use continues. In low-use areas, moderately impacted and pristine sites preferable; in high-use areas, moderately impacted sites preferable.
3. Lightly impacted	Ground vegetation worn away around the fireplace or center of activity.	USE ONLY IF NECESSARY Unless particularly resistant (sandy beaches, rocky rocky outcrops, dry meadows, or grasslands), sites will deteriorate if use continues. Moderately impacted sites always preferable. In low-use areas, pristine sites also preferable.
4. Moderately impacted	Ground vegetation worn away on most of the site, but humus, litter, decomposing leaves, and needles usually present on much of site.	USE WHERE POSSIBLE Sites not prone to further damage. They retain most desirable attributes; site impact not irreversible. Choose screened, forested sites, out of sight and sound of other parties. Do not damage overstory trees. Collect only dead and down firewood, broken by hand. Avoid trampling seedlings.
5. Highly impacted	Ground vegetation, humus and litter worn away on most of site, exposing gritty, dusty, or muddy mineral soil. Tree roots may be exposed if stock have been tied to trees. Firewood is usually scarce near the campsite. Campsites may overlay.	USE ONLY IF NECESSARY Never use in low-use areas; moderately impacted and pristine sites preferable. Encourage closure and rehabilitation. In high-use areas, moderately impacted sites preferable. But in some places, such sites must be accepted. Avoid practices that enlarge site; avoid wood fires.

Source: Adapted from Cole and Benedict 1983.

found in 37 percent of wildernesses. But of these areas, only 16 percent have a program to actively assist the revegetation of closed sites (Washburne and Cole 1983). Moreover, these programs are usually run by highly committed but untrained volunteers. Experimentation, documentation, and communication of what does and does not work is lacking, with a few notable exceptions: Lester and Calder 1979; Miller and Miller 1979; Schreiner and Moorhead 1981; Van Horn 1979. Finally, suitable techniques

and materials can be highly area- and site-specific. For all of these reasons, generalization about site rehabilitation is difficult. Cole and Schreiner (1981) provide an annotated bibliography on the subject; Hartmann and Kester (1975) provide a useful text on plant propagation.

The first step in any rehabilitation program is to effectively close the site to all use. Even day use, where horses are tied to trees or people inadvertently walk across the site, can frustrate a rehabilitation

attempt. This is one of the real problems with rehabilitating closed sites close to lakes. Even if people do not camp there, they may use the site for picnicking or walk across it to go fishing or swimming.

The most effective approach to closure consists of helping people understand the reasons for closures and letting them know about other desirable places to camp. It is best to get this information to visitors before they enter the area so they can adjust plans. Violations are sure to be more common if visitors learn of a closure only after they reach the campsite, probably weary and unsure of the distance to the next site. In a number of cases, rope or string between stakes or trees has been honored. A sign declaring the site closed, the reason for the closure, and the location of alternative open sites in the vicinity promotes compliance (fig. 16.13).

Once closed, the site should be cleaned up, eliminating firerings, charcoal, excess firewood, and trash. Where active revegetation is to be undertaken, the soil needs to be prepared. Compacted soil should be cultivated to a depth of about 4 inches. In conifer forests, where native plants prefer acid soils, peat moss or raw organic matter can be mixed with the cultivated soil. This is not desirable in grasslands because grasses generally prefer more neutral soils. At this stage it may also be desirable, depending on the nature of the undisturbed environs, to "plant" large rocks or decaying logs on the site. These can provide suitable microhabitats for seed germination and discourage use of the site. Finally, fertilizers can be added at this stage. Caution should be used, however. Fertilization has seldom improved revegetational success (Beardsley and Wagar 1971), tends to favor exotic species, and could lead to eutrophication of nearby waters.

Fig. 16.13. This campsite has just recently been revegetated. String and a small sign are being used to keep people out of the area. Photo courtesy of David Cole, USFS.

Under some favorable circumstances, natural revegetation may occur without much assistance within a short period of time. In the West, at least, natural revegetation is likely to be most rapid at lower elevations, on more productive soils, and in areas that receive plenty of light and moisture. Elsewhere, revegetation is likely to require decades, if not centuries (Parsons 1979; Willard and Marr 1971). In these places, revegetation can be facilitated by transplanting whole plants or plant cuttings, or by seeding.

Transplanting, a technique used frequently and successfully, is time consuming and can disturb adjacent areas from which plants are removed. Consequently, in a number of areas, cuttings of plants grown in nurseries are transported to the backcountry for transplanting (Miller and Miller 1979). Experience in the Pacific Northwest suggests the following procedure for transplanting:

1. Select species adapted to grow on the site. Species that naturally colonize disturbed sites are good choices, as are plants that reproduce vegetatively. Obtain transplants from some distance away and, if several plants are needed, take them from scattered locations to disperse damage. Choose relatively short plants with healthy looking foliage.
2. Water both the plants to be transplanted and the area to be transplanted one day before transplanting.
3. Dig around the plant, vertically rather than in toward the plant, so roots are not damaged. If possible, excavate sections of turf 8 inches in diameter rather than individual plants. Lift the plant or turf out by supporting it under the root ball (roots and soil) rather than by pulling on the stem. Plant as soon as possible, being careful to always keep plants cool, moist, and out of direct sunlight.
4. Place the plant upright in a hole slightly larger than the root ball. Make certain that roots are not doubled over on themselves. Fill in the excess space with organic matter and soil. When tamped down firmly, the top of the root ball should be slightly below the ground to facilitate watering and to reduce the risk of damage from frost heaving.
5. Water thoroughly. If the weather is very warm, it may be necessary to water the plants daily or to shade them. Where this is not feasible, survival rates can be increased by pruning some flowers, leaves, and branch tips and by providing large root balls. Campers will often water plants if requested. "Please water me" signs can work wonders.
6. Add a 1-inch layer of mulch over the transplanted area and around the base of the transplants. This can be leaves, pebbles, excelsior matting, jute netting, decaying wood, grass, or any other material that insulates yet allows free movement of air and moisture. Lightweight mulches may have to be anchored by limbs, stones, or similar objects.
7. Repair damage around the holes from which the transplants were taken. Fill the holes with soil and mulch the area.

Seeding is less complicated. Again, seed should be gathered from plants adapted to the site. In some cases, nonnative species have been used because seed is more readily available and it was thought that such plants would be replaced by native species. In Mount Rainier National Park, for example, red fescue, a nonnative species, was planted as a cover crop to reduce erosion, soil temperatures, and frost action, and to increase the organic matter of disturbed area. In four years, native plants did not invade red fescue sites; bare areas that were not planted with red fescue showed better revegetation (Van Horn 1979). To us, seeding with nonindigenous plants is an unacceptable alteration of natural conditions; the finding that it is frequently unsuccessful confirms this belief.

When seeding, it is important to become familiar with special germination requirements, such as scarification or stratification, of the species used. Seeds should either be scattered over the prepared soil and covered with one-half inch of soil or dropped into holes one-half inch deep. Soil should be tamped, mulched, and watered.

Site rehabilitation is an appropriate means for correcting past abuses, but it should be used judiciously. In addition to being costly, it interjects horticulture and landscaping into the wilderness. As a general principle, we believe rehabilitation should be used to restore sites that could then be protected through a new management program. Rehabilitation should not be used to bandage sore spots where no other change in management is implemented.

MONITORING CAMPSITE CONDITIONS

Effective campsite management required detailed knowledge of campsite location and condition. Sites should be inventoried to identify locations and problems that need attention, and to plan the types of corrective actions that will be required. If done carefully, the inventory can provide a baseline for camping trends in campsite number and condition to changes in visitor traffic and to management actions. Finally, the inventory and monitoring system can be a critical part of the Limits of Acceptable Change (LAC) planning process. Ideally, an inventory would include sites that visitors might use if they were

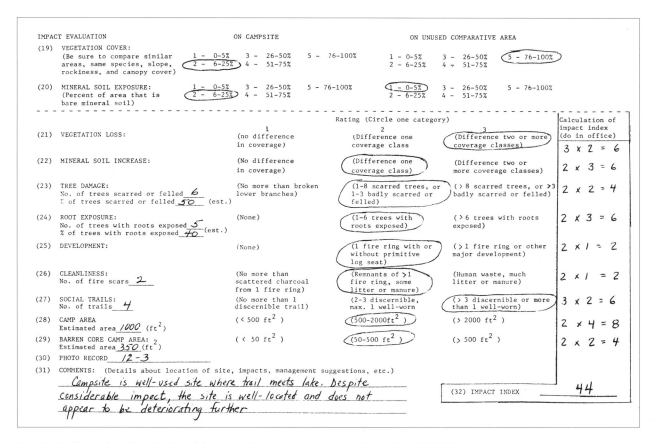

Fig. 16.14. Completed back side of form used to inventory campsites in the BMWC.

aware of them. Knowledge of potential sites would be useful in implementing a dispersal system or establishing new campsites if poorly located ones were closed.

Despite its importance, very little systematic campsite monitoring has been done. Moreover, what has been done has often been done with little purpose in mind. Perhaps the most widely used system is the *Code-A-Site system* originally proposed by Hendee and others (1976). Important information about each site is recorded on edgepunch cards that facilitate data retrieval and manipulation. Other systems consist of either visual estimates of impact (Frissell 1978; Parsons and MacLeod 1980) or more time-consuming but more precise measurements of conditions (Bratton and others 1978; Schreiner and Moorhead 1979). Either of these types of data can be stored on a Code-A-Site form or in any other convenient manner.

Another common monitoring method uses photographs. Photographs can be compared from year to year, but one must record date, time of day, the precise location of the photopoint, distance and direction to subject, height of the camera above the ground, camera make and model, focal length of the lens, filter, and film type. These conditions should be replicated to as great an extent as possible when subsequent photographs are taken. One interesting application of photographs, used in the Selway-Bitterroot Wilderness, is the recording of panoramas—full 360-degree views obtained by carefully leveling the camera and rotating it a specific amount for each photo. From experience, photographs have not proven to be reliable substitutes for field measurements or estimates of parameters, such as vegetational cover or tree damage. Patches of sunlight and shade often make interpretation of ground cover difficult, and it is seldom possible to distinguish features beyond the closest trees. Nevertheless, as supplementary documentation, photos can be quite useful. They can help identify the site for future remeasurements, record campsite features not measured in the field, and provide a visual supplement to collected data. A good source of further information on the use of photography is Brewer and Berrier (1984).

Most wildernesses have so many sites—Kings Canyon and Sequoia National Parks have more than 7,400 sites—and funding levels are so low that a system using visual estimates will be most practical. Cole (1983b) describes such a monitoring system based on the strongpoints of earlier systems. Fig. 16.14 shows one side of a form, based on this system, used to inventory all campsites in the Bob Marshall, Great Bear, and Scapegoat Wildernesses in Montana.

The form takes five to 10 minutes to complete. Modifications of this system are currently being applied in many other USFS wildernesses.

Nine impact parameters are used to evaluate campsite condition:

1. Loss of vegetation is expressed as the difference in vegetational cover between the campsite and its undisturbed surroundings. A vegetational cover class (percent cover of vegetation) is circled for both the campsite and an undisturbed comparative area. This undisturbed comparative area should be as similar as possible to the campsite in slope, canopy cover, and the composition of plants growing in protected places. The vegetation loss rating is based on the difference between these cover classes.
2. Mineral soil increase is a similar comparison between the campsite and an unused comparative area. In this case areas of mineral soil, devoid of vegetation and organic litter, are compared.
3. The number of trees that have been damaged (trunk scars, nails, stumps, and so on) is noted and used to rate tree damage. Large scars and felled trees are especially significant.
4. The number of trees with pronounced root exposure is noted.
5. The presence or absence of such facilities as firerings, log or stone seats, and more elaborate structures is used to rate level of development.
6. The presence and amount of charcoal, blackened logs, other campfire evidence, litter, toilet paper, human waste, and horse manure is used to rate level of cleanliness.
7. The number of informal trails providing access to water sources, the main trail, or adjacent campsites is noted. Well-worn trails are considered to be more significant than faint, barely discernible trails.
8. The total area of the campsite, including satellite tent areas and stock-holding areas, is paced off or tape measured.
9. The area devoid of vegetation, centered around the firering, is estimated.

In addition to measuring many of these parameters, each is rated on a scale of one to three. These ratings can simply be summed to arrive at the impact index or, as in Fig. 16.14, they can be multiplied by weighting factors reflecting the perceived relative importance of each parameter. These weights are the second column of numbers in the calculation box. In this case the impact index becomes the sum of the weighted ratings (the product of rating times weight). Although not strictly appropriate mathematically, such a procedure provides a useful relative index of impact.

Both the impact index and the individual parameter ratings can be mapped. Fig. 16.15 shows the location and overall condition (impact index) of campsites in a portion of the Bob Marshall Wilderness. Such a map is valuable for identifying problem areas

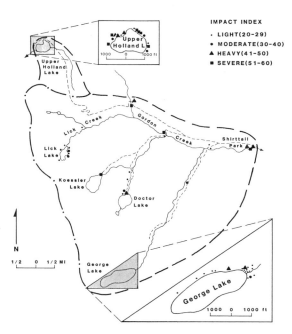

Fig. 16.15. This map of a portion of the Bob Marshall Wilderness displays the location and overall condition (impact index) of each campsite. This provides a graphic overview of campsite conditions at one point in time.

and specific types of problems. This makes it much easier to tailor a campsite management plan to the area. Obviously, different management strategies are necessary for Upper Holland Lake, with many highly impacted sites; Koessler Lake, with only one site, but a highly impacted one; and George Lake, with many sites, none of which are highly impacted.

Periodically, perhaps every five years, the area should be reinventoried. This will show whether the number of sites is increasing or decreasing and whether conditions on individual sites are improv-

ing or deteriorating. If standards have been established for campsite condition, the ratings can be related to specific standards to determine where and what type of management. By relating documentation of existing conditions (through monitoring) to specific objectives (standards) and then carefully choosing solutions from the array of possible management strategies described above, campsite management should become more effective and efficient.

MANAGING TRAIL IMPACTS

COMMON PROBLEMS AND MANAGEMENT

Impacts on and along trails result from the trampling of hikers and packstock and the effects of trail construction and maintenance. As discussed in more detail earlier in this chapter, these impacts include loss of vegetation and shifts in species composition, exposure of bare mineral soil, soil compaction, and changes in microhabitats, including changes in drainage.

Where trail construction is carefully planned, most of these changes are of little concern; although pronounced, most changes are localized and deliberate. Most wilderness trails were originally constructed to provide administrative access, particularly for firefighters, but currently are maintained primarily for recreational purposes. Most trail impacts only warrant concern when they provide obtrusive evidence of human use, become difficult to use, or require large amounts of money and manpower to maintain. Although trail problems are usually highly localized, maintaining and relocating trails usually costs more than any other aspect of wilderness management.

Table 16.4. Common trail impact problems and strategies and techniques for mitigating each problem.

Problem	Strategy	Technique (example)
Erosion	Improve location and/or design	Build water bars
Muddiness	Improve location and/or design	Route trails around boddy areas
Multiple trails	Improve location	Relocate trails
Shortcutting switchbacks	Change user behavior	Convince visitors to stay on existing trails
Informal trail systems	Reduce use	Reduce use quotas

Fig. 16.16. Deeply eroded trails tend to deteriorate because water is channeled down the tread. Such trails are a substantial disruption to the environment and can be difficult to use. Photo courtesy of the USFS.

The most common problems with trails are (1) excessive erosion, (2) muddy stretches in areas of water-saturated soils, and (3) development of impromptu trails, either adjacent to existing trails or in areas where no trails were planned. The first two problems make the trail difficult to use; all three suggest either "overuse" or improper use to visitors (table 16.4). Two other problems result from attempts to correct the three primary ones: excessive engineering and the proliferation of open and closed trails where trails have been frequently relocated. Both of these situations provide abundant evidence of human use and manipulation of the resource—evidence that cannot be eliminated but should be kept to a minimum.

Erosion

Although erosion can be significant on parts of a trail system, at least one study, in the Selway-Bitterroot Wilderness, showed that little erosion is occurring over the entire trail system (Cole 1983c). Material eroded from trail "banks" or the tread itself is usually deposited elsewhere on the trail. Soil is lost only where water drains off the trail, and much of that can be compensated for by sediment washed onto the trail from above by overland flow. Although trail troughs often change—either deepening through erosion or being filled in through deposition—trail systems as a whole usually exhibit a relatively steady state.

What is critical, however, are those stretches where erosion is pronounced. On badly eroded sections of trail in the Adirondack Mountains both trail width and depth were increasing by 1 inch per year (Ketchledge and Leonard 1970). Severe erosion can make a trail difficult to use, either because it is too deep and narrow or because exposed roots and rocks make footing difficult. This tempts people to leave the trail and make a new trail. Deeply rutted trails also exacerbate their own erosion problems by more effectively channeling water (fig. 16.16).

Although trampling can cause limited amounts of erosion, the primary effect of trampling is to make a trail susceptible to erosion by churning the soil, reducing infiltration rates, and removing vegetation. Running water is the principal agent of erosion (Root and Knapik 1972). Streams, snowmelt water, and water from springs all cause erosion when channeled down the trail. In some places rainfall can also be intense enough to erode trails. For this reason the main factors that determine degree of erosion damage are trail grade, orientation, and drainage—factors that affect the channelization and erosive force of water in the trail—and soil texture, the primary factor determining how readily the soil is detached and carried away.

Amount and type of use are generally less important than the locational and design features. Three studies in the northern Rocky Mountains concluded

Fig. 16.17. The effect of a horse's hoof is very different from the effect of a hiker's boot. Hikers tend to compact the soil; horses can punch holes in the soil, leaving soil detached and easily eroded. Photo courtesy of David Cole, USFS.

that trails were not substantially deeper where use levels were high (Cole 1983c; Dale and Weaver 1974; Helgath 1975). This is not to say that a 1,000 hikers per day would not cause more erosion than only one hiker per day. Rather, it means that beyond a low threshold of use—the amount of use required to eliminate vegetation and render the trail vulnerable to water erosion—location and design are more important determinants of erosion than amount of use. Therefore, to prevent erosion, use levels would have to be so low that bare trails do not form, and that is unfavorable since the public uses wilderness.

It has been suggested that type of footwear is an important determinant of amount of damage. Bainbridge (1974) wrote, "Indications are that Vibram lug soles may be 50 to 100 times more destructive than tennis shoes or flat soles but the conclusive research has not been completed." Three separate studies—all done in the East—conclude that lug soles are not substantially more destructive than other types of footwear (Kuss 1983; Saunders and others 1980; Whittaker 1978). Kuss, for example, found no significant difference in the volume of soil eroded from a stretch of trail after being trampled by lug-soled and corrugated rubber-soled boots. This lack of difference was found despite increases in soil yield, after 600 and 2,400 trampling passes, that amounted to 1.4 and 1.7 times the yield of undisturbed trail, respectively.

Whether trail use is by hikers or by parties with pack and saddle stock is an important indicator of potential erosion problems. A small bearing surface carrying heavy weight, a horse's hoof can generate pressures of up to 1,500 pounds per square inch (Bainbridge 1974). These pressures, along with sharp shoes, cause stock to break up, not compact the trail surface. Detached soil is more easily eroded, and makes trails dustier when dry and muddier when wet. Hooves also tend to punch holes through meadow turf and disrupt wet soils (fig. 16.17). Use of stock on frequently used, properly located, and well-maintained trails is unlikely to aggravate problems. But on little-used trails that are steep, pass through wet meadows, and are seldom maintained, stock use can be much more damaging than hiker use. Limiting stock use in such areas could therefore reduce trail problems. Some 25 percent of wildernesses with regular stock use have closed certain trails to stock use, presumably because these trails and the areas they access are particularly prone to damage (Washburne and Cole 1983). In many areas off-trail stock use is also prohibited because a single packtrain can leave tracks that will last for years (Laing 1961).

For most trails, the most effective solution to erosion problems lies in locating the trail where it is resistant to erosion and where this is not possible, designing it to minimize erosion. Studies have found that erosion is most severe where trails are located in soils of homogeneous texture and that lack rocks. Erosion-prone soils consist primarily of sand, silt, or clay, rather than a combination of these different particle sizes; fine sand and silt soils are particularly prone to erosion (Bryan 1977; Root and Knapik 1972). Such soils are frequently encountered in glacial deposits, particularly in valley bottoms and enclosed basins. Meadows also often have homogeneous, fine-textured soils. Meadow soils can also be highly organic, and organic soils are particularly prone to deterioration (Bryan 1977). Steep slopes and places where drainage or snowmelt run down the trail are also prone to erosion. Streambanks, with steep slopes, abundant moisture, and, in many places, fine-textured soils, can frequently experience excessive erosion.

For these reasons, in the mountainous West, at least, erosion problems are frequently avoided by locating trails on ridges, talus slopes, and bedrock, away from alluvial plains and the glacial deposits of valley bottoms. South- and west-facing slopes are preferred locations because snow melts earlier there. Where trails receive regular use, trails are best located in forests outside of meadows. Although the vegetation in meadows is relatively resistant (Cole 1979), regular trail traffic use will eliminate even resistant vegetation and expose soils that are highly prone to erosion.

It is important to avoid steep grades by locating trails on sidehills and by providing switchbacks where necessary. To divert water off the tread, trails are usually outsloped and often incorporate dips and rises (often called a rolling grade) rather than long, continuous downslope stretches. Water bars—logs, boards, timbers, or rocks installed across a trail, usually on an angle and sloping out—are common means of directing water off the tread and minimizing erosion. Water bars must be spaced closely enough so that water cannot build up excessive speed and erosive power. They must be securely anchored and large enough to keep water from running around or over them, forming destructive little waterfalls; and they must be maintained frequently because they cease to function when dislodged or buried in the sediment deposited behind them. Finally, all of these techniques need to be part of the original trail design; once a deep trough has eroded, none of these techniques will be effective. Proudman (1977) provides good how-to instructions on these techniques.

It will also be necessary to keep water from flowing onto the trail. The most common devices used are cross

ditches (rock- or log-armored ditches crossing the trail), culverts (wood, metal, or fiberglass drainages buried underneath the trail), and parallel ditches (depressions that carry water adjacent to but lower than the trail tread). All of these devices must be carefully placed and maintained or they can aggravate problems.

Erosion of streambanks can be minimized by locating stream crossings where banks are low, gentle, and stable. Where this is not possible, angling the trail across rather than directly up the bank and incorporating drainage devices can help minimize damage.

Muddiness

Muddy stretches are particularly disturbing to recreationists; both hikers and stock balk at walking through quagmires. In an attempt to skirt the problem, hikers and stock enlarge the muddy area until it can be hundreds of yards long and occasionally almost as wide. These quagmires usually result from trampling water-saturated soils. Again, amount and type of use are of little importance because it takes only a little trampling to do most of the damage; however, damage is much more rapid with stock use than with hiker use (Stanley and others 1979). Muddiness can be a season-long problem in places where the water table is always close to the surface, or it can be temporary, occurring during snowmelt or when heavy rains fall on trails that have been churned to dust. The solution is to either locate trails on dry soils or shield the wet soils from trampling through trail engineering (fig. 16.18). Relocation is preferred, if a better location exists.

Snowfields that do not melt until late in the season should be identified, and trails should be located away from meltwater channels. Identifying areas where the water table is close to the surface is

Fig. 16.18. Trails through areas of water-saturated soils develop into ever-larger bogs. In many cases the only solution is to bridge the area. It is best to bridge the entire bog, rather than just part of it—the problem with this trail. Photo courtesy of the USFS.

more difficult. By noting the plant species and plant communities that grow in places along existing trails where muddiness is a problem, one can identify reliable vegetational indicators of potential problems. In the Selway-Bitterroot Wilderness, for example, more than two-thirds of the muddiness problems in one trail system were found in one vegetation type, which, along with vigorous growth of four individual species, can be used to identify sites to avoid (Cole 1983c).

Where trails must be built through water-saturated soils, some sort of bridging is necessary to shield the vulnerable soil from trampling. By far the most common type of bridging is log decking, commonly known as corduroy. More elaborate designs involve elevated trails, with earth or gravel fill supported either by logs or flat rocks. These may or may not be ditched on either side or may use culverts to facilitate drainage. Although such a trail is a permanent improvement and shows a "substantially noticeable imprint of man's work," huge quagmires are also noticeable and undesirable. Therefore it is our opinion that such engineering is appropriate where necessary to cope with mud as long as (1) relocation is not feasible, (2) the design fits the environment, and (3) the practice is not carried to the extreme where every miniscule wet place is bridged.

Impromptu Trails

The three most common types of undesirable impromptu trails are multiple, parallel, or braided trails; shortcuts on switchbacks; and informal trail systems to popular attractions or in popular destination areas. Each of these situations is the result of a unique set of circumstances; consequently very different management approaches are required for each. The one element they have in common is that they are caused by people leaving the existing trail system—either out of dissatisfaction with the trail itself or a desire to go someplace else. Therefore, understanding visitors' behavior and possibly accommodating their desires, as well as informing them of the damage they are doing, are common means of dealing with these three situations.

Multiple trails are common in areas that are poorly drained or have homogeneous fine-grained textures. Trails in such places present difficult footing due to their slippery, muddy surface or their being deep and narrow. In either case, hikers and horses walk beside the trail, forming a new one (fig. 16.19). Multiple trails also tend to form in open areas where it is easier for users to spread out, therefore they are a particular problem in meadows. Other than educating people to stay on existing trails, the best solution to multiple trailing is relocation. Currently, a strong

trend is to get trails out of meadows into adjacent forested areas. Abandoned trails usually need to be actively rehabilitated or they may continue to erode and may take centuries to recover.

In some places, such as Yosemite National Park, it has been very difficult to get people to stop using trails in the meadows or along other preferred routes. In these cases engineering solutions, such as surfaced, elevated trails, have been employed to overcome the problems that encouraged users to form multiple trails. Although engineering may be preferable to doing nothing, we feel it should be a last option.

Shortcutting switchbacks is a common problem that has received considerable attention and it is usually dealt with by changing visitor behavior and trail design. Whether through education or regulation, visitors are asked not to shortcut switchbacks. In some places signs have been erected along the trail; this is an undesirable intrusion and should not be used unless absolutely necessary. Designs that can effectively reduce shortcutting include screening one switchback from another, building barriers of rock or vegetation, avoiding the use of numerous short switchbacks, and using wide turns.

Informal trail systems indicate too much use of an area and are difficult to control. In popular destination areas managers should develop an "official" trail system based on existing use patterns and encourage its use. This strategy should control the size of the informal trail network and keep trails out of fragile environments. Unnecessary and poorly located trails will cooperate. When laying out an official trail it is critical to provide access to the places visitors seek to go. If this is not done, the informal system will continue to be used, frustrating this management strategy.

Informal trails can also be controlled by reducing use, closing and rehabilitating trails, and persuading visitors to spread out. This is probably only realistic in remote, lightly used parts of the wilderness where management objectives are to keep the area trailless. Once trails begin to develop, use must be reduced. Although it may seem inappropriate to reduce use in lightly used places—particularly if use is not limited in much more heavily used destination areas—this may be the only means of meeting the objective of "no trails." Several actions can be taken at an early stage to make such an action less likely. Users of such areas should be educated about the need to travel in small parties, to spread out rather than follow in each other's footsteps, and to avoid using incipient trails. Of particular importance, management should not attempt to disperse use from heavily used destination areas to these lightly used areas unless they are willing to accept trails in these places.

Fig. 16.19. Multiple trailing is a common problem, particularly in meadows. Such trails tend to form where the trail tread is difficult to use; note the water flowing down the main tread of this trail. The most common solution has been to relocate trails in the forest or at the edge of the meadow where soils are drier and less erodible. Photo courtesy of Randel Washburne, USFS.

Engineering

As much of the preceding discussion concludes, next to proper trail location, engineering—surfacing, bridging, ditching, and so on—is the most effective means of avoiding trail problems. Problems that cannot be reduced or avoided by trail relocation will generally require an engineering solution. Although engineering is an appropriate means of providing for use without excessive resource damage, it is also undesirable and therefore should be kept to a minimum.

Visitor surveys (Lucas 1980) have indicated little support for high-standard trails, but strong support for low-standard trails. Likewise, visitors favor bridges where rivers cannot be crossed safely, but not where they merely prevent wet feet. In response to this sentiment and the wording of the Wilderness Act itself, trail designers should resort to engineering only where necessary and then should choose unobtrusive designs.

Excessive Relation

Frequent relocation can produce a maze of closed trails. Managers must therefore exercise restraint when relocating trails. This problem can be reduced by actively rehabilitating trails. A good rule of thumb, however, is not to relocate a trail unless (1) the new section is in a more resistant environment or is better designed, and (2) hikers can be kept off the old section of trail (Proudman 1977). Unless both these

conditions are met, relocation will only compound problems by disturbing new sites.

MONITORING TRAIL CONDITIONS

Monitoring of trails can be used to ascertain trends in trail condition, where and how to locate and design trails, and whether trail management programs are working. To be most useful, a monitoring system should be based on written standards that describe unacceptable conditions. Written standards tell the manager what data to collect and how to collect it. The manager must decide which types of trail deterioration are of concern and whether to monitor the severity of individual problems (trail width), the frequency of problems (such as the number or length of excessively wide trail segments), or both.

Rapid survey techniques exist that require little time and are sufficient for most monitoring purposes. For example, if a standard states trails should not exceed 1 foot in depth, monitoring simply requires walking the trails, noting segments where the depth exceeds 1 foot. If the standard states that no more than 1 percent of the trail will be deeper than 1 foot, systematic sampling may be more efficient. Rather than census the entire trail system, depth could be measured periodically, say every 0.2 mile. Other measurements that might be taken are width of the trail (either the tread or the entire disturbed zone), width of bare ground, and the presence or absence of such "problems" as rutting, gullying, lateral erosion, and poor drainage. Some monitoring systems (such as one devised by Bratton and others 1979) use rating systems based on a number of trail features. More detail on these and other techniques can be found in Cole (1983c).

As mentioned earlier, it can be quite useful to census problem trail segments and look for associations between deterioration problems and environmental indicators such as vegetation type. These indicators, once identified, can be used to guide trail location and relocation and to indicate where engineering and maintenance are necessary. Although such a survey involves an initial outlay of funds, the investment will be recovered quickly in reduced trail relocation, maintenance, and rehabilitation costs. It is not necessary to survey all trails. Just choose a few examples that represent the range of conditions in the area of concern, develop guidelines for these conditions, and extrapolate the results elsewhere.

REHABILITATION

Much of the information about rehabilitating camp-

sites also applies to trails, particularly the techniques available for reestablishing vegetation and the need to eliminate all use. The major difference is the need, in many places, to stop erosion and to replace the soil lost by erosion. It also may be more difficult to keep people from using the trail if it leads where they want to go.

To minimize use of a trail one must first provide a desirable alternative route. This may require observation of use patterns and visitor behavior, and even some questioning of users about their itinerary and what alternative routes might be acceptable. Once the alternative has been provided, one should try to mask the old trail. Careful selection of a starting point for the relocation can make it easier to hide the old trail. If it cannot be hidden, block it with logs, rocks, or brush. Finally, if this does not work it will be necessary to erect signs such as "Please stay on the trail to prevent damage" or "Trail closed for repairs." It is important to explain why the trail is closed (Dalle-Molle 1977).

Avoiding further trail erosion starts with looking for its source. Sometimes runoff has been directed down the trail and it must be diverted elsewhere. Ditches and water bars across the trail can be used to keep water off the trail. It is often also useful to place rock or log check dams in the trail to reduce water velocity and therefore erosion of the trail, and to allow backfilling of sediment. Specifications used in Mount Rainier National Park are to space dams no more than 25 feet apart on slopes up to 20 degrees, no more than 15 feet apart on slopes of 20 to 30 degrees, and no more than 10 feet apart on slopes in excess of 30 degrees.

Material used to fill in trail troughs—other than what is deposited behind check dams—must be judiciously selected. Where the trail follows the contour, it is often possible to move material deposited below the trail, as a result of construction, back into the tread. Other good sources of material include soil from streambeds and rock from other trail work, talus slopes, and rocky riverbeds. It is best not to remove too much material from any single place and to make sure the source area is blended into its surroundings and masked from view. Regardless of where the material comes from, revegetation will be most effective if the trough is filled with soil.

One of the few documented tests of rehabilitating multiple trails was tried along a section of trail in Tuolumne Meadows in Yosemite National Park (Palmer 1979). Of 22 techniques tried, the most successful one involved cutting off the sod ridges between the multiple trails at the level of the trail tread and stacking it in the shade (fig. 16.20). The soil

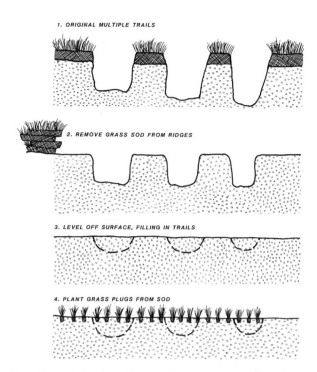

1. ORIGINAL MULTIPLE TRAILS

2. REMOVE GRASS SOD FROM RIDGES

3. LEVEL OFF SURFACE, FILLING IN TRAILS

4. PLANT GRASS PLUGS FROM SOD

Fig. 16.20. Multiple trails have been revegetated by removing sod, leveling the soil surface, and transplanting sod plugs.

beneath both the trails and the ridges was dug up to eliminate compaction, and sand was added to bring the trail up to the level of the surrounding meadow. Finally, the sod was divided into transplant plugs and planted. While this technique will work only in certain environments, it is well-suited to multiple trails in meadows—a very common problem in many areas—and is not extremely time-consuming.

MANAGING PACK AND SADDLE STOCK

Although the backpacking "boom" of the late 1960s and 1970s has relegated pack and saddle stock to a minority use in all but a few wildernesses, stock use is still an accepted tradition throughout most of the National Wilderness Preservation System (NWPS). This is in contrast to some other Nations, such as Australia, where use of stock in wilderness is not allowed. As of 1980, about one of every 10 parties entering wilderness traveled with stock. Although packstock accompanied more than 2 percent of parties in only 72 wildernesses and more than 50 percent of parties in only six areas, packstock impacts were reported to be a problem in 76 wildernesses (Washburne and Cole 1983).

Despite the prevalence of such problems, the published literature on packstock impacts and their management is sparse. Certain impacts are similar to those caused by hikers and can be managed similarly; others are qualitatively different and require very different sorts of management techniques.

TYPES OF STOCK IMPACT

Generally the impact of stock on trails is similar to that caused by hikers except that it is more pronounced. Weaver and Dale (1978) examined the effects of controlled amounts of use by horses and hikers on trail width and depth, percentage of bare ground, and soil compaction (bulk density). Trails produced by 1,000 horse passes were 2 to 3 times as wide and 1.5 to 7 times as deep as trails produced by 1,000 hiker passes. Compaction increased about 1.5 to 2 times as rapidly on horse trails as on hiker trails. Finally, one-half of the vegetation was lost after 1,000 hiker and 600 horse passes on a grassland, and after 300 hiker and only 50 horse passes in a forest. An experimental trampling study in a grassland in Waterton Lakes National Park, Canada, found that trampling by horses destroyed vegetational cover four to eight times as rapidly as trampling by hikers (Nagy and Scotter 1974). These experimental results suggest that the creation of multiple trails and new trails in trailless areas will occur much more rapidly with stock use than with hiker use. The trails created will also be wider, deeper, more compacted, and less vegetated.

The effect of stock on existing trails, which can differ from their effect on undisturbed sites, was examined experimentally in Great Smoky Mountains National Park (Whittaker 1978). Again, horse use caused more pronounced increases in trail width, trail depth, and litter loss than hiker use. But while hiker use generally tends to increase soil compaction on the trail, horse use loosens the soil, making it more susceptible to erosion (fig. 16.17). McQuaid-Cook (1978) has commented that this tendency for shod hooves to loosen soil leads to more pronounced incision of equestrian trails. Trail widening is accentuated by the tendency for stock to walk on the downslope side of the trail. This breaks down the outer edge of the trail so that new soil must be brought in to rebuild the trail. The result is a wide trail, a much wider area of disturbance, and an ongoing trail maintenance problem (Whitson 1974).

Equestrian trails require considerably more maintenance than hiking trails. They must be "brushed-out" to a greater height and width. Fallen trees must be quickly removed or detour trails will rapidly develop. Stock often break or dislodge

drainage devices such as water bars. Stock disturbance of muddy trail sections can be particularly
severe and can be corrected only with some type of
bridging more elaborate than required for foot travel.

On campsites, differences in the magnitude of
impact caused by hikers as opposed to stock parties
are even more pronounced than on trails. Moreover,
stock parties cause a number of impact types that
other parties do not. Unfortunately, very little data
on differences between these two types of use are
available. Unpublished data from Dr. Sidney Frissell's
work in the early 1970s, in what is now the Lee
Metcalf Wilderness, indicate that campsites used by
stock parties were, on the average, 10 times as large
and had 7 times as much exposed mineral soil as sites
used primarily by backpackers.

A more complete picture of differences in amount
of impact between stock and backpacker campsites
comes from a comparison of six sites of each type in
the Bob Marshall Wilderness (Cole 1983a). When
compared to backpacker sites, stock sites are much
larger, have many more damaged trees, have been
more extensively invaded by exotic species, and
have experienced much more profound soil disturbance (table 16.5).

Stock parties, generally being larger than backpacker parties, consequently disturb a larger area, to
which is added an adjacent area where stock are kept
(fig. 16.21). The animals are usually tied to trees,
resulting in a large number of damaged trunks and
exposed roots. Because stock parties usually carry
saws and axes to clean windfalls from trails, trees are
often felled for tent poles to support large canvas
tents and for firewood.

Although stock are usually kept adjacent to the

Fig. 16.21. Stock-holding areas adjacent to campsites greatly
enlarge the area of disturbance. Such areas often experience serious tree damage, loss of vegetation, and soil
erosion. Photo courtesy of the USFS.

camp, they occasionally are brought into the central
camp area. Here, the action of their shod hooves will
cause rapid deterioration of the site. Loss of organic
soil horizons, increased compaction, and decreased
infiltration rates typical of all campsites are particularly pronounced on sites used by stock parties.
Seeds of exotic plants contained in horsefeed readily
germinate and grow on such disturbed sites.

In areas where stock are grazed or confined for
the night, impacts result from both trampling and
defoliation of plants. These impacts, described in the
earlier section on grazing impacts, are unique to

Table 16.5. Differences in amount of impact between sites used primarily by backpackers and sites used
primarily by parties with stock, Bob Marshall Wilderness, MT.

	Backpacker sites	Stock sites
	(Median)	
Disturbed area (m²)	76	456
Area devoid of vegetation (m²)	3	13
Number of damaged trees	5	56
Number of felled trees	0	8
Number of trees with exposed roots	1	25
Seedling loss (%)	100	100
Ground cover vegetation loss (%)	26	33
Relative cover of exotic plants (%)	5	43
Increase in mineral soil exposure (%)	4.6	9.3
Depth of organic horizons (cm)	2.2	1.2
Penetration resistance (kg/cm²)	2.6	4.0
Infiltration rate (cm/min)	1.0	0.1

Source: Cole 1983a.

parties with stock and often affect a much larger area than all other recreational impacts combined. In a portion of the Eagle Cap Wilderness, an estimated 1.8 percent of the area had been significantly altered by recreational use. About three-fourths of this disturbed area consisted of areas used only by stock for grazing (Cole 1981a). Moreover, in comparison to the forests, the meadows and grasslands used for grazing are often both rare ecosystems and aesthetic attractions; therefore their disturbance is particularly undesirable.

Meeting parties traveling with stock or finding evidence of stock use, such as manure or corrals, also detracts greatly from the experience of many wilderness users. This is particularly true in the majority of wildernesses where stock use is a small minority. For example, in the Bridger Wilderness, Wyoming, where backpacking is the norm, 59 percent of parties preferred not to meet horse users; in the Bob Marshall Wilderness, where stock use is common, only 21 percent of parties preferred not to meet horse users (Stankey 1973). In the Rawah Wilderness, Colorado, where only 4 percent of the respondents to a survey used horses, 57 percent of those questioned wanted to see no horse users at all, not even small parties close to the trailhead. Only 23 percent wanted to see no other hiking parties at all. The only situation wherein a party of hikers would be considered more objectionable than even a small party of horse users seen near a trailhead, would be a large party of hikers walking or camped near the respondent's destination (Badger 1975).

In addition to dissatisfaction with meeting horse users, problems stem from finding evidence of horse use or dealing with inconveniences caused by their use. For example, in Yosemite National Park, Lee (1975) found that the presence of horse manure or facilities such as hitch rails were key sources of dissatisfaction with campsites. Unpublished results of a study by M. F. Trahan in Rocky Mountain National Park, Colorado, show that a majority of day hikers who disapproved of horse use—57 percent of all users—did so because they disliked horse manure and urine, and the flies and other insects attracted to it. Less common reasons for disapproval were concern with the damage stock do to trails, the dust they cause, and the large size of most stock parties. Fewer still disapproved because they disliked moving off the trail to let horse users pass or because they disliked the general idea of some people riding while others walked.

In addition to those that would rather not meet stock-equipped parties in the wilderness, many visitors believed that use of stock in wilderness is inappropriate. For example, about one-fourth of the visitors to Bridger Wilderness did not feel that "both backpacking and horseback travel are entirely appropriate ways to travel in wilderness areas" (Stankey 1973). In the Sierra Nevada less than 15 percent of the parties surveyed approved of horses as a means of recreational travel; 60 percent thought that use of stock was inappropriate even to render emergency aid (Absher and Absher 1979).

MANAGEMENT STRATEGIES AND TECHNIQUES

Despite the strong tradition of stock use in wilderness, management needs to come to grips with the inescapable conclusion that social, environmental, and administrative costs associated with stock use are much more pronounced than those associated with comparable amounts of hiker use. This situation is aggravated by the large number of backpackers who feel that use of stock and its impacts are inappropriate. In many areas the solution is complicated by a strong tradition of stock use by administrative agencies. In areas where use is already highly restricted due to ecological and social impacts, management must strive, particularly, to minimize those impacts associated with stock use.

As with campsite and trail impact, a number of factors influence the *severity of stock impacts*. The most important are frequency and amount of use, party size and behavior, time of use, and location of use. These define *four primary management strategies: (1) limiting or reducing use, (2) encouraging less damaging behavior, (3) discouraging use during times of the year when the potential for damage is high, and (4) encouraging use of particularly resistant environments.* Because stock cause more impact than hikers, *a fifth strategy, containment*, is particularly valuable in controlling the spread of stock impact (table 16.6).

Limiting Use
Numerous studies have concluded that impacts on trails and campsites are unlikely to be greatly diminished merely by reducing use, unless use levels are cut to almost nothing (e.g., Cole and Fichtler 1983; Grabherr 1982; Helgath 1975). Because stock use causes impact even more rapidly than hiker use, this conclusion has even more serious implications for managing stock use. Unless all stock use is eliminated, there will be few situations where reducing stock use will produce substantial benefits in improved trail and campsite conditions. Reducing use can help minimize social and aesthetic impacts (horse user-hiker conflicts, manure, and so on), but other less drastic actions can also be taken. Except in cases

Table 16.6. Factors that influence packstock impacts. Each factor defines a strategy and set of specific techniques (of which only one example is provided here) for managing impacts.

Factor	Strategy	Technique (example)
Amount/frequency of use	Reduce use	Close overgrazed meadows
Party size/behavior	Change behavior	Promote low-impact use
Season of use	Change timing of use	Prohibit use during spring
Environmental/ site conditions	Increase site resistance	Reinforce trail with log cribbing
Use distribution	Contain use	Provide corrals

where all recreational use must be limited, or where management objectives indicate that all stock use and impact are inappropriate—and all stock use is prohibited—there seems to be little justification for limiting the amount of stock use. Better solutions to stock-caused problems exist. One exception to this is the institution of limits on the use of specific meadows to avoid overgrazing. Managers of Sequoia and Kings Canyon National Parks, for example, are trying to implement a management plan with specific limits for use of certain meadows with a history of being overgrazed. If the limit is reached, the meadow is temporarily closed. The need for closure is evaluated by monitoring meadow condition or by determining use levels from posttrip itineraries that each stock party is required to submit. Some of these meadows have length-of-stay limits so that more users can share the limited resource.

Just as it is inequitable to ration stock use when hiker use is unlimited, it is also inequitable, where rationing is instituted, not to recognize that stock cause considerably more damage than hikers. In terms of comparable impact, more hikers than horse users can use an area. Consequently, where use is rationed, an equitable allocation system will issue far fewer stock permits than hiker permits.

Encouraging Less-Damaging Behavior
Promoting minimum impact stock use has much promise for reducing impact, particularly on and around campsites. Outside of malicious or thoughtless chopping of trees, most tree damage—a particularly severe problem on stock sites—results from felling trees for firewood or tent poles and tying horses to trees. Available techniques and equipment (USDA FS 1981) can largely eliminate these practices and their resultant impacts. Also, stock do not need to be in camp areas after unloading; if stock were kept off campsites, soil disturbance and horse manure would

also be greatly reduced. If these ideas were adopted by stock users, campsites used by stock parties should suffer no more damage than sites used by comparably sized groups of backpackers.

Rather than rely on education, many areas have established regulations designed to prevent inappropriate behavior. As of 1980, 27 percent of the areas with regular stock use prohibited tying stock to trees and 15 percent prohibited stock in camps (Washburne and Cole 1983). The number of stock affects both the disturbed area around campsites and loss of solitude. A large party detracts much more from visitor satisfaction than a small party (Stankey 1973). Although a limit on party size is currently the most common packstock management technique in wilderness— almost one-half of all areas have a limit—the number allowed ranges from five to 50 animals per party, with 20 the most common limit (Washburne and Cole 1983). Such high limits will have very little beneficial effect; both social and campsite impacts are unlikely to be reduced unless limits are 10 animals or less. In the Desolation Wilderness in California and Spanish Peaks Primitive Area in Montana, Stankey (1980) found that most visitors who supported limits favored four animals or less. Where studied, visitors usually support such limitations on party size (Lucas 1980; Manfredo 1979).

Stock impacts could also be reduced by requiring parties to carry stock feed, thus virtually eliminating grazing damage. Twenty-nine percent of wildernesses have taken this action (Washburne and Cole 1983). In many places, parties bring only enough feed to supplement grazing. Many more areas ask but do not require stock parties to bring stock feed. Where deterioration is not yet critical, this approach may be more acceptable to users and may postpone or avoid the need for regulations. It is important, however, that the feed not contain exotic weeds. Other possibilities include the prohibition of grazing

where areas have been overgrazed.

Managing the Timing of Use

Although only 5 percent of areas prohibit stock use during certain seasons of the year, the impact of both grazing and trampling is highly dependent on seasonal variables, particularly the phenology or stage in the annual cycle of development of plants, and the moisture content of the soil. Generally, plants and soil are most vulnerable to disturbance during spring when plants are using stored nutrients for growth and when soils are water-saturated. This has led Sequoia and Kings Canyon National Parks—the backcountry area with the longest history of research and management of packstock impact—to make their primary management tool "a system of opening dates that would vary depending on the type of hydrologic year and the vegetation and soils in question" (DeBenedetti and Parsons 1983). A research program examined the composition and distribution of the parks' major forage areas as well as their susceptibility to differing intensities, frequencies, and times of use. Opening dates are prescribed for three types of hydrological years (wet, normal, and dry), allowing the user to predict when use will be allowed. The adequacy of this system will be checked by a monitoring system.

Controlling Location of Use

A common action is to keep stock away from streambanks and lakeshores, where trampling can be particularly destructive and, in some cases, cause accelerated erosion. This will also reduce the risk of water pollution. Thirty-five percent of all areas have this regulation, making it the second most common restriction on use of packstock (Washburne and Cole 1983). Many more areas encourage this practice through educational programs.

Containment of Impact

Stock impacts can often be most effectively minimized by containing their areal spread. Reasons for this include (1) the high potential for damage wherever stock use occurs; (2) the high environmental, social, and maintenance costs of stock use that, in most areas, benefits only a small proportion of users; (3) the large numbers of impacts that are caused exclusively by stock; (4) the area affected only by packstock, mostly grazing areas, is often much larger than the area affected by hikers; and (5) grazing impacts are concentrated on meadows that are often a rare and aesthetically important ecosystem type. In those few areas where stock use is the norm, confining use may be less justifiable and will be a less important strat-

egy than changing behavior and practices.

Many wildernesses prohibit stock use of certain trails or areas, or restrict stock use to certain trails or areas. Sequoia and Kings Canyon National Parks, for example, are seeking to prohibit stock use in places that have never received regular stock use and in certain meadows being maintained as representative examples of pristine ecosystems (DeBenedetti and Parsons 1983). Such a policy avoids degradation of currently undamaged areas and provides protection for some representatives of meadow types that might be entirely altered by unrestricted grazing. It also provides places for hikers to go where they know they will not see stock parties. Where certain trails are closed to stock use, trail maintenance costs can be substantially reduced.

Confining use and impacts within destination areas also can be advantageous. NPS areas often require that stock parties camp at certain sites specifically designated for their use. This confines damage to one site in a particularly resistant area. In Yellowstone National Park, Wyoming, grazing is allowed only in designated meadows that are periodically closed to allow recovery. Corrals, drift fences, and hitch rails can also be used to confine the spread of impact (fig. 16.22). Where studied, most visitors support both restricting stock use in certain areas and requiring stock parties to use certain campsites (Badger 1975; Lucas 1980; Manfredo 1979).

THE CHALLENGE OF STOCK MANAGEMENT

Managing stock and its impacts is a difficult and serious problem. The damage caused by stock is

Fig. 16.22. Hitch rails, like corrals, serve to concentrate the impact of stock use in a small area. Photo courtesy of David Cole, USFS.

generally much greater than that caused by hikers, many types of impact can be attributed solely to stock, and in most areas only a very small proportion of visitors benefit from and are associated with this impact. Many hikers consider this to be an inappropriate impact on the wilderness resource and this along with other inconveniences, such as exposure to horse manure and moving off the trail to let horse users pass, creates conflicts between backpackers and horse users. On the other hand, some stock use is a generally accepted, traditional type of wilderness use. Managers must grapple with the questions of how much of this impact is acceptable and where should it be allowed. A particularly difficult question is whether to allow stock use in places now suffering from too much use. Where impacts are excessive, managers can implement programs to reduce them. Stock users can be educated to use low-impact camping techniques, or be confined to certain trails and campsites. The most effective management programs will use a variety of techniques to reduce damage resulting from use of stock.

SUMMARY

This chapter has identified the various environmental effects of recreational use and described many techniques for managing them. Several general points can be made in summarizing this material.

First, impact is inevitable wherever recreation use is allowed. Therefore, consistent with the goal of providing recreational opportunities, management can only limit impact, not prevent it. Nevertheless, to prevent impact from increasing incrementally, with little ability to keep track of cumulative impacts, it is imperative to set specific objectives, standards, or LAC that will place a limit on impact. Then, through monitoring of conditions, managers will be able to more clearly identify when specific impacts have become so pronounced as to demand management attention.

Second, many available strategies and techniques help managers deal with each type of impact. Too often managers try only one technique—often the one they are most familiar with or one the neighboring manager is using. In most cases, however, using several techniques simultaneously will be much more effective than using one. The proper procedure is to identify the source of the problem, to formulate actions that can eliminate the problem at its source, to implement a preferred set of actions, and, most importantly, to monitor results.

Managers have been preoccupied with "too much" use as the major cause of problems and limit-ing use to a "carrying capacity" as the principal solution. Amount of use is just one of many factors influencing amount of impact; often it is one of the less influential factors. Likewise, limiting use to a carrying capacity is only one of many alternative management techniques, and often it is not very effective. Because limiting use also limits recreational opportunities, use should be limited only where it will clearly solve problems or is the only means of avoiding excessive regimentation.

Finally, managers must show equal concern for both quality of experience and environmental impacts. The two are inextricably bound together; actions that affect one will affect the other—sometimes in positive and sometimes in negative ways. Therefore managers must clearly define problems and how alternative actions will deal with them. Managers must also consider how an action to correct a problem in a specific place will affect other places and other wilderness conditions. Only through more effective integration of ecological and experiential concerns, both in research and management, can we develop the more holistic approach that will make wilderness management more than the continual putting out of brush fires.

STUDY QUESTIONS

1. Select two impact "situations" (type of impact, environmental type, and location) that represent substantial alterations of natural conditions and two situations that do *not* represent substantial alterations. Defend your choices.
2. Provide a detailed description of at least one example of (a) direct, (b) indirect, and (c) cyclic effects of trampling on vegetation and soil.
3. Suggest three actions that managers might take to influence the amount of use that campsites receive and, thereby, reduce impact. Contrast the appropriateness of each action on campsites in popular destination areas and campsites in lightly used remote places in the wilderness.
4. Compare and contrast the magnitude and nature of impacts caused by (a) small parties and large parties and (b) hiker parties and stock parties. Describe where impacts are similar and where they differ. Suggest and defend management actions that might be taken to minimize differences.

REFERENCES

Absher, Jim; Absher, Ellen. 1979. Sierra Club wilderness outing participants and their effect on Sierra Nevada wilderness users. In: Stanley, J. T., Jr.; Harvey, H. T.; Hartesveldt, R. J., eds. A report on the wilderness impact study. Palo Alto, CA: Sierra Club: 31-60.

Badger, Thomas J. 1975. Rawah Wilderness crowding tolerances and some management techniques: an aspect of social carrying capacity. Fort Collins, CO: Colorado State University. 83 p. Thesis.

Bainbridge, David A. 1974. Trail management. Bulletin of the Ecological Society of America. 55(3): 8-10.

Bayfield, Neil G. 1971. Some effects of walking and skiing on vegetation at Cairngorm. In: Duffey, E.; Watt, A. S., eds. The scientific management of animal and plant communities for conservation. Oxford: Blackwell Scientific Publications: 469-485.

Beardsley, Wendell G.; Wagar, J. Alan. 1971. Vegetation management on a forested recreation site. Journal of Forestry. 69: 728-731.

Bradley, Jim. 1979. A human approach to reducing wildland impacts. In: Ittner, R.; [and others], eds. Recreational impact on wildlands: Conference proceedings. R-6-001-1979. Portland, OR: U.S. Department of Agriculture, Forest Service, Pacific Northwest Region: 222-226.

Bratton, Susan P.; Hickler, Matthew G.; Graves, James H. 1978. Visitor impact on backcountry campsites in the Great Smoky Mountains. Environmental Management. 2: 431-442.

Bratton, Susan P.; Hickler, Matthew G.; Graves, James H. 1979. Trail erosion patterns in Great Smoky Mountains National Park. Environmental Management. 3: 431-445.

Bratton, Susan P.; Stromberg, Linda L.; Harmon, Mark E. 1982. Firewood-gathering impacts in backcountry campsites in Great Smoky Mountains National Park. Environmental Management. 6: 63-71.

Brewer, Les; Berrier, Debbie. 1984. Photographic techniques for monitoring resource change at backcountry sites. Gen. Tech. Rep. NE-86. Bromall, PA: U.S. Department of Agriculture, Forest Service, Northeastern Forest Experiment Station. 13 p.

Brickler, Stan; Tunnicliff, Brock; Utter, Jack. 1983. Use and quality of wildland water: the case of the Colorado River corridor in the Grand Canyon. Western Wildlands. 9(2): 20-25.

Brown, J. H., Jr.; Kalisz, S. P.; Wright, W. R. 1977. Effects of recreational use on forested sites. Environmental Geology. 1: 425-431.

Brown, Perry J.; Schomaker, John H. 1974. Final report on criteria for potential wilderness campsites. Suppl. No. 32 to 12 ~ 204-3, unpublished. Conducted through: Institute for Study of Outdoor Recreation and Tourism, Utah State University, Logan, UT. 50 p.

Bryan, Rorke B. 1977. The influence of soil properties on degradation of mountain hiking trails at Grovelsjon. Geografiska Annaler. 59A(1-2): 49-65.

Cole, David N. 1979. Reducing the impact of hikers on vegetation: an application of analytical research methods. In: Ittner, R.; [and others], eds. Recreational impact on wildlands: Conference proceedings. R-6-001-1979. Portland, OR: U.S. Department of Agriculture, Forest Service, Pacific Northwest Region: 71-78.

Cole, David N. 1981a. Vegetational changes associated with recreational use and fire suppression in the Eagle Cap Wilderness, Oregon: some management implications. Biological Conservation. 20: 247-270.

Cole, David N. 1981b. Managing ecological impacts at wilderness campsites: an evaluation of techniques. Journal of Forestry. 79: 86-89.

Cole, David N. 1982a. Vegetation of two drainages in Eagle Cap Wilderness, Wallowa Mountains, Oregon. Res. Pap. INT-288. Ogden, UT: U.S. Department of Agriculture, Forest Service, Intermountain Forest and Range Experiment Station. 42 p.

Cole, David N. 1982b. Wilderness campsite impacts: effect of amount of use. Res. Pap. INT-284. Ogden, UT: U.S. Department of Agriculture, Forest Service, Intermountain Forest and Range Experiment Station. 34 p.

Cole, David N. 1982c. Controlling the spread of campsites at popular wilderness destinations. Journal of Soil and Water Conservation. 37: 291-295.

Cole, David N. 1983a. Campsite conditions in the Bob Marshall Wilderness, Montana. Res. Pap. INT-312. Ogden, UT: U.S. Department of Agriculture, Forest Service, Intermountain Forest and Range Experiment Station. 18 p.

Cole, David N. 1983b. Monitoring the condition of wilderness campsites. Res. Pap. INT-302. Ogden, UT: U.S. Department of Agriculture, Forest Service, Intermountain Forest and Range Experiment Station. 10 p.

Cole, David N. 1983c. Assessing and monitoring backcountry trail conditions. Res. Pap. INT-303. Ogden, UT: U.S. Department of Agriculture, Forest Service, Intermountain Forest and Range Experiment Station. 10 p.

Cole, David N. 1985. Recreational trampling effects on six habitat types in western Montana. Res. Pap. INT-350. Ogden, UT: U.S. Department of Agriculture, Forest Service, Intermountain Research Station. 43 p.

Cole, David N. 1986. Recreational impacts on backcountry campsites in Grand Canyon National Park, Arizona, USA. Environmental Management. 10: 651-659.

Cole, David N.; Benedict, Jim. 1983. Wilderness campsite selection—what should users be told? Park Science. 3(4): 5-7.

Cole, David N.; Schreiner, Edward G. S. 1981. Impacts of backcountry recreation: site management and rehabilitation—an annotated bibliography. Gen. Tech. Rep. INT-121. Ogden, UT: U.S. Department of Agriculture, Forest Service, Intermountain Forest and Range Experiment Station. 58 p.

Cole, David N.; Dalle-Molle, John. 1982. Managing campfire impacts in the backcountry. Gen. Tech. Rep. INT-135. Ogden, UT: U.S. Department of Agriculture, Forest Service, Intermountain Forest and Range Experiment Station. 16 p.

Cole, David N.; Fichtler, Richard K. 1983. Campsite impact in three western wilderness areas. Environmental Management. 7: 275-288.

Cole, David N.; Ranz, Beth. 1983. Temporary campsite closures in the Selway-Bitterroot Wilderness. Journal of Forestry. 81: 729-732.

Dale, D.; Weaver, T. 1974. Trampling effects on vegetation of the trail corridors of north Rocky Mountain forests. Journal of Applied Ecology. 11: 767-772.

Dalle-Molle, John. Resource restoration. 1977. Unpublished report on file at: U.S. Department of the Interior, National Park Service, Mount Rainier National Park, WA. 23 p.

DeBenedetti, Steven H.; Parsons, David J. 1979. Mountain meadow management and research in Sequoia and Kings Canyon National Parks: a review and update. In:

Linn, R., ed. Proceedings, first conference on scientific research in the National Parks. Washington, DC: U.S. Department of the Interior, National Park Service Trans. and Proc. Series No. 5, Vol. 2: 1305-1311.

DeBenedetti, Steven H.; Parsons, David J. 1983. Protecting mountain meadows: a grazing management plan. Parks. 8(3): 11- 13.

Dickman, M.; Dorais, M. 1977. The impact of human trampling on phosphorus loading to a small lake in Gatineau Park, Quebec, Canada. Journal of Environmental Management. 5: 335-344.

Fardoe, Brian K. 1980. An evaluation of backcountry horse use and recreation impact in the proposed Kakwa Provincial Park. Calgary, AB: University of Calgary. 202 p. Thesis.

Fazio, James R. 1979. Communicating with the wilderness user. Bull. 28. Moscow, ID: University of Idaho, College of Forestry, Wildlife and Range Sciences. 65 p.

Fenn, Dennis B.; Gogue, G. Jay; Burge, Raymond E. 1976. Effects of campfires on soil properties. Ecol. Serv. Bull. 5. Washington, DC: U.S. Department of the Interior, National Park Service. 16 p.

Ferguson, Michael A. D.; Keith, Lloyd B. 1982. Influence of nordic skiing on distribution of moose and elk in Elk Island National Park, Alberta. Canadian Field-Naturalist. 96: 69-78.

Foin, T. C., Jr.; Garton, E. 0.; Bowen, C. W.; [and others]. 1977. Quantitative studies of visitor impacts on environments of Yosemite National Park, California, and their implications for park management policy. Journal of Environmental Management. 5: 1-22.

Frissell, Sidney S. 1978. Judging recreation impacts on wilderness campsites. Journal of Forestry. 76: 481-483.

Frissell, Sidney S., Jr.; Duncan, Donald P. 1965. Campsite preference and deterioration in the Quetico-Superior canoe country. Journal of Forestry. 63: 256-260.

Geist, Valerius. 1970. A behavioral approach to the management of wild ungulates. In: Duffey, E.; Watt, A. S., eds. Scientific management of animal and plant communities for conservation. Oxford: Blackwell Scientific Publications: 413-424.

Godin, Victor B.; Leonard, Raymond E. 1979. Management problems in designated wilderness areas. Journal of Soil and Water Conservation. 34: 141-143.

Grabherr, G. 1982. The impact of trampling by tourists on a high altitudinal grassland in the Tyrolean Alps, Austria. Vegetatio. 48: 209-217.

Hammitt, William E.; Cole, David N. 1987. Wildland recreation: ecology and management. New York: John Wiley and Sons. 341 p.

Hansen, R. M.; Clark, R. C. 1977. Foods of elk and other ungulates at low elevations in northwestern Colorado. Journal of Wildlife Management. 41: 76-80.

Hart, James B., Jr. 1982. Ecological effects of recreation use on campsites. In: Countryman, D. W.; Sofranko, D. M., eds. Guiding land use decisions: planning and management for forests and recreation. Baltimore: Johns Hopkins University Press: 150-182.

Hartley, Ernest Albert. 1976. Man's effects on the stability of alpine and subalpine vegetation in Glacier National Park, Montana. Durham, NC: Duke University. 258 p. Dissertation.

Hartmann, Hudson T.; Kester, Dale E. 1975. Plant propagation principles and practices. 3d ed. Engelwood Cliffs, NJ: Prentice Hall. 662 p.

Harvey, A. E.; Jurgensen, M. F.; Larsen, M. J. 1979. Role of forest fuels in the biology and management of soil. Gen. Tech. Rep. INT-65. Ogden, UT: U.S. Department of Agriculture, Forest Service, Intermountain Forest and Range Experiment Station. 8 p.

Heberlein, Thomas A.; Dunwiddie, Peter. 1979. Systematic observation of use levels, campsite selection, and visitor characteristics at a high mountain lake. Journal of Leisure Research. 11: 307-316.

Helgath, Sheila F. 1975. Trail deterioration in the Selway-Bitterroot Wilderness. Res. Note INT-193. Ogden, UT: U.S. Department of Agriculture, Forest Service, Intermountain Forest and Range Experiment Station. 15 p.

Hendee, J. C.; Clark, R. N.; Hogans, M. L.; Wood, D.; Koch, R. W. 1976. Code-A-Site: a system for inventory of dispersed recreational sites in roaded areas, backcountry, and wilderness. Res. Pap. PNW-209. Portland, OR: U.S. Department of Agriculture, Forest Service, Pacific Northwest Forest and Range Experiment Station. 33 p.

Hicks, Lorin L.; Elder, James M. 1979. Human disturbance of Sierra Nevada bighorn sheep. Journal of Wildlife Management. 53: 909-915.

Hinds, T. E. 1976. Aspen mortality in Rocky Mountain campgrounds. Res. Pap. RM-164. Fort Collins, CO: U.S. Department of Agriculture, Forest Service, Rocky Mountain Forest and Range Experiment Station. 20 p.

Holmes, Daniel O.; Dobson, Heidi E. M. 1976. Ecological carrying capacity research: Yosemite National Park. Part I: the effects of human trampling and urine on subalpine vegetation, a survey of past and present backcountry use, and the ecological carrying capacity of wilderness. Washington, DC: U.S. Department of Commerce, National Technical Information Center; PB-270-955. 247 p.

James, T. D. W.; Smith, D. W.; MacIntosh, E. E.; [and others]. 1979. Effects of camping recreation on soil, jack pine, and understory vegetation in a northwestern Ontario park. Forest Science. 25: 333-349.

Ketchledge, E. H.; Leonard, R. E. 1970. The impact of man on the Adirondack high country. The Conservationist. 25(2): 14-18.

Kuss, Fred R. 1983. Hiking boot impacts on woodland trails. Journal of Soil and Water Conservation. 38: 119-121.

Kuss, Fred R.; Vaske, Jerry J.; Graefe, Alan A. 1985. A review and synthesis of recreational carrying capacity literature. Final report to National Parks and Conservation Association. Washington, DC. 210 p.

Laing, Charles C. 1961. A report on the effect of visitors on the natural landscape in the vicinity of Lake Solitude, Grand Teton National Park, Wyoming. Unpublished report on file at: U.S. Department of the Interior, National Park Service, Grand Teton National Park, WY.

LaPage, Wilbur F. 1967. Some observations on campground trampling and ground cover response. Res. Pap. NE-68. Broomall, PA: U.S. Department of Agriculture, Forest Service, Northeastern Forest Experiment Station. 11 p.

Lee, Robert G. 1975. The management of human components in the Yosemite National Park ecosystem. Yosemite National Park, CA: Yosemite Institute. 134 p.

Legg, Michael H.; Schneider, Gary. 1977. Soil deterioration

on campsites: northern forest types. Soil Science Society of America Journal. 41: 437-441.

Leonard, R. E.; Plumley, H. J. 1979. Human waste disposal in eastern backcountry. Journal of Forestry. 77: 349-352.

Lester, William; Calder, Sue. 1979. Revegetating the forest zone of North Cascades National Park. In: Ittner, R.; [and others], eds. Recreational impact on wildlands: Conference proceedings. R-6-001-1979. Portland, OR: U.S. Department of Agriculture, Forest Service, Pacific Northwest Region: 271-275.

Liddle, M. J. 1975. A selective review of the ecological effects of human trampling on natural ecosystems. Biological Conservation. 7: 17-36.

Lime, David W.; Lucas, Robert C. 1977. Good information improves the wilderness experience. Naturalist. 28(4): 18-20.

Lucas, Robert C. 1979. Perceptions of non-motorized recreational impacts: a review of research findings. In: Ittner, R.; [and others], eds. Recreational impact on wildlands: Conference proceedings. R6-001-1979. Portland, OR: U.S. Department of Agriculture, Forest Service, Pacific Northwest Region: 24-31.

Lucas, Robert. C. 1980. Use patterns and visitor characteristics, attitudes and preferences in nine wilderness and other roadless areas. Res. Pap. INT-253. Ogden, UT: U.S. Department of Agriculture, Forest Service, Intermountain Forest and Range Experiment Station. 89 p.

Lull, Howard W. 1959. Soil compaction on forest and range lands. Misc. Publ. 768. Washington, DC: U.S. Department of Agriculture, Forest Service. 33 p.

MacArthur, Robert A.; Geist, Valerius; Johnston, Ronald H. 1982. Cardiac and behavioral responses of mountain sheep to human disturbance. Journal of Wildlife Management. 46: 351-358.

Manfredo, Michael James. 1979. Wilderness experience opportunities and management preferences for three Wyoming wilderness areas. Fort Collins, CO: Colorado State University. 113 p. Dissertation.

Manning, Robert E. 1979. Impacts of recreation on riparian soils and vegetation. Water Resources Bulletin. 15: 30-43.

Marion, Jeffrey L.; Merriam, L. C. 1985. Recreational impacts on well-established campsites in the Boundary Waters Canoe Area Wilderness. Bull. AD-SB-2502. St. Paul, MN: University of Minnesota, Agricultural Experiment Station. 16 p.

McDowell, Theodore R. 1979. Geographic variations in water quality and recreational use along the upper Wallowa River and selected tributaries. Corvallis, OR: Oregon State University. 199 p. Dissertation.

McEwen, Douglas; Tocher, S. Ross. 1976. Zone management: key to controlling recreational impact in developed campsites. Journal of Forestry. 74: 90-93.

McQuaid-Cook, J. 1978. Effects of hikers and horses on mountain trails. Journal of Environmental Management. 6: 209-212.

Merriam, L. C., Jr.; Smith, C. K. 1974. Visitor impact on newly developed campsites in the Boundary Waters Canoe Area. Journal of Forestry. 72: 627-630.

Miller, Joseph W.; Miller, Margaret M. 1979. Propagation of plant material for subalpine revegetation. In: Ittner, R.; [and others], eds. Recreational impact on wildlands: Conference proceedings. R-6-001-1979. Portland, OR:

U.S. Department of Agriculture, Forest Service, Pacific Northwest Region: 304-310.

Moen, Aaron N. 1976. Energy conservation by white-tailed deer in the winter. Ecology. 57: 192-198.

Monti, P.; Mackintosh, E. E. 1979. Effect of camping on surface soil properties in the boreal forest region of northwestern Ontario, Canada. Soil Science Society of America Journal. 43: 1024-1029.

Nagy, John A. S.; Scotter, George W. 1974. A quantitative assessment of the effects of human and horse trampling on natural areas, Waterton Lakes National Park. Edmonton, AB: Canadian Wildlife Service. 145 p.

Palmer, Rexford. 1979. Progress report on trail revegetation studies. In: Stanley, J. T., Jr.; Harvey, H. T.; Hartesveldt, R. J., eds. A report on the wilderness impact study: the effects of human recreational activities on wilderness ecosystems with special emphasis on Sierra Club wilderness outings in the Sierra Nevada. Palo Alto, CA: Sierra Club Outing Committee: 193-196.

Parsons, David J. 1979. The recovery of Bullfrog Lake. Fremontia. 7(2): 9-13.

Parsons, David J.; MacLeod, Susan A. 1980. Measuring impacts of wilderness use. Parks. 5(3): 8-12.

Parsons, David J.; Stohlgren, Thomas J.; Fodor, Paul A. 1981. Establishing backcountry use quotas: an example from Mineral King, California. Environmental Management. 5: 335-340.

Proudman, Robert D. 1977. AMC field guide to trail building and maintenance. Boston, MA: Appalachian Mountain Club. 193 p.

Ream, Catherine H. 1979. Human-wildlife conflicts in backcountry: possible solutions. In: Ittner, R.; [and others], eds. Recreational impact on wildlands: Conference proceedings. R-6-001-1979. Portland, OR: U.S. Department of Agriculture, Forest Service, Pacific Northwest Region: 153-163.

Ream, Catherine H. 1980. Impact of backcountry recreationists on wildlife: an annotated bibliography. Gen. Tech. Rep. INT-84. Ogden, UT: U.S. Department of Agriculture, Forest Service, Intermountain Forest and Range Experiment Station. 72 p.

Reeves, F. Brent; Wagner, David; Moorman, Thomas.; Kiel, Jean. 1979. The role of endomycorrhizae in revegetation practices in the semi-arid west. I. A comparison of incidence of mycorrhizae in severely disturbed vs. natural environments. American Journal of Botany. 66: 6-13.

Roggenbuck, Joseph W.; Berrier, Deborah L. 1981. Communications to disperse wilderness campers. Journal of Forestry. 79: 295-297.

Root, J. D.; Knapik, L. J. 1972. Trail conditions along a portion of the Great Divide trail route, Alberta and British Columbia Rocky Mountains. Rep. 72-5. Edmonton, AB: Resource Council, Alberta. 24 p.

Saunders, Paul Richard. 1979. The vegetational impact of human disturbance on the spruce-fir forests of the southern Appalachian Mountains. Durham, NC: Duke University. 177 p. Dissertation.

Saunders, Paul Richard; Howard, Gordon E.; Stanley-Saunders, Barbara Ann. 1980. Effect of different boot sole configurations on forest soils. Ext./Res. Pap. RPA 1980-3. Clemson, SC: Clemson University, Department of Recreation and Park Administration. 11 p.

Schreiner, Edward S.; Moorhead, Bruce B. 1979. Human

impact inventory and management in the Olympic National Park backcountry. In: Ittner, R.; [and others], eds. Recreational impact on wildlands: Conference proceedings. R-6-001-1979. Portland, OR: U.S. Department of Agriculture, Forest Service, Pacific Northwest Region: 203-212.

Schreiner, Edward S.; Moorhead, Bruce B. 1981. Human impact inventory and backcountry rehabilitation in Olympic National Park: research and its application. Pacific Park Science. 1(1): 1, 3-4.

Settergren, C. D.; Cole, D. M. 1970. Recreation effects on soil and vegetation in the Missouri Ozarks. Journal of Forestry. 68: 231-233.

Silsbee, David G.; Larson, Gary L. 1982. Bacterial water quality: springs and streams in the Great Smoky Mountains National Park. Environmental Management. 6: 353-359.

Silverman, G.; Erman, D. C. 1979. Alpine lakes in Kings Canyon National Park, California: baseline conditions and possible effects of visitor use. Journal of Environmental Management. 8: 73-87.

Speight, M. C. D. 1973. Outdoor recreation and its ecological effects: a bibliography and review. Discuss. Pap. in Conserv. 4. London: University College. 35 p.

Stalmaster, M. V.; Newman, J. R. 1978. Behavioral responses of wintering bald eagles to human activity. Journal of Wildlife Management. 42: 506-513.

Stankey, George H. 1973. Visitor perception of wilderness recreation carrying capacity. Res. Pap. INT-142. Ogden, UT: U.S. Department of Agriculture, Forest Service, Intermountain Forest and Range Experiment Station. 61 p.

Stankey, George H. 1980. A comparison of carrying capacity perceptions among visitors to two wildernesses. Res. Pap. INT-242. Ogden, UT: U.S. Department of Agriculture, Forest Service, Intermountain Forest and Range Experiment Station. 34 p.

Stanley, J., Jr.; Harvey, H. T.; Hartesveldt, R. J., eds. 1979. A report on the wilderness impact study: the effects of human recreational activities on wilderness ecosystems with special emphasis on Sierra Club wilderness outings in the Sierra Nevada. Palo Alto, CA: Sierra Club Outing Committee. 290 p.

Stoddart, L. A.; Smith, A. D.; Box, T. W. 1975. Range management. New York: McGraw-Hill. 532 p.

Stohlgren, Thomas John. 1982. Vegetation and soil recovery of subalpine campsites in Sequoia National Park, California. Fresno, CA: California State University. 49 p. Thesis.

Stuart, D. G.; Bissonnette, G. K.; Goodrich, T. D.; Walter, W. G. 1971. Effects of multiple use on water quality of high-mountain watersheds: biological investigations of mountain streams. Applied Microbiology. 22: 1048-1054.

Taylor, T. P.; Erman, D. C. 1979. The response of benthic plants to past levels of human use in high mountain lakes in Kings Canyon National Park, California, USA. Journal of Environmental Management. 9: 271-278.

Taylor, T. P.; Erman, Don C. 1980. The littoral bottom flora of high elevation lakes in Kings Canyon National Park. California Fish and Game. 66: 112-119.

Temple, Kenneth L.; Camper, Anne K.; Lucas, Robert C. 1982. Potential health hazard from human waste in wilderness. Journal of Soil and Water Conservation. 37: 357-359.

U.S. Department of Agriculture, Forest Service. 1981. Techniques and equipment for wilderness horse travel. 2300-Recreation, 8123 2403. Missoula, MT: U.S. Department of Agriculture, Forest Service, Missoula Equipment Development Center. 42 p.

Vale, Thomas R. 1977. Forest changes in the Warner Mountains, California. Annals, Association of American Geographers. 67: 28-45.

Van Horn, Joseph C. 1979. Soil and vegetation restoration at the Sunrise Developed Area, Mt. Rainier National Park. In: Ittner, R.; [and others], eds. Recreational impact on wildlands: Conference proceedings. R-6-001-1979. Portland, OR: U.S. Department of Agriculture, Forest Service, Pacific Northwest Region: 286-291.

Vankat, John L.; Major, Jack. 1978. Vegetation changes in Sequoia National Park, California. Journal of Biogeography. 5: 377-402.

Wall, Geoffrey; Wright, Cynthia. 1977. The environmental impact of outdoor recreation. Dept. Geogr. Publ. Ser. 11. Waterloo, ON: University of Waterloo. 69 p.

Washburne, Randel F.; Cole, David N. 1983. Problems and practices in wilderness management: a survey of managers. Res. Pap. INT-304. Ogden, UT: U.S. Department of Agriculture, Forest Service, Intermountain Forest and Range Experiment Station. 56 p.

Weaver, T.; Dale, D. 1978. Trampling effects of hikers, motorcycles and horses in meadows and forests. Journal of Applied Ecology. 15: 451-457.

Whitson, Paul D. 1974. The impact of human use upon the Chisos Basin and adjacent lands. Sci. Monogr. Ser. 4. Washington, DC: U.S. Department of the Interior, National Park Service. 92 p.

Whittaker, Paul L. 1978. Comparison of surface impact by hiking and horseback riding in the Great Smoky Mountains National Park. Manage. Rep. 24. Gatlinburg, TN: U.S. Department of the Interior, National Park Service, Southeast Region. 32 p.

Willard, Beatrice E.; Marr, John W. 1971. Recovery of alpine tundra under protection after damage by human activities in the Rocky Mountains of Colorado. Biological Conservation. 3: 181-190.

ACKNOWLEGMENTS

Dr. Sue Bratton, Research Ecologist, National Park Service, University of Georgia.

Dr. Bob Manning, Professor of Recreation Management, University of Vermont.

Dr. Jeff Marion, Research Scientist, National Park Service, Virginia Tech.

Charlotte Pyle, Ecologist, National Park Service, Great Smoky Mountains National Park.

Dick Spray, Recreation Staff (retired), U.S. Forest Service, Albuquerque, NM.

The quality of a wilderness experience is influenced by many biological, social, and managerial conditions. Managers can control to some extent many of these conditions and maximize the visitor's opportunities for a high-quality experience. Photo courtesy of the USFS.

17

THE WILDERNESS EXPERIENCE AND MANAGING THE FACTORS THAT INFLUENCE IT

Robert C. Lucas was lead author for this chapter.

INTRODUCTION

Chapter 16 discussed managing visitor use to protect natural conditions in wilderness. The biocentric view of this book emphasizes the importance of preservation of a natural environment "to secure. . . the benefits of an enduring resource of wilderness." But managers are more than stewards of the land. According to the Wilderness Act, wilderness management must provide "outstanding opportunities for solitude or a primitive and unconfined type of recreation." This opportunity for a special type of recreation—the wilderness experience—must also be managed and protected from the impacts caused by visitor use.

This chapter will describe the wilderness experience in terms of the factors that influence its quality. The management objectives implied by the relationship of these factors to visitor experiences will be

identified. The rest of the chapter will describe management techniques for achieving most of the experience-related objectives. Some objectives presented relate to previous chapters, such as those on wildlife, fire, and recreation's ecological impacts. They will not be covered again in the management techniques section, which will stress recreation management. The distinction between indirect and direct recreation management presented in chapter 15 will be used to classify specific management techniques.

As explained in chapter 15, which presents an overview of wilderness recreation management, managing recreational impacts and experiences are closely connected. Thus, some of the same management techniques are discussed both in the preceding chapter on impacts and in this chapter on experiences, but from different viewpoints.

THE NATURE OF THE DESIRED EXPERIENCE

The wilderness visitor's experience is a very special thing. It is delicate and subtle, and can be affected by a multitude of factors, many of which managers can control or influence.

The Wilderness Act's statement of policy says that wildernesses "shall be administered for the use and enjoyment of the American people in such manner as will leave them unimpaired for future use and enjoyment as wilderness." The act's definition of wilderness includes "has outstanding opportunities for solitude or a primitive and unconfined type of recreation" and a setting that "generally appears to have been affected primarily by the forces of nature."

Three main types of conditions affect wilderness visitor experiences based on the act's definition of wilderness: natural, social, and managerial conditions. By managing these conditions the quality of experience is managed. These three components are those used in the Recreation Opportunity Spectrum (ROS) system (USDA FS 1982). In addition, the issue of diversity in all three components is important. We will discuss each of the components and diversity as they influence the quality of the wilderness experience available to visitors.

INFLUENCE OF NATURAL CONDITIONS ON EXPERIENCES

The Wilderness Act clearly stresses natural conditions. The three conditions and deviations from them that will affect most visitors are: (1) human impacts to natural environmental conditions; (2) presence of wildlife; and (3) natural ecological processes, particularly fires started by lightning.

The most important of these for visitor experiences probably is the *impact caused by recreational use*; for example, devegetated campsites, stumps of felled trees, or improper shortcut trails that have developed. These impacts and their management are the focus of chapter 16. Some impacts also are caused by commercial livestock, usually cattle or sheep, permitted to graze in many wildernesses under terms of the Wilderness Act.

Little is known about how visitors perceive such impacts. Some of the more severe types of impacts (e.g., stumps or dead trees) probably detract from many visitors' experiences, but more common impacts—such as loss of much of the ground cover vegetation in the core of campsites or many lower branches on trees near campsites broken off for firewood—likely have little or no effect, positive or negative, on visitors'

experiences (Lucas 1979). Some evidence shows that many visitors may prefer modest levels of some campsite impacts rather than totally unmodified conditions (Shelby and Harris 1985, 1986). As described more fully in chapter 15, trail impacts are thought to be evaluated by visitors largely in terms of ease of travel rather than unnaturalness of vegetation changes or soil loss. Visitors probably dislike the presence of commercial livestock and their impacts, but this potential conflict has not been studied.

A second natural condition that affects visitor experiences is *wildlife observation* (fig. 17.1) and, in some cases, harvesting certain species. The types of wildlife observed, the frequency of observation, and the behavior of animals observed all are expressions of the degree of naturalness.

In this case, as for recreational impacts, truly natural conditions may not exactly match most visitors' current desires. Wilderness wildlife, as described in detail in chapter 11, includes many animal species besides the deer, elk, moose, eagles, and so on that most people particularly enjoy seeing. In certain wildernesses, some natural species are dangerous to visitors, especially grizzly bears, but also black bears, poisonous snakes, scorpions, bison, and moose. Visitors vary in their appreciation of dangerous animals and their willingness to share the wilderness with them. Natural wildlife populations often will not be of an optimum size for visitor preferences. For example, elk, prized by hunters in many western wildernesses, will usually not be as numerous under wilderness conditions as they could be if the area was managed to maximize elk, rather than for natural, dynamic ecological conditions. Also, some truly wild animals may be secretive and difficult to observe, rather than half-tamed and easy to see. For a nonwilderness example, efforts by managers of Yellowstone National Park, Wyoming, to reestablish truly wild, natural populations of black bears have largely eliminated the roadside observations of begging bears that many visitors greatly enjoyed, and this change has provoked complaints.

The third kind of natural condition likely to affect visitors' experiences results from *large-scale natural ecological processes*. By far the most important process in most places is natural fire (see chap. 12), although insects, diseases, windstorms, floods, landslides, and avalanches can also play a role. The type of vegetation, its patterns, and wildlife all are strongly influenced by fire in most wildernesses.

Few visitors are trained ecologists; most will not recognize species shifts, such as meadows invaded by trees, or aspen being replaced by spruce, as the unnatural result of fire exclusion. But in many cases,

Fig. 17.1. For many visitors, wildlife observation is an important part of the wilderness experience. Opportunities to see certain animals like this mountain goat and kid are largely confined to wilderness. Photo courtesy of the USFS.

visitors prefer conditions that result from fire playing its natural role, as is the case for the two examples cited above. Preference usually rises after several years of postfire recovery. On the other hand, when a fire is actually burning in a wilderness it can inconvenience visitors, temporarily closing some trails and occasionally posing a risk. More often, smoke that impairs visibility will be a problem, adversely affecting visitors' experiences during ongoing fires. Most visitors support policies to allow more wilderness fires to burn, and support has grown over time as a result of education and experience (McCool and Stankey 1986; Taylor and Mutch 1986).

For all natural conditions, it is apparent that more completely wild situations are not automatically good for many visitors' experiences. The authors propose that managers still should do all they can to achieve natural conditions even though recreation management, as contrasted to wilderness management, might sometimes indicate other actions. The challenge for managers is to use education to help visitors more fully understand natural processes, as presented in chapters 10, 11, and 12, and thus to increase appreciation of their experiences under wilderness conditions.

INFLUENCE OF SOCIAL CONDITIONS ON EXPERIENCES

Visitors' experiences are strongly affected by other visitors and their actions. Generally, *social conditions affect experiences more than the natural conditions. Solitude, visitor conflict, and some visitor behavior* are all elements of social conditions related to experiences.

Solitude as a management concern stems from the Wilderness Act, in which the definition of wilderness includes "outstanding opportunities for solitude," and also from much general writing and common conceptions about wilderness. Research on visitors' reasons for visiting wilderness (Stankey 1973; chap. 9 in this book) supports the importance of solitude to many visitors.

What visitors consider crowding or solitude depends on crowding norms, which are influenced by characteristics of the visitors themselves, of those they encounter, and of the situation or location in which encounters occur (Manning 1985, 1986). For example, Lucas (1964) found that canoeists in the Boundary Waters Canoe Area Wilderness (BWCAW) in Minnesota preferred much lower encounter levels than did motorboaters. Conflict, discussed in the following section, demonstrates how characteristics of those encountered affect experiences. The situation's effects on feelings of crowding or solitude are revealed in the greater importance most visitors attach to solitude at the campsite compared to on the trail (Badger 1975; Stankey 1973).

"Solitude" is perhaps something of a misnomer. The dictionary definition of solitude is "the state of being alone." Solitude in wilderness generally refers to a *group* of visitors meeting relatively few other *groups* of visitors. Meeting no other visitors at all is not as desirable to many visitors as meeting a few other parties, say one a day (Stankey 1973). Solitude is certainly not the only appeal of wilderness, and for many visitors it is not the most important. But it is one of the major appeals for most visitors, and, unlike some of the more highly rated factors, such as scenic beauty (Lucas 1985), it is largely subject to control by managers. Acceptable solitude levels are clearly an important wilderness management objective. Wilderness is the place where opportunities to experience solitude should be available to the greatest degree. ROS guidelines also support this position (USDA FS 1982).

Conflict also occurs in some places between recreational use and nonrecreational uses, such as grazing, and uses outside wilderness that create noise, air pollution, or visual distractions, including aircraft flights. Conflict between different types of

visitors with different styles of use is more common as a major part of the social setting. It may affect visitors' experiences more than sheer numbers of other parties. Conflict can take many forms (Manning 1985). A common form is conflict between groups traveling by different means. Where motorized use is allowed (e.g., outboard motor use in parts of the BWCAW), visitors not using motorized means of travel prefer not to meet those who are (Lucas 1964; Stanley 1973). It is a one-sided conflict; the motorized visitors do not object to the nonmotorized visitors (Adelman and others 1982). Horse-hiker conflict is usually not as severe, but may be increasing some places (Lucas 1985). It also tends to be one sided, with the hikers complaining most. Large parties are a source of conflict in the view of persons in the typical smaller groups (Badger 1975; Pfister and Frankel 1974; Stanley 1973). Sometimes conflict can arise between visitors with outfitters and those on their own, and between hunters and nonhunters. Reducing or avoiding visitor conflict should be a wilderness management objective.

Some kinds of visitor behavior affect visitor experiences directly (Manning 1985). Other behavior affects experiences indirectly through environmental impacts. Littering is one of the most important, with strong negative effects (Lee 1975; Stankey 1973). Some other problem behaviors managers need to deal with include: loud behavior and unfriendliness (Lee 1975); camping unnecessarily close (Heberlein and Dunwiddie 1979); failing to yield the right of way on the trail, especially by hikers when meeting visitors with stock; and failing to control dogs.

INFLUENCE OF MANAGERIAL CONDITIONS ON EXPERIENCES

How managers operate obviously can greatly affect wilderness visitors' experiences. Experiences can be damaged by management actions intended to solve other problems, poorly designed actions, or implementation that has not been well thought out. General visitor management issues discussed in chapter 15 bear directly on visitor experience quality. Direct types of management have more potential for adverse effects than indirect approaches. Reliance on regulation, in particular, can sometimes detract from the sense of "primitive and unconfined recreation" in the Wilderness Act's definition of wilderness. Managerial presence, if too prominent, can diminish the sense of experiencing wilderness and facing challenges on your own. This relates to the issue of location of management. As we said in chapter 15, contact with visitors is usually preferable outside the wilderness rather than inside it. Sensitively attuning managerial conditions to provide a wilderness experience opportunity while achieving other wilderness objectives probably is the greatest challenge facing most wilderness managers.

DIVERSITY'S INFLUENCE ON EXPERIENCES

All three sets of conditions—natural, social, and managerial— will vary from wilderness to wilderness and within each specific wilderness. This is inevitable because of variation in use levels related to differences in access and attractions, and because of variation in natural conditions.

This variation is also desirable, *as long as all conditions meet basic wilderness definitions and objectives.* Planned diversity is desirable for reasons identical to those on which the widely used ROS system is based (Clark and Stankey 1979; Driver and Brown 1978; Stankey and Brown 1981; USDA FS 1982). A basic assumption is that quality in recreation is best attained by providing a diverse set of opportunities so that people who vary in their desires and abilities can find what they want. Diversity avoids favoritism or catering to any special group. Different portions of a wilderness vary in capacity, durability, and suitability for various types of use. They also vary greatly in accessibility—from areas reached by easy trails close to a trailhead to very remote places with no trails.

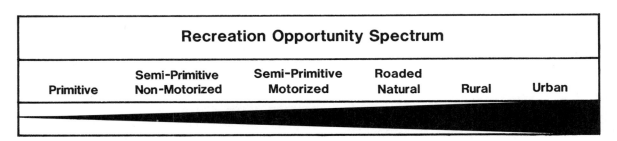

Fig. 17.2. The six classes of the ROS range from primitive to urban.

The complete ROS system has six classes (fig. 17.2). Existing wilderness fits within the primitive class and at least partly within the semiprimitive nonmotorized class (Stankey and others 1985). A few areas, and most Alaskan wildernesses, also have parts in the semiprimitive motorized class.

Objections are sometimes raised to applying the semiprimitive ROS class in wilderness because of a perceived contradiction between the names. "Semiprimitive" sounds like second-rate wilderness. This class could have been named better, but its characteristics accurately describe parts of many wildernesses, and we think it meets the legal definition of wilderness.

In the Limits of Acceptable Change (LAC) system described in chapter 9, step 2 is the definition and description of opportunity classes (Stankey and others 1985). This provides for managing diversity in wilderness recreation opportunities and in levels of protection of natural conditions in an explicit, planned fashion. Especially, it can provide very strict protection of the most pristine parts of a wilderness. The authors support this approach.

INDIRECT AND DIRECT MANAGEMENT TECHNIQUES

A variety of potential management tools and techniques are available to deal with specific recreation use situations. We will list the main ones, dealing first with indirect techniques and then with direct methods. (The concept of indirect and direct visitor management was explained in chap.15.) This section explains each technique, evaluates its effectiveness, presents what is known concerning visitor attitudes about each, and about the current extent of application of each method by wilderness managers. Some of the same techniques are also discussed in the previous chapter, but in relation to ecological impacts. Here the focus is on visitor experience quality.

INDIRECT MANAGEMENT TECHNIQUES

Indirect management techniques deal with factors that influence visitors rather than directly controlling them. Visitors are still free to choose. The main types of indirect management include: (1) physical design of the setting; (2) use of information and education; (3) eligibility requirements; and (4) fees.

Setting Design

Design affects access, trails, and facilities. All of these designed works of man need to be applied sensitively to avoid conflicting with the objective of wilderness as an essentially undeveloped area.

Modifying access to wilderness entry points can alter the amount and type of use. Because it takes place outside wilderness, legal constraints on development are lifted. Access roads could be shortened by closing the last section and making the trail longer. This would reduce the total amount of use reaching the wilderness boundary. Because of differences in the distance usually traveled in a day, access modification would tend to reduce day use more than camping use, and reduce hiking use more than horse use in areas with significant horse use. Reducing use can increase opportunities for solitude. Less day use inside wilderness may be desirable if it is felt to be not wilderness dependent (chap.14). The relative desirability of increasing horse use would depend on site-specific management objectives. The potential effect on visitor conflict needs to be considered.

Improving or extending roads, thus shortening trails, would have the opposite effect, increasing total use, raising the proportions of hiker and day use. This might direct some use away from other areas where use problems exist, especially if access was made more difficult in the problem areas. But access should be improved only with great care. Improved access might attract new users and create problems of impacts and displacement of some visitors with little offsetting gain elsewhere.

Modifying access to wilderness entry points is moderately common, although often the road changes stem from reasons other than modifying recreational use, such as logging near wilderness trailheads. Slightly more wildernesses reported improving road access (27 percent) in 1980 than rendering it more difficult (24 percent) (Washburne and Cole 1983).

In addition, design of access points and facilities provided can increase or decrease particular types of use and also total use. Horse facilities, such as unloading ramps, corrals, and hitch rails, encourage horse use. In water-oriented areas, such as the BWCAW, ramps for trailered motorboats result in more boat use and use by larger boats than would a portage from parking area to water. The portage will screen out large boats and reduce all boat use more than canoe use, with effect increasing as portages lengthen. The size of the parking area may have some effect on amount of use, although this usually is not a strong control on use. People will usually park somewhere, even if the parking lot is full, but, certainly, parking should not be expanded

where increased use is not desired.

Visitor acceptance of access modification is rarely studied. Lucas (1964) found little support for improving access roads. Stankey (1973) reported about 40 percent of the visitors in three western wildernesses opposed closing parts of roads, but more supported it later (Stankey 1980). Some visitors returning to the same access point they had used before would object to a longer trip to their destination. New visitors would usually be unaware of the modification if it had been done skillfully.

Trail design is a potentially powerful indirect management tool (fig. 17.3). Trails are an acceptable, unobtrusive way to influence use patterns. Some areas deliberately left without trails will be lightly used. Trails can be built or rebuilt either to be easy or to be steep and difficult, trail length from point A to B can usually be varied considerably, and bridges can be built to facilitate use or trails can ford streams to reduce or divert use. Some trails are too rough and rocky for horses, but hikers can scramble over them, unobtrusively separating these types of use.

Trail design can markedly influence the quality of the experience for the people who hike or ride horses over them. A trail can lead travelers to changing vistas or monotonously bore straight through dense forests. Trails can seek out varied vegetation, rock outcrops, glimpses of water, and perhaps increase chances of seeing wildlife. Trail design offers a unique opportunity for managers to subtly program visitors' experiences almost as though they could write a script that visitors had to act out. The sequence of visual experiences and level of challenge are strongly influenced by trail design.

A trail can pass right by popular campsites, thus encouraging their use, or swing around through trees or behind a ridge and shift camping use elsewhere. This can also reduce feelings of crowding by limiting campers' observation of trail traffic and vice versa. A winding, up-and-down trail cuts down on observation of other travelers just as long, straight, flat stretches increase sightings. Carefully thought-out trail loops or alternate routes can reduce encounters between users. Trail design also can facilitate or discourage off-trail travel and exploration.

Despite the potential power of trail design, its use is limited. Most trails were built more than 50 years ago, before areas were designated as wilderness, primarily as an administrative transportation system, especially for fire control. In the West, trails were intended mainly for horse travel, not hikers. Most trails were designed to get crews to fires quickly or service fire lookouts. Neither environmental protection nor visitor experiences were important objectives. Budgets for trail work have been low for many years, and maintenance of existing trails consumes most of the available funds. Most new trail construction is replacement of poorly located short sections of old trail. Washburne and Cole (1983) report that 22 percent of all wildernesses reported some new trail construction and 37 percent had upgraded some existing trails. Only 8 percent reported closing any trails, and 14 percent cut back maintenance on some trails to reduce use. Trailless zones were designated in 35 percent of the wildernesses.

Visitor acceptance of trail design changes is virtually unstudied. Stankey (1973) reported mixed reactions by visitors to a question about reducing the number of signs and trails. The sort of redesign discussed here would probably be well accepted by visi-

Fig.17.3. Trail design is a management tool that can indirectly influence amount, type, and location of use and can profoundly influence visitors' experiences. Fording a stream (left) will affect visitors differently than crossing it on a bridge (right). Photos courtesy of the USFS.

tors; probably most would be unaware of the action. This unobtrusiveness is a key characteristic of indirect management. If trails are skillfully laid out, visitors' experiences should be improved substantially.

In most wildernesses studied, visitors agree that trails are appropriate and desirable in wilderness (Stankey and Schreyer 1987). Support is stronger for simple, narrow, winding, low-standard trails than high-standard trails, and strong for leaving the trail system about as it is. Horse users prefer higher standard trails than hikers (Lucas 1980). But support for simple, low-standard trails and existing trail systems does not mean that badly eroded trails or numerous large mudholes are acceptable. A study of trends in recreational use of the Bob Marshall Wilderness Complex in Montana (BMWC), made up of three adjacent wildernesses, showed a sixfold increase in complaints about trail conditions from 1970 to 1982 (Lucas 1985). Maintenance, not expansion, of trail systems is desired by visitors. Support for bridges, especially over large streams, is strong and widespread (Stankey and Schreyer 1987).

Signs within the wilderness can affect visitor experiences in several ways. Directional signs, usually at trail junctions, make travel easier and perhaps a bit safer. They also are an obvious work of man and reduce the visitor's sense of adventure and reliance on map-reading and orientation skills. Almost all wildernesses have trail signs, but most managers strive for a balance, installing only limited, simple signs, particularly at confusing junctions (fig. 17.4). U.S. Forest Service (USFS) wilderness signs, for example, usually provide only one destination and do not give distances. Mile markers, formerly used some places, are no longer provided in national forest wilderness. Interpretive signs, explaining natural features or historic events, are rarely used in wilderness, and seem inappropriate to us. Other ways of conveying such information are available and preferable.

Visitors generally support directional signs and some complain if they are scarce (Lucas 1985), although most studies show a larger proportion is neutral about signs (Stankey and Schreyer 1987). Wood is the strongly preferred material (Hendee and others 1968).

Fig. 17.4. Simple directional signs, usually without distances, such as this sign in national park backcountry, are appropriate and are well accepted by visitors. Photo courtesy of the NPS.

Trail systems and associated bridges and signs are the main recreational facilities in most wildernesses, and in some they are the only ones. But some wildernesses have other facilities, almost all at campsites. These include fireplaces, outhouses, corrals, and hitch rails; a few areas have shelters and tables. Some Alaskan wildernesses have public cabins. As we discussed in chapter 15, the use of facilities should be carefully limited in wilderness to avoid changing visitor experiences to something other than primitive. Facilities should not be provided for the comfort and convenience of visitors, but rather primarily to protect wilderness resources. Generally, visitors seem to support little or no development of campsites and little increase in numbers of campsites. Attitudes seem to be shifting toward preferences for more primitive campsites (Stankey and Schreyer 1987).

Fireplaces are used mainly for fire control, and also to help identify designated campsites to limit the spread of impacts. About 10 percent of wildernesses have constructed fireplaces, most in national parks and in national forest wildernesses, but also in the BWCAW (fig. 17.5). Visitors tend to reject fireplaces (Hendee and others 1968; Lucas 1980)—more strongly in recent years (Lucas 1985), although studies have not been conducted in many places with fireplaces. Loose rock firerings are generally acceptable to visitors.

Tables, constructed of either split log or lumber, are a little less common than fireplaces. Most are in national parks and California national forest wilderness, and in a few eastern wildernesses. Tables might attract some use to certain places, but most visitors do not favor tables (Hendee and others 1968). Only 8 percent of visitors to the Desolation Wilderness in California were in favor of tables (Lucas 1980). Opposition to tables has grown over time (Lucas 1985). Tables would seem to detract from visitors' experiences and serve no wilderness resource protection role.

Outhouses vary from enclosed, roofed buildings such as found in developed campgrounds to simple boxes that rise only a few feet above the ground (fig. 17.6). About 15 percent of all wildernesses have enclosed toilets (Washburne and Cole 1983), and 19

Fig. 17.5. All established campsites in the BWCAW have fire grates. Similar fireplaces are found in other wildernesses, especially in CA and in national parks. Photo courtesy of the USFS.

percent have open box toilets. (A few places have both types.) Wilderness toilets are found in many parts of the country, but the greatest concentration seems to be in national forests in the Pacific Coast states and in national parks. In heavily used areas, toilets concentrate human waste and may reduce the chance of visitor contact with it, although decomposition is slower than with the individual burial system. In places with limited soil near campsites, as in the BWCAW, toilets can be carefully placed and probably reduce the chance of water pollution.

In a study in the 1960s, visitors favored toilets in areas with toilets (Hendee and others 1968), although more wilderness-oriented visitors opposed them. Opinions in 1970 were fairly evenly divided in some

areas and negative in others, especially in the Desolation Wilderness where visitors opposed toilets four to one (Lucas 1980). Toilets were opposed two to one in 1982 in the Bob Marshall where opinions had been about evenly divided in 1970 (Lucas 1985), suggesting a trend toward opposition. Attitudes about toilets seem to vary in relation to perceived need in each area, for example, support in the BWCAW, and to local practice, whether toilets are present or not (Stankey and Schreyer 1987). Thus, the effect of outhouses on the quality of visitors' experiences is mixed but probably negative on balance in many wildernesses. Toilets are an obvious sign of humans that intrudes on wilderness conditions; they should be used only where they are clearly essential.

Corrals for holding horses near camps are found in some western wildernesses, particularly at outfitter camps (fig. 17.7). They confine the impacts of horses to a selected area, which is usually devoid of vegetation, and avoid impacts elsewhere. Corrals are probably a good example of a "sacrifice area," as well as a work of humans, but may be the best solution to limiting impacts where parties with large numbers of stock camp, especially for long periods, such as during hunting seasons (see chap. 16). Visitors' experiences are affected by the presence of a structure, associated soil and vegetation impacts, and, for horse users, avoidance of the challenge of holding stock under primitive conditions. Horse users generally favor corrals; hikers oppose them (Hendee and others 1968; Lucas 1980, 1985). Stankey (1973), however, found a majority of visitors opposed to corrals and similar attitudes among horse users and hikers. Hitching posts or rails are less obtrusive facilities, useful for holding stock for shorter periods of time than corrals, with similar effects on visitor experiences.

Somewhat equivalent facilities in the BWCAW would be docks and canoe rests. Both are a convenience, but obtrusive. Most visitors rejected docks, while opinions were divided on canoe rests (Stankey 1973).

Fig.17.6. Toilets are provided in some wildernesses. Simple box toilets (left) are commonly used in the Pacific Northwest; (right) a toilet in the BWCAW. Photos courtesy of the USFS.

Shelters, usually open-fronted Adirondack types (fig. 17.8), are found in about 12 percent of all areas, mostly in national forests in the Pacific Coast states, the Northeast, and in national parks. Enclosed public cabins are common in Alaskan national forest wilderness, and are specifically authorized there by law. Shelters are a tradition in some places going back to the nineteenth century. They concentrate impacts and might have some advantages for that purpose (see chap. 15.) Visitor attitudes about shelters are almost unstudied. A 1960s study of three Pacific Northwest wildernesses with shelters found about two-to-one support for shelters, but opposition from more wilderness-oriented visitors (Hendee and others 1968). Nevertheless, shelters reduce the primitive character of the visitor's experience and can reduce solitude because a number of parties often wind up sharing a shelter overnight. Shelters function primarily as comfort and convenience facilities, with little or no wilderness protection role. Except in Alaska, where severe weather and bear danger confront visitors, and where cabins are legally authorized, shelters seem out of place in wilderness, and we favor their gradual elimination unless they have major historical significance.

Information and Education

Providing wilderness visitors and prospective visitors with information and education is a highly acceptable indirect management action. It does not alter the wilderness resource directly, as facilities do. It does not regulate or control visitors. Visitors retain freedom to choose, but their choices are made with more information. Thus, managers are helpful facilitators, not policemen. Good information and education enable visitors to have more rewarding experiences as they come closer to achieving the type of experience they are seeking, and have a deeper appreciation of the area. It can also help managers achieve objectives by influencing where visitors go, what they do, and how they do it.

Wilderness visitors provide a particularly good audience for information-education programs. As we pointed out in chapter 14, the most distinguishing socioeconomic characteristic of wilderness visitors is an extremely high education level. Most wilderness visitors also place a high personal value on wilderness, suggesting that most want to use it carefully. Information and education are widely used by wilderness managers. Former USFS Chief R. Max Peterson said wilderness management is "80 to 90 percent education and information and 10 percent regulations" (Peterson 1985). Visitor acceptance of educational programs is rarely a concern, but effectiveness often is a question, especially compared to regulatory approaches.

Fig. 17.7. Corrals are found in some western wildernesses, usually at outfitter camps. This corral is at an outfitter's camp in the Bob Marshall Wilderness. Photo courtesy of the USFS.

Fig. 17.8. The Adirondack Trail Shelter, this one in Maine, is provided in some national parks and national forest wildernesses in the Northeast and in Pacific Coast states. Some Alaskan wildernesses provide cabins to protect visitors from harsh weather and bears. Photo courtesy of George Bellerose, Adirondack Mountain Club.

Principles for Informing and Educating Visitors

Some general guidelines for the effective use of education and information are as follows:

1. *Carefully organize and design the message.* Fully explaining undesirable situations and the rationale for particular management actions probably causes visitors to modify their use patterns and behavior— but research confirmation is lacking. Dustin (1985) presents a useful analysis of how messages can be linked to six different stages of visitor morality,

ranging from fear of punishment to personal commitment to ethical values. An appropriate middle ground may exist for the level of detail—enough to adequately explain and motivate, but not so much that attention is lost. Messages need to be matched to settings; a simple, standardized message is appropriate for some types of behavior (e. g., littering), but some recommended actions need to vary with the setting (e.g., fire building procedures or campsite selection).

2. *Identify and understand the audience.* Make messages relevant to the specific audience. Consider the types of behavior and potential problems for each audience group, their motivations, and background experience. For example, horse users require a different message than backpackers.

3. *Time the message's delivery appropriately.* Visitor redistribution programs, described later, and minimum impact messages probably are most effective during the trip planning phase. For example, if a gas campstove, trowel for disposing of human waste, high lines for tying horses, or feed for stock are to be recommended, a message at the trailhead or in the wilderness has little influence on new visitors who do not have the recommended equipment.

4. *Closely related to timing is the choice of place for communication.* Home, club meeting place, school, ranger station or other office, trailhead, and the interior of the wilderness all may be appropriate, depending on the message and audience. Getting in a rut and relying on one location out of habit will be less effective. Few visitors voluntarily contact managers. Those who do present a valuable opportunity that should be used well. Poorly trained, poorly informed clerks, or managers too busy to communicate thoroughly and enthusiastically, whether in person, by telephone, or mail, waste these scarce chances to inform and educate the public.

5. *Select communication methods that fit the audience, message, and situation.* A variety of methods will probably be most effective. It has been commonly assumed that personal communication is superior to printed material. But some research suggests that printed matter can be almost as effective as face-to-face communication, at least for some messages (Roggenbuck and Berrier 1982).

Information and education are used for three main purposes: (1) to redistribute use, (2) to teach minimum-impact use, and (3) to educate about wilderness values.

Information to Redistribute Use
Managers of most wildernesses provide information to try to redistribute use (Washburne and Cole 1983),

usually within a particular wilderness and much less often to other areas outside the wilderness. Most efforts to redistribute use within a wilderness focus on shifting use among access points, but some have tried to alter visitors' choices of areas to camp.

Managers seek to shift use by making visitors more aware of alternative places to go and by providing descriptive information that makes some places more attractive and others less so. For all practical purposes, "secret" places do not exist. The many articles in outdoor magazines and numerous guidebooks attest to the public's interest in where-to-go information. This interest could be used to encourage use shifts. Conversely, articles that describe a fishing hotspot can accentuate overuse as well as attract users whose primary interest is a limit of fish rather than wilderness.

Use redistribution affects visitor experiences by altering opportunities for solitude. But the use of information to influence use distributions can have desirable effects even if overall distributions change little because information can help visitors better match their desires to the characteristics of the places they visit. It is possible for those who prefer lower levels of encounters to visit lightly used areas offering such opportunities, and those who prefer higher levels of contact to go to areas where such experiences are commonly available. Information can also help visitors develop realistic expectations and thus reduce dissatisfaction.

Shifting use within wilderness has met with varied effectiveness in the places studied (Lucas 1981). Effectiveness has been high for programs in Yellowstone National Park (Krumpe and Brown 1982), Shining Rock Wilderness in North Carolina (Roggenbuck and Berrier 1982), and the BWCAW (Lime and Lucas 1977). In each of these areas, about one-third of the people receiving information used it to pick entry points or campsites in line with managers' objectives. Together with lessons from the less effective programs, these studies suggest the following guidelines for making information a useful tool for redistributing visitor use:

1. Information campaigns must be geared to management objectives. As pointed out in chapter 14, managers must decide if they want to bring about a general redistribution (say from heavy- to light-use areas), or site-specific redistribution (probably a more appropriate objective), or help visitors match their desires and experiences better (a very appropriate objective and probably the easiest to achieve). Objectives should guide the design and conduct of the information campaign.

2. The information must be delivered to a large proportion of visitors.

3. The information must be available to visitors in the planning stage of their trip. After people have arrived at an access point it usually is too late to influence that trip, although later trips might be affected. If information does not reach many visitors early, its potential for improving experiences is severely reduced.

4. Information provided should cover a variety of attributes of the environmental, use, and managerial conditions. Different visitors have different objectives and will respond to various types of information in different ways. More complete information also will aid visitors in choosing places to visit best suited for the experience they are seeking.

5. Considerable detail is desirable and perhaps necessary to compete with previous knowledge and advice of friends. More detailed information also may improve the credibility of information, as well as helping visitors obtain the experience they prefer.

6. An information campaign cannot rely entirely on written material. Research (Fazio 1979) has shown that brochures are often a less important channel of communication than face-to-face communication. In the Shining Rock Wilderness (Roggenbuck and Berrier 1982), personal contact was no more effective than a brochure alone for redistributing total use, but it did increase effectiveness with some types of visitors. The difference in effect of personal versus written communication itself on visitor experiences is unstudied, but probably is mixed and not strong for most visitors. Some managers are now providing interactive computer programs and terminals to help the public select trails. Contact outside the wilderness may be preferred by some to contact inside. (Chap. 14 discusses location of management presence.)

7. Some ethical issues of truth in information campaigns need to be faced. Some overused areas may in fact be very attractive, with good fishing, easy trails, and so on. Certainly false information should never be used, but ethical guidelines are less clear on issues of selectivity, completeness, and emphasis. Such decisions clearly will affect visitor experiences.

8. Finally, managers must be sensitive to the danger of providing too much detailed information and taking away the sense of exploration and discovery that contributes to wilderness experiences for many people.

Information and education are promising tools for managing the distribution of wilderness use. Results are well worth the careful, skillful work such efforts require to help achieve the objectives of protecting wilderness and providing opportunities for wilderness recreational experiences.

Information is not a panacea for use distribution problems. In fact, unless used with care, information could stimulate use and create problems that would not otherwise occur. The USFS Recreation Opportunity Guides (ROG) generally omit information about wildernesses to avoid stimulating use. Some people feel that wilderness guidebooks can be destructive (Landrum 1976). Shifting use is a two-edged sword: it can help or hurt.

Information on Minimum-Impact Use
Only a few wildernesses, mostly wildlife refuges, do not have a minimum-impact education program (Washburne and Cole 1983). Many managers have emphasized such programs in recent years and devote substantial staff and budget to them. (The specifics of minimum-impact programs were discussed in chap. 16.)

Minimum-impact education programs reach the public through a variety of contacts: at schools and colleges; through organizations such as the Boy Scouts; at wilderness access points and on wilderness trails and campsites. Wilderness rangers do much of the educating. Some organizations, particularly Boy Scouts, are developing their own low-impact education program. The messages vary somewhat because some minimum-impact practices are based on judgment and assumptions and have not been objectively tested. Chapter 16 and Cole (1987) discuss this issue further. Most education focuses on camping behavior and stresses resource impacts rather than effects on other visitors' experiences. Some education, however, does relate to experiences. Recommendations to keep parties small, to camp out of sight of trails and other campsites, and to use subdued, natural-colored tents, packs, and clothing all can directly improve experiences. Reducing resource impacts also can indirectly improve experiences. Although education has rarely been used to attempt to reduce conflicts between different types of visitors (e.g., hikers and horse users), it might both reduce objectionable behavior and increase understanding and acceptance of differing users. Visitors clearly prefer information and education programs to being regulated, and wilderness rangers are well accepted (Stankey and Schreyer 1987).

Evidence of effectiveness of minimum-impact education is scarce because research and objective evaluations are rare, but a study of trends in the BMWC showed changes consistent with practices recommended in minimum-impact education programs. Visitors had increased knowledge of "pack-it-in, pack-it-out" handling of garbage, had increased knowledge that burying garbage was undesirable, had reduced littering, and made more use of

campstoves rather than wood fires. One study (Robertson 1982) also showed a positive relationship between visitors' knowledge of approved practices and their use in the Three Sisters Wilderness in Oregon.

At this stage, the large effort going into minimum-impact education is still based on faith, reinforced by the favorable subjective impressions of wilderness managers in the field. We think that both content and effective educational techniques need to be studied and strengthened, but we also share a deep faith in low-impact use education, in its appropriateness and potential effectiveness, as well as a preference for this type of education rather than regulation.

Wilderness Values
Wilderness managers occasionally try to educate visitors and the general public about wilderness values, purposes, and philosophy. One study showed that little information of this kind was included in printed material given to the public.

Information about wilderness values should be acceptable to almost all wilderness visitors. It should help improve the quality of visitors' experiences by deepening their appreciation of wilderness.

Eligibility Requirements
To drive an auto, a person must demonstrate knowledge and skill to obtain a license. In most states, youngsters must pass a course in firearms safety to obtain a hunting license. Although human life is not so directly at stake as in driving or hunting, a test or schooling in wilderness skills might be required of wilderness visitors. The course might be a few hours long and be conducted in a classroom, or it could last for days or even weeks in the outdoors. Several educational programs are designed to teach people how to use wilderness safely and sensitively, such as the National Outdoor Leadership School (NOLS) and college-level wilderness skills courses. Those affiliated with the Wilderness Education Association, which sets accreditation standards, are usually lengthy and thorough, and largely conducted outdoors. Shorter courses, perhaps using films or video, might present general principles.

The idea of eligibility requirements is far from new—J. V. K. Wagar suggested the need for certifying outdoor skills in 1940—but little has been tried. Some professional guides must pass tests, but not the general public (except for mountain climbers in a few places). A license requirement might be imposed only for heavily used areas, or only for those areas where use is actually rationed. In such places, wilderness permits might be issued only to visitors with licenses or to groups with a licensed leader, and others could gain experience by visiting other less-used areas. Obviously, the details could be complicated, but the general idea is worth considering.

Certainly, if skills, knowledge, and sensitivity to wilderness values could be raised, more people could enjoy wilderness without destroying it, the need for direct controls would be reduced, and actual rationing could be at least postponed. Increased skills and a deeper understanding of wilderness could raise the quality of visitor experiences. Such courses should reduce visitor conflict and resource impacts and thus further improve experiences.

Administrative costs could be high. Costs for visitors would vary with the length and demands of a course, but could be substantial. Training would have to be readily available; otherwise, eligibility requirements could foster elitism.

Fees
Fees are another technique for modifying use. We classify fees as an indirect technique because they do not directly control what visitors do, but this could be debated. The cost of the privilege of visiting an area is regulated, but the choice of paying or not is up to the visitor. Constant fees—that is, the same charge at all times and places—would tend to reduce use, with the degree of use reduction a function of the level of the fee. A flat entry fee would probably reduce short stays more than long ones, while a per-day fee would probably not have this effect. Ideally, a fee would encourage people who placed a low value on wilderness (those whose recreational interests lay mainly elsewhere) to seek an alternative for which no fee or a lower fee was charged. Unfortunately, persons who valued wilderness but whose incomes were low would also be discouraged. This is true, of course, for anything bought and sold, but the validity of this income effect for public goods and services is questioned by many people and raises again the issue of elitism. The income effect could be offset by free or lower priced entry permits for certain types of low-income visitors, such as inner-city Boy Scout troops. Prospective visitors might earn credit through work on trails, litter cleanup, or other service projects as an alternative to cash payments.

Variable fees would have a much more sensitive effect on the distribution and timing of use. Fees could vary between places, high at heavily used wildernesses and at overused entry points, and low or none at seldom-visited areas. (This is similar to high-priced theater tickets for front-center seats and inexpensive tickets for upper-balcony seats.) Fees could be raised at peak periods and lowered or dropped entirely during the off season. (Most resorts

have lower off-season rates.) Perhaps persons who had qualified for a "wilderness license" could pay a reduced fee on the assumption they would have less impact on the wilderness. Conceivably, a person's first visit in a year could be cheaper than subsequent visits to encourage spreading benefits among more people.

Administrative costs, especially for variable fees, could be moderate to high. Most wilderness visitors object to fees. Visitor studies usually show charging is one of the least popular methods of controlling use (Stankey and Schreyer 1987). Yet, visitor surveys show that fees at any reasonable level would not be beyond the incomes of many visitors. Support is greater for fees that are used to protect and manage the area visited, rather than going into the general treasury (Martin 1986). Congress would need to grant the wilderness-administering agencies the authority to use fees as a wilderness management tool. Perhaps later, when most potential wilderness has been either classified or allocated to other uses, and management needs are better recognized, the concept of wilderness user fees will seem more feasible.

DIRECT MANAGEMENT

Direct management techniques regulate and restrict individual choice. Management may be able to exercise a high degree of control, but generally with high administrative costs. To some extent, direct management requires less knowledge of visitors, their behavior, and likely responses to management actions than does indirect management. Some knowledge of use is needed; but if use is to be directly controlled to fit management objectives, less real understanding of it is required.

This means that direct management is usually somewhat easier than indirect management, and perhaps demands less professional skill. Direct management does, however, possess more potential for confrontations, conflict, and controversy than indirect techniques, and it carries higher costs for visitors. In any case, as we have explained before, direct techniques should be applied only after indirect methods have done as much as they can to solve management problems. Unfortunately, managers often leap directly from laissez faire, uncontrolled activity to tight regulation rather than adopting new controls only to the extent necessary, and using indirect methods as effectively as possible before employing direct management techniques.

Direct management can also include "strong suggestions," as well as regulating and rationing use. Many of the specific techniques discussed below can take the form of either regulations or strong suggestions. The distinction is basically whether noncompliance is considered a punishable violation or not. This distinction is probably significant to visitors. A suggestion, no matter how strong, imposes less on the quality of visitors' experiences than an enforceable regulation. Unfortunately, suggestions are more of a burden for conscientious visitors than for indifferent or careless visitors. A strong suggestion costs less for managers to implement than a formal regulation requiring field enforcement and followup. Objective data are not available on the effectiveness of the two approaches, although regulations are probably more effective, but often at considerably higher costs for both visitors and managers. Managers should strive to encourage visitors to adopt desired behavior as a social norm. To the extent this occurs, social pressure can become a substitute for agency regulations.

"Soft suggestions" or persuasion (involving less pressure than "strong suggestions") can be viewed as bridging the gap between direct and indirect visitor management on the continuum below:

Direct Visitor Management   Indirect Visitor Management

Enforcement — Regulations — Strong suggestions — Soft suggestions — Design — Education and information

All regulations and suggestions can either be uniform within a wilderness or vary from part to part. A number of types of visitor behavior can be managed directly. The main types of direct management include: (1) party size limits; (2) length-of-stay limits; (3) campfire restrictions; (4) prohibiting on certain types of use; (5) camping setbacks from water; rationing use intensity; and (6) restrictions on activities.

Party Size Limits
Setting a maximum party size (or trying to reduce the number of large parties through suggestions) has both social and environmental benefits. The social benefits are clearest; most visitors feel that large parties are out of place in wilderness and quality of experience suffers (Badger 1975; Pfister and Frankel

1974; Stankey 1973). Quality will be raised if contacts with large parties are reduced or eliminated. Environmental benefits are less well documented, but it seems obvious that unusually large parties expand the area impacted at campsites and probably intensify impacts in the core of the campsite. Slow recovery of impacted soil and vegetation means that the effects of a large party persist for a long time, probably for years, continuing to degrade visitor experiences (Cole 1987).

Maximum party size is set in an arbitrary fashion. About half of all areas limit party size; 10, 12, 15, and 25 persons are currently the most common limits (Washburne and Cole 1983). Maximum party size tends to vary with the character of an area. For example, large parties are appropriate where large rafts are needed to run rough, white-water rivers. But there seems to be a consensus that party size limits, perhaps six- to 12-persons, are reasonable in most places. Limits are most common in national forest wildernesses, least common in wildlife refuge wildernesses.

A little more than one-fourth of all wildernesses have a limit on numbers of horses or other stock, ranging from five to 50 head (Washburne and Cole 1983). Large parties and parties with large numbers of stock are not common (see chap. 13), so most visitors are not inconvenienced. Research has shown somewhat mixed attitudes about regulations on party size, but a majority of visitors in most wildernesses support a 12-person limit (Lucas 1980, 1985) and strongly support party size limits, particularly in more heavily used areas (Stankey and Schreyer 1987).

Length-of-Stay Limits

Although it can be regulated, length of stay usually does not contribute much to overuse. Few parties stay very long (chap. 13), and those who do usually remain in more remote, less used, and less impacted areas. Furthermore, the long, grand wilderness adventure to the most remote possible location seems particularly consistent with the purposes of the Wilderness Act and with the philosophy of wilderness.

General limits on stays appear to negatively affect experience quality for some visitors. Limits may diminish feelings of wilderness, even for visitors on short trips.

On the other hand, when an occasional party stays for a long time at one popular campsite, (A few parties almost homestead.) it is unfair to other visitors and hard on the site. Therefore, a reasonable limit on length of stay at any one campsite seems useful. Time spent at a particular location—not total time in the wilderness—is the factor with the greatest relationship to undesirable use patterns and adverse effects on experiences.

General length-of-stay limits are in effect in 28 percent of all wildernesses (Washburne and Cole 1983). In addition, almost half of all wildlife refuge wildernesses and a very few wildernesses managed by other agencies permit only day use. Stay limits are most common in national parks. The most common limit is 14 days. Enforcement is difficult without a permit system.

Limits on time allowed at any one campsite are not as common as general limits on visits to an entire area. This is true despite the fact that general stay limits are harder to enforce and, in our view, less useful than campsite limits. Again, 14 days is the most common campsite limit, especially in national forest wilderness. Hunting camps, usually set up in one place for a week or two in national forest wildernesses, may account for some of these long stay limits. National park limits usually range from one to three nights. Short limits, probably in the three- to five-day range, may be best for quality of experience, but shorter limits may be desirable for minimizing ecological impacts (chap. 16).

Campfire Restrictions

Campfires can be prohibited or discouraged throughout a wilderness, or at certain places, especially near timberline, where trees are scarce and slow growing. Campfires can be restricted to officially designated sites, sometimes to developed fireplaces. There is no question that campfires have substantial environmental impacts (Cole and Dalle-Molle 1982). The fire destroys vegetation where it is built (unless the sod removal techniques described in chap. 16 are successfully used), and it sterilizes soil. Fuelwood gathering causes more widespread and often severe impacts. Campfires and horse use often produce the most conspicuous impacts in wilderness.

The role of campfires in the wilderness experience is another matter. A campfire is a traditional and treasured part of a camping experience for most people. Three-fourths of the visitors to three wildernesses in Washington and Oregon agreed that "camping isn't complete without an evening campfire" (Hendee and others 1968). About 90 percent of the visitors to nine areas in the northern Rockies and California had campfires, often in addition to a campstove (Lucas 1980, 1985). Banning fires would require almost all visitors to change their behavior drastically, and would diminish the experience quality for most of them.

Carefully crafted compromises, matched to site-specific conditions, are the best approach. Educational efforts to encourage limited use of fires, small fires, minimum-impact fire-building and fuel-collec-

tion methods (discussed further in the previous chapter), and use of gas campstoves for most cooking must be a major part of a management program. Timberline or subalpine areas may require special education efforts or, in some cases, prohibition of campfires. Extreme fire danger may require temporary or seasonal prohibitions.

Campfire policies vary among wilderness-managing agencies. National park managers often prohibit campfires everywhere (43 percent of all areas), often require that fires be built only at designated sites (22 percent), sometimes merely discourage campfires (16 percent), but rarely ban fires only in subalpine areas (1 percent) (Washburne and Cole 1983). In contrast, less than 1 percent of national forest wildernesses have overall fire prohibitions, just 6 percent limit fires to designated sites (almost all in California or the BWCAW), 4 percent prohibit fires in subalpine areas, and 22 percent discourage fires. Managers of almost half of all wildlife refuge wildernesses ban campfires completely, but all other less restrictive policies are rare in refuges.

Presence of rock campfire rings also affects visitor experiences. In many wildernesses, especially in national forests, managers encourage visitors to remove all firerings and "naturalize" the site to remove all evidence of fire. The objective is to eliminate the visual impact of campfires; the ecological effects remain. Wilderness rangers remove the rings visitors do not obliterate, often over and and over again. Surveys indicate that visitors are not unduly disturbed by one reasonably sized ring (Lucas 1985; Shelby and Harris 1985). The common policies of leaving one well-located small firering per site, or removing rings only where fires or all camping is prohibited or discouraged, seem in line with visitor desires and require less work by wilderness rangers. Such policies also probably limit the spread of environmental impacts compared to total firering removal (see chap. 16).

Prohibiting Certain
Types of Use

Some types of recreational use conflict. Hikers sometimes dislike encountering horse users and their impacts (Shew and others 1986), and occasionally horse users are bothered by hikers. We have already mentioned that many people in small parties dislike meeting large parties. Canoeists usually resent the use of motorboats even in the few wildernesses where some motorized use is allowed. Prohibiting one type of use improves the quality of experience for one type of visitor but obviously eliminates or diminishes experiences for those whose use is prohibited.

Enforcement is relatively easy because prohibited uses are conspicuous.

Total prohibitions are rare. Prohibiting certain uses in some sections of a wilderness is far more common (fig. 17.9). Almost half of the NPS and about one-fifth of USFS wildernesses have portions closed to horses (Washburne and Cole 1983). Many areas have prohibitions on horses near lakes and streams. A few have seasonal prohibitions on horses. None ban hikers to provide exclusive horse-use zones. Much of the limited motorized use allowed under special exceptions is also zoned; for example, outboard motor use in the BWCAW is allowed only on certain waterways.

Excluding some uses from certain sections of a wilderness can be a valuable management tool, but it should be used with restraint. Associated education efforts to reduce objectionable behavior and to increase mutual understanding and acceptance are always essential. Often education can avoid the need to prohibit particular uses or reduce the area that must be closed for that type of use.

Camping Setbacks From Water

In many wildernesses, camping close to water is prohibited. A 100- or 200-foot no-camping zone is most common. Some restrictions refer only to lakes, some to lakes and streams, occasionally only to named streams. Such camping setbacks are most common in national forest wilderness, with 37 percent requiring setbacks. Similar regulations are applied in 22 percent of national park wildernesses and in 10 percent of wildlife refuge wildernesses.

Various reasons for setbacks are mentioned by managers. Some relate to reduced environmental impacts, but as chapter 15 describes more fully, shorelines are not necessarily more ecologically fragile, and water pollution depends on where wastes are disposed, not where camp is located. Benefits to quality of experience include: a reduced sense of crowding; keeping camps out of the foreground of the prime visual attraction; and keeping the lakeshore or streamside open to all visitors without disturbing the privacy of someone's camp.

Such regulations are unnecessary if only one party is present at a time. Crowding and visual intrusions might be reduced more effectively by encouraging people to select secluded sites, screened from view by topography and vegetation, rather than imposing a specific setback. Keeping shoreline areas available to all is a real benefit, but 200 feet is probably excessive.

Benefits to experience come at high costs to visitors and managers. Water is a powerful attrac-

tion. Most people want to be close to it, mainly for aesthetic reasons. Locations of existing campsites, developed by visitors' free choices over many years, clearly reflect this preference. For example, Brown and Schomaker (1974) found 44 percent of all campsites in the Spanish Peaks Primitive Area in Montana (now part of the Lee Metcalf Wilderness) within 50 feet of water, 63 percent within 100 feet and 85 percent within 200 feet. A 200-foot setback would require drastic changes in visitors' choices of campsites.

Besides reducing quality by forcing people out of preferred sites, the supply of potential places to camp is greatly reduced, and in steep, mountainous country, there will be *no* legal places to camp near many destinations because reasonably level ground is often confined to narrow strips close to water. About one-fourth of all wildernesses also prohibit camping within a certain distance of trails. Trail and water no-camping zones often overlap and close large areas to camping. If areas suitable for camping do exist, many new campsites will develop behind the setback, while the old ones closer to water typically persist, increasing total impacts considerably (Cole 1982).

Enforcement is difficult. Managers of one area with a 200-foot no-camping regulation reported that several years after enactment, about half of all campers were in violation. In most places with such regulations, the majority of violation notices are issued for camping too close to water (Swain 1986). Visitors are harassed, which is unpleasant for them and for wilderness rangers. Furthermore, Robertson (1986) found that wilderness campers were poor judges of distance from shorelines.

Camping setbacks may have been overused. Although this regulation may seem useful, it may have negligible effects on impacts and a negative effect on visitor experiences. Benefits are not clearcut and may not justify the full-scale enforcement campaign that is required. The regulation appears sometimes to have been adopted too quickly with insufficient analysis.

Rather than arbitrary setbacks, we recommend educating visitors in where to camp. The advantage

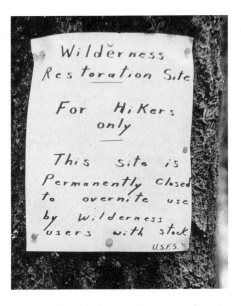

Fig. 17.9. Restricting certain types of use is more common than total prohibition. This campsite in the Bob Marshall Wilderness has been closed to horse traffic. Photo courtesy of the USFS.

of not camping too close to water should be explained, with perhaps 100 feet from water suggested as the minimum setback wherever possible. Reasons for picking a site screened from view should be explained. Concern for impacts may prompt choosing existing campsites as explained in the previous chapter. The relationship of impacts to campsite choices could be explained so that visitors could make reasonably good choices under varying conditions. This seems more effective than a rigid 200-foot setback that is widely violated, that is impractical at some places, and that is only indirectly related to the problems that actually concern managers.

Rationing Use Intensity

Rationing of use has major potential effects on quality of experience. Those permitted to enter, enjoy heightened solitude and quality of experience, but for others wilderness experience is denied. How use is rationed can further affect experiences.

Several techniques can be used to control use intensity. A daily limit can be set for the number of parties or individuals at all or certain entry points. Thereafter, travel itinerary is up to each party; they can make it up as they go. Limits could also be placed on the number of persons staying overnight in the entire area, in specific zones, or at individual campsites; in this case, numbers entering would depend on the planned lengths of stay of parties already in the area. If use were at capacity, numbers leaving would determine numbers admitted.

Several examples of use rationing systems are presented to help clarify the elements involved in such systems. The first four examples involve limits on numbers entering; the next four involve limits on overnight use; the last example involves limits on both entry and overnight use.

1. The USFS permits only seven parties per day to start float trips on the Middle Fork of the Salmon River in Idaho in the Frank Church-River of No Return Wilderness. Three permits per day are allocated to commercial guides; four are reserved for private parties and must be obtained through a lottery. A small application fee is charged.

2. Yosemite National Park rations camping use with a system of trailhead quotas, but visitors are free to travel and camp where they wish once they enter through the trailhead for which they have a permit. Quotas were established with the help of a simulation program that limits the number of parties entering so use of no travel zone exceeds a limit based on both ecological and social conditions. Reservations may be made from February 1 through Memorial Day and for Memorial Day through Labor Day. Half of each trailhead quota can be reserved; half is available on a first-come, first-served basis. Permits must be picked up by 10 a.m. on the first day of the trip or they are canceled and become available for drop-ins.

3. The main access to Mount Whitney in California, the highest peak in the conterminous 48 states, is by a trail through the John Muir Wilderness. Only 50 overnight campers (individuals) are admitted each day during the main use season, from late May through September. Advance reservations are accepted beginning March 1 for 100 percent of the quota; however, the large number of no-shows (about 30 percent in 1983) allows a substantial number of users to gain entry on a first-come, first-served basis. Day use is unrestricted. Reservations are handled by the Eastern Sierra Interpretive Association, a non-profit organization, in cooperation with the USFS. A $5 per person fee is charged.

4. The BWCAW requires permits for campers and some day-use motorized visitors between May 1 and September 30. Each entry point has a quota, derived from a computer simulation (Peterson and others 1977). Visitors are asked to list alternate dates and entry points. Reservations are accepted beginning February 1, by mail or telephone. The $5 reservation fee may be paid by credit card. Party size is limited to 10 persons and camping is limited to designated sites. Unreserved entries are available first-come, first-served 48 hours in advance, without a fee.

5. Camping use of Linville Gorge Wilderness in North Carolina, a small, very popular area, is limited to 40 parties per night on weekends and holidays only from May 1 through October 31. Party size cannot exceed 10 people. Reservations can be made beginning on the first working day of the month preceding the visit. Reservations can be made through the ranger station, by mail, telephone, or in person. Only one weekend permit per month will be issued to the same person or group to give as many people as possible a chance to visit the area.

6. Rocky Mountain National Park in Colorado also limits overnight camping. Permits are issued for 239 designated campsites, with wood fires permitted at only 41. Camping is limited to three nights at one site, and a total of seven nights per summer. The visitors must indicate where they will camp each night, with first and second choices, when requesting permits and are expected to adhere to this itinerary. Advance reservations can be made beginning January 1, in person, by mail, or telephone, except that no telephone requests are accepted after May 30. Permits must be obtained in person or by mail no more than 30 days before the visit. Permits not picked up by 10 a.m. of the first day of the scheduled trip are canceled. Party size cannot exceed seven in the summer or 15 in winter. Limited permits are also issued for more than 20 trailless cross-country zones in which visitors can choose their own campsites. They must move every day and can stay in each cross-country zone for only two nights. No fires or horses are permitted in cross-country zones.

7. The Indian Peaks Wilderness in Colorado requires permits for campers only, not day users, between June 1 and September 15. Visitors must indicate which of 19 travel zones they intend to camp in each night (with second choices). They receive a ticket for a specific zone for each night. Each zone has a daily quota for camper parties. Four zones have designated campsites that must be used; one is closed to camping; some prohibit wood campfires; and horses are banned from several zones.

About 90 percent of daily quotas can be reserved, and 10 percent are available for "last chance" permits on the day of entry or the day before. A $4 fee is charged for processing reservations, but no fee for "last chance" permits. Reservations can be made starting March 1 in person or by mail from the national forest or through a commercial reservation service, Datafix. The issuing agency checks for availability of the zones for the requested dates with a computer system. Parties normally are limited to 10 persons, but parties up to 25 may apply to the national forest for special, more restrictive permits.

8. The Great Gulf Wilderness in New Hampshire limits camping to 75 individuals per night between June 15 and September 15. Use is limited to four nights. Permits may be reserved no more than 30 days in advance. Party size is limited to 10 people, and camping is banned above timberline.

9. Both numbers of overnight parties and day users are limited in the San Gorgonio Wilderness in California. In the popular South Fork Basin, 22 overnight parties are permitted per night, and only 26 day-use parties may enter. Reservations are available. In addition to these quotas, experienced campers are permitted to use more remote sites away from trails and established campsites by the use of an "Explorer Permit" (Stankey and Baden 1977).

Limited entry permits are administered in a variety of ways, as these examples show. Some or all are usually available for advance reservations. Some proportion of the available permits often are held back for last-minute drop-ins on a first-come, first-served basis (sometimes called queuing from the similarity to waiting in line to be served). Usually these drop-in permits can be obtained one day ahead of entry. A mixture of reservation and drop-in permits seems to be fair. People who plan carefully far ahead, perhaps because of their need to schedule vacations and travel far from their home to the wilderness, need some advance assurance they will be able to visit the wilderness. Other people cannot or at least prefer not to plan so much, and operate in a spontaneous, spur-of-the-moment fashion. If they live close to the wilderness, they may react to last-minute weather changes. A mixed system gives each type of person a chance at a permit.

Limited permits could also be issued through a lottery, as is done for some big-game hunting permits. Handling such a lottery for entries on various dates is more cumbersome than assigning hunting permits for clearly defined hunting seasons, but it is done regularly for river floating permits. We are not aware of any lotteries for wilderness permits other than river floating, however. Most visitors surveyed reject the lottery concept. In fact, it is usually the least favored alternative, except on rivers where visitors have become familiar with lotteries and accept them better.

All of these and other approaches to rationing use—reservations; lottery; first-come, first-served; fees; and skill/knowledge—have different mixtures of advantages and disadvantages, which are reviewed in detail by Stankey and Baden (1977). They summarize the likely effects of each technique in table 17.1 at the end of this chapter.

Each system benefits certain types of visitors at the expense of others (cols. 1 and 2). Some are in wide use and others are untried (col. 3). Visitor acceptance varies from low to high, with some question marks (col. 4). Difficulty of administration varies, but only queuing (first-come, first-served) seems to be easy (col. 5).

Efficiency (col. 6) includes two concepts. First, how closely can use be matched to capacity? Second, how well does the system allocate permits to the people who place a higher value on the opportunity? The range is wide, from low to high. The different systems control use (col. 7) and affect visitor behavior (col. 8) in different ways.

Stankey and Baden (1977) provide five guidelines for managing wilderness rationing:

1. Start with an accurate base of knowledge about use, users, and impacts.
2. Use direct rationing only after less restrictive measures have failed to solve the problems.
3. Combine rationing techniques to minimize and equalize costs to managers and users.
4. Ration so the people to whom the experience is most valuable are more likely to get it.
5. Monitor all rationing programs so their effectiveness can be objectively evaluated.

With a reservation system there are usually no-shows, especially with free reservations. Generally, if a reservation has not been picked up and used by a certain time, such as 10 a.m., it is released for use by drop-in visitors. Some people might apply for a permit "just in case we decide we want to go," and this could be the cause of much of the problem.

Successful applicants for very scarce, hard-to-get permits might become ineligible for another permit for a time to give other people a chance. This is done in some states for certain limited big-game licenses, but Linville Gorge Wilderness is the only area we are aware of where such a system is used.

If permits are issued at several locations, a communication system is needed in order to know when the limit has been reached. A computer reservation system, similar to that used for airline ticket sales, would probably be the best solution. Generally, public acceptance of controlled entry seems to have been good, as shown both in studies (Fazio and Gilbert 1974; Hay 1974; Taylor 1972), and managers' experiences.

Some systems control travel routes or itineraries; for example, in Rocky Mountain National Park. Similar control of overnight visitors is common in other national park wildernesses. Usually, capacities are established for camp areas. Visitors applying for a permit must indicate the camp areas they want to use each night. This is checked against capacities and scheduled use by other parties. If space exists at each place each night, the permit is issued for this itinerary, and the party is expected to stick to it. If space is not available at one or more camps, an alternate route must be worked out. If this is possible, the permit is issued and the party is obligated to adhere to the revised route.

This system, which is analogous to a reservation system for a motel chain, has the potential for matching use to capacity very closely. It has some serious problems, however, particularly the loss of visitor freedom and spontaneity. For instance, at a trail junction there is no option to change plans because one way looks more fascinating than the originally planned direction. An unexpectedly beautiful camp might beckon for a second night, but if the schedule says "move," the party is supposed to leave.

Furthermore, many parties find it difficult or impossible to stay on schedule. Plans are often too ambitious, and travelers find they run out of energy before they reach their scheduled destination. Weather, blisters, illness, a camera forgotten hanging in a tree—all sorts of things can slow a party.

Whether a party is in the "wrong" campsite by choice or accident, it is likely to be an uncomfortable experience. Apprehensions could nag visitors. Will a ranger come along? Will he check their permit? Will he reprimand them, make them move, issue a violation notice, or what? If the camp quota is not full anyway, will the ranger take this into account? If the ranger ignores the violation, is this fair to the party that reluctantly passed a lovely, empty campsite late in the day and pushed on with aching feet until sunset to reach the campsite listed on their permit? The system can cause a loss of the sense of wilderness freedom and exploration, sometimes for a fairly small gain. It might transplant some of the "rat race" of most people's working world to the wilderness. In addition, it places the wilderness ranger in a particularly uncomfortable enforcement role. Backcountry camping has peaked and declined somewhat in most of the national parks, including those where controlled itineraries are used. This might suggest reconsideration of the need for such close control.

Perhaps some compromise might be considered for control of itineraries. Popular, heavily used zones or particular campsites might need to have controlled use, night by night, but parties going elsewhere, or promising not to use specified campsites, could be turned loose. Some of this is done in Rocky Mountain National Park and the San Gorgonio Wilderness.

Site-specific use management can create problems. Overuse problems may move from one place to another if managers approach management in an excessively fragmented way. Visitor use patterns are interconnected, and changing use at a few places can displace visitors to other places, perhaps conflicting with management objectives. Use-management plans need to consider larger areas that function as visitor use units, such as drainage basins in some areas, to avoid creating unintentional new problem areas.

Shenandoah National Park in Virginia considered a reservation system for designated camping areas in the park backcountry—the controlled-itinerary system—but rejected this approach because the managers saw it as being unduly restrictive of visitors, cumbersome in implementation, and unnecessary until all other alternatives have been tested (USDI NPS n.d.). Managers also thought that backcountry problems were not caused by visitors at large but

from a few destructive camping practices, some unthinking and some traditional, by backcountry users. The backcountry was classified as wilderness in 1976, shortly after this use management plan was put into effect. The system has remained essentially unchanged at least through 1986.

Instead, Shenandoah National Park adopted an innovative plan without rationing use. Permits are required for overnight use; maximum permitted party size is 10 people. Permits may be obtained ahead of time or after reaching the park. Visitors may camp where they want to, as long as they meet several conditions:

1. Camp out of view and at least 250 yards from any paved road.
2. Camp out of sight and at least one-half mile from any automobile campground, lodge, visitor center, or other developments.
3. Camp off and out of sight of any trail.
4. Camp out of sight of other camping parties.
5. Camp outside and out of sight of any trail shelter except when "essential" during "severely unseasonable weather."
6. Camp at least 25 feet away from any stream.
7. No wood or charcoal fires may be built, and campstoves are encouraged.
8. Camp at the same site no more than two nights.

The plan was developed with extensive public involvement and seems to be accepted by most visitors; it is a success in the eyes of park officials (Jacobsen 1975). The managers feel this approach is particularly appropriate in eastern deciduous forests where visibility is usually limited, but much of the system might have merit in some western areas as well.

Shenandoah managers developed this system to cope with heavy use that was severely damaging a limited number of designated camping sites, many with shelters, and producing a "country fair" atmosphere rather than a wilderness experience. They hoped it would provide visitors freedom, assure opportunities for solitude, open up (without deterioration) much of the park, and allow more use than would a site-reservation, controlled-itinerary system.

Shenandoah's campsite-spacing rules seem valuable because the visual isolation they produce is an important value to most wilderness visitors (chap. 9), but in the absence of specific guidelines or sanctions, campers often select campsites in such a way that visual isolation is impaired.

Unfortunately, to our knowledge, this management system has not been evaluated through monitoring. Backcountry camping in 1985 was only 36 percent of that in 1973. Whether some of this decline, common to many national parks (chap. 13), was

caused by the use-management program cannot be determined.

One interesting idea that has not been field tested calls for rationing use with the chance of obtaining a permit proportional to the use intensity in different parts of a wilderness—"risk zoning," as it has been called (Greist 1975). In other words, for those areas where use intensities were relatively high, the chance of getting an entry permit also would be high. Where use intensity was low (and where managers wanted to keep it low), the chance of getting a permit would be lower too. The advantage of this system is that it requires users to consider the risks associated with gaining entry and would, at least theoretically, accurately reflect the value placed on solitude by the user. Visitors who valued solitude little would usually be able to enter a wilderness rather than frequently being denied entry to maintain high solitude levels which they would not appreciate. At the same time, there would be places with high levels of solitude for those who prized it and who would rather take an occasional trip in such areas than frequent trips to more crowded areas.

In any place where use controls are needed, they should usually be applied at entry points, rather than to itineraries. With knowledge of normal use patterns and route choices, entry quotas could be set to keep overnight use within about the same campsite capacities of the route-control system. For example, if Arrow Lake has a four-parties-per-night limit, and use-pattern analysis shows (1) virtually all Arrow Lake campers enter from the Deer Creek trailhead and (2) about 10 percent of the Deer Creek parties choose to camp at Arrow Lake for (3) an average of two nights, about 20 parties per day could be permitted to enter at Deer Creek in order to keep use at Arrow Lake around four parties per night. (About two out of 20 would go to Arrow Lake, and if they stayed about two nights there would be two parties there from the day before.) To keep use below four parties a greater proportion of the time, fewer parties—maybe 15 per day—would be allowed to enter.

Some variation may occur; on some nights five or six parties might camp where only four were desired. But this happens with controlled itineraries also, with the added cost of guilt and worry for the campers. In Glacier National Park, Montana, where an itinerary system is in use, managers say most parties were found to be off schedule by about the fifth day of travel, although other areas report higher conformity.

The wilderness travel simulation models discussed later in this chapter are particularly useful in relating entry patterns to camp-use levels, especially when use from different entry points overlaps. Simulations can indicate the likelihood that any use level of a particular campsite will be exceeded.

Restrictions on Activities

Many specific activities can be prohibited or discouraged to reduce or eliminate various adverse impacts on the environment and experiences. Whatever restrictions managers impose, they must monitor results to decide whether to continue the restrictions, drop them, or modify them.

Hunting and fishing regulations offer considerable scope for affecting activities, varying use intensities, and altering impact on the wildlife and fish component of the ecosystem and thus affecting experience quality. The attractiveness of certain areas can be increased or reduced by varying the restrictiveness of seasons, bag limits, or both. Fish and game management, however, is a state responsibility except in national parks and wildlife refuges. State Fish and Game Departments usually object to controlling wilderness use by restricting hunting or fishing because they feel it unfairly discriminates against visitors who hunt and fish.

OTHER MANAGEMENT TOOLS AND TECHNIQUES

Several other management tools and techniques are means of carrying out either direct or indirect management. One of the most important of these tools is the wilderness ranger.

WILDERNESS RANGERS

Many of the management actions just discussed are carried out by wilderness rangers. Most patrol the wilderness during its use season, but some are stationed at busy trailheads to contact entering visitors (these people are often called Wilderness Information Specialists or WISs) (Schomaker and Lime 1986). The wilderness ranger often works during the summer only, or the summer and fall. A few are year-round employees who work on wilderness data tabulation and public education programs during the off season.

Wilderness rangers can be used as versatile field managers. They can gather field data on resource conditions, use, and visitor actions; influence visitor behavior by suggestions, advice, and information; enforce regulations; perform emergency trail repairs (but not the trail crew's job of major maintenance and construction); rehabilitate campsites; plan and direct or do cleanup (the garbage-collector role); and give

emergency assistance (Kovalicky 1971). As field managers, wilderness rangers can help solve site-specific problems (such as overuse of a popular camp area) by providing visitors with information and advice. In this way wilderness rangers can reduce both the need for areawide regulations and more direct controls.

The national parks have had wilderness rangers for some time, but they were rare until the 1960s in national forest wilderness. Now, almost all wildernesses and backcountry areas have wilderness rangers, although sometimes the large area patrolled by one person permits only superficial coverage. But in some areas great importance is placed on rangers as a major management tool. For example, the very heavily used Desolation Wilderness had nine wilderness rangers working in an area of about 65,000 acres until recently, when cutbacks were made. From all available evidence, wilderness rangers have proven to be very useful. Visitor surveys also indicate they are well accepted by the public (Hendee and others 1968; Lucas 1980; Stankey 1973).

Rangers should be selected for their interest and ability to work with people as well as their knowledge and concern for wilderness. Wilderness rangers are, in effect, people managers, and they are the agency's prime contact with the wilderness-using public. Volunteers have become increasingly common as wilderness rangers in recent years.

LITTER CONTROL

Litter cleanup and efforts to further reduce littering, usually through the "pack-it-in, pack-it-out" regulation, are essential in wilderness. Research indicates that litter detracts seriously from wilderness experiences (Lee 1975; Stankey 1973), and is a user complaint identified in several studies. Many believe that a clean site is more likely to be kept clean by users, although supporting evidence is scarce.

Litter does not all have to be removed by agency employees (fig. 17.10). In field tests in developed campgrounds, the "incentive system for litter control" reduced litter levels tenfold and at one-fifteenth the cost of standard cleanup procedures (Clark and others 1972a, 1972b). The incentive system in campgrounds consists of rangers contacting families with children and soliciting the help of children to clean the campground in return for fire prevention and environmental education type rewards—badges, comic and coloring books, and so on.

An adaptation of the incentive system has been developed for wilderness and backcountry (Muth and Clark 1978). It is actually an "appeal system" because it has not proven feasible for wilderness

rangers to carry a supply of incentive rewards, children are not as numerous, and many wilderness users objected to the notion of rewards—an appeal for visitors' help is all that is necessary. This is partly because the "pack-it-out" norm has become accepted.

In the BWCAW and adjacent Quetico Provincial Park in Canada, visitors are not permitted to take bottles or cans with them (reusable containers are permitted). This regulation is reported to have greatly reduced littering. Nevertheless, the regulation might be excessive, given that the "pack-it-in, pack-it-out" regulation is sufficient. Flattening an empty can and placing it in the bottom of the pack would directly solve the problem.

MONITORING QUALITY OF THE EXPERIENCE

Wilderness visitor management requires monitoring of important aspects of visitor experiences, just as much as resource condition monitoring. Visitor experiences are an ultimate product of wilderness management, and some measurement of product quality is essential. Unfortunately, monitoring methods for social conditions are not as well developed and tested as for resource conditions.

If the LAC system (chap. 9) is being used, monitoring of all indicators is essential. Some of these indicators usually will relate to visitor experiences. In any wilderness, whatever management system is being used, the identification of problems requiring management attention comes best from systematic, objective monitoring. Judging the effectiveness of management actions also requires monitoring.

To be most useful, information gathered by managers in the field needs to be collected systematically and accurately, and carefully recorded. Three important aspects of experience quality to monitor include: (1) encounter levels on trails; (2) campsite solitude; and (3) satisfactions/dissatisfactions.

Encounter Levels on Trails

The number of parties met per day by a group while traveling on trails or waterways is a measure of solitude that affects visitor experience quality, and it has been used as a LAC indicator. In one approach, wilderness rangers or volunteers tally how many parties they meet each day. To reasonably represent visitors' encounter experiences, the agency people must travel at about the same speed and for about the same distance that typical visitors do. Tallies might be adjusted slightly to compensate for unusually fast, long travel, or for coverage of only part of a typical day's travel. It is essential to keep formal

notes, preferably on a standard form, and to record the trail segments covered.

A second approach is for fieldworkers to ask visitors about their encounter experiences. "How many other parties did you meet yesterday?" (or "today" if late in the day). The visitor's route would be noted. More information could be obtained from visitors than in the first approach and thus results would be more valid. Answers should be recorded systematically in a notebook with date and location of travel noted.

Campsite Solitude

Most visitors place particular value on a campsite isolated from the sight and sound of other campers. How successful they are in achieving isolation significantly influences their experience quality. Therefore, all managers should monitor campsite solitude, and LAC systems will usually include it as an indicator.

Two approaches can be used to monitor campsite solitude. Because of their comparability, both could be used and the results combined with good accuracy. The first approach is *direct observation in the field*. A wilderness ranger could record how many other occupied camps were observable from each occupied camp. This must be done in the evening or early morning, when most people are in camp, which limits the number of observations possible.

The second approach can supplement the first. Again, it involves *asking visitors about their experiences* (surveying) during normal contacts. When a party is contacted in camp during the middle of the day, it would be common to ask: "Did you camp here or elsewhere last night?" Then, as appropriate: "Was anyone else camped nearby?" "How many groups?" Parties met on the trail who are obviously not day visitors would be asked: "Where did you camp last night?" The followup questions then would be the same: "Was anyone else camped nearby?" "How many parties?"

All the data need to be carefully recorded and the campsite identified as precisely as possible. Campsite environmental conditions should also be monitored, and a system of numbering campsites should be established to facilitate data recording and tabulation. Locating camps mentioned by parties on the trail may involve going over a map with them and sometimes will be imprecise, unfortunately. Data for a lake basin or general area are still useful, but the records should reflect this uncertainty.

Satisfactions/Dissatisfactions

Most managers would want some feedback from visitors on the things that satisfy or dissatisfy them,

Fig. 17.10. Litter control depends on cooperation between land managers and the public. Here, Sierra Club volunteers clean up litter in the Selway-Bitterroot Wilderness. The "pack-it-in, pack-it-out" regulation is the best solution to littering, and is being practiced by more and more visitors to most wildernesses. Photo courtesy of Richard Walker.

whether as part of a formal monitoring program or not. Reactions to trail conditions, campsite impact conditions, litter, specific management policies or regulations, and information provided by the agency are among possible topics managers might want to keep track of. There is no way to do this except by talking with visitors. Some of these topics are commonly discussed with visitors anyway, especially trail conditions. In these cases, it is just a matter of making careful notes after the conversation. To be most useful, the information should be collected in a standardized way. Recording spontaneous complaints and compliments is fine, but mixing such responses with answers to specific questions, such as "What do you think about our closure of camping at Summit Lake?" will produce a misleading, noncomparable mixture of information.

USE SIMULATION MODELS

In some wildernesses, visitor use must be reduced and/or redistributed to achieve specific management objectives. We have discussed a variety of techniques that can lower use levels and redistribute visitors away from critical sites. But the specific consequences of redistributing use are not entirely predictable. Until recently there has been no way to correlate

changes in the amount or distribution of overall use to resulting changes in the amount of use at particular sites and levels of solitude/crowding. For example, if a trailhead quota system is implemented, how will that affect the actual number of users present at a certain lake or on a certain trail within the wilderness? What will happen to numbers of trail encounters between parties or campsite solitude? The complexity of travel routes, which typically overlap, and the variability of travelers' decisions usually is so great that neither intuition nor formulas can accurately predict onsite use levels and distribution.

Rigid itineraries provide a more determinate result, at least for use of camp areas and encounters between camping parties, but not for encounters between parties while traveling on the trails. For many reasons, discussed above, not all parties adhere to their itinerary, so results are not as determinate as they might seem.

If use patterns and encounters resulting from any given total use level and entry-point distribution cannot be predicted, then trial-and-error experimentation cannot be used. Trial and error is very time consuming; managers would have to try a policy for at least a year to see how it worked. Results for any one year could be influenced by uncontrolled outside factors such as weather. Feedback about results is limited. Detailed information on use patterns and encounters would be available only if special, costly studies monitored users of the area. It would not always be possible to create the actual use pattern the managers desired to test; for example, how could twice as many visitors be attracted in any one year? Long-lasting or even irreversible damage to resources might result from tests of heavy use, visitor benefits could be sacrificed, and major changes in use policies could lead to controversy.

Systems that are too complex for analytic solutions and not suited to real-world experimentation are often approached by *simulation modeling*. Simulation models are simplified replicas of a particular real-world system, usually described so that they can be represented by a computer program. Simulation models are used widely in engineering and business. For example, a simulation model might be used to help decide, for an ocean port, how different combinations of additional cranes and tugboats alter the efficiency of loading and unloading ships.

One wilderness travel simulation model has been developed by Resources for the Future, Inc., in cooperation with the USFS, to provide a better way to formulate and evaluate use management policies (Lucas and Shechter 1977; Shechter and Lucas 1978; Smith and Krutilla 1976). This simulation model provides a practical way for managers to test use patterns quickly. Variability in visitor behavior is incorporated in the model, but in just a few minutes, use can be simulated for a number of seasons to average out variations. The model records and displays in appropriate tables the desired information on use and encounters. Because the experimentation takes place in the computer instead of the real world, the high resource and social costs are avoided. Even the most extreme patterns can be tested without damage to precious resources.

This wilderness use simulation model includes a replica of an area's travel system (entry points, trails, water or cross-country routes, and campsites), and provides for different types of parties (several sizes and methods of travel). The computer program for the model generates visiting parties of different kinds who arrive at the area at various simulated dates and clock times, enter at particular access points, select routes of travel, and move along them. The simulated parties may overtake and pass slower parties moving in the same direction (overtaking encounters), pass parties moving in the opposite direction (meeting encounters), or pass by parties camped in areas visible from trails or other travel routes, such as rivers (visual encounters). Parties that stay overnight select places to camp, which they may share with other camping parties (camp encounters). On a later day, camping parties leave the campsite and continue on their chosen routes, and eventually leave the area.

To make the model operational, data are needed on the area and its use. The travel network must be known, and also something about how different types of visitors behave within it—their patterns of arrival, various routes followed and relative popularity of each, travel speeds, and so on. This information is supplied to the model in probabilistic terms; for example, there might be one chance in 10 that a party entering at Deer Creek would select a route to Arrow Lake with a two-night stay there.

The simulator provides detailed output information for each simulation of a particular use "scenario." The model has the capability of producing summaries of a series or replications or runs of any such scenario, providing average values of the amount, character, distribution, and timing of use. For example, the number of parties of each type using each trail segment is provided. Additional information is available on the number of encounters by type of encounter, by type of party, and by individual trail segments and campsites.

The model is coded in the IBM-originated General Purpose Simulation System (GPSS) language, version V. The model has been successfully operated on IBM's 360 and 370 series of computers, Control Data Corporation's 6600 computer, and the Unisys com-

puter at the USFS's national computer center in Fort Collins, Colorado. A users' manual (Shechter 1975) is available.

To bring use impacts and solitude levels into line with management objectives for the area, managers might consider actions designed to alter numbers of parties entering at various trailheads or to reduce weekend peaks, or they might consider adding some new trails or campsites. Managers can test use patterns on the simulator and learn how closely the results agree with their objectives. If agreement is not close enough, the simulator's results will aid them in revising the use pattern to come closer.

Management objectives are critical in this process. The simulator will determine use distribution and encounter frequency for *any* use pattern, but whether this is acceptable or unacceptable must be a managerial decision based on management objectives. Which technique is chosen to shift the use pattern is also a managerial responsibility. Use might be rationed, a new trail might be built or another closed, or information supplied to visitors to change their location choices. The simulator is not concerned with *how* the use pattern is altered, but only with the *consequences* of the alteration. The simulator is an aid to the manager in decision making but it does not make the decisions. It is a way to play "What if?"—to try out a potential management plan before implementing it and to evaluate the results to help decide whether to proceed or modify the planned action. Both the actions to be tested and the evaluation of results depend on the manager's professional skill, not the computer. The simulation model could help put use modification plans on a sounder, more justifiable basis.

Applications of the simulator to test areas—the Spanish Peaks Primitive Area (Smith and Krutilla 1976), the Desolation Wilderness (Shechter and Lucas 1978), the Green and Yampa Rivers in Dinosaur National Monument in Colorado and Utah (Lime and others 1978), a 63-mile section of the Appalachian Trail (Manning and Potter 1984), and the Colorado River in Grand Canyon National Park in Arizona (Underhill and others 1986)—indicate that when the current existing use situation was simulated, the resulting use patterns and encounter experiences generally agreed with data from visitor surveys, indicating that the model was valid. Where there were discrepancies, they stemmed primarily from oversimplification of certain data describing typical use (e.g., including too few different travel routes to adequately reflect the variability of visitor movements), rather than inherent flaws in the simulation model itself. These shortcomings could be corrected in future applications of the model or accepted as reasonable approximations, suitable for policy deci-

sions. No simulation model totally mimics reality; simplification is always necessary. But all that is needed is reasonable representation of important factors to help guide decisions.

In the Desolation Wilderness (Shechter and Lucas 1978) and Dinosaur National Monument in Colorado (Lime and others 1978; McCool and Lime 1976) many simulation scenarios were tested. Use was increased and decreased by varying amounts, and uneven distributions were made more even by shifting use from popular entries to less-used access points and from heavily used weekends to weekdays.

Some clear relationships, not all expected, emerged. Changing the timing of visitor entries had little effect on use pressures or encounter levels. Changes in total use (all other things remaining the same) produced proportionate results. For example, if total use doubles, use of any specific location doubles, on the average, which, in hindsight, now seems obvious. Encounters, expressed in per-party-per-day terms, also double in this example, which was not expected.

This predictable, proportional relationship provides a base for comparing results of more complex scenarios in which use is redistributed against the same amount of total use but without any change in its distribution. Almost all use redistribution scenarios produced lower average daily encounters for visitors than the same total use without redistribution. Some use redistributions were much more effective in reducing average encounter levels than equivalent across-the-board decreases in total use. For example, one entry point redistribution plan required only a 9-percent reduction in total use, but reduced average trail encounters 16 percent and encounters in camp by 13 percent.

Average encounters do not tell the whole story, however. The frequency of extreme encounter levels, including both high levels and low or zero levels, changed substantially for different scenarios. In the example given, the proportion of party-days with high levels of solitude rose more than it would have, with an across-the-board cut in use, but this was not true of all scenarios. A manager probably would be more concerned about reducing or eliminating experiences of unsatisfactory quality than just altering averages. In addition, changes at key trouble spots were even more pronounced. This also would be more relevant to a manager's evaluation of the results of a scenario than overall averages.

A simulation model derived from this original model has been written for personal computers (Rowell 1986). It is interactive, very user-friendly, and provides graphic as well as tabular output. Graphics include use-flow maps drawn by the computer.

Another somewhat simpler simulation model has been developed for the BWCAW that presents only information on numbers of parties camping per night in each travel zone, based on numbers entering at various access points (Gilbert and others 1972; Peterson and others 1977). This has been used by managers to help set entry point daily limits that will not overtax available camping locations.

The use of computer-based simulation modeling in outdoor recreation management planning may arouse fears of depersonalization. On the contrary, modeling can help make it possible to maintain the traditional values of visitor independence, flexibility, and spontaneity as well as to protect resources and experience quality in the face of growing demands on limited resources.

VISITOR MANAGEMENT IN THE FUTURE

The apparent slowing rate of growth of wilderness recreation use presents managers with an opportunity to make major gains in solving wilderness management problems. The results of improved and intensified management are much less likely to be wiped out by skyrocketing use than seemed probable a few years ago. It would be a serious mistake to respond to short-term stabilizing recreational use with a reduced effort in wilderness management.

In the future, wilderness management should stress visitor education and information more and regulation less. Stable or lower use reduces the need to tightly control visitors. Visitor understanding of "wilderness ethics" and minimum impact use techniques is increasing. Benefits are apparent in many places: litter is less common; parties are smaller; tents are more often soft green or brown, rather than bright orange or blue; and so on. Continued emphasis on education can further improve visitor behavior and further diminish the need to rely on regulation.

Visitor education needs strengthening. It has been developed in a short time, and based mainly on intuition. Managers need to be self-critical of their educational efforts and need to evaluate the results of education programs to guide their improvement. Continuing familiar programs just because managers are comfortable with them or enjoy them will not be adequate. Management budgets will remain tight, in all likelihood, and programs must be cost effective.

Contents of messages directed at visitors need examination, and the future direction will tend toward more complete information geared more to variations in the situations visitors encounter. This will mean lengthier, more complex messages. How to communicate such messages most effectively, and how to reach key audiences that are the source of problem behavior, are challenges managers will need to meet successfully.

SUMMARY

This chapter has made several main points. First, many important values of wilderness depend on the quality of visitor experiences. Managers can influence factors that affect experience quality: natural, social, and managerial conditions. Natural conditions depend on management of user impacts, opportunities to view wildlife, and natural wildfires. Social conditions depend on management of solitude/crowding, user conflict, and certain types of problem behavior. Management conditions influence visitor experiences through style and tone, as well as specific actions. Diversity in all three conditions is desirable.

Second, indirect management should be the first choice over direct management. Indirect management involves two main techniques: design and information/education.

Design can include access, trails, and facilities to modify the amount, type, and distribution of recreational use. Most specific facilities, other than trails and bridges, have only a limited role to play in wilderness, receive limited support from visitors, and need to be used with restraint.

Information and education are essential tools for managing visitors and their experience quality. These tools can be used to redistribute use, to expand visitors' understanding of wilderness values, to reduce visitor conflict, and to increase visitors' skills in minimum-impact use. Guidelines for effective use of information and education that could help managers were presented.

Third, direct management also may be a necessary tool in some situations. Regulations and use rationing are the most common direct management approaches, but strong recommendations are a less-authoritarian alternative. Some types of regulations are more often appropriate than others. Party size limits, length-of-stay limits at campsites, campfire restrictions in some situations, prohibiting some types of use in parts of areas, and sometimes use rationing, all have their place in the manager's kit of tools. General length-of-stay limits, total prohibition of types of use allowed under the Wilderness Act, fixed itineraries, and blanket regulations prohibiting camping within a specified distance from water seem harder to justify. Rationing, when necessary, can be done many ways, and each way has different advantages and disadvantages. Usually a

combination of methods is preferable.

Fourth, we stressed the importance of monitoring visitor experience quality (as well as resource conditions), particularly encounters on trails and at campsites, and satisfactions and dissatisfactions. Use simulation models can provide a way to estimate results of alternative actions, and might be considered as "monitoring possible futures."

The future probably holds slower growth in recreational use of wilderness. This offers managers a valuable opportunity to get on top of the wilderness management challenge. It also provides a chance to back off on some tight visitor regulation, more and more replacing it with education and information. To achieve this, use of education/information needs to be strengthened.

STUDY QUESTIONS

1. How would you describe wilderness visitor experiences? What does the Wilderness Act say about visitor experiences?
2. What are the three main ways natural conditions affect wilderness experiences? How?
3. What three elements of social conditions relate to wilderness experiences? How does each one affect experiences?
4. Is diversity in all three types of wilderness conditions desirable? Why? Are there ways in which diversity could be undesirable?
5. How does the ROS system relate to wilderness experiences?
6. What are the four main types of indirect visitor management? How would each affect experiences? How commonly used are each?
7. What characteristics would an excellent wilderness trail have to contribute to high-quality experiences? Do these characteristics conflict with minimizing impacts (chap. 15), and, if so, how?
8. What sort of guidelines would you follow if you were planning to use education and information to manage wilderness visitor use? Outline a program to encourage use of campstoves instead of wood fires, or to discourage camping close to lakes, or to redistribute some use.
9. What aspects of use are most justifiably controlled with regulations? What are least suitably regulated?
10. What factors must be dealt with if recreational use must be rationed?
11. What would a wilderness manager monitor to keep track of experience quality? How?
12. How could simulation models of visitor use help management of quality of experience?

REFERENCES

Adelman, Bonnie Jane Eizen; Heberlein, Thomas; Bonnicksen, Thomas M. 1982. Social psychological explanations for the persistence of a conflict between paddling canoeists and motorcraft users in the Boundary Waters Canoe Area. Leisure Sciences. 5(1): 45-61.

Badger, Thomas J. 1975. Wilderness crowding tolerances and some management techniques: an aspect of social carrying capacity. Fort Collins, CO: Colorado State University. 83 p. Thesis.

Brown, Perry J.; Schomaker, John H. 1974. Final report on criteria for potential wilderness campsites. Supplement No. 32 to cooperative agreement 12-11-204-3. Unpublished report on file at: U.S. Department of Agriculture, Forest Service, Intermountain Research Station, Forestry Sciences Laboratory, Missoula, MT. 50 p.

Clark, Roger N.; Burgess, Robert L.; Hendee, John C. 1972a. The development of anti-litter behavior in a forest campground. Journal of Applied Behavior Analysis. 5(1): 1-5.

Clark, Roger N.; Hendee, John C.; Burgess, Robert L. 1972b. The experimental control of littering. Journal of Environmental Education. 4(2): 22-28.

Clark, Roger N.; Stankey, George H. 1979. The Recreation Opportunity Spectrum: a framework for planning, management, and research. Gen. Tech. Rep. PNW-98. Portland, OR: U.S. Department of Agriculture, Forest Service, Pacific Northwest Forest and Range Experiment Station. 32 p.

Cole, David N. 1982. Controlling the spread of campsites at popular wilderness destinations. Journal of Soil and Water Conservation. 37(5): 291-295.

Cole, David N. 1987. Research on soil and vegetation in wilderness: a state-of-knowledge review. In: Lucas, Robert C., compiler. Proceedings—national wilderness research conference: issues, state-of-knowledge, future directions; 1985 July 23-26; Fort Collins, CO. Gen. Tech. Rep. INT-220. Ogden, UT: U.S. Department of Agriculture, Forest Service, Intermountain Research Station: 135-177.

Cole, David N.; Dalle-Molle, John. 1982. Managing campfire impacts in the backcountry. Gen. Tech. Rep. INT-135. Ogden, UT: U.S. Department of Agriculture, Forest Service, Intermountain Forest and Range Experiment Station. 16 p.

Driver, B. L.; Brown, Perry J. 1978. The opportunity spectrum concept and behavioral information in outdoor recreation resource supply inventories: a rationale. In: Integrated inventories of renewable natural resources: Proceedings of the workshop; 1978 January 8-12; Tucson, AZ. Gen. Tech. Rep. RM-55. Fort Collins, CO: U.S. Department of Agriculture, Forest Service, Rocky Mountain Forest and Range Experiment Station: 24-31.

Dustin, Daniel L. 1985. To feed or not to feed the bears: the moral choices we make. Parks & Recreation. 20(10): 54-57, 72.

Fazio, James R. 1979. Communicating with the wilderness visitor. Bull. 28. Moscow, ID: University of Idaho, Forest, Wildlife and Range Experiment Station. 65 p.

Fazio, James R.; Gilbert, Douglas L. 1974. Mandatory wilderness permits: some indications of success. Journal of Forestry. 72(12): 753-756.

Gilbert, C. Gorman; Peterson, George L.; Lime, David W. 1972. Towards a model of travel behavior in the Boundary Waters Canoe Area. Environment and Behavior. 4(2): 131-157.

Greist, David. 1975. Risk zoning: a recreation area management system and method of measuring carrying capacity. Journal of Forestry. 73(11): 711-714.

Hay, Edwards. 1974. Wilderness experiment: it's working. American Forests. 80(12): 26-29.

Heberlein, Thomas A.; Dunwiddie, Peter. 1979. Systematic observation of use levels, campsite selection and visitor characteristics at a high mountain lake. Journal of Leisure Research. 11(4): 307-315.

Hendee, John C.; Catton, William R., Jr.; Marlow, Larry D.; Brockman, C. Fran. 1968. Wilderness users in the Pacific Northwest—their characteristics, values, and management preferences. Res. Pap. PNW-61. Portland, OR: U.S. Department of Agriculture, Forest Service, Pacific Northwest Forest and Range Experiment Station. 92 p.

Jacobsen, Robert R. 1975. Notes used by Superintendent Robert R. Jacobsen of Shenandoah National Park in a panel presentation at the Government use regulations along the Appalachian Trail workshop at the 20th meeting of the Appalachian Trail Conference; 1975 June 22; Boone, NC. On file at: U.S. Department of Agriculture, Forest Service, Intermountain Research Station, Forestry Sciences Laboratory, Missoula, MT; RWU 4901 files.

Kovalicky, Thomas J. 1971. The wilderness ranger concept. Naturalist. 22(3): 14-15.

Krumpe, Edwin E.; Brown, Perry J. 1982. Redistributing backcountry use through information related to recreational experiences. Journal of Forestry. 80(6): 360-362.

Landrum, Paul. 1976. Are guidebooks destructive? Eugene, OR: Free Country Times (University of Oregon Outdoor Program); Spring: 5.

Lee, Robert G. 1975. The management of human components in the Yosemite National Park ecosystem. Yosemite, CA: Yosemite Institute. 134 p.

Lime, David W.; Lucas, Robert C. 1977. Good information improves the wilderness experience. Naturalist. 28(4): 18-20.

Lime, David W.; Anderson, Dorothy H.; McCool, Stephen F. 1978. An application of the simulator to a river recreation setting. In: Shechter, Mordechai; Lucas, Robert C. Simulation of recreational use for park and wilderness management. Baltimore, MD: The Johns Hopkins University Press: 153-174.

Lucas, Robert C. 1964. Wilderness perception and use: the example of the Boundary Waters Canoe Area. Natural Resources Journal. 3(3): 394-411.

Lucas, Robert C. 1979. Perceptions of non-motorized recreational impacts: a review of research findings. In: Ittner, Ruth; Potter, Dale R.; Agee, James K.; Anschell, Susie, eds. Conference proceedings: recreational impact on wildlands; 1978 October 27-29; Seattle, WA. U.S. Forest Service No. R-6-001-1979. Portland, OR: U.S. Department of Agriculture, Forest Service, Pacific Northwest Region: 24-31.

Lucas, Robert C. 1980. Use patterns and visitor characteristics, attitudes, and preferences in nine wilderness and other roadless areas. Res. Pap. INT-253. Ogden, UT: U.S. Department of Agriculture, Forest Service, Intermountain Forest and Range Experiment Station. 89 p.

Lucas, Robert C. 1981. Redistributing wilderness use through information supplied to visitors. Res. Pap. INT-277. Ogden, UT: U.S. Department of Agriculture, Forest Service, Intermountain Forest and Range Experiment Station. 15 p.

Lucas, Robert C. 1985. Visitor characteristics, use patterns, and attitudes in the Bob Marshall Wilderness Complex, 1970-82. Res. Pap. INT-345. Ogden, UT: U.S. Department of Agriculture, Forest Service, Intermountain Research Station. 32 p.

Lucas, Robert C.; Shechter, Mordechai. 1977. A recreational visitor travel simulation model as an aid to management planning. Simulation and Games. 8(3): 375-384.

Manning, Robert E. 1985. Crowding norms in backcountry settings: a review and synthesis. Journal of Leisure Research. 17(2): 75-89.

Manning, Robert E. 1986. Density and crowding in wilderness: search and research for satisfaction. In: Lucas, Robert C., compiler. Proceedings—national wilderness research conference: current research; 1985 July 23-26; Fort Collins, CO. Gen. Tech. Rep. INT-212. Ogden, UT: U.S. Department of Agriculture, Forest Service, Intermountain Research Station: 440-448.

Manning, Robert E.; Potter, Fletcher I. 1984. Computer simulation as a tool in teaching park and wilderness management. Journal of Environmental Education. 15(3): 3-9.

Martin, Burnham H. 1986. Hikers' opinions about fees for backcountry recreation. In: Lucas, Robert C., compiler. Proceedings—national wilderness research conference: current research; 1985 July 23-26; Fort Collins, CO. Gen. Tech. Rep. INT-212. Ogden, UT: U.S. Department of Agriculture, Forest Service, Intermountain Research Station: 483-488.

McCool, Stephen F.; Lime, David W. 1976. The wilderness area travel simulator: applications to river recreation management. Paper presented to interagency whitewater management conference; Salt Lake City, UT; 1976 February 11.

McCool, Stephen F.; Stankey, George H. 1986. Visitor attitudes toward wilderness fire management policy—1971-1984. Res. Pap. INT-357. Ogden, UT: U.S. Department of Agriculture, Forest Service, Intermountain Research Station. 7 p.

Muth, Robert M.; Clark, Roger N. 1978. Public participation in wilderness and backcountry litter control: a review of research and management experience. Gen. Tech. Rep. PNW-75. Portland, OR: U.S. Department of Agriculture, Forest Service, Pacific Northwest Forest and Range Experiment Station. 12 p.

Peterson, George L.; de Bettencourt, James 5.; Wang, Pai Kang. 1977. A Markov-based linear programming model of travel in the Boundary Waters Canoe Area. In: Proceedings: river recreation management and research symposium; 1977 January 24-27; Minneapolis, MN. Gen. Tech. Rep. NC-28. St. Paul, MN: U.S. Department of Agriculture, Forest Service, North Central Forest and Range Experiment Station: 342-350.

Peterson, R. Max. 1985. National Forest dimensions and dilemmas. In: Frome, Michael, ed. Issues in wilderness management. Boulder, CO: Westview Press: 36-52.

Pfister, Robert D.; Frankel, Robert E. 1974. The concept of carrying capacity: its application for management of Oregon's Scenic Waterway System. Interim report to Oregon State Marine Board. Salem, OR: 112 p.

Robertson, Rachel D. 1982. Visitor knowledge affects visitor behavior. In: Lime, David W., tech. coord. Forest and river recreation: research update. Misc. Publ. 18. St. Paul, MN: University of Minnesota, Agricultural Experiment Station: 49-51.

Robertson, Rachel D. 1986. Actual versus self-reported wilderness visitor behavior. In: Lucas, Robert C., compiler. Proceedings—national wilderness research conference: current research; 1985 July 23-26; Fort Collins, CO. Gen. Tech. Rep. INT-212. Ogden, UT: U.S. Department of Agriculture, Forest Service, Intermountain Research Station: 326-332.

Roggenbuck, Joseph W.; Berrier, Deborah L. 1982. A comparison of the effectiveness of two communication strategies in dispersing wilderness campers. Journal of Leisure Research. 14(1): 77-89.

Rowell, Allen L. 1986. A wilderness travel simulation model with graphic presentation of trail data. In: Lucas, Robert C., compiler. Proceedings—national wilderness research conference: current research; 1985 July 23-26; Fort Collins, CO. Gen. Tech. Rep. INT-212. Ogden, UT: U.S. Department of Agriculture, Forest Service, Intermountain Research Station: 478-482.

Schomaker, John H.; Lime, David W. 1986. Wilderness information specialists at portals: information disseminators and gatherers. In: Lucas, Robert C., compiler. Proceedings—national wilderness research conference: current research; 1985 July 23-26; Fort Collins, CO. Gen. Tech. Rep. INT-212. Ogden, UT: U.S. Department of Agriculture, Forest Service, Intermountain Research Station: 489-493.

Shechter, Mordechai. 1975. Simulation model of wilderness-area use. Washington, DC: Resources for the Future. 172 p. (Available from National Technical Information Service, Springfield, VA. Manual order No. PB 251 635, Program tapes order No. PB 251 634.)

Shechter, Mordechai; Lucas, Robert C. 1978. Simulation of recreational use for park and wilderness management. Baltimore, MD: The Johns Hopkins University Press. 220 p.

Shelby, Bo; Harris, Richard. 1985. Comparing methods for determining visitor evaluations of ecological impacts: site visits, photographs, and written descriptions. Journal of Leisure Research. 17(1): 56-57.

Shelby, Bo; Harris, Richard. 1986. User standards for ecological impacts at wilderness campsites. In: Lucas, Robert C., compiler. Proceedings—national wilderness research conference: current research; 1985 July 23-26; Fort Collins, CO. Gen. Tech. Rep. INT-212. Ogden, UT: U.S. Department of Agriculture, Forest Service, Intermountain Research Station: 166-171.

Shew, Richard L.; Saunders, Paul R.; Ford, Joseph D. 1986. Wilderness managers' perceptions of recreational horse use in the Northwestern United States. In: Lucas, Robert C., compiler. Proceedings—national wilderness research conference: current research; 1985 July 23-26; Fort Collins, CO. Gen. Tech. Rep. INT-212. Ogden, UT: U.S. Department of Agriculture, Forest Service, Intermountain Research Station: 320-325.

Smith, V. Kerry; Krutilla, John V. 1976. Structure and properties of a wilderness travel simulator: an application to the Spanish Peaks area. Baltimore, MD: The Johns Hopkins University Press. 173 p.

Stankey, George H. 1973. Visitor perception of wilderness recreation carrying capacity. Res. Pap. INT-142. Ogden, UT: U.S. Department of Agriculture, Forest Service, Intermountain Forest and Range Experiment Station. 61 p.

Stankey, George H. 1980. A comparison of carrying capacity perceptions among visitors to two wildernesses. Res. Pap. INT-242. Ogden, UT: U.S. Department of Agriculture, Forest Service, Intermountain Forest and Range Experiment Station. 34 p.

Stankey, George H.; Baden, John. 1977. Rationing wilderness use. Gen. Tech. Rep. INT-198. Ogden, UT: U.S. Department of Agriculture, Forest Service, Intermountain Forest and Range Experiment Station. 20 p.

Stankey, George H.; Brown, Perry J. 1981. A technique for recreation planning and management in tomorrow's forests. In: Proceedings: XVII IUFRO world congress, division 6; 1981 September 7-12; Kyoto, Japan. Kyoto, Japan: International Union of Forestry Research Organizations: 63-74.

Stankey, George H.; Cole, David N.; Lucas, Robert C.; Petersen, Margaret E.; Frissell, Sidney S. 1985. The Limits of Acceptable Change (LAC) system for wilderness planning. Gen. Tech. Rep. INT-176. Ogden, UT: U.S. Department of Agriculture, Forest Service, Intermountain Forest and Range Experiment Station. 37 p.

Stankey, George H.; Schreyer, Richard. 1987. Attitudes toward wilderness and factors affecting visitor behavior: a state-of-knowledge review. In: Lucas, Robert C., compiler. Proceedings—national wilderness research conference: issues, state-of-knowledge, future directions; 1985 July 23-26; Fort Collins, CO. Gen. Tech. Rep. INT-220. Ogden, UT: U.S. Department of Agriculture, Forest Service, Intermountain Research Station: 246-293.

Swain, Ralph W. 1986. Colorado wilderness violators: who they are and why they violate. Fort Collins, CO: Colorado State University. 107 p. Thesis.

Taylor, Jonathon G.; Mutch, Robert W. 1986. Fire in wilderness: public knowledge, acceptance, and perceptions. In: Lucas, Robert C., compiler. Proceedings—national wilderness research conference: current research; 1985 July 23-26; Fort Collins, CO. Gen. Tech. Rep. INT-212. Ogden, UT: U.S. Department of Agriculture, Forest Service, Intermountain Research Station: 49-59.

Taylor, Ronald B. 1972. No vacancy in the wilderness. Sierra Club Bulletin. 57(1): 5-8.

Underhill, A. Heaton; Xaba, A. Busa; Borkan, Ronald E. 1986. The wilderness use simulation model applied to Colorado River boating in Grand Canyon National Park, USA. Environmental Management. 10(3): 367-374.

U.S. Department of Agriculture, Forest Service. 1982. ROS users guide. Washington, DC. 38 p.

U.S. Department of the Interior, National Park Service. [n.d.]. Exploring the backcountry. [Camping regulations for Shenandoah National Park issued in 1986.] Luray, VA: Shenandoah National Park.

Washburne, Randel F.; Cole, David N. 1983. Problems and practices in wilderness management: a survey of managers. Res. Pap. INT-304. Ogden, UT: U.S. Department of Agriculture, Forest Service, Intermountain Forest and Range Experiment Station. 56 p.

ACKNOWLEDGMENTS

Edward Bloedel, Division of Recreation, USFS, Washington, DC (at the time of review—now recreation staff, Sawtooth National Forest, ID).

James Browning, graduate student, College of Forestry, Wildlife and Range Sciences, University of Idaho, Moscow.

Dr. William Hammitt, Professor of Forest Recreation, Department of Forestry, Wildlife, and Fisheries, University of Tennessee, Knoxville.

Robert Jacobsen, Superintendent (retired), Shenandoah National Park, VA.

Dr. Stephen McCool, Professor, School of Forestry, University of Montana, Missoula.

Table 17.1. Summary of impacts and consequences of alternative rationing systems.

| | User evaluation criteria | | | |
Rationing system	(col. 1) Clientele group benefited by system	(col. 2) Clientele group adversely affected by system	(col. 3) Experience to date with use of system in wilderness	(col. 4) Acceptability of system to wilderness users[1]
Request (Reservation)	Those able and/or willing to plan ahead; e.g., persons with structured lifestyles.	Those unable or unwilling to plan ahead; e.g.,persons with occupations that do not permit long-range planning, such as many professionals.	Main type of rationing system used in both national forest and national park wilderness.	Good acceptance in areas where used. Users in areas not currently rationed prefer this system.
Lottery (Chance)	No one identifiable group benefited. Those who examine probablities of success at different areas have better chance.	No one identifiable group discriminated against. Can discriminate against the unsuccessful applicant to whom wilderness is very important.	None for general wilderness use. Commonly used for allocating white-water river permits and big-game hunting licenses.	Low.
Queuing (First-come, first-served)	Those with low opportunity cost for their time (e.g., unemployed). Also favors users who live nearby.	Those persons with high opportunity cost of time. Also those persons who live some distance from areas. The cost of time is not recovered by anyone.	Used in conjunction with reservation system in San Jacinto Wilderness. Also used in some national park wildernesses.	Low to moderate.
Pricing (Fee)	Those able or willing to pay entry costs.	Those unwilling or unable to pay entry costs.	None.	Low to moderate.
Merit (Skill and knowledge)	Those able or willing to invest time and effort to meet requirements.	Those unable or unwilling to invest time and effort to meet requirements.	None. Merit is used to allocate use for some related activities such as technical mountain climbing and river running.	Not clearly known. Could vary considerably depending on level of training required to attain necessary proficiency and knowledge level.

1. Based on actual field experience as well as on evidence reported in visitor studies in Stankey 1973.

Table 17.1. cont.

Administrative evaluation criteria

(col. 5) *Difficulty for* *administrators*	*(col. 6)* *Efficiency-extent to which system can minimize problems of suboptimization*	*(col. 7)* *Principal way in which use impact is controlled*	*(col. 8)* *How system affects user behavior*[1]
Moderately difficult. Requires extra staffing, expanded hours. Recordkeeping can be substantial.	Low to moderate. Less use can occur because of no-shows, thus denying entry to others. Allocation of permits to applicants has little relationship to value of the experience as judged by the applicant.	Reducing visitor numbers. Controlling distribution of use in space and time by varying number of permits available at different trailheads or at different times.	Affects both spatial and temporal behavior.
Difficult to moderately difficult. Allocating permits over an entire use season could be very cumbersome.	Low. Because permits are assigned randomly, persons who place little value on wilderness stand equal chance of gaining entry with those who place high value on the opportunity.	Reducing visitor numbers. Controlling distribution of use in space and time by number of permits available at different places or times.	Affects both spatial and temporal behavior.
Difficulty low to moderate. Could require development of facilities to support visitors waiting in line.	Moderate. Because system rations primarily through a cost of time, it requires some measure of worth by participants.	Reducing visitor numbers. Controlling distribution of use in space and time by number of persons permitted to enter at different places or times.	Affects both spatial and temporal behavior. User must consider cost of time of waiting in line.
Moderate difficulty. Possibly some legal questions about imposing a fee for wilderness entry.	Moderate to high. Imposing a fee requires user to judge value of experience against costs. Uncertain as to how well use could be fine tuned with price.	Reducing visitor numbers. Controlling distribution of use in space and time by using differential prices.	Affects both spatial and temporal behavior. User must consider cost in dollars.
Difficult to moderately difficult. Initial investments to establish licensing program could be substantial.	Moderate to high. Requires users to make expenditures of time and effort (maybe dollars) to gain entry.	Some reduction in numbers as well as shifts in time and space. Major reduction in per capita impact.	Affects style of camping behavior.

1. This criterion is designed to measure how the different rationing systems would directly impact the behavior of wilderness users (e.g., where they go, when they go, how they behave, etc.).

As the final lands are allocated to the NWPS, management of the system will receive increased emphasis. Primary objectives will be to maintain the qualities of natural ecosystems in settings such as, here, in the Spanish Peaks area of the Lee Metcalf Wilderness, MT. Photo courtesy of the USFS.

18

FUTURE ISSUES AND CHALLENGES IN WILDERNESS MANAGEMENT

Preparation of this chapter was shared by John C. Hendee, George H. Stankey, and Robert C. Lucas.

WILDERNESS PAST, PRESENT, AND FUTURE

The preceding chapters have traced the development of the wilderness idea from Biblical times to the present. We have discussed the various values of wilderness, the threats to these values, and the types of management actions that might be employed to protect them. In summary, wilderness, as a land-use concept, has evolved a great deal over the past years, particularly since passage of the Wilderness Act in 1964, as has our capacity to manage it.

But what about the future? Our experience with wilderness, in terms of defining and managing it, has derived from a particular set of environmental and sociopolitical conditions. To what extent will these conditions prevail in the future and, to the extent that they change, how will these new conditions affect wilderness—its use and its value to society, and needs for its management?

Looking into the future is always a risky business. Many forecasters predict major and fundamental changes for the world tomorrow. Toffler's *The Third Wave*(1980) foresees a profoundly different world;

Megatrends(Naisbitt 1982) similarly anticipates that the world of tomorrow will be a different place than it is today.

Significantly, most futurists and forecasters agree that the nature of the future rests largely on what happens today. What we do today (or fail to do) largely shapes the kind of future we will deal with tomorrow. The implications for thinking about wilderness as we approach the beginning of the twenty-first century are clear. The kind of wilderness system we will have a generation or even a century from now will depend greatly on the actions we take today. This kind of thinking underlies the concern of many for designating as much wilderness as possible now; tomorrow, many options may be gone. But in addition to this, it is our central contention that the quality of the wilderness system in the future is substantially dependent on the steps we take now to manage our existing areas, and to set high standards for such management. As we noted in the opening chapter, failure to implement adequate management today, could dilute wilderness tomorrow.

Fig. 18.1. Recreational experiences dependent on large tracts of wildland will one day be confined mainly to the NWPS. (above) Backpackers set up camp in the Endicott River Wilderness, AK; (below right) a packstring follows a trail high in the Marble Mountain Wilderness, northern CA. Photos courtesy of the USFS.

NEW PROBLEMS AND CHALLENGES

But the question still remains as to what new problems or changes in conditions in the future will confront and challenge wilderness managers and policy makers. Some foresee a highly regimented future, with wilderness recreation use controlled, computerized, and regulated in almost an Orwellian "Big Brother" sense. Others see wilderness as only a transitory fad, with use and interest diminishing in the future. Some see the wilderness resource increasing in importance and value, not only for its direct recreational values, but also as the repository of increased understanding about the world around us, and as a source of material values to humankind, such as for medicines and genetic stock for agriculture and forestry. And some see wilderness remaining as an important, even essential component of a spectrum of land uses, unique recreational opportunities and spiritual values (fig. 18.1).

Our view of wilderness in the future is optimistic. Little evidence supports the idea that public interest is waning, that wilderness is just a fad. To the contrary, wilderness has shown remarkable tenacity as an item on the public agenda, and we think public interest will continue. In fact, we would point to the growing international interest in, and support for, wilderness as one measure of the strength and resiliency of the wilderness idea. Whatever problems exist with the wilderness program in the United States, it nevertheless stands as an achievement that many other nations envy and hold up as a model to which they aspire, namely a special category of protection for lands with natural and wild values. Again, we see an interesting historical tie here; at the close of

the nineteenth century, wilderness and the protection of wild nature represented a cultural achievement that a young nation could point to as a source of pride and accomplishment. Now, a century later, wilderness continues to represent a major cultural achievement of American society.

Some wildernesses have experienced extremely high use pressures, necessitating intensive management, including rationing. Undoubtedly, this will remain the case in some areas. Nevertheless, we do not foresee a future in which the wilderness recreationist must book a time and route months ahead, where rangers lurk behind every tree, and where every step is monitored by sensors and satellites. Although the past 25 years have shown a generally steady increase in the level of recreational use of wilderness, more recently this trend has begun to alter, characterized by a growing stability, and in some cases, an outright decline in use. The reasons for this are not altogether clear, as we noted in chapter 14, but it is at least partially linked to the pervasive changes in the structure and composition of society—particularly in the age, distribution, and socioeconomic status of its people. As in all systems, growth could not simply go on forever.

A future of stabilizing use certainly offers some respite for managers constantly struggling to catch up. We may now be approaching a time when some of the seemingly intractable problems associated with managing use can be overtaken. In fact, we will now be able to engage in a kind of planning that is more proactive in nature, rather than continually reacting to the latest crisis to cross the desk. It may provide the opportunity for increased attention to the lighthanded, indirect approaches to management, which both managers and users alike prefer. The kind of "police state wilderness" some foresaw is not inevitable.

TRENDS IN WILDERNESS USE

The changing nature and levels of direct recreational use of wilderness may cause us to return to the question of "Why preserve wilderness?" In the past, we often spoke of the need to set aside more wilderness because of the seemingly endless recreational demands placed on such areas. Does a possible future of declining recreational use of wilderness mean that more wilderness is not needed? Not necessarily, by any means. But perhaps now we need to place greater emphasis on the establishment of a system that better provides a spectrum of environmental, scientific, and social values (fig. 18.2); ecosystem representation, protection of genetic diversity, and so on. During the 1960s, 1970s, and early 1980s, increasing recreational use of wilderness provided an important and immediately obvious justification for its protection; it has also been the source of many of the most pressing management challenges. A future of stabilized recreational use could lead to both an improved management situation and a refocused appraisal of needed additions.

MANAGEMENT FUNDING AND RESOURCES

The future may see increased public sector funding of wilderness management. Financial constraints, demand for cost effectiveness, and efficient delivery of services probably will characterize tomorrow, along with growing recognition that wilderness protection is possible only with adequate management. We think this portends new ways of accomplishing wilderness management. This includes alliances between different levels of government and among the public, private, and voluntary sectors of

Fig. 18.2. Wilderness provides a unique setting for educational, personal growth, and human development programs. A group under the supervision of the National Outdoor Leadership School plan a cross-country hike in the Popo Agie Wilderness, WY. Photo courtesy of the National Outdoor Leadership School.

society. Many of these changes are already well under way. In recent years, many crucial wilderness management jobs—trail construction and maintenance, campsite rehabilitation, visitor contact—have been accomplished only because of such action. Trails have been built by conservaion groups and local activity clubs. Volunteers have provided information to backpackers and have collected basic resource inventory data. These are but a few examples of accomplishing vital tasks using new thinking. If this sort of management characterizes the future, wilderness managers will have to develop new skills in the management and organization of people. Effective work by volunteers and other partners requires strong facilitation and guidance by professional wilderness managers. Volunteers must supplement professionals, not substitute for them, or quality control will suffer and continuity of programs will diminish (fig. 18.3).

THE WILDERNESS LEGACY

When the first edition of this book was published in 1978, less than 10 million acres of wilderness existed. Since then, the NWPS has grown more than ninefold. A 100-million-acre NWPS is a virtual certainty and will likely grow beyond that in the next decade. Few people, even among the most dedicated wilderness enthusiasts, foresaw such an outcome. It is further evidence, in our view, of the strength and breadth of support for wilderness.

Ironically, the rapid expansion of wilderness,

Fig. 18.3. Effective wilderness management requires long-term, adequately funded programs led by professionals. A wilderness manager gathers data for a campsite-condition study in the Selway-Bitterroot Wilderness, ID. Photo courtesy of the USFS.

Figure 18.4. The NWPS, constituting less than 2 percent of the conterminous 48 states, provides a degree of naturalness and solitude and many other unique values found only in wilderness. Shown here is the Everglades National Park Wilderness, FL. Photo courtesy of the NPS.

coupled with the many laws Congress has passed to create such a system, has raised fears about a gradual deterioration in standards, and perhaps even more serious, the slow, insidious creep of more lenient, less-demanding qualities for areas admitted to the NWPS. But by and large, the demanding standards of wilderness management described by the act have been endorsed by the words and actions of Congress. And although some areas admitted to the NWPS currently do not meet certain standards for wilderness, they provide an opportunity for managers to begin the process of restoring wilderness qualities. As the late Senator Frank Church (1977) has noted, this opportunity to restore wilderness qualities represents the "great promise of the Wilderness Act."

Finally, we believe that the future will further affirm the important symbolic values underlying the preservation of wilderness. Less than 100 years ago, the frontier of America officially closed. Today, the nation has been occupied and modified virtually from shore to shore. At 90.8 million acres, the wilderness system is, in one sense, vast and expansive (fig. 18.4). Yet, we must remember this constitutes only about 4 percent of the nation's total land area, and

less than 2 percent of the conterminous 48 states. How much more will be added—maybe another 1 percent? Beyond that, there is no more. Beyond that, the wilderness values that contribute to society—historical, ecological, recreational, spiritual, and inspirational—will be available only from what we have been able to preserve. With the supply fixed, only sensitive and judicious management will ensure the capacity of wilderness to supply such values into the future.

REFERENCES

Church, Frank. 1977. Wilderness in a balanced land use framework. Moscow, ID: University of Idaho Wilderness Research Center, Wilderness Resource Distinguished Lectureship 1. 18 p.

Naisbitt, John. 1982. Megatrends: ten new directions transforming our lives. New York: Warner Books. 290 p.

Toffler, Alvin. 1980. The third wave. New York: Morrow. 544 p.

APPENDIX A—THE WILDERNESS ACT OF 1964

Public Law 88-577
88th Congress, S. 4
September 3, 1964

AN ACT

To establish a National Wilderness Preservation System for the permanent good of the whole people, and for other purposes.

Be it enacted by the Senate and House of Representatives of the United States of America in Congress assembled,

SHORT TITLE

SECTION 1. This Act may be cited as the "Wilderness Act".

WILDERNESS SYSTEM ESTABLISHED STATEMENT OF POLICY

Sec. 2. (a) In order to assure that an increasing population, accompanied by expanding settlement and growing mechanization, does not occupy and modify all areas within the United States and its possessions, leaving no lands designated for preservation and protection in their natural condition, it is hereby declared to be the policy of the Congress to secure for the American people of present and future generations the benefits of an enduring resource of wilderness. For this purpose there is hereby established a National Wilderness Preservation System to be composed of federally owned areas designated by Congress as "wilderness areas", and these shall be administered for the use and enjoyment of the American people in such manner as will leave them unimpaired for future use and enjoyment as wilderness, and so as to provide for the protection of these areas, the preservation of their wilderness character, and for the gathering and dissemination of information regarding their use and enjoyment as wilderness; and no Federal lands shall be designated as "wilderness areas" except as provided for in this Act or by a subsequent Act.

(b) The inclusion of an area in the National Wilderness Preservation System notwithstanding, the area shall continue to be managed by the Department and agency having jurisdiction thereover immediately before its inclusion in the National Wilderness Preservation System unless otherwise provided by Act of Congress. No appropriation shall be available for the payment of expenses or salaries for the administration of the National Wilderness Preservation System as a separate unit nor shall any appropriations be available for additional personnel stated as being required solely for the purpose of managing or administering areas solely because they are included within the National Wilderness Preservation System.

78 STAT. 890.
78 STAT. 891.

DEFINITION OF WILDERNESS

(c) A wilderness, in contrast with those areas where man and his own works dominate the landscape, is hereby recognized as an area where the earth and its community of life are untrammeled by man, where man himself is a visitor who does not remain. An area of wilderness is further defined to mean in this Act an area of undeveloped Federal land retaining its primeval character and influence, without permanent improvements or human habitation, which is protected and managed so as to preserve its natural conditions and which (1) generally appears to have been affected primarily by the forces of nature, with the imprint of man's work substantially unnoticeable; (2) has outstanding opportunities for solitude or a primitive and unconfined type of recreation; (3) has at least five thousand acres of land or is of sufficient size as to make practicable its preservation and use in an unimpaired condition; and (4) may also contain ecological, geological, or other features of scientific, educational, scenic, or historical value.

NATIONAL WILDERNESS PRESERVATION SYSTEM—EXTENT OF SYSTEM

Sec. 3. (a) All areas within the national forests classified at least 30 days before the effective date of this Act by the Secretary of Agriculture or the Chief of the Forest Service as "wilderness", "wild", or "canoe" are hereby designated as wilderness areas. The Secretary of Agriculture shall—

(1) Within one year after the effective date of this Act, file a map and legal description of each wilderness area with the Interior and Insular Affairs Committees of the United States Senate and the House of Representatives, and such descriptions shall have the same force and effect as if included in this Act: *Provided, however,* That correction of clerical and typographical errors in such legal descriptions and maps may be made.

(2) Maintain, available to the public, records pertaining to said wilderness areas, including maps and legal descriptions, copies of regulations governing them, copies of public notices of, and reports submitted to Congress regarding pending additions, eliminations, or modifications. Maps, legal descriptions, and regulations pertaining to wilderness areas within their respective jurisdictions also shall be available to the public in the offices of regional foresters, national forest supervisors, and forest rangers.

(b) The Secretary of Agriculture shall, within ten years after the enactment of this Act, review, as to its suitability or nonsuitability for preservation as wilderness, each area in the national forests classified on the effective date of this Act by the Secretary of Agriculture or the Chief of the Forest Service as "primitive" and report his findings to the President. The President shall advise the United States Senate and House of Representatives of his recommendations with respect to the designation as "wilderness" or other reclassification of each area on which review has been completed, together with maps and a definition of boundaries. Such advice shall be given with respect to not less than one-third of all the areas now classified as "primitive" within three years after the enactment of this Act, not less than two-thirds within seven years after the enactment of this Act, and the remaining areas within ten years after the enactment of this Act. Each recommendation of the President for designation as "wilderness" shall become effective only if so provided by an Act of Congress. Areas classified as "primitive" on the effective date of this Act shall continue to be administered under the rules and regulations affecting such areas on the effective date of this Act until Congress has determined otherwise. Any such area may be increased in size by the President at the time he submits his recommendations to the Congress by not more than five thousand acres with no more than one thousand two hundred and eighty acres of such increase in any one compact unit; if it is proposed to increase the size of any such area by more than five thousand acres or by more than one thousand two hundred and eighty acres in any one compact unit the increase in size shall not become effective until acted upon by Congress. Nothing herein contained shall limit the President in proposing, as part of his recommendations to Congress, the alteration of existing boundaries of primitive areas or recommending the addition of any contiguous area of national forest lands predominantly of wilderness value. Notwithstanding any other provisions of this Act, the Secretary of Agriculture may complete his review and delete such area as may be necessary, but not to exceed seven thousand acres, from the southern tip of the Gore Range-Eagles Nest Primitive Area, Colorado, if the Secretary determines that such action is in the public interest.

(c) Within ten years after the effective date of this Act the Secretary of the Interior shall review every roadless area of five thousand contiguous acres or more in the national parks, monuments and other units of the national park system and every such area of, and every roadless island within, the national wildlife refuges and game ranges, under his jurisdiction on the effective date of this Act and shall report to the President his recommendation as to the suitability or nonsuitability of each such area or island for preservation as wilderness. The President shall advise the President of the Senate and the Speaker of the House of Representatives of his recommendation with respect to the designation as wilderness of each such area or island on which review has been completed, together with a map thereof and a definition of its boundaries. Such advice shall be given with respect to not less than one-third of the areas and islands to be reviewed under this subsection within three years after enactment of this Act, not less than two-thirds within seven years of enactment of this Act, and the remainder within ten years of enactment of this Act. A recommendation of the President for designation as wilderness shall become effective only if so provided by an Act of Congress. Nothing contained herein shall, by implication or otherwise, be construed to lessen the present statutory authority of the Secretary of the Interior with respect to the maintenance of roadless areas within units of the national park system.

(d)(1) The Secretary of Agriculture and the Secretary of the Interior shall, prior to submitting any recommendations to the President with respect to the suitability of any area for preservation as wilderness—

(A) give such public notice of the proposed action as they deem appropriate, including publication in the Federal Register and in a newspaper having general circulation in the area or areas in the vicinity of the affected land;

(B) hold a public hearing or hearings at a location or locations convenient to the area affected. The hearings shall be announced through such means as the respective Secretaries involved deem appropriate, including notices in the Federal Register and in newspapers of general circulation in the

Classification.

Presidential recommendation to Congress.

Congressional approval.

78 STAT. 891.
78 STAT. 892

Report to President.

Presidential recommendation to Congress.

Congressional approval.

Suitability.

Publication in Federal Register.

Hearings.

Publication in Federal Register.

area: *Provided*, That if the lands involved are located in more than one State, at least one hearing shall be held in each State in which a portion of the land lies;

79 STAT. 892.
78 STAT. 893.

(C) at least thirty days before the date of a hearing advise the Governor of each State and the governing board of each county, or in Alaska the borough, in which the lands are located, and Federal departments and agencies concerned, and invite such officials and Federal agencies to submit their views on the proposed action at the hearing or by no later than thirty days following the date of the hearing.

(2) Any views submitted to the appropriate Secretary under the provisions of (1) of this subsection with respect to any area shall be included with any recommendations to the President and to Congress with respect to such area.

Proposed modification.

(e) Any modification or adjustment of boundaries of any wilderness area shall be recommended by the appropriate Secretary after public notice of such proposal and public hearing or hearings as provided in subsection (d) of this section. The proposed modification or adjustment shall then be recommended with map and description thereof to the President. The President shall advise the United States Senate and the House of Representatives of his recommendations with respect to such modification or adjustment and such recommendations shall become effective only in the same manner as provided for in subsections (b) and (c) of this section.

USE OF WILDERNESS AREAS

Sec. 4. (a) The purposes of this Act are hereby declared to be within and supplemental to the purposes for which national forests and units of the national park and national wildlife refuge systems are established and administered and—

16 USC 475.
16 USC 528-531.

(1) Nothing in this Act shall be deemed to be in interference with the purpose for which national forests are established as set forth in the Act of June 4, 1897 (30 Stat. 11), and the Multiple-Use Sustained-Yield Act of June 12, 1960 (74 Stat. 215).

16 USC 577-577b.

(2) Nothing in this Act shall modify the restrictions and provisions of the Shipstead-Nolan Act (Public Law 539, Seventy-first Congress, July 10, 1930; 46 Stat. 1020), the Thye-Blatnik Act (Public Law 733, Eightieth Congress, June 22, 1948; 62 Stat. 568), and the Humphrey-Thye-Blatnik-Andersen Act (Public Law 607, Eighty-fourth Congress, June 22, 1956; 70 Stat. 326), as applying to the Superior National Forest or the regulations of the Secretary of Agriculture.

16 USC 577c-577h.
16 USC 577d-l,
577g-l, 577h.

(3) Nothing in this Act shall modify the statutory authority under which units of the national park system are created. Further, the designation of any area of any park, monument, or other unit of the national park system as a wilderness area pursuant to this Act shall in no manner lower the standards evolved for the use and preservation of such park, monument, or other unit of the national park system in accordance with the Act of August 25, 1916, the statutory authority under which the area was created, or any other Act of Congress which might pertain to or affect such area, including, but not limited to, the Act of June 8, 1906 (34 Stat. 225; 16 U.S.C. 432 et seq.); section 3(2) of the Federal Power Act (16 U.S.C. 796(2)); and the Act of August 21, 1935 (49 Stat. 666; 16 U.S.C. 461 et seq.).

39 Stat. 535.
16 USC 1 et seq.

41 Stat. 1063.
49 Stat. 838.

78 STAT. 893.
78 STAT. 894.

(b) Except as otherwise provided in this Act, each agency administering any area designated as wilderness shall be responsible for preserving the wilderness character of the area and shall so administer such area for such other purposes for which it may have been established as also to preserve its wilderness character. Except as otherwise provided in this Act, wilderness areas shall be devoted to the public purposes of recreational, scenic, scientific, educational, conservation, and historical use.

PROHIBITION OF CERTAIN USES

(c) Except as specifically provided for in this Act, and subject to existing private rights, there shall be no commercial enterprise and no permanent road within any wilderness area designated by this Act and, except as necessary to meet minimum requirements for the administration of the area for the purpose of this Act (including measures required in emergencies involving the health and safety of persons within the area), there shall be no temporary road, no use of motor vehicles, motorized equipment or motorboats, no landing of aircraft, no other form of mechanical transport, and no structure or installation within any such area.

SPECIAL PROVISIONS

(d) The following special provisions are hereby made:

(1) Within wilderness areas designated by this Act the use of aircraft or motorboats, where these uses have already become established, may be permitted to continue subject to such restrictions as the Secretary of Agriculture deems desirable. In addition, such measures may be taken as may be necessary in the control of fire, insects and diseases, subject to such conditions as the Secretary deems desirable.

(2) Nothing in this Act shall prevent within national forest wilderness areas any activity, including prospecting, for the purpose of gathering information about mineral or other resources, if such activity is carried on in a manner compatible with the preservation of the wilderness environment. Furthermore, in accordance with such program as the Secretary of the Interior shall develop and conduct in consultation with the Secretary of Agriculture, such areas shall be surveyed on a planned, recurring basis consistent with the concept of wilderness preservation by the Geological Survey and the Bureau of Mines to determine the mineral values, if any, that may be present; and the results of such surveys shall be made available to the public and submitted to the President and Congress.

(3) Notwithstanding any other provisions of this Act, until midnight December 31, 1983, the United States mining laws and all laws pertaining to mineral leasing shall, to the same extent as applicable prior to the effective date of this Act, extend to those national forest lands designated by this Act as "wilderness areas"; subject, however, to such reasonable regulations governing ingress and egress as may be prescribed by the Secretary of Agriculture consistent with the use of the land for mineral location and development and exploration, drilling, and production, and use of land for transmission lines, waterlines, telephone lines, or facilities necessary in exploring, drilling, producing, mining, and processing operations, including where essential the use of mechanized ground or air equipment and restoration as near as practicable of the surface of the land disturbed in performing prospecting, location, and, in oil and gas leasing, discovery work, exploration, drilling, and production, as soon as they have served their purpose. Mining locations lying within the boundaries of said wilderness areas shall be held and used solely for mining or processing operations and uses reasonably incident thereto; and hereafter, subject to valid existing rights, all patents issued under the mining laws of the United States affecting national forest lands designated by this Act as wilderness areas shall convey title to the mineral deposits within the claim, together with the right to cut and use so much of the mature timber therefrom as may be needed in the extraction, removal, and beneficiation of the mineral deposits, if needed timber is not otherwise reasonably available, and if the timber is cut under sound principles of forest management as defined by the national forest rules and regulations, but each such patent shall reserve to the United States all title in or to the surface of the lands and products thereof, and no use of the surface of the claim or the resources therefrom not reasonably required for carrying on mining or prospecting shall be allowed except as otherwise expressly provided in this Act: *Provided*, That, unless hereafter specifically authorized, no patent within wilderness areas designated by this Act shall issue after December 31, 1983, except for the valid claims existing on or before December 31, 1983. Mining claims located after the effective date of this Act within the boundaries of wilderness areas designated by this Act shall create no rights in excess of those rights which may be patented under the provisions of this subsection. Mineral leases, permits, and licenses covering lands within national forest wilderness areas designated by this Act shall contain such reasonable stipulations as may be prescribed by the Secretary of Agriculture for the protection of the wilderness character of the land consistent with the use of the land for the purposes for which they are leased, permitted, or licensed. Subject to valid rights then existing, effective January 1, 1984, the minerals in lands designated by this Act as wilderness areas are withdrawn from all forms of appropriation under the mining laws and from disposition under all laws pertaining to mineral leasing and all amendments thereto.

(4) Within wilderness areas in the national forests designated by the Act, (1) the President may, within a specific area and in accordance with such regulations as he may deem desirable, authorize prospecting for water resources, the establishment and maintenance of reservoirs, water-conservation works, power projects, transmission lines, and other facilities needed in the public interest, including the road construction and maintenance essential to development and use thereof, upon his determination that such use or uses in the specific area will better serve the interests of the United States and the people thereof than will its denial; and (2) the grazing of livestock, where established prior to the effective date of this Act, shall be permitted to continue subject to such reasonable regulations as are deemed necessary by the Secretary of Agriculture.

(5) Other provisions of this Act to the contrary notwithstanding, the management of the Boundary Waters Canoe Area, formerly designated as the Superior, Little Indian Sioux, and Caribou Roadless Areas, in the Superior National Forest, Minnesota, shall be in accordance with regulations established by the Secretary of Agriculture in accordance with the general purpose of maintaining, without unnecessary restrictions on other uses, including that of timber, the primitive character of the area, particularly in the vicinity of lakes, streams, and portages: *Provided*, That nothing in this Act shall preclude the continuance within the area of any already established use of motorboats.

(6) Commercial services may be performed within the wilderness areas designated by this Act to the extent necessary for activities which are proper for realizing the recreational or other wilderness purposes of the areas.

Mineral leases, claims, etc.

78 STAT. 894.
78 STAT. 895.

Water resources.

78 STAT. 895.
78 STAT. 896.

(7) Nothing in this Act shall constitute an express or implied claim or denial on the part of the Federal Government as to exemption from State water laws.

(8) Nothing in this Act shall be construed as affecting the jurisdiction or responsibilities of the several States with respect to wildlife and fish in the national forests.

STATE AND PRIVATE LANDS WITHIN WILDERNESS AREAS

SEC. 5. (a) In any case where State-owned or privately owned land is completely surrounded by national forest lands within areas designated by this Act as wilderness, such State or private owner shall be given such rights as may be necessary to assure adequate access to such State-owned or privately owned land by such State or private owner and their successors in interest, or the State-owned land or privately owned land shall be exchanged for federally owned land in the same State of approximately equal value under authorities available to the Secretary of Agriculture: *Provided, however,* That the United States shall not transfer to a State or private owner any mineral interests unless the State or private owner relinquishes or causes to be relinquished to the United States the mineral interest in the surrounded land.

Transfers, restriction.

78 STAT. 896.

(b) In any case where valid mining claims or other valid occupancies are wholly within a designated national forest wilderness area, the Secretary of Agriculture shall, by reasonable regulations consistent with the preservation of the area as wilderness, permit ingress and egress to such surrounded areas by means which have been or are being customarily enjoyed with respect to other such areas similarly situated.

Acquisition.

(c) Subject to the appropriation of funds by Congress, the Secretary of Agriculture is authorized to acquire privately owned land within the perimeter of any area designated by this Act as wilderness if (1) the owner concurs in such acquisition or (2) the acquisition is specifically authorized by Congress.

GIFTS, BEQUESTS, AND CONTRIBUTIONS

SEC. 6. (a) The Secretary of Agriculture may accept gifts or bequests of land within wilderness areas designated by this Act for preservation as wilderness. The Secretary of Agriculture may also accept gifts or bequests of land adjacent to wilderness areas designated by this Act for preservation as wilderness if he has given sixty days advance notice thereof to the President of the Senate and the Speaker of the House of Representatives. Land accepted by the Secretary of Agriculture under this section shall become part of the wilderness area involved. Regulations with regard to any such land may be in accordance with such agreements, consistent with the policy of this Act, as are made at the time of such gift, or such conditions, consistent with such policy, as may be included in, and accepted with, such bequest.

(b) The Secretary of Agriculture or the Secretary of the Interior is authorized to accept private contributions and gifts to be used to further the purposes of this Act.

ANNUAL REPORTS

SEC. 7. At the opening of each session of Congress, the Secretaries of Agriculture and Interior shall jointly report to the President for transmission to Congress on the status of the wilderness system, including a list and descriptions of the areas in the system, regulations in effect, and other pertinent information, together with any recommendations they may care to make.

Approved September 3, 1964.

LEGISLATIVE HISTORY:

HOUSE REPORTS: No. 1538 accompanying H. R. 9070 (Comm. on Interior & Insular Affairs) and No. 1829 (Comm. of Conference).
SENATE REPORT No. 109 (Comm. on Interior & Insular Affairs).
CONGRESSIONAL RECORD:

Vol. 109 (1963):	Apr. 4, 8,	considered in Senate.
	Apr. 9,	considered and passed Senate.
Vol. 110 (1964):	July 28,	considered in House.
	July 30,	considered and passed House, amended, in lieu of H. R. 9070.
	Aug. 20,	House and Senate agreed to conference report.

The National Wilderne
1964–

WILDERNESS AREA GRAPHICS BY LIZ BOUSSARD

reservation System 1964–1989

Wilderness Area	Acres	Year Designated	Agency	Public Land Unit
NEW JERSEY				
Brigantine	6,681	1975	FWS	Brigantine NWR
Great Swamp	3,660	1968	FWS	Great Swamp NWR
State Total: 10,341				
NEW MEXICO				
Aldo Leopold	201,966	1980	USFS	Gila NF
Apache Kid	44,650	1980	USFS	Cibola NF
Bandelier	23,267	1976	NPS	Bandelier NM
Bisti	3,968	1984	BLM	Albuquerque District
Blue Range	30,000	1980	USFS	Apache, Gila NFs
Bosque del Apache	30,287	1975	FWS	Bosque del Apache NWR
Capitan Mountains	34,513	1980	USFS	Lincoln NF
Carlsbad Caverns	33,125	1978	NPS	Carlsbad Caverns NP
Cebolla	60,000	1987	BLM	Albuquerque District
Chama River Canyon	50,260	1978	USFS	Carson, Santa Fe NFs
Cruces Basin	18,000	1980	USFS	Carson NF
De-na-zin	23,872	1984	BLM	Albuquerque District
Dome	5,200	1980	USFS	Santa Fe NF
Gila	557,819	1964 1980	USFS	Gila NF
Latir Peak	20,000	1980	USFS	Carson NF
Manzano Mountain	36,650	1978	USFS	Cibola NF
Pecos	223,333	1964 1980	USFS	Carson, Santa Fe NFs
Salt Creek	9,621	1970	FWS	Bitterlake NWR
San Pedro Parks	41,132	1964	USFS	Santa Fe NF
Sandia Mountain	37,028	1978 1980 1984	USFS	Cibola NF
West Malpais	38,210	1987	BLM	Albuquerque District
Wheeler Peak	19,661	1964 1980	USFS	Carson NF
White Mountain	48,366	1964 1980	USFS	Lincoln NF
Withington	18,869	1980	USFS	Cibola NF
State Total: 1,609,797				
NEW YORK				
Fire Island	1,363	1980	NPS	Fire Island National Seashore
State Total: 1,363				
NORTH CAROLINA				
Birkhead Mountains	4,790	1984	USFS	Uwharrie NF
Catfish Lake South	7,600	1984	USFS	Croatan NF
Ellicott Rock	4,022	1975 1984	USFS	Nantahala NF
Joyce Kilmer—Slickrock	13,181	1975 1984	USFS	Nantahala NF
Linville Gorge	10,975	1964 1984	USFS	Pisgah NF
Middle Prong	7,900	1984	USFS	Pisgah NF
Pocosin	11,000	1984	USFS	Croatan NF
Pond Pine	1,860	1984	USFS	Croatan NF
Sheep Ridge	9,540	1984	USFS	Croatan NF
Shining Rock	18,450	1964 1984	USFS	Pisgah NF
Southern Nantahala	10,900	1984	USFS	Nantahala NF
Swanquarter	8,785	1976	FWS	Swanquarter NWR
State Total: 109,003				
NORTH DAKOTA				
Chase Lake	4,155	1975	FWS	Chase Lake NWR
Lostwood	5,577	1975	FWS	Lostwood NWR
Theodore Roosevelt	29,920	1978	NPS	Theodore Roosevelt NP
State Total: 39,652				
OHIO				
West Sister Island	77	1975	FWS	West Sister Island NWR
State Total: 77				
OKLAHOMA				
Black Fork Mountain	4,583	1988	USFS	Ouachita NF
Upper Kiamichi River	9,371	1988	USFS	Ouachita NF
Wichita Mountains	8,570	1970	FWS	Wichita Mountains NWR
State Total: 22,524				
OREGON				
Badger Creek	24,000	1984	USFS	Mount Hood NF
Black Canyon	13,400	1984	USFS	Ochoco NF
Boulder Creek	19,100	1984	USFS	Umpqua NF
Bridge Creek	5,400	1984	USFS	Ochoco NF
Bull of the Woods	34,900	1984	USFS	Mount Hood, Willamette NFs
Columbia	39,000	1984	USFS	Mount Hood NF
Cummins Creek	9,300	1984	USFS	Siuslaw NF
Diamond Peak	52,337	1964 1984	USFS	Deschutes, Willamette NFs
Drift Creek	5,800	1984	USFS	Siuslaw NF
Eagle Cap	358,461	1964 1972 1984	USFS	Wallowa-Whitman NF
Gearhart Mountain	22,809	1964 1984	USFS	Fremont NF
Grassy Knob	17,200	1984	USFS	Siskiyou NF
Hells Canyon	130,095	1975 1984	USFS	Wallowa-Whitman NF
Hells Canyon	1,038	1984	BLM	Vale District
Kalmiopsis	179,700	1964 1978	USFS	Siskiyou NF
Menagerie	4,725	1984	USFS	Willamette NF
Middle Santiam	7,500	1984	USFS	Willamette NF
Mill Creek	17,400	1984	USFS	Ochoco NF
Monument Rock	19,800	1984	USFS	Malheur, Wallowa-Whitman NF
Mount Hood	46,520	1964 1978	USFS	Mt. Hood NF
Mount Jefferson	107,008	1968 1984	USFS	Deschutes, Mt. Hood, Willamette NFs
Mount Thielsen	55,100	1984	USFS	Umpqua, Winema, Willamette NFs
Mount Washington	52,516	1964 1984	USFS	Deschutes, Willamette NFs
Mountain Lake	23,071	1964	USFS	Winema NF
North Fork John Day	121,400	1984	USFS	Wallowa-Whitman, Umatilla NFs
North Fork Umatilla	20,200	1984	USFS	Umatilla NF
Oregon Islands	5	1978	BLM	Coos Bay District
Oregon Islands	480	1970 1978	FWS	Oregon Islands NWR
Red Buttes	3,750	1984	USFS	Siskiyou NF
Rock Creek	7,400	1984	USFS	Siuslaw NF
Rogue-Umpqua Divide	33,200	1984	USFS	Umpqua, Rogue River NFs
Salmon-Huckleberry	44,560	1984	USFS	Mount Hood NF
Sky Lakes	116,300	1984	USFS	Rogue River, Winema NF
Strawberry Mountain	68,303	1964 1984	USFS	Malheur NF
Table Rock	5,500	1984	BLM	Salem District
Three Arch Rocks	15	1970	FWS	Three Arch Rocks NWR
Three Sisters	285,202	1964 1978 1984	USFS	Deschutes, Willamette NFs
Waldo Lake	39,200	1984	USFS	Willamette NF
Wenaha-Tucannon	66,375	1978	USFS	Umatilla NF
Wild Rogue	25,658	1978	USFS	Siskiyou NF
Wild Rogue	10,160	1978	BLM	Medford District
State Total: 2,093,888				
PENNSYLVANIA				
Allegheny Islands	368	1984	USFS	Allegheny NF
Hickory Creek	9,337	1984	USFS	Allegheny NF
State Total: 9,705				
SOUTH CAROLINA				
Cape Romain	29,000	1975	FWS	Cape Romain NWR
Congaree Swamp National Monument	15,010	1988	NPS	
Ellicott Rock	2,809	1975	USFS	Sumter NF
Hell Hole Bay	1,980	1980	USFS	Francis Marion NF
Little Wambaw Swamp	5,000	1980	USFS	Francis Marion NF
Wambaw Creek	1,640	1980	USFS	Francis Marion NF
Wambaw Swamp	5,100	1980	USFS	Francis Marion NF
State Total: 60,539				
SOUTH DAKOTA				
Badlands	64,250	1976	NPS	Badlands NP
Black Elk	9,824	1980	USFS	Black Hills NF
State Total: 74,074				
TENNESSEE				
Bald River Gorge	3,887	1984	USFS	Cherokee NF
Big Frog	7,972	1984 1986	USFS	Cherokee NF
Big Laurel Branch	6,251	1986	USFS	Cherokee NF
Citico Creek	16,000	1984	USFS	Cherokee NF
Cohutta	1,795	1975	USFS	Cherokee NF
Gee Creek	2,493	1975	USFS	Cherokee NF
Joyce Kilmer—Slickrock	3,832	1975	USFS	Cherokee NF
Little Frog Mountain	4,800	1986	USFS	Cherokee NF
Pond Mountain	6,665	1986	USFS	Cherokee NF
Sampson Mountain	8,319	1986	USFS	Cherokee NF
Unaka Mountain	4,700	1986	USFS	Cherokee NF
State Total: 66,714				
TEXAS				
Big Slough	3,000	1984	USFS	Davy Crockett NF
Guadalupe Mountains	46,850	1978	NPS	Guadalupe Mountains NP
Indian Mounds	9,946	1984	USFS	Sabine NF
Little Lake Creek	4,000	1984	USFS	Sam Houston NF
Turkey Hill	5,400	1984	USFS	Angelina NF
Upland Island	12,000	1984	USFS	Angelina NF
State Total: 81,196				
UTAH				
Ashdown Gorge	7,000	1984	USFS	Dixie NF
Beaver Dam Mountains	2,597	1984	BLM	Cedar City District
Box-Death Hollow	26,000	1984	USFS	Dixie NF
Dark Canyon	45,000	1984	USFS	Manti-Lasal NF
Deseret Peak	25,500	1984	USFS	Wasatch-Cache NF
High Uintas	460,000	1984	USFS	Ashley, Wasatch-Cache NFs
Lone Peak	30,088	1978	USFS	Uinta, Wasatch NFs
Mount Naomi	44,350	1984	USFS	Wasatch-Cache NF
Mount Nebo	28,000	1984	USFS	Uinta NF
Mount Olympus	16,000	1984	USFS	Wasatch-Cache NF
Mount Timpanogos	10,750	1984	USFS	Uinta NF
Paria Canyon—Vermilion Cliffs	19,954	1984	BLM	Cedar City District
Pine Valley Mountain	50,000	1984	USFS	Dixie NF
Twin Peaks	13,100	1984	USFS	Wasatch-Cache NF
Wellsville Mountain	23,850	1984	USFS	Wasatch-Cache NF
State Total: 802,189				
VERMONT				
Big Branch	6,720	1984	USFS	Green Mountain NF
Breadloaf	21,480	1984	USFS	Green Mountain NF
Bristol Cliffs	3,738	1975 1976	USFS	Green Mountain NF
George D. Aiken	5,060	1984	USFS	Green Mountain NF
Lye Brook	14,621	1975 1984	USFS	Green Mountain NF
Peru Peak	6,920	1984	USFS	Green Mountain NF
State Total: 58,539				
VIRGINIA				
Barbours Creek	5,700	1988	USFS	Jefferson, George Washington NFs
Beartown	6,375	1984	USFS	Jefferson NF
James River Face	8,903	1975 1984	USFS	Jefferson NF
Kimberling Creek	5,580	1984	USFS	Jefferson NF
Lewis Fork	5,802	1984 1988	USFS	Jefferson NF
Little Dry Run	3,400	1984	USFS	Jefferson NF
Little Wilson Creek	3,855	1984	USFS	Jefferson NF
Mountain Lake	8,253	1984	USFS	Jefferson NF
Peters Mountain	3,326	1984	USFS	Jefferson NF
Ramseys Draft	6,725	1984	USFS	George Washington NF
Rich Hole	6,450	1988	USFS	George Washington NF
Rough Mountain	9,300	1988	USFS	George Washington NF
Saint Mary's	10,090	1984	USFS	George Washington NF
Shawvers Run	3,665	1988	USFS	Jefferson, George Washington NFs
Shenandoah	79,579	1976	NPS	Shenandoah NP
Thunder Ridge	2,450	1984	USFS	Jefferson NF
State Total: 169,453				
WASHINGTON				
Alpine Lakes	305,407	1976	USFS	Mount Baker-Snoqualmie, Wenatchee NFs
Boulder River	49,000	1984	USFS	Mount Baker-Snoqualmie NF
Buckhorn	44,474	1984 1986	USFS	Olympic NF
Clearwater	14,300	1984	USFS	Mount Baker-Snoqualmie NF
Colonel Bob	12,120	1984	USFS	Olympic NF
Glacier Peak	576,648	1964 1968 1984	USFS	Mount Baker-Snoqualmie, Wenatchee NFs
Glacier View	3,050	1984	USFS	Gifford Pinchot NF
Goat Rocks	105,023	1964 1984	USFS	Gifford Pinchot, Mount Baker-Snoqualmie NFs
Henry M. Jackson	102,671	1984	USFS	Wenatchee, Mount Baker-Snoqualmie NFs
Indian Heaven	20,650	1984	USFS	Gifford Pinchot NF
Juniper Dunes	7,140	1984	BLM	Spokane District
Lake Chelan-Sawtooth	150,704	1984	USFS	Okanogan, Wenatchee NFs
Mount Adams	46,776	1964 1984	USFS	Gifford Pinchot NF
Mount Baker	117,580	1984	USFS	Mount Baker-Snoqualmie NF
Mount Rainier	216,855	1988	NPS	Mount Rainier NP
Mount Skokomish	13,015	1984 1986	USFS	Olympic NF
Noisy-Diobsud	14,300	1984	USFS	Mount Baker-Snoqualmie NF
Norse Peak	50,902	1984	USFS	Wenatchee, Mount Baker-Snoqualmie NFs
Olympic	876,669	1988	NPS	Olympic NP
Pasayten	529,850	1968 1984	USFS	Mount Baker-Snoqualmie, Okanogan NFs
Salmo-Priest	41,335	1984	USFS	Kaniksu Colville NF
San Juan Islands	353	1976	FWS	San Juan Islands NWR
Stephen Mather	634,614	1988	NPS	North Cascades NP
Tatoosh	15,720	1984	USFS	Gifford Pinchot NF
The Brothers	16,682	1984 1986	USFS	Olympic NF
Trapper Creek	6,050	1984	USFS	Gifford Pinchot NF
Washington Islands	485	1970	FWS	Washington Islands NWR
Wenaha-Tucannon	111,048	1978	USFS	Umatilla NF
William O. Douglas	166,603	1984	USFS	Wenatchee, Gifford Pinchot NFs
Wonder Mountain	2,320	1984	USFS	Olympic NF
State Total: 4,252,344				
WEST VIRGINIA				
Cranberry	35,864	1983	USFS	Monongahela NF
Dolly Sods	10,215	1975	USFS	Monongahela NF
Laurel Fork North	6,055	1983	USFS	Monongahela NF
Laurel Fork South	5,997	1983	USFS	Monongahela NF
Mountain Lake	2,500	1988	USFS	Jefferson NF
Otter Creek	20,000	1975	USFS	Monongahela NF
State Total: 80,631				
WISCONSIN				
Blackjack Springs	5,886	1978	USFS	Nicolet NF
Headwaters	19,950	1984	USFS	Nicolet NF
Porcupine Lake	4,195	1984	USFS	Chequamegon NF
Rainbow Lake	6,583	1975	USFS	Chequamegon NF
Whisker Lake	7,345	1978	USFS	Nicolet NF
Wisconsin Islands	29	1970	FWS	Wisconsin Islands NWR
State Total: 43,988				
WYOMING				
Absaroka-Beartooth	23,750	1984	USFS	Shoshone NF
Bridger	428,169	1964 1984	USFS	Bridger-Teton NF
Cloud Peak	195,500	1984	USFS	Big Horn NF
Encampment River	10,400	1984	USFS	Medicine Bow NF
Fitzpatrick	198,838	1976 1984	USFS	Shoshone NF
Gros Ventre	287,000	1984	USFS	Bridger-Teton NF
Huston Park	31,300	1984	USFS	Medicine Bow NF
Jedediah Smith	116,535	1984	USFS	Targhee NF
North Absaroka	350,538	1964	USFS	Shoshone NF
Platte River	22,230	1984	USFS	Medicine Bow, Routt NFs
Popo Agie	101,991	1984	USFS	Shoshone NF
Savage Run	14,940	1978	USFS	Medicine Bow NF
Teton	585,468	1964 1984	USFS	Bridger-Teton NF
Washakie	703,981	1964 1972 1984	USFS	Shoshone NF
Winegar Hole	14,000	1984	USFS	Bridger-Teton NF
State Total: 3,084,640				
U.S. Total: 90,760,106				

NATIONAL WILDERNESS PRESERVATION SYSTEM
Summary Data

Agency	No. of Units	Acreage
U.S. Forest Service	354	32,457,616
National Park Service	43	38,502,565
Fish and Wildlife Service	66	19,332,976
Bureau of Land Management	25	466,949
TOTAL	488	90,760,106

TOTAL UNITS IN NWPS: 474—of the 488 units noted above, 14 are managed by more than one agency.

Fourteen wilderness areas lie in more than one state—13 areas are in two states and one area in three.

AREAS IN MULTIPLE STATES:

Absaroka-Beartooth (MT,WY)—USFS
Beaver Dam Mountains (AZ,UT)—BLM
Big Frog (GA,TN)—USFS
Cohutta (GA,TN)—USFS
Ellicott Rock (GA,NC,TN)—USFS
Hells Canyon (ID,OR)—USFS
Joyce Kilmer-Slickrock (NC,TN)—USFS
Mountain Lake (VA,WV)—USFS
Paria Canyon-Vermilion Cliffs (AZ,UT)—BLM
Platte River (CO,WY)—USFS
Red Buttes (CA,OR)—USFS
Selway-Bitterroot (ID,MT)—USFS
Southern Nantahala (GA,NC)—USFS
Wenaha-Tucannon (OR,WA)—USFS

AREAS MANAGED BY MORE THAN ONE AGENCY:

Arizona: Kanab Creek (USFS,BLM)
California: Ansel Adams (USFS,NPS)
Ishi (USFS,BLM)
Machesna Mountain (USFS,BLM)
Santa Lucia (USFS,BLM)
Trinity Alps (USFS,BLM)
Yolla Bolla-Middle Eel (USFS,BLM)
Colorado: Indian Peaks (USFS,NPS)
Mount Massive (USFS,FWS)
Idaho: Frank Church—River of No Return (USFS,BLM)
Montana: Lee Metcalf (USFS,BLM)
Oregon: Hells Canyon (USFS,BLM)
Oregon Islands (FWS,BLM)

ABBREVIATIONS

USFS—U.S. Forest Service
NPS—National Park Service
FWS—Fish & Wildlife Service
BLM—Bureau of Land Management
NF—National Forest
NP—National Park
NWR—National Wildlife Refuge
NM—National Monument

The Wilderness Society, founded in 1935, is a non-profit membership organization devoted to preserving wilderness and wildlife, protecting America's forests, parks, rivers, deserts, wildlife refuges, and shorelands, and fostering an American land ethic.

The Wilderness Society
1400 Eye Street, NW
Washington, D.C. 20005
(202) 842-3400

The National Wilderness P

Wilderness Area	Acres	Year Designated	Agency	Public Land Unit
ALABAMA				
Cheaha	7,490	1983 1988	USFS	Talladega NF
Sipsey	25,906	1975 1988	USFS	Bankhead NF
State Total: 33,396				
ALASKA				
Admiralty Island National Monument	937,396	1980	USFS	Tongass NF
Aleutian Islands	1,300,000	1980	FWS	Alaska Maritime NWR
Andreafsky	1,300,000	1980	FWS	Yukon Delta NWR
Arctic	8,000,000	1980	FWS	Arctic NWR
Becharof	400,000	1980	FWS	Becharof NWR
Bering Sea	81,340	1970	FWS	Alaska Maritime NWR
Bogoslof	175	1970	FWS	Alaska Maritime NWR
Chamisso	455	1975	FWS	Alaska Maritime NWR
Coronation Island	19,232	1980	USFS	Tongass NF
Denali	1,900,000	1980	NPS	Denali NP
Endicott River	98,729	1980	USFS	Tongass NF
Forrester Island	2,832	1970	FWS	Alaska Maritime NWR
Gates of the Arctic	7,052,000	1980	NPS	Gates of the Arctic NP
Glacier Bay	2,770,000	1980	NPS	Glacier Bay NP
Hazy Islands	32	1970	FWS	Hazy Islands NWR
Innoko	1,240,000	1980	FWS	Innoko NWR
Izembek	300,000	1980	FWS	Izembek NWR
Katmai	3,473,000	1980	NPS	Katmai NP
Kenai	1,350,000	1980	FWS	Kenai NWR
Kobuk Valley	190,000	1980	NPS	Kobuk Valley NP
Koyukuk	400,000	1980	FWS	Koyukuk NWR
Lake Clark	2,470,000	1980	NPS	Lake Clark NP
Maurelle Islands	4,937	1980	USFS	Tongass NF
Misty Fjords National Monument	2,142,243	1980	USFS	Tongass NF
Noatak	5,800,000	1980	NPS	Noatak N Preserve
Nunivak	600,000	1980	FWS	Yukon Delta NWR
Petersburg Creek-Duncan Salt Chuck	46,777	1980	USFS	Tongass NF
Russell Fjord	348,701	1980	USFS	Tongass NF
Selawik	240,000	1980	FWS	Selawik NWR
Semidi	250,000	1980	FWS	Alaska Maritime NWR
Simeonof	25,855	1976	FWS	Alaska Maritime NWR
South Baranof	319,568	1980	USFS	Tongass NF
South Prince of Wales	90,996	1980	USFS	Tongass NF
St. Lazaria	65	1970	FWS	Alaska Maritime NWR
Stikine-LeConte	448,841	1980	USFS	Tongass NF
Tebenkof Bay	66,839	1980	USFS	Tongass NF
Togiak	2,270,000	1980	FWS	Togiak NWR
Tracy Arm-Fords Terror	653,179	1980	USFS	Tongass NF
Tuxedni	5,566	1970	FWS	Alaska Maritime NWR
Unimak	910,000	1980	FWS	Alaska Maritime NWR
Warren Island	11,181	1980	USFS	Tongass NF
West Chichagof-Yakobi	264,747	1980	USFS	Tongass NF
Wrangell-St. Elias	8,700,000	1980	NPS	Wrangell-St. Elias NP
State Total: 56,484,686				
ARIZONA				
Apache Creek	5,420	1984	USFS	Prescott NF
Aravaipa Canyon	6,670	1984	BLM	Safford District
Bear Wallow	11,080	1984	USFS	Apache-Sitgreaves NF
Beaver Dam Mountains	17,003	1984	BLM	Arizona Strip District
Castle Creek	26,030	1984	USFS	Prescott NF
Cedar Bench	14,950	1984	USFS	Prescott NF
Chiricahua	87,700	1964 1984	USFS	Coronado NF
Chiricahua National Monument	10,290	1976 1984	NPS	Chiricahua NM
Cottonwood Point	6,500	1984	BLM	Arizona Strip District
Escudilla	5,200	1984	USFS	Apache-Sitgreaves NF
Fossil Springs	11,550	1984	USFS	Coconino NF
Four Peaks	53,500	1984	USFS	Tonto NF
Galiuro	76,317	1964 1984	USFS	Coronado NF
Grand Wash Cliffs	36,300	1984	BLM	Arizona Strip District
Granite Mountain	9,800	1984	USFS	Prescott NF
Hellsgate	36,780	1984	USFS	Tonto NF
Juniper Mesa	7,600	1984	USFS	Prescott NF
Kachina Peaks	18,200	1984	USFS	Coconino NF
Kanab Creek	68,250	1984	USFS	Kaibab NF
Kanab Creek	8,850	1984	BLM	Arizona Strip District
Kendrick Mountain	6,510	1984	USFS	Coconino, Kaibab NFs
Mazatzal	251,912	1964 1984	USFS	Tonto NF
Miller Peak	20,190	1984	USFS	Coronado NF
Mount Baldy	7,079	1970	USFS	Apache-Sitgreaves NF
Mount Logan	14,600	1984	BLM	Arizona Strip District
Mount Trumbull	7,900	1984	BLM	Arizona Strip District
Mount Wrightson	25,260	1984	USFS	Coronado NF
Munds Mountain	18,150	1984	USFS	Coconino NF
Organ Pipe Cactus	312,600	1978	NPS	Organ Pipe NM
Paiute	84,700	1984	BLM	Arizona Strip District
Pajarita	7,420	1984	USFS	Coronado NF
Paria Canyon-Vermilion Cliffs	90,046	1984	BLM	Arizona Strip District
Petrified Forest	50,260	1970	NPS	Petrified Forest NP
Pine Mountain	20,061	1972	USFS	Prescott, Tonto NFs
Pusch Ridge	56,933	1978	USFS	Coronado NF
Red Rock-Secret Mountain	43,950	1984	USFS	Coconino NF
Rincon Mountain	38,590	1984	USFS	Coronado NF
Saddle Mountain	40,600	1984	USFS	Kaibab NF
Saguaro	71,400	1976	NPS	Saguaro NM
Salome	18,950	1984	USFS	Tonto NF
Salt River Canyon	32,800	1984	USFS	Tonto NF
Santa Teresa	26,780	1984	USFS	Coronado NF
Sierra Ancha	20,850	1964	USFS	Tonto NF
Strawberry Crater	10,140	1984	USFS	Coconino NF
Superstition	159,757	1964 1984	USFS	Tonto NF
Sycamore Canyon	55,937	1972 1984	USFS	Coconino, Kaibab, Prescott NFs
West Clear Creek	13,600	1984	USFS	Coconino NF
Wet Beaver	6,700	1984	USFS	Coconino NF
Woodchute	5,600	1984	USFS	Prescott NF
State Total: 2,037,265				
ARKANSAS				
Big Lake	2,144	1976	FWS	Big Lake NWR
Black Fork Mountain	7,568	1984	USFS	Ouachita NF
Buffalo National River	10,529	1978	NPS	Buffalo National River
Caney Creek	14,344	1975	USFS	Ouachita NF
Dry Creek	6,310	1984	USFS	Ouachita NF
East Fork	10,777	1984	USFS	Ozark-Saint Francis NF
Flatside	10,105	1984	USFS	Ouachita NF
Hurricane Creek	15,177	1984	USFS	Ozark-Saint Francis NF
Leatherwood	16,956	1984	USFS	Ozark-Saint Francis NF
Poteau Mountain	10,884	1984	USFS	Ouachita NF
Richland Creek	11,822	1984	USFS	Ozark-Saint Francis NF
Upper Buffalo	11,746	1975 1984	USFS	Ozark-Saint Francis NF
State Total: 128,362				
CALIFORNIA				
Agua Tibia	15,933	1975	USFS	Cleveland NF
Ansel Adams	228,669	1964	USFS	Inyo Sierra NF
Ansel Adams	665	1984	NPS	Yosemite NP
Bucks Lake	21,000	1984	USFS	Plumas NF
Caribou	20,625	1964 1984	USFS	Lassen NF
Carson-Iceberg	160,000	1984	USFS	Stanislaus, Toiyabe NFs
Castle Crags	7,300	1984	USFS	Shasta-Trinity NF
Chanchelulla	8,200	1984	USFS	Shasta-Trinity NF
Cucamonga	12,981	1964 1984	USFS	San Bernardino, Angeles NFs
Desolation	63,475	1969	USFS	Eldorado NF
Dick Smith	65,130	1984	USFS	Los Padres NF
Dinkey Lakes	30,000	1984	USFS	Sierra NF
Dome Land	94,686	1964 1984	USFS	Sequoia NF
Emigrant	112,191	1975 1984	USFS	Stanislaus NF
Farallon	141	1974	FWS	Farallon NWR
Golden Trout	303,287	1978	USFS	Inyo, Sequoia NFs
Granite Chief	25,000	1984	USFS	Tahoe NF
Hauser	8,000	1984	USFS	Cleveland NF
Hoover	48,601	1964	USFS	Inyo, Toiyabe NFs
Ishi	41,600	1984	USFS	Lassen NF
Ishi	240	1984	BLM	Ukiah District
Jennie Lakes	10,500	1984	USFS	Sequoia NF
John Muir	580,675	1964 1984	USFS	Inyo, Sierra NFs
Joshua Tree	429,690	1976	NPS	Joshua Tree NM
Kaiser	22,700	1976	USFS	Sierra NF
Lassen Volcanic	78,982	1972	NPS	Lassen Volcanic NP
Lava Beds	28,460	1972	NPS	Lava Beds NM
Machesna Mountain	19,880	1984	USFS	Los Padres NF
Machesna Mountain	120	1984	BLM	Bakersfield District
Marble Mountain	241,744	1964 1984	USFS	Klamath NF
Mokelumne	104,461	1964 1984	USFS	Eldorado, Stanislaus, Toiyabe NFs
Monarch	45,000	1984	USFS	Sierra, Sequoia NFs
Mount Shasta	37,000	1984	USFS	Shasta-Trinity NF
North Fork	8,100	1984	USFS	Six Rivers NF
Phillip Burton	25,370	1976 1985	NPS	Point Reyes National Seashore
Pine Creek	13,100	1984	USFS	Cleveland NF
Pinnacles	12,952	1976	NPS	Pinnacles NM
Red Buttes	16,150	1984	USFS	Rogue River NF
Russian	12,000	1984	USFS	Klamath NF
San Gabriel	36,118	1968	USFS	Angeles NF
San Gorgonio	56,722	1964 1984	USFS	San Bernardino NF
San Jacinto	32,040	1964 1984	USFS	San Bernardino NF
San Mateo Canyon	39,540	1984	USFS	Cleveland NF
San Rafael	150,610	1968 1984	USFS	Los Padres NF
Santa Lucia	18,679	1978	USFS	Los Padres NF
Santa Lucia	1,733	1978	BLM	Bakersfield District
Santa Rosa	20,160	1984	USFS	San Bernardino NF
Sequoia-Kings Canyon	736,980	1984	NPS	Sequoia-Kings Canyon NP
Sheep Mountain	43,600	1984	USFS	Angeles, San Bernardino NFs
Siskiyou	153,000	1984	USFS	Six Rivers, Klamath, Siskiyou NFs
Snow Mountain	37,000	1984	USFS	Mendocino NF
South Sierra	63,000	1984	USFS	Sequoia, Inyo NFs
South Warner	70,385	1964 1984	USFS	Modoc NF
Thousand Lakes	16,335	1964	USFS	Lassen NF
Trinity Alps	495,377	1984	USFS	Klamath, Six Rivers, Shasta-Trinity NFs
Trinity Alps	4,623	1984	BLM	Ukiah District
Ventana	164,144	1969 1978 1984	USFS	Los Padres NF
Yolla Bolly-Middle Eel	145,404	1964 1984	USFS	Mendocino, Six Rivers, Shasta-Trinity NFs
Yolla Bolly-Middle Eel	8,500	1984	BLM	Ukiah District
Yosemite	677,600	1984	NPS	Yosemite NP
State Total: 5,926,158				
COLORADO				
Big Blue	98,320	1980	USFS	Uncompahgre NF
Black Canyon of the Gunnison	11,180	1976	NPS	Black Canyon of the Gunnison NM
Cache La Poudre	9,238	1980	USFS	Roosevelt NF
Collegiate Peaks	166,654	1980	USFS	Gunnison, San Isabel, White River NFs
Comanche Peak	66,791	1980	USFS	Roosevelt NF
Eagles Nest	133,325	1976	USFS	Arapaho, White River NFs
Flat Tops	235,035	1975	USFS	Routt, White River NFs
Great Sand Dunes	33,450	1976	NPS	Great Sand Dunes NM
Holy Cross	122,037	1980	USFS	San Isabel, White River NFs
Hunter-Fryingpan	74,250	1978	USFS	White River NFs
Indian Peaks	70,374	1978	USFS	Arapaho, Roosevelt NFs
Indian Peaks	2,922	1980	NPS	Rocky Mountain NP
La Garita	103,986	1964 1980	USFS	Gunnison, Rio Grande NFs
Lizard Head	41,189	1980	USFS	San Juan, Uncompahgre NFs
Lost Creek	105,090	1980	USFS	Pike NF
Maroon Bells-Snowmass	181,138	1980	USFS	Gunnison, White River NFs
Mesa Verde	8,100	1976	NPS	Mesa Verde NP
Mount Evans	74,401	1980	USFS	Arapaho, Pike NFs
Mount Massive	27,980	1980	USFS	San Isabel NF
Mount Massive	2,560	1980	FWS	Leadville Fish Hatchery
Mount Sneffels	16,505	1980	USFS	Uncompahgre NF
Mount Zirkel	139,818	1964 1980	USFS	Routt, Roosevelt NFs
Neota	9,924	1980	USFS	Roosevelt, Routt NFs
Never Summer	13,702	1980	USFS	Arapaho, Routt NFs
Platte River	770	1984	USFS	Routt NF
Raggeds	59,519	1980	USFS	Gunnison, White River NFs
Rawah	73,020	1964	USFS	Roosevelt, Routt NFs
South San Juan	127,690	1980	USFS	Rio Grande, San Juan NFs
Weminuche	459,804	1975 1980	USFS	Rio Grande, San Juan NFs
West Elk	176,092	1964 1980	USFS	Gunnison NF
State Total: 2,644,864				
FLORIDA				
Alexander Springs	7,700	1984	USFS	Ocala NF
Big Gum Swamp	13,600	1984	USFS	Osceola NF
Billies Bay	3,120	1984	USFS	Ocala NF
Bradwell Bay	24,602	1975 1984	USFS	Apalachicola NF
Cedar Keys	379	1972	FWS	Cedar Keys NWR
Chassahowitzka	23,617	1976	FWS	Chassahowitzka NWR
Everglades	1,296,500	1978	NPS	Everglades NP
Florida Keys	6,245	1975 1982	FWS	Florida Keys NWR
Island Bay	20	1970	FWS	Island Bay NWR
J.N. "Ding" Darling	2,619	1976	FWS	J.N. "Ding" Darling NWR
Juniper Prairie	13,260	1984	USFS	Ocala NF
Lake Woodruff	1,066	1976	FWS	Lake Woodruff NWR
Little Lake George	2,500	1984	USFS	Ocala NF
Mud Swamp/New River	7,800	1984	USFS	Apalachicola NF
Passage Key	36	1970	FWS	Passage Key NWR
Pelican Island	6	1970	FWS	Pelican Island NWR
St. Marks	17,350	1975	FWS	St. Marks NWR
State Total: 1,420,420				
GEORGIA				
Big Frog	83	1984	USFS	Cherokee NF
Blackbeard Island	3,000	1975	FWS	Blackbeard Island NWR
Brasstown	11,405	1986	USFS	Chattahoochee NF
Cohutta	35,247	1975 1986	USFS	Chattahoochee NF
Cumberland Island	8,840	1982	NPS	Cumberland Island National Seashore
Ellicott Rock	2,181	1975 1984	USFS	Chattahoochee NF
Okefenokee	353,981	1974	FWS	Okefenokee NWR
Raven Cliffs	8,562	1986	USFS	Chattahoochee NF
Rich Mountain	9,649	1986	USFS	Chattahoochee NF
Southern Nantahala	12,439	1984	USFS	Chattahoochee NF
Tray Mountain	9,702	1986	USFS	Chattahoochee NF
Wolf Island	5,126	1975	FWS	Wolf Island NWR
State Total: 460,215				
HAWAII				
Haleakala	19,270	1976	NPS	Haleakala NP
Hawaii Volcanoes	123,100	1978	NPS	Hawaii Volcanoes NP
State Total: 142,370				
IDAHO				
Craters of the Moon	43,243	1970	NPS	Craters of the Moon NM
Frank Church—River of No Return	2,361,767	1980	USFS	Bitterroot, Boise, Challis, Nezperce, Payette, Salmon NFs
Frank Church—River of No Return	720	1980	BLM	Coeur d'Alene District
Gospel Hump	205,900	1978	USFS	Nezperce NF
Hells Canyon	83,800	1975	USFS	Nezperce, Payette NFs
Sawtooth	217,088	1972	USFS	Boise, Challis, Sawtooth NFs
Selway-Bitterroot	1,089,017	1964 1980	USFS	Bitterroot, Clearwater, Nezperce NFs
State Total: 4,001,535				
ILLINOIS				
Crab Orchard	4,050	1976	FWS	Crab Orchard NWR
State Total: 4,050				
INDIANA				
Charles C. Deam	12,935	1982	USFS	Wayne-Hoosier NF
State Total: 12,935				
KENTUCKY				
Beaver Creek	4,756	1975	USFS	Daniel Boone NF
Clifty	13,300	1985	USFS	Daniel Boone NF
State Total: 18,056				
LOUISIANA				
Breton	5,000	1975	FWS	Breton NWR
Kisatchie	8,700	1980	USFS	Kisatchie NF
Lacassine	3,346	1976	FWS	Lacassine NWR
State Total: 17,046				
MAINE				
Moosehorn	7,386	1970 1975	FWS	Moosehorn NWR
State Total: 7,386				
MASSACHUSETTS				
Monomoy	2,420	1970	FWS	Monomoy NWR
State Total: 2,420				
MICHIGAN				
Big Island Lake	5,500	1987	USFS	Hiawatha NF
Delirium	11,870	1987	USFS	Hiawatha NF
Horseshoe Bay	3,790	1987	USFS	Hiawatha NF
Huron Islands	147	1970	FWS	Huron Islands NWR
Isle Royale	131,880	1976	NPS	Isle Royale NP
Mackinac	12,230	1987	USFS	Hiawatha NF
McCormick	16,850	1987	USFS	Ottawa NF
Michigan Islands	12	1970	FWS	Michigan Islands NWR
Nordhouse Dunes	3,450	1987	USFS	Manistee NF
Rock River Canyon	4,640	1987	USFS	Hiawatha NF
Round Island	378	1987	USFS	Hiawatha NF
Seney	25,150	1970	FWS	Seney NWR
Sturgeon River Gorge	14,500	1987	USFS	Ottawa NF
Sylvania	18,327	1987	USFS	Ottawa NF
State Total: 248,724				
MINNESOTA				
Agassiz	4,000	1976	FWS	Agassiz NWR
Boundary Waters Canoe Area	798,309	1964 1978	USFS	Superior NF
Tamarac	2,180	1976	FWS	Tamarac NWR
State Total: 804,489				
MISSISSIPPI				
Black Creek	4,560	1984	USFS	DeSoto NF
Gulf Islands	1,800	1978	NPS	Gulf Islands National Seashore
Leaf	940	1984	USFS	DeSoto NF
State Total: 7,300				
MISSOURI				
Bell Mountain	8,817	1980	USFS	Mark Twain NF
Devil's Backbone	6,595	1980	USFS	Mark Twain NF
Hercules Glades	12,314	1976	USFS	Mark Twain NF
Irish	16,500	1984	USFS	Mark Twain NF
Mingo	7,730	1976	FWS	Mingo NWR
Paddy Creek	6,728	1983	USFS	Mark Twain NF
Piney Creek	8,087	1980	USFS	Mark Twain NF
Rockpile Mountain	4,089	1980	USFS	Mark Twain NF
State Total: 70,860				
MONTANA				
Absaroka-Beartooth	920,310	1978 1983	USFS	Custer, Gallatin NFs
Anaconda-Pintlar	157,874	1964	USFS	Beaverhead, Bitterroot, Deerlodge NFs
Bob Marshall	1,009,356	1964 1978	USFS	Flathead, Lewis & Clark NFs
Cabinet Mountains	94,272	1964	USFS	Kaniksu, Kootenai NFs
Gates of the Mountains	28,562	1964	USFS	Helena NF
Great Bear	286,700	1978	USFS	Flathead NF
Lee Metcalf	248,944	1983	USFS	Gallatin, Beaverhead NFs
Lee Metcalf	6,000	1983	BLM	Bear Trap Canyon, Butte District
Medicine Lake	11,366	1976	FWS	Medicine Lake NWR
Mission Mountains	73,877	1975	USFS	Flathead NF
Rattlesnake	29,824	1980	USFS	Lolo NF
Red Rock Lakes	32,350	1976	FWS	Red Rock Lakes NWR
Scapegoat	239,296	1972	USFS	Helena, Lolo, Lewis & Clark NFs
Selway-Bitterroot	248,893	1964	USFS	Bitterroot, Lolo NFs
UL Bend	20,819	1976 1983	FWS	UL Bend NWR
Welcome Creek	28,135	1978	USFS	Lolo NF
State Total: 3,436,578				
NEBRASKA				
Fort Niobrara	4,635	1976	FWS	Fort Niobrara NWR
Soldier Creek	8,100	1986	USFS	Nebraska NF
State Total: 12,735				
NEVADA				
Jarbidge	64,667	1964	USFS	Humboldt NF
State Total: 64,667				
NEW HAMPSHIRE				
Great Gulf	5,552	1964	USFS	White Mountain NF
Pemigewasset	45,000	1984	USFS	White Mountain NF
Presidential Range—Ery River	27,380	1975 1984	USFS	White Mountain NF
Sandwich Range	25,000	1984	USFS	White Mountain NF
State Total: 102,932				

ss Preservation System
989

Isle Royale

Boundary Waters Canoe Area

Huron Islands · McCormick · Rock River Canyon · Delirium · Mackinac
Sturgeon River Gorge · Seney · Horseshoe Bay · Round Island
Rainbow Lake · Big Island Lake
Porcupine Lake · Blackjack Springs · Headwaters · Whisker Lake · Michigan Islands
Sylvania
Wisconsin Islands

MINNESOTA

WISCONSIN

Nordhouse Dunes

MICHIGAN

MAINE · Moosehorn

Great Gulf · Dry River
VT. · Presidential Range · Sandwich Range
Pemigewasset · NEW HAMPSHIRE
Bristol Cliffs · Breadloaf
Big Branch · Pine Peak
Lye Brook
George D. Aiken · Monomoy
MASS.
CONN. · R.I.

NEW YORK

IOWA

ILLINOIS

INDIANA

OHIO

Charles C. D.

Clifty

West Sister Island

Allegheny Islands · Hickory Creek

PENNSYLVANIA

NEW JERSEY

Great Swamp

Fire Island

Brigantine

MARYLAND
DELAWARE

W.VA.
Otter Creek · Dolly Sods · Shenandoah
Laurel Fork North · Ramseys Draft
Laurel Fork South · Rich Hole · VA.
Cranberry · Rough Mountain · Saint Mary's
Shrevers Run · James River Face
Mountain Lake · Thunder Ridge
Laurel Mountain · Barbours Creek
Kimberling Creek · Mountain Lake
Beartown · Little Dry Run
Lewis Fork · Little Wilson Creek
Big Laurel Branch · Swanquarter
Unaka Mountain · Pond Mountain
Sampson Mountain · Linville Gorge
Citico Creek · Joyce Kilmer-Slickrock · NORTH CAROLINA
Bald River Gorge · Shining Rock · Birkhead Mountains · Sheep Ridge
Gee Creek · Middle Prong · Catfish Lake South · Pocosin
Little Frog Mountain · Pond Pine
Big Frog · Southern Nantahala
Cohutta · Ellicott Rock
Rich Mountain · Tray Mountain
Brasstown · Raven Cliff
SOUTH CAROLINA
Congaree Swamp National Monument

MISSOURI
Bell Mountain · Crab Orchard
Paddy Creek · Rockpile Mountain
Devil's Backbone · Irish · Mingo
Hercules Glades
Piney Creek · Buffalo National River
Leatherwood · Big Lake
Upper Buffalo · Richland Creek
Hurricane Creek · East Fork
Poteau Mountain · Dry Creek
Flatside
Rock Fork Mountain · Black Fork Mountain
Upper Kiamichi River · Caney Creek
ARKANSAS

KENTUCKY
Beaver Creek

TENNESSEE

Sipsey

Cheaha

MISSISSIPPI · ALABAMA

GEORGIA

Hell Hole Bay · Wambaw Creek
Wambaw Swamp
Little Wambaw Swamp · Cape Romain

Blackbeard Island
Wolf Island
Cumberland Island

Okefenokee
Big Gum Swamp

Big Slough · Kisatchie
Turkey Hill · Indian Mounds
Upland Island
Lake Creek · Breton
Lacassine
LOUISIANA

Leaf
Black Creek

Gulf Islands

Bradwell Bay
Mud Swamp/New River · St. Marks

Cedar Keys · Billies Bay
Chassahowitzka

Little Lake George
Juniper Prairie · Lake Woodruff
Alexander Springs

FLORIDA

Pelican Island

Passage Key

Island Bay
J. N. "Ding" Darling · Everglades

Florida Keys

Legend

- National Park Wilderness
- National Forest Wilderness
- National Wildlife Refuge Wilderness
- Bureau of Land Management Wilderness
- ◇ Areas less than 20,000 acres in size.

Wilderness25

APPENDIX D—LAND AND RESOURCE MANAGEMENT PLAN—
MT. BAKER-SNOQUALMIE NATIONAL FOREST

GOAL

Preserve and protect the wilderness character. Allow for naturalness and provide opportunities for solitude, challenge, and inspiration. Within these constraints, and following a policy of non-degradation management, provide for recreational, scenic, educational, scientific, and historical uses.

This prescription is applied to those acres classified as Wilderness, including: Glacier Peak, Mt. Baker, Noisy-Diobsud, Boulder River, Henry M. Jackson, Clearwater, and Norse Peak. Refer to the Alpine Lakes Management Plan for management direction for the Alpine Lakes Wilderness. (See Management Prescription 27).

Common to all 10A, 10B, 10C, 10D, 10E

The Recreation Opportunity System (ROS) concept emphasizes that quality in outdoor recreation can best be achieved by providing a diversity of opportunities, consistent with resource limitations, to satisfy varying preferences of users. Wilderness ROS and their standards apply to all designated wilderness on the Forest (for specific direction regarding Alpine Lakes, consult the Alpine Lakes Area Land Management Plan).

Within each Wilderness Recreation Opportunity Sprectrum (WROS) Class there are Limits of Acceptable Change (LAC) which presuppose that certain areas (transition for example) of the wilderness will be allowed to receive relatively higher levels of use than other areas (trailless), and thus will receive higher levels of resource change or impact. Decisions about management of WROS Classes are aimed at making a conscious choice about the changes that will be allowed to occur. LAC should not be confused with a management objective that one is attempting to achieve. LAC is a maximum limit of change allowed. Managers try to achieve the best conditions possible rather than allowing conditions to deteriorate until this threshold is reached.

Wilderness must be managed to prevent degradation. The nondegradation principle directs that each Wilderness must essentially be as wild as it was at the time of classification, or if conditions are not known and cannot be reconstructed for the time of classification, the first Wilderness condition inventory should be used as the benchmark for maintaining Wilderness conditions. Nondegradation applies to all values of Wilderness: social, physical, and biological. Additionally, conditions shall be improved in situations where natural processes are not operating freely, and where the values for which a Wilderness was created are impaired.

The standards were (summarized in the following table) derived from field study and professional judgement.

CARRYING CAPACITY

Carrying capacities have been developed to estimate the amount of recreation visitor use that a wilderness or portion of wilderness, could support without degradation of resource values. Carrying capacity is commonly expressed in Recreation Visitor Days (RVDs) per year or people-at-one-time (PACT).

In the ROS system, coefficients have been developed that help in the estimation of carrying capacity. These coefficients are the estimated RVDs per average acre per year that a WROS class can support. Different coefficients are identified for each class and are a theoretical estimate of capacity based on average conditions.

For the Land and Resource Management Plan for the Mt. Baker-Snoqualmie National Forest, the following carrying capacity coefficients were developed in coordination with adjacent Forests sharing management of the Washington State Cascade Range Wilderness:

Zone	RVD/Acre/Year	RVD/Sq. Mile/Year
Transition	15.000	9600
Trailed	3.750	2400
General Trailless	0.250	160
Dedicated Trailless	0.078	50

LIMITS OF ACCEPTABLE CHANGE

Recreation visitor use of wilderness cannot occur without some degree of impact on wilderness resources. Impact occurs on the physical and biological features of wilderness as the quality of the recreation experience of other visitors. There is a point at which increasing impact of visitor use will result in unacceptable degradation outside the intent and direction of the Wilderness Act.

The LAC concept is a system to establish limits on the change that can be permitted within the nondegradation policy, before management actions must be taken to reverse trends of change. These actions can be either directed to improve the knowledge and abilities of the users or to reduce the numbers of visitors in impacted areas during critical time periods, or both.

The LAC levels or standards are different for each WROS Class. The standards for the *Dedicated Trailless* tolerate the least impact in order to achieve the most pristine wilderness conditions and the least evidence of man's activity. The *Transition Class* standards are more tolerant reflecting management of the area for a semiprimitive recreation experience and physical evidence of man's activity.

The following table summarizes the key indicators that will be measured in monitoring the physical, biological, and social conditions and the standards for each WROS Class, i.e., transition, trailed, general trailless, and Dedicated Trailless.

There is a high probability that initial monitoring results in some areas will indicate impact conditions in excess of standards established for particular WROS Classes. In this event, monitoring efforts will need to be

APPENDIX D—LAND AND RESOURCE MANAGEMENT PLAN—
MT. BAKER-SNOQUALMIE NATIONAL FOREST

intensified to establish the current trends. The objectives in these situations will be to institute management actions to achieve an improving trend. Downgrading the Wilderness Recreation Opportunity Class to a class more tolerant of impact will not be an option.

Over the long term, wilderness management activities should lead to an improving trend in the effects of man's activity on wilderness resources in all WROS classes.

DESCRIPTION OF WILDERNESS RECREATION OPPORTUNITY CLASSES

This trailed class includes system trails and may include user-made trails that have a travel way worn to mineral soil over long distances, and is characterized by having a large proportion of day-users who are often mixed in with overnight and long distance travelers. This area is usually adjacent to trailheads and extends into the wilderness a distance that is typically traveled in one day by a hiker. This class includes areas accessed by trail, around lakes or other attractions used by people, or pack stock within the day-use influence area. The class extends at least 500 feet on either side of a trail, but this may be wider around lakes or heavily used areas. The length of this trail class will be established for each trail depending on ease of travel, distance from trailhead outside wilderness, and destination attractions inside wilderness. This generally will be 3 to 5 miles inside the wilderness boundary. If the day-use activity occurs entirely outside wilderness, the trail will have no Transition Class.

Opportunities for exploring and experiencing isolation contrast with adjacent, more developed areas outside the Wilderness, though the visitor can expect the greatest number of people compared to other wilderness classes. The class introduces users to the Wilderness setting and normally provides relatively low challenge or risk in using outdoor skills compared to other classes.

This class includes all managed system trails extending beyond the Transition Class, and extends at least 500 feet on either side of the trail but may be wider around lakes or heavily used areas.

A moderate to high degree of opportunity exists for exploring and experiencing isolation (from the sights and sounds of civilization), independence, closeness to nature,

tranquility and self-reliance through the application of no trace skills in a natural environment that offers a moderate to high degree of challenge and risk as one travels further from trailheads. Visitors must be prepared for overnight camping, outdoor living, and changes in weather. A variety of user restrictions may be implemented to control use impacts as the need arises.

This class is characterized by area not falling into the other classes, and generally attracts lower use because of the lack of constructed trails and relative lack of attractions. The area is unmodified and user-made trails are not encouraged, but they may exist. If obvious user-made trails become well established, or are causing resource damage, consideration will be given to restricting use or reconstructing these trails in order to protect the wilderness resource from further damage. Reclassification from general trailless to trailed requires a supplement of the Forest Plan, which shall include full public involvement. This class is available for new trail construction only to protect resources or meet management objectives by dispersing use. If this should occur, the trail will be constructed to no higher than "more difficult" or "most difficult" standards.

This class provides an outstanding opportunity for isolation and solitude, mostly free from evidence of human activities and with very infrequent encounters with others. The user has outstanding opportunities to travel cross-country using a maximum degree of outdoor skills, often in an environment that offers a very high degree of challenge and risk. No-trace camping skills are strongly encouraged and any user built "improvement" is undesirable and shall be removed.

This class is managed forever trailless; obvious user-made ways are not permitted. The class may include way trails and routes not discernible as human related; the condition to be avoided is vegetation and soil loss along a continuous tread. The class may include popular attractions accessed only by cross-country travel. Human impact and influence is, by design, minimal, and user restrictions may be necessary to insure that trailless experiences remain. Areas chosen for Dedicated Trailless should be of a size that will allow for a meaningful experience and can be reasonably protected for the experiences and remoteness identified. Generally the class is a least 2,000—3,000 acres in size and contain whole drainages or basins out of sight and sound of trails, or areas outside the wilderness.

Classes under the Concept of Limits of Acceptable Change.

	Transition	Intensities General Trailed	Dedicated Trailless	Trailless
Capacity coefficient RVD's/acre/year	15.000	3.750	0.25	0.078
Vegetation loss at campsite (sq. feet) (or 3% from any acre)	1,000	1,000	500	0
Mineral soil exposed (sq. feet)	200	200	100	0
Trees scarred or felled or percent of trees on a site scarred or felled	15 (50)	15 (15)	7 (25)	0 (0)
Average number parties encountered when traveling day/snow-free season	8	5	2	1
Maximum encounters on any day	30	10	4	1
Unit size limit (people and stock together) unless otherwise authorized under Special Use Permit	12	12	12	12 (strongly encourage 6 people, 0 stock)
Number of campsites per 160 acre area	20	10	5	2
Occupied campsites visible from other campsites	4	3	2	0

Source: USDA Forest Service. June 1990. Land and Resource Management Plan. Pacific Northwest Region. Mt. Baker-Snoqualmie National Forest. pp. 4-207-213, 217.

APPENDIX E—SUMMARY OF AGENCY WILDERNESS MANAGEMENT POLICIES RELATING TO WILDLIFE[1]

	Agency			
	U.S. Forest Service	*National Park Service*	*Fish and Wildlife Service*	*Bureau of Land Management*
Source	FS Manual 2323.3 Wildlife and Fish	NPS Management Policies; II Animal Populations	Refuge Manual 6RM1.3 Habitat Management Refuge Manual 7RM1.3 Populations Management	BLM Manual 8560.34-Fish and Wildlife
Summary of wildlife management	Objectives 1.Provide an environment where the forces of natural selection and survival rather than human actions determine numbers and species of wildlife. 2.Consistent with objective one, protect wildlife and fish indigenous to the area from human caused conditions that could lead to federal listing as threatened or endangered. 3. Provide protection for known populations and aid recovery in areas of previous habitation, of federally listed threatened or endangered species and their habitats.	Strive to maintain the natural abundance, behavior, diversity, and ecological integrity of native animals as part of natural ecosystems. Protect native animal life against harvest, removal, destruction, harassment, or harm from human action. Natural processes shall be relied upon to regulate populations of native species to the greatest extent possible Unnatural concentrations of native species, caused by human activities, may be regulated if those activities cannot be controlled. Non-native species shall not be allowed to displace native species if this displacement can be prevented by management. Results of regulation of all animal populations shall be evaluated by research studies.	Fish and wildlife populations of a particular refuge will be maintained at levels consistent with sound wildlife management principles and in-conformance with that refuge's objective and will contribute to the wildest possible natural diversity of indigenous fish and wildlife and habitat types. Habitat management planning will consider the full range of management alternatives available and the impacts of each on the wildlife and habitat resources of the refuge and its ecosystem. Management will favor natural processes or require minimal, direct, artificial manipulation of the land, water, and vegetative cover.	Seek a natural distribution, number and interaction of indigenous species. Natural processes will be allowed to occur as far as possible without human influences, and wildlife species allowed to maintain a natural balance with their habitat and with each other. Special exceptions allowed where necessary to control disease epidemics or other health hazards in which wildlife species are involved as carriers.

	Agency			
	U.S. Forest Service	*National Park Service*	*Fish and Wildlife Service*	*Bureau of Land Management*
PUBLIC USE				
Hunting	Legal sport hunting allowed. Legal subsistence hunting permitted in Alaska.	Sport and commercial hunting prohibited. Legal subsistence hunting permitted in Alaska	Legal sport hunting allowed. Commercial hunting prohibited. Legal subsistence hunting permitted in Alaska.	Legal sport hunting allowed. Commercial and subsistence hunting prohibited.
Fishing	Legal sport fishing allowed. Emphasis is on quality and naturalness in fisheries management. Legal subsistence fishing permitted in Alaska.	Legal sport fishing allowed. Commercial fishing prohibited. Legal subsistence fishing permitted in Alaska except where permitted by law.	Legal sport fishing allowed. Commercial fishing prohibited. Legal subsistence fishing permitted in Alaska.	Legal sport fishing allowed. Commercial and subsistence fishing prohibited.
Trapping	Legal sport trapping allowed. Legal subsistence trapping permitted in Alaska.	Sport and commercial trapping prohibited. Legal subsistence trapping permitted in Alaska.	Legal sport trapping allowed. Commercial trapping prohibited. Legal subsistence trapping permitted in Alaska.	Legal sport trapping allowed. Commercial and subsistence trapping prohibited.
Grazing	Permitted where established prior to wilderness designation. Managed under guidelines for protecting both the wilderness and range resource.	Permitted where established prior to wilderness designation.	Permitted where established prior to wilderness designation.	Permitted where established prior to wilderness designation.
Domestic animals	Controlled packstock and pets allowed in most wildernesses. Some areas may be closed to either and where not compatible with the wilderness resource.	Same.	Same.	Same.
Research	Wildlife and fish research is a legitimate activity in wilderness when conducted in a manner compatible with the wilderness environment.	Same.	Same.	Same.

APPENDIX E—SUMMARY OF AGENCY WILDERNESS MANAGEMENT POLICIES RELATING TO WILDLIFE[1] *(cont.)*

	U.S. Forest Service	National Park Service	Agency Fish and Wildlife Service	Bureau of Land Management
POPULATION MANAGEMENT				
Native species	Reintroduction of wildlife species indigenous to the area which were extirpated by human-caused impacts, and to perpetuate or recover a threatened or endangered species.	Reintroduction of native wildlife species only for rehabilitation of human-caused impacts or to perpetuate wilderness character.	Reintroduction of native wildlife species only to enhance natural diversity and productivity, but not to increase recreational use.	Reintroduction of native wildlife species only for rehabilitation of human-caused impacts.
Exotic species	Introduction of exotic fish or animals prohibited.	Introduction of exotics only for nearest living relative of lost natural species or to control other undesirable exotics.	Introduction of exotic species prohibited.	Introduction of new species prohibited. Established desirable exotics may continue. Undesirable exotics may be controlled.
Stocking	Stocking of indigenous or native fish allowed to reestablish or maintain an indigenous species adversely affected by human influence or to perpetuate or recover a threatened or endangered species.	Stocking barren lakes prohibited. Stocking of native fish only to re-establish native species.	Stocking of native fish where extirpated only to enhance natural diversity and productivity, but not to increase recreational use.	Stocking of native fish species only where an established practice prior to wilderness designation. Previously nonstocked waters may be stocked on case-by-case basis (threatened and endangered species receive primary consideration). Manual and aerial methods preferred.
Predators, rodents, and insects	Control other wildlife damage to protect threatened and endangered species, prevent transmission of diseases or parasites, and prevent livestock losses. Control nonindigenous species to reduce conflicts with indigenous species, especially threatened or endangered. Allow indigenous insects to perform natural role. Control insects to protect adjacent lands. Control predators and rodents, only to protect threatened and endangered species, public safety, or to prevent livestock losses on case-by-case basis.	Control of predators only to protect nonwilderness resources, threatened and endangered species, and public health and safety.	Control of predators, rodents, and insects only to protect health, safety or non-wilderness property. Control should be accomplished with the least possible impact.	Control of predators to protect threatened and endangered species or livestock. Control of rodents and insects only for protection of wilderness values and nonwilderness property. No poisons will be used.

	Agency			
	U.S. Forest Service	*National Park Service*	*Fish and Wildlife Service*	*Bureau of Land Management*
Threatened and endangered species	Management actions must be necessary for perpetuation of species or recovery using necessary methods.	Visitors may be controlled to protect threatened and endangered species.	Protected as necessary.	Protected as necessary.
Culling	Not allowed.	Control of populations only to protect visitors.	Not covered.	Not covered.
HABITAT MANAGEMENT				
Supplemental feeding and watering	Only permitted under stringent guidelines.	Not covered.	Watering holes may be developed for refuge purposes .	Not covered.
Vegetation	Seeding only to rehabilitate human-caused impacts, or to maintain livestock grazing operations (where seeding was practiced prior to designation). Plant control only to protect grazing opportunities or nonwilderness property.	Not explicitly covered.	Not explicitly covered.	Clearing only to protect threatened and endangered species or rehabilitate human-caused impacts. Manual and aerial seeding preferred. Spraying only on case-by-case basis to protect threatened and endangered species or rehabilitate human-caused impacts.
Watershed	Watershed improvements allowed to rehabilitate human-caused impacts or protect wilderness values.	Not explicitly covered.	Not explicitly covered.	Development allowed only to rehabilitate human-caused impacts or protect non-wilderness property.
Fertilization and irrigation	Irrigate and fertilize only where grazing was established prior to designation and where needed to maintain grazing. Fertilization may also complement seeding operations for revegetation of areas.	Not explicitly covered.	Not explicitly covered.	Irrigation and fertilization only to rehabilitate human-caused impacts or to maintain grazing established prior to designation.

APPENDIX E—SUMMARY OF AGENCY WILDERNESS MANAGEMENT POLICIES RELATING TO
WILDLIFE[1] *(cont.)*

	Agency			
	U.S. Forest Service	*National Park Service*	*Fish and Wildlife Service*	*Bureau of Land Management*
Fire[2]	In some areas, lightning-caused fires are allowed to burn under carefully prescribed conditions in fire management plans. Deliberately ignited prescribed fires may also be used to meet specific objectives (reduce fuel accumulation, restore and maintain the natural role of fire, and protect life and property). Unplanned human-caused fires will be suppressed.	For areas where fire has been a historic part of the environment, naturally occurring fires and deliberately ignited prescribed fires are permitted to restore a more natural condition of fire hazard and occurrence, and to reduce the risk of fire damage to improvements within these areas, and to improvements and resources on adjacent lands.	Deliberately ignited prescribed fire and natural fires may be used when consistent with refuge objectives and contingent upon the existence of a current, approved fire management plan for the wilderness.	Use of prescribed fire is conducted almost exclusively through planned management ignitions. Prescribed natural fire is seldom used.
Other structures	Fish ladders, weirs, and fish hatcheries possible in Alaska. Established airfields and cabins allowed where included in wilderness management plans.	Not explicitly covered.	Temporary cabins, fencing, and aircraft landing facilities may be developed.	Not explicitly covered.

1. Original summary prepared by Pat Reed while he was a doctoral student at Colorado State University, 1985.

2. As a result of the severe fire season of 1988, fire management policies in all agencies are under review (USDA, USDI 1989). This table summarizes policies in effect during the 1988 season.

APPENDIX F—SECTION 1: U.S. FOREST SERVICE—DESIGNATED WILDERNESS AREAS

Wilderness Area Name	Administrative Unit Name(s)	Wilderness Acres	Wilderness Area Name	Administrative Unit Name(s)	Wilderness Acres
ALABAMA	**TOTAL ACRES:**	**33,396**	Sycamore Canyon	Coconino NF	23,325
Cheaha	Talladega NF[1]	7,490		Kaibab NF	7,125
Sipsey W. B.	Bankhead NF	25,906		Prescott NF	25,487
			West Beaver	Coconino NF	6,155
ALASKA	**TOTAL ACRES:**	**5,453,429**	West Clear Creek	Coconino NF	15,238
Admiralty Island	Tongass NF	937,459	Woodchute	Prescott NF	5,600
Coronation Island	Tongass NF	19,232			
Endicott River	Tongass NF	98,729	**ARKANSAS**	**TOTAL ACRES:**	**114,705**
Maurelle Islands	Tongass NF	4,937	Black Fork Mountain	Ouachita NF	7,576
Misty Fiords	Tongass NF	2,142,243	Caney Creek	Ouachita NF	14,460
Petersburg CR-			Dry Creek	Ouachita NF	6,310
Duncan Salt CK	Tongass NF	46,777	East Fork	Ozark NF	10,777
Russell Fiord	Tongass NF	348,701	Flatside	Ouachita NF	10,105
South Baranof	Tongass NF	319,568	Hurricane Creek	Ozark NF	15,057
South Prince of			Leatherwood	Ozark NF	16,735
Wales	Tongass NF	90,996	Poteau Mountain	Ouachita NF	10,884
Stikine-Leconte	Tongass NF	448,841	Richland Creek	Ozark NF	11,817
Tebenkof Bay	Tongass NF	66,839	Upper Buffalo	Ozark NF	10,984
Tracy Arm-Fords Terror	Tongass NF	653,179			
Warren Island	Tongass NF	11,181	**CALIFORNIA**	**TOTAL ACRES:**	**3,921,218**
West Chichagof-Yakobi	Tongass NF	264,747	Agua Tibia	Cleveland NF	15,933
			Ansel Adams	Inyo NF	78,775
ARIZONA	**TOTAL ACRES:**	**1,345,405**		Sierra NF	151,483
Apache Creek	Prescott NF	5,420	Bucks Lake	Plumas NF	21,000
Bear Wallow	Apache NF	11,080	Caribou	Lassen NF	20,546
Castle Creek	Prescott NF	26,030	Carson-Iceberg	Stanislaus NF	77,993
Cedar Bench	Prescott NF	14,950		Toiyabe NF	80,635
Chiricahua	Coronado NF	87,700	Castle Crags	Shasta NF	8,627
Escudilla	Apache NF	5,200	Chanchelulla	Trinity NF	8,200
Fossil Springs	Coconino NF	22,149	Cucamonga	Angeles NF	4,200
Four Peaks	Tonto NF	61,074		San Bernardino NF	8,581
Galiuro	Coronado NF	76,317	Desolation	Eldorado NF	63,475
Granite Mountain	Prescott NF	9,800	Dick Smith	Los Padres NF	67,800
Hellsgate	Tonto NF	37,440	Dinkey Lakes	Sierra NF	30,000
Juniper Mesa	Prescott NF	7,600	Dome Land	Sequoia NF	93,781
Kachina Peaks	Coconino NF	18,616	Emigrant	Stanislaus NF	112,277
Kanab Creek	Kaibab NF	63,760	Golden Trout	Inyo NF	192,765
Kendrick Mountain	Coconino NF	1,510		Sequoia NF	110,746
	Kaibab NF	5,000	Granite Chief	Tahoe NF	19,048
Mazatzal	Tonto NF	252,390	Hauser	Cleveland NF	7,547
Miller Peak	Coronado NF	20,190	Hoover	Inyo NF	9,507
Mount Baldy	Apache NF	7,079		Toiyabe NF	39,094
Mount Wrightson	Coronado NF	25,260	Ishi	Lassen NF	41,099
Munds Mountain	Coconino NF	24,411	Jennie Lakes	Sequoia NF	10,289
Pajarita	Coronado NF	7,420	John Muir	Inyo NF	228,366
Pine Mountain	Prescott NF	8,609		Sierra NF	351,957
	Tonto NF	11,452	Kaiser	Sierra NF	22,700
Pusch Ridge	Coronado NF	56,933	Machesna Mountain	Los Padres NF	19,760
Red Rock-Secret			Marble Mountain	Klamath NF	241,744
Mountain	Coconino NF	47,194	Mokelumne	Eldorado NF	60,154
Rincon Mountain	Coronado NF	38,590		Stanislaus NF	22,267
Saddle Mountain	Kaibab NF	40,539		Toiyabe NF	16,500
Salome	Tonto NF	18,531	Monarch	Sequoia NF	24,152
Salt River Canyon	Tonto NF	32,101		Sierra NF	20,744
Santa Teresa	Coronado NF	26,780	Mount Shasta	Shasta NF	33,845
Sierra Ancha	Tonto NF	20,850	North Fork	Six Rivers NF	7,999
Strawberry Crater	Coconino NF	10,743	Pine Creek	Cleveland NF	13,480
Superstition	Tonto NF	159,757	Red Buttes	Rogue River NF	16,150

APPENDIX F—SECTION 1: U.S. FOREST SERVICE—DESIGNATED WILDERNESS AREAS *(cont.)*

Wilderness Area Name	Administrative Unit Name(s)	Wilderness Acres	Wilderness Area Name	Administrative Unit Name(s)	Wilderness Acres
Russian	Klamath NF	12,000		Routt NF	6,659
San Gabriel	Angeles NF	36,118	Platte River	Routt NF	743
San Gorgonio	San Bernardino NF	56,722	Raggeds	Gunnison NF	43,062
San Jacinto	San Bernardino NF	32,248		White River NF	16,457
San Mateo Canyon	Cleveland NF	38,484	Rawah	Roosevelt NF	71,606
San Rafael	Los Padres NF	150,980		Routt NF	1,462
Santa Lucia	Los Padres NF	18,679	South San Juan	Rio Grande NF	87,847
Santa Rosa	San Bernardino NF	13,787		San Juan NF	39,843
Sheep	Mountain Angeles NF	39,482	Weminuche	Rio Grande NF	164,715
	San Bernardino NF	2,401		San Juan NF	294,889
Siskiyou	Klamath NF	75,680	West Elk	Gunnison NF	176,172
	Siskiyou NF	5,300			
	Six Rivers NF	71,700	**FLORIDA**	**TOTAL ACRES:**	**72,582**
Snow Mountain	Mendocino NF	36,370	Alexander Springs	Ocala NF	7,700
South Sierra	Inyo NF	53,865	Big Gum Swamp	Osceola NF	13,600
	Sequoia NF	28,219	Billies Bay	Ocala NF	3,120
South Warner	Modoc NF	70,614	Bradwell Bay	Apalachicola NF	24,602
Thousand Lakes	Lassen NF	16,335	Juniper Prairie	Ocala NF	13,260
Trinity Alps	Klamath NF	77,860	Little Lake George	Ocala NF	2,500
	Shasta NF	102,821	Mud Swamp/New River	Apalachicola NF	7,800
	Six Rivers NF	25,400			
	Trinity NF	292,060	**GEORGIA**	**TOTAL ACRES:**	**88,898**
Ventana	Los Padres	164,178	Big Frog	Chattahoochee NF	83
Yolla Bolly-Middle Eel	Mendocino NF	98,323	Brasstown	Chattahoochee NF	11,195
	Six Rivers NF	10,813	Cohutta	Chattahoochee NF	35,247
	Trinity NF	37,560	Ellicott Rock	Chattahoochee NF	2,181
			Raven Cliffs	Chattahoochee NF	8,562
COLORADO	**TOTAL ACRES:**	**2,587,137**	Rich Mountain	Chattahoochee NF	9,489
Big Blue	Uncompahgre NF	98,463	Southern Nantahala	Chattahoochee NF	12,439
Cache La Poudre	Roosevelt NF	9,238	Tray Mountain	Chattahoochee NF	9,702
Collegiate Peaks	Gunnison NF	48,986			
	San Isabel NF	82,248	**IDAHO**	**TOTAL ACRES:**	**3,960,221**
	White River NF	35,482	Frank Church-River	Bitterroot NF	193,703
Comanche Peak	Roosevelt NF	66,791	of No Return		
Eagles Nest	Arapaho NF	82,743		Boise NF	331,611
	White River NF	50,582		Challis NF	515,421
Flat Tops	Routt NF	38,870		Nez Perce NF	110,698
	White River NF	196,165		Payette NF	791,675
Holy Cross	San Isabel NF	9,489		Salmon NF	421,433
	White River NF	112,899	Gospel Hump	Nez Perce NF	205,764
Hunter Fryingpan	White River NF	74,399	Hells Canyon	Nez Perce NF	59,900
Indian Peaks	Arapaho NF	40,109		Payette NF	23,911
	Roosevelt NF	30,265	Sawtooth	Boise NF	150,071
La Garita	Gunnison NF	79,822		Challis NF	12,020
	Rio Grande NF	24,164		Sawtooth NF	54,997
Lizard Head	San Juan NF	20,802	Selway-Bitterroot	Bitterroot NF	270,321
	Uncompahgre NF	20,387		Clearwater NF	259,165
Lost Creek	Pike NF	105,090		Nez Perce NF	559,531
Maroon Bells-Snowmass	Gunnison NF	19,194			
	White River NF	161,768	**INDIANA**	**TOTAL ACRES:**	**12,935**
Mount Evans	Arapaho NF	40,274	Charles C. Dean	Hoosier NF	12,935
	Pike NF	34,127			
Mount Massive	San Isabel NF	27,980	**KENTUCKY**	**TOTAL ACRES:**	**17,183**
Mount Sneffels	Uncompahgre NF	16,505	Beaver Creek	Daniel Boone NF	4,756
Mount Zirkel	Routt NF	139,818	Clifty	Daniel Boone NF	12,427
Neota	Roosevelt NF	9,657			
	Routt NF	267	**LOUISIANA**	**TOTAL ACRES:**	**8,700**
Never Summer	Arapaho NF	7,098	Kisatchie Hills	Kisatchie NF	8,700

Wilderness Area Name	Administrative Unit Name(s)	Wilderness Acres	Wilderness Area Name	Administrative Unit Name(s)	Wilderness Acres
MICHIGAN	**TOTAL ACRES:**	**91,875**	Boundary Peak	Inyo NF	10,000
Big Island Lake	Hiawatha NF	5,840	Currant Mountain	Humboldt NF	36,000
Delirium	Hiawatha NF	11,870	East Humboldt	Humboldt NF	36,900
Horseshoe Bay	Hiawatha NF	3,790	Grant Range	Humboldt NF	50,000
Mackinac	Hiawatha NF	12,230	Jarbidge	Humboldt NF	113,167
McCormick	Ottawa NF	16,850	Mount Charleston	Toiyabe NF	43,000
Nordhouse Dunes	Manistee NF	3,450	Mount Moriah	Humboldt NF	82,000
Rock River Canyon	Hiawatha NF	4,640	Mount Rose	Toiyabe NF	28,000
Round Island	Hiawatha NF	378	Quinn Canyon	Humboldt NF	27,000
Sturgeon River Gorge	Ottawa NF	14,500	Ruby Mountains	Humboldt NF	90,000
Sylvania	Ottawa NF	18,327	Santa Rosa - Paradise Peak	Humboldt NF	31,000
			Table Mountain	Toiyabe NF	98,000
MINNESOTA	**TOTAL ACRES:**	**799,276**			
Boundary Waters			**NEW HAMPSHIRE**	**TOTAL ACRES:**	**102,932**
Canoe Area	Superior NF	799,276	Great Gulf	White Mountain NF	5,552
			Pemigewasset	White Mountain NF	45,000
MISSISSIPPI	**TOTAL ACRES:**	**6,006**	Presidential Range-		
Black Creek	Desoto NF	5,012	Dry River	White Mountain NF	27,380
Leaf	Desoto NF	994	Sandwich Range	White Mountain NF	25,000
MISSOURI	**TOTAL ACRES:**	**63,198**	**NEW MEXICO**	**TOTAL ACRES:**	**1,388,063**
Bell Mountain	Mark Twain NF	8,977	Aldo Leopold	Gila NF	202,016
Devils Backbone	Mark Twain NF	6,595	Apache Kid	Cibola NF	44,626
Hercules-Glades	Mark Twain NF	12,314	Blue Range	Apache NF	28,104
Irish	Mark Twain NF	16,117		Gila NF	1,200
Paddy Creek	Mark Twain NF	7,019	Capitan Mountains	Lincoln NF	34,658
Piney Creek	Mark Twain NF	8,087	Chama River Canyon	Carson NF	2,900
Rockpile Mountain	Mark Twain NF	4,089		Santa Fe NF	47,400
			Cruces Basin	Carson NF	18,000
MONTANA	**TOTAL ACRES:**	**3,371,630**	Dome	Santa Fe NF	5,200
Absaroka-Beartooth	Custer NF	345,589	Gila	Gila NF	557,873
	Gallatin NF	574,738	Latir Peak	Carson NF	20,000
Anaconda-Pintler	Beaverhead NF	72,537	Manzano Mountain	Cibola NF	36,875
	Bitterroot NF	41,162	Pecos	Carson NF	24,736
	Deerlodge NF	44,175		Santa Fe NF	198,597
Bob Marshall	Flathead NF	709,356	San Pedro Parks	Santa Fe NF	41,132
	Lewis & Clark NF	300,000	Sandia Mountains	Cibola NF	37,877
Cabinet Mountains	Kaniksu NF	44,320	Wheeler Peak	Carson NF	19,661
	Kootenai NF	49,952	White Mountain	Lincoln NF	48,208
Gates of the Mountains	Helena NF	28,562	Withington	Cibola NF	19,000
Great Bear	Flathead NF	286,700			
Lee Metcalf	Beaverhead NF	108,350	**NORTH CAROLINA**	**TOTAL ACRES:**	**101,273**
	Gallatin NF	140,594	Birkhead Mountains	Uwharrie NF	4,790
Mission Mountains	Flathead NF	73,877	Catfish Lake South	Croatan NF	7,600
Rattlesnake	Lolo NF	32,844	Ellicott Rock	Nantahala NF	3,930
Scapegoat	Helena NF	80,697	Joyce Kilmer-Slickrock	Nantahala NF	13,132
	Lewis & Clark NF	84,407	Linville Gorge	Pisgah NF	10,975
	Lolo NF	74,192	Middle Prong	Pisgah NF	7,900
Selway-Bitterroot	Bitterroot NF	241,676	Pocostin	Croatan NF	11,000
	Lolo NF	9,767	Pond Pine	Croatan NF	1,860
Welcome Creek	Lolo NF	28,135	Sheep Ridge	Croatan NF	9,540
			Shining Rock	Pisgah NF	18,450
NEBRASKA	**TOTAL ACRES:**	**7,794**	Southern Nantahala	Nantahala NF	12,096
Soldier Creek	Nebraska NF	7,794			
			OKLAHOMA	**TOTAL ACRES:**	**14,274**
NEVADA	**TOTAL ACRES:**	**798,067**	Blackfork Mountain	Ouachita NF	4,583
Alta Toquima	Toiyabe NF	38,000	Upper Kiamichi	Ouachita NF	9,691
Arc Dome	Toiyabe NF	115,000			

APPENDIX F—SECTION 1: U.S. FOREST SERVICE—DESIGNATED WILDERNESS AREAS *(cont.)*

Wilderness Area Name	Administrative Unit Name(s)	Wilderness Acres	Wilderness Area Name	Administrative Unit Name(s)	Wilderness Acres
OREGON	**TOTAL ACRES:**	**2,079,212**	Hell Hole Bay	Francis Marion NF	2,180
Badger Creek	Mt. Hood NF	24,000	Little Wambaw Swamp	Francis Marion NF	5,154
Black Canyon	Ochoco NF	13,400	Wambaw Creek	Francis Marion NF	1,937
Boulder Creek	Umpqua NF	19,100	Wambaw Swamp	Francis Marion NF	4,767
Bridge Creek	Ochoco NF	5,400			
Bull of the Woods	Mt. Hood NF	27,427	**SOUTH DAKOTA**	**TOTAL ACRES:**	**9,824**
	Willamette NF	7,473	Black Elk	Black Hills NF	9,824
Columbia	Mt. Hood NF	39,000			
Cummins Creek	Siuslaw NF	9,173	**TENNESSEE**	**TOTAL ACRES:**	**66,632**
Diamond Peak	Deschutes NF	34,413	Bald River Gorge	Cherokee NF	3,721
	Willamette NF	19,772	Big Frog	Cherokee NF	7,986
Drift Creek	Siuslaw NF	5,798	Big Laurel Branch	Cherokee NF	6,251
Eagle Cap	Wallowa NF	212,699	Citico Creek	Cherokee NF	16,226
	Whitman NF	145,762	Cohutta	Cherokee NF	1,795
Gearhart Mountain	Fremont NF	22,809	Gee Creek	Cherokee NF	2,493
Grassy Knob	Siskiyou NF	17,200	Joyce Kilmer-Slickrock	Cherokee NF	3,832
Hells Canyon	Wallowa NF	118,247	Little Frog Mountain	Cherokee NF	4,684
	Whitman NF	11,848	Pond Mountain	Cherokee NF	6,625
Kalmiopsis	Siskiyou NF	179,700	Sampson Mountain	Cherokee NF	8,319
Menagerie	Willamette NF	4,800	Unaka Mountain	Cherokee NF	4,700
Middle Santiam	Willamette NF	7,500			
Mill Creek	Ochoco NF	17,400	**TEXAS**	**TOTAL ACRES:**	**36,020**
Monument Rock	Malheur NF	12,620	Big Slough	Davy Crockett NF	3,584
	Whitman NF	7,030	Indian Mounds	Sabine NF	10,917
Mount Hood	Mt. Hood NF	46,520	Little Lake Creek	Sam Houston NF	3,810
Mount Jefferson	Deschutes NF	32,734	Turkey Hill	Angelina NF	5,286
	Mt. Hood NF	5,021	Upland Island	Angelina NF	12,423
	Willamette NF	69,253			
Mount Thielsen	Deschutes NF	5,911	**UTAH**	**TOTAL ACRES:**	**774,328**
	Umpqua NF	21,480	Ashdown Gorge	Dixie NF	7,000
	Winema NF	27,709	Box-Death Hollow	Dixie NF	25,751
Mount Washington	Deschutes NF	14,116	Dark Canyon	Manti-La Sal NF	45,000
	Willamette NF	38,622	Deseret Peak	Wasatch NF	25,500
Mountain Lakes	Winema NF	23,071	High Uintas	Ashley NF	276,175
North Fork John Day	Umatilla NF	107,058		Wasatch NF	180,530
	Whitman NF	14,294	Lone Peak	Uinta NF	21,166
North Fork Umatilla	Umatilla NF	20,435		Wasatch NF	8,922
Red Buttes	Rogue River NF	350	Mount Naomi	Cache NF	44,350
	Siskiyou NF	3,400	Mount Nebo	Uinta NF	28,000
Rock Creek	Siuslaw NF	7,472	Mount Olympus	Wasatch NF	16,000
Rogue-Umpqua Divide	Rogue River NF	6,850	Mount Timpanagos	Uinta NF	10,750
	Umpqua NF	26,350	Pine Valley Mountain	Dixie NF	50,000
Salmon-Huckleberry	Mt. Hood NF	44,560	Twin Peaks	Wasatch NF	11,334
Sky Lakes	Rogue River NF	75,695	Wellsville Mountain	Cache NF	23,850
	Winema NF	40,605			
Strawberry Mountain	Malheur NF	68,700	**VERMONT**	**TOTAL ACRES:**	**59,421**
Three Sisters	Deschutes NF	92,706	Big Branch	Green Mountain NF	6,720
	Willamette NF	192,496	Breadloaf	Green Mountain NF	21,480
Waldo Lake	Willamette NF	39,200	Bristol Cliffs	Green Mountain NF	3,738
Wenaha-Tucannon	Umatilla NF	66,375	George D. Aiken	Green Mountain NF	5,060
Wild Rogue	Siskiyou NF	25,658	Lyle Brook	Green Mountain NF	15,503
			Peru Peak	Green Mountain NF	6,920
PENNSYLVANIA	**TOTAL ACRES:**	**8,938**			
Allegheny Islands	Allegheny NF	368	**VIRGINIA**	**TOTAL ACRES:**	**89,459**
Hickory Creek	Allegheny NF	8,570	Barbours	Jefferson NF	5,600
			Beartown	Jefferson NF	6,043
SOUTH CAROLINA	**TOTAL ACRES:**	**16,847**	James River Face	Jefferson NF	9,086
Ellicott Rock	Sumter NF	2,809	Kimberling Creek	Jefferson NF	5,580

Wilderness Area Name	Administrative Unit Name(s)	Wilderness Acres	Wilderness Area Name	Administrative Unit Name(s)	Wilderness Acres
Lewis Fork	Jefferson NF	5,802	The Brothers	Olympic NF	16,682
Little Dry Run	Jefferson NF	3,400	Trapper Creek	Gifford Pinchot NF	5,970
Little Wilson Creek	Jefferson NF	3,855	Wenaha-Tucannon	Umatilla NF	111,048
Mountain Lake	Jefferson NF	8,253	William O. Douglas	Gifford Pinchot NF	15,880
Peters Mountain	Jefferson NF	3,326		Snoqualmie NF	152,408
Ramseys Draft	George Washington NF	6,725	Wonder Mountain	Olympic NF	2,349
Rich Hole	George Washington NF	6,450			
Rough Mountain	George Washington NF	9,300	**WEST VIRGINIA**	**TOTAL ACRES:**	**80,631**
Saint Mary's	George Washington NF	10,090	Cranberry	Monongahela NF	35,864
Shawvers Run	George Washington NF	95	Dolly Sods	Monongahela NF	10,215
	Jefferson NF	3,510	Laurel Fork North	Monongahela NF	6,055
Thunder Ridge	Jefferson NF	2,344	Laurel Fork South	Monongahela NF	5,997
			Mountain Lake	Jefferson NF	2,500
WASHINGTON	**TOTAL ACRES:**	**2,571,380**	Otter Creek	Monongahela NF	20,000
Alpine Lakes	Snoqualmie NF	117,776			
	Wenatchee NF	244,845	**WISCONSIN**	**TOTAL ACRES:**	**42,172**
Boulder River	Mt. Baker NF	48,674	Blackjack Springs	Nicolet NF	5,886
Buckhorn	Olympic NF	44,258	Headwaters	Nicolet NF	18,108
Clearwater	Snoqualmie NF	14,598	Porcupine Lake	Chequamegon NF	4,250
Colonel Bob	Olympic NF	11,961	Rainbow	Chequamegon NF	6,583
Glacier Peak	Mt. Baker NF	283,252	Whisker Lake	Nicolet NF	7,345
	Wenatchee NF	289,086			
Glacier View	Gifford Pinchot NF	3,123	**WYOMING**	**TOTAL ACRES:**	**3,080,371**
Goat Rocks	Gifford Pinchot NF	68,690	Absaroka-Beartooth	Shoshone NF	23,283
	Snoqualmie NF	35,951	Bridger	Bridger NF	428,087
Henry M. Jackson	Mt. Baker NF	27,985	Cloud Peak	Bighorn NF	189,039
	Snoqualmie NF	47,446	Encampment River	Medicine Bow NF	10,124
	Wenatchee NF	27,242	Fitzpatrick	Shoshone NF	198,525
Indian Heaven	Gifford Pinchot NF	20,960	Gros Ventre	Teton NF	287,000
Lake Chelan-Sawtooth	Okanogan NF	95,021	Huston Park	Medicine Bow NF	30,588
	Wenatchee NF	56,414	Jedediah Smith	Targhee NF	123,451
Mount Adams	Gifford Pinchot NF	46,626	North Absaroka	Shoshone NF	350,488
Mount Baker	Mt. Baker NF	117,528	Platte River	Medicine Bow NF	22,749
Mount Skokomish	Olympic NF	13,015	Popo Agie	Shoshone NF	101,870
Noisy-Diobsud	Mt. Baker NF	14,133	Savage Run	Medicine Bow NF	14,940
Norse Peak	Snoqualmie NF	51,343	Teton	Teton NF	585,238
Pasayten	Mt. Baker NF	107,039	Washakie	Shoshone NF	704,274
	Okanogan NF	422,992	Winegar Hole	Targhee NF	10,715
Salmo-Priest	Colville NF	29,386			
	Kaniksu NF	11,949	**GRAND TOTAL:**	**368 AREAS:**	**33,275,432 ACRES**
Tatoosh	Gifford Pinchot NF	15,750			

Note: National Forest System Lands source of information is *Land Areas of the National Forest System as of September 30, 1989*, Forest Service Publication FS-383. Additional information for the State of Nevada came directly from P.L. 101-195.
1. NF = National Forest.

APPENDIX F—SECTION 2: NATIONAL PARK SERVICE—DESIGNATED WILDERNESS AREAS

Wilderness Area Name	Administrative Unit Name(s)	Wilderness Acres	Wilderness Area Name	Administrative Unit Name(s)	Wilderness Acres
ALASKA	**TOTAL ACRES**	**32,979,370**	**GEORGIA**	**TOTAL ACRES:**	**8,840**
Denali	Denali NP[1]	2,124,783	Cumberland Island	Cumberland Island NSS	8,840
Gates of the Arctic	Gates of the Arctic & Preserve NP	7,167,192	**HAWAII**	**TOTAL ACRES:**	**142,370**
Glacier Bay	Glacier Bay NP & Preserve	2,664,840	Haleakala	Haleakala NP	19,270
Katmai	Katmai NP & Preserve	3,384,358	Hawaii Volcanoes	Hawaii Volcanoes NP	123,100
Kobuk Valley	Kobuk Valley NP	174,545			
Lake Clark	Lake Clark NP	2,619,550	**IDAHO**	**TOTAL ACRES:**	**43,243**
Noatak	Noatak National Preserve	5,765,427	Craters of the Moon	Craters of the Moon NM	43,243
Wrangell-St. Elias	Wrangall-St. Elias NP &Preserve	9,078,675	**MICHIGAN**	**TOTAL ACRES:**	**131,880**
			Isle Royale	Isle Royale NP	131,880
ARIZONA	**TOTAL ACRES**	**443,700**			
Chiricahua	Chiricahua NM[2]	9,440	**MISSISSIPPI**	**TOTAL ACRES:**	—
Organ Pipe Cactus	Organ Pipe Cactus NM	312,600	Gulf Islands	Gulf Islands NSS	—[4]
Petrified Forest	Petrified Forest NP	50,260			
Saguaro	Saguaro NM	71,400	**NEW MEXICO**	**TOTAL ACRES:**	**56,393**
			Bandelier	Bandelier NM	23,267
ARKANSAS	**TOTAL ACRES**	**10,529**	Carlsbad Caverns	Carlsbad Caverns NP	33,125
Buffalo Natl. River	Buffalo National River	10,529			
			NEW YORK	**TOTAL ACRES:**	**1,363**
CALIFORNIA	**TOTAL ACRES**	**1,990,034**	Fire Island	Fire Island NSS	1,363
Joshua Tree	Joshua Tree NM	429,690			
Lassen Volcanic	Lassen Volcanic NP	78,982	**NORTH DAKOTA**	**TOTAL ACRES:**	**29,920**
Lava Beds	Lava Beds NM	28,460	Theodore Roosevelt	Theodore Roosevelt NP	29,920
Phil Burton (NSS)[3]	Point Reyes	25,370			
Pinnacles	Pinnacles NM	12,952	**SOUTH CAROLINA**	**TOTAL ACRES:**	**15,010**
Sequoia-Kings Canyon	Sequoia-Kings Canyon NP	736,980	Congaree Swamp	Congaree Swamp NM	15,010
Yosemite	Yosemite NP	677,600	**SOUTH DAKOTA**	**TOTAL ACRES:**	**64,250**
			Badlands	Badlands NM	64,250
COLORADO	**TOTAL ACRES**	**55,647**			
Black Canyon of the Gunnison	Black Canyon of the Gunnison NM	11,180	**TEXAS**	**TOTAL ACRES:**	**46,850**
			Guadalupe Mountains	Guadalupe Mountains NP	46,850
Great Sand Dunes	Great Sand Dunes NM	33,450			
Indian Peaks	Rocky Mountain NP	2,917	**VIRGINIA**	**TOTAL ACRES:**	**79,579**
Mesa Verde	Mesa Verde NP	8,100	Shenandoah	Shenandoah NP	79,579
FLORIDA	**TOTAL ACRES**	**1,298,300**	**WASHINGTON**	**TOTAL ACRES:**	**1,678,138**
Everglades	Everglades NP	1,296,500	Mount Ranier	Mount Ranier NP	216,855
Gulf Islands	Gulf Islands NSS	1,800	Olympic	Olympic NP	826,669
			Stephen Mather	North Cascades NP	634,614
			GRAND TOTAL:	**42 AREAS**	**39,075,415 ACRES**

1. NP = National Park.
2. NM = National Monument.
3. NSS = National Seashore.
4. All acreage reported under Florida listing.

APPENDIX F—SECTION 3: FISH AND WILDLIFE SERVICE—DESIGNATED WILDERNESS AREAS

Wilderness Area Name	Administrative Unit Name(s)	Wilderness Acres	Wilderness Area Name	Administrative Unit Name(s)	Wilderness Acres
ALASKA	**TOTAL ACRES:**	**18,676,320**	**MAINE**	**TOTAL ACRES:**	**7,392**
Aleutian Islands	Alaska Maritime NWR[1]	1,300,000	Baring Unit	Moosehorn NWR	4,680
Andreafsky	Yukon Delta NWR	1,300,000	Birch Islands Unit	Moosehorn NWR	6
Arctic	Arctic NWR	8,000,000	Edmunds Unit	Moosehorn NWR	2,706
Becharof	Becharof NWR	400,000			
Bering Sea	Alaska Maritime NWR	81,340	**MASSACHUSETTS**	**TOTAL ACRES:**	**2,420**
Bogoslof	Alaska Maritime NWR	175	Monomoy	Monomoy NWR	2,420
Chamisso	Alaska Maritime NWR	455			
Forrester Island	Alaska Maritime NWR	2,832	**MICHIGAN**	**TOTAL ACRES:**	**25,309**
Hazy Island	Alaska Maritime NWR	32	Huron Islands	Huron NWR	147
Innoko	Innoko NWR	1,240,000	Michigan Islands	Michigan Islands NWR	12
Izembek	Izembek NWR	300,000	Seney	Seney NWR	25,150
Kenai	Kenai NWR	1,350,000			
Koyukuk	Koyukuk NWR	400,000	**MINNESOTA**	**TOTAL ACRES:**	**6,180**
Nunivak	Yukon Delta NWR	600,000	Agassiz	Agassiz NWR	4,000
Saint Lazaria	Alaska Maritime NWR	65	Tamarac	Tamarac NWR	2,180
Selawik	Selawik NWR	240,000			
Semidi	Alaska Maritime NWR	250,000	**MISSOURI**	**TOTAL ACRES:**	**7,730**
Simeonof	Alaska Maritime NWR	25,855	Mingo	Mingo NWR	7,730
Togiak	Togiak NWR	2,270,000			
Tuxedni	Alaska Maritime NWR	5,566	**MONTANA**	**TOTAL ACRES:**	**64,535**
Unimak	Alaska Maritime NWR	910,000	Medicine Lake	Medicine Lake NWR	11,366
			Red Rock Lakes	Red Rock Lakes NWR	32,350
ARKANSAS	**TOTAL ACRES:**	**2,144**	UL Bend	UL Bend NWR	20,819
Big Lake	Big Lake NWR	2,144			
			NEBRASKA	**TOTAL ACRES:**	**4,635**
CALIFORNIA	**TOTAL ACRES:**	**141**	Fort Niobrara	Fort Niobrara NWR	4,635
Farallon	Farallon NWR	141			
			NEW JERSEY	**TOTAL ACRES:**	**10,341**
COLORADO	**TOTAL ACRES:**	**2,560**	Brigantine	Edwin B. Forsythe NWR	6,681
Mount Massive	Leadville NFH [2]	2,560	Great Swamp	Great Swamp NWR	3,660
FLORIDA	**TOTAL ACRES:**	**51,253**	**NEW MEXICO**	**TOTAL ACRES:**	**39,908**
Cedar Keys	Cedar Keys NWR	379	Chupadera Unit	Bosque del Apache NWR	5,289
Chassahowitzka	Chassahowitzka NWR	23,580	Indian Well Unit	Bosque del Apache NWR	5,139
Florida Keys	Great White Heron NWR	1,900	Little San Pascual Unit	Bosque del Apache NWR	19,859
	Key West NWR	2,019	Salt Creek	Bitter Lake NWR	9,621
	National Key Deer Refuge	2,278			
Island Bay	Island Bay NWR	20	**NORTH CAROLINA**	**TOTAL ACRES:**	**8,785**
J.N. "Ding" Darling	J.N. "Ding" Darling NWR	2,619	Swanquarter	Swanquarter NWR	8,785
Lake Woodruff	Lake Woodruff NWR	1,066			
Passage Key	Passage Key NWR	36	**NORTH DAKOTA**	**TOTAL ACRES:**	**9,732**
Pelican Island	Pelican Island NWR	6	Chase Lake	Chase Lake NWR	4,155
St. Marks	St. Marks NWR	17,350	Lostwood	Lostwood NWR	5,577
GEORGIA	**TOTAL ACRES:**	**362,107**	**OHIO**	**TOTAL ACRES:**	**77**
Blackbeard Island	Blackbeard Island NWR	3,000	West Sister Island	West Sister Island NWR	77
Okefenokee	Okefenokee NWR	353,981			
Wolf Island	Wolf Island NWR	5,126	**OKLAHOMA**	**TOTAL ACRES:**	**8,570**
			Charons Garden Unit	Wichita Mountains NWR	5,723
ILLINOIS	**TOTAL ACRES:**	**4,050**			
Crab Orchard	Crab Orchard NWR	4,050	North Mountain Unit	Wichita Mountains NWR	2,847
LOUISIANA	**TOTAL ACRES:**	**8,346**			
Breton	Breton NWR	5,000			
Lacassine	Lacassine NWR	3,346			

APPENDIX F—SECTION 3: FISH AND WILDLIFE SERVICE—DESIGNATED WILDERNESS AREAS *(cont.)*

Wilderness Area Name	Administrative Unit Name(s)	Wilderness Acres	Wilderness Area Name	Administrative Unit Name(s)	Wilderness Acres
OREGON	**TOTAL ACRES:**	**495**	**WISCONSIN**	**TOTAL ACRES:**	**29**
Oregon Islands	Oregon Islands NWR	21	Wisconsin Islands	Gravel Island NWR	27
Three Arch Rocks	Three Arch Rocks NWR	15		Green Bay NWR	2
		459	**GRAND TOTAL:**	**71 AREAS**	**19,332,897 ACRES**
SOUTH CAROLINA	**TOTAL ACRES:**	**2 9,000**			
Cape Romain	Cape Romain NWR	29,000			
WASHINGTON	**TOTAL ACRES:**	**838**			
San Juan Islands	San Juan Islands NWR	353			
Washington Islands	Copalis NWR	60			
	Flattery Rocks NWR	125			
	Quillayute Needles NWR	300			

1. NWR = National Wildlife Refuge.
2. NFH = National Fish Hatchery.

APPENDIX F: SECTION 4: BUREAU OF LAND MANAGEMENT—DESIGNATED WILDERNESS AREAS

Wilderness Area Name	Administrative Unit Name(s)	Wilderness Acres	Wilderness Area Name	Administrative Unit Name(s)	Wilderness Acres
ARIZONA	**TOTAL ACRES:**	**272,520**	**NEW MEXICO**	**TOTAL ACRES:**	**128,900**
Aravaipa Canyon	Safford District	6,670	Bisti	Albuquerque District	3,946
Beaver Dam Mountains	Arizona Strip District	17,000	Cebolla	Albuquerque District	62,800
Cottonwood Point	Arizona Strip District	6,500	De-na-zin	Albuquerque District	22,454
Grand Wash Cliffs	Arizona Strip District	36,300	West Malpais	Albuquerque District	39,700
Kanab Creek	Arizona Strip District	8,850			
Mount Logan	Arizona Strip District	14,600	**OREGON**	**TOTAL ACRES:**	**16,703**
Mount Trumbull	Arizona Strip District	7,900	Hells Canyon	Vale District	1,038
Paiute	Arizona Strip District	84,700	Oregon Islands	Coos Bay District	5
Paria Canyon-Vermilion Cliffs	Arizona Strip District	90,000	Table Rock	Salem District	5,500
			Wild Rogue	Medford District	10,160
CALIFORNIA	**TOTAL ACRES:**	**13,861**			
Ishi	Ukiah District	240	**UTAH**	**TOTAL ACRES:**	**22,600**
Machesna Mountain	Bakersfield District	120	Beaver Dam Mountains	Cedar City District	2,600
Santa Lucia	Bakersfield District	1,733	Paria Canyon-Vermilion Cliffs	Cedar City District	20,000
Trinity Alps	Ukiah District	4,623			
Yolla Bolly-Middle Eel	Ukiah District	7,145	**WASHINGTON**	**TOTAL ACRES:**	**7,140**
			Juniper Dunes	Spokane District	7,140
IDAHO	**TOTAL ACRES:**	**720**			
Frank Church-River of No Return	Coeur d'Alene District	720	**GRAND TOTAL:**	**28 AREAS**	**474,902 ACRES**
MONTANA	**TOTAL ACRES:**	**6,000**			
Lee Metcalf-Bear Trap	Butte District	6,000			
NEVADA	**TOTAL ACRES:**	**6,458**			
Arc Dome	Battle Mountain District	20			
Currant Mountain	Ely District	3			
Mount Moriah	Ely District	6,435			

APPENDIX F— SECTION 5: NATIONAL WILDERNESS PRESERVATION SYSTEM SUMMARY

Agency	*National Wilderness Preservation System*		
	Units	*Federal Acres*	*(%)*
Forest Service, USDA	367	33,275,432	(36)
National Park Service, USDI	42	39,075,415	(42)
Fish and Wildlife Service, USDI	71	19,332,897	(21)
Bureau of Land Management, USDI	28	474,902	(1)
GRAND TOTAL	**492**	**92,158,646**	**(100)**

Agency	*National Wilderness Preservation System (excluding Alaska):*		
	Units	*Federal Acres*	*(%)*
Forest Service, USDA	353	27,822,003	(79)
National Park Service, USDI	34	6,096,045	(18)
Fish and Wildlife Service, USDI	50	656,577	(2)
Bureau of Land Management, USDI	28	474,902	(1)
TOTAL	**449**	**35,049,527**	**(100)**

Agency	*National Wilderness Preservation System (Alaska):*		
	Units	*Federal Acres*	*(%)*
Forest Service, USDA	14	5,453,429	(10)
National Park Service, USDI	8	32,979,370	(57)
Fish and Wildlife Service, USDI	21	18,676,320	(33)
TOTAL	**43**	**57,109,119**	**(100)**

Note: Detailed breakdowns by wilderness within each state and agency jurisdiction can be found in the Annual Wilderness Report to Congress. Some acreage values are estimates, pending final mapping and surveys. Total number of units for all agencies is 492; this is not additive from information above because of overlapping responsibilities.

Glossary

abiotic environment. Includes climatic conditions such as temperature and moisture regimes, and inorganic substances supplied by mineral soil.

acid-neutralizing capacity (ANC). The scientific indicator of buffering capacity (see *buffering capacity* and chap. 13).

acid rain. A phenomenon which occurs when sulfur dioxide and nitrogen oxides are chemically transformed into acidic sulfates and nitrates during atmospheric transport and are subsequently deposited downwind as acid precipitation (either rain or snow), acid fog, or as acidic particles (see chap. 13).

activity plan. Used by the BLM. A wilderness management plan prepared for a specific wilderness area, or two or more closely related areas. They help implement the BLM's wilderness management policy (see chap. 8).

ANC. See *acid-neutralizing capacity*.

anthropocentric. A philosophical viewpoint which sees wilderness primarily from a human-oriented perspective. The naturalness of the wilderness is less important than facilitating human use and convenience. Programs that would alter the physical and biological environment to produce desired settings are encouraged (see chap. 1).

autotrophs. Organisms that are green plants and provide the ecosystem's entire energy base by fixing solar energy and by using simple inorganic substances to build complex organic substances.

Bailey-Küchler System. A system using Bailey's ecoregion concept and Küchler's system of potential natural vegetation for classifying ecosystems in the United States and Puerto Rico. The system considers both physical environment factors, such as climate and soil, and biological environment factors, such as vegetation.

biocentric. A philosophical viewpoint which emphasizes the maintenance of natural systems at the expense of recreational and other human uses, if necessary, because wilderness values depend on naturalness and solitude. The goal of this philosophy is to permit natural ecological processes to operate as freely as possible, because wilderness values for society ultimately depend on the retention of naturalness and solitude (see chap. 1).

biological oxygen demand. The oxygen used in meeting the metabolic needs of aerobic microorganisms in water rich in organic matter (as in water polluted with sewage).

biome. A major type of terrestrial community, e.g., tropical rainforests, deserts, etc., which are recognizable by the characteristic structure of the dominant vegetation in that community.

Biosphere Reserves. Designated areas in an international network of representative protected areas. Biosphere Reserves are representative examples of the world's major biomes, which help complete a portrait of the world's ecosystems, and they often contain areas where environmental conditions are actively managed and accommodate human activity, as well as natural areas. Ideally, Biosphere Reserves contain a natural or core zone where minimal human impact is present and surrounding zones with human activity and natural resource use (see chap. 3).

biota. Fauna and flora together.

biotic environment. Biological members of an organism's habitat that interact with it, including competitors, predators, and parasites.

buffering capacity. Soil's ability to neutralize acids without a change in pH (see chap. 13).

bulk density. The weight of soil packed into a given volume (see chap. 16).

carrying capacity. The maximum level of use an area can sustain without exceeding the LAC in social and environmental conditions. As applied to recreational use of wilderness, often includes the effects of such use on experience quality due to crowding and conflict (see chaps. 7 and 9).

classified wilderness. Areas formally protected by the Wilderness Act of 1964 and its extension to eastern lands by the so-called Eastern Wilderness Act, to public lands by the Federal Land Policy and Management Act of 1976, and to Alaska by the Alaska National Interest Lands Conservation Act of 1980.

common wildlife. In wilderness, species that happen to be found in wilderness, but that also live in more modified environments. Their relationship to wilderness is incidental (see chap. 11).

de facto **wilderness.** Public lands that are wilderness in the general sense of the term, roadless and undeveloped, but which as wilderness have not been designated by Congress. Lands potentially available for wilderness classification.

de jure **wilderness.** Wilderness areas, officially designated and protected under provisions of the Wilderness Act of 1964, and belonging to the NWPS.

direct management. Management which emphasizes regulating peoples' behaviors; individual choice is restricted and managers aim at directly controlling visitor behavior with regulations and use requirements (see chap. 15). Contrasts with indirect management.

ecosystems. Includes all the organisms of an area, their environment, and the linkages or interactions between them; all parts of an ecosystem are interrelated. The fundamental unit in ecology, containing both organisms and abiotic environments, each influencing the properties of the other and both necessary for the maintenance of life (see chaps. 10 and 11).

ecotones. A habitat created by the juxtaposition of distinctly different habitats; a transitional zone between habitat types, containing species of both habitats.

ecotypes. A genetically differentiated subpopulation that is restricted to a specific habitat.

EIS. See *Environmental Impact Statement.*

Environmental Impact Statement (EIS). A required report for all federal actions that will lead to significant affects upon the quality of the human environment. The report must be systematic and interdisciplinary, integrating the natural and social sciences as well as the design arts in planning and in decision-making. The report must identify (1) the environmental impact of the proposed action, (2) any adverse environmental effects which cannot be avoided should the proposal be implemented, (3) alternatives to the proposed action, (4) the relationship between local short-term uses of man's environment and the maintenance and enhancement of long-term productivity, and (5) any irreversible and irretrievable commitments of resources which would be involved in the proposed action should it be implemented.

environmental modification spectrum. A concept that describes a continuum of settings which range from the totally modified landscape of a modern city to those remote and pristine reaches of a country (see chaps. 6 and 7). Related to the Recreation Opportunity Spectrum (ROS) and Wilderness Opportunity Spectrum (WOS) (see chap. 8).

exotic pathogens. Non-indigenous pathogenic organisms introduced into an ecosystem which may have potentially profound effects on otherwise pristine landscapes. Because ecological interactions are unknown, and host species may lack mechanisms for resistance, effects may be permanent (see chap. 10).

exotic species. Includes species introduced into a wilderness that may have adapted to wilderness ecosystems and compete with resident native (indigenous) wildlife species (The term *alien species* is also being used because "exotic" may connote something fascinating or wondrous.) (see chap. 11).

feral. Having returned to a wild state from domestication, such as feral horses, goats, pigs, and dogs.

fire dependent. An ecosystem evolving under periodic perturbations by fire and which consequently depends on periodic fires for normal ecosystem functioning (see chap. 12).

fire regime. The kind of fire activity (frequency and intensity). that characterizes a specific region (see chap. 12).

Forest Land and Resource Management Plan. Also know as the Land Management Plan (LMP) or Forest Plan used by the USFS. These plans translate national and regional direction into forest and wilderness goals, a description of the lands where prescriptions apply, a statement of the desired future condition, and a set of standards and guidelines for meeting the goals (see chap. 8).

forest structure. Often divided into four conceptual aspects: age structure, species composition, horizontal structure or mosaic pattern, and vertical structure or fuel ladders (see chap. 12).

gene. Generally, a unit of genetic inheritance. In biochemistry, gene refers to the part of the DNA molecule that encodes a single enzyme of structural protein unit.

gene pool. All of the genes present in a population of organisms. A population includes all members of a species living in a particular area and breeding together.

General Management Plan (GMP). Required for each national park under the National Parks and Recreation Act of 1978 (P.L. 95-625). A GMP describes the basic management philosophy for the entire national park and provides the strategies for addressing issues and achieving identified management objectives over a five- to 10-year period and sometimes longer (see chap. 8).

giardiasis. An intestinal disease caused by the protozoan pathogen, *Giardia lamblia*, which has become common in wilderness waters over the past 30 years (see chap. 16). It is commonly called *Giardia.*

GMP. See *General Management Plan.*

grazing. Foraging for food by domestic livestock (sheep, cattle, horses) and allowed in wilderness under grazing permits.

habitat. Place where an animal or plant normally lives, often characterized by a dominant plant form or physical characteristic, for example, a forest habitat.

hard release. Lands permanently released for other multiple use purposes, including resource development, following their consideration and non-selection for wilderness classification.

heterotrophs. Organisms which use the complex substances produced by autotrophs as a food base and rearrange or decompose them. For example, heterotrophs include: animals, microbes, and fungi. They may be either ingestors or decomposers (see chap. 10).

Implementation Plans. Sometimes called action plans, are the NPS's second level of planning. They deal with portions of a park, such as a wilderness or backcountry area, and are prepared for topics not adequately covered in the GMP or for topics addressed later (see chap. 8).

indigenous. Living or occurring naturally in an area; native, endemic people, flora, or fauna (see chap. 3).

indirect management. Management which emphasizes modifying peoples' behaviors by managing factors and situations that influence their decisions; visitors retain their freedom to choose. A "light-handed" approach to wilderness management (see chap. 15). An example would be retaining a low standard access road to help limit use of a popular wilderness trailhead. Contrasts with direct management.

Individual Wilderness Management Plans. Used by the FWS for each refuge wilderness in the National Wildlife Refuge System (see chap. 8).

inholding. A tract of land under private ownership within public lands, such as, a wilderness area.

interim management. The management of areas under study or consideration for wilderness classification during their review period, in a way that does not degrade their

wilderness qualities or preclude their being classified by Congress as units of the NWPS. In other words, the decision to study an area for possible wilderness designation is also a decision to temporarily manage that area as a wilderness.

intrinsic processes. Amelioration or preparation of severe sites by pioneering species and their eventual elimination by the less hardy climax species through competition, invasion, succession, and displacement (see chap. 10).

L-20 Regulation. The first systematic program of wilderness protection promulgated by the USFS in 1929. It was primarily a list of permitted and prohibited uses for designated roadless areas on national forests (see chap. 2).

LAC. See *Limits of Acceptable Change.*

Limits of Acceptable Change (LAC). A planning framework that established explicit measures of the acceptable and appropriate resource and social conditions in recreation settings as well as the appropriate management strategies for maintaining and/or achieving those conditions.

minimum tool rule. Apply only the minimum impact policy, device, force, regulation, instrument, or practice to bring about a desired result (see chap. 7). Achieve results using the most "light-handed" approach.

monitoring. Systematic gathering, comparing, and evaluation of data (see chap. 7).

National Environmental Policy Act of 1969 (NEPA). A federal law establishing as national policy that all federal agencies give full consideration to environmental effects in planning their programs. To implement this policy, the act requires specific "action-forcing" procedures which agencies must observe (See *Environmental Impact Statement*).

NEPA. See National Environmental Policy Act of 1969.

nondegradation. A concept that calls for the maintenance of existing environmental conditions if they equal or exceed minimum standards, and for the restoration of conditions below minimum levels (see chap. 7).

odor. As related to air quality, is caused by hydrogen sulfide from natural gas wells or gas sweetening plants, and by emissions from other industrial operations such as pulp and paper mills, metal-smelting plants, and gas and oil refineries (see chap. 13).

omnibus bill. A wilderness classification act designating several wilderness areas or WSAs.

opportunity class. Designates the availability of a particular quality or kind of experience that is appropriate to the conditions.

organic acts. A law providing original or basic direction to an agency. For example, the Federal Land and Policy Management Act of 1976 is regarded as an organic act for the BLM because it gives basic direction to the agency.

paper park. A derogatory term referring to a designated national park or similar area with limited management and protection (i.e., It is a park only on paper.) (see chap. 3).

pH. A measure of how acidic or alkaline (basic) a solution is on a scale of 0-14 with 0 being very acidic, 14 being very alkaline, and 7 being neutral. The abbreviation stands for the potential of Hydrogen (see chap. 13).

potential of Hydrogen. See *pH.*

primary succession. A process usually slower than secondary succession because it involves amelioration (improvement). of extreme site conditions by gradual alter-

ations brought about by the organisms (see chap. 10).

primitive areas. (1) USFS areas set aside under administrative regulation L-20 between 1929 and 1939. Nearly 14 million acres were set aside under the L-20 Regulation, but the lack of strict enforcement and its permissive acceptance of other forest management activities, including logging, led to its replacement in 1939 by the U Regulations. (2) An administrative designation formerly used by the BLM to manage lands for wilderness preservation purposes. It was superseded by the FLPMA in 1976. (3) Refers to an administrative category of protected areas on the national forests prior to the Wilderness Act of 1964, and either classified as wilderness or identified for subsequent wilderness consideration by that act.

Ramsar Sites. A designation for wetland areas of international importance, such as the Everglades in Florida. As with Biosphere Reserves and World Heritage Sites, areas on the Ramsar list have no legal standing as a result of such listing, but the international recognition may support their protection.

RARE. See *Roadless Area Review and Evaluation.*

RARE II. See *Roadless Area Review and Evaluation II.*

Recreation Opportunity Spectrum (ROS). A planning approach identifying a range of recreational environments across a spectrum ranging from urban recreation areas, rural countryside, highly developed campgrounds, intensively managed multiple-use forests, national parks, recreation and scenic areas, roadless wildlands, and wilderness. The ROS defines six classes: Primitive, Semiprimitive Nonmotorized, Semiprimitive Motorized, Roaded Natural, Rural, and Urban (see chaps. 1 and 8).

Refuge Management Plans. Used by the FWS, these plans are used for each refuge unit, which can include separate plans for management of hunting and fishing, grazing, public use, fire control, and other important activities (see chap. 8).

Regional Plans. Used by the USFS, they apply Forest and Rangeland Renewable Resources Planning Act-related program goals and standards to the national forests within each region and coordinate national forest planning with the planning of other agencies (see chap. 8).

Renewable Resources Assessment and Program. Required for the USFS by the Forest and Rangeland Renewable Resources Planning Act (RPA), as amended by the National Forest Management Act. The RPA calls for (1) preparation of an assessment of the supply and demand for the nation's forest and rangeland resources, and (2) development of a management program for national forests that considers alternative management directions and the role of the national forests (see chap. 8).

Research Natural Area (RNA). Areas set aside to preserve representative ecosystems for scientific study and educational purposes (see chap. 6).

Resource Management Plans. Used by the BLM. They are a type of land-use plan designed to guide the management of an entire resource area (see chap. 8).

RMP. See *Resource Management Plans.*

RNA. See *Research Natural Area.*

Roadless Area Review and Evaluation (RARE). A USFS effort in the early 1970s to systematically inventory, review, and evaluate the relative values for future uses of existing roadless areas. The RARE process identified the extent of roadless lands remaining on the national forests and recommended each area for wilderness consideration, further study, or release for other mul-

tiple use (see chap. 5).

Roadless Area Review and Evaluation II (RARE II). The second Roadless Area Review and Evaluation in 1977-1979 incorporated new roadless area criteria and the requirements of the National Forest Management Act. The final RARE II inventory list included 2,919 roadless areas including 62 million acres in national forests and national grasslands in 38 states and Puerto Rico. Each area's resources were estimated, site specific information was reviewed, and potential for uses was assessed (e.g., potential timber, harvesting, grazing, and mineral extraction). RARE II also sought to assess how each area might contribute to qualities of the wilderness system, such as ecological diversity (see chap. 5).

ROS. See *Recreation Opportunity Spectrum.*

secondary succession. Fairly rapid changes following cutting or burning of a forest or removal of grazing animals from a depleted range (see chap. 10).

silviculture. The cultivation of forest trees; forestry.

simulation model. Simplified replica of a real-world system, usually described so that it can be represented by a computer program, and the effects of changes simulated (see chap. 17).

soft release. Also known as "Colorado release." First included in the Colorado Wilderness Act, soft release provides for the release of areas considered for but not classified as wilderness, to the same treatment as other lands in the national forest planning process. Thus, soft released areas may be considered again as to their wilderness potential during the next cycle of forest planning and ultimately classified as wilderness (see *hard release*).

successional changes. Long-term, predictable trends of an ecosystem, as opposed to short-term cyclical changes. An orderly process of community development involving changes in species structure and community processes with time.

sustainable development. Natural resource utilization that does not exceed the permanent productive capacity of the ecosystem. Thus, a level of development use that can be permanently sustained (see chap. 3).

synecology. The relationship of organisms and populations to biotic factors in the environment.

trampling. Walking on vegetation and soil by humans and packstock which may cause: abrasion of vegetation, abrasion of surface soil organic layers, and compaction of soils (see chap. 16).

transactive planning. A strategy used by wilderness managers which incorporates the concept of societal guidance, wherein people are willing and able to construct and guide their own future if given the opportunity to do so. It recognizes the importance of social interaction among those affected by a decision. Small working groups of citizens are the basis of the transactive planning process, and they interact with a planner. Transactive planning has been used in coordination with the LAC process (see chap. 9).

untrammeled. Not subject to human controls and manipulations that hamper the free play of natural forces. A word describing desired wilderness conditions used in the Wilderness Act.

U Regulations. Regulations U-1, U-2, and U-3(a) replaced the L-20 Regulation in 1939 as the authority under which unroaded lands in the national forests were administratively protected. Regulation U-1 established wilderness areas, tracts of land of not less than 100,000 acres. Regulation U-2 defined wild areas as tracts of land between 5,000 and 100,000 acres that could be protected, modified, or eliminated by the chief of the USFS. Regulation U-3(a) established roadless areas for recreational use under natural conditions (see chap. 4).

visibility. An air quality-related value Congress has singled out for protection in the Clean Air Act.

visibility impairment. Caused by the scattering of light by particles or gases, or by the extinction of light by particles, between the viewer and the scene being viewed (see chap. 13).

WARS. See *Wilderness Attribute Rating System* used in RARE II.

wilderness. The legal definition is found in the Wilderness Act of 1964 Section 2c (P.L. 88-577): "A wilderness, in contrast with those areas where man and his own works dominate the landscape, is hereby recognized as an area where the earth and its community of life are untrammeled by man, where man himself is a visitor who does not remain." This legal definition places wilderness on the "untrammeled" or "primeval" end of the environmental modification spectrum. Wilderness is roadless lands, legally classified as component areas of the NWPS, and managed so as to protect its qualities of naturalness solitude and opportunity for primitive types of recreation (see chap. 1).

wilderness allocation. All processes and activities of government agencies and interested publics to identify areas for potential protection as wilderness and for their classification by Congress under the Wilderness Act.

wilderness-associated wildlife. Includes species commonly associated with wild habitat characteristics of wilderness (see chap. 11).

Wilderness Attribute Rating System (WARS). A system used in RARE II to document and assess the wilderness attributes of roadless areas (see chap. 5).

Wilderness Classification Act. Legislation that designates an area or areas as part of the NWPS.

wilderness dependent. Dependent on the wilderness conditions of naturalness and solitude (see chap. 7).

wilderness-dependent wildlife. Species dependent on conditions of naturalness and solitude and thus species whose continued existence is dependent on and/or reflective of wilderness conditions (see chap. 11).

wilderness management. Government and citizen activity to identify—within the constraints of the Wilderness Act—goals and objectives for classified wildernesses and the planning, implementation, and administration of policies and management actions to achieve them. Involves the application of guidelines and principles to achieve established goals and objectives, including management of human use and influences to preserve naturalness and solitude.

Wilderness Opportunity Spectrum (WOS). A spectrum of wilderness conditions including finer gradations of naturalness and solitude, i.e., primitive conditions. The WOS includes, for example, pristine, primitive, and portal designations, indicating decreasing degrees of naturalness and solitude. Like the ROS, WOS is a kind of zoning, which delineates particular areas where different management prescriptions or restrictions on visitor behavior apply (see chap. 8).

wilderness parity. A phrase used to describe a very stringent orientation to managing wilderness for naturalness

and solitude, with little compromise to accommodate human use.

Wilderness Study Area (WSA). Areas found to possess candidate characteristics for wilderness designation and designated for formal study to assess their suitability for wilderness classification. WSAs were designated during the BLM's wilderness review process (during the inventory phase) begun in 1978 and ending in 1980. WSAs have also been identified in wilderness legislation that mandates their study (see chap. 5).

WOS. See *Wilderness Opportunity Spectrum*.

WSA. See *Wilderness Study Area*.

World Heritage Sites. An international classification system to recognize and designate areas which represent: a major stage of the earth's evolutionary history; significant ongoing geological processes, biological evolution, and man's interaction with his natural environment; superlative natural phenomena, formation, or features; and has natural habitats where threatened or endangered species of animals or plants of outstanding universal value can survive (see chap. 3).

Acronyms

ANCSA. Alaska Native Claims Settlement Act of 1971

ANILCA. Alaska National Interest Lands Conservation Act of 1980

BLM. Bureau of Land Management, U.S. Department of the Interior

BMWC. Bob Marshall Wildernss Complex, Montana

BWCAW. Boundary Waters Canoe Area Wilderness, Minnesota

CEQ. Council of Environmental Quality

CNPPA. The Commission on National Parks and Protected Areas

CONCOM. Council of Nature Conservation Ministers, Australia

CPS. Canadian Park Service

DOC. Department of Conservation, New Zealand

EA. Environmental Assessment

EIS. Environmental Impact Statement

EPA. Environmental Protection Agency

FAO. Food and Agricultural Organization

FLPMA. Federal Land Policy and Management Act of 1976

FMC. Federated Mountain Clubs, New Zealand

FWS. Fish and Wildlife Service, U.S. Department of the Interior

IUCN. International Union for Conservation of Nature and Natural Resources

IWLF. International Wilderness Leadership Foundation

LAC. Limits of Acceptable Change

MAB. Man and Biosphere Program

NAAQS. National Ambient Air Quality Standards

NEPA. National Environmental Policy Act of 1969

NFMA. National Forest Management Act of 1976

NGO. Nongovernmental organization

NOAA. National Oceanic and Atmospheric Administration

NPS. National Park Service, U.S. Department of the Interior

NZFS. New Zealand Forest Service

NWPS. National Wilderness Preservation System

ORRRC. Outdoor Recreation Resources Review Commission

P.L. Public Law

RAWS. Remote Automated Weather Station

RIM. Recreation Information Management (system)

RNA. Research Natural Area

ROS. Recreation Opportunity Spectrum

RPA. Forest and Rangeland Renewable Resources Planning Act of 1974

SAF. Society of American Foresters

TNC. The Nature Conservancy, a non-profit organization

UNEP. United Nations Environmental Program

UNESCO. United Nations Educational, Scientific, and Cultural Organization

USFS. U.S. Forest Service, U.S. Department of Agriculture

VIM. Visitor Impact Management

WARS. Wilderness Attribute Rating System (RARE II)

WOS. Wilderness Opportunity Spectrum

WSA. Wilderness Study Area

WWC. World Wilderness Congress

INDEX